SWEDEN

•Uppsala

•Stockholm

TEUTONIC
ORDER

Kalmar

Gotland

BALTIC SEA

•Riga

•Moscow

ARK

•Lund

Copenhagen

Rügen

LITHUANIA

R U S S I A

Danzig
TEUTONIC
ORDER

Vistula

POLAND

Oder

•Warsaw

•Kiev

Dnieper

Elbe

MAN

nsburg

Cracow

Carpathian Mts.

Dniester

C U M A N S

Danube

Vienna

•Gran

•Buda

HUNGARY

Belgrade

Danube

BLACK SEA

OF VENICE

LES

ADRIATIC SEA

SERBIA

BULGARIA

Balkan Mts.

GDOM

THE

SICILIES

nnines

EPIRUS

Adrianople

•Constantinople

SULTANATE

OF

ICONIUM

EMPIRE OF
NICAEA

rmo

AEGEAN SEA

•Athens

ACHAIA

SEA

Crete

Cyprus

J.P.T.

EUROPE IN RENAISSANCE AND REFORMATION

S. HARRISON THOMSON
UNIVERSITY OF COLORADO

EUROPE

IN

RENAISSANCE

AND

REFORMATION

HARCOURT, BRACE & WORLD, INC.

NEW YORK · BURLINGAME

FRONTISPIECE: *Adoration of the Magi,* detail from wood altar-screen sculptured by Veit Stoss, *ca.* 1485, in the church of St. Mary in Cracow, Poland [PHOTO BY STANISLAW KOLOWCA].

MAPS BY LOUIS M. KOBBÉ AND JEAN PAUL TREMBLAY

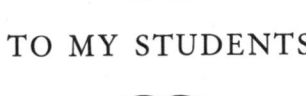

TO MY STUDENTS

Library of Congress Catalog Card Number: 63–14421

PRINTED IN THE UNITED STATES OF AMERICA

PREFACE

THE NEED for a volume covering the period from the extinction of the Hohenstaufen line of emperors of the Holy Roman Empire to the end of the religious wars on what is academically known as the upper-division level has been evident for some years. Each generation sees history in its many facets differently from its predecessor. The present book is an effort to portray this middle period of our European tradition within the framework of the accepted results of recent study and research. It does not claim to present startling new conclusions. Good history has been written for a long time and by many honest and competent scholars. Some aspects of the story told in this book may therefore appear to be quite conventional history. Others may be, in proportion or in obvious relationship, novel or unaccustomed. In the nature of the use to which such a book may be put in college and university teaching, the instructor will be, and certainly should be, free to adapt, reinterpret, or refocus the material here offered.

The basic assumption upon which I have proceeded is that this period, from Dante to Westphalia, is peculiarly an epoch of endings and beginnings in almost every area of European life: society, economy, religion, art, education, and letters. It has been my effort, therefore, to present an overall picture. This will explain the title: "Europe *in* Renaissance and Reformation." The book is not a history of the Renaissance in its usual sense or of the Reformation, Catholic and Protestant. These great movements take their important place in the narrative, but other things of great moment were happening at the same time all over the European scene and their history must be told. Within the covers of one book only selected aspects of the whole concourse of human life can be recounted. Another selection than the one here presented could easily have been made. It is my hope and indeed assumption that the instructor who guides a group of students in this study will, in lectures or readings, fill the gaps that are only too evident in this account.

The author of any serious work of history owes a tremendous debt to the painful labors of other scholars, some still alive and active, others now long gone to their reward. The collections of documents, monographs, and works of synthesis from which we all must draw are both a warning and an encouragement. They warn us that we are bound by the work of those who preceded us.

They encourage us to hope that those who come after may be grateful for our modest efforts. In the academic pursuit both teacher and student are joined in an endeavor to spread the knowledge of our roots, our *via vitae,* and our search for the truth about ourselves and our institutions. It is in the conviction that this middle period of European history is of living and suggestive value to the modern world in its restless quest for understanding that the present book has been written. I owe much to the generations of students, graduate and undergraduate, at a number of colleges and universities who have, by their interest and frequent questioning, taught me along with themselves the pleasures and profits of capturing the spirit and worth of their cultural heritage. My appreciation of their part in this common enterprise is barely measured by the dedication of this book.

I wish to acknowledge special debts of gratitude to a number of colleagues to whose word in various areas covered by this book I am proud to defer. Professor Roland H. Bainton read the whole manuscript, made many useful suggestions, and saved me from many mistakes. The late Professor Sidney Painter read a number of the earlier chapters, with great profit to the account. Professor Ernest Hatch Wilkins gave me generously the benefit of his profound knowledge of Dante and the early humanistic Renaissance, and Professor Berthold L. Ullman read the chapters on earlier and later humanism, saving me from many infelicities in expression and from factual errors. I am fully aware that there may be some slips that remain; they are mine and mine alone. I am indebted to Professors Allen D. Breck, Walter G. Simon, and Robert Hawkins for allowing me to impose on their time with specific questions. My debt to my wife Zome cannot easily be described. She has held me mercilessly to clarity and sequence when I might have wandered from Dante's *diritta via.* The text has also profited from numerous valuable suggestions of my son, Williell. Mrs. Aline B. Stone has been most patient with the tedious task of typing and retyping a longish manuscript.

All translations except those otherwise indicated are my own.

S. HARRISON THOMSON

Boulder, Colorado
January 1963

CONTENTS

vii

CONTENTS

Contents

MAPS

EUROPE IN RENAISSANCE AND REFORMATION

CHAPTER ONE

THE WORLD OF DANTE

T HE lifetime of Dante Alighieri (1265-1321), one of the supreme poets of the Western world, spanned a period in which many crucial changes took place in politics, society, religion, economics, and art. It would be difficult to conceive of a more significant phase of history than the latter part of the thirteenth century and the beginning of the fourteenth. The significance lies not only in the happenings of this period, but fully as much in the less palpable changes in spirit and motivation that underlay these events. It shall be our purpose in this study to describe the occurrences, and, perhaps more important, to try to get behind them to the spirit, which outlives the events and often brings forth new ones.

Papacy and Empire

FOR centuries before Dante's birth the whole Italian peninsula had been torn by bewildering and incessant strife. The most dramatic and spectacular aspect of this chronic contentiousness was the battle between the Holy Roman Empire and the Papacy. No less bitter, if much less consistent and comprehensible, was the strife within the manifold political subdivisions of Italy,* in which the old feudal aristocracy was pitted against the rising commercial bourgeoisie. This internecine struggle was not unrelated to the larger contention between Empire and Church. Indeed, the shibboleths and the pattern of alignment of the larger tended to be carried down into the lesser struggle; the partisans of the Papacy, called Guelphs since the early thirteenth century, faced the Ghibellines—those who favored the imperial cause. The papal-imperial issue died down after the papal victory over the house of Hohenstaufen, but the animosities remained; the field of battle was merely transferred to the social and economic arenas. The old feudal aristocracy, forced to give way, joined the ranks of the upper bourgeoisie. The aristocracy and their partisans tended to be Ghibellines. The rising commercial classes, including the artisans, were

---

* In this period such terms as "Italy," "Spain," "Germany," and "Russia" indicate geographical areas, not political entities.

3

usually Guelph. But such lines were often obscured by local rivalries and family disputes.

After the death, in 1250, of the brilliant Emperor Frederick II, the Papacy determined to crush the Hohenstaufen family, which had consistently opposed papal expansion. The Pope called in Charles of Anjou, younger brother of the French king Louis IX (St. Louis), offering him the Sicilian crown in exchange for his help. Charles invaded southern Italy. At the decisive battle of Benevento (1266) the French forces, supported by the Papacy, defeated the heirs of Frederick, led by Manfred, his natural son, who was legitimate regent and self-styled king of Naples and Sicily. Charles assumed the title of King of Naples and Sicily, ruling as Charles I of the Kingdom of the Two Sicilies (1266–82).

The Papacy soon found that it had rid itself of one antagonist only to put in his place another, potentially just as troublesome. The story of the next half century is in large measure that of the Papacy's efforts to rescue itself from this dilemma. In its attempt to gain independence from outside domination, the Papacy succeeded only in preventing Italy from achieving any kind of unity. Dante was a witness and in a sense a victim of this struggle; all the leading protagonists appear on the vast stage of his *Divine Comedy*.

The grandson of Frederick II, Conradin, made a gallant, vain attempt to regain the heritage of the Hohenstaufen in Italy but was defeated by Charles of Anjou at the battle of Tagliacozzo (1268) and executed shortly thereafter. The Holy Roman Empire was in dark eclipse. During the so-called Great Interregnum (1250–73) there was no imperial rule in Italy. It was not until 1273 that a real effort was made to elect an emperor who might bring firmness into the shambling structure. Rudolf of Habsburg, elected in October of that year (Rudolf I, 1273–91), was a prince whose very inconspicuousness was his principal recommendation to the imperial electors. He proved to be something of a surprise and was the founder of a dynasty that, with minor interruptions, retained its imperial title for more than five centuries. Yet during Dante's lifetime the Holy Roman Empire, once the dominant force in Italian political life, ceased to play any significant role in the area south of the Alps; it became in reality the Holy Roman Empire of the German Nation.

The Rise of National States

THE Papacy had won its centuries-long battle with the Empire, but it was destined to suffer defeat in a very short engagement at the hands of a less extensive, if more intensely conscious and powerful, antagonist: the national state. The wise rule of Louis IX (St. Louis, 1226–70) had done much to unify the French nation and make France the leading power in Europe. Louis' grandson, Philip IV (the Fair, 1285–1314), took the country still farther along the road to national unity. A nationally awakened France under his rigorous leadership broke the political power of the Papacy in a bitter struggle lasting only seven years. To make victory more sure, Philip then took the Papacy captive (see p. 53), and for almost seventy years (1308–76) the center of Christendom was at Avignon on the Rhône River. This humiliating captivity, with its grave consequences for the Church and its prestige among the common

people, was a source of bitterness and grief for Dante. He bemoaned the degradation into which the once majestic Rome of the Caesars and the martyrs
had fallen. Philip was the first ruler in modern times to introduce into international relations the element of nationwide, popular support of a monarch.
There was at that time no adequate counter to that support. In the face of the
power of a nation's unity, the traditional defenses of the Papacy were completely outdated and useless.

In Spain and Portugal unification was gradually but inevitably proceeding.
The Moors had been forced far to the south of the peninsula. Out of many
petty kingdoms—León, Castile, Aragon, Catalonia, Navarre, Galicia, the Asturias—the process of consolidation was beginning to make larger and more
viable political units. Two important events mark the latter part of the thirteenth century in Spain, one internal, the other external. The first was the
striking growth of parliamentary institutions throughout Spain, a growth that
came sooner than it did anywhere else in Europe. The second was the intervention in Sicily of Peter III of Aragon (see p. 10). Thus, after centuries of
virtual isolation from events in the rest of Europe, Spain again became a factor
in the international affairs of the Continent. The arrival in Italy of still another
foreign conqueror made the tribulations and uncertainties of the Italian people
even more painful and introduced an additional element of discord into the
already tense and disturbed peninsula.

In England the changes that took place late in the thirteenth century were
similar to those in France and Spain, although perhaps not so striking in their
manifestations. Parliamentary institutions, representing the voice of a great
section of the people, came into effective existence, and the personal power of
the monarch was sharply circumscribed. The country was relatively prosperous,
and commerce and urban organization were noticeably on the increase. By
virtue of various marriage alliances and his vast feudal holdings in France,
the king of England was playing a significant, if at times confused, role in
Continental politics, just as the French and Spanish dynasties were deeply involved in Italy. The political and commercial rivalry with France soon erupted
in a long and crippling war. But it is possible to discern, late in the thirteenth
century, the sure foundations of the English state, based on a national administration and the common law, which was to be an example to the rest of Europe
of national unity and orderly development for centuries to come.

That part of the Empire north of the Alps, which, until the extinction of
the Hohenstaufen, was bound to Italy and Provence by the accident of dynastic
union, went its separate way from the time of the Great Interregnum (1250–
73). Dante and Petrarch were to deplore in vain the withdrawal of the bearer
of the imperial title from the seat of the Caesars. But the facts of geography
and growing national differences were decisive. The Empire north of the Alps
was as disunited as Italy, and the separate principalities and imperial and free
cities had accommodated themselves so successfully to living on their own that
no emperor, however ambitious or strong, could possibly be more than a titular
ruler. The best illustration of this situation was the Hanseatic League, a federation of north German cities for commercial purposes. The League included
among its members at one time or another about one hundred cities and had
outposts and "factories" from Novgorod in Russia to London. For almost two

centuries it was virtual ruler of the Baltic and the whole eastern shore of the North Sea. It regulated commerce, coined money, controlled ports and prices, waged war, and frequently dictated to monarchs what they should or could do.

Although the royal, or imperial, crown remained in theory elective, the princes of Germany, both lay and ecclesiastical, had grown in power until, by the middle of the thirteenth century, they were sovereign in their own right. The history of Germany in this period, and for centuries to come, is one of separatism and decentralization to the point of disintegration. There was as yet no semblance or sign of German nationalistic sentiment as we have come to understand the term. Yet this absence did not indicate any loss in national vigor. Indeed, the contrary seems to be the case. For it was precisely in these centuries of constitutional separatism that the Germans pushed eastward in a tremendous wave of colonization—along the shores of the Baltic into Prussia, to the Gulf of Finland, southeastward into Poland, along the Carpathians, into Bohemia, down the Danube, and into the plains of Hungary and south Slavonia —taking with them their town laws and organization, their technical skills, their commercial and industrial proficiency.

The parallel between the developments in Germany and in Italy in these centuries is striking. Both were politically decentralized and individualistic; both were economically and culturally extraordinarily vital and imaginative. There is, however, the considerable difference that, whereas Italy was prey to much foreign invasion and interference, no foreign conqueror set foot on German soil.

On the eastern borders of the Empire lay a number of considerable and even imposing kingdoms. For them the thirteenth century was a period of troubled uncertainty. They had their own difficulties, arising either from their geographical situation or from constitutional or dynastic growing pains, but in addition they had to adjust themselves to the pressure of the German movement eastward and to undergo, at the same time, occasional attacks originating in the East. The invasion (1240–41) of the Tartar hordes crossing southern Russia, Poland, and then, after a defeat at Liegnitz in southern Silesia, Moravia and Austria into Hungary, left an indelible memory of terror and devastation with the inhabitants of these countries. Repeated later threats of invasion from the East kept these vivid impressions alive. This fear was compounded by the vague rumblings of the almost equally terrible power of Muscovy, which, in the winter of 1242, crushed the vaunted might of German knighthood. The tough but hardly civilized Lithuanians were the only barrier left between the Western-oriented Polish kingdom and the scourges from the East.

Poland had been able, in large degree, to absorb the German influx and utilize the new blood for strengthening of the stock. But Russia's reaction to the Mongol invasion was less successful. The profound difference between the cultural potential of the Polish people and that of the Russians in later centuries can probably be traced to this period. Only toward the end of the century was there any demand in Poland for a strong central authority. The twelfth century in Poland had been a sad period of increasing dynastic dissolution, reminiscent of the worst days of the do-nothing kings of Merovingian Gaul. But a reaction set in, and with it the rise of a national Polish spirit. The fourteenth century witnessed the impressive achievement of a united nation under a strong monarch who was at the same time a political and administrative architect of great ability.

The kingdom of Bohemia occupied a unique position in the Empire; although her king was cupbearer of the Empire and an elector, the emperor could not even set foot in the kingdom without invitation and had no rights of any sort within her boundaries. This snugly situated kingdom made great progress in the thirteenth century. She was economically and politically strong, rather more centralized than the Western kingdoms, and was led, for most of the century, by two exceptionally able monarchs of the native hereditary dynasty, the Přemyslids: Přemysl Ottokar I (1197–1230) and Přemysl Ottokar II (1253–78). Perhaps even the latter was too strong, for he excited the envy of other princes of the Empire. At the end of the century they united against him and crushed the Přemyslid state, to the advantage of the new Habsburg dynasty.

The lands of the Crown of St. Stephen of Hungary reached from the eastern limits of the Carpathians to the Dalmatian coast, including the regions later known as Slovakia, Transylvania, the Banat, Croatia, Slovenia, Bosnia, and Herzegovina. The rulers of Hungary prided themselves on their friendly relations with Western courts, and during the twelfth and thirteenth centuries the passage of tens of thousands of crusaders and pilgrims down her beautiful Danube had had a determinative influence on Hungary's blood, her economy, and her culture. Her western boundary, the Dalmatian coast, was in constant contact with the Venetian colonies that dotted the Adriatic, and there is ample evidence that Hungary's relations with the Papacy and with the commercial cities of Italy were close and lively.

The states of the Balkans are generally regarded as having been, during most of this period, on the periphery of Western civilization. But this concept scarcely does justice to the facts. By the eleventh century the Byzantine Empire, or Roman Empire (of Greek language), was in control of the Balkans to the Danube, the Drava, and the Dalmatian coast. In the course of the twelfth and thirteenth centuries Greek rule was pushed back by the growing power and aggressiveness of the ruling house of Serbia, the heirs of Stephen Nemanya (d. 1200), and by the resurgence of Bulgarian nationalism. Two external circumstances contributed to the weakening of Byzantine control over southeastern Europe: the growth of Venetian commercial activity, which always involved political interference, and the disturbances incident to the Crusades. From this latter circumstance arose the conquest of Constantinople by the Frankish crusaders (1204) and the establishment of the Latin Empire of Constantinople, which lasted, somewhat precariously, until 1261. Peninsular Greece, in the meantime, had become a feudalized French subkingdom, subject to all the uncertainties and disorganization to be expected when one political society is forcibly imposed upon another of quite dissimilar base. Contemporary with the subsidence of Frankish vigor and influence in the peninsula, which would have appeared to strengthen the Byzantine cause, there occurred the rise of a hitherto unnoticed people north of the Danube—the Vlachs, or Wallachs, more recently known as the Rumanians. Their origins are a matter of dispute, but it is certain that their speech was predominantly Latin and their orientation

Byzantine. By resisting Bulgarian expansion northward, they obliged the fiery Bulgarians to press southward against the Byzantine Empire. The Bulgarian threat to the defense of the Byzantine Empire prepared the way for the Ottoman conquest in the fifteenth century.

The significance of the Balkans, peninsular Greece and the islands of the Aegean, and the Byzantine Empire itself in Western political and cultural history has been underestimated by modern scholars; it was certainly not underestimated in the thirteenth century. The two most powerful commercial states of Italy, Venice and Genoa; the Angevin ruler of the Kingdom of the Two Sicilies, the largest political unit in the Italian peninsula; the house of Aragon; the Papacy; the royal house of France; and numberless French feudal nobles were all profoundly interested in events along the eastern coasts of the Mediterranean, whether for religious, economic, or political reasons. Frequently their interest was a compound of all three. The student of Western history should try to see these centuries through the eyes of the men of the time. We shall, in the course of this study, have frequent occasion to relate the history of the West to the less familiar history of the area of the Byzantine heritage, as well as to the almost equally unfamiliar history of the area between the West and the Byzantine Empire.

The Political Structure of Italy

WE HAVE in very general fashion passed in review the major events in the world outside his native land in the years when Dante was preparing to write the great *Divine Comedy,* a work which, it has been said, "rested upon the entire evolution of the Middle Ages." In order to grasp the complex interplay of men and ideas, institutions and forces, which characterized this period and which contributed so much to the structure and complexion of our modern world, we shall need to be more curious about the details of political and social life, the doctrines and methods of the Church, the changing positions of buyer and seller, peasant and worker, soldier and saint, artist and poet—that is, the dreamer and the doer—and the avenues of cultural transmission from one tongue to another and from one age to the next. In order to understand the atmosphere in which the beginnings of the Renaissance appeared in their most obvious form, we shall start with a description of the political structure of several larger units in Italy itself.

It is hardly necessary to justify the choice of the year 1300 as the focal point of our introduction. Dante himself called this year the "middle of the way of this our life." Because of the important events that took place immediately before and after that year, it can be regarded as the "hinge of history," dividing the medieval from the beginnings of the modern world. The reasons for this appellation will become clear in the course of our narrative.

In the year 1300 the Italian peninsula was broken up into almost countless petty sovereignties, the heritage, in part, of the Lombard conquest of the sixth and seventh centuries. These many states, or political units, may be grouped according to their political structure: kingdoms, republics, hereditary duchies

Italy, ca. 1250

or counties, the lands of the Church, and despotisms of innumerable degrees
of absolutism or potential freedom and democracy. By the end of the thirteenth
century there were at least a half-dozen powers that could be called the leading
Italian states, although none of them gained or maintained its eminence without challenge.

The largest of these powers in territorial extent was the kingdom of Naples,
the mainland part of the Angevin Kingdom of the Two Sicilies, ruled by the
ambitious Charles of Anjou. Charles had grandiose plans for becoming the

9

most powerful ruler in the whole Mediterranean area. He was senator of Rome, which meant that he had control of that city and its surrounding countryside. As Imperial Vicar of Tuscany, he was the leader of the Guelph, or papal, cause in northern Italy. He exacted heavy tribute from the Emir of Tunis and in 1267 assumed the title of King of Jerusalem. In that same year he took possession of Corfu and, shortly thereafter, of the kingdom of Albania. At about the same time he acquired the suzerainty of Achaia, which then included the northwestern part of the Morea (the ancient Peloponnesus), from the Greek emperor of Constantinople, and eleven years later (1278) he assumed the title of Prince of the Morea. In 1271 Charles was able to dictate the election of a friendly Italian prelate as Pope Gregory X. Gregory died five years later; but after a succession of short-lived popes, Charles was able again (1281) to secure the election of a pope who was favorable to his cause—Martin IV, a Frenchman. As his plans grew and took shape, Charles' relations with southern Slavs, Serbs, and Bulgars, opponents of Byzantium, became closer. It was clear that he intended to build a vast empire covering the whole eastern basin of the Mediterranean, from Sicily and Tunis in the west to the Black Sea and the Danube.

Charles seemed invulnerable, and his successes were overpowering. But trouble had been brewing for some time, and his very successes had multiplied his enemies. Among the native Sicilians, long-smoldering resentment erupted on Easter (March 31) 1282 in Palermo in a wholesale massacre of French soldiers and officials. This holocaust, known as the Sicilian Vespers, marked the end of French domination in that half of the kingdom. The victorious Sicilians offered the throne to Peter III of Aragon, who could claim, through his wife, Constance, daughter of the late King Manfred, to be the defender of Hohenstaufen tradition in Italy. Peter, who may have been working for such a break between the Angevin and his Italian subjects, quickly accepted the offer. A naval war broke out between the Angevin forces, supported by the Papacy, and Aragon; it dragged on for several years, but no clear-cut decision was ever reached.

Both Charles and Peter died in 1285, as did Pope Martin IV. Peter's second son, James II of Aragon, wished to relinquish Aragon's claim to Sicily, but the Sicilians refused to return to Angevin rule and invited James' younger brother Frederick to be their king (Frederick II, 1296–1337). Open warfare gave way to negotiation, and peace was finally arranged at Caltabellotta in August 1302. Sicily and the mainland were separated; an Angevin continued to rule the kingdom of Naples with the title of King of Sicily, but the island was ruled by an Aragonese prince with the title of King of Trinacria.

By the time Charles of Anjou died, it had become clear that any effort to unite Italy was doomed to failure not only because of chronic outside interference in Italian affairs but also because of strong Italian individualism. Centuries were to pass before integration was attempted again, and then it was under quite different circumstances. The Papacy, which had struggled so grimly with the Hohenstaufen in order to avoid being crushed by the Empire, had been saved from Angevin domination by the Sicilian Vespers. The defeat and death of Charles of Anjou gave the Papacy a breathing space it could readily use.

Rome and the Papacy

TO SPEAK of the Papacy is, of course, to speak of Rome. Yet in the later Middle Ages the two were far from synonymous. Rome seethed with the same political and social countercurrents that made all the cities of central and northern Italy the scenes of unceasing civil strife in these centuries, although for a number of reasons the struggle was never so sharp or the outcome so decisive as in cities north of the Tiber. The old distinction between Guelph (papal) and Ghibelline (imperial) interests which had had some consistent meaning in the twelfth century, no longer corresponded to the issues in the Angevin and post-Angevin period. The Empire had ceased to be a reality in Italy and there was no longer any point in either attacking or defending it.

The issues had shifted and with them the interests of the various elements of Italian society. Throughout the peninsula, the growth in power and influence of the working classes and the lower bourgeoisie, the *popolo* (in which we do not, of course, include the peasantry), and the consolidation in spirit of the upper commercial classes with a sprinkling of commercially minded nobility, together constituting the *grandi,* made conflict between these groups inevitable. The differentiation between rival groups thus came to be based largely on social and economic factors rather than on the question of whether the spiritual or the temporal power should predominate in local politics. In Rome itself, on several occasions in the thirteenth century, the people rose against the Papacy and supported the Ghibelline cause for a time. Yet the presence of the Papacy, the fact that Rome was not a commercial or an industrial center, and the inescapable conclusion that the prosperity of the individual citizen, whatever his status, depended in great measure upon the general peace in the city, all tended to make Rome somewhat less subject to the sharp upsets which marred the history of all the other leading communes of central and northern Italy.

Since the days of Innocent III (1198–1216), the Papacy had claimed to control in full secular fashion the States of the Church, which included the Patrimony of St. Peter and lands north of Rome, as well as the duchy of Spoleto, the March of Ancona, and the Romagna. In fact, however, control was more often lax than not. In 1275 the Habsburg Emperor Rudolf I, upon demand of Pope Gregory X, made specific grant to the Papacy of these lands (adding Ravenna), and thenceforth the Papacy became one of the most considerable states of Italy. The strategic position of these Papal States, sitting athwart central Italy from the Tyrrhenian Sea to the Adriatic, made it possible for the Papacy to nullify any move from any quarter to bring all of Italy under the sway of a single power.

Although the city of Rome itself was administered by a senator, theoretically chosen by the people of Rome, the several Papal States were administered by papal rectors or locally elected *podestàs,* whose authority and effectiveness varied greatly from commune to commune. The dominant phenomenon of medieval Italian life was the instability of political rule. The leading noble houses of Rome, particularly the Orsini and Colonna families, strove incessantly for control. The Roman people were notoriously changeable and subject to new and sudden enthusiasms. The successive popes varied markedly in their ability to dominate the anarchy which prevailed, and the Papacy was severely handicapped by the complete lack of continuity in policy or leadership during these critical decades. From 1261 to 1294 there were eleven popes, and for six of those thirty-three years the Papal See was vacant. Considering the pressures from outside Rome or Italy, in addition to this collection of domestic uncertainties, it is somewhat surprising that any papal policy in Italian politics can be discerned at all. Within the College of Cardinals, there was a sharp cleavage in orientation. One group of cardinals was strongly pro-Italian, perhaps antiforeign might be more accurate; another group, sometimes larger in number, was French either in origin or in sympathy. This cleavage, with predominance swinging from one side to the other, accounts for the long periods of vacancy on the papal throne and the frequent paralysis of Church policy.

Florence

IN THE twelfth century Florence became the pre-eminent commercial city of Tuscany, in the face of determined opposition from the other Tuscan communes of Siena, Pisa, Pistoia, and Lucca. The political complexion of Tuscany, and particularly of Florence, tended to reflect the conclusions of the Church-Empire struggle. On the death of Frederick II in 1250, as the result of a popular revolt, the city was divided into six sections (*sestieri*), each of which named two "good men" to a body of twelve "old men" (*anziani*). It was the function of this council to be a check on the *podestà*, the ranking magistrate of the city, who was actually brought in from the outside. The city militia of twenty companies was put under the command of a captain of the people (*capitano del popolo*) who, under the *anziani,* was the representative of the popular will. These two, *capitano* and *podestà,* ruled side by side, each responsible to the *popolo* who had made the revolt. In later times Florentines looked back upon this, their first democracy, with deep nostalgia.

The passions of the Florentines for independence and for commercial profit are evident at every point in their history. Florentine democracy turned out to be no less aggressive toward commercial rivals than the rule of the Ghibellines had been. After four years of war, Pisa, Siena, and Pistoia were forced to submit. In such intercommunal wars it was customary to expel from a conquered city the leaders and many of the rank and file of the opposite party. Those whom Guelph Florence had driven out of defeated cities stirred up willing Ghibellines elsewhere in Tuscany and won a resounding victory at the battle of Montaperti in 1260, forcing Florence to become Ghibelline. Six years later, however, when the forces of Charles of Anjou defeated Manfred at the battle of Benevento, Florence once again became a Guelph city. The supremacy of the city for ten years was offered to Charles. He, in turn, sent a vicar to govern the city, with the help of the twelve *anziani* and of another, more broadly based, legislative Council of Ninety. Yet democratic governance was bound to be experimental; we can easily trace a dozen constitutional changes in Florence in the next generation, intended to protect the city from capricious despotism, from corruption, or from outside control. In none of the rapid political changes, however, did the *popolo minuto,* as the common people came to be called, count for anything. Poverty, unemployment, and inequities were rife, while the Guelphs were intent on eradicating vengefully every trace of Ghibelline power and wealth. The most pleasant prospect of this game was the pillaging and razing of Ghibelline towers and houses.

The distinction between Guelph and Ghibelline after the death of Frederick is not always easy to draw, but it is fairly accurate to say that by the end of the thirteenth century the Ghibellines throughout Italy tended to be the aristocratic party, and the Guelphs to represent the interests of the commercial classes. Once Guelph dominance in Florence was a fact, it became apparent that the primary interest of the city was its commercial success. This success, in turn, was the work of the seven leading merchant guilds (*arti maggiori*). Beginning in 1282, the functions of government were assumed by six "priors," each representing a section of the city, and also, by common understanding, one of the leading guilds and each elected for two months. The framework of this government by priors lasted for over two centuries, although not without some stormy interruptions. Early in 1293 popular resentment against the magnates (*grandi*) resulted in the issuance of the Ordinances of Justice, which clipped the power of the *grandi,* named a new presiding official for the six priors, the gonfalonier of justice, and raised nine lesser guilds (*arti minori*) to greater participation in the affairs of the city. Severe punishment was decreed for magnates who committed any act of violence. It was under this system of government that Florence grew and prospered until the early sixteenth century. While representing the commercial interests of the city, it was flexible enough to permit the benevolent and indirect dictatorship of the Medici in the fifteenth century and to allow a general atmosphere of democracy to pervade the republic. To say that it solved all problems of civic strife would, however, be going too far.

There is much in the story of Florentine communal development that applies to dozens of lesser Italian cities from the thirteenth to the sixteenth centuries— the struggle between rich and poor and between the nobility and the commercial classes; the institution of the foreign *podestà* as chief magistrate for a limited period of time; the establishment of a communal militia under a professional and salaried soldier (the *capitano*) and of a council representing more or less widely the various elements in the population; the tendency toward excluding the nobility from civic position; the apparent possession of all the attributes of political sovereignty, most frequently exercised by the waging of brutal and sanguinary wars against neighbor communes; and, very essentially, an atmosphere of independence and individualism, not to say communal truculence. And yet, although this skeleton of government was usually discernible elsewhere in Italy, quite often it was hardly more than a form; many a *podestà* or *capitano,* legally or by force, converted his temporary position into a life rule and, in not a few cases, established a dynasty.

Lesser States of Northern Italy

WHILE Florence maintained the semblance of a democratic regime, the maritime Republic of Genoa fluctuated between control by four leading families and democratic choice of a *podestà,* who usually contrived to become a despot.

The importance and wealth of Genoa, like that of her rival, Venice, were out of all proportion to her rather meager land territory. She managed to take full advantage of the security afforded by the line of mountains behind her, parallel to the coast. While she never had to face the constant threat of attack which was the curse of the cities of the Tuscan and Lombard plains, hers was still a turbulent life. In the early thirteenth century she had a bitter struggle with Pisa for supremacy on the western Mediterranean from which she finally emerged victorious. Her victory made war with Venice inevitable; control of foreign markets in the seas and along the coasts of the whole eastern Mediterranean was at stake. This was a longer contest, and the peace concluded in 1299 found both combatants nearly exhausted. A few years later, the Emperor, Henry VII, found it relatively easy to take over control of a city weakened by long warfare far from home and convulsed by domestic squabbles. Before Genoa could recover, Venice, disposing of greater reserves of trade and wealth, had forged ahead in her drive to dominate the commerce of the Mediterranean and the outlets for that commerce through the passes of the Alps.

To the northeast of Genoa lay the strategically situated lands of the counts of Savoy, the family of the Sabaudi. Transit from the Ligurian coast or from the outposts of Milan at Alessandria or Vercelli over the passes of the Jura Mountains had to be through the territories of Savoy. The principal city of the county, Turin, was on the direct line of east-west transport between France and Italy, and the counts were well aware of the significance of their control of the "saddle of the Alps." Their mountainous lands were not conducive to the growth of great commercial centers, nor, save for the prosperous capital of Turin, were there any powerful cities in their realms. The rule over this hilly country remained distinctly feudal, but during the thirteenth century, under the long and vigorous reigns of Counts Thomas I (1189–1233) and Amedeus IV (1233–53), several strategically located nuclei of Sabaudo strength were effectively exploited. By the usual methods—purchase, marriage, feudal inheritance, conquest, or negotiation and persuasion—the holdings of the family soon began to assume the character of an integrated territory. In the fourteenth century, under the firm and aggressive leadership of Amedeus VI (1343–83), the rule of the house of Savoy reached south to the Ligurian coast at Nice, east well into the Lombard plain to include Vercelli, and west to the Rhône north of Lyons. The essentially noncommercial basis for the power of the house of Savoy and the freedom of these lands from most of the bitternesses of the Guelph-Ghibelline strife go far to explain their growth in structural unity precisely in those centuries when other Italian cities and states were exhausting themselves in fruitless and almost suicidal strife.

East of Savoy and northeast of Genoa, in the upper reaches of the Po valley, there were many communes—among them Alessandria, Pavia, Novara, Piacenza, Bergamo, and Brescia—which had been fighting, both inside and outside their walls, for or against powerful emperors, since early in the eleventh century. The situation was in many ways similar to that of the Tuscan plain. There were many independent cities which had alternately allied with and fought against one another. In Milan, next to Venice the greatest commercial center in northern Italy, the head of the Guelph party, Martin della Torre, forced his own election as *anziano del popolo* in 1258 and that of a friend and fellow-sympathizer with the popular cause, Pelavicini, as *capitano* for five years. Thus the two halves of the government, civil and military, were under the control of one man, a Guelph. When Martin della Torre died, in 1263, his brother Philip became *anziano,* while the leadership of the Ghibelline party was assumed by the newly named archbishop Otto Visconti. Both parties had alliances with lesser communes outside Milan, in each of which, in turn, there was either civil war or tension following or leading up to civil war. This precarious balance was maintained until 1277, when, by a sudden reversal of fortune, the Ghibellines took over. The Visconti, able, vigorous, and ruthless, were destined to rule in Milan and frequently in nearby communes for more than two centuries—one of the relatively few cases in Italian history in which a despotism was converted into a fairly durable dynasty. Under the Visconti, Milan expanded its rule, just as Florence was doing, by conquest, by negotiation or marriage alliances, by trickery, by absorption of a smaller town that could not defend itself against a neighbor, or by imperial appointment to the vicariate of dependent communes. By 1315 Matteo Visconti was *signore* or lord of Milan, Como, Pavia, Tortona, Alessandria, and Bergamo. But such accumulation of power did not proceed without numerous setbacks and violent upsets. The della Torre were able to recover a large part of their control in Milan in 1302 and kept it until 1311 and the Visconti were later several times driven from Milan.

The Lombard communes were as passionately devoted to their freedom as were those of Tuscany, and many a despot, thinking himself secure in his power, found himself suddenly faced with eviction or death. Yet, though the similarities between the Lombard and Tuscan communes were considerable, there were also some differences. The Lombard towns had practiced democracy against pope and emperor as early as the eleventh century, two hundred years earlier than the Tuscan towns. They were also to lose the passion for freedom a century or more before the Tuscan cities. Further, as one examines the struggles within the Lombard towns, it is clear that the parties in conflict were differently constituted from those that split the Tuscan communes. In the latter it was the *grandi,* or *popolo grasso* as they came to be called, the upper bourgeoisie with only a sprinkling of the nobility, against the *popolo minuto,* the craftsmen and common people. The nobility was not a political factor except for those individual noblemen who had joined the bourgeoisie. In Lombardy, on the other hand, the struggle was between the nobility and those under their command on the one side, and the artisans and craftsmen on the other. The fact that almost all the *capitani del popolo* were of the nobility also helps to explain the universal willingness of the *popolo minuto* to desert or expel them in favor of other captains who, they thought, would give them a more acceptable government. It should also be noted that Lombardy's geographical situation, nearer Germany and thus more easily accessible to the German emperors on their way to Rome to be crowned, made it inevitable that imperial politics should play a large part in Lombard history. There was less imperial interference in Tuscany than in Lombardy—conceivably because the emperors had learned something from their unhappy experiences with Italian communes in the north and, by the time they reached Tuscany, were willing to let well enough alone.

To the east and northeast of the territory of the Visconti stretched the lands of Verona, from near the Po northward into the Alps, on both sides of Lago di Garda. Verona was the capital city of the scourge of northern Italy, Ezzelino da Romano for twenty-three grim years, until his death in 1259. Then in 1277, Alberto della Scala, like Romano a Ghibelline, became captain and rector of the *gastaldi* (handicrafts) and of "all the people" of Verona. Della Scala maintained an alliance with other Ghibelline *capitani,* particularly the Visconti at Milan and the Bonacorsi at Mantua. It was a later heir of this della Scala house (the Scaligeri), Can Grande (d. 1329), with whom Dante sought refuge in 1316 and to whom he dedicated the third part of the *Divine Comedy,* the *Paradiso.* Verona under the Scaligeri is another example of a despotism which became a dynasty; the Italians of the age regarded Verona as committed to the principle of monarchy. The Scaligeri were renowned for their own culture and for their munificent support of the cause of humane letters.

Southeast of the lands of the Visconti, in the fruitful valley of the Po, lay proud Mantua, the city of Virgil. During the long struggle between the popes and the emperors, the city and surrounding countryside had at various times been in the possession of both sides. The strategic location of the city enabled her to gain favorable terms from popes as well as emperors, and a tradition of civic freedom was even fed by her somewhat detached history. Mantua had opposed Frederick II and tenaciously fought the tyrant Ezzelino da Romano. In 1274, fifteen years after the latter's capture and death, the city, confused by civil strife, decided to name two *capitani.* One of these, Pinamente Bonacorsi, had his colleague quietly murdered and took over the rule of the city and its outlying territory, assuming the title of Captain-General of Mantua. The Bonacorsi family ruled until 1328, allying themselves with the Ghibelline Visconti of Milan and the Scaligeri of Verona. This alliance went contrary to the basically Guelph sentiments of the city and led to much popular discontent. In a sudden attack in 1328, the Gonzaga family, whose position had been growing stronger during the Bonacorsi tyranny, killed or captured all the Bonacorsi. Luigi Gonzaga was immediately recognized as head of the state. The new lord of Mantua set the tradition of firm and, for the period, just rule. The dynasty made notable contributions to Italian culture in the succeeding centuries and endured in power until the early eighteenth century.

East of Mantua lay Ferrara, which had joined the Lombard League in the twelfth century. The city was the scene of bitter strife between its two leading families, the Este and the Salinguerra, until, in 1240, it formally accepted the lordship of Azzo VII d'Este. His successor expanded the territory under Ferrarese rule to the southwest; in 1288 Modena and in 1289 Reggio were obliged to acknowledge the rule of the Este. Their ambition brought them, in the north, close to Paduan territory, and, southward, into a prolonged war with Bologna (1296–98), which was stopped only after active intervention by Pope Boniface VIII. The terms of peace (1299) allowed the Este to retain most of their conquest. But, since they were now impinging on territory which the Church had long claimed, the Este were put on the defensive; upon the death of Azzo VIII (1308), papal troops were sent into Ferrarese territory by orders of Pope Clement V. The city's powerful neighbor to the north, Venice, having no desire to see papal claims come any closer, hurried to the rescue of the Este. Internal troubles prevented any stable settlement until 1317, when Robert of Anjou, king of Naples (1308–43), who had been invited into the city as a *capitano,* was driven out and five Este brothers were proclaimed *signori* of the city. Making peace with a distant Papacy, the Este family were invested (1332) with the *signoria* (lordship) of the city by the Pope. They were to be the lords of Ferrara for several of the most glorious centuries in the city's history. This city is typical of northern Italy in these years in that the *popolo* seemed only too glad to sign away the independence they had not known how to use. They were more fortunate than some other communes in that their masters were benevolent, moderate, just, and able to survive in a world in which casualties among *signori* were high.

Just forty miles north, close to the coast and to Venice, lay Padua. Partly because of her eastern location and traditionally close relations with powerful Venice, Padua had been spared some of the tragic civil strife which had had such dire consequences in most Italian communes. She had won her freedom from Ezzelino da Romano and was proud of her Guelph independence. Consuls ruled the commune until the end of the twelfth century, when there was a rapid transition to the *podestà* form of government. Yet the city's democratic traditions had remained vigorous, so that in the political calculations of the time Padua was assumed to represent the cause of republicanism. Her democracy went so far that she attempted to demonstrate and protect it by an annually elected Council of One Thousand. This device led to chaos, and in 1318 the city gave up her freedom in an orderly manner by allowing Jacopo di Carrara to become *signore.*

South of the Po and southwest of Ferrara were the city and tributary territory of Bologna, which, located at a crossroads of the principal commercial routes from the four points of the compass, had shared the fortunes of most Italian communes. As a free imperial city in 1112, Bologna had been ruled by four consuls, chosen by a *consiglio maggiore.* But the city was unable to resist the general trend away from democracy and toward concentration of power in the hands of one man. She suffered perhaps more than most from the complex of commercial growing pains and political squabbles between the Ghibelline aristocracy and the Guelph democracy. A civil war between the leading Guelph family, the Geremei, and the leading Ghibelline family, the Lambertazzi, resulted in a Guelph victory (1274). The commune had grown notably in wealth and cultural vigor, centered naturally around the ancient and famous university. But when, between 1274 and 1278, the new Habsburg Emperor Rudolf I renounced imperial control of the whole exarchate of Ravenna and gave Bologna to the Church, the city entered upon a new phase of its history. It was thenceforth regarded by the Papacy as a part of the States of the Church. But the city tended to have other ideas and not unwillingly accepted Taddeo Pepoli, an ambitious local noble, as *signore* in 1337. The sons of Pepoli, to whom he left his rule, were unable to maintain their power. In subsequent years, the *signoria* changed hands several times, and the ancient independent spirit of the city seemed to grow dim in the process.

The Republic of Venice

VENICE, busy with her commerce and safe in her lagoon, stood aloof from Italy's exhausting civil wars during much of the turbulent twelfth and thirteenth centuries. While others fought, she bought and sold at fabulous profit in all the marts of the known world. Her proud galleys, singly or in fleets, had come to dominate most of the eastern basin of the Mediterranean. During the Crusades she had vastly increased her power. The Adriatic was virtually a Venetian lake. Her doge, Enrico Dandolo, was able to divert the Fourth Crusade (1204) to effect the conquest of Constantinople, with the result that Venetian trade extended into the Black Sea, and the produce of Muscovy, the eastern Balkans, Armenia, and the steppes was borne to the West in Venetian ships. When the Frankish conquerors were driven out of Constantinople in 1261, Venice stayed on under favorable conditions, and even increased her Levantine trade. Her wealth was prodigious.

During most of these years, as we have pointed out, Venice paid little heed to the furious civil strife in the cities west of her on the mainland. Her longstanding and fierce rivalry with Genoa came to a head in 1298, when Genoa won a naval victory resulting in a temporary truce. But she had been forced to reconsider her aloofness from the land cities to the west when, during a famine in 1268, her neighbors refused to sell her necessary food. And in the early years of the fourteenth century, the noise of battle and the boastful threats of the victorious *capitani* began to be annoying. The *podestàs* in the Lombard plain, driven by ambition or inability to woo peace successfully, were trying to increase their dominions. This policy of expansion meant inevitably that the quiet security of Venice would now be disturbed from the mainland. In self-defense, therefore, she began to be increasingly active in Lombard and even in Tuscan politics, and, by the middle of the fourteenth century, she was clearly on the way to becoming a land as well as a sea power.

The development of the unique constitution of the city on the lagoon involved several centuries of gradual restriction in two directions. On the one hand, the plebeians were step by step removed from active participation in the control of the city because the more important businessmen wished to avoid the chaos of the frequent revolutions taking place in other Italian cities. On the other hand, the power of the doge was steadily lessened, to avoid the possibility that he might aspire to establish a dynasty or become a despot. A political crisis in 1289 resulted in the choice of Gradenigo, an aristocrat, as doge, but subsequent dissatisfaction led to the formulation of an extremely elaborate electoral system intended to protect the city from the caprice and uncertainty to which the Lombard towns were only too painfully subject. In 1297 the Great Council, in whose hands rested the sovereignty of the state, was "closed"; that is, eligibility for membership was limited with a few possible exceptions to those who had been members of the council during the preceding four years (1293–97). In 1312 the new arrangement was formalized; membership in the Great Council was restricted to those whose ancestors' names were on a list (drawn up in 1315) of men who had been members of the Council at some time since 1172. This list came, in 1506, to be called the Golden Book.

After an attempted *coup d'état* in 1310, a Council of Ten, at first temporary but made permanent in 1335, was established, with power to act quickly against dissident elements. The Council served to stabilize the city, and order and prosperity, shared by all elements of the citizenry, were the measure of the effectiveness of Venetian bourgeois government. Yet it should be made quite clear that Venice was seldom if ever unsettled by the stormy winds of democracy; the city was strictly a patrician oligarchy, ruled by successful merchants, not nobles. Order and prosperity were what Venice wanted, and they were what she got, at least until order became decay and prosperity became paralysis.

There were many other, lesser political units in Italy at the end of the thirteenth century, a few of which loomed larger in the next two or three centuries than some we have treated here. Nowhere in Europe did small states rise or fall so rapidly as in Italy. Coalitions, combinations, alliances, unions, and separations often occurred with lightning-like rapidity, and with little regard for logic or consistency. Yet a gradual settling down of the over-all political tumult into a relatively stable association of larger and viable independent states was discernible. We shall have occasion to note this process of stabilization in our study of the next three centuries.

DANTE

THE first of the great Florentine trio of Dante, Petrarch, and Boccaccio was undoubtedly the greatest of the three in intellect, in imagination, in intensity of passion. He is also the most difficult to place in his proper niche in cultural history. It has been said that he was primarily a medieval man—indeed, the quintessence of the Middle Ages—because of the theological cast of his thought, the assumptions he accepted from the Age of Faith, and his universalism. Others regard him as one of the harbingers of the modern world, by reason of his secularism, his reverence for the vernacular, and his appreciation of nature. Whichever position one takes, and there is much to be said on both sides, it is clear that Dante was of his time. He was also much more. He did not feel completely at home in his own century; had he been exclusively a product of his time, he would not have challenged the mind and heart of every generation since. To the extent that he had his roots in the whole of Western culture in the thirteenth and early fourteenth centuries, he shared the fate of the humanistic Renaissance which made its appearance during his lifetime. And like the Renaissance, Dante's life and work cannot be understood apart from the chaos, the pettiness, the cynicism, the instability, the hypocrisy, the tragic sense of life, and the faltering alliance between sacred words and diabolical deeds of which this period offered so many grim examples. But no more can he be understood apart from the fair hopes, the saintly lives, the great charities, the celestial dreams, and the noble devotions in which this same age was so rich. Whether as poet or as man, as prophet or as philosopher, as mirror of his world or as image of the world then in birth, Dante has more to say to us than any other person of his age.

Life

DANTE ALIGHIERI was born in Florence in 1265 of ancient and gentle lineage. His family was not inordinately rich, but they possessed a house in Florence and farmlands in the *contado,* the territory surrounding the city. We do not know much of Dante's education, save that he had the training of any young gentleman, in letters, music, sport, and drawing. He speaks of the famous Brunetto Latini as of a master, although we are not told how formal the relationship was. Nor do we know precisely how extensive was his reading in the Latin classics at this early stage of his life, although it is certain that manuscripts of most of the Latin classics were abundantly available in late thirteenth-century Florence.

Dante was a soldier in at least one campaign—the battle of Campaldino in 1289, when the Florentines defeated the forces of the neighboring city of Arezzo —and perhaps in several others, for he speaks of military matters with a first-hand familiarity. He fell deeply in love with a certain Beatrice Portinari, the daughter of a Florentine *grande,* when he was nine and began writing lyrics in her honor at eighteen. Beatrice, the inspiration of his life and poetry, was married to a Florentine noble, Simone dei Bardi, and died at the age of twenty-four, sometime soon after 1292. Dante himself, after a period of moral laxity and experiment for which he was later remorseful, married Gemma Donati, of the leading Guelph family of Florence, to whom he had been affianced in 1277.

He had by this time become interested in Florentine politics. Since participation in political life and the holding of any civic office were dependent upon membership in one of the seven greater guilds of the city, about 1295 Dante joined the guild of physicians and apothecaries. His natural abilities, combined with the influence of his wife's family, brought him rapid advancement, and he was elected one of the six ruling priors of Florence for the two-month term from June 15 to August 15, 1300.

Florence was then embroiled in one of her chronic internal struggles for power. A feud between the two leading families, the Cerchi (popularly called the "Whites") and the Donati (the "Blacks"), both basically Guelph, involved not only the whole city but Pope Boniface VIII, the latter on the side of the Blacks. Dante, despite his marriage to a Donati, declared for the Whites. When the Blacks, with the help of Boniface, won out (November 1, 1301), Charles of Valois, a French prince, entered the city as papal vicar, and Dante had to flee, leaving his wife and four children behind. On January 27, 1302, Dante and four other leading Whites were tried on obviously trumped-up charges of peculation and extortion and were sentenced to be banished for two years. Dante's wife, since she was a Donati, was left in peace. On March 10 a more drastic sentence was issued: Dante and fourteen other Whites were permanently exiled from Florentine soil, to be burned alive if they ever returned. Among the six hundred Whites sentenced to banishment or death within the next few months was a friend and literary intimate of Dante, Ser Petracco, a Florentine notary, whose then unborn son, Francesco Petrarca, was to become Florence's greatest poet after Dante.

The exiled Whites, despite the fact that they were for the most part Guelph in their sympathies, were welcomed by the Ghibellines in a number of Tuscan cities that were ancient enemies of Florence. Feeling the need for some kind of organization, the exiles appointed twelve counselors, of whom Dante was one, to serve as a sort of directory. But Dante soon became disgusted with the instability and senseless wrangling of his fellow Whites. It was difficult for a man of his high intelligence, upright principles, and acute sensitivity to be at home in any "practical"-minded political group. He therefore left the group, determined, as he remarked later in the *Paradiso,* to form a party "by himself." What he meant, of course, was that he wanted to leave party politics completely to devote himself to study and writing.

The period of exile, which lasted from 1302 to his death in 1321, was for the most part a calvary of bitter agony of spirit for Dante. He felt the pitiful chaos of his beloved land in every breath and thought while he wandered the earth. He deeply resented the treatment he had received from his native city and, quite naturally, expressed this feeling in his writing. "I have unjustly suffered punishment," he said in the *Convivio.* ". . . through almost all the lands to which our tongue extends, I have wandered, virtually a beggar, showing, against my will, the hurt which people look for in one who has been unjustly mistreated. . . . I have been a ship without a sail and without a rudder, driven into strange ports and on many a shore by the dry wind of poverty."

There are many blank spots in Dante's unhappy pilgrimage, although some dates and places are reasonably certain. In 1303 he was probably in Forlì, in 1304 in Bologna, and in 1306 in Padua. He was in Verona several times and in the Lunigiana in 1309 and 1311. He probably spent some time in Paris during his exile, but it is highly unlikely that he went to England and studied theology at Oxford, as Boccaccio seems to assert. Dante probably began the *Inferno,* the first part of his *Divine Comedy,* between 1307 and 1313, in the midst of his travels.

Whether from France or England, the plans of the new Emperor, Henry VII, for an expedition to Italy brought Dante back to his homeland. Henry had given enthusiastic public utterance to great plans for the revitalization of the Roman Empire. This promise, we may assume, aroused Dante's hopes that here at last was a leader who could bring that peace he so ardently desired, and with it the renewal of Roman glory. It was in connection with the rosy future he envisaged for Roman peace under an inspired Emperor that Dante wrote his most important treatment of political theory, the *Monarchia.* He also sent the Emperor, in April 1311, a fervent pledge of his personal loyalty. But Henry was not successful, although he did receive the obedience of a number of Italian cities and conquered a few more. His coronation in Rome (June 1312) was almost furtive, for half the city was occupied by his enemies, and the cities of Tuscany and many in Lombardy stoutly and successfully rejected his demands. He died of a fever in August 1313 at Siena.

Dante had sensed Henry's failure months before the end. Profoundly depressed, he fled for refuge and solace to the convent of Santa Croce di Avellana, in the mountains of Gubbio, where he devoted himself to writing the *Comedy,* his monument to the Christian plan of salvation. But even in this mountain retreat the poet did not enjoy peace for long; by 1316 he was again a wanderer. In that year Florence offered the White exiles a kind of amnesty. According to its terms, Dante was to walk through the streets of the city as a penitent, pay a fine, and serve a short term in prison. He rejected the offer indignantly, saying to the Florentine friend who had served as intermediary:

Why should a man who believes in justice pay money to those who inflict injury upon him as though they were his benefactors? . . . If this is the only way I can return to Florence I will not return. Can I not look on the face of the sun and the stars anywhere in the world? Can I not think noble and sweet thoughts anywhere in the world without making myself ridiculous and ignominious to the people of Florence? I shall not starve either.

In that same year Dante accepted the generous hospitality of Can Grande della Scala, the Ghibelline ruler of Verona. The best years of his life were spent under that roof, where his two sons, Pietro and Jacopo, came to join him. In 1319 he moved to Ravenna, as the guest of Guido da Polenta, and in the beautiful forests facing the Adriatic he continued work on the *Paradiso*, the third part of the *Comedy*. Although his paths lay in pleasant places, his love and longing for Florence remained unstilled. It was in Ravenna that he wrote:

> If it ever comes to pass that the sacred poem
>   To which both heaven and earth have laid a hand
>   So that for many a year I have been ahungered
> But conquers the cruelty that bars me out
>   Of the sheepfold fair where I slept as a lamb,
>   Enemy to the wolves that waged war upon it,
> Now, with altered voice, with altered hair,
>   Shall I return a poet and take the
>   Chaplet above the font of my baptism.
>   *Paradiso* xxv.–8

He may have sensed the appropriateness of his near completion of the *Paradiso*. The grand poem was his life. Sent by da Polenta to Venice on a diplomatic mission, he caught a fever on the marshy way back to Ravenna and died in that city on September 14, 1321.

Writings

DANTE's principal works are *Vita Nuova* (*The New Life*), *Convivio* (*The Banquet*), *De vulgari eloquentia* (*On the Possibilities of the Vernacular*), *Monarchia* (*Monarchy*), and the *Divine Comedy*. There are also extant eleven letters from various periods of his life, and a philosophical *Questio de aqua et terra* (*Question concerning Water and Earth*), the authenticity of which is not beyond dispute.

The *Vita Nuova*, Dante's first serious work, was completed after the death of Beatrice, sometime before 1295. It is a collection of thirty-one Italian *canzoni* (sonnets) and one ballad, written about Beatrice or about the spiritual experi-

Dante and His Poem, fresco attributed to Domenico di Michelino (1465), in the Duomo, Florence [ALINARI].

ences stemming from Dante's love for her which had enriched his life. Each poem is preceded and followed by a prose explanation of its meaning and the circumstances surrounding its composition. Perhaps the central *canzone,* around which the whole work is symmetrically planned, is the *Donne che avete intelletto d'amore,* which begins:

> To you ladies who understand what love is
> I wish to speak of the lady of my heart.
> I could never compass all her praises;
> Yet must I talk of her to clear my thoughts.

The *Vita Nuova* is a confession of the inner struggle that the poet's love for Beatrice had set up in his mind and heart. The "new life" derived from his resolve to devote the rest of his days to an explanation of the effects of love, in its highest form, upon humanity.

Dante did not claim that the experience or the thought were original with him; indeed, he gave generous credit to the poet Guido Guinicelli, whom he called "the father of me and of my betters," for suggesting some of the concepts of love. Guinicelli had, simply put, made troubadour love sincere. This tremendous departure from the traditions of the Sicilian school of poetry, which had mastered all the techniques of love poetry but had left its spirit still sensual, Dante called the *dolce stil nuovo,* the "sweet new style." In northern Italy the influence of Provençal love poetry was strong, and Dante acknowledged that he had learned much from these northern poets, particularly from a certain Provençal poet, Arnaut Daniel. More significantly, in the *Vita Nuova* Dante revealed his intention to create a drama of all Christian life, centered around the ennobled love which Beatrice had evoked in him. He had been moved to "write of her what had never been written of any woman."

The *Convivio* was composed some time later, between 1305 and 1308, in the more unsettled years of his exile. Painful memories of the death of Beatrice, years of stormy immersion in Florentine politics, and the bitterness of defeat and exile made this period, as Dante himself admits, a time of moral decline. By 1305, when he had broken with the feuding Whites and made his decision to devote his life to thought and writing, the *canzoni* and ballads he had written only a few years before made him uneasy, and he set out to re-present them in purified form. He could not call them back, for too many people had read them. He planned to offer fourteen of them as a kind of philosophical banquet with each *canzone* interpreted allegorically and commented upon in such a way as to lend some elevated meaning to the text. His decision to use the vernacular arose from his conviction that it was fully capable of expressing the loftiest sentiments and was in some respects richer in meaning than scholastic Latin. His purpose was to present Dame Philosophy as the object of his love instead of the more obvious ladies for whom the poetry had originally been written. "I fear the infamy," he remarked in the introduction, "of having pursued so great a passion as anyone reading these odes would have thought had ruled me. . . . And as my true purpose was different from what these odes apparently show, I intend to explain them allegorically after discussing the literal account." He got no further than four treatises, the introduction and the first three *canzoni*. These first four sonnets are on a high plane. In all probability he found the remaining *canzoni* too sensual to allegorize and gave up the whole project at that point. The significance of the work lies primarily in its demonstration of Dante's growing interest in philosophy and theology, and the wide and thoughtful reading he had already done in these areas. The vast erudition that graced the *Comedy* had its foundation in these years.

De vulgari eloquentia was begun in about 1305 but never finished. It was written partly in response to critics who had taken him to task for using the lowly vernacular, the language of servants and cowherds, to discuss such noble themes as divine philosophy and pure love, and partly in an attempt to rationalize and systematize the great variety of dialects and speech patterns to which his wanderings had exposed him. Dante's effort to create a "science of the vernacular tongue" was the first of its kind and is of cardinal importance and value to modern philologists. He preserved and critically analyzed specimens of old Italian which would otherwise have been lost. Dante's criticisms of the various Italian dialects and his judgment that the common speech, if purged of its defects in pronunciation and "rude words," could become the most beautiful, noble, and expressive language in the world were only partially correct. The history of linguistic development demonstrates that any artificial and "rational" modification of a language will not last, whereas priority among dialects

DANTE, *Divine Comedy,* first page of MS No. 289, folio 1, in the Pierpont Morgan Library, New York [PIERPONT MORGAN LIBRARY].

is likely to be achieved by the innate vigor of a single one. In the case of Italy it was Dante's own Tuscan dialect that won out. The poet himself, in his own inspired writing, demonstrated how the speech of his native Florence, properly used, was superior to the other dialects of Italy.

Political exiles have always been prone to give thought to the theoretical bases of the state, and Dante was no exception. There is frequent reference in the fourth treatise of the *Convivio* to questions of political theory, the authority of the state, the opinion of the multitude, and the need for a single head to ensure a "life of felicity." Dante's *Monarchia* treats the Holy Roman Empire as heir to the ancient empire of the Romans, in which the whole world lived at peace under a rule of law. Furthermore, he claimed, the ancient Roman order must have had God's approval, for He allowed His Son to be born, live, and be judged under Roman law. The unified and universal rule of a monarch above the strife of city or nation, exercising a benevolent control, under law, over the peoples and states of the world, will ensure the just aim of universal peace and the reconciliation and coordination of Church and State, the spiritual and the secular, revelation and reason. The function of the Church in this millennium will be so to permeate society with Christian teachings that men will come to approve and support the Church and the State, giving to each its due and deriving from each the maximum benefit, and thus live a full and satisfying Christian life. Dante's state, for his own time, at least, was a grandiose but vain dream. His conception has been called the epitaph of the Empire. Dante knew and understood much history, but he was too close to the politics of his own time to perceive that the Holy Roman Empire had received a fatal blow with the death of Frederick II in 1250 and that the death of Henry VII in 1313 had sealed its demise. Before his eyes the new European reality, the national state, had already made its appearance.

In each of Dante's earlier works we observe traits and qualities that were to reach full fruition in his greatest work, the *Divine Comedy*. His attempts to master various media and develop various themes, the declaration of ideal love in the *Vita Nuova*, the forced allegory and the philosophizing of the *Convivio*, the rationalization of the vernacular and the mastery of its potentialities in *De vulgari eloquentia*, all enriched his mind and his technical equipment for the consummation of his intellectual and artistic creativeness. The *Comedy*, called the *Divine Comedy* only some time after Dante's death, was completed between the death of Emperor Henry VII in 1313 and the poet's death in 1321. There is no doubt that Dante had worked at it many years earlier, but neither the resources nor the impulse to finish it came until his hopes in a new Roman world of peace and order were proved false.

The work is divided into three main parts: *Inferno* (Hell), of thirty-four cantos; *Purgatorio*, of thirty-three cantos; and *Paradiso*, of thirty-three cantos, making in all one hundred cantos, the square of the perfect number ten. The poem is an allegorical portrayal of Dante's journey through the three kingdoms of the world-after-death. Through Hell and Purgatory his guide is Virgil. Hell is a deep hole of nine circles or levels in which Dante and Virgil find all the great sinners of history, suffering pain and punishment appropriate to their sins. Dante meets a notable collection of popes and kings, writers and statesmen, traitors and murderers on his way. At the bottom, three-faced

Lucifer, the father of all sin, is stuck breast high in ice, his six wings flapping cold and helpless. After taking Dante through to the other side of the earth, Virgil guides him up the sunlit, cone-shaped Mount of Purgatory, with its seven concentric ledges, each reserved for cleansing transgressors from one of the seven sins. In Purgatory Dante meets the Latin poet Statius, as well as those Christians who, though sinners, yet have hope of finally attaining Paradise.

The Earthly Paradise begins at the summit of the Mount of Purgatory; the Celestial Paradise is beyond. Virgil, being a pagan, cannot enter Paradise, and at the top of Purgatory, where the Garden of Eden meets their gaze, Beatrice encounters Dante and acts as his guide. She explains many theological mysteries that had puzzled him and, as they move higher in the heavens, Dante has visions beyond his power to relate. The angels and the saints, in the presence of the Prime Mover of all things, convey to Dante the ineffable blessedness of union with the Divine Essence, "the love that moves the sun and other stars," in ecstatic contemplation.

The *Comedy* is an allegory of man's pilgrimage toward salvation, but, unlike the conventional medieval allegories, it does not focus upon personified abstractions. Dante uses actual historical persons to convey, in a figurative context, the realities of Christian doctrine: sin and retribution, remorse and repentance, God's love and mercy shown through His sending of His Son. The poem is the consummation of Dante's years of searching and experience.

It is customary to regard the *Comedy* as the *summa,* the summation, of medieval life and faith. It is all of that. But there are several aspects of the work that do not fall within this category. It breathes an individualism that was completely at odds with the medieval mind. It rejects the claim of the Church to rule every part of man's life and, by implication at least, denies the centricity of the sacramental powers of the Church. When popes and cardinals are consigned to Hell by a layman, a revolution in authority and doctrine is on the way. The poem is also well ahead of the Middle Ages in its rejection of the sacred Latin of the Church, the schools, and the wandering scholars in favor of the vernacular, the language of the bourgeoisie, the businessman, the craftsman, and the peasant, who together were to make the modern world.

SUGGESTIONS FOR FURTHER READING

COMPAGNI, DINO, *Chronicle*. London, 1906. Temple Classics
COULTON, G. G., *From St. Francis to Dante*. London, 1907. A paraphrase of the *Chronicle of Salimbene of Parma*
DANTE, *Divine Comedy*. Many translations. E.g. Modern Library (Carlyle-Wicksteed). Most convenient translation of all Dante's works, Latin and Italian, in Temple Classics, 6 vols., London, 1899–1906, with Latin or Italian and English on facing pages
DANTE, *Monarchy and Three Political Letters,* ed. D. Nicholl. London, 1954
VILLANI, GIOVANNI, *Selections from the First Nine Books of the Croniche fiorentine,* Westminster, 1896

BROWN, HORATIO, *The Venetian Republic*. London, 1902. Temple Classics
COTTERILL, H., *Medieval Italy*. London, 1915
D'ENTRÈVES, A. P., *Dante as a Political Thinker*. Oxford, 1952

FLETCHER, J. B., *Dante.* New York, 1916
GILSON, E., *Dante the Philosopher.* New York, 1948
GREGOROVIUS, F., *History of Rome in the Middle Ages.* 8 vols. London, 1894–1902
MOORE, L., *Studies in Dante.* 4 vols. Oxford, 1899
RUNCIMAN, S., *The Sicilian Vespers.* London, 1958
SCHEVILL, F., *History of Florence.* New York, 1936
SEDGWICK, H. D., *Italy in the Thirteenth Century.* 2 vols. New York, 1933
SISMONDI, S., *History of the Italian Republics,* ed. W. Boulting. London, 1906
TOYNBEE, P., *Dante Alighieri: His Life and Works.* London, 1910
VOSSLER, K., *Medieval Culture: An Introduction to Dante and His Times.* 2 vols. New York, 1929

AMARI, M., *Storia della guerra del Vespro Siciliano.* 1886
BARBI, M., *Dante, vita, opere i fortuna.* 1940
CIPOLLA, C., *Storia delle signorie italiane dal 1313 al 1530.* 1881
COSMO, U., *Vita di Dante.* 1930
GIANNINI, F., *I comuni 1000–1300.* 1909
LABANDE, E. R., *L'Italie de la renaissance.* 1954
NARDI, B., *Dante e la cultura medievale.* 1949
RENAUDET, A., *Dante humaniste.* 1952
RENUCCI, P., *Dante, disciple et juge du monde gréco-latin.* 1954
SALVEMINI, G., *Magnati e popolani di Firenze 1280–1295.* 1899
SCHNEIDER, FR., *Dante. Eine Einführung in sein Leben und Werk.* 1940
SIMEONI, L., *Le Signorie.* 2 vols. 1950
VEZIN, A., *Dante. Seine Werke und seine Zeit, sein Leben und Werk.* 1949
VOLPE, G., *Medio Evo italiano.* 1923
ZINGARELLI, N., *Dante. La vita, i tempi e le opere.* 2 vols. 1947

CHAPTER TWO

THE CHURCH, THE STATE,
AND THE CITY

I N ORDER to grasp the full import of the events of the fourteenth and fifteenth centuries as they affected the institutions of Western society, it is necessary to review, at least briefly, the framework of the most powerful single factor of that society, the Roman Catholic Church.

The Foundations and Organization of the Medieval Church

SINCE its foundation the Church had gone through a long and exacting course of growth and development, surviving many crises from within and without to achieve a unity of teaching and a solidity of structure that went far to explain its great power and tremendous influence. The Church claimed to have been specifically founded by Christ in His charge to the apostle Peter: "And I say also unto thee, That thou art Peter, and upon this rock (*petré* in Greek) I will build my church and the gates of hell shall not prevail against it. And I will give unto thee the keys of the kingdom of heaven: and whatsoever thou shalt loose on earth shall be loosed in heaven" (Matthew 16:18, 19). This broad commission was the cornerstone of the Roman Church, for it was accepted without question in the Middle Ages that Peter had been the head of the Christian community in Rome for twenty-five years, until his martyrdom in 67 A.D. The Roman successors of Peter had not only maintained this claim to a kind of primacy—not always accepted by other patriarchates and bishoprics—but had gradually come to exercise it. The very repetition of the claim added its effect to Rome's central location and her aura of the ancient *caput mundi*.

But the Church possessed more than tradition. Emphasis on doctrine as a firm defense against the pagan world and the numerous heresies that swarmed in the Mediterranean world marked the history of the Roman see. This steady and unrelenting orthodoxy not only strengthened the position and prestige of the Church, but also resulted in the gradual formulation of a distinctive body of theological doctrine and, in the absence of adequate civil administration throughout Europe, of a body of law to guide the Christian in his life in society. The accumulated doctrine of the Christian faith was succinctly expounded by Peter Lombard, bishop of Paris, in his *Four Books of Sentences* (*ca.* 1150). At about the same time, the civil and legal aspects of the Christian's life were systematized and codified by Gratian, a law professor at Bologna, in his *Decretum,* or *Concordia discordantium canonum* (*ca.* 1140). The *Sentences* became the theological textbook of the Roman Church for the next four centuries, even the definitive formulation of the Church's doctrine by St. Thomas Aquinas in the thirteenth century did not modify its basic positions. The *Decretum,* or canon law, supplemented in later centuries by legal-minded popes, regulated the operation of the Church as an organization and the life of the Christian in all its aspects. The Church thus had in its hand instruments for the complete control of the believer: a doctrinal system to which his assent was necessary for salvation in the next world and a well-integrated system of law and practice for his guidance and discipline in this world.

The Church regarded itself as the custodian of the Scriptures and the Creeds, which had been won and maintained through arduous intellectual battles and sealed in the blood of martyrs. The doctrine of the Trinity, the dual rule of faith by Scriptures and Church tradition, man's sinfulness and need for salvation, the efficacy of the sacraments as channels of grace, the Church's absolute custody of both salvation and sacraments—these were the most significant heads of Catholic doctrine.

The four books of the Lombard's *Sentences* will show the order in which the mysteries of the faith were presented: Book I, "On the Mystery of the Trinity"; Book II, "Concerning the Creation and Formation of Corporal and Spiritual Things and Many Other Items Pertaining Thereto"; Book III, "Concerning the Incarnation of the Word and Other Matters Relating Thereto"; Book IV, "Concerning the Sacraments and Sacramental Signs." From the point of view of the Church's power, with which we are here primarily concerned, the fourth book is perhaps the most significant, for it was from the Church's absolute control of the sacraments, the sacred and visible signs of an invisible grace, that its power over the believer chiefly derived. The number of sacraments varied in the early centuries from two to a great many, but seven came to be accepted in the late twelfth century, and the Catholic Church has not since changed that number. The seven sacraments of the medieval Church were baptism, confirmation, the Eucharist, penance, ordination, matrimony, and extreme unction. It will be noticed that each of the crucial stages in human life, from birth to death, was protected by a sacrament. By thus enveloping its children under its protective cloak, the Church bound them inseparably to itself.

The sacrament of baptism, which must precede all other sacraments, had to be properly administered by a priest (or, in case of necessity, by a lay person) to a new-born infant or, exceptionally, to an older person. By this sacrament, the original sin with which all descendants of Adam are charged is washed away, and the recipient is incorporated into the mystical body of Christ. The sacrament of confirmation, whereby the gifts of the Holy Spirit are bestowed upon the believer, follows baptism after a period of instruction. This sacrament normally may be administered only by a bishop. The believer is then prepared to partake of the Eucharist (from the Greek word for thanksgiving). The Eucharist, also called the Holy Communion or the Lord's Supper, has come to be regarded as the central feature of the Mass. Through this sacrament, says the Lombard, "we are perfected in that which is good." It "restores us spiritually, whence it is properly called Eucharist, that is "good grace," for in this sacrament not only is there an increase of virtue and grace, but He who is the Fount and Origin of all grace is taken in his entirety." Baptism and the Eucharist were the most important of the seven sacraments. In a period when the Church was universal throughout central and western Europe, the power of excluding a person from participation in the Eucharist, a rite to which all claimed or needed access, constituted excommunication and therefore was a tremendous and dreaded weapon in the hands of the Church. The words of Christ's institution of this sacrament, "This is my body . . . this is my blood," gave rise to much philosophical speculation in the Middle Ages. How was it possible for such simple things as bread and wine to be transformed into the body and the blood of Christ, dead on the Cross and then departed to heaven over a thousand years ago? After long hesitation and much debate, the Church accepted, at the Fourth Lateran Council in 1215, the doctrine of transubstantiation. According to this doctrine, the physical elements (*substantia*) behind the accidents (weight, size, color, taste, etc.) of the bread and the wine were changed by a miracle into the true body and blood of Christ, and were so received by the ministrant priest and the believer. Only the accidents of the bread and wine remain. The union of the believer with Christ and with all other believers was thus consummated. The Eucharist (the Mass) was regarded as a sacrificial rite, in which the whole people partook by their presence and participation in the forms of the service. The doctrine of transubstantiation has been challenged in details by some churchmen, but it has continued to be the official doctrine since the thirteenth century. Questions also have arisen as to whether the sacrament is valid and salutary for the believer regardless of the personal character of the ministrant. The Church early took what is called the "objective" view of this and the other sacraments, that the sacrament properly administered was valid *ex opere operato,* quite independently of the priest who administered it. This position ensured that the Church's primary authority and its contact with the believer could not be broken.

The fourth sacrament, penance, consists of three elements: contrition, confession, and, after satisfaction or in anticipation of it, absolution. At the Lateran Council of 1215 this sacrament was clarified so as to bind the individual Christian irrevocably to the Church. It was decreed that every Christian must go to confession at least once a year if he did not wish to be excluded from the sacrament. This meant confession to the parish priest, who thus came to represent the power of the whole Church. With this sacrament there came to be associated the indulgence—that is, a remission of a part or the whole of the earthly or purgatorial punishment (satisfaction, or *pena*) specified for a sinner by a proper authority. Abuses arose, and the Church on several occasions had to restrain the clergy from overenthusiastic use of the power to absolve the sinner from punishment. From early in the fourteenth century the conviction grew that the power of the Church to absolve from punishment

31

(*pena*) and guilt (*culpa*) came from its control of the treasury of merits of Christ and the saints, through the power of the keys. In later medieval practice, indulgences were frequently represented as valid in anticipation of the sin mentioned. They thus became a highly marketable commodity, and a highly profitable one to the Church, to churchmen, and to their agents. The Crusades greatly increased the use of indulgences. In order to attract people to so dangerous an enterprise, the popes offered plenary indulgences (forgiveness of all sins, even, by clear implication, of those not yet committed) to those who would "take the cross," and partial forgiveness to those who contributed to the costs of the Crusade. It is not difficult to see to what lengths such a relaxation of the original concept of true penance could and, indeed, frequently did go.

The sacrament of ordination to the state of deacon or priest, like confirmation, could be administered to an ordinand only by a bishop. The laying on of hands by the bishop bestowed a certain sacramental character upon the recipient that was normally indelible and, like baptism, could not be repeated. The sacrament of matrimony, acknowledged to possess a "minimum of spirituality," was really regarded by the Church as a concession to the passions of the flesh, for the unmarried life (the monastic ideal) was greatly to be preferred. This sacrament could be validly administered but once. Divorce was not permissible, but in certain circumstances a marriage might be annulled.

Extreme unction, the anointing of the believer with consecrated oil when *in extremis,* or at the point of death, was instituted for the remission of sins, and if expedient, for the return of bodily health.

All these sacraments in the exclusive hands of the Church constituted an awesome body of controls, reaching into all the critical areas of a Christian's life. Certainly on the earthly pilgrimage there was no escape from the care of the Church, and the entrance into the next world—hell, purgatory, or heaven—was also, the Middle Ages thought, in the sure hands of that same universal Church. As far as the individual believer could see, both the Church and his own final destiny were personified in the parish priest.

Bishop, Priest, and Monk

THE original administrative unit of the Church was the bishopric, with its cathedral, usually located in the principal city of a province. During the Middle Ages, the bishoprics began to be grouped into larger units, with a city chosen as the metropolitan see (from the Latin *sedes,* or seat) of the archbishopric. These larger units naturally varied somewhat in size. In the Empire, for example, there were seven archbishoprics by 1400: at Cologne, Mainz, Trier, Bremen, Magdeburg, Salzburg, and Prague. The number of bishoprics constituting the archdiocese varied greatly: Magdeburg had four, and Mainz twelve. In Italy there were thirty archbishoprics and a correspondingly larger number of bishoprics, all loyal to and dependent upon the pope. In England there were only two archbishoprics, in France eleven, in Poland one, in Hungary one, and in Scandinavia three.

The Papacy claimed the prerogative of choosing the bishop, but in practice he was usually elected by the clergy, or chapter, of the cathedral, sometimes on the nomination of the ruling prince. Final approval rested formally with the pope. The duties of administration and supervision, both of the considerable property that belonged to the bishopric and of ecclesiastical matters, were so great that the bishop had a large corps of assistants who made up the cathedral chapter and performed religious and secular functions at his order. Each of these functionaries, or members of the bishop's family, was allotted an office as the gift of the bishop, with an appropriate stipend, called variously a prebend or a benefice.

The bishop was powerful in his diocese, but he had no lack of jurisdictional problems. Not the least of his worries was the independence, gradually but surely acquired, of the chapter, led by a dean who held office for life and thus gained great power in the administration of the "fabric" of the cathedral. In addition, the various monastic and mendicant orders were constantly attempting to enlarge their independence and generally succeeded in freeing themselves from bothersome episcopal visitation. Members regarded themselves as owing obedience directly to the head of their order, who in turn was responsible solely to the pope. Conflicts over the cure of souls arose between these orders and the parish priest, who had to account to the bishop; and the bishop was usually unable to enforce his authority over the regular orders.

The wealth in the hands of the Church, much of it by purely feudal title, had grown to immense proportions by the later Middle Ages. In the thirteenth century the income of the bishop of Paris far surpassed that of the king of France. In the fourteenth century the Church owned at least one-third of the land of England, upon which no tax was paid to the royal treasury. In addition to the tithe, the faithful had bestowed upon the Church their treasures of gold and silver and their lands and possessions out of loyalty or trepidation at the thought of the pains of hell, and the Church never willingly gave any of its wealth to secular powers.

The religious work of the Church (the *cura animarum,* or care of souls) was performed by the priesthood (priest and deacon) and the monastic and mendicant orders. The average parish priest in Europe during the thirteenth and fourteenth centuries was not very literate. He could read and write a little Latin, he knew by rote the *Pater noster,* the *Credo,* and most of the Mass and the Litany. But, since much of his learning had been by ear, his reading of the services was far from exact. The sermons and exhortations of bishops and conscientious clergy of that age are full of denunciations of the ignorance and negligence of the parish clergy in such matters. But among the higher ranks of the clergy there were many who were guilty of the same shortcomings, and with less excuse, since they had the advantages of schooling and the means with which to obtain the necessary books. The parish clergy were frequently charged with moral laxity. On balance, however, the parish clergy toward the end of the Middle Ages were probably no worse in morals and no more negligent of the essentials of their task than were the higher clergy.

It would be difficult to make out so favorable a case for the monastic and mendicant orders. They had grown immensely wealthy, and the records of episcopal visitations and disciplinary prescriptions eloquently attest to the moral decline of the whole monastic establishment without much distinction of order or country. In addition, in the fourteenth and more obviously in the fifteenth century, the monasteries felt free to disregard the bishop's disciplinary actions. Their numerous immunities gave them an increasing sense of luxurious security that could only result in laziness, cynicism, arrogance, and immorality. Efforts of individual monastic reformers to direct the attention of their orders to the primitive and noble ideals which had originally inspired and justified the origins of the order seldom if ever had lasting effect. The mendicant orders, the Franciscans (Friars Minor, or Grey Friars) and the Dominicans (Order of Preachers, or the Black Friars), had begun as devout and austere reactions against the current of laxity so prevalent in the early thirteenth century and had maintained this idealism into the fourteenth century in a high degree. But they too became wealthy, and by the mid-fifteenth century, throughout Europe as a whole, there was little difference between them and the older orders. In parts of Europe, indeed, the decline in mendicant morality set in even earlier but primitive idealism was frequently strong enough to maintain a generally high level of monastic life through the fourteenth century.

One of the leading defenders of the Papacy against the Empire in the early fourteenth century was the Spanish Franciscan Álvaro Pelayo, who had traveled much throughout Europe. Writing about 1330, he put the monks and the mendicant friars on the same level of laxity. "They [the monks] buy jewels, corals, and knives with silver and ivory handles . . . they buy soft and delicate garments, clothing themselves softly because they are royal. . . . Some religious are stouter and more insolent litigators than lay folk." Of his own friars he asserted: "Some of them are in more abundance than other religious because people's devotion is commonly turned more toward them and the people give them more, which is to them an occasion of transgression, since they turn all this to gain whatever their holy and apostolic rule may say." Criticism of both monks and friars grew even sharper as their wealth, arrogance, and moral laxity became more ostentatious.

Thus we see that the Church in the fourteenth century was a highly integrated system of control. By persistence and the accumulation of tradition, wealth, and political and psychological power, it had become a sort of benevolent monopoly throughout Europe, transcending the boundary lines of kingdoms and the Empire and claiming the allegiance, under threat of condign discipline, of all classes of society, from emperor to serf. It possessed a clearly elaborated rationale in its impressive doctrine. It had acquired, partly by reason of the failure of temporal government to fill the gap left by the collapse of the Roman Empire, a determinative position as legislator for Western society. It had accumulated enough property and wealth of all sorts in all of Europe to be the dominant economic power in the thirteenth century. In the fourteenth century, it perfected the administration of its resources in a degree unsurpassed even by the genius of the Medici in Florence.

The Church and the National State

THROUGHOUT the Middle Ages a bitter struggle between the Papacy and various secular governments was either imminent or active. The secular government might be the Empire, an aggressive monarch, an independent-minded city far from Rome, the recalcitrant nobility of Rome, or even the people of the city of the popes. Instances of resistance to the claims of the Papacy came and went, but the claims remained, confirmed by time and frequent victory. The essence of these claims, as it became clear under Gregory VII (1073–85) and Innocent III (1198–1216), was universality. The ancient test of orthodoxy—*quod semper, ubique et ab omnibus creditum est* (what has been believed always, everywhere, and by everyone)—was also the key to the scheme of universal dominion which the Roman Church, from the late eleventh century, regarded as its mission. In all its political and cultural action and teaching, the Church adhered to this theme.

In the thirteenth century the Church supported the university movement and encouraged the international character of the instruction and curricula. The fact that the medium of instruction was Latin, the official language of the Church for a thousand years, gave an added element of permanence and universality to the patronage of Rome. Indeed, the Church attached so much importance to this universal language, ecclesiastical Latin, that it resisted the rise of the vernaculars by stringent measures. Ecclesiastical persecution of Peter Waldo (d. *ca.* 1215) and his followers, the Waldensians, for daring to preach without episcopal permission and to translate portions of Scripture into the vernacular, began late in the twelfth century and was confirmed by a synod at Toulouse in 1229 and another at Tarragona in 1234. The first of these synods forbade the laity, and the second the clergy, to possess the Bible in the vernacular under pain of excommunication. Through these and other measures the Church clung tenaciously to the symbol of its universal dominion, the sacrosanct Latin of the Vulgate, the liturgy, and canon law.

In opposition to this universality was the growing use of the vernacular tongues throughout Europe, in the home, in the market place, and in social intercourse. That the opposition to Latin was quite unguided and even perhaps unconscious did not in the least detract from its vigor. By the end of the twelfth century there was a considerable literature in French, Spanish, and German, and in the next century the mass of widely disseminated poetry, drama, history, and devotional writing in these languages and in Italian, the West Slavic tongues (Czech and Polish), and Hungarian was imposing. A vernacular language is far removed from any idea of universality. It is something local, intimate, and restrictive. Use of the vernacular sets off the user from those who do not know it and groups together those who do. The language and the nation march together.

France may be the best example of growth in the consciousness of national "otherness," but it is not difficult to trace the same development in other lands. However torn and divided the Spanish peninsula may have been, the growth of a Spanish spirit ran parallel with unification and was accurately reflected in the native literature of Spain. Germany had the Empire, which, though it did not unite all Germans, nevertheless allowed their feeling of uniqueness to grow. The Western Slavs, the Poles and the Czechs, had a long history of anti-German sentiment, voiced in their native tongues. To them the Germans were *niemcy,* the "mute," inferior beings because they could not speak the Slavic tongue. Nationalism, bound to the vernacular speech, was winning its battle against the universal language of the universal Church. The issues of this battle came to their sharpest focus in the struggle between the Papacy, headed by an astute, aggressive, and determined pope, Boniface VIII (1294–1303), and France, under the leadership of an equally determined king, Philip IV (the Fair, 1285–1314), aided and supported by ministers who shared his beliefs in national sovereignty and by a nobility and a people who responded to an appeal to their French national sentiment. The conflict is so typical and so important that its background and course will be traced (pp. 37–42, 53–55) in some detail.

Popes of the Later Middle Ages

AS AN organized force, the Christian Church in the West reached the zenith of its power under Pope Innocent III (1198–1216). Motivated by ideals of papal power and responsibility, Innocent easily disciplined the kings of England and France, named or deposed three Holy Roman emperors, and took most of Italy under his personal care. His activities reached far beyond the sphere of secular politics. Himself a brilliant canon lawyer, he made many decisions that were taken over intact into the body of canon law, by means of which the Church encompassed all human life. His interest in doctrine culminated in the Fourth Lateran Council of 1215, one of the monuments of ecclesiastical order, which was completely his work in organization and decisions. In large measure, the glory and power of the Church in the thirteenth century, the Age of Faith, were the result of the extension and realization of the ideals and methods of Innocent III.

The Church was fortunate in this century in having a number of other popes of extraordinary ability and energy. Gregory IX (1227–41), a nephew of Innocent III, was almost his uncle's equal in intellect, energy, and purposefulness. Much of his pontificate was devoted to the struggle with Emperor Frederick II (1212–50), the organization of a Crusade to retake Jerusalem from the infidel Saracens, the support of the mendicant orders, and the organization of the papal Inquisition. Innocent IV (1243–54) gave much attention to the Crusade, the addition of his collection of decretals to the body of canon law, the uprooting of heresy, and missionary activity among the Tartars and in the Far East; but he was fully as determined as his predecessors to crush the recalcitrant and slippery Frederick. He called a council—the Thirteenth General or Ecumenical Council—which met at Lyons in 1245 and declared the Emperor deposed. On the death of Frederick in 1250, Innocent could regard the battle as won. The Papacy had thus attained one of its goals: it had subjected the Empire to its will. But the alliance with France, formed when Innocent IV asked Charles of Anjou to subdue the heirs of Frederick in exchange for the rule of the kingdom of Sicily, was to cause later popes much embarrassment and affect profoundly the position of the Church in Europe.

After the death of Innocent IV, there followed four decades of short pontificates. Although some of the popes were able and well-intentioned, the Church made no great gain in these years, for which the Papacy was primarily responsible. Its immersion in petty Italian politics, the flagrant nepotism of many of the popes and cardinals, the growth of the power of the Inquisition, the subservience of the papal *curia* to France, the growing cynicism of large sections of the clergy in the discharge of their religious duties, the continued failure of the crusading idea, which the Papacy supported, to bring anything but grief and severe economic demands—all these and more combined to lower the prestige of the Papacy. Yet at least some of the prestige of the Church lost by the Papacy in Italy was being rewon in the outer reaches of Christendom, where these same decades are marked by countless high and devout ventures of true religious fervor, and the faith delivered to the saints was being nobly lived and eloquently preached in village and hamlet, on the byways and passes, by monk and friar, priest and bishop. Christianity was being taken seriously by numberless individuals, and the century is quite rightly known as the Age of Faith.

The last of the rather inconsequential popes of the latter half of the thirteenth century was Celestine V, elected in 1294, largely because the Sacred College, which then consisted of twelve cardinals, was deadlocked on the issue of a pro-French or a pro-Italian policy. Despite public dissatisfaction with the delay, twenty-two months went by before the cardinals were able to agree on a successor to the late Franciscan Pope, Nicholas IV (1288–92). The final choice, although unanimous, was fully as unfortunate as the vacancy had been. Peter del Morrone, a saintly and widely revered hermit monk from the mountain country of the Abruzzi, had founded, about 1258, the order of Benedictine hermits later called Celestines, after his pontifical name, Celestine V. He was not a cardinal and had had no administrative experience. His incapacity for administrative and political guidance of the vast papal machinery made the cardinals regret their choice almost immediately. Charles II, the Angevin king of Naples (1285–1309), dominated and used the Pope for his own purposes in southern Italy. Celestine was as unhappy in his high office as the cardinals were with his performance; and on December 13, 1294, he finally abdicated to return to his beloved asceticism. Dante condemns him as the Pope who "through base cowardice made the great refusal."

Boniface VIII and Philip the Fair of France

IT HAS been suggested, although not proved, that one of the most positive of the cardinals, Benedict Gaetani, was in some way especially responsible for Celestine's almost unprecedented renunciation of the papal tiara. Gaetani was elected pope eleven days later and took the name of Boniface VIII. In his first pronouncements he emphasized his hope and desire that Christendom should find peace. But his nine-year pontificate was among the most stormy and catastrophic in the history of the Papacy.

Boniface was an excellently trained canon lawyer. Both before and after becoming a cardinal in 1281, he had been active in papal policy-making and had been sent as papal envoy to the Emperor and the kings of Sicily, England, and France, as well as to many Italian cities. Successive popes had trusted him and rewarded him with many benefices in Italy, France, and England; his fellow cardinals had respected him. He had indeed grown old in the service of the *curia;* he may have been more than seventy when he became pope in 1294. With age, Boniface had taken on an arrogance and an irascibility that, along with his sharp tongue, were ill calculated to smooth the path of any delicate negotiations with a determined or powerful opponent.

The Pope's first pressing task was to bring some order out of the addled confusion Celestine had left. This he did with firmness and dispatch. He knew every detail of curial procedure, and soon the machinery was again functioning smoothly. He then became involved in a number of critical problems, among them an acrimonious struggle with the powerful Roman family of Colonna, sharp disputes with many cities and rulers in all parts of Italy from Naples to Lombardy, and an unsuccessful attempt to obtain from Edward I of England a confirmation of King John's feudal homage for the kingdom of Scotland. Boniface filled the coffers of the *curia* with the money brought by pilgrims to Rome during the jubilee of 1300. With dubious success, he made extensive demands on kings and princes in outlying Denmark, Poland, and Hungary to submit their thrones to him and repeated the ancient papal claims to control of the Empire, meeting the envoys of the Emperor Albert, seated on his pontifical throne, sword in hand, with the words: "I, I am the Emperor." But the most spectacular, and for the Papacy the most disastrous, aspect of Boniface's pontificate was his bitter controversy with Philip IV (the Fair, 1285–1314) of France over the king's right to levy taxes upon the French clergy.

Philip was at war with Edward I of England, and needed money. He claimed from the clergy of France a levy of a tenth of their annual income to support his military effort. The clergy immediately complained to Boniface, and on February 24, 1296, the Pope issued the bull *Clericis laicos,* which declared that the state was unequivocally subject to the Holy See and that no secular power or prince had any jurisdiction over the property or persons of the Church. Any violation of this law was punishable by excommunication. The bull was couched in general terms, and Edward was affected as much as Philip. Edward, in fact, had forced the English clergy to grant him a fifth of their annual income by threatening to seize all their lands and manors, over which his feudal rights were indisputable, and to imprison any ecclesiastic who resisted. In his stand the king had the complete support of the English laity. Boniface backed down. In France, however, the conflict was not so easily decided. Philip answered the *Clericis laicos* by forbidding the entry into France of any foreigners, meaning papal envoys and collectors as well as Englishmen. He then forbade the exportation of gold or silver or any military provisions, thus cutting off the Papacy's supply of these goods from its most substantial contributor. Boniface, wounded in a sensitive spot, replied in somewhat conciliatory tones in the bull *Ineffabilis amor* (September 25, 1296), saying that he was not forbidding the French clergy to contribute to the defense of the realm; he wanted only to have his prerogatives recognized. In the next few months he made further efforts to mollify Philip, ordering the French clergy to pay the tenth into the royal treasury. But Philip, relying upon experts in the law, stated his position in an anonymous pamphlet, *Antequam essent clerici,* published in the autumn of 1296. In this pamphlet, the theory is clearly set forth that the rule of the secular prince antedates any clerical claims to control the laity; on the contrary, the clergy must be obedient to lay rulers in all temporal matters. "The clergy," the pamphlet says, "like the laity, form a part of the state, and whoever refuses to aid the latter is a useless member."

Although the king's position seemed irreconcilable with papal theory, Boniface, in difficulties with the stubborn Colonna in Rome and the Campagna, moved further in the direction of appeasement. In the bull *Etsi in statu* (July 31, 1297), he went so far as to make a formal disavowal of the claims set forth in the *Clericis laicos*. But Philip did not respond to this overture. Annoyed by what he regarded as interference in the conduct of his foreign relations by the Pope, who in 1298 had declared a truce between Edward of England and Philip, the French king in 1299 welcomed at his court members of the Colonna family who had been driven out of Rome by Boniface.

Victorious in his pursuit and expulsion from Rome of the Colonna family, Boniface prepared a glorious jubilee in 1300. The jubilee was a huge success. The attractions of the Eternal City, heightened by generous indulgences, brought hundreds of thousands of eager pilgrims from all over Europe. Boniface was gratified by this evidence of the loyalty of the faithful and also by the replenishment of the depleted papal coffers, for the withdrawal of French financial support during the previous four years had been a serious blow to the papal budget. The chroniclers tell us that the contributions of the pilgrims

Pope Boniface VIII, by Arnolfo di Lapo (sometimes attributed to Andrea Pisano), in the Grotte Nuove, Vatican Basilica [ALINARI].

during the jubilee were so great that two servants were kept busy day and night with large rakes gathering in the coins before the altar of St. Peter's.

It was probably in this year that Philip received "A short summary . . . of the shortening of the wars of the Kingdom of the Franks" (*Summaria brevis*), well calculated to confirm him in his independent policy toward the Papacy. The author, Pierre Dubois, was a lawyer "of royal causes" at Coutances in Normandy and proctor of the university in that city. He was thus a minor official not necessarily in favor at court. But he urged the king to regard himself as the principal Christian power. This was the same doctrine that Philip's own legal advisers had been expounding, and Dubois' work can only have confirmed the king in his course. On the other side, Boniface, relying upon canon law and the teaching and actions of Gregory VII and Innocent III, was further encouraged in his course by the success of the jubilee and his victory over the Colonna. Between two such convinced opponents, the universal Church and the national state, only a battle to the death could be expected.

There was quiet during most of the year 1300, but the conflict broke out again late in 1301, when Boniface, having indisputable evidence that Philip was keeping the incomes of vacant bishoprics, abbacies, and benefices of other churches not covered by specific papal permission, sent Bernard de Saisset, bishop of Panniers in Languedoc, to protest and negotiate with the king. Bernard was known at Philip's court, where his open opposition to the king had made him quite unpopular. Boniface's choice, therefore, was unfortunate, for it exacerbated the already bitter distrust and antipathy on both sides. On July 13, 1301, friends of Philip took Bernard into custody, and three months later serious charges were brought against him before the king. It must be said in Philip's defense that, although he disliked Bernard intensely, and for good reason, he treated him with formal correctness, and after a time allowed him to return to Rome. But Boniface, feeling his strength, was unrelenting. On December 4, 1301, he withdrew all previous concessions he had made to Philip. The next day he issued the bull *Ausculta fili,* in which he claimed supremacy over kings and empires, warning Philip: "Let no one persuade you, my dear son, that you have no superior on this earth and that you are not subject to the supreme head of the ecclesiastical hierarchy." This bull was read to the king on February 10, 1302. Philip's entourage was enraged at the assertion that their king was not his own master. When it became apparent that the council of French clergy which Boniface had called for November 1, 1302, in Rome was intended to pronounce Philip's guilt and perhaps even to depose him, Philip countered by calling on the three estates of France, the clergy, the nobility, and representatives of the bourgeoisie, to meet on April 10, 1302.

This historic assembly, the first meeting in France of all three estates, later called the Estates General, provided a platform from which one of the king's advisers, Chancellor Pierre Flote, made an eloquent appeal to French national feeling. Flote presented to the assembly what he asserted was a bull from Boniface, *Deum time,* now recognized as a falsification worked out in the chancery of the king. This "bull" was a much stronger and more brutal attack on Philip than the real papal bull, *Ausculta fili,* strong as that was.

Philip's reply to the *Deum time* was then circulated. Its intent and tenor may be gathered from the opening sentences: "Philip, by the grace of God, King of the Franks, to Boniface, who calls himself Pope, little or no greeting. Let your very great fatuity know that we do not submit to anyone in temporal things; that the collation of benefices and vacant prebends belongs to us by right of our crown." The war of invective, propaganda, and partial truth got hotter. The estates stood by the king enthusiastically. French national feeling was aroused.

At the synod in Rome that autumn, Boniface presented the bull *Unam sanctam,* which stated categorically the doctrine of papal supremacy over every lay ruler and anathematized all who did not accept that doctrine. Gregory VII and Innocent III may have thought in such terms, but, in spite of all their power, they never dared or thought it wise to express such thought unequivocally. This momentous bull begins:

We are compelled to believe and hold, and we do firmly believe and quite simply confess that there is one holy catholic and apostolic church, outside of which there is no salvation or remission of sins . . . there is of this one and unique church one body, one head, not two as if it were a monstrosity, and that head is Christ, and Peter the vicar of Christ, and the successor of Peter. . . . In his power, as we are taught by the words of the gospel, there are two swords, the spiritual and the temporal. . . . Either one of these swords is in the power of the church. . . . The spiritual is in the hand of the priest, the material in the hands of kings and soldiers, but to be used at the nod and sufferance of the priest. . . . We declare that it is absolutely a necessity of salvation that every human creature be subject to the Roman pontiff.

Upon receipt of this uncompromising declaration of papal policy and the theory of universal dominion, the king sent pairs of speakers over the country to present the case for French independence from the profligate Italian Papacy to the people of his kingdom. It was an extremely clever propaganda appeal to French national sentiment; and it was a very effective one, for the response was uniformly favorable to the French king. Measure quickly followed countermeasure. The Pope declared (April 13, 1303) that Philip had rendered himself subject to excommunication. Philip had an assembly of dignitaries, civil and ecclesiastical, lay twenty-nine serious if hardly convincing charges against Boniface. William of Nogaret, who had become the king's chief adviser after the death of Pierre Flote, laid plans, with the help of the Colonna, experts in Italian intrigue, to bring the Pope from Rome to Lyons and try him there on these charges. It was known to the king's friends that Boniface had prepared a bull of excommunication and deposition of Philip, to be published on September 8, 1303. On September 7 Nogaret and Sciarra Colonna, with a troop of knights, rode into Anagni, the Pope's summer residence. They stormed the doors of the papal palace and faced the old Pope, fully robed on his throne, with threats and abuse. Boniface was dignified and firm, and in the presence of his courageous and impressive bearing Nogaret realized that he could not carry out his plan to take the Pope all the way to France. Indeed, if Nogaret had done Boniface any bodily violence it is probable that he would not have got out of Anagni alive. As it was, on September 9 the citizenry of Anagni raised such a commotion around the palace on behalf of Boniface that Nogaret and Sciarra Colonna fled. But the shock of the indignity was fatal to Boniface. He died in Rome a month later, on October 11, 1303.

The incident at Anagni has come to be regarded as the end of an era for the Papacy. This hallowed institution of the Papacy, fresh from a glorious victory over the Empire after two centuries of struggle, had crumbled in the face of attack from a hitherto unnoticed force—the national state—and that in a short seven years. The captivity of the Papacy at Avignon (see Chapter 3) was the ultimate measure of the humiliation of the Papacy. These issues are vastly more important than the personalities of the principal protagonists, interesting as they are. The defeat of the Papacy cannot be blamed on Boniface's stubbornness, arrogance, tactlessness, pettiness, and rigid legalism, however he may have been guilty on all these scores. Nor can the victory of Philip be explained by his cleverness, the ability of his advisers, or the integrity of his policy. He was in fact vindictive, deceitful, and cynical. But he happened to represent a new force in European history, one that would brook no obstacle: the force of national sentiment. The men who supported and gave voice to this idea were a new tribe, the secular-minded *chevaliers du roi,* drawn from the lower and middle bourgeoisie. Their outlook on life was anticlerical, anti-ecclesiastical, this-worldly, and deeply rooted in their native soil.

The next few years were but an anticlimax to Anagni. With Rome in the control of the troops of Charles II, the Angevin ruler of Naples, the cardinals quickly elected as pope the irenic general of the Dominican Order, later canonized as Benedict XI (1303–04). The cardinals were unanimous in feeling that peace with the powerful French king was the most pressing need of the Papacy. To this end, Benedict canceled most of the decrees of Boniface against Philip and the Colonna and absolved all Philip's agents save Nogaret, at the same time preaching eloquently against the perpetrators of the crime of Anagni. He died after a pontificate of only eight months. His successor, elected after an interval of ten months, was the archbishop of Bordeaux, Bertrand de Got, who, as Pope Clement V (1305–14), was never to set foot in Italy. The Avignonese captivity of the Papacy had begun; the dominance of the national idea was established.

Secularism and the Rise of Towns

NEXT to the defeat of the Papacy by a nationally awakened France, the phenomenon of greatest importance in early fourteenth-century Europe was the irresistible upsurge of the towns and the bourgeois spirit, taking the place of feudal society and economics, then in a late stage of decomposition. From the point of view of subsequent history, the growth of the towns is perhaps even more important than the capture of the Papacy. For out of the towns came the bourgeois spirit, and the bourgeois spirit was predominantly secular. In increasing measure, secularism is the dominant characteristic of the modern age, with the beginnings of which we are here primarily concerned.

Like most important developments in human history, the appearance of the urban bourgeoisie can be traced over several centuries, but certainly by about

1300 future trends were clear and a general secularization of life and thought in Europe seemed to be well advanced. Both the Church and feudal society throve in an agrarian culture. The great spokesman of Church doctrine, St. Thomas Aquinas, regarded the city as basically evil and the people on the land as by nature better and more moral. In the thirteenth century, adherents of the Papacy had made much of the doctrine of the fullness of power (*plenitudo potestatis*) as a support for the Church's claims to absolute control over the whole of society, secular and religious, civil and ecclesiastical. The mere fact that this polemic took place indicated that the Church had sensed the growing tendency among the people away from ecclesiastical authority in secular matters and toward a concept of the separate sovereignties of convenient secular organisms.

The town movement spread throughout Italy earlier than elsewhere. The decline of Islam as the ruler of the Mediterranean was first noticeable in Italy, and Italian merchants took the lead in developing techniques of manufacture and exchange and in cultivating new markets for their wares. Italy was dotted with despotisms and cities that, even in the twelfth century and to an increasing extent in the thirteenth, had claimed and for long periods exercised full or almost full sovereignty. They had made war, joined and left leagues, made and unmade their own laws, elected their own magistrates and judges, levied their own taxes, coined money, and in some cases actually chosen their own bishops and clergy. This was heady wine. The appetite grew with its use. The battles between the Papacy and the Empire in Italy frequently flowed around and over these urban centers, but the cities never lost for long the control of their own affairs. Emperors and popes, prudently and realistically accepting the facts, grew accustomed to leaving these cities strictly alone. Bartolus of Saxoferrato, a great Italian legist and political analyst of the fourteenth century, spoke of these cities as "entities recognizing no superior" (*universitates superiorem non recognoscentes*). Their predominant feature, apart from their independence of the Church, as well as of any other higher authority, was their secularism. They were not necessarily antireligious, although they were frequently anti-Church, but they existed primarily for secular purposes—for security, trade, commerce, and profit.

An antipathy to ecclesiastical suzerainty and control was thus characteristic of the Italian cities and republics. Their location near the seat of the Papacy, their ever present potential antagonist, obliged them to adjust themselves to the fact of that antagonism. But elsewhere in Europe the situation was different, and the town spirit was correspondingly different from that in Italy. In the rest of Europe the enemies of urban success were not primarily the Papacy or the Church.

The Romans had built military towns at strategic points in Spain, ancient Gaul, England, and along the Rhine and Danube rivers. Many of these well-placed *castra* continued to be inhabited in the fifth to the eighth centuries, though by a relatively small population. In Gaul and along the Rhine, there were also settlements that were somewhat more than rural villages, probable survivals from the ancient Roman *latifundia,* or large estates. But these seemed to lose their population in the early feudal era, from the eighth to the tenth centuries. The towns that began to spring up all over Europe from the eleventh to the fifteenth centuries had little or nothing to do with these earlier foundations, even when located on the same sites. The great upsurge of population of the tenth and eleventh centuries, amplified by the dislocation of individuals and groups during the Crusades, resulted in an increased demand for goods and services and created an atmosphere of hope and adventure. This exciting atmosphere was at the root of the phenomenon of rapid urbanization.

Most towns grew up at fords on the principal rivers, at key crossroads and natural harbors, around castles on easily defended hills and mountains, and around ecclesiastical or industrial centers. The coasts of southern France and the many rivers in the area north of Paris were especially favorable to the growth of towns, which began there in the tenth century. Some French and English towns developed around old Roman *castra*. In the Holy Roman Empire north of the Alps some 2500 towns were founded between the eleventh and the fifteenth centuries, many of them around episcopal centers or alongside monastic establishments. Beginning in the thirteenth century, German colonization eastward founded cities in Poland and Bohemia under laws formulated by Magdeburg and, by reason of their adaptability, widely copied in northern Europe. The Polish and Czech kings at first favored this colonization which brought commerce and the commercial classes to their kingdoms. The anti-German reaction was slow in developing.

Once the towns became established, expansion by clearly definable steps continued for centuries. At the beginning of the town period, approximately in the tenth and eleventh centuries, probably less than 5 per cent of the population of Europe dwelt in towns. Three centuries later this proportion had grown to 20 per cent. In addition to the vast increase in the number of towns—there were perhaps ten times as many in the fourteenth century as in the two previous centuries—many of the established cities doubled or trebled in population, and consequently in size. The map of a typical German city, Munich, shows the extent and tempo of this expansion. Although most of these commercial centers built their last walls before 1300, their growth continued after that time. The cities usually controlled an area of a league outside their walls, so that citizens could live in the faubourgs (from *forisburgum,* outside the castle [*Burg* in German]) of the city and yet do business within the walls and enjoy the rights of protection and share in their own government. Some medieval cities, favorably situated, grew to considerable size, but exaggerated estimates of their populations have been made. In 1450 Nürnberg had fewer than 25,000 inhabitants, Frankfurt-on-the-Main about 9000. Cologne was the largest city in Germany, with a population of 52,000. Ypres in Flanders in 1430 had about 11,000, Basel around 8000. Brussels and Liége were larger, about 20,000 and 30,000, respectively. Ghent and Bruges, among the largest cities of northern Europe, at the same period probably counted around 50,000 and 40,000 population, respectively. Florence's population has been estimated at about 75,000, while Venice in the same period probably contained between 90,000 and 100,000 inhabitants.

In their early stages the towns were usually controlled by the local feudal lord (*seigneur*) or churchman whose territory bordered or surrounded the

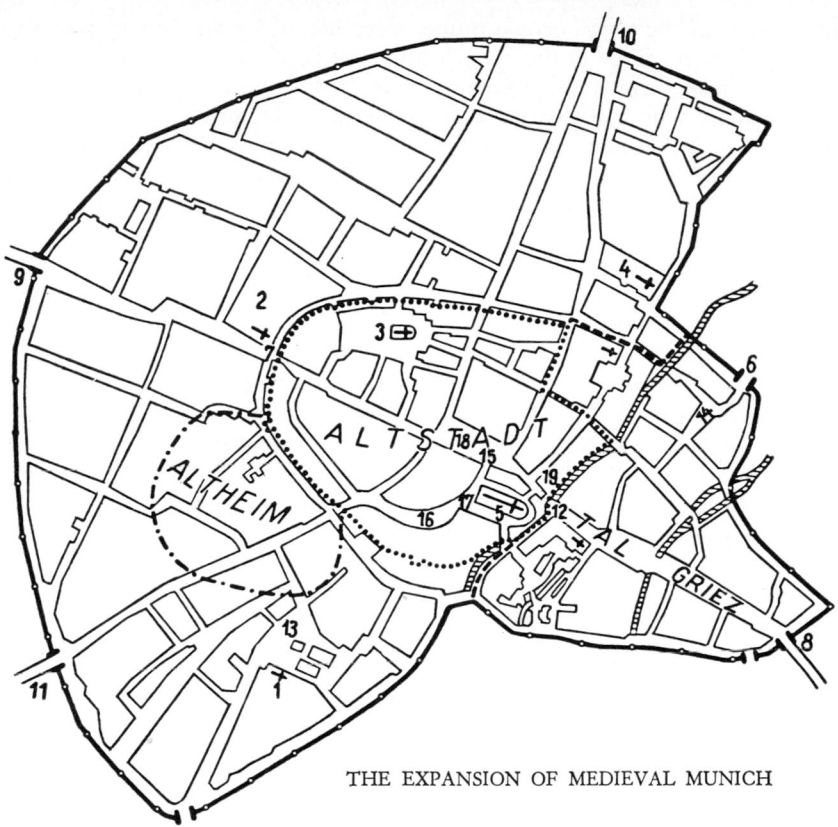

THE EXPANSION OF MEDIEVAL MUNICH

Founded by Heinrich der Löwe (Henry the Lion) in 1158. • • • wall of 1164; — — wall added *ca.* 1255 to include the sections of Tal and Griez; • — the wall around the Altheim section; —○— the great wall, begun *ca.* 1310.

1 Monastery in the meadow *(Angerkloster)* dedicated to St. Clara and Jacob's Church. 2 Augustinian monastery. 3 Church of Our Lady. 4 Franciscan monastery. 5 St. Peter's Church. 6 Grakkow gate. 7 Kaufinger gate. 8 Lower gate *(Niederes Tor)*. 9 Upper gate *(Oberes Tor)*. 10 Schwabinger gate. 11 Sendlinger gate. 12 Talburg gate. 13 Fairground *(Dultplatz)*. 14 Graggenau. 15 Grain market. 16 Cattle market. 17 Horse market. 18 Hall *(Dinghaus)*. 19 Town Hall.

Medieval Munich, from *Die deutsche Stadt im Mittelalter,* by Hans Planitz, Böhlau-Verlag; Graz-Köln, 1954.

town or by the monarch (see Chapter 9). But the invariable goal of the townsmen was independence from any immediate outside control, save perhaps a formal loyalty to the monarch, who was generally remote and therefore less likely to exert annoying pressure and make frequent demands than a noble whose proximity made daily contact and some friction inevitable. The townsmen wanted the right to their own courts, freedom from capricious tax levies by the local lord, and, as symbols of autonomy, a bell and belfry, a seal, a wall and gates they could close, and a town hall. Most of all they wanted a charter, or agreement with the lord or monarch, acknowledging their rights.

The citizens of the town, or commune, were bound by an oath of mutual defense and loyalty. Some of the French towns were known as *communes jurées;* the citizens who formed the governing body of the commune being called *jurés* —that is, those who had sworn (*jurer,* to swear) such an oath. From this oath, called an *Eid* in German, came the term *Eidgenossenschaft* (oath community) by which the German city dweller identified his peculiar status.

Since the cities were primarily commercial and industrial organizations, their governing bodies were usually selected from among the leading businessmen. In Italy the members of the magistracy were not uncommonly chosen from wards or quarters of the city, but it was more usual for the councils, by whatever name they went, to consist of representatives of the dominant merchant guilds. Only later, after this limited representation had given rise to civil strife in the cities, were the craft guilds permitted any direct representation. The council usually chose its presiding officer (there were several), sometimes a mayor, called a *magister civium,* or in Germany a *Bürgermeister.* The mayor represented the city on ceremonial occasions, spoke for it in its relations with other cities and sovereignties, and served as presiding judge when the council acted as a judicial body.

While in Germany and Italy the city officials were usually chosen by the burghers, either directly or through the guild organization, towns in France and the Lowlands frequently had the office of *échevin* (*scabinus*), which originated in the days of Charlemagne. The *échevin* apparently represented the law of the sovereign or the state, quite separate from the autonomy granted the town in its charter. Very rarely do we hear of a French or Lowlands city gaining the express right to choose its own *échevin;* usually he was named by the king or the ruling prince. This feature, indicating the determined retention of royal sovereignty over the chartered city, is one of the structural differences between the cities of France and the Lowlands and those of Germany. In the Holy Roman Empire north of the Alps, the sovereigns of the Middle Ages were not strong enough to maintain their sovereignty in the face of the persistent demands of the cities. The imperial cities (*Reichsstädte*) won almost complete independence, whereas the cities to the west (England included) were never able to obtain more than a partial and easily revoked measure of self-government. The fact is that the western kingdoms were farther advanced along the path to unification and centralized state structure. In the two areas in which the cities achieved the greatest liberty in the later Middle Ages, Italy and Germany, national unification came centuries later than in France, England, and Spain, where the prerogatives of royal power were clung to more tenaciously and more successfully. The height of this communal movement in France was in the first half of the thirteenth century, somewhat later than in Germany, but its decline began almost immediately thereafter. It is almost impossible to find a grant of a new commune in France after 1215, whereas hundreds of new imperial or royal charters can be found in Germany after that date. By about 1300 the communal movement had perceptibly weakened in France, while in Germany it continued to gain strength and momentum.

By 1300 a number of French kings, from Philip II (Augustus, 1180–1223) to Philip (IV) the Fair, had followed a consistent policy of unification and centralization. They had no desire to promote the existence of a potential rival, and they were quite aware of the danger inherent in leagues, such as those which the German cities had formed—the League of the Rhenish Cities, the Swabian League, and the more widely known Hanseatic League (see Chapters 6 and 9). These leagues in Germany were strong enough to defy electors, the Church, kings, and emperors. In France no leagues of cities were permitted. Indeed, cities were disciplined and deprived of their privileges for mistreatment of royal officials or for rising against episcopal authority. Philip Augustus, to punish the city of Étampes, simply declared in 1199: "We have herewith obliterated the commune and have granted to the churches and knights that there will never again be a commune at Étampes." A century later, in 1296, Philip the Fair punished the city of Laon for an uprising in somewhat more elaborate terms: "We find them guilty . . . and take from them the characters and privileges . . . the clock, the seal, the common archive, and the other things that belong to a commune . . . absolutely and forever." In Germany no emperor dared to discipline any city. He was more likely to court the favor of the bourgeoisie and, when in need of money, to sell the cities even greater privileges than they already had.

This sharp difference between the course of urban development in France and in Germany helps to explain much of the later political history of the two countries. France was tending toward centralization. In Germany a spirit of bourgeois separatism in opposition to the nominal central authority was not only allowed to exist but even encouraged. Late in the fourteenth century the greater nobility in Germany began to find the leagues of cities too powerful and, by various pressures, even by war, reduced them to submission. Yet it must be pointed out that it was not imperial but princely action against the independence of the cities that broke the power of the leagues.

In the Lowlands, where the bourgeois spirit was strong, there were three parties to the development of towns: the burghers, interested in manufacturing and trade and eager to have complete freedom from interference; the ecclesiastical authority, the bishop or his representative, who had ancient proprietary and feudal rights in the principal towns; and the feudal prince. The last named might be, for example, the count of Flanders, the count of Hainault, or the duke of Brabant, or he might be the king of France, who from time to time revived his interest in old claims to border areas. The struggle for supremacy among these three forces was not decided in the Middle Ages but intermittently produced high tension and open warfare for several centuries thereafter.

In Spain the development of the urban movement was affected in large measure by the nature of the *reconquista,* the gradual recovery of Christian sovereignty from the Moors. The Christian inhabitants of cities under Moorish control who often formed a majority of the population were cut off from contact with fellow Christians beyond the city borders and had to learn to live by themselves, developing a spirit of self-sufficiency. But as the Christian kingdoms regained territory from the Moors, the cities, again under royal sovereignty, demanded and received charters from the kings of Aragon and Castile. Almost without exception, the kings insisted on placing in the towns royal officials under various titles—the *alcalde del rey* (the royal mayor), the *adelantado* (royal deputy), or the *merino mayor*—men trained in royal law and faithful to the royal cause. In some respects this group of officials was similar in spirit and function to the *chevaliers du roi* of Philip the Fair of France, who had a vision of a unified state based on law and efficiency. But there is an important distinction. The primary enemy of French royal strength at the beginning of the fourteenth century was the Roman Papacy; in Spain the enemy of union at this time was not an outside power but the inertia of Spanish separatism, brought on by centuries of division and subjection to Moorish conquest. The leagues of Spanish cities, known as *hermandades,* were not comparable to the German leagues, for they restricted themselves to mutual defense against local disorders and brigandage on the roads. There was no thought of organized opposition to royal authority. Thus the Spanish tendency toward national centralization at the level of the bourgeoisie was, as in France and England, well advanced by the fourteenth century, although modified by the circumstances of dynastic and political development. The Spanish town had its liberties, but it remained unquestionably a part of the kingdom, subject to the royal administration and royal authority.

In its origins, the town movement had made much of the concept of *communitas,* a common aim, and the idea that every citizen should "treat his neighbor as his brother." Yet the towns were hardly models of peace and mutual love and forbearance. The very vigor of the movement, its dynamic urge toward wealth and power, created bustle and tension, rivalry and bitter competition. The strong and the weak, the fast and the slow, soon found their natural places. The results were sharp cleavages among the patriciate, or the rich burghers who were in commerce on a grand scale, concerned mostly with export and international trade; the craftsmen who owned their little businesses and had a local clientele; and the skilled or unskilled day laborers, who were at the mercy of their employers for their daily bread. The fourteenth and fifteenth centuries are full of accounts of friction among these classes. We shall have occasion to return to that story (see Chapter 4). At this point it is necessary only to point out that almost all the social and economic manifestations of our own times are implicit in the rise and early vicissitudes of the town. Administration, jurisdiction, the drive for a strong central government, the inequities of chance and birth, the cost in human values of spirited competition, the sense of local pride, the frequent accesses of civic unity in the face of an outside threat, and all the pains of civic growth—these experiences the towns and citizenry of the later Middle Ages tasted to the full.

The basic motives behind the growth of the cities everywhere in Europe remained secular. The merchant intent upon profit in this world was seldom equally intent upon laying up treasure in heaven. The hold of the Church upon his thoughts and interests was bound to be weak. Commercial profit brought with it prestige and other trappings of worldly success with which the Church's ideal of the monastic life could not compete. Thus the secular ideal presented a threat to the Church which had to be combatted with every possible weapon. But to combat, one must understand; therefore the thirteenth century abounded in discussions of the essential nature of the secular state.

All this discussion, even when it favored the secular power, was based on the premises of Aristotle, whose works on ethics and political theory were widely read in the universities of that century. According to Aristotle and his commentators, the state was a natural outgrowth of the family which could take, for various reasons, any one of three forms: monarchy, autocracy, or timocracy. These forms, in turn, might degenerate, respectively, into tyranny, oligarchy, or democracy. Aristotle's emphasis was on the practical, natural, pragmatic aspects of the development. His great authority in these centuries made it almost impossible to reject his naturalistic premise. To explain it away by theological interpretation was hardly possible; the proofs for the natural origin of the state were too simple and evident. St. Thomas Aquinas wrote an elaborate treatise *On the Rule of Princes* (*De regimine principum*), which was left unfinished at his death in 1274, and completed by a pupil, Ptolemy of Lucca, about 1310. Giles of Rome (1285) and James of Viterbo (1300) dealt with society as a natural phenomenon, in their writing, even though they spoke of a "prince" instead of the state as a collective concept. One finds such expressions as "man is a social animal," "the community of the state," "the perfect society," which show clearly that they were discussing the problem of the organization of society on a broad base. These writers may all be said to favor ecclesiastical primacy, whereas Dante's *Monarchia* (*ca.* 1311) favors a secular solution. Yet to all these thinkers the civil organism originated in the natural order. They differed primarily on the auspices under which the perfect society could be best achieved, the Church or the civil secular organism.

This point of divergence was a burning issue in the early years of the fourteenth century. The Church instinctively and uncompromisingly opposed the secular concept, insisting that both secular and religious matters came within the bounds of ecclesiastical direction and control; the adherents of the secular view bitterly and aggressively fought against the claims of the ecclesiastical party. It is easy to identify the protagonists of the ecclesiastical concept: churchmen and scholar-clerics, convinced of the scriptural and canonical sanction of their cause. It is not so easy to determine from what group or class the spokesmen of the secular cause came, nor what was precisely the nature of their support among the population. Whatever may have been the roots of the ideas and the support it could count upon we can see quite readily that it was the secular cause that won out.

We have mentioned the sudden increase in population in the tenth and eleventh centuries and the corresponding upsurge in the spirit of trade and commerce, particularly in Italy, as a result of the weakening hold of the Moslems on the Mediterranean. The Crusades hastened these processes, so that by the end of the thirteenth century there had developed not only a well-articulated system of commercial interchange, with specialization in production, distribution and capital manipulation, banks and international credit, but also a recognizable commercial class. The social origins of this class throw light upon the decline of feudal society, which began in this same period.

The merchants and entrepreneurs came originally from among the footloose surplus thrown up by the rapid growth in population. Mostly from the land, they were men who naturally gravitated to the bustling urban centers in search of a better life. Some of these newcomers, more intrepid than others, saw possibilities of gain from taking products finished in a town to distant areas where such goods would command high prices. From modest and individual beginnings the natural development was toward more extensive and adventurous undertakings, until Europe was covered by a network of routes of commerce and exchange between the Baltic–North Sea area and the Mediterranean, from the plains of Poland to the marts of Cordova. The North had wool, furs, pitch, and herring; the East had spices, fine tapestries, and delicate metal work. An exchange was natural, welcomed by both parties, and profitable to the middlemen. Italy, midway between northern Europe and the Near East, was ideally situated to take full advantage of this growing trade. As a simple consequence, the commercial city, the commercial class, and the commercial or bourgeois spirit in the twelfth to fourteenth centuries were best exemplified in the Italian peninsula. This simple economic and social fact is of prime importance in any consideration of the unique social and cultural manifestation we call the Renaissance.

Yet the similar, though spectacular, changes that were taking place elsewhere in Europe should not be ignored. Wherever there was a favorable concourse of raw products, skilled workmen, and means of communication and transportation, commercial and industrial centers grew up. We shall have more to say about their economic developments in a later chapter (9), but it is necessary to emphasize here this tremendous growth in urban population and wealth in order to explain the rise of the bourgeois spirit and its inevitable penchant for the secular. When a society is daily and hourly immersed in competition for profit through the haggling of the market place, it is unrealistic to expect its members to entertain lofty spiritual ideas. Where the Church had offered salvation in the next world in return for self-denial, discomfort, poverty, humility, and absolute obedience, success on this new scene of adventure and activity offered a sort of salvation in this life, with comfort and joy thrown in. To human nature, now coming back into its own, the alternatives seemed weighted in favor of the secular, bourgeois ideal. Sermons by leading clerics of the time reflect to an unusual degree their anxiety lest the things of the Kingdom of God be forgotten or slighted. The lay spirit, an overweening concern for the successes of this world, the absorption in things of time and sense (*in hoc saeculo*)—what we call secularism—had begun to dominate the social and intellectual scene in Europe by the early fourteenth century. Any effort to stem the trend was foredoomed to failure.

SUGGESTIONS FOR FURTHER READING

BETTENSON, H., *Documents of the Christian Church*. New York, 1943
COULSON, H. H., *A Source Book for Medieval Economic History*. Milwaukee, 1936
COULTON, G. G., *Life in the Middle Ages*. 4 vols. in 1. New York, 1930
Peter Lombard and the Sacramental System, trans. E. Rogers. New York, 1917
MIRBT, C., *Quellen zur Geschichte des Papsttums und des römischen Katholizismus.* 1924
ROSS, J. B., and M. M. McLAUGHLIN, *Portable Medieval Reader*. New York, 1949

Boissonade, P., *Life and Work in Medieval Europe*. New York, 1927

Cambridge Economic History. 2 vols. Cambridge, 1941, 1952

Carlyle, R. W. and A. J., *History of Medieval Political Theory in the West*. 6 vols. London, 1903–36

Clarke, M. V., *The Medieval City State*. London, 1926

Coulton, G. G., *Five Centuries of Religion*. 4 vols. Cambridge, 1923–50

Coulton, G. G., *Social Life in Britain from the Conquest to the Reformation*. Cambridge, 1919

Lewis, E., *Medieval Political Ideas*. 2 vols. New York, 1954

Lopez, R. S., and I. W. Raymond, *Medieval Trade in the Mediterranean World*. New York, 1955

Mumford, L., *The Culture of Cities*. New York, 1938

Mundy, J. H., and P. Riesenburg, *The Medieval Town*. New York, 1958

Pirenne, H., *Belgian Democracy*. Manchester, 1915

Pirenne, H., *Medieval Cities*. Princeton, 1949

Schnürer, G., *Church and Culture in the Middle Ages*. Paterson, N.J., 1956

Smith, A. L., *Church and State in the Middle Ages*. Oxford, 1913

Thompson, J. W., *Economic and Social History of Europe in the Later Middle Ages*. New York, 1931

Ullman, W., *Medieval Papalism*. London, 1949

Wood-Legh, K. L., *Studies in Church Life in England under Edward III*. Cambridge, 1934

Below, G., *Der deutsche Staat des Mittelalters*. 1925

Below, G., *Territorium und Stadt*, 1923

de Lagarde, G., *La Naissance de l'esprit laïque au déclin du moyen age*. 6 vols. 1946

Ercole, F., *Dal Comune al principato*. 1929

Espinas, G., *Les Origines du capitalisme*. 4 vols. 1933–49

Lavedan, P., *Histoire de l'urbanisme*. 3 vols. 1926–52

Lestocquoy, J., *Les Villes de Flandre et d'Italie sous le gouvernement des patriciens*. 1952

Petit-Dutaillis, C., *Les Communes françaises*. 1947

Planitz, H., *Die deutsche Stadt im Mittelalter*. 1954

Rörig, F., *Die europäische Stadt im Mittelalter*. 1955

CHAPTER THREE

THE AGE OF AVIGNON
1305–78

T HE period from 1305 to 1378, during which the Papacy was either moving about in southern France or settled at Avignon, was one of the most eventful and significant in the whole history of the Church. It was not unprecedented for the pope and his *curia* to be absent from Rome. Indeed, the popes during the seventy years before the death of Benedict XI in 1304 had resided in some place other than Rome for an aggregate of more than half those years. Nor was it without precedent for a pope and his court to reside in French territory for a considerable period. Innocent IV, one of the ablest and strongest popes of the thirteenth century, was established at Lyons in France for all but a year of his eight-year papacy and for more than half his episcopate; he even held the thirteenth General Council of the Church Universal (1245) in Lyons. But the Papacy's stay in Avignon in the fourteenth century differed notably from earlier temporary absences from the city of St. Peter and St. Paul.

The seven popes who headed the Church during these seventy-odd years of "captivity" were all Frenchmen, as were most of the cardinals, yet this preponderance of French personnel at the top of the administrative ladder is not the only characteristic that sets the Avignonese era apart from the periods before and after it. The fourteenth century, as we have seen, was an age in which the old Rome-centered civilization was passing away in the mind of most of Christendom and a new world of individualistic, nationalistic, and secular interests and loyalties was being formed. The Papacy's absence from Rome for so long a time can only have contributed to the birth and early growth of this new world. Rome, despite its aura of the Caesars, the apostles, and the martyrs, could no longer be associated with the Papacy since the popes were not there. The Papacy became, at least in the opinion of the French, the English, and the Germans, a French institution and, as such, subject to suspicion and criticism on other than traditional religious grounds. Neither an England at war with France nor a Germany whose emperor (Louis IV) had been excommunicated by a French pope was likely to render the reverent obedience that the successor of St. Peter should properly have expected. Thus the separation of the Papacy from the ancient and hallowed center of Christendom precipitated a tendency to distinguish and divorce the Christian religion from the ancient Church and Rome. The ultimate result was that Christianity became national, individual, or both in the Protestant Reformation.

There were many conscientious and loyal churchmen of the fourteenth century, among them several of the Avignonese popes themselves, who sensed the tragic error of keeping the *curia* away from Rome. They may not have known how far reaching the ill effects of this separation could be, but their sound religious instincts told them it was wrong.

Clement V (1305–14)

AS WE have seen, the election of Bertrand de Got, who assumed the name of Clement V, took place only after ten months of deadlocked wrangling in the College of Cardinals (see p. 42). It was a victory for the pro-French party in the College. The Pope was crowned at Lyons in the presence of the kings of France and Aragon, the cardinals, and other notables. The influence of Philip IV on the new pope was soon evident in Clement's decision to remain in France, as well as in his creation of nine French cardinals out of ten at the first promotion. True, Clement was a sick man, unable to muster the physical stamina to resist the demands of so cool and tough a ruler as Philip. Against other opponents, the Pope showed occasional and laudable firmness. By training a jurist, his additions to the canon law, known as the Clementines, were both substantial and significant. On the other hand, he was most kind to his relatives: five of them were made cardinals and others received rich bishoprics.

Aside from the decision not to return to Rome, the most notable events of Clement's reign were his modification, under pressure from Philip, of the decrees of Boniface against the king and his aides, the suppression of the Order of the Templars, and the ecumenical Council of Vienne.

Philip was determined to erase from the record every trace of the actions of Boniface VIII against him and his advisers. He demanded that Clement not only withdraw all of Boniface's bulls against him but also that he try and condemn the dead Pope for heresy. Clement delayed as long as he could, but eventually he had to comply to a considerable degree with the king's demands. In 1306 he granted Philip permission to receive the tithe from ecclesiastical properties in France for five years, abrogated the bull *Clericis laicos,* and declared that there was no intention that France should suffer from the bull *Unam sanctam.* At the same time he restored the two Colonna cardinals to their places in the College of Cardinals. To Philip's demands that Boniface VIII, now dead four years, be tried, Clement replied that so delicate a matter could be handled only by a competent council, which Philip knew would take some years to arrange for. However, the Pope had to purchase the delay by promising to suppress the Templars, a quasi-military order founded in Jerusalem in 1119, with rich possessions in France. The charges, of all manner of heresy and vice, intended to justify the suppression of the order, were hardly credible. Some of the members of the order may have been as lax as the average French parish priest, but for the most part, the order maintained a high standard of discipline and behavior. With the decline of the crusading movement, the Templars' reason for existence had virtually disappeared. Their worst sin appears to have been their wealth and their financial genius; Philip needed money.

On October 13, 1307, on Philip's order, every Templar in the kingdom was suddenly arrested. The king asserted that he was thereby defending the true Christian faith, and he called upon the other rulers of Europe to join him in purging Christendom of this nefarious brood. He forced confessions from the leaders of the order and, when Clement protested, turned his expert corps of publicists and vilifiers upon the Pope. A papal commission appointed in August 1308 seemed to guarantee the legality of the trial, but the commission was made up of clerics who favored the king's cause. Yet Philip, wanting even faster action than this might have brought, arranged to have a provincial synod of French clergy called at Sens on May 11, 1310. The synod found fifty-four Templars guilty on all counts as charged. They were burned the next day. Five days later nine more were executed at Senlis. Elsewhere in Europe—in England, Germany, and Spain—the order was investigated but found innocent of the extreme charges.

In March 1309, Clement established himself and his *curia* in the pleasant city of Avignon on the Rhône, the property of the kingdom of Naples, surrounded by the Venaissin, a papal territory held in fief from the king of France. In March of the next year the trial of Boniface VIII for heresy, murder, and immorality began, with William of Nogaret, Philip's chancellor, in charge of the prosecution. As a counterpoise to the pressure under which Philip had put him, Clement had invited the newly elected Luxemburg emperor, Henry VII (1308–13), to go to Italy and attempt to bring order to that turmoiled land. The prestige of Henry's early successes enabled the Emperor to persuade Philip, at Clement's urging, to withdraw his demands for a trial of the dead Pope and permit the case of the Templars to be put in the hands of a council to meet in the fall.

The council finally met on October 6, 1311, at Vienne, on the Rhône twenty miles south of Lyons. It was in session, with long interruptions, for almost seven months. Clement told the council that there were three matters on the agenda: the case of the Templars, the Crusade, and the reformation of abuses in the Church. The last item, although urged by several prelates, received no real attention, and the crusading movement was everywhere moribund. But the case of the Templars was very much in every churchman's mind. The council would have wished to hear the Templars in their own defense, but Philip and Clement united to force the summary suppression of the order (March 22, 1312) and soon after transferred its possessions to the Order of the Hospitalers. The tragedy was not yet played out. The Grand Master, Jacques de Molay, and several other high officials of the order were tried, found guilty, and sentenced to life imprisonment. But Philip, not satisfied with the verdict, had de Molay and his next in command, Guy of Auvergne, master of Normandy, burned at the stake on March 18, 1314. The story was current that de Molay, the flames alight around his feet, summoned Clement and Philip to meet him within the year before the judgment seat of God. Whether or not they answered his call, Clement died a month later, and Philip five months later. Philip's conduct throughout this affair, as well as in the prosecution of

Palace of the Popes at Avignon [FRITZ HENLE, MONKMEYER].

the dead Boniface, can only be labeled vindictive, dishonorable, and deceitful. Further, there is no evidence that either he or the cause of French unity gained anything by the suppression of the order. Nor did Clement's conduct honor the best traditions of the papal office. Although occasionally astute, he was not of heroic stature. The nine years of the pontificate of Clement V were, for the Papacy, unhappy ones. The decision to remain in France and not return to Rome, the city of the martyrs and the seat of the Papal See, was in itself fateful. Beyond that the Pope, perhaps against his will, set precedents of submission to secular pressures, and allowed the affairs of the Church in Italy to fall into a disorder from which recovery was almost impossible.

John XXII (1316–34)

FOR more than two years after the death of Clement V, the twenty-three cardinals, split into three groups, French, Italian, and Gascon, were unable to decide upon his successor. It was again a French king, this time Philip V (1316–22), who forced the cardinals to make a decision, although he did not dictate the choice. The new pope, selected on August 7, 1316, was a Gascon, as Clement had been, Jacques Duese, from Cahors, who took the name of John XXII.

Already seventy-two years old, and in delicate health, John faced the formidable task of restoring the prestige of the Papacy, which Clement's subservience to the French king had greatly reduced. The papal treasury was also seriously depleted, for Clement had bequeathed a large part of the papal treasure to relatives as if it were his personal property. The long vacancy before the election had seriously impaired the efficiency of papal administration There was chaos in Italy, and in Asia Minor the threat of the Turks was becoming more serious. In the course of his eighteen-year pontificate John XXII was the center of some of the most bitter controversies in the history of the Church; he was also largely responsible for the elaboration of a papal administration and judicial and fiscal machinery so efficient that they have needed little basic modification to the present time. The major events of his reign were the dispute within the Franciscan Order, the conflict between the Papacy and the Wittelsbach Emperor Louis IV (Louis of Bavaria, 1314–47), the deterioration of papal rule in Italy, and John's descent into near-heresy. No less important were John's active participation in the systematization of the administrative procedure of the Papacy and in the revision of canon law and his patronage of letters and art.

The Franciscan Dispute

SINCE its foundation in 1216, the Franciscan Order (Friars Minor) had been faced with the agonizing problem of how to grow in numbers and influence without at the same time losing its primary aim of absolute and high-minded poverty. In 1279 Pope Nicholas III had attempted to solve the problem in the bull *Exiit qui seminat,* a compromise that protected the concept of poverty and yet assured the order of its continued existence in a "practical" world. The issue split the order into two groups, one commonly called the Spirituals, which favored a strict interpretation of the rule of St. Francis, the other called the Conventuals, which held that, though the individual friar could not own anything, the convent to which he belonged could possess property which the friar could use and enjoy. Pope Celestine V, himself an ascetic hermit monk, had favored the Spirituals and had given them the rule of his own order, the Celestines. Boniface VIII had revoked this arrangement, preferring a more lax interpretation of the Franciscan rule; yet he did not go so far as to legislate drastically against the Spirituals. By the time of the Council of Vienne (October 1311), there had been much bitter polemic within the order on both sides of the question of poverty. Added to this conflict was the growing acuteness of the dispute concerning the relation of the mendicant orders to the parish clergy. The latter protested that wandering clergy, hearing confessions, accepting alms, and giving absolution, were obstructing the ordinary work of the Church. The Franciscan problem was thus a live issue, reaching to the remotest parish of Europe.

Clement V had brought the matter before the Council of Vienne and issued a bull, *Exivi de Paradiso* (May 6, 1312), which favored the Spirituals, permitting the use of property only so far as absolutely necessary. But this solution was unsatisfactory to both sides, and John XXII had to face a problem which had grown in bitterness because of a long series of half-measures. His predisposition to see all problems administratively and "practically" made him favor the Conventuals against the Spirituals, whom he regarded as vain, obstinate, and unreasonable dreamers. In two bulls of December 10, 1317, he listed the errors of the Spirituals and deprived them of all convents under their control; he then turned more than a score of their leaders over to the Inquisition. Within the next year, fifty Spirituals (by then commonly called Fraticelli) * were burned as heretics in southern France, and in following years the number of martyrs reached many hundreds.

The resistance of the Spirituals to John was determined. By 1322, the whole order, in a chapter general at Perugia, formally reiterated the Spiritual concept of poverty, defending the doctrine of the poverty of Christ and His disciples, and denied the Pope's right to change the constitution of the order. John was furious at this denial of his supremacy. He promptly threw Bonagrazia of Bergamo, who had been delegated to carry the order's conclusions to the Pope, into prison and, on November 12, 1323, issued a bull, *Cum inter nonnullos,* in which he condemned the position of the Spirituals as heretical. In an effort to prevent the spread of Spiritual doctrines, John ordered William of Ockham, the English nominalist philosopher and an active Spiritual, to remain in Avignon. Most of the order formally submitted, but there was much grumbling, for Michael of Cesena, the general of the order, in 1325 publicly urged its members not to speak ill of the Pope. Sensing that the opposition had not been crushed, in June 1327 John ordered Cesena to come to Avignon. Once Cesena was there, the Pope, suspecting his loyalty, charged him with heresy and in a public hearing on April 9, 1328, angrily forbade him to leave. Seven weeks later (May 26, 1328), Cesena, accompanied by Bonagrazia, Ockham, and two other Spirituals, escaped from Avignon at night by boat. They reached Pisa on June 7, where they were warmly welcomed by officials of Emperor Louis IV. The cause of the Spiritual Franciscans thus became involved in the struggle between John XXII and the Emperor.

Pope John and the Empire

ON THE death of the Habsburg Emperor, Albert I, in 1308, Philip the Fair had urged the candidacy of his brother Charles of Valois. But the electors, fearful of French designs on Germany, elected a prince of minor significance, Henry of Luxemburg (Henry VII), on November 27, 1308. Pope Clement V, as we have seen, was pleased to have a counterpoise to the French king's embarrassing pressure upon him and encouraged Henry's somewhat romantic plans to unite Italy and be crowned in Rome. Yet he did not want Henry to

* It is, however, proper to distinguish between the two groups. Some Spiritual Franciscans had close sympathy and associations with Fraticelli throughout the fourteenth century, but many of them resented being identified with this essentially antiecclesiastical and separatist group.

be too successful, for the memory of a strong emperor in Italy, Frederick II, still lingered in papal circles. Thus, once Henry was in Italy, Clement supported Robert of Anjou, king of Naples, and was delighted when Henry met determined opposition from Florence and other Guelph cities. In the decretal *Pastoralis cura* Clement freed Robert from Henry's ban of deposition, by virtue of "the incontestable supremacy which the Holy See possesses over the Empire," a clear restatement of the position of Innocent III and Innocent IV. Clement's successor, John XXII, was to make telling use of this papal claim against Henry's successor, Emperor Louis IV.

On October 19, 1314, two electors of the Empire chose a Habsburg, Frederick the Handsome, duke of Austria, to succeed Henry VII. The next day, the remaining five electors elected Louis, duke of Bavaria, as Emperor (Louis IV). There were thus two Emperors and, on November 25, two simultaneous coronations, Louis' at Aachen (Aix-la-Chapelle) and Frederick's at Bonn. Since the Papal See was vacant at the time and remained so until the election of John XXII in August 1316, the new Pope, ascending the papal throne almost two years after the imperial elections, was faced with the problem of deciding which of the elected Emperors to recognize. Choosing to temporize, he recognized neither but ordered the two rivals to present their claims to him for decision. John's order was not obeyed, for the two were fighting a desultory war. In the autumn of 1322, Louis won a decisive battle at Mühldorf in Bavaria, with the substantial help of King John of Bohemia and Frederick of Hohenzollern, burgrave of Nürnberg (see Chapter 6). Louis was wisely lenient in victory, and the Habsburg cause quickly collapsed.

As victor and generally acknowledged choice of the German people, Louis asked Pope John for his approval. But John could not forget that most of Italy was in theory at least a part of the Empire, or that Louis' predecessor, Henry VII, had in fact ruled for a time much of the peninsula. A victorious and energetic emperor with Germany solidly behind him was a serious threat to papal domination in Italy. John therefore refused to accept Louis' interpretation of the battle of Mühldorf as decisive and in October 1323 ordered Louis to give up his rule within three months, to present himself at the *curia* at Avignon to have his case heard, and not to exercise any royal or imperial authority until the Pope gave his approval. In the meantime, John declared, the imperial throne was and had been vacant. He added that the choice of the electors of the Empire was not binding upon him. The tenor of Clement's bull *Pastoralis cura* was fortified and confirmed by this reiteration. To Louis' vigorous protest the Pope responded by excommunicating the Emperor (March 23, 1324). It is clear that John was using the disputed German election as a basis for weakening Louis so that he would not venture into Italy. No one paid much attention to John's fulminations; about all the Pope achieved at this stage of the conflict was to convince the Germans that he was in the French camp. Even most of the high German clergy remained friendly to Louis after the papal excommunication and interdict. John was thus unwittingly one of the principal unifiers of German national sentiment.

In March 1327, Louis set out for Italy, to receive the Iron Crown of Lombardy in Milan in May. He entered Rome on January 7, 1328. In his suite there were two scholars who had fled from the University of Paris in the spring of

1326 and joined Louis' court at Munich. Marsilio of Padua and John of Jandun were thenceforth identified with the cause of the secular state in its conflict with universal ecclesiastical claims. The book which they wrote jointly in 1324, entitled *Defensor pacis (Defender of the Peace)*, is one of the great documents in the history of Western thought on the subject of the state and its foundation in the will of the people.

At the coronation ceremony, and, in fact, throughout his rule in Italy, Louis gave the appearance of recognizing the key part played by the Roman people in imperial affairs. Yet Louis, a German, was quite aware of the essential validity of his election by German electors, and never for a moment gave support to any possible claim that the Roman *populus* had a voice in his election. It was, furthermore, obvious that the Pope had nothing to do with either Louis' election or the formal coronation. The representative of the Roman people who placed the crown on Louis' head was none other than Sciarra Colonna, that practiced and determined foe of papal supremacy, whom we have met at Anagni.

Three months later (April 18, 1328), in answer to John's proclamation of a crusade against him, Louis declared the Pope deposed as a heretic. A Franciscan monk, Peter de Corbara, was chosen by a committee of clergy and laity in Rome and invested by Louis as Pope, taking the name Nicholas V. There was obviously no ground for such an election, either in canon law or in valid tradition, and this part of Louis' Italian venture verges on the absurd, despite the fact that the anti-Pope received a surprising amount of support both in Rome and elsewhere in Italy. As his vicar in Rome, Louis appointed Marsilio of Padua. Marsilio may have derived some ironic amusement from his work, but the severity of his rule cooled the feeling of the Romans for the secular theories the Emperor seemed to be supporting. Louis finally thought it best to return to Germany, where he arrived in January 1330, having shed the anti-Pope Nicholas on the way. Nicholas made his peace with John and lived on in Avignon on a comfortable pension, doubtless much better off than he would have been as a Franciscan in Rome.

Louis took back with him to Munich Michael of Cesena, Bonagrazia of Bergamo, and William of Ockham, three of the Spiritual Franciscans who had escaped from Avignon in the spring of 1328. From this point on, Louis' struggle against the Pope was closely interwoven with the ideals and theories of the Spiritual Franciscans. They lost no opportunity to accuse Pope John of denying explicit statements of the Gospel and were delighted to add their voices to the accusations of heresy hurled against John in the last years of his life. Any mistake of John was grist for their mill. It was evident from the outset that the reasoning of Louis' Franciscan and secular defenders was quite beyond the Emperor's own comprehension; he was no trained philosopher or theologian, and their arguments were exceedingly abstruse and scholastic. This does not, of course, mean that their arguments were ineffective. If they had been, the Pope's defenders would not have had such difficulties in answering the charges and dismissing the evidence. They could do neither.

Once Louis was re-established in his native Bavaria, with his court and publicists around him, the battle of propaganda, negotiation, plot, and counterplot went on with renewed vigor. In attempts to gain papal approval and thus strengthen his political position, Louis made several gestures of conciliation toward the Pope, even agreeing to abdicate under certain conditions; but John was inflexible. Acting on a suggestion from Cardinal Napoleon Orsini, a member of one of the leading families of Rome, Louis appealed to a general council for its support against the Pope. Before this appeal could lead to any new development in the struggle, John XXII died (December 4, 1334). It was widely hoped that a peaceful settlement was now possible; but in fact the death of the Pope closed only one phase of the conflict, which was destined to continue for another fourteen years.

The Troubled States of Italy

THE Papacy had been gone from Italy for twelve years at the time John XXII became Pope. In the eighteen years of his presence in Avignon it was natural that papal prestige in Italy and the effectiveness of papal rule in the contentious and undisciplined peninsula should deteriorate. Clement V had had to fight a war *in absentia* against Venice to keep Ferrara, a part of the papal northern marches, from falling into the hands of the merchant republic. Clement, like all popes after him, had trouble with those whom he had appointed vicars. If French, as many of them were, they were hated as greedy and brutal foreigners by the Italians whom they ruled. If native Italians, they had to face the impossible task of quelling the bitter Guelph-Ghibelline feud, which was always either in progress or on the verge of breaking out.

In central Italy the campaign of Henry VII had aggravated this delicate situation by introducing a second foreign element into the complex of animosities. But in northern Italy Henry's policy of naming able and wise Italian princes or despots as imperial vicars had a stabilizing effect. Matteo Visconti of Milan and Can Grande della Scala of Verona were notable examples of this policy. The rich Lombard plain was thus strongly and largely voluntarily Ghibelline, and the efforts of John XXII to win the region back to the papal cause, notably by engaging in a war which erupted immediately upon his ascension to the Papacy, were not welcomed. Papal excommunications and interdicts, once powerful weapons to compel obedience, were entirely futile. The two cardinals whom John sent as his legates negotiated with everyone, but the situation only grew worse for the Guelphs, and the legates returned to Avignon disillusioned.

The absence of the Papacy from Rome, in addition to reducing considerably the population of the city, withdrew whatever stabilizing effect the *curia* might have had upon a restless and mercurial *populus*. Ancient feuds flared anew; the Colonna and the Orsini battled in the streets and from their hills and palaces for control of the city; order and peace were at the mercy of unoccupied soldiery and grasping rabble. Outside the city the Papal States were infected with the individualism that characterized the early stages of the era of the *condottieri* (professional military captains), then rampant throughout Italy. The pope's control over papal territory vanished, and the cities of central Italy joined leagues of Guelph or Ghibelline communes in complete disregard of their supposed primary allegiance. When the popes, relying upon the ancient bond between the Holy See and the Angevin house, appointed kings of Naples or their sons or brothers as papal vicars in central Italy, they only increased the resentment of the native Italians under their jurisdiction for they now not only had a foreign pope but were ruled by foreign soldiery.

John was happier than usual in one of his legates to Italy, his nephew Cardinal Bertrand du Poujet, who was charged in 1319 with the task of winning Lombardy back from the Ghibellines, then led by Matteo Visconti and Can Grande della Scala. Partly by patience, partly by persuasion, and partly by military action, du Poujet was able, over a period of ten years, to make significant inroads on Ghibelline power, so that when the Emperor Louis made his trip to Italy his support proved far less wide and durable than he had hoped for, and when he left, in 1330, it had almost disappeared. The cardinal's hold on Bologna, the principal city in the northern part of the Papal States, was so firm that in 1329 John XXII announced his intention of moving the *curia* there within the year.

The projected move never took place. The year 1330 marked a decisive change in the direction of Italian history. The failure of Louis' venture was all that was needed to show the Italians, as well as the Germans and, indeed, the whole world, that the Empire had no longer any meaning for Italy. The imperial effort had failed, not primarily through the opposition of the Papacy, absent in Avignon, or through any brilliant military successes of the leading military power of the peninsula, the kingdom of Naples, but because the idea of the Empire had lost its appeal to a substantial segment of the Italian people. Those who called themselves Ghibellines were among the first to rejoice at Louis' failures. The terms "Ghibelline" and "Guelph" no longer had any ideological content, and their battle slogans had ceased to arouse enthusiasm.

The Papacy profited at least momentarily from Louis' failure, and with him the failure of the imperial idea, for many Ghibelline cities and despots soon made their peace with Cardinal du Poujet. But some of them seemed to favor another answer to the problem they faced with the dissolution of imperial prestige in northern Italy. King John of Bohemia, son of the late Emperor Henry VII and adherent of Emperor Louis, was invited (October 1330) by the city of Brescia to defend it against Mastino della Scala, tyrant of Verona. John, always ready to ride to a rescue, accepted the invitation and on December 24 led his troops into the city. The Pope quickly expressed his displeasure at King John's independent entry into north Italian affairs, but within a very short time the cities of Bergamo, Cremona, Crema, Como, Pavia, Vercelli, Novara, Lucca, Milan, Parma, Modena, and Reggio had accepted the king as their ruler. King John made it clear that he was not acting for the Emperor, at the same time assuring the Pontiff that he would be glad to cooperate with the Papacy. By the spring of 1331 the Pope had decided that it would be easier to deal with a single successful overlord who was anxious to collaborate with the Papacy than to carry on an expensive war with many fractious cities—and wiser to turn a successful and popular conqueror into a willing friend than into a determined enemy. He therefore came to terms with King John through Cardinal du Poujet at Castel Franco near Modena on April 17, 1331.

The vacuum caused by the withdrawal of Louis and the general failure of imperial suzerainty in northern Italy had, for the moment at least, been filled. King John obviously felt that he was carving out a new and rich kingdom for himself, with the support of the Pope. For his part, Pope John judged that he had accomplished in northern Italy what his predecessors had done in the south by giving the kingdom of Naples to the house of Anjou: that is, he had destroyed the Ghibelline resistance to papal dominance. Several factors, not at first clear to the signatories at Castel Franco, were to nullify the plans of everyone involved. The king of Bohemia was quite incapable of sticking to any idea or plan for long. As early as August 1333, he was eager to return to Germany and Bohemia. Italy had lost its attraction for him, particularly since he was unable to hold the cities of the Lombard League—fully as restless as himself—in check. Furthermore, the Pope had not properly assessed the political realities of Italy. Naples was feudal and completely without commercial or communal tradition. Northern Italy was separatistic, commercial, and communal; no uniform pattern of treatment was possible for several cities in the League. The projected kingdom of northern Italy therefore failed to materialize.

In the process of its failure, a young man of whom we shall hear more learned much about Italy that was to shape the future course of the Empire. Prince Charles of Luxemburg (later Emperor Charles IV), the sixteen-year-old son of John of Bohemia, was with his father in these years and was put in charge, as his father's regent, of the cities which had given John their *Signoria*. Charles acquired, during almost two and a half years, valuable firsthand experience of Italian individualism, caprice, and unpredictability.

Papal Administration and Finance at Avignon

IT WAS at Avignon that the administration of the vast interests of the Church reached its highest efficiency. Although no single Avignonese pope can claim exclusive credit for the effective reform and centralization of the papal court, all seven popes contributed to it. Yet the reforms effected by John were of paramount significance in papal administrative history. His successors at Avignon carried on his reforms under the compulsion of necessity. The longer the Papacy stayed away from Rome, thus giving credence to the common charge that it had become a servant of the French monarchy, the weaker its hold became on an Italy disturbed by civil war, a Germany openly anti-French, and an England engaged in a bitter struggle against the Capetians and their successors (see Chapter 5). Efficiency in administration therefore had to take the place of general Europe-wide support. The reforms seldom involved innovation; rather they meant the perfecting of long-existing techniques and agencies.

The activity of the papal court was carried on in four principal departments: the apostolic chamber (*camera apostolica*), the chancery (*cancellaria*), the judicial branch, and the penitentiary. The *camera apostolica* was headed by a chamberlain, or *camerarius,* who had the rank of bishop and was responsible only to the pope. This department was a kind of financial ministry, charged with the collection, disbursement, and auditing of all papal revenues. Because it exercised the power of taxation throughout Christendom, it tended to become the key department in the whole administration, almost determinative in papal policy. The papal chamberlain virtually controlled the functioning of the whole personnel of the *curia*.

Finance looms large in any consideration of the Avignonese Papacy. The machinery the Papacy worked out to solve the serious financial problems arising from its presence in France offered abundant ground for criticism of the venality and cynicism of the whole institution. The Papal States had been, before 1305, the source of a large income to the Papacy. After 1305 this income steadily dwindled until 1353, when Rome and the Papal States were reconquered by Cardinal Albornoz (see below, p. 72). The Papacy was also owed contributions by the monarchs of Naples, Spain, and England as feudal dues; but these dues were always in arrears and were sometimes refused altogether. The Papacy had therefore to shift for itself.

The largest single source of revenue was the so-called *servitia communia,* or the taxes which had to be paid the *curia* by every ecclesiastic, from canon to archbishop, ostensibly to defray the clerical costs of arranging his appointment or promotion. The amounts to be paid were proportionate—roughly 35 to 45 per cent of the annual income of the benefice. Probably as a recognition of the Papacy's indebtedness to France, Urban V (1362-70) and Gregory XI (1370-78) reduced the rate for benefices in France by half. The revenue was divided equally between the pope and the cardinals, and nonpayment brought excommunication. These transactions are faithfully recorded in the archives of the *curia.* That they were a substantial source of income is attested by the fact that in the first ten years of the pontificate of John XXII a total of almost 900,000 gold florins—approximately equal to $2,500,000 a year—was paid into the papal *camera* as *servitia communia.* This rate of income from this source was at least maintained for the rest of the Avignon period. There were other established fees, varying with the wealth of the diocese, to be paid by archbishops for the privilege of receiving the pallium * in Rome directly from the hands of the pope. In the case of Mainz this fee ran as high as 26,000 gulden (equivalent at least to $2,000,000).

There were numerous other gratuities to be distributed. Every official who was even remotely concerned with the process demanded his share. Many churchmen complained of the practice; some have left exact records of the bribes they were forced to pay to all and sundry at Avignon. Álvaro Pelayo, a Spanish Franciscan and papal penitentiary under John XXII and a defender of the Papacy in its struggle against Louis IV, condemned the venality of the *curia* in terms as bitter as those employed by any enemy of Avignon. In his work *On the Plaint of the Church (De planctu ecclesie)*, written in 1340, he said:

Today every prelate is loaded with gold and silver . . . the church is filled with gold and silver. . . . Though they put lead on the bulls, the gold they give for that bull weighs more than the lead, sometimes 50, 70, or 100 gold florins. . . . Where is there called for today any purity of heart or a clean conscience, or a genuine faith? . . . The church has gold and it keeps its gold, or else gives it to relatives. The sacraments are bought with gold.

* The pallium is a circular wool band fitting over the shoulders, given by the pope to archbishops (and a few bishops), to symbolize the authority of the office. The archbishop may not exercise his jurisdiction without the pallium.

From the annates, the income from the first year of less lucrative benefices, and from reservations, the fee exacted from clerics who wished to be put on the waiting lists (expectancies) for prebends and Church offices, grew the papal practice of keeping all the income yielded by the benefice of any cleric who died while at the *curia*. The practice was later applied to almost any benefice that became vacant, and to any that the pope might declare vacant. The pope also claimed the right to "provide" or appoint a cleric to fill any vacant benefice anywhere in Christendom. In view of this claim, suppliants who wished to be put on one or more waiting lists were willing to pay considerable sums for the privilege. Vast sums were also realized from the systematized sale of offices at the *curia,* the standard price being ten times the annual salary. There were many other lesser sources of papal revenue. The total income was tremendous, but the moral effect of such commercialization of the sacred cure of souls was shocking, even to loyal friends of the Papacy. In spite of the large expenses to which his Italian wars and his struggle with Louis exposed him Pope John left a surplus of 500,000 florins on his death in 1334.

The papal chancery, headed by the vice-chancellor, was charged with the copious administrative detail which the Church had assumed: the examination of all applications (*supplicae, supplicationes*) for benefices and the correct formulation, authentication, issuance, and final registration of letters and grants.

The judicial functions of the Church had grown immensely with the expanding claims of powerful popes and the inevitable increase in conflicts of jurisdiction as various secular powers gained in strength and became conscious of their potential rights. There was therefore a series of judicatories, from the pope himself and the Rota, the cardinals in consistory sitting as a court of appeal, to several audiences (*audientiae*) with authority in specific kinds of cases. The *audientia litterarum contradictarum,* for example, had the special task of handling cases in which two suppliants had letters granting them the same benefice, from equal or perhaps the same authorities. Individuals, cardinals, or qualified trained jurisconsults could be designated to act as a court whose decisions might be accepted by the litigants or, sometimes, appealed to a higher court, the Rota, or to the pope himself.

The penitentiary, headed by the grand penitentiary, had the task of pronouncing the termination of an ecclesiastical disciplinary act. After an individual had been sentenced by a qualified ecclesiastical authority to a certain penance (*penitentia*), upon his supplication, the penitentiary was empowered to ascertain whether satisfaction had been made. The absolution or dispensation could then be granted. The suppliants were of all grades of importance. If, for example, Emperor Louis IV had sought to quash the excommunication which John XXII had hurled against him, he would have had, as a matter of form, to present himself personally or through a procurator before the grand penitentiary, who would have referred so important a case to the Pope himself.

Letters and Art in Avignon

THE astounding activity of John XXII was not limited to the areas of political affairs in Germany and Italy, doctrinal disputes over the principle of poverty for the mendicant orders, or administrative reform and initiation, important as these matters undoubtedly were. His interest in the cultural possibilities of his position and the encouragement he gave to artists and men of letters were of great significance for the future intellectual and artistic development of Western Europe. John enlarged and adorned the palace he chose for the papal residence in Avignon. In 1317 he added a tower, a meeting room for the consistory, and a large study for himself. Two years later he built two large rooms for audiences. In successive years, summer residences and churches in Avignon and environs were built or rebuilt. For all this construction John brought in well-known French architects and builders and took a personal interest in the planning and building. For the most part the style was developed French Gothic, often with more than a touch of soberness or even heaviness. In these residences and churches John favored large murals, and the records of his accounts show that much money was spent on wall paintings and frescoes, almost all of which have unfortunately since disappeared or been effaced. The painters who did this work were all Frenchmen; it was not until the reign of Benedict XII (1334–42) that a flood of Italian painters invaded the court. Later Avignonese popes also encouraged creative men, but it was John who established the tradition of having a large contingent of active artists at the *curia*.

This octogenarian Pope deserves even more credit for his attitude toward learning. In view of his own high competence in the field, his encouragement of the study of canon law is not surprising, but his founding of a papal library and his orders to have copies made, at his personal expense, of the writings of classical authors—the works of Vegetius, the declamations and tragedies of Seneca, the *Almagest* of Ptolemy, the *Natural History* of Pliny the Elder— reveal an aspect of the spirit of Avignon different from that of graft and cynical disregard of the Christian virtues. Petrarch, who lived in or near Avignon for some of these years, made many derogatory remarks about that "sink of iniquity"; he nevertheless stayed there and enjoyed the benefits of the formidable concourse of the great and the learned from all over the world.

Later Avignonese popes, almost without exception, continued the tradition of welcoming, encouraging, and supporting men of letters. Nowhere else in Europe in the fourteenth century, with the possible exception of Paris, were so many of the intellectual and cultural leaders of the Western world to be found. In addition to the four hundred highly competent and mostly worldly officials of the *curia* itself, at one time or another there were at Avignon world-renowned artists, theologians, philosophers, returned missionaries from Asia and Africa, the cultured representatives of the Greek Patriarch of Constantinople, the leading diplomatic envoys from every royal or princely court in Europe, and, for shorter visits, princes and kings. On several occasions, the talented Emperor Charles IV (1346–78) himself visited the court. The papal library, of which we have three carefully composed catalogues (1339, 1369, and 1375), contained around two thousand extremely precious volumes in philosophy, science, theology, and history, reflecting a high degree of sophistication and broad intellectual interests. By making the court the cultural center of Europe under such favorable circumstances, the Avignonese popes did much to prepare the channels of intellectual exchange without which the international movement of humanism would have been impossible.

John and the Beatific Vision

IN THE last years of his reign, John XXII stumbled into a sharp controversy which has become a source of embarrassment to later papal apologists. In several sermons late in 1331 and early in 1332, he expressed an opinion concerning the Beatific Vision of the saints in Paradise that shocked the *curia* and gave ammunition to his enemies. He asserted that the saints, in the interval between their physical death and the day of the Last Judgment, when their souls would again be joined to their bodies, do not see God face to face, and that during this same period the souls of the damned are not yet in hell. He would have been better advised not to venture into the field of theology, in which he was not thoroughly trained. Ockham and the other Spiritual Franciscans made quick and telling use of this error in doctrine, and the accusation of heresy could not be refuted. It was ironic that the Pope who had been so vigorous in his pursuit of heretics early in his reign should end his days under a cloud of heretical doctrine. The cause of the Papacy suffered considerably. The University of Paris protested the Pope's view as heretical and, in the face of the clear dictates of orthodox theology, John made a qualified retraction just before his death.

John XXII died on December 4, 1334, at the age of ninety. His death marked the end of an epoch in papal history, the age of the great canon lawyers, whose claims to world dominion were based on a strict construction of that great instrument of human governance, the *corpus iuris canonici,* and the thesis that this governance was in the power of the successors of St. Peter.

Benedict XII (1334–42)

NINE days after John's death the cardinals met in conclave to choose his successor, and on December 20 they unanimously elected Cardinal Jacques Fournier, who took the pontifical name of Benedict XII. An austere Cistercian, a trained theologian with appropriate administrative experience as bishop and frequent negotiator for John XXII, and an enthusiastic heresy-hunter, Benedict had had some preparation for the arduous tasks before him. Yet in some respects he was not equal to the challenge of the office, lacking at times firmness and the ability to translate ideas into deeds. Before the death of John, Benedict, then a cardinal, had been charged with the examination of John's pronouncements on the Beatific Vision. He found them without support in Church tradition, and soon after becoming Pope he made a pronouncement that clearly labeled them heretical.

The new Pope's first significant act was to scold the Franciscans publicly for their laxness and general lack of proper discipline. He tried thereafter to reform all the monastic orders along the idealistic lines of his own Cistercian Order. Aware of the commerce in ecclesiastical offices that disgraced the *curia,* he sent home great numbers of clerics of high and low degree, who were at Avignon when they should have been tending their flocks in their own dioceses or parishes. He demanded that only suitable clerics be granted papal provisions, and he was a bitter enemy of nepotism on the part of the pope as well as of lesser authorities. He is reported to have said: "A pope has no relatives." His zeal frightened the benefice-seekers who crowded Avignon, and there was a sudden and noticeable exodus from the city.

Benedict's economies and his scrupulous attitude toward the systematized sale of papal favors that had made his predecessor and his court so wealthy brought on a decline in papal revenues. But Benedict counterbalanced this loss by stopping, through viable compromises, the expensive wars in Italy that John had pursued throughout his pontificate. He declared that the Church, the great protagonist of peace and love, would only lose by resorting to war. As a net result, the *curia* during Benedict's reign was fully as solvent as during the pontificate of John, though not so rich in gross income.

In his relations with secular powers, Benedict was conciliatory, more concerned with the spiritual mission of the Church than with its temporal dominance. Knowing of Benedict's conciliatory temper, the Emperor Louis IV entered into negotiations looking toward a settlement of the long conflict. Terms satisfactory to both sides were arranged, but King Philip VI of France (1328–50) did not welcome a settlement that would have left intact the ancient imperial title to the kingdom of Arles and other lands along the Rhône. Furthermore, Robert of Anjou, king of Naples, enjoyed being papal vicar of Italy and therefore did not welcome a settlement with the Empire, whose ancient title to northern Italy would inevitably be reactivated by an agreement between the Emperor and the Pope. These two loyal allies urged Benedict not to accept Louis' terms. The pressure was greater than the Pope could withstand, and Louis' representatives left Avignon in frustration early in 1336.

Further negotiations were nullified by the outbreak of full-scale war in 1337 between Edward III of England and Philip VI of France. In order to carry on what promised to be a difficult and costly enterprise, Edward naturally sought allies; and who was a more likely friend than Emperor Louis IV, a long-time enemy of the French Papacy and therefore of France? An alliance was actually contracted on August 26, 1337. Benedict's instinctive desire to come to terms with the Emperor while there was still time had been sound, but it was frustrated by the petty ambitions of the kings of France and Naples.

The next significant step in the papal-imperial conflict was the proclamation by the imperial electors at Rense, July 16, 1338, that the imperial dignity derived directly from God, and that he who was elected by all or a majority of the electors was legally and immediately the king and, when crowned at Aachen, could function as emperor without the approval or confirmation of the Pope or anyone else. This declaration of imperial independence became a law of the Empire by Louis' edict *Licet iuris* of August 6, 1338. It marks a significant epoch both in imperial constitutional history and in the relations between the Empire and the Papacy. In the course of the next few years Louis, now in a much stronger position, made gestures of reconciliation; but the king of France still believed that it was against the special interests of France to permit friendly relations between Germany and the Papacy, and French intrigues prevented any consummation of Louis' attempts.

The prolonged absence of the *curia* from Rome had brought that city to a sad and dilapidated state. In 1337 Benedict was elected senator and urged to bring the Papacy again to the city of St. Peter and St. Paul. Petrarch added his eloquent voice to the plea. But the insistence of Philip VI of France, then just becoming involved in the English war, added to the open reluctance of the cardinals to leave their native France, forced Benedict to decide against the move. In 1335 he had begun in earnest to construct a palace that would be suitable to the dignity of the papal court, building on to the palace which John before him had enlarged. The work of addition and embellishment was continued under his three successors, for the massive structure was thirty years in the building. The cardinals followed their leader's example and built handsome, substantial winter homes in the city and delicate, artistic summer residences in the lush countryside of the Venaissin. All the architects were French; no influence of Italian Renaissance architecture can be traced in the Avignon of this early period, either in the buildings or in the many tombs, which normally express architectural form and motif sooner than do larger structures.

Benedict XII did not discourage the beginnings of the Italian or humanistic Renaissance. The papal library, begun in 1317 by John XXII, was further enriched at Benedict's orders by the addition of some valuable manuscripts of the classics. The atmosphere of the *curia,* according to the accounts which Petrarch has left us, was congenial to the furtherance of polite learning, and in 1335 Petrarch himself was granted a canonry at Lombez * in Gascony in a letter that praised his love of literature. Petrarch obtained some of his most precious copies of the classics in these years, probably in Avignon itself. As a center of cosmopolitan culture Avignon was no less effective under the monastic Benedict XII than under the canon lawyer John XXII. Benedict died on April 25, 1342, probably one of the best-intentioned and at the same time most reviled and hated of the medieval popes.

Clement VI (1342–52)

UPON the death of Benedict, Philip VI of France, who apparently regarded the affairs of the Papacy as his personal concern, sent an emissary to Avignon to urge the election of Cardinal Pierre Roger, archbishop of Rouen. By the time the embassy reached Avignon, Pierre Roger was already Pope Clement VI. Everyone was happy, including Clement, an active-minded, energetic, affable, eloquent cleric. The cardinals had had enough austerity.

The reign of Clement VI was an eventful decade in European politics. The dispute between the Papacy and Emperor Louis IV came to an end, and with it were stilled the voices of the most vehement Spiritual Franciscans. The line of Henry VII (of Luxemburg) was reinstalled on the imperial throne. The Papacy had once again to go to war in north Italy; the city of Rome exploded in the tragicomedy of Cola di Rienzo; the Black Death, originating in the Far East, spread from the port of Marseilles to the remotest corner of Europe, bringing wholesale death in its wake; the bitter war between France and England passed through a decisive crisis; the city of Rome enjoyed a jubilee in 1350; and Clement bankrupted the Papacy almost beyond recovery.

Clement believed that the pope should be a generous and benevolent prince, remarking that his predecessors had not known how to be popes. He invited

* The bishop of Lombez was one of the Colonna and a friend of Petrarch. Petrarch continued to live at Vaucluse after receiving the benefice.

the clergy to ask for benefices; then, to satisfy the resulting demand, he had to increase the reservations on a large scale. This procedure took from the bishops throughout Christendom the right to make appointments to benefices and livings in their dioceses. In 1344 Clement declared that "the right to dispose of all churches, dignities, offices, and ecclesiastical benefices" belonged to the pope. Centralization of ecclesiastical administration at Avignon, already a source of widespread complaint, was thereby greatly increased.

Emperor Louis made several attempts to conciliate the Papacy, once again offering to abdicate, but both Clement and the imperial Diet (September 8, 1344) refused to accept the proposed arrangement. The German electors were not especially favorable to Louis—they even planned at that time to supplant him as ruler—but their pride in the Empire would not allow them to accept the humiliation the Pope demanded of the Emperor. Clement was patient; and on April 13, 1346, after a shift in the electoral college favorable to his cause, he issued a bull deposing Louis from the imperial office. Eight days later, in Avignon, the young Prince Charles of Moravia,* grandson of the Luxemburg Emperor Henry VII and son of King John of Bohemia, solemnly promised the Pope that if he were made emperor, he would withdraw all imperial decrees unfavorable to the Papacy, would never enter any papal domain without express permission, and would go to Rome only to be crowned, leaving on the same day. In short, he promised to be a good boy. On July 11 at Rense the five electors present unanimously chose him Emperor. He took the title of Charles IV. It was not an election that the German people accepted with wild enthusiasm, and many of them called Charles *Pfaffenkönig,* priest's king. Charles hardly deserved this epithet. Although Clement had been his tutor when Charles was a boy in Paris and had continued to be a personal friend, Charles did perhaps more to free the Empire from papal domination than Louis had done with all his belligerence. The new Emperor's methods were different, and his political sense was keener; his concept of his office was more clear-cut, his patience greater, his assessment of issues more realistic and effective.

The idea of the Crusade as a general and permanent Christian obligation was never absent from papal policy. Pope John had made efforts to bring the Eastern Church back into the fold, hoping to persuade the French king to head a Crusade against the infidel Turk, but the involvement of France in a war with England eliminated her from the Pope's armory of weapons. Clement engineered an alliance among those French and Catalonians still in strategic positions in the East, in Greece, and in Cyprus, and the Hospitalers scattered along the coast of Asia Minor and Venice. This combination took Smyrna in October 1344 and drove the Turks out of the Greek islands of the Aegean.

Cola di Rienzo

MEDIEVAL Rome, with or without the popes in residence, had always been fickle, tempestuous, and irrational. The nobles fought among themselves and against the common people. Anarchy was continuous, the temper of the people mercurial. Into this chaos came a magnetic demagogue who brought at least

* Charles of Luxemburg, since 1333 margrave of Moravia.

temporary order. Cola (Niccolà) di Rienzo, a man of obscure origin, had taught himself classical Latin from the inscriptions that dotted the ancient city and fed his eager imagination on the history of Rome's vanished grandeur. He had achieved some prominence in the city by his learning and fervid oratory and was sent to Avignon in the spring of 1343 as a member of a legation to ask the Pope to return the *curia* to Rome. While in Avignon he made the acquaintance of Petrarch and favorably impressed Pope Clement. By Easter 1344 he was back in Rome, where he displayed open enmity toward the nobility. Three years later, on May 19, 1347, the opposition to the power of the great families broke out in an enthusiastic if bloodless popular uprising. Rienzo was its vibrant voice. The people approved his program, and the senators were driven out of the city. Rienzo, as the popular leader, had almost absolute power. Order was restored, justice was equitably meted out, and Rome recovered some self-respect. Rienzo, apparently inflated by his success, then summoned all the rulers of the world to bring their titles and documents to Rome for his inspection and approval. He called himself Candidate of the Holy Spirit, Friend of the World, Tribune Augustus, and Knight Nicholas, and had himself crowned with five crowns. Seven months of his caprice revised the opinions of the people of Rome, ever willing to change their minds; as suddenly as he had seized power, Rienzo abdicated (December 15, 1347) and fled to the mountains of the Abruzzi.

Avignon had watched these curious events with mixed feelings. Petrarch was enthusiastic in Rienzo's praise. He saw the revolution as a great overture to Rome's return to the leadership of the world. More politically experienced heads thought otherwise, correctly assessing Rienzo as a fool and a coward. These men rejoiced when the noble party was able, on Rienzo's flight, to take over command of the city.

The rest of the papal territory in Italy had lost some of its feeling of direct dependence on the Papacy under the lax and pacific rule of Benedict XII. By the time Clement VI came to the throne, papal control of the March of Ancona and the Romagna—a very considerable territory—had virtually disappeared. In 1337 Taddeo dei Pepoli had forced the city of Bologna, proud of her long struggle for independence, to accept him as *signore*. The death in 1343 of King Robert of Naples, long the papal vicar in northern Italy and mainstay of the Guelph cause, meant the virtual ruin of that cause in the Piedmont. Clement's involvements in France and Germany kept him from taking a strong line in Italy. Ambitious despots whose lands bordered upon papal territory had begun to nibble off substantial chunks of areas which owed allegiance to the distant *curia*. By 1350 the position of the Papacy in northern Italy was so desperate that the militant and quite unchurchly Giovanni Visconti, who had purchased the archbishopric of Milan from financially harassed Clement VI for fifty thousand florins, controlled seventeen cities in the Piedmont and then proceeded to add the usually papal city of Bologna to his domain by chicanery and outright purchase. The Scaligeri of Verona, formerly stout defenders of the Guelph cause, were sadly degenerate and unable to stop the expansion of the city of the Visconti; Milan was supreme in north Italy, protesting firm loyalty to the Papacy yet blandly defying every order from Avignon. It was several years before the Papacy was once again a leading force in Italian politics.

The Black Death

THE world of the West soon found something else to talk about than the Rienzo incident and the tribulations of the Papacy in Italy. Late in the autumn of 1347, the Black Death, later identified as the bubonic plague, appeared at Genoa and Marseilles, brought from the Far East by way of Constantinople or Syrian ports. It broke out in Avignon in January 1348 and in seven months claimed 62,000 victims. Seven thousand dwellings were emptied by deaths. From March 14 to April 27 eleven thousand corpses were buried in the Pope's newly purchased cemetery. Clement took personal charge of the fight against the plague, encouraging those engaged in service to the sick, the dying, and the dead. When the severest stage of the plague had passed, the panicked people throughout Europe struck out blindly and accused the Jews of poisoning wells and springs. In one of the most creditable acts of his pontificate, Clement took the Jews under his special protection, threatening to excommunicate anyone who molested them. The effects of the Black Death on every aspect of European life were tremendous, and we shall frequently cross its grim path as we speak of war and commerce, art and religion.

In 1348 Clement bought outright the city of Avignon from Joanna, queen of Naples, for the relatively modest sum of eighty thousand florins. Joanna was indebted to Clement for pronouncing her innocent of the murder, just outside her bedroom door, of her husband, Andrew of Hungary. Although most chroniclers inclined to think that she had some responsibility in the matter, Petrarch, Boccaccio, and the Pope believed her not guilty.

Pope Clement VI died at Avignon on December 6, 1352. He had directed the affairs of the Church with a certain diplomatic skill, but rather as a realistic secular prince than as a spiritual leader. He was more clever than wise. His freedom from the trammels of careful economy left the Papacy bankrupt.

Innocent VI (1352–62)

CLEMENT'S successor, Innocent VI (Etienne Aubert), had a distinguished legal mind and wide experience in papal administration; at the time of his election he was the grand penitentiary. In great sincerity, he set out to reform some of the lax practices that Clement VI had allowed, and there was another exodus from Avignon of clerics who had hoped to collect fat prebends all over Christendom and live in ease at the papal court. The mendicant orders were particularly unhappy at the strictness and reforming zeal exhibited by the new Pope, although he was equally severe with the Spiritual Franciscans, the Hospitalers, and the Fraticelli (see p. 57). The Inquisition was active, and two Spiritual Franciscans were burned at the stake in Avignon. St. Birgitta of Sweden had welcomed Innocent's election, but with the increasingly severe enforcement of his reforms she became disillusioned and heaped bitter words upon his head: "He has been more hateful than the Jewish usurers, more of a traitor than Judas, more cruel than Pilate."

In foreign affairs the pontificate of Innocent was not fortunate. His election had been favored by King John II of France (1350-64); but Innocent, a poor judge of the value of a king's word, was repeatedly deceived and bitterly disappointed by the rulers of France, England, Navarre, Castile, and Aragon. In Italy, however, he was blessed with success, owing solely to his choice of a legate to administer the States of the Church and to recall to proper obedience those cities that had accepted papal sovereignty. Cardinal Gil Albornoz, who had had experience in the Moorish wars in Spain, set out for Italy late in 1353. He was soon joined by Cola di Rienzo, whose erstwhile prestige in Rome, it was hoped in Avignon, would help Albornoz to recover papal power in that troubled city. They entered Rome in August 1354, amid great popular enthusiasm. But Rienzo behaved like a tyrant, and his rule this time lasted only two months. On October 8, 1354, a mob set fire to Rienzo's castle, and when he attempted to escape, he was caught and murdered. Albornoz was nevertheless able to enforce order in Rome, and elsewhere in the Papal States he was most persuasive. With scant funds and few troops, he won the support of the rulers of numerous north Italian towns and then proceeded to show a military capacity astonishing in a prince of the Church. By the summer of 1357 he had forced the recalcitrant cities and despots of the Papal States to sue for peace. But at the very time that he was restoring the authority and prestige of the Papacy in Italy, jealous intrigues at Avignon brought about his recall. His successor as legate, Androin de la Roche, abbot of Cluny, was so ineffectual that Albornoz was sent back to Italy, where, with inadequate forces as usual, he worked wonders by diplomacy, coolness, and resourcefulness. In November 1363, he was once again relieved of his power, this time by Urban V, who had become Pope in the preceding year. Urban had been influenced by jealous prelates, particularly by Bernabò Visconti, lord of Milan, whose plans for expansion into the area of the Church's possessions Albornoz had blocked so effectively.

It was during the pontificate of Innocent that Emperor Charles IV made his first journey to Rome, to be crowned (1354-55). Innocent had insisted that Charles fulfill his promise to Clement VI, to enter, be crowned, and leave Rome on the same day. The Pope may have gained somewhat in popular esteem from this restriction on the action of an emperor, but it was scant consolation for his lack of success elsewhere.

Innocent's relations with Spain were typical of his diplomatic failures. Peter I the Cruel (1350-69), king of Castile, had married Blanche of Bourbon, sister-in-law of Charles V of France (1364-80), but left her almost immediately to return to his favorite mistress, Maria de Padilla. Because of this repudiation, which was an affront to the French king, Peter was excommunicated (1355) and Spain laid under an interdict. Peter promised to mend his ways, but his promises were promptly forgotten, and repeated efforts of papal legates to bring him into line were futile.

The war between France and England (see Chapter 5) reached the end of a phase during the pontificate of Innocent. Attempts early in 1356 by a papal legate to act as intermediary were vain, and in the definitive negotiations from which the Peace of Brétigny (1360) resulted, the Pope's representative, Androin de la Roche, abbot of Cluny, served only as an occasional errand boy, without influence on the terms of peace. The conclusion of the truce of Bordeaux (March 23, 1357) had released great numbers of former soldiers from service and left them without means of livelihood. Many formed themselves into bands called Free Companies which found the country around Avignon an agreeable site of operations. Innocent's emergency measures of defense kept the marauders out of the Venaissin; but three years later, after the conclusion of the Peace of Brétigny, a new wave of discharged mercenaries threatened to engulf the Papal State. Innocent collected some voluntary soldiery but ended by paying the marauders 14,500 gold florins to leave. They went on south into Italy.

To add to the Pope's troubles, Avignon was visited in 1361 by a recurrence of the Black Death: seventeen thousand people, including nine cardinals, died of the plague in the papal city in that year. Innocent himself died on September 12, 1362.

While the sincerity and reforming zeal of Innocent VI are generally recognized, external circumstances and his own instability and frequent indecision made his reforming efforts and good intentions of no avail; the prestige of the Papacy during his pontificate suffered accordingly.

Urban V (1362–70)

UPON the death of Innocent, the cardinals elected as pope William of Grimoard of Marseilles, who took the name of Urban V. Urban was a scholarly, ascetic, and sincere monk. He was led to make the drastic decision to return the Papacy to Rome by three circumstances. First, the king of France, the protector of the Avignonese Papacy, was, after the Peace of Brétigny, either a prisoner of the English or so weak that his protection meant nothing. Second, the situation of the Church's possessions in Italy was grave, despite the heroic work of Cardinal Albornoz, and it appeared to be easier to rule the Patrimony from Rome than from distant Avignon. Finally, there was moral pressure from various sources, including St. Birgitta of Sweden, St. Catherine of Siena, and Petrarch, the leading man of letters of the Christian world, all demanding the return of the Papacy to its rightful seat; to this pressure Urban, a sincerely pious churchman, was forced to respond. The king of France, Charles V, the Wise, sent an embassy to Avignon protesting the proposed departure. The cardinals almost unanimously objected to going. Life in Avignon was pleasant and, to Frenchmen, far preferable to the stormy life that the fickle Roman populace would certainly lead them. But Urban was not to be deterred. He left Avignon on April 30, 1367, accompanied by the wails and even threats of the cardinals, and, journeying over land and sea by leisurely stages, arrived in Rome on October 16. In the meantime, the only one of his lieutenants who might have made the return to Italian soil a success, Cardinal Albornoz, restored to favor in 1364 and named legate to Naples, had died (August 22).

Rome revived quickly with the *curia* in its midst. There were royal visitors; Emperor Charles IV came to the city to pay his respects to the Pope. But the acrimonious strife of nobles and cities in and around the Papal States was too much even for a man with Urban's good intentions. He was not at home in a world of intrigue, murder, and deceit, particularly now that there was no Albornoz to dominate the scene. After three years he admitted his error and returned to Avignon, arriving in September 1370. He survived his return by only three months, dying on December 19, 1370.

Gregory XI (1370–78)

URBAN'S successor was another Frenchman, Pierre Roger de Beaufort, a nephew of Clement VI. Gregory XI was pious, conscientious, affable, and a trained canonist. The prompt fulfillment of St. Birgitta's prophecy to Urban V that his death would soon follow his desertion of Rome for Avignon made a deep impression on Gregory, who himself was of frail health. Both St. Birgitta and, after her death in 1373, St. Catherine of Siena reported to the Pope their messages and visions from God that demanded the final and irrevocable return of the Papacy to Rome. Gregory determined to follow this advice at the earliest possible moment, but the war between France and England engaged his attention; he was influential in arranging the truce of Bourges (1375) between the two monarchs. No sooner was this accomplished than a revolt of north Italian cities erupted against papal rule, and Florence and Bologna had to be disciplined. The task was carried out under the direction of Cardinal Robert of Geneva, who turned out to be as ruthless as the *condottieri* with whom he had to deal.

Despite these interruptions, Gregory's decision to return remained firm. St. Catherine strengthened his hand against the cardinals who would have preferred to stay on in Avignon and friends who tried to persuade the Pope not to leave the safety of the now handsome city on the Rhône. On September 13, 1376, the Pope left French soil, arriving in Rome on January 17, 1377. Gregory did not live long enough to feel established in Rome, but his decision to return had ended an era in the history of the Papacy during which time, despite the high personal morality of the popes who ruled the Church from French soil, the Papacy suffered profoundly in the opinion of the Christian world.

SUGGESTIONS FOR FURTHER READING

Cambridge Medieval History, Vol. VII

COSENZA, M., *Francesco Petrarca and the Revolution of Cola di Rienzo*. Chicago, 1913

CREIGHTON, M., *A History of the Papacy during the Reformation*. 5 vols. London, 1882–94

DUBOIS, P., *Recovery of the Holy Land*, trans. W. I. Brandt. New York, 1956

FLICK, A. C., *Decline of the Medieval Church*. 2 vols. New York, 1930

GARDNER, E. G., *St. Catherine of Siena*. London, 1907

GASQUET, A., *The Black Death*. London, 1908

GEWIRTH, A., *Marsilius of Padua: The Defender of the Peace*. 2 vols. New York, 1951, 1956

GREGOROVIUS, F., *History of Rome in the Middle Ages*. London, 1894–1902

HUGHES, P., *History of the Church*, Vol. III. New York, 1947

OKEY, T., *The Story of Avignon*. London, 1926. Medieval Towns Series

ORIGO, I., *Tribune of Rome: Cola di Rienzo*. London, 1938

PASTOR, L., *History of the Popes from the Close of the Middle Ages*, Vol. I. London, 1891

SCHAFF, P. and D. S., *History of the Christian Church,* Vol. V, part 2. New York, 1910

YOUNG, N., *The Story of Rome.* London, 1926. Medieval Towns Series

FINKE, H., *Papsttum und Untergang des Templerordens.* 1907

GUIRAUD, J., *L'Église romaine et les origines de la renaissance.* 1911

HALLER, J., *Papsttum und Kirchenreform.* 1903

HAUCK, A., *Kirchengeschichte Deutschlands,* Vol. V. 1920

HEFELE, C. J., and H. LECLERCQ, *Histoire des conciles,* Vol. VI. 1914, 1917

LIZERAND, G., *Clément V et Philippe IV le Bel.* 1910

MIROT, L., *La Politique pontificale et le retour du Saint Siège à Rome en 1376.* 1889

MOLLAT, G., *Les Papes d'Avignon.* 1949

MÜLLER, K., *Der Kampf Ludwigs des Baiern mit der römischen Curie.* 2 vols. 1879

PAPENCORDT, F., *Rienzi et Rome à son époque.* 1845

PIUR, P., *Cola di Rienzo.* 1931

RIEZLER, S., *Die literarischen Widersacher der Päpste zur Zeit Ludwigs des Baiers.* 1874

RODOCANACHI, E., *Cola di Rienzo. Histoire de Rome de 1342 à 1354.* 1888

SCHOLZ, R., *Die Publizistik zur Zeit Philips des Schönen und Bonifaz VIII.* 1903

WURM, H. J., *Cardinal Albornoz.* 1892

CHAPTER FOUR

EARLY HUMANISM

THE term "Renaissance" has been applied to a number of periods in European history. The "Carolingian Renaissance" refers to the great outburst of intellectual activity at the time of Charlemagne and his direct heirs, largely in France and western Germany. The "Ottonian Renaissance," a perhaps less widely used term, designates the literary and artistic movement east of the Rhine which began under the vigorous rule of Otto the Great (d. 973). "Renaissance" also describes the twelfth-century complex of revived interest in the classics and the rise of universities, centering, again, for the most part in France. The names of Bernard Silvester, John of Salisbury, and Peter Abélard suggest the peculiar genius of this movement.

But historians of Western culture have not regarded the following century as a continuation of the twelfth-century Renaissance. In the thirteenth century, commonly called the Age of Faith, the appeal of men like Abélard to the criteria of human reason and the traditions of ancient classical letters was ignored or engulfed in the passion of the scholastics to fit all human thought into theological patterns. The university foundations of Paris and Oxford dominated thought and learning in these years, and their curricula were founded on philosophical and theological dispute and speculation within the framework of Christian dogma. After the death of St. Thomas Aquinas (1225-74), the method and subject matter of the schools—that is, scholasticism—began to decline in vitality and in its response to the interests of the time. A new renaissance supervened, generally called the humanistic or Italian Renaissance. It is usually accepted that this period extends from Petrarch (1304-74) to Erasmus (1466?-1536) or, on the Continent at least, to Montaigne (1533-92).

All these renaissances have been the subject of much discussion and reexamination in the light of new or forgotten facts and approaches. We are here concerned with the last period, that of the humanistic Renaissance of the fourteenth and following centuries. But it should be clearly understood that any sharp delimitation of an intellectual movement or cultural current is a falsification of history. The so-called mind of an age is never precisely the mind of everyone living in that age. Such a "mind" may impose itself by its coherence or relative popularity, or because some, perhaps only a few, of its adherents are eloquent, striking, dramatic, or merely fortunate in their biographers. While Bernard Silvester, Abélard, and John of Salisbury, all good churchmen, are clear illustrations of these possibilities in the twelfth century, many of their contemporaries did not share either Abélard's confidence in human reason or Bernard's and John's love of the Latin classics. Likewise, during the thirteenth century, there were many who were not convinced by St. Thomas' approach to the *summum bonum* and many who cultivated the Latin classics.* Hundreds, if not thousands, of manuscripts of works of Ovid, Statius, Horace, Seneca, Lucan, Donatus, Priscian, Virgil, Cicero, Suetonius, Pliny the Elder, Valerius Maximus, Quintus Curtius, and many other writers of Rome were either written or used and annotated during the thirteenth century. These manuscripts testify that interest in ancient letters had not completely died out during the scholastic period. The glory of Rome was never completely forgotten where Roman legions had marched. This tradition emerged from time to time under the impulse of some brilliant and appealing exponent or when, as in the case of declining scholasticism, an opposite tendency lost momentum or faltered in its leadership. It should hardly be necessary to remark that the frequently repeated statement that in the Middle Ages man lived "enveloped in a cowl" is more false than true. Human values, human interests, human passions have seldom been subjected to more thoughtful examination than during the thirteenth century, at the height of the Age of Faith. For these reasons, the break between the mind of the thirteenth-century scholastic and that of the fourteenth-century or the twelfth-century classicist should not be overemphasized. Change and development certainly took place; but the alteration of cultural direction was not so violent as we have often been led to think.

Forerunners of Petrarch

IT IS both conventional and accurate to regard Italy as the seat of the Renaissance. Italy's connection with the movement in every field of human activity is, as we shall see, beyond question. On the other hand, to give Italy sole credit for the rise of a continent-wide redirection of the human spirit in letters, art, music, society, and politics is hardly justified. Europe was very much of a cultural entity, and there was continuous movement from one country to another, particularly on the part of the churchmen, who were the intelligentsia of the time. That the members of the literate class shared a common tongue, Latin, made communication among men of all nationalities simple; such communication was, indeed, more general than it is today. There was hardly a serious university student in the thirteenth century who did not study at more than one institution; if, by chance, he did remain at one university, his friends and colleagues came from several countries. It was a truly international age. This fact must be kept in mind in any assessment of origins and development. Any cultural movement, of course, draws on many sources for its origins and development. This is particularly true of the humanistic Renaissance.

* For the sake of argument, the fact that fully half the total work of St. Thomas was commentary on Aristotle need not be taken into account. What St. Thomas would have been without the classical heritage is difficult to imagine.

The University of Paris was the intellectual capital of Europe in the thirteenth century; scholarly minded and intellectually ambitious men from all over the Christian world flocked to the left bank of the Seine. Currents of thought and exchange of ideas beamed out from Paris to every corner of the Continent and to England. This radiation was especially significant for Italy. As the theological bastion of orthodoxy, the University of Paris was taken under the special protection of the Papacy in 1231. The traffic of men and ideas between Paris and Rome, in view of the Papacy's direct interest in this capstone of the whole European educational system, was heavy. The route between the capital of the Church and that of learning lay through the Rhône valley and Provence, the home of the troubadours with their poetry of love and the delights of nature. There were Provençal poets at the courts of the princes and despots of northern Italy from the end of the twelfth century, and their influence upon both the form and the content of the freshly awak-ened vernacular literature of the Lombard valley was remarkable. Brunetto Latini (d. *ca.* 1295), whom Dante revered as a teacher, wrote his encyclopedic *Li Livres dou Tresor* in French, which he termed the most excellent language. His ideas and techniques may indeed be traced to French models. Plentiful use and adaptation were made in northern Italy in the late thirteenth and fourteenth centuries of the French *Chanson de Roland, Roman de Troie,* and *Roman de la Rose,* and of the whole body of legend about Alexander the Great. There were, furthermore, many translations from Latin into French, both poetry and prose, by north Italians who found French a more poetic, flexible, and harmonious medium than their own vernacular. These were cer-tainly not spiritual voices in the usual sense of that word, nor did their works reflect the theological interests of the University of Paris. The subjects were purely classical, or rather pseudoclassical: secular love lyrics, encyclopedias, epic and heroic poems, and, in a few cases, works on science, medicine, and travel.

It is not difficult to see in this flood of markedly nonreligious themes and variations, all showing admiration for human emotions, a preparation for the secularism and cosmopolitanism of the age we know as the Renaissance. These tendencies built up, over a century or two, a most favorable background for the classical revival. The secularism of the pagan classics needs no emphasis. What was so compelling was the fact that their expression of the qualities of human character and the glories of nature was so much more noble, plausible, urbane, and eloquent than that found in either the Latin texts of pseudo-classical works or in their vernacular translations. The true classics could satisfy where the pseudoclassics could not.

The first real fruits of the classical revival were borne precisely in that area of Italy through which the current of transit between Paris and Rome had been passing and in which the luxuriant Provençal literature had received so warm a welcome in the thirteenth century—the plains of Lombardy and the valley of the Po. Padua and Verona were the homes of the first scholars whom we can call classical humanists in the strict sense of the term. In Padua there were three men who deserve to be called forerunners of Petrarch: Lovato de' Lovati, Geremia da Montagnone, and Albertino Mussato.

We know of Lovato de' Lovati (1241-1309) from his lively correspondence with a certain Bellino, who had criticized Lovato for championing the works of the ancients. Bellino objected to classical Latin poetry as abstruse, obscure, and irrelevant, while claiming that the vernacular poetry was realistic, flexible, living, and comprehensible. Lovato's answer was to deny his critic's premises. He added the prophetic barb: *Mox quota pars tecum?* "Soon, how many will be on your side?" There is more here than meets the eye; Lovato could hardly have appealed to the future if his own experience and observation had not led him to sense some growth of public interest in the classics of ancient Rome. This interchange of views probably took place in the last decade of the thirteenth century. Lovato's own creations, epic poems based on Tristan and Isolde and on the struggles between the Guelphs and the Ghibellines, are now mostly lost; but enough of his writing survives to indicate that he appreciated classic style and shared the ideas of the Roman writers.

Concerning Geremia da Montagnone (*ca.* 1260–1321) we know considerably more. A judge by training, he wrote some legal treatises and was active as an examiner of law graduates at the University of Padua. Over a period of years, probably between 1295 and 1310, as relaxation from his judicial labors, he compiled an elaborate *Compendium moralium notabilium,* a collection of sayings from the Bible, the ancients, the Fathers of the Church, and medieval authors of worth, classified according to subject matter. The list of authors from whom he culled is most impressive. He must have had, in his own possession or within access, a rich collection of manuscripts. He quotes, for example, many lines of Catullus, the most delicate lyric poet of the Golden Age of Rome, barely known until Montagnone's time.* What we have of Montagnone's own Latin prose is in the rather stilted style of the legal profession, showing little influence of the classical models he read so carefully for his *Compendium.*

The third of the Paduan prehumanists, Albertino Mussato (1262–1329), was a more active humanist than either Lovato or Montagnone. Of humble origin, he rose to eminence by his own energy and ability. In 1296 he was made a knight and became a member of the Great Council of Padua. He was an active supporter of the ill-fated plans of the Emperor Henry VII for Italy and was frequently chosen for embassies to Henry, who liked him, as well as to other Italian cities, princes, and popes. He wrote both prose history and drama. The prose style of his *De gestis Henrici VII* (1313) reveals his close reading of Livy's Roman history and Julius Caesar's *De bello gallico.* Like Caesar, he spoke of himself in the third person; like Livy, he introduced speeches and documents into the narrative; and he adopted Roman nomenclature for local offices and titles. Of his other works—letters, soliloquies, elegies, some epic fragments, and a tragedy—the last, the *Eccerinis* (1315), was his most notable effort. This tragedy and the *De gestis Henrici VII* were specified by the city of Padua when he was honored with the laurel crown of the poet in 1315. When the *Eccerinis* was first performed, a public holiday was declared in the city. The drama is classical in structure, modeled on Seneca's tragedies, and has nothing in common with religious drama as the Church knew and pro-

---

* One poem of Catullus exists in a ninth-century MS in Paris (lat. 8071), and scattered references may be traced from then until Montagnone, but none had quoted so extensively as he did in the *Compendium.*

moted it. It tells the story of Padua's heroic resistance to the brutality of Ez-zelino da Romano and, by implication, to all tyrants—notably Can Grande della Scala of Verona, who was attempting to take Padua under his wing. There was some irony in Mussato's high patriotism, for he was destined to die in exile from his native city when the political situation in Padua changed.

In his poetry Mussato was something of an artist, although he could not be accused of originality. Many of his best lines are only paraphrases of Ovid, Catullus, or the *Eclogues* of Virgil. From his correspondence we gain an insight into his motivation. He ardently opposed the naturalistic scholasticism (see pp. 153–54) then dominant at the University of Padua and appealed to the citizenry of the city to appreciate the beauty and nobility of their Roman past. He has an important place in the preparation for Petrarch. Although the scholastic tradition was too deeply entrenched for him to uproot it, his work and its popularity were significant harbingers of the new learning.

Meanwhile, at Verona, the riches of the library of the cathedral, which contained many of the classics in old manuscripts, were being explored by several scholars, while in Bologna many professors of grammar, rhetoric, and poetry were discovering the potentialities and the delights of the classics. One of these Bolognese, Giovanni del Virgilio, soon after 1320 was producing poetry modeled on Ovid and Virgil which far surpassed in quality the medieval doggerel that was called poetry in the fourteenth century. There was also a lively enthusiasm for the cult of classical letters among certain student groups. This same current of interest can easily be traced in most of the larger cities of Italy in the early years of the fourteenth century. In Florence, Arezzo, Milan, Pavia—wherever there was a public chair or a school of rhetoric or grammar—there was a growing interest in Latin letters; the soil was being spontaneously prepared for the first powerful flowering of the study of antiquity in Petrarch.

PETRARCH

FRANCESCO Petrarca (Petrarch, 1304–74) has frequently been called the first modern man. That is much too broad an appellation. Yet, although he could not have been what he was without Dante and the humanists who preceded him, he looms above his humanist predecessors and contemporaries in stature, in finish, in immediate effectiveness, and in the extent of his influence upon posterity. He quite properly occupies the place of honor in the long line of pioneers of the modern spirit.

Life

PETRARCH's father, Ser Petracco, of an old and respected Florentine family, was a notary of the republic who had joined the party of the Whites (Guelphs), of which Dante was a prominent member, and had been banished from the city by the same decree that sent the poet on his long wanderings. The result of the party's effort to regain power in Florence from the Blacks (another Guelph faction) was a pitched battle under the walls of the city on July 20,

1304. The contest went against the Whites, and Petracco had to flee from the territory of the Florentine Republic. At sundown of the day of the battle, a son was born to Petracco's wife in her home in Arezzo, about fifty miles up the valley of the Arno. Petracco fled, but his wife, Eletta, stayed on for seven years unmolested. In 1311 the father took his family to Pisa; the next year they moved to Avignon, where the papal court had but recently settled and where trained notaries were needed. In the crowded city of the *curia* accommodations for a family were not obtainable or even desirable, and Eletta and the children, Francesco and his younger brother, Gherardo, were moved to the pleasant city of Carpentras, fifteen miles northeast of Avignon. Here Francesco received his first instruction in grammar and rhetoric from a local teacher, Convenevole da Prato, who, although somewhat eccentric, still gave the boy sound training. In 1316, when the boy was barely twelve, his father sent him to the nearby University of Montpellier, which had a reputable faculty of law. Francesco was fairly successful in his studies although, to his father's annoyance, he already preferred Cicero and Virgil to the heavy law compends.

In 1320 Petracco arranged for both sons to go to Bologna, then the mecca of those who wished to study either civil or canon law. Francesco spent probably the most carefree years of his life at Bologna, not always studying. He later remarked of himself that he would have made great progress in his studies if he had persevered. But at the end of several years there was little doubt in his mind that the law held much less appeal for him than classical letters. He had found other men who shared his enthusiasms, and much time and probably much of the limited means of the young men in this group were spent in acquiring, copying, reading, and discussing the great Latin writers.

In April 1326, the death of their father recalled Francesco and Gherardo to Avignon. There was not enough of a patrimony left to start Francesco on any career, and he seems to have drifted in uncertainty for a time, until, on April 6, 1327, he met Laura de Sade. His life and thought were never, to his dying day, to be free of the impress of his love for her. Personable and friendly, an ideal courtier, he was soon taken into the establishment of the powerful Stephen Colonna, the head of the great Roman senatorial family which had been opposed to Boniface VIII and had therefore moved to Avignon under French protection. Stephen's youngest son, Giacomo, had known Petrarch in Bologna; and when they met again in Avignon, they became fast friends. Petrarch's material worries were thus at an end, and his interests in learning and letters could now be confidently pursued. He traveled in northern Europe, Flanders, and western Germany at the Colonnas' expense in 1333, making more friends and interesting them in his quest for manuscripts of ancient Roman writers. Late in 1336 he set out on a journey to Rome, which he had dreamed of seeing from his earliest childhood. He walked eagerly the length and breadth of the city, following maps and asking questions. To his disappointment, he found the Romans ignorant of the history of their own city, but he wrote to Cardinal Giovanni Colonna that he was more than pleased with what he saw: "In truth Rome was more imposing and her relics are greater than I had thought." His interest was drawn to the monuments of Rome's Christian history and the sites of martyrdom, as well as to her ancient pagan glories. He returned to Avignon in August 1337 and soon moved to Vaucluse, an idyllic spot along the river Sorgue, about twelve miles east of Avignon. He lived at Vaucluse, with his precious books, one faithful servant and her husband, with some interruptions, from 1337 to 1353. There he had his greatest inspirations, wrote his most eloquent love lyrics to Laura, and experienced his purest and most intense passion for her.

Petrarch's fame for learning was Europe-wide. Avignon was the center of culture and art in Europe, and through his close connection with the great Colonna family he met all the illustrious visitors. His personality was so winning, his gift for friendship so magnetic, that favors inevitably came his way. He asked for nothing more than that his acquaintance send him a manuscript of the Roman classics, if any were to be found when the visitor returned to his home. In September 1340, both the University of Paris and the Roman Senate—strangely enough, on the same day—offered him the laurel crown of the poet. In the citation, *Africa,* his epic poem of the life of Scipio Africanus, was mentioned as deserving the crown. He had enlisted the support of friends in both places so as to be sure of getting the offer. He decided to accept the Roman crown and, reputedly on his way to Rome, went to Naples to visit King Robert, highly literate and interested in the new learning. It was on this occasion that Boccaccio, then a young gallant at King Robert's court, saw and heard Petrarch for the first time. The coronation, bringing with it Roman citizenship, took place on the Capitol on April 8, 1341. This was undoubtedly the high point of Petrarch's public life. On the way back to Avignon he stopped at Parma, for about a year, as a guest of the lords of Correggio, and during his sojourn made further progress on the *Africa.*

Back in Avignon in the spring of 1342, he immersed himself in study, correspondence, and writing, interrupted by occasional embassies for the Pope. This same year he began the study of Greek with Barlaam of Calabria. Since Barlaam's Latin was very poor Petrarch profited little from the instruction; yet he gave the study of Greek no little impulse simply by recognizing its cultural superiority over Latin. In 1354 a friend, Nicollò Sigero, sent him from Constantinople a handsome copy of Homer. Petrarch was moved to tears at the sight of the pages of the divine Greek master of his own beloved Virgil, but he confessed that he could not read a line of the poem.

In 1343 an embassy, headed by the eloquent young Cola di Rienzo, came to Avignon to urge the return of the Papacy to the city of the Caesars. Rienzo's fire and classical learning attracted Petrarch, who supported the Roman's appeal to the Pope with all his powers of persuasion. The revolt of Rienzo in Rome four years later seemed to Petrarch a laudable movement promising a revival of the spirit and idea of Rome. But, since the Roman nobility was the primary object of Rienzo's attacks, the Colonna family, one of the two leading noble houses of Rome, was bitter against the self-styled tribune. The long friendship between Petrarch and his generous patron was thus grievously strained, and the poet withdrew almost entirely from the court.

In the next year, 1348, the Black Death struck. It was particularly severe in Avignon, and the love of Petrarch's life, Laura, was a victim, dying on April 6, the anniversary of the date on which they first had met in 1327. Avignon and

Vaucluse could never from that time be the same to him. In 1353 the Visconti of Milan invited him to their court, on terms that were both munificent and considerate. Petrarch felt no twinges of conscience at accepting the bounty of a despot, for he was left free to go on with his own study and writing; being required only to make occasional appearances at court, provide a few speeches, and compose polished epitaphs for members of the Visconti family and entourage. His friend Boccaccio reproached him for denying all his ideals of freedom and human dignity by accepting the hospitality of a tyrant, but for eight years, until 1361, Petrarch was a contented guest of the ruler of Milan.

Rienzo's pitiful failure to recreate the Roman Republic (see pp. 69–70), both in 1347 and on his second attempt in 1354, the latter time with papal support, obliged Petrarch to look elsewhere for some dynamic force that might restore to the name of Rome its former power and glory. The Emperor Charles IV had made several visits to Avignon since his election in 1346. Petrarch certainly knew of Charles' wide and informed interests and admired his firm intelligence and diplomatic skill. The poet wrote to him first in 1351 and had a long and gratifying conversation with him in Mantua in December 1354, as Charles was on his way to Rome to be crowned. At this meeting Petrarch expounded his great hopes for the revival of Rome's glory and the

Petrarch, school of Bellini, in the Borghese Gallery, Rome [ANDERSON].

FRANCISCVS PETRARCHA

Emperor listened sympathetically. In 1356, at the Emperor's invitation, Petrarch visited the imperial court at Prague, where he was deeply impressed by the high level of culture. He later remarked in a letter: "I have never seen anything less barbarous, nor anything more humane than the Emperor and a number of the most eminent men around him—I will mention no names— but I repeat, leading men and men of high station, yet worthy of even greater honors, and as a matter of fact so mellow and urbane that one would think they were Athenians born and bred." Needless to say, Charles, as a practical politician, was polite to Petrarch and attentive to his lofty ideas of what the Holy Roman Empire should be and do in the fourteenth century; he even made Petrarch a count palatine of the Empire in 1357. But the poet in politics has seldom been a success, and Petrarch was no exception.

In 1361 he left the hospitality of the Visconti for Padua and Venice, in order to be near his daughter Francesca, who had recently married. His last years were full of honor, but not a little dispute as well. Five times a papal secretary-ship, promising security and influence, was offered to him, and five times it was refused. The *Signoria* of Florence asked him to return to the city and accept both the properties that had been confiscated from his father and a lucrative post at the university. The offer was conveyed to him by Boccaccio in person in 1351; refusal was immediate and notably courteous. While living in Venice, he made arrangements to leave his rich library to that city in return for a residence on Venetian territory. In 1370 he chose the town of Arquà, in the gentle Euganean hills, a few miles from Venice. However, his health was failing; nor was he to find complete freedom from attack and controversy even at the end of his life. Some of his ventures into politics had made him enemies, and there were those who impugned his Latin style and his scholarship as well. His pen had lost none of its cunning, and his part in these polemics was as sharp and telling as ever. He never recovered from a heart attack in 1370 and spent the following years putting his work and library in order. Feeling the end near, he wrote to Boccaccio of his hope that death would find him "either reading or writing, or better still, if God will, praying and weeping." Early in the morning of July 19, 1374, his servants found him dead in his study, his head bent over his precious Augustine.

Vernacular Poetry

BY REASON of his long life, his wide travel, his faithfulness to the passion for learning, and his fortunate connections with princes and prelates, scholars and statesmen, Petrarch may be said to have had more influence upon the mind of his time than any other single person. This amazing influence was exercised in many directions. His was a complex and many-sided personality, and his interests were wide, manifold, and presented to his time and to posterity with conviction. His place in our cultural heritage might be considered in relation to the guiding passions of his life and work: his admiration for Cicero and for all classical letters, his love for Laura, his deep Italian patriotism, his conviction that he and Italy shared Rome's past glory and were its proper custodians, his veneration for Augustine, his hatred of sham and quackery in all forms, and, not least, his desire for his own fame. Each of these motivations found copious voice in literary creation. Cicero was his earliest love. As an adolescent he preferred reading Cicero to all other pleasures. He formed his style and thought on Cicero and encouraged his friends and acquaintances to refresh their minds at that pure fount. He almost persuaded himself that Cicero, had he lived later, would have been a Christian, and his devotion to Augustine was heightened by the knowledge that the great bishop of Hippo had been trained as a Ciceronian rhetorician. So pervasive a passion could hardly be other than infectious.

Petrarch's love for Laura invites comparison with Dante's love for Beatrice. Petrarch's was perhaps less noble. Being at once physical and spiritual, it inspired him to write lyrics unsurpassed in any vernacular for beauty and constancy to one object of affection. There is no doubt that the influence of Provençal courtly lyric upon his sensitive imagination was profound, rooted in a boyhood and early manhood spent in the heart of Provence. But his love poetry goes beyond the art of the troubadours in its spiritual quality and even in its technical excellence and diversity of form. Guiding himself also by his beloved classical models that he admired so greatly, he never consciously violated the laws of rhetoric and rationality. The great collection of his Italian poetry, known as the *Canzoniere,* contains all his poems to Laura, divided into two sections, "To Laura in Life" and "To Laura in Death," and, in addition, many ballads on political, patriotic, and personal themes. The section "To Laura in Life" recounts the course of his love for Laura, of their meetings and their effect upon him, sometimes almost day by day. The collection, as he left it, begins with the sonnet *Voi ch'ascoltate,* in which he confesses how vain his passion has been.

> O ye who in scattered verse the echoes hear
> Of all those sighs with which I fed my heart
> When I, by youthful error first misled,
> Quite another man from what I now appear,
> Uncertain 'twixt frantic hope and vainer fear,
> In diverse style from what I presently complain,
> Throughout my song by hopes and griefs but vain
> I strive to find, if not a pardon, then a tear.
> But well I see that years on end to all
> My name has been a byword and a jest
> And even to me I count myself a shame
> And of my folly the fruit has been but blame
> And sad repentance and the knowledge clear
> That what may please the world is but a passing dream.

Strangely enough, the two best-known poems in this collection are not directed to Laura. *Italia mia,* an apostrophe to the land of his birth, and *Spirto gentil,* addressed to Cola di Rienzo, present two other aspects of Petrarch's complex personality. In *Italia mia* Petrarch expressed what might be called Renaissance nationalism. He appealed to God to bring peace, and to the rulers of Italy to take thought of the great mission of Italy and the lives of their subjects. The first of eight stanzas is the appeal to God.

O Italy, my Italy. Words cannot heal the mortal wounds
Thy precious body has had to bear.
Yet I take some consolation
That I can bewail the woes
Of the Tiber, the Arno
And the Po, where I wander sad and troubled.
O ruler of the universe, I pray
That that mercy which led thee
To dwell awhile on earth
May bring thee to look upon this thy beloved land.
See, God of love,
How petty a thing gave rise to this cruel war.
Those hearts which haughty and fierce Mars
Has hardened
Open thou, O Father, to tenderness and peace.

The eight-stanza *canzone* (VI) addressed to Rienzo in 1347, *Spirto gentil,*
expresses Petrarch's deepest hopes that Rome may recover her leadership in
Italy and the world and his admiration for Rienzo's efforts to revive the
grandeur of the city out of its despair and decay. The first stanza sets the
tone and reveals Petrarch's passion for Italian unity.

O noble spirit who with fire divine
Enkindles those members awhile which as a pilgrim hold
On earth a Lord, gracious, wise, and brave;
Now that the staff of state is in thy hand
Rome and her errant children to confine
And call her to her ancient way,
To thee I speak, for elsewhere not a beam
Of virtue do I see—here in the world it is lost—
Nor anyone who is ashamed of evil.
What faces Italy or what she can hope for
I do not know; she seems not to know her own good,
She is old, weak, lazy, and slow.
She will sleep forever, and there's none to awake her.
Would that my hands could wind through her tresses.

Many of Petrarch's sonnets, ballads, and *canzoni* are rich in scriptural al-
lusions and in direct borrowings from Virgil, Seneca, Ovid, and Horace. He
fused his classical bent and his expressive genius with the native language to
a degree matched by no other humanist.

Later in life, Petrarch added to this collection *I Trionfi,* a long poem in
six sections: "Triumph of Love," "Triumph of Chastity," "Triumph of Death,"
"Triumph of Fame," "Triumph of Time," and "Triumph of Eternity." Left
unfinished at his death, the poem nevertheless represents a vast panorama of
Roman and Christian ideals through which his own experience, his love for
Laura, and his hopes for a noble civilization are displayed. The poem is very
uneven in quality and at times monotonous and turgid, but it contains many
passages of striking beauty and exalted vision.

Petrarch's work was of the highest significance for the development of
Italian vernacular literature. We shall hear, in the fifteenth and sixteenth cen-

turies, of Petrarchism: that is, direct imitation of his lyric and even epic style and mode. But he was of greater import for the humanistic revival. His exaltation of Cicero, Seneca, and Virgil, as well as of some of the lesser lights of ancient Latin literature; his search for manuscripts, which was a stimulus to the rediscovery of works either lost or forgotten in the Middle Ages; his appreciation of the glories of Rome's past and of Italy as the repository and guardian of those glories—these enthusiasms, assembled in a single determined genius, marked an epoch in the cultural history of Europe.

Latin Works

PETRARCH's Latin works, much more voluminous than his Italian poetry, include a pretentious epic poem, *Africa,* a vast correspondence reaching to the remote corners of the Continent, historical biography, dialogues, polemics against individuals and groups, and religious and introspective works. The *Africa,* begun in 1339 at Vaucluse and never finished, was intended to be the story of Rome's great victory over Carthage. The hero was Scipio Africanus. Petrarch wanted the poem to be the master work of his life, and it was for this ambitious undertaking that the laurel crown of the poet was offered to him. Ironically, the poem's artificiality has condemned it to virtual oblivion, for epics must almost write themselves in the blood of a vigorous people.

Petrarch's correspondence, in Latin, was perhaps his principal means of spreading his enthusiasm for humane letters in the quarters where such fervor would be likely to do the most good. He wrote letters to close friends, to kings and popes, to the Emperor and various despots; nor did he limit himself to writing to the living. He maintained a serious, if one-sided, correspondence with Cicero, who was his idol and yet not above criticism, with Homer, Livy, Virgil, Horace, and Seneca—indeed, with every classical author whose style or thought he considered important. In a manner of speaking, he seemed to assume that they replied to him through their writings, and in his own to them he freely offered criticism and advice. He kept revising and polishing his epistles to the end of his life, organizing them into *Familiar Letters, Letters of Old Age, Letters to Posterity, Metrical Letters,* and *Letters without Titles.* About 550 letters written by Petrarch are extant, but it is probable that this is less than half of all he wrote. In 1353 he decided to clear away the "rubbish" collected over the years at Vaucluse, and almost none of his correspondence before that time has come to light. Thereafter he carefully kept copies of his correspondence, and the collection from 1353 to the end of his life is nearly complete.

As any appeal to what seems good in the past is inevitably an appeal to the muse of history, so Petrarch was conscious of the call. The *Africa* was an attempt to immortalize Roman courage and Roman history. With his widening horizon of knowledge, Petrarch also undertook to provide his own age with an adequate dictionary of illustrious ancients. His *De viris illustribus* was drawn from the works of Julius Caesar, Pliny, and Livy and from Suetonius' *Lives of the Caesars,* the abridgment of *Pompeius Trogus* by Justinus, and other, less reliable Roman historians. Petrarch was at work on this treatise when he met the Emperor Charles IV in Mantua in 1354. To Charles' request that he dedicate the work to him, Petrarch answered that he would do so if the Emperor proved himself worthy of such an honor. Petrarch was essentially attempting to write a history of Rome by means of biographies of her leading men. Compilation though it certainly was, Petrarch intended it to be factual, even scientific, as a counterpoise to the *Africa,* which was a poetic presentation of a great crisis in Roman history.

Petrarch was no mean disputant and polemist. At least three of his later compositions are invectives: *Apologia contra gallum* (*Defense against an Anonymous Frenchman*), of uncertain date, perhaps 1355; *Invectiva contra medicum* (*Attack on a Doctor*), 1355; and *De sui ipsius et multorum aliorum ignorantia* (*On His Own Ignorance and That of Many Others*), written in 1367, revised in 1370. The *Apologia* was apparently a response to some Frenchman, of unknown identity, who had attacked Petrarch for his praise of everything Roman and for urging the return of the Papacy to the Eternal City. Petrarch answered at some length that, having seen what France had to offer —her tumult, her barbarity, and her filth—he much preferred Rome and Italy. The *Invectiva* expressed his low opinion of doctors in general—"that noxious and useless breed of men"—against whose quackery he had waged a mordant campaign since 1353. In this invective he warned Pope Innocent VI to beware of doctors, since they were all fakes. The *De sui ipsius ignorantia* was an answer to four young Venetians who, in his last years, had enjoyed the hospitality of his house in Venice, then set themselves up as judges of his learning and general scholarship, qualifying him with bumptious condescension as "a good fellow but quite illiterate, really, you know" (*sine litteris*). The young men, of the fashionable Averroist school of naturalism,* ridiculed Petrarch's religious turn of mind. The poet might have borne with amusement an attack upon his learning, but an attack upon his religious sincerity was another thing. In the final version of the *De sui ipsius ignorantia,* published in 1370, he reviewed his long life of study, showing complete familiarity with the curricula of the universities, and labeled the Averroistic tendency as a false way, destructive of human values. Real enlightenment and profit to the soul, he claimed, were to be found in the Christian faith and in those luminaries of antiquity whose lives and philosophy were near to those of the Christian tradition. This polemic is perhaps the sharpest and most devastating work the essentially gentle and tolerant humanist ever composed.

Christian Motivation

THE religious bent was an important part of Petrarch's nature. In his own assessment of his spiritual growth, he looked upon the year 1342 as the date of his religious conversion. He had been strongly drawn to St. Augustine before, as is revealed by his moving account of his ascent of Mont Ventoux

---

* Averroës, a Muslim philosopher (d. 1198) was accepted in the medieval universities as "The Commentator." He taught the eternity of the world, the complete separation of God from His universe, and that there was only one intellect, in which each individual participates. His teachings attracted some Christian philosophers and were condemned, several times as heretical. See also below, Chapter 7.

(Windy Mountain) with his brother Gherardo on April 26, 1336. He wrote to his friend Dionigi di San Sepolcro in Paris of his arrival at the summit:

While I was admiring this panorama in detail, now losing myself in a certain physical ecstasy, now lifting my soul, like my body, to the heights, it occurred to me to glance at the *Confessions* of St. Augustine, a gift of your affection, which I keep in memory both of the author and of the giver, and which I always carry with me . . . I opened it to read whatever might strike my eye. What wouldn't I find in it which would not be meet for pious devotion? By chance the tenth book of the work fell open before me. My brother, anxious to hear me read something from Augustine, stood up, all attention. I take God to witness, as well as my brother, the passage which first caught my attention was: "Men go about to admire the heights of the mountains and the vast waves of the sea, the long courses of rivers, the circuits of oceans and the orbits of the stars, and they neglect themselves." I was struck, I admit. I asked my brother, who wanted me to read on, not to bother me more. I closed the book, irritated at myself for prizing the things of this world when I should have learned even from the philosophers of the Gentiles that nothing is to be prized but the soul, and that for the soul, when it is large and noble, nothing is of moment.

Some time after Petrarch's return from Italy and his acceptance of the laurel crown, a change took place in his estimate of himself and of the value of fame, and in his own humility and awareness of a need for God. Many of his Italian poems, particularly the *Triumphs,* are rich in religious feeling. But in several of the longer works which he wrote in his later years an even more religious attitude is dominant, particularly in the *Secretum* (also known as the *De contemptu mundi*), begun in 1342 and finished some years later, and the *De vita solitaria,* begun in 1346 and finished perhaps as late as 1366. The *Secretum,* which must have arisen out of the spiritual crisis through which he passed in 1342, is in the form of a three-day-long dialogue between the poet and St. Augustine, with Truth as the arbiter. It is a document of complete self-revelation, certainly modeled after the *Confessions* of St. Augustine. On the third day Augustine puts Petrarch's crisis to him bluntly: "You are bound by two unbreakable chains, Love and Fame." The poet cannot deny the truth of the analysis; he can only attempt to understand how great the power of each of the chains upon him really is: his love for Laura, now increasingly spiritualized; and his insatiable need for fame, in life and with posterity. The work on the life of solitude is perhaps less religious and more humanistic; in it he appears to seek the solitude of the scholar, not for contemplation of the goodness and being of God, but to be away from the noise of the crowd and free of the responsibilities of society. Yet even here spiritual and specifically Christian strains are easily discernible.

Although, as we have seen, Petrarch cannot correctly be called the first humanist, yet we must consider him the father of humanism as an active movement. His genius was so inclusive and touched the life of his time at so many points and with such stimulating impact that the intellectual life of Western Europe could never be the same after him. As a classicist and manuscript collector he set new standards. As a friend he won countless warm-hearted men of influence to his beloved pursuit of humane letters. As an

Italian patriot he set a tone and a fashion that others were to follow. While not an original thinker, he was a courageous opponent of the materialistic Averroism of the Italian universities and of the aridity of current scholasticism. As a political figure he was too single-minded in his passion to revive the grandeur of Rome to be wholly successful. As a Christian he was a fervent Augustinian and quite unmedieval. In the area of historiography he exercised great influence through his study of the Roman historians and re-evaluation of their relevance to his time. Humanism was centered around the greatest event in the history of the mind of the West, the achievement of Rome; without history there was no humanism. Petrarch's whole endeavor was to revive a history. Petrarch the vernacular poet, in style, inventiveness, artistry, and sincerity, had no equal in his century and perhaps, after Dante, in all of Italian literature.

BOCCACCIO

ALTHOUGH Petrarch never lived in Florence, he is known as the second of the great Florentine trio of which Dante was the first, both because his ancestors were Florentine and because it was in Florence that his most noteworthy successors flourished. Florence, for somewhat elusive reasons, was more sensitive than any other city in Italy to the currents of thought that Petrarch embodied and encouraged. Petrarch's best-known successor and, in a degree, his heir, the third of the Florentine trio, was his close friend and great admirer Giovanni Boccaccio.

Boccaccio was born in 1313, probably in Paris, the son of Boccaccio di Chellino, a traveling Florentine merchant connected with the powerful Bardi family, and a Frenchwoman of gentle birth. In 1315 or 1316 the father returned to his small estate in the town of Certaldo, in the Val d'Elsa, about twenty miles from Florence, bringing the child with him; Giovanni always regarded himself as a Florentine, or a Certaldese. When he was about twelve years old, he was apprenticed to a business friend of his father in Naples. After six years of this life, which Boccaccio later regarded as completely useless and lost, his father, disappointed in the boy's lack of enthusiasm for commerce, allowed him to study law at the University of Naples and even employed a private teacher for him. Both Giovanni and the tutor were wasting their time. The disgusted father in 1333 ordered his son back to Florence to work in his own store. But Giovanni had seen enough while in Naples to know what he really wanted to do. He had made friends in the court circles of the enlightened King Robert. The royal chancellor, Barbato, well versed in the classics, became a friend of Boccaccio, and the royal librarian, Paul of Perugia, was drawn to the young Florentine and opened to him the treasures of the rich royal library. Boccaccio profited from this opportunity to the full. From boyhood he had been aware of his own proclivity to tell stories and write poetry, and this natural bent was strengthened by the opportunities he had had to learn the poetry of ancient masters under such pleasant circumstances. He was deeply impressed by his visit to the ivy-covered tomb of Virgil, on the height of Posilippo, from which there was a clear view of the Bay of Naples with Sorrento and the blue isle of Capri in the distance. He came to regard this experience as the turning point of his life.

For most of the first forty years of his life, Boccaccio wrote in the vernacular; yet his plot and themes, and even the names of his characters, were drawn in large measure from classical mythology. His thoughts were constantly fixed upon ancient culture.

At the age of twenty or soon thereafter, Boccaccio met and fell in love with a lady long supposed to have been Maria d'Aquino, a natural daughter of King Robert and the wife of a noble at the royal court. This was no high and exalted passion such as Dante's for Beatrice or even Petrarch's for Laura but a banal and almost sordid liaison. Yet Maria sensed Boccaccio's gift and urged him to write. In the years from 1336 to about 1350, a long succession of stories, plays, and imaginative pieces came from his pen, all in the vernacular. These constitute a body of literary inventiveness and adaptation hardly matched in the history of Italian letters. The *Filocolo* (1337–39) is a prose version of the story of Flore and Blancheflore, an original French romance current in an Ital-

Boccaccio, fresco by Andrea del Castagno, in the Convent of Sant' Appolonia, Florence [ALINARI].

ian form in the preceding century. Boccaccio wove into the story all kinds of classical and medieval lore on geography and astronomy, as well as biblical tales. Boccaccio's ladylove appears in the story as Fiammetta, queen of the tournament of storytelling. Some of the techniques that he later developed in the *Decameron* appear in this romance.

Boccaccio's next work was the *Filostrato* (1339-40), an Italian romance in octave rhyme, virtually the story of the medieval *Roman de Troie* reshaped into the story of Troilus and Criseida brought together by Pandaro, an accommodating friend to both parties. Thus employing a classic theme adorned by three distinctive character types—the hesitant lover, the lady, and the helpful friend—Boccaccio told a story superior to the *Filocolo* in dramatic form and content. The octave rhyming scheme is regarded as virtually Boccaccio's invention.

The *Filostrato* was followed by *Teseida* (1340-42), an epic poem, also in octave rhyme. No Italian before had attempted an epic in the vernacular, and the *Aeneid* of Virgil and the *Thebaid* of Statius challenged imitation. Love and war are mingled around the story of Arcite and Palemon, two Theban friends who loved the same Athenian princess, Emilia. There followed the *Ameto* (1341-42), a pastoral romance; the *Amorosa visione* (ca. 1342), an unsuccessful allegory in the *terza rima* so tellingly used by Dante in the *Divine Comedy;* *Fiammetta* (1344-46), in which Boccaccio tells how much his *inamorata* missed him when he left Naples to return to Florence; the *Ninfale fiesolano* (1346-49), a pastoral idyll in octave rhyme, perhaps the most delicate, lucid, and sensitive of all his vernacular works.

The Decameron

THIS was a most impressive body of literary creativity, much of it original and pioneering. Yet most of it would have become the object of purely antiquarian interest were it not for the *Decameron*. In this work, written between 1348 and 1353, Boccaccio's genius reached its maturity. The scene is Florence during the Black Death of 1348. Seven young women and three young men decide to leave the pest-ridden city for purer country air. To pass the time, they tell stories. They agree that over a period of two weeks each of the ten will tell a tale every day. Since Saturdays and Sundays are to be devoted to rest and devotions, a hundred stories will result.

Each day's storytelling is to be guided by a theme, assigned on the previous day by the one appointed queen or king of that day's activity. The scheme is not adhered to consistently, but it serves as a point of departure. The rare value of this, the most famous collection of short stories in world literature, resides in its air of composure, its smooth movement, its unerring if at times ironic mastery of human psychology—that is to say, human frailty—and its profound revelation of the culture of the time in all its manifestations. There is not a European literature in which stories told by Boccaccio in the *Decameron* have not reappeared. In English literature particularly, from Chaucer to the twentieth century, one can find traces of Boccaccio's genius. The *Decameron* is very much of its time: it is Italy and particularly Florence in the mid-fourteenth century. Yet in every characterization, in the organization and presentation of each story, in every situation, Boccaccio's familiarity with classical models is evident. The dignity, objectivity, and humanity of the Ciceronian ideal all stand forth in the *Decameron*. It is humanistic in the full sense of the term.

Boccaccio as Classicist

ABOUT 1353, perhaps as a result of conversations with Petrarch, who stopped off in Florence in the summer of 1350 on his way to the jubilee in Rome, Boccaccio decided to devote himself to Latin letters. Apparently his previous work in the vernacular now seemed to him merely entertaining trash, unworthy and unsuitable. He began to feel apologetic about the *Decameron* and regretted his inability to withdraw it from circulation. His passion for manuscripts of the Latin classics became almost a mania. He kept himself poor buying, having copied, or copying himself manuscripts of Terence, Livy, Tacitus, Cicero, Varro, Boetius, and others. He traveled widely in search of manuscripts of the classics and would gladly have stolen them if all other means of acquiring them had failed. Indeed, he certainly did add some codices to his library without benefit of payment. His enthusiasm for things classical led him to learn Greek and to undertake to have Homer translated into Latin. He heard from Petrarch of a certain Calabrian, Leonzio Pilato, who claimed to know Greek and had him brought to Florence in 1359 by the city fathers, engaging to keep him in his own home. Leonzio's Greek was dubious, his Latin weak, his manners worse, his disposition that of a disgruntled bear. But Boccaccio endured him for three years and got out of him something resembling a Latin translation of the *Iliad* and the *Odyssey*.

In the last twenty years of his life Boccaccio projected some informative and scholarly works in Latin, among them *De casibus virorum illustrium* (*On the Vicissitudes of Famous Men*), *De claris mulieribus* (*On Famous Women*), *De genealogiis deorum gentilium* (*On the Genealogies of the Pagan Gods*), and *De montibus, sylvis, fontibus, lacubus, etc.* (*On Mountains, Forests, Springs, Lakes, etc.*). Although his intent was to write history in Latin about illustrious men and women, preferably of classic times, he could not avoid spinning entertaining stories. The *De genealogiis* is Boccaccio's most scholarly work. It reflects fully the years he had spent, even while writing light literature in Italian, reading the great Latin masters. It is a kind of encyclopedia of classical mythology and, toward the end, a defense of poetry as a mirror of man's best thought and endeavor, not only sanctioned but vouchsafed to a few men by God Himself. The treatise *De montibus* was Boccaccio's attempt to help the student to understand the geography of the ancient world, much of which, because of the change of geographical names or the general disregard for geography, had become quite unfamiliar to men of the Middle Ages. Much serious and careful work went into this dictionary, and indeed it proved to be tremendously useful to later readers of the classics.

In the 1360's Boccaccio was employed by the Republic of Florence on several important diplomatic missions. His income from his property at Certaldo was hardly adequate to support him, and these official assignments added substantially to his resources. In 1362 he went to Naples at the invitation of a

Florentine friend. He soon found that the situation had been misrepresented to him; the apartment assigned to him was so filthy that he left in anger and bitterness, returning to Certaldo and thence going to Venice to stay with Petrarch in the spring of 1363. For most of this decade, however, he remained on his modest estate at Certaldo. In 1373 he was asked by the *Signoria* of Florence to lecture on Dante's *Divine Comedy,* and he set about composing a commentary on the work. Although his health was failing, he gave a course of lectures from the fall of 1373 to the early spring of 1374. These lectures are of historical value to this day, for he had talked to many individuals who had known Dante and thus was able to add richness and immediacy to his interpretation of the *Divine Comedy.* Unfortunately, he was able to finish his commentary only through Canto 17 of the *Inferno.* The news of Petrarch's death in July 1374 was a great blow to him; although he was nine years younger than his master and friend, his own infirmities brought release in death on December 21, 1375.

Not the least important aspect of the story of Boccaccio and his place in the broad movement we call the Renaissance is the fact that he was a complete layman and had never had any connection with the Church. The unqualifiedly secular character of his scholarly activity is indicative of the tendency humanistic learning was henceforth going to manifest.

Boccaccio's own judgment of his place in literature and cultural history differed from that of posterity. We honor him today for being the initiator of Italian prose literature, the greatest storyteller of the modern world, the forerunner of Chaucer, Rabelais, and La Fontaine. That should be glory enough for any man. But Boccaccio depreciated his vernacular production, priding himself rather on having introduced Greek to Italy. He wrote in the *De genealogiis:*

It is my pride and my glory to have enjoyed, the first among the Tuscans, Greek poetry. . . . I was certainly the first to bring to Etruria, at my own expense, the books of Homer and some other Greeks . . . not to Etruria only, but to the whole of Italy. It was I who, first among the Italians, heard in private the *Iliad* from Leonzio Pilato. It was I, furthermore, who arranged to have these Homeric songs read in public. And if I may not myself have gone deeply enough into these matters, yet I learned what I could, and certainly if that feckless man had stayed any length of time with us I would have learned much more.

OTHER FLORENTINE HUMANISTS

FLORENCE seemed peculiarly receptive to the ideals which Boccaccio so energetically and prolifically advocated. Petrarch had refused the invitation to return to the city of his birth, but his refusal was based on personal reasons, not on any lack of interest at Florence in the new learning. For the contrary was the case. Among Petrarch's closest friends in the early 1330's were Florentines who shared his deep interest in classic letters. Many of these men, among them Lapo da Castiglionchio, Giovanni da Strada and his son Zanobi, and Francesco Nelli, were schoolmasters or heads of monastic estab-

lishments and therefore in ideal positions to spread that interest. A few generations of pupils schooled in the classics built up a broad basis of civic support
for the new learning and created an atmosphere of interest and sympathy that
was almost unique in Italy. Indeed, by the last quarter of the fourteenth century there had already emerged a whole circle of competent scholars, some
connected with the university, some belonging to monastic orders, others
simply literate laymen with cultural interests. Although some of these scholars
moved elsewhere in Italy, temporarily or permanently as employment or ex-
pediency dictated, Florence was and remained the natural center of this
circle.

There was, for example, Giovanni Malpaghini (sometimes known as
Giovanni da Ravenna), who had worked for Petrarch as his scribe and secretary and who, gifted with a remarkable memory, had acquired an exceptional knowledge of classical learning. After a few years in this subordinate
capacity (1364–68), he left Petrarch to try his own fortunes elsewhere, only
to return and then leave again. His wandering foot took him as a secretary or
an independent professor of Latin rhetoric and eloquence to Rome, Florence,
Avignon, and Ragusa. At Florence, where he spent the last years of his life,
his enthusiasm served well the cause of humane letters. Although he himself
wrote almost nothing, many scholars who later became leaders in the movement were his students. Among those who studied under him in one city or
another were Roberto Rossi, Francesco Barbaro, Leonardo Bruni, Poggio
Bracciolini, and Jacopo d'Angelo da Scarparia—all significant figures in the
subsequent history of humanism.

At Florence, largely but not exclusively under the stimulus of Boccaccio's
enthusiasms, interest in the new learning grew noticeably from about 1350.
Efforts had been made to found a university (*studium*) there in the early part
of the fourteenth century, but without any real success. In 1349 Pope Clement
VI gave the city a bull permitting the establishment of a university with all
faculties. Progress was slow, both in the recruitment of able professors and in
competition for students with the *studia* at Pisa, Bologna, and Siena; and the
subsequent success of the university was only mediocre, partly because of its
late establishment and partly because of the wealth of Florence, which made
the cost of living for poor students—and students were always poor—almost
prohibitive. Nevertheless, the city's interest in its own university was strong.

The *Paradiso* of Alberti

EDUCATION and culture throughout the Middle Ages had been in the hands
of the Church. There was no other group or institution in European society
that could have assumed that charge. But in fourteenth-century Florence the
shift from ecclesiastical to lay patronage of education became quite marked.
In the middle of the century a sort of circle of culture, known to contemporaries
as the *Paradiso* of Alberti, was established in Florence. Antonio degli Alberti
was a wealthy merchant who made his spacious villa, *Paradiso,* available to
guests, both men and women, nobles and burghers, churchmen and laymen,
who were interested in lofty conversation and intellectual stimulation. He spread

an enticing table, opened his gracious gardens, brought in musicians, and occasionally arranged informal lectures or the reading of poetry by one or another of the group. He asked only that his guests should enjoy themselves discussing matters of nonmundane interest. Augustine, Plato, Dante, and Frederick II, the Roman poets and historians, the prophets and seers of old—these were the subjects of their converse. While the adults were engaged in such intellectual pursuits, their children were encouraged to join in sports and games in a meadow just outside the gardens.

The Circle of *Santo Spirito*

THIS was only one such group. There was another, equally frequented but less ostentatious, centering around Luigi de' Marsigli, a monk of the Order of the Augustinian Heremites. Marsigli made his Church of the Holy Spirit (*Santo Spirito*) the center for a group of devotees of the new learning. Many of them were close friends of Boccaccio, who had encouraged the organization of this coterie of enthusiasts. Indeed, Boccaccio asked to be buried in the cemetery of the church and left his precious books to the library of the convent.

Marsigli had a great reputation as an eloquent preacher and in his sermons mingled quotations from the Scriptures and the Fathers of the Church with sayings from Cicero, Seneca, and Virgil, proclaiming the divine nature of truth and morality wherever found. He shared Petrarch's low opinion of the papal *curia* at Avignon and inveighed against the immorality of "Babylon" in many of his sermons and writings. His leadership of the group determined the tenor of the discussions, which was both religious and highly learned. More than half the members of the circle of *Santo Spirito* were laymen, a fact that emphasizes the trend of the new learning. Churchmen participated as lovers of the classics, not as custodians of the traditions of the Church. The general level of discussion was in a more serious vein than that at the *Paradiso* of Alberti, although some of the members of Marsigli's group—indeed, Marsigli himself—were also frequent or regular guests of Alberti.

The circle of the *Santo Spirito* resembles in everything but name the better-known Platonic Academy of the late fifteenth century. It is even frequently called the Academy of *Santo Spirito*. This group continued as a force in the humanistic movement in Florence until the death of Marsigli in 1394. By that time the new learning had gained powerful momentum in the Republic, independent of the Church and of the university, although it had adherents in both organizations. It was already a predominantly nonclerical movement, inseparable from the burgher spirit and the cultural impulse that naturally follows upon economic success.

SALUTATI

ONE of the regular participants in both the *Paradiso* group and the circle of *Santo Spirito,* a great admirer and correspondent of Petrarch and a close friend of Boccaccio, became the leading figure in the further extension of humanism in Florence. Coluccio di Piero de' Salutati (1330–1406) was secretary of the Republic of Florence for thirty years, from 1375 until his death; but he is more important in our story as the connecting link between the first stage of humanism—the age of Petrarch and Boccaccio, the period of the discovery of the Latin classics—and the glorious second stage, when Greek, Latin, and even Hebrew were cultivated, when the fashion for classical learning extended to countries outside Italy and profoundly affected the vernacular languages and literatures.

Salutati was born in Stignano, a small town between Florence and Lucca. His father, a Guelph, was driven out of his city by the victorious Ghibellines in 1334 and settled in Bologna at the invitation of Pepoli, then the *podestà* of that city. The young Coluccio grew up in the atmosphere of the famous university, where he studied law. In 1351, at the age of twenty, he became a notary of the commune of Pescia in Tuscany. His career from 1351 until 1375 was that of a moderately successful bureaucrat. In 1367 he was chancellor of Todi, a small town in Umbria. In 1368 he was with the papal court during the temporary stay of Pope Urban V at Rome. He formed a low opinion of what he with some heat called a "Frenchified" Papacy. In 1370 he was chancellor of the *anziani* at Lucca, only to be forced out of office by a political upset the following year. He had registered in Florence as a notary in 1370, probably taking temporary assignments in order to get acquainted with conditions in that city.

Salutati had educated himself along classical lines, but he admitted indebtedness for his literary style and polish to no one. We know that he was in correspondence with scholars throughout Italy from the 1360's on and that without ever meeting Petrarch, he became one of his most enthusiastic and loyal admirers. He first wrote to the poet at Arquà in 1368 and received a gracious if short note in reply, complimenting him on his fine Latin style. He must have met Boccaccio early, for by 1369 they seem to have been on intimate terms for some time.

In 1374 Salutati was an official notary in the office of the *Signoria,* the College of Priors; and when the chancellor, Niccolò Monaci, was deposed for fraud, Salutati was promoted to the office for a term of one year. Every successive appointment for the next thirty years was likewise for a single year at a time. The office of chancellor of the *Signoria* was extremely important. All decrees and decisions of the *Signoria,* all documents concerned with the foreign affairs of the Republic, went through his hands. He was at the same time an employee, a servant, of the *Signoria* and its guide and adviser.

In these decades Florence was torn by profound disturbances, civil wars, and the uncertainties attendant upon social adjustments and class tensions. In 1378 a revolt of the *ciompi* ("ragbags"), drove the burghers and nobles out of office and put in their places representatives of the proletariat, who soon formed two new guilds and thus joined the fourteen then-active *arti minori,* composed of the craftsmen of the city. Salutati's integrity was so respected that the new masters of Florence, quite inexperienced in administration, kept him on as chancellor and deferred to his counsel in their policies. With courage and dignity he tempered the iconoclasm of the radicals so that the affairs of the state did not suffer during the tumult. When, in 1382, a more conservative element came to power, Salutati was retained in office, and his services in keeping a steady hand on the wheel were openly recognized. The humanist was now influential in politics. His prestige, gained at a critical juncture in Florentine history, redounded to the credit of the movement of which he was a leading representative. Classical learning had proved itself in the eyes of the people, and in subsequent years in Florence there was almost no opposition to the patronage of that learning by the Republic.

Salutati's personal prestige and the permanence of his public office were reflected in the increasing importance attached to the style of diplomatic documents. In a day when all chanceries throughout Europe, civil and ecclesiastical, composed their documents in Latin, it was natural that attention should be given to the quality of the composition. The better the Latin, the more effective the document. It will be remembered that Petrarch was employed on several diplomatic missions by various princes and despots who valued his eloquence as an effective diplomatic weapon. Salutati, as the first leading humanist to hold a key public post, added to the repute the new learning was winning for itself. It was, then, not really surprising that so acute a political realist as Gian Galeazzo Visconti of Milan should have assessed correctly the place of classical eloquence in diplomacy when, as the humanist Vergerio reported in 1406, "He was often heard to say that the writings of Coluccio had done him more harm than a thousand Florentine horsemen." Precisely because Salutati's state documents commanded respect and were therefore effective—they were spread throughout Italy and frequently copied by other chanceries—other cities and states, tyrants, princes, and democracies felt the need of similarly trained literary statesmen. The market, so to speak, for the humanists was growing. There were soon more places for men schooled in the classics than there were competent candidates. No Italian court was respectable without at least one humanist. Salutati and his success can be largely credited with having created this condition.

But Salutati's activity went beyond this important initiation. He wrote lives of Dante, Petrarch, and Boccaccio, maintained a prodigious correspondence, encouraged younger scholars in their endeavors, and collected manuscripts of the classics that had hitherto escaped notice and carefully collated them with other and sometimes better copies, thus making a notable contribution to the science of textual criticism. He composed a number of important treatises on classical subjects, such as *De laboribus Herculis* (1400). This work, although not original, yet shows a thorough control of large areas of classical learning, particularly the world of Virgil, and marks the end of a stage—the most advanced before the arrival of Greek in Italy—in the humanistic absorption of Latin learning. This was as far as the West could go without Greek. Salutati was not himself a Greek scholar; but he realized that Greek was necessary to a complete recovery of antiquity, and he encouraged young and ambitious scholars to master the language so as to be able to translate the great Greek works into Latin. He sponsored unselfishly, among others, the young Poggio Bracciolini and Leonardo Bruni, who were destined to be among the most brilliant ornaments of the whole humanist movement.

Among Salutati's few formal writings outside the field of classical scholarship was a short treatise, *De tyranno* (*On the Tyrant*), written in the form of a letter to a friend at Padua, in which he advocated tyrannicide:

Anyone who sets up a tyranny may lawfully be resisted, not merely by a party of the people, but by an individual, and such a monster may be put down by force, even to the point of murder.

It was perhaps safe for an official of the Republic of Florence to hold such ideas, just as it was a fact that the life of an Italian despot was always in danger, but it nevertheless took some hardihood to proclaim tyrannicide as a reasoned doctrine.

Probably the high point of Salutati's career was the arrival in Florence of Manuel Chrysoloras, the leading scholar of the Byzantine Empire. Chrysoloras, already advanced in years, had first been sent to Italy with a colleague, Demetrius Kydonios, to solicit aid from the West for the defense of Constantinople against the Turks. The two Greeks landed at Venice in 1394. The news of the arrival of two such distinguished Greek scholars spread rapidly in Italy, and a pair of young Florentine noblemen, Roberto Rossi and Jacopo d'Angelo da Scarparia, both protégés of Salutati, hurried to Venice at his suggestion to meet the celebrities. The Greeks, disappointed in their hopes of obtaining military help from the West, returned to Constantinople the following year. The young Florentine nobles had apparently made a favorable impression, for they took d'Angelo with them. Rossi returned to Florence, bringing glowing accounts of the profound learning of the Greek savants. As a result of these reports, Salutati, seconded by Palla degli Strozzi, a wealthy burgher, and Niccolò Niccoli, who was influential with the administration of the university, persuaded the *Signoria* to invite Chrysoloras to teach Greek to any who might wish to learn. The terms of the offer were generous: a house and 150 florins a year for five years, later raised to 250 florins. Chrysoloras accepted the invitation and arrived in Florence in January 1397. His teaching was brilliant, the response was enthusiastic. The West now possessed the key to the other half of the treasures of antiquity, and a new epoch in the maturing of the mind of Europe had been opened.

SUGGESTIONS FOR FURTHER READING

BLANCHARD, H. H., *Prose and Poetry of the Continental Renaissance*. New York, 1955

BOCCACCIO, GIOVANNI, *Amorous Fiammetta,* trans. B. Young. New York, 1926

BOCCACCIO, GIOVANNI, *Decameron.* Many editions, e.g. in Modern Library and Everyman's Library

BOCCACCIO, GIOVANNI, *Filostrato,* trans. N. E. Griffin and A. B. Myrick. Philadelphia, 1929

BOCCACCIO, GIOVANNI, *On Poetry.* Books XIV and XV of *Genealogia deorum gentilium,* trans. C. G. Osgood. Princeton, 1930

CASSIRER, E., *et al.,* ed. and trans., *The Renaissance Philosophy of Man.* Chicago, 1948

PETRARCH, FRANCESCO, *The Sonnets, Triumphs and Other Poems,* trans. Thomas Campbell. London, 1859 (Bohn). Frequent reprints. Other translations

PETRARCH, FRANCESCO, *Letters to Classical Authors,* trans. M. Cozenza. Chicago, 1910

PETRARCH, FRANCESCO, *The Life of Solitude,* trans. J. Zeitlin. Urbana, 1924

PETRARCH, FRANCESCO, *Petrarch at Vaucluse: Letters in Verse and Prose,* ed. E. H. Wilkins. Chicago, 1958

SALUTATI, COLUCCIO, *On Tyranny*, in E. Emerton, Humanism and Tyranny. Cambridge, 1925
SCHEVILL, F., *The First Century of Humanism*. New York, 1928

BURCKHARDT, J., *Civilization of the Renaissance in Italy*. Many editions
COSENZA, M., *Francesco Petrarca and the Revolution of Cola di Rienzo*. Chicago, 1913
FLETCHER, J. B., *Literature of the Italian Renaissance*. New York, 1934
HOLLWAY-CALTHROP, H. C., *Petrarch: His Life and Times*. London, 1907
JERROLD, M. F., *Francesco Petrarch, Poet and Humanist*. New York, 1909
SYMONDS, J. A., *The Renaissance in Italy*. 7 vols. London, 1875–81. Vols. I–III. Anchor paperback
TATHAM, E. H. R., *Francesco Petrarca*. 2 vols. London, 1925–26
TOFFANIN, G., *History of Humanism*. New York, 1954
ULLMAN, B. L., *Studies in the Italian Renaissance*. Rome, 1955
WHITFIELD, J. H., *Petrarch and the Renascence*. Oxford, 1943
WILKINS, E. H., *Life of Petrarch*. Chicago, 1961
WILKINS, E. H., *The Making of the Canzoniere and Other Petrarchan Studies*. Rome, 1951
WILKINS, E. H., *Studies in the Life and Works of Petrarch*. Cambridge, 1955

BILLANOVICH, G., *Petrarca letterato. Lo scrittoio del Petrarca*. 1947
DAVIDSOHN, R., *Geschichte von Florenz*. 4 vols. 1896–1927
EPPELSHEIMER, H. W., *Petrarca*. 1934
GEIGER, L., *Renaissance und Humanismus*. 1882
KOERTING, G., *Petrarca's Leben und Werke*. 1878
MONNIER, P., *Le Quattrocento*. 2 vols. 1924
DE NOLHAC, P., *Pétrarque et l'humanisme*. 2 vols. 1907
NORDSTRÖM, J., *Moyen Age et renaissance*. 1933
ROSSI, V., *Il Quattrocento*. 1933
SABBADINI, R., *Le Scoperte dei codici latini e greci ne' secoli XIV e XV*. 2 vols. 1905, 1914
SAITTA, G., *Il Pensiero italiano nell' umanesimo e nel rinascimento*. 3 vols. 1949–51
SAPEGNO, N., *Il Trecento*. 1938
VOIGT, G., *Die Wiederbelebung des classischen Altertums*. 2 vols. 1893
WEISS, R., *Il Primo secolo del umanesimo*. 1949

CHAPTER FIVE

FRANCE AND ENGLAND:
THE HUNDRED YEARS' WAR
TO 1380

FRANCE UNDER THE LAST OF THE
CAPETIANS AND THE FIRST VALOIS

Louis IX (1226–70), better known to history as St. Louis, is widely regarded as the greatest medieval king of France. The conventional picture of him sitting under a tree at Valenciennes, dispensing justice to men of high and low estate, has caught the spirit of the man and his rule. A pious and faithful son of the Church, he led, at great personal sacrifice, the last two medieval Crusades; yet he would brook no papal interference with the rights of the kingdom of France. He was a staunch feudalist; yet he furthered the growth of the burgher class by giving special privileges to towns and merchants. Indeed, he attached the rising bourgeoisie to the crown, an attachment that was most significant in the subsequent social adjustments of the period before the French Revolution. He refused to weaken the power of the Emperor Frederick II by accepting the imperial crown from the Pope; yet he withstood the Emperor with equal firmness when Frederick detained some French ecclesiastics on their way to Rome, and he later supported his youngest brother, Charles of Anjou (Charles I of the kingdom of Sicily), in his efforts to wreck the imperial power in Italy. He left a tradition of royal dignity, concern for his people, and devotion to justice that solidified the monarchical principle among the French so firmly that it survived the caprice and ineffectiveness of many of his successors.

During his reign, France was the center of Western culture, and the University of Paris was the home of the giants of Christian thought. St. Thomas Aquinas, St. Bonaventura, Albert the Great, Roger Bacon, William of Auvergne, Alexander of Hales, and hundreds of lesser lights lectured and disputed on the Left Bank in the days of St. Louis. The king was proud of his university and made many gifts to it. It was his chaplain, Robert of Sorbon, who founded the college which has loomed so large in the history of French and European culture from that day to the present.

In domestic affairs, the primary development in medieval France was the continuation of the process of centralization begun by Philip II (Augustus, 1180–1223) and Louis VIII (1223–26). The growth of towns and commerce involved an increase in the importance of money. Though the social system was still predominantly feudal, based on the land, the efficient and responsible administration of the kingdom, wars, justice, and a growing bureaucracy demanded that the king have access to ready cash. Furthermore an impartial justice, which would enhance the unity and strength of the realm, could best be administered if the judges were paid from the royal treasury and thus were not dependent upon the fines that they might assess or upon the whims of a local seigneur.

St. Louis used the powers and agencies built up by his two predecessors with decision and persistence. The *curia regis,* or royal court, of the Capetian kings had certain similarities to that of the Plantagenet kings in England, though it was somewhat more flexible, and its constituency less easily defined. It was probably in the reign of St. Louis that the *parlement* of Paris grew up out of the *curia regis* and took on its judicial, as opposed to legislative, character, which differentiates it from the English Parliament. In essence, the *parlement* of Paris was the *curia regis* functioning in its judicial aspect. The *parlement* came to consist of employees of the king who had specialized in the law, and were consequently of bourgeois origin with a legalistic and critical attitude toward all vested rights. They could hardly be expected to favor the cause of the nobility above that of the king, from whom they received their positions and their pay. Soon called *clercs du roi* or *chevaliers du roi,* the king's clerks or knights, these legists constituted the core of the king's advisers, and, with the passage of time and under later rulers, they became more influential in making royal policy than the great feudal magnates. Chosen for ability and loyalty to the crown, they were natural opportunists, antiaristocratic in their social creed. They were to be even more powerful under critical circumstances as aides and counselors to St. Louis' grandson, Philip IV (the Fair), and were destined to set the tradition of French royal bureaucracy for centuries to come.

The *curia regis* handled the finances of the kingdom, a part of its activity which had long been known as the *chambre des comptes.* The accounts of royal officials throughout the kingdom, the bailiffs (in the north) and seneschals (in the south), had to be audited. Although some improvements were introduced, based on Norman models, during the reign of St. Louis, the great reforms in fiscal administration did not come until the following century, when circumstances demanded a thorough review of national finance. St. Louis' sources of income were essentially feudal, from the royal demesne, feudal aids, and donations (sometimes forced) from the clergy and the towns. He refrained from any debasement of the coinage, thus raising the credit of the royal currency in the whole kingdom. Following a conservative rather than an expansionist foreign policy, he had little occasion for extraordinary expenditures which would have called for new sources of income and a new tax policy. These were exigencies which confronted his successors.

In foreign affairs Louis IX had to fight with his strongest vassal, the Plantagenet duke of Aquitaine, who was at the same time Henry III, king of

England. In this long-drawn-out struggle Louis was victorious in foiling Henry's grandiose dreams to recover Normandy and other Plantagenet territories north of the Loire, but his success was due as much to Henry's complete lack of military capacity as to his own efficient leadership. At the treaty of Paris of 1259, after Henry rendered liege homage to the French monarch for his French possessions and renounced his claims to Normandy, Anjou, Touraine, Maine, and Poitou, Louis restored to him his possessions in the dioceses of Limoges, Cahors, and Périgueux, with the possibility of later restoration of the Agenais and Saintonge, which Henry's ineptitude had lost. This gesture of generosity, Louis felt, would achieve peace between France and England. To the south, Louis strengthened the bonds of friendship with Alfonso X of Spain, despite the urgings of his advisers that he claim the Spanish throne through his mother, Blanche of Castile.

By the end of his reign, St. Louis had greatly increased the royal domain, partly by outright purchase but mostly by utilizing provisions in feudal law and by marriage alliances. He had made France the greatest power in Europe. In later times, nostalgic Frenchmen looked back upon the reign of St. Louis as the "good old days." But it was the end of an epoch, the flowering of medieval France, graced and led by a king and saint whose justice and firmness, in union with his saintliness, gave France a character and an emotional tone no other country of Europe was ever to attain. It is the contrast between this atmosphere and the crude realities of a burgeoning secularistic and cynically bourgeois state that marks France's entry into the modern age.

Philip III

IN 1270 St. Louis died while on a Crusade against the Moslems in Tunis, and his eldest son, Philip III, ascended the throne. The fifteen years of Philip's reign saw no remarkable developments. The king was of slender stuff, and the government was almost entirely in the hands of the *clercs du roi* trained under St. Louis. The substantial increases in the royal domain during the reign of Philip III, mostly in southern France, were due to the feudal law providing for the reversion of lands to the king on the extinction of a vassal's line rather than to royal initiative. Philip was completely outshone by his uncle, Charles of Anjou, who had been enjoying many successes in Italy as king of Sicily and sought even greater prizes. It will be remembered that after the Sicilian Vespers (1282), when the French in Sicily were massacred by the natives, King Peter III of Aragon accepted the crown offered by the Sicilians. To punish the effrontery of this prince, who dared to stand up against his uncle, Philip set out on a campaign to discipline the house of Aragon. In the meantime Charles had died (January 1285). Nevertheless, acting as if on a crusade, Philip laid siege to the Aragonese city of Gerona. But the Spanish resistance foiled Philip for ten weeks, and his hard-won victory was more costly than a quick defeat would have been. His fleets were destroyed, his army decimated. He himself fell ill and died at Perpignan (October 7, 1285) on the way back from an ignominious campaign.

The year 1285 was significant for the deaths of King Charles I of Sicily, his friend and supporter Pope Martin IV, King Peter III of Aragon, and King

Philip III of France. The deaths of these Mediterranean rulers, all in one year, were certain to alter the directions of the conflicting policies in that area. France had dominated the western Mediterranean, but the death of Charles, the most ruthless and ambitious of them all, and the substitution of Spanish rule in Sicily obliged the French ruling house to seek an outlet for its energy in another direction. In some degree, the French effort to drive the English out of France, although at times it gave the impression of a civil war, represented the transfer of French energy from Italy to France itself, from uncertain conquest of a foreign and distant land to the consolidation of a natural geographical unity into a national state.

Philip IV, the Fair

ANY such tremendous movement as the consolidation of a people into a national state demands much time and suffers many setbacks, but the reign of Philip IV (the Fair, 1285-1314), son of Philip III and grandson of St. Louis, marked a long step forward. The character of Philip the Fair has always puzzled historians. Accounts by his contemporaries are contradictory. Some chroniclers regard him as personally responsible for the measures and policies of his reign. Others regard him as pliable in the hands of his counselors. Just before his death, he is reported to have taken upon himself the burden of the great and fateful decisions made in his name during his thirty-year rule. The truth probably is that he chose his counselors because of their tested agreement with his own aims and then supported them in the exercise of their duties, never letting broad policy get out of his own hands.

The vigor with which, from the early days of his reign, Philip followed up all advantages accruing to the crown was certainly the king's own, as was the decision to withdraw from the profitless Spanish wars in which his father had become involved. For several years after his accession at the age of seventeen, he gave no indication of the aggressive plans he certainly early had in mind. He maintained in positions of trust the legists trained by his grandfather, St. Louis, but he kept his own counsel. He wanted his realm in order before engaging in a life-or-death struggle with so strong and able an opponent as Edward I of England. Edward, the son of Henry III, had been his father's lieutenant in Gascony, and his high abilities were well known and respected by the French.

The reasons for the coming struggle were quite simple. If Philip looked at a map of France in about the year 1290 he saw several sore spots. Gascony was in the possession of the duke of Aquitaine—that is, King Edward I of England. In the northwest tip of France lay Brittany, with its traditional leaning toward England. On the northeastern border were the counties of Flanders, Artois, and the bishopric of Lille, all with close commercial relations with England, source of the wool from the weaving of which they made their living. The counts of these three provinces regarded themselves as virtually independent rulers and had no intention of changing their status. Philip thus found himself under English pressure from three sides. In effect, he faced the necessity of war on at least three fronts.

In order to wage such a struggle with any hope of success, the king must be strong at home and assured of administrative and fiscal control of the kingdom. From the early years of Philip's reign, all the royal officials, as if by general instructions, pushed the royal rights and feudal privileges to their extreme limits. The nobility, the feudality, resisted; but the royal pressure was not to be stopped, and the agents of the king, themselves of low or bourgeois birth, were only too pleased to be able to subject the haughty nobles to annoying restrictions in the name of the monarch. By these means Philip made rapid progress at the beginning of his reign toward consolidating royal power, vastly increased the sources of the king's revenue, and confirmed the policy of royal favor for the rising bourgeoisie. Philip, even more than St. Louis, cast his lot with the middle class, the class of the future. In the actual administration of the business of the kingdom, he allowed the *curia regis* to continue to develop along the lines laid down by his father and grandfather. The lawyers increased in number in his Great Council, while his provincial officials, chosen for their efficiency and loyalty to him, were members of the *parlements*. The proportion of peers and nobles in the *curia regis* diminished under Philip, and trained bureaucrats began to take their place. The Court of Inquest functioned both through roving commissions sent to the provinces and as a court of appeal. The king's justice was quick and satisfactory. There is no doubt that Philip wanted absolute power, but he knew that such power must be based on satisfactory service to the kingdom.

The struggle with the king of England that was implicit in the English possession of Gascony in fief to the king of France had smoldered during the reign of Philip III and was only temporarily appeased in the early years of Philip the Fair. Edward I was busy with Welsh and Scottish concerns, Philip was strengthening his control over France. But in the spring of 1293, after preliminary incidents that aggravated the bad blood on both sides, 200 English ships met and defeated 225 Norman ships off the coast of Brittany. Philip summoned Edward, as duke of Aquitaine, to appear before the *parlement* of Paris; when he failed to appear, the court declared his lands in France confiscated. Edward, then engaged in Wales, played for time and made gestures of compliance. Philip meanwhile poured troops into Gascony and the Agenais and refused to withdraw them on Edward's demand. It was clear that the French king was determined, at all costs, to recover Aquitaine. There was deceit and fraud on both sides. Since both monarchs were strong, war was inevitable. In a very real sense this was the beginning of the Hundred Years' War, although the date of its outbreak is conventionally set over forty years later, under Edward III and Philip VI.

Edward I was well aware of the magnitude of the issues at stake. In Aquitaine he could count on the support of the towns and the lesser nobility. The upper nobility, wishing to embarrass their direct overlord, the duke of Aquitaine, sided with *his* overlord, the king of France. Edward proceeded to make the most of diplomatic possibilities, seeking allies among other enemies and restive vassals of Philip. Within a year, the duke of Brabant, the count of Bar, the duke of Guelders, the archbishop of Cologne, the counts of Savoy and Juliers, and even the Emperor of the Holy Roman Empire, Adolf of Nassau (1292–98), had declared against Philip. The aged count of Flanders, Guy de Dampierre, chronically in financial straits, was won over to the anti-French side by a marriage contract between his daughter and Edward's eldest son, and a large sum of money. But Philip could play this game almost as well as Edward. He sent substantial support to John Balliol, the king of Scotland, then fighting his English overlord, and ordered Guy de Dampierre to bring his daughter to Paris with him. He had no intention of allowing the daughter of one of his vassals to become queen of England.

A French fleet attacked Dover unsuccessfully, whereupon an English fleet raided the coast of Gascony and was welcomed by the citizenry. But on land French arms had the advantage. Robert d'Artois, Philip's brilliant general, defeated Edward's Gascon forces at Bonnegarde in southwestern Gascony on January 30, 1297, and some months later (August 20, 1297) routed the forces of Guy de Dampierre and his German allies at Furnes, near the coast of Flanders. Guy submitted abjectly, and he and his two sons were imprisoned by Philip in separate castles, where people could come to see how the king treated vassals who dared to rebel. The king of France won this round without much question. A truce between Edward and Philip was arranged in October 1297 by Pope Boniface VIII on the basis of the territory then held by each party to the conflict. Since Philip was at the time occupying Flanders and Aquitaine, the truce was favorable to him.

Edward held strong points in northern Gascony, the town of Bayonne and most of the southern part of the duchy of Aquitaine. With a view to maintaining his position, he kept a formidable army of mercenaries in the field. Reverses at the hands of the burghers of Flanders induced Philip to sign a treaty at Paris, May 20, 1303, which restored to Edward all the territory that had been his before the outbreak of hostilities. By the terms of the peace, Prince Edward, son of the English king, was to marry Philip's daughter Isabella. Edward gave over to the prince the whole duchy of Aquitaine in 1306, "to have and to hold . . . as we and our progenitors have held it." Edward's policies of firmness, justice, and efficiency were maintained until his death in 1307, and English prestige and favor stood high among the Gascons in these years.

After Philip's successes in Gascony in 1297, he turned his attention to the struggle with Pope Boniface VIII which has been related in Chapter 2, and, since Edward's troubles with the Scottish succession had broken out afresh, there was a temporary lull in the Anglo-French war. Edward's son and successor, Edward II (1307-27), was of such feeble stuff that France had nothing to fear from him.

But gains of the French monarch on the northern and northeastern front were not so easily held. He had defeated and humiliated Guy de Dampierre, count of Flanders, and had quartered French troops in key Flemish cities. The tough and independent-minded Flemings broke out in the "Matins de Bruges" on the morning of May 18, 1302, when all Frenchmen quartered in Bruges were massacred. The rest of Flanders rose in sympathetic revolt, and the army sent to Flanders by Philip to discipline the rebels was roundly defeated at Courtrai on July 11, 1302. By June 1305, French arms were victorious, but Flemish spirit and pride were not broken.

The three wars in which Philip had been engaged—the war against Spain, which had broken out again in 1293; the war against the king of England,

and the war against Flanders—in addition to his bitter conflict with Pope Boniface, had been frightfully expensive, and, despite his victories over the English and the Pope, he was in dire financial straits. The costs of his modernized administration were outrunning his feudal sources of income. His destruction of the Order of the Templars (1307–14) was another phase of his effort to balance his budget (see above, Chapter 3). The cumulative effect of his unbalanced budget was to oblige him once again to appeal, as in 1302, to the Estates General. He summoned the representatives of the three Estates to meet at Tours to hear his requests for increased levies. There was no pattern of refusal available to them, and when they met, in 1314, they had no alternative to obeying the monarch's orders. By this time the most powerful person in the kingdom, after Philip himself, was the minister of finance, Enguerrand de Marigny, who had risen to that high position by sheer administrative ability. To the people of France, it was de Marigny who seemed to be the oppressor, and he was generously hated. But, since the king supported him, Philip was the ultimate object of the widespread resentment at royal exactions and levies. At the meeting of the Estates in 1314, when de Marigny finished his eloquent speech calling for acceptance of further taxes, Philip immediately came forward and thanked the assembled nobility and citizens for their generous response to his needs. There was little for them to do but accept his thanks. The king was certainly not asking for the consent of the people to be taxed. In reality, at all the meetings of the three Estates, the king or his minister simply told them what they were to offer, then without waiting for any discussion, thanked them politely for their compliance and dismissed them. The spirit of these meetings of the Estates General was somewhat different from that of the truculent English Parliament in the same decades.

The last year of Philip's reign, 1314, was fraught with disappointments for him. The wives of his three sons were accused of immoralities, and two of them had to be imprisoned for life. Their lovers were executed with exaggerated cruelty. There was almost universal reaction against the king's heavy taxation and severe rule, and the two higher Estates, the nobility and the clergy, joined in protests against royal oppression. Prominent among the signatories of these protests was the nonagenarian and venerable Sire de Joinville, who had faithfully served Philip's grandfather, St. Louis. The king was taken aback at the strength and bitterness of the opposition, and this shock, added to what was probably a heart attack while hunting, is believed to have led to his death, at forty-six years of age, on November 29, 1314. In his long and vigorous reign, he had consolidated French power on all fronts, internal and external; substantially increased the territory of the kingdom; and, realizing the growing importance of the bourgeoisie, favored them and their spirit, thus preparing the ground for the financial strength of the France of Francis I. He has been accused of debasing the coinage, a charge only partly true. His manipulation of the currency might more properly be called an adjustment that corresponded to the new conditions of general inflation. In this regard, he was more conservative than most modern governments. Philip was not only the first modern king of France; he was one of the greatest kings of her whole history. By the time of his death he was hated by most of his subjects.

The Last Capetians

PHILIP IV was succeeded by his three sons in turn: Louis X (the Quarrelsome or the Stubborn, 1314–16); Philip V (the Tall, 1316–22), and Charles IV (the Fair, 1322–28). The fact that none of them had a male heir accounts for the succession of brothers and also occasioned the discussion that led to the so-called Salic law of France. As it was stated by Philip V to justify his seizure of the throne, this was a modification of an ancient tribal law of the Salian Franks to the effect that a woman could not inherit landed property. Whether the throne of a nation is "property" or not is a dubious point.

None of the three sons of Philip IV was in any respect the equal of his father. The resurgence of the nobility that broke out in the last year of Philip's reign gained momentum under the weaker and more inexperienced hands of his sons; it is not surprising, therefore, that this decade and a half saw the collapse of the feudal monarchy in France. In the reign of Louis X, the League of the Nobility, working through the intriguing and ambitious Charles of Valois, younger brother of Philip IV and uncle of the twenty-year-old monarch, secured the dismissal of the more able and therefore objectionable ministers of the late king. Some were tortured; de Marigny, the only person in the kingdom who might have been strong and astute enough to maintain the royal primacy over a baronial revolt, was given a mock trial on many charges, including sorcery, and was tortured and hanged (April 30, 1315). The nobles reassumed the feudal prerogatives which Philip had taken from them. Royal judges were deposed, and trial by battle and private wars again became the practice. The clock was turned back. A feudal French army sent against the stubborn Flemings stuck in Flanders mud and was cut to pieces. French pride and prestige sank to the level the nobility seemed to prefer. The one good measure for which the king was responsible, a decree permitting serfs to buy their freedom, was intended to bring the crown some income. It remained almost a dead letter because the serfs were so poor that they could not afford the purchase price of their freedom.

When Louis the Quarrelsome died (June 5, 1316), after just over eighteen months of a feckless reign, his queen was expecting a child. If it turned out to be a boy, he would of course succeed to the throne under a regency. Meanwhile, Louis' young brother, Philip of Poitiers, acted as regent. When the son who was born to Queen Clementine died, only five days after his birth, Philip proclaimed himself king (Philip V, the Tall) and had himself crowned at Paris (January 9, 1317). An assembly of high churchmen, nobles, some of the citizenry of Paris, and doctors of the University of Paris in February 1317 confirmed the action of Philip and declared that "women do not succeed to the throne of France." Opposition to Philip on the ground that Jeanne, the four-year-old daughter of the deceased Louis X, should have succeeded to the throne soon died down. Under the conditions of a threatened war, a long regency would probably have been disastrous for France.

Philip V set out to put the kingdom back on the path of efficiency and legalism which Philip IV had perhaps too energetically trod. Relations with Flanders were delicate and at times almost reached open war. With Edward II of England he had no trouble, largely because Edward was in no position to take the offensive. Philip avoided war when diplomacy would gain his ends, and persuaded where others might have threatened.

Philip V, like his brother Louis, died (January 2, 1322) without leaving a male heir. His younger brother, Charles, the third son of Philip IV to be king of France, ruled for only six years (1322–28) and was the last of the long line of the Capetians. Charles IV became involved in the affairs of the Empire through his second marriage, to Mary of Luxemburg, daughter of the late Emperor Henry VII and sister of the knightly King John of Bohemia. Meanwhile developments in both Flanders and Gascony were somewhat to France's advantage. The troubles of Edward II at home were reflected in his operations in Gascony, and a halfhearted war from 1324 to 1326 led to a treaty, signed in Paris in 1327, by which Edward accepted humiliating terms as to the English holdings in Gascony and paid Charles a large indemnity. The kingdom of France was stronger than it had ever been, owing, in great measure, to the weakness and difficulties of her enemies, actual or potential, as well as to the steady nationalistic policy of the French kings, intended to reclaim for their country all territory which could even remotely be called French.

The Valois Succession

ALTHOUGH Charles was married three times, he had no male issue when he died (February 1, 1328), and there were no more sons of Philip IV. The succession was therefore in doubt. There were three possibilities: Jeanne of Navarre, the daughter of Louis X; Edward III of England, whose mother, Isabella, was the daughter of Philip IV; and Philip of Valois, son of Charles of Valois and hence a nephew of Philip IV. Edward III, who had succeeded to the throne of England upon the abdication of Edward II in 1327, as the only direct male descendant of Philip IV, was nearest to the throne, whereas Philip of Valois was a grandson of a previous king, Philip III. The thought of having an English king as ruler of France was repugnant to the French. On his deathbed, therefore, Charles IV called Philip of Valois to him, appointed him guardian of the queen and of the child whom she was then expecting, charged him with seeing to it that "the twelve peers of France and the high barons should consult as to the succession and give the crown to him who had the right thereto." The child was a girl. Without hesitation, the assembly of nobles gave the crown to Philip of Valois, who took the royal title of Philip VI. The year 1328 thus marks the end of the Capetian line and the beginning of the related line of Valois.

Feudalism had been a long time on the throne, and the last of the Capetians had done their share to bring it to an end. Philip the Fair had looked ahead to the new days of the bourgeois state, in which those who controlled business and industry would determine national policy. Yet this was a revolution in statecraft that could not happen overnight, or even in a century. The processes that combined to bring it about can be traced back several centuries to the rise of the towns and the bourgeoisie and to a corresponding diminution in the wealth and power of the landed nobility. Both movements were reflected in the court and administration of the kings of France, who came to rely in increasing measure upon able servants and counselors recruited from the bourgeoisie and trained in the law. The internal tensions caused by the drive toward French unification, heightened by the struggles of the French monarch against the Papacy, Flanders, and England, in actuality strengthened the forces of French national unity by keeping the issue clearly before the people. Greater and more distressing trials lay ahead for the French people and the cause of national integration.

From the first, Philip VI insisted that Edward III render homage for his French possessions. After some delay and with obvious reluctance, Edward came to France in 1329 and gave a qualified homage, withholding liege homage until 1331. It was clear that the king of England had not given up his hopes to rule in France but was simply biding his time. Philip, on the other hand, was determined to retain every gain made by his predecessors. A revolt of the townspeople in Flanders was put down by a massacre of twelve thousand Flemings in 1328, and the democratic spark seemed to be quenched. There followed a kind of peace. Robert d'Artois, a peer of France of royal blood and brother-in-law of the king, demanded that the county of Artois, which had been given to his aunt, be turned over to him. A long-drawn-out dispute in feudal courts ensued, enlivened by some forgeries and several sudden deaths, commonly thought to be due to poison. The forgeries were discovered, and the case was decided against Robert in 1332. He fled to Flanders, whence, when the pressure became too great so close to France, he crossed over to England. There he was welcomed warmly at the court of Edward III and remained to take an active part in Edward's planning and campaigns in Flanders and France.

By this time, it will be remembered, the Papacy was well established at Avignon on the Rhône, and Philip maintained cordial relations with Pope John XXII. King John of Bohemia spent much time at Philip's court, and their common interest in the form and ceremony of feudal knighthood kept them close friends. The romantic and pious Philip decided to take the cross in July 1332, and a year later the Crusade was formally announced by Pierre Roger, archbishop of Rouen. By 1336 all preparations seemed complete, but the realization of the plans was to be nullified by a new outbreak of the long war with England.

During the reign of Philip VI the kingdom of France was more prosperous than at any period in the Middle Ages, and the national spirit was high. Yet the personality of the king did not augur well for the immediate future. Philip, too concerned with the trappings of feudal knighthood for those stern times, showed no disposition to adapt himself to the tasks confronting the kingdom. The royal finances were inadequate and poorly organized; little had been done to improve the financial structure since Philip IV. The military establishment of the country was still feudal and essentially haphazard. France faced the long strain of the coming war with England so poorly prepared that the course of the first stages of that conflict should cause no surprise.

ENGLAND TO 1338

THE thirteenth century in England was marked by a series of severe constitutional crises, accompanied by an upsurge in national spirit and by economic and cultural progress. King John had been forced to grant the Great Charter to rebellious barons in 1215. When he died, in the following year, much of his land was in the hands of a French army called in by the barons, who had resented John's efforts to annul the Charter. His son Henry III, who succeeded him at the age of nine, had one of the longest and most unsatisfactory reigns in all English history (1216–72). Yet Henry was in no small degree responsible for the progress in popular sovereignty that took place in these years, even though it was achieved principally against his will. He was impulsive and unstable, capricious and deceitful, and lacking in loyalty, administrative courage, foresight, and patriotism. These deficiencies created opportunities for the baronial opposition to demand and get promises of reform in the royal administration and, when promises were violated, as they almost always were, to oblige the king by force of arms to accept councilors and officials named by the barons, to have his finances controlled by their committees, and to submit all his actions to their approval. There were uprisings of the barons against Henry and his advisers in 1233, 1241, and 1250, and a protracted baronial revolt from 1258 to 1265. Henry's subservience to the Papacy and his support of the unbearable papal exactions aroused resentment in all classes of society. He added insult to injury by giving rich benefices and honors to the relatives of his wife, Eleanor of Provence, and accepting them as his personal advisers in preference to the English nobles, who regarded themselves as the natural counselors of the monarch and objected violently to the foreigners at court.

In 1257 Henry's brother, Richard of Cornwall, was elected King of the Romans, at a cost to himself of 28,000 marks, an enormous sum for the time. Richard had previously (1252) refused the offer of the Sicilian crown, but Henry, less realistic, had begun to conceive of himself as a factor in European politics and, under the influence of his wife's uncles, was dabbling in Italian affairs. In 1254 Henry accepted the crown of Sicily for his second son Edmund from the pope, and as a consequence found himself obliged not only to send troops to Sicily but also to pay 135,000 marks for papal expenses incurred in the war against the Hohenstaufen. Such consummate vainglory was a shock to the barons and the English clergy. They had hardly realized Henry's capacities. When in 1258 the treasury was depleted, Henry asked the Great Council to help meet a payment on his indebtedness; the Council thereupon demanded new appointments to important offices and, in order to assure future control of expenditures, set up a baronial council of fifteen to represent their interests. The council of fifteen was in turn to be supervised by a council of twelve. The formalized demands of the baronage are known as the Provisions of Oxford (1258). The king, thus deprived of his power of initiative, could only submit. But the barons were unused to ruling, and factions developed in the Council and among their followers, with the result that Henry was able to regain power. At that point, because of the will of the baronage not to yield to Henry's caprice and incapacity, civil war became inevitable. It broke out in 1263.

The baronial cause was led by Simon de Montfort, a brilliant and high-minded brother-in-law of the king and a son of the French leader of the Albigensian Crusade. De Montfort, though a native of France, had identified himself with the cause of the English barons and played a leading role in formulating the Provisions of Oxford. It was he who led and inspired the younger barons, a majority of the townspeople, and some of the clergy in the struggle against royal chicanery and oppression.

The battle of Lewes in 1264 between the baronial forces and the forces of Henry III was a resounding victory for the popular side. Henry and his brother Richard were captured and obliged to accept a government similar in principle to the one the king had undermined after agreeing to the Provisions of Oxford in 1258. A baronial council of nine, headed by de Montfort, was the virtual ruler of the kingdom. The following year, 1265, de Montfort called a meeting of the Great Council, to which each shire was invited to send two knights and each city and borough two representatives. This meeting was the first time in English history that the knights and the towns were represented on this broad scale in the Great Council in which representatives from the shires and from the cities and boroughs sat together to consider and legislate national policy, and it is therefore extremely significant in the story of English growth toward the modern bourgeois state. Significant as it was, however, it proved to be premature. Some barons thought de Montfort had gone too far and too fast in displacing the king, and Henry certainly gained some adherents from among these malcontents. At the battle of Evesham in 1265, brilliantly won by Henry's son Edward, which put the king back in power, there were few barons fighting on the side of de Montfort, and the royal victory meant the abolition of the baronial council. Nevertheless, it had been shown that popular discontent could limit the power of the monarch, and the barons were not likely to forget that they had once ruled England. De Montfort, perhaps the only one of the barons who realized exactly what he was doing, died on the field at Evesham, but his vision of a constitutional monarchy was to become an actuality sooner than his failure indicated.

Edward I

THE tumultuous events of 1258–67 were not without their clear lesson for Henry's oldest son Edward, who succeeded his father in 1272 and ruled until 1307. At the time of his father's death Edward was on a Crusade, and there was such order in England that he delayed his return until 1274. Edward is variously known as the Unifier and the Legislator; both epithets are justified. He subjugated Wales early in his reign and Scotland toward the end, although the latter conquest was subsequently lost under his incompetent son, Edward II. He called many parliaments and through them regularized the royal prerogative in the all-important matter of the levying of taxes. By increasing the prestige of the itinerant justices he broadened the legal power of the crown and tightened the royal jurisdiction in all feudal matters. He restricted the powers of the Church over the transfer of land (Statute of Mortmain, 1279), and in the three Statutes of Westminster (1275, 1285, 1290) took full and ruthless advantage of feudal law to provide that as much land as possible should revert to the grantor or the highest overlord, the king himself.

The subjugation of Wales was arduous and bitter. Welsh resistance was stubborn and skillful, and it took two major campaigns (1277–78 and 1282–83) to bring the territory under the English rule. Alexander III of Scotland died in 1286, leaving no direct heir. After several years of indecision and the death (in 1290) of Margaret, Alexander's granddaughter, some thirteen claimants to his throne appeared. Edward, asked to adjudicate the claims, first demanded recognition of his own overlordship of the Scottish kingdom. Under previous Scottish kings this overlordship had frequently been acknowledged, and though they expostulated, all the claimants and the Scottish nobles renewed the recognition in 1291. Edward's decision, in 1292, was in favor of John Balliol, who then swore fealty to the English king.

In some ways this was the high point of Edward's reign: Wales subdued, laws promulgated and obeyed at home, Scotland a vassal kingdom. But trouble was brewing on another front. We have already sketched the beginnings of the struggle with France. As the clouds over the Channel darkened, the Welsh took advantage of Edward's difficulties and revolted (1294). Edward had then to lead an expedition against the Welsh rebels, at the cost of military losses in Gascony; he could not be in two places at once. The next year (1295) the Scottish nobles rejected Balliol, whom they regarded as too compliant toward Edward, and effected an alliance with Philip IV of France, an international relationship that was destined to endure, at least sentimentally, for more than three centuries. Under the threat of French attack from the sea, Edward convoked what has come to be called the Model Parliament late in 1295. This group included not only the baronage and the high clergy but two elected knights from each shire and two elected burgesses from each borough. In addition, some elements of the clergy who had not been invited to earlier parliaments were included. The representation was broader and more systematic than in any previous parliament. They were summoned, professedly, to grant taxes, which, meeting separately—nobles, clergy, and commons—they proceeded to do. ,

Thereupon Edward invaded Scotland and brought back to England the coronation Stone of Scone, only to meet aristocratic opposition from the Archbishop of Canterbury, who, following the policies of Boniface VIII, objected to an increased levy on the Church. The king was able to extricate himself from this involvement with some success but then became embroiled in the war in Flanders, while on his northern frontier his troops were humbled by the Scottish leader, Sir William Wallace, at Stirling in 1297. Edward avenged this defeat in person the following year at Falkirk, but without quelling all Scottish resistance.

The years from 1296 to his death in 1307 were trying for Edward, now attempting to maintain military supremacy on three fronts—Scotland, Gascony, and Flanders—and at the same time to combat the recalcitrance of a small group of leading English barons. He was also determined to resist the demands of Pope Boniface VIII. The pressures on him were heavy and complex; yet through it all he maintained his firmness and eventually had the satisfaction of winning the support of the barons and of seeing his mortal enemy, Philip IV of France, defeated by the Flemings at Courtrai in 1302. The last year of his life was darkened by the revolt of Robert Bruce, the newly crowned king of Scotland. Determined to crush the rebellious Scots once and for all, Edward assembled a powerful force in June 1307. Already broken in health, he failed to reach the Scottish border before death overtook him on July 7, 1307.

Edward II

EDWARD II, the son of Edward I, was tall and handsome and sat his horse like a man, but he was far from the cut of his father. His rule was in fact so ignominious as scarcely to deserve the telling. He had little stomach for war and, when goaded into it, showed not even mediocre talent for leadership. The Scots under Robert Bruce defeated the forces of Edward II at Bannockburn, June 23-24, 1314. The king fled the field as fast as his mount would take him. That was the end of the Scottish problem for three centuries. The Scots were free.

In the meantime Edward, showing himself the heir of the weakness and folly of his grandfather, Henry III, rather than of the wisdom of his father, dismissed his father's advisers, heaped riches and honors upon a glib favorite, Gaveston, who delighted in insulting the nobles of the court, and disregarded virtually all the precepts of responsible rule. And yet, largely because of his indolence and incompetence, the period of his reign (1307-27) is one of the most important in the whole course of English political development. The barons, who had suffered curtailment of their power and prestige through the firmness and independence of Edward I, sensed immediately that his son was of a lesser breed and proceeded to take advantage of the fact. In 1310, after a number of sharp disagreements with the king and his advisers, the barons came to a parliament in full armor, demanding the right to reform the government. They named a commission of twenty-one Lords Ordainers who drew up the Ordinances of 1311, the basic purpose of which was to increase the participation of the baronage in government. But the Ordinances were not easy to execute, and the barons, in addition to being divided among themselves, were less interested in the public good than in their own power. In 1322 Edward was able to defeat the baronial leader, Thomas of Lancaster, in battle, whereupon the Ordinances of 1311 were revoked, about thirty barons were executed, and the king recovered his authority. This success, however, was only a temporary reprieve for Edward. When his queen, Isabella, turned against him (1325) and rallied the opposition to the king, a parliament (1327) demanded and obtained his deposition.

The rule and fall of Edward II were a tragic revelation of how ignoble, reckless, and derelict the son of a great father could be. The successful baronial opposition to Edward II was a significant step toward limited and constitutional monarchy, but the motives of the baronage should not be too unreservedly lauded. There was in this case, as in the case of the similar uprising against Henry III, little regard on the part of the nobility for any broad ideals of representative popular government. They were concerned with their own privileges and prerogatives. However, in the process of limiting the absolutism of the monarch, they demonstrated that such power could be so circumscribed, by pressure of various sorts, threat of armed revolt, or withholding of financial grants, as to force the monarch to rule "according as it hath been hitherto accustomed."

EDWARD III AND THE HUNDRED YEARS' WAR

THE rule of Edward III (1327–77), who succeeded his father at the age of fourteen, under a regency, was an eventful half-century in English history. The regency proved not very satisfactory, and the young king ended it in 1330 simply by declaring himself of age. His first moves as an independent monarch were rather experimental, but he soon showed some of his grandfather's sense of responsibility. He was handsome, gracious, personally popular, and notably adept in handling his subordinates. The royal household, his advisers and officials, was chosen with some circumspection and was kept within appropriate bounds. His friendly relations with the towns and the rising burgher class were responsible for much of the prosperity that England enjoyed in the period before the scourge of the Black Death in 1348. The Commons in Parliament were beginning to learn their power, the power of the purse, and, as the costs of the French war mounted, the frequent exercise of that power set patterns and precedents of bargaining between the crown and the representatives of the towns which were to be followed into modern times. Edward used Parliament in governing more than any previous ruler—partly, of course, because he was obliged to do so—and, whether as a judicial or as a legislative body, in its entirety or through commissions, as a body in control of taxation or as a legislative assembly with power of initiation, Parliament began in this period to assume the determinative position in English political life which has set England apart from the other states of Europe. The last years of Edward's reign were marred by his physical and mental deterioration, but by that time parliamentary rule and the concept of the responsibility of the government to elected representatives had been in effect for some decades, and a return to absolutism, real or attempted, was hardly possible.

Although the internal political and structural developments of Edward's reign were of tremendous and lasting importance, they seem undramatic, compared with the Hundred Years' War, much of which took place in this period. As we have seen, the struggle between England and France was inherent in the geopolitical situation: the king of England, as the heir of the Norman and Plantagenet kings, held vast territories in France as a feudal vassal of the king of France. As long as the king of France was weak or unaggressive there was no trouble. But as soon as a strong French king, such as Philip Augustus, attempted to consolidate territory over which he was feudal suzerain, conflict was inevitable. King John had lost Normandy (1204), and Henry III lost more. Edward I maintained a precarious position in Gascony but was unable, because of other commitments and the craftiness of Philip IV, to retake any former Plantagenet possessions or improve the conditions of feudal vassalage under which he held his lands. Under Edward II there was little but uncertainty and friction. Philip IV of France, prey to domestic difficulties, did not follow an aggressive policy toward Edward's holdings, but the Gascons, generally pro-English, were frightened lest the English king give them up entirely. In 1324 there was a species of war, and the French took the Agenais from the English. The situation changed after the accession of Edward III in 1327; it was soon evident that the new king had every intention of making good his claims to Gascony, the Agenais, Périgueux, and Saintonge. He put a new group of officials in charge to set the economy and administration in order while the Gascon nobles of dubious loyalty were handled with notable delicacy and tact.

Upon the death of Charles IV of France (February 1, 1328) Edward III of England claimed the French throne by virtue of his position as the only direct descendant of Philip IV. The French, unwilling to be ruled by an English king, accepted Philip of Valois, whereupon Edward decided to reopen the war.

The English monarch had several reasons, quite apart from his dynastic claim to the French throne, which contributed to his decision to go to war against Philip VI. The French were openly supporting Scotland against England; in Flanders, which was economically important to England as a market for her raw wool and a source of finished cloth, Louis de Hervert, count of Flanders, had asked for the active support of King Philip to crush the Fleming burghers at the battle of Cassel in August 1328. He had since been ruling his land in close dependence upon the French king. This meant a severe reduction in English trade in her most important staple, and Edward was, by training and native perception, very much aware of the facts of England's economic health. Further, Edward's wife, Philippa, was the daughter of the count of Holland and Hainault, between whom and the king of France no love was lost. From about 1332 Edward was making preparations for a conflict which he saw to be inevitable. He set out to gain the favor, if not the formal alliance, of most of the feudatories of the Lowlands, Hainault, Guelders, and Brabant. The bait—English trade—was attractive. Emperor Louis IV, because of his bitter conflict with the Avignonese Papacy, was glad to support Edward against Philip, as was Robert d'Artois, Philip's brother-in-law. As we have seen (p. 110), Robert sought refuge at the English court after having been convicted of treason to the French crown. He naturally wished to embarrass his wife's brother and urged Edward to claim the French throne as his right. Although this urging was not the cause of the war, Robert's position as a trusted adviser of the English king was surely of some significance.

Edward had to face the fact that his father's incompetence and misrule had ravaged the royal administrative machinery, and the young king needed time to gather up the loose ends left by that rule and the three years of ineffectual regency. The sources of royal income had also been weakened, and the military structure was in disarray. Edward's annoyance with the French for aiding his opponents during the Scottish wars (1330–33) certainly contributed to his decision to attack Philip and recapture the Plantagenet inheritance; his postponement of the attack until 1337 can be understood in the light of his need for time to make the necessary repairs in his own realm. He temporized by listening to emissaries of Pope Benedict. The French Pope naturally wished to forestall an attack upon the French king by prolonging negotiations between Edward and Philip. Edward protested against Philip's occupation of his

French fiefs and stirred up trouble for Philip in Flanders, already in turmoil because of the chronic rebellion of the Flemish burghers against the French king. This rebellion was complicated by feuds and tensions between ruling houses in various parts of the Lowlands. The burghers, interested in commerce, would have preferred to remain neutral and do profitable business with both France and England, whereas the nobility were moved by chivalric ideals, hopes of dynastic favor, or gentlemanly bribes from one side or the other. It would have been difficult to reconcile the two varieties of motivation and discover a united Lowlands.

Philip's reply to Edward's provocative preparations was to redeclare, in the late summer of 1337, Edward's fiefs of Gascony and Ponthieu forfeit. His soldiery moved farther into these lands. Hostilities broke out in the Channel between English and Norman sailors, and some English coastal towns were sacked.

The legates of the Pope sought to pacify the principals in the impending conflict, and Philip seemed inclined to fall in with their efforts. But Edward had almost completed his preparations for war and was determined to claim his heritage. On October 7, 1337, he formally renewed his claim to the French throne. He listened politely to the papal legates, hastening his final preparations for war as they talked and argued. In July 1338, Edward landed at Antwerp with a large force. He went on to Coblenz to receive from the Emperor (September 5), in an impressive ceremony replete with all the pomp of a decadent chivalry, the title of Vicar-General of the Empire. The Emperor formally declared the fiefs held by Philip in the Empire forfeit. There was now no withdrawal possible on either side.

The Hundred Years' War, First Period, 1337–80

EDWARD's preparations had been costly; his alliances had been even more so. He had guaranteed or given "subsidies" to all his allies, who were almost uniformly more interested in English gold than in the military support they had so blithely pledged to give the English king in return. When Edward was ready, in the late summer of 1339, to march into France across Flanders, his allies simply did not move, and the five-weeks' campaign was a fiasco. Edward accepted a personal challenge from Philip to single combat or to a pitched battle between their respective armies, but Philip did not appear.

Edward's expenses had already outrun his resources, and he had to seek help. His former "noble" allies had taken his money quite chivalrously, but had given no aid. The burghers of the Lowlands seemed more substantial. They were now led by Jacques van Artevelde, wealthy and respected merchant of Ghent. The burghers were at odds with their count, Louis de Nevers, as well as with with his suzerain, King Philip, who had joined de Nevers in suppressing the popular revolt of 1328. Their bitterness was deep; yet they were sufficiently realistic to want to protect themselves from the charge of treason against their overlord and the king. Van Artevelde therefore offered Edward the support of the burghers of Ghent (January 1340) on condition that Edward declare himself king of France. The burghers would thus be able to justify their support of Edward by claiming that they were only being loyal to their feudal overlord. Edward complied in a hurry, for he was so deeply in debt that he had to pawn his crown to the archbishop of Trier in order to get back to England.

Once in England, he set about raising funds for the campaign of the coming summer. French raids on a number of English coastal towns led up to the naval battle of Sluys, off the estuary of the Scheldt, between two hundred French, Genoese, and Spanish ships and Edward's two hundred English merchantmen and men-of-war (June 23 and 24, 1340). It was a decisive English victory. Edward had given some attention to the formation of a kind of royal navy, and although some of his own ships had been previously captured and were used by the French at this engagement, organization and discipline on the English side were superior to those of the enemy. The subsequent land campaigns in Flanders were a failure, and many of Edward's adherents in England and on the Continent were indignant at his waiting game; the truce of September 25, 1340, which marked Edward's failure, cost the French king almost nothing. In Brittany, which naturally leaned away from France and toward England, Edward was more fortunate; the more determined native resistance to Philip enabled Edward to keep a foothold in the peninsula.

By 1345 the situation was looking much worse for Edward. He was still penniless, and the Emperor had deserted him for Philip. This may have been a blessing for Edward; it was certainly no boon to Philip. The burghers of Flanders repudiated van Artevelde's leadership and murdered him in July 1345. The count of Flanders was again master in his own lands. Edward's whole strategy of entry through a Flanders supposed to be pro-English had failed. Another opportunity, however, had been gradually taking shape. A dynastic dispute in Brittany brought an appeal from Joan of Flanders, the wife of one claimant to the title, to Edward. At first reluctant to take on another dubious cause when his own looked so forlorn, Edward finally decided to try his fortune. His first military efforts were dismal, but Philip matched Edward in lack of military aptitude. Another truce (March 1343), imposed by the papal legates, brought two years of uneasy peace, during which Edward occupied strongholds in Brittany and improved his financial position somewhat. Gascony, the cause of the whole struggle, was relatively quiet; Edward was unable, until 1345, to send much help to his lieutenants there, and Philip contented himself with minor but steady encroachment.

On the expiration of the truce, Edward was again on the Continent with a picked army of about ten thousand horsemen and archers. In July 1346, he landed in Normandy and moved eastward parallel to the coastline. Foolishly, Edward ravaged the country, making the provisioning of his own troops difficult; without some unearned luck and Philip's slowness, he would surely have lost his whole army. Philip finally caught up with the English between Abbeville and the village of Crécy on the southern bank of the Somme on August 26, 1346. The English were deployed with a gentle descending slope below them, at the bottom of which they had dug irregular pits. The French, confident in the efficacy of their great superiority in numbers, probably more than thirty thousand in all, their fine armor, and their impetuous charge, were eager to engage the enemy; Philip seemed unable to restrain his knights. The French vastly misjudged the potentialities of the English position, as well as the effectiveness of English weapons. The Genoese bowmen, of which Philip had six thousand, might have been useful in close operations, but they were pitifully overmatched by the firepower, range, and accuracy of the English longbows in the hands of English yeomen. The contemporary French chronicler Jean Froissart tells of the meeting between the Genoese bowmen and the English archers:

When the Genoese were somewhat in order they approached the English and sent up a loud shout, in order to frighten them; but the English remained quite quiet and did not seem to attend to it. They then sent up a second shout, and advanced a little forward; the English never moved. They said "Boo" still a third time, advancing with their crossbows presented, and began to shout. The English archers advanced one step forward and shot their arrows with such force and quickness that it seemed as if it snowed. When the Genoese felt these arrows . . . all turned about and retreated quite discomfited.

The English bowmen had a pleasant afternoon. Froissart concludes his account of the battle with the comment, "There is no man, unless he had been present, that can imagine or describe truly the confusion of that day, especially the bad management and confusion of the French, whose troops were numberless."

After this astounding victory Edward marched northward to besiege and, after a long and stubborn resistance, take Calais, thus giving England control of the Strait of Dover and a powerful commercial hold on all northern trade. Philip asked for a truce, and Edward returned to England as a great conqueror. The whole kingdom shared the king's elation at his victories.

England had but a short time to enjoy her amazing, if expensive, triumph, and the humiliation of France and of Philip was soon buried in a deeper suffering. The Black Death struck France early in 1348, England in late August of the same year. Cities were decimated, the poor and clergy suffering the heaviest losses. The pestilence raged in England through 1349, and in Wales, Ireland, and Scotland the following year. The total population loss on both sides of the Channel probably reached one third, although contemporary estimates run much higher. Under such conditions it is remarkable that agriculture, business, administration, law, and religion could function at all. In the face of the loss among the laboring class and the natural desire of landowners and employers to continue their work, the government imposed strict regulations on the wages that could be paid workers and restrictions on the movement of workers (Ordinance of 1349 and Statute of Laborers of 1351). More will be said of this crisis in another connection, but it is proper to mention it here as a backdrop for the pursuit of the war within a few years of the plague's severest outbreak.

Certainly for several years large-scale war was out of the question. There were, however, sporadic local engagements, at sea, along the Gascon frontier, and along the Norman and Breton coasts. English arms could count some modest gains in these exchanges. In an effort to support the house of France, Charles d'Espagne, a cousin of the French king, assembled a fleet and attempted to invade England in 1350. The ensuing naval engagement with the English fleet took place off Winchelsea and was again a decisive victory for King

Edward, who commanded in person with noticeable pleasure and even bravado. Several years' recovery from the plague was sufficient to permit increased action in the north of France. After the death of Philip VI in 1350, his son John, called the Good, continued the policy of unrelenting opposition to Edward's claims, and the renewal of full-scale war seemed certain to everyone.

Negotiations for peace were by now habitual, but since neither side was willing to make any major concessions, they came to nought. Edward was urged on in his plans for another invasion by Charles the Bad, king of Navarre, an intriguing and intermittently treasonous cousin of the French king. At times Edward was led to hope for help from discontented nobles within France. But the king of France had at least a partial deterrent to an English attack on his northern coast in the form of the Scots, who were always glad of an excuse to raid northern England. These raids became so serious that Edward was obliged to direct the campaign against the Scots in person while his son, Edward, the Black Prince, was having some success in Gascony.

In midsummer 1356, the Black Prince was moving northward from Bordeaux on a routine and even leisurely harrying expedition. On September 3 he heard that King John of France was on the north side of the Loire with a large army. The prince was in great danger and knew it. He therefore veered south, trying to avoid capture. King John, scenting a victory, turned after the English army not far from Poitiers on the evening of September 18. A papal delegate who had been trying to keep up with one or the other army chose this moment to suggest that the two leaders come to terms. He was wasting his breath. The next morning the prince, still trying to avoid direct contact with the French, managed to maneuver his troops into an advantageous position, mostly on a height, with his archers well protected behind a hedge. The French cavalry made the first charge, only to retire beneath a rain of English arrows from above. They were replaced by armed foot soldiers, less vulnerable to the archery barrage. But the English archers poured the deadly hail of their shafts into their midst, until finally English mounted bowmen flanked the French from both sides, and the battle was over. The French king was taken prisoner and courteously transported first to Bordeaux and thence to London, where he was honorably and pleasantly detained while awaiting his ransom. In his absence the dauphin, Charles, became regent of the kingdom.

By now France, the arena in which armies had marched, fought and ravaged, was in a deplorable state. The nobility had been decimated by the two costly battles of Crécy and Poitiers; those who had survived were divided in their judgment as to the responsibility for the catastrophe, a goodly proportion of them blaming it on the king and his counselors. There was much unrest among the peasantry and the townsfolk. Agriculture and trade had suffered tremendously from the war and its dislocations and costs. In the absence of any firm hand—and even if King John had been in residence, the situation would hardly have been much better—the country was disorganized and dispirited. The Estates General met on October 17, 1356, and appointed a commission of eighty to investigate the record of the government and the causes of France's humiliation. Each class denounced the others. The young dauphin,

Charles, was about the only balanced and reasonable person in the assembly, yet even he was powerless in the face of the forces of emotion and bitter recrimination.

To add to the disaster, Paris was the scene, early in 1357, of a bourgeois revolt under the leadership of Etienne Marcel, a leading cloth merchant and provost of the Paris guilds. Marcel was virtual dictator of the capital for over a year. He has been hailed as the advocate of democracy in France, and he regarded himself as the spiritual heir of van Artevelde, but his record is somewhat questionable. He allied himself first with the shifty and ambitious Charles the Bad of Navarre, participated in a number of planned murders, then made common cause with the Jacquerie, a revolt of the peasantry in the provinces against war taxes. The ambition and demagoguery of Marcel, the opportunism and deceit of Charles the Bad, and the undisciplined vengeance of the Jacquerie were poor foundations on which to build a reformed government. The excesses and intemperance of this combination alienated the mass of the French people, while the firm conduct of the young dauphin commanded their respect. On July 31, 1358, Marcel was killed by the citizens of Paris as he was inspecting the defenses, and on August 2, the dauphin was welcomed enthusiastically in the city. This part of the crisis was over.

The Peace of Brétigny

THE king, John the Good, between jousts and pleasantries in London, was negotiating a peace. The English demanded a high cash ransom for him and the cession of almost all of the ancient Plantagenet empire in France. When these conditions were scornfully rejected by the French, Edward crossed the Channel to negotiate directly—with an army at his back. The French could also negotiate, and Edward decided to settle for less than he had at first demanded. By the Peace of Brétigny (May 8, 1360), King John ceded to the English king Poitou, Saintonge, the Angoumois, Limousin, Périgord, the Agenais, Quercy, Rouergue, Bigorre, Calais, La Rochelle, Guines, and Ponthieu. Other details of the treaty were not fulfilled by either side, but perhaps neither party expected them to be. All the English holdings in France were placed under the control and administration of Edward, the Black Prince, and heavy levies were laid on the rest of France to pay the ransom for King John. The required amount could not be raised, and King John returned as a prisoner to England, where he died on April 8, 1364. He was a feudal gentleman, but expensive as a king.

His son, Charles V (1364-80), known as Charles the Wise, used the next few years to strengthen the position of the crown in preparation for the renewal of the war, for he had no intention of accepting the decision of Brétigny. He was a ruler of quite modern dimensions; literate and a supporter of culture, a calculating economist, a clever negotiator, a good judge of men, firm in his decisions, and able to wait for the right moment, he commanded wholesome respect from friend and foe alike. The English who dealt with him remarked: "He's no gentleman, he's a lawyer."

Charles the Bad of Navarre was up to his old tricks again in 1364, and

France after the Peace of Brétigny, 1360

Charles V acted quickly. His new Constable of France, Bertrand de Guesclin, was a soldier first and a gentleman, if necessary, thereafter; du Guesclin captured some of Navarre's cities, and Charles V was able to impose (March 1365) a peace that kept his rival out of northern France. In Flanders, with its history of sympathy and commercial connection with England, Charles had the satisfaction of breaking the engagement of the Flemish heiress to a son of Edward III and substituting (1369) his own brother, Philip of Burgundy, as prospective bridegroom. The Pope, Urban V, was of no little help in arranging this transfer of affections.

By 1368 Charles felt strong enough to renew hostilities against the English. The French countered the usual English tactic of laying waste the land by mobile harassment and the erection of impregnable fortresses, which the English had to bypass. The English thus had no chance to meet in the field and defeat an inferior French force. The French military establishment had not yet been able to readjust to the English superiority in the field; delaying tactics were necessary. The English found, as a consequence of the French policy, that they were beating the air. The serious illness of the Black Prince and the death of the leading English general, Sir John Chandos, critically handicapped the English effort. In December 1370, du Guesclin caught an English army tired out from a campaign, attacked it briskly, and crushed it near Le Mans. The English defeat of the Spanish fleet off Winchelsea in 1350 was avenged in the summer of 1372, when the Spaniards off La Rochelle attacked and destroyed an English fleet bearing reinforcements to the dwindling English forces in Gascony. The following year, Edward's younger son, John of Gaunt, duke of Lancaster, led a campaign in Artois and Auvergne, with no military success at all. Du Guesclin's forays and steady pressure whittled away at the English possessions until, by his death in 1380, the English territory was reduced to about what it had been in 1333. The illness and death of the Black Prince (1376), Edward III's steady decline in vigor and determination, and the struggle between John of Gaunt and the rest of the baronage for control of the government

Edward, the Black Prince, effigy on tomb at Canterbury Cathedral [THE TIMES, LONDON].

made any concentrated effort at defense of the royal lands in France quite unlikely.

From the high position of victory England had occupied at Brétigny in 1360 to the low point of disorganized and flaccid defense of what was left of those gains in 1380 was a sorry descent. Brittany was the only area in which the English position in 1380 was as strong as it had been twenty years earlier. On the other hand, France, under a subtle and determined monarch, Charles V, aided by a vigorous and relentless military leader, du Guesclin, had shown astonishing recuperative powers. The roles of victor and vanquished had been reversed. By 1380 the principal protagonists had left the stage. Edward III died in June 1377, unmourned in England. Three years later du Guesclin (July 13, 1380), and a bare two months after that (September 16) Charles V, followed him in death. The king of France in his last years had lost his queen, then his daughter, finally his powerful allies, Pope Gregory XI (1378), King Henry II of Castile (1379), and Emperor Charles IV (1378). In spite of his recent gains against English arms, no peace had been achieved, and the hatred between France and England had only grown in bitterness with the prolongation of the war. Charles was, furthermore, leaving his troubled and divided kingdom in the hands of a twelve-year-old boy. The domestic troubles in which England was involved, about which we shall learn more later (Chapters 7, 9, and 10), made it certain that there would be no effective resumption of the war in the last decades of the century. From about 1380 to the end of the century, the "peace" was no more than a temporary truce of exhaustion and diversion of energy. Although the struggle had been going for almost a century, no real conclusion had been reached. On this somber note we may record the end of the first period of the so-called Hundred Years' War.

SUGGESTIONS FOR FURTHER READING

Annals of Ghent (Annales Gandenses), trans. Hilda Johnstone. London, 1951

COULTON, G. G., *Social Life in Britain from the Conquest to the Reformation*. Cambridge, 1919

FROISSART, *Chronicles*. Many editions. Everyman's Library

JOINVILLE, *Memoirs of the Crusades by Villehardouin and de Joinville*. Everyman's Library

ARMITAGE-SMITH, S., *John of Gaunt*. Westminister, 1904

Cambridge Medieval History, Vols. VI–VIII

DUNN-PATTISON, R. P., *The Black Prince*. London, 1910

FUNCK-BRENTANO, F., *The Middle Ages*. London, 1926

LEVETT, E., and A. BUMARD, *The Black Death*. Oxford, 1916

LODGE, E., *Gascony under English Rule*. London, 1926

MACKINNON, J., *History of Edward III*. London, 1900

MCKISACK, M., *The Fourteenth Century 1307–1399*. Oxford, 1959

OMAN, C., *History of the Art of War in the Middle Ages*. 2 vols. London, 1924

PERROY, E., *The Hundred Years War*. London, 1951

PETIT-DUTAILLIS, C., *The Feudal Monarchy in France and England*. London, 1936

POWICKE, F. M., *The Thirteenth Century,* Oxford, 1953

RAMSAY, J., *Genesis of Lancaster, 1307–1399.* 2 vols. Oxford, 1913
TOUT, T. F., *The History of England from the Accession of Henry III to the Death of Edward III.* London, 1905
TOUT, T. F., *The Place of Edward II in English History.* Manchester, 1914
VICKERS, K. H., *England in the Later Middle Ages.* London, 1921

LAVISSE, E., *Histoire de France,* Vol. IV, parts 1 and 2. 1902
LUCE, S., *La France pendant la guerre de cent ans.* 2 vols. 1890–93
LUCE, S., *Histoire de Bertrand du Guesclin et de son époque.* 1876
PERRENS, F. T., *Etienne Marcel, prévôt des marchands.* 1874
PIRENNE, H., *Histoire de Belgique,* Vols. I and II. 1929
PIRENNE, H., E. PERROY, *et al., La Fin du Moyen Âge.* 2 vols. 1946. Vol. VII of *Peuples et civilisations*

CHAPTER SIX

SPAIN AND THE EMPIRE TO 1437

O UR account thus far has centered for the most part on Italy, France, and England. This focus is both natural and conventional. Italy had the Papacy, and, in the time of Dante, the Papacy was the central institution of Europe—indeed, of all Western civilization. France had the University of Paris, the most influential cultural and educational organ of the European continent, frequented by students and scholars from all parts of Christendom. The kingdom of France, furthermore, with her recent history of forceful leadership—no other country could boast so able a line of kings as Philip Augustus, St. Louis, and Philip the Fair—was the most populous, unified, and advanced state in Europe. Across the Channel, England had benefited from her isolation by strengthening her institutions, uniting the native English and Norman French strains into an English people, and broadening the base of her social and political structure by giving legislative representation to the rising bourgeoisie. In the course of the long war between France and England, the science of war changed, and the political systems of both kingdoms underwent great modifications. By the end of the war, about 1450, the economy and the culture as well as the balance of social power in both countries were substantially different from what they had been at the outbreak of hostilities in the 1290's.

But the fact that these three lands, Italy, France, and England, were active, wealthy, populous, and in the van of "progress" toward the modern world does not mean that events of future significance were not taking place elsewhere. It is with these other regions that we are now concerned.

SPAIN

T HE Moslem conquest of the Spanish peninsula in the early years of the eighth century had been sudden and almost complete. Only a narrow strip along the mountainous northern coast maintained its independence, as the kingdom of the Asturias. Charlemagne's attempt to recapture the land for Christendom had been a notable failure. But within a short time a life of comfort and internal squabbles weakened the Moslem hold, and the *reconquista* (reconquest) of the peninsula by Spanish Christians proceeded relentlessly, if slowly and unevenly. The eleventh century saw three kingdoms well established in the north: the kingdoms of Castile and León united for the first time in 1037 under Ferdinand I of Castile, extending to the Guadarrama Mountains; the smaller kingdom of Navarre; and, to the east of it, the, at first, minute kingdom of Aragon. Reaching from the Pyrenees to the eastern coast, the strong county of Barcelona protected the eastern flank of Spanish Christendom. A century later, the Christian area had almost doubled, and in the west, along the Atlantic seaboard, the new kingdom of Portugal (from 1140) reached to the Tagus River. León and Castile captured the stronghold of Toledo in 1085 and then in 1147 took the fortress of Calatrava from the Almorávides, Mohammedan tribesmen from north Africa. The middle of the upper Guadiana River became the southern frontier. The kingdom of Aragon expanded until, united with the county of Barcelona in 1137, it controlled both banks of the Ebro River and a substantial coastline facing the Balearic Islands. Navarre, hemmed in by Aragon and Castile, was to play only a minor role in Spanish political life until the end of the reign of Ferdinand the Catholic.

The next stage of the reconquest appeared early in the thirteenth century. The most significant military action was the Christian victory at Las Navas de Tolosa in 1212, when Alfonso VIII of Castile, aided by contingents from all the Christian kingdoms, defeated the Almohades.* Within a few decades various Moslem kingdoms submitted to the powerful Christian advance— Cordova in 1236, Jaen in 1246, Seville in 1248. Thus the kingdom of Castile and León by the middle of the century stretched from the Bay of Biscay on the north to the Mediterranean Sea on the south; Portugal had reached her present southern shore at almost the same time. Aragon had also made advances, though less striking ones, southward along the eastern coast south of Valencia. More important, she had conquered the Balearic Islands by 1232. These significant conquests had been carried out under two remarkably able and energetic rulers, Ferdinand III of Castile† (1217-52) and James I of Aragon (1213-76). Christian Spain, although divided into a number of kingdoms frequently at war with one another, was thus master of the western portion of the western basin of the Mediterranean. All that was left in Moslem hands was the small kingdom of Granada, along the southern coast from Gibraltar to near Cartagena, which paid a substantial yearly tribute to the king of Castile. The *reconquista* had demanded a tremendous effort on the part of the Christians, and there seemed no need to expend the energy to conquer so small and harmless a state as the Moslem kingdom had become. Consequently, for two centuries and more thereafter Granada was left almost undisturbed. The Christian states of Spain began a period of adjustment and consolidation which reached its climax in 1469, in the union of Castile and Aragon by the marriage of Isabella the Catholic of Castile and Ferdinand II of Aragon, later Ferdinand V of Castile, known as the Catholic.

* The Almohades, a reforming Moslem sect from the Atlas mountains, had defeated the Almorávides in northern Africa and crossed to Spain in 1146, soon subjecting other Moslem groups to their rule.

† León and Castile had separate rulers from 1157 to 1230. From this time "Castile" may be assumed to include León.

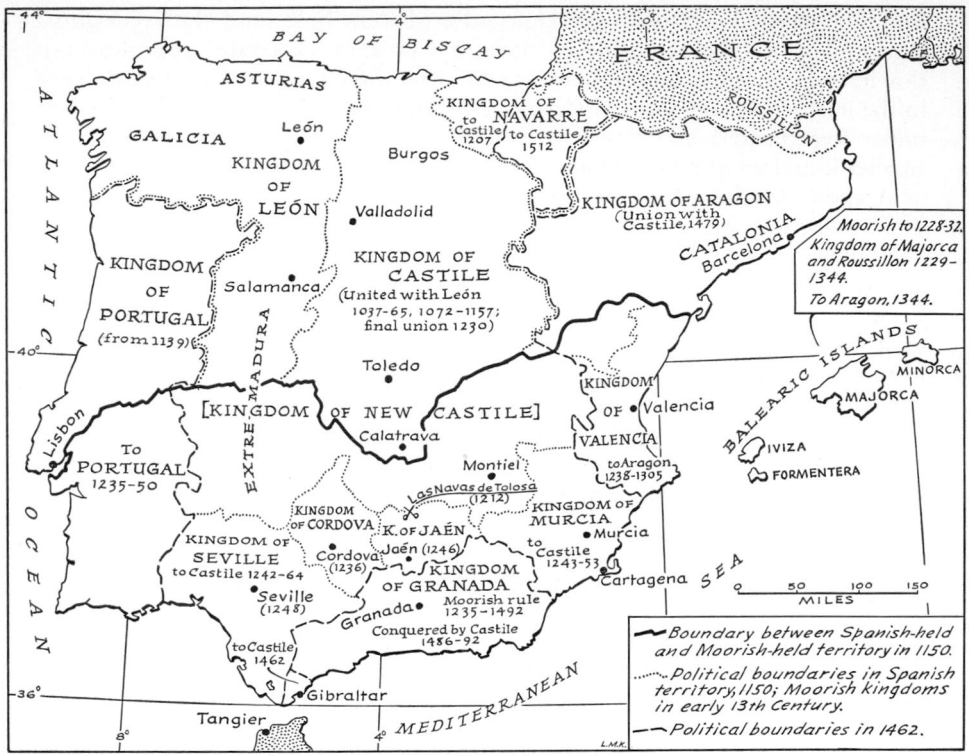

Map content:
BAY OF BISCAY
FRANCE
ASTURIAS
ATLANTIC
GALICIA
León
KINGDOM OF NAVARRE
to Castile to Castile
1207   1512
Burgos
ROUSSILLON
KINGDOM OF LEÓN
Valladolid
KINGDOM OF ARAGON
(Union with Castile,1479)
CATALONIA
Barcelona
Moorish to 1228-32.
Kingdom of Majorca and Roussillon 1229-1344.
To Aragon, 1344.
KINGDOM OF PORTUGAL
(from 1139)
Salamanca
KINGDOM OF CASTILE
(United with León 1037-65, 1072-1157; final union 1230)
EXTREMADURA
Toledo
[KINGDOM OF NEW CASTILE]
Calatrava
KINGDOM OF VALENCIA
to Aragon 1238-1305
KINGDOM OF • Valencia
BALEARIC ISLANDS
MINORCA
MAJORCA
IVIZA
FORMENTERA
Lisbon
To PORTUGAL 1235-50
Montiel
Las Navas de Tolosa (1212)
KINGDOM OF MURCIA
• Murcia
KINGDOM OF CORDOVA
K. OF JAÉN
Cordova (1236)
Jaén (1246)
to Castile 1243-53
Cartagena
SEA
KINGDOM OF SEVILLE
to Castile 1242-64
• Seville (1248)
KINGDOM OF GRANADA
Granada •
Moorish rule 1235-1492
Conquered by Castile 1486-92
to Castile 1462
Gibraltar
Tangier
MEDITERRANEAN
0 50 100 150
MILES

Boundary between Spanish-held and Moorish-held territory in 1150.
Political boundaries in Spanish territory, 1150; Moorish kingdoms in early 13th Century.
Political boundaries in 1462.

The Reconquest of Spain from the Moors, 1150–1492

In the two Christian kingdoms, Castile (and León) and Aragon, the hundred years following the mid-thirteenth century were characterized by diverse developments. Castile and León, reunited under Ferdinand III in 1230, had expanded with extreme rapidity, and the process of unification involved serious conflicts of law and administration. There were perpetual dynastic struggles, and the nobility resisted any efforts of the monarchy toward order and centralization which would have curtailed their liberties. Alfonso X the Scholar (*el Sabio*) succeeded Ferdinand III as king of León-Castile in 1252. The territorial extent of the kingdom did not call for further conquest, and he found such a chaotic diversity of custom in the several parts of his kingdom that he set about codifying and uniformizing the law. The result of his work, *Las Siete Partidas,* was a great achievement, based on the absolutist concepts of Roman law. But Alfonso was more scholar than politician. In the area of practical politics, he was faced by a turbulent, proud, resistant nobility, unaccustomed to restraint in any form and even contemptuous of the king's plans for a united monarchy. Alfonso made his own path more difficult by poor management of the royal economy and by chasing the will-o'-the-wisp of the imperial crown. Careless in money matters, he twice debased the coinage, allowed the Moslem kingdom of Granada to reduce its tribute to the royal treasury, gave up the rights of Castile in Portugal without any real compensation, and made overgenerous gifts to favored courtiers.

The extinction of the Hohenstaufen line of emperors of the Holy Roman Empire with the death in 1254 of Conrad IV, son of Frederick II, tempted Alfonso to become involved in imperial politics. William of Holland, elected to succeed Conrad IV in 1254, died two years later. Since Alfonso's maternal grandfather, Philip of Swabia, had been German king and emperor from 1200 to 1208, the king was easily persuaded to claim the imperial crown by right of inheritance. Much Spanish gold was spent in attempts to persuade the German electors to make Alfonso emperor, although the Spanish people had a low opinion of the project and particularly of the expenditures involved. A bare and temporary majority of the imperial electors did in fact elect Alfonso on April 1, 1257, but in the meantime, Richard of Cornwall, brother of Henry III of England, had accepted election by the remaining electors (one of whom voted for both candidates) and was actually crowned at Aachen by the archbishop of Cologne. Alfonso had paid handsome bribes and had a title, but he never set foot on German soil. Pope Gregory X obliged him, in 1275, to renounce the title.

That same year Alfonso's eldest son, Ferdinand de la Cerda, heir to the throne, died, leaving the Castilian succession in doubt. In *Las Siete Partidas* Alfonso had prescribed the principle of primogeniture for the Castilian succession. Now, under pressure, he violated his own principle and named his younger son, Don Sancho, as his successor. Then, to make matters worse, Alfonso tried to correct his mistake by creating a new kingdom for Ferdinand's son. When, in 1282, Don Sancho refused to accept that solution, a war between Alfonso and his son broke out. On the death of Alfonso X in 1284, Don Sancho was recognized by the majority of the nobility and the towns as

Alfonso X Reading His Cantigas, a collection of 420 lyric poems in praise of the Virgin Mary, from the manuscript in the Escorial [MAS, BARCELONA].

Sancho IV, but the turmoil of the kingdom continued throughout the eleven years of his reign. Aragon welcomed the sons of Ferdinand de la Cerda and supported their claims, with resultant tension and intermittent war between the two kingdoms. It was into this dispute that Philip III of France plunged when he came to Spain and laid siege to Gerona in 1285. Ostensibly he came to support the de la Cerda heirs, but it was not clear which side in the conflict his policy really favored. His troops attacked and pillaged both sides with equal brutality.

Aragon's drive for dominance of the western Mediterranean made a decisive advance in 1282, when the Sicilians offered the crown of Sicily to Peter III after the bloody Sicilian Vespers and the expulsion of the French. Peter's acceptance was immediate. Aragonese influence, thus strengthened, came to rival and at times surpass that of the French in the western Mediterranean. Roger de Loria, the great Aragonese admiral, made Aragon the leading naval power in those waters until his death in 1302. This rise of the house of Aragon to power was accompanied by a twenty years' war between the French interests on one side, sporadically supported by the Papacy, and the Aragonese and Sicilians on the other. The Peace of Caltabellotta in 1302 was a victory for the Sicilians. The ending of hostilities freed large numbers of soldiers, and the king of Sicily (the Aragonese Frederick II), anxious to be rid of these troublesome soldier-brigands, suggested that they go to the aid of the hard-pressed Emperor Andronicus of Constantinople. They were only too glad to get into another war. Thus Aragonese imperialism did not stop with control of Sicily. At one time or another, the house of Aragon, or Catalan freebooters from the ports of Catalonia, acting independently but frequently using the name of the king of Aragon, their nominal ruler, ruled in southern Greece, Sicily and southern Italy, Sardinia, and the Balearic Islands and held several cities in Asia Minor. The duchy of Athens, under the Aragonese king of Sicily, lasted from 1311 to 1387. In the mid-fourteenth century Aragon was the strongest single power in the entire Mediterranean basin.

Within Spain there was no clear pattern of development. In each of the kingdoms the nobility was unruly, the towns independent. The de la Cerda heirs were growing up and being fought over. Peace between the kingdoms was intermittent. At Campillo in 1304 Castile and Aragon agreed to cease fighting between themselves and made joint war on the Moors. This war was a fiasco, but the peace it was intended to initiate between Castile and Aragon lasted for almost forty years. Alfonso XI (1312–50) may be credited with keeping Castile intact. He had firmness and ruthlessness, both necessary qualities in a turbulent age. He managed the nobles, whether by diplomacy or deceit, by sending them to engage in frontier raids against the Moors, or by encouraging them in their chivalric pursuits; at least he kept them reasonably busy. He favored the towns, improved the administration of justice, and restored a great measure of confidence and stability to the people and the monarchy.

The reign of his successor and only legitimate son, Peter I the Cruel (1350–69), was more eventful if less constructive. Alfonso XI had left a number of sons by his favorite mistress, Leonora de Guzmán. One of these, Henry (Enrique) of Trastamara, won support among the discontented nobility and eventually from Charles V of France, and a dynastic struggle impended. Peter complicated the situation by rejecting, then imprisoning his wife, Blanche of Bourbon, almost immediately after their marriage in 1350, thus angering her French relatives. Henry meanwhile gained further support from Aragon, whose king, Peter IV, was eager to cause his neighbor trouble. The Aragonese king employed for this purpose a large number of the Free Companies, soldiers and freebooters out of work because of the Peace of Brétigny between France and England. We have met some of them before (see pp. 72–73) as they massed on Avignon, which seemed to them rich and therefore fair game in their quest for booty. These companies, led into Spain by Bertrand du Guesclin, succeeded in subduing most of Castile; in 1366 Henry was crowned king at Burgos. His half brother, Peter the Cruel, appealed to the Black Prince, then in Gascony, and persuaded him, against the better judgment of his advisers, to enter the Spanish war on the side of legitimacy. The forces of the Black Prince won the battle of Najera in 1367, but after the victory the brutal performance of Peter so disgusted Edward that he took his troops back to Bordeaux. Peter was soon defeated in the battle of Montiel and killed in a personal tussle with Henry (1369), who subsequently reigned as Henry II until his death in 1379. One fortunate outcome of the battle of Montiel was the high mortality among the Free Companies, some of which were on both sides of the conflict; fewer of them were left to pillage the countryside, in Spain or in France. Henry's rule was not peaceful; he was able to weather the storms only by considerable concessions to the nobles and the towns. Much of the constructive program of Alfonso XI was undone during the civil and dynastic wars of Peter I and Henry II. Even John of Gaunt, a son of Edward III, claimed the throne of Castile, through his wife Constance, daughter of Peter the Cruel. This claim added to Henry's eagerness to give aid to Charles V of France in his war with England. Castilian naval forces, as we have seen, defeated an English fleet off La Rochelle in June 1372.

Henry was succeeded by his son, John I (1379–90). After the death of his first wife, Eleanor of Aragon, John married Beatrice, the heiress of Portugal (1383), in the hope of bringing about a union of the two kingdoms. Instead, war broke out, which resulted in a Castilian defeat at Aljubarrota in August 1385 and confirmed Portuguese independence. The next year Portugal made an alliance with England, thus initiating a tradition of friendship which has lasted to our day. Two minorities followed in Castile, those of Henry III (1390–1406) and John II (1406–54), with the troubles incident to regencies. However, John II was fortunate in his regent and, later, in his minister, the Constable Álvaro de Luna. The jealous nobility plotted against de Luna constantly, and in 1427 he was exiled. Without his firm hand affairs were soon in such chaos that he had to be recalled. After some years of success, he was again exiled in 1439, once more to be recalled. Although de Luna gave solid prestige to the royal power, the queen, Isabella of Portugal, herself led the plotting against him. This time it was successful and, with the ungrateful king's consent, de Luna was executed in 1453 on charges of sorcery. His crime was apparently efficiency and effective support of the royal authority.

In 1410 the son of John I of Castile and Eleanor of Aragon became Ferdinand I of Aragon. The reign of a Castilian prince over Aragon was a first step toward a union. Ferdinand's son and successor, Alfonso V the Magnanimous of Aragon (1416–58), married the daughter of King Henry III of Castile. This was the second step toward dynastic union. The next step, the marriage in 1469 of Ferdinand the Catholic, heir to the throne of Aragon, and Isabella of Castile, marked the culmination of the logical trend of Spanish history. In 1474 Isabella succeeded her brother, Henry IV, as ruler of Castile, and in 1479 Ferdinand inherited all of Aragon and her Mediterranean possessions. Despite all its disheartening chapters, union of the leading powers of the peninsula was simply a matter of time.

Growth of the Spirit of Spanish Unity

OUR story has been almost exclusively a political and dynastic account. This has been necessary because of the peculiar nature of the developments in the peninsula. France also passed through a period of division and then unification, but the division was caused by the presence of a non-French power, the king of England, on what was naturally French territory, commanding resources for resistance and even aggression over which the French ruler had no actual control. There was some parallel in Spain at the beginning of our period, since the Moorish principalities were at least connected with their coreligionists in north Africa. But as the Spanish *reconquista* became more vigorous, north African support for the Moors dwindled. Then for two full centuries the troubles of Spain were of her own creation. Progress toward centralization was made virtually impossible by a turbulent and proud nobility with no concept of national unity and no desire to collaborate with a strong monarch or to support sound legislation in the interest of the nation as a whole. Inner dynastic squabbles, frequent minorities of monarchs, romantic attachments and consequent illegitimacies, overweening royal ambitions, and the chivalric customs of the time—all these retarded the process of unification for which geography and culture so obviously intended the peninsula.

But underneath the surface events a sense of *hispanidad* ("Spanishness") was growing in the cultural and intellectual life of Spain—in the language, the common concepts, the coin of cultural exchange, the awareness of common elements in history, and the vision of a common future.

From the twelfth century a tendency toward general acceptance of the Castilian dialect can be traced, and even Portuguese writers in the thirteenth and fourteenth centuries wrote in Castilian. The greatest literary monuments of this early period, the *Crónica general* of Alfonso X, the Scholar, the *Poema de mio Cid, El libro de Apolonio, Los siete Infantes de Lara,* and the *Poema de Fernán González,* are all of Castilian origin, and by their originality and vigor exerted a powerful influence on cultural concepts and literary expression in all other parts of the peninsula. In education Spain was not behind the rest of Europe. Indeed, without the collaborative work of Spanish, Moslem, and Jewish scholars in twelfth-century Spain, notably at Toledo and Seville, the northern universities would not have had the tools with which to work. Aristotle and his great Arab and Jewish commentators came to the West mostly through Spain and in translations made in Spain by Spanish scholars. Without Avicenna (Ibn Sina, d. 1037) and Averroës (Ibn Rushd, d. 1198), Aristotle would have been incomprehensible. The works of Avicenna and Averroës were translated into Latin in Spain, and thence carried to Paris and Oxford. The early universities at Palencia (founded 1208–09), Valladolid (*ca.* 1250), Salamanca (1228), Lisbon (1290), Lérida (1300), and Huesca (1354) were all national institutions founded by the kings of Castile, Portugal, or Aragon without waiting for papal charters. Their existence was sometimes precarious, their financial situation often difficult. Their curriculum was similar to that of the universities at Paris, Bologna, and Oxford, yet with an emphasis on the Arabic and Hebrew languages which the northern centers could not match, and a leaning toward the study of canon and civil law. Students and teachers alike have always been congenital wanderers, and those in medieval Spain were no exception. Scholars came to Spain from distant parts of Europe, and Spanish students and masters went to Italy and France to study and lecture. The currents of intellectual exchange on an academic plane were thus added to the exchanges on a political, military, and commercial basis between Spain and Italy, Provence, France, England, Greece, and the Byzantine Empire. It is a commonplace that Dante was influenced by Provençal poetry. The Provençal poets in turn were profoundly influenced by Arab-Spanish verse forms and motifs. In compensation, Dante's *Divine Comedy* was known, translated, and imitated in Spain in the fourteenth century. Petrarch's Italian lyrics were avidly copied by Spanish poets, and some of Boccaccio's works were translated into Catalan within a few decades of his death. Many French pilgrims and soldiers came to Spain either to visit the shrine of Santiago de Compostela or to join in the crusades against the Moors. Troubadours and minstrels were obviously among these travelers, bringing with them their music and their stories, which were eagerly listened to and became the property of the people, then taking back to France motifs from the Arab-Spanish society which they had seen and come to appreciate.

Administration, the Orders, and the Church

NEXT to the king, the most important element in Spanish political life was the *Cortes.* From Visigothic times, the king had had a *concejo,* or royal council of advisers. The functions of government in the later Middle Ages, however, became so complex that of necessity there grew up a separate body or bodies of clergy and nobility, rather local in nature, which came to be called the *Cortes.* From time to time the king would call these *Cortes* to advise him. As the progress of the *reconquista* gave rise to independent cities which were centers of commerce and therefore wealthy, the king began to invite representatives of the towns to the *Cortes.* This practice began in Aragon in 1162 and in León in 1188; in Castile also it appeared before the end of the twelfth century. Thus Spain was the first European power to evolve a rudimentary parliamentary government in which the Third Estate was recognized and represented. Since the kings in Spain faced a hostile nobility in these centuries, it is not surprising that they welcomed the support of the municipalities and paid for it by granting them substantial favors, such as the right to elect their own magistrates, implying virtual self-government. Later kings were to try with some success to nullify these liberties, but the fact of their early existence is quite clear and significant.

The *Cortes* was not specifically a legislative body, but late in the thirteenth century the *Cortes* of Castile gained the right to present to the king petitions, which, if accepted, became law. In order to enforce acceptance of their petitions, the *Cortes* could withhold grants of money to the king. Although the king had many sources of income "of his own," he was continually asking for special gifts or levies; the *Cortes* therefore wielded some power. Furthermore, the *Cortes* had much to say about the selection of the regent in the case of a minority. It could even refuse to accept the oath of a new sovereign, although a sufficiently strong king might disregard this refusal and gain general acceptance.

The Military Orders

IMPORTANT as the king, the nobility, the *Cortes,* and the cities were in the future development of Spain, there were other elements that contributed to the uniqueness which has always characterized the peninsula. Among them were the great military orders, the position of the Church and the clergy, and the idea of empire.

The crusading orders of the Hospitalers and the Knights Templar were not Spanish foundations, but in the course of the Crusades they acquired more lands and wealth in Spain than in any other country in Europe. We have seen (Chapter 3) how Pope Clement V suppressed the Templars in 1312 at the demand of Philip IV (the Fair) of France. The effect of the suppression in Spain was that most of their vast properties passed to the Spanish crowns and many of the members joined the three native military orders: the Orders of Calatrava, of Santiago, and of Alcántara.

The founders of the Order of Calatrava were two Cistercian monks who had volunteered to take the fortress of Calatrava from the Moors in 1158. Their efforts, financed by the archbishop of Toledo, were successful. The crusaders, organized under a military leader, took the Benedictine rule and were approved by the Pope. Their labors and enthusiasm brought members and rewards, and two lesser orders were joined to them by papal bulls.

The Order of Santiago was founded at about the same time, but of a different stock—converted brigands. They made excellent crusaders. They associated chaplains with them and regarded themselves as defenders of the faith and the scourge of the infidel. They certainly were the latter. They wore the special insignia of St. James, a sword with its hilt red, as with the blood of the infidel. Their clerical members followed the rule of St. Augustine. By the time of the union of Castile and Aragon, this order had about two hundred commanderies spread throughout the peninsula and vast properties in land and treasure.

The Order of Alcántara also arose in the late twelfth century in León as a defense against the Moor. Cistercian monks were allowed to join it and to devote "as much time as they could spare from their primary obligation, war against the infidel, to religion."

All three orders had as their prime object to make war against the Moslem. But since they all existed by royal grant, approved by a papal bull, they were nominally under the king's orders and in fact fought for their monarch in the field against other Christian princes in the thirteenth and fourteenth centuries. The Grand Masters of these orders were absolute rulers within their constitutions; all the members, usually of the nobility, took vows of obedience, poverty (interpreted to mean that any gifts to the orders were not to be appropriated by any single member), and chastity (which allowed marriage but demanded fidelity to the marriage vow). These orders were so powerful in Spain that several popes used them or tried to use them to curb the independence of the Spanish kings. At other times their semireligious nature, coupled with their wealth and independence, induced other popes to endeavor to abridge their privileges. Such efforts the knights resisted firmly. Occasional weak rulers gave the orders a chance to increase their independence from royal control. In the fifteenth century the Grand Masters of these orders had become the most powerful subjects of the kings of Spain. Each had at his absolute command not only great wealth but also what was virtually an independent army. Small wonder that Ferdinand II of Aragon felt it necessary to take the orders under tight royal control by securing from Pope Innocent VIII a bull (1489) granting him for life the administration of all three orders.

The Church

THE Church in Spain was extremely influential. Fabulously wealthy from gifts and highly privileged by numerous exemptions and immunities in all the kingdoms, it nevertheless presented a framework of Spanish unity. It was one church, whether in Aragon, in Navarre, in León, in Castile, or even under Moorish domination in Granada. But the Church was not always in accord with the various monarchs. Popes, kings, and cathedral chapters not infrequently engaged in three-cornered disputes over the nominations of bishops, of which there were twenty-four in Castile alone. Gradually, however, the papal right to name bishops won out. In the fourteenth century, particularly in Aragon, papal priority was no longer questioned in such matters. The frequency with which the popes appointed non-Spaniards to rich benefices—"to the great prejudice of our people and the common weal," as the *Cortes* phrased one complaint to the pope—obviously enhanced the growing feeling of *hispanidad*. On the other hand, the kings clung jealously to their rights. Some papal bulls were forbidden publication, some prelates were chased out of the country, and the immunities of the clergy, reaching as high as bishops, were curtailed in secular matters and even in certain religious matters. The attempts of ecclesiastical courts to handle secular cases were quickly quashed, while, at the same time, the disciplinary authority of the ecclesiastical courts in purely religious matters was, in principle, supported. The steady and repeated assertion of the spirit of Spanish royal and ecclesiastical independence through these centuries laid the foundation for the almost antipapal Catholicism which can be observed under the later *reyes católicos* of the sixteenth century, Charles I (Emperor Charles V) and Philip II.

The Spanish Idea of Empire

IN THE sixteenth century the Spanish Empire stretched around the globe. The Spanish monarch was the master of the most far-reaching realm the world had ever known. But this situation was not a complete novelty to the Spanish mind. From earliest Christian times there had been propagators of universal ideals among the Spaniards. They held one end of the Great Sea— the Pillars of Hercules were theirs—and on their other flank they looked west and north over the waters. They had driven the great Charlemagne back across the mountains in headlong flight. They had driven the Moor into the sea. Who else had done as much? Charlemagne had humbled the Germans, the wild Avars, and the Italians. They, the Spaniards, had humbled him. Islam had enslaved the Christians in the east to the Danube, and none could check its course. The Spaniards, singlehanded, had pushed Islam back to Africa. Who had taken over Sicily and southern Italy from the French and held their territory? Who ruled in Greece and the isles of the sea? Who was to say that the Spaniard's *orgullo,* his pride, was not amply justified by performance? Who was better fitted to rule the world than the Spaniard? There was no answer. God had been especially gracious to Spain, and Spain and the Spaniards meant to prove that confidence well placed.

Through all the vicissitudes of Spain's internecine dynastic difficulties, the bonds of union, isolation from the rest of Europe, and self-sufficiency grew tighter until, by the end of the fifteenth century, Spain was prepared in mind and heart to assume the burden of her mission.

THE HOLY ROMAN EMPIRE

THE death of the Emperor Frederick II in 1250 marked the end of an epoch in the idea of a Christian Empire. The grandest and most inclusive period had been that of Charlemagne's reign. His heirs had been unable to keep his conquests together. The center of gravity under Charlemagne had been France and northern Italy. By the treaty of Verdun in 843 the Empire was split into three parts: western France; to the east, something vaguely resembling central and southern Germany; and between them a monstrosity reaching northwest from the Alps to the Lowlands and southeast to Rome, bulging westward from the Alps to take in the valley of the Rhône. This division represented acceptance of the inherent impossibility of holding together the vast and diverse creation of a political genius. From that time France went her separate way, while the German kings from Otto I (962–73) on attempted to re-establish the unity and integrity of Charlemagne's creation out of the two eastern parts. Frederick II was one of the most powerful, intelligent, and determined of these rulers, but he was unable to control both slopes of the Alps. Therein lies the clue to the subsequent history of the Empire. Italy and Germany, by the simple facts of their location, their ethnic, social, and economic structure, the tremendous barrier of the Alps looming between them, and the tenuousness of the ties that brought them together, should not have been expected to fit in the same harness. If we add to these natural obstacles the firm determination of the Papacy to control the state in any form, the outcome of the empire of the German kings from Otto to Frederick was certain to be failure.

We have recounted in Chapter 1 the vain efforts of Frederick's heirs, Manfred and Conradin, to keep even his Italian possessions intact, and we have seen how quickly Charles of Anjou, with papal approval and help, disposed of them. In Germany, the princes received this news almost with indifference; they had grown accustomed to a great degree of independence from an emperor who was almost always in far-off Italy and were not interested in bringing him or his governance any closer.

It is true that the landgrave of Thuringia, Henry Raspe, had been elected emperor in 1246 by the three ecclesiastical electors, the archbishops of Mainz, Cologne, and Trier,* on orders from Pope Innocent IV, who had deposed Frederick II at the Council of Lyons in 1245. But nobody paid much attention to Henry, or to his successor (elected in 1247), another obscurity, William of Holland, who quite prudently spent almost all his time until his death in 1256 at home in Holland and Friesland. The next election was split; three electors voted, in return for heavy bribes, for Richard of Cornwall, brother of Henry III of England, and three for Alfonso X of Castile, also in return for generous gifts. The seventh elector, King Ottokar II of Bohemia, himself too strong to be a good candidate, impartially voted for both candidates, thus creating two different majorities out of the same electoral body. Alfonso never set foot in Germany, whereas Richard made four ceremonial visits to Aachen and up the Rhine to Cologne, leaving imperial politics strictly alone. His death in 1272 closed what is usually called the Great Interregnum (1250–73), a period during which there was no effective German Emperor of the Holy Roman Empire of the German Nation, and "imperial" affairs did not, in any real sense, exist.

Rudolf I of Habsburg (1273–91)

THE electors were quite well aware that the Empire could not afford another absentee and uninterested ruler. Yet they had no desire to give up any of the property or prerogatives they had acquired during the Interregnum and were therefore unwilling to select a prince known to be rich and aggressive. Impelled somewhat by public opinion, as well as by the urging of Pope Gregory X, now anxious to find a counterweight to the too-ambitious Charles of Anjou, the electors finally (October 1, 1273) chose Count Rudolf of Habsburg. Rudolf, then in his middle fifties, had shown qualities of courage and consistency in the process of increasing the very modest inheritance of the Habsburgs in eastern Switzerland. But he was not one of the great princes

---

* The electoral college of the Empire was a slow growth from the late ninth century. By the mid-thirteenth century the pre-eminence of seven great princes in the choice of the German king-emperor was generally recognized. In addition to the three ecclesiastical electors above mentioned they were: the king of Bohemia, the only kingdom in the Empire, the count palatine of the Rhine, the margrave of Brandenburg, and the duke of Saxony.

of the Empire, and the electors reasoned that he could be counted on not to try to bring back the days of a Barbarossa or even a Frederick II.

Yet Rudolf, it transpired, had no intention of letting good opportunities pass. As he assessed the situation, the most vulnerable of the princes of the Empire was the powerful King Ottokar of Bohemia. Not only had Ottokar refused to recognize Rudolf's election, but his very successes and wealth incited the jealousy of his neighbors, the Wittelsbachs in Bavaria, the nobility of Austria, which he had conquered, and Ladislas IV of Hungary. When, therefore, Ottokar resisted Rudolf's demands for feudal vassalage for Austria, the Emperor united Ottokar's enemies and surprised him at the Marchfeld near Vienna, August 26, 1278. Ottokar died on the field of battle. Now Rudolf's policy became clear. He took posssession of Austria and Styria, thereby making his family the richest and strongest in Germany. He obviously intended to build up a powerful hereditary empire in southern Germany.

Such a sudden rise to predominance was a shock to the German princes, and opposition greeted Rudolf's next moves. He wanted to have his son crowned during his own lifetime, but the electors refused his request. Papal policy, favorable to Rudolf under Nicholas III (1277–80), was reversed under Nicholas' successor, Martin IV, a creature of Charles of Valois. Rudolf's presentation of Romagna to the Papacy in 1279 was therefore a futile gesture.

The ancient territory of the kingdom of Burgundy, intermittently known as the kingdom of Arles, stretching southward along the eastern bank of the Rhône River from Lorraine to the sea, wavered between imperial and French influence. The Hohenstaufen emperors had kept it safely in the Empire, but on the extinction of that line in the mid-thirteenth century French influence began to predominate. Rudolf, desirous of bolstering his family power, set out to recover Burgundy for the Habsburgs. He had some initial diplomatic successes, but eventually met opposition both from the German princes, who feared lest he become stronger than they wanted any emperor to be, and from the count palatine of Burgundy (Franche Comté), who wanted to transfer his feudal allegiance to the king of France. Rudolf brought an army into Burgundy in 1289 and succeeded in exacting the appropriate homage from the count and from the cities of Lausanne and Besançon. It proved a short-lived gain.

Yet the record of Rudolf of Habsburg stands up well under examination. He brought a spirit of order to the Empire. He aided the burgher class by quelling brigandage in northern Germany, which had disturbed both the free and the imperial cities and harmed their trade. On the other hand, these same cities had occasion to complain of his harshness in collecting taxes from them by armed agents. With the aim of raising the prestige of the imperial government, so grievously damaged during the Interregnum, he established "local peaces" (*Landfrieden*) throughout the Empire and appointed royal governors to see that they were maintained. Needless to say, the princes were irked at this invasion of their control of their own lands. At the end of Rudolf's reign, the Empire was once again a political organism pointed in the direction of unity, although that destination was still far distant. The Empire had been beset by separatism too long for the miracle of concord and integration to take place in a short span of years.

Adolf of Nassau (1292–98)

WHEN Rudolf died (July 15, 1291), at the advanced age of seventy-two, the electors rejected his son Albert, duke of Austria, whom his father had so earnestly recommended. Albert was rich and powerful; he was also known to be firm to the point of tyranny. The electors had had enough of firmness and, at the urging of the archbishop of Cologne, chose Adolf, count of Nassau. Adolf was a minor prince who matched the greed of the electors by the facility with which he made the promises they demanded. However, he turned out to be more ambitious than was expected. In 1294 he declared war against Philip IV (the Fair) of France, hoping thereby to gain territory in the west. This step cost him much German support. Duke Albert of Habsburg, resentful of his rejection by the electors, headed the opposition, which included, in addition to many of Adolf's former adherents among the princes, most of the German clergy, whose immunities Adolf had consistently violated. The inevitable war was on the way in the spring of 1298, when the princes of the Empire solemnly deposed Adolf for arbitrariness, violation of the peace, spoliation of the Church, and persecution of religion. At the same meeting the electors chose Albert as German king. Adolf met Albert and his forces near Worms on July 2, 1298, and died bravely in battle. The Habsburgs were back on the imperial throne.

Albert I of Habsburg (1298–1308)

ALBERT made an alliance with Philip IV in 1299 in hopes of maintaining cordial relations on his western frontier, even at the expense of relinquishing some imperial lands close to France. Pope Boniface VIII forced him, by threats of excommunication, to modify this pro-French stand. As a reward for compliance, or at least a promise of compliance, Boniface recognized him as King of the Romans in 1303. Boniface's death in October of that year meant France's victory in the contest between the French king and the Italian Pope; Albert's reaction must have been an ambivalent one: relief at the death of a demanding pope, embarrassment at having broken an alliance with the now triumphant Philip.

But there were other troubles to bedevil the Emperor. The king of Bohemia, Wenzel (Václav) II, son of Přemysl Ottokar II, was elected king of Poland in 1300, and his young son Wenzel was elected king of Hungary that same year on the extinction of the native Árpád line. The danger to the security of the Empire and to the Habsburg dynasty of a dynastic combination of Poland, Bohemia, and Hungary was perfectly evident to Albert and more serious than the wide possessions of Ottokar II had been to Albert's father, Rudolf I. However, fortune was with Albert, although his first military effort —he took an army into Bohemia in 1304—was a failure. In 1305 Wenzel II died, and with him the union of Poland and Bohemia. His son Wenzel III, king of Bohemia and Hungary, was murdered in 1306. He was the last male member of the long line of the Přemyslids who had ruled in Bohemia since early in the tenth century. Albert was able to force the Bohemian Estates to elect his son Rudolf king. This solution proved to be only temporary, for Rudolf died in 1307 and the Estates then chose Henry of Carinthia instead of another Habsburg. Albert's plans were meeting all sorts of opposition when he was murdered (May 1308) by a group of discontented nobles led by his nephew Duke John of Swabia.

Henry VII of Luxemburg (1308-13)

THE electors were now obliged to decide between a strong imperial policy pointing toward the east, represented by the Habsburg family, and a softer, western, pro-French orientation. The Papacy, then at Avignon under French dominance, obviously favored the latter choice. After months of discussion, intrigue, and generous bribery, Count Henry of Luxemburg was elected emperor. He was gentle, kindhearted, temperate, romantic, and moderately stupid. One act of his reign—the imposition of his thirteen-year-old son John upon Bohemia as her king—seemed to indicate Henry's interest in keeping the center of gravity of the Empire in the east. At the time there was no active opposition from the Habsburgs to this invasion of their zone of influence. The establishment of the house of Luxemburg in Bohemia was to have momentous consequences. Once this was arranged, Henry set out for Rome to be crowned and, on the way, to bring peace and order to Italy. He died of a fever at Buonconvento, near Siena, in August 1313. During his short rule he had made no effort to follow Rudolf's policy of strengthening the central power of the Empire, choosing instead to give back to the German princes powers and privileges which furthered separatism. The lessons from the rule of Frederick II, that Italy and Germany could not be forced into the same mold, were completely lost on Henry. He weakened the centralizing forces which his predecessors had rallied, wasting imperial prestige on a vain, romantic, and inane Italian adventure. It would have taken more than Dante's paeans of praise to make Henry an effective emperor of the Holy Roman Empire of the German Nation in the fourteenth century.

Louis IV of Bavaria (1314-47)

THE suddenness of Henry's death in the prime of life caught the electors unprepared to choose his successor immediately. There were several candidates put forward in the next few months by various electors, principally Henry's son, the young John of Bohemia, Frederick the Handsome of Austria, the eldest surviving son of the late Emperor Albert, and Louis, duke of Upper Bavaria, head of the house of Wittelsbach. Louis, engaged in defending his lands against the Habsburgs, won a brilliant victory at Gammelsdorf in November 1313. This gave him a certain advantage, and since most of the electors were reluctant to strengthen either of the two more prominent houses, Luxemburg or Habsburg, Louis received a majority of the electoral votes in October 1314. But two of the votes were contested, and by Habsburg count there were four votes for Frederick. Both Louis and Frederick were crowned by their respective supporters on the same day, November 25, Louis at Aachen, Frederick at Bonn. The sequel was eight years of war—fortunately for northern Germany, fought exclusively in Austria and southern Germany. Louis had more general support in Germany than Frederick, but for the most part central and northern Germany were content to watch and hear about the war. There were almost no pitched battles, and the fortunes of war were largely those of position and occasional forays. Finally, on September 28, 1322, the forces of Louis, supported by John of Bohemia and Frederick of Hohenzollern, met the army of Frederick of Austria at Mühldorf on the Inn and routed it, taking Frederick and his brother prisoner. Louis treated Frederick with exceptional generosity, thus winning a friend who stood by him in the rough years ahead.

Louis' next years were troubled by his dispute with Pope John XXII, who refused to recognize the validity of the imperial election (see p. 58). Louis also met with domestic difficulties as he tried to increase the holdings of his family. The direct line of the house of Ascania, which had held the mark of Brandenburg, died out in 1320. Louis, in his capacity as Emperor, conferred the mark on his son Louis in 1323, although it was generally believed that John of Bohemia had been promised this territory in payment for his services at the battle of Mühldorf. Louis' position in Germany now appeared to be quite strong; his excommunication by the irascible Pope John XXII in 1324 left most Germans unmoved. Excommunication had lost its edge as a political weapon. But the struggle dragged on, and Louis determined to attack the Avignonese Pope John where he was vulnerable—that is, in Italy. He put matters in order in Germany and, sure of the loyalty of Frederick of Austria, named him joint king. Louis' clemency and dignity won the support even of much of the German clergy; although the archbishops publicly sided with the Pope, they remained on near-friendly terms with Louis. The towns in general were favorable to him. Thus feeling reasonably safe in Germany, he set out early in 1327 for Rome, where he was ceremonially crowned in January 1328 by four syndics of the Roman *populus*. An imperial coronation in which the Papacy had no part was an implicit denial of the right of the Pope to any part in imperial affairs. Louis was careful, while in Rome, to make it clear that he regarded his prior election by the imperial German electors as final and incontrovertible. The Italians were quite unimpressed by Louis and his claims. In the late summer of 1328, he left Rome and was back in Germany in 1330. The Roman venture had turned out to be a diplomatic liability. Feeling that the tide of battle was running against him, he spent the next few years in a fruitless attempt to balance the Habsburgs against John of Bohemia. This juggling act was complicated by the bitter opposition all his plans and efforts at reconciliation met from the Papacy, not only from John XXII, who died in 1334, but also from his successor, Benedict XII. In this fracas Louis, unable to achieve any substantial increase in the domains of his family, ended by alienating both the Habsburgs and John of Bohemia. Yet the very bitterness of the papal opposition worked in Louis' favor with the German people and even with the clergy.

In these dynastic struggles Louis sought support wherever he could find it. His best ally was the German cities. For almost two centuries, from the first days of German separatism and the weakening of the imperial power through dynastic squabbling and governmental anarchy, the cities and their commerce had been subject to disturbances and annoyances from a robber baronage. The absences of Frederick II from Germany, the chaos of the Interregnum, Rudolf's concentration upon the affairs of his house, and the weakness of his successors had aggravated the situation of the cities. Their defense was to league together regionally for mutual protection. Thus we find a Westphalian League and a League of the Rhine in the thirteenth century, the latter including almost eighty cities in the Rhineland. Practice in cooperation brought success; success brought attention and imitation. Many lesser leagues were formed, some of them temporary. In 1327 there was formed a league of twenty-two Swabian and Swiss cities, to which Louis extended imperial approval in 1331. It was to Louis' advantage to favor the growing commercial classes for their support might easily outweigh the opposition of an elector or many petty princes and they were also a possible source of needed loans.

The long-drawn-out struggle between Louis and the Papacy was a source of irritation to the German princes. They considered the refusal of John XXII and his successor Benedict XII to recognize the majority vote of the electors an affront to their dignity and prerogatives. This feeling was formalized by the Declaration of Rense, signed by a group of princes in July 1338, and confirmed by the ordinance *Licet iuris,* which was promulgated by the Diet of Frankfurt on August 6, 1338. This decree proclaimed the principle that the imperial title was in the sole and final gift of the electors and that the pope had no power whatsoever in the matter. It declared

that the imperial dignity and power proceeded in the beginning immediately from God alone, and that God has given laws to the human race through the Emperor and the kings of the world, and that the Emperor is made very Emperor solely by the election of those entitled to elect him and does not need the confirmation or approbation of any other person, since in temporal matters he has no superior on earth, but all nations are subject to him, and the Lord Jesus Christ Himself commanded that what was God's should be rendered to God and what was Caesar's to Caesar. . . . By the law and ancient approved custom of the Empire, when anyone is elected Emperor or king by the imperial Electors, unanimously or by majority, at once by the mere fact of election he is to be considered and entitled very King and Emperor of the Romans . . . nor does he need the approbation, confirmation, authority, or consent of the Pope or the Apostolic See or of any other person.

The declaration was enthusiastically received by every element of the German people. It may be premature to speak of an upsurge of German nationalism —Germany for the Germans—at this point, though it is difficult to resist the impression that the roots of that sentiment were present, in greater or lesser degree, in large sectors of the population. The legal phraseology of these two decrees might be cold and matter-of-fact, but the enthusiasm with which they were welcomed was ardent.

Soon thereafter Louis concluded an alliance with Edward III of England against the French king. This was probably the high point of his reign. For the moment Louis was popular and enjoyed an aura of success. But his opportunistic shifts of position in the next years and his heedless manipulations to get Tyrol and Carinthia for his son cost him popular support and encouraged his enemies among the princes.

The new pope, Clement VI (1342–52), declared Louis deposed in April 1346 and put forward for the imperial dignity a rival candidate who would both satisfy a majority of the electors and promise appropriate obedience to the Papacy. This obliging prince was the Luxemburger Charles of Bohemia, son of King John of Bohemia and thus grandson of the Luxemburg Emperor Henry VII. Brought up in Paris, Charles had been tutored by Pierre Roger, who later became this same Pope Clement VI. The friendship between the prince and his former tutor certainly contributed to his election, early in July 1346. But Louis, undiscouraged by the election of a rival emperor, remained on the offensive quite successfully until his death in October 1347. There was no Wittelsbach able to carry on the fight, even though at the end of Louis' life the family was vastly richer and more powerful than before his election. Louis had given the imperial title more prestige than it had enjoyed at least under his two predecessors, and by going to Rome had brought to the office and indeed to the whole Empire an international significance they sorely needed.

Charles IV (1346–78)

WITH the reign of Charles IV, Luxemburg king of Bohemia and emperor, the Empire entered upon a new phase of its history, the roots of which are clearly traceable to the period of the Interregnum and Rudolf of Habsburg. It became almost entirely a Germanic kingdom, with minor appendages in Burgundy and the Lowlands, and including, in a special relationship, the Slavic kingdom of Bohemia, Charles' own favorite land. Charles ruled for thirty-two extremely busy years. So many issues and crises arose, internal and external, that his actions and decisions have inevitably aroused controversy. Historical judgments of him range from very unfavorable to highly laudatory.

Before becoming emperor, Charles had had administrative experience in Italy, as the lord of a number of cities of the Lombard plain, and in Bohemia, as margrave of Moravia and lieutenant for his father, King John. In his early twenties he was already known as able and efficient. His first years as Emperor and king of Bohemia were occupied in bringing a degree of peace and order to both the Empire and his hereditary domain. He wished, naturally, to be crowned in Rome, for such a ceremony would signify a degree of cooperation between Church and Empire that had been lacking for many decades. The thirty years of animosity between Papacy and Empire under Louis IV had not benefited either party, or the cause of law and order. Clement VI, otherwise friendly toward Charles, was unwilling to have his plans for reordering Italian politics complicated by Charles' presence. Ancient Ghibelline sentiments might too easily revive. It was not, therefore, until Clement's death (1352) and the election of a less positive successor, Innocent VI (1352–62), that Charles' plans for a Roman coronation were realized.

With Innocent's blessing, Charles left Prague in September 1354, attended by a train of only three hundred knights. On November 10 he arrived in Mantua, where, a few weeks later, he listened politely to Petrarch's fervid urgings that he restore the glory of the Caesars. He then went on to Milan, where he was enthusiastically welcomed by the Visconti and received the Iron Crown of the Lombards. The Visconti seemed anxious to pay him handsomely (200,000 gulden) for the imperial vicariate of Milan. Moving on to Florence, he confirmed that city's independence for another eagerly paid price. He arrived at the gates of Rome on April 2. The elaborate coronation at the hands of the papal legate, the cardinal of Ostia, took place on Easter Sunday, April 5. Charles left the city at sundown, in accordance with his promise to the Pope (see p. 69), and set out on the return journey the next day. At Pisa he put down an uprising with some severity; then, as quickly as possible, moved on northward. He reached Augsburg on July 3, and on August 15 he re-entered his beloved Prague. He had conferred knighthood upon fifteen hundred suppliants in Italy and had accepted large sums of money pressed on him by Italian cities and despots for confirming privileges which they would have exercised in any case, with or without his permission. It is clear that he had no desire to stay in Italy or to become involved in the pointless politics of communes and petty tyrants, having had his fill of them as a young man.

As a result of his consideration of the problems of the Empire as he left the Lombard valley and took a last look at Italy, the graveyard of so many German ambitions, Charles brought forth a series of imperial regulations for discussion by the Diet at Nürnberg on November 25, 1355. These regulations, accepted by the Diet, were promulgated on January 10, 1356. At a Diet at Metz in December of the same year, they were issued, with supplementary clauses, as what later came to be known as the Golden Bull of 1356, a sort of constitution of the Empire. Intended to prevent disputed elections, the Golden Bull designated the seven electors heads of indivisible principalities and prescribed the manner of their selection of an emperor. It granted the electors increased powers within the Empire, rights of coinage, and judicial control of their own subjects. It called for annual meetings of all the electors, to consult and advise the emperor. In essence, the document recognized the existing degree of independence of the great princes and, by implication, the fact that the days of a highly centralized Empire were gone. The Empire thus became, in effect, a sort of federation of great princes, presided over by an emperor who, despite his high estate, exercised his authority at the will of these princes. In one respect the Bull was conservative: by declaring the electoral lands indivisible, it arrested the disintegration of hereditary lands which was proceeding at an alarming pace. By confirming the Declaration of Rense and the *Licet iuris* of 1338, the Bull eliminated the Papacy from imperial politics for all time and recognized the deep separation in the Empire between Germany, where the Pope could exercise no authority, and Italy, where his influence and authority were potentially, if not actually, paramount.

The Bull was in no sense an effort to unite Germany. However, by forbidding the formation of leagues of imperial cities unless directly under the emperor's patronage, it did attempt to lessen causes for strife between the rising burgher class and the princes. The cities naturally felt this prohibition to be directed at their independence, and there was some resistance to the Bull from that quarter in the years following its promulgation. It seems probable that, given the conditions Charles had to face, any effort on his part to eliminate the separatism inherent in German history from the time of Charlemagne might have driven the anciently divided parts of Germany still farther apart.

All things considered the Golden Bull was probably the best answer possible at the time to the problem of German disunity. Charles had intermittent trouble with the Habsburgs and the Wittelsbachs, the heirs of Louis IV. His policy was to appease such outbreaks by persuasion, patience, diplomacy (bribery or "gifts"), or, in the last resort, by force. An able general when necessary, he still preferred less costly and drastic measures. The prosperity of Germany under his rule showed how beneficial this policy was for the country.

Charles was accused by some of his contemporaries, and by not a few subsequent historians, of subservience to the Papacy. It is true that he owed his election, at least in part, to the favor of his friend and former tutor, Clement VI. But a close examination of his relations with the various popes who ruled during his thirty-two years as Emperor reveals quite clearly that he was his own master. He refused many requests and suggestions from Avignon; in German affairs he took no guidance from the Papacy at any point. He was uniformly courteous to the popes but it was the courtesy of a man strong in his own rights and sure of his own enlightened aims. From this point of view, then, this was

Charles IV, detail from votive picture, tempera on wood, by a Czech master after 1370 [National Gallery, Prague].

a period during which the German church and the German monarch were thinking and acting primarily as Germans. The belligerent nationalism of the sixteenth century was implicit in the policy and performance of Charles toward the Papacy.

The mark of Brandenburg had not fared well under the Wittelsbach heirs of Louis IV. In the late 1350's Charles had begun to look upon the mark with increasing interest. It offered both commercial and political opportunities for the prosperity of his kingdom of Bohemia and the expansion of his house. In 1365 Brandenburg was turned over to Charles to administer for six years. The nobles of the mark rose against Charles' officials, and the Emperor had to take the matter in hand. The result was that in 1373, by the treaty of Fürstenwald, Brandenburg became the property of the Luxemburg house.

Charles' interest in the area of the Empire north of his Bohemian kingdom was not limited to the mark of Brandenburg. With that powerful league of northern German cities, the Hansa, the Emperor's relations were, if less direct, not less realistic. Before his accession, this league had been allowed to grow in power and wealth, free from imperial interference. Since Barbarossa no emperor had set foot in a north German city, or indeed anywhere on the Baltic coast. In 1369 Charles took the city of Hamburg under his personal care. He regarded the Hanseatic League as an element of strength to the Empire, and spoke of it as a "society of merchants." He made no move to force it to disband as he might have done under the provisions of the Golden Bull. On the contrary, he maintained a friendly understanding with the Hansa, which did not meddle in internal imperial affairs. After Brandenburg became a land of the Bohemian crown in 1373, Charles made an official state visit to Lübeck, the leading city of the Hansa. Although the visit was not unrelated to Charles' desire to influence the Danish succession, his treatment of the Lübeckers as almost independent allies and friends was nevertheless indicative of the Emperor's calculatedly benevolent policy in northern Germany.

One of the first acts of Charles' reign had been the foundation of the University of Prague in 1348, modeled in part on the University of Paris, with which he had become familiar as a youth, and in part on the University of Bologna. This was the first university east of the Rhine and north of the Alps. The professors were both Czech and German; the students came from all over the Empire as well as from the Slavic lands of Bohemia and Poland. The first chancellor was the learned and influential archbishop of Prague, Ernest of Pardubice, who should perhaps be called the cofounder of the university. In 1372 the faculty of law, with a natural leaning toward the organization at the University of Bologna, separated from the three faculties of arts, medicine, and theology.

Charles had set up to make his beloved Prague a worthy capital of the Empire. He built the handsome stone bridge across the Moldau which still bears his name; carried on the construction begun under his father of the imposing St. Vitus Cathedral on the Hradčany, the height west of the river; established a monastery observing the Slavic rite; and guided the expansion of the city east of the river by donating the royal vineyard for settlement. Deeply interested in the spiritual life of the kingdom, he actively favored both monastic and secular reforms in the Bohemian church. He gathered around him, as officials of his court, both royal and imperial, Czech and German scholars who made that court a center of vigorous cultural impulses. In the chancery there was developed a *Kanzleisprache* which, as a supple and vigorous High German dialect, was to develop into the literary German of modern times.

The last important action of Charles' busy life was to secure the election in 1376 of his eldest son, Wenzel (Václav), as King of the Romans and therefore his successor as emperor. It will be remembered that the electors had in the past avoided establishing any such continuity of the title in a single family. But Charles, by his usual methods, obtained the requisite electoral votes and later the full approbation of Pope Gregory XI.

In the process of gaining the votes necessary for the election of his son, Charles had exacted heavy contributions from the imperial cities and had pledged several of them to powerful princes in return for their support. The cities resented this disregard of their traditional rights; in defiance of the Emperor and in open violation of the Golden Bull, the Swabian League was revived in 1376. In the military action which followed, Charles was unsuccessful, and Ulrich of Württemberg, who had taken over the leadership of the imperial and noble forces against the cities, was humiliated in battle at Reutlingen (1377). Charles was obliged to recognize the League and confirm its members in their traditional rights not to be sold or hypothecated and to be allowed to join in a league. Before his death in November 1378, Charles bequeathed Brandenburg to his second son, Sigismund, and a part of Lusatia and the New Mark to his third son, John. He also parceled out parts of the family estates to his brother John Henry and his nephew Jošt. Charles recognized only too acutely the separatism that was deep in the structure of Germany. Nevertheless, he had shown the direction in which Germany could and should move if any workable unity were to be achieved. In the circumstances of the mid-fourteenth century no ruler could have completely reversed the trend toward fragmentation that had set in under the successors of Charlemagne five centuries before. But, by liberating Germany from papal tutelage and from the incubus of costly involvement in Italy, Charles did free the land from burdens that had proved unbearable and thus encouraged its growth as a national entity. Charles, French by education and Czech by preference, was one of the nurturers of the German national idea.

Wenzel (1378–1400)

THE son and successor of Charles IV, Wenzel (Václav IV) of Bohemia, has enjoyed a bad reputation among historians. He may indeed not have been the equal of his father in some respects, but at least some of the reasons for Wenzel's lack of success were outside his control. By splitting up the family lands, Charles certainly made Wenzel's task more difficult. The Swabian League, to which leagues of Rhenish and Alsatian cities were soon added, grew in strength and pretensions, and Wenzel was unable to force it to disband. Nor could he utilize the conflicts between the guilds and the patriciate in these cities in order to assert imperial power over them, as his father might have done. The Great Schism in the Church (see below, Chapter 11), which broke out in the spring of 1378, soon after the return of the Papacy to Rome, was a source of no little trouble to Wenzel. Charles had decided to support the Roman pope, Urban VI, against Clement VII, a Frenchman of the Avignon line. Wenzel's decision to continue his father's policy disturbed his relations with Charles V and Charles VI of France, who naturally adhered to Clement. His decision to support one of the popes against the other made him vulnerable to any prince or elector who might seek an excuse to act independently of the emperor. His father had been perhaps too successful, and the princes were just biding their time until they could free themselves from a strong emperor's control. Their disposition toward a young successor is thus not difficult to imagine. Furthermore, it must be remembered that, in view of the elective nature of the imperial dignity and the certainty of dissipation of the feudal prerogatives of the emperor under heedless or absentee rulers, the power of an emperor was in direct proportion to his personal fortune. Charles had been able to start from a strong position: for more than a decade before his father's death and before becoming emperor, he had virtually ruled the rich kingdom of Bohemia for whose wealth and order he was largely responsible. In the course of his thirty-two-year reign over the Empire he had been able to increase greatly the property of which he was personal ruler and, by marriage, diplomacy, and purchase, raise his house to the dominant position in the whole Empire. But at that point Charles made an error that his successors were to regret bitterly. Having amassed so great an estate, he divided it up among several members of his family. Wenzel, in possession of only a minor part of the Luxemburg family inheritance, was therefore as Emperor put in a position of weakness from which he was never able to recover.

But Wenzel's own contributions to his ultimate failure were substantial. He did not follow his father's example of interesting himself consistently and steadily in imperial affairs. In fact, from 1387 to 1395 he did not set foot in the Empire. He remained in Prague and rejected the suggestions, made to him as early as 1380, that he appoint an imperial vicar to take over the affairs of Germany. He gained the animosity of the cities by siding with the nobility of southern Germany in a war between the Swabian League, now consisting of forty towns, and the Wittelsbachs with their princely allies (1388–89). German opinion was alienated by his too active interest in securing the Hungarian throne for his brother Sigismund. His effectiveness in enforcing order in German affairs was greatly diminished by his protracted struggle with the Bohemian nobility and feudal clergy. During the 1390's his two brothers Sigismund and John, to both of whom he had been generous, were leaders in plots against him. By championing the Roman line of the Papacy, Wenzel deprived himself of a chance to act as arbiter and end the Schism, which was an offense to every Christian and a burden to those who counted the cost of maintaining two papal establishments. Since his stand with regard to the Papacy aligned him against France, he was led to make a marriage alliance with England, sending his sister Anna to marry the young Richard II in 1382. The few occasions on which Wenzel made gestures of ruling in Germany were ridiculed and disregarded. In an effort to retrieve some prestige for the office he held, he met with the king of France, Charles VI, in 1398 to discuss the possibility of concerted action to end the Schism. But Charles was intermittently insane, and Wenzel was more than intermittently drunk.

The conviction grew among the princes that Wenzel must be deposed. The suggestion was first made formally at a meeting at Pforchheim in 1399 and agreed upon at a meeting of five electors at Frankfurt in May 1400, attended by many other princes. The selection of a successor was not difficult. Rupert of the Palatinate, the only layman participating in the election, was chosen emperor. Wenzel refused to recognize the electors' right to depose him but found his erstwhile friends of little help. The decree of deposition (August 20, 1400) specified Wenzel's shortcomings: his laziness, his loss of imperial lands, his dismemberment of the Empire by the creation of the duchy of Milan, his lack of energy in ending the Schism. On the basis of such charges, many of the emperors in history should have been deposed. The signatories of the decree must have had tongue in cheek when they affixed their names to the document, for they had personally profited from all Wenzel's "misdeeds" and were careful to choose a successor who would do even less than Wenzel to make the Holy Roman Empire look and function like an empire. There was no provision in the traditions of the Empire for the action of the electors, and the whole procedure was of dubious legality. Yet Wenzel, beyond blustering, did nothing to reverse their decision, and Germany accepted the situation with hardly a murmur.

Rupert of the Palatinate (1400–10)

UNDER Rupert, the Empire returned to its usual condition of chaotic separatism and frequent war among princes and between cities and princes. Rupert made himself ridiculous by starting out for Milan and Rome in 1401 without sufficient funds. In Lombardy he had to pawn his crown in order to pay his way back to Germany. In 1408–09, in a dispute over recognition of the authority of the Council of Pisa (see below, Chapter 11), Rupert sided with the Roman pope, Gregory XII, whereas Wenzel, now deposed as emperor but still king of Bohemia, recognized the Council, which gratefully returned the compliment. Wenzel's course was the more popular in Germany; Rupert lost the support of many who formerly favored him. A civil war between Rupert and Wenzel was avoided only by Rupert's death in May 1410.

Sigismund (1411–37)

AFTER some months of wrangling and maneuvering—at one time there were three princes, Wenzel, Sigismund, and Margrave Jošt of Moravia, who claimed to have been elected emperor—five of the electors, including Wenzel, chose (July 21, 1411) Wenzel's younger brother Sigismund, since 1387 king of Hungary, as emperor. Wenzel claimed to retain the title of King of the Romans, but no one paid much attention to him. Sigismund's reign of twenty-seven years was an eventful era in European history. Tall, handsome, gracious, witty, fluent in seven languages, he began his reign with much in his favor, but he faced exceptionally trying problems throughout his occupancy of the throne: the disorder that had only increased under Wenzel and Rupert, the Schism in the Church which was crying for solution, the heresy of John Hus and his followers in Bohemia, the conflict between the Teutonic Order and the kingdom of

Poland, the Hussite Wars, and the Turkish attacks on his own kingdom of Hungary (we shall learn more of these problems in Chapters 7, 8, and 11). Sigismund was kept jumping from one issue to the next, with occasional good intentions, but never with any real success. His failures were in large part those of his own character. Although he undoubtedly had good qualities, he was also fickle, vain, cruel, licentious even for a monarch, capricious, unable to pursue a given policy to its conclusion, and chronically improvident. In 1411 Sigismund had pawned his hereditary mark of Brandenburg to Frederick of Hohenzollern, then burgrave of Nürnberg, for 100,000 gulden. Frederick was a firm and able administrator who brought order among the unruly Brandenburgers where Sigismund had failed. In 1415, unable to repay the loan, Sigismund made a new arrangement; two years later he invested Frederick with the electorate in perpetuity. Sigismund was thus responsible for bringing a new and powerful dynasty into German history.

Some time before Sigismund became emperor, certain scholars and rulers had begun to argue that a general council is superior to a pope, can be called by a king, and is competent to judge a pope. Sigismund was involved in the Conciliar Movement (see Chapter 11), an attempt to apply these theories to end the Schism, as the head of the Empire, and, for a time, as the presiding officer of the Council of Constance (1414-18). While at this Council he held two meetings of the imperial Diet, in 1415 and 1417, and made Constance the virtual capital of the Empire.

Sigismund was impressed by his own role at the Council of Constance, believing that he had been responsible for effecting a solution of the Schism in the Church. He was thus easily persuaded that he might bring peace between France and England, then locked in a bitter and complex phase of the Hundred Years' War. Sigismund went to Paris in March 1416, but no one at the French court was ready for peace. He therefore went on to England, where on August 15 he signed a defensive and offensive alliance with Henry V. Such an alliance was not without precedent; at the beginning of the wars with France, Edward III of England had made an alliance with Louis the Bavarian. But in 1416 this connection appeared to be a reversal of the traditional Luxemburg-French alliance which had been consecrated by the blood of John of Bohemia at Crécy. In reality, like most instances of Sigismund's opportunism, it had no noticeable effect on European politics. The Emperor himself did an about-face in 1422, when he again favored the French side in the person of the new king, Charles VII.

Sigismund's relations with John Hus and his followers will be treated in detail in Chapters 7 and 11, in connection with religious developments and the Conciliar Movement. The Bohemian people never forgave the Emperor for his refusal to honor the safe-conduct he had given to the reformer at the Council of Constance. In permitting Hus' death at the stake on July 6, 1415, Sigismund had failed to realize that he was not dealing with a mere theological issue and that Hus was, rather, the conscience of a whole people. Aroused, that conscience proved stronger than Sigismund's "crusaders."

Upon the death of his brother Wenzel in 1419, Sigismund assumed the title of King of Bohemia and was recognized by a rump meeting of the Estates and even crowned by the Catholic nobles in St. Vitus Cathedral. But he chose not to follow counsels of moderation and, as a consequence, for seventeen years was refused entrance to the royal city. He had started out with a determination to "exterminate" the Hussite heresy. For fifteen years, from 1419 to 1434, the Hussite "Warriors of God" defied and defeated the troops of the Emperor, reinforced by foreign "crusaders" recruited in Germany, England, France, Italy, Hungary, and the Lowlands. After Sigismund's first military threats to Bohemia and an inglorious siege of Prague in 1420, there were thereafter three principal crusades against the Hussites, in 1421, 1427, and 1431, and several lesser attempts. They were all failures. The leadership of the Czechs —under John Žižka until his death in 1424, thereafter under Prokop the Great—was superior to that of the Germans, their organization and spirit better, and their military inventiveness frightening to the mixed army of Sigismund. The high costs of the campaigns against the Hussites forced the electors and Sigismund to seek means of raising funds. Sigismund was of no use in fiscal matters. But the English Cardinal Beaufort, acting as papal legate in Germany, had a Diet of the Empire called in December 1427 and persuaded it to levy a general tax on imperial lands. The plan was, for the time, excellent and the rate of taxation bearable. The only trouble was that almost everyone taxed refused to pay. The cities were in the business of making, not disbursing, money; the nobility claimed their exemptions; the peasantry had no money. When Sigismund was finally (1436) allowed to enter Prague, it was only after guaranteeing all the freedoms of the Bohemian Estates and accepting the *compactata* won from the Council of Basel by the Hussites (see Chapter 11).

As arbiter of the dispute between the Teutonic Order and the kingdom of Poland (see p. 194), in 1419 Sigismund decided for the Order, thereby alienating the Polish king, Jagiello, and his powerful cousin and ally, Grand Duke Witold of Lithuania.

While still king of Hungary, Sigismund had led a crusade, widely proclaimed and supported by the popes of both the Roman and Avignon lines, against the Turks under Murad II. Leading a mixed army of German, Magyar, French, Burgundian, and a few English knights, Sigismund captured the fortress of Nicopolis Minor from the Turks in 1395. The next year, however, his forces were decisively defeated at Nicopolis Major, and he barely escaped with his life from the field of battle. Again, in 1428, he was engaged in military operations against the Turks on the Hungarian frontier, but his fortunes were little better than before. The Turkish pressure was not to be relaxed for several centuries.

Sigismund was no more fortunate in his defense of his possessions in the southwest. The Venetians had bought the Dalmatian coast for 100,000 ducats from Ladislas of Naples, who had recently driven out Sigismund's troops from a province that had been Hungarian territory for almost three centuries. Sigismund's campaign to recover these lands from Venice in 1412 and 1413 were fiascos. In 1431 and 1432 he led another campaign to recover Dalmatia, with the same result. To finance these two expeditions he had pawned sixteen north Hungarian cities to Jagiełło of Poland. Hungarian resentment at this expedient was understandably deep and vocal. It is difficult to find any act in Sigismund's life that combined integrity with either intelligence or consistency, or was graced by either honor or success.

Albert II (1438–39)

SIGISMUND had made some sort of plan for the succession. Having no son, he had arranged a marriage for his only daughter, Elizabeth, with Albert of Habsburg, and on his death bed (d. December 9, 1437) had persuaded the Czech and Hungarian Estates to name Albert king. The electors, following the example of the Estates, unanimously elected Albert emperor on March 18, 1438. His reign was short and almost eventless: he died on October 27, 1439. For the next five centuries the Habsburgs were in almost uninterrupted possession of the imperial crown.

SUGGESTIONS FOR FURTHER READING

ALTAMIRA, R., *History of Spain*. New York, 1949
ALTAMIRA, R., *History of Spanish Civilization*. London, 1930
BARRACLOUGH, G., *Origins of Modern Germany*. Oxford, 1947
BERTRAND, L., *History of Spain*. London, 1934
BRYCE, J., *The Holy Roman Empire*. New York, 1907. Many editions
Cambridge Medieval History, Vols. VI–VIII
CARSTEN, F. L., *The Origins of Prussia*. Oxford, 1954
CASTRO, A., *Structure of Spanish History*. Princeton, 1954
CHAPMAN, C. E., *History of Spain*. New York, 1918
CHAYTOR, H. J., *History of Aragon and Catalonia*. London, 1933
DENHOLM-YOUNG, N., *Richard of Cornwall*. Oxford, 1947
HENDERSON, E. F., *A Short History of Germany*. 2 vols. New York, 1902
LANE-POOLE, S., *The Story of the Moors in Spain*. New York, 1903
LEA, H. C., *The Moriscos of Spain: Their Conversion and Expulsion*. Philadelphia, 1901
LIVERMORE, H. V., *A History of Portugal*. Cambridge, 1947
MERRIMAN, R. B., *The Rise of the Spanish Empire*, Vols. I and II. New York, 1918
NOWELL, C. E., *A History of Portugal*. New York, 1953
PEERS, E. A., *A Companion to Spanish Studies*. London, 1929
PROCTER, E. S., *Alfonso X of Castile*. Oxford, 1947
STUBBS, W., *Germany in the Middle Ages, 1200–1500*. London, 1908
THOMPSON, J. W., *Feudal Germany*. Chicago, 1928
THOMSON, S. H., *Czechoslovakia in European History*. Princeton, 1953
VALENTIN, V., *The German People: Their History and Civilization*. New York, 1946

ALMEIDA, F. de, *História de Portugal*. 6 vols. 1922–29
ASCHBACH, J., *Geschichte Kaiser Sigmunds*. 4 vols. 1838–45
BLEYE, S. AGUALDO, *Manual de historia de España*. 2 vols. 1927–33
CALMETTE, J., *Formation de l'unité espagnole*. 1946
HEIMPEL, H., *Deutschland im späteren Mittelalter*. 1953
KRAUS, V., *Deutsche Geschichte im Ausgange des Mittelalters*. 1905
LINDNER, T., *Deutsche Geschichte unter den Habsburgern und Luxemburgern*. 2 vols. 1890–93
LINDNER, T., *Geschichte des deutschen Reiches unter König Wenzel*. 2 vols. 1875–80
PETIT-DUTAILLIS, C., *L'Essor des États d'Occident*. 1937
SOLER, A. G., *La Edad media en la corona de Aragón*. 1930
WERUNSKY, E., *Geschichte Karls IV. und seiner Zeit*. 3 vols. 1880–92

CHAPTER SEVEN

PHILOSOPHERS, MYSTICS, AND HERETICS

PHILOSOPHERS

For many centuries, Western Christendom had wrestled with the age-old philosophical questions of being and becoming, of the eternal and the transient, of the actual and the ideal. Since the greatest fact in the life of the West was the Christian faith, all non-Christian or pre-Christian concepts and patterns of thought had somehow to be measured against the faith once delivered to the saints and preserved in the Scriptures and the writings of the Fathers. This measuring resulted inevitably in further difficulties and confusions. There seemed to be only one great Church Father—St. Augustine of Hippo (d. 430)—who was able either to absorb the confusions or to offer an intellectually convincing way out of the difficulties.

Augustine came to be the dominating factor in the thought of the West and remained so, supported by the authoritative writings of the anonymous late-fifth-century sage erroneously called Dionysius the Areopagite (the Pseudo-Dionysius) and St. Anselm of Canterbury (d. 1109), well into the thirteenth century. Both of the latter were in the Platonic tradition of idealism. Briefly and crudely put, the essence of this Augustinian-Platonic trend of thought is that God is the supreme Idea, that the pattern and cause for the universe and all its particulars are eternal ideas and reasons whose seat is in God's mind, that our knowledge comes from illumination and not from sense perception, that mind and body are not one but two entities. By the late thirteenth century this set of beliefs, reworked and recast, had become the leading school of thought in opposition to another great philosophy: the persuasive and tightly integrated system of St. Thomas Aquinas (d. 1274), which is known as the Aristotelian-Thomistic synthesis. These two were by no means the only currents of philosophical thought in this crucial century, but they stand out in clear relief against the confusing multiplicity of doctrinal and philosophical dissension and debate.

The late twelfth and early thirteenth centuries saw the discovery and translation, usually through previous Jewish or Arab renderings, of the works of

Aristotle, accompanied by the elaborate commentaries of the Moslem sages Avicenna (d. 1037) and Averroës (d. 1198). These newly discovered works were at first disturbing to Christian thought. Fresh ideas of causation and new estimates of the power of human reason to grapple with the problems of cosmology and metaphysics soon captured the imagination of leading thinkers in the West. The thought of Averroës was rationalist, based on an acceptance of the data of sense as a starting point for all knowledge. Averroës postulated the existence of an active intellect (*intellectus agens*), separate from the individual soul and one and the same in all men. He argued for the eternity of the world and of motion and for the concept of the double truth—the truth of theology and the truth of philosophy. The subtlety of his reasoning and its avoidance of some of the difficulties in traditional Christian thought attracted many scholars of the thirteenth century.

The leading voices in the presentation of the Averroistic explanation of the puzzles of man and the universe were a Fleming, Siger of Brabant (d. 1284?), and a Dane, Boetius of Dacia (d. *ca.* 1280), both masters at the University of Paris. Siger insisted that he submitted his conclusions, derived from reason, to the test of Christian revelation. But Boetius, it appears, went farther along the path of Averroistic (naturalistic) rationalism. Carried to its logical extreme, Averroism would discard Christian revelation as a source of knowledge.

This naturalistic trend was directly and firmly opposed by the Franciscan St. Bonaventura (1221–74), a determined and eloquent Augustinian. St. Bonaventura used the Aristotelian method of rational investigation and proof, but only to support his advocacy of the Augustinian doctrine that knowledge comes from illumination and the earlier Platonic doctrine, accepted by Augustine, that ideas have objective reality outside the individual mind. There was much of the mystic in St. Bonaventura. He believed that God is to be apprehended directly from man's inner experience, from the traces of God in the human soul, the vestiges of His creation of man in His own image. Bonaventura's influence in his own order was great, and the Franciscans in general labored in the Augustinian-Platonic tradition.

St. Thomas Aquinas and Christian Rationalism

ST. THOMAS Aquinas (1225–74) now entered the controversy. Following the lead of his teacher, Albert the Great (d. 1280), who had made a specialty of the works of Aristotle, Thomas subjected the writings of The Philosopher, as Aristotle was called, to minute examination. Not satisfied with the text as he found it, he commissioned a fellow Dominican, William of Moerbeke, to translate the Aristotelian corpus afresh from the Greek. Point by point, he attacked the Averroist positions in a heated polemic that lasted for years. The victory finally lay with Thomas. He showed that it was impossible to say, as did Siger and Boetius of Dacia, that there were two truths, one arrived at by reason and the other by faith. One cannot be of two minds, both a Christian and a pagan (i.e., a naturalist), at the same time. Largely as a result of Thomas' work, thirteen philosophical propositions, key teachings of Averroism, were condemned in

1270 by Stephen Tempier, bishop of Paris. In 1277, 219 propositions, many of them extracted from the works of Siger of Brabant, were expressly condemned by the same authority.

St. Thomas' supreme achievement was to show that reason and revelation need not be contradictory, as Siger and Boetius held or clearly implied. In the great dispute as to the priority of reason or revelation, the Augustinians, without any hesitation, decided in favor of revelation, while the Averroists decided in favor of reason. Thomas demonstrated the dispute itself to be quite unnecessary. There is one truth, he argued, as there is one God, the source of all truth. There is thus no possible conflict between any supposed two truths. Reason is necessary and proper when it speaks within the area of its competence. But there is a limit to its competence—the realm of the data on which reason must be based. At that point revelation takes over. Its authority is direct from God, who has chosen two appropriate media to convey His one truth. Both media are valid, each within its sphere.

In his *Summa theologica* and *Summa contra Gentiles,* St. Thomas showed that the Christian need have no fear of the consequences which the application of reason would have upon his faith. Rational inquiry, if properly conducted, can only support the principles of revelation. Christianity now had a philosophy, embodied in these two great *Summae.* Until then it had had a theology, founded exclusively upon revealed truth, but not, in any strict sense, a systematic and rationally based philosophy. By accepting and defending both the basic conclusions of centuries of Augustinian thinking and, on the other hand, the Aristotelian method of rational investigation and proof, St. Thomas effected a compromise—or, perhaps more accurately, a synthesis—which has endured to this day. Starting from Augustinian premises he so ordered the thought of Aristotle as in effect to Christianize him where possible, and, where not possible, to reject him.

In his own day and in the following generation, St. Thomas was attacked by both parties to the dispute. The Augustinian tradition remained strong and had able and persuasive advocates. Naturalistically inclined minds still preferred their position, and although Averroism was condemned along with its protagonists, Siger and Boetius, its attraction persisted. By the early fourteenth century, three main currents of Christian philosophic thought could be distinguished: (1) the right wing—that is, the Augustinian tradition—which was defended by St. Bonaventura, Duns Scotus, and in general the Franciscans and all those whom we can properly call "realists": * (2) the center, led by St. Thomas and the Dominicans, including those whom we call the "moderate realists"; and (3) the left wing, the Averroists and the *via moderna* of the fourteenth and fifteenth centuries, best represented by William of Ockham and the growing school of

---

* The term "realist" may be applied to the adherents of Augustinian-Platonic idealism mentioned earlier in this chapter. To the realist, all things perceived by our senses are actually reflections, indicators, or offshoots of an "idea," or archetype, or "universal" existing in the mind of God. Thus the particular man, horse, or tree that we perceive is modeled, in varying degrees of perfection, after the original "idea" or "universal" Man, Horse, or Tree. The universal is therefore always more "real" than the particular; a particular tree approaches but can never equal the perfect quality of "tree-ness" that exists in the ideal Tree.

"nominalists." There were, of course, many thinkers who cannot easily be fitted into these categories, but these are the broad lines of differentiation.

Rigorous adherence to the rules of formal Aristotelian logic and dialectical proof, together with the body of doctrine that developed from the twelfth through the fourteenth century, is known loosely as scholasticism. This method-*cum*-doctrine had its shortcomings. As Albert the Great, himself an adept in the use of the scholastic method, put it: "Many at Paris have followed, not philosophy, but sophisms." Method and technique tended to become paramount over substance and ultimate purpose. In the decades following the victory of Thomas' middle-of-the-road synthesis over the naturalism of the Averroistic school, no clear pattern of development can be traced. Theology and philosophy were still intertwined. There were criticisms and treatises of "correction," analyses and rephrasings, and many attempts at compromise and synthesis, but nothing constructive or original evolved.

This highly analytical phase of medieval thinking was exemplified in the Franciscan John Duns Scotus (1266–1308), a Scot who studied and lectured at Oxford and Paris. Although in general Duns Scotus accepted St. Thomas' basically rational theory of knowledge, on many points he took direct issue with the "Angelic Doctor." Perhaps the sharpest difference is reflected in Dun Scotus' doctrine of voluntarism. Whereas Thomas had stressed the primacy of intellect in God and man, Duns Scotus believed that God's will is the final and only determinant of good. His power is unlimited and absolute, not bound by, and therefore not related to, man's merits. He may save whom He wills. Thus Scotus arrived at the doctrine of predestination. In other connections, however, he ascribed great independence to man's free will. He never, in fact, resolved the contradiction between these two views, and students of this period have found it difficult to form a clear picture of his over-all philosophy. His critical analyses of the arguments of other philosophers—including Thomas—were frequently elaborate and fine-spun, but they often reveal little of his own thought. He was called the "Subtle Doctor," and with good reason. His very subtlety and his habit of carrying analysis to extremes pointed up a major weakness in scholasticism: they showed that the dialectic method applied to either theology or philosophy could lead only to opinions, not to certainty. The years after Duns Scotus are properly known as the period of the deterioration of scholasticism.

William of Ockham and the *Via Moderna*

THE generation that followed Scotus was distinctly inferior to him, but then a new and fresh personality appeared who set his mark on the development of Western thought and modern science in general in a most significant way. William of Ockham was born in Surrey between 1290 and 1300, became a Franciscan about 1310, and studied and lectured at Oxford between 1318 and 1324. His lectures must have been provocative, for in 1324 he was summoned to Avignon to answer charges of heresy brought by the chancellor of the University of Oxford. The dispute between the Spiritual Franciscans and Pope John XXII was then at its height, and William, as we have seen, identified himself with the Spiritual party. The Pope forbade him to leave the city, but on the night of May 26, 1328, he escaped from Avignon with Michael of Cesena, General of the order, Bonagrazia of Bergamo, and several other Spiritual Franciscans. He fled to Pisa and joined forces with the Emperor Louis, and then engaged in a bitter struggle with the Pope on quite other issues. For his contumacy in escaping from Avignon, William was immediately excommunicated. He is reported to have said to the Emperor: "You defend me with your sword, and I will defend you with my pen." He became Louis' leading publicist, and his political writings from 1328 to his death in 1349 or 1350 were powerful defenses of the imperial theory against those who favored the Pope. He is thus of significance in the field of political philosophy as well as in that of logic and metaphysics. After the death of Louis in 1347, William made an effort to become reconciled with his order and the Church—with what result is not known.

In the field of formal philosophy Ockham is regarded as the refounder of nominalism, perhaps more accurately called terminism. As we have pointed out, this philosophy was known as the *via moderna* as contrasted with the *via antiqua,* of which St. Thomas had come to be regarded as the leading protagonist. Ockham believed that logic could reveal the truths of nature, but he posited a God high above all knowledge. We cannot apprehend Him by reason, as the Thomists believed, or by illumination, as the Augustinians consistently held, but only by faith. Thus Ockham once again separated the truth of reason and the truth of faith, which Thomas had labored to unite. God to him was even above the universals on which St. Thomas and, *a fortiori,* the extreme realists based their theories. Ockham's doctrine of economy *—known as "Ockham's razor"—discarded the universals simply because they were not necessary to an understanding of the particulars. What are called universals exist only in our minds, as abstract terms (*termini*) or generalizations; they have no existence in the particular thing. The particular object perceived by our senses has finality, uncomplicated by any possible connection with a universal that is outside it and not subject to the limitations to which the particular must be subject. This position was of great significance for scientific thought, for it suggested that natural phenomena were susceptible to rational investigation unimpeded by considerations of metaphysics and theology. It has been said that Ockham's pioneering work in developing a logic based upon and purely applicable to natural objects was the most important advance in scientific thought since the Greeks.

Ockham had many followers in England and on the Continent. Indeed, the *via moderna* virtually monopolized university teaching in philosophy and theology for the next century and a half. Alan Woodham, Nicholas of Autrecourt, and especially John Buridan and Nicholas of Oresme, all accepted the terminism of the "Venerable Inceptor" and applied it to problems of cause and effect, mechanics, gravity, and motion. The individualistic trend—the emphasis on the particular object—was attractive and powerful. It brought the focus of man's attention from high abstractions and metaphysical hypotheses down to individual, sensible, and measurable things. Its emphasis on the tangible attracted practical minds. Ockham's thought was the beginning of a whole school which was preparing the logical and philosophical bases for the new world. In the

---

* *Entia non sunt multiplicanda praeter necessarium:* beings should not be multiplied beyond what is necessary. As between two explanations of natural phenomena, the simpler is always to be preferred. The sentence does not appear in Ockham's work in precisely this form, but it correctly represents his thought.

spheres of his direct influence, philosophy and political theory, areas in which the humanists were sorely deficient, Ockham must be counted a modern man. His work in the fields of logic and metaphysics paralleled the work of Petrarch and his followers in literature, poetry, and critical scholarship.

Several years before Ockham's escape from Avignon, two secular scholars, John of Jandun and Marsilio of Padua, had fled from Paris as a result of the uproar caused by a book of which they were thought to be joint authors, the *Defensor pacis (Defender of the Peace)*. The fact that both had been lecturing at the University of Paris on Aristotle and that Marsilio had once been rector of the University was no protection. From Munich, to which they escaped, Marsilio went with the Emperor on his Italian trip and was for some months the imperial lieutenant in the city of Rome. He must have been too vigorous because the Romans were glad to see him go. We know little of him after 1328, but he looms large in the history of political philosophy.

Defender of the Peace appeared in two books. The first, intended as a discussion of the broad principles of political theory, is virtually a commentary on Aristotle's *Politics*. The second, more specific, presents the application of these principles and the opposition they may be expected to meet. According to the author, the state exists for the highest good of its citizens. Rulers must be obedient to law, and law must be rooted in the will of the whole citizenry, voiced by a majority vote. Marsilio envisaged popular sovereignty as functioning through responsible representatives, not in a fully democratic fashion. He seemed to accept the principle of a multiplicity of states, divided according to choice, language, and common interests. He admitted that there were difficulties in the way of this ideal state: opposition from Rome, the pettiness of princes, and ignorance and lack of understanding on the part of the citizenry. He analyzed the opposition he anticipated from the Church at some length and presented some very clear ideas as to how it could be met. Control of the Church, according to Marsilio, was in the wrong hands. The pope and the hierarchy were protected by a falsely defended tradition, the power of the keys, and a canon law which perpetuated the evil conditions. They must be sharply limited in the exercise of their power—and here Marsilio pioneered—by the authority of a general council representative of the whole Church and its lay membership. The later Conciliar Movement owed much to Marsilio's theories.

It should be pointed out that the principle of representative government had been familiar for many decades when Marsilio composed his work. The English Parliament was already representative of a fairly wide segment of the people; the French Estates General had met several times (in 1302, 1308, and 1314) before Marsilio wrote his book; the Spanish *Cortes* had been meeting for well over a century. But none of these was the actual ruler of its state. These bodies were, as yet, mere counselors of the ruler, with only incipient power to influence his decisions or to refuse him money.

Marsilio was far ahead of most ecclesiastical thinking, as well as of the performance of civil government. In the belief that the Church should be governed by a general council with the pope as simply the presiding officer, Marsilio and Ockham were in almost perfect agreement. Yet as metaphysicians the two thinkers were poles apart. Marsilio was a naturalist, a student of medicine, a rationalist in the strict Averroist tradition. To Ockham, on the other hand, faith was so important that its dictates were above any reasoning or questioning. In their attitudes toward the problems of government they both saw the need for recognition of the voice of the people as a corrective to the ills of unbridled monarchy. Each in his own way was a pioneer of the modern spirit.

Revival of Augustinianism

THE *via moderna* was having its triumphs, but the *via antiqua* still commanded the loyalty of many able and vigorous thinkers throughout the fourteenth and well into the fifteenth century. The old antagonism between Augustinianism and Aristotelianism did not disappear; it merely changed in form and emphasis. The lines of loyalty were no longer those of the two mendicant orders, the Franciscans as Augustinian followers of St. Bonaventura and the Dominicans as supporters of St. Thomas. In Ockham's native England there was a firm background of opposition to a naturalistic view of the world and a steady inclination toward acceptance of the older Augustinian positions as against the Aristotelianism of St. Thomas. Robert Kilwardby, Archbishop of Canterbury from 1272 to his death in 1279, was a Dominican and yet an adherent of the predominantly Augustinian Oxford school of thought. The heir of Grosseteste and Adam of Marsh, Kilwardby not only attacked the teachings of his fellow Dominican, St. Thomas, but went so far as to forbid the teaching of certain Thomistic doctrines in England. Kilwardby's successor as Archbishop of Canterbury, the Franciscan John Pecham (1279–92), was also a fervent follower of Augustinian idealism and an opponent of St. Thomas' middle way. On the other hand, there were Franciscans in England and on the Continent who, like Ockham, found the *via moderna* more acceptable.

Paris remained a center of intellectual activity during the fourteenth century, and in the many new universities in all parts of Europe there was a great emphasis on discussions of philosophy, theology, and political theory. Yet the most provocative and original thinking in this century was that of Englishmen. After Duns Scotus and Ockham, there were, to mention but a few, Walter Burley (d. 1346), Thomas Bradwardine (d. 1349), Richard FitzRalph (d. 1360), and John Wyclyf (d. 1384). Each of these thinkers made a notable contribution to the current of intellectual life, and each played a part in the transformation of European thought from the rigidity of scholasticism into a freer synthesis. Their contributions range from metaphysical and political innovations or reemphases to innovations in mathematics and mechanics.

Walter Burley taught at Oxford, was then a fellow of the Sorbonne at Paris (by 1324), and was later tutor to the young Edward III. His many commentaries on Aristotle became popular all over Europe and were required reading in Italian universities until late in the fifteenth century. In his noncommentarial works he defended the realist position—"that universals have an objective existence outside the mind"—in direct opposition to the nominalist thesis. Burley made several trips to Avignon and Italy, where he saw ancient manuscripts that he could not have seen in England. He there became convinced that not enough was known of the lives and thought of the ancients. Relying on such classical writers as Seneca and Diogenes Laertius and some medieval compilations, he composed a kind of encyclopedia entitled *De vita et moribus philosophorum* (*On the Life and Thought of the Philosophers*). In this work he presented biographical and bibliographical data about some 150 ancients, including astronomers and statesmen as well as philosophers. The work tends to be anecdotal, but it was the best and practically the only available source for such biographical information during the fourteenth century. It was widely copied all over the Continent and by the early years of the next century had been translated into German, Italian, Spanish, and Czech, and a part of it into French. The work of Burley is of especial significance as evidence of the growing curiosity about Latin and Greek culture which was a background for the more elevated aspects of the Renaissance.

Thomas Bradwardine (*ca.* 1290–1349), who was consecrated Archbishop of Canterbury just a few months before he succumbed to the Black Death, is of interest from several points of view. In his many works on mathematical subjects—*De arithmetica practica, De arithmetica speculativa, De proportionibus velocitatis motuum, De geometria speculativa, De continuo,* and astronomical tables—Bradwardine did not go beyond what was known to the Arabs, although even this knowledge was an advance over his contemporaries. In other works, however, he attempted to use principles of mathematical deduction to resolve theological problems. An advocate of the Oxford (Augustinian) position, he was disturbed by the implications of the Scotist teachings concerning the all-encompassing will of God. Ockham's followers, who were numerous, had begun to argue that God was responsible for evil as well as for good. Bradwardine set about to combat this doctrine. In 1344 he published *De causa Dei contra Pelagium* (*Concerning the Cause of God against Pelagius*), in which he defended the absolute sovereignty of God and the necessity under which man, led by grace, is moved to do what God has willed. He rejected the Ockhamists' position concerning the freedom of man's will, a position to which they were led by their assumption that there was a sharp separation between the absolute, unknowable God and the experience of man's mind. He puts forward the paradox that God decrees that man shall be free at the same time that He decrees that man shall act, thus determining both man's freedom and his action. Both the decreed act and the freedom have the same source. Contingency and necessity are thus compatible. Although Bradwardine's treatise did not immediately attract widespread notice or attack, it was of great influence later in the century. His doctrine was accepted and taught by FitzRalph and Wyclyf, and through them reached a much larger circle. The ancient issue of Augustinian predestination and Pelagian freedom of the will was being fought out once again—and not for the last time.

Richard FitzRalph (d. 1360), archbishop of Armagh in Ireland, was prominent in the attack on the privileges of the mendicant orders and spent much of his time at Avignon as the head of the seculars (parish priests, as opposed to members of orders), who wished to recapture for the secular clergy the cure of souls. He wrote a number of purely philosophical works in the Augustinian tradition, but his most important writing, *De pauperie Salvatoris* (*On the Poverty of the Savior*), is an elaborate argument against the mendicant orders, in the form of a theological and philosophical treatment of dominion and grace on purely Augustinian lines. His debt to Bradwardine is evident throughout.

His position is that lordship (*dominium*)—that is, ownership of property or office—is grounded in grace, and that grace is in the gift of God, quite apart from the Church or any human ordering. If Church office and the enjoyment of property are thus taken from the control of the Church and made dependent solely upon the grace of God, it is obvious that the Church will soon lose its power. FitzRalph's target was the mendicant orders alone, whose exercise of their lordship he found wanting. In the hands of John Wyclyf his doctrine was later extended to the whole ecclesiastical establishment, with what results we shall observe.

John Wyclyf (*ca.* 1320–84) is noted more for his political thought and for his translation of the Bible into English than for his philosophical work. But his true stature as a philosophical thinker has not yet been properly assessed. While at Oxford he may have heard lectures by Bradwardine or FitzRalph. He certainly regarded them both with great respect and borrowed from them freely. He was, from the beginning, a realist of the Platonic-Augustinian cut. Universal ideas, he held, are real, from the mind of God, creative archetypes of other entities. His was, indeed, an extreme realism—"he who denies universal ideas is an infidel"—in direct opposition to the Ockhamist *moderni doctores,* whom he ridiculed. He followed Bradwardine's theory of grace and predestination— an easy step for a realist who emphasized the unity of creation as emanating from God's mind—and FitzRalph's not-unrelated doctrine of dominion through grace. In his thinking about the natural world he advanced ideas about the transmission of light which closely resemble the modern quantum theory. He wrote two voluminous *Summae,* one, the *Summa de ente,* purely philosophical and metaphysical, and the *Summa theologie.* The latter is not a systematic treatment of the whole field of theology but concentrates upon those doctrines on which Wyclyf questioned the position of the Church. We shall meet Wyclyf again, as a heretic in theology (see below, pp. 173–77), but it can be said here that his whole system of thought, as it reached into the related fields of philosophy, theology, cosmology, ethics, and political theory, was more consistent and unified than that of almost any other man of the fourteenth century.

On the Continent in these years there were no minds to match the originality and vitality of the English thinkers. The ablest were two Frenchmen, Nicholas of Autrecourt (d. after 1350) and John Buridan (d. *ca.* 1366), both followers of Ockham. Both men carried Ockham's method and assumptions further in an effort to work out a philosophical basis for the natural sciences quite independent of Aristotle.

The end of this century and the early years of the next saw the rise to prominence and influence of two French schoolmen whose names and careers are closely linked. Peter d'Ailly (1350–1420) and John Gerson (1363–1429) were both, successively, chancellors of the University of Paris, both cardinals of the Avignon line of the Papacy, both leaders in the Conciliar Movement, and both advocates of the *via moderna* in philosophy. Gerson and d'Ailly regarded the nominalist doctrines of Ockham as the best framework for theology and laid much stress on mysticism as the natural and truest form of theology. Their vigor of expression, their great learning, and their collaboration in so strategic a post at the University of Paris gave these two ecclesiastics tremendous prestige throughout the Western world and helped to make nominalism the dominant philosophy in most of the universities of the fifteenth century. Of the two, Gerson, who from 1383 was d'Ailly's pupil, was slightly more interested in mysticism, and his writings in this field were copious and popular. So widely was he known as a mystical thinker that the *Imitation of Christ* of Thomas à Kempis was often ascribed to him. D'Ailly was also interested in astronomy and geography. His voluminous treatise *Imago mundi* (*On the Shape of the World*) had a notable influence on Columbus, and a commentary he wrote on the *Meteora* of Aristotle is known to have been carefully read and quoted by Amerigo Vespucci.

These two cardinals were vigorous thinkers and prolific writers, but they were hardly creative minds. The early fifteenth century was not a strikingly original period in the usual disciplines of philosophy. For originality in this century we must follow the mystic way, which reached its culmination in the life and thought of Nicholas of Cusa. To understand Nicholas and his significance we must retrace our steps to the end of the thirteenth century, for it was then that the mystic movement began to take on a clear and distinguishable shape.

MYSTICS

THE tradition of Christian mysticism—the longing of the individual soul for direct union with God—is so old as to seem inherent in the Christian faith. From New Testament times on, the mystic way has never lacked devotees. But it did not play a leading role in Christian thought and action until St. Bernard of Clairvaux lent it his full support and the Augustinian school of the Victorines in twelfth-century Paris gave it the sanction of systematic expression. In this same century, there were a number of movements throughout Europe that exhibited characteristics akin to mysticism. The Albigenses * and Waldenses, the latter sometimes called the "Poor Men," rose up to challenge the established Church in the late twelfth and early thirteenth century. These laymen rejected the Church's monopolistic control of the Scriptures in Latin and of the sacramental means of grace, and the reservation to the ordained priesthood of the right to preach. They claimed, in short, the rights of the individual to direct access to God, without the intermediacy of the organization. Quite obviously, the Church could not suffer this independence. If the individual could enjoy a full religious life without benefit of the Church's instrumentation, there might soon be no need for the Church at all. The Church's persecution of these and similar groups was determined and partially successful.

The thirteenth century witnessed the rise of the mendicant orders of St. Francis and St. Dominic. The former in particular was a kind of orthodox revolt against institutionalism and its works. It supplanted the theology of books with the theology of personal religion, of direct experience, of the simple and receptive heart crying out for its Creator. God's love, which St. Francis felt in his inmost being, was dearer to him than the world and even the Church,

* It is, of course, almost certain that the Albigenses should not be called Christian. They were, however, frequently grouped by the Church with other sects as heretics.

save as the Church served to keep men ready to receive that love. His true followers were the Spiritual Franciscans. The conservative Conventuals preferred the way of organization and order. The thirteenth century was the century of system and order, from Innocent III in the Church to St. Thomas Aquinas in philosophy. From the Albigenses to the Spiritual Franciscans almost a century later, the movements of individualism, mysticism among them, found the road rough. But the repression, like almost all repressions, only drove the urge underground. In the fourteenth century it erupted with such violence that the Church was completely unable to curb the movements that arose and had to adapt itself to their existence and try to absorb them into its fabric. With no background of independent religious experience and thought, groups arose that went far beyond Christian orthodoxy. Some of them even embraced pantheistic teachings, carrying the concept of mystic union so far as to believe that God and His creature are one, that man, being divine, is no longer subject to law.

Not all manifestations of the deep-rooted drive for freedom were in the area of individual religious experience and expression. There were sects of laymen in Italy, France, and Germany which represented the antisacerdotal social consciousness that monasticism had failed to nurture. In Italy, particularly in Umbria, the few remaining intimates of St. Francis who refused to accept the rule imposed on their primitive spirituality by the Church dispersed as individuals to mountain retreats and formed new contemplative and mystical groups. The beliefs of these scattered groups were highly diverse, ranging from orthodox to radical. Their membership was both lay and religious, but the element of separation from the organized Church was always present. The very spread of the movement indicated the existence of a feeling among the people that institutional religion no longer answered their needs. The poetry of Jacopone da Todi (1228–1306) reflected much of the fervor, the deep and vibrant religious passion, that found no outlet in the established Church. His best-known poem tells the story of the Crucifixion, with the characters speaking in the first person. The Virgin Mary cries out:

> Oh, my son, my son, my son—son, belovèd lily
> Son, who can console my anguished heart?
> Son, those joyous eyes—son, why dost thou not answer?
> Son, why dost thou hide from me, from the breast that nourished thee?

Jacopone, as if present at the sad event, speaks in his own person.

> Never again do I wish the company of man.
> Rather would I know the beasts of the field.
> Men intrude too much upon my life
> From which I have lost my Redeemer.

A mystic of a quite different sort entered upon the Italian scene later in the fourteenth century. St. Birgitta of Sweden (1303–73) had come to Italy determined to purify the Church and effect the return of the Papacy from Avignon. Urban V, partly in response to her appeals, did return to Rome. But before her death he gave up in despair and returned to Avignon. St. Catherine of

Siena (1347–80), only twenty-six when Birgitta died, assumed the task in which the Swedish saint seemed to have failed. The burden of St. Catherine's frequent ecstatic visions was that she should use whatever influence and persuasion she possessed to return the Papacy to Rome and bring about a reform of life and motive in the whole Church. She was thus, as it were, a political and activist mystic. Her earnest efforts and her instinctive response to human needs, from peasant's to pope's and king's, had some effect, for the Papacy, as we have seen, did return to Rome in 1378. But the Schism was more than she could bear. She came, at the end, to regret her part in bringing the Papacy back from Avignon. Urban VI, whom she had supported, had failed to live up to her hopes. She died on her thirty-third birthday, in agony of spirit over the Church. She had successors, but there was hardly a movement to carry on her work.

Spain did not escape the impact of the lay religious movement. The Catalonian Arnold of Villanova (*ca.* 1240–1311), remarkable for his medical and scientific learning, became interested, about 1290, in the mystical and apocalyptic ideas of Joachim of Flora. Arnold aggravated his offense by attacking, as a layman, the morals of the clergy, some of whom, he asserted, were members of Antichrist. The clergy's reaction was immediate. Arnold made a kind of retraction before the University of Paris and then went to Rome to appeal to Boniface VIII. The Pope treated the theological aspects of the case lightly; he formally confirmed the adverse judgment rendered in Paris but made Arnold his private physician. "Stick to your medicine and forget theology and we will grant you our favor." But Arnold continued to write, and his writings must have been read, for in November 1316, at the instigation of several Dominicans of Aragon, fourteen of his propositions and numerous treatises were condemned by an inquisitor at Tarragona.

The records of the Catalonian Inquisition show that there were Beghards and Waldensians, Fraticelli, and other heretical groups in fourteenth-century Spain, as there were throughout Europe. In the north of Europe, particularly in northern France and the Lowlands, the Beghards and the Beguines were the best known of these lay groups from the late twelfth century through the fifteenth century. Founded by Lambert de Bégue of Liége in about 1180, these groups of devout men and women banded together to follow Christ, to minister to the sick and the needy, to pray and worship, to work, and, if need be, to beg together in ordered humility. The Church strove to bring them under the control of the Franciscans or the Dominicans, whose popularity they had substantially undermined. In the fourteenth century severe edicts were issued against them, restricting their work and preaching, and some tragic incidents are recorded. The Inquisition was looking for heresy, and when pantheistic doctrines—frequently in the air during periods of religious dissatisfaction—made inroads among the Beghards or Beguines, it was not difficult to find something that could reasonably be called heresy. Furthermore, there is no doubt that there was some, if not much, license and libertinism. The Beghards not infrequently became associated with the Fraticelli, an offshoot of dubious orthodoxy of the Spiritual Franciscans, and Beguines were to be found in close relations with the Brethren of the Free Spirit, a group which was pantheistic and often libertine.

In England in the later Middle Ages there were individual mystics, but there was never a movement of mysticism such as that in Germany and the Lowlands. The *Ancrene Riwle* (*Rule for Anchoresses*), a comprehensive guide for the pious life written for three ladies of the upper class around 1200, was widely circulated and read in the following century, but it precipitated no school. With Richard Rolle of Hampole (*ca.* 1290–1349) the current of mystic thought grew stronger. He wrote both in Latin and in English, praising the life of contemplation and denouncing the vice and luxury of the world. His *Incendium amoris* (*The Fervor of Love*) and *De emendatione vitae* (*On the Emendation of Life*) were frequently copied. A century after Rolle's death (in 1434 and 1435) they were translated into English by Rich Misyn. The story of Rolle's first mystical access has its own charm.

I was sitting in sooth in a chapel, and as I was delighting in the sweetness of prayer and meditation, on a sudden I felt a pleasant and unknown warmth overtake me. At first I knew not what, doubting whence it could come. After a long while I became certain it was not from man but from my Maker, for I felt it even warmer and more pleasing. . . . For as I sat in that chapel, and in the night before supper as I was singing psalms, as well as I could, I heard, as it were, a tinkling of somebody talking or rather singing. . . . All this remained long in my ears and memory.

Some years later Walter Hilton (d. 1396), an Augustinian canon of Nottingham, wrote the *Scale* (ladder) *of Perfection*. Hilton, like Rolle, was not primarily interested in the ecstatic manifestations of the mystic way and illustrates clearly the English tendency toward sobriety in personal religion. Other contemplatives, such as Julian of Norwich (d. *ca.* 1420) and Margery Kempe (1373–*ca.* 1430), were active in the England of Wyclyf and Chaucer, but they are isolated phenomena which do not indicate a great popular demand for escape from the oppressive uniformity of the ecclesiastical organization. Their influence was not such as to start a movement, nor were they at any time in danger of falling into heresy.

The Rhenish Mystics

WHILE these various mystical groups and movements all over Europe were struggling both with their own religious concerns and against the Inquisition, a notable focusing of mystic genius was taking place along the Rhine, particularly at Cologne. Mysticism was not unknown in Germany in the earlier Middle Ages, but it reached its height in the fourteenth century, in the religious inspiration of such men as Meister Eckhart (*ca.* 1260–1327), John Tauler of Strassburg (*ca.* 1300–61), Henry Suso (*ca.* 1295–1366), John of Ruysbroeck (1293–1381), Gerard Groote (1340–84), and other members of the group known as the Friends of God.

Meister Eckhart was a Dominican at Cologne, trained in the school whose most brilliant lights were Albert the Great and St. Thomas Aquinas. Eckhart also studied at Paris in 1302 and 1311, and rose to be provincial of his order for Saxony, Vicar-General of Bohemia (in 1307), and finally provincial of Germany (in 1310). He preached and taught with great effectiveness and popularity both in Latin and in the vernacular at Strassburg, Frankfurt, and, for the last six years of his life, Cologne. The writings of the Pseudo-Dionysius and John Scotus Erigena as well as the current Neoplatonism had profoundly affected him. Although he had every intention of remaining completely orthodox, his speculative mind was led into paths bordering dangerously on pantheism. He was trained in the scholastic method but attempted to avoid an appeal to the intellect alone, preferring to speak to the soul and the will. Starting from a concept of God in two aspects—an "unnatured Nature," or the "Ground and Essence" of the Godhead, and the "natured Nature," or God in His personal aspect—Eckhart paralleled this duality of divine essence in the nature of man. "There is in the soul," he wrote, "something above the soul, divine, simplex, unnamed rather then named." This "oversoul" he called a *scintilla,* or small spark, which, corresponding to God's "Ground" or "Essence," permits communication between man and God in a sort of unity. "God with His own nature, His essence, His Godhead, is in the soul, yet He is not the soul. The soul returns a divine reflection to God, so that they are both the same light." Eckhart was careful, at least later in his life, to insist on the difference between God and man and thus avoid the pitfalls of pantheism. God remains God, and man remains man. Their "unity" is one of communication, not of nature.

But Eckhart's elevated words were not always clearly understood. In 1325 charges of heresy were lodged against him by Henry of Virneburg, archbishop of Cologne, who had burned a number of Beghards in 1322 and 1325 on similar charges of heresy. The charges were quashed by the Inquisitor in Germany, Nicholas of Strassburg, a fellow Dominican and friend of Eckhart. But the archbishop was not discouraged. In 1327 he renewed the attack, this time including the Inquisitor himself. Both parties appealed to John XXII. In February 1327, Eckhart made a public statement that he had always opposed heresy and stood willing to retract any errors that might be found in his writings. He died in the same year. Two years later John XXII declared, in the bull *In agro dominico,* that of the twenty-eight articles with which Eckhart had been charged, seventeen were heretical and the remaining eleven were suspect. The Pope's judgment in matters of doctrine proved in other cases to be somewhat dubious and his understanding of spirituality in any form very tenuous. But from another point of view John was quite right. Eckhart's emphasis upon the close and primary relation of the individual soul with its Creator would make the intervention of the Church through the sacraments, particularly penance, unnecessary. There was in Eckhart not a little of the evangelical spirit. His authority was the Scripture, and his speculation was always tested by the Bible and personal experience. He preached a practical religion, fed by the warmth of contemplation. He advocated not withdrawal from the world but, rather, active participation in human society.

Among Eckhart's friends and admirers were two men destined to carry the mystic torch through the century, John Tauler and Henry Suso. Tauler was born in Strassburg about 1300, became a Dominican about 1315, and somewhat later went to study at Cologne, and perhaps thereafter to Paris. Basel, Bavaria, Cologne, and again Strassburg were all to hear him before he died in his native city in 1361. His fame rests primarily on his preaching; his simple, direct, and evangelical sermons have retained their popularity well into modern times. Tauler laid great emphasis on man's *Kehr,* the work of the Holy Spirit, and on the divine light that illumines man and guides him to union with God. He wrote of the soul:

The image [of God] lies in the soul's powers, the likeness in its virtues, the divine color in its union; and thus its union becomes so intimate that it does not work its works in the form of a creature, but in its divine form, wherein it is united to God, nay that its works are taken from it, and God works all its works in His form. And then, while it beholds God and thus becomes more united with Him, the union may become such that God altogether pours Himself into it and draws it so entirely into Himself that it no longer has any distinct perception of virtue or vice, or recognizes any marks by which it knows what it is itself. But God regards the soul as a creature. Therefore let the light of grace overpower the light of nature in you; for the higher the knowledge the soul attains in the light of grace, the darker does it deem the light of nature.

It will be noticed how Tauler avoided pantheism by the clear statement, which he frequently repeated, that "God regards the soul as a creature"; a creature, of course, can never rise to equality or real union with its Creator.

In many of his sermons, Tauler made approving references to certain "divine men" who had responded to the "eternal Light" and had attained an "enlightened understanding." These were the Friends of God. Tauler first came into contact with this lay movement when he went to Basel in 1324. He was so impressed by its spirit and thought that he became identified with it and is accounted its leading preacher. The sources of the thought of the group as it spread from Switzerland down the Rhine were various: the apocalyptic-prophetic literature of earlier German mystics such as St. Hildegard of Bingen and St. Elizabeth of Schönau, the more intellectual mysticism of Eckhart and his disciples, and the echoes of Spiritual Franciscanism, several of whose most prominent leaders, William of Ockham and Bonagrazia of Bergamo among them, were at the court of the Emperor Louis IV in Munich during these years. The Friends of God were not a radical, iconoclastic group. They regarded themselves as a church within the Church, reverencing the sacraments and respecting the institution which they hoped to be able to purify by their own devout lives and the resources of a renewed faith.

From this group came the great German mystics of the later fourteenth and fifteenth centuries as well as the anonymous author of the *Theologia Germanica (German Theology)*, the single most influential German religious writing before Martin Luther. We know of the author only that he was once a member of the Teutonic Order at Frankfurt. His teaching, influenced by Eckhart and Tauler, exercised a tremendous influence on Luther: "Next to the Bible and St. Augustine, no book has ever come into my hands from which I have learned more of what God and Christ and man and all things are." The author's mysticism is clear and strong:

God and man should be wholly united so that it can be said of a truth that God and man are one . . . where the truth always reigneth, so that true perfect God and true perfect man are at one, and man giveth place to God, that God Himself is there, and this same unity worketh continually . . . without any I or me or mine—then there is Christ and nowhere else.

Henry Suso (*ca.* 1295–1366) was different in temper from both Eckhart and Tauler, although he was a pupil of the former and a companion of the latter. Born near Lake Constance of a noble family, he became a Dominican at thirteen, and before his twentieth year he began a life of austerity hardly equaled even in that enthusiastic century. He tells of his rigorous self-discipline in his *Autobiography*. He pricked *IHS* * into his chest, wore a hair shirt and an iron chain, and then replaced the hair shirt with a garment in which 150 sharp tacks were imbedded. This punishment he replaced after sixteen years with a wooden cross from which thirty spikes protruded. The blood from this grim instrument covered his body. He never, at any time of the year, entered a room in which there was a fire. These and other tortures which he inflicted upon himself are difficult for our age to justify or even understand. Yet out of this rigor came writings that speak of sweet faith, profound and self-effacing love, and a burning conviction of the presence of the Holy Spirit in his heart. In his book *The Eternal Wisdom* Suso stressed the dignity and the eternal value of suffering. But however much and however eloquently he may represent the mystic movement, Suso was more medieval, closer to the monastic and physically ascetic ideal, than his teacher Eckhart or the Friends of God, with which movement he is usually associated.

John of Ruysbroeck, a friend of Tauler and Suso and also of Gerard Groote, was born near Brussels in 1293, entered the secular priesthood, and became at the age of almost sixty an Augustinian monk and prior of the abbey of Groenendael, near Waterloo. His long life (he died at the age of eighty-eight) brought him into contact with several generations of mystics. He was not a philosopher like Eckhart, whom he may have heard preach in Cologne, nor a violent ascetic like Suso, nor even a great preacher like Tauler. His life and thought were gentle, almost passive. Eschewing heresy and particularly the pantheism to which mystics are so prone, he worked out a scale of mystical experience. In his *Spiritual Marriage* he described the three stages of the soul's search for God: the active, the inner, and the contemplative. In the first, active stage, the soul practices the Christian virtues and makes its faith evident to the world. In the second stage, the soul looks inward to meditate on the love of God. This is as far as most men can go. The third stage, contemplation, calls for deep immersion in the further darkness unknown to the ordinary creature. Here the soul finds unity with God, yet without losing its individual identity. Some of Ruysbroeck's expressions go beyond orthodox formulae, but his more ecstatic states were not meant for general practice; else there would have been an outbreak of emotional excesses with no corresponding growth in faith.

The Brethren of the Common Life

OF THE friends of Ruysbroeck, the one who was destined to have the widest and most enduring influence was Gerard Groote. Groote spent his early life as a wandering scholar at Paris, Cologne, and Prague, living on two generous

---

* Medieval scribes frequently wrote the name Jesus as *Ihesus* and abbreviated it *IHS*. The more learned were aware that the abbreviation might also refer to the *in hoc signo* which inspired the Emperor Constantine before the battle of the Milvian Bridge in 312.

benefices. He took the degree of master of arts in Paris in 1358 and thereafter studied law for several years, spending a total of eight years in Paris. During an illness at the age of thirty-four (1374), he experienced a sudden and deep conversion. Still a layman, he began to wander about and preach. The substance of his message was repentance. Then, after a retirement of three years to a monastery for contemplation, he emerged as a missionary preacher in many cities and towns in the Lowlands. People came from miles around to hear him "lay the axe at the root of the tree" of immorality and sloth, in the words of Thomas à Kempis. He preached to the clergy in Latin and to the common folk in the vernacular. The Franciscans, who were the principal object of his attack, secured a prohibition of his preaching on the ground that he was not ordained. The bishop of Utrecht, although personally friendly to Groote, decreed that deacons—that is, clerics not yet ordained as priests—should not be allowed to preach in his diocese. Groote died of the plague in August 1384 without receiving an answer to his appeal to the Pope from this decree.

Groote's greatest work was accomplished during the last months of his life, when, with the help of Florentius Radewyns (1350–1400), vicar of a church in Deventer, he founded the Brethren of the Common Life. This was a semi-monastic organization consisting largely of lay folk, men and women, who lived and worked together, conducting schools, copying manuscripts, and supporting themselves by their own daily toil. The movement was at first almost informal. With time and increase in numbers it took on a more precise organization. In the next century it grew in influence, spread to many centers in the Lowlands and along the Rhine, and came to hold a most important place in the history of Christian humanistic education. Its members taught from the classics of Latin literature and so furthered the cause of learning throughout the Rhineland and Germany. Erasmus was the greatest but not the only eminent name to come from the schools of the Brethren. Graduates were in constant demand as teachers wherever the young needed sound instruction. But education was only one phase of the activity of the Brethren of the Common Life. Their purposes are well stated in the statutes regulating the life in their houses. The statutes of the community at Herford declared:

For the promotion of our soul's salvation as well as for the edification of our neighbor in the purity of the true Christian faith and the unity of our Mother, the holy Christian Church, we will and intend to live a pure life, in harmony and community, by the work of our own hands, in true Christian religion and the service of God. We purpose to live a life of moderation, without beggary; to render obedience with reverence to our superiors; to wear a simple and humble habit; diligently to observe the canons of the holy Fathers, in so far as they are of profit; diligently to apply ourselves to the virtues and other holy exercises and studies; and not only to live a blameless life, but to give a good pattern and example to other men.

The principal establishments of the Brethren were at Deventer, the mother house at Zwolle, Hoorn and Amersfoort, Delft, Gouda, 's Hertogenbosch, Utrecht, and Nymegen. But there were many other centers, both in the Lowlands and in Germany, where members of the group or their pupils devoted their lives to the ideals of Groote. The house at Cologne was active until 1802, when it was secularized by the French under Napoleon. The core of the life of the Brethren was the *devotio moderna,* the desire to abase the self, to commune with God, to scorn temporal things, and to maintain the progress that had been achieved by habits of devout and humble submission to God's will.

Next to the founder of the movement, Groote, the greatest personality of this school of mystics was Thomas à Kempis, author of the *Imitation of Christ.* After the Bible, this work has been more frequently printed and translated than any other writing in European history. Almost 2500 editions in many languages have appeared. The authorship of the *Imitation* has been disputed for centuries, the most serious claimants for the honor being, besides Thomas, Cardinal John Gerson and Gerard Zerbolt of Zutphen, the latter a member of the Brethren at Deventer. Thomas' authorship, however, by now seems quite certain.

À Kempis was born in 1380 at Kempen, near Cologne. He was educated, from the age of twelve, at the school of the Brethren at Deventer under the personal guidance of Radewyns, whom he called "my good father and sweet master." Thomas joined the community of the Brethren at Mt. St. Agnes in 1400 and spent the next seventy years there, dying in his own room at the venerable age of ninety-one. His life was spent in contemplation, depreciation of the things of this world, and striving for the perfect life in union with God. There is much in the thought of à Kempis that we would regard as negative —its passiveness, its contempt for the values of this world. His emphasis on the need for the human soul to refresh and revive itself by communion with the Divine and on return to simple Christlike goodness and abnegation of self must be seen in the context of the worldly and hypocritical fifteenth century. The *Imitation* alternates between prayer and objurgation to the inward life.

I will hearken what the Lord will speak in me. Blessed is the soul which heareth the Lord speaking within her, and receiveth from His mouth the word of consolation. Blessed are the ears that gladly receive the pulses of the Divine whisper, and give no heed to the many whisperings of this world. Blessed indeed are those ears which listen not after the voice sounding without, but for the Truth teaching within. Blessed are the eyes which are blind to outward things, but intent on things within. Blessed are they that enter far into inward things, and endeavor to prepare themselves, more and more, by daily exercises, for the receiving of heavenly secrets. . . . O Lord my God! Thou art to me whatsoever is good. And who am I, that I should dare to speak to Thee? I am Thy poorest, meanest servant, and a most vile worm, much more poor and contemptible than I can or dare express. Yet do Thou remember, O Lord, that I am nothing, have nothing and can do nothing. Thou alone art good, just, holy; Thou canst do all things, Thou accomplishest all things, Thou fillest all things, only the sinner Thou leavest empty. Remember Thy mercies, and fill my heart with Thy grace, Thou who wilt not that Thy works be void and vain.

Nicholas of Cusa

THE work of a younger contemporary of Thomas à Kempis has, after long neglect, come to be recognized as the most original and significant synthesis of the fifteenth century. Nicholas of Cusa (1401–64) was born near Trier along the middle Rhine, attended the school of the Brethren at Deventer, and then studied Greek, Hebrew, law, mathematics, and astronomy at Padua. He represented the archbishop of Trier, who was of the antipapal party, at the Council of Basel in 1432 (see Chapter 11); then in 1437 changed sides and defended the papal position. Because of his learning and linguistic attainments, he was entrusted by popes with delicate diplomatic missions, promoted to the cardinalate in 1448, and made bishop of Brixen in 1450. For some years, as virtual supervisor of the Church in Germany, he held synods and worked to reform the clergy. In his own diocese of Brixen his reforms met opposition and he was even imprisoned by the Habsburg archduke of the Tyrol. He spent his last four years studying and writing in Italy. He wrote copiously on mathematical as well as philosophical questions, but his best-known work is *De docta ignorantia* (*On Learned Ignorance* or *Not-Knowing*), in which he tried to bring the finite and the infinite into their right relation. Previous philosophies had set them in opposition, but Cusa conceived of the infinite as the absolute maximum which, because it is one, is also the minimum. The opposites thus coincide in the infinite, which is God alone. Since man could not know the infinite, he could apprehend truth only by learned ignorance, that is, comprehension beyond reason. This idea was a categorial rejection of the Aristotelian attempt to understand diversity in terms of the tension between opposites and required a return to the Neoplatonic positions of the Pseudo-Dionysius and the Platonic tradition which both St. Thomas and Ockham had repudiated. Cusa's dependence on the intuitive approach of Eckhart is everywhere apparent, and many of Eckhart's expressions and questions appear in his writings. Indeed, he, like Eckhart and his followers, was accused of pantheistic tendencies, in that he came close to identifying the finite and the infinite. He argued that coincidence of the finite in the infinite means not identity but participation.

The philosopher and the mystic met in Nicholas. Almost equally important, humanistic freedom and intuition appeared to grace and form the whole man. In Cusa the Neoplatonic philosophical tradition, more at home in the schools of the twelfth century than in the universities of the thirteenth and fourteenth centuries, joined the mystic way of Eckhart and Suso, and a step was taken toward the Augustinianism of the Reformers.

HERETICS

WE MUST again retrace our steps to the times of Innocent III. The Fourth Council of the Lateran (1215), called and controlled by Innocent, marked a major stage in the formulation of religious ideas and teachings. There was from the time of the Council an accepted authority in matters of doctrine: the Church, speaking through the popes. Since the Church was convinced that it was in possession of final truth in all matters, it demanded conformity to its pronouncements. The papal Inquisition was established and supported, and the secular authority was obliged to enforce its findings. The first object of the Inquisition's activity was the Albigensian heresy in southern France (1208–16). This heresy was soon crushed, but in the years that followed, as we have seen, there were similar manifestations of popular dissatisfaction with sacerdotalism throughout Europe which eluded such prompt and complete elimination. In Italy, France, the Lowlands, England, Austria, and Bohemia, many small movements of nonconformity or overt opposition sprang up as answers to the Church's extreme repression of dissent. Toleration was something that no one, orthodox or heretic, considered for a moment, and heresy could appropriately be punished only by burning. The good king of France, St. Louis IX, had another treatment for heresy. He declared that when a layman heard the faith spoken against, he should draw his sword and thrust it into the offender's body up to the hilt.

Some of those called heretics by the Church were predominantly evangelical, such as the Waldenses, the Humiliati, and perhaps the Arnoldists. They appealed to the authority of the Scriptures, which they wanted in the vernacular, and challenged the Church, with its elaborate hierarchy, luxury, and sacerdotal exclusivism, to be judged by God's word. Other groups were pantheistic and libertarian, led astray by an exclusive emphasis on some aspect of Christian thought. Most of the vagaries can be traced to movements that arose or first became noticeable in the twelfth century; they frequently reappeared during the thirteenth century, usually over a wider area than before the institution of the Inquisition. We are thus led to conclude that the efforts of the Church to uproot the heresies only served to drive them underground temporarily and in the end spread them more widely throughout Europe, as dissatisfaction with the Church's custody of the Christian faith increased.

The Church energetically—one might say frantically—pursued its policy of repression; the *bullaria* of every pope from Innocent III on for centuries are full of decrees against specific heresies and heresy in general. The very vigor of their procedure and the frequency with which the subject appears in the records bear witness to the vitality of the issue—the failure of the Church to fulfill its simple religious mission. All the heresies point to the yearning of the common people—they were all essentially lay movements—for a simple and pure exercise of religion and a return to apostolic ideals. There is little evidence that the higher clergy understood the nature of this yearning.

The mendicant orders were designed by their founders, St. Francis and St. Dominic, to provide this kind of evangelical ideal for the common people. The hierarchy, however, almost immediately forced the orders into its organizational mold. The Franciscan Order was split into two factions: the strict party, called Observantists and later Spirituals, which insisted on the ideal of poverty; and the laxer members, or Conventuals, who were willing, as the hierarchy wished, to become as worldly as the rest of the clergy. The Spirituals fought against the hierarchical trend for decades, but the weight of the organization was thrown into the scales in favor of the Conventuals. In a number of bulls Pope John XXII decided against the Spirituals. Many were imprisoned; four were burned at Avignon in 1318. We have seen how certain leaders among the Spirituals sought refuge from papal persecution at the court of Emperor Louis IV (the Bavarian).

But papal repression could not settle the basic problem of the failure of the hierarchical organization of the Church to satisfy the religious needs of the common folk. After papal decisions had gone against the Spirituals, and wherever the Franciscans had been active, sects of lay groups arose almost spontaneously, proclaiming in some form or other the ideals of the stricter party of the Franciscans. Southern and central Italy, southern and northern France, Spain, Flanders, parts of Germany, even parts of Asia Minor and Egypt, all witnessed cases of this heresy throughout the fourteenth and well into the fifteenth century. In almost every recorded instance, the populace showed open sympathy with the heretic and disapproval of the inquisitor or the Church official who conducted the trial and condemnation. In northern Europe, wherever these antiecclesiastical movements appeared, they seemed to coalesce with or be absorbed into the lay mystic groups; the Beghards and Beguines, and the Brethren of the Common Life. The urge for independence from the Church and the priesthood is a fact of European experience in the fourteenth and fifteenth centuries which must be kept in mind in any attempt to explain the later outbreak of the Protestant Reformation.

John Wyclyf

MOST of the lay movements that we have described originated among the common people. Their leaders were rarely persons of education or social status, and the authorities were usually able to restore discipline without great difficulty, simply by burning a few leaders and imprisoning other suspects. But in two countries, England and Bohemia, the revolt against ecclesiasticism got out of hand. The movements led by John Wyclyf (*ca.* 1320–84) and by John Hus of Prague (1370–1415) had much in common and some connection, although the later was hardly a transplantation of the earlier, as has frequently been asserted.

John Wyclyf was the eldest son of the squire of Wyclyf-on-Tees, in the north of England. He studied at Oxford in the days of Burley, Bradwardine, and FitzRalph and was master of Balliol College in 1361–62. He lectured in arts in the 1360's, rose to some eminence as a philosopher, and took his doctor's degree in 1372. He had chosen the Augustinian line, in the tradition of Grosseteste and Kilwardby, and was recognized in Oxford as the leading exponent of the realist (Platonic) philosophy even before he took his final degree.

England was then involved in the wars with France, and when, in 1365, the Papacy at Avignon demanded payment of the Peter's Pence (an ecclesiastical tax on the kingdom of England amounting to £200 a year, then some years in arrears), English opinion was united in supporting the king and Parliament in their refusal to pay. Wyclyf then, or some time shortly thereafter, apparently went beyond simple agreement with the official refusal and openly voiced doubts about the theoretical basis of the papal claim. Since he was the leading scholar at Oxford, whatever he said was noticed, and he became known as a strong nationalist, opposed to papal encroachments.

In 1374 he was named to a small commission sent to Bruges to treat with representatives of the Papacy on a number of disputed matters. The negotiators met in the summer of that year; the results were negligible. Wyclyf was not a member of the later commission which continued negotiations with the papal envoys. From the time of his return from Bruges—September 1374— Wyclyf's opposition to the Papacy was overt. His first-hand experience of papal diplomacy must have had some effect upon his attitude: the papal envoys at Bruges had expressed an interest in bribes to modify their views. Whether the other representatives of the English king were any more scrupulous than the papal envoys we may doubt. But from this time onward, Wyclyf devoted his thought and energy to a thorough examination of the bases of spiritual and temporal authority. From this period came his works *De dominio divino* (*On Divine Dominion*), *De civili dominio* (*On Civil Dominion*), and *De officio regis* (*On the Office of the King*), in which he echoed FitzRalph's assertion that dominion is inextricably related to grace. To the righteous man God gives everything; to the unrighteous man, not a farthing. From this Augustinian concept, it was a logical step to question the clergy as to the vast property they possessed and the power they exercised in virtue of their office. If the high clergy (or the low, for that matter) are not living morally and therefore are not in grace, they have no right to their property and power. The function of the king is to sit in judgment on the morals of the clergy if their conduct calls for such action. Wyclyf came to his conclusions over a period of time, but his completed doctrine of dominion would have put the clergy completely at the mercy of the monarch.

Wyclyf's teaching happened to coincide with the plans of John of Gaunt, the ambitious younger son of the ailing King Edward III. Gaunt's position was anticlerical, in large part because of his desire to shift some of the burden for supporting the war in France onto the rich but tax-exempt Church. Thus began an alliance between the theologian and the prince which augured trouble for the clerical cause. The new bishop of London, William Courtenay, moved against Gaunt by calling Wyclyf before him in London in February 1377. There was no trial, nor even a questioning, but a brawl precipitated by John of Gaunt. Wyclyf had not uttered a word. However, Pope Gregory XI, prompted by Courtenay, issued a series of bulls (May 22, 1377) against Wyclyf's teaching as presented in the *De civili dominio*. These bulls were not published in England until mid-December. There was another species of trial at Lambeth Palace before the bishops early in 1378, but the mother of the young Richard II forbade any decision against Wyclyf, who was still favored by John of Gaunt.

In September of that year, the Great Schism broke out. Wyclyf, like most other Englishmen, at first supported the Roman Urban VI; then, as the Schism proceeded, he came to despise both sides of the unsavory controversy. He was writing his voluminous treatise *De ecclesia* (*On the Church*) during this and the following year. In the course of his disputes, and from his study of the roots and sanctions of the Church's teaching, he had begun to question the official doctrine of the Eucharist, which explained the miracle of the change in substance of the elements, bread and wine, into the body and blood of Christ at the moment of consecration by the ministrant priest. Wyclyf, as a realist philosopher, found that the dogma of transubstantiation, laid down in the Fourth Lateran Council of 1215, clearly meant that the substance of the bread and wine was annihilated in order that the substance of the body and blood of Christ might take their place. He argued that annihilation was impossible. The substance of bread and wine is God's creation; God's creation is the extension of a universal idea in the mind of God; annihilation of a substance therefore means that God is annihilating a part of Himself—a terrible thought and manifestly impossible. On this basis Wyclyf concluded, sometime in 1379 or 1380, that the doctrine of transubstantiation was not in accordance with the

Scriptures or with Christian doctrine. Early in 1381, Wyclyf's teachings on the Eucharist were examined in Oxford by a commission appointed by the chancellor of the university and condemned by a narrow majority. John of Gaunt, who had no stomach to defend a heretical doctrine on so important a matter, urged Wyclyf to accept the decision of the commission, but Wyclyf felt unable to repudiate the logic of his position and soon after left Oxford, retiring to his church at Lutterworth. There he maintained his literary activity and kept in touch with former students and colleagues who were carrying on the reform movement. In May 1382, Courtenay, then Archbishop of Canterbury, convened a meeting of clerics at Blackfriars Hall in Oxford, which condemned 24 conclusions from Wyclyf's writings (10 as heretical and 14 as erroneous), without mentioning Wyclyf by name. A few dons who attempted to defend him were quickly forced to submit. The meeting was ended by an earthquake, to which Wyclyf and the Archbishop gave divergent interpretations.

With Wyclyf thus deserted by his princely protector and his Oxford sympathizers silenced, there was no possibility that his movement would succeed. He suffered a paralytic stroke on December 28, 1384, and died three days later. He had not been excommunicated and thus was able to be buried in consecrated ground. The Council of Constance pronounced him a heretic in May 1415. In 1428, at the order of Pope Martin V, Wyclyf's bones were exhumed, burned, and cast into the little stream that flows by the churchyard of Lutterworth.

In his last years, probably beginning as early as 1379, Wyclyf had begun to make his appeal to the common people of England. His plan was simple. He organized small preaching missions, made up of Oxford students, which he sent out in pairs to towns over the countryside. The effectiveness of these enthusiastic young men must have been great. A chronicler, quite anti-Wyclyf in his attitude, relates that every second person he met on the highway was a follower of Wyclyf. These "pore prestis" preached in the vernacular, using, as we must conclude from the wide spread of the manuscripts, English translations of Wyclyf's tracts and sermons, or his own vernacular versions of pithy discourses on points of doctrine or attacks on the vices of the friars and the secular clergy. It was this aspect of Wyclyf's campaign that gave it the name of Lollardy, a term then commonly applied to wandering sectaries and exhorters. The Lollards were classed with the Beghards and the Fraticelli as at best undesirable citizens, and at worst subversive heretics.

In addition to guiding the work of the "pore prestis," Wyclyf saw the need to get the Scriptures to the people. His demand for reform was based on the Bible, and his great treatise *De veritate sacre scripture* (*On the Truth of Sacred Scripture*), written in 1379–80, was a monument to his conviction. Probably in 1382 he began to make his own translation of the Bible into English. It is not certain whether he finished the New Testament before his death, but the work was revised and carried to completion in 1388 by his younger colleagues, especially John Purvey and Nicholas Hereford. It had a wide circulation beyond purely Lollard circles. About two hundred manuscript copies have survived.

Wyclyf's principal heretical teachings may be grouped into four categories:
1. He rejected the authority and even the validity of tradition. The title of

Doctor Evangelicus, given him by his English followers and later adopted by his Bohemian admirers, represented his belief that the individual Christian and the whole *ecclesia,* the assembly of the faithful, should be guided solely and finally by Scripture. The Roman Church, regarding itself as the custodian of sacred tradition handed down from Christ to Peter and from him to all his successors, and regarding this tradition as equal in weight to Scripture, could not endure this rejection of its charge. In thus proclaiming the sufficiency of Holy Scripture, Wyclyf was announcing for the first time in doctrinal history the formal principle of the Protestant Reformation, which a century and a half later Luther, unaware of his predecessor, was to make so prominent a part of his teaching.

2. Wyclyf regarded as immoral the immunity of the ecclesiastical hierarchy from control and correction by the civil authority, basing his reasoning on the doctrine of dominion by grace. The authority and perquisites that the clergy enjoy must be subject to examination by the king or his representatives, who are appointed by God to that function. The Roman Church could not submit to any such program, for this would have meant the creation of national churches and the absolute denial of Petrine supremacy.

3. In his works *On the Church* and *On the Power of the Pope* (*De potestate pape,* 1379–80), Wyclyf maintained that the Christian Church was the congregation of the predestinate, whose sole head was Christ, and that the hierarchical organization—the pope, the cardinals, and the prelacy—were not warranted in their claim to control that Church. Further, he asserted that members of the hierarchy not only could err in their doctrine but might themselves not be among the predestinate. If such a doctrine were to gain currency the Roman Church would cease to exist.

4. Wyclyf rejected the Church's doctrine of transubstantiation on philosophical grounds. The Mass, of which the Eucharist is the principal component, was the most important sacrament of the medieval Church; rejection of the miracle of transubstantiation, which was in the power of the ministrant priest, would mean that the Church's control over the individual believer would be irreparably weakened.

Wyclyf had arrived at all these beliefs gradually, struggling through the maze of historical and philosophical development which lay behind the fixed dogmas he came to question or reject. A close examination of his writings in chronological order makes it clear that his final opinions were arrived at slowly and that he was led on, step by step, by two impulsions: the logic of his realist philosophy, which forced him to deny what he felt to be the unwarranted claims of the hierarchy to power; and his conviction that the people of England were being prevented by this same hierarchy from gaining a knowledge of the true gospel message. Both positions inevitably entailed opposition to the Church.

Wyclyf's followers were relentlessly persecuted and almost stamped out. Some of them remained at Oxford for a while after his death but were finally forced to recant or flee during the next few years. Some were turncoats. The suggestion has been made that Wyclyf or Wyclyf's teachings had borne some responsibility for inciting the Peasants' Revolt of 1381. One of the leaders of the Revolt, John Ball, is supposed to have admitted attending Wyclyf's lectures, but there is no proof even of this, and no evidence has been found to connect Wyclyf in any way with the uprising. Lollardy, however, did not completely disappear. In the decades after Wyclyf's death, it persisted, if we may judge from occasional trials for heresy in western England, among the middle and lower classes. A Lollard manifesto affixed to the doors of St. Paul's and Westminster Hall in London was treated by the high clergy as a very serious matter. In 1401 Parliament passed a statute *De heretico comburendo* (*On the Burning of a Heretic*), aimed specifically at Lollards, and England caught up with the Continent in its treatment of those who dared to dispute the official faith.

The figure of Wyclyf looms over his age and his colleagues at Oxford. The university declined after he left its halls. There were, of course, other reasons for this decline than his passing. But the fact is that in England he was not followed by any original and provocative thinker for a whole century, until the humanistic revival and the golden age of the "Oxford Reformers," Colet, Erasmus, and More.

The Hussite Movement

MORE than seven hundred miles away from England, on the banks of the gentle Moldau, a storm had been brewing for decades, since before the name of Wyclyf was heard in the schools of Oxford. Charles IV, king of Bohemia and Emperor of the Holy Roman Empire from 1346, was deeply interested in the religious life of his country and lost no opportunity to further the cause of reform. There was much that was wrong in the Bohemian church, as in the Church everywhere else in Europe during the age of Avignon: simony, widespread concubinage, plurality of benefices, absenteeism, a slothful clergy, and lax monastic orders. In 1363 the Emperor invited to Prague Conrad Waldhauser (d. 1369), a fervent member of the Augustinian Order who had lately been most effective in preaching reform in Austria. Charles urged Conrad to settle in Prague and, a few years later, supported the eloquent and ascetic Czech Milíč of Kroměříže (d. 1374), who took up Conrad's mantle. Milíč preached against the vice and laxity of the clergy, thus drawing upon himself the wrath of the Prague authorities. The large crowds which came to hear him inveigh against clerical abuses were some index of public opinion of the clergy. He was obliged to make two trips to the papal see to answer charges of heresy brought against him by the Prague clergy.

In the 1380's and 1390's the call for a higher morality among the secular clergy and the monastic orders persisted, but it was not the only focus of contention in Prague. The university, founded by Charles in 1348, had become the scene of violent altercations between German and Czech professors and students. Smoldering for some time, the dissension erupted in brawls in 1384 and 1385, then subsided for some years only to break out again with heightened bitterness in the early fifteenth century. This deep-seated antagonism throughout these decades must be kept in mind, since it enters into matters of allegiance in theology and philosophy.

The combination of the movement for reform in clerical morals and the nationalistic tension between Czechs and Germans was personified in John Hus and perpetuated in the Hussite reformation. Born in the south Bohemian town of Husinec about 1370, Hus studied at the University of Prague in the days when the reform movement and the growing anti-German tension were active. He took his bachelor of arts degree in 1393, and began to lecture in philosophy in 1398. By this time the struggle over the two philosophical currents, realism and nominalism, was open and acrimonious. The German "nations" were almost solidly nominalist, the Czechs as solidly realist. A convinced realist, Hus was prominent in the polemic. He combined lecturing at the university with frequent preaching, and in 1402 he became the regular preacher of the Bethlehem chapel, founded in 1391 by two wealthy Prague laymen for preaching in the vernacular. His sermons were popular. Queen Sophia often came from the royal castle across the river to hear him.

In 1403 there was the first sharp altercation in Prague over the spreading of Wyclyf's doctrines. Forty-five articles and statements from the English reformer's works were condemned by the university, then dominated by German professors, against the opposition of the Czech members of the faculty. The conflict revolving around the German-Czech antipathy, Wyclyf's realistic philosophy, and his antiecclesiasticism grew more bitter with the passing years. Finally, in January 1409, King Wenzel sided with the Czech opposition to the Germans and issued, at Kutná Hora, a decree giving the Czech "nation" at the university three votes to the Germans' one, a reversal of the situation that had obtained until that time. Several thousand German professors and students left Prague for Leipzig, where they founded a university in the Saxon city. Hus, who was generally recognized as the leader in the nationalistic struggle as well as in the reform movement, was thereupon elected rector of the University of Prague (October 17, 1409).

The German-Czech problem was thus eliminated for the time being, but the contention between the conservatives and the reform party remained. Archbishop Zbyněk finally sided with the conservatives, ordered Wyclyf's books burned (July 16, 1410), and excommunicated Hus. Prague was laid under an interdict (June 20, 1411) which stopped all religious services. At the king's suggestion, Hus left the city in October 1412, after publishing an appeal to Christ against the interdict, in order to relieve the people of Prague of the effects of the decree. He spent the next two years in southern Bohemia, preaching in the open and writing, while, in Prague, his opponents carried on an active campaign against him and his followers. They finally preferred charges of heresy and contumacy against him at the papal court. Hus appealed to a general council against what he held were false allegations, and when such a council was actually set for Constance late in 1414, he set forth to present his case. The Emperor Sigismund, as we have seen, sent a safe-conduct, but later, as presiding officer of the Council, repudiated his own guarantee of safety.

The result of Hus' trial was certain from the outset. He was condemned, almost solely on the basis of statements alleged to have been made in his work *De ecclesia* (*On the Church*). The leaders of the prosecution at the Council were, in addition to Czech and German clerics from Prague, the two eminent French cardinals, Peter d'Ailly and John Gerson, of whom we have heard as fervid and widely read philosophers and mystics. Whatever may have been the technical grounds of the condemnation and "relaxation to the secular arm," the essential fact was that the hierarchy could not tolerate Hus' concept of the Church as the congregation of the faithful, those predestined by God to be saved. On this basis the pope and the cardinals were not only superfluous but a hindrance to the Gospel. The hierarchy, in council assembled, could hardly be expected to permit such reasoning. Hus was burned at the stake in Constance on the morning of July 6, 1415. Burning for heresy was far from uncommon. This case was different and, as it turned out, fraught with grave consequences for the Roman Church, for it was not the thought of one man that was being repressed but the sense of right of an entire nation. The immediate answer to the burning was an indignant protest to the Council on September 2, 1415, signed by 452 Bohemian nobles and knights. Three days later the signatories defied the Council to meddle in the religious affairs of their country. This rebellion was something new. There was no pattern by which a council or the *curia* could adequately discipline a whole Christian nation.

In Bohemia, during Hus' absence, his friends and followers had continued their reform agitation. But new factors were entering the drama. Jacobellus of Misa, Hus' leading collaborator, was a strong advocate of communion by the laity "in both kinds" (*sub utraque specie*)—that is, the bread and the wine; hitherto the cup had been withheld from the laity. This novel teaching was immediately popular, and the chalice (*calix*) became a symbol among all classes of Czech society, from peasant to magnate, of the popular and national revolt against the control by the clergy of the means of grace. In this revolt we see further evidence of the growing feeling that the Church had failed to fulfill the spiritual needs of the layman.

The fourteenth century was an era in which the foundations of the unitary and exclusive hierarchical organization of the universal Church were being shaken from below. The Church's acceptance of the ordered philosophy of St. Thomas Aquinas was being challenged and rejected by many. Regimentation in speculation was no longer possible; philosophical thought was becoming independent. The mystics, rooted in the life of the common people, by their very basic approach to the sources of religious truth, the impulses and sensitivities of the individual soul, were dispensing with the mediation of the organized and sacramental Church. God and the soul of man could meet and commune. As for the heretics, almost all of them shared the tenet that the sacraments were not the exclusive possession of the Church and that the individual layman had the right of access to the Scriptures, to read and understand for himself. The two most potent of the later medieval heretics, Wyclyf and Hus, carried these presuppositions to their logical conclusions, rejecting the Roman Church, with the pope and the cardinals at its head, as the true Church of Christ. Wyclyf flatly pronounced the pope to be Antichrist, and Hus did not deny the assertion. His followers certainly acted as if they believed it. The established institution could not accept such fundamental divergence from its ancient and hallowed tradition. These portents of the secular age, when a man would be free to be outside the Church if he wished, are part and parcel of what we call broadly the Renaissance. Why the older methods were not effective in repressing this divergence we shall see when we treat of the Great Schism and the Councils.

SUGGESTIONS FOR FURTHER READING

D'Arcy, M. C., *Thomas Aquinas: Selected Writings.* Everyman's Library
Fairweather, E. R., *A Scholastic Miscellany: Anselm to Ockham.* Philadelphia, 1958
Hus, John, *The Church,* trans. D. S. Schaff. New York, 1915
The Letters of John Hus, trans. H. B. Workman and R. Pope. London, 1904
À Kempis, Thomas, *The Imitation of Christ.* Many editions
McKeon, R., *Selections from Medieval Philosophers.* 2 vols. New York, 1931
Petry, R. C., *Late Medieval Mysticism.* Philadelphia, 1957
Spinka, M., *Advocates of Reform, from Wyclyf to Erasmus.* Philadelphia, 1953
Suso, Heinrich, *The Life of the Servant,* trans. J. M. Clark. London, 1952
Theologia Germanica, in English. Many editions
Wyclyf, John, *Select English Writings,* ed. H. E. Winn. Oxford, 1929
Wyclyf, John, *Tracts and Treatises,* trans. R. Vaughan. London, 1845

d'Aygalliers, A. W., *Ruysbroeck.* London, 1925
Carré, M. H., *Realists and Nominalists.* Oxford, 1946
Clark, J. M., *The Great German Mystics: Eckhart, Tauler, and Suso.* Oxford, 1949
Faggin, G., *Meister Eckhart e la mistica tedisca preprotestante.* 1946
Gebhart, E., *Mystic Italy,* trans. E. M. Hulme. New York, 1922
Gilson, E., *History of Christian Philosophy in the Middle Ages.* New York, 1954
Gilson, E., *The Spirit of Medieval Philosophy.* New York, 1936
Hyma, A., *The Brethren of the Common Life.* Grand Rapids, 1950
Jones, R. M., *Studies in Mystical Religion.* New York, 1909
Kettlewell, S., *Thomas à Kempis and the Brothers of the Common Life.* 2 vols. London, 1882
Lechler, J., *John Wycliffe and His English Precursors.* London, 1884
Lücker, M. A., *Meister Eckhart und die Devotio Moderna.* 1950
Lützow, F., *Life and Times of Master John Hus.* London, 1909
Macfarlane, K. B., *John Wycliffe and the Beginnings of English Non-Conformity.* New York, 1953
Pantin, W. A., *The English Church in the Fourteenth Century.* Cambridge, 1955
Schaff, D. S., *John Hus.* New York, 1915
Underhill, E., *Mysticism: A Study in the Nature and Development of Man's Spiritual Consciousness.* New York, 1930
Underhill, E., *Mystics of the Church.* New York, 1926
Underhill, E., *Ruysbroeck.* London, 1914
de Vooght, P., *L'Hérésie de Jean Huss.* Louvain, 1960
Workman, H. B., *John Wyclif,* 2 vols. Oxford, 1926
de Wulf, M., *History of Medieval Philosophy.* 2 vols. New York, 1935–38

CHAPTER EIGHT

NORTHERN AND EASTERN EUROPE

NTIL recent times the northern and eastern areas and peoples of Europe have suffered from neglect on the part of historians and others interested in cultural development and interrelations. The beaten path for students of Western culture has lain, for the most part, west of the Rhine, in Italy, France, England, and, to a lesser degree, Spain. This preference for the western periphery has had its justifications in the past, but in the light of twentieth-century re-evaluations of cultural roots and patterns of political interaction, it is necessary to revise our perspectives. The north of Europe—Scandinavia and the Baltic basin—stands as a barrier between the great Eurasian power, Russia, and the West for almost a thousand miles. Directly south of the Baltic, reaching in an uneven line to the eastern Mediterranean for another thousand miles, lie the lands of the Slavic, Latin, Magyar, and Mediterranean peoples, who also have had to submit to attack, infiltration, and conquest from both sides. Their blood, their society, their institutions, their art, and their language all bear witness to the various pressures they have had to withstand. During the period of interest in this book, the tide flowed both ways, westward and eastward, and the resulting mixture and overlay of cultures and political patterns have left us a complex and puzzling set of historical problems.

The Scandinavian people, somewhat isolated from their southern neighbors by geography and climate, were converted to Christianity late. Although we know that there were missionaries in the north as early as 700 and that King Harald I (945–85) was baptized in 960, the eleventh century saw missionaries still contending with pagan religion. Denmark, close to the German bishopric of Hamburg-Bremen and influenced by her close relations with England, did not enter into formal relations with the Papacy until 1060. Norway and Iceland were Christianized under King Olaf (d. 1030), who became Norway's patron saint. In Sweden the work went more slowly; not until the mid-twelfth century was the whole of the country converted to the faith of the rest of Europe. An archbishopric was established at Lund in 1103 or 1104 with jurisdiction over Denmark and Sweden. In 1152 a separate archbishopric was established in Nidaros (later Trondheim) in Norway. Many of the early priests in these archbishoprics were Germans.

DENMARK TO THE UNION OF KALMAR

THE political history of the Scandinavian peoples is one of almost chaotic turbulence until the thirteenth century, when a semblance of order became discernible. The dynasties of Denmark, Sweden, and Norway had intermarried, with the usual results: disputed succession, wars and assassinations, regencies for minor children, and revolts of ambitious nobles fomented from within and without. Denmark, the most advanced of the three counties as well as the most populous and prosperous, had a long history of expansion behind her by this time. The southern part of Sweden, Skania, was Danish territory, as were parts of the southern and eastern coasts of the Baltic (the Pomeranian coast, Livonia, and Esthonia) and the Orkney and the Faeroe Islands. By early in the thirteenth century, Denmark, under Waldemar II (1202–41), had conquered Holstein and taken possession of the territories on the right bank of the Elbe. But in 1223 Waldemar was taken prisoner by Count Henry of Schwerin and forced to give up Hamburg and Lübeck, an imperial city. Danish control of the southern shore of the Baltic, excepting the island of Rügen, was broken. The Danish possessions on the eastern coast of the Baltic were simply allowed to go by default.

Internally, Denmark in the middle of the century was torn by conflicts among the kings, the Church, and the magnates. When Archbishop Jacob, who opposed the royal house, was deprived of his temporalities (1257), by King Christopher I (1252–59), Pope Alexander IV excommunicated the king (1259) and laid the country under an interdict. A civil war, lasting intermittently until 1273, resulted in a qualified victory for Jacob, to whom Christopher's son and successor, Eric V (Klipping, 1259–86), paid damages of fifteen thousand marks. A few years later, in 1282, the magnates forced King Eric V to grant a charter that specified their extensive rights and limited royal action against the nobility. Once the relationship of the magnates and the crown had been agreed upon and fixed in a document, the nobility apparently found that their interests lay on the side of the king in his disputes with the Church. Eric Klipping was assassinated in 1286, the third Danish king within thirty years to meet such an end.

The disputes that disturbed the kingdom for several decades after 1282 were between the Church and the monarchy. Archbishop Jens Grand, who was probably involved in the murder of King Eric Klipping, was captured, chained, and thrust into a dungeon, where he was kept almost immobile for two years. He finally escaped, swearing terrible oaths and vowing vengeance on the new king, Eric VI (Menved, 1286–1319). It was not what we would call a genteel society. Pope Boniface VIII, as a matter of course, put the kingdom under an interdict until the king paid a heavy fine, but the archbishop, for his health, was transferred to Riga. The distance from Denmark was thought to be salutary for him.

The relations between the Church and the monarchy did not improve in the next years. At the same time, the state was further weakened by depreciation of the coinage, by the king's hypothecation of numerous Danish lands to German nobles, and by heavy borrowing on the royal revenues of Skania (1318). Eric then used the moneys thus collected to wage costly wars to the south, in Mecklenburg and Pomerania. Just what could have been gained from the wars was never quite clear. The country entered on a period of internal anarchy which lasted to the middle of the fourteenth century. The German Count Geert III of Holstein gained almost complete ownership of Schleswig and, possessed of large holdings in Denmark, was for a decade the virtual ruler of the kingdom. German nobles and settlers streamed into Schleswig, which was lost to Denmark. The Danish monarchs were weak and defeatist. In 1332 large parts of Danish territory in southern Sweden were ceded to Magnus Eriksson, then king of Sweden (as Magnus II, 1319–65) and Norway (as Magnus VII, 1319–43). This was probably the lowest ebb of Danish national history. The Black Death, which hit Scandinavia late in 1348, was a further blow to the national spirit.

But the next half century saw a marked revival of spirit and vitality. King Waldemar IV Atterdag (1340–75) was ambitious and clever. He consolidated Danish holdings, reorganized the royal administration, out-negotiated the counts of Holstein, and took advantage of an uprising in Sweden to regain Skania, Halland, and Blekinge (1360). Perhaps the most important single act of his long reign was his arrangement of a marriage between his daughter Margaret and Haakon, heir to the crowns of Norway and Sweden. At one time he planned an invasion of England as an ally of France, to re-establish ancient Danish claims to the throne of England. His last years were less happy. He was at war with the Hanseatic League, consisting at that time of about eighty merchant cities of north Germany, from 1361, when he attacked and took the key Hansa city of Wisby on the island of Gotland, until 1370. At the end of the first four years of this war he was victorious; the Hansa had to ask for a truce (1365). But, regrouping its forces and gaining the support of the counts of Holstein and Albert of Mecklenburg, then king of Sweden, the Hansa attacked Waldemar in 1368, took Copenhagen, and forced the king to sue for peace. By the Peace of Stralsund (May 1370), the Hansa won both a naval and a diplomatic victory, gaining the right for its merchants to travel and trade freely in Denmark and Skania, to collect two-thirds of the revenues in certain ports for fifteen years, and to exercise a veto over Waldemar's successor if he failed to guarantee their liberties.

Shortly after the death of Waldemar in 1375, his five-year-old grandson, Olaf, was elected king of Denmark as Olaf II (1375–87). Olaf's father, Haakon VI, king of Norway (1355–80), and his mother, Margaret (Waldemar's daughter), ruled in his name. Haakon died in 1380, and since Olaf, thus king of Denmark by election and of Norway (as Olav V, 1380–87) by right of inheritance, was only ten years old, Margaret, herself queen of Norway, ruled over Denmark in her son's name. In 1385 Margaret proclaimed her son "rightful heir to Sweden." He died unmarried, at the age of seventeen, in 1387, thus eliminating the possibility of a union achieved by hereditary right. Nevertheless, the idea of such a union was still strong in all three countries. Within months of the death of Olaf, Margaret was elected by the diets of Denmark and Norway as "powerful lady and rightful ruler" of the two kingdoms. Later, in 1388, the Swedish diet elected her queen of Sweden. Her idea of a northern union was realized; it became a fact in her person. As a ruling sovereign she was charming, firm, and persuasive; but she was astute enough to realize that such a union had to be formalized if it was to have any permanence. She therefore called the notables of the three kingdoms to a meeting at Kalmar in 1397. The notables crowned her grandnephew, Eric of Pomerania, king in all three lands (Eric VII of Denmark, Eric XIII of Sweden, 1397–1437), and then signed a document that was a sort of constitution for the Union of Kalmar. The three kingdoms were to retain their distinct entities but, having a monarch in common, would act in consultation and for their mutual interests. The document was never ratified by the several diets but as long as Margaret lived the union which it so hopefully described was an actuality.

NORWAY

NORWAY, more remote than Denmark from the centers of Western culture, was less advanced in society and institutions than her southern neighbor. Just as Denmark, obeying the urge to expand, had made settlements in Esthonia and Courland and along the southern shore of the Baltic, so Norway had looked across the North Sea and sent her ships toward the setting sun. Norwegians had settled in the islands off Scotland, the Faeroes, the Hebrides, the Orkneys, and the Shetlands. Farther west, Iceland was a Norwegian settlement, although she resisted incorporation into the mainland kingdom until 1263, when she accepted Norwegian sovereignty. Greenland was discovered in about the year 1000, and a few hardy Norwegians remained, for a short time, on its southern coast, but there was no formal recognition of Norwegian sovereignty until 1261.

The era from 1130 to 1228 in Norway has quite properly been called the Age of Civil Wars. The nobility in these years was perhaps more turbulent and unruly than that in any other Scandinavian kingdom. The twelfth century was a period of violence, intrigue, frequent royal murders, and wars of revenge. Yet the age was not without some gains in governmental structure and social and economic growth. It was followed by a period (1228–1318) which has been called, by contrast, Norway's Age of Greatness. During these years, peace was maintained, royal power was consolidated, and the aristocracy was confident and contented in its favorable social and political position. The merchant class, though increasingly affected by the rivalry of English traders and, toward the end of the century, by the aggressive competition of the merchants of the German Hansa, made substantial gains. The kings of this century and a royal council of leading magnates, lay and ecclesiastical, established a machinery for government as efficient as any in western Europe at that time. Perhaps as important as any other event in this age was the change that took place in the legal structure. King Haakon IV (the Old, 1217–63) undertook to codify the ancient laws of the kingdom; and his son, Magnus VI (the Lawmender, 1263–80), with the assistance of counselors trained in Roman and canon law, brought the ancient laws into general accord with the most advanced legislation in the West. A significant feature of this legislative reform was that the king and not the people was assumed to be the source of law. Although there was as yet no clear distinction between the king as an individual person and the king as the crown, comprehending the total will of the realm, the ground was laid for this important concept.

The cities of the western and southern coasts continued to prosper. Nidaros, the site of the archbishopric, remained a cultural center but lost the economic race to Bergen, which became the largest and richest city of the kingdom. As the center of North Sea trade, Bergen was completely cosmopolitan. Traders from England, Spain, France, the Lowlands, the Baltic, and the Hanseatic cities were so numerous that they threatened to crowd the Norwegians out of business in their own city. After a series of dynastic involvements with the Danish and Swedish ruling houses, Norway, at the end of the century, was ruled by a foreign king. There was, however, a measure of economic and political autonomy remaining, owing in great part to the efficient machinery of local and state government set up by Magnus the Lawmender, which continued to function in spite of a foreign monarch and a partially foreign court. The measures taken by Haakon V (1299–1319), who excluded foreigners from participating in internal trade, were also a reason for the survival of Norwegian economic and political integrity. By the early fourteenth century, Norway's foreign trade was essentially in German hands, which augured ill for the political independence of the Norwegians. Concurrently, there was sharp deterioration in Norwegian political vigor.

Haakon VI, son of Magnus II of Sweden (VII of Norway), held the Norwegian throne for thirty years (1350–80), five years under his father's regency, the rest as direct ruler. He was ten years of age at his accession. The Black Death (1349–50), transmitted through the sea traffic to Bergen and Stavanger, had struck Norway heavily; but a well-trained bureaucracy kept the ravages from turning into a catastrophe. Grown to manhood, Haakon strengthened the administration, gathered around him the ablest advisers in the kingdom, and was respected and loved by all classes of his people. In 1363 by his marriage to Margaret, daughter of King Waldemar IV of Denmark, Haakon was drawn, somewhat reluctantly, into the struggle for power in Sweden and Denmark. His father, the king of Sweden, was not a strong monarch, and the pro-German faction of the Swedish nobility brought in Albert of Mecklenburg as king in 1363. Haakon was defeated in the brief war that ensued and withdrew to Norway. In the revival of the Danish war with the Hansa, Haakon allied with his father-in-law and shared in Waldemar's defeat. But since Haakon was not the direct object of the Hanseatic drive, the terms he was obliged to accept were mild, a simple truce for five years. He stood firm against the more extreme demands and came to a workable agreement with the League in 1376. He reasserted his claims to the throne of Sweden and did in fact rule in the western part of that kingdom. The wars had been expensive, and he was driven to borrow heavily and to debase the coinage.

We have seen how Olaf, already heir to Norway, was elected king of Denmark in 1375, and how the Union of Kalmar was formed in 1397. It is easy to understand how the history of each of the three kingdoms became inextricably involved in that of the others. Their problems overlapped, their enemies were frequently identical, and the intermarriages of their ruling families bound them even more closely together. The Union of Kalmar, therefore, was only an attempt to formalize a situation whose actuality was familiar and widely accepted among the Scandinavian peoples.

The Union was not destined to have a long life as a constitutional arrangement. There were many factors working against its permanence. Margaret had made some mistakes that, under successors of less prestige and winsomeness, made total cooperation impossible. Denmark was the most populous, the most advanced, and the most powerful of the three countries. Margaret (herself a Dane) chose Danes as her advisers and officials in Norway and Sweden. She also made a Dane archbishop of Lund in Sweden. She never called together the national council of either Sweden or Norway. She occasionally gave fiefs in Norway and Sweden to Danes and Germans. She failed, in spite of great political sagacity, to see that she was thus affronting national feelings in both countries, at a time when nationalism was a growing force all over Europe.

The young Eric of Pomerania, who was Margaret's choice to succeed her, was not without preparation for his task. But his very ambition to retake Schleswig from the counts of Holstein exposed him to attack from recalcitrant Swedish nobles. He was, in fact, opposed in both Norway and Sweden, and a rebellion in 1434 headed by Engelbrekt Engelbrektson, centered in the mining area of Dalecarlia, and supported by the miners and the merchants as well as by the nobles, led, after fighting, negotiation, and broken royal promises, to the deposition of Eric (1439) in Denmark and Sweden. In 1440 these two countries chose Christopher of Bavaria (Christopher III of Denmark, d. 1448) as Eric's successor. Norway also accepted Christopher in 1442, thus again establishing the union.

Upon the death of Christopher, a new line, the house of Oldenburg, appeared on the Scandinavian thrones in the person of Christian I. Christian, chosen king of Denmark in 1448 and of Norway in 1449, ruled until 1481, paying most attention to increasing the possessions of his house. Although he did not lack ability, he was wasteful, grasping, and capricious. After defeating the Swedes, he was recognized as king of Sweden in 1457, and thus the union was once more in effect, for the third time in twenty years. But Sweden wanted no Danish rule, and there was strong, if intermittent, support for the marshal of the kingdom, Karl Knutsson. Knutsson was three times in actual possession of the throne (as Charles VIII) and twice driven out before establishing his line in power. The late fifteenth century, when Sweden was ruled by Knutsson's nephew, Sten Sture the Elder, as regent, was a period of quiet and recovery unknown since the days of Margaret.

SWEDEN

WE HAVE seen how the Scandinavian kingdoms were from earliest times closely related by language, culture, geography, and interest. The closeness of their political and economic relationships varied from time to time, as internal dynastic accidents incident to marriage alliances and external pressures such as German commercial expansion caused a temporary shifting of political alignments. But the fact remains that the history and development of these three kingdoms were naturally and inseparably entwined. Thus, in sketching the stories of Denmark and Norway in the later Middle Ages, we have told much of the story of Sweden. It remains only to make certain aspects of that story more distinct.

Norway, which faced mostly west, had colonies in the islands north of Scotland, in Iceland, and in Greenland and had ancient and close ties with England and Scotland. Denmark, next door to Germany, was engaged in a running struggle to protect her southern frontier from the German counts of Holstein. Culturally, she was also close to Germany, and her literature and language show unmistakably this proximity. Sweden, on the other hand, faced east and south. Her natural areas of expansion lay in Finland and along the eastern Baltic coast. The Swedish island of Gotland was an obvious middle point for the whole Baltic area, of which Wisby was one of the most important ports. Sweden was thus tightly involved with German trade with Novgorod and was open to pressures from Muscovy. At the end of the thirteenth century, Sweden was greatly weakened by factional strife, but she gained headway under Magnus II Eriksson (1319–63, d. 1374). During his long reign, Magnus made some progress toward centralization of royal power, abolished the remnants of slavery (1335), codified civil and criminal law, became involved in a war between the Hansa and Waldemar IV of Denmark, had to face a rebellion led by his son (1356–58), was excommunicated by the Pope, lost Wisby to Waldemar, and was forced to fight Albert of Mecklenburg, to whom the Swedish magnates offered the crown in 1363. Albert, who claimed the throne of Sweden from 1363 to 1389, had his difficulties, too. The Swedish nobility had no love for the German officials whom Albert brought with him, and when Margaret, widow of Haakon VI and daughter-in-law of their own king Magnus II Ericsson, was made queen of both Denmark and Norway, they invited her to accept a similar title for Sweden (1388). The three kingdoms were, at this point, united under a single ruler, and the Union of Kalmar of 1397, was, as we have seen, only a formalization of the fact. From this time the history of the three kingdoms, though there was no little tension and misunderstanding among them and the Union itself was seldom an actuality, must be considered together.

Literature and Art

SCANDINAVIA in the later Middle Ages and the Renaissance cannot be regarded as a great center of cultural development or artistic creativity. All three countries were too close to their primitive state. It has been estimated that as many as sixty students a year went to Paris from Scandinavia in the early fourteenth century, including a few from Finland. But this stream was soon diverted to universities nearer home, at Prague, Cracow, Heidelberg, and Erfurt. Some completed the circle and added Paris to their curriculum. But when universities were founded in 1419 at Rostock on the Baltic and in 1456 at Greifswald, the majority of young Scandinavian scholars were satisfied to study nearer home. Some years later (1475), Queen Dorothea obtained a papal charter for a university at Copenhagen, which opened in 1479 with a predominantly German faculty. The Swedes could do no less; in 1477 a university was founded at Uppsala. Apparently Swedish students still wished to get their education outside of Scandinavia, for in 1498 King John decreed that no Swedish student might study abroad before spending three years at either the University of Copenhagen or the University of Uppsala. In any event, on the eve of the Reformation, Scandinavia had institutions for instruction at the highest level. The first printing press in Scandinavia was established at Odense in 1482, but the art made very modest progress.

Literature in the period of the union was neither original nor brilliant. There was a fashion for native translations from Latin sources, such as Geoffrey of Monmouth, and from some of the medieval French romances. Of more historical significance but of a hardly higher literary quality were the vernacular rhymed chronicles, both Swedish and Danish. Nothing can be found in Scandinavia resembling the atmosphere of fifteenth-century Latin humanism or the art of the Renaissance. In the plastic arts, German, or rather Hanseatic, Gothic style dominated. Scandinavia as a whole went directly from the Gothic Middle Ages to the Protestant Reformation without passing through the Renaissance in the form and with the ideals usually associated with that term.

THE EASTERN BALTIC

THE eastern shore of the Baltic Sea was inhabited by small groups of native peoples—the Finns, the Esths (related to the Finns), the Kurs, the Livs, the Letts, and the Lithuanians. The first two groups were of Mongolian origin; the last four were indigenous Baltic peoples, to whom the *Borussi* (original Prussians) should be added. Sweden early took possession of Finland. The Danes had established trading posts along the southern coast of the Gulf of Finland in the twelfth century but relinquished their hold in the middle of the fourteenth century. The greatest colonizing element along the coast was the German merchant and missionary. Until the arrival of the Germans in the late twelfth century, the Baltic peoples were under constant pressure from the Slavs of Novgorod and environs. The bishopric of Riga was established in 1186 by Meinhard, an Augustinian monk who had been sent from Bremen as a missionary; and the crusading order of the Knights of the Sword followed almost immediately. This order, which occupied itself with building castles and bringing in German peasant farmers, was absorbed in 1237 by the Teutonic Knights, whose seat, from 1230, was in Prussia. The inevitable struggle between the Knights, pressing eastward, and the Slavs, pushing westward under the leadership of Prince Alexander Nevsky, resulted in a titanic battle on the ice of Lake Peipus early in 1242. The battle was won by Slavs, but the German drive kept on relentlessly. The gaps in the line of German control of the littoral were closed by 1253, when Memel was founded at the mouth of the Niemen River. However, the resistance of the native Kurs and Zemgallians (a tribe of the Letts) to Germanization continued with savage brutality on both sides until 1290. In this year, the Zemgallians migrated southward in a body to join the Lithuanian Samogitian princes (dukes) in their perpetual war against the Teutonic Knights. Since this Order was under the special care of the Papacy, the whole Baltic conquest, the result of a crusade, became virtually a papal state. The Prince-Archbishop of Riga, Albert II, became the ruler of the Baltic, although the Order was not a very obedient subordinate.

In the West the fourteenth and fifteenth centuries saw the feudal system weaken its hold on the land and the peasant. In the Baltic empire of the Teutonic Order, this same period witnessed the tightening of the grasp of the German knights on the land and the peasantry. The native nobility had been either annihilated in the resistance to Germanization or forcibly assimilated. The effort to bring German peasants to till the sandy soil of the coast had failed, and the native peasantry became a serf class, working for the German lords. The manorial system, with all its rigors, was introduced. As it turned out, the conquest was a transfer from military oppression to social and economic subjection. This thralldom was not effected without resistance and bloodshed. In Esthonia in the spring of 1343 a peasant revolt resulted in the death of more than eighteen hundred German and Danish nobles. Reval was besieged by a great mob of peasants, and the Knights were able to restore order only at heavy cost to themselves and the peasants.

Riga, ideally situated for commerce, near the mouth of the Daugava (Dvina) River, became a member of the Hanseatic League in 1282, and the Hansa and the Teutonic Order were soon in business together, sharing the Russian trade and profitably marketing their own farm surpluses. The natives who remained in the city were reduced to small retail businesses, the crafts, and menial labor. These same natives hoped in vain to profit from the struggle for power that broke out in 1297 between the German merchant class, supported by the archbishop of Riga, and the aristocratic Order. This struggle did not end even in 1330, when the Order gained a victory, which was confirmed by Emperor Louis IV in 1332. Some years later, under Emperor Charles IV, who was more commercially minded than his predecessor, the decision was reversed in favor of the archbishop and the merchants. At the height of its power, in 1346, the Order bought Esthonia from King Waldemar IV of Denmark, and with that acquisition reached its greatest territorial extent.

The Grand Principality of Lithuania

IN THE meantime, to the south, the Teutonic Order, which had come to Prussia in 1230, had been carrying on an implacable crusade against the *Borussi*. By 1283 the Order had crushed all resistance in Prussia, and the *Borussi* soon thereafter vanished from history. The Order continued its push toward the east against the Lithuanians of Samogitia, but this effort was less successful than that against the *Borussi*, for the Lithuanians were fortunate in their leadership. The Grand Princes of the late thirteenth and the fourteenth centuries, Mindaugas (d. 1263), Vytenis (d. 1316), and Gedyminas (d. 1341), were men of courage and political sagacity who were determined to limit German control to the bare coastline of the Baltic.

Gedyminas was especially tenacious in his opposition to the Order and fought with diplomacy as well as with the sword. He made extensive conquests to the east and to the south, until White Russia and much of Little Russia formed parts of his dominions. He even threatened the rule of the Tartar Khan Uzbeg,

Northern and Eastern Europe, ca. 1350

ruler of the Golden Horde. These conquests achieved and his eastern frontier
secured, he turned his attention to his western antagonist, the Teutonic Order,
whose treacheries and injustices he was determined to avenge. In 1323 he invited the archbishop of Riga and other churchmen to Vilna and there signed
a treaty of peace, obviously aimed at the aggressive policy of the Order. The
Order, indignant at this consolidation of its enemies, renewed hostilities. The
Germans were thus forced to wage war on two fronts—to the north along the
coast, against the opposition of the Church and the merchants of Riga, in order
to widen their narrow hold on Memel and the mouth of the Niemen; and to

the southeast in the direction of Grodno, against Gedyminas and his Lithuanians. For the next sixty years, this campaign was at least an annual effort, and occasionally there were three or four expeditions in a single year, against the heathen Lithuanians, who sometimes returned the compliment. In 1362 the Order captured Kovno; in 1362 the Narew River was crossed. In 1370 the Lithuanian Grand Prince Olgierd sent a boastful notice to the Grand Master of the Order, telling him that he, Olgierd, was going to attack the German fort at Memel. The Order's forces were too strong and well disciplined for so brazen an attack on the heart of its defense system to succeed, but it was a narrow escape.

This was the last such attack from the east. A decade or more of disputes among claimants to the rule of Lithuania encouraged the Order in its hope of taking over the principality by negotiation or treachery. Olgierd was succeeded (1377) by his son Jagiełło, but the latter's cousin Witold refused to accept his leadership and joined forces with the Order for an invasion of his own country. Jagiełło weaned Witold away from this alliance in 1384 by giving him Samogitia to rule. The Order was still strong and determined, however, and Jagiełło thought it prudent to take advantage of the circumstances of the Polish succession to solve his own problem. The crown of Poland had rested on the head of a young princess, Jadwiga, since the death in 1382 of her father, Louis I, king of Poland and Hungary. Jagiełło sought her hand, and the magnates—against her will, as she was in love with a childhood playmate, William of Habsburg—decided in favor of the Lithuanian marriage, which took place in 1386. Jagiełło accepted Christianity for himself and for his country and became king of Poland as Władysław II (1386–1434). The Teutonic Order was thwarted, for its repeated claim that it was leading a crusade against a heathen country now became implausible. The dynastic union of the Grand Principality (Duchy) of Lithuania and the kingdom of Poland thus deprived the Order of its original and basic reason for existence and was a landmark in Baltic history.

POLAND UNDER THE LAST PIASTS AND THE JAGIELLONIANS

POLAND in 1386 could look back upon a troubled past. Christianized in the tenth century, Poland had had close relations with the West, especially with the Holy Roman Empire, since the days of Otto III (d. 1002). The geographical location of the Polish state, with no natural frontiers on the east or west, presented her rulers with several difficult problems. The Germans pushed into Poland from the west; the original Prussians on the Baltic shore obstructed access to the sea on the north; Lithuanians, Little Russians, and, from the early thirteenth century, Tartars made onslaughts on her southeastern boundaries. Dynastic divisions also contributed to the process of fragmentation. During most of the thirteenth century, Poland was divided into four principal sovereignties: Silesia, largely Germanized, prosperous, and progressive; Great Poland, the western part; Little Poland, around the capital of Cracow; and Mazovia, covering the middle Vistula basin. These were not stable territories, and there were other subdivisions.

It was a period of political misfortunes; yet there were compensations. German merchants and craftsmen, clerics and colonists, came to the towns and country-sides in great numbers. They brought Western culture and institutions with them with the result that the cultural level of Poland at the beginning of the fourteenth century was higher than that of any other Baltic power, excluding the Empire as such. Furthermore, the Polish church, unlike the temporal state, had retained its unity, so that an important emotional factor tending toward integration remained, awaiting only the impulse of a national leader to contribute to the reunification of the state. Toward the end of the thirteenth century and at times early in the fourteenth century, a large part of southern Poland was ruled by the Czech king of Bohemia who claimed the title of King of Poland. However, the Přemyslid line, which had reigned in Bohemia for almost four centuries, died out in 1306, and Poland was ready to set out again on the rocky road to unity.

Władysław I Łokietek (1306–33) saw clearly Poland's need for access to the Baltic along her main river, the Vistula. The Teutonic Order, then in possession of Pomerania, the city of Danzig, and Prussia, was the obstacle. It was obvious to Łokietek that, in order to recapture her natural coastline to the west, Poland must have peace and allies in the east and moral justification for an aggressive policy toward the Order. The Papacy made a decision in favor of Poland's claim to Pomerania in 1321; Łokietek then began a series of wars with the Order to implement that decision. The first wars were moderately successful, but John, the king of Bohemia, took over much of the duchy of Silesia in 1331, and Łokietek ended his reign in 1333 with less territory than he had had ten years before. Nevertheless, his aims became those of his successors: one Polish king-dom, with access to the sea; limitation of the power of the Teutonic Order; and expansion to the south and east.

Casimir III (the Great, 1333–70) was a worthy successor to his father. Seeking allies to counteract the diplomatic and military strength of the Teutonic Order and John of Bohemia, who claimed the Polish crown, he found them in Emperor Louis IV (Louis of Bavaria) and King Louis I of Hungary, and was soon able to persuade King John to abandon his claims. Casimir's hopes of regaining Pomerania, pursued by patient and deft diplomacy, were doomed to disappoint-ment, but he did contrive to increase Polish domains in the southeast. By 1349 he was the ruler of the territory around Lwów, which remained a part of Poland for many generations. He joined Podolia to his kingdom in 1352.

Casimir was a ruler of exceptional breadth of vision and intellectual capacity. There was not an aspect of national life on which he did not leave a deep impress. Not only did he have a vast over-all plan for Poland's political life, but he recog-nized the need for organizational efficiency. He reorganized the royal chancery and codified Polish law—a tremendous task because of the irregular history of the country—into the "Statutes of Casimir the Great." He was an intelligent patron of the arts and ordered the construction of many churches in the later Gothic style. In the course of reorganizing his chancery and staffing his bureau-cracy, Casimir was made aware of the need for advanced study and learned officials. In the thirteenth and early fourteenth centuries numbers of Polish students had gone to foreign universities, at Bologna, Padua, and Paris. After the foundation of the University of Prague by Charles IV in 1348, young and ambitious Poles streamed across the mountains to Bohemia. Casimir, hoping that a Polish university would attract and train his subjects who might otherwise have gone to Prague to study, founded a university at Cracow in 1364 modeled after the University of Bologna. The king manifested his desire to support the cultural growth of his land by his continued interest in the work of the university, his concern for the improvement of conditions in the Church, and his patronage of art and letters. He built hundreds of castles and public buildings, including the royal castle of the Wawel on a hill overlooking Cracow.

Casimir's relations with his neighbor, Charles IV, king of Bohemia and Holy Roman Emperor, were an improvement over his relations and those of Łokietek with Charles' father, King John of Bohemia. Charles respected Casimir's high sense of duty and his cultural interests. A treaty of mutual aid and friendship was signed between them in November 1348 and reaffirmed in 1356. Casimir's consistent firmness and dignity in his dealings with friend and foe, hardly less than the soundness of his policies in bringing law, prosperity, and order to his state and in increasing her territorial extent, won him respect throughout Europe and raised Poland to the honored position of a European power.

Casimir had no male heir and was therefore destined to be the last of the Piast dynasty. On his death in 1370, he was succeeded by the husband of one of his daughters, King Louis I (the Great) of Hungary (king of Poland 1370–82), a descendant of the Angevin house which ruled in southern Italy and Sicily. The Polish magnates obtained from Louis at a diet at Košice in 1374 some material concessions as to finance and taxation, thus setting in motion the machinery of "capitulations" which was to contribute heavily to the ultimate downfall of Poland. Louis was able to raise the intellectual and artistic level of the court at Cracow; he had in his train not a few Italian scholars and artists of competence. But the Poles were not used to being ruled by a foreigner, and Louis was not popular. The fact that the Piasts had been a national and hereditary dynasty had tended to hold the kingdom together. This natural unity was disturbed by the election of a non-Polish monarch. During his reign, Louis spent most of his time outside Poland. After Louis' death, the acceptance of Jagiełło, Grand Prince of Lithuania, as king, in 1386, involving a dynastic union between Poland and the vast territory and various peoples over whom Jagiełło ruled, put a dangerous strain upon the forces of unity within the Polish state.

Nevertheless, the two countries, Poland and Lithuania, had at least two potent concerns in common: both were threatened by the Teutonic Order, both looked with yearning upon lands that they had lost to the Order. Related to these concerns was the fact that Lithuania, extending far into Russian territory, needed the assurance of substantial support in the rear, and Poland, not completely sure of her southern border on Bohemia and Hungary, also needed support. The dynastic union, therefore, in spite of some disadvantages, was a boon to both parties.

After the dynastic union of 1386 between Lithuania and Poland, the Teutonic Order was faced with what appeared to be a united enemy on its eastern and southern flanks; yet it maintained an aggressive attitude. But Jagiełło, by tact or by firmness, managed to keep the peace on his eastern and northwestern borders as long as Jadwiga lived. The queen, on her part, showed statesmanlike qualities perhaps superior to those of her brilliant husband. She initiated constitutional changes in the monarchy which, if carried out, would have markedly improved the structure of the state. Educated at the highly sophisticated courts of Buda and Vienna under Italian and French influences, she had religious and intellectual interests which raised the cultural level of Poland above that of any previous era. Almost unaided, she revived the University of Cracow, which had almost vanished, and supported reform in the Church and initiative in art and letters. She was, simply put, one of Poland's greatest rulers.

After Jadwiga's death in 1399, Jagiełło's principal problem was to maintain royal authority in the two divergent parts of his realm. The Polish nobles felt themselves superior to this less cultivated prince, while the Lithuanian nobles were irritated at Jagiełło's prolonged absences in effete Cracow. They needed little encouragement to use their independence to increase their lands eastward and southward. Jagiełło's cousin Witold, as Grand Prince of Lithuania, had ambitious visions of subjecting Moscow to his rule, but the eastern reaches of his far-flung conquests were very difficult to maintain and the task exceeded his military forces. While he was campaigning in southern Red Russia and beyond the Dnieper, the Teutonic Knights were overrunning Samogitia and the valley of the Niemen. They were unwilling to accept as genuine the conversion of pagan Lithuania to Christianity at Jagiełło's order in 1386, and a major war was inevitable. Jagiełło, supported by Witold, who had returned from his eastern campaign with some other lesser princes and a few Czech mercenaries, met the Knights between Tannenberg and Grunwald in southern Prussia in July 1410 and crushed the army of the Order. The treaty signed at Toruń (Thorn) the next year was lenient toward the Order. Undoubtedly Poland lost a great opportunity to repossess her Baltic littoral, a recovery which had been the dream of her more farsighted monarchs for centuries. Two years later Jagiełło signed with Witold the Union of Horodło, which bound Lithuania and Poland more closely together. It was, in fact, an effort on Jagiełło's part to forestall the diplomacy of the Emperor Sigismund, who was attempting to entice Witold into the anti-Polish camp with promises of a royal crown.

In the remaining years of his reign, Jagiełło saw the Polish magnates (upper nobility) rise to claim their ancient privileges, and his own prestige and authority diminish. In 1424 a son, Władysław, was born of Jagiełło's fourth marriage, but a group of the nobility, while recognizing that the young prince had prior hereditary rights to the succession, nevertheless insisted upon their right to *elect* him as Władysław III (1434-44). Witold died in 1430, and Jagiełło four years later, at the great age of eighty-six. Despite the rise in the power of the magnates and the decline of royal authority in Jagiełło's last years, his long reign had made Poland-Lithuania powerful. His descendants were to rule in Poland through her period of greatest glory, until 1572, in Bohemia for two generations, from 1471 to 1526, and in Hungary from 1490 to 1526. A federated state of Central Europe was never nearer realization than under the Jagiellonian dynasty.

For a decade after the death of Jagiełło, Zbigniew Oleśnicki, bishop of Cracow and leader of the magnates in their movement to regain power, dominated Polish policy. A devout churchman, he rigorously disciplined the lesser nobles and bourgeoisie who sympathized with the Hussite movement. He supported Sigismund against his rebellious Czech subjects and then sided with Albert of

Habsburg (Emperor Albert II, 1438–39), during his brief occupancy of the imperial and the Bohemian thrones. In 1443 Oleśnicki recovered a part of Silesia from Bohemian possession.

The ancient struggle between Slav and German had not, in the meantime, lost any of its bitterness. Humiliated at Grunwald in 1410, the Teutonic Order took some years to lick its wounds, but the concentration of the armies of Poland-Lithuania on the eastern marches, as well as the absence from Poland of a large Polish-Lithuanian army fighting in Bohemia on the side of the Hussites against Emperor Sigismund, encouraged the Order to take the offensive again. At first, in the 1420's, there was guerilla warfare on both sides that, while laying Prussia waste, brought no decision. On the death of Witold in 1430, Lithuania's position was difficult, and Witold's successor as Grand Prince, Jagiełło's frustrated brother, Swidrigiełło, was an intriguing and ambitious character who made matters worse. He rejected the sovereignty of Poland and allied with the Order. The Knights, welcoming this disastrous split in the Polish-Lithuanian state, invaded Polish land, only to be defeated decisively in 1431 and again in 1433. The settlement of the dispute between the two Christian states was brought before a Church council at Basel (see Chapter 11), without a clear decision for either side.

The Order, it seems, had learned little from its previous defeats. In 1435 the Knights once again invaded Poland. This time they were allied, incongruously, with Russian Orthodox forces; with Korybut, who had learned Hussite tactics in Bohemia; and with Swidrigiełło; they were blessed hopefully by Emperor Sigismund. When the armies, large for those days, met north of Vilna, the Knights and their mismated allies were outmaneuvered and outfought. In the negotiations for peace the Poles won an important point: the Empire was henceforth to refrain from interfering, directly or indirectly, in Polish relations with the Order. From his firm conduct of the war the Polish king, Władysław III, gained some needed prestige in Lithuania, whose struggle for independence was a constant source of concern to the Polish monarchy.

The interests of the neighboring states of Central Europe—Poland-Lithuania, Bohemia, and Hungary—were sufficiently similar to inaugurate what might be called an era of federalism, of dynastic alliances among the states that faced the growing power of Muscovy in the east, and, as we shall see, of the Ottoman Turks in the southeast and south. These eastern pressures had taken the place of the German pressure from the west, which subsided at about the same time, and had the additional effect of inducing the Central European states to place more emphasis upon their Western, Latin connections and traditions. In these centuries, the Latin language, Latin education, the Roman Church, with all its powerful moral and emotional appeals, and Western trends in thought and custom gained an irrevocable hold on the peoples of Central Europe. There was much truth in the saying that the Pole, the Czech, and the Magyar of the late Middle Ages were more Roman than the Holy Roman Empire and more Catholic than the pope.

Oleśnicki's plans for collaboration between Poland and Hungary led to Polish support of Hungary in her war against the Turks. The disastrous defeat of the

Hungarian forces under Władisław III (who ruled Hungary as Wladislas I) at Varna in 1444 spelled the end of these hopes.

Casimir, the younger brother of King Władysław III of Poland, was already Grand Prince of Lithuania. In 1447 he accepted the crown of Poland as Casimir IV on favorable terms and ruled until 1492. He aligned himself with the party that had opposed Oleśnicki and showed remarkable tact and firmness, both in internal affairs and in the international arena. Against the opposition of the magnates of Poland as well as of Lithuania, he regained for the crown rights and territories which his father, Jagiełło, had been obliged to surrender.

The Ottoman Empire had its most spectacular success—the capture of Constantinople—in 1453, during the long reign of Casimir IV. Since Turkish resources were thereafter freed for further action elsewhere, the pressure from the south on Poland's possessions of Podolia and Moldavia increased immeasurably. At the same time the aggressive temper of the Teutonic Order made war on the northwestern frontier certain. Casimir had to choose which front he would defend: that facing the Baltic or that on the southeast, along the Black Sea. He decided first to settle matters with the Order. There followed the tedious Thirteen Years' War (1453–66) which, according to the terms of the Second Peace of Toruń (1466), resulted in the final humiliation of the Order, the incorporation of Royal Prussia (or Polish Pomerania) and the mouth of the Vistula, with Danzig, as an integral part of the Polish kingdom, and the reduction of ducal Prussia * to the status of a feudal fief of the Polish king, for which the Grand Master should give homage. Thus Casimir achieved what his predecessors had sought in vain to compass: he put Poland firmly on the Baltic Sea, in full control of her own natural waterway, the Vistula, and the precious port of Danzig. The Teutonic Order subdued, Casimir devoted his energies to the southeastern frontiers and waged campaigns against the Tartars and the Turks, but with less favorable results. The Polish frontiers had to be withdrawn from the Black Sea, and the Turks took control of the coastline to the Dnieper River.

Upon the death of the Hussite king, George of Poděbrady, in Bohemia, Casimir secured the Bohemian crown for his son Władysław, who ruled as Vladislav II of Bohemia. Two decades later, when the elective king of Hungary, Mathias Corvinus, died, Władisław was elected King Wladislas II of Hungary as well. A third son, John Albert, succeeded Casimir as king of Poland (1492–1501), and a fourth son, Alexander, was chosen Grand Prince of Lithuania. Thus the Jagiellonian dynasty ruled in all three kingdoms. On the death of Vladislav II in 1516, his nine-year-old son Louis II succeeded to the throne of Hungary and Bohemia. There was no constitutional union among the three states; nevertheless, a kind of Jagiellonian empire of Central Europe did exist. Since the days of the Roman Empire there had never been in Europe a peacetime domain so extensive or so crucially placed. Its life-span, however, was destined to be short, its impress on history only minor. Its sudden dissolution in 1526, as a result of the death of the young King Louis II of Hungary and Bohemia, demonstrated how fragile this structure actually was.

* This territory would correspond roughly to what has been called, since 1701, East Prussia.

Detail from *The Battle of Grunwald,* wall painting by Jan Matejko, Polish Romantic painter (1838–93), in the National Museum, Warsaw [J. NIKIFOROW].

Governmental Institutions

IT WILL by now have become clear that the organization of the immense Polish-Lithuanian state was loose and its governmental institutions in flux. There were, however, some features sufficiently constant to merit description.

197

Poland had for centuries suffered from separatism, and only periodically, under a strong monarch, were these centrifugal forces brought under control. The concept of the crown, therefore, had never really dominated Polish thought. The *szlachta* (lower nobility) and the Church, both of which were strongly nationalistic in orientation, had grown in power and prestige in the fourteenth and fifteenth centuries. The death of the last of the traditional Piast dynasty, Casimir III (the Great) in 1370, and the accession of a foreigner, Louis I of Hungary, to the Polish throne profoundly affected the position of the crown in Poland. Louis, as we have seen, was obliged to grant the nobility as a class a Charter of Rights in 1374. Thenceforth Poland was, explicitly or implicitly, a state in which the nobility represented the will of the whole people. No king could rule or reign without its consent. The king's Council of State was made up of a few magnates, including the ruling officials of the kingdom. The magnates were usually allied with the ecclesiastical hierarchy, most of whom came from the leading families. The lesser *szlachta* found their interests running parallel with those of the bourgeoisie, who were growing in numbers, wealth, and influence throughout the fifteenth century.

The earliest records of Polish administration speak of the *wojewody* as military commanders, appointed by the king and attached to his court. As the king steadily lost power from the twelfth century onward, the *wojewody* became almost independent princes, and lost interest in acting as agents of the monarch. A new official, the *starosta* (literally "caretaker") then appeared. In the meantime, a subordinate military official, the *kasztelan* (from the Latin *castellanus*) had taken over the military functions of the *wojewody*. By the fourteenth century, however, this latter official had lost some of his authority and the *starosta* began to control civil, military, and even judicial representation of the army. There were generally about a half-dozen *kasztelanaty* in each *wojewódstwo*. All these officials came to be selected by the royal Council of State, although a strong king might be able to influence the nominations in his own favor.

The Council of State gradually developed into the *Sejm* or diet, a body in which the magnates sat together with the higher royal officials and the prelates of the Church. As their economic power began to make itself felt, representatives of the lesser nobility and a few delegates from the royal cities, who together formed a Chamber of Deputies, joined the *Sejm*. Those who sat in this lower house were representatives of the provincial *sejmiki*, or dietines, and were bound to vote as they had been instructed in mandates from the *sejmiki*. The *sejmiki* had great power in financial matters, for all tax measures had to be approved by them or by the cities directly. By the second half of the fifteenth century, the central *Sejm* was functioning as three estates or orders: the king; the Senate (that is, the magnates, royal officials, civil and military, and the high prelates); and the Chamber of Deputies. The representation of the bourgeoisie in the latter body was not great, but it was gaining in importance with the growth of commerce and the power of money. It is something of an anomaly that while centralizing tendencies were on the increase in western European states—for example, in Spain, France, and England—and the crown was increasingly gathering power into its own hands, the tendency in Poland was toward control of the organs of the state by a representative parliamentary body, which in effect led to dispersal of power. If we look several centuries ahead, we can see that all these trends continued without substantial modification. The West tended toward absolute monarchy; Poland, toward a figurehead monarchy and an absolute parliamentary body. It was Poland's misfortune in the eighteenth century to be surrounded by three absolute monarchies that found her parliamentarism easy to manipulate.

Religion

THE Catholic Church in Poland had from its very beginnings shown a spirit of independence from papal domination. On many occasions Polish kings had disregarded or defied orders and disciplinary actions from Rome, with the support of the people and the Polish clergy. Heretical movements made their appearance in Poland in the thirteenth century and more prominently in the fourteenth; they met much popular sympathy and relatively little effective opposition from the authorities. John of Schweidnitz, an inquisitor, who attempted to repress a popular heretical preacher, John of Pirna, in Breslau in 1341, was murdered by the populace.

The reform movement of John Hus in neighboring Bohemia was warmly welcomed in Poland, not only because it was a nationalistic anti-German movement, and therefore congenial to the Poles, but also because its religious aims aroused wide sympathy among the bourgeoisie, the lesser nobility, and the parish clergy. The Polish delegation at the Council of Constance (1414–18) sided with Hus, and in subsequent years this sympathy was confirmed and strengthened. In 1420 the Czech Hussites offered the crown of Bohemia to Jagiełło and, on his refusal, to Witold; they had refused to grant it to Sigismund. Witold delegated his nephew, Prince Korybut, to accept the crown as regent. Korybut in fact acted intermittently as the head of the Hussite state for over five years (1422–27). From 1422 to the battle of Domažlice (Taus) in 1431, he led Polish soldiers, fighting beside Czech Hussites, against the crusaders of the Emperor Sigismund in many engagements. In Silesia and southern Poland there was much Hussite activity and sympathy with Hussite aims for decades after the outbreak of the Hussite wars. In return, Hussite soldiers joined the Polish forces in the wars against the Teutonic Order in 1433. At the Council of Basel (1431–49) the Polish delegation took a stand opposing the papal party, favoring the conciliar position.

In fields other than church polity, the effects of Polish participation in the two great councils of Constance and Basel were of momentous significance. The councils gave Polish scholars and churchmen an opportunity to meet and argue with delegates from other lands who were already committed to the new humanistic learning. It would have been impossible for men as intelligent and open-minded as the leaders of the Polish delegation—such as Paul Włodkowicz and Stanisław of Skarbimierz at Constance, and Stanisław Ciołek, Nicholas Błonie, and Nicholas Lasocki at Basel, all eminent scholars, well read, and competent Latinists—to associate for months and years with the leading minds of Europe without becoming infected with the virus of humanistic learning. The Polish church, in fact, was profoundly influenced throughout the remainder of the fifteenth century by the ideas and ideals brought back from Constance and Basel by the scholars and churchmen who represented Poland.

The eastern half of the Polish-Lithuanian state presented a completely different picture. Whereas Poland had had a Christian church and culture since the mid-tenth century, the Grand Principality of Lithuania comprised a heterogeneous assemblage of peoples and cultures, from Samogitia (on the borders of the territory of the Teutonic Knights), Poland proper, and Red Russia in the west, to the Tartar khanates on the south and the east and the Russian and Muscovite principalities in the northeast. The grand princes and their Lithuanian subjects were pagan until 1386, and Christianization thereafter, though formal, was slow. The Slav subjects—White Russian, Ruthenian, or Little Russian—who made up a majority of the Lithuanian state, were of the Eastern Orthodox faith, with which religion the grand princes had never cared to interfere. The Lithuanian state around 1400 reached southward almost to the Black Sea, at the mouth of the Dnieper, and northeastward to within a hundred miles of Moscow. In all this area the Eastern Orthodox Church predominated, and relations with Constantinople were steadily maintained. When Lithuania, by the union with Poland, became nominally Roman Catholic, the Orthodox metropolitanate at Kiev was favorably disposed toward a union between the Roman and Eastern Churches. Suggestions for such a union became more frequent as the pressure of the Ottoman Turks on Constantinople and what was left of the Eastern Empire grew more uncomfortable. A delegation to the Council of Constance in 1415, led by the Greek Emperor John Paleologus in person, discussed the project of union with the Western Church without any result. At the Council of Ferrara-Florence in 1438–39, another delegation, in desperate need of Western help, made doctrinal concessions to the Latin Church which resulted in a union, signed on July 5, 1439. The effects of the union among the Slavs were minimal. As a chiefly political measure, it had too many enemies. The point at which the two churches and their cultures came into closest contact was in the Polish-Lithuanian state, where a large segment of the population was Eastern Orthodox and the ruling element Latin Christian.

Culture and Western Influences

BUT Polish culture did not look only to the East. Churchmen and traveling scholars, of whom perhaps more than a hundred studied in Italian universities in the fifteenth century alone, were not the only Poles who talked reform before the Reformation. Jan Ostrorog (d. 1501), whose father had once acted as regent of the kingdom of King Władysław III, was himself *wojewoda* of the province of Poznań. A layman who had studied in Padua, Ostrorog, was an independent political thinker of stature. In 1459 he presented to the *Sejm* a well-thought-out program for the reform of the state, the *Monumentum pro rei publicae ordinatione* (*Suggestion for the Ordering of the Commonwealth*). In this proposal he advocated a national state whose entity would be symbolized by the king, a national church of which the king would be head, taxation for all, church and clergy included, and universal military service. He objected to the vast contributions sent to Rome from the people of the Polish kingdom and suggested that the annates should henceforth go into the national treasury.

He repudiated the sale of indulgences, adding, "After Rome, our own country is the greatest sink of simony and deceit." He called for preaching and the liturgy in the Polish language, rejecting German for the Polish clergy as well as for the merchant class. "Whoever wants to live in Poland should speak Polish." It is not difficult to trace the influence of Hussite nationalism and anticlericalism in his thought and expression.

Of hardly less cultural significance was the massive historical work of Jan Długosz (1415–80), secretary to Bishop Oleśnicki, tutor to the sons of Casimir IV, and later archbishop of Lwów. He was not humanistically minded, yet wrote excellent Latin, deeply influenced by the Roman historian Livy. His patriotic fervor hardly obscures the prime value of his *Historia Polonica* (*History of Poland*). Written from the documents, it took twenty-five years and twelve large volumes to bring the story of his native land up to a few years before his death. He made the Poles more than ever conscious of their glorious past and thus contributed greatly to their national spirit in the times of trouble that lay ahead. At the same time he brought to the Western world in the universal language of learning, Latin, the record of Polish history and her contribution to the security of the West from the Eastern forces that she had so steadfastly withstood.

BOHEMIA

THE kingdom of Bohemia, consisting of the crown lands, Bohemia, the margravate of Moravia, and the lands of Eger, Lusatia, and Upper Silesia added under King John (1310–46), formed a part of the Empire since the tenth century and has thus been summarily treated in an earlier chapter. But its relationship to the Empire was quite special, as stipulated in the Golden Sicilian Bull of Frederick II in 1212, in which the Emperor agreed that the king of Bohemia owed him only one feudal duty: to accompany him, with three hundred men-at-arms, to Rome to be crowned, an obligation which could be commuted by a nominal cash payment. Aside from this obligation, Bohemia was essentially independent of imperial jurisdiction. When, however, John, son of Emperor Henry VII, was elected king of Bohemia and became involved in imperial affairs, it was natural that Bohemia should draw closer to the German world. The towns were already Germanized to a degree that roused Czech resentment, and during John's reign more Germans came to trade, to mine, and to settle. This German influx caused a Czech pamphleteer, writing about 1325, to exclaim:

Just look around you and see how this clever and deceptive people insinuate themselves into the richest church livings, the choicest prebends and the best paying grafts, even into the inner circles of the princes. . . . In the German cities their craftsmen of every kind have combined so that everybody must sell his goods at a price they set. If he sells for less, he is in for rough handling or a heavy fine, and sometimes he may even have to give up his trade completely. . . .

The writer's anger and indignation make him eloquent:

Good God, the foreigner gets all the breaks, the native is crushed. The normal and proper thing is for the bear to stay in his forest, the wolf in his cave, the fish in the sea, and the German in Germany. That way the world would have some peace.

The Poles were accustomed to accusing the Czechs of having sold out to the Germans. They failed to consider that the Czechs, hemmed in by Germans on three sides, were exposed to a pressure that the Poles, faced by Germans on only one side, could not know; and they underestimated the anti-German sentiment that persisted among the Czechs.

King John began his rule in Bohemia with good intentions; but his German advisers were not welcome among the Czech nobility, and, after a few years, he found more absorbing interests in expensive military adventures elsewhere in Europe. For example, he made several forays into southern Poland to give substance to his claim to the Polish crown. Wherever there was a war, John could be counted on to put in an appearance. In spite of his romantic proclivities, however, this knightly king was not without some political acumen, and he was able to add a few territories to the crown lands: Egerland in 1322, much of Upper Lusatia in 1327–29, scattered principalities in Upper Silesia in 1327–35. In the latter year King Casimir acknowledged John's claims to Silesia in return for John's surrender of his claims to the Polish crown. But the royal government and the royal income suffered from his lack of consistent attention to the business of ruling. John was exceedingly careless about crown property. The royal palace in Prague was in such disrepair that his son Charles had to rent a citizen's house for his residence in Prague until he could make the castle livable. When, finally, John called his son from Italy to Prague in 1333 and, giving him the title of Margrave of Moravia, set him to rule as regent, order slowly reappeared. Charles had a sure hand, and the nobility soon felt its firmness. While still only regent for his father, he secured from Pope Clement VI, his former tutor in Paris, the separation of the bishopric of Prague from the German archbishopric of Mainz and erection of Prague as a separate archepiscopal see (1344). He planned the beautification of the city and invited artists and architects to come to the court to help him make the capital of Bohemia the most attractive city on the Continent.

When, upon John's death on the field of Crécy in August 1346 (see above, Chapter 5) Charles ascended the throne of Bohemia (1346–78), he had been virtual ruler of the country for thirteen years. He had brought a measure of efficiency to the administration, but much remained to be done. Charles' election as Emperor of the Holy Roman Empire had a profound effect upon Bohemian culture, particularly upon the development of the city which was now both the capital of the kingdom of Bohemia and the capital of the Empire. Prague, snugly astride a picturesque elbow of the Moldau River, immediately became the leading capital of northern Europe. During his long reign Charles overlooked no opportunity to embellish the city, raise its cultural level, and make his kingdom orderly, proud, and self-sufficient. Not only did he bring artists and architects from abroad, but he also encouraged local craftsmen and artists, supported men of letters, both native Czechs and Germans, and gave his approval to reform among the clergy. He took a direct and personal interest in efficient government and a capable bureaucracy, guarding jealously the economy of the country. His own experience, as regent for his father, with the free-spirited and restless nobility convinced him that the kingdom needed a written constitution. He put before the Estates in 1355 such a document, since called the *Majestas carolina*. The first part prescribed the powers and responsibilities of all the elements in the kingdom, the king, his officials, the nobility, the cities, and the free citizenry. The second part was a legal code. The nobility would have none of it; the constitution would have clipped their wings and limited their "ancient liberties." Charles, rebuffed, never brought the matter up again. He nonetheless used his power much as if the *Majestas* had been accepted, and the nobility were kept within reasonable bounds, somewhat to their frustration.

Charles' rule as Emperor has been sketched earlier (Chapter 6). He worked hard and successfully at that complex task, but his beloved kingdom of Bohemia came first in his affections. In his constitution for the Empire, the Golden Bull of 1356, he recognized the unique position within that framework occupied by Bohemia and even recommended to all the electors that their sons should learn Czech. In 1373 he added Brandenburg to the lands of the Bohemian crown. With perfect right the thirty years of his rule are known as the golden age of Bohemian history.

Charles' oldest son succeeded him, both as king of Bohemia (Václav IV, 1378–1419) and as Emperor (Wenzel, 1378–1400). Wenzel gave as much time and trouble to getting his younger brother Sigismund firmly placed on the Hungarian throne as to almost any other enterprise. Sigismund was betrothed in 1379 to Maria, the daughter of Louis the Great of Hungary and Poland; but there was opposition to this alliance among the Hungarian magnates, and the marriage was not performed until 1385. Sigismund was not crowned king of Hungary until 1387. There was bitter irony in Wenzel's efforts on his brother's behalf, since Sigismund proved a born ingrate who was later to intrigue to take Wenzel's imperial crown from him. At home in Bohemia Wenzel's rule was at first moderately successful. There was peace, a measure of prosperity, and no adventures. He retained most of his father's tried advisers; as long as they lived, the efficient administration of the kingdom was maintained. Nevertheless, the magnates who had been kept in line by the firm hand of Charles IV soon became restless under Wenzel, and from the last decade of the century to the end of his life, he was to have trouble with them. He had neither the nature nor the resources to force them to submit to his will. During most of this time his brother Sigismund was plotting against him and encouraging the nobility in their resistance to royal authority.

The great event of Wenzel's reign was the outbreak of the Hussite movement. We have given some attention to the nationalistic roots and the course of this movement in Chapter 7. Wenzel, with his queen, Sophia, was sufficiently in tune with the spirit of the Bohemian people to support Hus as far as he was able, and in 1409 he issued the Bull of Kutná Hora, which resulted in the departure of the German students and professors from Prague. Both in this dispute and in his relations with the hierarchy of the Church in Bohemia, Wenzel aligned himself with the masses of the Czech people, who were and had been for decades demanding reform in the Church. The nationalistic complexion of the pre-Hussite movements, from the early fourteenth century, is clearly discernible. The towns of Bohemia that had been predominantly German in population, had, by the mid-fourteenth century, become increasingly Czech. When, therefore, Hus, following after other reformers in Bohemia, joined his demands for reform in the Church to a campaign to take control of the university in Prague from the Germans, the great mass of the people supported him. The king was quite aware of the breadth and depth of the sentiment behind Hus. The angry reception of the news of Hus' martyrdom at Constance in 1415 confirmed Wenzel in his earlier opinion.

The Hussite Wars

WENZEL died on August 16, 1419, from a stroke brought on by anger at a popular demonstration held in defiance of his orders. His had been a troubled reign, and at its end even greater disturbances were on the way. The struggles between the followers of Hus and the adherents and foreign allies of the Catholic party were just breaking out. For fifteen years Bohemia and the adjoining lands were to be the scene of one of the most bitter and dramatic wars in European history. The followers of Hus, who called themselves the "Warriors of God," were led for five years by Jan Žižka of Trocnov, called John of the Chalice. They repelled crusades against Bohemia led by Emperor Sigismund, who, as heir of his brother Wenzel, was titular king of Bohemia and who was supported by the Papacy and the German princes. The Hussites were always outnumbered and always victorious. Žižka was a military genius who utilized new principles of mobility and surprise, as well as what would now be called psychological warfare, with such success that opposing forces would not infrequently flee in disorder at the news that the Hussite troops were in the region. Žižka's first great victory was a defense of the city of Prague. Taking position on a hill, since called Žižka's Hill, near the river (July 1420), he repulsed repeated attacks by Sigismund's superior forces and finally forced them to raise the siege. Soon Sigismund was obliged to leave the soil of Bohemia.

Sigismund led four separate crusades against the Hussites, in 1420, 1421, 1427, and 1431, each one carefully prepared, well financed, and participated in by contingents from all over the Empire and even from England. They uniformly resulted in ignominious defeat for Sigismund. The war was waged ruthlessly on both sides from the very first. Fields were laid waste, cities burned, prisoners executed. The record is quite clear that the imperial forces initiated this ferocity, but the Hussites learned fast.

In October 1419, the leaders of the Hussite movement had proclaimed their program in a form later to be known as the Four Articles of Prague. This key document demanded the free preaching of the Gospel; the communion for all believers in the two kinds (*sub utraque specie,* that is, both the cup and the bread); the deprivation of the clergy of their temporal possessions; the suppression of slanderous statements against the kingdom; and the punishment of offences against God's word. These demands remained the Hussite principles throughout the fifteen years of war and indeed may be recognized as a central force in all Bohemian history into modern times. But there was a split within the Hussite ranks. The bourgeois group, including a few nobles, known variously as the Praguers, the Calixtines (from *calix,* cup), and the Utraquists, stood on the conservative side, while on the more radical side stood the Taborite (from Tabor, their headquarters in southern Bohemia) party, whose membership was predominantly the peasants and craftsmen, with a sprinkling of knights, clergy, and university men. As long as Žižka lived, he was able to prevent a definitive break between the two Hussite factions, but after his death in 1424, there was no leader with sufficient prestige or power to prevent the schism from becoming permanent. The lines of separatism between the parties were never clear, and many shifts of allegiance took place during the wars.

The Hussites refused to allow Sigismund to be crowned in Prague and sought a king from another land. They offered the Bohemian crown first to Jagiełło, king of Poland, then to his nephew, Witold, Grand Prince of Lithuania. Witold temporized and in 1422 sent his nephew Prince Korybut to be his regent. Korybut brought some troops with him, accepted the Four Articles, and found favor with both parties of the Hussites. Although Korybut was under pressure from Jagiełło (also his uncle), the Emperor, and the Papacy to desert the Hussite cause, he remained loyal to his Bohemian friends. As late as 1431 he stood before Jagiełło in Cracow, expressing indignation at a petty insult by the powerful Bishop Oleśnicki to Hussite envoys to the Polish court, and challenging the bishop to personal combat. In August of that same year, at Domažlice, there occurred the sensational defeat of the invading crusaders by the Hussites under the leadership of Prokop the Great, a former lieutenant of Žižka; over 100,000 crusaders fled in terror at the approaching sound of the Hussite war-hymn, "O ye who are the warriors of God."

Three months later an invitation from the Council of Basel to the Hussites to send representatives to discuss a possible agreement between the Catholic Church and the Bohemians reached Prague. The invitation and the conditions under which the Hussites agreed to go to Basel were themselves a moral victory. Fifteen representatives, chosen from both camps of the Hussites, with Prokop the Great at their head, arrived at Basel early in 1433. The Utraquists were eager to compromise; the Taborites were more resistant to the arguments and promises of the Council. The Council wanted the Czechs to return to the Church. The Czechs wanted, first, full recognition of the Four Articles of Prague. The negotiations dragged on. In the meantime, back in Bohemia, the partisans of the two Hussite factions, the Utraquists, supported by the Catholic nobility, and the Taborites, had finally come to blows. The decisive battle took place at Lipany, May 30, 1434, and was won by a Utraquist stratagem. This battle between Czechs has been called the "saddest day in Czech history." Czechs did to the Czech cause what the whole Empire, backed by the Catholic Church, had been unable to do.

At Basel, two years of so-called negotiations went by. Finally, on July 5, 1436, at Jihlava (Iglau), in the presence of the Emperor, representatives of the Utraquists signed the *Compactata* (*Compacts*) with the representatives of the Council. The *Compactata* brought the Czech nation back into the fold of the Church, with certain special privileges. The conditions conformed almost literally to the Four Articles of Prague. Sigismund was soon thereafter admitted to the city of Prague, into which, for sixteen years, the Hussites had refused him entrance. Sigismund died in December 1437, worn out by much futile campaigning and even more love-making and duplicity. His son-in-law, the Habsburg Archduke Albert, became king of Hungary, Emperor (Albert II, 1438–39), and king of Bohemia. Albert died after an eighteen-month reign, leaving his queen to bear a posthumous son, known to history as Wladislas Posthumous. The Bohemian crown was considered to be elective (see Chapter 6), and the Estates took their time in choosing the next monarch. For a few years, while the Catholic and Utraquist parties were jockeying for position, no decision was made. Finally, in 1444, a young Utraquist noble, George of Poděbrady, became the recognized head of the Hussites, with broad popular support. After some military engagements against the Catholic nobility, who wanted Church lands returned to Roman obedience, he was elected by the Bohemian Estates on April 27, 1452, as administrator of the land for a period of two years. In the meantime Hussitism had become, from force of circumstance, perhaps more political than religious, although the religious head of the Utraquist party, John Rokycana, elected archbishop of Prague, was a person of high spiritual and intellectual stature. The radical Taborite movement had lost its power. Opinion in the kingdom had come to favor the principle of legitimacy and the recognition of Wladislas Posthumous as king, and George accepted this solution. It was made quite clear to Wladislas that he was to be king on the basis of election by the Estates, not by hereditary right. Wladislas accepted this condition, immediately confirmed George as administrator of the kingdom, and was crowned in Prague on October 28, 1453. The relations between the young, warm-hearted king and his administrator were affectionate and loyal.

George of Poděbrady, Hussite King

GEORGE set himself the task of achieving unity and security in a land so long troubled by civil and religious strife, and the return of order under a confident and firm administration brought with it prosperity. Finances were stable, crops were good, the prestige of the kingdom was improving. In religious matters, however, the country did not fare so well. The *Compactata* had not really brought peace with the Roman Church, and the Catholic party, influential at court, and in close concert with the papal *curia,* labored to force Bohemia into unconditional accord with Rome. But the temper of the Czech people was not yet ready for such a radical change of policy. George conducted negotiations on the religious issue for years, gaining the wholesome respect of the papal court. Through it all, however, he insisted on the basic Bohemian position as presented in the *Compactata*. In this stand he had the unqualified support of the great majority of the people of Bohemia and Moravia. When young Wladislas died of the plague in November 1457, George's position was so strong that, although there were other candidates, he was elected king (1458–71) by the Bohemian Diet in March 1458, without a dissenting vote. Moravia, Lusatia, and Silesia, including Breslau, which held out longest against the king's rule, were soon brought into line, and from 1460 George ruled over a united kingdom. He was a convinced Hussite, yet maintained an attitude of tolerance toward the Bohemian Catholics, until Pope Pius II in 1462 repudiated the *Compactata,* thus changing the official attitude of the Church toward the kingdom of Bohemia. In 1464 George was summoned to Rome to answer charges of heresy. Pius died before the summons could be enforced, and it was not until 1466 that Paul II, Pius' successor, denounced George as a relapsed heretic. The break between Rome and the kingdom of Bohemia was complete.

From early in his public life, George of Poděbrady was accustomed to thinking in large terms. He appears to have entertained ideas of forming a great Central European dynastic union, perhaps under his leadership. But experience in governing broadened his views, and by 1462 he had formulated, with the assistance of a German diplomat, a plan of a European union of princes to assure peace, repel the Turkish advance, and provide for arbitration of disputes between Christian monarchs. The plan was urged on the kings of France, Poland, and Hungary, notably by George's advocate, Antoine Marini, and on the Republic of Venice. It met its most determined opposition from the Papacy, since any such union of princes would have minimized its position as the bond between all the Christian states of Europe. George had many friends among the rulers of Europe, including the Habsburg Emperor Frederick III and the king of France, Louis XI. Furthermore, none of the German princes, who had vivid memories of the Hussite wars, wished to fight for the Pope against Bohemia. The decree of Pope Paul II in 1466, declaring George a relapsed and perjured heretic, was generally disregarded throughout the Empire. The universities of Leipzig and Erfurt went so far as to declare it null and void. But Mathias Corvinus, king of Hungary, whose territories faced the southern border of Moravia, was eager to defend the faith and destroy the heretic. In the process he might gain some territory. The first attacks were easily successful, and Moravia, Silesia, and Lusatia fell into Mathias' hands in 1468. Then George, supported by the Czech people, quickly retaliated, defeated Mathias near Kutná Hora in February 1469, and took him captive. George, more generous than wise, released Mathias on the latter's promise to intervene for him in Rome. He should have known better. Three months later (May 3, 1469), Mathias had himself crowned king of Bohemia at Olomouc in Moravia by George's Catholic enemies, and George answered by having the Bohemian diet (June 1469) offer the crown to Władysław, the fifteen-year-old son of King Casimir IV of Poland. As Władysław was a Catholic, Mathias could no longer count on exclusive Catholic support for his claims.

George's sudden death on March 21, 1470, brought an end to the perennial negotiations with Mathias. The Papacy sided with the Hungarian king, and in 1478 by an agreement between him and Władysław (Vladislav II of Bohemia, 1471–1516) he was given the eastern part of the lands of the Bohemian crown, and Vladislav was given Bohemia for his lifetime. This division brought no peace. Vladislav was aggressively Catholic; his Bohemian subjects were equally fervent Utraquists. He was unpracticed in dealing with a diet in which the Third Estate, the burgesses, had a firm voice, and especially antagonized this powerful Estate by trying to limit its time-sanctioned rights. The king's flagrant disregard for the rights of the Utraquists brought on a violent uprising in Prague in 1483; he was obliged to agree, in 1485 at Kutná Hora, that the two faiths, Utraquist and Catholic, would be treated as equals. In 1490, on the death of Mathias, Vladislav was elected king of Hungary as Wladislas II, and chose to live thereafter in Buda. This withdrawal of their king was a relief to the Bohemians, but it had both good and bad effects. The parts of the lands of the crown that had been ceded to Mathias by the agreement of 1479 were returned to the crown, but the government of the kingdom now lay in the hands of the selfish and tyrannous magnates. In political matters at least, these decades (1485–1526) are among the saddest of the whole history of Bohemia. Economically the country enjoyed reasonable prosperity, and in artistic creativity there were bright spots. But the period from the end of the golden age of Charles IV, when Bohemia was the center of the Empire, and Prague, next to Avignon, the capital of European culture, to the collapse of the Jagiellonian monarchy at Mohács was a lamentable descent and a source of chagrin to every patriotic Czech.

Art and Culture in Late Medieval Bohemia

THROUGH its close relations with the Empire from as early as the tenth century, Bohemia had been involved in all the main currents of European culture. The Czech kings of the thirteenth century had brought Germans into the kingdom in great numbers, and the urban civilization and ideals of these immigrants made Bohemia one of the most progressive and prosperous lands of Europe. When John of Luxemburg became king, the current of Western ideas and contacts moved even faster; in the arts, literature, social customs, and economic techniques, the kingdom was well on the way toward its leadership of Europe under Charles IV.

The many stone churches and monasteries built in the thirteenth and fourteenth centuries show the gradual increase in popularity of Western architectural styles. The influence of both Byzantine and Roman models, built particularly for the Carthusian and Cistercian orders, appeared as early as the 1250's and 1260's. With the arrival of the Luxemburgers (1310), Western artists and architects found quick, widespread acceptance of their architectural norms; they were astonished to learn that Czech artists were the equals in some respects of their fellows in the West. The handsome Prague Cathedral of St. Vitus, begun in 1316 under King John and carried on under Charles IV by Matthew of Arras and Peter Parler from Swabia, was one of the architectural glories of Charles' reign. The Gothic tradition was followed in many monastic and ecclesiastical structures in the period before the storms of the Hussite wars isolated Bohemia from the cultural currents of the rest of Europe. In the fourteenth century, Czech painting reached a high degree of vigor and originality. Influences from Italy prevailed over those from northern Europe, especially in realistic portraiture, as it was used in manuscript illumination and in wall painting. In this field the Czech school produced some notable masterpieces.

We have in another connection (Chapter 7) remarked upon the great literary activity that accompanied the reform movement before and after the time of Hus. But other fields than theology challenged the interest of Bohemian intellectuals. During the reign of Charles, many historical works of great value, in prose and verse, in Czech, German, and Latin, were written and copied for wider use. There were numerous translations of Latin handbooks, dramas, allegories, and romances into Czech and German throughout the fourteenth century and into the fifteenth. As an instance of this absorption into the vernacular of the cultural property of the Latin West, we may cite the *History of Alexander the Great*. This "history" was well known in Italy and France in its Latin form, and there were many redactions and translations of it into Western languages. It was translated into Czech in the fourteenth century, as was the immensely popular work of the Englishman Walter Burley (d. 1346), *De vita et moribus philosophorum* (*On the Life and Thought of the Philosophers*), which appeared in Prague by about 1360. Early in the next century the *Travels of Sir John Mandeville* was also translated into the vernacular. The University of Prague was the leading intellectual center of the Empire until the Hussite wars.

Shortly after the end of these wars, there arose a religious movement somewhat similar in temper to that led by Hus, but less theological and aggressive and more socialistic and pacifistic. This movement, known as the Unity of Czech Brethren (*Unitas fratrum bohemorum*), was led by a devout layman, Peter Chelčický (d. *ca.* 1460), about whose personal life little is known. His numerous writings breathe a desire for withdrawal from the world, a hatred of violence, a deep dislike of institutionalized religion, and a distrust of the feudal nobility. The fervent desire to recapture the spirit of primitive Christianity is evident on every page of his works. The Unity was to play an important role in the history of the Czech people down to modern times, acting, as it were, as the leaven in the loaf.

The latter part of the fifteenth century in Bohemia, disturbed though it was by the vicissitudes of King George in maintaining the integrity of the kingdom against Mathias Corvinus of Hungary and the ambitious Bohemian Catholic nobility, witnessed a strong growth of interest in humanistic studies. There was already a wide knowledge of the Latin classics and a long tradition of interest in humane letters, which the sanguinary Hussite wars and their aftermath had not been able to quench. Czech students began again to travel to Italian universities and brought back with them prized manuscripts and the ideals of the new learning. The best known of these missionaries of ancient classical learning was Bohuslav Hasištein of Lobkovice, who returned from his Italian studies in 1482 to inspire others with his experience. It was significant that his enthusiasm received eager and knowledgeable response.

HUNGARY

THE history of Hungary, a powerful and far-flung bastion of Christianity against the Tartars of the thirteenth century and the Ottoman Turks of the four centuries that followed, has been touched upon from time to time during the discussions of the western Slav states, Poland-Lithuania and Bohemia. The kingdom of Hungary was inhabited mostly by an Asiatic race related to the Finns, called Magyars. Christianized about 1000 A.D., the Magyars maintained close relations with Italy across Croatia, Styria, Carniola, and the Adriatic Sea. The native dynasty, the Árpáds, became extinct in 1301; and after a prolonged struggle the house of Anjou, a branch of the French royal house, then ruling in Naples, ascended the throne in the person of Charles Robert of Anjou (Charles I, 1309–42).

The Angevin kingdom of Hungary began as a kind of feudal monarchy, with a few great families holding most of the power and wealth. But the Angevins were temperamentally incapable of enduring a nobility that was too strong, and they gradually recovered for the crown some of the power it had lost in the thirteenth century, creating, in large measure, a new nobility from their foreign followers. As this new nobility owed its existence and hence loyalty to the ruling house, it could be relied upon not to bite the hand that fed it.

The second Angevin ruler of Hungary, quite justly known as Louis the Great (Louis I, 1342–82), encouraged and guided the economic expansion of the country and brought the nobility under the control of the law. Strong at home, he followed an expansionist foreign policy, adding Dalmatia (1381) and forcing his suzerainty, at least for a time, on Serbia, Moldavia, and Wallachia. He decisively defeated a large Turkish army in 1365 at Widdin on the Danube. Some of his conquests were later taken from him by the Ottoman Turks, who had annihilated the army of his allies, the Serbs, in 1371. Thereafter, the Turks, highly organized and fed by successes, were on the offensive all along the frontiers of the Christian Balkan states.

As we have seen, Sigismund, the second son of Emperor Charles IV, married Louis' daughter Maria and became king of Hungary in 1387. With his accustomed clumsiness he lost much of Louis' gains. Urged on by the Pope, Sigismund prepared a crusade against the Turks in 1395, and was shamefully defeated the next year at Nicopolis Major. The Turkish pressure did not lighten, although it was applied at different places: at one time the Poles would feel it along their southeastern frontier; then Croatia and then Transylvania or the lower Danube would feel it. But in the 1430's there appeared a Hungarian military leader, John Hunyadi, of the lesser nobility, who was a match for the Turk. During the short Hungarian reign of Albert of Habsburg (Albert II, 1437–39) no decision was reached; but under his successor, Wladislas I (1440–44, also king of Poland as Władysław III), Hunyadi drove the Turks back, defeated several massed armies, and made many raids into Turkish territory. Wladislas accepted the peace offered by the sultan and then, at the papal nuncio's instance, treacherously violated its terms. In the subsequent campaign the young king, contrary to the advice of Hunyadi, attacked the sultan's army of 100,000 men at Varna (1444) and lost his life on the field. The Hungarians were defeated, the papal nuncio, Cardinal Cesarini, was assassinated by his own men, and Hunyadi barely escaped with his life. For six years during the minority of Wladislas V (Posthumous, 1446–52) Hunyadi was regent of the kingdom with almost royal powers. Although unsupported by the magnates he went on to win other battles against the Turks. He died in 1456.

Mathias Corvinus, Soldier and Patron of Learning

SOME years later Hunyadi's son Mathias Corvinus was elected king (1458–90). We have met Mathias in his quest for the Bohemian crown against George of Poděbrady. Mathias was criticized for this ambition by the Magyar nobility, who felt that he should have carried on his father's policy of aggressive opposition to Turkish expansion. He probably realized that Hungary could not defeat the Turk single-handed, and he may have wished to form a coalition of Christian states which under his leadership would be able to repulse Turkish aggression. In any event he did not live to achieve the union he sought.

Mathias' reputation for brilliance as a military leader, gained over years of campaigning, was equalled by the breadth of his cultural aims and achievements. He was a true prince of the Renaissance. He made his court at Buda the most brilliant in Europe outside those of the Medici at Florence and the Este at Ferrara. His amazingly rich library of the classics and the Christian philosophers, both Greek and Latin, was the admiration of scholars the world over. Himself well and widely read, he joined as an equal the circle of learned men he supported at his court. He brought artists and works of art from Italy, patronized artists and writers, and decorated his palace with priceless paintings and tapestries from East and West. The king's court poet, young Janus Pannonius (1434–72), was lauded in extravagant terms by humanists from all over the West and was perhaps the best Latin poet of the century; Guarino of Verona, the great humanist educator who had taught Janus, asserted that the world had not seen his equal. Janus enjoyed royal patronage as bishop of Pécs (Fünfkirchen) for a few years, only to fall into disfavor and have to flee for his life. Mathias also had at his court the astronomer Regiomontanus (1436–76), whom he placed in charge of the library and the astronomical observatory at a lavish salary. In 1473, only two years after the first printing press was used in France and five years before Caxton printed his first book in England, Mathias invited a Roman printer to set up his press in Buda. It is worthy of remark that humanistic influences came to Hungary direct from Italy, not mediated through German or French scholarship as they were in other courts of Central Europe in these centuries. This direct influence may well account for the enthusiastic erudition of the court of Mathias.

The last decade of Mathias' rule (1480–90) was probably, from the point of view of the intellectual atmosphere of the court, the most brilliant of his long reign. Continual and close contact with Italy, especially with the Medici and the Platonic Academy at Florence, was maintained by Italian scholars in Buda and Hungarian students and scholars in Italy. The amazing richness of cultural achievement at Florence, Ferrara, Verona, and Milan was reflected in the circle of humanists around Mathias, and the tributes to Mathias' initiative from the whole Western learned world attest the high esteem in which Hungarian culture was held.

BYZANTIUM AND THE BALKANS

THE Byzantine Empire never really recovered from its capture by the Latin adventurers of the Fourth Crusade, who ruled in Constantinople from 1204 until 1261. The Greeks, although they retook Constantinople in 1261, were never able to revive Byzantine vigor. Any suzerainty which had ever been exercised over princes or areas in Bulgaria, Macedonia, or Greece disappeared completely. The Bulgarian Empire shared this decline and barely maintained a show of independence in the face of the aggressiveness of the neighboring south Slav state of Serbia. This principality, wedged between Hungary in the north and east and the Venetian settlements on the Dalmatian coast, had learned from both; under several energetic rulers it had pushed south to Saloniki and virtually controlled Bulgaria. Out of a series of dynastic contests there emerged a dominant figure, Stephen Dushan (1331–55), of the ancient Nemanya dynasty, quite modern in his rule. His father, Stephen Uroš III, defeated the Bulgarians in 1330, thus preventing their alliance with Byzantium. The next year the son rose against the father and took the Serbian throne. His goal was to occupy the throne at Constantinople. He almost succeeded, conquering by war or ruse nearly all the European territory then belonging to the Eastern Empire. He took Albania, the whole Vardar valley, Epirus, and most of Thessaly, and in 1345 he assumed the title of Tsar of the Serbs and the Greeks. He stopped at that point in his conquests to organize his widespread lands. In 1349 he issued a law code, the *Zakonik,* providing uniform justice and, thereby, stability to a mixed population.

The last years of his reign were complicated by the fact that his successes had won him three major enemies: the Catholic king of Hungary to the north and east, the Orthodox ban (governor) of Bosnia to the west, and the Orthodox Greek Emperor at Constantinople to the south and east. Dushan's own religious convictions were adjustable. He expelled the Greek priests from his domains and at one time intimated to the Papacy that he might be converted to Roman Catholicism; at another time he supported the Bogomile * party in Bosnia but ended by remaining in the Orthodox Church, to which he had given a national Serbian organization and a Serbian patriarch. The closest western relations of both Serbia and Bosnia, as well as of Bulgaria, were with Venice. Both sides were realistic, and their common interests along the Adriatic coast led to cooperation instead of conflict. Both sides profited economically from the association. Late in 1355 Stephen was leading his army against Constantinople; he had reached Diavoli, a few leagues from the imperial city, when he caught a fever and died. If he had succeeded in his campaign, it is possible that the Turkish conquest would never have taken place. His own genius had built an empire, but it hardly survived his death. His successors were not of his caliber.

The Turks first settled on European soil at Tzympe in 1354 and found conquest so easy that in 1366 Sultan Murad I moved his capital from Brusa in Asia Minor to Adrianople on the Maritza. The Turkish advance was along a wide front, from Albania in the west to the Danubian principalities and the Black Sea coast in the east. The two Roumanian principalities, Wallachia and Moldavia, ruled by native hereditary *voevody,* were for the most part under the suzerainty of the kings of Hungary, but, whereas Hungary adhered to the Roman Church, the Roumanians were Orthodox and were ministered to by Greek priests. The Turks reached the Danube in a few places without much difficulty by about 1365; they found it difficult to get any foothold on the northern bank until 1394. The defeat suffered by the crusaders under Emperor Sigismund at Nicopolis in 1396 opened the way for the Turks to move northward into Moldavia and along the coast to the mouth of the Danube in the early years of the fifteenth century.

The tragic defeat of Serbian and Bulgarian forces by the Ottomans on the

* A dualistic sect which arose in Bulgaria in the tenth century and flourished in the Balkans for several centuries before being absorbed by Islam.

plain of Kossovo in June 1389 marked the end of the great empire of Stephen
Dushan and the beginning of over three centuries of Ottoman domination of
the Balkans. From the Adriatic to the Black Sea, the Christian civilization south
of the Danube was rudely submerged and deprived of connections with the
West. Bosnia, under the aggressive if brief leadership of Tvrtko I (1353–91)
and the kingmaker, Hrvoje, duke of Spalato (d. 1416), led the south Slavs
against the Turks, until, beset by Sigismund from the north, the national
Bosnian party called in the Turks to expel the Magyar forces. The Ottomans
stayed to ravage and to rule. A few Bosnian kinglets survived intrigue and civil
war for a time, but, in 1463, the kingdom ended with the decapitation of King
Stephen Tomašević by Sultan Mohammed II. Kings of Hungary retook a part
of northeastern Bosnia from the Turks, but it was not until late in the seventeenth century that the Turks began to withdraw from southern Croatia, Bosnia,
and Herzegovina. The three centuries of Turkish occupation made an ineradicable impression upon the Balkan people and their culture.

The vast area from Scandinavia to the Bosporus and the Adriatic, inhabited
by many and diverse peoples, presented some striking developments during
the last three centuries of the Middle Ages. In some respects the trends were
the same as those in the West; in others, they seemed to be in the opposite
direction.

As in the West, national states were taking shape in northern and eastern
Europe, and national feeling was keeping pace with the growth of native
languages and literatures. The Scandinavian states, despite a common dynasty
for a part of this period, began to find divergent interests, leading, in the next
century, to sharp conflict and separation. The Polish-Lithuanian state was too
extensive in its eastern reaches for nationalistic sentiment to gain ground, but
in the West where it faced the Germans, Slav-Teuton antipathy became sharper.
The separatism of the Bohemians grew, in spite of several attempts to form
a central European non- (and even anti-) German group—Poland, Bohemia,
and Hungary. The Balkan peoples suffered submergence under the Ottomans
and were unable to retain, to any appreciable extent, a national existence.

In contrast to the West, where states like France, Spain, and England were
becoming more centralized and pointing toward the absolutism of the sixteenth
and seventeenth centuries, the principal states with which we have dealt in this
chapter were allowing the central power to become more dissipated. The nobility was encroaching at an increased rate on the royal prerogative. The consequent dispersion of authority was to have sad results in later centuries, and the
states were to suffer conquest and dismemberment at the hands of more centralized and predatory powers. "Democracy" under these conditions was a
luxury that proved very costly.

In matters of culture, the countries of northern and eastern Europe made
rapid progress. Whereas about 1200 their cultural level was almost primitive,
by the end of the fifteenth century they had caught up with their western
contemporaries in art, science, letters, education, and social and political thought.
They could quite easily compete on equal terms with Italy, France, and Germany.

In social and economic development as well, great changes had taken place.

In the thirteenth century the economy of the Baltic, along the Carpathians and the Danube, was in the hands of the Germans and the Jews. By about 1500 the Scandinavian merchants were their own masters; Poland's towns, once German, had, in many cases, become Polish; in Hungary the native Magyars were actively engaged in commerce in competition with the Venetians and the Greeks; and the Hussite wars had driven the Germans out of their entrenched positions of economic power in most of Bohemia. Northern and eastern Europe thus faced modern times, weak in political organization but strong in national temper and in those elements that foster national pride and tradition. The peoples of this buffer-land were destined to need these qualities to weather the storms that were to break upon them from all sides in subsequent centuries.

SUGGESTIONS FOR FURTHER READING

ALLEN, W. E. D., *The Ukraine: A History.* Cambridge, 1941

BAIN, R. N., *Slavonic Europe: A Political History of Poland and Russia from 1447 to 1796.* Cambridge, 1908

BILMANIS, A., *History of Latvia.* Princeton, 1951

BOYESEN, H. H., *The Story of Norway.* London, 1886

Cambridge History of Poland, Vol. I. Cambridge, 1950

GIBBONS, H. A., *Foundations of the Ottoman Empire.* Oxford, 1916

GJERSET, K., *History of the Norwegian People.* 2 vols. New York, 1915

HALECKI, O., *Borderlands of Western Civilization.* New York, 1952

HALECKI, O., *History of Poland.* New York, 1942

IORGA, N., *History of Roumania.* London, 1925

JURGELA, C., *History of the Lithuanian Nation.* New York, 1949

KNATCHBULL-HUGESSON, C. M., *Political Evolution of the Hungarian Nation.* 2 vols. London, 1908

KOSARY, D., *History of Hungary.* Cleveland, 1941

LARSEN, K., *History of Norway.* Princeton, 1948

LÜTZOW, F., *Bohemia: A Sketch.* Everyman's Library

MILLER, W., *The Balkans.* New York, 1896

OSTROGORSKY, G., *History of the Byzantine State.* Oxford, 1956

SCHEVILL, F., *History of the Balkan Peninsula.* New York, 1922

SETON-WATSON, R. W., *History of the Czechs and Slovaks.* London, 1943

SETON-WATSON, R. W., *The Roumanians.* Cambridge, 1934

SÖRENSON, S., *Sweden.* New York, 1899

SPEKKE, A., *History of Latvia.* Stockholm, 1951

STROMBERG, A. A., *History of Sweden.* New York, 1931

TEMPERLEY, H. W. V., *History of Serbia.* London, 1917

THOMSON, S. H., *Czechoslovakia in European History.* Princeton, 1953

VERNADSKY, G., *The Mongols and Russia.* New Haven, 1953

ZAREK, O., *History of Hungary.* London, 1939

BRETHOLZ, B., *Geschichte Böhmens und Mährens.* 4 vols. 1921–25

CARO, J., and R. ROEPELL, *Geschichte Polens.* 5 vols. 1840–86

DENIS, E., *Fin de l'indépendance bohême.* 2 vols. 1890

DOMANOVSZKY, A., *Die Geschichte Ungarns.* 1923

HANTSCH, H., *Die Geschichte Oesterreichs,* Vol. I. 1947

IORGA, N., *Histoire des états balcaniques.* 1925

JIREČEK, K., *Geschichte der Serben.* 2 vols. 1911, 1918

KRABBE, L., *Histoire de Danemark.* 1950

MAILÁTH, J. N. VON, *Die Geschichte der Magyaren.* 5 vols. 1852–53

MAKKAI, L., *Histoire de Transylvanie.* 1946

PALACKY, F., *Geschichte Böhmens.* 5 vols. 1836–67

REIMERS, E., *Der Kampf um den deutschen Osten.* 1942

SAYOUS, E., *Histoire générale des Hongrois.* 1900

SCHIEMANN, T., *Russland, Polen und Livland bis ins 17. Jahrhundert.* 2 vols. 1886–87

SCHUMACHER, B., *Geschichte Ost- und Westpreussens.* 1937

SERAPHIM, E., *Geschichte Liv- Esth- und Kurlands.* 2 vols. 1897–1903

SOBIESKI, W., *Der Kampf um die Ostsee.* 1933

STADTMÜLLER, G., *Geschichte Südosteuropas.* 1950

UHLIRZ, M., *Handbuch der Geschichte Österreichs und seiner Nachbarländer Böhmen und Mähren,* Vol. I. 1927

WOJCIECHOWSKI, Z., *L'État polonais au moyen âge.* 1949

XENOPOL, A. D., *Histoire des Roumains,* Vol. I. 1896

CHAPTER NINE

ECONOMIC AND SOCIAL REVOLT

THE economy of the Middle Ages had been largely agricultural. Medieval society had been for the most part one of fixed classes—the nobility, the clergy, the worker on the land. There was essential truth in the three-fold grouping of the "dwellers in God's house" as those whose respective duties were *pugnare, orare, laborare* (to fight, to pray, to work). When the nobleman bore arms, the priest or the monk took care of men's souls, and the peasant or the serf supported them both by his toil and sweat. This division of function with its accompanying social classification was hardly disturbed from the chaotic period of the Germanic invasions in the fifth and sixth centuries until the period of the Crusades.

By the end of the eleventh century, however, a basic change had begun to appear. It was not so much the crusading movement itself which affected European social and economic development, though the Crusades did exert a powerful influence on European life, as it was other forces and events which had themselves helped to precipitate the crusading movement. Perhaps the most radical element in this complex was a tremendous population increase in every part of the Continent and in all classes of society. A second condition, of less extent but certainly of great significance, was the diminishing of Moslem vigor and a consequent relaxation of Moslem control of the Mediterranean. The Italian coastal cities took immediate advantage of this slackening to push their trading ventures to north African and Asia Minor ports. As a result, there was an enrichment of the stock of luxury goods that they could offer to their European customers, who for centuries had had to be satisfied with their own almost primitive products.

The initiative and success of the Italian towns were contagious, and within a century the town was established throughout Europe as a center of trade and as a new factor in the social and economic structure. The records of the slow and at times precarious conquest of the rights to trade must be read in the light of the natural reluctance of the nobility and the monarchy to admit a third independent body into their company. At the same time, account must be taken of the need of the whole state for what the townsman and the trader alone seemed to possess—the ability to create wealth. The rulers were always in need

216

of money; the ancient sources of wealth were steadily dwindling; and the nobles, dependent upon the soil and the peasant for support, found it difficult to maintain their extravagant estate in an age that was beginning to prize things other than vain pageantry and foolish wars.

The Prelude to Capitalism

THE phenomenon of capitalistic enterprise can be traced in every age. There have always been adventurous individuals aware of the nature of profit and the methods of amassing wealth. In the early centuries of the Christian era, under the Roman Empire, there was large-scale, capitalistic, specialized industrial production, with highly organized export reaching out a thousand miles from Rome. When the Germanic invasions annihilated this commercial network, Europe was reduced to small-scale, local craft production. The agricultural economy of the Middle Ages, in which little or no movable wealth was available, did not encourage capitalistic enterprise as we usually conceive of it, but with the growth of the towns the spirit of enterprise and profit became a pervasive factor in all social and economic life. The political implications of this new manifestation were not immediately evident. We shall see how important they came to be as we follow the story into modern times.

We are not here concerned with theories that attempt to explain the rise of the towns. Many factors certainly entered in. Whatever the reason for their origin and growth, by the middle of the thirteenth century Europe was dotted with cities and towns which presaged our modern urban civilization. The town was the cradle of democracy and progress in a world committed to a philosophy of status and repression. Our present hopeful concepts of a free economy and developing society are all rooted in the medieval town.

By the middle of the thirteenth century, the town movement had been in progress for well over two centuries, and the patterns of organization had become fairly clear. There were considerable divergences in administration and control between an Italian city such as Florence and an English borough such as Chester, but there were also differences between cities within Italy or within the German-language area. The early history of much of the town movement focused around two poles of a line of tension: at one extreme, the feudal regime, represented by the lord of the region in which a town arose or revived; and at the other extreme, the merchants and artisans, who may have originally clustered around the lord's castle or burg for protection or convenience. The tug of war between these two extremes may have begun in an arrangement quite acceptable to both parties. The lord saw a chance to profit by collecting a tax for the use of his land and for protection. He could even have had one of his own officials act as a sort of supervisor of the growing cluster of merchants. As he saw the group grow, he envisaged a greater income from the merchandising and from the need for his justice (which had to be paid for). He welcomed to the outskirts of his castle fairs, weekly or seasonal, that attracted the country folk from miles around as well as merchants with wares from strange lands. The community around the castle became a thriving settlement, a *foris burgum* (outside the castle), later known as *faubourg*. The noble needed money, and towns brought and made money. The merchants needed the security which the feudal noble could provide and a central location to market their wares. The relationship was as simple as that.

Yet friction inevitably arose as the number of merchants and artisans and the volume of business increased while the noble continued to exercise his supervision, enforce his justice, and collect his taxes. As a result of sustained disputes, the townsmen gradually won an agreement from the lord acknowledging their "liberties"—to be free of any seigneurial supervision or interference within the limits of their town. This charter was the townsmen's special pride, and the symbols of their liberty—the town hall, a bell, their own court and magistrates, and the right to close the gates to the town, which the lord or his official could not enter without permission—were to the townsmen the ultimate glory and the reward for their perseverance.

This development accounted for a considerable proportion of the new towns in Europe. Some towns were awarded charters by monarchs who, at odds with their vassals, wanted support from a class which had reason to dislike or distrust the feudality. These royal charters usually provided for a royal official (in France an *échevin* or a seneschal, in England a sheriff, in Germany a *castellanus*) who would represent royal authority and justice. The towns sought, with unequal success, to free themselves from all such control, and their records for centuries are full of petitions, refusals, and concessions from one side or the other.

In Italy there was no effective feudal or royal power to obstruct communal development. In Spain the crown counted the cities its allies against the obstreperous nobility and was therefore paternally lenient toward urban liberties. In France the crown kept a firm hand on the towns and, as we have seen (Chapter 2), early in the thirteenth century even recovered some of the concessions it had previously made.

In Germany the imperial cities enjoyed a large measure of freedom. The looseness of the imperial organization and the ambitions of great territorial princes left the emperors no choice but to favor the commercial class of the cities as a counterweight to the independence of the feudal barons. It is possible to trace the expansion of the German cities from the eleventh to the fifteenth century by the successive enlargements of the city walls. As the population increased, the old walls were either torn down, built onto, or encircled with new ones constructed to accommodate the new demands. In the absence of a firm national government, there were often alliances, with temporary goals, among neighboring cities. Because the cities were frequently faced by anarchy or harassed by robber barons, many of them felt obliged to join in leagues for mutual protection and commercial security. Thus a league of Rhenish cities (1226, revived in 1254), a league of Westphalian cities (1253), a league between Strassburg, Basel, and Freiburg (1285), and, oldest and best known of all, a league of Hanseatic cities (1188?) were formed. The leagues were loose and frequently short-lived, but they indicated a recognition of common interests—political and military defense against the feudality and furtherance of commercial aims. The introductory articles of the Foundation of the Rhenish League of 1254 illustrate the spirit and purpose of these associations:

In the name of the holy and indivisible Trinity Amen. Judges and consuls and all the citizens of Mainz, Cologne, Worms, Speier, Strassburg, Basel, and other cities, bound together in a solemn league of peace, to all the faithful in Christ, greeting in Him who is the author and source of salvation.

(1) Since the dangers of the land and the perils of the roads have long brought many good men and true to ruin, so that the innocent are oppressed without any reason, it has been necessary to seek a way to eliminate this sort of scourge, so that justice may not be lost and our territory and our district may return to their ancient peace and order.

(2) It is for this reason that we desire, by this present document, to inform all men that we, with the help of our Lord Jesus Christ the author and lover of peace, through whom every good thing takes its rise and course, agree with one accord in order to preserve peace and the observance of justice, and, having taken our oaths, bind ourselves mutually from now for the next ten years.

(3) This obligation will be observed . . . so that all, young and old, great and small, Jews, laymen, and all clerics, secular and regular, shall enjoy the tranquility of this holy peace.

(4) In cases of discord or disagreement among members of the league now or in the future, . . . four men of high repute shall be chosen to decide, with full authority, all questions in dispute by an amicable compromise or a just settlement . . .

At the meeting of the League at Worms on October 6, 1254, several months after its formation, the prologue to the *acta* of the session included the phrase "to the Glory of God, holy mother Church and also the Holy [Roman] Empire, over which our most serene lord William, King of the Romans, presides." The addition of William's name and auspices was significant in that it illustrated the desire of the cities to be free of any local feudal involvement.

In addition to noble and royal patrons, from whom they sought incessantly to work free, the cities of the Middle Ages had recognized a third type of suzerain: the ecclesiastical lord—bishop, archbishop, or monastic establishment. The Church was the greatest single landholder in Europe in the thirteenth century, and many cities grew up on Church land. Although such cities appeared less frequently in Germany than in England or Italy, they were still numerous, particularly along the Rhine in the period of eastern colonization, in which the Church was a leading factor. Missionary activity and the foundation of towns went hand in hand. The ecclesiastical overlords were more tenacious of their ancient rights than the lay suzerains. The townsmen, for their part, resented the fact that their hard work supported the monks or canons in luxury and sought, at every possible juncture, to get relief from galling feudal obligations. The history of the relations between towns and their bishops and abbots is full of bitter struggles, riots, attacks upon the clergy, and repeated violence. The law was usually on the side of the ecclesiastical personages, and the townsmen were frequently forced by the royal court to accept an inferior position. The deep resentment of the townsmen under ecclesiastical jurisdiction in part explains the strong appeal of the Protestant faith to the bourgeoisie in the sixteenth century.

The City and Class Conflict

BY THE beginning of the fourteenth century the town structure was well established. The towns had expanded to limits that they would not exceed for several centuries. Their rights as against their feudal overlord, whether church, king, emperor, or lesser suzerain, were clearly understood and accepted. At about this time we note another line of development. Reasonably safe from further compulsions, the cities began to show signs of internal upheaval. The whole fourteenth century was, indeed, torn by convulsions in the urban centers. In every country of Europe, even in remote Poland and Hungary, more or less violent civil disturbances centered in the cities or arose over issues related to class warfare and the demands of city workers for a share in the new prosperity attendant on urbanization. The feudality was involved in this new set of disturbances to only a minor degree. In essence, it had lost most of its importance in the preceding century, when it had yielded to the monarchy above it and to the new bourgeois class below it. True, in many sectors of national life the feudal nobility retained many of the trappings and some of the substance of power. There were even instances in which the nobility appeared to gain in power, as in England, where, in this century, two kings were deposed by the magnates. But closer examination of these cases would show that the power wielded by the baronage was due to their representation of the nation as a whole, and not of their class alone. Everywhere in Europe the nobility was on the defensive or in retreat before the growing significance of money and the money-making class.

It is necessary to examine the social and economic structure of this new and dominating institution, the city, in order to understand why its internal history in the fourteenth century was so turbulent and why it became so powerful in modern times. Obviously the towns had prospered through the initiative and sagacity of individuals. As opportunity offered, these individuals established themselves as leaders in their trade or occupation and consolidated their positions. A local merchant who developed good connections with traveling merchants, so that he could buy his goods at a satisfactory price and sell them at a profit, would naturally wish to maintain control both of his source of goods and of his market. Competition established him, but, once established, he would naturally not want too much of it. The result of this attitude was the organization of merchant guilds, consisting of entrepreneurs trading in a single article or group of related products, such as wine, corn, wool, meat, wood, leather goods, or salt.

As commerce grew in volume and variety, a need arose for the organization of trade on a national and an international scale. Wholesale trade required—and produced—large quantities of capital. Profits were impressive. Those who were fortunate or aggressive enough to get in at the beginning of this trade became the upper crust of the mercantile class. The center of the international groups was northern Italy; the Lombards—the Genoese, Florentines, Sienese, and Lucchese financiers—had branch offices and warehouses in all the principal cities of northern and eastern Europe and of England. In Paris alone there were, at the end of the thirteenth century, sixteen branches of various Italian mercantile houses. This monopoly was broken during the fourteenth century when Catalans, southern Frenchmen, and Lowland German merchants, having learned the tricks of international commerce and finance from the Italians, invaded the field and captured generous portions of the trade.

The growth of international trade was not without its effect upon the social and economic life of the towns. As the richer merchants organized for greater profit and for protection against local competition into what came to be called in Italy the *arti maggiori,* and in the north the *lignages,* they gradually created a class which separated itself from those citizens who were dependent upon the large mercantile houses for their wages. In Paris the select group consisted of the drapers, the furriers, the spice merchants, the mercers, the money-changers, and the goldsmiths. The first defense of the craftsmen was to organize into craft guilds. But this grouping, which came to be called in Italy the *arti minori,* did not include the unskilled worker, who was dependent for his living upon his daily wage. The growing population of the cities showed a steadily increasing proportion of these unskilled workhands. It required more than a generation for a peasant fresh from the soil to accustom himself to town life and to learn a trade. Thus before 1300, in various parts of Europe, particularly in the Lowlands, a situation arose which was potentially highly dangerous. The ancient aristocracy of blood and the sword had, in the towns, given way to a new aristocracy of commercial monopolistic control. In all the mercantile cities of Europe there was a patriciate, made up of the ruling merchant families, frequently closely connected by common interests with corresponding families in other mercantile centers. As the members of this urban patriciate grew more wealthy, they became more conscious of their position of eminence. They could even buy titles of nobility or marry into the ancient aristocracy. In a not unfamiliar pattern of behavior, they became more aristocratic—arrogant is perhaps a more accurate word—in bearing and attitude than the nobles whose places they were now able to take. The feudal nobility was getting poorer, while the urban patriciate, the upper bourgeoisie, was growing richer. In the cities, furthermore, the patriciate had more than the power of money. By virtue of having organized their merchant guilds before the artisans joined together in their craft guilds, the members of the patriciate had acquired political power as well, and had formally excluded from town office all those whom they contemptuously called "blue nails"—that is, those who worked with their hands.

At the other end of the scale, the small merchant whose home was his shop, the artisan day laborer, and the unskilled worker saw the gap widening between themselves and the "fat" merchants, and saw their dependence upon the patriciate becoming hopelessly complete. The tension between the patriciate and the lower strata of the economic structure increased to the point of inevitable explosion. In the thirteenth century, violent outbreaks at Douai in 1245, at Liége in 1253, at Ghent in 1275, at Bruges and again at Douai in 1280, and again at Bruges in 1281, and less serious uprisings in the Lowlands were a foretaste of what the fourteenth century was to bring. In this later period not a country of Europe escaped the effects of the uneven development from the agricultural organization of the feudal age to modern industrial society. The struggle in the various countries assumed somewhat diverse forms, and the occasions precipitating open conflict were quite varied. But the strain arising out of the growing distance between the upper bourgeoisie and the working class was the same everywhere, and the possibility of strife only grew with time. Out of this tension and resultant struggle was to emerge our modern society, with a new focus on the right of the individual and a balance, albeit somewhat precarious, between status and progress, between the individual and the state.

The Low Countries

SINCE the first notable outbreaks occurred in the Lowlands, thereafter the course of the struggle for democracy in the cities of Flanders, Brabant, and Hainault and throughout the bishopric of Liége was followed with close attention by the rest of Europe. The Lowlands offered a sort of experimental case for other cities where similar tensions were ready to erupt. This impassioned social conflict was complicated by the political situation. The Capetian kings of France, in their perennial struggle with their fractious vassals, the Plantagenet kings of England, followed a consistent policy of enlarging their base of attack upon England along the coast by moving into Flanders. In a day of complex feudal relationships, the claim of the French king to Flanders was difficult to dispute. Force was the final recourse, and the king of France usually had more of it than any count of Flanders. On the other hand, Flanders was in close and profitable commercial contact with England. The English market, both for export and for import, was the source of raw materials and profitable sales for Flanders. Instinctively the Flemings resisted any effort to make them a pawn in the contest between the king of France and the king of England, but the situation was not simple. The Countess Margaret of Flanders (1244–80) favored the craftsmen in their disputes with the patriciate; the patriciate, in return, allied themselves with her overlord, the king of France. In 1275 the Thirty-Nine of Ghent (a rotating magistracy made up exclusively of members of the patriciate), displaced by Margaret, appealed to the Paris *parlement*. Margaret's successor, Guy de Dampierre, went further in favoring the working proletariat and thus cemented the alliance between the French king, then Philip the Fair, and the patriciate. The common people of Flanders had every reason to hate the French monarchy, since, through its great power, it was burdening them with the heavy load of an oppressive oligarchy from which they had, by their own efforts and with the help of their count, almost freed themselves. They called the patriciate the *Leliaerts* (men of the lilies, the Capetian symbol) and took for themselves the nickname of *Clauwaerts* (men of the claw which the Flemish lion flourishes). With passions running high, the commons united behind Count Guy. He, however, misjudged the power and ruthlessness of Philip and overestimated the ability of Edward I of England to help him quickly. As we have seen (Chapter 5), he had to surrender in 1300 to Philip, who then confirmed the union of Flanders to the French crown.

The Flemish patriciate, allied with Philip, enjoyed its moment of triumph. It did not last long. The commons, humiliated and desperate, awaited only a leader to rouse them to fanatic revolt. An almost unknown weaver of Bruges, Peter de Coninck, who had great native gifts of eloquence, was the man of the hour. Under his leadership, the craftsmen and workers of Bruges suddenly attacked the sleeping French soldiers, but recently quartered on the town, in the early morning hours of May 18, 1302. The Flemish password, *schild en vriendt* (shield and friend), was the giveaway. The French soldiers could not pronounce it and were dispatched almost to a man along with their patrician supporters. This massacre, the "Matin of Bruges" (Chapter 5), brought about a quick revival of democratic and national feeling throughout the Lowlands. The

French invader and the patrician oppressor were the objects of popular and brutal vengeance.

The anger of the people next turned against the French king. To avenge the massacre of his soldiers at Bruges, Philip sent an army against Flanders under the command of Robert d'Artois. The Flemish commons gladly accepted the challenge of invasion. Led by two sons of Count Guy de Dampierre, then a prisoner in Paris, the unsoldierly fullers and weavers, carpenters and masons, met the proud French army under the walls of Courtrai on July 11, 1302. This was an array of "rabble" to which the splendidly caparisoned knights of Philip were not accustomed. The Flemings compensated for not being gentlemen by standing fast, armed only with pike and halbert. Knowing their own soil, they dug a network of ditches into which the French knights, unable to stop because pressed from behind, rode their charges and foundered. The Flemish chronicler Hocsem reported that "the French knights were stacked up in the ditches like beeves for the slaughter." The encounter has been called the battle of the Golden Spurs, from the 602 pairs of knightly spurs the rabble collected from the field after the battle was over. Philip's decisive defeat came as a shock to crowned heads everywhere.

For several years the French king tried to retrieve some of his lost military prestige by conducting forays against the cities of Flanders, but it was not until June 1305, by the treaty of Athis, that he was able to make a peace with the Flemings that was at all satisfactory to him. The terms he imposed were hard upon both the count of Flanders and the towns. The very severity of the treaty kept alive the spirit of indignant resistance, and the peace proved to be only a truce. For another fifteen years the commons of Flanders withstood French advances. After Philip's death in 1314, his successor, Louis X, sent another army against the Flemings. It bogged down in the mud of Flanders' fields, to the mocking amusement of the Flemish commons.

Perhaps more important for the future than Flemish resistance to the kings of France was the course of events within the towns of Flanders, Brabant, and Liége. Everywhere the commons—that is, the proletariat or the crafts—won recognition, as against the patriciate, the bishop, and the princes, of their right to participate in the governance of the towns. Henceforth, when a town made an agreement with a bishop, count, or king, it was clear that the "leading citizens" had renounced, however unwillingly and temporarily, their exclusive control and that the magistracy in the towns represented, in a very real sense, the proletariat as well as other elements of the population. Furthermore, the struggle in which the people of the Lowlands were engaged had acquired nationalistic undertones. A royal chaplain in Paris declared that fighting the Flemings was as praiseworthy as fighting the Saracens. By the peace of 1320 Flanders surrendered the Walloon (French) parts of the county. But this loss was not without compensation, for the Flemish part of Flanders had won its freedom from the crown of France. The victory was in great part the work of the laboring townsmen, who had rejected the leadership of the "fat" oligarchy in the towns as well as of the counts of Flanders, most of whom would have been willing to accept the suzerainty of the kings of France provided that their personal feudal rights were guaranteed. The Flemish gains were formalized in an agreement known as the peace of Fexhe, signed on June 18, 1316, by the townsmen on one side and by the Prince-Bishop of Liége, Adolphe de la Marck, supported by the patriciate, on the other. The bishop later repudiated his agreement, laid an interdict on Liége, and waged a partially successful war against the townsmen. But the struggle only postponed the decision on the question of feudal rights over the town.

A similar struggle was going on in other areas of the Lowlands. In the middle 1320's around Bruges and, indeed, throughout maritime Flanders, the peasantry, actively supported by the crafts in the city, rose against the feudal seigneurs. At times the conflict became violent, and atrocities were frequent on both sides. In 1328 the count of Flanders, Louis de Nevers, called on the French king, Philip VI, for help. In the subsequent battle of Cassel (August 23, 1328), the rebels were caught between the French, advancing from the south, and the army of the count of Flanders, advancing from the north, and were crushed. Punishment for rebelling against their feudal lord was cruel, and the patriciate, which had sided with the count, enjoyed its revenge. The century-old feeling among the Flemish common people that France was their natural enemy received further confirmation. However humbled, the commons remembered that they had once governed themselves. In the circumstances, democracy became identified with nationalism, and the sum of Flemish thought and feeling was anti-French. Thus it is not surprising that the Flemish people inclined toward the English side in the French-English controversy, especially since every Flemish weaver and dyer knew that without the English wool he handled every day and the English market to which he sold, he would be out of employment.

We have seen (Chapter 5) how Edward III of England and Philip VI of France came to blows in 1337, and how Edward began his campaign through Flanders. The count of Flanders, Louis de Nevers, who was loyal to the French king, had arrested two English merchants in the late summer of 1336, and confiscated their goods and the ship belonging to one of them, then ordered the cessation of all trade with England, thus depriving the Flemish weavers and dyers of their raw materials and markets and driving them into the arms of Edward. The spokesman and leader of the Flemish commons at this time was a substantial citizen of the city of Ghent, Jacques van Artevelde. This tribune of the people was not himself of the proletariat, but a wealthy merchant, the owner of considerable properties and of sufficient means to be able to advance moderate sums of money to Edward. The conflict between the proletariat and the patriciate of Ghent had earlier been compromised, and most of the merchants had joined the craft guilds, so that the two classes, instead of being at sword's point, had found it to their interest to work together. This situation explains van Artevelde's position as the recognized leader for the whole of the national element in the southern Lowlands. For eight years (1337–45), van Artevelde, given the title of Captain-General of the city of Ghent, spoke for the people of Flanders. The fact that Ghent, which until 1333 had favored Count Louis against Bruges and Ypres, had turned against their suzerain and his demands indicated a crystallization of national Flemish feeling against the French cause, of which Louis was only an agent.

Soon after the initiation of serious hostilities between Edward and Philip, the English king took measures of reprisal against the adherents of Philip in the Lowlands which wrought havoc with the Flemish economy. The English blockade of the coast prevented the delivery of necessary foodstuffs. After a number of conferences with the representatives of the leading cities of Flanders, the duke of Brabant, and envoys of King Philip, van Artevelde persuaded the people of Ghent to accept a policy of neutrality. Bruges and Ypres quickly followed Ghent's lead. The position of these three industrial cities was so strong that the policy was next accepted by the count of Hainault and the dukes of Brabant, and Guelders, and, subsequently, although reluctantly, by both Edward and Philip. The blockade was raised, raw wool and foodstuffs flowed in, and van Artevelde was essentially the ruler of the Lowlands. Yet distrust of France remained rooted in the masses of the people, and as the war between England and France progressed, neutrality was gradually abandoned. In 1340 troops from the Flemish cities were fighting alongside the English against the French. From this time the story of Edward's campaigns may be separated from the story of the class struggle in the Lowlands.

Although the antagonism between the patriciate and the commons may have lessened in intensity during the rule of van Artevelde and with the threat of French aggression, it did not disappear. Indeed, it took all the dexterity and tact of which van Artevelde was capable to keep the tension from breaking out into civil war. In proportion as the Lowlands ceased to be a principal theater of international war, the ancient discord between the classes increased. Both parties began to find van Artevelde's firm hand and moderate policy irritating. In January 1343, a revolt against the captain's rule led by Jan van Steenberghe, a prominent bourgeois of Ghent, was put down only by a show of military force. Two years later, a conflict was imminent between two of the crafts, the weavers and the fullers. The weavers had refused the wage demands of the fullers. In addition, the deans of the two crafts were personal rivals. Van Artevelde, after vainly trying to bring the parties together, pronounced in favor of the weavers, and the battle was on. It burst out on May 2, 1345. Outnumbered, the fullers were crushed, and hundreds were killed in the encounter. The victory of the weavers made future disturbances certain, for other crafts, overshadowed by the weavers, resented their domination of the affairs of the city.

The bloody brawl and smoldering bitterness in his own city endangered van Artevelde's position as Flemish leader. On Sunday, July 17, 1345, the captain returned to Ghent from a meeting with Edward to find his house surrounded by a mob of textile workers. As he sought sanctuary, he was assassinated. His policy of compromise and cooperation between the burghers and the craftsmen on the one hand, and between the various crafts and the day laborers on the other, had eventually failed.

The following years were marked by more civil strife among the crafts. The Black Death, which reduced the population regardless of class or craft, brought a measure of peace, but the only groups that profited from this lugubrious calm were the bourgeoisie, returning to the cities from exile, and the nobility. From 1349 the weavers and other textile crafts in the Flemish cities were obliged to submit to a moderate revival of bourgeois rule. Nevertheless, the long struggle on the part of the commons in the cities of the Lowlands for participation in their governance was not completely in vain. In a famous document, the *Joyeuse Entrée* of Brabant (1354–56), the duke recognized in several specific stipulations

225

the right of his subjects to their municipal privileges and their direct interest in all basic decisions touching the rule of the duchy.

In Flanders the situation was less happy than in Brabant. The successor to Count Louis de Nevers, Count Louis de Mâle (1346-84), supported the patriciate, and the resentment of the artisans flared up repeatedly. In 1379 there was a final and serious outbreak. A not-insignificant factor in these disturbances was the presence in the Lowlands of dissident and heretical groups—Beghards, Beguines, Flagellants, "Dancers," and Lollards—groups which were antiecclesiastical, semianarchical, and in some degree communistic. By the late 1370's, the basic character of the revolutionary movement was different from that of the 1326-38 uprisings. Whereas the peasantry and the artisans were allied in the earlier movement, the revolt of 1379 was exclusively an urban revolt. The peasants even applauded its brutal suppression. Philip van Artevelde, a son of the Captain-General of Ghent, having only modest capacities for leadership, could hardly succeed where his father had failed. The rebellious Flemings were disastrously defeated in battle at Roosebeke in 1382 by the forces of the king of France, and there followed a period of repression during which many craftsmen —weavers, fullers, and dyers—fled the Lowlands for England. Yet the memory of popular government and a cause fought and bled for remained. After the death of Louis de Mâle in 1384 none of the Flemish rulers and none of the house of Burgundy that began to unite the Lowlands early in the fifteenth century were able to reinstate full feudal rule. The citizens of the cities had won municipal rights, and intended to keep them. Neither the prince, nor nobility, nor patriciate was ever able to take these rights away from them again. The story of Belgian bourgeois liberties is a significant chapter in the larger drama of the liberation of the common man from medieval physical constraint. From this physical liberation to the freeing of man's spirit was only a short step.

Elsewhere in Europe during the fourteenth century there were similar uprisings of the common people against long-established constraints. Although some of these revolts met partial success, most of them were quickly and ruthlessly put down.

France

ANY analysis of social and economic developments in France is complicated by the overwhelming disasters incident to the Hundred Years' War with England. Cities and countryside in the paths of armies of both sides were devastated and their populations decimated or scattered. Trade routes were broken, crops went unplanted or unharvested. The Black Death was a further disturbing factor with its effects especially grave in the wake of war. Nevertheless, both before and during the long war, tendencies toward a popular rejection of the rule of the merchant oligarchy were alive in France as well as in the Lowlands. Conditions were not identical. France's economy was more nearly self-contained than that of the Lowlands; the welfare of the worker was thus more nearly a local affair than in Flanders, where trade with a foreign country, England, was a necessity of life. Furthermore, the political relationships were different. The French kings were allied with the bourgeoisie against the feudality. The Flemish commons, on the other hand, had to face an alliance of feudality and patriciate, supported by the French king. The French kings, unlike the Flemish rulers, favored the cities and incorporated them, in a measure, into their political programs. Yet within the cities of France in the late thirteenth and early fourteenth centuries, that is, on the eve of the war with England, dissension erupted between the patriciate, or the merchant corporations, and the workers, the craft journeymen and the unskilled day laborers. Our records of these outbreaks are incomplete because the upper bourgeoisie, who kept the records and supported the chroniclers, saw no reason to give publicity to such regrettable and unseemly occurrences as street brawls among the lower orders.

In Provins there were seditions against the commercial aristocracy in 1310, 1324, and again in 1349, when the king, convinced of the bad management of the mayor (who was, of course, of the ruling patriciate), suppressed the communal constitution. From 1295 to 1321 Laon was disturbed by perennial strikes and rebellions against the upper bourgeoisie, and in 1322 Charles IV renewed the suppression of that commune. From 1285 to 1305 Arras was in constant turmoil; the commons were enraged at the cynical disregard by the patrician *échevins* of simple rules of political honesty. There were several popular insurrections in Rouen against the merchant aristocracy in the late thirteenth century, and in 1321 Philip V, recognizing that the complaints of the working class were justified, revised the city's constitution in their favor. These instances are typical of a broad movement of revolt against the merchant aristocracy, which had usurped control in the cities of France and had unjustly shifted the burden of taxation from their own shoulders, which might have been able to bear it, to those of the craftsmen, small shopkeepers, and unskilled laborers, who were already living at a bare subsistence level.

After the Black Death in 1348 and 1349 the uprisings were even more violent and determined. Famines in 1351 and 1359 in France worsened the already tragic conditions of the working class. In Paris alone, well over 100,000 deaths from pestilence and famine were reported. In answer to the tremendous dislocation of population and values, the royal administration attempted to control skyrocketing prices and wages. In 1351 King John II (the Good) issued a detailed decree of 262 articles, fixing wages for field hands (for reapers and sowers, two sous a day), unskilled domestic labor, and guild artisans. The whole scale of wages and the cost of necessities were increased by about one third, and the cost of membership in the guilds was also increased. This legislation had several effects. The guilds, once strictly regulated by royal decree, were weakened, and prices did in fact decline from the heights reached in the period of panic just following the Black Death. A previous tendency toward a cash nexus between employer and employee was hastened, and yet, since wages were not allowed to rise as fast as prices, the condition of the peasants and the town proletariat was soon as bad as it had been before the plague.

In Paris, the uncertainties of trade and industry in the years after the Black Death, coupled with the wastefulness of the favorite-ridden government of King John II, brought to the top a certain Etienne Marcel, a rich cloth merchant with demagogic gifts. Marcel, elected to the powerful post of Provost of the Merchants of Paris in 1355, by appealing to the ill-fed and ill-paid working class of the city, came to be the unquestioned dictator of Paris. With the help of the sinister Charles the Bad, king of Navarre, Marcel dominated the Estates General that met in Paris in October 1356. It will be remembered that King John II had been decisively defeated by the Black Prince near Poitiers on September 19 and had been taken prisoner to London. John's son, the dauphin Charles (who later ruled France as Charles V), acting as his father's lieutenant, was hard beset by the intrigues of Charles of Navarre and the ambitions of Marcel. At the next meeting of the Estates General, in February 1357, the dauphin's request for a general tax was refused, save on condition that the Estates control the government's policy and use of the money. Marcel was the master of the Estates. He had grand phrases about his desires to "protect the rights of the people," and many historians have considered him a noble tribune of the people who wished to establish democratic and representative government in France. Later reflection, however, has considerably modified this judgment, and a more realistic evaluation of his aims compels us to regard this controversial figure as a very clever demagogue who would have liked to be ruler of France. In the light of his alliance with Charles the Bad of Navarre, already notorious for his duplicity and frequent treasonable acts, Marcel's appeals to the commons of Paris and his programs of "reform" must be judged as hardly more than rabble-rousing. Yet his rise is significant as a clear indication of the mounting power of the underprivileged proletariat, a growing element in the population to whom, fifty or a hundred years earlier, no one would have thought of paying the slightest attention.

When the Estates met again, early in January 1358, conditions throughout France had worsened. English troops were on French soil; the nobility was undisciplined; bands of marauders, released mercenary soldiery, were roaming and ravaging at will; crops went untended; a debased coinage added to the insecurity of life; and the government bureaucracy was helpless in the face of a sadly divided monarchy. On February 22, Marcel, at the head of a mob almost three thousand strong, decked out in revolutionary colors, red and blue, marched to the royal palace, threatened the dauphin, and killed before his eyes the marshals of Champagne and Normandy. The blood of the marshal of Champagne soaked the robe of the dauphin. Soon thereafter Charles slipped out of Paris to organize resistance to the revolution. He found the countryside seething with unrest. The plight of the peasant was tragic, and his patience long since exhausted. "Jacques," as the peasant was called, meant to do something about it. His complaints were not entirely the same as those of the proletariat of the towns, particularly of Paris. The urban masses were rebelling against a wasteful and ineffective monarchy; for the peasantry, the villains were the nobles, who had insisted on keeping them in a condition close to slavery. But too many of the peasants or their sons had tasted the free air of the towns. It took only a single incident to set the conflict ablaze: the revolt of the peasants, called the Jacquerie, broke out in March 1358. Led by a certain William Carle, the enraged peasants burned, ravaged, murdered, and plundered. One nobleman was stuck on a spit and roasted alive in the presence of his wife and children. Carle sought to enlist the turbulent townsmen in his support, but, except in a few scattered towns, the urban proletariat saw the struggle in a different light. Marcel, frightened by an unfavorable turn of events in Paris, was misguided or vicious enough to welcome the invitation from the peasants. Charles of Navarre, cynical and calculating though he was, could not accept this alliance, and he and Marcel split on the issue. The dauphin weaned Charles farther from Marcel, and the end of the rebel was in sight. The Paris mob, never noted for its consistency or loyalty, turned against him; on July 31 he was killed at the gate of St. Antoine. It took the dauphin all of the two years until the Peace of Brétigny (May 8, 1360) to bring a semblance of order into the government of France.

Both the Paris revolt under Marcel and the Jacquerie were ended, but the basic ills which caused the resentment of the peasantry toward the nobility and that of the town proletariat toward the patriciate and the monarchy to burst out in violence were not removed. Furthermore, both townsmen and peasantry distrusted and detested the monarchy for the heavy taxes it had imposed, particularly the *gabelle,* on salt, the *fouage,* a hearth tax, and various and onerous *aides,* some of them invented, some revived from early feudal dues. The war with the English continued under Charles V (1364–80), and more taxes had to be levied. Despite the improved administration that Charles demanded of his officials, the poorer classes inevitably felt the burden of taxation more than the merchants and the nobility. Revolts against the patriciate, the nobility, the clergy (who escaped taxation almost entirely), and the royal officials broke out in most of the leading French cities from 1378 to 1382, and were particularly brutal and sanguinary in Paris, Rouen, St. Quentin, and Lyons. Heads rolled on both sides. Other cities, such as Laon, Orléans, and Amiens, were heavily fined or lost their communal rights. But the bitterness was too widespread to be repressed by fines or penalties, however ruthlessly applied. Disaffection on the part of the workers toward the ruling class, whether the upper bourgeoisie (the "fat" merchants), the grasping royal officials, or a greedy clergy, seemed to cover the whole Continent. Apparently it took little to start a rebellion almost anywhere. There were simultaneous popular uprisings in these years in England, France, the Lowlands, and Italy, along the Rhine, and in German cities east of the Rhine. The occasions for the outbreaks were somewhat different in each case, related to local conditions. But a Continent-wide feeling of bitter discontent with things as they were and as the privileged classes wanted to keep them was painfully evident.

Italy

IN ITALY, the scene of almost chronic political disturbances during the fourteenth and fifteenth centuries, social and economic factors were inextricably involved with politics. At some time during this period nearly every Italian commune was subjected to angry uprisings rooted in social, economic, or political tensions. The only outstanding exception was Perugia, which seems to have enjoyed a calmer and saner development than its neighbors. The reason was simple. The artisans successfully held the balance between the nobility and the proletariat and maintained a tradition of evenhanded justice for the good of the whole commune.

Rome: Cola di Rienzo

ONE of the most spectacular manifestations of social disturbance was led by Cola (Niccolà) di Rienzo in the city of Rome. Self-educated, eloquent, convinced that he was born to recreate the "glory that was Rome" and lead her to resume her position as the capital of the world, he rose to become "Tribune" on May 20, 1347. Cola set about to crush the entrenched nobility of Rome. He carried the common people with him and, for seven months, was absolute master of the city, where, early in August, he ceremoniously crowned himself with six crowns; summoned the kings and princes of the earth to bring him the documents by which they ruled; called himself "Nicholas, by the authority of Our Most Gracious Lord Jesus Christ, Tribune of Freedom, Peace and Justice, Eminent Liberator of the Holy Roman Republic"; and presided at lavish banquets celebrating the foundation of an Italian federation. He was somewhat premature. Pope Clement VI, in distant Avignon, at first approved of Rienzo's actions; but, as the tribune's dreams led him on, the Pope became alarmed and withdrew his support. The Roman nobility, in the meantime, were gaining strength and outside allies. By December Rienzo had begun to lose his nerve. The Roman mob sensed the weakening of their idol, and he thought it safer to leave the city. Late in December he fled to the mountains of the Abruzzi, taking refuge from the ban of the Church with hermits living in the hills. The significance of his tribuneship is that it was a sort of republican revolt against the vested power of the nobility. The common people of Rome had sufficient grounds for complaint against the wealthy feuding nobility to rejoice at their abasement. On the other hand, the Roman mob has throughout history seldom commanded respect for its consistency or devotion to principle. This revolution, then, adds little to the story of the emancipation of the common man.

Florence

IT WAS quite different with Florence, the commercial and industrial capital of Italy. The Guelph victory over the Ghibelline party at Florence after the battle of Benevento in 1266 (see Chapter 1) coincided with an economic boom that favored particularly the greater merchants. This group, made up of the seven merchant guilds (*arti maggiori*),* seized political power in Florence in 1282 and established a system of government by six priors, chosen every two months, who were always of the upper merchant class. Professedly antinobility, the merchant aristocracy was none the less of the same exclusive caste of mind, and what is sometimes called Florentine "democracy" was so close to a rule by the commercial aristocracy that it would have been difficult to tell them apart. The decade after 1282 was a period of tension. The small businessmen and the crafts, organized at this time in at least twenty-five guilds (*arti minori*), had been until now unable to raise one of their members to the priorate; yet this group was growing in numbers, cohesiveness, and power to such a degree that it became a threat to the "fat" merchants, the *popolo grasso*. There were thus two distinct struggles going on at the same time: the Guelph-Ghibelline controversy, declining in sharpness yet still significant, inasmuch as Florence

---

* The seven *arti maggiori* were (1) the guild of judges and notaries, (2) the *Calimala*, dealers in imported wool, (3) the *Cambio*, the money-changers, (4) the *Lana*, dealers in locally made wool, (5) the Por Santa Maria guild, retailers in the shopping district, (6) Physicians and apothecaries, specializing in herbs and oriental spices, (7) furriers, importers and manufacturers of fur garments.

was traditionally Guelph and some of her neighbor cities, such as Arezzo and Pisa, were staunchly Ghibelline; and the social and economic conflict, increasing in explosive potential within Florence, between the merchant aristocracy, ensconced in positions of political power, and the small merchants, the craftsmen, and the laboring class. These two struggles, which crossed lines of interest and traditional allegiance, confused the total picture for decades and make the history of Florence exceedingly difficult to trace with clarity.

The *arti maggiori,* aware of the growing power and influence of the *arti minori,* decided to make a gesture of compromise instead of open challenge and invited the five strongest of the lesser guilds to join them in the government. These five *arti* (butchers, shoemakers, blacksmiths, builders, and secondhand dealers) came to be known as the middle guilds (*arti mezzi*). Twelve guilds were thus represented, but the majority of seven wielded by the *arti maggiori* never left any doubt as to who controlled the government of the city. The magnates, still strong in their wealth and military power, aggressively maintained their prerogatives, while the populace resented their arrogance.

The growing discontent among the *popolani* found a voice and a leader in Giano della Bella, a respected member of the *Calimala*. The priory, supported by the nine *arti minori,* issued a revised constitution, the Ordinances of Justice (January 18, 1293). Its provisions were directed pointedly against the magnates. They were now specifically excluded from the priorate and put under heavy restrictions in their daily and commercial life. Each member of a magnate family—about 150 magnate families in all—was requested to swear a special oath of allegiance to the priory and to post a heavy bond that he would not disturb the peace. The patriciate struggled to break free of these restraints with a measure of success. But the Ordinances, frequently amended and more frequently disregarded, remained a living document which the *popolani* always regarded as the charter of their liberties.

Florence prospered in the first half of the fourteenth century, largely because of improved methods of handling textiles, and also because in these decades the big merchant houses became international bankers. Such families as the Peruzzi, the Bardi, the Frescobaldi, and the Acciaiuli became fabulously rich, but the *arti minori* and the *popolo minuto*—that is, the craftsmen and the unskilled laborers who did the work—gained little from this prosperity. In 1340 the city was visited by an epidemic, which worsened the lot of the poor. When a political upheaval of 1342–43 brought in a foreigner, Walter de Brienne, duke of Athens, as *capitano di guerra,* the common people, along with the archbishop and the nobility, hopefully supported him. The common people believed that any change would be an improvement; the *grandi* believed that an outsider's rule would offer them their only chance to recover the power they had lost to the *arti maggiori*. When Walter was granted the sovereignty of the city (September 8, 1342), he assumed that he had been given a mandate to rule Florence according to his own whim, without regard to the ancient liberties of the citizens. He signed his letters "Duke and Lord of the Florentines." In a few months all his previous supporters were angered at his arbitrary rule and the brutality of his soldiery and were scheming to drive him out. On July 26, 1343, city-wide indignation erupted, and Walter, with three hundred of his soldiers, was besieged in the palace by a united and determined populace. He traded his sovereignty for his life and was escorted to the edge of Florentine territory.

The government that ruled Florence after the departure of Walter de Brienne was more representative of the whole populace than any that had preceded it. All three groups of guilds, the *arti maggiori* (great), the *arti mezzi* (middle), and the *arti minori* (lesser), were represented in the *Signoria,* or city magistracy. The presence of the artisans must have galled the patriciate, who had grown used to their dominant position. Both the historian Giovanni Villani and the storyteller Boccaccio have words of bitter sarcasm for the riffraff that was pushing its way into the high offices of the state. But still the working class below the *arti minori* had not yet achieved any political status.

From 1343 to 1346 Florence was beset by the failure of several of its greatest banking houses, among them the Bardi and the Peruzzi. These firms had lent Edward III of England large sums of money (totaling almost £450,000) which his expensive wars in Scotland and France prevented him from repaying. Edward's repudiation of these debts caused a panic in Florence that deeply affected the working man through the stoppage of production. Quite naturally the worker blamed the great merchants for his unemployment and consequent distress. The effects of this catastrophe were still being felt when the Black Death struck. Florence lost perhaps two-thirds of its population of 120,000 in 1348. The complaints of the workers during this period were aggravated by the efforts of the patriciate to force the artisans and day laborers to work at less than half the wages they could get on the free market. Although the Ordinances of Justice of 1293 and the democratic success of 1343 had provided a framework for a kind of democracy, the records of the next thirty years tell of many minor outbreaks of strikes or violence by workers against their employers. The patriciate was almost exclusively Guelph and the city was involved in wars with neighboring cities, such as Arezzo and Pisa, which leaned to the Ghibelline cause. The arrogance and repressive measures of the Guelph party made the working man even more inclined to blame the oligarchy for his hardships; political, economic, and social issues became confused in the minds of the poor and oppressed.

The growing tension in Florence between the merchant oligarchy and the craftsmen was not an isolated phenomenon in Italy. When Emperor Charles IV was on his way to Rome in 1355 to be crowned, there were bloody revolts in Siena and Lucca, near Florentine territory, which he had to settle, with drastic discipline to both sides. In 1368 there was an uprising of the *popolo minuto,* who demanded higher wages. The masters protested that because of a famine in the land they did not have the money for the increases. Four years later the Guelphs (magnates) decreed a prohibition of popular action of any sort. For the next six years, while Florence engaged in a desultory war against the papal legate in Tuscany, both sides of the struggle within the city were nursing their grievances and laying their plans. The final and most serious outbreak came in June 1378. By a coup the *popolani* took over the *Signoria,* and for a time it looked as if peace might prevail. But the *popolani* were either too moderate or too slow in reforming the government, and the *sottoposti* (those dependent on the *arti,* or guilds) massed to demand more action.

This mass of the lowest level of workers was now commonly called the *ciompi* (ragbags). The mob took over Florence, robbing and burning wantonly. For three days, from July 21 to 24, the *ciompi* controlled the city. To consolidate their victory, they set up three new *arti,* added to the previous 21 (7 *maggiori* and 14 *minori*) : the *tintori* (dyers), *pettinatori* (jerkin makers), and *ciompi* (all the rest of the laboring class). Their enthusiasm outran their judgment. The merchants locked their stores, and the *ciompi* faced starvation. After several fitful recurrences of violence the revolution collapsed. The first two new *arti* (dyers and jerkin makers) were allowed to exist for a while, but the *arte* of the *ciompi* was suppressed. By 1383 the forty-years' experiment in democracy had ended. The *arti maggiori* and the *arti minori* again shared seats in the *Signoria,* but the officials of the city were mostly from the oligarchical *arti maggiori.*

During the next forty years the Florence of the guilds gradually became the Florence of the Medici. The forms remained and a kind of republic existed, but it must be understood that the proletariat, although it shared in the great prosperity of Tuscany, had not improved its political and constitutional position in the slightest degree. From 1402, or perhaps more precisely from 1434, the history of Florence for almost a century is the history of the benevolent despotism of the Medici family. It began in a struggle for supremacy between the Albizzi, a rich and established merchant and banking family, and the Medici, a newcomer to the ranks of the oligarchy, acting as the leader of a group of *nouveaux riches.* The victory of the Medici in 1434 under the head of the family, Cosimo de' Medici, brought no sudden change in the constitution of Florence. The new power functioned smoothly simply by using the old state mechanism to advance its interests. The key to Medici control was a single new law that provided for a commission of ten electors who would select the six new priors every two months. The Medici then chose these ten electors, who in turn chose the members of the *Signoria.*

We have thus far considered social transformations in three countries of western Europe: the Lowlands, France, and Italy. They have many features in common and many points of difference. But in all of them the lower working classes, suffering from economic pressures and an inability to make their needs and desires known by peaceful political expression, took refuge, in final desperation, in open and violent revolt. It is thus not possible to separate political from economic action or economic condition from social consciousness.

Germany, Bohemia, and Poland

IN GERMANY the political situation of the cities differed from that in France and the Lowlands in that the royal or imperial power was much weaker. The German cities therefore enjoyed a large measure of independence. Relatively free of the Guelph-Ghibelline antagonisms that convulsed the Italian communes, they frequently banded together in leagues, such as the Hanseatic League, the League of the Rhine Cities, and the Swabian League, and thus achieved a degree of stability and security. Nevertheless, they were not completely immune to disturbances rooted in social and economic inequalities. In Nürnberg, Cologne, Magdeburg, Frankfurt, Augsburg, and smaller cities of the Empire, there were uprisings of the lesser guilds or the lower working classes against the patriciate on several occasions in the fourteenth and early fifteenth centuries.

In Bohemia, owing to the great immigration of craftsmen from German towns in the thirteenth century, the national antipathy of Slav to Teuton complicated the class conflict. In many of the cities of the kingdom the Germans were allowed to live according to the city law (*Stadtrecht*) which they had brought along with them, usually modeled after that of Magdeburg. With this independence the Germans usually dominated the Czechs economically and socially. It is not surprising that the native element resented the Germans and that there were numerous and violent disputes in Prague and in the smaller cities of the kingdom between the "fat" merchants, who were mostly German, and the increasing numbers of Czech handworkers over wages, depreciated money, and a voice in the city government.

In Poland also there was a large increase in the German element in the cities during the thirteenth and fourteenth centuries, and again the national question of ancient Polish-German antagonism played a crucial role. The Polish cities, far removed from the centers of urbanism in Italy, the Lowlands, and western Germany, were retarded about half a century in the mechanics of municipal development. But by the mid-fourteenth century the masters of craft guilds were claiming a position of equality with the merchants. In 1368 King Casimir III decreed that a city council must consist half of merchants and half of craftsmen. The decree was premature and was only occasionally obeyed. In Cracow the tension between craftsmen and day workers, on the one hand, and the merchants on the other, reached its height in the years 1406 to 1410. In an effort to make their desires known, the handworkers (*commune vulgus*) met in separate parts of the city and elected representatives to meet with the council, then consisting only of members of the merchant guilds. This procedure set a precedent; a council of sixteen members, half merchants and half commoners, governed for many years in Cracow and other Polish towns. In 1435 the eight highest executive officers of the city joined the sixteen members of the council, and a council of twenty-four members was thereafter accepted. The representation of the proletariat on the council did not mean that there was no further disagreement between the classes. But it did establish the principle of equal representation and elevate the disputes from street brawls and strikes to the level of more or less reasonable discussion, sometimes resulting in appeals to the king. The national problem found a gradual solution as the merchant members, originally of German blood and speech, gradually became Polonized, and by the mid-sixteenth century one element of potential friction was minimized.

The Hanseatic cities of Germany were motivated solely by the desire for security and commercial profit. Virtually independent of territorial princes and even of the emperor, their administrations (*Stadträte*) were completely in the hands of the merchant class, whose rule was purposeful and firm. Any handworker or craft journeyman who came to one of these cities to live and work knew quite well who controlled its government and what he could expect. Yet in the late fourteenth century there were uprisings of the proletariat against the rigid rule of the merchants in several Hanseatic cities, notably Bremen (1365), Brunswick (1374), Lübeck (1376, 1380, 1384), Stralsund (1391), and

Cologne (1396). In every case the League took a hand to protect the old order. In Stralsund, uneasy since 1370, the revolt succeeded and a new council, led by a commoner, Karsten Sarnow, was installed. The League forced the city to recall the former council and execute Sarnow. Disturbances broke out again in the early years of the next century, particularly in Lübeck, the principal city of the League. In 1408 fifteen of the twenty-three members of the council thought it prudent to leave the city, whereupon, without much violence the townsmen took over. But this was insubordination; the German emperor, Rupert of the Palatinate, laid a ban on the city. His death soon thereafter prevented any active pursuit of the disciplinary action, and the new council of Lübeck sought allies. In Wismar and Rostock bloodless revolutions similar to that in Lübeck had driven out the old oligarchic councils. Consequently, Lübeck, Wismar, and Rostock formed an alliance, ostensibly of like-minded proletarian-controlled cities. This novelty, if it succeeded, would obviously be a threat to the aims of the League. After four years of litigation, in June 1416, Jordan Pleskow, former mayor of Lübeck, and the old council were reinstated by order of Emperor Sigismund. Pleskow, too wise to disregard the significance of the revolt of the commoners, added to the council five new members from among the guild officials and the lesser guild citizenry. The revolt had been a healthy shock for the whole Hansa; the membership, previously declining, almost doubled at the next meeting of the League in 1418, at which thirty-five cities and the Emperor were represented.

England

IN BRITAIN the course of social development in these centuries was somewhat different from that in any of the areas thus far considered. Since the days of William the Conqueror, it had not been possible for any involved feudal situation to appear such as obtained in the Lowlands, where there were rival claims to royal suzerainty which were in turn disputed by the feudality or the communes. In England there was no doubt who was king, and there was no question as to who gave the boroughs their charters. Furthermore, the history of the English towns, in contrast with the story across the Channel, in Italy, and east of the Rhine, is notable for the relative absence of bitter interclass struggles. There were, indeed, some such disputes leading to violence and bloodshed, but few that indicate the sharp cleavage between the classes found in the Lowlands and in Italy. A partial explanation lies in the fact that, aside from London and Bristol, the English towns were not so industrialized as the towns on the Continent. The English boroughs maintained an atmosphere more nearly agricultural, so that the onset of a capitalistic and industrial age caused no sudden wide divergence between the profits of the entrepreneur and the wages of the daily worker. It was industrialization that made the Flemish merchants quickly rich, leaving the day laborer far behind. Capitalism came more slowly to England, so that prices and wages and security for the worker adjusted gradually to the new conditions.

England, nevertheless, was not free from social problems rooted in economic changes. Even before the Black Death struck, there was tension between the rich merchants of London and the craftsmen. In 1346 all but "the better classes of citizens" were excluded from city elections. In addition to the mass of citizens who, by the middle of the century, no longer had any hope of rising out of their position as employees, there was an increasingly large number of floating unskilled persons whom we can only call a mob. This group was tinderbox material in a large city. The countryside was in a hardly better condition. Rising prices, coupled with the incidence of the demands of Edward III for money to carry on his French war, were beginning to hit the peasant, the small landowner, and, through the larger landowner, the serf. The land was, in the words of William Langland, "full of folk"; the roots of discontent were established.

The Black Death made its first grim appearance in England on the coast of Dorsetshire on August 1, 1348. It spread north and eastward to Oxford and London, which it reached on November 1, and thence northward into Scotland in the spring of 1349. Its ravages were terrible, carrying off probably a third of the population and striking all ages and classes, although it is certain that the poor suffered most heavily. There was therefore a scarcity of labor and a sudden rise in wages asked and offered. Many crops were left unharvested for want of reapers. Royal edicts limiting wages to the level prevailing before the pestilence were universally disregarded, nor did fines and imprisonment for violations bring obedience. The next Parliament (1351) issued a Statute of Laborers which made more specific and formal the government's insistence that the pre-Black Death standards of prices and wages for peasant and artisan be maintained. The Statute proved almost unenforceable. Manor courts as well as employers, who needed the good will of the worker above all else, virtually conspired to circumvent the provisions of the law. On the average, wages increased about 80 per cent over 1346 levels, and the prices of most consumer goods, such as salt, lime, iron, wheelwright products, and linen, more than doubled. The wage earner was thus actually worse off than before the Black Death, and his outlook for the future even less hopeful. The victory of the Black Prince at Poitiers (1356) and the favorable Peace of Brétigny (1360) may have pleased Edward III, but there was small consolation in such glories for the farmhand, the cotter, the thatcher, the carpenter, or the mason. The laborer knew that it was the sweat of his brow and the blisters on his hands and feet that paid for the king's claims to a distant land.

How generally the provisions of the 1351 Statute of Laborers were evaded may be inferred from the severity of a statute passed by Parliament in 1361, which provided that laborers who moved from place to place in search of better wages were to be branded with a red-hot iron. The only effect of this drastic measure was to increase the resentment of the working man against the government which prevented him from making a living wage. There were few judges brave enough to enforce this statute.

It is not often in these centuries that we get a true view of the feelings of the common man, for most of the literature of the period comes from the courts and the clerical class. But in William Langland we hear the voices of the peasant and the poor. Langland was a cleric in minor orders who lived among the people and recorded their plight in the form of a poetic vision. The first version of *The Vision of Piers Plowman* was written in 1362. Like the two subsequent versions, it depicts the hardships of the poor in starkly realistic terms.

The most needy are our neighbors, and we take good heed
As prisoners in pits and poor folk in cots,
Loaded down with children and heavy landlords' rent,
What they win by their spinning, which should be for porridge
Milk, and meat, to feed their babes—
The babes that are always crying for food—
Aye, and themselves go hungry
With woe in winter, rising at night
In a narrow room to rock the cradle,
Carding, combing, clouting, washing, rubbing, winding, peeling rushes,
It is pitiful to read the woe of these women.
Many a one puts a good face on it,
Ashamed to beg, abashed to tell a neighbor
How deep their need may be—day and night.
Many the children, and only one man's hand
To clothe and feed them, and only a pittance to do withal,
Bread and thin ale for them are a banquet,
Cold flesh and cold fish are like venison.
On Fridays and fast days, a farthing's worth of mussels
Or as much of cockles a feast would be.
To comfort such cotters, to help would be charity in sooth.

But Langland did not see only the poverty and woe. It is significant that he went beneath the surface and sensed, as he moved about among the common folk of England, their deep discontent with the structure of society. This discontent was traceable not only to economic inequalities but also, in large degree, to social injustice and the arrogance and wanton luxury of the nobility and the rich merchants. Jean Froissart, who generally regarded the lower classes with the scorn of the social climber, also recognized the bitter animosity of the peasantry and the town proletariat toward the ruling classes; nor did he venture to deny its justification.

The last years of the reign of Edward III were marked not only by frequent clashes in London between the citizenry (*plebs*) and the nobility (*domini*) but also by a number of conflicts in other parts of the kingdom (for example, at St. Albans, Bangor, Evesham, Bury St. Edmunds, Dunstable, and Lynn) between the common people and either the nobility or the heads of some of the richer abbeys with proprietary rights over the towns. The bishop of Rochester doubtless had these encounters in mind when he told the assembled people, during the coronation ceremonies of Richard II on July 17, 1377, that "the dissensions and discords that have arisen and have lasted so long between the people and the nobility (*inter plebem et dominos*) should be abated. . . . He urged the lords," continued the chronicler, the Monk of St. Albans, "that they should not vex the people with such heavy loads (*taxationibus*)." Given, on the one hand, the restrictive temper of the lords and the merchant oligarchy and, on the other, the pent-up resentment of the common folk at depressed wages and rising prices, an open and decisive struggle was inevitable.

The administration of the finances of the kingdom in the first years of the reign of Richard II was unfortunately clumsy, and a serious deficit faced Parliament in 1380. It was decided that a poll tax was necessary; every person fifteen years of age and older was to pay a shilling. On this basis the poor bore a burden completely out of proportion to their ability to pay. This levy was the last straw. The government had kept wages down, but prices for the necessities of life had been allowed to double and treble.

The Peasants' Revolt

THE long-smoldering resentment finally broke out into open revolt in Essex on May 30, 1381, when a collector of the poll tax was driven out by the men of the town of Fobbing. Although the rebellion seemed spontaneous it is more than likely that it had been planned for some time. First blood was shed in Essex a few days later, and simultaneously in Kent a certain Wat Tyler assumed the leadership of the uprising. At his side was John Ball, an excommunicate priest with a long career as an agitator for the rights of the common folk, who inflamed the already angry mob with apocalyptic talk about the justice of their cause and the brighter future, when there would be no rich or poor. The men of Essex and Kent, whose leaders had agreed to make common cause, marched on London *en masse*. On June 12 they encamped outside the gates and found that there were elements within the city eager to join them. At the moment, the King's Council was in a weak position to offer resistance. There was a war on the Scottish border, and troops were not plentiful. Some of the insurgents burned the palace of the bishop of London at Lambeth and the Marshalsea and King's Bench prisons, where those who had failed to pay the poll tax were usually sent. All three of these buildings were on the south side of the Thames and therefore accessible to the rebels.

The rebels would speak with no one but the king, and a parley was set for the next day. But this first meeting, with the fourteen-year-old monarch and his ministers standing on a barge in the middle of the Thames, led to no real discussion of the issues and was broken off. The next day, Thursday, June 3, the rebels entered London in good order, from two sides, to be welcomed by two aldermen of the city and by many sympathetic citizens. The crowd methodically destroyed the recently finished Savoy Palace of John of Gaunt, for it represented the oppression of the government. They burned other symbols such as the Fleet and Newgate prisons, then marched to the Tower, where the king and his ministers were cowering, and camped. The rebels, perhaps too easily, were in undisputed possession of the city. They presented to the king their program of demands, as follows:

1. Servitude should be abolished.
2. All who had participated in the uprising should be pardoned.
3. All men could buy and sell in every country, town, fair, or market in England.
4. All land held in service should not be held at more than fourpence per acre, and if previously held at less, that rate should not be increased.

The leader of the uprising appeared to wish simply for recognition of the common people as free men, with rights to free trade, cheap land, and ordinary justice. The king, after trying to put the rebels off with fair words, agreed to meet with them early the next morning at Mile End. At the meeting, faced by the rebels in battle array, Richard granted all requests and summoned thirty clerks to write the charters providing for civil emancipation and amnesty for participants in the revolt. The king thus in effect annulled the Statute of Laborers. Many of the insurgents, relying on the royal word, went home, bearing what they thought was good news of relief from oppression. Meanwhile, in London, the crowd proceeded to the Tower and seized and beheaded Simon of Sudbury, Archbishop of Canterbury, whom, as the king's chief minister, they held responsible for their plight. Robert Hales, treasurer of the kingdom, and a number of lesser officials were also executed. The king had expressly given the rebels permission to execute "traitors," knowing quite well whom the people regarded as such.

The government, however, still commanded resources and obedient soldiery. The king's ministers had no intention that the charters which Richard had given should be honored, nor that the demands to which he had acceded should be met. The rebels had to be dispersed, either by guile or, if that failed, by force. Guile was tried first. Wat Tyler was told that the king would meet him at Smithfield, outside the northern walls of London, at vespers on Saturday, June 15. When the king and his retinue arrived, Tyler, all unsuspecting, advanced unarmed from the line of his followers to greet them. He read out to the king and his ministers and knights the further demands of the insurgents, demands addressed as much against the clergy—"since we are oppressed by so vast a horde of bishops and clerks"—as against the villeinage they wanted abolished. The king granted all the demands so far "as consistent with the regality of my crown" and asked that the commons go home. Tyler, pleased with the success of his mission, mounted his horse and was turning to rejoin his supporters when he was attacked by the mayor of London, surrounded by men-at-arms. Mortally wounded, he clung to his mount and attempted to escape. As Tyler, spent and dying, fell from his running horse, Richard rode to the line of the rebels, too far away to see what had happened to their leader, and assured them that he was their king and told them they should, like loyal subjects, disperse to their homes. Richard and his retinue then returned to the city, where royal troops had been collecting. The redoubtable mayor of London traced Tyler to St. Bartholomew's hospital, where his friends had brought him to die, pulled him from his bed, and had him dragged on the ground to Smithfield; there he cut off his head and, sticking it on his lance, rode to greet the king. Without their leader, the rebels were shattered. They were easily induced, by assurances that their king's charters were good and that they had gained some liberties, to leave London. They quickly learned otherwise. That night the king's soldiery took bloody revenge on the peasantry still in the city. The streets ran red with blood, and London was safely in the king's hands. On July 15, at St. Albans, center of the revolt at Hertfordshire, the rebellion was put down with great brutality. John Ball, the prophetic and eloquent voice of the people, was hanged, disemboweled, and quartered. The King's Council in a few days had spread its control to surrounding counties. Those who claimed the king's charters of emancipation soon knew the bitter truth. At Stowe in Essex Richard declared before a large crowd of commons:

O most vile and odious by land and sea, you who are not worthy to live when compared with the lords whom ye have attacked . . . you were and are serfs, and shall remain in bondage, not that of old, but in one infinitely worse, more vile without comparison. For as long as we live and by God's help rule over this realm, we shall attempt by all our faculties, power, and means to make you such an example of offence to the heirs of your servitude that . . . you may supply them with a perpetual ground for cursing and fearing you and fear to commit the like.

Yet a rebellion that had been in the making for thirty years, since the Statute of Laborers, could not be quelled in a few days. Disturbances continued as far north as York, as far west and south as Devonshire, in Sommersetshire, in Lancashire, and in many other areas. In the eastern counties the uprisings were perhaps best organized and longest lasting. At Bury St. Edmunds, as at St. Albans, there was a long tradition of tension between town and abbey. In June 1381, John Wrawe, who had been in touch with Wat Tyler, had no difficulty in arousing the peasants and townsmen against the chief justice, who represented royal discrimination against the commons, and the prior of the abbey, who embodied the oppressive rule of the abbey over the town. Both were beheaded. A charter of liberties for the city was drawn up, and the subprior was forced to sign it. However, the commons did not enjoy these liberties for long. The earl of Suffolk brought royal justice, accompanied by many hangings, to the town within a week. In other centers the story was very similar. It is estimated that royal justice accounted for about fifteen hundred executions of leaders of the peasant and proletarian movement. Yet it took months for the government to restore complete order. Late in September the town of Maidstone was taken over by the people, and some of the wealthier citizens were executed. When Parliament met in November 1381 and in January of the next year, there was still talk of unrest and bitterness among the common folk. In subsequent years there were renewed flare-ups of peasant discontent. The memory of the temporary success under Wat Tyler and John Ball, fed by frustration and hope, could not be expected to die in a people who loved liberty as passionately as did the English.

The peasant had now to bend his back to rougher and longer toil. The townsman was forcefully reminded that the rights of abbey, cathedral, and feudal lord bound him as firmly as ever. On the gates of every walled city there gaped down at him the fixed grimaces of the shriveling heads of townsmen, peasants, or priests who had dared to lead the commons against authority. The social program of fourteenth-century England was, or so it seemed to be, a successful one of forceful repression and victimization of the commons, urban and rural.

We have stated earlier (Chapter 7) that there is no reason to connect John Wyclyf with the Peasants' Revolt. But his movement for reform of the Church, in head and members, and the revolt of the peasantry and the town proletariat had certain things in common. Both were rooted in the concept of individual rights—the one to physical freedom from feudal servitude and the other to religious individualism, the right of the individual to read and understand his Bible, free to a degree from an entrenched priesthood which had forgotten, for the most part, the terms of its commission. That these two movements appeared in England at about the same time and met opposition from the same quarters—

the ecclesiastical hierarchy and the King's Council—is also not without significance. But of even more striking import is the breadth of the movements in
England, their simple earnestness, the precision with which their demands were
stated, the primitive humility of the leaders, and the candid confidence of their
followers. The success of the barons and the Church hierarchy had an appearance of ease that was deceptive. Archbishop Sudbury was dead, and within a
few years Chief Justice Tresilian was hanged at Tyburn; the earl of Salisbury,
too, adorned the end of a hangman's rope, the earl of Suffolk died in futile
exile, and King Richard, so glib with promises and so quick to repudiate them,
lost his crown and ended his life in ignominy.

The story of the age-old struggle of the common people for the simple rights
of human beings fills the pages of history. In the fourteenth century this struggle became a Continent-wide phenomenon, transcending lines of climate, race,
and language. In some respects it was the most important event of the whole era.
It is conservative to assert that if this revolt had not taken place when and where
it did, subsequent centuries could never have been called modern.

Despite all the differences in the essential characteristics of the social and economic revolts in the several countries, their basic character as rebellions against
unreasonable and authoritarian vested interests is unmistakeable. This also is
Renaissance: a new hunger and a vision of freedom and of a happier day.

SUGGESTIONS FOR FURTHER READING

COULSON, H. H., and R. C. CAVE, *A Source Book for Medieval Economic History.*
Milwaukee, 1936
COULTON, G. G., *Life in the Middle Ages.* 4 vols. New York, 1930
MONROE, A. E., *Early Economic Thought.* Cambridge, 1924
POWELL, E., and G. M. TREVELYAN, *The Peasants' Rising and the Lollards: Docu-
ments.* London, 1899

BEER, M., *Social Struggles in the Middle Ages.* London, 1924
BOISSONADE, P., *Life and Work in Medieval Europe.* New York, 1927
Cambridge Economic History. 2 vols. Cambridge, 1942, 1952
CHADWICK, D., *Social Life in the Days of Piers Plowman.* Cambridge, 1922
COULTON, G. G., *Chaucer and His England.* London, 1930
COULTON, G. G., *The Medieval Village.* Cambridge, 1931
GILLIAT-SMITH, E., *Story of Bruges.* London, 1921. Medieval Towns Series
LINDSAY, P., and R. GROVES, *The Peasants' Revolt 1381.* London, 1950
LUCAS, H. S., *The Low Countries and the Hundred Years' War.* Ann Arbor, 1929
MARTIN, A. VON, *Sociology of the Renaissance.* Oxford, 1944
PIRENNE, H., *Belgian Democracy.* Manchester, 1915
RENARD, G., and G. WEULERSSE, *Life and Work in Modern Europe.* New York, 1926
ROGERS, J. T., *Six Centuries of Work and Wages.* London, 1912
SHEEDY, A. T., *Bartolus on Social Conditions in the Fourteenth Century.* New York,
1926
STRIEDER, J., *Jacob Fugger the Rich.* New York, 1931
TAWNEY, R. H., *Religion and the Rise of Capitalism.* New York, 1926
THOMPSON, J. W., *Social and Economic History of Europe 1300–1500.* New York,
1931

VAN DER ESSEN, L., *Short History of Belgium*. Chicago, 1920
ZIMMERN, H., *The Hansa Towns*. New York, 1889

BLOCH, M., *Les Caractères originaux de l'histoire rurale française*. 1952
BORKENAU, F., *Der Übergang vom feudalen zum bürgerlichen Weltbild*. 1934
DOEHAERD, R., *L'Expansion économique belge au moyen âge*. 1946
HAUSER, H., *Les Débuts du capitalisme*. 1927
HAUSER, H., *Ouvriers du temps passé, XVe et XVIe siècles*. 1927
HAUSER, H., *Travailleurs et marchands dans l'ancienne France*. 1920
LAVISSE, E., *Histoire de France*, Vols. III and IV. 1920
LEFEBVRE, YVES, *Etienne Marcel et le Paris des marchands au XIVe siècle*. 1927
LEVASSEUR, E., *Histoire des classes ouvrières et de l'industrie en France avant 1789*. 2 vols. 1903–04
PAGEL, K., *Die Hanse*. 1943
PETIT-DUTAILLIS, C., *Les Communes françaises*. 1947
PIRENNE, H., *Histoire de Belgique*, Vols. I and II. 1903
VAN WERWEKE, H., *Jacques van Artevelde*. 1943
VERCAUTEREN, F., *Les Luttes sociales à Liége aux XIIIe et XIVe siècles*. 1946

CHAPTER TEN

FRANCE AND ENGLAND: THE HUNDRED YEARS' WAR (1380–1453) AND BEYOND

T HE year of the death of Charles V (1380), although it marked the great decline in the English position in France, nevertheless opened one of the most unfortunate epochs in the history of the French nation. Under Charles' determined and clever leadership, the country had recovered much of her unity and confidence. Had he survived only a few years longer, the consolidation of French society and political integrity would certainly have been greatly advanced. His death at the age of forty-three was a heavy loss to the country.

FRANCE FROM 1380 TO 1415

T HE heir to the throne, Charles VI, was then a boy of twelve, and the actual rule fell into the hands of the dukes of Anjou, Berry, and Burgundy, his father's brothers, and the duke of Bourbon, his mother's brother. All four of these royal princes were vicious, crassly self-seeking, and avaricious. The country was in a state of unrest. In many cities and some areas of the countryside, there were outbreaks of violent resentment against the heavy taxes necessary to maintain the war against the English. The dukes were not the men to handle such a situation. Faced with angry demonstrations in Paris in October 1380, the Royal Council suppressed the principal taxes, but since the government had to have money, new ones were immediately levied. The indignation of the populace in Paris and in the provincial centers was consequently doubled. In the capital the fury of the people reached its height in March 1382, when a mob broke into the city hall, armed themselves with the lead mallets which had been stored there for defense of the city against the English, and ran amok. The *maillotins* (malleteers) ruled Paris for a few days, but the dukes were finally able to quell the uprising. They promptly executed some leaders and fined others heavily. In Rouen, Amiens, Rheims, Laon, and other cities of northern France there were similar outbursts. But the most formidable was in Flanders, led, as we have seen, by Philip van Artevelde, son of Jacques van Artevelde, who had been leader of the Lowlands for almost a decade earlier in the century. The revolt in Flanders was really directed against the count. But he appealed for help to his son-in-law, Philip the Bold, duke of Burgundy, who in turn persuaded the young Charles VI to take the field against the rebels. The resulting battle of Roosebeke (November 22, 1382) was a decisive French victory. More than twenty thousand Flemings lay dead on the field. The Flemish revolt had failed, the prestige of the royal cause had risen, and rebels elsewhere were cowed. Paris was punished for its fractious spirit—hundreds of heads rolled, bourgeois property was confiscated, heavy fines were levied, and the guilds were stripped of much of their privileges. Provinces where there had been rebellions were similarly disciplined. For the moment the Royal Council, led by the princes, of whom the duke of Burgundy was the strongest, was supreme.

In 1388 Charles VI, then twenty years of age, announced that he would rule by himself. His uncles were thanked for their services and, grumbling, left the court. Former ministers of Charles V, who had been chosen for loyalty and efficiency rather than for their noble titles, were brought back into office. They introduced some sound reforms, and it began to look as if the *marmousets,* as the nobility contemptuously called them, would repair the ravages of eight years of misgovernment. But in 1392, on a campaign into Brittany, the king suddenly went mad; immediately two of the royal dukes, Berry and Burgundy, took charge. The king's younger brother, Louis, duke of Orléans, though named regent, lost power to his uncles except during the king's intermittent periods of sanity. The uncertainty of the king's mental health, added to the bitter rivalry between his uncles and his brother, made these years a period of governmental chaos. The war with England had not been pursued seriously on either side. The minorities of Richard II and of Charles VI virtually coincided, and in both countries rival relatives of the king were striving for control of the income and the perquisites of power. In both countries there were revolts against authority—the Peasants' Revolt of 1381 in England and the disturbances of 1378-82 in France. After 1388 the "war" became a series of long truces, half-heartedly interrupted by minor coastal raids, and the relative positions of the two sides underwent no real change.

In his periods of relative sanity Charles VI showed more interest in the pleasures of the court than in the problems of governing the state. The nobles, without a war to keep them busy, sought relief from inactivity in knightly adventure. The duke of Bourbon went to Spain to fight for the king of Castile and then to the Barbary Coast. John the Fearless, duke of Burgundy, in 1396 joined a crusade against the Turks on the lower Danube. At Nicopolis in 1396 he was captured and held for high ransom. Others went to Italy to lend their swords to the Avignonese pope and to Italian cities and despots, always anxious to have someone do their fighting for them. Louis of Orléans, although more interested in France than were his uncles, was nevertheless ambitious for himself. He had married Valentina Visconti and thus gained a kind of claim to the duchy of Milan, which later French monarchs were to use as an excuse for invasion of the peninsula. France's involvement in Italian affairs, already more than a century old, was thus renewed. It was destined to be a very costly involvement.

In spite of the ambitions and popularity of Louis of Orléans among the aristocracy and the upper bourgeoisie, the duke of Burgundy managed to retain his position of predominance in the government until his death in 1404. Louis, then just thirty-two years of age, felt that his time for glory had come. It soon became certain that the rivalry between the houses of Burgundy and Orléans, which, while Philip the Bold was alive, was kept short of open conflict, would erupt in civil strife. At this point political aspirations and decisions became involved with the Great Schism in the Western Church (see below, Chapter 11). England had originally supported Pope Urban VI and his successors at Rome. The people of Flanders took the same line. Soon after the duke of Burgundy became lord of Flanders in 1384, he declared that he would not force the Flemings to desert their Roman allegiance. When, therefore, the University of Paris in January 1394 declared for a settlement of the Schism by the *via cessionis,* resignation of both popes, Burgundy supported this policy. On the death of Clement VII in 1394 a new pope was elected at Avignon and the Schism was thus prolonged. The duke welcomed the growing coolness of Paris and the university toward Avignon. In July 1398, France finally and formally withdrew its support from the Avignonese pope so that, in the absence of a titular head of the Church in France, ecclesiastical administration was in confusion.

During the Schism the duke of Orléans had consistently supported Avignon. The sharp divergence between Orléans and Burgundy on this issue, added to the long and tense struggle for power, only served to hasten intrigue at court and prepared the way for the final open break between the supporters of Burgundy and the Orléanists. In October 1407, there was a show of reconciliation between Philip's successor, John the Fearless, and the duke of Orléans, brought on by the renewal of the English war. Yet only a few weeks later, on November 2, 1407, Louis of Orléans was attacked and murdered in a Paris street. The Parisians received the news of the murder calmly. Orléans had not endeared himself to the populace of Paris. Duke John admitted having ordered the assassination and promptly left Paris for the safety of his own lands. When he returned to the capital a few months later, a prominent theologian, Jean Petit, defended the crime in a four-hour speech before a public assembly as justifiable tyrannicide. The defense was largely specious, but Burgundy was so strong that no one at that time dared to go beyond verbal condemnation of his act.

After the death of Louis, the count of Armagnac—whose daughter married Charles, Louis' son and successor—took up the Orléanist cause, and the party thenceforth became known as the Armagnacs. Around Armagnac rallied the dukes of Berry, Bourbon, and Brittany, as well as substantial elements from southern and central France. Burgundy's supporters were the Flemish nobles, some German lords, the city and University of Paris, and groups from northern France which had connections with England. By 1411 both sides were ready, and a bitter civil war began. The king, most of the time sick or incapacitated, was generally disregarded, although he was constantly under Burgundy's control. From the murder of Orléans in 1407, Paris was in perpetual disorder and unhappy under the increasingly irritating rule of the royal officials. The townspeople's demands for reforms had little effect until April 1413, when street rioting broke out. Under the leadership of a butcher, Caboche, the mob captured the Bastille and great numbers of royal officials were imprisoned. Three weeks later the royal palace was invaded for the purpose of appealing to the king in person. The detailed ordinance (*Ordonnance cabochienne*) presented to the king and *parlement* on May 26 and 27 was a model of moderate constitutionalism. It was, of course, too good to be applicable. A reaction took place immediately, and the "better" elements of Paris joined the government in calling for peace. Early in August it looked as if a compromise settlement between the court party and the bourgeoisie of Paris would bring order. Burgundy had misjudged the course of events. When the people of Paris showed that they leaned to the Orléanist cause, he fled to his own territory in northern France. His attempt, in February 1414, to re-enter Paris failed, and a short struggle ended a year later (February 7, 1415) in the peace of Arras between Burgundy and Armagnac. The victory lay with the king and the Armagnacs, for Burgundy was excluded from the city of Paris. But by this time Henry V, who had succeeded his father Henry IV as king of England, was preparing to take the crown of France as well.

ENGLAND FROM 1380 TO 1415

WE HAVE seen in Chapter 9 that the results of the Black Death were over thirty years in making themselves fully felt. When the Peasants' Revolt ended in a decisive victory for the royal authority, the position of the peasant and the town laborer was worse than before. During Richard II's minority no one was desirous of pursuing the French war, which, in the last years of Edward III, had been going badly for the English. There was too much trouble at home: the perennial struggle among the great nobles for influence at court; economic and social difficulties resulting from a lowered peasant population; and the aftermath of the Peasants' Revolt. Added to these distractions there were Scottish border incursions which the French took delight in encouraging. Thus England's disinclination to continue the French war matched that of France, although for somewhat different reasons.

Richard II

THE rule of Richard II (1377–99) is of considerable importance in English history. During his minority, which lasted until 1389, the government was in the hands of a royal council that was split by jealous factional strife. The principal rivals for power among the twelve councilors of the king were the king's uncle, John of Gaunt, duke of Lancaster, and his enemies, Bishop Courtenay of London and the earl of March. Because of the financial straits into which the costly wars of Edward III had brought the monarchy, Parliament, the source of money, exercised an unusual degree of control over policy. In 1377 Parliament forced a recasting of the Royal Council, and in 1380 they proclaimed their right to name the five principal ministers of state. But Parliament as yet lacked the practice—and, indeed, the capacity—necessary to control broad policy, and no leader competent to advise the king arose from parliamentary ranks. Richard, who had begun to surround himself with ministers of his own choosing, in 1385 gave an indication of his concept of the kingly office by curtly refusing Parliament's demand that he change his ministers. The king's lavish gifts to some of his favorites and consequent heavy taxation brought protests from leaders of Parliament, resulting, in 1386, in a crisis between Parliament and Richard. When he bluntly rejected the suggested guidance of Parliament, preferring that of his present councilors, he was as bluntly threatened with deposition. In November 1388, five leaders of the opposition, by now known as the Lords Appellant, accused five of Richard's councilors of treason. Two of the five councilors were caught and executed, along with other less prominent members of the court party, and for a year the Lords Appellant ruled the country for the king. In May 1389, Richard informed the Council that, as he was now twenty-two years of age, he would henceforth rule in his own person.

For the next eight years there was relative calm in the kingdom. Richard's uncle, John of Gaunt, in favor as the king's adviser, brought a measure of stability and accord. Parliament warmed to the king and thanked him for his "good governance and gracious lordship," although there were murmurs about his gifts to his friends. The internal peace, however, was more apparent than real. The opposition, led by the earls of Arundel and Warwick and the duke of Gloucester, was simply biding its time.

After the death of his beloved queen, Anne of Bohemia, in 1394, Richard became more open in his extravagance and arbitrary rule. In 1397, accused by the opposition of bringing England to ruin, he met the charges with quick arrests and trials. Arundel was executed, Gloucester died in prison, probably put to death, and Warwick, by craven confession, saved his life if not his honor. A packed Parliament approved Richard's behavior, even granting him for life the duties on wool, woolfells, and leather—a quite unusual concession. English popular opinion was incensed at Parliament's subservience, and Richard made matters worse by declaring that his subjects and their possessions were his chattels and that he was above the laws of the land. It has been seriously suggested that from this year, 1397, Richard was no longer completely sane. His reckless actions from this point on to the end of his reign hardly seemed those of a rational and responsible man. He squandered much of his income on display and revelry, he extorted huge sums from subjects apparently by caprice, he threatened whole counties with all kinds of retribution if they did not supply the large amounts he demanded immediately, and he left his just debts unpaid. In March 1399, on the death of John of Gaunt, he sequestered the Lancastrian estates in violation of a solemn promise that Gaunt's son, Henry of Bolingbroke, duke of Hereford, should succeed to the lands and title, and at the same time extended a previous ten-year banishment to exile for life. He then unwisely set out to quell a rebellion in Ireland.

In Richard's absence the indignation of all England at his exactions and deceit boiled over. When Henry, leaving his exile in the Netherlands, landed in Yorkshire, the country flocked to his standard. Richard returned from a failure in Ireland to find little support; even his own men began to desert him. He was forced to surrender to Henry. There is uncertainty as to Richard's last acts. On September 29, 1399, he signed a deed of abdication, probably under duress;

he was not allowed, in any case, to appear before Parliament. Some members of Parliament objected that he had not abdicated freely, but their objections were quickly quashed and on the next day he was formally declared deposed. On the same day Henry claimed the throne on grounds of descent (he was a grandson of Edward III), conquest, and election. Parliament immediately voted to accept his claims. The "election" at least was correct. The constitutional position of Parliament was considerably strengthed by its deposition of one king and its election of a successor who was not a son of the deposed monarch. Richard was imprisoned secretly and died in late February 1400, perhaps from the effects of brutal treatment.

Henry IV of Lancaster

THE reign of Richard II ended almost as ignominiously as that of his great-grandfather, Edward II. And again, as in the earlier case, significant gains in constitutional government accompanied the royal misfortunes. The powers of Parliament in legislative and financial matters had become more clearly defined. Its control, by approval or disapproval, of the principal ministers had been frequently claimed on the floor of Parliament. It was beginning to be accepted that, in addition to the Royal Council, including the principal ministers of state, a body of trained administrators, attached to the court under the direct orders of the king but accountable to Parliament, was now indispensable. With its growth in size and complexity, the state was releasing itself from the dependence on the clergy for administrative personnel which had characterized the previous reigns. The policy of the Tudors, under whom the state took over the Church to make it serve the secular purposes of the kingdom, found precedent in the last years of the fourteenth century. As Henry of Bolingbroke, the first Lancastrian king (1399–1413), began his rule as Henry IV, he had to face the fact that the authority and prestige of the crown had suffered greatly in his success. The revolution of 1399 was a victory for the greater nobles and the parliamentary party, but a defeat for royal power.

Henry's position was weak, but he applied all his energies and his considerable talents to strengthening it. He promised to consult Parliament, he favored for a while the clerical party to whom he owed much, and he issued a general pardon for the followers of Richard. He was indeed so eager to please the Church party that early in 1401 he supported the vigorous measure of Archbishop Arundel of Canterbury against the Lollards and personally signed an order to burn a certain William Sawtre (or Chartyrs) at Smithfield for heresy. Sawtre became the first Lollard martyr. This execution was followed by the statute De heretico comburendo (March 10, 1401), which was rigid enough to satisfy the high churchmen and to precipitate a cruel persecution of the followers of Wyclyf. But within a very few years he tightened his control of the Church, secularized much monastic property, and kept bishoprics vacant.

Henry's first years as king were trying. Wales under Owen Glendower was in successful revolt in 1401; there was the usual trouble on the Scottish border; the people of England were grumbling at the heavy taxes; and late in 1401 malcontents among the magnates were spreading the rumor that King Richard was still alive and in Scotland. Rebellion spread in the north and west, led by Sir Henry Percy, earl of Northumberland, and his son Hotspur. In a hard battle at Shrewsbury (July 21, 1403), Henry defeated the largest detachment of the rebels and executed those of their leaders that did not escape or die on the field of battle. The Welsh war dragged on, as Glendower received help and encouragement from France, but Henry's persistence and the aggressive action of his son, the Prince of Wales, began to tell by 1405. By 1409 organized rebellion from that quarter was over. Meanwhile, the remnants of the English opposition to the Lancastrian line were gathering force. Not a few of the nobles who had welcomed Henry were disappointed at not receiving the rewards they had hoped for and were glad to intrigue against him, particularly when he was having difficulties with Parliament. Armed revolt broke out in April 1405. The highest ranking leaders of the revolt were the duke of Northumberland and Archbishop Scrope of York. The rebels issued a manifesto that appealed to the middle class rather than to the baronage, as had been characteristic of the earlier opposition to Henry. There is no doubt that the people of Yorkshire supported this uprising. A royal army met the rebels (Northumberland managed to be absent) at Shipton, and the leaders of the rebellion were induced, probably on false promises, to lay down their arms. Henry then had four leaders of the men of York, Archbishop Scrope, the earl of Nottingham, and two knights, executed without a trial. Drastic as it was, the suppression of this revolt secured Henry's throne. The opposition weakened and almost disappeared in the face of his firmness and consistent sagacity. In the spring of 1406, the heir to the Scottish throne, whom his father was sending to France for safety, was captured at sea by English sailors who turned him over to Henry. With such a hostage in his hands Henry had no more trouble with Scotland. Perhaps after all he was the strong man England needed.

Notwithstanding these successes, the last years of Henry's rule were not free from trouble. The Archbishop of Canterbury, Arundel, was determined to uproot Lollardy, which retained its hold on broad sections of the people and even on the lower clergy. Around the throne and in the Royal Council there was a continual battle for power, at this point between the baronial party, led by the earl of Arundel, and the Beauforts, half brothers of the king. The bitterness of this struggle presaged the dire animosity with which the Wars of the Roses were to be fought. From about 1411, the king and the Prince of Wales were frequently in disagreement. The son was headstrong and eager to rule. Impatient to get into the war in France, late in 1411, on his own initiative, he sent some troops to help the duke of Burgundy. There were even rumors that he was in a plot to usurp the throne. But, despite his failing health, Henry IV maintained his authority to the end (March 20, 1413).

Henry V and the Invasion of France

HENRY V began his rule by substituting his own ministers for those of his father. The choices he made reflected his intention to follow a more ambitious policy in foreign affairs than his father's. The Lollards, still strong in spite of the measures taken against them by Archbishop Arundel, found a leader in Sir

John Oldcastle, who succeeded in identifying some of Wyclyf's theological doctrines with the general middle-class dissatisfaction with the wealth, conduct, and hypocrisy of the clergy, from prelate to parish priest. Lollardy thus assumed a political tinge that forced the court to take a hand in its suppression. Oldcastle was seized, examined, and excommunicated. He escaped, led an abortive armed revolt, which was put down without much difficulty, and then disappeared, only to be caught and executed in December 1417. By becoming in part a political movement of opposition to the Church and thus to the crown which had taken the Church under its protection, Lollardy lost much support it might have retained if it had remained purely theological or even religious, and from this time until the Tudor reformation it existed as scarcely more than an underground movement with no pretense to intellectual respectability.

No one was surprised when Henry V renewed the war with France. Henry was young and self-confident, with notable military capacity and an obvious ambition to cut a figure in European politics. Both the Burgundians and the Armagnacs sought his support; yet, although he played with both sides, he made such extravagant demands that neither could accept his terms. Henry may have intended it that way. While the negotiations were going on, he was making elaborate preparations for war. The expenses of preparation were heavy, and all classes were taxed to the point of grumbling. A conspiracy of nobles, close to the king, apparently wished to take advantage of the general discontent and planned to put the Scottish pseudo-Richard or earl of March on the throne. Henry, warned, acted quickly and ruthlessly. The three ringleaders were executed with the bare formalities of a trial. Henry was not to be diverted from his projected conquest of France. He seemed to feel that a glorious foreign war would be enough to divert the minds of his subjects. In August 1415, he left Southampton with two thousand men-at-arms and six thousand archers and landed at the mouth of the Seine near Harfleur, to which he laid siege. Surrounded, the garrison surrendered on September 27, 1415, after five weeks of isolation and artillery bombardment. It was planned to garrison Harfleur and take the rest of the army back to England for the winter months. Henry insisted that the army should be transported from Calais. His advisers pointed out to him that such a move would require the English forces, which had suffered substantial losses from action and dysentery, to march overland at least 160 miles through territory occupied by French forces in great and growing numbers. Henry nevertheless decided to march and left Harfleur on October 8 for a fateful encounter with a vastly superior French army.

FRANCE FROM 1415 TO 1453

WE LEFT France recovering from a period of civil war between the Armagnacs, the court party, and John the Fearless, duke of Burgundy. After the peace of Arras (February 23, 1415), between the Armagnacs and the Burgundians, the duke of Burgundy left Paris, now in the hands of the Armagnacs, for his own lands, and bided his time. When news of Henry's landing reached the court at Paris, some troops were dispatched to the Norman coast. But there were no troops from Burgundy. As Harfleur was being besieged, feudal reinforcements were sent from northern France toward Rouen, under the command of the constable of France, Charles d'Albret. It was this force, probably at least four times the size of Henry's army, now strengthened to thirteen thousand * soldiers, that met the invader at Agincourt in Artois steadily for some days (October 23–25, 1415). The horses sank to their bellies in the mud, and the knights had to dismount and try to fight on foot. The English archers and lightly armed men-at-arms, more widely disposed than the tightly serried French feudal host, had the Frenchmen at their mercy. It was a dramatic victory, like Crécy and Poitiers in the preceding century. A French historian even remarked that the French had learned nothing since Crécy. Henry's welcome in England was as enthusiastic as the gloom in Paris was deep.

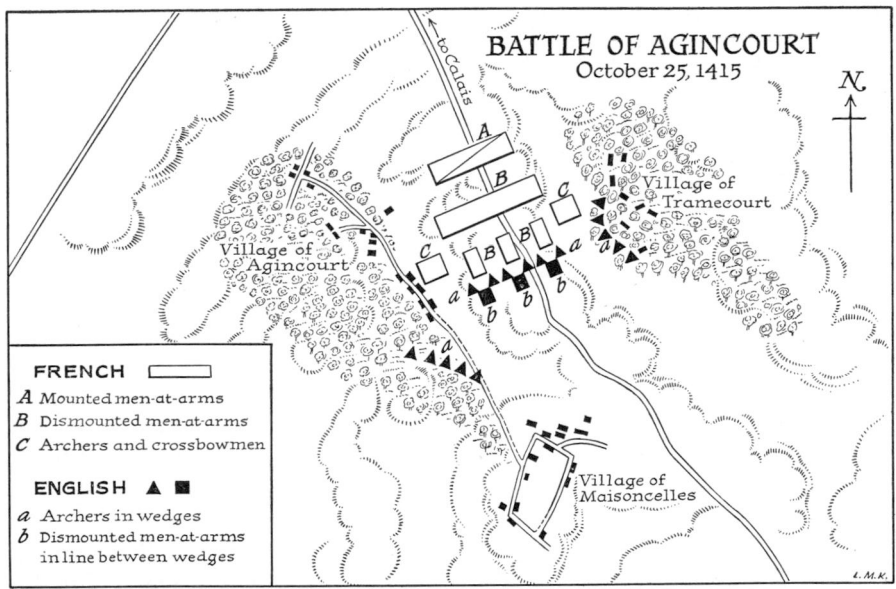

At this point the Emperor Sigismund, regarding himself as divinely appointed to settle all disputes in Europe, thought he could bring peace between France and England. He visited first Paris, stunned by defeat, and then London, gay and elated with victory. Henry wanted the terms of the Peace of Brétigny and more, but the best that could be got out of the negotiations was a series of truces between the two enemies. Sigismund signed an alliance for the Empire (the treaty of Canterbury) on August 15, 1416. He addressed Henry as "Our brother Henry, King of France" and promised to help him to recover the French crown. Sigismund's signature was at best worthless.

---

* Estimates, both contemporary and modern, of the number of troops involved, vary greatly according to the nationality of the writer. English historians may hazard a proportion of five or six to one, and the French, three or four to one, and a German historian has seriously argued that the English outnumbered the French. A proportion of four to one seems most probable.

The next year, 1417, saw a renewal of the military action. While English troops under Henry's personal command were conquering Normandy, the duke of Burgundy was preparing to take over the government of France. He proclaimed to the French that the humiliation the country had suffered was the fault of the Armagnac party and pledged that he would relieve the unjust tax burdens. He named Charles VI's wife, Queen Isabelle of Bavaria, then at Tours, as regent. Within Paris, the new Constable of France, Count Bernard of Armagnac, ruled harshly. The king was incapacitated, two dauphins had died by 1416, and the third, Charles, was only thirteen years old when he in turn became dauphin. Late in May 1418, the leading spirit of the Burgundian party in the city, Perrinet Leclerc, an iron merchant, opened the Porte St. Germain to the Burgundians. A thousand Armagnacs were massacred before sundown. A fortnight later, after a rumor had been spread abroad that the Armagnacs were planning to retake the city, another massacre of Armagnacs still in prison broke out, and almost two thousand were dispatched amid scenes of callous brutality. The cry in the streets was *"vive le roi et le duc de Bourgogne."*

The duke, John the Fearless, was at the moment enjoying life in Burgundy. He finally arrived in Paris, with Queen Isabelle, on July 14, 1418. The spirit of terror in the capital ran high, and it took the duke almost six weeks to bring order. Outlying cities and districts submitted to his rule, and by early October the duke, acting "in the name of the king," supported by Queen Isabelle and in possession of the person of the king, was master of most of France.

But the Armagnac party, to which the dauphin Charles had escaped from Paris, was not disposed to quit. The dauphin, now sixteen years of age, set up a government at Bourges and Poitiers and in October 1418 proclaimed himself regent of the kingdom for his father. Then, early in January 1419, after a long and agonizing defense to which Burgundy had refused assistance, Rouen fell to Henry V. Normandy was in English hands again. In the face of English successes, the Armagnacs and Burgundians drew together. Negotiations for a settlement which had been going on for some time between the two parties culminated in a series of meetings between the dauphin and the duke. At the third of these meetings, on a bridge at Montereau on September 10, 1419, hot-headed followers of the dauphin murdered the duke of Burgundy. The new duke, Philip the Good, then twenty-three years old, swore vengeance against the Armagnacs and allied himself with the king of England. Accordingly, on May 21, 1420, a treaty between Charles VI of France and Henry V of England was signed at Troyes. By its terms Henry married Charles' daughter Catherine and was declared Charles' son and heir to the throne of France. He was to share the government of France with the duke of Burgundy during Charles' lifetime. The so-called dauphin was disowned. Henry entered Paris on December 1 and was warmly welcomed by all classes. This second English success in the long conflict proved fully as ephemeral as the earlier success of Brétigny in 1360. Henry died at Vincennes on August 31, 1422, and Charles VI, two months later (October 21). Henry's son was then only ten months old. John, the duke of Bedford, the infant king's uncle, was named regent in the will of Henry V.

Charles VII

ON THE death of Charles VI, the dauphin proclaimed himself king of France (as Charles VII) at Bourges, where he made his capital and installed the offices which managed those parts of France that remained loyal to him. He came to be called the "King of Bourges." Faced with a choice between two crowned claimants to the throne—one a young man of nineteen, the son of a French king, and the other an infant of a year or less, the son of a foreign conqueror—most Frenchmen found that their sympathies lay with the former. Charles VII thus gained some popular support without having to fight for it. The English had difficulties in maintaining themselves in Normandy owing to the recovery of French spirit and the homesickness of English soldiers and settlers. Even the threat of severe punishment did not stop Englishmen from "escaping" to their homeland. Bands of "brigands" scouring the areas occupied by the English were fed and supported, like an underground army, by the native French. Men and women from all classes, the townspeople, the nobility, the clergy, and the peasantry, joined these bands, raiding, despoiling, and frequently hanging upon convenient trees English officials or Frenchmen who worked for the hated conqueror. This sort of dogged resistance was indeed more effective than that of the army of medieval knights whose refusal to learn from defeat at Crécy and Poitiers had almost destroyed their own class at Agincourt.

Whereas the English met stubborn resistance in the parts of northern France they occupied, in Paris their rule, or rather condominium with the Burgundians, was more successful. Henry V had been determined to bring order, and when he saw that Philip the Good of Burgundy had named capable officials to key offices in the capital, he made no attempt to interfere. The Parisians were thus ruled by Frenchmen, or at least Burgundians, and although there was no sweeping program of reform, there was stability and almost no evidence of foreign domination. The regent, the duke of Bedford, continued Henry's policy of quiet collaboration with the officials of Philip the Good.

In the next few years English and French forces fought a number of set battles, including those at Graville (September 26, 1423) and Verneuil (August 17, 1424). By the latter battle the English completed their conquest of all France north of the Loire, and on August 2, 1425, Le Mans fell into English hands. The next year, 1426, was quiet. The duke of Bedford had been called (November, 1425) to England to avert a civil war which the reckless ambitions and violent actions of his younger brother, Duke Humphrey of Gloucester, regent in England, had made almost inevitable. Not only had Gloucester quarreled with his uncle, Henry Beaufort, chancellor of the kingdom, irritated Parliament and most of the nobility into consistent opposition, but his marriage in February 1423 to Jacqueline, countess of Hainault, Holland, and Zeeland, and former wife of Duke John of Brabant, had involved him in a harebrained project to claim her territories for himself. As they were part of the lands of Burgundy, such a claim would have meant war between England and Burgundy, close allies in France since the battle of Agincourt.

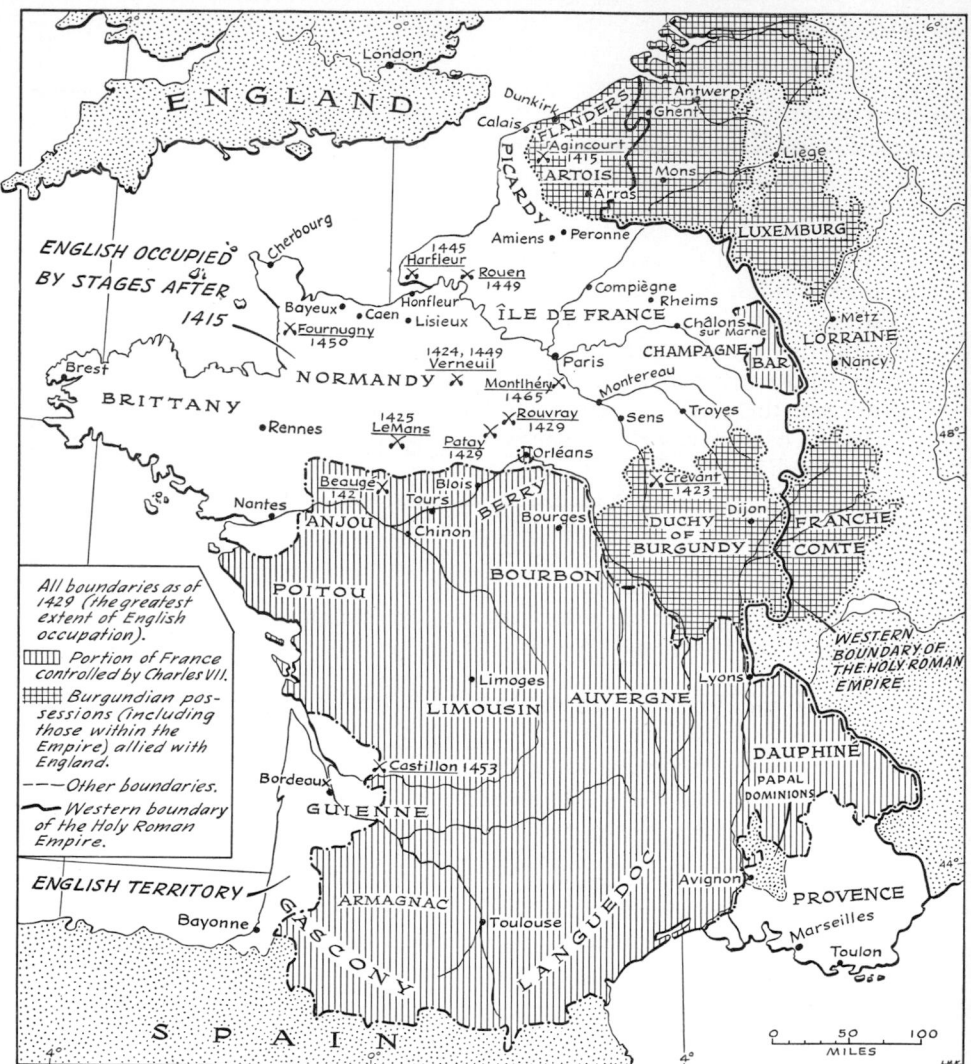

ENGLAND

London

ENGLISH OCCUPIED
BY STAGES AFTER
1415

Dunkirk
Calais
FLANDERS
Antwerp
Ghent
Liège
Agincourt
1415
PICARDY
ARTOIS
Arras
Mons
LUXEMBURG

Cherbourg
Amiens
Peronne
1445
Harfleur
Rouen
1449
Compiègne
Rheims
Metz
LORRAINE
Bayeux
Caen
Honfleur
Lisieux
ÎLE DE FRANCE
Châlons
sur Marne
Nancy
Fournugny
1450
1424, 1449
Verneuil
Paris
CHAMPAGNE
BAR
Brest
BRITTANY
NORMANDY
Montlhéry
1465
Montereau
Sens
Troyes

Rennes
1425
LeMans
Rouvray
1429
Patay
1429
Orléans
Crevant
1423

Nantes
Beauge
1421
Blois
Tours
BERRY
Bourges
DUCHY
OF
BURGUNDY
Dijon
FRANCHE
COMTE
ANJOU
Chinon

All boundaries as of
1429 (the greatest
extent of English
occupation).
▥ Portion of France
controlled by Charles VII.
▦ Burgundian pos-
sessions (including
those within the
Empire) allied with
England.
——— Other boundaries.
—— Western boundary
of the Holy Roman
Empire.

POITOU
BOURBON

LIMOUSIN
Limoges
AUVERGNE
Lyons

WESTERN
BOUNDARY OF
THE HOLY ROMAN
EMPIRE

DAUPHINÉ
PAPAL
DOMINIONS

Bordeaux
Castillon 1453
GUIENNE

ENGLISH TERRITORY

Bayonne
GASCONY
ARMAGNAC
Toulouse
LANGUEDOC
Avignon
PROVENCE
Marseilles
Toulon

S P A I N

0   50   100
MILES

France, 1415-61

The adventure, as might have been expected of Gloucester, was badly handled. He had antagonized Burgundy and damaged English prestige. He returned to England in March 1425, leaving his wife cooped up in the city of Mons. It was his continued intrigues and threats to peace that led the Royal Council to urge Bedford to return to England to assure peace. Bedford remained in England for sixteen months while English campaigns in France stood still. In order to complete the conquest of northern France, the English needed to extend their lines westward. In 1427 Bedford requested of Parliament heavy reinforcements for the campaign of 1428, and Parliament voted a substantial grant. It was decided to take Orléans, a key fortified outpost in the obedience of Charles VII. A quite inadequate force of four thousand to five thousand men invested Orléans on October 12, 1428. Unable to encircle completely the city and thus reduce it to starvation, the English troops could only annoy by occasional assaults and artillery bombardment. During six months of this futile siege Charles VII sent no help. His treasury was empty, he had few resources in himself, and his advisers were of little use.

Joan of Arc

THEN on March 6, 1429, a young girl came to the castle at Chinon where Charles VII was living, and demanded audience. She was Joan of Arc, a peasant girl from Domrémy, on the border of Lorraine. Although ridiculed at first, Joan soon persuaded the king that she had a special message and divine direction for him which would free Orléans and lead him to Rheims to be crowned. From the age of thirteen Joan had heard voices and seen visions. She had said little of these experiences to anyone, but when she was eighteen, in 1429, her visions began to be of French victories over the English invader. She was ordered by the saints who spoke to her to go to the king and lead him to save Orléans and then on to Rheims to be crowned. Joan's good sense and modesty were convincing, and Charles was finally won to her plan. She was examined by four bishops and learned men at Poitiers who attested to her orthodoxy and uprightness. On April 21, in white armor, a white banner borne before her, she set out from Blois at the head of a small force to free Orléans from the English besiegers.

On April 29 Joan reached Orléans and by night came into the city. Her presence and confidence worked a miracle in the minds of the defenders. They wanted suddenly to take the offensive. On May 3 a sortie took one of the English positions, and in another three days the English were driven out of all the redoubts from which they had surrounded the city. The English raised the siege on the 8th. The next step was the coronation at Rheims on July 17. Joan stood at Charles' side, her mission accomplished. Nevertheless, she counseled the king to go straight to Paris. French cities on the way declared for Charles, and the environs of Paris might have done so if they had been free to choose, but Bedford stood ready to resist. On September 8 Joan led an attack on the Porte St. Honoré of Paris, but the capital was too well fortified to be taken by direct assault. Charles had little real desire to carry on an aggressive war such as Joan urged, and his advisers were even pleased that the assault led by Joan had failed. From this time her influence waned and she had no direct hand in the conduct of the war.

It must be admitted that Joan's military capacities were not her greatest asset. But her ability to inspire confidence and enthusiasm when they were lacking or dormant was remarkable. It was solely due to her that the English were driven out of the valley of the Loire and that Champagne and many towns in the Île de France declared for Charles. If Charles had been more perspicacious or even moderately courageous the English might have been driven out of Paris after the coronation at Rheims. Unfortunately, however, he was both lazy and craven, and his counselors were worse. Yet in spite of

Charles' character the current of national sentiment was flowing in his favor. The duke of Burgundy was wavering in his loyalty to the English alliance; Bedford was toying with the idea of withdrawing from Paris and settling the English line in Normandy.

As the campaign of 1430 took shape, Joan boldly led a small detachment into Compiègne, where, on May 23, she was overpowered and captured by the Burgundians. She was sold to the English for ten thousand gold francs. Bedford planned to discredit her and counteract her influence by proving that she was a sorceress, which would at the same time mean the stake. The bishop of Beauvais insisted that she be tried by his court. From February to April 1431 she was examined by a court of high ecclesiastics and theologians, all Frenchmen. Her answers were direct and brave. She reiterated firmly the story of the "voices" that had directed her and told how, even in prison, they had counseled her to answer all questions forthrightly. Her coolness, her evident and unfailing trust in God, and her high intelligence won grudging admiration even from her inquisitors. Nevertheless, conviction was a certainty from the outset. On May 23, 1431, the judgment of the court was announced: that she was a sorceress and her visions the work of Satan. The next day, confronted with a threat that she would be burned that day, and in grievous physical condition from brutal treatment during her long imprisonment, Joan weakened and admitted the truth of the charges. Four days later, however, she was declared to have "relapsed." She was hastily condemned, and at high noon on May 30 she was led to the stake in the old marketplace of Rouen by English soldiers. The trial summaries left by the judges read more like attempts to justify their decision than a court record. Obviously they felt themselves in the wrong. The University of Paris, always interested in anything related to the faith, and the bishop of Beauvais, were under English control, and might plead that excuse for the shameful miscarriage of justice. Charles VII, however, who owed his recent triumphs and the resurgence of French national feeling to the inspiration of the Maid of Orléans, did nothing to save her life. Although he had many high-ranking English prisoners whom he could have used to ransom her, he made not a single gesture in that direction. The French people as a whole were much more patriotic than their king. The death of Joan, condemned by a French court acting under English orders, was almost immediately regarded by all classes in France as a martyrdom,* and it crystallized French determination to be rid of the invader.

What Joan had thus won for the French national cause, which Charles so poorly headed, was not to be lost. The English hoped to counter some of the psychological benefit which Joan's leadership and martyrdom had given the French by bringing the young King Henry VI to be crowned at Paris. The results, however, were not encouraging. Although Charles' military aids were of poor quality, resistance to the English from peasants and the bands of partisans in the years 1431–35 was effective. The English cause was so weakened that Philip the Good of Burgundy, unhappy at an alliance with a losing cause, shifted sides, and by the treaty of Arras (September 21, 1435) joined the party of

---

* In 1450 a process of rehabilitation of Joan of Arc was begun, and in July 1456 Pope Calixtus III revoked the condemnation by the court at Rouen. She was proposed for canonization in 1903 and canonized by Pope Benedict XV on May 16, 1920.

Charles VII. The next year the Parisians drove the English out of Paris; other cities hitherto in English hands fell to Charles. The tide of war was clearly running against the English and it appeared as if, with a little more aggressiveness on the part of Charles, the English could have been driven out of all of France. But because the long war had exhausted all elements of society in those parts of France which had been occupied by the English or exposed to military action famine, disorder, and lawlessness prevailed. Hence an active campaign of expulsion presented great natural difficulties. Yet everywhere in France it was recognized that it was only a matter of time before the English would have to withdraw.

Almost concurrently with the signing of the treaty of Arras, the duke of Bedford, who had acted with great ability as regent in France and occasionally in England, died. Both the English cause in France and the cause of the Lancastrian monarchy in England were to suffer from his demise. Henry VI, declared of age in 1437, was weak and ineffective.

From about 1438 Charles VII, till then a passive and almost spineless figure, began to act like a king. He crushed rebellious nobles, reorganized his military as an active standing army by the *Ordonnance* of 1445, cleaned France of the *écorcheurs,* brigand gangs who made the countryside insecure for peasant or townsman, and appointed and listened to ministers and advisers whose first concern was France rather than their own purses. It is probable that some part of this transformation was the work of Agnes Sorel, the king's mistress, who is credited by all the chroniclers with a fine mind, political sagacity, and fervent patriotism, as well as great charm and beauty. It is also at about this time that we begin to hear much of the activities of the dauphin Louis, whose nervous energy and determined craft caused his father much concern but also presaged the political genius of the future Louis XI.

The Pragmatic Sanction of Bourges

ONE of the greatest economic factors in France for centuries had been the Church, whose power and independence had been a source of annoyance to the monarchy from Carolingian times. Even the victory of Philip IV over Boniface VIII had not perceptibly weakened the position of the ecclesiastical organization. Charles VII utilized the dissatisfaction felt throughout France at the sad performance of the Church during the Great Schism (see below, Chapter 11) and at the Councils of Constance and Basel to induce the French clergy, assembled at Bourges (June–July 1438), to condemn the *curia* and accept a statute of the Church in France. This statute, thenceforth known as the Pragmatic Sanction of Bourges, accepted most of the decrees of the Council of Basel, declaring a general council supreme over the Church, and, more important for France, affirmed the independence of the French church from papal control, forbidding appeals to Rome, abolishing annates (save a portion during the lifetime of Pope Eugenius IV), and placing the election of French bishops in the hands of the cathedral chapters and the king. The king then issued the whole declaration of the synod over his name as a royal ordinance. The general impression was that there was now a Gallican church with the king replacing the pope as its head. This declaration must be kept in mind when we come to discuss the Reformation in France, for it is one reason why there was no great impulse in France, comparable to that in Germany or in England, for separation from Rome. The French church had its independence for a century before the Reformation.

In 1444 a two-year truce was signed between England and France, but the English claimed at that time only Normandy and a part of Guienne. In the spring of 1448, Maine was finally given up to France. In October 1449, Rouen fell to the French, and in the spring and summer of 1450, the English were forced out of all Normandy. In June 1451, Bordeaux fell to the French. A gallantly led English expedition in October 1452 recaptured the city, but a year later it was again lost. Charles VII entered Bordeaux in triumph on October 19, 1453. England had had enough, and the long war ended without a treaty. Only Calais, of all the conquests in France of the kings of England, remained in English hands. Both France and England profited by the English withdrawal: England because she was now free from the terrific drain of maintaining an expensive establishment, civil and military, in an unfriendly land and could henceforth concentrate her energies on developing her own natural strength, her insular position; France because the path of unification within her natural frontiers could now be firmly entered upon. The future greatness of both England and France may be said to have begun with this fortunate, if to the English temporarily humbling, outcome of a long and exhausting struggle.

ENGLAND: LANCASTER AND YORK

IN ENGLAND the last years of the war were marked by disorder and dissension among the nobles who made up the Royal Council. Humphrey, duke of Gloucester, named Protector of the Realm during the minority of his nephew, Henry VI, was allowed little actual power. His aspirations to greater authority were opposed by the Council, led by Henry Beaufort, bishop of Winchester, a son of John of Gaunt. The conflict within the Council continued after the coronation of the king in 1429. Beaufort was vulnerable in popular opinion because he had accepted a cardinal's hat and a papal legateship, and Gloucester harped on the fact that his opponent was taking orders from a foreign ruler, the pope. The dissension became so bitter that Bedford, Gloucester's elder brother, had to return again (July 1433) from his post as regent in France to compose the differences and reduce Gloucester's power. To add to the complications of personal squabbles, the government was in debt and the exchequer empty. Bedford, the only high-ranking magnate who was universally respected, imposed a spartan regime on the treasury and, had he lived, might have brought some order into the chaos that Gloucester's unbusinesslike administration had produced. Bedford's death (September 1435) was a disaster. Soon thereafter Beaufort, a more clever intriguer than Gloucester, regained the ascendancy in the Council; the majority of King Henry VI, declared in 1437 when he was fifteen years of age, only confirmed the dominance of Beaufort and his friends.

Gradually the structure of governmental control changed. The old Council lost its predominance to the ministers of the king, career officials whose daily contact with affairs gave them power which the members of the Council could not match. Beaufort had warm supporters among these officials and passed this advantage on to his successor, the duke of Suffolk. Gloucester's influence in government declined. He was removed from the Council in 1446. But his popularity remained high. As policies concerning the conduct of the war in France clashed and as charges of mishandling the defense of English possessions were hurled from both sides, Suffolk's party summoned Gloucester to attend a special Parliament called at Bury St. Edmunds in February 1447. It was a cruel trap. He was immediately arrested on charges of treason and died five days later. It was never determined whether he died of natural causes, but his friends and followers believed that he had been treacherously done to death.

The Wars of the Roses

THE mantle of Gloucester's leadership fell on his cousin Richard, duke of York, an able general and resolute antagonist. York, descended both paternally and maternally from Edward III, became the first leader of the Yorkist faction in the Wars of the Roses. Two of his sons were to wear the crown, as Edward IV and Richard III, during the period of bitter civil strife. Suffolk must have sensed the potential strength of the duke of York, for he had him sent into virtual exile as the King's Lieutenant in Ireland. Suffolk himself proved to be an inefficient minister, and as the fortunes of the war in France went against England the blame was laid at his door. Early in 1450 he was impeached by Parliament. He stood his ground but was banished from the kingdom for five years. On the way to Calais, he was intercepted in the Channel (May 1450) and beheaded by a self-appointed executioner. For three years the Lancastrian court party experienced a measure of success, but when, late in 1453, the king became temporarily insane the pendulum swung to the other side. In March 1454, York was named Protector by the spiritual and temporal lords. With the king's recovery York was dismissed (February 1455) and withdrew from London to begin preparation for what seemed to all parties an inevitable civil war. His forces engaged and defeated the court party near St. Albans on May 22, 1455. The Wars of the Roses between the house of Lancaster (whose standards carried a red rose) and the house of York (whose emblem was a white rose) had begun.

From 1455 to 1461 the advantage shifted from one side to the other. The middle class in the cities and the peasants on the land watched the parade of armed knights with little enthusiasm. To them, both sides were equally hateful; they plundered, destroyed crops, disrupted communication and business, and extorted from the common man. York was killed in a minor skirmish near Wakefield on December 30, 1460, and his son Edward carried on the fight with the help of the powerful earl of Warwick. Together they went to London (February 26, 1461) where, a week later, the young duke was accepted by the people as King Edward IV. Henry VI fled to Scotland, and the Lancastrian cause was more or less in eclipse for years. Warwick was actual ruler of England until about 1464, when the king began to resent the tutelage.

Warwick favored an alliance with Louis XI of France, while Edward, annoyed by Louis' petty interferences in English politics, preferred to side with the duke of Burgundy. Anxious to recover his influence over the king, Warwick led a rebellion against him in 1468 and even took him prisoner. When Edward refused to accept Warwick's guidance, the earl joined forces with Margaret of Anjou, the energetic wife of Henry VI, drove Edward from England, and put Henry, who after being captured on the Scottish border had been imprisoned for five years (1465–70) in the Tower, back on the throne (November 1470 to March 1471). Warwick enjoyed his position but briefly. Edward, with Burgundian help, soon returned, defeated Warwick's forces at Barnet (April 14, 1471), and left Warwick dead on the field of battle. Henry VI, an unwilling guest of Edward at the battle, was recommitted to the Tower, where he soon died, probably at the orders or at the hands of Edward's brother, Richard of Gloucester.

From 1471 to 1483 Edward reigned in relative peace. An expedition to France in 1475 was a fiasco, but Edward collected a fat pension from Louis XI for bringing his soldiers back to England. He took an effective interest in commerce and industry, kept a tight rein on royal officials, both those of the baronage and those of the commons, whom he raised to favor and office, and prevented what was left of the nobility from meddling in affairs of state. He used working officials, mostly lawyers, chosen for their brains and their loyalty, as his advisers. Parliament was convoked only six times during his reign, and he was independent of parliamentary financial aid, as he got much of his income from "benevolences"—a euphemism for forced gifts to the royal exchequer. Edward was not capricious in "persuading" rich subjects to make these "gifts," and it is probable that the burden of support of the government was more equitably spread by this system than by any other previously in use, particularly since favoritism or bribery had, in the past, allowed the richest to escape paying any taxes at all. Edward's practicality went far to explain the content and prosperity of the last years of his rule.

Upon the death of Edward IV in 1483, his brother Richard of Gloucester placed Edward's two sons, Edward V, then twelve years old, and his brother Richard, duke of York, eleven years old, in the Tower and took the title of Protector. By deceit and by chicanery he gained from a Parliament that he had chosen acknowledgment of his claim to the throne (as Richard III) and had his young nephews smothered to death. Many even of those who had supported Richard during his cynical and bloody career were so shocked and disgusted by what was generally assumed to be the murder of two innocent and harmless lads that they deserted him to join in cabals and plots against him. As the rumors of the murder spread abroad, large segments of both the Yorkist and Lancastrian factions united in support of Henry Tudor, a distant claimant, through his mother, to the throne. Henry was then living at the court of the duke of Brittany. Apprised of his wide support, he landed in Wales after a rebellion against Richard had broken out in England and took immediate charge of the campaign. He met Richard and his followers at Bosworth Field on August 22, 1485. Richard died fighting gallantly on the field of battle, where most of his captains were killed or taken captive. The Wars of the Roses were over.

FRANCE FROM 1453 TO 1491

THE last years of the reign of Charles VII (d. 1461) were fully as disturbed as the earlier ones. Nevertheless, with most of France freed from English occupation, Charles was able to pursue policies of rehabilitation and extension of French control toward what had already begun to be called France's "natural frontiers"—the Rhine, the Pyrenees, the Mediterranean coast west of Marseilles and the Atlantic coast. The administrative reforms which Charles had begun in the middle 1430's made it possible for France to take advantage of the gradual withdrawal of the English to resurrect trade and commerce, both domestic and foreign.

Much of the economic progress of the country in the latter part of the reign of Charles VII was due to the financial and administrative genius of Jacques Coeur (1395–1456), a merchant-financier of Bourges who rose by his own ability from the lower bourgeoisie to be the royal commissioner in southern France and a member of the Great Council. He dominated French trade in the Mediterranean and amassed a tremendous fortune by methods more familiar in the nineteenth century than in the fifteenth. He owned factories in many cities, made commercial treaties with foreign powers, purchased vast lands in France, financed Charles' reconquest of Normandy in 1449–50, gave the king sixty thousand *écus* to take Cherbourg, operated mines and minted money for the king, made many generous gifts to the Church, married his daughter into the nobility, and placed his sons high in the ecclesiastical hierarchy. He was too rich and successful to escape jealousy, and in 1453 Charles, influenced by vicious gossip, condemned him first to prison and then to banishment and loss of all his goods and possessions. Escaped from prison, he was welcomed at the court of Pope Nicholas V and given command of a fleet against the Turks. He died on the expedition at Chios in November 1456. But he had shown France what enterprise could do. The very considerable success of French sea trade in the next century was in great measure attributable to his initiative.

On his eastern frontier Charles had to contend with the expansionist policy of Philip the Good, duke of Burgundy. Philip was adroit, ambitious, rich, and lucky. Marriage alliances had increased his territories, and the profitable commerce of the Lowlands and the Burgundian hereditary lands had made his court the most lavishly magnificent in all Europe. Philip had two aims. The first was to acquire the territory lying between his southern possessions, Burgundy and Franche Comté, and his northern lands, much of what we now know as Holland, Belgium, and Luxemburg. For a large part of his possessions he was a vassal of the king of France; the rest lay within the bounds of the Empire. His second unconcealed aim was to use this dual allegiance to build a separate kingdom, independent both of the Empire—where independence was easy—and of France. Charles was well aware of Philip's purposes. Philip had allied with the English and was strong when they were strong. But after Joan of Arc led Charles to his coronation and the English began to be on a nervous defensive, Philip thought it wise to forget the English alliance and make a deal with Charles. The treaty of Arras (1435) read like an arrangement between equals. But after the reconquest of Normandy and the expulsion of the English in 1453, Charles was able to deal with Philip as king with vassal. Their relations were tense and became more so when, in August 1456, the dauphin Louis, facing discipline from his father for several instances of disobedience, fled to Philip's court. The duke welcomed the runaway prince with smiles and feasting. He had a hostage. Charles, knowing his son better than Philip did, remarked that the duke was sheltering a wolf that would eat his sheep.

Philip's ambitions to consolidate his various territories into a kingdom were almost realized. The Emperor's envoy did in fact suggest to the duke that he accept the title of King of Brabant or of Frisia. But Philip, who wanted to establish a compact area along the Rhine from Switzerland to the sea, a virtual revival of the kingdom of Lothair in the ninth century, refused. Neither the Emperor nor Charles could permit the rise of so powerful a neighbor as Burgundy would be if his aims were attained, and so Philip's plans remained a dream.

The years of English occupation of France and the absence of a strong central government had left a heritage of feudal separatism. In 1440 Charles had quelled a revolt of the nobility in southern France, known as the *Praguerie,* in which the dauphin was involved. But the spirit of rebellion was not dead. John II, duke of Alençon, in the north, and John V, count of Armagnac, in the south, both set themselves against Charles in 1455. The king took decisive action. Alençon was arrested, and his property was confiscated. Armagnac had to flee to Spain. Charles' remaining years were saddened by the treasonous attitude of the dauphin. He lived in continual fear that his son would succeed in poisoning his food and at the end refused all nourishment. Yet Charles had well prepared the land for the masterful rule of his successor, and the son, although indecently impatient for his father to die, was to be a great king of France as long as he continued his father's policies.

Louis XI, the Spider King

LOUIS XI began his reign on July 22, 1461, with decrees of severity. The feudal nobles, pleased that the king had given them an excuse to rebel, formed a League of the Public Weal (*Ligue du bien public*), ostensibly to restore justice and equity to the kingdom. Burgundy's son Charles, count of Charolais, and Louis' brother, the duke of Berry, headed the League, which fought the king's forces in an indecisive battle at Montlhéry in July 1465. However, Louis calculated that the leaders of the League would not trust one another, and he soon succeeded, by bribes and promises, in splitting the coalition against him. He made treaties, which he certainly did not intend to keep, with the League in order to gain time; individual nobles he won over by gifts of land or office; and he made attractive concessions to the burghers of Paris. In 1467 the duke of Brittany, allied with Charles (the Bold), now duke of Burgundy, invited the English to recapture Normandy. Louis retaliated by calling the Estates General, which, in April 1468, at his suggestion, declared Normandy an integral and inalienable part of the kingdom of France. Louis then undertook to persuade in person the duke of Burgundy to agree to terms of permanent peace. He went to meet Charles at Péronne (October 9, 1468) but had the misfortune to arrive just as an insurrection erupted in Liége against the duke's appointee as bishop. Messengers from Liége informed Charles that the bishop and the governor of Liége had been murdered at Louis' instigation. Charles was so furious that for several days even Louis' life hung by the slender thread of Charles' anger. The reports were somewhat exaggerated; the bishop and the governor had only been imprisoned and treated courteously. But Louis, in order to save his life, made every promise demanded of him. Once out of Charles' power, of course, he began to organize the ruin of this too powerful vassal. The task took some years and several wars and conspiracies.

In the meantime Charles had been pursuing the aim that had ruled the counsels of his father, the creation of a compact kingdom stretching from Burgundy and the Franche Comté along the Rhine to the sea. To unite the extremities of his territory, he needed to add Lorraine or Champagne or both. By 1473 he had made some minor gains by purchase or by threat of force, but in so doing he had alerted all his neighbors to the dangers of his plans and had disturbed the security of the Rhine cities and the Swiss cantons. Both the latter had no intention of losing the independence they had enjoyed for so long and at great cost. In 1473 Emperor Frederick III appeared on the point of conferring a crown on Charles when news of the formation of a league of Rhenish and Swiss cities allied with the king of France came out. Charles replied to this direct challenge by invading Lorraine and taking Nancy in November 1475. He then attacked the town of Grandson on February 18, 1476, and induced the defenders to surrender by promising them their lives. When they surrendered, he had them hanged or drowned. Indignant at this treachery, the Swiss allies fell on Charles' army near the town and drove the Burgundians from the field. The despised "cowherds," as Charles called them, had the laugh on the redoubtable duke. In June, thirsting for revenge, Charles besieged Morat on the way to Bern. The Swiss, mobile and crafty, fell on his carelessly deployed army and almost annihilated it. At Nancy on January 5, 1477, while leading a foolhardy attack on the larger forces of the Swiss and their allies in the pay of Louis XI and Duke René II of Lorraine,* Charles was killed. Thus ended the Burgundian threat to the unity and safety of France. Yet not quite, for Charles had left an only daughter, Mary, then twenty years of age. She chose to marry Maximilian of Austria, heir to the Habsburg lands, in August 1477. One of the offspring of this union was Philip the Handsome, and from his marriage (1496) to Joanna of Castile and Aragon was to stem one of the longest and bitterest dynastic rivalries in European history.

When Louis had organized Charles' enemies against him, and was sure that their interests would force them to fight to the bitter end, he felt free to bring the other recalcitrant noble houses of France to heel. The first great noble to be disciplined was John II, duke of Alençon (1473), who was sentenced to death, then reprieved by Louis. Next was John V, count of Armagnac, who was killed in his own castle by an archer of Louis' attacking army. Then the purge was interrupted for a time. In August 1475, Edward IV of England, invited by Charles of Burgundy to reclaim his French "inheritance," landed in Calais with an army but no supplies. Louis blandly bought him off with some

---

* Grandson of René I (see p. 265).

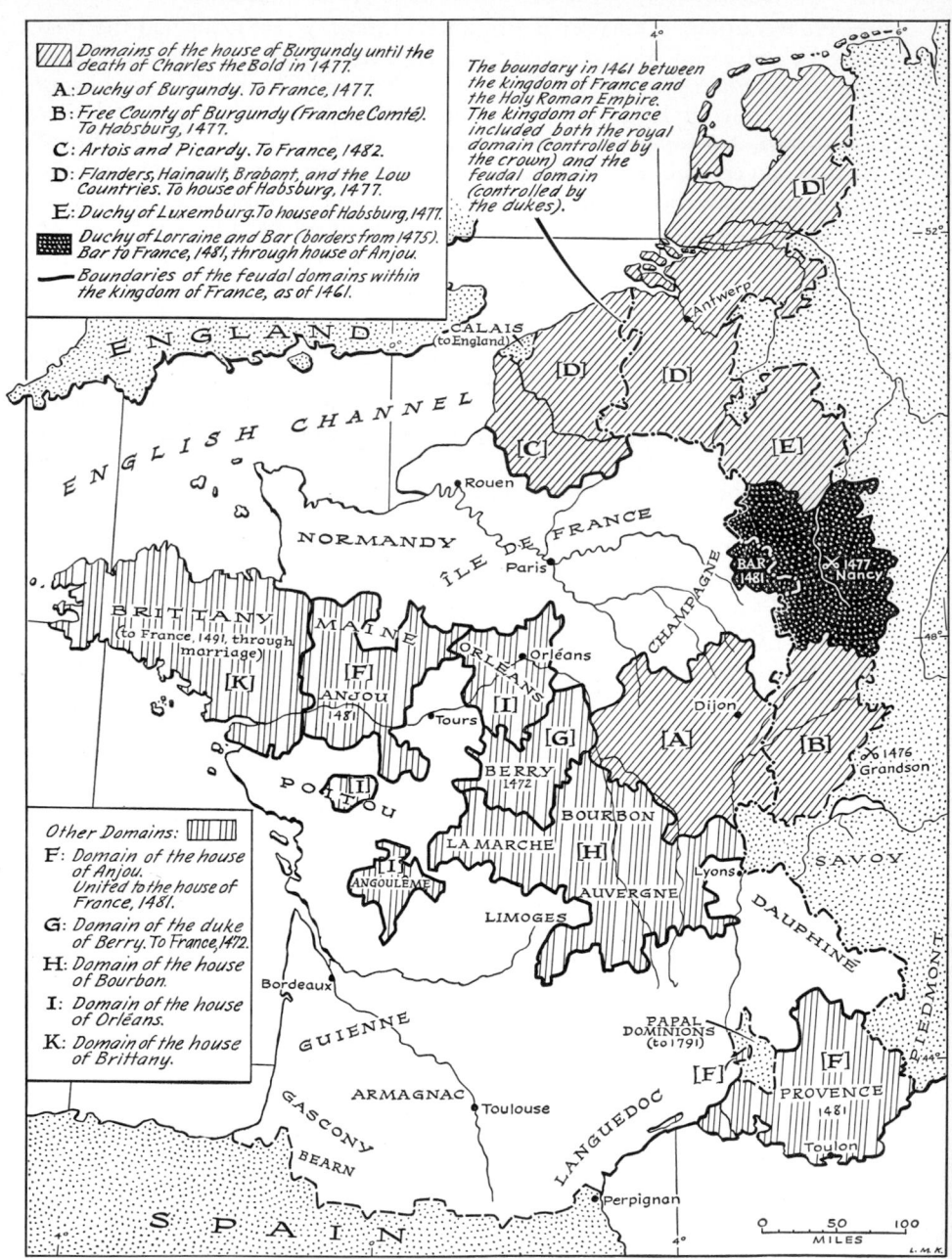

Domains of the house of Burgundy until the death of Charles the Bold in 1477.
A: Duchy of Burgundy. To France, 1477.
B: Free County of Burgundy (Franche Comté). To Habsburg, 1477.
C: Artois and Picardy. To France, 1482.
D: Flanders, Hainault, Brabant, and the Low Countries. To house of Habsburg, 1477.
E: Duchy of Luxemburg. To house of Habsburg, 1477.
Duchy of Lorraine and Bar (borders from 1475). Bar to France, 1481, through house of Anjou.
Boundaries of the feudal domains within the kingdom of France, as of 1461.

The boundary in 1461 between the kingdom of France and the Holy Roman Empire. The kingdom of France included both the royal domain (controlled by the crown) and the feudal domain (controlled by the dukes).

Other Domains:
F: Domain of the house of Anjou. United to the house of France, 1481.
G: Domain of the duke of Berry. To France, 1472.
H: Domain of the house of Bourbon.
I: Domain of the house of Orléans.
K: Domain of the house of Brittany.

France, 1461–91

cash, a few promises, and generous feasts for his soldiers. Edward was glad to return to England, and Louis resumed the more serious business of eliminating treasonous French nobles. In January 1476, the duke of Nemours was arrested and in the following year tried for treason. He had written an abject plea to Louis which influenced the judges in his favor, but Louis overruled their moderate sentence by changing the membership of the court, and had him summarily beheaded on August 4, 1477. Lesser members of the various coalitions that had plotted against Louis and given aid and comfort to his enemies followed these leaders in death or disgrace.

Louis was fortunate also in the natural deaths of his rivals and relatives. In 1480 the aged Duke René I of Anjou and count of Piedmont and Provence * died. The next year René's nephew and heir, Charles IV, count of Maine, died leaving Maine, Anjou, Bar, and Provence to Louis. In March 1482, Mary of Burgundy died from the effects of a fall from her horse. In the negotiations that followed this last death (peace of Arras, December 23, 1482), Louis gained for the crown of France the duchy of Burgundy, Picardy, and the Somme towns. The counties of Burgundy (Franche Comté) and Artois came as the dowry of Mary's infant daughter when she was affianced to the dauphin Charles. The Comté was soon occupied by French troops, followed by ten thousand immigrants to replace natives who fled from French occupation. Although Charles did not carry out the marriage contract, the claim to the Comté was never abandoned. Of the great feudal holdings of France, only Brittany successfully resisted incorporation into the royal domain by Louis' ruthless drive for centralization of royal power.

In his last years Louis suffered two paralytic strokes, but his mind and will remained unaffected until the end (August 31, 1483). His was a character to challenge description. Cruel, deceitful, suspicious, calculating, tyrannical, cynical, tenacious, and persuasive, he was nevertheless one of the greatest rulers in all French history. His visions of French unity, French natural boundaries, French power in Europe, and French stability never wavered, and he allowed nothing to stand in the way of their realization. With him feudal France receded into the background, and modern France emerged. The later accomplishments of Henry IV and Richelieu, of Louis XIV and Napoleon, would have been unthinkable without the stern, ruthless discipline to which Louis XI, the Spider, subjected *la doulce France,* the "sweet land of France." France liked the discipline little; yet her wealth and power were directly traceable to it.

Charles VIII

THE death of Louis XI brought to the throne his son Charles VIII, an ungainly, unprepossessing, inept youth of thirteen. Charles' oldest sister, Anne, with her husband, Pierre de Bourbon, lord of Beaujeu, acted as regent. Almost at once the repressed nobles and princes of the blood, in reaction against the rule of Louis XI, attempted to gain control of the Royal Council and the government. An Estates General called in January 1484 proved less than compliant with the wishes of the princes, however, and even freely discussed the claims

---

* He had also been king of Sicily and of Jerusalem and duke of Lorraine and Bar.

of the Estates themselves to a larger voice in the government. Anne, who had all her father's artistry in manipulation, induced Charles to remove most of the princes from the Council so that her husband might preside. The duke of Orléans, thus deplaced as head of the Council, plotted at home and abroad to recover his power, but Anne forestalled his moves until, finally, what the French called the Fools' War (*la guerre folle*) developed. The princes were leagued and had the help of both Maximilian, King of the Romans, and the duke of Brittany. Charles' forces under Anne's command defeated the allies easily in July 1488, captured the duke of Orléans, and imprisoned him for three years in Bourges.

Brittany's participation as a leader in the revolt emphasized the need for some measure to counteract Breton independence. Brittany had been a disturbing factor in French history for at least two centuries and was now the only part of France's natural landblock that was not an organic part of the kingdom. The duke of Brittany, Francis II, died in 1488, leaving only a fourteen-year-old daughter, Anne, for whose hand there arose a flock of aspirants. Brittany's geographical position made marriage of the heiress to a potential or actual enemy of France a matter of grave concern to the kingdom. Consequently, at the urging of Anne de Beaujeu in October 1491 Charles VIII, then twenty-one, occupied some Breton towns with his soldiery and went on to Rennes to talk with the princess. He was apparently persuasive, for they were publicly affianced three days later and married on December 6, 1491. This marriage implied the physical unification of France and can conveniently be regarded as marking the end of an epoch of gradually lessening separatism. Removal of the threat of princely separatism was the most important step in the elimination of feudalism in its most pernicious form. Herein lay the secret of much of the strength of France in succeeding centuries. With the unification of France and the consolidation of royal authority, we step over the threshold into modern political history.

ART AND LETTERS

England

THE fourteenth century was a period of great artistic activity in many regions of Europe—in Bohemia, in southern Germany, in Italy, and in parts of France. But England seems not to have been so affected. The perennial wars with France or with Scotland and sometimes with both, the Black Death, and the continued preoccupation with economic problems prevented any great creative urge that might otherwise have made this century an age of inspired art. Nevertheless, in architecture the century was not completely barren. In the time of Edward I (1272–1307) there was a fashion known as Decorated Gothic, which treated conventional Gothic freely and richly, doubling the resilient curves of thirteenth-century Gothic to form a series of elongated *s*'s. This style, however, soon gave way to a less free and imaginative design, Perpendicular Gothic, which is best illustrated in Gloucester Cathedral. Eschewing the additional curves of the Decorated Gothic, it enhances the quadrangular designs in the walls, and uses the ogival arch as little as is congruent with sound structural demands. The over-all effect is one of height and light. Even the ribbings in the vaults seem angular and efficient, as if dictated by the engineer and not the artist. This style was followed in parish churches and a few cathedrals for a good century or more after 1340.

When, in January 1381, the young Richard II married Anne of Bohemia, the daughter of the Emperor Charles IV, the way was opened for Continental influences to flow into England. The imperial court at Prague had been a cosmopolitan center of art and letters, and Anne certainly influenced Richard in that direction. His successors, the Lancastrians, in some ways more Continental than English, encouraged the building of handsome palaces and churches, colleges, hospitals, and guildhalls. They promoted as well the lesser arts, the design and manufacture of jewelry, stained glass, illuminated manuscripts, wood carvings, and fine gold and silver work. It would, however, be a mistake to credit the rulers of England with the sole impetus in these artistic and architectural developments. The people of England—the guildsmen, the gentry, the nobility, the monastic orders, and the secular clergy—were all interested in the amenities of life, whether in church, castle, guildhall, or home, and the testimony they have left us speaks loudly of the vigor and grace of their conception and their craftsmanship. In the midst of the wars with France and the civil Wars of the Roses, a lively interest in art and architecture pervaded all levels of English society. But the decades of concern with war and with dynastic rivalries that inevitably deranged civil and commercial life finally had their dire effect on cultural expression. Before the advent of the Tudors and stability, English originality declined noticeably, while Flemish techniques and style became prominent factors in English art.

In literature and learning the fourteenth century was a period of transition from a Latin- or French-dominated scene to one in which the English language and temper took command. In the days of the first two Edwards, at least, the ruling class still prided itself on its Norman-French culture; it was not until 1365 that English came to be the language of debate on the floor of Parliament. The literature was thus composed mainly of the traditional romance and allegory which adorn medieval French literary history. But by the middle of the century the native English element was struggling for recognition and had already given evidence of its strength and individuality. The creations of the end of the century—sensitive poetry such as *The Vision of Piers Plowman,* referred to earlier (Chapter 9) in connection with the social unrest after the Black Death, *The Pearl, Sir Gawain and the Green Knight* (this latter quite in the French romance tradition), the many anonymous love lyrics—are remarkable for their expert handling of verse form and for the sureness with which they carry a message. No less significant was the English prose of the pre-Chaucerian era. Richard Rolle wrote moving homilies in English prose though he also wrote much in Latin. John Wyclyf, whose complete Latin works would fill over forty large volumes, not only wrote much in English and stimulated massive Lollard vernacular literature but also organized and began the translation of the Bible from the Vulgate Latin into English. He probably completed the New Testament himself about 1382, and his colleagues and pupils finished the work and revised it a few years later. Its immense popularity and therefore its great influence among the people are attested by the survival—in spite of a rigorous persecution of the Lollards in the fifteenth century—of almost two hundred manuscript copies.

These vernacular works, prose and poetry, were evidence of the growing national consciousness of the English people and their deliverance from the leading strings of French models. The eventual expulsion of the English from France was to parallel the creation of their own literary medium, without which no people becomes a nation. But halfway through the French wars the English produced one of their greatest national geniuses, Geoffrey Chaucer.

Chaucer

CHAUCER (1340–1400) was the son of a prosperous London vintner. He served in the army in France, was captured, and was ransomed by Edward III in 1360. For many years thereafter he served the crown as negotiator or messenger abroad for the king or some member of the royal family. He made at least two trips to Italy, in 1372, when he may have met Petrarch and Boccaccio, and in 1378. In 1386 he was a member of Parliament. He served as controller of the customs at London for some years and attained a degree of material comfort, but with the decline of power of John of Gaunt he lost or sold his offices, and from 1388 his fortunes waned. He was in such difficulty that he was once (1398) sued for debt. The accession of the son of John of Gaunt, Henry of Lancaster, to the throne in September 1399 brought a reversal of Chaucer's situation, but he lived only a few months after Henry had granted him a pension of forty pounds.

Chaucer's literary activity was the avocation of a busy bureaucrat and man of affairs. He translated from both French and Latin, and some of his poetry shows a close familiarity with known Italian works. His most finished artistic production, the tragic story of two lovers, *Troilus and Criseyde,* is in large measure an adaptation of Boccaccio's *Filostrato*. But his greatest and most English work is the *Canterbury Tales*. Thirty pilgrims on the way from London to the shrine of Canterbury meet at an inn and agree to pass the time on their way by telling stories. The pilgrims come from every social group: knight, squire, lawyer, monk, sailor, clerk, merchant, cook, sheriff, parson, miller and housewife. The whole is thus an unequaled mosaic of English medieval life. For humor, pungency, tolerance, realism, and correspondence to the essential temper of the English people then and later, the *Canterbury Tales* have never been matched in English or, indeed, in any other European language.

Other Writers: Relations with the Continent

THE fifteenth century as a whole could not hope to come up to the level of Chaucer. There were poets and dramatists of significance, but they lacked the concentrated Chaucerian realism and innate power; nor did they show compensatory superiority in other areas. There were imitators, both Scottish and English, of Chaucer, but imitation is always deterioration. John Lydgate (1370–1449), for a time prior of Hatfield Broadoak in Essex, was a prolific author of allegories and translations. Known as a facile versifier, he composed poems on demand for almost every conceivable occasion. But his facility left little room for profundity. Thomas Hoccleve (1369?–1450?) was a person of convivial tastes who made some translations and adaptations from French and Latin originals. One of these, *The Regiment of Princes,* was written in 1412 for the young Lancastrian prince Henry, later Henry V. There were other writers, less notable, who contributed literate verse and prose throughout this century. The demand for literary pabulum was growing, and the reading public, now more lay than clerical, required a greater variety of reading matter. We find titles as varied as *The Dicts and Sayings of the Philosophers* in translation (*ca.* 1455), John Capgrave's *Chronicle of England* (1464), the *Babees Book* (*ca.* 1450), a manual of good manners, and, most popular of all, Thomas Malory's *Morte Darthur* (*ca.* 1469), a masterly compilation of the whole Arthurian legend, the source and inspiration of Tennyson's *Idylls of the King.* The spirit of most of these and similar works produced in the fifteenth century is essentially medieval. Indeed, much of what was produced after Chaucer was more medieval in its romantic naïveté and limited outlook than the works of Chaucer himself. England was not completely unaffected by Continental currents of thought, of which in another connection the Renaissance element will be emphasized, but during the French war and the subsequent civil wars of Lancaster and York, there was little time or energy left for the refined, or recondite, pursuit of humane and classical learning.

A thin thread of contact existed between the Italian humanistic Renaissance and England. At the Council of Constance in 1417 Cardinal Beaufort, uncle of Henry V, met Poggio Bracciolini, the brilliant Florentine humanist who had come to the Council as secretary to the Roman Pope, John XXIII. Beaufort was so impressed by Poggio that he invited him to England as his guest. Poggio accepted and spent almost four years, 1418–22, in England, where he found no one with whom he could converse on any subject but the miserable weather and the intolerable food. He left, bored with the English. The disinterest was mutual, and his visit precipitated no widespread, sudden access of enthusiasm for humanism. The most notable English patron of the new humanistic learning was Duke Humphrey of Gloucester (d. 1447), uncle of Henry VI and for a time incompetent regent of the kingdom. On several occasions he made generous gifts of money and books to Oxford and took an especial interest in the encouragement of the classics at his beloved university. Of the almost three hundred manuscripts that he gave to Oxford, a large proportion were of the classics. Unfortunately only sixteen of those he gave are now known to exist.

A few English scholars visited Italian centers in the next decades. Four English churchmen, Robert Flemming, dean of Lincoln (d. 1483), William Grey, bishop of Ely (d. 1478), John Free, bishop of Bath (d. 1465), and John Gunthorpe, dean of Wells (d. 1498), traveled widely in Italy and studied, at one time or another, with the great Guarino da Verona. They all brought back manuscripts to England and advanced the knowledge of the Latin and Greek classics. Several of them were already in a position to extend patronage to younger scholars for study and travel to humanistic centers. Many others, after studying in Italy, returned to England where they rose to high ecclesiastical position, and then used that position and their wealth to support younger scholars in travel and study. By the last decades of the century, when the wars had ceased, there was an atmosphere congenial to the pursuit of classical learning, and a number of private schools boasted excellent instruction in Latin and Greek. But the names of Thomas Linacre (d. 1524), William Grocyn (d. 1519), John Colet (d. 1519), William Lyly (d. 1522), and Thomas More (d. 1535), the leading lights of English humanism, all of whom were born in the mid-fifteenth century and studied in Italy before 1500, belong to the Tudor period rather than to the period now under study.

France

IN THE thirteenth century France dominated the cultural and intellectual life of Europe. The University of Paris was the mecca of scholars everywhere. French literary themes in prose and poetry were praised, repeated, copied, and adapted along the trade routes of the known world. French society was the model of good living from the Gulf of Finland to the Pillars of Hercules. And French Gothic art was the envy of the world. This reputation carried over into the next century. But the substance behind the reputation had diminished. Other universities, in Italy, Spain, Germany, and England, were attracting and holding students and professors who would earlier have gone to Paris. The lands outside France were developing their vernacular literatures and finding satisfaction in their native *genres*. They realized, furthermore, that they had their own contributions to make to the culture of Christendom. French chivalric ideals and feudal society began to lose their appeal to peoples for whom feudalism itself no longer corresponded to the realities of economic and social life. Conditions different from those in France, such as the sunnier climate in Spain and Italy, or the ingrained ideas of what constituted suitable public buildings in Germany and the Baltic regions, or a retarded economy that could not afford the outlay involved in elaborate Gothic structures, as in many parts of Europe—all these factors modified the otherwise pervasive influence of French Gothic art. The fourteenth century thus saw a lowering of France's cultural prestige.

Notwithstanding this decline in the external significance of French culture, the fourteenth century was one of the most eventful in all the history of France. The century began with the great victory of Philip the Fair over Boniface VIII. As we have seen (Chapter 2), it was more than a personal victory. It was the triumph of the idea of a secular national state over the universalism of a supranational theocracy. The far-reaching implications of the struggle were not lost on the intellectuals of the time, and the pamphleteering, on both sides, was prodigious. For the first time, on a large scale, nonclerical intellectuals stood up to the hitherto dominant churchmen and, in not a few cases, proved themselves more learned than the clerics. The end of the monopoly of learning, long exclusively in the hands of the clergy, was in sight. When a layman could argue successfully with a doctor of theology on matters of Church doctrine or government, and quote Scripture, St. Augustine, St. Gregory, or canon law to his opponent's confusion, the Church's monopoly on culture was tottering. The beginnings of a transformation can be so clearly traced in this century that we must speak of the gradual secularization of the state, of society, and of culture as characteristic of the age.

The great work of Jean de Meun (d. 1308), the continuator of Guillaume de Lorris' *Roman de la Rose,* dates from late in the thirteenth century, but its anti-clerical spirit of criticism and its rational approach to every question, whether it concerned monarch or priest, were characteristic of the new temper. Much of the drama and literature of entertainment, the *fabliaux,* the *lais,* the *jeux,* was purely bourgeois in origin and purpose. The *chansons de geste,* intended for the courts of the nobility, were going out of style. Yet the upper bourgeoisie, ambitious to break into the ranks of the nobility, patronized the aristocratic poets, among whom Guillaume de Machaut (d. 1377) and his disciple Eustache Deschamps (d. 1405) were the best known and most prolific. De Machaut and Deschamps produced quantities of ballads and allegorical poems which abundantly revealed the temper of the time. Both of them were interested in the events of the day and might be called journalist-poets.

Jean Froissart (d. 1405) was a poet of the same school, but his greatest work was his prose *Chronicles of England, France, Spain, Brittany, Flanders and Other Countries Adjoining.* Of north French bourgeois birth, he attached himself to the courts of princes, as secretary or court historian, and lived at various times in England, Gascony, Milan, Avignon, Paris, and the Lowlands, collecting by personal interview or through documents available to him the material for his story. His sympathies were all with the feudal world; the common people barely interested him. His snobbery is all the more obvious in that he was himself a barefaced social climber who did not realize that the world of chivalry he painted in such glowing colors had had its day. In the *Chronicles,* which he corrected, reworked, and expanded for over fifty years, he has left us one of the great monuments of medieval historical writing.

The generalization that the whole period of the Hundred Years' War was one of cultural decline for France, particularly serious in its effects upon literary creation, is only partially true. Northern France and parts of Gascony were intermittently ravaged. Paris suffered from internal tumult, and all of France was visited by the Black Death and the recurrences of the plague. The University of Paris, the intellectual voice of France, lost in public esteem by taking sides in the civil wars between Burgundy and the Armagnacs. The situation was discouraging. But there was no complete eclipse of learning. Royal and aristocratic patronage of art and letters was at times generous. Philip VI bought many books for the royal library; his wife, Jeanne of Burgundy, was widely known as a patron of artists and writers, and a number of scholarly works were dedicated to her. Charles V, deeply interested in learning, built a great royal library. The duke of Berry, his brother, was lavish in his support of art, artists, and scholars. Some of the manuscripts that he ordered and had illuminated are to this day regarded as unmatched in the finesse and richness of their decoration. Charles VII was, according to the chronicler Chastellain, a "great historian and a fine Latinist." Philip the Good of Burgundy, and Duke René I of Anjou * proved amazingly liberal patrons of learning and the arts. Philip had a whole army of highly trained translators, scribes, illuminators, and bookbinders whose task it was to make his library

* For his other titles see above, p. 265.

the most comprehensive and scholarly in northern Europe. René, although not so rich as Philip, made up in zeal and discrimination what he lacked in wealth.

By the middle of the fifteenth century, the vernacular literature had assumed a distinctive character. The romance of chivalry had almost disappeared. There was a new bourgeois interest in politics, prompted by the logic of events, the struggle with England, the civil wars, the revolts of the peasantry and the artisans, and the conflict between church and state. A new realization of the importance of history and chronicle and of French history in particular emerged. The rising tide of French nationalism called for and created a new current of historical writing that reached its height at the end of the century in the works, some in prose, some in poetry, of Georges Chastellain (d. 1475), Jean Mechinot (d. 1491), Henri Baude (d. 1491), Thomas Basin (d. 1491), Robert Gaguin (d. 1501), Martial d'Auvergne (d. 1508), and, perhaps best known to posterity, Philippe de Commynes (d. 1511) (see below, p. 277).

Important as the growing secularism in government and culture undoubtedly was, and revealing as was the accompanying burgeoning of the national spirit with its interest in historical literature in any form, these were not the only significant cultural manifestations in France of the late Middle Ages. It has long been conventional to assert that the Renaissance did not come to France until the sixteenth century. The Renaissance, taken as a European movement, defies precise definition. It differed in different countries; nor did it show itself simultaneously throughout Europe. Without examining too closely the meaning of the term as it relates to France, we may still fairly safely present three leading characteristics which we should expect to find in some degree in any society before we use the term "Renaissance": (1) secularism, or a minimization of the clerical influence in church, state, and literature; (2) a bourgeois, antifeudal social element; and (3) classical humanism, an interest in the Latin and Greek factors in education and art as well as in literature.

The national secular state is typical of the modern world. We meet it first in France under Philip the Fair. The self-awareness of a bourgeois society is accepted as perhaps the dominant mark of modern social structure. Although this does not emerge in France earlier than in several other countries, particularly Italy, we do find that the bourgeoisie was conscious of itself and aggressive in fourteenth-century France. We have discussed at some length, in this and preceding chapters, the existence of these two Renaissance characteristics in France of the fourteenth and fifteenth centuries. (See above, Chapters 5 and 9.)

It is quite true that France had no humanistic revival like that in Florence, no trio like Dante, Petrarch, and Boccaccio who adorned the glorious history of that Athens of the western world. Nevertheless, France had some notable advocates of humanism. For almost seventy years in the fourteenth century, Avignon, the seat of a French Papacy, surrounded by French territory was, if we may judge from the roster of visitors, the meeting place of the intelligentsia of Europe. The influence of the court of Avignon on the intellectual and artistic life of the Christian world was incalculable. Although the outbreak of the English wars had some dampening effect upon the development of humanistic studies, France was not far behind Italy in this interest. In the fourteenth century there was much copying of manuscripts of the Latin classics, and the manuscripts were read and commented upon close to the time of copying. Not only were Cicero and Ovid, Seneca and Virgil, Horace and Livy frequently copied by French scribes during the first part of the war period, but other and less prominent Latin authors were also known and revered.

Early French Humanism

A QUARTET of French lovers of antiquity illumined the last decades of the fourteenth century and the early years of the fifteenth century: Gontier Col (*ca.* 1350–1418), his younger brother Pierre Col (*ca.* 1360–1418), Jean de Montreuil (1354–1418), and Nicolas de Clamanges (*ca.* 1355–1437). The four were close friends, if differently employed, and their correspondence over almost forty years reveals their enthusiastic reading of the Latin classics and their earnest desire to perfect their knowledge of antiquity and to propagate their passion among their numerous acquaintances. Gontier Col was a member of the rich bourgeoisie of Sens who became a clerk—"receiver of aids"—in the royal establishment in 1379 and soon thereafter secretary to the duke of Berry, from which position he entered the royal chancery. He was rapidly promoted until in 1388 he became secretary to Charles VI. He was entrusted with many important and responsible posts and was a confidant of the king during the trying years of the Burgundy-Armagnac tension.

Jean de Montreuil was also a professional bureaucrat. He was successively secretary of finance under Charles V and chancellor of Charles VI, and was often sent as special envoy to Avignon, Scotland, Germany, and to various Italian courts. He was a friend of Coluccio Salutati, the great Florentine secretary and humanist, and attended the Council of Constance. Unlike Gontier Col, he was a cleric possessing several lucrative prebends. He acknowledged his indebtedness to Gontier for "turning his attention to classical studies." We know him well through his copious correspondence, which he collected and edited. Although considered grasping and ungracious, he was passionately fond of the great Latin writers, whom he quoted continually in his letters to all and sundry.

Nicolas de Clamanges, of modest origins, studied at Paris and early gained a reputation as a brilliant humanist. Called to Avignon by Pope Benedict XIII, he remained for ten years as papal scriptor and secretary. A sensitive soul, the bitter polemic between Benedict and both the king of France and the University of Paris induced him to retire to an Augustinian priory in Champagne, there to devote himself to scholarship, correspondence with his friends, and writing.

Less is known of Pierre Col, Gontier's younger brother. He traveled widely, to Egypt, Sicily, and Spain, became a royal secretary, and attended the Council of Constance in 1416. He is best known for his part in the controversy that arose over Jean de Meun's position toward women in the *Roman de la Rose*. Christine de Pisan, the leading woman poet of France, in 1399 attacked the *Roman* as unjust to women and, furthermore, as "encouraging vice, comforting dissolute life and prone to shame and error." Her charges were seconded by

Jean Gerson, chancellor of the University of Paris. Naturalism was not yet acceptable. The humanists, led by Jean de Montreuil, Clamanges, the Col brothers, and some like-minded friends, struck back. The points in dispute multiplied considerably, and despite the great prestige of Christine and Gerson, the humanists appear to have had the better of the argument. The significance of the quarrel lies in the fact that it was the first case in French intellectual history in which the theological presuppositions of the Middle Ages and the naturalism of the Renaissance met head-on. Although both Christine and Gerson were acquainted with the ancient authors, they were limited in their outlook and concepts by their deep medievalism and could not come to grips with the newer and freer terms and ideas to which the humanists were committed and fervently loyal.

France and the Church: the Schism and the Councils

THE French monarchy was intimately involved in the vicissitudes of the Church. From a selfish point of view the Avignonese Papacy had been a boon to France. But the English war had nullified much of that benefit. Then the return of the Papacy to Rome, followed by the unfortunate *schisma* (the Greek word for "split") * and the revival of a counter-Papacy at Avignon, brought in its wake disturbance and dissension among all elements of the French church. At the University of Paris the Schism became a topic of heated debate almost from the moment it began in 1378. In November 1378, King Charles V declared the adherence of the kingdom of France to Clement VII (1378–94) in Avignon. The university hesitated to choose between the rival popes, uncertain as to the legality of the papal elections. Two German scholars there, Conrad of Gelnhausen (*ca.* 1323–90) and Henry of Langenstein (*ca.* 1335–97), early advanced the idea that the only way to heal the regrettable "rent in the seamless robe of Christ" was by a general council of the whole Church. In May 1380, Conrad, a learned canon lawyer, wrote a letter (*Epistola concordiae*) to Charles V, asking him to call such a council as the only means of settling so sharp a division. He urged that the king of France, as the leading monarch of Christendom, should take the initiative. Conrad may be considered the originator of a doctrine of conciliar government of the Church. In September 1381, Henry of Langenstein, then vice-chancellor of the university, published the *Epistola concilii pacis,* calling for a council to heal the breach and purify the Church. The new king, Charles VI, found the hesitation of the university intolerable and forced the "nations" to accept the Avignonese pope. The Anglo-German "nation" of the university, to which both Conrad and Henry belonged, voted against accepting Clement, and in 1382 and 1383 Henry and a number of the German masters † and students left Paris in the interests of safety and comfort.

The subject of the Schism and how this scandalous perversion of the principle of union and universality could be righted occupied the minds of all conscientious Frenchmen, both churchmen and laity, for decades. The university

---

* See below, Chapter 11.
† It is not certain whether Conrad left Paris in 1381 or with Henry in 1383. He became first chancellor of the University of Heidelberg in 1386.

had been restless ever since the king had forced it to accept the Avignonese line. In 1391 Jean Gerson, in a sermon before the royal court, called for a review of France's position, and the conviction that both popes should resign gained wide support. In June 1394, after a sort of referendum, the university recommended that the king demand double cession, that is, resignation of both popes. Soon after Clement received news of this decision, he died of a stroke (September 16, 1394). His successor, Benedict XIII (1394–1423), was quite unamenable to the idea of cession. In August 1396, the university proposed that France end its adherence to the Avignonese pope. On July 28, 1398, after a synod of French clergy had voted by a majority to withdraw its obedience and the king, temporarily sane, had given his approval, a royal decree to that effect was promulgated. There was now, for Frenchmen, no pope. In a Catholic country such a situation was serious. But a reserve concept was quickly adopted, that was based on the idea of an ancient and independent French church, a concept later to be known as Gallicanism. At the time there was even talk of the "restoration of the ancient liberties of the church of France." In fact, and to a degree in theory, the king was for a while head of the Church in France.

Through the University of Paris and her leading theologians, from Geln-hausen to Gerson and d'Ailly (see above, Chapter 7), France had taken a leading part in the disputes over the Schism and Conciliar Movement which resulted, in spite of great difficulties, in composing for a short time the rift in the Church. But the Conciliar Movement, which France officially supported, was a grand failure. This movement, and France's role in it, is the subject of Chapter 11. In the course of the councils, the promise of French initiative was unfulfilled. That France failed to produce either the issues or the leaders to dominate the movement may have been a commentary on the decline in the temper of the French mind. Perhaps the shock of the humiliation to French arms at Agincourt precipitated this decline, but for whatever reason the French spirit remained stunned for several decades. There was no continuation of the humanism instituted by the circle around Montreuil, Clamanges, and the Col brothers, nor was there much noteworthy vernacular literature. Few great works of art were conceived and executed during the first half of the fifteenth century; nor indeed was the pride of France, the University of Paris, sufficiently alive to shake itself free of the cloying inanities of an outworn scholasticism.

About the middle of the century, however, the cultural life of France began to revive. This new phase coincided with the end of the war with England and, perhaps less significantly, with the extinction of the Conciliar Movement. The cost of France's involvement in a protracted civil war and an English occupation was terrific, bearing particularly sorely upon the arts and letters, education, and national pride. The way back from virtual silence and inaction to a leading position in the race for intellectual eminence in Europe was difficult and long. The general reaction in France at mid-century was relief at the release from the violence and uncertainty of a hundred years of war and governmental chaos. But relief precipitated no new ventures in positive thinking. True, some universities had been founded in the mid-fifteenth century; at Caen,

Angers, and Poitiers in 1432, at Bordeaux in 1441, at Valence in 1451, and at Nantes in 1460. But good faculties and good student bodies are slow growths. Without enough well-prepared scholars to guide their development, these foundations produced no new departures in science or learning. Their curricula were painfully and conventionally medieval, and even in that conservative line they did not soon attain even to mediocrity. We must look outside the schools and the universities for originality and significance in these years.

The leading names in French letters in the latter part of the fifteenth century were François Villon (1431–65?), Philippe de Commynes (1445–1511), the anonymous author of the devastating *Farce of Master Pierre Pathelin,* written about 1465, and the author of the informative *Goodman of Paris.* Of these, only Villon and Commynes really loom large on a European stage. For artistic creativity we have to look to the Burgundian court—only partially French— and the Flemish geniuses. The single French artist who merits being named in this period, Jean Fouquet (1415–*ca.* 1480), was deeply indebted to the Flemish painters, though he probably visited Italy and learned from the Italian masters.

Villon is probably the greatest medieval poet of whom France can boast. His life was a long and agonizing story of poverty and misfortune, of painful and even criminal degradation, out of which, by some peculiar miracle, there issued the purest poetry. While a student at the University of Paris, he killed another student in a quarrel and had to flee. Pardoned, he returned, only to get into further trouble. We next find him in prison at Meun-sur-Loire. Somehow he was freed and wrote poignantly in the *Grand Testament,* of his suffering, hunger, and humiliation. Into the *Testament* are interwoven some *ballades.* One of them, the "Ballad of the Hanged," written when Villon thought he himself would be swinging from the noose, is the most touching and powerful of all his verses.*

You brother men, who after us remain,
　Be not more hard to us than is our due,
For if you feel some pity for our pain,
　The sooner God shall show his ruth to you.
　Here, five and six, we hang before your view,
Our flesh, that all too lavishly we fed,
Long since devoured and rotted to a shred,
　While we, the bones, to ash and dust decay;
Let no man mock us, us so sore bestead,
　But pray that God will wipe our sins away.

Do not, though we were by man's justice slain,
　Scorn us that in a brother's name we sue;
Not every living man is wholly sane:
　Can you not then, knowing that this is true
　Make it your plea for us whose lives are through,
To Him who in the Virgin's womb was bred,
That His grace fail not at the fountain-head,
　But save us when the infernal lightnings play?
Let no soul vex us now that we are dead,
　But pray that God will wipe our sins away.

* Translation by H. B. McCaskie.

We have been washed and laundered by the rain
   The sun has blacked and dried us through and through:
Crows have picked out our eyes, and daws have ta'en
   The hairs that in our beards and eyebrows grew;
   Our bodies know no rest, ever anew
At the wind's changing pleasure buffeted
This way and that; and where the birds have fed
   Our cheeks are pocked like thimbles. See you may
Into no brotherhood like ours be led.
   But pray that God will wipe our sins away.

Prince Jesus, Lord of all, out from the dread
Empire of Hell grant that we may be sped,
   Deal with it not, to it no tribute pay,
Men, here let no light mocking words be said,
   But pray that God will wipe our sins away.

Philippe de Commynes was higher on the social scale than Villon. He was of a Flemish bourgeois family that had been raised to the nobility in the fourteenth century. Philip the Good, duke of Burgundy, was his godfather, and he was brought up at the Burgundian court. From 1468 he leaned toward King Louis XI and engaged in international intrigue in England, Brittany, and Spain. In 1472 he entered Louis' service, receiving a generous pension and titles for his abandonment of Charles the Bold, then duke of Burgundy. On the death of Louis in 1483 Commynes' position was less certain; at one point he spent eight months in an iron cage, at another twenty months in prison in Paris, but he was intermittently in favor under Charles VIII and Louis XII. His *Mémoires,* in twelve books, cover events from the battle of Montlhéry (July 1465) to the coronation of Louis XII in 1498. They are first-hand history. Commynes knew the principal characters of the drama and was present at most of the crucial events. He had access to documents and other means of satisfying his passion for truth. His history could not be called impartial. He favored royal power when it was directed toward crushing the selfish separatism of the great vassals. He saw the progress of the masses of the people, through the agency of the Estates General, toward representation in government. He approved heartily of the political structure of England as he saw it function on various visits to the island. Commynes' *Mémoires* introduced a period of historical writing that is essentially modern. He was a historian who thought like a statesman and felt like a moralist.

One of the greatest disseminators of learning in early modern Europe was the printing press. Invented about 1450 by John Gutenberg, a German in Mainz, the art of printing from movable type spread first through Germany and Italy. It came to France somewhat later. In 1470, at the instance and with the encouragement of Louis XI, the first printing press in France was set up at the Sorbonne in Paris by Johann Stein, a German master of the university, cooperating with Guillaume Fichet, a French scholar known to Louis. Louis gave French citizenship to three German journeymen who completed the atelier. The first book printed (1470) in France was an edition of the letters of the Italian humanist Gasparino da Barzizza. In the next two years nine editions of the Latin classics saw the light in Paris. France was striving to make up for lost time in humanistic studies, and the printing press was a mighty aid in that effort.

The end of the fifteenth century saw a new France and a new England. The institutions and the ideals which had advanced and guided the nations on both sides of the Channel when they entered upon the long war were no longer alive at the end of that struggle. Great forces had arisen which were to change the face of Europe.

The France that emerged victorious from the century-long struggle with England was vastly different from the France of the first half of the fourteenth century. The monarchy was strong and aware of its need for centralized power. The Church had survived the Schism and the Councils, and learned to live and labor by its own standards. The nobility had lost not only much blood and wealth, but also much of their usefulness. The bourgeoisie, on the other hand, had made tremendous gains in status and self-confidence. In cultural respects, the progress had been less noticeable, but a steady secularization of learning was producing a new class of literate laymen who would eventually usurp the clergy's monopoly of media of communication and political influence. In art and letters, a new spirit of inquiry and imagination, open to foreign ideas and motifs, enriched the fare placed before the subjects of Louis XI and his immediate successors. Joan of Arc's appeal to every Frenchman to live or die for "sweet France" continued to inspire a people hungry for a cause to espouse and a standard to follow.

In the following century France was to be forced to stand almost alone against the most powerful ruler since Charlemagne. She withstood the enemy successfully. That success was rooted in the remarkable recovery achieved during the middle and late fifteenth century under Charles VII and Louis XI.

SUGGESTIONS FOR FURTHER READING

See bibliography to Chapter 5.

BARRETT, W. P., *The Trial of Jeanne d'Arc*. London, 1931
COMMYNES, PHILIP DE, *Memoirs*. 2 vols. London, 1885–86. Bohn Library
Goodman of Paris (*Le Ménagier de Paris*), trans. E. Power. London, 1928
MONSTRELET, E. DE, *Chronicles*. 6 vols. London, 1810

BRIDGE, J. S. C., *A History of France from the Death of Louis XI,* Vol. I. Oxford, 1921
CHRIMES, S. B., *English Constitutional Ideas in the XVth Century*. Cambridge, 1931
COULTON, G. G., *Chaucer and His England*. London, 1921
DARWIN, F. D. S., *Louis d'Orléans 1372–1407*. London, 1936
EVANS, J., *English Art 1307–1461*. Oxford, 1947
HAGGARD, F. C., *Louis XI and Charles the Bold*. London, 1913
JACOB, E. F., *Henry V and the Invasion of France*. London, 1947
JACOB, E. F., *The Fifteenth Century*. Oxford, 1961
KINGSFORD, C. L., *English Historical Literature in the 15th Century*. Oxford, 1913
KINGSFORD, C. L., *Henry V*. London, 1923
KITCHIN, G., *History of France,* Vol. I. 1899

LOWELL, F. C., *Joan of Arc*. Boston, 1896

MOWAT, R. B., *Henry VI*. London, 1932

MOWAT, R. B., *The Wars of the Roses*. London, 1914

OMAN, C. W., *History of England from the Accession of Richard II to the Death of Richard III, 1377–1485*. London, 1910

PERROY, E., *The Hundred Years War*. London, 1959

SACKVILLE-WEST, V. M., *Joan of Arc*. London, 1948

SCOFIELD, C. L., *Life and Reign of Edward IV*. 2 vols. London, 1923

STEEL, A., *Richard II*. Cambridge, 1941

WYLIE, J. H., *History of England under Henry the Fourth*. 4 vols. London, 1884–98

WYLIE, J. H., and W. T. WAUGH, *The Reign of Henry the Fifth*. 3 vols. Cambridge, 1914–29

D'AVOUT, J., *La Quérelle des Armagnacs et des Bourguignons*. 1943

DE BEAUCOURT, G. DU FRESNE, *Histoire de Charles VII*. 6 vols. 1881–91

BONENFANT, P., *Philippe le Bon*. 1955

BOSSUAT, R., *Le Moyen Age*. 1931

CALMETTE, J., and L. G. PÉRINELLE, *Louis XI et l'Angleterre, 1461–1483*. 1930

CHAMPION, P., *Louis XI*. 2 vols. 1927

LUCE, S., *La France pendant la guerre de cent ans*. 2 vols. 1890–94

MICHELET, J., *Jeanne d'Arc*. 2 vols. 1925

VALOIS, N., *La France et le grand schisme d'occident*. 4 vols. 1896–1902

CHAPTER ELEVEN

THE GREAT SCHISM AND
THE COUNCILS

T HE last of the Avignonese popes, Gregory XI (1370–78), had brought the Papacy from its "captivity" on foreign soil back to Rome in January 1377. The pressure of public opinion against a further postponement of the return to the ancient see of the apostles and the heads of the Church had been more than any pope could withstand. The Roman populace, furthermore, after seventy years without their precious *curia,* was determined that the Papacy henceforth should be as Italian as it had been in former times. Gregory was disturbed at the prospect of a new conflict, and before his death, in an effort to assure an acceptable choice of successor, relaxed some of the customary restrictions upon the manner of election. Immediately after his death, the cardinals began to feel the pressure of the Roman populace. Their houses were guarded, their servants roughly handled; if they ventured into the streets, they were accosted by raucous reminders that they had better choose a Roman or at least an Italian for pope. This was the common street cry which soon became an official demand from the officers of the city of Rome.

Election of Urban VI

THE cardinals, only sixteen in number, for six were absent in Avignon and a seventh on a mission, met in conclave on April 7, 1378. The clamor of the crowd outside the Vatican was quite audible, and their own guards informed them with trepidation that they were in great danger of physical harm from the mounting anger of the mob. When the conclave met the next morning it became evident that the French majority was unable to agree among themselves upon a French pope, and as the noise of the mob outside crying, almost in unison, "Give us a Roman or at least an Italian," bore in upon them, and the solemn, almost sinister tolling of the bells of St. Peter's dinned on their ears, the cardinals quickly agreed upon Bartolommeo Prignano, archbishop of Bari. Prignano was not a cardinal, but had been vice-chancellor of the *curia* under Gregory XI and was known as an energetic official and an enemy of vice and corruption in the Church. The question of the validity of the election, in view of the disturbances throughout the city of Rome, in the square outside St. Peter's, and even before the doors of the room in which the conclave was meeting, was raised by several of the cardinals at the time, but the majority disregarded the question and proceeded with the enthronement of Prignano as Urban VI.

Election of Anti-Pope Clement VII: the Schism

URBAN soon showed himself arbitrary, ill-tempered, suspicious, tactless, and brutal. He publicly insulted the cardinals, ordered them around like menial servants, and attacked their perquisites and prerogatives. Reaction came quickly. By June 21 all the French cardinals had left Rome, using the excuse that the heat was unbearable, and in a few days three of the four Italian cardinals joined them at Fondi. The cardinals who had elected Urban now decided to depose him and elect another pope. On August 9 they issued a *Declaratio* accusing Urban of apostasy, claiming the election was void because of duress, and declaring the Holy See vacant. Urban, now without a single cardinal in his *curia,* created a completely new college of twenty-eight cardinals on September 18. Two days later the old college elected Cardinal Robert of Geneva pope, as Clement VII. There were now two popes and two colleges of cardinals. It was obvious that Urban would insist on staying in Rome. It was also obvious that Clement, a Frenchman, with his French cardinals, would return to Avignon.

To place blame at this point for this unheard-of split in the headship of the Church is perhaps unrealistic. The pronouncements of both sides, Urban and the defecting cardinals, are full of contradictions, inconsistencies, and irrelevancies. They were nevertheless carefully read in the chanceries of Europe to which they were sent, and there conclusions were reached on quite different grounds. The king of France was at first inclined to take a neutral position, but by mid-November, upon the strong recommendation of the French clergy, he declared for Clement VII. To the aging Emperor Charles IV, by nature strongly disposed to consistency and a legal point of view, the contradictory actions of the cardinals seemed untenable, and he supported Urban without condoning the tactlessness which had precipitated the breach. He wrote to other princes, to King Charles of France, Queen Joanna of Naples, and others, in an effort to form a diplomatic bloc strong enough to bring order out of the Schism. Had he lived, he might have succeeded. There was no subtler and more effective diplomat in all of Europe than the Emperor. His death in November 1378 left the Empire in the very young and uncertain hands of his son Wenzel. Some princes in the western reaches of the Empire, however, leaned to the side of Clement. The influence of the French court had always been strong along the Rhine. England, still at war with France, declared, as might have been expected, against Clement rather than for Urban, who did nothing to inspire English confidence. Scotland, naturally, took sides against England and with France. Castile, at first neutral, by mid-1381 declared for Clement. Aragon decided formally in the same sense somewhat later, in 1386. Portugal, at first pursuing a line similar to that of Castile and Aragon, was persuaded by England in 1381 to switch to Urban. Hungary, outside the Empire, sided with Urban from the early days of the division. Since the king of Hungary, Louis, was also king of Poland, the latter kingdom was also in the camp of Urban.

Thus Europe was about evenly divided in allegiance to the Roman and Avignonese lines. The evenness of the political alignment did not minimize the chaos. Both popes claimed universal jurisdiction; many ecclesiastical preferments had two occupants, many abbeys had two abbots, many bishoprics had two bishops and two completely different sets of officials. The bitterness and confusion, the sinister effect upon the ministry of the Church, the economic stress put upon the laity who were called upon—on penalty of dire punishment from both sides—to support two occupants of an ecclesiastical benefice, can hardly be imagined. Because the disaster reached into the pocket of the modest individual, everybody was obliged to give thought to the sad state of the Church. Everybody, high and low, agreed something must be done to bring peace and unity to the "robe of Christ" rent between rival claimants, each of whom was cursing, anathematizing, and excommunicating the other in a spirit of keenest hatred.

The first, almost spontaneous, suggestion was that a general council of the whole Church be called to compose the issues. There had been general (ecumenical) councils of the Church since apostolic times, and they had always spoken with authority. But it was not clear, under the conditions obtaining after 1378, how such a council could be called. If one pope summoned it, the other would refuse to attend or recognize it and the whole purpose of the council would be frustrated. There was, furthermore, no recent precedent for a secular prince to call a council. Yet it was almost universally agreed that there should be a council. This view reached its height when, on May 20, 1381, the four faculties of the University of Paris, theology, law, medicine, and arts, unanimously agreed that the way of a general council should be adopted. However, in spite of the powerful urging of Henry of Langenstein, vice-chancellor of the university, Conrad of Gelnhausen, a leading theologian of the university, and other earnest men at Paris in the years from 1378 to 1382, this view gradually lost its attractiveness (see above, p. 274). It seemed plainly impracticable for anyone except a pope to convoke, constitutionally, a general council of the whole Church. When this avenue appeared blocked another was tried, the *via cessionis,* the way of cession or resignation. It was now urged that both popes be persuaded, in the interests of the peace and purity of the Church, to resign and allow a completely new and unencumbered election. Each of the popes protested his willingness, nay his earnest desire, to sacrifice himself for the peace of the Church, but was perhaps more sure that peace could best be attained by his remaining as pontiff: the other so-called pope should resign. Thus between vain hope and increasingly desperate confusion a whole decade passed without relief.

England, technically in the obedience of the Roman pope, was in fact less concerned with the sordid strife between the popes than with her own ecclesiastical affairs. England had the protection of her statutes of Provisors and *Praemunire,* which prevented the Papacy from exacting from the English church the vast levies of which the Church in other countries complained so bitterly. Here and there in the Empire, particularly in the west and south, individual prelates and princes favored Avignon, but general sentiment favored the Roman line. The universities were uniformly pro-Urban. But the political weight of an Empire with so loose a structure and headed, after 1378, by a weak figurehead soon (1400) to be deposed, was quite insufficient to overbalance the pro-Avignon strength of France and the Spanish kingdoms. In face of this stalemate of power, the issue would have to be settled on other bases. The arena of struggle was to be not political, but administrative.

The last years of Urban VI were lamentable. He became foolishly embroiled in the dynastic struggles of the kingdom of Naples, executed five of his own cardinals on charges of treason, and died in 1389 from the effects of a fall from a donkey. His successor, elected by the remnant of the Roman college of cardinals, was a Neapolitan, Boniface IX, who ruled from Rome until his death in 1404. An abler diplomat than his predecessor, allied with Ladislaus of Naples, he crushed the French faction in southern Italy, subdued the Colonnas in Rome, and united Italy under his obedience. In his relations with foreign states, England and the Empire, he regained some of the prestige that Urban had lost. His very firmness, however, hardened the purpose of those who sought to reunite all Christendom. In France, where discussion of the problems of the Schism raged the most ardently, the conviction was gaining ground that something had to be done and that the crisis in the whole of Christendom was so serious as to override national prejudices and delicate constitutional prerogatives. There was some hope that Boniface might be willing to accept the *via cessionis,* but he soon showed himself no less stubborn than Urban, regarding himself as the true and only pope, and refusing flatly any suggestion that he should resign. On January 1, 1394, a ballot was taken at the University of Paris to find out which of three possible solutions of the Schism was preferred. The way of cession, calling for resignation of both popes, received the majority of the votes; the way of a special council (*via compromissi*), involving submission of the two popes to a commission of high-minded men for adjudication, was next; the way of a general council (*via synodi*) was the least popular. The whole ballot was a kind of repudiation of Clement, who, from Avignon, angrily condemned the proceedings and forbade the university to meddle further in the matter.

On the death of Clement in September of that year, the French king, reflecting the changed temper of the leaders of the university and the French clergy, urged the Avignonese cardinals not to elect a successor, in order that a union between the colleges of cardinals might be possible. The Avignonese cardinals put off opening the royal letter until after electing a Spaniard, Pedro de Luna, as Pope Benedict XIII. Benedict was sixty-six at his election and in calmer times would have made a distinguished record as a pope. He was learned, adroit, courageous. But these qualities at this juncture in papal history only made a solution of the crisis more difficult. Benedict, committed to the idea that only a conference between him and Boniface could be profitable for union, bustled about with preparations to meet the Roman pope, Boniface IX, somewhere or other. Little progress was made. When delegations from the French king pressed him brusquely to accept the *via cessionis,* he put them off. After so many promises from all sides had proved vain, the French clergy, at a number of synods, decided that they favored substraction (withdrawal) of obedience to the pope at Avignon (1398), and their decision was issued as a royal ordinance. When Benedict was deserted by his own cardinals, a French adventurer, Geoffrey Boucicaut, brother of Marshal Boucicaut, besieged him in his castle. Benedict's resistance won sentimental support among the French people to such an extent that a national parliament of 1403 canceled the substraction and reaffirmed their obedience. Benedict was not without some conquests in his early years. Peter d'Ailly, famous theologian and chancellor of the University of Paris, accepted in April 1394 the bishopric of Puy from Benedict, and two years later the more important see of Cambrai. Nicholas de Clamanges, the leading humanist scholar of France, became Benedict's secretary and librarian in 1397. The support of these two high and respected ecclesiastics was a definite gain to Benedict's cause. But for the five years from 1398 to 1403 France recognized no pope and was in actual fact a national Gallican church. Internally, the absence of a real head of the Church was unfortunate. France was not yet ready for a national church with the king as head.

This amiable gesture of annulment of the substraction did not, however, mean that there was any diminution of the general demand in France, and indeed in other Christian states, for the abatement of the Schism. Richard II of England, in the last troubled years of his reign, had broad support among the English people for his efforts toward a common papal policy with France. The English were veering away from Rome, the French had withdrawn their support from Avignon, they were thus for a time on almost identical ground. The University of Oxford, asked by the University of Paris in 1395 to join forces to enforce the *via cessionis,* agreed that the present situation was impossible, but contended that a general council would be the only agency that could end the Schism and bring peace and union. The atmosphere at Paris and at other university centers in France, in Spain, and in Germany was tense.

After a tumultuous reign of twenty-four months, during which he barely managed to retain control of the city of Rome, Innocent VII, the successor of Boniface IX, died in November 1406. Many felt that the death of one pope offered a good opportunity for a reconciliation of the cardinals of the two obediences, and a consequent agreement on the surviving pontiff. When, however, the Roman cardinals persisted in electing a successor to Innocent and chose a Venetian, Angelo Corrario, as Gregory XII, popular indignation rose and talk of the immediate use of force to bring the popes and the cardinals to their senses was heard everywhere. The University of Paris was by now aggressively anti-Benedict. The French king was anxious to be advised as to what should be done. By royal decree a meeting of over two hundred prelates and doctors was called for November 18, 1406, to discuss openly and thoroughly the basic question: should France and the French church continue in the obedience of Benedict XIII (renewed in 1403), or should that obedience once again be withdrawn. The detractors of Benedict, mostly from the university, spoke first, attacking the Pope for his bad faith and emphasizing the failure of the *via cessionis* to achieve unity and peace. Some of the speakers were more voluble and violent than reasonable and logical. The defenders of Benedict had their say a few weeks later. The most effective was d'Ailly, who remained cool, urbane, and statesmanlike in the presence of emotion and provocation. While he urged the *via cessionis* as, on all counts, the best solution, he saw many advantages in the idea of a council, the *via synodi*. He defended Benedict, who, he pointed out, had acted in full accordance with tradition and canon law. The conclusion of the assembly was a compromise. France should retain her obedience to Benedict in spiritual matters and reject obedience in temporal matters, that is as to collation to benefices and ecclesiastical dignities involving property. On February 11, 1407, the king approved the decision and it became law.

In the meantime the two popes, sensing the pressure of public opinion, had begun to show signs of life. They both protested their deep desire to end the Schism, and, after long negotiations, hypocritical on both sides, made arrangements to meet at Savona in northern Italy late in September 1407. They both started out in good time, but, though Benedict disembarked at Savona on September 24, and later pushed on to Porto Venere, Gregory refused to proceed farther north than Lucca. At this point barely forty miles separated the rival popes. Offering all kinds of trivial excuses, neither would move from where he was. The farce, dragged out over seven months, disgusted everybody, most particularly the French, who had put so much, perhaps too much, interest and effort into bringing the popes together. Even the cardinals, whose cowardice and shortsightedness had made them partners in the crime thus far, were revolted at the deplorable spectacle. Seven of Gregory's cardinals left him (May 11, 1408) and went to Pisa, issuing a proclamation justifying their actions. Two more followed soon thereafter. These nine cardinals sent letters to Gregory and to Christian rulers, explaining their actions and declaring their intention to join with cardinals of the opposite college in an effort to end the Schism. Four of Benedict's cardinals soon joined these nine, and later in June there came six more from the Avignon college. The united colleges signed a statement (June 29, 1408) proclaiming their intention to bring peace in the Church independently of the popes, who had so lamentably failed to do their sworn duty.

In the meantime Benedict had issued a general bull of excommunication (dated May 19, 1407, but delivered to the king of France only on May 14, 1408) against any who should withdraw obedience to him. The bull had an effect quite opposite to what Benedict intended. All France boiled with indignation, and Charles VI immediately proclaimed France's neutrality between the two popes. Benedict, thinking it best to leave French territory, took refuge in Perpignan (June 15, 1408), then a part of the kingdom of Aragon. In desperation, both popes issued calls for a general council, Benedict for Perpignan and Gregory for Aquileia. The united cardinals, condemning any such council called by popes whose word had so often proved worthless, issued on July 14 a call to all bishops to a council of the whole Church which would convene at Pisa on March 25, 1409, the feast of the Conception.

The *via cessionis* and the *via compromissi* had both failed to bring peace and unity to the Church. The *via synodi,* the conciliar method, had now to be tried. At Perpignan Benedict did in fact hold a sort of council, but it was sparsely attended and soon melted away. Gregory's council hardly met. Of the three, Perpignan, Aquileia, and Pisa, the first two had every color of legality, being convoked by duly elected popes. Yet they were without result. Pisa, on the other hand, was convoked by cardinals, an initiative for which there was no provision in canon law. Yet Pisa met, had a measure of success, and, even if its immediate result only added confusion to the already sad plight of the Church, launched the Conciliar Movement.

THE COUNCIL OF PISA

IN THE months before the Council met at Pisa, Benedict tried valiantly to hold his support, now reduced to a few cardinals and Spanish prelates. Those who had come to his council at Perpignan advised him to deal with the cardinals at Pisa and send a representative authorized to pledge his abdication; then they gradually slipped away. Gregory lost his scattered support even more rapidly and by January 1409 had only three powers, Carlo Malatesta, lord of Rimini, the Republic of Venice, and Ladislaus of Naples, who still recognized him as pope. He was reduced to pitiful disguise and flight. With the two popes in such straits, all Europe was hopeful that the forthcoming council at Pisa would be successful in its quest of union and peace.

The Council at Pisa opened on the day set, March 25, 1409, and was the most impressive meeting of dignitaries Europe had seen since the Fourth Council of the Lateran in 1215. Twenty-two cardinals, 84 bishops (and proctors for 102 other bishops), 87 abbots, 41 priors, the generals of the Dominican, Franciscan, Carmelite, and Augustinian orders, some 300 doctors, ambassadors of 17 secular princes including the Emperor, the kings of England, France, Bohemia, and Poland, and hundreds of other high clerics and secular lords graced the deliberations, which lasted from March 25 to August 7, producing emotion, flights of oratory, and great and important pronouncements.

The proceedings were not without their humor. On the second day proctors and beadles were sent to the portals of the cathedral to stand and summon the two "schismatic" popes to appear and answer the charges against them. This mummery was repeated four more times in the first month of the sessions. On April 15 ambassadors from Rupert of the Palatinate, who had been elected Emperor to succeed the deposed Wenzel in 1400, appeared before the Council to defend Gregory and protest the action of the cardinals in calling a council without Gregory's prior action. The arguments they presented were legalistic and familiar, and the manner of their presentation was so crude as to arouse the Council's resentment. The ambassadors soon realized the futility of further discussion and left (April 21) without waiting for a formal answer from the Council. About the only real advocate Gregory still had was Carlo Malatesta, who appeared before the Council to speak with courage and subtlety, but to no better purpose than the ambassadors of Rupert.

These diversions past, the Council declared itself legally convoked and competent to judge the two popes. The inquiry into the careers and performances of the two pontiffs took about a month. Finally, at the fifteenth session on June 5, the sentence of deposition of both popes was read out. The deposition read:

These two pretenders are schismatics, approvers and authors of schism, notorious heretics, guilty of the horrible crime of perjury and the violation of their vows, the source of contumely and open scandal to the Church. In consequence they are declared unworthy of the sovereign pontificate, deposed from their functions and dignities and even driven out of the Church.

Such solemn formal deposition of a pope by a college of cardinals had never before taken place, and the members of the Council were quite aware of the revolutionary nature of their act. Just as they were enjoying their success, envoys of the king of Aragon arrived. They brought a conviction and a message. The message was to the effect that Benedict would resign if Gregory would. The offer was late, and the Council laughed the envoys out of countenance. Their conviction, that Benedict was the only true pope, was equally unwelcome. Sensing the hostility of the Council, they asked for safe-conduct to return to their king. Cardinal Balthasar Cossa, of whom we shall soon hear more, then master of Bologna, told them rudely that, safe-conduct or no, if he caught them he would burn them alive. Benedict had been deposed; his answer was the creation of twelve new cardinals. Far from being healed, the Schism was now consolidated.

The Council, however, was committed to the course it had set out upon. Having solemnly deposed both "schismatic" popes, it had to elect a successor. The Church must have a head. The twenty-four cardinals went into conclave. All was not harmony, but Cardinal Cossa, to whom the tiara was offered, maneuvered opinion so that the aged Cardinal Peter Philargi, a native Cretan, was unanimously chosen on June 26, 1409, and took the name of Alexander V. The Council rejoiced that it had ended the Schism and that its members could now go about their business. The rejoicing was premature. Before the Council disbanded on August 7, 1409, Alexander's generosity was being widely drawn upon and abbacies and benefices were being copiously granted to all suppliants. The reform so earnestly desired and promised by the cardinals was assuming a strangely familiar aspect. As the Council dissolved it was decreed that a new council should convene in April 1412 to consider reform of the Church "in head and members."

Malatesta and Ladislaus of Naples still supported Gregory XII, so that the efforts of Cardinal Cossa, more at home on the battlefield than before the altar, to master Italy on behalf of Alexander V, were only partially successful. Rome was taken by Cossa, but Alexander died (May 3, 1410) before he was able to set foot in the Vatican. Outside Italy, Gregory continued to be recognized by Bavaria, Poland, and some parts of Germany, while Spain and Scotland remained faithful to Benedict XIII. It is true that Alexander was accepted as the true pope by a majority of Christendom, but it soon became tragically evident that instead of the two popes which the Council of Pisa had deposed, there were now three. Hopes that the death of one pope might lead to the consolidation of all the cardinals and the recognition of the single pontiff were soon dissipated. A short conclave (May 17, 1410) elected Cossa to succeed Alexander, and he took the title of John XXIII. Whether as Cossa or as John XXIII the cardinal of Bologna is a controversial figure. According to his many enemies, his youth was lurid, his young manhood brutal and blood-spattered beyond description. He was reported to have been a highwayman, a pirate, a multiple murderer, a malevolent and calculating scoundrel beyond even the usual Italian standard.

This picture is certainly highly exaggerated. He was undoubtedly an active, ambitious, brilliant, wily, and persuasive person whose scruples were under control. The papal chair was the obvious culmination of his ambitions. His life before reaching the throne of St. Peter had been one success after another. Once seated in that throne, however, he seemed to lose the magic touch which had brought him this far.

John tried to wean the kings of Aragon, Castile, and Navarre from their support of Benedict, but without success. He approached Malatesta with the aim of inducing him to desert Gregory, only to have Malatesta declare war against him. Louis of Anjou's fleet, sent to support John in his Italian campaign, was defeated and scattered by Ladislaus of Naples. In supporting the candidacy of Sigismund of Hungary for the imperial crown to succeed Rupert (1411), John was more fortunate. Sigismund, who thought of himself in large terms, was to play a notable role in the affairs of the Church and particularly in the Conciliar Movement over the next twenty-six years until his death in 1437.

The Council decreed by the Council of Pisa to be convened within three years was called for April 1, 1412, in Rome. Since reform was to be its principal task, John fortified his own position by creating fourteen new cardinals, among whom were d'Ailly, the powerful and energetic Zabarella, bishop of Florence, and Robert Hallam, bishop of Salisbury. John obviously sought, in anticipation of the meeting of the Council, the favor of the University of Paris and of English opinion. He was to be disappointed in both aims. Few prelates had arrived in Rome by April 1412, and the Council did not begin to function until early in 1413. The delegates who were anxious to discuss reform, particularly the French prelates, came prepared with a detailed program for the purification of the Church. They found John singularly uninterested in the subject. The Council, whose only real accomplishment was a condemnation of the writings of Wyclyf, was thereupon prorogued.

As the existence of three popes and the nonperformance of the Council at Rome combined to outrage public opinion, the Emperor Sigismund became convinced that a general council with more authority than that exercised by Pisa would have to be called. He therefore urged John to issue the call. John's reluctance was natural. The clear implication of Sigismund's reasoning was that Gregory, Benedict, and John were on the same level of legitimacy, whereas John held that the depositions of the two rivals at Pisa, and consequently his own position as pope, were final. However, chased out of Rome by Ladislaus, barely welcome anywhere else in Italy, John was in no position to argue with the Emperor. After further negotiations, he issued a call for a general council of the Church to meet at Constance on November 1, 1414. John would of course have preferred an Italian city, but as Constance was a free imperial city on the Swiss frontier, and therefore easy of access from Italy as well as from the Empire and the north, he could not refuse Sigismund's request. Because of John's lack of success in Italian politics, the initiative had passed to Sigismund. The imperial negotiators listed the subjects which, in the Emperor's view, must be on the agenda of the coming council: the reform of the Church "in head and members," the extirpation of heresy, the reconciliation of the Greek and the Latin churches, and, more specifically, a decision as to which one of the three popes was legitimate and should therefore consecrate the Emperor. The representatives of the French king protested that their monarch accepted the decisions of the Council of Pisa, the depositions of Gregory and Benedict as definitive and the elections of Alexander and John as canonical and proper. France, however, was torn by civil strife and Charles VI was unable to hold to a strong line. His envoys were finally obliged to accept the program of Sigismund. John, on the other hand, had a stroke of luck. His determined adversary, Ladislaus of Naples, died suddenly on August 6, 1414, and the Pope was vastly relieved. He would have liked to prorogue the Council until he could have brought all Italy, or at least the States of the Church, under his effective control; but it was too late for so ambitious an undertaking. Nevertheless, he could now go to Constance in a stronger position than before the death of Ladislaus.

THE COUNCIL OF CONSTANCE

THE Council of Constance (1414–18) was not only one of the most important councils in the whole history of the Church, it was an event of international moment unmatched in the whole of the later Middle Ages. Interest in its progress ran high in all corners of Europe. It was a new and unprecedented effort to settle the troubled affairs of a confused world by a representative meeting of the best minds of every nation.

After problems of organization and agenda were decided, the work of the Council fell into three larger areas: (1) the liquidation of the work of the Council of Pisa and the deposition of all three popes; (2) the question of heresy in England and Bohemia; (3) reform of the Church "in head and members."

John XXIII entered Constance in pomp on October 28, 1414, accompanied by a large retinue of Italian prelates and officials. Thereafter ecclesiastics of every rank and country drifted steadily into the city. The first official session took place on November 16, and the next day Cardinal Peter d'Ailly, the dominating personality of the whole Council, arrived with a modest retinue of forty-eight persons. At its most frequented, the chroniclers tell us, Constance entertained over 100,000 visitors and 30,000 horses, including a substantial proportion of riffraff. Some of the princes, ecclesiastical or lay, had ostentatiously large trains. The Archbishop Elector of Mainz had an escort of 500 persons. The city fathers handled the influx efficiently and justly, controlling prices and maintaining order.

The Italians had an agenda prepared, the execution of which would have simplified procedure immensely and allowed the delegates to return home quickly, leaving Pope John in undisturbed possession of the field: the essential matter was to affirm the decision of the Council of Pisa and have the secular princes enforce these decisions by force of arms. D'Ailly pointedly remarked that they had come to the Council to heal the rifts in the Christian Church, not to make them worse. He insisted that Gregory and Benedict be given a chance to take part in the Council. When the English delegation arrived (January 21, 1415), and the German delegation got together, early in the year, they both sided with the French as to the purposes of the Council and its treatment of the two dissident popes. As the Council faced long discussions and weighty decisions, the question of who had the right to vote inevitably arose. The Italians held that only bishops and mitred abbots should be allowed to vote. This view had strong precedents. But at Constance it meant that John, with more bishops in his obedience than all others combined, would control all decisions. The Germans demanded that proxies of absent bishops, doctors of divinity, delegates of cathedral chapters and universities, and representatives of ruling princes should also vote. It was quickly seen that if this view were to obtain the votes would be hopelessly confused, and bribery and distrust would creep into all deliberations. It was decided, early in February, to group all delegates by four "nations," English, French, German, and Italian, roughly as at the University of Paris. By this arrangement each "nation," however small its total representation at the Council, would have equal weight with every other. It was then decided that matters on the agenda would be taken up in separate meetings of the various "nations" and their decisions brought together in a plenary session of the whole Council. Sigismund had made his ceremonious entry into the city on Christmas day, 1414; soon after his arrival the Council reached its greatest attendance: 29 cardinals, 3 patriarchs, 33 archbishops, almost 150 bishops, 100 abbots, 50 provosts, 300 doctors of theology, more than 100 dukes and earls, 2400 knights, and 116 envoys of cities. Entertainment was not overlooked. There were, besides the ecclesiastics, professional comedians, 1500 prostitutes, 1400 flute-players, and many professional gamblers.

By mid-February John had suffered two defeats: the agenda of the Italians had been quickly rejected, and the traditional voting procedure by bishops and abbots only, by which he could have controlled the Council, had been replaced by the vote by "nations." A third and double blow hit him on February 15. A proposal was made on that day in a meeting of the French, German, and English nations that all three popes should abdicate, and he heard of an anonymous memoir listing all the sins and crimes of which he was supposed to have been guilty from his childhood. John, shaken by the charges, took counsel with several of his own cardinals and wished to defend himself; but his counselors advised him that he would save everybody trouble if he resigned. He tried to qualify his resignation but was soon forced to accept a formula promising that he would resign if, as, and when Gregory and Benedict also resigned. He read this formula in public on March 1. This was a defeat for John. Yet he was not without some support. Sigismund seemed to have taken over control of the Council, and the French, particularly, who had borne the burden of the whole conciliar agitation, resented the highhanded manipulations of the Emperor. John could therefore count on some support from that quarter. He hoped desperately for this division among his enemies to grow sharper, but later in March this dispute between Sigismund and the French was pacified, and John had to give up hope for a breach in the opposition which would save his crown. One last recourse was left: John could flee from Constance and thus, by canon law and ancient tradition, dissolve the Council. During the afternoon of March 20, while a jousting tourney outside the walls of Constance was entertaining the royal party and the townspeople, a groom and a boy, on a scrawny nag, rode out of the city gate toward Ermatingen. That night Frederick of Austria, no friend of Sigismund, rode in haste to his own castle of Schaffhausen to meet the Pope, who had ar-

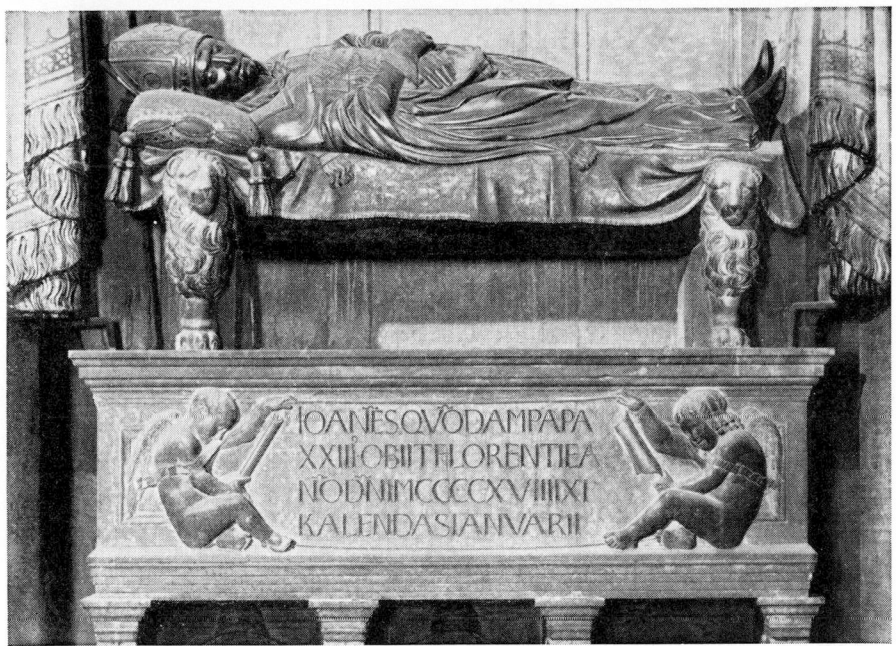

Pope John XXIII, by Donatello, on the wall of the Baptistery of San Giovanni Battista, Florence [ALINARI].

rived there on horseback but an hour or two before him. When the escape of John was learned the next day, the Council was in consternation. Its decision, not to disband but to place itself above the Pope and papal tradition, marked a new departure in the history of the Church.

The Trial and Condemnation of John Hus

JOHN's sensational flight was the end of the road for him. After this futile effort to escape the logic of events, he is of no further significance in history. His formal deposition, after much discussion, on May 29, 1415, was an anticlimax, unregretted by anybody. We must return to the case of a single Czech priest, whose trial at Constance was to have repercussions lasting for centuries. We have placed John Hus (see above, Chapter 7) in his Czech milieu as the culmination of almost a century of a reform movement in Bohemia. Hoping to convince the Council of Constance of his complete orthodoxy, he arrived at that city on November 3, 1414. Within a few days he was imprisoned and over a period of eight months was treated badly, being much of the time in chains in a damp and unlighted cell. From his stay in Constance came his letters, over sixty in number, to friends and officials, which have been accepted by his countrymen as Hus' testament to the nation. Their tone is tender, fervent, trustful, and inflexible. He was visited in his cell by committees of ecclesiastics and by individual inquisitors, and given two public hearings before the whole Council: on June 5, 7, and 8, and a final hearing on July 5.

Hus was quite aware of the long list of charges against him but he had faith that he could prove either that the charges were false or that his position could be supported by Scripture or the Fathers of the Church. The result of Hus' trial was certain from the outset. The safe-conduct which the Emperor had given him was later repudiated by the Emperor when he presided over the Council. The leaders of the prosecution at the Council were, in addition to Czech and German clerics from Prague, the two eminent French cardinals, Peter d'Ailly and John Gerson, whom we have met as fervid and widely read philosophers and mystics. When, at the first hearing on June 5, Hus was shown copies of his works, he declared that he would gladly retract any statement he had made in them that could be shown to be false or heretical. When he began to reply to the charges as they were read, quoting Scripture and the Fathers in defense of his position, he was interrupted by cries and objections. The Council had no desire to listen to a defense. "Answer yes or no," was their demand. When he stood silent, he was told he assented to the errors with which he was charged. The next session of this hearing was held in the presence of the Emperor. D'Ailly presided and attempted to prove that Hus, as a realist, could not accept the Church's doctrine of transubstantiation. In this he failed completely, as Hus had never accepted Wyclyf's position on the sacrament and had on this doctrine always been consistently orthodox. The rest of this session was not very fruitful. At the end d'Ailly advised Hus to submit to the Council, which would deal mercifully with him. The Emperor ventured the helpful suggestion that he should recant his errors even if he had never made them. On the next day, June 8, thirty-nine articles drawn from the *De ecclesia* and two other recent works were read out and discussed. It was quite clear that Hus held that the Church was the "congregation of the predestinate," whose head was Christ, and not the pope, the cardinals, and the clergy. Such a concept, if followed to its logical conclusion, would remove any need for the physical organization of which the prelates were high officials and from whose power and emoluments they profited. Hus asked for another hearing to explain his views in greater detail. Most of the Council objected to giving him that opportunity, on the grounds that it was not the function of a Council to argue, but to pronounce. He was to be given a chance to abjure his errors in writing, or the Council would act according to its judgment and authority. Sigismund privately advised members of the Council not to let Hus go free: "If he does not abjure let him be burned." The Emperor was overheard by three Czechs; the Czech people were later informed of this pronouncement and they never forgave him for his desertion of Hus. Hus realized that the cause was decided against him, but, as he declared in letters to his friends and in conversations in prison:

Would you abjure errors which you know for certain you had never held? . . . If I knew that I had written or preached anything erroneous, contrary to the law and the Church, God is my witness that I would in all humility retract. But my wish always has been that better doctrine be proved to me out of Scripture, and then I would be most ready to recant.

To a Council which had just deposed the pope who had convoked it, had forced the resignation of a second and was soon to depose a third, and had firmly declared itself superior to the successor of Peter, such doctrine—an appeal to Scripture as superior to the Council—was both heretical and profoundly dangerous. On July 5 Hus was given another chance to recant to a group of prelates, but declined to abjure what he had not said, or what he felt to be true. The next day, in full session, the charges were read. When he tried to answer, he was commanded to be silent. As the reading of the charges went on he protested that he had come to Constance of his own free will, trusting in the safe-conduct of the Emperor. Sigismund blushed. Then the sentence: his works to be burned, Hus to be degraded from the priestly office and "committed to the secular arm." At the end of the ceremonial defrocking, the archbishop of Milan, attended by five bishops, said: "We commit thy soul to the devil." Hus rejoined: "And I commit it to the most holy Lord Jesus Christ." The morning was nearly spent when the fire was lit around him. His ashes were cast into the Rhine.

The trial and death of John Hus have occasioned much dispute. Seen from a modern point of view it is clear that he was not allowed to defend himself. It is equally clear that from the point of view of the medieval Church his views were subversive of discipline and organization; that is, they were heretical. And the only recognized punishment for heresy was death at the stake. Sincerity was not the issue. Thousands of sincere people died at the stake in the Middle Ages and the period of the Renaissance, and little was said or done about it. What made the death of Hus different from the common run of punishment for "heretical pravity" was the fact that a whole people, almost to a man, felt that he had been unjustly, wantonly, and treacherously murdered, when they knew from personal experience and conviction that he was a true and enlightened Christian priest. The Czech people therefore rose in revolt against an Emperor and a Church that had committed so foul a crime. The fact that this people, five centuries after Constance, freely chose the day of Hus' death at the stake for their national holiday is an unmistakable index of the depth of that national conviction.

The Deposition of John XXIII

IT HAS been remarked above that after Pope John's vain effort to escape he was personally of no real significance. Nevertheless, it was necessary to formalize the position the Council had won. The Council prepared with great care a list of seventy-two charges against John, of which sixteen were later dropped as too shameful for public reading. The fifty-six remaining charges were presented to the Council on May 25, and after John was given a chance to answer, which he declined, the sentence of deposition was pronounced on May 29. The theoretical implications of the deposition were quite clear to everyone. The Council had shown itself superior to the pope, who was simply an elective presiding officer of the Church. The ancient tradition that the pope, the successor of Peter, the rock upon which the Church was founded, was the sole and effective head of the Church, was no longer to be accepted. The pope had been the sign of the Church's unity, its guarantee of orthodoxy; now the Council had taken over all these symbols and functions. This was revolution. The classic statement of this conciliar theory was contained in the four articles proposed by the French, German, and English nations on March 29, 1415, to the fourth session of the Council, and voted a week later (April 6). Taken together, these articles are known as the decree *Sacrosancta,* which has been called by a great authority in this area "probably the most revolutionary official document in the history of the world." * Of these four articles, the first two proclaim the conciliar theory in all its rigor:

1. The Council of Constance, legitimately assembled in the Holy Spirit, constituting a general council and representing the Catholic Church, holds its power directly from God, and everyone, of every status and dignity, including the pope, is obliged to obey it in matters of faith, the extinction of the Schism, and the reform of the Church in head and members.

2. Anyone, even the pope himself, who should refuse consciously to conform to the decrees, statutes, and ordinances of the holy council or of any other general council canonically assembled, on these points or others related to them, shall be submitted to penitential action and shall suffer the appropriate punishment, even if it becomes necessary to resort to means other than those of canon law.

Meantime, negotiations for the resignation of Gregory had been carried on between the Council and Gregory's loyal supporter, Carlo Malatesta. Cardinal John of Ragusa represented Gregory in spiritual and theological matters. The resignation was read and accepted at a session of the Council on July 4, 1415, which had, by a face-saving fiction, been called by Gregory himself. Gregory was thereupon named cardinal-bishop of Porto and papal legate of Ancona. He died in his diocese on October 18, 1417. There remained Benedict XIII. He was not disposed to accept the Council's suggestion that he resign. When missions of cardinals had failed to persuade him it was thought that the Emperor might have more success. Sigismund went to meet Benedict at Narbonne on August 15, 1415, and conversations there and at Perpignan dragged on for four months. The old Pope, one of the more learned of the popes of the later Middle Ages, was sure of his rights and of his duty to defend his office. His own cardinals deserted him and on December 13, 1415, declared him deposed. In January 1416, the king of Aragon withdrew his obedience and Castile and Scotland followed soon after.

Reassembled in Constance by the early autumn of 1415, the Council felt free to get on with the agenda. Pope John had been deposed, Pope Gregory had resigned, heresy in the form of John Hus had been properly disposed of. There remained the important and controversial matter of reform. Each element or faction in the Council was certain that every other element or faction seriously needed purging and renewal. The cardinals were satisfied with the college of cardinals, but wanted reform elsewhere. The French, who had suffered from the

* J. Neville Figgis, *From Gerson to Grotius* (Cambridge, 1923), p. 31.

[FACING] *John Hus at the Stake in Constance,* from the Leitmeritz *Cancionale,* an early sixteenth-century painting, in the State Institute for Care and Preservation of National Treasures, Prague [STÁTNÍ ÚSTAV PAMÁTKOVÉ PÉČE A OCHRANY PŘÍRODY, PHOTO BY V. FYMAN].

En ppmi vatk dnisalonima saens   Monb'optanit meliore redr dertn
Edenir ilanes cotens ena viros   Vnitr ut pnlan relligrone huma
Ordnus antiq no ur lar thr superbus Cterla monet antes romain; ania ler
Ciret pon sue ir cruina romatini   Er vate slanis ges male scta credir
Onnas suerath no elle ntuilstri   dumena vatis vidit coltana mortis
Sednog olan ii latue ferre dnus   Adlia mts celos ingemiug; petit

exercise of the system of annates, wanted them abolished, while the cardinals, who realized that these substantial payments supported the pope and the *curia,* wanted the annates continued and enforced. Other subjects for reform related to simony, ecclesiastical taxation, the papal *curia,* the morals of the clergy, and the Benedictine Order, which was much too prosperous. A commission of reform was named to organize and prepare the whole subject for the consideration of the Council. Many sermons were preached during the summer and autumn of 1415. The French were the most vehement in their charges of vice and laxity, and in their demands that the Council do something radical to purify the Church.

The Church was still without a head, nor could the Council canonically elect a new pope until Benedict resigned or was formally deposed and his cardinals joined forces with Constance. Early in February 1416, the Council heard of the failure of Sigismund's mission to Perpignan and of the substraction of obedience to Benedict by Aragon, Castile, and Scotland. But aside from accepting the report, in the absence of the Emperor, who was traveling about, bringing peace to embattled Europe, the Council could go no further. Jerome of Prague, a follower of Hus who had traveled much stirring up conservative opposition at Prague, Vienna, Paris, and Cracow, had, under inquisitorial treatment, retracted his Hussite teachings on September 11, 1415. In prison he repented of his recantation, and at a second trial on May 23, 1416, he bravely and eloquently revoked his retraction. A papal secretary, the eminent humanist Poggio Bracciolini, has left us a moving account of Jerome's trial and defense. He was burned, as a relapsed heretic, on the same spot as Hus, on May 30, 1416.

After the delegates from Castile, Aragon, Navarre, and Portugal had been received, and the Spanish prelates and nobles recognized as a fifth "nation" at the Council (October 15, 1416), a commission was named (November 5) to try Benedict XIII. In three weeks it brought in its report, which accused him, in twenty-seven articles, of having furthered the Schism and therefore of being a heretic and a schismatic. He was summoned to appear within one hundred days before the Council.

Deposition of Benedict XIII and Election of Martin V

WHEN Sigismund returned from his travels on January 27, 1417, the important matter of the deposition of Benedict XIII could be carried to completion. Benedict was formally summoned three times more: March 8; May 25, 1417; and finally, in the presence of the Emperor, declared deposed amid great celebrations and ceremonies on July 26, 1417. Without supporters, without a church, keeping court with a few faithful retainers in the impregnable family castle of Peñiscola on the rocky coast near Valencia, he died in 1423, still calling himself the only true pope.

After the deposition of Benedict the Council was free to proceed to the next necessary step—the election of a pope who would bring that peace and unity of which the Church universal stood in such great need. The preliminary discussions were not carried on in harmony. The five nations distrusted one another, and within the nations there was wide diversity of opinion and no little petty quarreling. But there were able prelates, anxious to get things done. On October 9, 1417, the decree *Frequens* was issued, providing for the next general council of the Church to meet within five years, another seven years thereafter, and subsequently a council every ten years. A month later the election of the next pope was held. There were fifty-three electors, of whom a majority represented the Council rather than the cardinals. There were six electors each from the five nations in addition to the twenty-three cardinals. After three days of deliberations, on November 11, 1417, Cardinal Odo Colonna, a highly respected prelate, was chosen pope and took the pontifical name of Martin V. It had been a long time since secular power had had a predominant voice in the selection of the Vicar of Christ. There was great rejoicing in Constance and throughout Christendom. The Church once again had a single head, recognized by all princes and prelates. Martin, as the creation of the Council, declared his acceptance of all decrees and the program of reform which the Council had proclaimed. Martin thus agreed formally to the principle of conciliar supremacy. But reform was still to be taken up, and many suggestions and projects of reform lay before the Pope. The future of the Council, however, was to be more brief than its past. Many delegates, after three years of tense wrangling at Constance, were tired and anxious to get back to their homes and tasks. Projects of reform, however necessary and attractive, received little real attention. On February 22, 1418, Pope Martin V issued the bull *Inter cunctos,* which was intended to guide the Church in its struggle with the Hussite heresy. The bull listed forty-five articles of Wyclyf and thirty articles taken from the works of Hus which were labeled heretical. On March 6 seven decrees of reform, all that the five nations could agree on, and therefore very moderate, were published. This was the last serious work of the Council. On April 22 the Council was dissolved, at its forty-fifth session, in the presence of the Pope and the Emperor.

Debate still rages, within and without the Catholic Church, on the subject of the Council of Constance. The central question is as to whether it was in law and in fact a general council. Canon law until this time had always required that for a council of the Church to be an ecumenical council, it must be presided over by a pope or his legate, and that means, of course, a properly elected and consecrated pope. The last four sessions were under the presidence of Martin V, which leaves no doubt as to the validity of that part of the Council. Although it can be argued both ways, it seems proper to conclude that, by accepting the decrees of the Council before he became pope, Martin gave an ecumenical character to the whole assembly. Whether this extends to the decrees of the fourth and fifth sessions, especially the *Sacrosancta,* may be variously answered. We shall see that Martin's successor, Eugenius IV, explicitly accepted in 1446 all the decrees of the Council of Constance "without, however, prejudice to the rights, dignity and primacy of the apostolic see." The Council distinctly revived some of Europe's confidence in the Church. It had wrestled courageously with the disorganization and division which had disgusted and angered the common man as well as the princes who had to deal with the realities of Church property, taxes, transfers of prelates, and benefices. The Church was the most wealthy and powerful force in every land of Europe, and confusion and counterclaim in the Church affected the whole social and economic structure. Europe therefore breathed a vast sigh of relief when the Schism was finally ended and the princes and prelates were agreed on accepting the decisions of the Council.

The theory of the superiority of the council over the pope, a revolution in the doctrines that had guided the Church thus far, disturbed very few people. Practically speaking, the monarchistic theory of an absolute pope was seen to have failed. The theory of absolutism had begun to weaken in secular government; why should it not likewise fail in ecclesiastical government? Men were already accustomed to the growing power of representative bodies. Parliaments, diets, and *cortes* had been tried in various countries for almost two centuries, and had proven fairly successful. Why should not the same system work in the case of the Church? This reasoning was widespread, if not consciously revolutionary. This plausible parallelism between the representative governance of a nation-state such as France or England, and the governance of an international or supranational organization like the Church seemed so obvious that it was to take decades of experience to convince those who ruled the Church that it was false and unworkable.

Martin V and the Revival of the Papacy

UPON the dissolution of the Council of Constance, Martin was faced with the decision as to where he should establish the papal seat. Sigismund urged him to settle somewhere in the Empire; Basel, Strassburg, and Mainz were suggested. The French, as might have been expected, strongly favored Avignon. But Martin wisely decided that Rome, the city of the martyrs, was the only place where the *curia* could maintain its capital position in Christendom. It took him over two years to reach the Eternal City. There was much to do on the way. The States of the Church, in the absence of a pope in Italy, had fallen into various usurpers' hands, and Martin needed time, money, and deft diplomacy to regain papal dominance in naturally turbulent areas. Rome received him enthusiastically on September 30, 1420. But the city of the Caesars and the popes was a sad sight. The streets were in filth and dilapidation, many churches were roofless or used as stables, robbers infested the alleys and public places by night and by day. Many public monuments had been demolished or carted away piecemeal. Parts of St. Peter's lay in ruins. Wolves preyed on the outskirts of the city, digging up corpses even in the Vatican cemetery. Martin set to work immediately to clean up the mess and bring order. He was firm and constructive, enlisting the help of nobility, citizenry, and the cardinals. He restored his own churches, the Lateran and the Vatican, and employed noted artists, such as Gentile da Fabriano, Pisanello, and Masaccio, to beautify the walls. All this work, which Martin rightly thought so important for reasons of efficiency and morale, took time, energy, and, what was of equal importance, money. There was therefore some excuse for his neglect of the reform measures which the Council had enjoined upon him and to which he had so unhesitatingly subscribed. However, when he set about systematically and on a wholesale scale to enrich his family (the Colonna) by bestowing Church possessions and lush fiefs on brothers and cousins, he went beyond the limits of equity or propriety. No question of his personal morality and probity has ever been raised, but even his own adherents and defenders have objected to his nepotism.

Pursuant to his desire to re-establish Rome in the mind of Christendom as the center of the devotional life of the whole Church, he proclaimed for the year 1423 a jubilee which brought many pilgrims to Rome. The great humanist Poggio, whom we met at Constance, affronted by the great numbers of non-Italians who came to the city, remarked that Rome was "inundated by barbarians." In his relations with the secular princes of Europe Martin was fairly successful. Both England and France treated him with respect and his consistent firmness with other states gained prestige for the Papacy. He acted and spoke with the confidence and precision of a pope of the thirteenth century. It soon became clear that he had no intention of following the dictates of the Council of Constance which had created him if he could possibly avoid it. Yet he could not openly flout the specific provisions of the decree *Frequens* which he had himself proclaimed. According to that decree, the pope had to convoke a council within five years after Constance. Martin therefore called such a council to meet in Pavia in April 1423. It was poorly attended—the rest of the world being at war—and transferred itself to Siena in June. The Council, small as it was, was conciliar in spirit and therefore hostile to a strong-minded pope. The delegates wished to begin their reformatory program with reforms of the pontifical office and the *curia*. Martin's answer was to dissolve the Council (March 7, 1424).

The next council, set for Basel in 1431, was seven years away. Martin could easily have given thought to the problem of reform. He could have reasoned that some reform of the abuses in the curial organization would have taken the wind out of the sails of the conciliar party and would, in anticipation, have left them with nothing to complain of at the next meeting. All that Martin did was to issue a reform bull on May 16, 1425. It was not taken very seriously. Nobody expected much from papal bulls in any case. There had been too many of them and too little action. Rome continued to be hated for its greed. An agent of the Emperor wrote from Rome to Sigismund in 1429, "And as you know at the Roman court you can get anything you want with money." Martin was fortunate in the cardinals who served him. Cesarini, Capranica, Antonio Correr, and Albergati were all men of piety, great learning, and impressive breadth of culture. Vespasiano da Bisticci, the Florentine bookseller, who knew everybody and to whom we are indebted for so much information about personalities of the period, wrote: "The cardinals that Martin made during his pontificate were all men of exceptional gifts." Although Martin tasted success in persuading Alfonso of Aragon to desert Clement VIII, the dim successor of Benedict XIII, thus making the restoration of the unity of the Church complete, in a more serious matter he suffered humiliating defeat. As early as 1420 he had proclaimed a crusade for the "extirpation of the Wyclyfites, Hussites and other heretics." This and subsequent crusades against the Hussites had been disasters for papal prestige and imperial arms (see above, Chapter 8). He had issued a call for the next council to meet at Basel on March 7, 1431, but he died just a fortnight before the opening date (February 20, 1431), and his successor, Eugenius IV, was left the problem of the Hussites, with whom Martin had been disinclined to treat under any circumstances. Eugenius, believing it best to deal with the Hussites by defeating them in battle, sent Cardinal Cesarini to supervise the campaign of the summer of 1431. The imperial forces crossed the Bohemian border in the southwest part of the country and at Domážlice (Taus) the 130,000 crusaders were put to rout. Thereafter the Hussites had to be treated as at least equals. This negotiating was to occupy much of the time of the Council for some years.

THE COUNCIL OF BASEL

THE Council of Basel began gradually, as attendance was at first scanty. Cesarini had been named by Martin to preside, with power to prorogue or dissolve, and he made every effort to attract prelates to Basel but with only indifferent success. It soon became evident that the Pope was not enthusiastic about the Council and that the Council was determined to go on with its tasks. The impression was general very early in Basel that the Pope wanted to dissolve the Council or transfer it to some city under his control. Under such conditions mutual confidence was impossible. The Council invited the Hussites to come to Basel to discuss, as between equals, the issues that kept them apart. Eugenius was immediately angered at the tone of the invitation to condemned heretics and on November 12 gave Cesarini power to dissolve the Council. The letter with this instruction was not published, but news of the Pope's wishes leaked out. A month later, on December 14, the Council met in its first formal session to lay out its program: (1) to uproot heresy; (2) to bring peace among Christian peoples; (3) to reform morals in the Church "in head and members." A week later the Pope's bull of dissolution arrived, and after much talk and rumor was published on January 13, 1432. The Council was furious and affirmed the necessity for conciliar action. The same day, Cesarini, disgusted with the Pope's dissembling, wrote Eugenius a letter of reproof and advice, which unfortunately was disregarded by the Pope. The Council meanwhile took its stand and proclaimed anew on February 15 in caustic terms the principle of conciliar superiority over the Pope. Emperor Sigismund, although primarily anxious for peace in the Church, nevertheless accepted the conciliar position and urged the Council to disregard the Pope's order to dissolve and to get on with its work of reform.

The Council organized itself somewhat differently from that at Constance. Instead of nations, four committees of twenty members each were set up: on faith, on reformation, on unity and peace, and on general business. Free and open discussion of issues was encouraged, and, to prevent control by a clique, the membership in the committees was changed every four months. If three of the four committees approved an issue or a decree, it was brought before the whole Council in general session. In spite of this formal organization by committees, however, the nations played a considerable part in the working of the Council and came to be recognized as organs parallel with the committees. At all events, thus fortified and functioning, the Council forced Eugenius to withdraw his bull of dissolution and to recognize the Council. His handling of relations with the Council had been both inept and dishonest; opinion even among his former supporters was swinging against him. Six of his cardinals left him to join the conciliar side. This was one phase of a battle that was to last another twenty years. The first engagements went to the Council, as by the bull *Decernimus* (January 30, 1434) Eugenius admitted the legality of the Council and gave his complete adherence to it, which meant, of course, acceptance of the conciliar theory. The Council could claim to have won its case. But it was to be a short-lived victory.

Apart from the running battle with Eugenius on the basic question of conciliar or papal sovereignty, much of the activity of the Council was concerned with the negotiations with the Hussites. The letter of invitation of October 15, 1431, found the Czechs divided between the more conservative Hussites, known variously as Utraquists, Praguers, or Calixtines, and the radical groups, the Taborites and the Orphans (the soldiers who had been especially close to the blind Žižka) (see above, Chapter 8). The conservatives were anxious to negotiate with the Council, as they would have preferred to stay in the Church if a few concessions were made; whereas the Taborites and the Orphans would have been quite content to continue their own separate sectarian existence. The spiritual head of the Calixtines, John of Rokycany, was enthusiastic over the prospect of negotiating directly with the fathers at Basel. There was, however, some hesitation among the Hussites to deal with Sigismund or his envoys. They remembered the short shrift Hus had been given with Sigismund's safe-conduct in his hand. They therefore demanded clear guarantees of the safety of their delegates before setting out for Basel. Preliminary negotiations at Cheb (Eger) between representatives of the Council and the Hussites took place in May and satisfactory safeguards for the Czech envoys were offered. In December a large embassy, representing the various shades of Hussite opinion, set out for Basel, arriving, three hundred strong, on January 4, 1433. They were welcomed with a mixture of warmth and curiosity. The dreaded general Prokop the Great who had demolished the army of the crusaders at Domážlice, one of the leaders of the delegation, was a fierce and forbidding reminder of the Hussite threat. The discussions were remarkably reasonable in tone, though Cardinal Cesarini had on several occasions to exercise his gifts of compromise and mediation. It was agreed that the Four Articles of Prague (see above, Chapter 8) should form the core of the discussions and that each side should be allowed four speakers and several days each, if required, to present its case in full. Rokycany, in a defense of the first article that lasted three days, was conciliatory and impressively learned. Prokop, who followed him, was brief, and so convinced of the rightness and strength of the Hussite position that he urged the Council to accept God's word while there was yet time. Nicholas of Pelhřimov, the Taborite bishop, was abrupt and antagonizing. Peter Payne, known to the Czechs as Peter the Englishman, defended the fourth of the Four Articles. He had left Oxford soon after 1411 and come to Prague, attaching himself to the radical wing of the Hussites and acting as their most voluble advocate. His vehement three-day defense of both Wyclyf and Hus was ill received by the Council. Again Cesarini and Rokycany had to pour oil on the troubled waters.

Discussions pro and con, scholarly and rhetorical, continued through February and March; somewhat to everybody's surprise, personal relations between the fathers of the Council and the Hussites were almost amicable. By that time it had become evident that the Hussites would not give up the Four Articles and that the Council, unable to force them to do so, would have to make some concessions. The Council, naturally, wished to make as few concessions as possible. The Hussites, on the other hand, had to report back to the coming meeting of the Czech Estates and left Basel on April 14, accompanied by representatives of the Council, reaching Prague on May 8. The diet listened to Rokycany's report, then to the arguments of the envoys of the Council. The conservative Utraquists were the most anxious for peace, but were nevertheless adamant in refusing to give up the communion in both kinds (*sub utraque*). On other points the Taborites and the Utraquists were far apart. The envoys of the Council skillfully played upon the divisions they found, hoping to divide the Hussites even more sharply. A small Hussite delegation returned to Basel, where, on August 11, it presented to the Council the draft of an agreement which the Czechs would accept. It was essentially the Four Articles of Prague of 1420 with slight modifications, known henceforth as the Compacts (*Compactata*). These articles were as follows:

1. The Sacrament is to be given freely in both kinds to all the faithful in Bohemia and Moravia and to any elsewhere who accept the faith of these lands.
2. All mortal sin shall be punished by those whose office it is to do so.
3. The word of God is to be freely and truthfully preached by the ministers of the Lord and by worthy deacons.
4. The priests during the dispensation of grace shall own no worldly possessions.

Without going further than secretly to decide to permit communion in both kinds, the Council sent another embassy to discuss these demands in Prague. They arrived at the Czech capital on October 22. The city of Pilsen, loyal to Catholicism and encouraged by the Council, was under siege by the Taborite army under Prokop's leadership. But Taborite discipline had become seriously relaxed, and the long-drawn-out siege was a failure. The conciliar envoys realized that the divisions among the Hussites, added to the failure to take Pilsen, so weakened the Czech position as to make it unnecessary for the Council to make any further concessions at that time.

Later in November the Council's envoys made a counterproposal to the diet, allowing communion in both kinds to those in Bohemia and Moravia who wanted it and calling for further definition and discussion of the other three articles. Reluctantly the diet accepted these proposals as a basis for further negotiations, which were carried on at Basel in February 1434. The nub of the controversy was now the Hussites' insistence that all Bohemians should be compelled to accept communion in both kinds, whereas the Council refused to abandon those in Bohemia who, like the city of Pilsen, wished to retain their ancient Catholic usages. The Council sought, furthermore, to strengthen this Catholic party, which included some of the leading nobles of the land, and thus weaken the Hussite cause. This aim involved interference in Bohemian affairs, which was resented by the Taborites and the Orphans as well as by some of the Utraquists. The two Bohemian factions, the conservative Utraquists, led by the nobles and the bourgeoisie of Prague, and the now-united Taborites and Orphans, led by Prokop, were drawing farther apart. The conservatives were attracted by the proposals of the Council; the radicals were becoming more resolute in the refusal to accept any compromise. Both sides began to think of resort to force. Armed conflict was inevitable.

The decisive battle took place near Lipany, twenty-five miles east of Prague, on May 30, 1434. The Utraquist forces numbered 25,000, the Taborites about 15,000. It was Czech against Czech; on both sides there were those who had fought under Žižka and knew his tactics well. Prokop's forces were surrounded; for a whole day and a night the battle raged. Numbers were finally decisive. Prokop and several thousand of his men lay dead on the field, with as many of the Utraquists beside them. The consequences of the conservative victory at Lipany were far-reaching. At Basel the Council was elated, and a *Te Deum* was sung. The informants of the Council had counted perhaps too much on what separated the Hussite factions, and not enough on what they all had in common, a devotion to the Four Articles of Prague together with a general desire for peace. After Lipany the Bohemian diet undertook a conciliatory pacification of the kingdom and named delegates to discuss Sigismund's recognition as king of Bohemia with him at Regensburg. The Council's envoys were also invited to the conference. Sigismund, for whom recognition and coronation at Prague, denied him since his brother Wenzel's death in 1419, was assuming greater importance as he grew older, encouraged the Bohemian envoys, against conciliar pressure, to stand fast on the issue of the Compacts. At the same time, with his usual high sense of honor he told the envoys of the Council: "Just wait until I am crowned as king in Bohemia and then we will take care of this pestiferous heresy." At this stage of the negotiations, popularity with the Bohemians was of more moment to him than the uncertain favor of the Council. The envoys of the Council were surprised to find the Bohemians quite united and firm in their position. The Regensburg conference broke up on September 3, without any tangible results. Negotiation, proposal and counterproposal between the Council, the diet, and the Emperor continued for months. By the summer of 1435 the Bohemian envoys were asking Sigismund to grant in his own name, as king and Emperor, what the Council was refusing them. Sigismund acceded and urged the conciliar envoys in private to make the same concessions. The latter, however, would not go so far as to accept the Bohemians' interpretation of the Compacts. Sigismund's conduct was opportunistic and deceitful. By assuring each side that he favored their cause he induced them to agree to a meeting for late May 1436 at Iglau (Jihlava), where they were to sign an agreement between the Council and the Bohemian envoys. The Compacts were formally signed, in the presence of the Emperor, at Iglau on July 5, whereupon everybody joined in singing the *Te Deum*. But the very next day there was a sharp dispute over Rokycany's celebration of Mass in the Bohemian fashion, and the Czech delegates protested that they had been tricked. They would have left for home that same day if Sigismund had not begged them to stay to discuss his return to Prague. The Compacts, the objects of years of discussion and negotiation, were no real doctrinal agreement. There was an outward peace: the Bohemians were recognized as being in the Catholic Church; but the basic differences remained. The fact that there was a form of peace was due in part to fatigue, on both sides, as well as to the fact that the Council had passed the peak of its power and prestige. In the struggle between pope and council the next victories were to fall to Eugenius.

The question of reunion of the Eastern and the Western churches had been uppermost in the minds of many recent popes. Hardly a pope in the thirteenth and fourteenth centuries had failed to bring the matter before Christendom. It had been mentioned as recently as Constance. Cardinal Cesarini remarked to Eugenius, soon after the latter became pope in 1431, on the question of reunion with the Greeks: "That is an old story, which has been going the rounds for three hundred years, and every year it comes up all over again." Now, with the Turks pressing hard on the gates of Constantinople, the initiative was finally coming from the East. The Eastern Emperor, John VIII Paleologus (1425-48), knew the West, having spent 1422 seeking military aid against the Turks at various Western courts. He knew from personal observation that the ancient crusading zeal was dead. As early as 1431 he expressed a willingness to pay the price for Western help by bringing the Eastern Orthodox Church into union with the Church of Rome. Because of the tension between Pope and Council at Basel, the question of Greek union received only scanty attention from the Council. The Pope, however, persevered and sent his secretary Garatoni to Constantinople in 1434 to arrange for a conference at the Eastern capital to bring the two churches together. But as the Council, in the intervening years, gained confidence in its power and precedence over the Pope, the prospect of adding to its prestige by achieving what no pope had been able to do proved attractive. An embassy therefore was sent to Constantinople to arrange for representatives of the Byzantine Empire to meet with the Council. Garatoni and the conciliar envoys were dealing with the Byzantines at the same time, and the Greeks were subtle enough to carry on two sets of contradictory negotiations simultaneously. The Council issued a decree on September 7, 1434, without either asking Eugenius' permission or even informing him, setting alternative places where the Greeks could come to join formally the Western Church. The Greeks remarked that the Pope's presence and approval were necessary, in their opinion, for the union to be ecumenical, that is, legal and effective. Eugenius made the correct gestures of accord with the Council, so as to avoid giving the Greeks the impression that they were dealing with a Church that was irreconcilably split. Since the Greeks objected to coming as far as Basel, discussion of alternatives occupied some months. Emperor John and the Patriarch of Constantinople approved the decree of September 7, 1434, only in November of 1435. The cost of transporting and housing a large Byzantine delegation was a disturbing matter, and the efforts to get various cities—Avignon, Strassburg, Venice, or Florence—to guarantee the large sums necessary for this purpose took time and patience. The choice was put to a vote in the Council on December 5, 1436, and the order of preference came out as follows: Basel; then, if the Greeks refused to come to that city, Avignon as second choice; if that was unacceptable, somewhere in Savoy. The Council misjudged the deciding factors in the problem. The Greeks had never agreed to go to Avignon, and had repeatedly said they did not want to cross the Alps. Furthermore, Eugenius made it clear in April 1437 that for reasons of health he could cross no mountains. Public opinion in Europe, as well as among the Greeks, was getting a little tired of the pettiness and indecision of the Council. Yet the Council seemed unable to read the signs of the times, and continued to plan on Avignon. The latter city was reluctant to advance great sums to guarantee the transportation and maintenance of the Greeks. A determined minority in the Council, led by Cesarini, urged the majority to live up to its own decree and, because within the term fixed Avignon had not advanced the necessary guarantee-money, choose another city for the conference with the Greeks. Antagonistic feelings in the Council in the month of April ran so high that the burghers of

Basel had to move into the cathedral in armed force to keep a degree of order and to prevent the spilling of blood. Some of the saintly delegates came wearing daggers and swords beneath their vestments. The minority, fortified by the support of the Pope, his legates, and a feeling of moral probity, to which the majority could lay no claim, had prepared a decree naming Florence, Udine, or some other Italian city agreeable to the Greeks and the Pope. The two decrees, that of the majority naming Avignon, and that of the minority were read at the same time. The bishop of Oporto, reading the minority decree, outyelled the bishop of Albenga, who intoned the majority decree. The majority decree received the seal of the Council, but several members of the minority bribed the guardian of the seal and had their decree also sealed. This minority decree, naming Florence as the meeting-place of the Council with the Greeks, was hastily taken by the Greek ambassador, Dishypatos, to Eugenius, then at Bologna, and the Pope solemnly approved it, May 30, 1437. Eugenius had always wanted the Council on Italian soil. The Greeks, furthermore, had consistently objected to going anywhere else than to an Italian city. The minority decree visibly bore the Council seal. On July 17 Dishypatos declared that he recognized only the minority as the true Council, and that they could now get on with the arrangements for the early arrival of the Greeks from Constantinople.

Meanwhile, the Council at Basel, angry at being outwitted by the papal party, summoned the Pope (July 31) to appear before them within sixty days. They charged him with about every fault and shortcoming they could imagine. Eugenius answered with a bull (September 18) transferring the Council to Ferrara. The Council then declared him contumacious, and threatened him with deposition (October 12). All this division was confusing to the Greeks; but, faced with a decision, Emperor John accepted the legitimacy of Eugenius and the minority and embarked (November 1437) on the ships Eugenius had sent. The Emperor Sigismund, who might have helped to avoid the worsening of the breach between Council and Pope, did not live to witness its deplorable eventuation. He died at Znojmo in Bohemia on December 9, 1437, and with him the line of the Luxemburgers.

THE COUNCIL OF FERRARA-FLORENCE

THE legate of the Pope, Cardinal Albergati, opened the Council at Ferrara on January 8, 1438, charged by Eugenius to propose three principal matters for the agenda: (1) the union of the churches, Greek and Roman; (2) ecclesiastical reform; and (3) peace among the Christian peoples. The Council set to work, better attended by high ecclesiastics than Basel had ever been. On January 10 it annulled all acts of the Council at Basel passed since the transference by Eugenius of the Council to Ferrara. At Basel, what was left of the Council suspended Eugenius from his office (January 24, 1438) and forbade all princes and prelates to obey him henceforth. Eugenius had the Council at Ferrara approve his bull (February 15, 1438) excommunicating those who remained at Basel. At about this point in the exchange of suspensions and excommunications, the Greeks arrived in Italy.

Headed by the Emperor and the Patriarch of Constantinople, the delegation of seven hundred Greeks—bishops, scholars, priests, monks, and nobility—made a deep impression upon the Latins. There were details of precedence and protocol (for example, whose throne, the Pope's or the Emperor's, should be the higher) to be decided or compromised. The Greeks' bargaining position was weak. They were receiving their living allowances from the Pope, and they wanted Western military aid. But once these details were ironed out, generally by compromises that saved somebody's face, the Greeks and the Latins could get down to the business of their meeting. Commissions, consisting of Greek and Latin scholars and prelates, were set up to examine points of disagreement, theological and political, and to make recommendations. Some of the Greeks knew Latin; very few of the Latins knew Greek, but there were competent humanist interpreters who edited the reports of these commissions in both Greek and Latin. The leading Greek negotiator was Bessarion (1403–72), archbishop (metropolitan) of Nicea, the brilliant young confidant and adviser of the Emperor who had been for some years active in the preliminary negotiation at Constantinople as efficient advocate of the cause of union with the Roman Church. On the Roman side, the leading negotiators were Cardinals Albergati and Cesarini, the Spanish Dominican Juan de Torquemada, envoy of the king of Castile, and Nicholas of Cusa, philosopher and mystic, previously an advocate of the conciliar theory but since 1436 a believer in papal supremacy.

The first doctrinal agreement, on the dogma of purgatory, was reached in mid-July, when a commission of Greeks and Latins discovered that there was less difference in doctrine than in personality and attitude. The second doctrinal point, taken up in October, was more involved: the procession of the Holy Spirit. Eastern Orthodoxy had maintained with the Nicene Creed (325 A.D.) that the Holy Spirit proceeds "from the Father." The Latin Church had added "and from the Son" (*filioque*). The subtler East held that the addition made the Holy Spirit of dual origin, thereby disturbing the unity in the Trinity. This difference of opinion had been a part of the reasons for the split between the East and the West in the ninth century, made permanent in 1054. The discussions were long and tedious. For two months the disputants wrangled to no purpose, usually on points quite beside the basic issue.

While this issue was still being discussed, news came of fresh Turkish attacks on Constantinople. Eugenius, who was beginning to feel the financial pinch of supporting the numerous Greek delegation, urged the transference of the Council from Ferrara to Florence. Florence had offered a substantial loan to the embarrassed Pope. In February 1439, after a trying trip over the Apennines in winter, the Council was established in the city of the Medici. By now the Greek Emperor had lost some of his earlier hopefulness that he could outbargain the West. He realized that the Pope had gained immeasurably at the expense of the Council at Basel, and that the Latin theologians could not be diverted from their traditional positions. To satisfy pride and vanity on both sides there were several weeks of further intense debate, but both the Pope and the Emperor, closer together than their supporters, were putting pressure upon their respective disputants to bring their arguments to a close with a compromise formula. On June 4 a declaration was drawn up by the Greeks to be presented the next day to the Emperor, Eugenius, and to the ailing Patriarch of Constantinople. It read: "We agree with you and unite with you and acknowledge that the Holy Spirit proceeds from the Father and from the Son as from one sole origin and cause." A few days later (June 10) the Patriarch lay dead; further doctrinal questions were for a time in abeyance. But the Emperor thought the time had come to discuss practical matters, and asked Eugenius just what material aid he could count on in his life-and-death struggle with the Turks. Eugenius promised 300 soldiers and two galleys for the defense of Constantinople, and, when the city was under siege, 10 additional galleys for a year or 20 for six months. He further promised to have a crusade preached throughout all the West against the Turk. A few theological points remained to be defined and compromised, which, in view of everybody's fatigue and the desire of the Greeks to be on their way home, was not difficult. The final question of the primacy of the Papacy, however, raised a storm. By June 23 it looked as if the whole of the Council's work would be wrecked on this one point. Yet Bessarion refused to abandon hope; while the Emperor and the Pope were dining together he had a commission appointed to find a formula upon which both parties could agree. In a few days a statement was formulated to which the Latins could subscribe. The Greeks said: "We recognize that the Pope is the sovereign pontiff, . . . the representative and vicar of Christ, that he rules and governs the Church of God, saving all the privileges and rights of the Church of the East." With this formula agreed upon (June 26), there remained only the necessity to combine the various agreements and compromises into one decree of union to be signed and sealed by both parties. The ceremonial signing took place on July 5, 1439; the next day, in the cathedral of Florence, whose majestic cupola the architect Brunelleschi had finished but three years before, at the last official session of the Council the solemn decree was read to the public, in Greek by Bessarion, in Latin by Cesarini. It was an impressive and moving spectacle: the Christian Church reunited after six centuries of Schism.

When the Greek delegates, returned to Constantinople, reported the results of their negotiations, the people quickly saw that little had been gained and a good deal given up. The Emperor lost much popularity, and those in the delegation who had opposed concessions to the West were heroes. Fanatical Greek nationalism wanted nothing to do with the despised, barbarous West. The union of the Church at Florence was thus devoid of the intended results. Yet it was not completely lost motion. The two cultures had, for the first time in many centuries, stood face to face and discovered something to justify mutual respect. The most learned and esteemed of the Greeks, Bessarion, decided to remain in the West. He realized that the days of Constantinople were numbered and that the future of Christian culture lay in the West. He believed in the union. Returning to Constantinople for a short time, he endeavored to defend the actions of the delegation, and in his absence was made a cardinal by Eugenius. Bessarion returned to Italy late in 1440 to become one of the most useful and devoted members of the *curia,* acting as intermediary between the Roman court and the East, and as legate for the Pope on many important missions in Italy and abroad. He was also prominent in the humanistic movement, as we shall see in the next chapter. Another member of the Greek delegation, Isidore of Moscow, was also elevated to the cardinalate, but he did not remain in Italy.

The Council of Ferrara-Florence recovered for Eugenius almost all the prestige that the Papacy had lost in the early years of the Conciliar Movement. Its decisions met with the united approval of the Italian people. An Italian pope was again pope in fact, and the seat of the papal authority was once more at Rome. The reluctance of France and much of Germany to recognize the fact of revived papal primacy was to be expected, as in both France and the Empire national and separatist impulses had been in existence for many generations.

Although the Council at Basel was completely discredited, the rump attendance refused to acknowledge the fact. After suspending the Pope and threatening to depose him, there was nothing to do but carry out the "deposition," (June 25, 1438). Most of the next year was taken up by discussions with various princes. Of those approached, the German Emperor (Albert of Habsburg), the king of France, and the king of Castile followed what they called a neutral line, but seemed to the Council more hostile and opportunistic than neutral. The "neutrality" of France was profitable to the monarchy. King Charles VII, heartened by recent successes against the English, called an assembly of the French clergy at Orléans for May 1, 1438, then transferred it to Bourges. The great achievement of this assembly was its solution of the relation of France to the Council and the Pope. It accepted most of the decrees of the Council, which was fast losing its prestige, and declared that the Pope could not nominate to French benefices save when an incumbent died at the Roman *curia*. This arrangement was then issued as a royal decree, the so-called Pragmatic Sanction of Bourges (July 7, 1438). It created a Gallican church under the control of the crown and the upper nobility.

Duke Amadeus of Savoy, a widower, was elected pope by the Council on November 5, 1438, and took the name of Felix V. He was not recognized outside his own duchy. As the prestige of Eugenius grew, more princes of Germany came over to his side, and in June 1448, when the Emperor, Frederick III, withdrew his support of the Council at Basel, it moved to Lausanne, where Amadeus was quietly living. In the spring of 1449 the king of France persuaded Amadeus that it would be better to resign as pope. The Council—a ghost of its former confident self—made the face-saving gesture of electing as pope Nicholas V, who was already (since 1447) Pope at Rome. There was left, of the brave pronouncements of Pisa and Constance, almost no ghost to lay. What there was was laid by Pius II in 1460, who, as Aeneas Silvius Piccolomini, had been one of the loudest and most eloquent advocates of conciliar supremacy in the earlier years of the Council of Basel. He had been convinced by the successes of Eugenius that the papal theory was superior to the conciliar theory. Henceforth the Papacy was to be monarchical, as it had been in the days of its glory. The effort to transfer the assumption of parliamentary representative government from the marketplace, the guildhall, and the royal administration to the Church had failed. The Church apparently was of such a nature that free and open discussion and disagreement, resulting in concession and compromise, would not work. In a world pointed toward separatism and the fragmentation of power, the Church held steadfastly to the principle of a single, central, and absolute authority.

Central authority had won a victory; but that victory, dramatic and convincing as it undoubtedly was, coming at the end of over forty years of bitter struggle, left the combatants fatigued. There was no energy left for the task which, at the beginning of the struggle, all parties had recognized as of paramount need and importance: reform of the Church "in head and members," purging it of the evils by now evident to the lowest and most obscure layman. The Reformation was almost a century in the future, but its outbreak is directly related to the failure of the Conciliar Movement, too busy with the struggle against papal primacy to purify the Church and cleanse it of its abuses.

SUGGESTIONS FOR FURTHER READING

See bibliography for Chapter 3.

BRUCE, H., *The Age of Schism*. London, 1907
FIGGIS, N., *From Gerson to Grotius*. Cambridge, 1916
GILL, J., *The Council of Florence*. Cambridge, 1959
JACOB, E. F., *Essays on the Conciliar Epoch*. London, 1952
JORDAN, G. J., *The Inner History of the Great Schism of the West*. London, 1930
KITTS, E. J., *In the Days of the Councils*. London, 1908
McGOWAN, J. D., *Pierre d'Ailly and the Council of Constance*. Washington, 1936
ULLMANN, W., *The Origins of the Great Schism*. London, 1948

BLIEMETZRIEDER, F., *Literarische Polemik zu Beginn des grossen abendändischen Schismas*. 1909
DE BOÜARD, M., *La France et l'Italie au temps du grand schisme d'Occident*. 1936
CHRISTOPHE, J. B., *Histoire de la Papauté pendant le XVᵉ siècle*. 2 vols. 1863
FINKE, H., *Forschungen und Quellen zur Geschichte des Konstanzer Konzils*. 1889
HEFELE, C. J., and H. LECLERCQ, *Histoire des Conciles,* Vols. VI, pt. 2, and VII. 1915–16
KNEER, A., *Die Entstehung der konziliaren Theorie*. 1893
LAZARUS, P., *Das Basler Konzil*. 1912
LENFANT, J., *Histoire du Concile de Basle*. 2 vols. 1731
LENFANT, J., *Histoire du Concile de Constance*. 2 vols. 1727
LENFANT, J., *Histoire du Concile de Pise*. 2 vols. 1724
PERROY, E., *L'Angleterre et le grand schisme d'Occident*. 1933
SALEMBIER, L., *Le grand schisme d'Occident*. 1921
SCHWAB, J. B., *Johannes Gerson*. 1858
THUDICHUM, F., *Papsttum und Reformation im Mittelalter*. 1903
TSCHACKERT, P., *Peter von Ailli*. 1877
VALOIS, N., *La France et le grand schisme d'Occident*. 4 vols. 1896–1902

CHAPTER TWELVE

HUMANISM IN FLOWER:
THE *QUATTROCENTO*

I N A previous chapter we have described the growth of "the more humane studies" (*studia humaniora*) in Italy from the time of Dante to the death of Salutati, the famed chancellor of the Republic of Florence. The great names of the early phase of this movement are Petrarch and Boccaccio, who, with Dante at the beginning of the fourteenth century and Salutati at the end, constitute the Florentine quartet. There is no doubt that Florence can claim to have given birth or haven to the founders of the humanistic Renaissance. And, as we shall see, her primacy in the republic of letters and art was not challenged until the middle of the fifteenth century, when the humanistic popes employed the vast resources of the Church in an effort to make Rome the mecca of scholars throughout the world.

HUMANISM IN *QUATTROCENTO* FLORENCE

B Y THE time of the death of Salutati (1406) there were several active centers of the new learning in Florence, among them the *Paradiso* of Alberti and the circle of the *Santo Spirito* (see above, Chapter 4). This latter group, founded by Luigi de' Marsigli, was maintained after his death in 1394 by Salutati and his younger friends. Among these rising humanists already recognized for their brilliance were Niccolò Niccoli (1364-1437), Leonardo Bruni Aretino (1374-1444), Ambrogio Traversari (1386-1439), Poggio Bracciolini (1380-1459). Two still younger men were soon added to the group, Carlo Marsuppini Aretino (1398-1453) and Giannozzo Manetti (1396-1459). These were men of diverse talents and temperaments, whose personal relationships ran the gamut from intimate and lasting friendship to jealous and at times petty animosity. They were not the only humanists in Florence; they were simply the most widely known of a large company of scholars and propagators of the new movement in education and culture whose work and works carried on to high perfection the earlier pioneering labor of Petrarch and Boccaccio. There was, indeed, not a single one of these half-dozen who could not have improved upon the Latin prose of both Petrarch and Boccaccio or who did not have a better critical knowledge of the Latin classics than that possessed by their two forerunners. Furthermore, most of them were at home in Greek and were thus better equipped to present the best of the ancient world to the mind of their age. Yet they all took inspiration from the lives and writings of their spiritual forebears and devoted their talents to the same end with passionate zeal. To them the cultivation of the humane letters, best exemplified in the writings of the Greek and Latin masters, was the chief end of life.

We have met Niccolò Niccoli before when he cooperated with Salutati to bring Manuel Chrysoloras, the famed Greek scholar, to lecture at the University (*studio*) of Florence in 1396. His father, a very successful Florentine merchant, had left Niccolò a substantial and going business. But the son, disliking commerce, sold his share of the business and devoted his life and his fortune to the pursuit of letters. Instead of marrying he collected manuscripts and added to what codices he could buy fully as many which he copied out in his own hand. By the end of his life he had amassed, from near and far, a remarkably large library of eight hundred codices, well chosen, carefully collated and corrected, and cared for with the devoted tenderness of a lover. Nor was he miserly about his precious books. He loaned them, perhaps too freely, to scholars and students. At his death his executors found that two hundred of the eight hundred were out on loan, and it took some time to get them back. Niccolò's collecting had been expensive, and, when he was thinking about the disposal of his treasures, he found he had not enough of his fortune left to build suitable bookcases for the tomes. Cosimo de' Medici stepped in and purchased the whole collection, which he installed in the monastery of San Marco.

Niccolò had broad classical interests. His house was furnished with all sorts of relics of ancient life: porcelain, silver trays, cups, goblets, coins, vases, and gems; and he enjoyed inviting friends and acquaintances to eat from dishes which Cicero or Seneca might have used. It was no uncommon occurrence for him to appear, handsomely dressed in crimson, on the square before the Duomo, greet old friends, then get into conversation with some stranger to the city and take him home to dine and see his collections. Vespasiano da Bisticci, from whose memoirs we learn so much about Florentine personalities, said of him: "Just to see him presiding at table, that was really a delight." His imposing presence and his passion for ancient art and letters were a boon to the whole movement. His influence was great, but he wrote almost nothing. He was perhaps too aware of the discrepancy between what he might have written and the lofty style of the ancients to wish to profane the language they used. Yet he gave encouragement and helpful criticism to others who did feel the urge to write, and there were many who owed their start to him. He was, on the other hand, not above jealousy. He had been active in bringing Chrysoloras to Florence, but within the year had begun to make the Greek's work difficult. The gentle Guarino of Verona, Aurispa, and the tougher Filelfo were to feel his sharp tongue and his sharper intrigue when they dared to disagree with him. All had eventually to leave Florence.

Leonardo Bruni Aretino

LEONARDO Bruni (1374–1444), called Aretino from his birthplace of Arezzo, a dependency of the Republic of Florence, had a quite different career from that of Niccoli. Of modest birth, he rose by his own abilities and hard work to positions of eminence and cultural recognition. Petrarch was his early ideal. He soon came to Salutati's notice and was taken under the Florentine secretary's affectionate protection. The arrival of Chrysoloras in Florence early in 1397 was a great boon to the brilliant young student, and his quick mastery of Greek as well as his wide knowledge of both Greek and Latin literatures marked him for rapid promotion. For a while he was taken into the home of the Medici as a tutor for the young Nicola de' Medici, with such good effect that the pupil came to be known as the most cultured of all the Florentine nobility.

In 1405, upon the recommendation of both Salutati and Poggio Bracciolini, he was appointed secretary to Pope Innocent VII, and joined the *curia* at Rome. These were the days of the Schism, and Bruni was uncomfortable in the acrimonious atmosphere he found at the papal court. Homesick for Florence, he was happy to be chosen chancellor of the *Signoria* in 1410. The conditions of employment, however, were not so favorable as they had been for Salutati, and Bruni soon returned to the papal *curia,* now under Pope John XXIII, who offered him an attractive future in the Church. But Bruni preferred to remain a layman, and married in 1412. Nevertheless, he accompanied John to Constance in 1414, only to leave him in March of the next year and return to Florence. He had saved enough money from his generous salary as a papal secretary to devote all his time for the next ten years to his *History of Florence,* which he had begun while still at Constance. His scholarly work was interrupted on several occasions by election to the Council of Ten and to the priorate; he was also sent on several diplomatic missions for the Republic. He labored at his *History* for the last thirty years of his life, leaving the twelfth and last book unfinished at his death. Bruni was convinced that history and rhetoric could and should be combined. He weighed the great historians of antiquity, Polybius, Caesar, and Livy, with their attention to truth and detail, against the broader, philosophical view of Cicero that history should be presented as the guide of life, the wisdom of the ages. Without minimizing in any degree the need for accuracy and critical handling of the sources, he leaned to the Ciceronian position. The story of Florence offered opportunities for remarks on the nature of liberty and tyranny, and Bruni, doubtless influenced by Salutati, made his own views quite clear. To him the pursuit of liberty is the central theme of human history, and in his own day the history of beloved Florence illustrated that pursuit as eloquently as had the history of Greece and Rome in ancient times. The *History* was doubtless Bruni's most important work, but his production, translations into Latin of Xenophon, Plutarch, Aristotle, and Plato, ten volumes of letters, invectives, essays, orations, and finally lives of Dante and Petrarch—in all seventy-four volumes—was prodigious.

In 1427 Bruni was again made chancellor of the Republic, this time on the same liberal terms Salutati had enjoyed. He was highly esteemed both in Florence, where he was one of the glories of the city, and abroad. Travelers from as far away as Spain and Portugal would come to Florence just to catch a glimpse of him, robed in majestic scarlet, browsing in his favorite bookshop, or walking sedately from the Piazza della Signoria to his home. His funeral was a state ceremony. A copy of his *History of Florence* was placed upon his chest with his hands folded over it. Giannozzo Manetti, in the presence of the fathers of the city and high dignitaries of the Church, pronounced the funeral oration: "Now, O most worthy star of the Latins, we crown thy fortune-favored holy sleep, as a testimony of thy vast learning and thine unmatched eloquence, a gage both to those now living and to coming generations, with the high meed of the laurel," and with trembling hands placed a laurel crown upon the brow of the aged chancellor.

Ambrogio Traversari and Giannozzo Manetti

BRUNI had died in the arms of his closest friend, the monk Ambrogio Traversari (1386–1439), who, born near Florence, joined the Camaldolese Order at the age of fourteen. These were the days of the enthusiasms of Niccoli and the teaching of Chrysoloras. To Ambrogio, who had begun to learn Greek on his own before Chrysoloras came, that great event served only to confirm his interests. He learned Hebrew in the same independent way. In the succeeding years he joined the group of humanists who maintained the circle of *Santo Spirito* which Marsigli had founded. Traversari, as the only monastic member in a group of scholars indifferent to religious motivation, had some difficulty in adapting himself to their critical attitude. He scrupulously avoided quoting profane authors in his sermons, yet the language of his preaching was a good approximation of Ciceronian Latin. His knowledge of these same profane authors was at least equal to that of the other members of the group, and of the Greek writers it was superior. He dedicated himself to the translation of the Greek fathers into Latin; we have from his hand excellent translations of many lives of the Greek saints, sermons of St. Chrysostom, the works of the Pseudo-Dionysius the Areopagite, and the *Lives of the Ancient Philosophers* of Diogenes Laertius. This last work, begun reluctantly at the urging of Cosimo de' Medici, was as close as Ambrogio could bring himself to handling a heathen work. Made general of his order in 1431, the last years of his life were busy with ecclesiastical politics. He was insistent in his appeals for reform in the Church, and was active at the Council of Ferrara-Florence (see above, Chapter 11). With Bessarion, he was responsible for editing the acts of the Council in Greek and Latin. Traversari was an anomaly in the Florence of the *quattrocento*. His Christian piety and his austere monastic life seemed out of tune with the humanistic temper. Yet in many ways he was a better humanist than those friends who loved him for his mildness, smiled at his devoutness, and tolerated his scruples.

Among those in Florence who were influenced by Traversari, Giannozzo Manetti (1396–1459) must be mentioned. Of a noble Florentine family, he had been destined by his father for commerce and public affairs, but at the age of twenty-five he suddenly found himself attracted to the study of letters. He stole time from his sleep to read the philosophers and historians of Greece and Rome without telling his father of his new passion. Joining the circle at *Santo*

Spirito, he found himself more sympathetic to Traversari than to the less Christian minded humanists. He learned Greek with Traversari and then Hebrew. For the latter, he brought a certain Rabbi Manuel into his house and read the Old Testament through in Hebrew with his help. Then he had two Greeks in his house with whom he conversed only in Greek. His equipment and humanistic scholarship were recognized to be of the best; his motivation was primarily religious and philosophical. Respected in business circles as well as at the university, which interested him more than it did most of the humanists, he was occasionally involved in local politics as well as in foreign affairs, having been sent on numerous diplomatic missions. For some reason not quite clear to us, he left Florence in 1453, to spend his last years between the court of Pope Nicholas V at Rome as papal secretary and that of King Alfonso of Naples. He may have incurred the displeasure of Cosimo de' Medici for dedicating a philosophical work *On the Dignity of Man* (*De dignitate et excellentia hominis*) to Alfonso and not to Cosimo. Traversari and Manetti must be grouped together as avowedly Christian humanists at a time when that approach was already exceptional. Manetti's fame never matched that of Traversari and fell far short of that of Leonardo Bruni. He may have been their equal in massive learning, but the elements of originality and singlemindedness which turn learning into art were lacking.

Poggio Bracciolini (1380–1459) was perhaps the most distinguished of the Florentine scholars. He came to Florence about 1395 to work in the secretariat as a scribe and notary under Salutati, but the latter quickly recognized the qualities of the young man and obtained for him a post at Rome as apostolic scriptor. For the next fifty years his story is not directly connected with his native Florence, but with the Roman *curia* and his amazing discoveries of manuscripts of works believed lost which he made while in papal employ. In spite of his absence in Rome, Poggio always considered himself a Florentine; when he returned to the Arno as chancellor in 1453 he felt he was coming home.

A colleague and a successor of Bruni as chancellor of Florence, Carlo Marsuppini Aretino (1398–1453), and his pupil Matteo Palmieri (1406–75) were both highly regarded by their contemporaries; from our vantage point, they appear of somewhat less significance. Marsuppini, a facile versifier in Latin, was not a major poet. His most useful contribution lay in his teaching activity at the university in Florence, where, from 1431 on, he had large classes in Latin and Greek rhetoric and philosophy. The post of chancellor was given him in 1444 upon the death of Bruni. He had, however, none of the warmth and dignity which made Bruni and Traversari so influential, nor the deep enthusiasm for the classics which Niccoli exuded. In 1452 Pope Nicholas V commissioned him to translate Homer into Latin. Only Book I and a part of Book IX were completed. Palmieri, his pupil, was one of the first humanists to popularize the humanistic ideals by writing in the vernacular. The aim of his *On the Life of a Citizen* (*Della vita civile*) was to present Roman ideals of citizenship in current Italian. He could speak from personal experience, as he had held many public offices in the Republic, including that of prior and gonfalonier of justice.

These men, Niccoli, Bruni, Traversari, Manetti, Marsuppini, and Palmieri, whose periods of active participation in the field of the "more humane letters" covered more than a half-century, from about 1390 into the second half of the fifteenth century, formed the core of what we must call the early Medici circle. Many lesser lights worked faithfully at the same studies, but it was essentially these scholars who, generously supported by Cosimo de' Medici, gave Florence the precedence in the new learning in Italy. Dante, Petrarch, Boccaccio, and Salutati were of course Florentines, but two of them had lived in exile and the effect of the work of the remaining two might easily have been lost if there had not followed them this group of devoted and productive lovers of ancient letters.

The Medici and the New Learning

THE patronage of the Medici is one of the most remarkable maecenates in the history of the modern world. The Medici were a trading family first heard of in the late twelfth century. Their wealth grew with that of Florence during the thirteenth century, and by the mid-fourteenth they were one of the wealthier merchant houses, along with the Bardi, the Strozzi, the Albizzi, the Capponi, the Peruzzi, the Pucci, the Rinucini, and the Rucellai. The Medici were registered in two of the seven major guilds (*arti maggiori*), the guild of the cloth merchants (*calimala*) and that of the bankers or money-changers (*cambiali*). Of all the Florentine banking firms, the Medici, partly because they were not yet the leaders, were the least affected by the nonpayment by Edward III of England (1339–40) of debts owed to various Italian bankers, especially the Bardi. Several rival houses were completely ruined by this catastrophe, but the Medici profited from the disasters of others. At the time of the revolt of the Ciompi in 1378, the Medici, alone of the leading merchant families, were sympathetic to the popular cause. The real eminence of the Medici began with the work of Giovanni di Bicci de' Medici (1360–1429), a financial and administrative genius. Quiet and retiring by disposition, he was yet chosen for public office on several occasions and in 1401 was one of the judges who chose Ghiberti over Brunelleschi to execute the north door of the Baptistery just outside the Duomo. He became banker for Pope John XXIII and sent his son Cosimo to Constance with the Pope. He paid a large sum to Duke Louis of Bavaria for John's release from captivity in 1418 and gave the ex-Pope shelter in Florence until his death the next year. This was the beginning of the relationship of the Medici with the Papacy, a connection profitable for both parties. The Papacy was always in financial straits; the Medici both systematized papal finances and made a steady if reasonable profit from handling large sums for the *curia*. On the death of Giovanni di Bicci in 1429, Cosimo, then thirty-nine years of age, with broad experience in all branches of the family's far-flung financial empire and in international diplomacy, took over. By this time the Albizzi were the only house that could rival the Medici, and the inevitable war for commercial and political supremacy in the Republic came to a head in 1434, when the Albizzi won the first round and the Medici were exiled. Cosimo, escaping a prison sentence by the judicious distribution of substantial sums, went to Venice, where the family had interests. Florence, without Cosimo's financial genius, was lost, and the Florentines soon realized this. The Pope, Eugenius IV, intermittently residing in Florence, well aware from past experience of the indispensability of the Medici and particularly Cosimo, helped the Florentines to see the error of sending the Medici to another city which their genius would certainly enrich at Florence's expense. Cosimo was recalled in September. The Albizzi and eighty of their supporters were exiled; for the next three centuries with hardly a break Florence was the city of the Medici.

Without for a moment losing control of his commercial and banking affairs, Cosimo nourished scholarly interests. While still in his teens, he was spending large sums in support of scholars and learning, paying Chrysoloras' expenses, and ordering Greek books from Constantinople. As he took command of the house of Medici he provided libraries for collections of manuscripts, supported artists and sculptors who executed works the whole city could enjoy, persuaded Pope Eugenius IV to bring the Council to Florence in 1438, and personally advanced the guarantee of 100,000 florins to house the Greeks. He then implemented the suggestion of the venerable Greek Gemistos Plethon that he found a Platonic Academy in Florence. This takes us a few years ahead of our story, but it is important to realize that when we speak of the Medici "circle" we are speaking of a group of scholars who were carefully selected, intelligently encouraged, and amply supported by a great and powerful man who was not the founder of a commercial dynasty but its ablest head. We shall meet Cosimo in connection with art and architecture, politics, and the brilliant revival of Platonism later in the century. When he died in 1464 the city of Florence quite appropriately gave him the title of *Pater Patriae*—Father of His Country.

HUMANISM AT ROME

WHILE Florence, impelled by generous Medici patronage and the genius of her humanist sons, was leading the rest of the Western world in the recapture of classical eloquence, the Papacy was suffering the shocks of the Schism and the Conciliar Movement. The papal court was frequently in flight before mob rule in Rome or the caprice of princes, and the greater part of the energy of the popes in the early fifteenth century was devoted to political maneuvering and the crude struggle for survival. Yet in spite of this absorption in quite mundane matters, there was a steadily growing interest in the concerns which excited the humanists. Poggio Bracciolini was employed in 1403 because of his fine command of classical Latin style, and re-employed by four successive popes with increased emoluments, for the same reason. Pope John XXIII employed Leonardo Bruni as a secretary in 1410 and he could have stayed with the *curia* indefinitely if he had so desired. It was as John's secretary that Poggio, from Constance, made excursions to Swiss, French, and German monasteries in which he made such amazing discoveries of classical manuscripts. Martin V (1417–31) undertook the badly needed physical restoration of Rome, but he also supported Poggio handsomely, realizing the prestige the most famous living humanist brought to his court.

There were other eminent humanists at Martin's court: Agapito Cenci de' Rustici (d. 1464), Bartolommeo de Montepulciano (d. 1429), and Antonio Loschi (d. 1441), all with excellent training, wide travel, and notable scholarly production. Martin tried, furthermore, in 1428, to attract Francesco Filelfo (1398–1481), just returned from Constantinople, into his entourage; however,

Filelfo found an offer to teach at the University of Florence more to his liking. All these humanists made sure, in the papal chancery, that the correspondence of the papal *curia* was in impressively good Latin; they also acted as heads of diplomatic missions, in which learning and eloquence were effective. Eugenius IV (1431–47) retained all four of these officials in their posts, thus giving continuity to the tradition of learning at the *curia*. This tradition was supported by a number of the cardinals residing in Rome who both practiced the new learning themselves and gave generously to artists, schools, and scholars. There were other cardinals, such as Capranica, legate at Bologna, and Albergati, bishop of Bologna, who were ambitious to make their cities centers of intellectual activity. Capranica had a vast personal library of two thousand volumes which he turned into what we would call a public lending library. From the group of humanists whose origins lay in Florence one at least was to carry his intellectual tastes to the papal throne. Thomas Parentucelli of Sarzana, bishop of Bologna, was a widely recognized humanist who became Pope Nicholas V (1447–55). During his pontificate Rome easily challenged Florence for the leadership of the humanistic revival.

Pope Eugenius IV, as we have seen (see above, Chapter 11), spent much of his pontificate at war with the Council of Basel. He had been a Franciscan monk, and his personal life was so austere that he was commonly nicknamed "Abstemius." Some of his contemporaries, and indeed some historians since, have belittled his support of the new learning. But it was this monk who raised Traversari to the generalship of his order largely because of his learning and who gave him great responsibilities in the negotiations with the Greeks for the union of the churches. Eugenius went further. He urged Traversari to continue his scholarly work. He was so interested in Traversari's work that he made specific suggestions of writings of the Greek fathers that should be translated into Latin. He then put manuscripts, funds, and copyists at Traversari's disposal.

Maffeo Vegio, a lover of Virgil, was a prominent professor of law at the University of Pavia, with deep classical interests until the Pope called him to the Roman *curia* in 1431 or 1432, where he remained as "abbreviator" until his death in 1458. Influenced by his study of St. Augustine and by the preaching of San Bernardino of Siena, his interests became increasingly Christian, even reformatory. Vespasiano says of him: "He valued immortal treasures more than the perishing ones of earth, and set his face toward that true end which every Christian should seek. . . . His good deeds were so many that he deserves to be kept in memory by all learned men." Aeneas Silvius, no praiser of other men, wrote of him that his fame and station (*fortuna*) were much below his worth.

Eugenius was able to induce Giovanni Aurispa (d. 1459), one of the most distinguished of the pupils of Guarino da Verona, to join his staff as a secretary before 1437. His knowledge of Greek was to be valuable during the subsequent negotiations with the Eastern Church. He was frequently given permission to be absent from the *curia* in search of manuscripts and on diplomatic missions, during which he kept fresh his friendships with other humanists throughout Italy. Another pupil of Guarino da Verona who joined the staff of Eugenius IV was Ermolao Barbaro. Younger than Aurispa, he was distantly related to the Pope, which would explain why he was soon (1437) named bishop of Bergamo and later (1443) translated to the more important bishoprics of Treviso and Verona.

Of even greater significance for the reverence paid Roman grandeur was the work of Flavio Biondo (Flavius Blondus) of Forlì, the historian and archeologist (1388–1463). He was almost self-taught, and, until the age of thirty-five, only a town clerk in Forlì. But his reading had been thorough, and when banned from his native city after a local upheaval, he obtained (in 1427) a post as secretary to the Venetian *podestà* in Padua and Brescia. He owed his successful Venetian career to the friendship of the humanist Francesco Barbaro, uncle of Ermolao Barbaro, who probably recommended him to the Pope. At all events, in 1433 Eugenius appointed him a notary and the next year apostolic secretary. In 1436 he was made apostolic scriptor. Being married and the father of ten children, he was not eligible for ecclesiastical preferment. He was neither courtier nor flatterer. He substituted for flattery hard and faithful work, remaining loyal to Eugenius in the Pope's tribulations, and continued the painstaking labor which resulted in his first notable work of antiquarian research, the *Roma instaurata,* dedicated to the Pope (1446). In this great work he traced, step by step, block by block, ancient Rome and her monuments, comparing it with the Rome of his own day. Having, as it were, described the two ends of Roman history, the Rome of the Caesars and that of the popes, he next set about describing the Italian peninsula, whose conquest was Rome's glory and whose reunification under the Church was the dream of every pope. This work, *Italia illustrata,* was finished in 1453. The amount of detailed information about the eighteen regions into which he divided the peninsula was tremendous; however, not a little of it was trivial, and there was no poetic lift to his writing. This was the first serious attempt to treat the history and geography of the whole peninsula as a unit. His last work, *Roma triumphans* (1459), dedicated to Pope Pius II, was an institutional and social history of ancient Rome such as had never yet been attempted. The scholars of the Renaissance had up to this point been inspired by an enthusiasm for letters which had about run its course. To justify further cultivation of the literature of Rome, a more realistic and accurate appreciation of social, political, geographical, and economic relationships was imperative. This need Biondo sought to supply, and the very pedestrian quality of his work, for which he was then and later criticized, was perhaps the most valuable element in his contribution.

The leading humanist attached to the papal *curia,* and probably the most eminent in all Italy, was Poggio Bracciolini, a Florentine who received his early training under the protective care of Salutati. Joining the *curia* in 1403, for fifty years he remained its brightest humanistic light. He served under five popes, from Boniface IX to Nicholas V. His fame rested about equally upon his own copious compositions and his amazing discoveries of works of Roman writers. The manuscripts of these works had lain unnoticed in monastic and episcopal libraries for centuries. They were in older scripts which were unfamiliar to the scholastic world and copies of works whose strange titles had held no attraction for the monks of the earlier Middle Ages or the clergy of the thirteenth and fourteenth centuries. It was only from Petrarch on that a few scholars began to be curious about works which, mentioned in the few writings of such authors as Cicero, Seneca, Ovid, and Virgil, had been copied in sufficient numbers to be widely known. Salutati had discovered the whole corpus of the *Epistolae familiares* of Cicero in 1392; Guarino da Verona had found some additional letters of Pliny in 1408. Other works of the Latin authors began to be identified in the next few years. The hunt was on. Poggio, fortunate in being attached to the papal court, profited by its frequent movement. Between 1405 and 1410, for example, the *curia* was, for varying periods of time, at Viterbo, Lucca, Siena, Pisa, Pistoia, Bologna, and Rimini. Wherever the *curia* stopped, Poggio made a point of searching in the local archives, the library of any nearby monastery, or the library of the cathedral for manuscripts that might contain hitherto unnoticed works of the Latin writers. He copied out whole codices when he could not buy or beg, and thus came into possession of a priceless library of the Roman classics. The discoveries he made during the Council of Constance were the sensation of the learned world. While Pope John XXIII, whom he was serving as secretary, was either being tried or in prison, Poggio made four trips to nearby libraries in search of manuscripts, as he said to a friend, "to liberate the ancient fathers from their prisons." On the first trip, to Cluny in France, he found two unknown orations of Cicero. On the second trip, he found in the ancient monastery of St. Gall in Switzerland the first complete copy of Quintilian's *Institutio oratoria,* the first three books and half the fourth book of Valerius Flaccus' *Argonautica,* and Asconius' commentary on five orations of Cicero. Later on this exploratory journey he found the *Silvae* of Statius. A third trip uncovered the *Astronomicon* of Manilius, the *Punica* of Silius Italicus, the *Historia* of Ammianus Marcellinus, the *De rerum natura* of Lucretius, and other lesser works. On a fourth expedition, into Germany, he found the *De re rustica* of Columella and eight further orations of Cicero. In 1418, at the end of the Council, Cardinal Beaufort invited Poggio to England. The experience was depressing for him.* Returning to Rome in 1423, he took up again his work at the *curia,* and began the composition of the *Dialogues,* which were, in a fashion, his answer to the problems of life as he observed it. There is a certain bitterness and frustration evident throughout this work. The titles of some of the essays betray this spirit: "On Nobility," which insists that performance and not blood is the true measure of nobility; "On Fickleness of Fortune"; "On the Misery of the Human Estate"; "On the "Unhappiness of Princes." The clergy were the especial object of his scorn and invective, and the fact that he was in the service of the Church seems to have made no difference to him or to the popes who continued to employ him. Secure in his position at the *curia,* Poggio engaged in personal polemics, and was so savage in his invectives that, as Vespasiano da Bisticci remarked, "the whole world was afraid of him." He was involved in a quarrel with Filelfo over a period of nine years, each calling the other the vilest names he could dig up from Latin literature and inventing some new terms of abuse. This was thought to be quite normal, as indeed it was. Among his other writings was his *Book of Jokes (Liber facetiarum)*, barbed and bawdy, directed mostly against the clergy, a copious correspondence, a few translations from the Greek, and attacks on the Council of Basel.

* For Poggio's English experience see above, Chapter 11.

In 1435, at the age of fifty-five, already the father of fourteen children by a patient mistress, Poggio put her aside and married an eighteen-year-old girl who then bore him four more. In 1453 at the age of seventy-three, on the death of his friend Carlo Marsuppini, he was called to Florence to become chancellor of the Republic. He was also chosen prior and a member of the *Signoria.* The business of the chancery was carried on by trained subordinates so that Poggio was left free to devote his energies to a *History of Florence,* which was to cover the period from 1352 to his own day. It was left unfinished at his death. His historical work is subject to the criticism that he was too interested in showing his superiority to Bruni as a stylist. His merits as a historian were minor.

The year 1447, in which Nicholas V came to the pontifical throne, was a red-letter one for the devotees of classical learning. Nicholas, who had himself received a thorough humanistic training at Florence, knew personally all the leading scholars of Italy. He tried to get many of these humanist friends attached to his court, and rewarded them generously for their translations and original compositions. He always carried a purse or two full of money to give to some ambitious scholar who might stop the Pope on the street in Rome and read him his latest effusion. Much of this volunteer scholarship was quite worthless, but the Pope was serious about his patronage, and the encouragement he gave from papal funds, the searches for manuscripts he directed and financed, and the papal library of almost five thousand manuscripts which he established and generously enriched made Rome the leading center of the new learning in all Italy, and therefore in all the Western world during Nicholas' pontificate. The Pope was fortunate to have reigned during a period of relative peace and therefore of prosperity for the Papacy. The glory of the Florence of the Medici was still bright at the mid-century, but Rome was even more glorious. The brilliant society of the learned known as the Roman Academy, led by Pomponio Leto for the Latins and Cardinal Bessarion for the Greeks, was more solidly rooted than the Platonic Academy in Florence and, precisely because it made no sweeping philosophical pretensions, received a more sympathetic welcome from the fraternity of scholars.

The Spread of Humanism in Italy

FLORENCE and Rome were only the leading centers of the humanistic Renaissance. There were competent and even superlative students of the classic literatures and ideals at many other cities and courts in Italy. Petrarch had traveled widely. His correspondence was even wider, and his enthusiasm for the beauties of ancient culture, as shown in its language and the monuments of its thought, was infectious. Without being a professional teacher, he nevertheless had many followers who looked to him as their master. In Milan, Venice, Padua, Naples, Verona, Bologna, and Mantua the seeds of his gospel had taken root and matured so that by early in the fifteenth century there were trained and competent classicists either well established at various courts, employed by the cities as professors, or the owners of successful private schools, patronized by the bourgeoisie, the nobility, or ambitious students making their living by manual labor or by working as copyists.

Milan

IN MILAN, raised from a county to a duchy in 1395 by Emperor Wenzel, the Visconti ruled with an iron hand. Petrarch had lived in Milan as the honored guest of Giovanni Visconti for eight years. The nephews of Giovanni had little or no interest in letters, but their heir, Gian Galeazzo (1352–1402), ambitious to become king of Italy and even emperor of the Holy Roman Empire, would have welcomed the aid and sanction of the humanists whose laudatory verses could be bought. He spared no expense in building handsome churches, such as the Certosa of Pavia, and in collecting saints' relics, paintings, or manuscripts of the classics; yet his interest in such matters was not that of the humanist, but rather that of the unfocused amateur become suddenly rich. His son Filippo Maria (d. 1447) was a political intriguer and, fortunately for his neighbors, an unsuccessful one. Culture was of quite secondary interest to him. He does, however, have the merit of having invited Gasparino da Barzizza to Milan in 1418 to head a Latin school for boys. Filippo Maria read the poetry of Dante and Petrarch, mixing it indiscriminately with French romances of chivalry and translations from the Latin. It is doubtful if he understood much of what he heard or read. He is more important for having married his daughter to the captain-general of his soldiery, Francesco Sforza (1401–66), who soon took over the rule and became duke of Milan. At various times the humanists Francesco Filelfo and Pier Candido Decembrio (1392–1477) and the architect Antonio Filarete were in his employ as tutors for his children or as court officials. His son Galeazzo Maria (d. 1476) continued the policy of having humanists at court, as tutors, secretaries, or experts in vilification, as a part of his political defense organization. The humanists knew more words, and words were important in propaganda wars. Both Galeazzo Maria and his brother and successor Ludovico the Moor (*il Moro*) supported the neighboring University of Pavia, where humanists were chosen for the chairs of Latin rhetoric and Greek. Milan was rich and powerful, and its rulers, Visconti and Sforza, had humanists and artists at their court, yet the duchy always trailed behind Florence, Rome, and even Venice as a center of the new learning.

Florence seemed to the men of the Renaissance the capital of the world's republic of arts and letters, and there was no one to dispute for long that primacy. The republic on the Arno lived by and for *humanitas*. In Rome, on the contrary, however interested any pope or cardinal might be in the revival of the excellencies of Greek and Roman culture, it was never allowed to become more than a means or a façade. Rome was the head of the ecclesiastical organization of the known world, with all its involvements; such a basic commitment could not yield to the fancy of style. In Milan, humanism and the humanists were hardly more than a fad or a plaything, to be used by the Visconti and the Sforza in their diplomacy abroad or as a diversion for their subjects. Humanism had no deep roots among the people of Milan.

Venice

IN VENICE, however, the situation was somewhat different. The loyalty of the Venetians was peculiarly focused on their city. Its oligarchic government, the highly restricted citizenship, and the steady commercial prosperity made such an attitude natural. It seemed unlikely that this smugness would be disturbed by what, to a native Venetian, would appear to be a passing fad imported from Florence. Yet the humanist movement owed much to Venice. Petrarch had honored the city by five years of residence on her territory (1362–67) and frequent later visits, had formed many friendships with leading citizens, and had at one point arranged to leave his precious library to the city— an arrangement he later canceled. The intellectuals of Venice treasured their connections with humanists on the mainland, and we find a copious correspondence continuing between eminent scholars everywhere in Italy and their colleagues in Venice. Those Venetian scholars who were of the aristocracy were able to offer hospitality to famed humanists passing through the city on their way to other centers. Chrysoloras, Vergerio, Guarino, Traversari, and Bessarion, among others, were entertained in the palaces of Venetian nobles turned humanist scholars, and the atmosphere in the city, with its intimate connections with Constantinople, apparently warmed toward the new learning.

Yet, in spite of all these opportunities and the wealth and favorable location which the city enjoyed as the western port of émigrés from Constantinople, Venice never really took humanism seriously. Scholar after scholar, after being invited to settle in Venice, left in disgust or anger. Gasparino da Barzizza tried to make a living in the city in 1407, and then again in 1411, but had to depart penniless. Guarino da Verona arrived in 1408 from Constantinople with many Greek manuscripts and an impressive mastery of Greek language and literature. He stayed in Barbaro's house and in 1414 founded a school, but this was a failure and he left in 1419 and never returned. His most famous pupil, Vittorino da Feltre, also tried to support himself by a school, only to be obliged to leave. These last two, Guarino and Vittorino, are the most famous educators of the whole humanist movement, and both had to turn their faces away from Venice. Filelfo served as secretary to a Venetian embassy to Constantinople. On his return in 1427, bringing his Greek bride, the daughter of Chrysoloras, as well as many Greek manuscripts and a fresh competence in Greek, he was invited by a few wealthy individuals to set up a school. A plague hit the city and his sponsors fled. They wrote him warm letters of appreciation but enclosed no money. In a few months, embittered, he departed for good. Georgios Trapezuntios of Crete was the next to be invited (1433) by private persons to come to Venice to establish a school. He left for Florence in a few months.

Padua

THE fate and fame of Padua was, in this period, closely tied to that of Venice. Under the benevolent despotism of the Carraras, the university had been rather more open-minded than most Italian universities; the early Paduan school of humanists (see above, Chapter 4) had already prepared the soil for the work of Petrarch and his followers. Venice absorbed Padua in 1405, and the university, already famous for its teaching of canon and civil law and medicine, was generously favored by the city. It became in fact the Venetian university. The scriptor of the city from 1405 to his death in 1447 was Sicco Polentone, who composed, in eighteen books, a history of Latin writers from

Livius Andronicus to Petrarch. He furthered the cult of his fellow Paduan, Livy, and one of the notable events of this century in Padua was the discovery in 1413 of what were reported to be the bones of the great historian. The remains were in a remarkable state of preservation. Polentone was summoned to examine the remains, and while he hurried off to the *Signoria* to start a collection for an appropriate mausoleum, somebody stole all the teeth from the body. The students, of course, were blamed. The abbot of the monastery in which the bones were found was so angry that the Paduans should honor the remains of a pagan more than a saint that he took a hammer and smashed the skull to bits. But the city fathers ceremoniously buried the bones with due reverence. A whole series of eminent humanists had posts at the university, which was greatly frequented by students from north of the Alps, from Germany, the Lowlands, Poland, Hungary, and the British Isles. We find at Padua at various times Guarino, Filelfo, Vittorino da Feltre, Gasparino da Barzizza, and, later, Ermolao Barbaro and Giovanni Marcanova, who amassed a great collection of books and antiquities which he gave in 1467 to a Paduan monastery. A chair of Greek was established at the university in 1463 and the Athenian Chalcondylas was named its first occupant.

Verona and Mantua

VERONA, also a dependency of Venice, in 1420 invited Guarino, a native of the city who had gained a great reputation in Venice and Padua as a teacher of Latin and Greek, to return to his home and teach. He lived at a distance from the city on an idyllic estate with lawns, orchard, domestic animals, and vineyards, near a gentle stream. Some of his students lived in his house, others were day pupils of various ages. There was so much local opposition to him that in 1429 he accepted an invitation from the Marquis Niccolò d'Este to tutor his son Leonello. Guarino moved to Ferrara, where he was to spend the rest of his long life, teaching, lecturing, and writing. The city, supported by the Este family, founded a university out of the body of scholars attracted by Guarino's fame and learning. He remained active until his death at the advanced age of eighty-six in 1460. His was a nature both winsome and exciting, learned and warm. These traits of Guarino seemed to be transmitted to the Este family and persisted among the traditions of Ferrara for centuries after his death. Vittorino da Feltre (1378–1446), Guarino's pupil and junior by only a few years, occupied a similar post at Mantua as tutor to the children of the Gonzaga, the rulers of that city, from 1423 until his death. The Gonzaga built him a spacious villa, well set in a garden, which he called *La Giocosa* (The Happy Home), where he was free to take paying as well as nonpaying pupils. Though the eulogies of Vittorino at his death were fulsome, the highest tribute was paid during his lifetime when both Poggio and Filelfo sent their sons to be taught by him. Both Guarino and Vittorino ennobled the teaching profession by a twofold devotion: love for the subject taught and love of the student.

Naples

THE court of the kingdom of Naples had a tradition of interest in learning under both the dynasties that ruled southern Italy in the later Middle Ages, the houses of Anjou and Aragon. In 1341, on his way to Rome to receive the laurel crown, Petrarch had visited King Robert at Naples; the king discussed Petrarch's work with him with intelligent interest (see above, Chapter 4). Boccaccio, then a young courtier at Naples, saw Petrarch on that occasion and began his life-long admiration and friendship with the poet. Petrarch found at Robert's court an atmosphere favorable to learning though admittedly somewhat partial to scholasticism. The king had assembled a remarkable library, the first princely collection of note in Europe, and had in his service a number of scholars with foreign travel and study behind them. Robert, however, died too soon (1343) to have been able to carry out ideas and suggestions Petrarch surely gave him, and the disturbed conditions under his successors were not favorable to the new learning. Alfonso I (Alfonso V of Aragon), called the Magnanimous, who finally conquered the kingdom in 1435 after a war lasting over twenty years, was ambitious to be recognized as a great and munificent Italian prince. The Medici, the Gonzaga, the Este, and the Sforza families had gained great renown from their support of the arts and classical studies. Alfonso followed the same course. He called into his service several of the leading humanists of Italy, treated them liberally, and gave them his protection when they were attacked. The most notable of these scholars were Beccadelli, known as Panormita from his birthplace Palermo, and Lorenzo Valla. Beccadelli (1394–1471), a typical wandering scholar, had studied at Siena, Florence, Bologna, and Pavia. In 1426 he published a collection of pornographic verse, the *Hermaphroditus,* which made him immediately famous. In 1433 at Siena he was crowned with the laurel wreath of the poet by Emperor Sigismund, then on a visit to Italy. Rejected by several cities and courts as official Latinist, he was finally employed by Alfonso at Naples in 1435. He composed a history of the reign of Alfonso, wrote many of the king's diplomatic documents, and was sent on a number of diplomatic embassies to other courts. His prose style was facile and effective, his verse resonant and harmonious. Where he really excelled, however, was in his ability to communicate his enthusiasm for classical studies to large groups of people. He popularized humanistic learning by founding an academy whose doors were open to the public and to whose meetings the passers-by were invited. It was the opposite of an ivory tower of recondite learning. Alfonso shared the enthusiasm and gave generously to its support. Beccadelli was Alfonso's guide in building up the already rich library of the Aragonese kings until it was widely regarded as the equal of the library of Nicholas V in Rome. Alfonso named him royal secretary the year before his own death in 1458 and Beccadelli stayed on under Alfonso's successor, Ferdinand I, until his death in 1471.

Lorenzo Valla (1407–57) had a wider experience and enjoyed a higher repute than Beccadelli. He grew up in Rome and credited Leonardo Bruni for help in Latin and Aurispa for guidance in Greek. He knew Poggio and all the scholars at the papal court, and profited from these connections. His critical genius, however, was his own, as was his acid and contentious temperament. Failing to get a papal appointment in 1431, he left Rome to shuttle for several years between Pavia, Milan, Genoa, Ferrara, and Mantua. He came to be known everywhere, feared and disliked for his sharp aspersions on everybody else's Latin style. At last, in 1437, we find him at Naples as secretary to King Alfonso. He alternated with Beccadelli in reading and explaining the classics to Alfonso in open sessions every evening in the royal library. The king consulted with him in all cultural matters, and he wrote many of the royal official letters. His own compositions, however, were of more lasting importance. His early (1431) dialogue *On Pleasure* (*De voluptate*) had made clear his Epicurean philosophy. Although he wrote other treatises of a philosophical nature, his genius lay in philological and literary criticism. In 1440 he published his attack on the Donation of Constantine, which he showed, by methods of inner historical criticism, to have been a forgery. In fact, the Papacy had paid little attention to the Donation for some time, and Cardinal Cusa had, a few years previously, shown the document to be an anachronism. But the pitiless tone of Valla's attack aroused resentment in Church circles. Pope Eugenius ordered the Inquisition in Naples to make an effort to try him (1444), but Alfonso forbade any further action and nothing came of the trial. Another work of Valla, *The Elegancies of the Latin Tongue* (*Elegantiae Latinae linguae,* 1444), was an effort to restore Latin, purged of its medieval blemishes, to its proper primacy over the vernacular. The Latin which he hoped would thus displace the vernacular was rather the tongue of Quintilian than that of Cicero. Most of his contemporaries considered this slight to their patron saint Cicero unforgivable treason. As might be expected of a scholar so positive, confident, violent, and gifted as Valla in an age of individual opinions, he was involved in many battles. The dispute with Poggio, lasting two full years (1452–53), ran the gamut from personal insults to serious and subtle discussion of philosophical and cultural questions. From 1447 to his death in 1457 Valla was at Rome, called by Nicholas V to be apostolic secretary. The anomaly presented by Valla's occupancy of this high position in the Church and his consistent and open attacks upon many key tenets of the organization seems to have disturbed only the friars who had tried to set the Inquisition upon him. The Renaissance Papacy was singularly tolerant.

The removal of Valla to Rome left Beccadelli the leading humanist established at Naples. But many eminent scholars came to visit the court at Alfonso's request for longer or shorter periods: Fazio from Genoa, Manetti from Florence, Aeneas Silvius from Siena, Theodore Gaza from Rome, and other lesser lights who were eager to share the warmth of the welcome extended to all humanists by Alfonso the Magnanimous. Alfonso's successor, Ferdinand I (1458–94), had little if any pure humanistic interest. Some scholars remained in his employ, but as officials, not as humanists.

The Platonic Academy

COSIMO DE' MEDICI had been urged by Gemistos Pletho, a distinguished member of the Greek delegation to the Council of Florence in 1439, to found in the city an academy on the Athenian model, which would be the promulgator and arbiter of the new studies for the whole of the Western world. It was already obvious that Constantinople could not hold out much longer against the Turk, and that Greek studies would have to be carried on, if at all, in the West. That very year Cosimo chose a six-year-old boy, Marsilio Ficino, the son of his physician, to be the ultimate head of the academy. The course of the boy's study was set in accordance with Gemistos' suggestion, which meant that he was to be raised a Platonist. Cosimo gave much attention in the following years to collecting manuscripts of the works of Plato and Plotinus, a third-century interpreter of Plato, against the time when his academy would undertake their translation into Latin. Pletho was almost alone among the Greeks in the West in placing Plato above Aristotle, and a bitter polemic raged for many years between the Greek and Italian adherents of Plato and the defenders of Aristotle, until Bessarion persuaded the participants that they were wasting their time and energies and, in addition, making themselves ridiculous. Cosimo had made his choice, and was undisturbed by the barrage of epithet and argument that filled the air over the respective merits of Aristotle and Plato. His academy was to be Platonic.

At eighteen Ficino became a member of the Medici household, and began to study Greek under a pupil of Vittorino da Feltre. He made such progress, in both Greek and philosophy, that in 1456, at the age of twenty-three, he presented to Cosimo a work entitled *Outlines of Platonic Thought* (*Institutiones ad Platonicam disciplinam*). In 1462 Cosimo gave Ficino one of his villas, Careggi, a few Greek manuscripts, and the specific commission to translate Plato. Ficino spent much of the rest of his life (d. 1499) at this task. His studies confirmed for him the validity of the Christian faith; in 1473, at the age of forty, he took priestly orders. He found the thought of Plato essentially in concord with Christian thought, attributing any apparent divergence to a failure on our part to understand fully either Plato or the Christian Scriptures.

The villa of Careggi, which Ficino called "The Academy," became a center for the humanists and scholars of Florence. Ficino's life was completely dedicated to philosophy; he never married and had no time for the amusements common to the time. Day and night he worked at the texts, asking only for more time to study and understand the truths they held. On Cosimo's death in 1464 his son and successor Piero the Gouty (1416–69) continued his support of the villa and Ficino's work. After Piero, Lorenzo the Magnificent (1449–92) took special pride in the work of the Academy, asking only to be allowed to join the group that met with Ficino around the bust of Plato in their friendly discussions. The group was a very diverse cross section of Italian life: Agli, bishop of Fiesole; Accolti, chancellor of the Republic; Leone Battista Alberti, the architect; Benivieni, a poet; Vespucci, a Dominican; Angelo Poliziano, a humanist; Cristoforo Landino, professor of rhetoric; Pietro Leone, the physician of Lorenzo; some members of the patriciate of Florence; and, at various times, many others from all walks of life, obscure and famous, rich and poor, both in and around Florence. The one requirement for acceptance was a humble desire to learn from Plato and his followers. The Academy was already well established in the intellectual life of Florence and Italy when, in 1484, a gracious and wealthy young man of twenty-one spent some months in Florence. This was Pico della Mirandola.

Born prince of Mirandola in 1463, at ten years of age he had been named apostolic notary by Pope Sixtus IV. That early nomination was not purely gratuitous: he was precocious. After studying at several university centers in Italy and at Paris, by the age of sixteen he was at home in both Latin and Greek and known for his fabulous memory. He went to Padua in 1480 and studied there for two years under strongly Averroistic philosophers and with Jewish rabbis who exposed him to the mysteries of the *Cabbala,* which had a deep influence upon him. At Florence in 1484 Pico sensed the strong contrast between the naturalistic tendencies of the scholastic studies he had absorbed at Padua and the Platonic and Neoplatonic thought of Ficino and the Academy. Both seemed to him to contain some truth; he became convinced that all that was necessary was to uncover the basic concord and bring the two together. As the Christian Scriptures were in large measure of Hebrew origin he decided to master Hebrew in order to make the Christian-Platonic synthesis complete. There were learned Jews in Florence and he was soon studying the text of the *Cabbala.* He went to Paris in 1485 for a year to deepen his understanding of the great scholastic teachers. On his return to Italy in 1486 he published in Rome nine hundred *conclusiones,* theses which he offered to defend publicly against all comers. He even offered to pay the traveling expenses of any challenger who might come from a distance. The public disputation was a quite conventional scholastic device. But the vast number and range of these *conclusiones* was striking, and some of the assertions were immediately suspect. Pope Innocent VIII condemned (August 1487) thirteen of the theses as heretical. Pico's *Apologia* defending the orthodoxy of the thirteen condemned theses so angered the Pope that Pico had to flee Italy. He was caught in France and imprisoned at Vincennes (February 1488). Released, probably at Lorenzo de' Medici's request, Pico was soon safe in Florence. His further publications, particularly his work *On the Dignity of Man (De dignitate hominis,* 1489) in the true humanistic spirit exalted the creative potentialities of man beyond the usual Christian conception. At Lorenzo's request he began a treatise—*De ente et uno*—which would show that Plato and Aristotle, the two great protagonists of ancient thought, were in essential accord, but Pico's untimely death (1494) at the age of thirty-one prevented the conclusion of this ambitious undertaking. To the last Pico devoutly believed that Christ, Plato, Aristotle, Moses, and Mohammed were in basic agreement and that all truth and knowledge are one. Religious sensitivity was prominent in his nature; at the end of his life, influenced by Savonarola, he was contemplating entrance into a monastic order.

Marsilio Ficino and Pico della Mirandola were two of the most well-equipped, devoted, and hard-working scholars of the whole fifteenth century. They were the dominant spirits in the Platonic Academy, and its best thought was theirs. The conditions under which the Academy existed were the most favorable that could have been conceived. There was no lack of funds; there was no lack of encouragement and sympathy from the authorities of the Republic. The head of the Republic was a member of the Academy. There was no dearth of books on which scholarly activity depended; Lorenzo got the members of the Academy everything they needed or asked for. They suffered no lack of scholarly assistance and had complete freedom in every way, yet the Academy created no philosophical tradition and had no heirs. The reason for this sterility is not far to seek: the thought of the Academy was synthetic, an effort to manufacture a living philosophy out of fragments borrowed from other systems of thought. This method has often been tried in the history of man's efforts to understand himself and the universe, always with the same negative result. Not all the resources of the Medici and the best minds of the fifteenth century could breathe life into an artificial conglomeration of Hebrew, Christian, Greek, Hellenistic, Arabic, and humanist platitudes.

The end of the fifteenth century saw the humanist movement well established and universally accepted throughout Italy. The classics, Greek and Latin, and in a lesser degree, Hebrew, had proven themselves a good school for society. Access to the masterpieces of Roman and Greek thought had broadened and deepened the variety of man's enjoyment and satisfactions. Somewhere in this mass of new literature now available to every literate person was to be found the answer to all social, political, artistic, and ethical problems. So thoroughly had classical culture permeated the life and thought of Italy that the vernacular was beginning to show the influence of classic models. Many humanists, remembering that their great prototype Petrarch had used his native tongue freely, began to write in Italian, and what they wrote was surprisingly parallel, in theme and style, to what they read and wrote in Latin or Greek. The vernacular thus grew in prestige as well as in substance and flexibility. Among the members of the Academy who used the vernacular effectively were Lorenzo de' Medici, author of many musical lyrics, Cristoforo Landino, Girolamo Benivieni, Angelo Poliziano, and Pico della Mirandola—all serious and competent scholars of the classics who illustrate the intermingling of the ancient and the contemporary that marked the end of the century. The erudite humanist would never again be able to scorn the vernacular. He could only add to its vigor and naturalness the richness of ancient theme and the precision of classic form.

THE NORTHERN RENAISSANCE

THUS far the story of the revival of learning has been focused almost exclusively on Italy, whose primacy in this revival cannot be challenged. The rest of the world had other problems. But there were curious minds from north of the Alps who traveled to Italy, met and sometimes studied with Italian humanists, then returned to their native lands as teachers or court officials. Their number, however, was small, and the difficulty they met in propagating the new learning in their native lands was often great. With the passage of time the situation improved; and the number of foreigners studying at Italian universities or with some humanist teacher grew steadily during the fifteenth century. Poggio Bracciolini spent almost four years in England without apparent result, yet within twenty years of his departure for Italy there was a considerable circle of English humanists in England, and a respectable number of Englishmen (and some Scots) studying in Italy. Duke Humphrey of Gloucester (see above, Chapter 10), younger brother of King Henry V, eagerly furthered the new learning. He not only had several trained Italian humanists in his service, but he collected manuscripts of the classics which he later presented to Oxford University. By the middle of the century there were probably two score Englishmen studying in Italy, most of whom were well connected, so that on their return to England they moved into important and influential positions in Church or state: William Grey (d. 1478), bishop of Ely; Robert

Flemming (d. 1483), dean of Lincoln and founder of Lincoln College, Oxford; John Free (d. 1465); John Gunthorpe (d. 1498), dean of Wells; John Tiptoft (d. 1470), better known as the earl of Worcester, all spent time in Italy as students of some Italian humanist. Free, Gunthorpe, and Tiptoft studied with Guarino da Verona. They enthusiastically spread the thought and ideals of the new learning in England, preparing the ground for the further work of Grocyn, Linacre, Lyly, Colet, and More, a work whose effects thoroughly impressed Erasmus when he visited England in 1499 and again in 1505 (see below, Chapter 15).

Humanism in the Empire

THE relations between Italy and that part of the Empire north of the Alps were, in the fourteenth century, intermittently close and uncomfortable. Emperor Charles IV was at home in Italy, but took care not to wear out his welcome. His sons, Wenzel and Sigismund, were so busy with the Schism, the Councils, and the Hussite wars that cultural matters were relegated to the background. It is only with the rule of the Habsburg Emperor Frederick III (1440-93) that we can speak of any concerted support of the new learning in the Empire. Before this time a few German students had traveled to Italy and brought back with them enthusiasm, improved Latin and some Greek, interesting ideas about life and wine, and perhaps a few precious manuscripts of the classics. Their welcome, either in monastery or university, was distinctly cool. The Brethren of the Common Life, whom we have met before as a semimonastic brotherhood dedicated to teaching, in their schools had favored good Latin and were not antagonistic to the humanistic skills. Their motivation was, of course, purely Christian. Their influence on the direction the humanistic Renaissance was to take north of the Alps was powerful. But this movement was in general independent of Italian humanism.

About the middle of the fifteenth century, however, the complexion of the humanistic revival in the north changed noticeably. In 1444 Peter Luder (1414-74) was appointed professor of Latin and expositor of the ancient authors at Heidelberg. He had studied in Rome and Padua and was a good Latinist. But he had a sharp and irritating tongue, and was immediately in trouble with his colleagues. As a consequence he had to keep on the move. We find him teaching successively at Ulm, Erfurt, Leipzig, then (1462) back in Padua to study medicine, which he thought would get him in less trouble. He was later in Basel and finally in 1474 in Vienna. He was a character, carefree, convivial, without conventional moral scruples. The theologians found him unwelcome; he formed no school and had few followers. He was, nevertheless, the founder of humanistic studies in Germany. There were a few others of this sort, Italian-trained apostles of the new learning, who wandered from university to university or from free city to free city. Nicholas of Cusa (1401-64), whom we have met (see above, Chapter 7) as a philosophical mystic and bishop of Brixen from 1450, a competent scholar in Latin and Greek and interested in astronomy and mathematics, supported and encouraged German scholars who wished to broaden their knowledge of the ancient philosophers. His thesis was that all true knowledge (*scientia*) was of God and that it therefore behooved the Christian to understand and appropriate that knowledge wherever it might be found.

The greatest name in this earlier period of the German humanist quest was that of Rudolf Agricola. Agricola (1443–85), a native of Groningen in Holland, studied at Erfurt, Louvain, and Cologne. At the age of twenty-three he went to Italy to study law, but at Pavia he found that the law held no interest for him compared with the study of the ancients. He then proceeded to Ferrara to learn Greek at the court of Ercole d'Este, where he stayed for the next seven years. Returning to Germany, he settled at Heidelberg to be near his friend von Dalberg, bishop of Worms. He made some progress in Hebrew before his early death as he returned from a trip to Rome. His principal work was the *De formando studio,* which might be freely translated *On the Educational Process.* It is not easy, from a reading of this very pedestrian and commonplace description of the new learning, to understand the great reputation Agricola enjoyed in pre-Reformation Germany. But he was among the first to transfer the best of the Italian movement to Germany in such a way as not to offend German pietistic sensibilities.

It was thus into an atmosphere that had been partially prepared that there came an active and influential Italian humanist, Aeneas Silvius Piccolomini (1405–64) of Siena. Trained at Siena and Florence under Filelfo, he attracted the attention of Cardinal Capranica, who took him in 1432 to the Council of Basel as his secretary. His eloquence made him a marked man and the Council appointed him its Chief Abbreviator, then sent him on several diplomatic missions. He accepted the conciliar view of the Papacy and wrote fervently, that is acidly, against Pope Eugenius IV. Yet by 1439, or perhaps earlier, he realized the weakness of the conciliar position, and when, in 1442, Emperor Frederick III, who, while technically neutral, leaned to the cause of the Pope, offered him a post in the imperial chancery at Vienna, he accepted with alacrity. His life until this time had been full and interesting. He had written much, some of it on a level with Beccadelli's *Hermaphroditus,* and had had an unspecified number of natural children in the various capitals of Europe that he had visited on missions for the Council. A change supervened when he was about forty years of age. Declaring that Venus had deserted him, he took priestly orders (1446) at Vienna. He wrote to a friend: "Ah John, I have done evil enough and indeed too much. But I have come to myself. Oh I pray it may not be too late." At Vienna he rose to be the Emperor's chief diplomat. He was primarily responsible for restoring good relations between the German Emperor and the Papacy after years of tension during the Council of Basel, and received the bishopric of Trieste as a reward (1447). Of greater importance was the influence he had upon letters and learning in Germany through his connections at the court of the Emperor. He encouraged young princes in attendance at court to try to write better Latin, and he exchanged letters with scholars and students, both in Italy and in Germany. In Vienna he met with small groups of friends eager to spend their evenings in good companionship and discussion. While in the Emperor's employ he wrote some verse, but more pamphlets on the conciliar theory and on the rise of the Roman Empire. He collected material which he later worked into a history of Bohemia, the story of the reign of Frederick III, and a long essay on Germany as he knew it, which is the best description of fifteenth-century Germany that we have. His historical writing was brilliant, cynical regarding human nature, contemptuous of the "barbarian" (i.e., the non-Italian), and reflected his desire to achieve fame as a stylist. He sometimes allowed himself to praise where he found courage and sincerity. His account of the Hussite wars in his *Historia Bohemica* was tinged with admiration, and this work of Piccolomini, later Pope Pius II, was eventually put on the *Index*.

About 1450 an event of great significance for all educational and cultural development in the Western world occurred in Mainz. A certain John Gutenberg perfected a process of printing by movable type. This meant that where it had taken one trained scribe a month or two to copy out a single book, now a thousand or more could be made at one time and sold at a price which, compared with that of a handwritten book, was incredibly cheap. The first great book printed by this process was a large copy of the Latin Bible, probably about 1454. The type was cut to imitate as closely as possible the liturgical Gothic script then in wide use. The new art took some time to spread, but within twenty years there were books being printed in Italy, France, Switzerland, and in at least a dozen towns in Germany. In Germany the Gothic type retained its hold; elsewhere the so-called roman type, clearer and neater in appearance, was generally adopted. By the end of the century over 36,000 separate book titles had been printed, often in editions of 2000 to 3000. In Venice alone in the 1490's there were 150 printing establishments. The first books printed were predominantly of religious content, but editions of serious historical and literary works of ancient Latin and Greek authors began to appear quickly. This art worked a revolution in the spread of the new learning, and brought the literature of the ancient world within the reach of the ordinary man.

Humanism under Civic Patronage

AMONG the princes of the Empire before the end of the century one stands out as a sponsor of the new learning and the arts of the Renaissance. Eberhard of Württemberg (1445–96) was sufficiently known for his favorable attitude toward the new learning to have had a work by Marsilio Ficino dedicated to him in fulsome phrases. He was not a scholar; his education had not included Latin. He did, however, have works of the ancients translated for him into German, and he valued the wisdom he found in Livy, Sallust, Xenophon, Demosthenes, and Josephus. He kept at his court Augustin Tünger, who made a collection of moralizing stories in German, somewhat like the *Facetiae* of Poggio but without the vulgarity, directed against the immorality of the monks and the clerics.

The favorable reception given the study of the ancient literatures in Germany was not limited to the courts of princes in the fifteenth century. We have seen that many of the free imperial cities sought teachers for their grammar schools from the Brethren of the Common Life. By about 1450, there must have been several dozen such schools, conducted by men who had gone through the course of studies at Deventer, 's Hertogenbosch, or Zwolle in the Lowlands. Strassburg, Augsburg, and Nürnberg were leading centers of the new learning in many genuinely German manifestations.

Jacob Wimpheling (1450–1528) was a typical German Christian humanist. He was a secular cleric who delighted in attacking the monastic orders. More at home with the early Christian fathers than with the pagan writers, he once declared: "The study of the heathen writers is not of itself harmful to the Christian faith; what is harmful is the false understanding and use we might make of them." When a Strassburg theologian was attacked by a certain obscure humanist, Jacob Locher, Wimpheling came to his defense. His *Defensio theologiae* was accepted as the program of the German Christian humanists. In other polemics he was extremely nationalist and particularly anti-French. His German verses against France, at best stodgy, when sent to the French scholar Robert Gaguin nevertheless precipitated a war of words. His own *Germania* (1501) was so strongly nationalistic in its description of all the areas that lay on the border between France and Germany as to expose him to well-aimed ridicule from the French side. He claimed that Germany, not France, was the true heir of the Roman Empire, that Alsace and Lorraine had always been German, and supported his contentions with a great body of documentation. His conclusion, as a native Alsatian, is unmistakably clear: "We are Germans, and not Frenchmen, and our land must be called Germany and not France, because Germans live in it." The work was quickly answered by Thomas Murner (1475–1537), a German Franciscan scholar with no pretensions to humanistic learning. Yet Murner had little trouble showing that Wimpheling's "proofs" were flimsy and partial. Murner took his unpopular position so that, as he said: "The Germans may not become ridiculous because of not knowing the simplest facts of our own and French history." In 1505 Wimpheling attempted to justify his earlier position by publishing a concise outline of German history. Like most other German humanists he was interested in the problems of education and wrote several treatises aimed at raising the standards in German schools.

More significant in German intellectual history was Sebastian Brant (1457–1521), who had been a professor at Basel but in 1500 returned to his native city of Strassburg as secretary of the city. He was a reputable humanist who had published an edition of Terence and had learned Greek. But his genius lay in his German poetry and in his ability to reflect the popular temper. His satirical poem, *The Ship of Fools (Das Narrenschiff)*, was published in Basel in 1494. It was immediately popular, and all Germany chuckled and laughed at his barbs at all classes of society. The clergy were the particular butt of his sarcasm, and to a degree Brant may be regarded as a forerunner of the Reformation. Somewhat different was Johann Geiler of Kaisersberg (1445–1510), a close friend of both Wimpheling and Brant. Geiler was the leading preacher of Strassburg from 1478 to his death in 1510. His approach was scholastic and medieval; his reforming fervor was completely orthodox, his sermon technique that of St. Bernard. Yet he was a force in Germany and his sermons (in German) were frequently reprinted and widely used. The coincidence of these three quite different men at Strassburg, none of whom had studied abroad, contemporaries and fast friends, well illustrates the several trends of the time: the dominantly religious and patriotic aspects of German humanism, the urge for education, and the conservative pietism which emanated from the German pulpit.

In Augsburg the atmosphere was somewhat different. This ancient city had long-standing commercial relations with Venice and Florence, and the lines of cultural dissemination could be expected to flow easily between this center and Italy. The great name in humanistic learning at Augsburg is Conrad Peutinger (1465–1547), who returned from Italy with a doctor's degree in law in 1485. He was no indigent student, but a merchant of substance, a scholar by inclination and a public official by demand of the city of Augsburg and Emperor Maximilian. The Emperor came almost every year of his reign (1493–1519) to Augsburg for stays of several weeks. He frequently asked Peutinger to undertake diplomatic missions for him to distant courts and to write his speeches or speak for him. Peutinger was also the Emperor's adviser in cultural affairs; with the Emperor's help he assembled a great collection of old coins, antiquarian documents, maps, and manuscripts from Roman and ancient German times, which he hoped to expand until it represented graphically the whole history of medieval Germany. His was a fundamentally religious nature, and he sympathized with Luther's early pronouncements, welcoming him as a guest in his home in 1518. A few years later (1521) he urged Luther to retrace his steps and not to leave the Church. There was a humanist circle in Augsburg of which Peutinger was the center, but this circle of scholars, most of whom knew Greek, never produced any ranking humanist. In the storms of the Lutheran revolt the group lost its unity: some went with Luther, some fought the Reformation. After 1517 in Germany there could be no peaceful or ivory-tower pursuit of the learning of the ancients. No one could stay aloof from the battle Luther had begun.

Nürnberg, like Augsburg, received the first impulses of the Renaissance from Italy. Hartmann Schedel (1440–1514) had studied in Leipzig under Peter Luder and, probably at Luder's suggestion, had gone to Italy to study medicine, returning to Nürnberg in 1480. He brought back with him copious notes and extracts which he had copied out in his own hand from Roman and Italian historians. He continued to collect manuscripts and printed books, from which he was able to produce the massive and justly famous Nürnberg *World Chronicle,* which appeared in both German and Latin in 1493 with two thousand woodcut portraits (only eight hundred different ones), maps and plans of cities. An immediate sensation, it served as a model of world history for some centuries. Schedel was not alone in his interest in science and scholarship. Regiomontanus (Johann Müller of Königsberg, 1436–76), the most famous German mathematician and astronomer of the century, had come to Nürnberg from the court of King Mathias of Hungary. He had spent years in Italy, knew Bessarion and other humanists, and had produced editions of Seneca's tragedies as well as some translations from the Greek. He sensed that not only the "more humane" letters but also the natural sciences were about to be revived and reviewed as a part of the whole renewal of man's mind, and he valued particularly the hitherto unutilized contributions of the Greek and Hellenistic scientists.

One of the greatest of all German humanists was a native Nürnberger, Willibald Pirckheimer (1470–1530). His father, a man of means and culture, had encouraged the son to interest himself in the new studies, and when he took the lad on business trips taught him from Cicero, Seneca, Terence, and Virgil. Willibald was then sent to Italy to study music, the classics, and some jurisprudence at Padua and Pavia for seven years (1488–96). On returning to Nürnberg he became councilor of the city and was called upon to advise the

Emperors Maximilian I and Charles V. In view of the press of his official duties, his scholarly activity was impressive. He did numerous translations from Greek into a very competent Latin, not only of works of Xenophon, Euclid, Ptolemy, and Plutarch, but of the Greek Christian fathers. He put his large library at the disposal of those who could profitably use his treasures. He followed Luther for some years, but before his death in 1530 he came to feel that the reformer had gone too far, and he remained within the Church. Pirckheimer and Peutinger had much in common. Both were employed as diplomats, were interested in history, were devout Christians and patriotic Germans. Both were active supporters of the humanist movement and offered the riches of their library collections to colleagues and friends. Pirckheimer, however, was much the more competent and productive scholar, whose writings on many subjects were read with great interest by Germans of every class.

It is not possible to leave Augsburg and Nürnberg without mentioning two notable Renaissance artists: Hans Holbein the Younger (1497–1543) and Albrecht Dürer (1471–1528). Holbein, although he spent most of his life away from home, was the artistic glory of Augsburg. Dürer, born in Nürnberg, spent most of his life in his native city. Neither was, properly speaking, a humanist; yet both understood the purposes and meaning of the movement. Holbein's portrait of Erasmus, like Dürer's woodcuts to illustrate editions of the classics, reveals the artist's understanding of the new and liberating spirit motivating the men who constituted the new course.

The universities, where scholasticism was still dominant, became less antagonistic to the new concept of scholarship about the turn of the century, although the change did not come without many academic battles. There were new universities founded: Greifswald in 1456, Freiburg and Basel in 1460, Ingolstadt in 1472, Mainz and Tübingen in 1476, Wittenberg in 1502, and Frankfurt-on-the-Oder in 1506. At the newer foundations the conservative tradition had a less strangling hold on the curriculum. There was, therefore, some future for the humanist, and in the course of the first half of the sixteenth century we find able Greek and Latin scholars occupying appropriate chairs at these as well as at the older universities and a growing support of and pride in their achievements among the people.

The Reuchlin-Pfefferkorn Controversy

OF ALL the battles fought over the new learning and its spirit around the beginning of the sixteenth century, and there were many, none is more dramatic or more ridiculous than the Reuchlin-Pfefferkorn controversy. John Reuchlin (1455–1522) had studied Greek at Paris and Basel and jurisprudence at Orléans. He went to Italy with Duke Eberhard of Württemburg, and later (1484) became a magistrate at Tübingen and in 1502 at Stuttgart. In his spare time he studied Hebrew, both privately and with rabbis. The *Cabbala* challenged his interest and in 1494 he published a study *On the Wonder-Working Word* (*De verbo mirifico*) in which he contended that God and Man met through the miraculous letters of the Hebrew word JHVH (Jahweh, Jehovah) for God. The mystical tendencies in this and other similar works of Reuchlin may be traced to Pico della Mirandola, for whom Reuchlin had a great admiration. In

1506 he published a Hebrew grammar and later several other books on the Hebrew language and Hebrew thought. The modern world owes its system of instruction in Hebrew to Reuchlin. Between 1505 and 1507 several German churchmen attacked his position exalting Jewish thought. A Dominican of Cologne, Hoogstraten, who was soon (1508) to be the inquisitor for the Rhine area, led this early attack, but the real battle was yet to come. In 1509 the path of Reuchlin, the greatest living Gentile scholar of Hebrew, crossed that of Johann Pfefferkorn (1469–1522), a converted Jew who had taken it upon himself to destroy the vestiges of his former religion. He had obtained a mandate from the Emperor (August 1509) ordering all Christians to help him in his cleansing work and commanding all Jews to bring their anti-Christian books to Pfefferkorn. The books were then to be examined by Reuchlin, the inquisitor Hoogstraten, and the four universities of Mainz, Cologne, Erfurt, and Heidelberg. The decision was that the Jews could retain the Bible but not the Talmud, a valued compilation of Jewish spiritual writings. The Emperor neglected to act on the decision so that, for the moment, the Hebrew books thus collected were untouched. In the course of the discussions Reuchlin and Pfefferkorn locked horns, the latter holding that all Hebrew books were vicious and should be destroyed, the former contending that there was both cultural and religious value in much Hebrew literature. Insults were exchanged and clerics and humanists lined up on one side or the other. All Germany relished the feud. At first Reuchlin was conciliatory and wrote (October 28, 1511) the theological faculty at Cologne that he would gladly retract whatever was erroneous in his theology, but a few months later he took an almost defiant line. Reuchlin's *Augenspiegel,* a German pamphlet attacking Pfefferkorn in strong terms, was condemned by the Emperor on October 7, 1512. In answer to the condemnation the humanist published in the spring of 1513 a violent *Defense against All Calumniators.* His opponents, he said, were "stupid sheep, foxes, bucks, sows, pigs, children of the devil." In July of that year the theological faculties of Louvain, Cologne, Mainz, Erfurt, and Paris joined in the condemnation of the *Augenspiegel.* Reuchlin appealed to Pope Leo X, and the young bishop of Speier to whom the Pope referred the matter decided (April 1514) that the book was harmless and that the inquisitor should be fined and kept silent. In June both Reuchlin and Hoogstraten were summoned to Rome. Neither went. Instead, a commission of twenty-four was appointed, which was disposed in Reuchlin's favor. The case dragged on for several years; a decision was about to be announced when the Pope intervened (June 1520) and condemned the book. Obscurantism had won a very hollow victory. The controversy had, at its end, been of much less interest than the outbreak of the revolt of Luther, already three years old, and the issues between Reuchlin and Pfefferkorn were already outdated by new conflicts. The most important, or at least the most enduring, result of the controversy was a by-product, the *Letters of Obscure Men,* a devastating satire on the opponents of Reuchlin, written (1515, 1517), at least in large part, by Ulrich von Hutten and Crotus Rubeanus, two of the younger German humanists who had rallied to the defense of Reuchlin.

The humanistic movement in Germany was, as we have seen, quite different from its progenitor in Italy or indeed in any other country of Europe. It lasted barely a half-century, and was, during its short existence, predominantly Christian, valuing the pagan classics for what they could contribute to Christian knowledge. Whereas in Italy the Greek and Latin classics were esteemed and studied for themselves, in Germany they were merely aids to the study of Christian documents. There is a world of difference between the two views.

Humanism in Hungary

OF THE lands bordering on the Empire, only Hungary, under the stimulus of her Renaissance King Mathias Corvinus, had a humanist movement at all comparable to that in Germany. We saw (pp. 210–11) how Mathias supported learning, collected an impressive library, and had at his court two distinguished Hungarian humanists, John Vitéz and his nephew Janus Pannonius. Hungarian humanism, unlike that in most of Germany, was directly derived from Italy. There were, at various times, several score Italian scholars at the royal court at Buda, and between 1480 and 1490 the influence of Medicean Florence was so pronounced that there was almost a replica of the Platonic Academy on the banks of the Danube. Mathias' successor, Wladislas II, continued his favor to the court scholars, but the defeat of the Christian forces at Mohács in 1526 by the Turks and the partition and occupation of the kingdom spelled the end of an intellectual movement, until then largely imported from Italy. A few more decades would have been necessary for its roots to go deep into the native soil.

Bohemia

BOHEMIA was effectively cut off from the humanistic Renaissance by its Hussite isolation until the latter half of the fifteenth century. During his service at the court of Frederick III at Vienna, Aeneas Silvius Piccolomini visited Bohemia several times and established personal relations with a number of Czech scholars, several of whom had already visited Italy. Aeneas' influence, through correspondence, was substantial. It is, however, remarkable that the Czech humanists with whom Aeneas corresponded so regularly did not share the pagan amoralism which characterized his earlier years. Early Czech humanism had a religious base, similar to much of the German humanism we have observed. The greatest Czech humanist of the next generation was a highly placed noble, Bohuslav Hasištein of Lobkovice (1460–1510). On his return from seven years' study in Italy (1475–82) he gathered around him a group of friends devoted to the study of ancient letters. He was well connected at court and was made provost of the Vyšehrad in 1483 by King Vladislav, only to leave for a long trip to the Orient to view the scenes of the ancient empires with his own eyes. His personal fortune was ample, and his library was exceptionally rich in the classics, both in manuscripts and in the printed books just then coming off the presses in Italy and Germany in great numbers. His passion for things classical led him to give up his place at court and attempt to imitate the rustic life of a Horace or a Virgil at his family estate of Hasištein. This artificiality was of a piece with his depreciation and rejection of the vigorous native Czech

language in favor of a resuscitated Latin. Many among his friends and followers maintained contacts with Italian humanists and, hardly less, with scholars
at the cities and courts in Germany. Erasmus was in touch with several of
Lobkovice's younger colleagues. The total of Czech interest in the classics from
the middle of the fifteenth to the end of the sixteenth century was considerable.
Some of the later Czech humanists enriched their native literature by translations into Czech of some of the more prominent classical writers; several of
the works of Petrarch and Erasmus' *Praise of Folly* were rendered into Czech.
The first book printed in Bohemia (Pilsen, 1468) was a Czech translation of
the *History of Troy.*

Poland

POLAND, dynastically united with Lithuania, was the largest kingdom in Europe in the fifteenth century. Although not well known in the West, it was not
immune to ideas and movements in the rest of the Continent. The Polish delegation at the Councils of Constance and Basel had met the humanists from
Italy and had entered into friendly relations with them. Almost one hundred
Polish students have already been traced who studied and took degrees at
Italian universities during this century. Virtually all of them returned to Poland to take their places in the ecclesiastical hierarchy or at the royal court as
secretaries and diplomats. Nevertheless, the most significant personality in
early Polish humanism was an Italian, Philip Buonacorsi (1438–96), known as
Callimachus. He had grown up within the circle of humanists at the papal
curia under Nicholas V and Pius II, then, having incurred the displeasure of
Pius' successor Paul II (1464–71), he set out on his travels, earning his living
as best he could. A business commission took him to Cracow, and once there
he accepted the position of tutor to King Casimir's children (1470). The king
came to rely upon this widely traveled and deeply cultured Italian. He composed, for the king's guidance, a book of *Secret Counsels,* which could almost
be substituted for Machiavelli' *Prince.* In one matter he was prophetically right.
He advised Casimir to trim the privileges of the Polish nobility. The nobility,
however, were furious when they heard of his suggestions, and, on the death
of Casimir, Buonacorsi had to flee from Poland until tempers cooled. King
John Albert, who had been his pupil, recalled him and made him his *magister
epistolarum,* or personal secretary. He was in fact the king's principal minister.
This energetic and versatile foreigner brought to the crude Polish court a cosmopolitan polish it had never before possessed. He maintained a wide correspondence with his Italian humanist friends, particularly Lorenzo the Magnificent, Poliziano, Marsilio Ficino, and Pico della Mirandola. He could have returned to Italy and been warmly welcomed; instead he stayed on in Poland until his death in 1496, encouraging younger scholars in their studies, guiding
Poland's defense against the Turks, and writing some historical works which
describe the reigns of which he had personal knowledge. His is a good case of
the humanist as statesman, and as such he was impressively foresighted, honest,
and intelligent. The next century, the sixteenth, is properly the century of
humanism in Poland, but its brilliance would have been impossible without the

preparatory work of the Polish scholars who wandered to Italy and of Calli-machus, an Italian who reversed the current and wandered to Poland, and his direct disciples.

France

CLASSICAL humanism as we found it in fifteenth-century Italy and, later in the century, in Germany, Bohemia, and Hungary, does not appear in France until after the French invasion of Italy in 1494. In spite of some sporadic Greek instruction at Paris and a few isolated scholars with humanist interests, one looks in vain for humanist circles or groups, usually the first step in the development of a full-fledged humanism. Another generally reliable index of interest in the Latin and Greek classics, the number of books containing the works of classical authors published by the new printing process, would indicate that there was as yet no real demand for the Roman or Greek authors in the original languages. Of the 17 known editions of Cicero's orations published before 1501, 14 were printed in Italy, 2 in Germany, and only 1 in France. Of the 20 editions of Livy's *Roman History,* 18 were printed in Italy, 1 in Spain, and 1 in France. The Spanish edition was a translation into Spanish and the French edition was in French. Of the comedies of Terence there were 42 editions, of which 26 were printed in Italy, 8 in Germany (2 in German translation), 5 in France (4 in Latin at Lyons and 1 in French at Paris), 1 in Spain, 1 in Holland (in Dutch and Latin), 1 in England (in English and Latin). These examples, taken together, probably constitute a fair sampling of the relative intensity of interest in the new learning in France and Italy in the latter half of the fifteenth century. The early promise of humanist interest evinced by the spate of editions of classical authors printed at Paris in the first years of the printing press, 1470–72, was not fulfilled. There are several possible explanations for France's apparent backwardness. The long involvement in the war with England, followed by the struggle with Burgundy, though undoubtedly a distracting factor, should, however, not be given too much weight. Large parts of France were left completely untouched by the ravages of war, particularly in the south and the west, precisely where we might have expected contact with Italy to foster favorable cultural interchange. It seems more likely that the "backwardness" of France in taking up the new learning was a matter of choice or, perhaps more accurately, satisfaction with what she already had. The curriculum at the University of Paris had not changed in character in three centuries. Why should it? Every Frenchman knew that France had been the center of the world's culture since time immemorial, that everybody who wanted to be anybody or know anything came to Paris to study, and that the art and architecture of France, her drama, her poetry, and her music were imitated all over the world. Why should Frenchmen look elsewhere for guidance? The descent of thousands of French soldiers into Italy under Charles VIII in the campaign of 1494–95, of Louis XII in 1499–1500, and of Francis I in 1515–16 shook French confidence in the primacy of their land in cultural matters. Once the French had seen and experienced the comfort and urbanity of Italian life, the new freedoms in thought and society, French leaders were led to emulate Italian advances. As a consequence the spirit of literary and philosophical inquiry soon spread among the educated classes. Italian professors of Greek and Latin rhetoric and, in a few cases, of Hebrew, were appointed to French universities. A new generation of French scholars was on the way, of so energetic and confident a stamp as to challenge effectively in the sixteenth century the primacy of Italy in classical studies.

The humanistic movement in Europe, as we have traced it, reached its point of highest integration and fruitfulness in the half-century from about 1475 to about 1520. Quite obviously it had advanced more rapidly and productively in some countries than in others, for reasons not difficult to grasp. Indeed the movement, for all its similarities and common basic documents, the classics of Greece and Rome, took on quite distinct and separate characteristics in each of the lands in which we find it. In Italy the movement was native in origin and international, or, rather, supranational in outlook. Anyone who could master the ancient tongues and literatures, write good Greek or Latin verse and prose, was admissible to the society of the elect. In Germany, on the other hand, the humanist movement was, for the most part, highly national, even patriotic. In the peripheral lands, Hungary and Poland, humanism was imported; whereas

Quintilian, *Institutiones Oratoriae,* first page of the first edition, Rome, 1470, in the Pierpont Morgan Library, New York [PIERPONT MORGAN LIBRARY].

339

in Bohemia, under constant German pressure, and at the same time with a longer history and tradition behind it than in Germany, it had a peculiar international character, and we find the Czech humanists reaching out beyond Germany to Italy, Switzerland, and France for contacts and moral support. In Italy, the site of the Papacy, the humanists succeeded in keeping their thought and writing free of the embarrassment of religion, though in their personal situations they were either employees of the Church or may have been dependent upon papal largess for their livelihood. In Germany the humanists were, in a majority, religious, but independent of the ecclesiastical establishment. In Hungary it was royal initiative that gave life to the movement, and the king did not hesitate to use the Church to pay the cost of his initiative. In Poland the movement was involved with the royal court and not closely tied to the Church; it also had reforming undertones which go far to explain the otherwise amazing spread of the Lutheran reform in Poland in the sixteenth century. In England, the key leaders of the movement were largely in Church positions and not radically reforming. In the early years of the movement in England it was not native, but was a product imported whole from Italy by a few adventurous patrons.

The movement does not cease to exist in 1520, the term we have set to the period of its flowering, but continues through the sixteenth and into the seventeenth century. Yet in some places it was stultified and lifeless, weighed down by its own limitations. In other lands, as we shall see, the movement was swamped or absorbed by the Protestant Reformation. In spite of its decline, however, we must expect other movements, such as the Protestant Reformation and the Catholic Counter-Reformation, to accept humanism and utilize to the full the gains it had made over the narrower outlook and cultural resources of the medieval world.

SUGGESTIONS FOR FURTHER READING

See bibliography to Chapter 4.

DA BISTICCI, VESPASIANO, *Memoirs. Lives of Illustrious Men*. London, 1926

BRACCIOLINI, POGGIO, *The Facetiae,* trans. E. Storer. New York, 1928

BRANT, SEBASTIAN, *Ship of Fools,* trans. E. H. Zeydel. New York, 1944

HUTTEN, ULRICH VON, *Letters of Obscure Men,* trans. F. G. Stokes. London, 1925

PICCOLOMINI, AENEAS SYLVIUS, *The Commentaries,* trans. F. A. Gragg. Northampton, Mass., 1937

Ross, J. B., and M. McLAUGHLIN, *Renaissance Reader*. New York, 1953

VALLA, LORENZO, *On the Donation of Constantine,* trans. C. B. Coleman. New Haven, 1922

WHITCOMB, M., *A Literary Source-Book of the Italian and German Renaissances*. Philadelphia, 1900

ADY, C. M., *Pius II (Aeneas Sylvius Piccolomini)*. London, 1913

BOULTING, W., *Aeneas Sylvius: Orator, Man of Letters, Statesman, and Pope*. London, 1908

Cambridge Medieval History, Vol. VIII

EINSTEIN, L., *The Italian Renaissance in England*. New York, 1902

FLETCHER, J. B., *Literature of the Italian Renaissance*. New York, 1934

JERROLD, M. F., *Italy in the Renaissance*. London, 1927
MITCHELL, R. J., *John Tiptoft, 1427–1470*. London, 1938
SCHEVILL, F., *History of Florence*. New York, 1936
SCHEVILL, F., *The Medici*. New York, 1949
SHEPHERD, W., *Life of Poggio Bracciolini*. New York, 1837
TILLEY, A., *Dawn of the French Renaissance*. Cambridge, 1918
VICKERS, K. H., *Humphrey Duke of Gloucester*. London, 1907
WEISS, R., *Humanism in England During the Fifteenth Century*. Oxford, 1941

ANAGNINE, E. G., *Pico della Mirandola*. 1937
AUBENAS, R., and R. RICARD, *L'Église et la Renaissance (1447–1517)*. 1951
BATTAGLIA, F., *Enea Silvio Piccolomini e Francesco Patrizi*. 1936
BRANDI, K., *Die Renaissance in Florenz und Rom*. 1909
COVILLE, A., *Gontier et Pierre Col et l'humanisme en France au temps de Charles VI*. 1934
FIRMIN-DIDOT, A., *Alde Manuce et l'hellénisme à Venise*. 1875
GARIN, E., *Filosofi italiani del Quattrocento*. 1942
KNEPPER, J., *Jakob Wimfeling (1450–1528)*. 1902
RUEGG, W., *Cicero und der Humanismus*. 1946
SAITTA, G., *Marsilio Ficino e la filosofia dell' umanesimo*. 1954
TOFFANIN, G., *Il Cinquecento*. 1935
DELLA TORRE, A., *Storia dell' Accademia platonica de Firenze*. 1902
VAST, H., *Le Cardinal Bessarion*. 1878
WALSER, E., *Poggius Florentinus, Leben und Werke*. 1914

CHAPTER THIRTEEN

SCIENCE AND TECHNICS;
EXPLORATION AND DISCOVERY

UNTIL recently it has been conventional to speak of the "scientific revolution of the sixteenth and seventeenth centuries" as the beginning of the modern world view. The uncanny inventiveness of Leonardo da Vinci (d. 1519), the meticulous anatomical analysis of Vesalius (d. 1564), and the imaginative cosmological thinking of Copernicus (d. 1543) were thus regarded as "revolutionary" and sharply divergent from the thought that preceded them. But the present generation of historical scholarship, closer to the sources than the last, has revised this long-accepted assumption. Deeper reading in the writings of these "revolutionaries" with a view to ascertaining the sources of their thought, and a more careful analysis of the trends among scholars and thinkers of the later Middle Ages have shown us that many of the tenets of the scientific "revolutionaries" of the sixteenth to the eighteenth century were either clearly and explicitly based upon the speculative suggestions and specific findings and figures of their medieval forerunners or were incomprehensible unless seen as extensions or supplements to earlier scientific investigation.

The Latin Christian Heritage

THE stock of scientific (*scientia* was a general term for knowledge of any sort) knowledge possessed by medieval man had come to him largely by inheritance, and that from two sides, of which the earlier was his Latin Christian legacy. For centuries there had been no possibility for him to enlarge upon it. Rather it may have shrunk a little. Many of the writings of the Latin scientific thinkers had either dropped from sight and use or were known to very few of the clergy, whose interests were primarily in the salvation of men's souls and only secondarily in physical or cosmological thought. Their number, their time, and their energies were limited, and the means at hand for spreading what knowledge of the world about them they had were tragically primitive. St. Isidore, bishop of Seville (d. 636), made a great collection (the *Etymologies*) of details of geographical and natural science that was accepted in his day as authoritative. We would call most of it pseudoscience or old wives' tales—although he did know the earth was round. The Venerable Bede of England (d. 735) had a mathematical turn of mind, but for him mathematics was useful only insofar as it facilitated the intricate computations of the church calendar. His curiosity, however, ranged still wider, and, knowing Pliny better than Isidore had before him, he recorded his careful observations of the tides and connected them with the phases of the moon. Alcuin of York (d. 804) and a German churchman, Rabanus Maurus (d. 856), hardly did more than recast the knowledge transmitted by Isidore and Bede. These four, known as the encyclopedists, were the predominant scientific authorities of Europe until the late eleventh century.

The Greco-Arab Tradition

LIKE many other aspects of European life and thought, the course of scientific development was profoundly influenced by the Crusades. Contact with a highly advanced Islam was bound to have great effect. The twelfth century—the century of the Crusades—saw a sudden and amazing growth in the number and variety of Arabian scientific works made available to the West in Latin translation. In the fields of astronomy, geology, optics, medicine, and mathematics, the names of Arab scientists of the previous four centuries, till then completely unknown in the lands of Latin Christendom, became almost household words among the educated classes. At the same time some ancient Greek medical works and the philosophical and scientific works of Aristotle began gradually to appear in Latin form, either through Arab and Jewish mediation or directly from the Greek. The body of scientific knowledge which thus came to the West was Greek and Hellenistic. The Arabs were primarily transmitters, but in the transmission, by translation from the Greek and contact with the West, whether in Greece, Sicily, Italy, or Spain, they not infrequently added their own thought and experience in original works or in extensive commentaries on their Greek models. This Semitic or Islamic element is the second side of the scientific inheritance of the later Middle Ages.

It is necessary to keep this dualism of scientific thought and tradition in mind as we proceed, for the juxtaposition of the two traditions, Christian-Western and Greco-Arab, inevitably set up a cultural ferment from which was to result the scientific revolution of the sixteenth and seventeenth centuries. That later revolution was marked not so much by specific bits of revolutionary information, or even by the development of specific experimental techniques, as it was by a new attitude of mind, a broader world view, a philosophy of questioning curiosity. This attitude and philosophy were a gradual growth over the four centuries from the beginning of the Crusades to the age of Leonardo da Vinci, Galileo, and Vesalius. It is easy for the man of the twentieth century to smile with a consciousness of his own superior knowledge at the works of natural "scientists" of these early centuries. They have left us treatises called bestiaries, or *physiologi,* which were hardly more than catchalls of many sorts of current lore, containing descriptions of the unicorn and his habits, authoritative discourses on the sirens, centaurs, and frightening sea monsters. There were also *herbaria,* encyclopedias of botanical knowledge, with, to us, weird classifications of plants, and medical receipt books whose recommendations would, if exactly followed, have quickly decimated the population of Europe. But somehow they survived their science. The spirit of inquiry was the hopeful aspect of this interest, and the interest itself was one of the signs of the new age. It can hardly be emphasized too strongly that the second half of the curriculum of the schools, the quadrivium, was exclusively scientific: arithmetic, geometry, astronomy, and music. In the Middle Ages theology may have been the Queen of the Sciences, but the handmaidens of the Queen, the sciences, were quite untheological, and with the passage of time came to occupy a major portion of the interest and attention of the court of knowledge.

The two strains in the European scientific tradition, the Christian-Western and the Greco-Arab, disagreed on many points. The principal battlefield upon which the struggle between them was fought was the university. The universities were the centers for the exchange of ideas, and it was to these centers that newly discovered texts were brought to be tested by the methods of logical analysis then in style. Aristotle, the "master of those who know," as Dante called him, and known to the schoolmen as "The Philosopher," dominated the curriculum in the universities of Europe, save perhaps at Bologna, which had a special interest in canon and civil law. Aristotle was as much a natural scientist as he was a logician and metaphysician. His works on animals, on physics, on the meteors, and on astronomy were available to the West in Latin translations from about 1200, and every scholastic philosopher was familiar with their ideas. As the Arabs had accepted most of Aristotle's basic positions, their influence upon the West was confirmatory of his thought; it was thus perfectly natural that his views on the universe and its details should have formed the structure of all medieval scientific thought.

At the universities of Oxford and Paris the ideas of Aristotle and the Arabs were examined, discussed, reworked, and, where necessary, corrected or revised to accord with Christian doctrine. One of the great ecclesiastics of the thirteenth century, Robert Grosseteste (d. 1253), was the first chancellor of Oxford and later (1235–53) bishop of Lincoln, the largest bishopric in England. He illustrates admirably the spreading of the intellectual interest of his time into the field of natural science. He learned Greek and translated some works of Aristotle into Latin and wrote comments on others. He was familiar with the latest Arab scientific work, using Arabic numeration as early as 1215. He was a firm advocate of experiment as a method. Primarily a theologian and a philosopher, he nevertheless interested himself in the whole area of natural science. He wrote on astronomy and cosmology, optics, light and the rainbow, the calendar, comets and meteorology, and weather and the tides, urging the more methodical and inductive employment of observation and greater use of mathematics in all scientific work. He was the actual founder of an experimental-mathematical tradition which was to dominate English thought for almost two centuries after his death. Roger Bacon (d. 1294), a Franciscan friar until recently better known than Grosseteste, looked to the great bishop of Lincoln as his master. Going somewhat further along the lines of mathematical inductive thought than Grosseteste, he described the nerve system of the human eye, and in his researches into the nature and properties of light he made magnifying glasses, using plano-convex lenses, without understanding clearly their function. It was partly his investigations into the nature of things but fully as much his sharp criticism of everybody else that got him into trouble with his own order to such an extent that he spent fourteen years in confinement. In spite of this temper of repression, however, the current of speculation on natural questions had set in, not to be reversed.

Albert the Great (1193–1280), the leading commentator on Aristotle of the century, was particularly interested in the Philosopher's scientific works, and his comments on the works *On the Animals, On Plants, The Physics,* and *The Heavens and the Earth* display an articulate appreciation of scientific methodology and its philosophical basis. "We cannot," he said, "understand particular organisms by syllogisms. Experimentation alone can give us certain results." In his descriptive studies of plants and animals Albert was especially concerned to work out an adequate system of classification, the key to any advance in the science; though largely guided by Aristotle, he introduced some corrections and many refinements into the data left by the Philosopher.

By the end of the thirteenth century we may notice a great broadening of the field of scientific inquiry. The practice of frequent and public discussion and theorizing in all areas of knowledge at all the universities of Europe resulted in many heated disputes; and these in turn stimulated thought and experimentation. Witelo, a Polish scholar, about 1280 wrote an elaborate treatise, *De perspectiva,* on a basis of detailed experiments which he described with great precision. In the area of botany and zoology, where Albert the Great had labored so methodically, there were others to follow. Matthew Sylvatico compiled (*ca.* 1320) a dictionary of plants he had seen in his travels, collected, and cultivated in his own garden in Salerno. The studies of Roman naturalists were reread and brought up to date, and about the middle of the century Conrad of Magdeburg, a German naturalist, wrote a *Book of Nature* (*Das Buoch der Natur*) which, partly borrowed, partly original, was the first scientific treatise written in German, and retained its popularity until well into the sixteenth century.

Anatomy

HUMAN anatomy was approached from the points of view of Galen and Aristotle, who did not always agree. To Galen the brain was the center of the nervous system, while Aristotle thought the heart was. The blood, Galen held, was made in the liver, then got into the veins where it pulsed or moved backwards and forwards, whence most of it reached the right side of the heart. Some of the blood seeped through the septum into the left ventricle of the heart where, purified and mixed with "vital spirits," it passed out through the arteries into the parts of the body. The heart, the center of the arterial system, dilated under the expansion of innate heat and gave rise to the "animal spirits" which caused movement. This, and much more, was not just idle speculation. Much dissection and observation had been going on since the end of the thirteenth century, and the structure of the human body, the bones and tissue, and the muscular and veinous systems were accurately described in a number of educational centers. A professor at Bologna, Mondino de Luzzi (d. 1326), wrote an elaborate treatise, *Anatomia,* in 1316 which was to be a standard work for over two centuries. Post mortem examinations to determine causes of death, though forbidden by the Church, were frequent as early as the year 1300. The great number of cadavers provided by the Black Death normalized the practice of dissection and spread the knowledge of human anatomy. Much practice in dissection by many physicians produced improvements in medical science. Nerves, tendons, and ligaments, for instance, were traced and named, and gall-stones were described by various Italian scholars by the mid-fourteenth century. Advances in medical science being impossible without a control of basic anatomy, this early stage of the development was obviously necessary. More than most of the sciences, medicine had been associated with the Church for centuries. From the days of the Emperor Constantine, Christian ethic had favored hospitals; under monasticism ministration to the sick was regarded as obligatory for the Christian. The hospitals managed by the monastic orders were remarkably clean and well ordered. Much empirical knowledge was gained from this sort of practice, and considerable expertness in the therapy of some diseases, mental as well as physical, was achieved.

Chemistry

THE chemistry of the later Middle Ages was mostly alchemy—the pursuit of the secret of transforming baser metals into gold. The origins of alchemy were probably in Egypt, where practical chemistry blended with philosophical ideas about prime matter as that to which all else could be reduced. In the course of experimentation much practical knowledge of chemical processes was acquired, and many alchemical treatises of the time reveal how persistent and observant these practitioners were. Metals were refined and acids were employed in many combinations, and the results were carefully recorded. The specific gravities of many metals and alloys were accurately measured. Earlier claims of transmutation of metals, such as from lead to gold, however, were gradually dropped by the more serious investigators without there being any real advance in chemical theory. That had to wait until the sixteenth century and Paracelsus. In one important chemical technique, the later Middle Ages made a great advance. The process of distillation was perfected to the point where a volatile substance like alcohol could be condensed. The perfection of this process, by which stills could produce efficiently *aqua vitae* (96 per cent alcohol), must be credited to two theologians, the Catalan mystic Raymond Lull (d. 1315) and the Franciscan John of Rupescissa (d. after 1356).

Cosmology

THE principal scientific interest of the scholastic world was the universe and its motions. The scholastics were quite unafraid to tackle the whole cosmos with a syllogism. The earlier Middle Ages had regarded the whole of the world of nature, the sun, the moon, and the stars, not primarily as of intrinsic interest, but rather as unities by which moral and spiritual truths could be demonstrated. The heritage of Greek astronomical and cosmological ideas did nothing to disturb this view. To the Greeks the relations between the earth and the other heavenly bodies were fixed and stable. Ptolemy (d. *ca.* 170 A.D.), who gathered together and systematized Greek thought and calculations in astronomy, worked out a scheme according to which the center of the universe was not far from the center of the earth. The moon, the sun, and the planets Mercury, Venus, Mars, Jupiter, and Saturn moved in concentric orbits; outside of these the crystalline globe of the heavens and the fixed stars made the panoply of the firmament. Encompassing all was fixed the ninth globe, the prime mover of the universe. Ptolemy must have been aware of many difficulties in his system, since he made adjustments to try to explain the periodic movements of stars, which the system of concentric spheres and orbits by itself could not do. But those who came after him did not, for centuries, improve upon his formulations. It was his system, unaltered and perhaps not even fully understood, that framed the thought of the Middle Ages concerning the riddle of the universe.

It was not very difficult to bring the universes of Ptolemy and Aristotle together, and the eighth book of Aristotle's work on *The Physics* was studied and commented upon with the Ptolemaic system in mind. The question as to what made the planets move in their orbits was hotly debated. It became involved with the question of the tendency of objects to move toward the center of the earth. Motion, in whatever direction, linear or "downward," was an increasing interest of thinkers from the time of the transmission of Greek science to the West on into modern times. St. Thomas Aquinas constructed his most convincing argument for the existence of God upon the principle that for motion, the most obvious and unescapable fact in the universe, to exist, there must be a prime mover, and that must be God.

As the major concepts of this philosophical system developed and were applied to the explanation of details, it was held that the planets and stars were moved in the heavens by angelic beings, each assigned to a particular job of keeping a celestial body in motion. The theory behind this was that the thrust behind a body in motion must be given by direct and continuous physical contact. Thus an arrow sent from a bow is propelled by the air which rushes from in front of the arrow to the rear and there exerts propulsive power.

But while Petrarch was still a young man this theory of continuous propulsion had begun to be challenged by a group of scholars at Oxford, most of them connected with Merton College, and at Paris. They argued that an impetus could be imparted to a body by a mover which would act for a while, then might die away and the body gradually come to rest. This was in accordance with visual observation. In the case of the heavenly bodies, however, God had given them an impetus which was of a permanent nature, and furthermore, in the heavens there was no air resistance. About the precise nature of this impetus there was much discussion, which yielded no consensus beyond the thought that there was something, such as "impetuosity," inside the body which kept it in motion after the physically observable mover was no longer in contact. The acceleration of falling bodies was explained as being due to the increased heaviness (*gravitas* or gravity) gained by the body as it moved downward. To us it frequently sounds as if these thinkers were saying that a body was heavier because it weighed more. But it was not quite so simple. They were hammering out a new approach to and understanding of the universe around them, and the tools they had to work with were still those of the age of dialectic analysis. They were committing themselves to the gospel of observation and explanation, whereas their predecessors had been content to repeat and restate ancient dogmas. There could be no theoretical advances in science without this new attitude toward knowledge and understanding of the data of the natural world.

The theory of impetus was not universally accepted in the fourteenth century. In some form or other William of Ockham (d. 1349), whom we have met as an opponent of papal power and as the leading nominalist philosopher (see above, Chapters 3 and 7), was sympathetic to this rejection of the traditional Aristotelian-Ptolemaic world view. More active protagonists of the new view of motion and consequently precursors of Leonardo da Vinci, Copernicus, Galileo, and Giordano Bruno, were Walter Burley (d. 1346), who taught at Oxford, then at Paris, and defended his views in public disputations at Toulouse and Bologna, and Walter Heytesbury (d. 1371), a leading Oxford mathematician. At Paris John Buridan (d ca. 1367), rector of the university, opposed the Aristotelian contact theory of motion, and suggested the relation of mass and velocity to impetus. Among his successors was Nicholas Oresme (d. 1382), who insisted that the world rotated on its axis daily. This conclusion was reached on philosophical grounds, not by observation. The value of the theory was therefore largely doctrinal and not scientific. The fifteenth century saw a partial eclipse of the theory of impetus. There was no technical equipment, no telescopes or instruments, nor indeed any body of applied mathematics which could corroborate or correct the theory, and though the great Cardinal Nicholas of Cusa (d. 1464) accepted and elaborated upon it, its full implications and its modification, by way of correction, into the modern theory of inertia had to wait another century and a half before techniques and observation could catch up with and correct theory.

Leonardo da Vinci, Scientist and Engineer

THE greatest master of the technics of the late Middle Ages and the Renaissance was at the same time one of the supreme artists of all time: Leonardo da Vinci (1452–1519), of Florence, about whose artistic creativity we shall have much to say in the next chapter. The illegitimate son of a Florentine notary of moderate means, his precocious versatility was early recognized. The professional artist in the Renaissance had to be much more than just an artist. He had to be an engineer, a builder, and master of materials and dynamics as well. The workshop of a busy artist was an admirable place for a curious young man to meet and study the practical problems of nature: the elements, physics in all its branches, organic and inorganic nature, design, geometry and proportion, and their applications to the practical needs of his society. To these studies Leonardo added a deep interest in pure and applied mathematics. Somewhere he came upon a copy of the works of Archimedes; and he knew the *Elements* of Euclid by heart. He was so convinced of the primacy of mathematics in all scientific work that he wrote in his *Notebooks* that "no one should bother to read my Principles who is not a mathematician." In 1483 he moved to Milan, probably invited to the court of Ludovico Sforza for his musical ability. But Leonardo went beyond the purpose of his invitation and offered his services in the design and construction of instruments of war, in building bridges, canals, and locks, and in all sorts of military and naval engineering. He claimed that he was also able to build for peace, and he added, "I can furthermore execute sculpture in marble, bronze or clay, and in painting I can do as well as anybody else, no matter who he may be." He remained in Milan for sixteen years, employed by Sforza on all kinds of artistic and engineering work. His notebooks, copiously illustrated in his own hand, describing in great detail the machines and devices he invented, show the incredible resourcefulness of his mind. From the period of his stay at Milan came the idea for suburban cities with a population of thirty thousand to relieve the crowded conditions of Milan itself, elaborate plans for draining the swampy regions along the Po, the construction of aqueducts to supply the city with needed water, and through highways into and out of the city.

In 1499, as the armies of Louis XII of France approached Milan, Leonardo started on his travels. He spent a while in Venice, where he gave advice on how the city might be defended against the Turks, and went on to Florence. And then almost unaccountably we find Leonardo, peaceful, gentle, and highly moral, in the employ of Cesare Borgia, Machiavelli's ideally cynical and cruel despot-prince, as his "servant, architect and engineer-in-chief." His notebooks for these years (1501–02) show his inventiveness at work on problems of defense, engines of war, wagons, artillery, and mobile fortifications. For the next three years (1503–06) he was in the employ of the Republic of Florence, mostly engaged in sculpture, or consulted on various artistic matters. He had found time, however, to survey and design a canal with locks and sluices which would have taken the water of the Arno from its headwaters to Pisa.

Before the king of France, Louis XII, took over Milan in 1507, Leonardo had been recalled by Louis' lieutenant. He stayed in the French service, as artist and engineer, for the next six years with headquarters in Milan, designing armored wagons for the city of the king, military defenses, hydraulic mechanisms, aqueducts, and machinery for digging canals and lifting heavy weights, gun mountings, and even repeating machine guns. But his interest in, to him, deeper questions of the mysteries of nature never flagged. His notebooks contain a wealth of anatomical drawings, human and animal, based on careful and extended dissections and observation, minute studies of the motion of birds and animals, studies of light and shadow, flying machines in elaborate detail, helicopters, and parachutes. He also conceived of devices that would allow men to walk underwater to make submarine studies possible. The number of practical applications of his studies on the nature of power and its transmission, gears, pendulums, improvements in textile and weaving machinery, and large hole-boring machinery that he drew in his notebooks and accompanied with lucid explanations, runs into the hundreds. Of his inventiveness there seemed to be no end. After an unhappy period of three years, spent mostly at Rome (1513–16), Leonardo accepted an urgent invitation from Francis I of France to accompany the king to Amboise. Recent studies have shown that for much of his free approach to physical principles he was indebted to the venturesome speculative mathematical thinkers of the thirteenth and fourteenth centuries we have mentioned earlier in this chapter, such as Roger Bacon, Buridan, Walter Burley, and Nicholas Oresme. It is equally certain that he could hardly have made the advances in application of his inventive ideas without the considerable progress made by the fifteenth century in mechanics and the perfection of tools of all sorts. But above and beyond his unquestioned indebtednesses to his predecessors, both theoreticians and mechanics, his own universal gifts of curiosity, observation, and accurate artistic reproduction make his place in the history of science unique and secure.

Late Medieval Technical Advances

THE mention of techniques and scientific instruments brings us face to face with one of the great parallelisms of our history: that between the feudal way of life and the derivative or static concept of science. Under feudalism, based upon and satisfied with an agricultural and pastoral regime, there seemed to be no call for technical advance. The old ways were adequate, novelty was disturbing. We have seen in previous chapters how this economic and social stability began to be shaken at the time of the Crusades and the attendant mass movement of peoples of every nation. New places, new faces, and new customs could only stimulate curiosity and emulation in the minds of wandering Westerners. Out of the wide travel, the exchange of ideas, certain technical advances appear in the West which go far to account, over the centuries of transition to our modern world, for the fall of feudalism, the rise of a new world view, and the success of the capitalist economy. At some time in the later Middle Ages certain significant inventions became common property, and with their acceptance and development the way to the scientific revolution of the sixteenth and seventeenth centuries was opened. These inventions—the horse collar, the water mill, the compass, the sternpost rudder, the clock, gunpowder, the lens, paper, and printing by movable type—seem prosaic to us; to their age they were world-shaking.

The advance of agricultural productivity necessarily depended upon the cultivation of the soil. The earlier draught animals were oxen, strong but exceedingly slow, pulling under a yoke resting on their necks. The horse was, until about the year 900 A.D., of little use in heavy farm work. About this time the stiff horse collar made its appearance, and with this appliance the weight of the horse's effort was borne squarely by his shoulders. Ploughing became more rapid, while the plough could go deeper and turn over more soil. The consequent phenomenal increase in the productivity of the land was reflected in the great growth in population that took place in the eleventh and twelfth centuries. The rapid rise of towns as well as the whole crusading movement may in part be traced to this mechanical improvement which increased the amount and quality of available food.

This improvement in basic agricultural technics was accompanied, during the last centuries of the Middle Ages, by an increase in the utilization of water power. Late in the eleventh century in England five thousand water mills were listed in the Domesday Book. They were used for grinding corn and other grains. These were undershot mills, slow and not powerful. It was not until the early fourteenth century that we hear of overshot water mills, by which time the principle of the gear was well known, so that by a combination of gears and an overshot structure great power, as much as forty to sixty horsepower, and speed were generated. They were adapted to cut wood, operate forge hammers, turn grindstones, and run triphammers to crush oak bark for tanning leather. Windmills came into use in the fourteenth century, at first to grind corn, but, because they had to be rotatable to catch the varying winds, they at first remained small. They were most useful in flat areas where there was inadequate waterfall for a water mill, and where the movement of winds was relatively constant and predictable.

The magnetic compass had a long history before it came to be widely used in the West. The qualities of the lodestone, which points toward the Lodestar (the North Star), were known in the early Middle Ages, but it was not until the thirteenth century that the magnetic compass became a usable aid to navigation. As the Mediterranean skies were usually clear, navigation by sun and stars raised no great difficulties; on northern seas, frequently overcast, the compass was a great improvement. In his *Epistola de magnete* (1269) Petrus Peregrinus of Maricourt described the mechanism known to him in some detail. The early compasses were crude affairs, consisting of a magnetized needle in a straw or attached to a small piece of wood floated in a basin of water. Once the compass was established as a reliable navigational aid, enterprising tool-makers in Italy as well as in Flanders made whole assemblies which simplified its directional use. In the early fourteenth century the compass-box and the compass card, setting off the points of the compass, were in common use. By the early fifteenth century some of these same craftsmen knew enough to allow for the deviation of the magnetic north from the true north.

Of almost equal significance for navigation was the adoption, early in the thirteenth century, of the sternpost rudder for sailing vessels. Before this time steering had been by an oar or an oar-shaped rudder hung over one side of the ship near the stern, that is, on the quarter of the vessel. By attaching a rudder to the sternpost much greater control of the ship's action could be achieved, and in practice, the shipbuilders found that ships with the sternpost rudder could be built larger than those with a rudder on the quarter. The helmsman soon came to occupy a favored place in the sterncastle built up over the stern of the ship where the rudder tiller had to be manipulated. To accompany these improvements, great progress was made in the sailor's guide, the map. The first sea maps, based on an accumulation of compass readings, were called *portolani*. These charts, which first came into use somewhat before 1300, showed the direction and distance between known coastal points, so that the sailor knew, e.g., that if he sailed 20 degrees south of east for 120 Catalan leagues from where he was, he would reach a certain port. The resultant coastline as laid out by these fixed points was remarkably near to the true delineation. Commerce and communication throughout all of Europe benefited immeasurably from the consolidation and verification of geographical facts resulting from the use and continual improvement of these charts.

Improvements in the techniques of map making were not limited to the *portolano* charts for mariners. The thirteenth and fourteenth centuries saw many adventurous spirits traveling to far-off China and India. The vision of the habitable world thus expanded greatly. The stories of their travels prompted new maps of the distant world which shrank the old Roman orbit in comparison. Marco Polo, a Venetian merchant, is only the best known of a long series of Westerners who traveled to Cathay and lived to tell the tale. But the map makers were often better than imaginative. There was presented to King Charles V of France in 1375 a scientifically drawn map of the world (*Mappemonde*), the work of a Catalan draughtsman, which represented with amazing accuracy the location of rivers, cities, and coastlines of China and India. Naturally there were errors and confusions that make the modern student smile, but in view of the fragmentary nature of his information the map maker was uncannily near the precise truth. The great Greek geographer Ptolemy was rediscovered early in the fifteenth century, and his *Cosmographia,* translated into Latin, was first published in Vicenza in 1475. Within the next few decades the maps of the whole world take on remarkably realistic outlines. The discovery and settlement of the New World would certainly have been impossible without the improvements in shipbuilding techniques and navigational aids that were developed in the late fourteenth and fifteenth centuries.

Most of the technical advances in navigational aids—the rudder, the compass, the perfecting of the astrolabe, the maps and charts that were so necessary in expanding man's physical horizon—were the work of Italian mechanics and toolmakers. The Italians were responsible for even more. The Egyptians had been able to measure time accurately by their water clock, and the hourglass was in early use in the Mediterranean area, but it was centuries before any substantial improvement was introduced into methods of measuring time. The monks of the Middle Ages had been adept at dividing the day and the night into "hours" according to which they performed their various religious exercises, but it was not until the early fourteenth century that there was developed a mechanical clock, operating on principles familiar to us: a series of geared wheels, impelled by a hanging weight or, later, by a coiled spring, in regular motion controlled by an escapement. Much preliminary trial and experiment must have preceded the first successful attempts, when James de Dondis of Padua, in 1344, designed a mechanical tower clock which, executed by another Paduan, Antonio, worked. John de Dondis, son of James, worked for sixteen years (1348–64) to complete a more complicated mechanism which was purchased by Gian Galeazzo Visconti and placed in the castle of Pavia. Within the next two decades a half-dozen more mechanical clocks were produced, often combined with astronomical plates or background. The first such clock in France was one commissioned by Charles V of Henry de Vick of Württemberg, begun in 1362 and finished in 1370. First installed in the Royal Palace, it was later moved to the Palace of Justice. It was accurate to within two hours in twenty-four. From this time clocks improved in accuracy and elaborate paraphernalia. The pocket watch, powered by a coil spring, did not come into use until the end of the sixteenth century. The usefulness of the clock for the facilitation of public and private life hardly needs emphasis. This advance came in response to a need for general agreement as to the measurement of time by the merchant and the official. Time was money, and the clock provided the means of saving both. It is to be observed that this invention arose as most of the others we have mentioned, precisely in that country which had shown the most business acumen and drive for commercial gain.

The invention which was to have the greatest effect on politics and science in the West was gunpowder. Probably originating in China, the use of nitre (potassium nitrate) as an explosive was known to the Arabs and the Greeks by the ninth century. But it was not until late in the thirteenth or early in the fourteenth century that technics in the Latin world had advanced to the point where cannon had any effectiveness. The use of gunpowder spread rapidly in the fourteenth century; ships, as well as land armies, began to be equipped with crude cannon, and, slightly later, hand guns. When feudal walls lost their impregnability, feudalism lost much of its political and economic usefulness. The man with the gun was the equal and perhaps the superior of the man on horseback. Gunpowder was thus the great leveler. From the scientific point of view gunpowder precipitated new interests in questions of combustion, as it seemed to burn without air, and the trajectory of the projectile in the air caused discussion and speculation which finally led to new theories of motion and dynamics.

Optics had been steadily studied in the West since the early eleventh century. The works of Arab scientists were translated into Latin and experiments with mirrors and lenses performed. Grosseteste, Roger Bacon, and Dietrich of Freiburg (d. 1311) had made the principle of the lens known to the curious. Its first practical use was for reading spectacles. We know of some of these in use in Italy by the middle of the fourteenth century. The spread of literacy was destined to bring with it an increased demand for reading aids, particularly among the old. The telescope, without which many physical astronomical conjectures could never have had any confirmation or correction, stemmed directly from these experiences with simple lenses of magnification.

For writing material the monk of the Middle Ages had used vellum or parchment—that is, carefully prepared sheep or calf skin. This was handsome and almost indestructible. But it was also expensive and usually hard to come by. The twelfth and thirteenth centuries were the era of the university, and great masses of students were writing whole books. Their number increased in the fourteenth century and even more in the fifteenth. The consequent increased demand for a cheaper writing material was natural and pressing. There was at hand something to satisfy, at least partially, this demand: paper, made of linen rags. Like many of the inventions we have just discussed, paper came from the East. It had been used in China centuries before, and by the Arabs probably during the tenth century. First used very sparingly in Italy late in the thirteenth century, paper spread steadily northward until we find it in fairly common use in England late in the fifteenth century. As England was a sheep-producing country, vellum was not difficult to obtain, and paper was late in displacing it for writing purposes. The Lowlands and Venice were the centers which produced most of the paper, which was then exported to all points of Europe. When printing by movable type was invented about 1450, paper was already produced so cheaply and in such quantity that thousands of books were put in the hands of students and scholars who would otherwise have been unable to purchase the expensive handwritten texts necessary for their studies. The increasingly literate bourgeoisie now found it easy to procure and enjoy printed copies of their favorite authors, both in Latin and in the vernacular. Printing itself was, obviously, a great boon to culture, but without paper its benefits would have been restricted to the few who could afford to purchase a book printed on vellum.

Over the three centuries, the thirteenth through the fifteenth, with which we are here concerned, we have noticed the eager concern of the philosophers with scientific theories. For the most part they pursued their inquiries with the only tool they knew, the syllogism. The results of their discussion had then to be brought into accord with Christian theology. The few original thinkers, like Grosseteste, Roger Bacon, and Albert of Saxony (d. 1390), who struck out on new lines and called for an experimental approach to scientific theory were in a great minority. Much experimental work would not, furthermore, have been possible with the very primitive technical equipment at their disposal. Thus real advances in scientific knowledge were almost in abeyance for several centuries. Nevertheless, the period of scholastic discussion of scientific subjects was far from wasted. These medieval thinkers were untrammeled by recalcitrant facts determined by limited experiment. Their imagination thus had free course, and later scientific theorists were greatly indebted to the speculative thought of the late scholastics.

In the meantime, techniques were able to make substantial progress. The growth of population and the consequent need for improvements in agriculture, transportation, and production of consumer goods inevitably brought about great changes in European life. The clock, the magnetic compass, new navigational aids and styles of ships, improved farm tools, water mills for power, distillation, paper and printing—these are only the most prominent among the inventions which were the offspring of mother necessity. By the end of the fifteenth century, with these inventions securely in hand, Europe was ready for the basic if delayed scientific revolution of the sixteenth and seventeenth centuries.

EXPLORATION AND DISCOVERY

THE brilliant and well-advertised success of Marco Polo's travels to the exotic court of Kublai Khan in Mongolia between 1271 and the end of the century precipitated a veritable rash of missionary and exploring activity in the next decades. A Franciscan, John de Monte Corvino, was sent to the various courts of Asia in 1289. He spent a year in southeastern India, winning about a hundred converts. In 1305 we find him in Peking, where, according to his later account, he had labored for eleven long years and had established a mission which survived him. There were other expeditions down the eastern coast of Africa which were looking for the fabled Christian kingdom of Prester John. This kingdom had appeared in legend from the twelfth century, and was then, by common consent, placed in India, adjoining the realm of the great Khan. From early in the fourteenth century it was thought to be in Ethiopia. It was not until 1391 that the true story of an ancient Christian kingdom of Abyssinia was known in the West, from reports of a Catalan priest who, after spending several years at the court of the Ethiopian king, gave King John I of Aragon an extended description of the land and its ruler.

Another Franciscan, John Marignolli, was a special legate of the pope to China and India from 1338 to 1353. From this time until well into the fifteenth century there were many travelers to the heathen lands beyond the Christian pale. The motives of these hardy souls were mixed. Some few were motivated by the highest missionary ideals. Some were merely curious as to the customs and peoples who were strange to the European. Others, probably the most numerous group, were in quest of trade. The commercial cities of Italy, Venice, Genoa, Pisa, and Florence carried on a steady trade in the eastern basin of the Mediterranean and the Black Sea. But there were obvious geographical limitations to their eastern expansion. At eastern ports they had to trade with oriental merchants, who in turn traded with merchants from the interior, India and China. Expansion of trade in that direction thus met with certain inherent difficulties which made these Italian merchants desirous of looking elsewhere for markets. In the fourteenth century, after the crusading movement had virtually died down, the Italian shipowners and traders began to look westward and northward for a large part of their trade. A whole fleet—the Flanders Fleet—of ships left Venice at least once a year for the Lowlands, loaded with goods from the East: spices, fine woven cloth, manufactured and luxury goods which were profitable to handle because of their relatively light weight, such as drugs, dyes, porcelain, and precious stones. This fleet had to pass through the Strait of Gibraltar and skirt the coast of Portugal, at one or more of whose ports they would regularly put in for supplies for the long voyage toward their destination on the North Sea. They returned the same way, laden with goods from the north, woolens, linen, woven silks, and such products as tallow, leather, hemp, and hides. Of course there were land routes which were used for the transport of these same commodities from Venice, Genoa, and Milan, through the mountain passes to cities like Basel, Augsburg, Salzburg, Marseilles, and London, but sea transport was cheaper and more characteristic of the new capitalism of wholesale, corporate merchandising.

Portuguese Ventures

THE frequent passage by the coasts of Portugal of these Italian fleets must have inspired the Portuguese to enter the lists contending for mastery of the sea. Portuguese rulers had fought the Moors at sea early in the twelfth century, and soon thereafter Genoese captains are found in Portuguese employ. In 1317 a Genoese, Manuel Pezagno, became admiral of the Portuguese navy. A few years later, probably in 1335, a Portuguese fleet under Genoese captains visited the Canary Islands, already known as the Fortunate Isles. Possession of the islands was disputed with Castile, finally in vain, but this expedition may be regarded as the beginning of Portugal's remarkable career of exploration. It is highly probable that during the fourteenth century Portuguese sailors set foot on Madeira and the Azores. In 1386 the treaty of Windsor joined England and Portugal in an alliance maintained into the twentieth century. The next year Philippa, daughter of John of Gaunt, duke of Lancaster, married King John I of Portugal. There were five sons from this marriage, the third of whom, born in 1394, is known to history as Prince Henry the Navigator.

The work of Prince Henry constitutes, almost by itself, a glorious era in Portuguese history. As viceroy of Algarve province, the southernmost part of the kingdom, he fitted out fleets to defend the coast against Moorish pirates. After capturing the port of Ceuta in Morocco, just opposite Gibraltar, he began systematically to send ships or small fleets along the western coast of Africa with instructions to explore as far southwards as they could go. In order better to prepare these expeditions he established at Cape St. Vincent a small city intended as headquarters for his school of navigation and exploration. His whole life was devoted with exemplary singleness of purpose to the study of geography and the records of all previous explorations and the preparation of the many expeditions which he sent out. His motivation was mixed. While he had the native curiosity of the born explorer, he was also anxious to spread the Christian faith. He was, furthermore, desirous to combat the Moors, ancient enemies of his people, who possessed much if not all of the continent of Africa. Finally he sought new routes and peoples with whom Portugal might trade on a competitive basis with the Italian commercial cities. One of his first successful operations after the conquest of Ceuta was the effective discovery of the island of Madeira and its proper colonization (1419-20). He brought to the island horses and sugar cane, both of which prospered. His expeditions, taken as a whole, met with varying degrees of success: storms and mariners' fears of shoals and currents turned some ships back. Prince Henry was aided by the improvements in navigational techniques taking place elsewhere in Europe. His brother Peter toured Europe procuring the latest maps and books on sailing and geography. The Portuguese shipbuilders had made of their caravel, originally a coastwise fishing vessel or trader, a faster and more manageable ship with three or more masts, rigged with lateen (triangular) sails, which could sail close to the wind in almost any weather.

Yet, in spite of Prince Henry's careful planning and generous support, it took twelve years—from 1422 to 1434—to get a Portuguese ship past Cape Bojador on the northwestern shore of Africa. This cape had been accepted as the ultimate limit of navigation, and mariners shuddered at the thought of passing it southward. In 1432 one of the Azores had been discovered by a Portuguese captain, and with the passage of Cape Bojador in 1434, progress from that point was rapid. In 1436 the Port of the Galley, three hundred miles beyond Cape Bojador, was reached. In 1443 a Portuguese admiral, Nuño da Tristão, reached Cape Branco. In the 1440's some natives were captured and brought back to Portugal and the prospect of cheap (slave) labor and easy profits induced enterprising merchants to engage in the traffic and to venture farther afield for native captives. Cape Verde had been passed in 1445. By 1448, 927 captives had been brought to Portugal. In 1448 and 1449 trading posts were established on the African coast, and Portuguese-African luxury goods were being sold on the European market. There was great hope that a southern route to India might be found.

In 1456, only three years after the fall of Constantinople, the captain of one expedition, Diogo Gomes, was given specific orders to proceed on to India if he could, and an interpreter who was supposed to be able to communicate with the inhabitants of that land was added to his crew. By the time of the death of Prince Henry, in 1460, his expeditions had reached as far as Sierra Leone. The gain in actual distance of coastline explored, perhaps a scant thousand miles, was less significant than the impetus he gave to exploration and the tradition he established of careful and objective study of geography and navigation as a necessary preparation for exploration and colonization. Of not less sig-

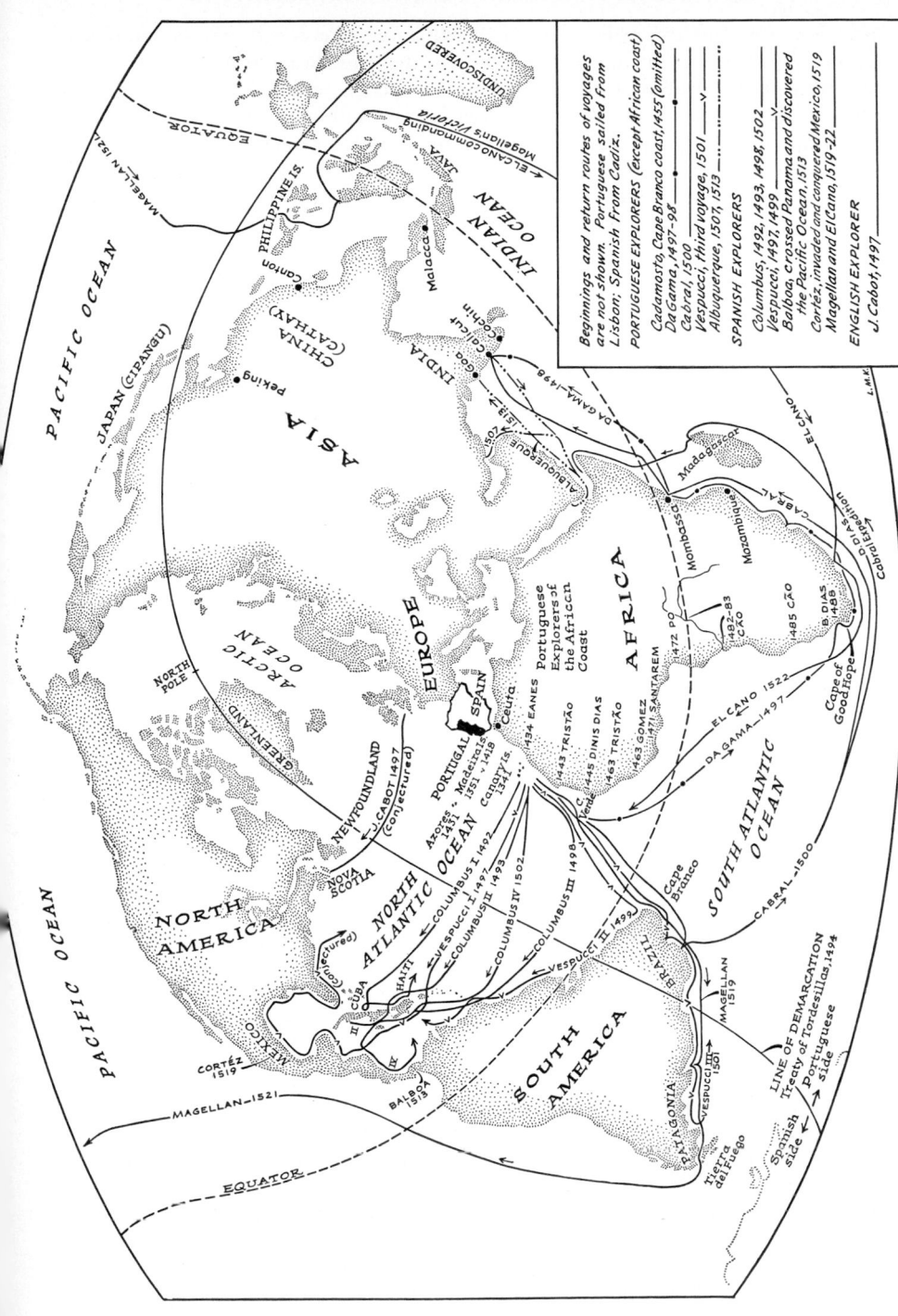

Explorations and Discoveries, 1341–1522

nificance for further exploration was what we may call his geographical philosophy. He was firmly convinced that the Indies could be reached by a southern route around Africa. The land route, it will be remembered, had been made more difficult and expensive by the fall of Constantinople to the Ottoman Turks in 1453 and the consequent enhancement of the power of Islam to bar the eastward routes. Prince Henry thereupon redoubled his efforts to find a route to the East that would not be dependent upon the consent of the Turks. In 1455 Cadamosto, a Venetian captain, came into Prince Henry's employ and made an extensive trading and exploring voyage to Madeira and the Canaries, and from thence southwards to the coast of Africa beyond Cape Branco. The next year he sailed even farther south, discovered the Cape Verde Islands, and, off the river Cacheu, the Bissagos Islands.

The death of Prince Henry in 1460 was not the end of Portuguese exploration. In 1463 Diogo Gomes identified the coast of Sierra Leone and Cape Mesurado, the modern Liberia. The successes of the Portuguese in discovery and in the establishment of trade in African merchandise brought Spanish competition; the dynastic war between Castile and Portugal that began in 1474 was to a considerable degree sparked by the rivalry for commercial supremacy in north and west Africa. In 1482 Diogo Cão, who had grown up as a member of Prince Henry's entourage, sailed some distance up the Congo River where a post was established which maintained friendly relations with the natives. Before his death in 1486 Cão had explored 1450 miles of the coastline of western Africa. In 1488 Bartholomew Dias turned the Cape of Good Hope, so called by King John II because of the "promise it gave of finding India." In 1497 Vasco da Gama, another Portuguese admiral, sailing on eastward beyond the Cape, put in at Mozambique, where he met some Arab merchant ships, and at Mombasa. He sailed on to Calicut on the Malabar coast of India in the spring of 1498. Moors had been there before the Portuguese and were able to turn the natives against the Christians. Da Gama was glad enough to turn back, reaching Lisbon in September 1499, with a greatly depleted crew. The eastern sea route to India was, after over a century of search, opened. But by this time the western route to the Indies had been followed by a Genoese captain by the name of Christopher Columbus, in the employ of their Catholic Majesties, Ferdinand and Isabella of Castile and Aragon.

Spanish Explorations

THE year 1492 was important in the history of the Spanish peninsula as well as in the history of the Western Hemisphere. In that year the Moorish kingdom of Granada, the last Moorish stronghold in the peninsula, was conquered by Ferdinand and Isabella. It had been, by reason of its position on the southern coast of Spain, a sort of guardian and deterrent of ship traffic in either direction to and from Gibraltar. Portuguese travel eastward to the marts of the Orient was effectively discouraged. It was thus easier and simpler for Portugal to devote her attention to the freely accessible western coast of Africa. On the other hand, Spain, during most of the fifteenth century disunited and often in anarchy, was in no position to undertake any program of exploration. But, by the marriage in 1469 of Ferdinand and Isabella, there arose a common Spanish dynasty and hopes of organic unification (see above, Chapter 6). Firm and vigorous rule brought quick recovery and the reconquest of what remained of Moorish territory was resumed. After a prolonged campaign the Moorish kingdom of Granada capitulated to the Spaniards in 1492; the whole Iberian peninsula was again, after almost eight centuries, entirely under Christian rule. This conquest freed the Spanish monarchs to join the search for a westward route to the Indies. In the course of this search, a new world was found, a new field for the westward expansion of European culture.

In this same year of 1492 Christopher Columbus (Cristóbal Colón he called himself when in Spanish employ), a Genoese captain in the service of the Catholic kings, commanding three caravels, sailed westward from the port of Palos on August 3 and landed, on October 12, on the Caribbean island of San Salvador. He thought he had compassed the westward route to India and that the islands he discovered lay just off the coast of China.

The career of Columbus before this voyage was a story of imagination, determination, disappointments, and frustrations. Born in Genoa in 1451, the eldest son of a wool weaver, he early left the family trade for the sea. When he was twenty-five, the Genoese ship on which he was a sailor was sunk in a battle with French ships off the southern coast of Portugal. Christopher, clinging to an oar, managed to reach shore. An elder brother, Bartholomew, was employed in Lisbon as a chart-maker, and Christopher went to join him. The two Genoese brothers soon set up in the chart-making business for themselves. Nourished by the reports and talks of the mariners, the idea of a direct westward route to India began to take shape. But practical sailing experience was necessary before any major enterprise could be undertaken. For several years Christopher served as a sailor in Portuguese ships, going beyond Ireland on one cruise, returning to Genoa on another, and south to Madeira, the Azores, and the Gold Coast on still others. By 1483 he was a respected mariner with good connections in the shipping world. His path for a westward sea route to the Indies had in the meantime been fortified by the calculations of a Florentine physician, Paolo Toscanelli, who, relying on Marco Polo's reports, had estimated the distance from Lisbon to Japan as about three thousand miles. Columbus, perhaps in communication with Toscanelli,* had received a copy of the chart of the route the Florentine had drawn. Miscalculating the length of a degree of latitude, Columbus was convinced of the correctness of Toscanelli's figures. Such an expedition would obviously be costly, and Columbus lost no time in asking John II, king of Portugal, to finance it. The king firmly rejected the idea. Columbus next tried Spain. He was unable to obtain an audience with Queen Isabella until 1486. Somewhat sympathetic to his plea for support, she appointed a commission to examine the project. No firm decision was reached, but Columbus was given a sort of retaining fee, which, unfortunately, was very irregularly paid. For over a year he waited in vain, then tried the Portuguese king again, only to be disappointed a second time. He then approached Henry VII of England through his brother Bartholomew, who, when this hope turned out to be vain, tried the French court, with the same negative result. Queen Isabella was still friendly, but her advisers were

---

* The story of Columbus' correspondence with Toscanelli, though quite old, is now regarded as doubtful.

flatly opposed to the whole idea. Late in 1491, as he was on the point of going to France with his plan, Isabella invited Columbus to court. His conditions were first refused, then, after he packed up his charts to leave Spain forever, accepted. In April 1492, the contract between Columbus and the monarchs, promising three outfitted ships, the title of Admiral and 10 per cent of the gold or produce from trade with the regions to be discovered, was signed. The *Santa Maria* of 100 tons, the *Niña* of about 60 tons, and the *Pinta* of about 75 tons, and a fleet complement of some 90 men under Columbus' command left the port of Palos on August 3. A month later the fleet dropped anchor in the Canary Islands. Most of the remainder of the trip was over pleasant seas, with favorable trade winds. There was grumbling after three weeks of sailing beyond the Canaries without sight of land, but Columbus held firm, and early in October land birds were seen flying in a southwesterly direction. On the 11th branches of trees began to be noticed in the water, and at two o'clock the next morning a lookout cried out "Land, land." At noon of October 12 the fleet found haven, dropped anchor in a cove in five fathoms of water, and Columbus placed the royal standard of Castile on a white beach, knelt on the ground and "gave this island the name of San Salvador—Holy Savior." It was not the India that he hoped to find, but what is now known as Watlings Island in the Bahamas. In the next few months Columbus sailed southwest and west, discovering many small islands and the northeastern shore of Cuba. This latter, Columbus was sure, was the Cipangu (Japan) of which Marco Polo had written as lying off the coast of Cathay. On Hispaniola (Haiti) he left a small colony of thirty-nine men at a point which he called Navidad. The small amount of gold he was able to obtain from the natives disappointed him, but between him and his lieutenants enough of the precious metal was collected, as dust, nuggets, or jewelry, to make a respectable gift for Queen Isabella. After the *Santa Maria* had foundered on a coral reef late in December he turned his two ships homewards on January 4, 1493, skirting the northern shore of Haiti. After a stormy and difficult passage he reached Lisbon on March 4, 1493.

When Columbus reached Spain he was greeted with great enthusiasm by both the people and the monarchs. The natives and the gold he brought were the evidence of his discoveries. He was named Admiral of the Ocean Sea and Viceroy and Governor of the Islands. His report of the voyage, printed and reprinted, translated into several languages, was soon widely known over the whole Continent. The monarchs obtained from Pope Alexander VI an acknowledgment of the discovery and possessions beyond the seas in a bull, dated May 3, 1493; a second bull, dated the following day, specified that a north-south line of demarcation, set at one hundred leagues west of the Azores, should divide the explorations of Portugal from those of Spain. The African coast, the Madeiras, the Canaries, and the Azores lay east of this line; the new world which Columbus had discovered lay to the west. Portugal protested that this line was too far east and the following year, on June 7, 1494, a compromise was reached. By the treaty of Tordesillas a line 270 leagues west of the papal line, that is, 370 leagues west of the Cape Verde Islands, was agreed upon. Since such measurements were necessarily somewhat vague, it is not surprising that some confusion as to just where the line was should have arisen.

In the meantime Columbus had set sail on his second voyage. The success of the first had brought many volunteers for the second, which was more of a colonizing venture than a voyage of discovery. The Admiral set out with seventeen ships and twelve hundred men. Following a more southerly course, he landed on the small island of Dominica on November 3. He discovered further small islands on the way to Haiti, where he found the settlement of Navidad abandoned, the colonists killed by natives. He established on the same island a new colony which he called Isabella under the rule of his younger brother Diego, then went on to explore much of the northern coast of Cuba. After almost three years of exploration and tribulation he reached Spain on June 11, 1496.

Compared with the first voyage, the return from the second was dismal. Columbus brought no proof that he had reached China. The colony at Isabella had proved a failure as a trading post, and the promised gold did not materialize. The hope that souls might be won for the Church, so prominent in earlier plans, was disappointed, as no conversions could be reported beyond the few natives brought back to Spain on shipboard. All in all Columbus' enemies had plausible grounds for their criticism after his second voyage. The monarchs, however, received him courteously, and confirmed his titles and honors. They were worried lest the king of Portugal find the fabled Antipodes, the "fourth part of the world," before they did, and Columbus was still their most competent navigator. He was outfitted, albeit rather skimpily, for a third voyage, and left for Haiti on May 30, 1498, at the head of a fleet of six caravels. Taking a southerly route, he was twice becalmed before reaching Trinidad, off the northern coast of South America on July 31. He was still expecting to meet Chinese mandarins, but the naked natives he saw hardly fulfilled his hopes. On August 5, 1498, Columbus and his men set foot on the Paria peninsula of South America, which he mistook for an island, revising his opinion after a fortnight's sailing and repeated assurances from the natives that it was the mainland. Turning northwards, he anchored in a safe harbor on the southern shore of Haiti on August 31. The colony he had left at Isabella was rent by dissension. There was trouble with the natives and among the Spaniards, and Columbus' authority was defied. Meanwhile, back in Spain, detractors made much of Columbus' failure as an administrator, with the result that a special royal commission was sent to Haiti. Quickly assuming that Columbus and his brothers were responsible for all the misfortunes, the royal commissioner put them in chains and sent them back to Spain. Although they were released from their fetters on royal order, the monarchs were by then busy with other matters. Columbus was hopeful not only of complete vindication but of being restored to his offices and properties. After long delays, in September 1501, he was informed that although he could continue to use the titles of Admiral and Viceroy, another was being appointed Governor of the Islands and the Indies. He swallowed his pride to the extent of asking for ships and money to make another voyage to the Indies. His request was granted with surprising speed. He sailed from Cadiz on May 11, 1502, and reached Haiti on June 29, just ahead of a hurricane. A fortnight later, having weathered the tempest, he sailed southwesterly, looking for the passage between what he thought was China (that is, Cuba), and the continent he had discovered in 1498 (South America). He reached Cape Honduras, skirted the coast of present-day Nicaragua and

Costa Rica, clear to the Isthmus of Panama, then eastward along the coast of Venezuela. He came very close to seeing the sea that led to China. Not understanding the natives, he never heard how close he actually was to the Pacific.

Columbus spent Christmas 1502 and New Year's 1503 in the present harbor of Cristóbal, Panama Canal Zone. On the return toward Haiti the hulls of his ships had become so worm-eaten that they had to be beached at Jamaica, where he and his crews were marooned for a year, June 25, 1503, to June 1504, before help was sent from the colony on Haiti. Columbus chartered another ship and sailed for home, to arrive November 7, 1504. Queen Isabella lay on her death bed, and breathed her last only three weeks after Columbus' return. Ferdinand was not now interested in the boring details of the new and thus far very unproductive new world. Columbus rejected offers to have his claims arbitrated, standing on the original promises made him. He spent his last days in near-poverty. But to the end he was confident justice would be done him; his will disposed of vast sums which were never to come into his possession. Ironically, to the day of his death, May 19, 1506, he was unaware of the greatness of his own accomplishment. He could not know that his intrepid and uncannily inspired seamanship had discovered the New World, and that the Atlantic, the great barrier which he had crossed, was to be the bond that holds together the old and the new European civilizations.

Other explorers, close to Columbus in time, deserve to be spoken of in the same breath. Another Italian, Amerigo Vespucci (1451–1512), who had represented the house of Medici in Spain since 1492, piloted in 1499 and 1500 for Ojeda, a Spanish gentleman, an expedition which set out to find the passage to India. They skirted the northern coast of South America from Surinam to Venezuela. In 1500 a Portuguese captain, Alvarez Cabral, bound for India by the route of da Gama, around the Cape of Good Hope, sighted the eastern coast of Brazil at Cape St. Roque, and sailed along the coast for five hundred miles before veering southeast to turn the Cape of Good Hope. He was convinced he had discovered a large island. A year later, in May 1501, Vespucci was sent out by the king of Portugal to explore the coast of Brazil and claim it for Portugal. He explored as far south as the La Plata River, traversing almost 50 degrees of latitude (3200 miles of coastline), and discovered islands in the south sea between Africa and Cape Horn. The extensive voyages of Vespucci made it certain, for the first time, that a new continent had been discovered. Further confirmation was to be the labor of Ferdinand Magellan (Magalhães). In 1507 a German humanist, Martin Waldseemüller, in a work entitled *Introductio cosmographiae,* which contained a translation of Vespucci's letter describing his four voyages, suggested that the New World be called America, after Amerigo. A Spanish soldier of fortune, Vasco Nuñez de Balboa, following the route of Columbus' fourth voyage, in 1513 stopped in the Gulf of Darien long enough to cross the Isthmus of Panama, see the Pacific Ocean, and claim it for the king of Spain. Settlements of Spaniards in Central America followed within a few years, culminating in the foundation of the city of Panama in 1519 and, that same year, the conquest of the Aztec empire of Montezuma by Hernan Cortés.

Portugal in the East

WHILE Spain was having such successes in discovering the New World to the west, Portugal was carrying on an active and lucrative campaign of discovery and colonization in the east. Rivalry between the two neighboring powers was natural and keen. In 1495 Manuel I of Portugal, the successor of John II, decided to send a fleet to India around the Cape of Good Hope. The fleet sailed in 1497, under the command of Vasco da Gama, who depended on the previous observations of Dias. Da Gama, after putting in for supplies at several ports on the eastern coast of Africa, proceeded across the Indian Ocean to the Malabar coast and its principal spice port, Calicut. He found the Arabs well entrenched in the trade and not anxious to share it with a stranger. But da Gama was able to get enough spices to prove that trade was possible, and returned to Lisbon with a greatly depleted crew in the fall of 1499. An effort by two emissaries of the king of Portugal to reach the spice coast of India in 1497 overland by Egypt and Arabia had shown that success by that route was clearly impossible. The sea route was the only hope. In 1500 Cabral, having skirted the coast of Brazil and rounded the Cape of Good Hope, reached Calicut, and went on to establish a trading factory at the nearby port of Cochin. Two years later another well-equipped fleet sailed, under da Gama, who found it necessary to show his military strength. He bombarded Calicut, then won a naval battle against the Arabs. Superior gunnery was decisive in both actions. The first Portuguese viceroy, Almeida, fought and won decisively a battle against a combined Moslem fleet of Egyptian and local ships in 1509, thus impressing the pattern of force upon Portuguese relations with the native princes and peoples. Such a policy would call for high organization and eternal vigilance. These qualities were possessed in a good degree by the greatest Portuguese colonial leader, Alfonso de Albuquerque.

Albuquerque was sent to India in 1506 but did not become viceroy until Almeida's retirement in 1509, ten years after the first Portuguese ships had sighted the spice coast. In the meantime the Portuguese had built an empire around the Indian Ocean. With Goa, Socotra off the Gulf of Aden, and Ormuz at the entrance to the Persian Gulf safely in their hands, the Portuguese controlled the western Arab trade routes and eventually extended their sway as far south as Ceylon. There remained the eastern coast of India, the routes to the China coast and to the Spice Islands, otherwise known as the Moluccas. In the six years of his viceroyship Albuquerque (d. 1515) was almost able to achieve his aims of political and commercial control of the whole eastern spice trade. He was energetic, far-sighted, and aggressive. In 1511 he took strategically placed Malacca, thus opening the way both to the China coast and to the rich Molucca Islands. Within two years a Portuguese ship reached Canton, and soon there was a Portuguese settlement at Macao, just south of the larger port. The Portuguese formula in their dealings with native rulers was first a show of force, then a negotiated treaty which allowed them to trade and build warehouses. Albuquerque was very astute in locating his bases at such points as to allow him to utilize readily his preponderant sea power. The interests of the

Portuguese being primarily commercial, the native princes were largely left alone in the exercise of their political power. Missionary activity was encouraged, but rather clumsily directed, so that achievement in this direction was modest.

Albuquerque's successors managed to extend Portuguese rule and to increase the quantity of spices sent back to Lisbon, but their successes were eventually costly. An increased supply of spices naturally lowered prices on the European market. Venice, which had long been dealing with the Arabs and had acted as intermediary for the sale of spices reaching the western market, was hard hit by the lowered price for that commodity. In 1504 a Venetian fleet returned empty from Alexandria. The Portuguese had already successfully excluded the Arabs from the spice trade. In protest, Venice withdrew her ambassador from the court of Portugal. But prices continued to decline as the quantity of imports grew. Though the profits from the trade were at first fabulous—as much as sixty times the cost of the expedition—Portugal soon found that the high cost of maintaining installations, depots, and troops at so great a distance from the home country almost canceled out any expected gains. The height of the Portuguese boom was reached about 1520. Within twenty years of that time the Asiatic and African colonial enterprise, what with lowered prices for the imports and the loss of many Portuguese ships to pirates on the high seas, was barely paying its way. By 1560 Portugal was on the verge of bankruptcy. This condition can be traced in the main to the moral decline resulting from sudden excessive wealth and the ruinous cost of maintaining an elaborate colonial establishment so far from home.

The regrettable effects of what the Portuguese had thought was good fortune are not the only aspect of the Portuguese African and Asiatic expansion. The importance to the common man in Europe of spices which could preserve food can hardly be exaggerated. So long as the source of spices was in the hands of the Moslems, the European had to pay heavily for his food preservatives. The poor—most of the population—could not afford the luxury of any preservative save salt. It was to the Arabs' advantage to keep the spices in scarce supply. Once the source of supply was wrested from Moslem control and this merchandise shipped in large quantities to the West, the whole European food budget was changed. With food easier to preserve, winter diets, even for the common man, became more varied and palatable. It would be safe to say that this improvement in diet contributed noticeably to the increased birth rate in Europe and to the general resistance to disease which the sixteenth century witnessed. From the standpoint of morale, furthermore, Portuguese successes were a tonic for the West. The fall of Constantinople to the Turks in 1453, even if of little strategic importance, had been a serious blow to Western pride. Portuguese conquest of a hitherto strictly Moslem area and the lucrative trade monopoly that resulted from it went far to even the score.

Columbus and his successors, flying the flag of Spain, had without doubt performed an heroic and imaginative work of discovery, though at the time they did not understand the significance of what they had done. Yet for the twenty-two years between da Gama's trip around the Cape of Good Hope to India and the sources of goods the West sorely needed, and the circumnavigation of the globe by Magellan and his captains, Portugal was ahead of Spain. She had tangible profits from the work of her sea captains, and Spain had only the glory of discovering some new islands that failed to produce gold. But after Magellan and the conquests of Cortés in Mexico and Pizarro in Peru the situation changed. Thereafter, for the next century Spain was to be the great exploiting power of Europe. The fabulous wealth Spain extracted from the Americas proved almost enough to choke her.

Magellan and the Circumnavigation of the Globe

BY 1519 the western route to the Spice Islands had not been found. There were still stout hearts that thought it could be discovered if one only went far enough. Ferdinand Magellan had made several trips for the king of Portugal to the East Indies by the eastern route, but had left Portuguese service for that of Charles I of Spain in 1517. He convinced Charles that the Spice Islands were west of the line of demarcation and thus in the Spanish sphere. It was necessary only to find the strait which led beyond the New World explored by Vespucci. With instructions from Charles that he "should straightway follow to the islands of Maluco" in search of spices, Magellan left Seville with a fleet of five vessels in August 1519, bound for South America. A year later he was slowly and painstakingly exploring the coast of southern Brazil and the barren shores of Patagonia. On November 28, having taken thirty-eight days to struggle through the stormy straits that now bear his name, he reached the wide ocean, which he immediately named the Pacific. His fleet now reduced to three vessels—one foundered, a second deserted—he steered northwestward, with the trade winds at his back. He missed the islands of the south Pacific, and, without new supplies of water and food, his crews had to survive on "old biscuits reduced to powder and full of grubs, and stinking, and we drank water that was yellow and stinking. We also ate the oxhides that were under the main-yard."

In mid-March they anchored at one of the islands of the Philippines, and early in April reached Cebu, a larger island of the archipelago. Here Magellan became involved in a native squabble and was killed, April 27, 1521. His men carried on and reached the Moluccas in a few weeks, where they loaded their ships with valuable spices and enjoyed the profusion of fruits and vegetables that the islands offered. The *Victoria,* the single ship which returned to Spain, left in December 1521 and, taking a southerly route to the Cape of Good Hope, reached the Bay of St. Lucar on September 6, 1522. It had taken slightly over three years to circumnavigate the globe.

In 1496 Giovanni Cabotto, an experienced Venetian mariner better known as John Cabot, in the employ of Henry VII of England, was commissioned "to seek out, discover and find whatsoever islands, countries, regions or provinces of heathens or infidels, in whatever part of the world they may be, which before this time were unknown to all Christians." He left the port of Bristol in May 1497 and returned in August. He appears to have set foot on the coast of Newfoundland or Nova Scotia. He made another voyage the next year, but where or even if he landed on the North American continent is not surely known. His son Sebastian made some voyages in search of a northwest passage to the Indies, without success. The expeditions of the Cabots aroused only scanty enthusiasm among the English.

The century preceding the triumphant return of one of Magellan's ships to Spain from circling the globe had indeed witnessed a revolution in man's ideas of the shape and size of the world. Whatever the motives of the monarchs and the explorers may have been—and gold, trade, slaves, and the spread of the Christian faith, in this order, were all present—the effect of the discovery of whole continents, new races, civilizations hitherto unimagined, was both humbling and explosive. The European could no longer count himself unique and exclusively blessed with God's favor. The discoveries were explosive in that they loosed a new series of wars among the states of Europe, wars for trade and treasure, and, hardly less disturbing, for national pride and glory.

The discoveries were to have vast and complex repercussions in every area of European thought and life. In the literatures of all European peoples the impact of these events upon the imagination of poets and political writers was forceful and cumulative. Modes and fashions, clothes and customs, were to reflect the new perspectives. Produce from the New World—tobacco, for example—was to have a tremendous physical and psychological influence upon Western society. In economics and industry gold from the New World and the spread of the trading network in the Western Hemisphere altered the focus of economic control in every European country, and hastened the culmination of the capitalistic revolution of the sixteenth and seventeenth centuries. The drive for colonies and the foundation of the great imperialistic powers, whose rivalries were to keep the development of the modern world in turmoil for centuries, had begun even before Magellan weighed anchor in the port of Seville and set out for the Spice Islands on that brilliant August morning in 1519.

SUGGESTIONS FOR FURTHER READING

ANDERSON, R. and R. C., *The Sailing Ship*. London, 1926
BAKER, J. N. L., *History of Geographical Discovery and Exploration*. New York, 1931
BEAZLEY, C. R., *The Dawn of Modern Geography*. 3 vols. Oxford, 1897–1906
BERNAL, J. D., *Science in History*. London, 1954
BUTTERFIELD, H., *The Origins of Modern Science*. London, 1949
CROMBIE, A. C., *Augustine to Galileo*. London, 1952
CRONE, G. R., *Maps and Their Makers*. London, 1953
DAMPIER, W., *A History of Science*. New York, 1932
DUHEM, P., *Études sur Léonard de Vinci*. 3 vols. 1906–13
DUHEM, P., *Le Système du monde*. 5 vols. 1913–17
FORDHAM, H. G., *Maps, Their History, Characteristics and Uses*. Cambridge, 1927
HART, H. H., *Sea Road to the Indies*. New York, 1950
JACOBS, J., *The Story of Geographical Discovery*. New York, 1913
KIMBLE, G. H. T., *Geography in the Middle Ages*. London, 1938
LACROIX, P., *Science and Literature in the Middle Ages*. London, n. d.
LEY, C. D., ed., *Portuguese Voyages, 1498–1583*. London, 1947. Everyman's Library
LOCY, W. A., *Growth of Biology*. New York, 1925

MARTINS, J. P. OLIVEIRA, *The Golden Age of Prince Henry the Navigator*. London, 1914

MASON, S. F., *A History of the Sciences*. London, 1953

McCURDY, E., *The Mind of Leonardo da Vinci*. New York, 1939

McCURDY, E., *The Notebooks of Leonardo da Vinci*. New York, 1938

NEWTON, A. P., *Travel and Travelers in the Middle Ages*. London, 1926

NORDENSKIÖLD, E., *A History of Biology*. New York, 1928

ROBERTSON, J. D., *The Evolution of Clockwork*. London, 1931

SARTON, G., *Introduction to the History of Science*. 3 vols. in 5. Baltimore, 1927–48

SARTON, G., *Six Wings: Men of Science in the Renaissance*. Bloomington, Ind., 1957

SINGER, C. G., *A Short History of Science to the 19th Century*. Oxford, 1941

SOMERVILLE, B. T., *The Chart Makers*. London, 1928

STEVENSON, E. L., *Portolan Charts; Their Origin and Characteristics*. New York, 1911

TAYLOR, E. G. R., *Tudor Geography 1485–1563*. London, 1930

THORNDIKE, L., *History of Magic and Experimental Science*. 6 vols. New York, 1923–41

THORNDIKE, L., *Science and Thought in the Fifteenth Century*. New York, 1929

CHAPTER FOURTEEN

THE ARTS

IN FEW areas of European life and growth has there been so clear a line of distinction drawn between what is commonly called medieval and what passes for Renaissance as in that of the arts. In political and economic organization, in social growth, in ecclesiastical structure and theological formulation, it is usual to speak of transition and development. But in treating of the plastic and representative arts it is conventional to emphasize the existence of a sharp break between the artistic product of the Gothic Middle Ages and the modern, scientific, realistic Renaissance. That is not the position taken here. Although there was no precise time at which the formal and symbolic suddenly ceased to dominate artistic creation and the realistic or naturalistic and scientific suddenly took over, it is true that changes took place in the techniques of artistic representation. Practice and experiment brought improvements in the handling of various media. The public for whom the works of the artist were intended grew wider as commerce, industry, and communication spread and as the bourgeoisie increased in number and wealth. The spirit of individualism, so important to some analysts of artistic motivation, had developed farther in some countries, notably Italy, than in others, and with greatly diverse effects upon man and society. The vast growth in educational facilities that took place in the fourteenth and fifteenth centuries gave rise to a new and demanding public, whose criteria and appetites were substantially different from those of a feudal or monastic society. These various factors basically affected the direction and content of the several arts, not only during these two centuries but for a long time thereafter.

There is a certain arbitrariness in breaking up the arts into sculpture, painting, and architecture. Almost all the great artists performed in more than one of these areas, and many of them in all three, with equal competence. But for the purposes of our present consideration the division has the advantage of tracing lines of development that took place over a period of several centuries without the interjection of terms and issues from another discipline. The artists of Italy must claim the major part of our attention. As John Addington Symonds has put it, "From the Pope upon St. Peter's chair to the clerks in a

Florentine counting-house, every Italian was a judge of art. . . . During that period of prodigious activity the entire nation seemed to be endowed with an instinct for the beautiful and with the capacity for producing it in every conceivable form." * Of no other European nation could this be said. However, some attention will be given later in the chapter to artistic production in other lands of Europe, if only to indicate, on broad lines, the direction their interests took and the continuity of their individual genius. In the following sections only a few of the leading representatives of the plastic arts can be discussed, and of these few, only a small portion of their works can be mentioned. The lush productivity of the age would defy anything even approaching a complete treatment, at least within the compass of this study.

SCULPTURE

THE court of the Emperor Frederick II in Sicily was the scene of an intellectual ferment unmatched elsewhere in Europe. It was not only the direct impact of Islam on Christianity, which, given favorable circumstances, would have been enough to bring about a revolution of the spirit and mind of Western man. In the field of art it was more. The Emperor himself, known as the *Stupor mundi,* the wonder of the world, whose mind, fertile and free, ranged over the whole gamut of human expression, demanded from his court imagination and creativeness. He added his own inspiration. He built castles, public works, and monuments which recall the days of the conquering Caesars. There is no art without artists, and Frederick discovered men to match his vision, though it might be more accurate to say that he found men who were capable of being channels of his own genius.

The Pisan School

ONE of these artists, Nicholas of Apulia, after years in Frederick's employ, surrounded by Byzantine, Islamic, French, and south Italian art—all these strains captive to the recreating genius of Frederick—stopped off in Tuscany, probably during one of Frederick's trips to northern Italy. Better known as Niccolò of Pisa (Niccolò Pisano, d. *ca.* 1280), he was the earliest master of plastic art in the Italian Renaissance. In 1254 he was invited to Padua to design and begin the construction of the basilica of St. Anthony. The result was a harmonious blend of Byzantine, Gothic, and native Romanesque, with decoration of bas-reliefs and sculptured figures which give abundant evidence of a new sense of the grouping of figures. He was thereafter given a number of architectural commissions in Arezzo, Cortona, and Florence which he executed satisfactorily in the Italian Gothic style then in vogue.

Sometime before 1260 Niccolò saw in Pisa a Roman sarcophagus, now in the Campo Santo and identified as that of a certain Roman matron of the second century A.D., the realism of whose decoration made a deep impression on him. In that same year he was commissioned to design and build the pulpit in the Baptistery at Pisa. On the crowded panels of this hexagonal pulpit, with

* *Renaissance in Italy. The Fine Arts.* London, 1877, Chapter 1, p. 3.

its varicolored marble columns and Gothic cusps, though scriptural scenes are depicted, the lifelike forms of many of the figures on the Roman sarcophagus may easily be recognized: the reclining matron, the servants waiting upon her, the eager children, and the heroic form of the gladiator. This pulpit marks the opening of an epoch in the history of the plastic arts. Once launched on this line, Niccolò confirmed his ideal and, training his son Giovanni and other pupils in his technique, built with them another pulpit in the cathedral of

Pulpit by Giovanni Pisano, in the Duomo, Pisa [ANDERSON].

Flight from Egypt, detail from Pisano's pulpit in the Duomo, Pisa [ANDERSON].

Siena (1266) which was a more finished work of art than the Pisa pulpit, and indeed shows some northern influence. Toward the end of his life he built a highly decorated nine-paneled fountain in the public square of Perugia, in front of the cathedral.

His son Giovanni (1250–1328) was his most brilliant pupil. Others were called to various cities of Italy to execute pulpits, reliefs, and tombs in the master's style, which thus spread to most of the peninsula. Giovanni Pisano was less influenced by the serene calm of the Roman models which had so impressed his father. His figures betray more emotion and in his works that depict scenes of passion, disorder and tumult dominate the picture. Though his control of classic line may not be questioned, there is a clear suggestion of Gothic religiosity in his figures. His most representative creations are the hexagonal pulpit at Pistoia (1302–10) and a hexagonal pulpit in the cathedral at Pisa only a few steps from his father's pulpit in the Baptistery, which by common agreement it excels in vigor, unity, and emotional stress. For fourteen years (1284–98) Giovanni was Master of Works of the cathedral at Siena. He also produced a monument to Pope Benedict XI (d. 1304) which has two angels drawing back the curtains from the recess in which the Pope's recumbent effigy lies. The design is Gothic, but the execution is classic. Giovanni had many pupils, and therefore much influence on the course of Italian sculpture. From his time Italian plastic art turns to nature for its lines and models, and nature gives life to form and substance.

Andrea Pisano (1270–1348) was a pupil of Giovanni, though his first work was in metal rather than marble. He was early called to Florence, where he kept busy under the direction of Giotto executing medallions for the Campanile and statues for the façade of the Duomo. The statues of the four Doctors of the Church—Ambrose, Augustine, Jerome, and Gregory—on the façade are his work. But without a doubt Andrea's most remarkable creation was the south doors of the Baptistery of St. John. The work was commissioned in 1330 and completed, after some difficulties in casting so large a piece in bronze, in 1336. Of the twenty-eight panels twenty are scenes from the life of St. John the Baptist and eight are figures of the Virtues. The composition is clear, the figures few, and the stories are told with direct simplicity. In 1337 Andrea succeeded Giotto as principal architect of the Duomo and remained in that position until 1343. So important a post could easily have absorbed all his time and energies. Yet, in addition to designing and building the lower section of the Campanile, we find him executing statues, altars, and tombs, designing public buildings, churches, towers, and city walls, and, in time of war, planning the city's defenses. His sculptures show a close and scientific observation of nature, warmed by a sympathetic regard for the beauty of the human frame and the dignity of classic restraint. Two of his sons, Tommasso and Nino, followed in his footsteps; the former completed the chapel in the Campo Santo at Pisa and the Campanile of the Duomo at Florence.

Pisa produced, albeit indirectly, yet another sculptor of note, Andrea di Cione Orcagna (*ca.* 1309–68), who, after years of the exacting discipline of the goldsmith's craft in his father's shop in Florence, studied sculpture under Andrea Pisano. He was a versatile artist, serving as architect and poet as well as sculptor. Under the influence of Giotto and in spite of his goldsmith's training, he was primarily a painter. Nevertheless, he is best known for the *Tabernacle of the Virgin* in the Or San Michele, close by the Duomo in Florence. This tabernacle, which gives the impression of an enlarged jewel casket, combined intaglio, mosaics, and panels in relief in varied but harmonious patterns. It bears witness to his training as a goldsmith in its mastery of detail, to his gifts as a painter in its Giottesque harmony, and to his practice as an architect in its structural congruity.

The Florentines

ORCAGNA was the last of the Pisan school, of which Niccolò had been the founder and inspiration. The leadership in sculpture during the fifteenth century—the *quattrocento*—passed to Florence. But the transition goes, as it were, from Pisa to Florence by way of Siena. Orcagna, trained by Giovanni Pisano, was influenced by Giotto and did his best work in Florence. The transition to Ghiberti would seem to be direct. Nevertheless, there comes between these two masters an artist whose powerful and versatile genius was to have weighty impact on the whole of the Florentine *quattrocento,* not least upon the last and greatest of that tradition, Michelangelo. Jacopo della Quercia (*ca.* 1375–1438) was born and trained in Siena by his father, a goldsmith. Vasari tells of his clever execution of an equestrian statue in Siena made of wood, cloth, glue, and clay. This was in 1396. In 1402 he competed unsuccessfully against Brunelleschi and Ghiberti for the bronze doors of the Florence Baptistery. We next find him in Lucca in 1406, sculpturing the marble tomb of *Ilaria del Carreto,* the wife of the tyrant of that city. For the rest of his life he went back and forth, as his commissions and not infrequently his caprice dictated, between Siena and Lucca, with shorter stays at Venice, Bologna, and Milan, frequently in search of the proper grade of marble for his works. His great merit was the range of his power: from the perfect repose, "sculptural arrest," shown in the sepulchral tomb of *Ilaria,* to the muscular, energetic vigor of the figures on the great door of San Petronio in Bologna and the equally virile figures on the three-sided fountain (*Fontegaia*) of Siena. Of this latter work only fragments remain, but there is ample evidence here as elsewhere of della Quercia's conviction that the human body should be represented in its muscular verisimilitude. He worked ten years on the portal of San Petronio and left it unfinished at his death. He designed it in thirty-three half-figures and fifteen reliefs, all in marble, some of which are his best work. The themes are all biblical: five over the door from the life of Christ; the ten reliefs on the right and left are from the Old Testament. He was able to blend Gothic and Renaissance elements in a number of his creations. But his forte was the depiction of spiritual states through attitudes of the body, as in the expulsion of Adam and Eve, sullen, broken, stooped, and sick, from Paradise. Della Quercia is the first sculptor of the Renaissance to express so powerfully the movement of which the human body is capable. Michelangelo, a whole century later, acknowledged his indebtedness to della Quercia in this portrayal.

In Lorenzo Ghiberti (1378–1455), closer in temper and genius to Orcagna than to della Quercia, Florence captured the primacy in Renaissance sculpture, hardly to be challenged during the *quattrocento.* Ghiberti was taught the goldsmith's art by his father, and his work in metal evidences the soundness of his early training. In his youth he also studied painting and tried his hand at other media as well. In 1400, because of a plague and civic disturbances at Florence, he left the city and entered the employ of Pandolfo Malatesta, the lord of Pesaro, as a painter and decorator of the ducal castle. In 1401, the plague over, the *Signoria* of Florence announced an open competition for bronze doors of the Baptistery. Seven contestants were accepted, among them Ghiberti, della Quercia, and Brunelleschi. The subject assigned for the competitive panel was the sacrifice of Isaac by Abraham. By common consent, not only of the judges but also of the contestants, Ghiberti's panel was adjudged the best, and he began work on the whole north door in 1403. The plan was similar to that of Andrea Pisano's south doors. The two parts of the door contained 28 panels, 20 from the life of Christ, the four evangelists, Matthew, Mark, Luke, and John, and the four Doctors of the Church, Ambrose, Augustine, Jerome, and Gregory. The technical problems of casting satisfactorily were great, and many of the panels had to be done over several times. The door was not completed until 1424, and at a cost to the city of Florence of 22,000 florins (equivalent to about $500,000). He had executed other works in the meantime, some at Florence and others in other cities, and he was in great demand throughout all of northern Italy. This north door shows, in the course of the years Ghiberti was engaged on it, development in the artist's con-

The Gates of Paradise, by Lorenzo Ghiberti, east doors of the Baptistery of San Giovanni Battista, Florence [BROGI].

The Sacrifice of Isaac, detail of Ghiberti's *The Gates of Paradise* [BROGI].

ceptions. The earlier panels, for example, the Annunciation and the Nativity, are similar in design and tone to the panel of the Sacrifice of Isaac with which he won the contest. They are closely related to the mode of Andrea Pisano's door, simple and direct, with few figures in the scene, and little or no complicated imagery. In later panels, for example in that of Christ carrying the Cross, Ghiberti speaks with more authority; the drama of the scene, the emotions conveyed, and the impact upon the viewer are more freely and powerfully depicted.

Sure of his medium and his own powers, Ghiberti accepted a contract to do a second door in 1425, originally intended to follow the earlier designs in twenty-eight panels. But the plan was changed, perhaps under the influence of Leonardo Bruni, to one of ten larger panels. This east door, described by Michelangelo as worthy of being the *porta del Paradiso* (the gate of Paradise), was not finished until 1452. On these spacious panels, several related incidents of biblical history are combined within one frame. To represent the various events, an illusion of spatial difference is created by a carefully calculated difference in the depth of the relief. For the first time in sculpture linear perspective is utilized to create an illusion related to time as well as to space. But even with these liberating advances in technique and concept Ghiberti faced some difficulties. The last panels, those of Moses and David and Goliath, are overcrowded. The artist has tried to tell too much. The rich borders of the door are decorated with smaller figures, full length or bust, of prophets, Old Testament characters, portraits of a few friends, and a portrait of himself. At various times in the twenty-seven years during which he was engaged on the Porta del Paradiso, upon which his fame primarily rests, he did a *St. Stephen* for the Or San Michele (1428), a shrine of *St. Zenobi* for the Florence Duomo (1432), a papal mitre for Pope Eugenius IV in Rome (1444), and worked for many years with Brunelleschi in the construction and decoration of the Duomo. About 1445 he wrote an autobiography which he called his "Commentaries," rare among artists until his time, in which he not only tells what he did, but goes into detail in describing his methods and his artistic purposes.

A younger Florentine contemporary and occasional collaborator of Ghiberti was, in the opinion of some historians of art, an even greater sculptor. He certainly produced more works of the highest quality. Donatello (1386–1466) is first heard of as a craftsman in Ghiberti's shop in 1403. His first independent creations were two small statues for the façade of the Duomo (1406–08). Until he left Florence for Rome in company with Brunelleschi in 1433 he was increasingly busy with commissions for statues, sepulchral effigies, and reliefs in marble and in bronze. Most of his commissions were for Florence, but he visited Siena, Pisa, and produced work for other cities as well. This period, from 1405 to 1433, may be called his first or Gothic period, as his execution and subjects would appear to have been influenced by Gothic models. Yet there was much flexibility in his expression, and statues like the *St. John the Evangelist* for the façade of the Duomo (1415) are full of character and power. The next year he completed the *St. George* for the Or San Michele, a highly intellectual and challenging figure of youth facing its destiny. After many works on the Duomo and the Campanile, in 1425 he finished a bronze *St. Louis of Toulouse* for the Or San Michele. It gives an initial impression of Gothic inspiration, but more careful inspection of the young figure would show that the artist was consciously presenting a medieval saint as a young and vital reality. Also from this period was the bronze *David* standing relaxed with Goliath's sword in his right hand and a stone in the left, over the severed head of the giant. It is completely natural. The model must have been a supple and graceful Tuscan shepherd boy. The works of the latter part of this first period exhibit a finished mastery of the possibilities of the human face and form.

Donatello's visit to Rome in 1433 began the second, classic period of his creative life, which lasted until 1443. The *cantoria* (singing gallery) for the Duomo in Florence, begun in 1434, was completed in 1438. Classic influences show most clearly in the architectural design. Five pairs of mosaic-filled columns with a continuous panel of singing cupids (*putti*) run the whole length of the structure. The whole impression is of the pure and unrestrained joy of children in singing and dancing.

The third, Paduan, period, from 1443 to 1454, was occupied in sculpting statues of saints, among them *St. Francis, St. Anthony, St. Louis,* and other religious subjects on the Basilica of St. Anthony in Padua. In 1447 he began work on an equestrian statue of Erasmo da Marni, nicknamed *Gattamellata,* larger than lifesize, to be placed just outside the Basilica. There is evident reliance on the equestrian statue of the Emperor Marcus Aurelius, which he must have seen in Rome. There had been no such statues made in the meantime. The detail in the statue, of both horse and rider, is fine. The rider's hands are ungloved, his armor elaborate, and the head haughty. Donatello was ever the portraitist, and here he depicted the tyrant ruler, hard, suspicious, astute, and successful.

In 1454 the sculptor left Padua for Mantua, where he did a few minor works, then returned to Florence. In this fourth period (1454–66) the power of his vision was undiminished, possibly even his ideas were too rich for his medium. He embarked upon a number of works but finished only a few. He began a pulpit for the Medici church of San Lorenzo in 1461, but died before it was finished. In some ways these last reliefs were Donatello's most powerful production. The mass of figures in the panels, by contrast with his earlier expression, individual portraiture, convey an impression of grotesque and demoniac disorder—all within the framework of the scenes of the Crucifixion and the

David, bronze, by Donatello, in the Museum of the Bargello, Florence [BROGI].

Resurrection, as if, now for the first time, and after so many years of thought, Donatello realized the horrendous tragedy of the Cross.

Among the contemporaries and friends of Ghiberti and Donatello, one artist, Luca della Robbia (1399–1482), saw his subjects in a different light. Whereas the two former were impressed with the tragic sense of life and the tense drama of destiny, Luca's work was suffused with the sweetness and serenity of confident faith. However, his fame, both in his own time and later, did not rest on this contrast between his artistic vista and that of his older colleagues. He began as a goldsmith and later in his career moved into bronze and marble. His first works may not be dated before 1428, when he was almost thirty years old, and are merely very good reliefs. His greatest work in marble was the *cantoria* or singing gallery in the Duomo in Florence, begun in 1431 and completed in 1438. The similar work of Donatello was to be placed on the opposite wall in the nave of the cathedral. Luca's *cantoria* consisted of separate panels which, together, represent Psalm 150, whose triumphant theme is "Praise ye the Lord." The mien of the youths and maidens is more serious than in the relief of Donatello; more attention is given to the music and the instruments and less to the exuberant movement of children which characterized Donatello's piece.

This creation alone would have been enough to mark Luca as one of the most significant artists of the *quattrocento*. After a few more marble pieces for the Campanile and the completion of a bronze door for the sacristy of the Duomo begun by Donatello, he apparently concluded, about 1440, that there must be a medium better suited to his artistic aims than marble or bronze. He began to work in clay, carrying his experimentation on to glazed terra cotta. Somewhere in his experimentation, probably accidentally, he came upon a process of firing the terra cotta in light colors, white, blue, flesh tints, and rose. Although majolica ware was known as early as the twelfth century, Luca's delicacy and precise handling of fine-grained terra cotta to catch his soft modeling was new. With this invention, which he improved upon with further experimentation, achieving in the process all the major colors, there began a series of remarkably exact and expressive medallions, plaques, and larger pieces, which, because of the plasticity of clay and the added effectiveness of natural colors, could not possibly have been matched in marble or bronze. Friezes, arches, and borders, even a sarcophagus, abounded in natural colored fruits and foliage. Through an incredibly productive period, from 1438 to his death in 1482, aided by his nephew Andrea della Robbia, he maintained an unchanging sculptural serenity. His many representations of the Madonna and Child, though all different, never failed to show a radiant mother and a happy and thriving child. The tensions that beset Donatello, and in lesser degree Ghiberti, never touched Luca.

Luca started a school. His nephew Andrea (1435–1525) inherited the technical secret of his polychrome glazing, but was inferior to him in artistic fervor. His best works were probably the equal of Luca's average. He in turn had seven sons, of whom five worked in the family atelier. By this time the della Robbia enamel technique had come to be applied to many household objects, such as tiles, bathrooms, and fountains. There were many imitators of the tech-

Cantoria by Luca della Robbia, in the Museum of Santa Maria del Fiore, Florence
[ANDERSON].

nique and the style. Daily living may thus have been made more artistic, but art had inevitably lost much of its spiritual motivation.

All these major artists had pupils and followers. The middle of the fifteenth century is rich in fine sculptors. The names of Desiderio da Settignano (1428–64), Antonio Rosselino (1427–79), Mino da Fiesole (1431–84), Benedetto da Majano (1442–97), and Andrea Sansovino (1460–1529) are illustrious, and occupy places of honor in the history of the plastic arts of the *quattrocento*. For our purposes, we may best limit the story of the period before Michelangelo to two, Antonio del Pollaiuolo (1429–98) and Andrea di Cione, better known as Verrocchio (1436–88).

Pollaiuolo, born in Florence and trained as a goldsmith, did his best work in Rome. As a young man he had worked for a time in Ghiberti's atelier while the Porta del Paradiso was being finished. He received commissions for fine bronze, silver, and gold pieces, remarkable for their finish and detail, and also worked in enamel. Later he studied painting with his brother Piero, who had made portraits of the leading humanists of Florence. Antonio achieved an almost equal competence, being engaged by Lorenzo de' Medici to paint both scriptural scenes and scenes from classical mythology. Sometime after the death of Pope Sixtus IV in 1484 he was invited to Rome by Sixtus' successor, Innocent VIII, to design and execute a bronze tomb for the deceased Pope. This work, showing the recumbent Pope surrounded by panels representing the Christian virtues, faith, hope, and charity, the ten arts and sciences, and the Roman virtues of fortitude, temperance, prudence, and justice, was perhaps his most impressive creation. After Innocent's death in 1492 Antonio set to work to make a monumental sarcophagus bearing a recumbent figure of the

379

Pope, which he completed just before his death in 1498. This tomb was unique in that there were two figures of Innocent, one recumbent and the other seated and speaking. Antonio ranks among the most versatile and finished of the Florentine artists. He created in gold, silver, and bronze as well as in stone. He was an accomplished armorer, engraver, designer, painter, and master of perspective. Controlling the mathematics and sciences auxiliary to his art, he was in all of them invariably competent, often brilliant.

Verrocchio was sixteen when Ghiberti's second door was mounted in the Baptistery at Florence. We must assume him to have been in the crowd at the ceremony on the Piazza del Duomo. He was almost the same age as Andrea della Robbia, whom, at least later, he knew quite intimately. Yet it was not until he was almost thirty that he appears as an independent worker in gold and other metals. His earliest known work was a *David* standing over the head of Goliath, the same theme Donatello had used thirty years before. Sometime in this decade the young Leonardo da Vinci labored and learned in Verrocchio's shop. He could hardly have had a better teacher. Verrocchio did at least fifteen pieces for the Medici, tombs for Piero and Giovanni, notable in that there is no suspicion of a Christian motif, busts of Lorenzo and Giuliano and of various women, members or friends of the Medici family. Most of Verrocchio's work avoided, in the late Renaissance spirit, any Christian touch. Yet the guild of the merchants commissioned him to do a large group of Christ and Thomas as the latter touches the wound in the Savior's side. The hands and the draping of the garments merit particular attention. The years 1465 to 1475 were almost exclusively occupied with work for the Medici. His commissions thereafter came from all over Italy. Venice invited him in 1481 to do an equestrian statue of their late general and benefactor, *Bartolommeo Colleoni*. At first angered by local jealousies, Verrocchio refused to touch his tools, but in 1485 he began work. The design and casting model were finished before his death in 1488, but finally had to be cast by his pupil Leopardi. It is a stern and forbidding warrior that sits so fiercely on a handsome charger. Every detail of eye, brow, chin, and bearing of the rider, and armor and harness is drawn in perfect naturalism. There is no better embodiment of the Italian age of the *condottieri* than Verrocchio's *Colleoni*.

Michelangelo

MICHELANGELO, however, was yet to come. The artistic genius of the Renaissance reached its peak in Michelangelo Buonarotti (d. 1564). It is difficult to keep this gigantic and terrible figure within any bounds. Born a Florentine in 1475 and apprenticed to the painter Ghirlandaio at the age of fourteen, Michelangelo Buonarotti soon found greater satisfaction in working in stone, and was taken into the family circle of Lorenzo de' Medici. Here where he associated daily with members of the Academy founded by Cosimo de' Medici and Marsilio Ficino, the beauty and poetry of Greece were presented to him under the most propitious circumstances. He also heard the preaching of Savonarola, and his serious and moral nature was deeply impressed with the message of divine indignation and coming retribution for a wayward and sinful

Bartolommeo Colleoni, designed by Andrea Verrocchio (1481), completed by Alessandro Leopardi, in the Piazza di Santi Giovanni e Paolo, Venice [ANDERSON].

world. His art was to express much of the awful fear of God's judgment which he absorbed in these early years.

When the Medici were forced out of power in Florence in 1494, Michelangelo left the city, and after a short stay in Bologna, went to Rome (1496), where his greatest work was to be done. His first substantial piece was a *Pietà,* which combined remarkably classic repose with Christian religious feeling. From 1501 to 1505 he was back in Florence. The Medici were still out of power, but Michelangelo's fame was such that he was given several valuable commissions, one of which, the *David,* is among his finest pieces. Julius II recalled him to Rome and commanded him to design and build a magnificent mausoleum for the Pope. It was to be so grand that a new and more spacious church would have to be built to house it. Thus arose the idea of the new St. Peter's. The mausoleum was to be almost a martyrdom for Michelangelo. He was torn between the demands of Julius and, after his death, those of his executors—in addition to suffering the obstruction of the later popes—for full forty years. He cried out: "I have lost all my youth tied to this tomb." Once, in 1506, he fled from Rome to escape Julius' demands, but returned two years later to undertake, still protesting, to paint the ceiling of the Sistine Chapel. The whole ceiling was done in the unbelievably short time of four years. He painted sculpture. Insisting that he was only a sculptor, he signed himself *Michelangelo Buonarotti scultore fiorentino*. Any comparison of Michelangelo with Phidias, sometimes adduced, would have to take account of the basic difference between the ages in which the two men worked. Between the Greece that produced Phidias and the age of Michelangelo the drama of Christianity had been lived. The sibyls and the prophets of the Old Testament as Michelangelo painted them were tired and troubled. The new dispensation of grace had aged all that went before, both Jewish and pagan.

In 1521, again under unwelcome compulsion, he began work on a new sacristy in the church of San Lorenzo in Florence that was to contain monuments of the Medici. In these years the city passed through tribulations and trials, and at one point Michelangelo took an active part in engineering its defense against imperial troops under the prince of Orange. In the meantime, also at the command of the Medici Pope Clement VII, he had begun (1524) the handsome Laurentian library. Soon after the settling of Florence's status in 1531 as a Medici duchy, Michelangelo returned to Rome. From 1534 to his death in 1564 he rarely left Rome. The new pope, Paul III (1534–49), obliged him to complete the planned decoration of the Sistine Chapel by painting the *Last Judgment* on the end wall. Grumbling at having to paint, he completed this tremendous work in 1542. In 1535 he had been named chief architect, sculptor, and painter of the Palace of the Vatican. He served without asking for compensation and painted a number of separate frescoes at the Pope's specification, the best known of which were the *Conversion of St. Paul* and the *Martyrdom of St. Peter*. His artistic labors, usually under compulsion from a pope or a pope's heirs, were no source of pleasure to him. The praise he got for his work interested him not at all, and he resented bitterly the frustrations and the interference from persons he did not respect. In spite of these disagreeable experiences he was able to find some compensation. During his years at Rome, at least until 1547, the year of her death, Vittoria Colonna, one of the remarkable women of the Renaissance, was his consolation and joy. They shared a fine common response to the stimuli of Christian Neoplatonism, and he was never happier than when reading his poetry or conversing with her whom he called

> The soul and heart of my fragile life
> Noble lady and gracious.

Poetry may not have been Michelangelo's best idiom, but inspired by his reading of Petrarch, by his sympathy for Ficino, and by the thought of the Academy, he nevertheless found it an outlet for sweet and powerful thoughts he was not free or able to express in stone.

> How can it be that I am no more my own
> O God, O God, my God?
> Who has torn me from myself?

or again

>These eyes of mine, fain to see the beautiful
>And my very soul, on salvation bent
>Will not prevail
>Unless heaven should come to him who looks on beauty.
>
>From the highest star
>There falls a splendor
>Which upward draws desire
>Nor does the warmed heart have else
>To bring it love and wise device
>Than a face whose eyes regard the soul.

Not only his poetry, but his letters as well, show the terrible forces which stirred in Michelangelo, struggling for expression, and it is not difficult to understand why his contemporaries spoke of his *terribilità*. His intense artistic power, the fire that burned in him, gave him no rest and caused men to shrink from him. His figures, painted on the Sistine ceiling or graven in marble, such as the *David* and the seated *Moses,* his lyrics, nervous yet bridled by his own austere will, all betrayed a nature eager to challenge the gods, yet humble before the great and simple truths of Christian revelation.

His last years were lonely. He had outlived friends and rivals. He occupied himself with poetry and contemplation, his tempestuous inner forces mellowed with time and the world's recognition of his supremacy in every field of art. In Renaissance art he towers, alone.

France

FRANCE had been the home of Gothic art, which had flowered in that congenial atmosphere. The cathedrals and public buildings had been richly decorated by Gothic statuary on portals and façades, and inside the sanctuaries chapels and aisles were adorned by tombs with elaborate recumbent effigies of kings, nobles, and prelates, while in panels around the base would appear figures of retainers or mourners, or in some cases iconography of patron saints. The theme of virtually all French sculpture of the late Gothic period, that is, the last two centuries of the Middle Ages, was religious. About the year 1300 a change in the manner of execution took place. Although the themes remained substantially what they had been in the glorious thirteenth century, a slight tendency toward realism, a recognition of movement and individualism emerges. More of the Gothic figures are obvious attempts at portraiture, and joy and grief, power and purpose, are no longer hidden from the beholder. The body has not yet been systematically studied, and drapery remained more important than an accurate representation of the human form. In the relief panels of the *Creation* on the north portal of the cathedral of Auxerre (early fourteenth century) Adam and Eve are conventional nudes, but God is fully clothed. Cain and Abel are both cowled. The tomb surmounted by an effigy of the occupant, frequently accompanied by his wife, became very popular in the course of the fourteenth century, and many "tomb-makers" grew expert in a sort of portraiture. The quality of stone, not always marble, was inferior to Italian marble. The coarser grain of French stone was less likely to tempt the mason to venture beyond a minimally true likeness of his subject.

Toward the end of the fourteenth century, however, a new current set in, precipitated largely by the arrival (1386) in Dijon, the capital of the dukes of Burgundy, of a Flemish artist, Claus Sluter (d. 1406). He took in hand the completion of the tomb of *Philip the Hardy,* for which he used alabaster and, for the platform on which the effigy was to rest, black marble from Flanders. Sluter died in 1406, but his nephew Claus de Werve (d. 1439), working in the same tradition, completed the monument in 1410. It is in this type of monumental statuary, and notably in Burgundy, that we will find the best examples of portraiture and movement in all of France. Nevertheless, the influence of Sluter and his pupils spread far beyond the confines of Burgundy. In France there were many statues of the Madonna and Child, and some efforts to portray life and movement, but the heavy drapery and the demands of conventionalism in posture and expression tended to obstruct freedom and experimentation.

In those parts of France under English control during the Hundred Years' War or devastated by the operations of the war, there was little or no artistic creation from the early fourteenth to mid-fifteenth century. When, about 1450, these areas were again free and French, the artists began where their predecessors had left off over a century before. Thus the façade of the cathedral of Rouen, completed in 1486, is basically a Gothic conception, although Flemish and Burgundian influences are clearly traceable. By the turn of the century a species of naturalism and attention to individualism and movement was noticeable throughout France, though the framework was still strongly medieval. It was not until after Charles VIII and his army returned (1495) from the Italian fiasco with new ideas and some Italian artists that the new realism and classical and secular motifs began to interest the French and dictate the direction artistic expression would thereafter take.

Germany

IN GERMANY, until the Black Death (1348), the plastic arts were in a heavy Gothic mold and the subjects were almost exclusively ecclesiastical. The relief felt by all classes at the passing of the plague showed in the statuary in the churches. There was more emotion portrayed, both joy and sorrow, and a degree of individualism appeared in monumental effigies for secular as well as for ecclesiastical personages. Heavy drapery, however, still concealed any anatomical precision. The court of the Emperor Charles IV at Prague was a lively center of international intellectual and artistic activity. Drawing upon his French experience, Charles first (1344) invited a north French architect, Matthew of Arras, to plan the cathedral of the newly created archbishopric on north French Gothic lines. On Matthew's death in 1352 a young Swabian architect and sculptor, Peter Parler, was invited to Prague. From 1353 to his death in 1399 Parler carried on the construction of the cathedral of St. Vitus, modifying slightly the plan, and established a school of sculptors who were responsible for

The Unicorn Is Wounded, sixth of the Unicorn Tapestries, in the Cloisters, New York [THE METROPOLITAN MUSEUM OF ART, THE CLOISTERS COLLECTION, GIFT OF JOHN D. ROCKEFELLER, JR., 1937].

busts, tombs, and ecclesiastical statuary in Bohemia until the devastating beginning of the Hussite wars in 1419.

In the rest of the Empire, at Vienna, Strassburg, Ulm, Nürnberg, Freiburg, Erfurt, and other centers, there was much sculpture being done in the fourteenth and on into the fifteenth century. But the content was strictly medieval Gothic, conventional, formal, unscientific, unanatomical, attitudinal, and symbolic rather than realistic. The second half of the fifteenth century sees some development in the direction of realism. At Nürnberg a distinct school of sculpture developed, of which the leaders were Veit Stoss (1447–1533), Adam Krafft (*ca.* 1460–1508), and Peter Vischer (1460–1529). Stoss worked in wood, and all his subjects are scriptural. The earliest dated work is the altar-screen in the church of St. Mary in Cracow, begun in 1477. Krafft worked exclusively in stone, and his most impressive work is the ornately decorated high (65 feet) tabernacle in the church of St. Lawrence in Nürnberg. His favorite decoration was from nature, leaves, trees, and flowers. Vischer's two sons had traveled and studied in Italy, and his own close attention to anatomical detail reflects the influence of Italian realism.

In central Germany Tilman Riemenschneider (1468–1531) was the leading sculptor, working both in wood and in stone. He was a careful workman, even in nudes, unafraid to portray sentiment, whether through design or in portraiture, but the content of his work is strongly Gothic. Nevertheless, even taking into account the progress achieved by Vischer and Riemenschneider, and it was considerable, no German made any real approach to the realism in which Italy, from Niccolò Pisano in the mid-thirteenth century, was so rich until Albrecht Dürer (1471–1538). Dürer did not work in the third dimension of sculpture, yet in his sketching and painting he not only faithfully delineated scientific observation but added to that linear precision the interpretation of character and emotion.

England

THE close political, as well as geographical, connection between England and France in the thirteenth century will easily account for similarities between English and French artistic tradition. Yet there were differences due to climate, social and political particularities, and a long history of ecclesiastical separation. In England, as in France, the thirteenth century was the great century of cathedral building. The magnificent cathedrals of Wells, Lincoln, Salisbury, York, Ely, Winchester, Worcester, and Westminster Abbey, if not begun in that century, were at least largely built and decorated in the period from Richard I (the Lion Hearted) to Edward II. Façades, portals, corners, capitals, and towers called for decoration, and stonemasons were only too pleased to try their skill. The motifs and the intricate designs employed are frequently impressive and not seldom graceful. But the sculpture is usually clumsy. More often than in France and Germany the subjects of the statuary were secular personages, kings and queens and noble patrons of the Church. Inside the churches monumental effigies, as often of knights as of bishops, crowd the aisles while the English penchant for wood-carving found a ready outlet in the decoration of choir stalls, screens, and pulpits.

The fourteenth century witnessed only a slight change, and that in the direction of greater ornateness, more elaborate borders, and finer attention to detail of hair, drapery, and ornament. It was in this period that, for example, at Lincoln, Wells, St. Albans, and Exeter, there appeared many heads of monarchs, bishops, abbots, master masons, placed right at the spring of the arches or as stops or corbels. The stonemason—for it was he and not a professional sculptor who did these heads—often gave a lively expression to these portraits. The total mass of this sculpture over all of England is tremendous. The façades of Exeter and Wells cathedrals alone must each count several hundred statues, half life-size and larger. In addition there was the work on the inside of the church, reredos, choir and altar, monumental effigies, and occasional pieces.

About the middle of the fifteenth century more emphasis was given to a portraiture in stone which made a determined effort to depict character and emotion. There are extant fine statues and busts of kings and prelates which lead directly to the great collection in Henry VII's Chapel in Westminster Abbey. They are still, of course, heavily draped, so that we have no means of knowing how far the mastery of anatomy and movement had progressed. As one looks back from about 1500 on English sculpture, the impression is not one of a vital artistic tradition. It is still determinedly English Gothic. The spirit of the Renaissance had not yet come to England.

Spain

THE Gothic influence came to Spain from France early in the thirteenth century and, with Spanish modifications, remained strong until the beginning of the sixteenth century. León and Castile, having close cultural ties with northern France, took to the Gothic with enthusiasm; the cathedrals of Burgos, León, Cuenca, and Ciudad Rodrigo are almost pure Gothic, while Toledo, farther south, shows strong French influence. Sculpture, in the Gothic period intimately connected with architectural structure, followed the same course, reflecting French motifs and concepts. In Catalonia, on the other hand, the importation of artistic ideas was from Provence and from southern Italy, which belonged to the crown of Aragon for some of this period. The cathedral of Barcelona, while undoubtedly Gothic in many respects, yet represents some features that recall the Romanesque of the cathedral of Narbonne. The transepts, for example, are undeveloped, and the arches of the vertical windows in the apse are almost semicircular. Again, ecclesiastical sculpture ran parallel to this composite in style. The favorite monument to a king or queen was a sarcophagus capped by a recumbent statue of the subject, frequently under a decorated canopy. In the fifteenth century, as techniques improved and Spanish artists gained confidence, the border decorations diverged from the Gothic and revealed a growing interest in natural forms, flowers, leaves, conceits, and designs of various sorts, some doubtless traceable to Moorish models. Although, as a usual thing, in the Gothic tradition, sculpture was anonymous, enough of these Spanish artists are known by name for us to distinguish a school of sculpture at Poblet in Catalonia, where the royal family had a burial place. About the middle of the fifteenth century Spain began to feel the influence of Flemish and Burgundian art. In sum, Spanish art was in large measure passive and receptive through the fifteenth century. The great age of Spanish artistic creativity, fanatically religious, awesome, proud and grim, was yet to come.

Looking back over the story of sculpture—of primary significance because of its emphasis on the third dimension which the painter strives to represent on a flat surface—it becomes clear that Italy, and particularly Florence, bred the initiators of the new course. The freedom and imaginative flair, the daring spirit that brooked no binding conventions, but had eyes only for the natural and the true, this we find only in Italy. Any comparison of the realistic, scientific sculpture that was accepted throughout Italy by the year 1400 with the stilted, formal, and stable styles which we find in France and spreading from there to Germany, England, or Spain, however well the artists in these countries may have commanded their own styles, might make the observer wonder what actually the northern artists thought they saw or were trying to represent. Obviously any comparison of artistic styles and conventions must take into consideration time and place, the assumptions and demands of the society toward which the artist can work. But in the case of the Italian plastic artists of the late Middle Ages, that is, the period of the early Renaissance, it must be accepted that they brought about a revolution in creative vision. After they had spoken in marble or bronze, sculpture and indeed all art could never be the same again.

PAINTING

THE art of painting did not suffer the near eclipse that befell sculpture in the centuries after the fall of the Roman Empire. The Byzantine tradition lingered on, particularly in southern Italy and in the areas such as Ravenna and Venice, where relations with Byzantium, commercial and cultural, persisted. Vasari, writing in the mid-sixteenth century of the artists of the early Renaissance, emphasizes the Byzantine tradition that, dominant throughout the thirteenth century, had so profound an influence upon the initiators of the new course. Vasari began his story of the painters whom he regarded as exponents of the "new method of design and painting" with an account of the life and work of Cimabue (1240–1302). But we now know that Cimabue had predecessors, formed and trained in the Byzantine tradition, who made altarpieces, painted frescoes on walls, or painted on wood. Indeed, we know the names of several of these artists who heralded the dawn of the new and living art: Giunta, who probably did some of the earliest paintings on wood of the Franciscan tradition, and the Roman artist Pietro Cavallini (ca. 1250–1330), who composed some mosaics which, while adhering to Byzantine subjects and techniques, yet succeeded in adding a note of personalism and life to the formalism of the Byzantine school. Cavallini was called to Assisi to decorate the new church of St. Francis, and may have met there the younger Cimabue. Other works of his have recently been discovered in Rome.

Cimabue and Giotto

CIMABUE, of a noble Florentine family, has left a renown beyond the catalogue of his authenticated creations. That he was deeply influenced by the Byzantine masters there is no doubt. Not only are most of his subjects in the Byzantine line, but the arrangement of the persons and objects in his frescoes in the Upper and the Lower Church at Assisi are quite Byzantine. On the other hand, the representation of individual characters in his works is as likely as not to be of quite distinguishable persons, clearly done from living models and not, as in almost all Byzantine work, a lifeless and conventional delineation. Cimabue's pupil and successor was Giotto (1276–1336). Vasari tells a de-

The Fire Test before the Sultan, fresco by Giotto, in the Church of Santa Croce, Florence [ALINARI].

lightful story of Cimabue's discovery of the young Giotto. Passing by on a country road, he saw a young shepherd boy drawing sheep on a slate. He forthwith got the boy's father's permission to take the lad into his home and shop. It was this gifted boy who was to grow up to be the real and productive initiator of the new painting of the Renaissance. Though trained by Cimabue and influenced by Giovanni Pisano the sculptor, Giotto went beyond his masters in the freshness of his inspiration. He was a lover of nature and of his fellow man. Thus rooted, it is small wonder that he and Dante—then an exile— should, when they met at Padua, have found much in common. Dante says of him in the *Comedy* while he was still alive that he had already displaced Cimabue as the leading painter of Italy. He worked in many places in Italy, Assisi, Florence, and Padua. At this latter place he decorated the walls of the Arena Chapel with frescoes drawn from the life of Christ and the lives of the saints (1305). He also worked at Naples, and probably stayed and worked for several years at Avignon, between the years 1309 and 1314. In each place he had pupils, who passed on his temper and techniques, so that all Italy felt, in greater or lesser degree, the impact of his appeal to nature. To such a child of nature the Franciscan spirituality would inevitably be congenial, and Giotto's warmest frescoes are those which have St. Francis as their center. The spirit of the *Little Flowers* (*Fioretti*) radiates from almost all of his creations, not only in the basilica at Assisi, but also in the Barbi Chapel in Florence and in other and smaller panels of scenes in the life of Christ and the saints. Some of his pupils approached his mastery of the portrayal of joy and sorrow, anxiety and pain, but none really reached his level. Orcagna, whom we met earlier as a brilliant sculptor, counted himself a pupil of Giotto and has left a number of powerful and at the same time charming frescoes, done about 1350. His painting of the *Last Judgment* on the wall of the Strozzi Chapel in Santa Maria Novella, finished in 1357, is especially striking.

Early Sienese Painting

CONTEMPORARY with Giotto there was growing up a school of painting at Siena, of which the most productive and influential leader was Duccio (*ca.* 1260–1319). He painted an altarpiece of the Virgin on wood (completed in 1310), which aroused such devotion that the whole town closed shop on the occasion of its installation. It is regarded as the masterpiece of the Sienese school. In his concept Duccio followed the Byzantine style, but in details of attitudes of the persons, both of the Virgin and of the angels surrounding her, he depicted grace and devout sentiment. Duccio was followed by his pupil Simone Martini (1284–1344), who became a friend of Petrarch at Avignon. Among his many works were frescoes in the basilica at Assisi and the *Assumption of the Virgin* in the Campo Santo in Pisa, some paintings on wood in Naples, and an altar now in the Uffizzi Gallery at Florence. Martini's technique was superb and his production prolific, but he lacked the warmth and inner grace of Duccio. After Martini, the leaders of the Sienese school were the Lorenzetti brothers, Pietro and Ambrogio, who, in addition to work in Siena, also took part in the decoration of the Assisi basilica. Ambrogio Lorenzetti (d. 1348) ventured into the field of civic and political art. The spacious walls of the Palazzo Pubblico of Siena called for a grandiose message. On one wall he painted an allegory of *Good Government,* lauding the classic virtues, Power, Prudence, Justice, Magnanimity, Peace, and so on; on the other wall he painted a corresponding representation of *Evil Government.* Facile rather than profound, he did other narrative works in tempera and fresco in Orvieto and Cortona. Vasari remarked of him that "his manners were more those of a gentleman and philosopher than of an artist."

The efforts of the Lorenzetti to keep Siena a leader in artistic creativity were only moderately successful; after them the school was somewhat isolated from the more vigorous trends of Italian painting. One of the later Sienese painters, Stefano di Giovanni, better known as Sasseta (1392–1450), might be excepted from this category of deterioration. His work was distinguished by tenderness and delicacy, combining deep emotion, technical perfection, and imaginative vitality. Seen in relation to other schools of painting, the emphasis of the whole Sienese group of painters, almost to the end of the fifteenth century, on legend, mysticism, and ostentatious detail indicated confusion in place of conviction, imitation instead of creative originality. It was not until the very end of the century that art at Siena showed any real inclination to catch up with the humanistic current of the Renaissance. Sienese medievalism had made a gallant stand, but the naturalism of Florentine and Umbrian painters and sculptors finally, inexorably, won the day.

The number of *trecento* artists, many of them competent and some excellent, who have not been mentioned, even in Florence and Siena, is legion. And elsewhere in Italy, as in Padua and Verona, Milan and Bologna, there are paintings from this period which, seen in isolation from the more significant currents of development we have suggested here, will impress by their control of the techniques of fresco and canvas, by the largeness of their concept, or the freshness of detail. The Renaissance in art, though pre-eminently a Tuscan and Umbrian movement, could be found elsewhere in Italy. In Venice, however, there was almost complete isolation from the rest of the peninsula. The Byzantine tradition was still weighing heavily on the Queen of the Adriatic. The period of Venetian artistic greatness was yet to come.

Florence in the *Quattrocento*

WE MUST now resume the story of Florentine painting where we left it, late in the fourteenth century. The next great landmark in Renaissance painting is the revolutionary work of Masaccio (1401–28), but two of his older contemporaries, Masolino (1383–*ca.* 1447) and Fra Angelico (1387–1455), are, as artists, of almost equal significance, and, by reason of their longer life-spans and the fact that their own work illustrates the changing concepts of artistic authenticity, more instructive. Both Masolino and Fra Angelico began to paint under the influence of the Gothic tradition. Of the two, perhaps Fra Angelico remained closer to the Gothic spirit. Although he studied the new naturalism and profited from it, to the end of his life his work retained a devout and emotional cast. His influence in this direction was felt well into the sixteenth century, not only in Florence and Umbria but in Rome as well, where, beginning with Pope Nicholas V (1447–55), this genre of painting was welcomed. His ablest pupil, Benozzo Gozzoli (1420–97), though highly regarded in his own day, has since often been called the last of the Gothic painters. For the development of the art toward its fullest expression he has only minor significance.

Contemporary with the beginnings of Masolino and Fra Angelico the new current of naturalism in sculpture was gaining ground and prestige. It will be remembered that Ghiberti and Brunelleschi competed in Florence in 1401 for the contract to do the Baptistery. The impulse thus given to a study of the forms of nature, perspective and light and shade, was soon transferred to painting, as the painters began to experiment in their medium to see how well they could reproduce on a flat surface the depth the sculptor was able to realize in his three-dimensional stone.

Vasari tells us that Masaccio was a pupil of Masolino. It is hard to understand how a painter who died when still a young man of twenty-seven could have "early" and "late" periods. Nevertheless, such is the case. Frescoes and panels ascribed to him show a whole gamut of change and development. His early works, dated in 1423 or 1424, already indicate his freedom from Gothic stiffness and a control of the laws of tactile impression. One almost expects the figures in the *Christ and the Tribute Money* to move and speak. Masolino and Masaccio worked together on the frescoes in the Brancacci chapel in Florence, but the scenes done after Masolino left are easily recognizable as the work of the younger and more expressive artist. He had followed his earlier line of thought and artistry and succeeded in giving a full impression of depth to forms and faces. His *Expulsion from Paradise* is so lifelike it can hardly be distinguished from the same subject done in deep relief by Della Quercia, to whom, as we remarked above (p. 373), Michelangelo was indebted. In others of his frescoes in Santa Maria Novella in Florence, Masaccio employed architectural design (here intimately influenced by Brunelleschi) as a framework for his enscenements. Formal perspective lining heightened the impression of depth and emphasized the tactile impression achieved by his delicate use of light and shade.

Of the notable Italian painters of the *quattrocento* between Masaccio and Leonardo da Vinci, and they were many and productive, we can mention only a few. Paolo Uccello (1396–1475), Castagno (*ca.* 1410–57) and Domenico Veneziano (*ca.* 1400–61) are classed as experimentalists whose subjects reached far beyond the conventional biblical and legendary scenes. Uccello, for example, who had worked as an apprentice in Ghiberti's shop, did an equestrian fresco of the English *condottiere* John Hawkwood and several battle scenes for the Medici palace. Castagno did a series of fresco portraits of famous men which revealed careful study of action and of human and equine musculature. Domenico felt that the chiaroscuro which other painters had been content to use really obscured significant details, and, in a number of profile portraits as well as in larger frescoes, he used shades of green, blue, pink, and white to emphasize or clarify not only perspective, but expression and concept. The painters of the new naturalist current, it would appear, whether traditionalists or experimentalists, achieved their effects by accident, by intuition, or by conscious trial and error. It took a nonpainter, the architect Leone Battista Alberti (1404–72), to apply mathematics and analysis to the problems of pictorial representation and put the results of scientific thought into some order. In the thought of Alberti mathematics and science are handmaidens of art. In a short treatise *On Painting* (*De pictura*) in 1435 Alberti analyzed mathematically perspective, color, and light and shade, insisting on the congruence of natural physical laws and the laws of vision. If the painter obeys these laws he will faithfully represent his subject and the eye will then see what is actually there. The influence of Alberti in advancing the use of mathematics in art portrayal was profound.

The primacy of Florence as a center of artistic creativity during the *quattrocento* was not really challenged until the end of the century, which corresponds to what historians of art call the High Renaissance. But during this brilliant century in other cities and at other courts there were artists of rich talent and serious purpose, the mere list of whose names and works would fill a volume.

Perugia had her Perugino (1450–1532), who did frescoes in Florence and Rome. Venice, breaking gradually out of the Byzantine tradition early in the *quattrocento,* learned the mysteries of the new naturalism at first from outsiders who were imported; but Jacopo Bellini (1400–*ca.* 1470) and his sons Gentile (1429–1507) and Giovanni (1426–1516) founded a tradition of realistic detail in portraiture which many artists of the sixteenth century tried to follow. The latter's portrait of the Venetian Doge Loredano is the best-known example of his refined naturalism. Padua, since 1405 a possession of Venice, maintained nevertheless a degree of cultural independence. Andrea Mantegna (1431–1506), a pupil of a Paduan artist, Squarcione (1394–1474), was employed at the court of the Gonzaga at Mantua and executed commissions in Verona, Florence, and Rome as well as in Padua. He also worked in copper, which showed better than the canvas or the fresco his exacting draftsmanship. Verona, Ferrara, Bologna, and Milan also produced artists whose best work might rank with some of these we have mentioned. Yet their average was much below that of the Florentines and the Umbrians. The rulers in these cities, however, were ambitious to have the sanction of the presence of distinguished artists, and we will find many of the Florentines and the Umbrians visiting the courts of the Gonzaga, the Este, the Sforza, or the Urbino families and influencing or inspiring the local artists by their work and instruction.

Piero della Francesca (dei Franceschi) (*ca.* 1415–92), a native of Borgo San Sepolcro in Umbria, owed much to his Florentine teachers, and in his person brings together much of the best of the Umbrian and the Florentine traditions. In 1439 he was an assistant to Domenico Veneziano when the latter was painting the frescoes in the church of San Egidio in Florence. There were active in the Florence of that time Uccello, Donatello, Brunelleschi, and Alberti. All of Piero's later painting reflects the influence of Alberti's mathematical ideas. He spent at least six years in Florence, then returned to Borgo San Sepolcro to paint an altarpiece—the *Madonna of the Confraternity of Mercy* (1445). The design is almost an isosceles triangle crowned by a semicircle. Thereafter he had commissions in Ferrara, at the Vatican, at Rimini, Urbino, and Arezzo. At Arezzo he finished in 1466 a memorable fresco on the spacious walls of the choir of the church of St. Francis: the whole *Legend of the Holy Cross* from Adam, the planting of the tree on Adam's grave—to the battle between Chosroës and Heraclius in the seventh century as told by James of Voragine in the *Golden Legend*. The fresco, in three horizontal bands and ten scenes, was heroic in concept and execution. Each of the ten scenes tells its story in rich if static detail. Piero avoids movement and his figures seem poised and serene. He is intent on control of light and shadow, mathematical balance in composition, and a use of color that would combine representation of nature with the inner meaning of the scene. The *Resurrection of Christ,* in the Town Hall of Borgo San Sepolcro may be his most striking work. A muscular and majestic Christ stepping out of the tomb is squarely in the middle of the picture. In the background both to the right and left are straight trees, in front of Him four Roman soldiers, asleep, grouped by twos to right and left. The flexible use of rose-pink, gold, cool gray, green, burnt orange, and purple to emphasize and project the painter's desire to make the figure of Christ dominate the scene is especially effective. Piero did some portraits and, late in life, wrote much about his theories of painting and architecture. He was more conscious of the developments in these fields than most of his contemporaries, and his penchant for a geometric and mathematical framework for all art creation runs parallel with the classic themes of the next century.

Back in Florence the ground was being prepared which was to bear its richest fruit in Leonardo da Vinci. The second half of the *quattrocento* pro-

The Resurrection, by Piero della Francesca, in the town hall of Borgo San Sepolcro [ALINARI].

duced several competent painters who continued the tradition of Masaccio and the experimentalists, fully attentive to the realism which accorded with scientific observation. Happy to profit by the advances made in the use of color, light, and shade, they nevertheless sought to give due place to the portrayal of emotion and psychological background to every scene. Baldovinetti (1425–99) and the brothers Pollaiuolo (Antonio, 1433–98, and Piero, 1443–96) are the leading representatives of this later line of development. The Pollaiuoli worked in Rome as well as in Florence, and branched out into work in bronze

The Expulsion of Adam and Eve from Paradise, by Masaccio, in the Brancacci Chapel, Santa Maria del Carmine, Florence [ALINARI].

and gold. Thus trained in observing detail, the brothers went on to a careful study of anatomical representation, and their canvases, panels, and frescoes, whether free or crowded, indicate their scrupulous attention to the human form. Andrea Verrocchio (1436–88) is most renowned for having been the teacher of Leonardo da Vinci, but his influence on Florentine painters was strong. The statue of *Colleoni* (see above, p. 381), so forceful, imposing, and harmonious, obliged all portrait painters—and all painters needed to paint portraits of their patrons—to re-examine their work in order to see if they were creating in their medium an effect upon the onlooker at all comparable to that made by the equestrian statue. The paintings known to be by Verrocchio reveal his concern for anatomical precision; in his atelier principles of careful observation were unequivocally demanded.

Two of the most popular and prolific painters of the late *quattrocento* were Domenico Ghirlandaio (1449–94) and Sandro Botticelli (1444–1510). Both were in the soft tradition of Fra Filippo Lippi, excelling in an agreeable utilization of techniques achieved by earlier experimentalists, so presented as to please patrons and avoid disturbing anybody's conscience. It may be of historical value to know what a mistress of a rich patron looked like; it is equally instructive to see her represented as a saint or the Virgin Mary. Christian themes were used as an excuse for grandiose exhibits of the painter's mastery of perspective, costume, and architectural detail. Botticelli's *Spring* and the *Birth of Venus* show how he conceived grace and curves, but he felt it unnecessary to obey the laws of physics. In the former, at least one of the Graces would have fallen over, and in the latter, Venus could not possibly have stayed erect another second without support. But perhaps Venus needed no support in Florence. However fragile and delicate his style may have been, tragedy was not beyond the scope of Botticelli. In his last works he speaks more shrilly, and in his pencil illustrations to Dante's *Divine Comedy* as well as in a late *Pietà* he reveals his understanding of the tragic sense of life. At the end he did much to redeem the early years of facile grace and little else. What Renaissance art of the late *quattrocento* needed was precisely what it got from Leonardo da Vinci, a recall to honest reality and a purposeful appeal to nature.

Leonardo da Vinci

LEONARDO we have met earlier as an engineer, musician, scientist, anatomist, and writer. He was truly the universal man of the Renaissance. He regarded painting as the highest art; yet, involved in the distractions of the life of a courtier at Milan at the beck and call of Giangaleazzo Sforza, and also congenitally disinclined to bring a work of art to arduous completion, he did not finish many paintings. Among the few he did complete, three, each in its genre, are probably the greatest in the world: the *Madonna of the Rocks,* the *Last Supper,* and the Louvre *Gioconda:* a devotional panel, a monumental fresco, and an oil portrait. The *Madonna* was done about 1480, the *Last Supper* (in the refectory of Sta. Maria delle Grazie in Milan, miraculously intact after a bomb hit during the Second World War) in 1498, the *Gioconda* finished in Florence in 1504. Leonardo's supreme mastery of the medium is evident in every stroke. His pencil sketches show how accurate was his anatomical eye, and how, above and beyond that, he was able to convey spirit and essence in physical movement. This basic dexterity, furthermore, was fitted into superbly divined design, executed with a sense of monumental proportion, as in the *Last Supper*. Where the magic and mystery of color were added to detail and design, the result beggars description. He has been probably the most influential painter in our European tradition. There were none to match him among those who came after. But a younger contemporary, who painted more, and also sculptured much, must be placed very near Leonardo.

While Leonardo preferred painting, Michelangelo spoke of himself as a sculptor, and when he painted, as on the ceiling of the Sistine Chapel, he was painting what he saw—sculpture. It was his genius that he was able to transfer his vision to a flat surface. He finished by 1512 the fresco which he had undertaken so reluctantly. He would have preferred never to touch a paintbrush again had not Pope Clement VII commanded him in 1533 to paint the *Last Judgment* on the altar wall of the same chapel. After this tremendous work was finished in 1541, he agreed to do the frescoes on two walls in the chapel of St. Paul in Rome for Pope Paul III. This last work lacked the unity and harmony of the *Last Judgment*. The last phase of Michelangelo's life, from *ca.* 1550 to 1564, was dedicated to the design and building of the church of St. Peter's in Rome, the seat of the popes and the leading sanctuary of Chris-

Self-portrait, by Leonardo da Vinci, in the Uffizi Gallery, Florence [ALINARI].

tendom. We must now turn briefly to the story of architectural change in these centuries.

ARCHITECTURE

THE Gothic style in ecclesiastical architecture first appeared in the Île de France, in the neighborhood of Paris, about the middle of the twelfth century, and spread steadily, in church and monastic building, throughout France and across her frontiers to England, to Spain, to Germany, and to the Lowlands, and, later and more slowly, to Italy. Of necessity we use the term Gothic somewhat loosely. The pointed arch, ribbed vault, flying buttress, and cruciform floor plan are generally accepted as the more distinctive characteristics of the style. But local or national modifications or tradition might alter the plan almost beyond recognition. With each remove from the region of its birth this style lost something of its original character and took on something of the land to which it had migrated. Spanish Gothic, for example, was noticeably different from French or German Gothic. Many factors entered into this differentiation: climate and the quality of light, the availability of proper building materials, the fancies of local or imported architects, the demands or the taste of the ecclesiastic or prince who let the contract and paid for the construction.

Whereas, in the case of the two sensitive arts that we have thus far considered, sculpture and painting, the nature of the medium allowed rapid responses to changes in techniques or style, in the case of architecture, the slow completion of a church or building lent a certain stability to style, which was lacking in the other arts and had the effect of retarding change. Scarcely a church of any size anywhere in Europe took less than sixty years to build, some took over a full century, a few were completed only in the nineteenth or twentieth century. Some indeed have never been completed. We are compelled, largely for these reasons, to accept a periodization of architectural styles quite different from that for the more responsive arts. We must speak of the dominance of the Gothic style in European building, ecclesiastical and civic, from about 1200 to about 1500. On the other hand, in Italy, and particularly in Tuscany, in Umbria, and in Lombardy, where building revived in the early fifteenth century, we must allow a Renaissance style beginning about 1400–20 and extending on into the sixteenth century, tapering off into the Baroque. This overlapping of style in architecture must be understood if we are to avoid false and misleading periodizations.

France

GOTHIC architecture in France, which led and inspired all Europe, passed through three generally recognized phases: (1) early or ogival, (2) radial or circular, and (3) flamboyant. The best examples of the earliest style are the monastic church of St. Denis in Paris, begun by the Abbot Suger in 1140, and the cathedrals of Sens (begun in 1143) and Senlis (begun in 1150). The cathedrals of Notre Dame in Paris (1163–1235), Laon (1160–1205), and Soissons

Amiens cathedral, planned by Robert de Luzarches, built chiefly between 1220 and 1288. Note the heavy façade, the massive towers, the delicate flèche at the crossing of the nave and transept, and the double flying buttresses [AEROFILMS, LTD.].

(1160–1212) all show some very early features, but have undergone modifications, either in proportion of height to base, the insertion of circular traceried windows in the façade or in the transepts, sometimes both, double or single aisles, in the degree of pointedness in the arches or the window framing, or perhaps in varying the number of stories in the nave from the conventional three, triforium, arcade, and clerestory, to four. The first period easily passed over into the second or circular period. The more prominent ecclesiastical edifices from this second period are the cathedrals of Rheims (1212–41), Amiens (1220–99), and Bourges (1190–1275). On the other hand, little alteration in plan or technique appeared in north French cathedrals until the middle of the next century, beyond a tendency to thin walls and an increase in the number of windows. French cathedrals, in many cases, have double aisles (e.g., Notre Dame in Paris and the cathedral of Bourges), semicircular apses with ambulatory east of the choir, and usually have two towers in the west and a slender flèche arising out of the crossing of the nave and apse. The height of the nave vault is great. In southern France many Romanesque traits persisted. The walls were heavy and much less windowed. The buttresses were inside, acting as partitions between chapels which opened on the nave. Triforia were felt to be unnecessary and seldom appeared. Finally the transept almost disappeared. We have mostly an aisled basilican floor plan, as at Albi, constructed at the end of the thirteenth century, and the church of the Jacobins in Toulouse, built about 1300.

The Hundred Years' War was almost disastrous for French architecture. What construction there was, even in areas not directly affected by the war, lacked vigor and conviction. But as soon as it was certain that the English were on the run, a new spirit emerged. French architecture, like nationalism, found fresh inspiration, and burst out in the exuberance and abandon of Flamboyant Gothic. It was perhaps poetic justice that, as the English were driven out of France, they left behind them with the French, as if in payment for damages, the heritage of their own Decorated Gothic style. The Flamboyant is little else than an adaptation of the richly sinuous style which at that very moment the English were beginning to desert for the more austere Perpendicular. The first trace of the new style may be noticed in a chapel in Amiens cathedral. It became popular only after 1400. By the mid-fifteenth century this joyous, flowing, and unrestrained style had spread to all parts of France. There was hardly a corner, a molding, a capital, a window, or a pinnacle that was not used by the masons to show their happy ingenuity. In addition to churches and cathedrals built or decorated wholly or partially in this style, there are many civic and domestic buildings in Flamboyant Gothic. The Palace of Justice in Rouen and the private mansion of Jacques Coeur, the financial wizard who served Charles VII, in Bourges, were both built around 1450. This was indeed the last flowering of French architectural and decorative genius until late in the fifteenth century.

Home of Jacques Coeur, built *ca.* 1450 in Bourges [GIRAUDON].

Château d' Azay-le-Rideau, in the Loire district [GEORGIA ENGELHARD, MONKMEYER].

Toward the end of the century traces of Italian Renaissance architecture may be found. This is especially true of secular architecture. The medieval fortress of king and noble gave way during the fifteenth century to the château of king, seigneur, and rich bourgeois. The valley of the Loire was soon dotted with these many-towered and richly decorated châteaux. Two years before he left on his Italian venture in 1494, Charles VIII had begun construction of his royal château at Amboise. Italian touches are already evident. When he returned from Italy he brought twenty Italian artists and artisans with him and the adaptation of Italian concepts of comfort and elegance to French requirements proceeded at a more rapid pace, as more châteaux were built. The château d'Azay-le-Rideau on the Indre is perhaps the most gracious from the period of Louis XII, while Chambord, begun by Louis XII and completed by Francis I (1524), may be regarded as the culmination of the style. This period in architecture is known as the first French Renaissance.

England

IN ENGLAND Gothic architecture went through three fairly distinguishable periods: (1) Early, known variously as Lancet or Early Pointed, from *ca.* 1189 to 1307; (2) the Decorated period, known also as Geometrical or Curvilinear, from 1307 to 1377; and (3) Perpendicular, or Rectilinear or Late Pointed, from 1377 to 1485. The dates are obviously somewhat arbitrary, corresponding to the periods of reigning monarchs. But the correspondence does have substantial foundation in fact. Gothic ideals were quickly accepted in England. Kings and prelates brought many French builders across the Channel, though the English masons soon adapted French formulae to their own taste and needs. Certain differences between English and French construction that immediately strike the eye arose in the earliest period of the transplantation of the style from France. The English cathedral floor plans are rectangular. The choir is rectangular instead of semicircular. The English cathedrals almost uniformly have two transepts, the eastern one slightly smaller. The vaults of the English churches are much lower, usually by half, than the French (Amiens, 140 feet; Salisbury, 84 feet). The west façades of English churches are never so imposing nor are the portals so large as in the French, and the English churches tend to have a tower over the crossing of the transept and the nave. The flying buttress so prominent in French Gothic is the exception rather than the rule in England, where neither the aisles nor the nave were so high as in France and the outward thrust was therefore less compelling as an engineering hazard.

The fourteenth century in England, as in France, was not a period of architectural progress. The continuing French war, the Black Death, and subsequent social unrest ending in the Peasants' Revolt of 1381 all helped to dampen enthusiasm for invention and adventure in building. The churches that were built in that and the subsequent centuries, such as Exeter cathedral, the nave of York Minster, or the Lichfield choir, all show a distinct loss of quality and a tendency to economies in labor and design. The end of the French war brought as much of a revival in architectural vigor to England as it did to France. The period from about 1450 to 1520 witnessed the end of Gothic architecture in England. A number of chapels were built in these seventy years which are the crown of English decorative craftsmanship. The chapels of King's College, Cambridge, and of Eton College, the chapel of Henry VII at Westminster, are all distinguished by harmonious proportions, massive fan vaulting, and rich decoration along the walls and traceried windows. Gothic was to expire in England under the Tudors, but its end was memorable.

Germany

GERMAN Gothic for the most part derived from the French. Many German artists had traveled to France during the early Gothic period and later some French master builders were called to Germany to plan and build churches. The church of St. Elizabeth at Marburg and the cathedrals of Magdeburg, Cologne, Freiburg, Strassburg, and Metz were directly influenced by Amiens or Rheims. Many of the German churches in this period as well as many in

Salisbury cathedral, built chiefly between 1220 and 1266. Note the double transepts, the tower at the crossing of the nave and transept, the modest façade, the cloisters, and the chapter-house [AEROFILMS, LTD.].

Poland were built of brick; stone was difficult to procure. The different medium undoubtedly effected some modifications in structure. Much of the craftsmanship in German building, in window screens and altars, was of a high quality, but the spirit which produced the French masterpieces could not be transferred by simple imitation. By about 1500 elaboration had taken the place of harmony and restraint. Germany's particular contribution to Gothic style was the "Hall-Church," in which an impression of spaciousness is achieved by making the nave and the aisle approximately the same height. The activities of the Dominicans and the Franciscans had made preaching popular, so that large congregations were common.

Many German churches have a single tower in the west, and this feature, coupled with the tendency of German builders to build small transepts, has given an appearance of narrowness to their churches which the floor measurements might not justify. There was, proportionately, in Germany and the Low-lands, more civic and domestic building in the Gothic period than in France. This fact resulted from the rapid growth of the towns and consequent bourgeois wealth. All the Hanseatic cities—and at one time or another there were almost a hundred of them—had money to build with, as well as a need for town halls, guildhouses, and chambers of commerce. The town halls at Bruns-

St. Vitus cathedral, founded in 930, rebuilt by Charles IV, on Hradčany Hill, Prague. Charles IV bridge in the foreground [MIRKO J. PITNER, FPG].

wick, Breslau, Münster, and Tangermünde are representative of the various adaptations of Gothic style to a civic building. The Cloth Hall at Ypres in Belgium (1200–1304, destroyed by the Germans in 1914) was perhaps the best example of secular Gothic design in all of Europe. Its central tower could quite well have been a cathedral tower. The town hall of Brussels (1401–55), the town halls in Bruges (1377) and Louvain (1448) could from the exterior easily be taken for developed and elaborate Gothic chapels. Many private residences had decoration, doors, or windows in a style that was quite certainly borrowed from church or cloister.

Italy

IN ITALY Gothic was never really at home. There are several reasons for this apparent rejection by the most artistic people of the West of the greatest single artistic creation of the French. One reason is climate. In the Île de France, where Gothic was born, it rains on about 275 days in the year. Where the sky is overcast so much of the time, light is precious, and much space must be given to windows. In Italy, on the other hand, intensity of the sunlight calls for small windows. The heavy high walls and small windows of the Romanesque thus suited the Italian situation perfectly, whereas the Gothic excess of window space would never have been acceptable. The second reason for Italian nonacceptance of Gothic was rooted in as simple a matter as economic history. It will be remembered that Mediterranean commerce had revived in the eleventh and twelfth centuries, and the cities of Italy had been the first to profit by this economic boom. In these centuries they began to use their

Apse of St. Vitus cathedral seen from the east [DEUTSCHE FOTOTHEK, DRESDEN].

new-found wealth in building churches. The only styles they knew were Roman and Byzantine. The resultant style is called Romanesque, with a basilican floor plan, semicircular arches and windows, heavy walls with solid buttresses. By the time French Gothic had developed sufficiently to be an export product, Italy had about reached the saturation point of ecclesiastical building, in a style appropriate to conditions in the peninsula. After the mid-thirteenth century it is as possible to find Gothic features in churches or public buildings that were not yet completed as it is to find pointed arches in the portals and in the nave of the Santa Maria Novella or the Duomo in Florence or in the whole west screen of the essentially Romanesque Duomo in Ferrara. The church of Sant' Angelo in Perugia, a quite Roman (sixth century) circular structure, now has a Gothic portal. The Duomo at Arezzo, begun in 1277, is completely rectilinear in floor plan. The west portals are ogival, the south portal is semicircular, and the six lancet windows on the north and south walls are all ogival. The five clerestory windows are circular. Of such a combination was Italian Gothic made. It was completely eclectic. The Italian builders had their own problems, and most Gothic features and devices did not apply. In Rome itself during this century there was built only one Gothic church, Santa Maria sopra Minerva (begun 1280). The extensive arcades of the Doge's Palace in Venice are Gothic of the fourteenth century, but of an ornateness that is quite unique and could never have been conceived by a reputable French architect.

The cathedral at Milan (built between 1385 and 1485), after Seville the largest medieval structure in the world, is remarkable rather by its completely non-Italian character. Some of the architects were imported by the Visconti and the Sforza rulers, mostly from Germany, but also from France. Italian masons and architects were able to modify certain of the Gothic features, yet while the high ornateness and excessive statuary (135 pinnacles and 2300 statues on the exterior) may add to its impressiveness, yet inevitably it strikes the viewer as a case of decadent exaggeration. It has none of the dignity of classic simplicity which Brunelleschi and his followers mediated to the builders of the Italian Renaissance.

Transition to Renaissance Architecture

ITALY's contribution to architecture in these centuries certainly does not consist in her quite arbitrary and selective employment of a few Gothic traits, superimposed on an essentially Romanesque architectural temperament. Italy rather was, in the fifteenth century, the scene of a real revival in architectural thought. The humanistic literary Renaissance of the fourteenth century had turned men's minds to the visible remains of ancient Rome. The first fruits of this redirection of attention appeared, as we have seen, in sculpture and painting. Architecture, dealing with larger bodies, came more slowly into focus, but none the less surely. Vasari tells us how, after the competition for the Baptistery doors had been won by Ghiberti, the young Brunelleschi, already established as a builder in Florence, suddenly dropped his work on the Duomo and asked Donatello to accompany him to Rome. Once there the two young men gave themselves for four years to a minute study of the remains and ruins of Roman sculpture and buildings. In a very few years after his return from Rome Brunelleschi had thought out the forms he conceived to be the logical heirs to Roman beauty, and he began, in 1419, the construction of the Foundling Hospital in whose portico round columns supported Corinthian capitals under round arches. It was the first structure in the new Renaissance style.

The next year Brunelleschi became chief builder of the partly built Duomo, with the difficult assignment of constructing the great cupola. The diameter of its base had to cover the space of the nave and the aisles, a distance of 140 feet. His solution of the problems involved in this construction was regarded as little short of miraculous. He designed the church of Santo Spirito from the ground up in 1435, in a rectangular style which is more Roman than Romanesque. The bays are square, the transepts are identical with the choir, and a dome covers the crossing—all in obedience to the newly discovered principles of perspective. In subsequent buildings, both ecclesiastical and secular, Brunelleschi drew upon Roman models to emphasize his independence of the God-centered Gothic and the growing conviction of the humanists that man was the measure of all things. He was asked to design a number of town palaces for rich bourgeois families, the first of which, for Cosimo de' Medici, was originally designed by him but built by Michelozzo. It is now known as the Riccardi palace. The Pitti palace he began in 1440, the Quaratesi a little later. The plan for all these palaces was in general rectangular, surrounding an inner cortile. They set the style; later palaces built by Leone Battista Alberti and his contemporaries followed the severe Roman lines so successfully used by Brunelleschi. In the churches he designed Alberti returned to the basilica floor plan, emphasizing the harmonious features of arcades and a spacious nave. The Strozzi palace, a massive and handsome building in the same tradition, was begun in 1489. Alberti was responsible for spreading the style, both for churches and for palaces beyond Tuscany to Mantua and Rimini, both as a builder and through his treatise *On Architecture,* which soon gained deserved popularity. His career was crowned by his invitation to Rome by the humanist Pope, Nicholas V. The pontiff asked Alberti to plan a new church of St. Peter, whose construction was actually begun by the time of the artist's death in 1472. Bramante, generally credited with the basic plan of St. Peter's, accepted Alberti's foundations.

The Renaissance style of architecture initiated by Brunelleschi and so capably propagated by Michelozzo and Alberti reached Milan and the Lombard valley about the middle of the century in the person of Filarete (1400–65), a Florentine who spent a dozen years in Rome, then, about 1445, came into the employ of Francesco Sforza, for whom he built a number of public and private buildings. About 1460 he wrote a treatise on architecture illustrated by 250 drawings of buildings and detail, actual or suggested, which reflect his preference for pure classic lines. His work bore fruit after his death. About 1480 a change in public taste made itself felt; the Gothic, which because of the proximity to France and French influences had gained a degree of popularity in northern Italy, disappeared virtually from Milanese building.

The leading figure in Milanese architecture of the end of the fifteenth century and, indeed, along with Brunelleschi and Alberti one of the three greatest Renaissance architects, was Donato Bramante (1444–1514). Born near Urbino, he began as a painter, in the workshop of Andrea Mantegna at Rome. He may have known Alberti later at Mantua, but he settled in Milan in 1472, where he worked until 1499 and was certainly influenced by Leonardo da Vinci, who had preceded him in the employ of the Sforza. The last fifteen years of his life, 1499–1514, he lived in Rome. In the city of the popes Bramante designed and built a number of churches and secular buildings, among them the Palazzo della Cancelleria (1495–1505), a three-storied palace with an imposing two-storied cortile annexed to the basilican church of San Lorenzo. The façade was regular, decorated with Corinthian pilasters to heighten the effect of the rectangular windows. He also built the Palazzo Guiraud (1503), in a strongly classic style, and several courts in the Vatican palace. The work for which Bramante is best known, however, is the basilica of St. Peter's. Pope Julius II selected him as the architect, and the work was begun in 1506. Bramante chose a central design based on Alberti's original conception, rejecting the usual longitudinal form, and planned the church in the shape of a Greek cross, with four apses and a large dome at the crossing. Upon the death of Julius II in 1513 work was brought to a standstill. Later chief architects substantially modified Bramante's plan, and it was not until 1547, when Michelangelo became the director of the work, that this plan was rescued and essentially put into effect. The basilica was finally consecrated only in 1626. It is still the largest church in the world.

We have traced in broad lines the changes that took place in the three principal arts—sculpture, painting, and architecture—between the days of Gothic splendor and the acceptance of its decline and supplantation. We have seen how the process and tempo of change differed in each of the larger areas of Europe. Local conditions, political and economic, as well as physical, climatic, and geological factors, influenced these processes of change and development. Individual men of genius precipitated modifications, changed the trends, or made crucial contributions to the new currents of thought and imagination. In the area of the arts technological advances were of less moment than in the domain of discovery and exploration. The fulfillment of Europe's artistic potential which marked these few centuries was a matter of the mind and the imagination. Seldom in our history has there been a time when so many supreme masters of vision and projection in all the media, whether stone, paint, or plaster, lived and created in the same atmosphere. From Florence, which bred most of the greatest of these geniuses, this enlivening air of liberation from the trammels of a convention-bound art spread all over Europe. By the beginning of the sixteenth century every land of the Western world had felt, and in many ways appropriated, the lessons Florence had to give.

SUGGESTIONS FOR FURTHER READING

ANDERSON, W. J., *Architecture of the Renaissance in Italy*. London, 1909
AUBERT, M., *La Sculpture française au moyen âge*. 1946
BERENSON, B., *The Italian Painters of the Renaissance*. New York, 1952
BODE, W., *Florentine Sculptors of the Renaissance*. London, 1909
BURCKHARDT, J., *The Cicerone: An Art Guide to Painting in Italy*. London, n. d.

DEWALD, E. T., *Italian Painting, 1200–1600*. New York, 1961

EVANS, J., *English Art 1307–1461*. Oxford, 1949

FAURE, E., *History of Art*. Vol. III, *Renaissance Art*. New York, 1923

FLETCHER, B., *A History of Architecture on the Comparative Method*. New York, 1924

FOWLER, H. N., *A History of Sculpture*. New York, 1916

FREEMAN, L. J., *Italian Sculpture of the Renaissance*. New York, 1927

GIELLY, L., *Jacopo della Quercia*. 1930

GOLDSCHEIDER, L., *Ghiberti*. London (Phaidon), 1949

HAUSER, A., *The Social History of Art*. 2 vols. London, 1951

HOLT, E. G., *Documentary History of Art,* Vol. I. New York (Anchor), 1957

KNAPP, F., *Italienische Plastik vom 15. bis 18. Jahrhundert*. 1923

MARQUAND, A., *Luca della Robbia*. Princeton, 1914

MATHER, F. J., *A History of Italian Painting*. New York, 1923

ORPEN, W., *Outline of Art*. 2 vols. New York, 1923

PEVSNER, K., *An Outline of European Architecture*. London (Pelican), 1951

PIJOAN, J., *An Outline History of Art,* Vol. III. New York, 1928

PINDER, W., *Die Deutsche Plastik vom ausgehenden Mittelalter bis zum Ende der Renaissance,* Vol. I. 1924

POPE-HENNESSY, J., *Italian Gothic Sculpture*. London (Phaidon), 1955

RICCI, C., *Baukunst und Dekorative Plastik der Hoch- und Spätrenaissance in Italien*. 1923

SCHMECKEBIER, L., *Handbook of Italian Renaissance Painting*. New York, 1938

SCHUBRING, P., *Luca della Robbia und seine Familie*. 1905

SIMPSON, F. M., *A History of Architectural Development*. 3 vols. London, 1913

THODE, H., *Franz von Assisi und die Anfänge der Renaissance*. 1904

VALENTINER, W. R., *Studies of Italian Renaissance Sculpture*. London (Phaidon), 1950

VASARI, G., *Lives of the Most Eminent Painters, Sculptors and Architects*. 8 vols. New York, 1900. Temple Classics. Other editions

CHAPTER FIFTEEN

THE EUROPE OF MACHIAVELLI

THE life-span of Niccolò Machiavelli, from 1469 to 1527, covered a period that for important happenings was fully as significant as had been the lifetime of Dante. Dante portrayed the great drama of human salvation as a manifestation of divine plan and understood it as a function of a unified theocratic empire. He did not or could not see that all around him the Christian empire as well as the imperial idea was already a thing of the past. In the next two centuries Western man began to enjoy freedom to think and build apart from the dictates of an all-enveloping combined church-state. Much real freedom was won. In state structure France and England, under the leadership of monarchs conscious of their national responsibilities, declared not only a measure of independence, but at times antagonism to the Church. In political thought, throughout all of Europe, there was manifold examination of the postulates underlying the Church's dogmatized supremacy. In education and culture, schools had grown up whose aims were not solely the training for the priesthood. The laity also began to demand a share in the enjoyment and propagation of culture. In law, the growth of representative and parliamentary governments in Spain, in England, and in France introduced new norms of justice and new sanctions. The old sanctions of canon law lost much of their force. In commerce, the ancient prescriptions of the Church, which regarded money as a dead thing and forbade the taking of interest, were discarded as men found that individual imagination and initiative would bring substantial and tangible rewards. In society, a whole new class had emerged—the bourgeoisie—whose strength the Church, having gained its primacy in a feudal and hierarchical age, was unprepared to resist, and the Empire, rooted in abstract and disparate allegiances, was unable to control. Marco Polo's adventures in the East were known to the contemporaries of Dante, but they were treated almost as science fiction. By the first decade of the sixteenth century thousands of Europeans had either seen the Spice Islands or reached the Western Hemisphere. In philosophy, previously the sole domain of the Church, these last centuries of the Middle Ages witnessed a revolt against that domination, and much of the philosophical and, indeed, theological thought, whether of clerics or of humanist scholars, was openly anticlerical or in implication disruptive of the established ecclesiastical order. Art, which had for centuries been a religious exercise and a visual sacrifice to God, left the path of conformity and convention in the portrayal of images for the new cult of individualism. The art of the thirteenth century was a theological matter. Much of the art of the fifteenth century was scientific and naturalistic. Man had displaced God as the measure of beauty and truth. In the vernacular literatures, by the end of the fifteenth century, motivation and subject matter had undergone a great measure of secularization. The poetry of Villon would have been impossible in the thirteenth century, just as Sebastian Brant's *Ship of Fools* (1495) could not have been written and well received two centuries before. In many important aspects of European life and thought the period from Dante to Machiavelli witnessed a revolution and a revaluation. Machiavelli's lifetime, furthermore, was to see, in almost as many respects, the beginnings of new trends which have been continued and intensified into our own day.

MACHIAVELLI AND FLORENCE

NICCOLÒ Machiavelli was born in Florence on May 3, 1469. Both his father, a respected lawyer, and his mother were of ancient and noble lineage. Of his early life we know little, but in 1494, the year of the fall of the Medici, when he was twenty-five years of age, he became a minor official of the newly reorganized Republic of Florence. He served the Republic as a secretary and diplomat from 1498 until 1512, when the Medici returned to power. Machiavelli, dismissed, imprisoned, then freed, went into exile on his small estate at San Casciano, near Florence, where he devoted himself to letters and writing. From this period come his reflections on ancient and contemporary history. *The Prince* (1513) is the best known of these writings, but his *History of Florence* (completed in 1525), the *Art of War* (1520), and *Discourses on the First Decade of Livy* (finished in 1518), are in some respects even more important documents. His final conclusions as to the aims and means of the ideal ruler remain a matter of considerable discussion. The reader can easily get two different views from *The Prince* and the *Discourses*. In *The Prince* Machiavelli appears to praise the cynical, grasping, ruthless, and ambitious ruler who uses easy promises, hypocrisy, deception, prison, the sword, and poison to attain his position and keep himself in power. In the *Discourses* the retributions of history are made plain. The history of Rome offers many examples of the ultimate futility of force and compulsion, and Machiavelli so emphasizes the sinister effects of the very means he seems to approve in *The Prince* as to sound like a stern moralist. Whichever of these two views he may really have held, he had, during his lifetime, seen much history made and had means of learning about much more. The Florence of his boyhood, under the brilliant leadership of Lorenzo the Magnificent, was the intellectual center of the Western world. For concentration of intellectual eminence and scholarly equipment there was no group in Europe that could compare with the Platonic Academy and its entourage. Machiavelli grew to manhood during the tense battle for the balance of power between the five great powers of Italy: the Papacy, Florence, Naples, Milan, and Venice. He witnessed the fall

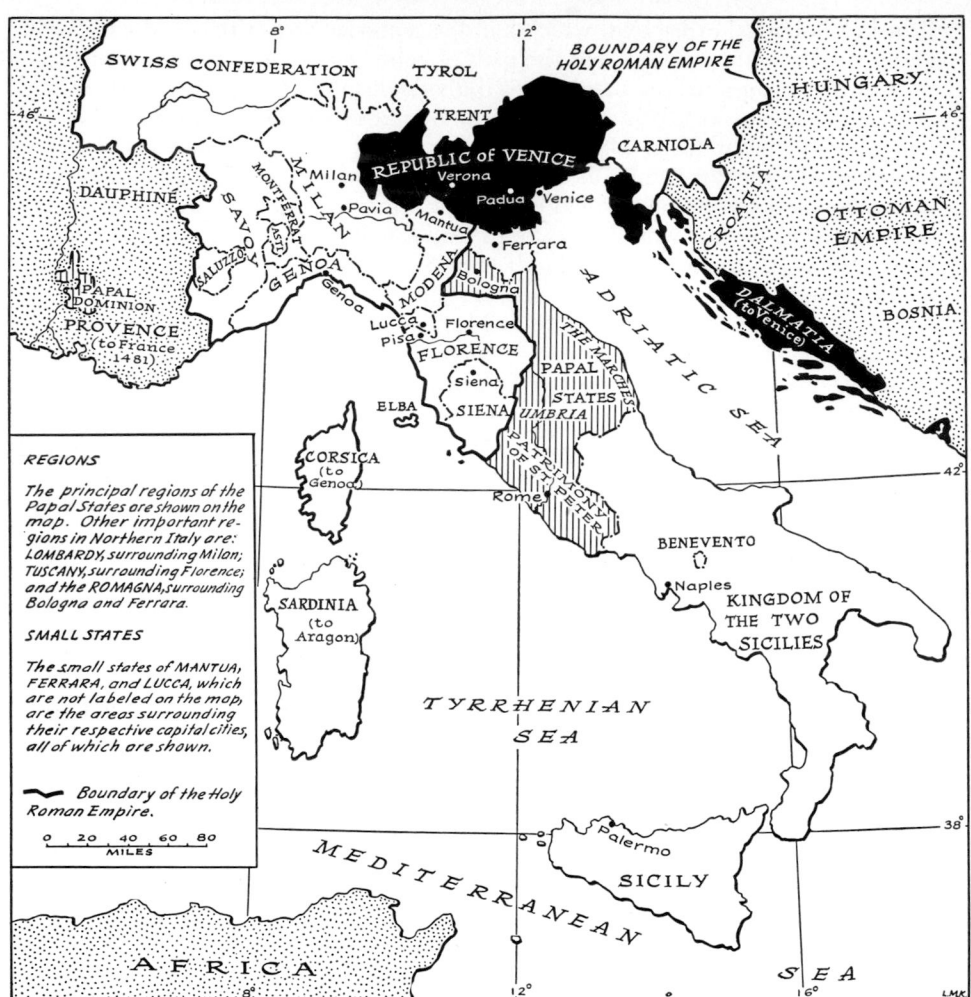

Italy, ca. 1500

of the Medici. Twenty-five when Charles VIII came conquering through Italy, he saw later French conquests vanish into thin air. He knew the story of the rise and decline of the Sforza and was directly aware of the decline of Venetian power. The political greed of the Papacy in the person of Alexander VI's son Cesare Borgia, who was the protagonist of *The Prince,* was well known to him. The subjection of Italy to the arms of Emperor Charles V, who ruled Spain, the Holy Roman Empire, and southern Italy, took place in the last years of Machiavelli's life. It would be difficult to find any reflective observer whose life-span and experience comprehended so many significant and suggestive crises.

The Benevolent Despotism of the Medici

THE Medici, one among many powerful families at the time of Dante, had, by business success and political acumen, become the leading family of the Republic early in the fifteenth century. (See above, Chapter 12.) The rivals of the Medici, the Albizzi, had been able to have Cosimo de' Medici exiled to Padua in Venetian territory, hoping thus to force him into bankruptcy. But the Albizzi could not control Florence, and in 1434 Cosimo was invited to return. From then until the establishment of the theocratic Republic under Savonarola in 1494, Florence was the city of the Medici. Cosimo acted as personal host to the Council of Florence in 1438–39 and to the Eastern Emperor and his retinue. Cosimo was a persuasive advocate of order and peace within the Republic, much of whose prosperity in the fifteenth century may be attributed to his influence and guidance. His foreign policy of peace and cooperation was remarkably successful in an Italy torn by ambitious faction. Upon the death of Filippo Maria Visconti, despot of Milan in 1447, who had ambitions to conquer all of northern Italy, he supported his son-in-law and successor, Francesco Sforza, but in such a way as to hold a balance between

Lorenzo de' Medici (the Magnificent), by Giorgio Vasari, in the Uffizi Gallery, Florence [ALINARI].

413

Milan and Venice. A few years thereafter Cosimo joined the other two great powers of northern Italy, Milan and Venice, in the Italian League of 1455. The negotiations had taken place under the aegis of Pope Nicholas V. The League was a milepost in Italian unity. Although the peaceful principles of the League were frequently violated, Italian thinking in later centuries never forgot this attempt to formalize the cooperative urge among these powers.

On his death in 1464, Cosimo was given the title of Father of His Country (*Pater Patriae*) by a grateful citizenry, and he passed on the great wealth of his house and his influence to his son Piero il Gottoso (Peter the Gouty). Piero was able, both in finance and in diplomacy, and maintained the policies of Cosimo, but his illness prevented great activity. On his death in 1469 his twenty-year-old son Lorenzo, well trained by Piero for his responsibilities, was recognized as the head of the family and the first citizen of the Republic.

In the twenty-three years during which he presided over the fortunes of Florence, although without public office, Lorenzo had to face several internal conspiracies and external crises. The bank and the family business, the source of most of their wealth and political power, were active but beginning to suffer from the competition of other banking houses, Italian and German, and from the diminution of trade from the East after the fall of Constantinople in 1453. Lorenzo followed the foreign policy of his father and grandfather, striving for amicable arrangements with the other great powers of Italy along lines of the League of 1455. In 1470 he supported a move by Pope Paul II to bring Venice, the Papacy, and Naples into a Triple Alliance for peace. Venice, now less aggressive on the mainland, was fighting for her eastern empire against the Turks and was glad to cooperate for peace on the mainland. Lorenzo's policy of pacification in Italy, essentially a recognition of the achievement of a nonaggressive balance of power among the five great states, was extended to relations with Louis XI of France, and until Louis' death in 1483, the ancient Angevin claims to Naples and Milan were not pressed.

The most serious challenge to Lorenzo's power was the Pazzi conspiracy of 1478. The Pazzi were a Florentine banking family whose rivalry to the Medici had turned to bitter hatred. A plot was formed to kill Lorenzo and his much loved younger brother Giuliano. Pope Sixtus IV, uncle of one of the conspirators and by now an enemy of Lorenzo, was told of the plans, and finally gave his approval to the plot, though objecting to murder. While Lorenzo and Giuliano, unarmed, were at mass in the cathedral, two renegade priests began the attack. Giuliano was killed; Lorenzo, wounded in the neck and arm, escaped. The people rallied around him, quickly hanging Francesco dei Pazzi and Salviati, archbishop of Pisa, whom they held responsible for the murder, and killing about eighty others, some doubtless innocent. Lorenzo's hold on Florence was strengthened by this attempted assassination. Pope Sixtus IV excommunicated Lorenzo, "that son of iniquity," and the Priors of Florence, but in the city the decree was disregarded. The Pope's invitation to Ferrante, king of Naples, to punish Florence was accepted, and war broke out. The papal initiative was not popular either in Italy or abroad, save in Naples. Nevertheless, Florence, unprepared for war, was in danger, and territory of the Republic was invaded from several directions. In 1479 Lorenzo, deciding on a bold move, went alone and unarmed to meet Ferrante. The king was persuaded that it was to everybody's interest for Florence and Naples to be at peace in the face of foreign threats, from the Turks or possibly from France. Peace was signed in February 1480; Lorenzo returned to Florence a diplomatic victor, although Florence had some indemnities to pay. Soon fortune smiled on Lorenzo. The Turks took Otranto in August 1480, and Ferrante needed help. Ferrante's need was Lorenzo's opportunity; the indemnities previously imposed on Florence were canceled and territories restored. In addition Lorenzo advanced a subsidy to Ferrante. The Turks withdrew. Naples remained a faithful ally of the Medici, and Lorenzo's repute among the Florentines reached its greatest height. Italy was once more at peace.

The twelve years remaining to Lorenzo were years of steady and strenuous work. The government of Florence was modified in the direction of efficiency and concentration of power. Florentine finances were suffering from the drains of war and expensive diplomacy; new taxes were necessary. They were levied as equitably as possible, though not without some grumbling on the part of the merchants and citizens. In foreign affairs Lorenzo consistently cast the weight of Florence, wherever possible, into the balance against war between the states of Italy. At times the policy was unrealizable, as in 1483 and 1484 when Ferrara was defeated by Venice and forced to give up some territory to her northern neighbor. In 1485 Lorenzo intervened between the new pope, Innocent VIII, and Ferrante of Naples, and though unable to prevent the short War of the Barons, did, by patient diplomacy, prevent it from spreading. Lorenzo's repeated, honest efforts for peace and order among Italian states were so convincing that public opinion throughout the peninsula was in general inclined to recognize him as the advocate and defender of Italian unity. A peace in 1492 between Pope Innocent VIII and Ferrante, long at odds, was in great part due to Lorenzo's persistent intermediacy. In his last years he suffered intensely from arthritis and rheumatic fever. The medication given him would have killed a less vigorous man. He had with him at the end his humanist friend Angelo Poliziano, and Pico della Mirandola visited him at Lorenzo's request. The reforming Dominican, Girolamo Savonarola, who had returned to Florence in 1489 and had become prior of San Marco in 1491, also came in response to a message from Lorenzo. The monk urged him to abide in his faith and to put his trust in the mercy of God, then gave him his blessing. The frequently retold story that Savonarola demanded that Lorenzo restore his ill-gotten wealth to the proper owners and give back to Florence her lost liberties is in all probability quite false. At peace with his soul, Lorenzo died on April 8, 1492, only forty-three years of age.

On Lorenzo's death, his son Piero was accepted by the *Signoria* to occupy his father's position. He soon showed he was not of the stuff of which rulers are made. The break between Milan and Naples and the actuality of invasion by Charles VIII of France, at the invitation of Ludovico Sforza of Milan—crises which would have taxed Lorenzo's diplomacy—were too much for Piero. Florentine opinion was against Naples and in favor of France and Milan. Piero showed himself unstable and the *Signoria* pronounced his primacy in the city void. The people then sacked the Medici palace. With his brother Giuliano, Piero fled (November 9, 1494) to Bologna, and sixty years of Medici rule in Florence were ended.

On November 17, Charles VIII, accompanied by Savonarola, entered Florence as conqueror, with great fanfare. He had over twelve thousand troops at his back, splendidly equipped, who were welcomed by the loud *Viva Francia*'s of the Florentine populace. In ten days he had overstayed his welcome. Savonarola told him to his face that if he did not leave promptly God would visit His anger upon him and all his host. On November 28 Charles led his troops out of Florence for Rome and Naples, loaded with an indemnity of 120,000 florins and the booty his army had baldly appropriated. Once the French were gone the Florentines set about to reconstruct their government without the Medici. A Greater Council of fifteen hundred members was set up on the Venetian model to name magistrates and approve laws. It was, in turn, to create lesser and special councils with appropriate powers and to act as a final court of appeals. At Savonarola's suggestion, the former *parlamento* was abolished. He regarded it as an agency by which power could be taken from the people. Savonarola, whose frequent visions were dramatically presented to the people, was now virtual dictator of the Republic. He intended to create an active theocracy in Florence, controlled at every step by boards, lists of eligibles, and an elaborate system of election by lot. It was not democratic or open, but it was a typically Italian system under which Florence was to function fairly satisfactorily and to live precariously, amidst the pressures of an ambitious Papacy and the power of France, until the return of the Medici in 1512.

Savonarola's course was soon run. At the beginning and for some time his prestige was so high that he had virtually alone written the Constitution of 1494. In 1496 he instigated the great bonfire of the Vanities, in which dice, cosmetics, trinkets, jewelry, false hair, and light literature went up in flames. But, in May 1497, Pope Alexander VI excommunicated the monk for defiance of previous warnings to temper his extreme reforming zeal. Savonarola, like any serious reformer, had many enemies. Now able to come out into the open, they capitalized on Savonarola's tactical errors. He was charged with having tried to overthrow the Constitution, and when the traditionally fickle popular support was no longer behind him, he was tried and condemned to death by hanging. The sentence was carried out in the Piazza on May 23, 1498; the body was then burned and the ashes were thrown into the Arno.

Machiavelli had entered the service of the state as a minor secretary in 1494. In 1499 he became chancellor and secretary to the Ten of Liberty and Peace, roughly equivalent to the office of foreign affairs. In the subsequent twelve years he served on a number of important diplomatic missions to the Papacy, to King Louis XII of France, to the Emperor Maximilian, and to numerous lesser courts. He was a close observer of political currents and the motives of princes and ministers. The summer and autumn of 1502 he spent at the court of Cesare Borgia, the brilliant son of Pope Alexander VI. Cesare was then at the height of his power and it appeared as if he would soon have control not only of all the Romagna and the Papal States but of Tuscany as well. Florence, without the guiding hand of the Medici and lacking even the civic conviction which Savonarola's righteous indignation might have provided, saw Cesare's conquests coming closer and was quite rightly anxious for her safety. Machiavelli's task as envoy to Cesare was to dissuade him from attacking Florence.

In the course of his association with Cesare, he conceived a great admiration for him, whom he put forward in his *Prince* as the ideal ruler. Florence was in the end saved by two extraneous developments, the fact that Louis XII did not wish Cesare to control Tuscany and obliged him to withdraw, and the death of Pope Alexander VI on August 18, 1503. Without his father's support Cesare was isolated and vulnerable, and Pope Julius II, elected in spite of Cesare's efforts at obstruction, took over all of Cesare's conquests by January 1504. Machiavelli's ideal prince retired to Naples and was taken a prisoner to Spain, to die three years later in battle.

For the next eight years, from Cesare's collapse to the return of the Medici in 1512, Florence had a degree of quiet, while the king of France was steadily tightening his hold on northern Italy. Not only was he lord of Milan and the protector of Florence, but from 1510 he was at war with Julius II. In 1511 his troops, under the brilliant leadership of Gaston de Foix, could easily have marched into Rome itself. French success brought the Italian states together again; and in October 1511 the Holy League, directed against France and consisting of the Papacy, Venice, and the kingdom of Naples, was formed. In the war which followed the French won the battle of Ravenna against the League (April 11, 1512), but de Foix was killed in action. Without his leadership the French campaign was hopeless. The Republic of Florence, which had been friendly to Louis of France, was ordered by the League to take the Medici back. In September 1512, Giuliano and his brother Cardinal Giovanni de' Medici entered the city as private and leading citizens, and the system of government was restored essentially as it had been under Lorenzo de' Medici. In 1513, on the death of the energetic if somewhat confused Julius II, Cardinal Giovanni de' Medici became Pope Leo X, thus fortifying the position of the Medici in Florence. They remained in power until, at the approach of the armies of Charles V in 1527, the people of the city revolted, drove them out, and restored the Republic as nearly as it was before the rule of the Medici. This restored Republic lasted only three years (1527–30).

Venice

THE late fifteenth century witnessed events which were fateful for Venice: the fall of Constantinople to the Turks in 1453 and the discovery of trade routes to the Far East and the New World. The monopoly of the city on the lagoons over eastern trade was broken. Thus, although still rich and vigorous, Venice was, in the last decade of the fifteenth century and the first part of the sixteenth, necessarily on the defensive, actively engaged in intrigues and diplomatic maneuvers in order to strengthen her own delicate position and dissolve coalitions against her. One tactical victory had been the acquisition of the island of Cyprus between 1468 and 1488. But there were also humiliations. Friuli was ravaged by the Turks. A Venetian fleet led by Antonio Grimani was disastrously defeated by the Turks in August 1499 and in the ensuing war Venice's allies left her to withstand the Turkish attack alone. She was forced to give up more territory on the Adriatic and in the Morea.

Venice reacted to these misfortunes along her eastern frontier by extending her western and southern fronts on the mainland. When the death of Pope

Alexander VI removed Cesare Borgia from the scene Venice moved southward into the Papal States and occupied Rimini and Faenza. Julius II, previously favorably disposed toward the island republic, now became the leader of states with Italian interests that felt themselves threatened by the expansionist moves of Venice, and in 1504 the Pope brought the Emperor Maximilian and Louis XII of France into a temporary alliance with the Papacy against Venice. As Venice maintained her aggressive attitude and the previous alliance had been too loose, the Pope consolidated the alliance, added Henry VII of England and some Italian states, forming what is known as the League of Cambrai (1508), which provided for the partition of Venetian territory among the signatories and Spain, Hungary, and the duke of Savoy if they would join the League. War naturally followed, but the Pope, Maximilian, and Spain left the fighting to Louis XII. When the French king defeated the Venetians at Agnadello (May 14, 1509) Venice was forced to retire from most of her conquests in the Po valley. The victors, however, were even less popular in the towns they took than the Venetians, and, by contrast, the easy yoke and stable justice of Venetian rule seemed far preferable to the capriciousness and frequent brutality of the French soldiery. When Julius II abandoned his allies in the League and absolved Venice (February 24, 1510), the Republic was already on the way to regaining most of her lost territories. Julius now realized that by calling in foreigners—the Empire, France, and Spain—he had affronted the incipient sentiment of Italian unity. From this time he reversed his policy and proclaimed himself the leader in the campaign to free Italy from the hated foreigner, by which was meant the French, "those barbarians," as he called them. The result of his efforts was the formation of the Holy League (October 1511) with Venice and Ferdinand as king of Naples. Henry VIII of England soon joined, and a year later Maximilian of the Empire. The death of Gaston de Foix at the battle of Ravenna (April 11, 1512) and the subsequent failure of French leadership allowed papal aims at least a temporary triumph. Julius was to die in 1513, Louis XII in 1515, and Maxmilian in 1519. Thus, for some years after Ravenna, Venice was left in relative peace, and the League of Cambrai, intended to destroy her, was forgotten.

Naples

BY THE middle of the fifteenth century the kingdom of Naples had seen many changes in rulers. The French house of Anjou, expelled from Sicily in 1282, had never renounced its claims, and the house of Aragon had intermittently ruled in Sicily or on the mainland ever since. In 1283 Peter III of Aragon had been invited by the Sicilians to be their king. During the fourteenth century Sicily and Naples went their separate ways, the former under Aragonese rulers, the latter ruled by the Angevins. Robert of Anjou (1309–43), a friend and admirer of Petrarch, had given Naples a period of cultural splendor; his granddaughter Joanna (1343–82) was not only ineffective but inordinately pleasure-loving and wasteful. Confusion, decay, and external intrigues, largely of papal inspiration, made Naples an uncertain element in Italian politics. In 1409, on the death of Martin of Aragon, king of Sicily, his cousin, Alfonso V of Aragon, became the first ruler to unite both crowns in one person.

In a few years Joanna II of Naples (1414–35), needing assistance against Louis of Anjou, offered to adopt Alfonso as her heir and successor if he would help her against her French adversary. He accepted the offer in July 1421. The end result of this bargain was that Alfonso, already king of Aragon and Sicily, after a prolonged military and naval struggle with the Angevin claimant to the throne, entered Naples in triumph as king in February 1443. That same year Pope Eugenius IV formally invested Alfonso with the kingdom of Naples. Until his death in 1458 he kept court in Naples, maintaining order and fostering culture. In 1455 he joined the general Italian peace. To Neapolitans he is known as Alfonso the Magnanimous. He left the kingdom of Naples to his natural son Ferrante (Ferdinand I) and the remainder of his possessions to his brother John. The dominance of the house of Aragon over the western Mediterranean was incontestable. The Balearic Isles, Sardinia, Sicily, and southern Italy were solidly in Aragonese hands. Such predominance on their southern horizon inevitably disturbed the peace of mind of the rulers of France and the rest of Italy. We shall see how this concentration of Mediterranean power in one ruler's hands was to be a large factor in precipitating a conflict between France and the Habsburg rulers that was to last for almost three centuries.

King Ferrante was not his father's equal. He barely managed to defeat a poorly organized Angevin attempt to regain the throne of Naples (1462), and by cruelty and caprice he so alienated public opinion in the kingdom that when the Moslems landed in 1480 at Otranto the population preferred them to Ferrante. When a revolt broke out in Naples in October 1485, Pope Innocent VIII sided with the rebels. Ferrante was saved only by the naval help of his cousin Ferdinand of Aragon and by distractions and rivalries among his enemies. The French claims to the crown of Naples had hitherto, at least since 1302, been represented by a cadet branch of the Capetians, the ruling house of France. Louis XI, busy with the tasks of consolidating royal power in France, had been content to extend his influence in Savoy and to maintain alliances with the Sforza in Milan and the Medici in Florence, studiously avoiding any interference in Neapolitan affairs. It was his son and successor, Charles VIII, who altered this policy of restraint with such fateful results. It is not necessary to discover any sparks of political genius in this sad figure of a king to explain the quick conquests of 1494 from the passes of the Alps to the Bay of Naples. From the Neapolitan side, the cruel and senseless rule of Ferrante could easily justify the tolerance with which the citizens of the kingdom welcomed the French conqueror.

SPAIN OF THE CATHOLIC KINGS

SPANISH history at the turn of the century summons up large vistas of adventure, success, pride, confusion, and decline. The dynastic union of Castile and Aragon (see map, p. 128), by the marriage of the "Catholic Kings," the conquest of the Moorish Kingdom of Granada, the expulsion of the Jews, the establishment of the Inquisition, the voyages of Columbus, the beginnings of the greatest empire the world had ever seen, the election of a Spanish king to be Emperor of the Holy Roman Empire—these are only the most obvious events of Spanish history on the threshold of the modern era.

The marriage of the Catholic Kings, Ferdinand and Isabella, in 1469 did not bring about a constitutional union of their two kingdoms. Castile retained its *Cortes* and traditions; Aragon continued to be a federal state. The marriage contract carefully protected each kingdom from interference by the ruler of the other. The undeniable progress toward Spanish unity which took place during their reigns was due to the forceful identity of purpose shared by the king and queen. From early in their reign Ferdinand and Isabella were determined to fortify political unity by religious uniformity. The court of the Inquisition had existed in Aragon since the early thirteenth century; in 1477, as a measure of handling the irritating problem of Jews who had become converted to Christianity, a royal decree set up such a tribunal in Seville, and Pope Sixtus IV, at Ferdinand's request, confirmed its establishment in a number of bulls during the next few years. In these bulls it was stipulated that the inquisitors should be subject to the king. In 1483 the Pope recognized that the Inquisition in Spain was a royal Inquisition, yet in Aragon the Holy Office met bitter resistance from the people before capitulating to the royal edict in 1487. Jews, both converts and nonconverts, escaped in great numbers, with disastrous results for the Spanish economy. In 1492, culminating years of persecution, all Jews still in Spain were ordered expelled. The Dominican Thomas Torquemada, the third Inquisitor General, by his ruthlessness earned a fearful place in the annals of human cruelty. Through the unholy work of the Holy Office, Spanish religious unity was preserved, but the loss of the only element in the population with any business competence was a blow from which Spain has never recovered.

One of the significant policies for which Ferdinand was largely responsible was that of widely spread marriage alliances. As early as 1486 there was talk of marrying his daughter Catherine to the young Arthur, eldest son of Henry VII of England. This marriage eventually took place in 1501. The next daughter, Joanna (the Mad), was married in October 1496 to Philip the Handsome of Austria (and Burgundy), son of Emperor Maximilian I. This alliance caused some internal trouble for Ferdinand, since Philip soon laid claim in his wife's name to the kingdom of Naples, control of which Ferdinand had no intention of relinquishing. The marriage was to result in binding Spain to the Empire, as the eldest issue of the union was to be Charles I of Spain and Charles V of the Empire. Quite obviously the two marriages, to Prince Arthur and Archduke Philip, heir to the Burgundian lands, were aimed at encircling France. But in 1505 Ferdinand reversed his position and sought an alliance with Louis XII of France. Ferdinand, with friends in both camps, could easily play one against the other, a sport he relished immensely.

Among Ferdinand's accomplishments must be listed his engineering of four considerable territorial acquisitions: Cerdagne, Roussillon, Granada, and Navarre. The first three were consummated while Isabella was still alive. The Moorish kingdom of Granada had led a precarious vassal existence for over two centuries when, in 1482, the Catholic Kings attacked it. Its subjugation came after a war lasting ten years and a final sanguinary siege of the two cities of Malaga and Granada. The terms of capitulation were generous, but after forced conversions had driven the Moors to revolt, they were obliged to choose between baptism and expulsion (February 12, 1502). Those who accepted baptism were called Moriscos. The ever suspicious Inquisition managed to make their lives miserable until final expulsion in 1609.

The acquisition of Navarre was accomplished as a pendant to the formation of the Holy League. Both French and Spanish monarchs had, for centuries, sought to absorb this small mountain kingdom straddling the Pyrenees. The ruling families of Navarre had at various times married into both Spanish and French royal houses. Ferdinand, after the death of Isabella, married (1505) as his second wife Germaine de Foix, niece of Louis XII, a granddaughter of Gaston IV, king of Navarre, and cousin of Queen Catherine of Navarre. As the Holy League, formed in 1511 by Julius II and Ferdinand, was pointed against France, Ferdinand, declaring the rulers of Navarre to be allies of France, his enemy, sent his troops into Navarre, and King Jean d'Albret fled to France (July 1512). Julius II helpfully issued bulls transferring the kingdom to Ferdinand (February 1513), who had conquered it in the name of the Church. Ferdinand broadened his claims by proclaiming his hereditary rights to the throne on behalf of his wife. There remained to the d'Albret family only the smaller part of the kingdom that lay on the northern slopes of the Pyrenees, safe within French protection.

Before his death in 1516 Ferdinand had consolidated the Spanish spirit, established the Spanish Inquisition, taken over from his cousin the kingdom of Naples, conquered Granada and Navarre, expelled the Jews, accepted most of the New World from Columbus, meddled successfully in Italian politics on both sides of a number of issues, violated almost every solemn promise and treaty which he made, and had withal made Spain, by marriages, opportunistic diplomacy, and luck, the strongest single power in Europe. The Spain which he turned over to his grandson Charles I was so rich, united, and fortified by location, alliance, colonies, and family possessions that Spanish preponderance in Europe was to last until the middle of the seventeenth century.

FRANCE

IN THE preceding account of developments in the various states of Italy and of Spain's involvement in Italian affairs, France and her rulers have been frequently mentioned. The France of the late fifteenth century was in fact deeply involved in Italy. It is conventional to explain the Italian wars of Charles VIII, Louis XII, and Francis I as the romantic ventures of capricious rulers mad for glory and the trappings of military conquest. This does less than justice to the realities. France had driven out the English by 1453, after a long and exhausting struggle. In the process she had found a national soul. The next generation was to see a powerful upsurge of energy and applied patriotism under a brilliant and tenacious taskmaster. Louis XI, King Spider (1461–83) (see above, Chapter 10), exacted obedience from unruly vassals and thus tightened and strengthened the internal bonds of unity and, more significantly, made the monarchy respected. He had humbled Burgundy and extended French sovereignty to the Pyrenees and to the Vosges in the east. He also meddled in Italian affairs, but more by diplomacy and bribery than by military action.

Louis' son and successor, Charles VIII, was a boy of only thirteen on his accession in 1483, and the conduct of affairs was in the forceful hands of Louis' favorite daughter, Anne de Beaujeu. So long as she was actual ruler, that is, from 1483 to 1491,* the country continued along the lines Louis had set, with equal firmness and even greater wisdom than her father had shown, and against the opposition of the princes of the blood and the Estates General. By the time Charles declared himself of age and began to make his own usually inept decisions Anne was ready to withdraw gracefully from public life. But before retiring she had arranged the marriage of Charles to Anne of Brittany, a union which brought into the hands of the king of France that duchy, whose frequently independent attitude had been a source of great irritation and even danger to the French monarchy. In this acquisition—as in the conquests of Louis XI—we see something similar to the Spanish conquest of Granada and Navarre. Both countries needed a political unity within natural geographical boundaries. But by the time Charles began to rule in his own right, new facts demanded new and revised analyses of international relations.

To the southwest, the remarkable unification of Spain under the Catholic Kings and the obvious military strength shown by the conquest of Granada in 1492 was disturbing. From 1486 there had been rumors of a Spanish-English marriage alliance, which would have caught France in a vise between two ancient enemies, an unpleasant reminder of the Hundred Years' War. To the east, the implications of Mary of Burgundy's marriage to the Emperor Maximilian I (1477) had been alarming. Burgundy, if backed by the Empire, might rise once again to disturb the French monarchy. In the early 1490's negotiations were already under way for the marriage of John, oldest son of Ferdinand and Isabella, to Maximilian's daughter Margaret of Austria, who had recently been repudiated by Charles VIII of France. Such a marriage would join two enemies of France on opposite frontiers, the Empire and Spain, and the figure of a vise is again apposite. By 1493 then, on four sides, France had actual or potential enemies, who were on suspiciously intimate and cooperative terms. As France looked south the prospect was even less promising. The western basin of the Mediterranean was really an Aragonese lake, with the Balearics, Sardinia, and Sicily under the king of Aragon, and the kingdom of Naples in the hands of another Aragonese prince. France faced actual or potential encirclement and strangulation. It is quite true that Charles VIII was vain, romantic, dissipated, and a sad figure of a king or a man, but that alone does not explain the French effort, sustained over more than thirty years, to break out of this threatening encirclement.

The Italian Wars

WHEN Ludovico Sforza, ruling in Milan for his minor nephew Giangaleazzo Maria Sforza, anxious to weaken the kingdom of Naples, invited Charles to

* The Estates declared Charles of age in 1484, when he was fourteen years of age, but he was content to allow Anne to rule for him for seven years more.

revive the ancient French claim to Naples, there were enough of Charles' advisers who favored the idea to persuade the king that he should set out across the Alps. In order to have peace at his back he made treaties with his three neighbors, Henry VII of England, Ferdinand of Aragon, and Maximilian of the Empire, giving to each the bribe of land or money in return for the assurance of peace while he was absent in Italy. To Henry he gave 745,000 gold crowns in cash (treaty of Étaples, November 1492). To Ferdinand he ceded Cerdagne and Roussillon (treaty of Barcelona, January 19, 1493). To Maximilian he returned Franche Comté and Artois (treaty of Senlis, May 1493). The whole procedure was tragically thoughtless and wasteful. The military expedition reached Milan in October 1494 and, after "borrowing" 60,000 ducats from Ludovico Sforza, Charles marched on to Florence (see above, p. 415). After Florence came Rome and the easy conquest of Naples (February 12, 1495), but Charles' success was short-lived. The League of Venice, between Spain, Venice, the Pope, Milan, and Maximilian, concluded on March 25, 1495, was pointed at him and he thought it wiser to go home. On the way back to France, at Fornovo at the foot of the Appenines (July 6, 1495), 40,000 of the allies met Charles with 10,000 and the French barely broke through, leaving behind them all their baggage and booty. Charles, himself remarked he had won "nothing but glory and smoke." Fortunately the expedition had cost the French state very little. The army had lived off the Italian cities and princes.

Charles' early death (April 1498) brought his cousin Louis, duke of Orléans, to the throne as Louis XII. While not robust, he was genial and popular at court and among the people. His intimate and leading adviser was the archbishop of Rouen, George d'Amboise, later a cardinal, whose barely concealed ambitions for the papal chair explained some of France's Italian policy under Louis XII. Since Louis' wife, Jeanne, daughter of Louis XI, was no longer necessary to his position, the marriage was annulled on newly discovered grounds of consanguinity and youth. Anne of Brittany, widow of Charles VIII, was his next bride. She brought with her the duchy of Brittany, thus confirming the addition to the French monarchy of this important and strategic corner of the French land mass.

Louis, descended from Valentina Visconti of Milan (see above, Chapter 10), decided soon after his accession to annex the duchy to the kingdom of France. Some diplomatic preparations ensued. Venice, the Swiss, and the Borgias were willing to profit from the ruin of another Italian state, and in August 1499 Milan was easily in Louis' hands. The conquest was indeed deceptively easy. When Louis left for France, Ludovico Sforza retook Milan (January 1500), and Louis had to fight to win it back (April 1500). The temptation to go on to Naples was irresistible. D'Amboise was doubtless anxious to be closer to Rome. By the treaty of Granada (November 11, 1500), Louis engaged to share the prospective conquest with Ferdinand of Aragon. The Pope gave his blessing and, late in July, Louis' troops marched into a Naples that had but recently welcomed another French army, only to see it leave with even greater enthusiasm. The present conquerors, French and Spanish, soon fell out; in the sequel the French suffered several disastrous defeats and, even after being heavily reinforced, had to surrender to Gonzalo de Córdoba (January 1, 1504).

The new pope, Julius II, used Louis against Venice in the League of Cambrai; then, reversing his position, formed the Holy League aimed at Louis in 1511. After a costly victory at Ravenna in April 1512, Louis realized that his Italian policy was a lost cause. To make the outlook more depressing, Henry VIII of England had routed a French army at Guinegate (the Battle of the Spurs) in August 1513. Furthermore, the Emperor and the Swiss were threatening. At the end of his reign Louis had to give up all his dreams of possessing the duchy of Milan. His second queen, Anne of Brittany, died, widely mourned, in January 1514. A third marriage was arranged, with the young and vital Mary Tudor, the sister of Henry VIII (May 1514). Her efforts to rouse the king from his grief and depression proved too much for an aged man of fifty-two and he died within a few months (January 1, 1515). His successor, Francis of Angoulême, under the title of Francis I was to lead his country's desperate struggle against even greater forces of encirclement than those which had faced Louis XI, Charles VIII, and Louis XII.

ENGLAND: THE BEGINNINGS OF TUDOR POWER

THE victory of Henry Tudor over Richard III on Bosworth Field (August 22, 1485) ended a period of civil dissension at home and indecision abroad. At the same time it opened an era of greatness and consolidation unequaled in English history. The Wars of the Roses had gone far to break the hold of feudalism upon the English political and social structure. The aristocracy had decimated its own ranks in war and undermined its prestige with the people, who, after years of disturbance and pointless war, had lost patience with the whole institution of nobility. The firmness with which Henry attended to the business of being king after Bosworth impressed the English people. Nevertheless, the first fifteen of his twenty-four years of rule were troubled by attempts of malcontents at home to unseat him, and, abroad, by diplomatic crises calling for coolness and sound thinking. The economy of England had suffered substantially during the chaotic Wars of the Roses and, although it was fundamentally firm, being based on wool, fish, and trade, the heightened tempo of competition from a revived France, a prosperous Low-lands, and an aggressive Hanseatic League made it necessary for Henry, not unwillingly, to interest himself in the commerce of his subjects. Their prosperity meant royal income.

Henry's claim to the throne was none too strong. He was a descendant of a mistress of John of Gaunt, duke of Lancaster, whose offspring were later legitimized. In order to strengthen his remote Lancastrian claim he engaged to marry Elizabeth of York, thus combining both lines. But he insisted that Parliament declare him king without mention of Elizabeth. He was crowned first alone and the marriage was performed after the coronation. The queen was not crowned until November 22, 1487. Many of the troubles he experienced in the first half of his reign were traceable to efforts of irreconcilable Yorkists to dethrone him. In 1487 Lambert Simnel, a youth of about the age of the older son of the late Edward IV, was put forward in Ireland as the young prince, said to have escaped from the Tower. Margaret of Burgundy, a sister of Edward IV, supported the claim. After being crowned in Dublin, Simnel, with a force of German and Irish mercenaries, landed in west England, only to be quickly defeated and taken prisoner (June 16, 1487). He was given a steady job in the royal scullery. This quick and decisive victory strengthened Henry's cause, but the Yorkists were not yet satisfied. Margaret of Burgundy's court was the center of more conspiracies, the best prepared of which was one aimed at putting a certain Perkin Warbeck, a young man of Flemish origin, on the throne of England. This hoax lasted six years. In 1491, after long coaching for his part, he landed in Cork, pretending to be Richard of York, the younger of the two sons of Edward IV that had been imprisoned in the Tower. The Irish were attracted to him and he was subsequently welcomed at the courts of Charles VIII, Margaret of Burgundy, the Emperor at Vienna, and James IV of Scotland. The latter gave him his daughter in marriage. Henry, who had spies within the conspiracy, was well informed of all moves. Several English conspirators were apprehended and beheaded. Finally, in 1497, after adventures in Ireland, Warbeck landed in Cornwall, and, failing to take Exeter, surrendered to Henry's mercy. His significance lay not in his own person, but rather in the circumstance that Yorkist opposition, headed by the earl of Warwick, could still stir some faint embers of civil war. The intriguing earl had finally to be beheaded in November 1499, a few days after Warbeck had been hanged on charges of conspiracy and treason. That was the end of such plots, although not of Henry's troubles.

Ferdinand of Spain had desired a marriage alliance with Henry as early as 1486, to help in the containment of France. The result of long negotiations was the marriage of the Prince of Wales, Prince Arthur, then fifteen years old, and Catherine of Aragon, then almost sixteen, in November 1501. Arthur died four and a half months later. At Ferdinand's suggestion Catherine was then engaged to Henry, the surviving younger son of the English monarch, then eleven years old. The marriage took place by proxy in 1503 and formally in June 1509, three months after Henry succeeded his father on the throne.

Henry VII had set the tone of Tudor government. He had an instinct for political efficiency. He wanted broad support among the lesser officials, and the justices of the peace who administered royal justice were of great value to him. He called Parliament eleven times in his entire reign, only once in his last twelve years. The function of Parliament was in actuality to give Henry the power with which to run the government. The execution and interpretation of the law he kept in his own hands, through the Council, a body made up of twenty or thirty advisers and officials, absolutely dependent on the king and bound by a special and personal oath of loyalty to him. They were a mixed lot, a few churchmen, mostly lawyers and laymen of the gentry or the burgher class, chosen for loyalty and efficiency. Henry rewarded them moderately with titles and estates, but more by his confidence and the power he allowed them to wield. Richard Fox, keeper of the privy seal from 1487 and bishop of Winchester from 1501, was the most important single member of the Council, but there was no one among Henry's ministers who exercized any preponderant influence over him. Henry was his own first minister and determined all the broad policies in every department of his government.

The success of his reign is the measure of his greatness. In domestic affairs he furthered the rule of law and the unity of the realm. This involved an increase in the authority of the crown, a decrease in the power of the greater nobility. Henry favored industry and commerce at home and abroad. In 1490 he forced the Hansa to allow English merchants to trade in Denmark and Iceland on equal terms with the Hanseatic merchants; in 1496 he made a business-like commercial treaty, the *Intercursus Magnus,* with the Lowlands. In foreign affairs he pursued a policy of peace and avoidance of adventures. The dignity and stability which his policies and firmness gave to the English realm made him a highly desirable partner or ally. Every Continental monarch at one time or another would have liked to involve Henry in an intrigue or a war, but he kept as free of such traps as good sense and his strong diplomatic, financial, and military situation could make him. He thus laid the firm foundations for England's later traditional function as the maintainer of the balance of power in Europe. With the Church Henry kept on friendly, even generous terms. He could the more easily do so because he was the virtual master of the Church in England. Favoring learning and education, he was munificent in benefactions to the universities of Oxford and Cambridge. He frequently had humanists, English or foreign, in his employ and commissioned the Italian humanist Polydore Vergil to write a history of England in the style of Livy. The years of Henry's rule were the years when Grocyn, Linacre, Colet, and More shone as the bright lights of English humanism. They were all welcome at the court of the king.

Henry VIII

HENRY VII's son and successor, Henry VIII, not yet eighteen years of age on the death of his father (April 21, 1509), came into possession of a soundly administered, peaceful, and prosperous kingdom blessed with a full treasury. The young king was handsome, accomplished, and popular. He was also ambitious to play a large role in European politics. He gladly joined the Holy League on the Pope's invitation and was soon sending detachments of troops to Spain and France in pursuance of a general anti-French campaign which was poorly planned and haphazardly executed. Henry did, however, have a taste of the glory he so ardently sought when his troops put the French to flight at Guinegate in August 1513, in the so-called Battle of the Spurs. The Scots, allied with France, declared war, and Henry's forces, under command of Surrey, defeated James IV disastrously on the field of Flodden (September 9, 1513), leaving the Scottish king dead on the field of battle. With English military prestige at a peak, a shift in alliances on the Continent was inevitable. Henry's leading adviser, Thomas Wolsey, astutely measured the forces and intentions of the shifty Ferdinand and the equally mendacious Maximilian, and a marriage of Henry's beautiful sister Mary Tudor with Louis XII of France was arranged (August 1514). The realignment of the powers, favorable to France, who needed security on her northern frontier, as well as to England, now no longer in need of Spanish support against France, came as a shock to Ferdinand and a surprise to most of Europe. It was now realized that England would make independent diplomatic decisions with her own advantages in view. When Louis' early death (January 1, 1515) largely invalidated the recent alliance, Francis I immediately let it be known that he had his own diplomatic aims. Furthermore, his success at Marignano over the Swiss (September 13, 1515) made Henry's recent victory at Guinegate look very small. The next few years were a time of indecisive jockeying for position. To the two young and mettlesome monarchs the struggle between their respective countries for primacy in European politics became almost a personal combat.

In the very important matter of the production of an heir to the throne, a subject on which the English, with memories of dynastic squabbles, were highly sensitive, Henry was not fortunate. Queen Catherine bore him only one child who survived, a girl named Mary (1516–58). The absence of a male heir was to be a matter of grave concern to Henry as well as the English people for many years and the precipitant of portentous events.

The career of Thomas Wolsey is one of the most remarkable in English history. In the first years of his reign Henry was more interested in sports and pastimes than in the drudgery of governmental routine. Wolsey, ambitious and energetic, took the drudgery off the king's shoulders, increasing his own power and wealth in the process. He accumulated numerous minor prebends and benefices, and became successively titular bishop of Tournai (1513), bishop of Lincoln (1514), Archbishop of York (1514), cardinal (1515), Lord Chancellor (1515), papal legate *a latere* (1518), in the meantime administering several vacant bishoprics with profit to himself. As legate *a latere* he was more powerful in the English church than the Archbishop of Canterbury; as Lord Chancellor he controlled the administrative and judicial structure of the kingdom, and, under the king, mostly quite content to let him carry the burden, determined foreign policy. Within the Royal Council his friends and creatures occupied all the key offices. Wolsey's power was at its height about 1520. By then he had begun to say "I shall do thus and so" rather more often than "The king will do thus and so." We shall see to what pass his ambition and overconfidence brought him. We now leave England and the Lord Chancellor at the zenith of his impressive career.

THE EMPIRE AND THE HABSBURGS

Following the short rule of the Habsburg Albert II (1438–39), his cousin Frederick of Styria was elected Emperor. The rule of Frederick III from 1440 to 1493 was one of the longest reigns in imperial history, and, from the viewpoint of the Empire, among the least successful. Frederick had three main interests, astrology, his collection of precious stones, and the aggrandizement of the Habsburg family. From 1444 to 1471—twenty-seven years—he did not bother to attend a meeting of the Diet, in spite of repeated and urgent appeals from the Electors and the cities that he should come and consult with them concerning reform in the structure and administration of the Empire. There were many plans put forward by individual princes and prelates, but in the absence of the Emperor nothing could be done. Lacking the leadership Frederick might have given, some princes took independent action. The duke of Bavaria, for example, in 1463 organized a regional Landfrieden League, a sort of federation to maintain peace and order in southern Germany. There were other such regional organizations by various groups of princes. Although such leagues could hold together for short periods, the net result of these regional attempts at maintaining peace was to strengthen the power of the greater princes who were strong enough to lead the movements and to give them a semblance of policy. Frederick was not the man to counter this tendency toward separatism or to inspire general confidence that he could bring peace and order to Germany.

Toward the Pope Frederick was obsequious, when German opinion would have preferred a policy of independence, similar to that of France after the Pragmatic Sanction of Bourges of 1438. By contrast, Frederick signed the Vienna Concordat with Pope Nicholas V in 1448, which gave the *curia* a dominant voice in the control of the German church. The Emperor's well-known disinclination to interfere in German affairs encouraged the princes and cities in their endless feuds. The cities of Franconia waged a long and exhausting war against their Brandenburg overlord Albert Achilles from 1449 to 1451 which involved most of south and middle Germany. The Emperor did nothing to stop the senseless conflict. For five years there was war between the archbishop of Cologne and the towns of Westphalia. Again the Emperor did almost nothing while parts of the Empire were being wasted. In 1460 there was war between the Hohenzollerns of Brandenburg and Nürnberg and the Wittelsbachs of Bavaria. Frederick favored the Hohenzollerns, but it was rather the diplomatic intervention of Pope Pius II in 1463 that brought about the defeat of the Wittelsbachs than any active help from the Emperor. In the struggle between Poland and the Teutonic Knights the Emperor again did nothing, and the defeated Knights came under Polish control at the Second Peace of Toruń (1466). (See above, Chapter 8.) These and many lesser quarrels reduced royal authority and prestige to a shadow. Anarchy prevailed. Demands for reform in imperial organization began to be heard from every quarter. But these demands were not to bear fruit until Frederick's successor, Maximilian I, assumed the power in 1486.

In matters which directly concerned Habsburg possessions, however, Frederick was more active. When Charles the Bold of Burgundy attempted in 1474 to seize territory adjacent to Habsburg lands along the Upper Rhine Frederick took a hand. He took advantage of Charles' desire to arrange a marriage between his (Frederick's) son Maximilian and Charles' heir Mary. Soon after the death of Charles in the battle of Nancy (1477) the marriage was performed and the rich heritage of Burgundy, including the Franche Comté and the Lowlands, came into Habsburg possession. It was the house of Habsburg, not the Empire as such, that profited from the inheritance. Bohemia, under the Hussite king George of Poděbrady, had freed itself from the rule of the Emperor, and Hungary, under Mathias Corvinus, was consistently an enemy of the Habsburgs. When Mathias captured Vienna in 1485, Frederick fled, penniless and pitiful, reduced to begging help and even board from German princes. The next year Frederick was obliged by the electors to consent to the election of his son Maximilian as king of the Romans. From this time until his death in 1493 Frederick was largely disregarded and the government was in the hands of Maximilian.

Maximilian was a man of action. Many in Germany thought the young prince, handsome, vigorous, and covered with knightly glory from military action against the French, the Burgundians, and Hungary, would be the one to bring peace and unity to Germany. Nevertheless, numerous difficulties faced this energetic ruler. Imperial finances were precarious. The banking houses, the Welsers, the Fuggers, and other lesser firms, on whom the Emperor had to rely when he needed ready cash, demanded high rates of interest and kept the imperial plate in pawn. War with Charles VIII of France broke out in 1493; in February 1495, to counteract Charles' victories in Italy, Maximilian joined the League of Venice with Pope Alexander VI, Venice, Milan, and Ferdinand. At home demands for reform in imperial administration were becoming more insistent. Maximilian himself would have accepted reform, provided it increased the imperial revenues needed to carry on his wars. The princes and the cities (recognized in 1489 for the first time and summoned to the Diet as the Third Estate) wanted their own kind of reform. At the Worms Diet in 1495 Maximilian requested a continuing grant of taxes for ten to twelve years for the defense of Germany against France and the Turks, warning the Diet that such defense was a matter of life or death for the Empire. Accusing Maximilian of not having fulfilled his promises of reform to previous Diets, the Diet countered with a specific proposal, formulated by Berthold, Archbishop Elector of Mainz, which stipulated that imperial policy should be determined by a council of the greater princes, led by the electors, that the imperial army be under the control of this council, and that the costs of government be defrayed by an imperial tax, the Common Penny (*allgemeiner Pfennig*), at the rate of one tenth of 1 per cent on property values, to be collected by the priests and administered by a commission named by the imperial council. Naturally Maximilian rejected this severe restriction of his rights and power. Long negotiation followed, and a compromise of sorts, favorable rather to the Emperor than to the Estates, was worked out. A *Landfriede* or public peace was proclaimed, forbidding private wars. A Supreme Court of the Empire (*Reichskammergericht*), whose sixteen members were to be nominated by the Estates, and only the presiding officer, the *Kammerrichter,* by the Emperor, was established to administer the Roman law. The *allgemeiner Pfennig* was approved, though now to be collected by the princes or the cities, and administered by imperial treasurers. The Emperor's gain was that the idea of a supreme imperial council was abandoned.

On paper, great progress toward a workable imperial constitution had been made, and the Diet of Worms of 1495 is rightly judged an important landmark in German history. But in operation, the new arrangements met many obstacles. The princes were reluctant to collect money for the Emperor, the *Landfriede* was violated, the Church objected to the imposition of Roman law where it had previously had its own jurisdiction, and Maximilian had no intention of submitting to direction from his subjects. At Freiburg im Breisgau in 1497 Maximilian told the Diet he would no longer be "bound hand and foot" as at Worms, and, despite patient work by Berthold, any semblance of cooperation between Emperor and Diet vanished for the time being. At the Augsburg Diet in 1500 a new compromise was reached. Maximilian, having suffered some military and diplomatic setbacks, was in a relatively weak position to resist the demands of Berthold and the princes. A Council of Regency (*Reichsregiment*) of twenty-one members was established. The presiding officer and two other members were to be royal nominees. Of the remaining 18 members, 12 represented the electors and the princes, and 6 were from the 6 principal areas (circles or *Kreise*) into which Germany was divided for administrative purposes, roughly Franconia, Bavaria, Swabia, Lower Saxony, Westphalia, and the Upper Rhine.* Once again the arrangement seemed the best possible compromise, and once again it failed to work. Maximilian was indignant at the Council for trying to follow a foreign policy opposite to his own. The princes refused to forego their ancient privilege of making war on their neighbors whenever they wished. The Common Penny was forgotten in the confusion.

In reality Germany was not yet ready for the federalism which Berthold was advocating. The knights, a powerful class, resented their exclusion from representation. The break between Emperor and princes was open and bitter. Maximilian's countermeasures, the establishment of a permanent Imperial Council and a degree of unified administration for his Austrian lands, had some success, so that by the time the Diet met in Cologne in 1505 Maximilian's position was very strong. Berthold had died in 1504. Maximilian's son Philip, married to Joanna of Spain in 1496, had become king of Spain on the death of Isabella in 1504, and his infant son Charles was thereby heir apparent to both Spain and Burgundy. Maximilian's prestige was perhaps higher than at any other time in his reign. The Diet, awed and leaderless, was compliant. The Emperor's foreign policies and entanglements were expensive, and successive Diets offered sometimes vocal, sometimes sullen and silent opposition to his demands for money or soldiers. The division of the Empire into ten circles in 1512 was of some administrative benefit, but no real or organic advance toward the unification of Germany was achieved in the last years of Maximilian's reign. By his death in January 1519 the imperial structure presented no semblance of unity; the trend toward separatist rule by the princes was decided.

SCANDINAVIA

WE HAVE seen in an earlier chapter (8) how the three Scandinavian kingdoms, Denmark, Norway, and Sweden, had followed a stormy course of union, war, separation, and, under strong rulers, further attempts at reunion. The Union of Kalmar (1397) under Queen Margaret had seemed for a while an ideal solution to the problems of the Scandinavian states, but it was a reality for only a short period. The revivals of the Union in 1442 and 1457 aroused nationalist opposition in all three countries, particularly in Sweden, and only served to show that their sense of separateness was stronger than their common traditions. Heavy taxes and brutal enforcement of royal decrees produced among the Swedish peasantry a growing antipathy to Danish rule. This anti-Danish

* In 1512 the Diet added to these six four new circles; the Austrias, the four Rhenish electorates joined into one area, Burgundy and the Lowlands, Saxony and Brandenburg. By including the Austrias he was going somewhat outside Germany proper. The system of circles did not function until some years later, after Maximilian's death.

trend brought the Swedish nobility and the peasantry closer together. While the Danish king, Christian I (1448–81), was promptly (1449) recognized as king in Norway and extended his rule to the south over Schleswig and Holstein in 1460, a military campaign was necessary to gain the Swedish throne (1457). For the most part the Oldenburg dynasty ruled their dominions as if they were all Danish property. In 1471 Sten Sture the Elder, regent of Sweden, defeated King Christian in battle near Stockholm; he then ruled Sweden, not without difficulties, until 1497, maintaining his quasi-royal power by favors to the cities and by forcing grants of money from an exceedingly rich church. With both the Church and the magnates leaning to the Danish court, Sture in 1497 was compelled to accept the Danish king, Hans (John), as king of Sweden. But Sture, his power and popularity great among the common people, succeeded in deposing Hans in 1501. On Sture's death in 1503 a distant cousin, Svante Sture, became regent, and in 1512 Svante's son Sten Sture the Younger after him.

A crisis in Scandinavian affairs began the next year. The Stures' versatile counselor, Hemming Gadh, had won allies among the Hanseatic cities, and the subsequent war between Denmark and the cities relieved Danish pressure on Sweden, so that on the death of King Hans in 1513 and the election of Christian II (1513–23) Sten Sture was firmly in control of Swedish affairs. But trouble lay ahead. Christian was learned, ambitious, and ruthless, a ruler in the Machiavellian tradition. Soon after being firmly established as king in Denmark and Norway he set out to force acceptance by Sweden. In Sweden there were two parties. The leader of the nationalist party was the regent, Sten Sture; the leader of the party favoring union with Denmark was Sture's bitter enemy, Gustavus Trolle, archbishop of Uppsala. Sture had had Trolle deposed and imprisoned in 1516, and had in turn been excommunicated by the archbishop of Lund. The latter called upon Christian II of Denmark to come to Stockholm and free the Swedish archbishop. Christian made three invasions of Sweden. The first two expeditions were failures, but the last in 1520 was successful and Sten Sture died from battle wounds. The Swedes were demoralized by the loss of their leader, and Christian was crowned in Stockholm on November 4, 1520. While coronation festivities were going on, the Swedish magnates and high officials of Stockholm were summoned into the royal castle, accused of heresy, imprisoned, and the next day, by Christian's order, beheaded in the public square. Ninety-four corpses lay for three days where they had fallen. Christian left Sweden soon after, convinced that the Swedes were crushed and his rule secure. The opposite was the case. This Stockholm Blood Bath was in fact the end of Danish rule in Sweden. Revolt was universal in the land among all classes, and soon, under the inspiring leadership of Gustavus Vasa, a young nobleman whom Christian had once taken to Copenhagen as a hostage and who had subsequently escaped to Sweden, the land was independent, cleaned of Danish troops.

At home in Denmark Christian was for a while more successful. Favoring the burgher and peasant classes, he strove to break the power of the national diet (*Rigsraad*) by heavy taxation and abrogation of their ancient privileges. Much of his legislation was enlightened and progressive, fostering learning, commerce, ecclesiastical reform, and solid finance. As early as 1519 he was favorably inclined toward the reform teaching of Luther, although at this early stage nothing definite came of the interest. Christian's vigorous and harsh measures, coupled with his cynical disregard of oaths and solemn engagements, brought revolt. Early in 1523 many groups of nobles and some burghers renounced allegiance to the king, and his uncle, Frederick of Holstein, assumed the leadership of the uprising against him. Discouraged, Christian fled to Flanders, remaining in exile or prison until his death in 1559.

The atmosphere in the three Scandinavian kingdoms was now favorable to change. The spirit of independence of outside control, whether of the Roman Church or of a king from another country, or indeed of a native king who sought to initiate drastic reforms, had become a national passion.

RUSSIA: "MOSCOW THE THIRD ROME"

EUROPEAN civilization as we know it had little direct or prolonged contact with Russia until about the middle of the fifteenth century. Along the northern reaches the Hanseatic League had established profitable commercial relations through its factory (depot) at Novgorod from the twelfth century. At Constantinople merchants from the west had dealings with traders from the north. Missionaries from the Eastern Empire had carried Christianity to the principality of Kiev as early as the late ninth century. Kings of Poland had at various times been at war with Kievan or Muscovite princes or occasionally allied with Russian Slavic princes against the Turks along the Dnieper or the Black Sea coast. The Teutonic Knights and the German Knights of the Sword had been roundly defeated by Prince Alexander Nevsky on Lake Peipus in 1242, so that they knew quite well the mettle of the Russians to the east of the Baltic coast. Yet taken together all these occasional contacts were only on the margin of European experience; and to the man of the West, Russia remained remote, barbarous, drear, and uncouth.

The area of Russia was, in the Middle Ages, unbounded and ununified. From the tenth century to late in the twelfth the Slavic princes of Kiev built a kind of empire by subduing surrounding rulers. Close relations with Constantinople and relative stability brought about a high level of culture in which art and letters flourished. But in 1169 Kiev was taken and sacked by the army of a neighboring prince. The decline of this southern capital was followed by three centuries of dispersion of Russian vigor. Three centers may be distinguished: Galicia, Novgorod, and Suzdal, which fitfully prospered and declined until Muscovy in the fifteenth century emerged as the dominant Russian state. The waves of Mongol invasion, from 1223 to 1327, which covered all of southern Russia, made any sort of unification impossible. But to the north, about the middle of the thirteenth century, there arose a line of determined rulers of the small principality of Muscovy, who, by conquest, marriage, or compact, spread their rule over Novgorod, Pereiaslavl, Smolensk, Tver, and the lands in between. Expansion to the south and west brought, in the mid-fourteenth century, conflict with the vigorous Lithuanian state, led by Olgierd (1345–77), son of the great Gedyminas. Olgierd took Kiev in 1361 and reached the Black Sea. Moscow recovered the initiative for a while around 1380 under Grand Duke

Dimitri, but Basil I (1389–1425), beset from the east by Tamerlane and his host and from the west by Vitovt (Witold) (1388–1430), the Lithuanian prince, was able to hold Muscovite territory only with difficulty.

It was during the rule of Basil II (1425–62) that Russia was first represented at a conference in the Western world. Isidore, Metropolitan of Russia, with about a hundred clerics and laymen, attended the Council of Ferrara-Florence in 1439, in the train of the Byzantine Emperor John VIII. It was at this Council that the Orthodox and Roman Catholic churches were formally united. Basil was ruling when, in 1453, Constantinople fell to the Turks, and there arose in Russia and particularly in Moscow the feeling that the custody of imperial Roman tradition had devolved upon the Great Russian people. "Moscow the Third Rome" became, under Ivan III (1462–1505), the official slogan of court and clergy.

Under the rule of Ivan many neighboring princes voluntarily recognized the suzerainty of Moscow. The changes in feudal allegiance were sometimes the work of the boyars, the nobility of the various principalities, who, impressed by Ivan's rule and the stability of the Muscovite state, proffered their loyalty directly to Ivan, over the heads of their local princes. The latter were thus forced to follow the lead of their boyars. In this way Yaroslav (1463), Novgorod, the largest Russian state (1478), Tver (1485), and Vyatka (1489) were brought under Ivan's rule. He also freed Muscovy from any obligation to pay tribute to the Tartar Khan, and wrung from the Lithuanian Grand Prince Alexander the recognition of his title of Autocrat of All Russia (1494). Ivan initiated a policy of participation in West European affairs. He had diplomatic and commercial relations with Denmark, Hungary, Emperor Maximilian, and Ottoman Turkey, and the Venetians were anxious to have Ivan on their side in their continual wars with the Turks.

Consonant with the expansion of his political and military prestige, Ivan tightened the administration of his court and his control over the hitherto semi-independent princes and boyars, enforcing their direct loyalty to him by personal oaths. His second wife, Sophia (Zoe), the niece of John VIII, last Byzantine Emperor, not only brought with her Byzantine ideas of absolutism and elaborate court ceremonial which tended to set the ruler apart from his people, but she also served as a symbol of the connection of Moscow with the Byzantine tradition. The Church did everything possible to enhance and exploit the mystique of the new and rigid absolutism, and the theory of the divine right of kings was soon enounced by the hierarchy in a more extreme form than was ever to be known in the West. Church and state were united in propagating the unquestioned supremacy of the Tsar.

THE OTTOMANS IN EUROPE

THE Ottoman Turks were well established in the Balkans, with their capital at Adrianople, in the second half of the fourteenth century (see above, Chapter 8) and, after crushing the Serbian Empire at Kossovo (1389) and the crusaders of King Sigismund at Nicopolis (1396), were pressing on the frontiers of Hungary in the early decades of the fifteenth century. Then at

Varna on the Black Sea in 1444, the Christians once again suffered humiliating defeat. To the peoples of the Danubian area the Turk was already only too familiar. The fall in 1453 of a scantily populated and desperately defended Constantinople, surrounded on all sides by Turkish positions, hardly came as a surprise to the people of the Balkans. The West, however, was shocked out of its ignorance and complacency and was suddenly deeply concerned about the inexorable advance of the infidel. The situation had its ironic aspects. Emissaries to Western courts from the Christian states which had sought help in order to face the Turk had received short shrift. In 1464 Pope Pius II launched a crusade to recover Constantinople, but died just as it was setting out from Venice. His successor had no interest in carrying out Pius' plans. Indeed, the only real and successful opposition to the Turk was to come from the native leaders of the Balkan peoples, first the Hungarian John Hunyadi until his death in 1456, then the Albanian Scanderbeg until his death in 1467. Hunyadi's son, Mathias Corvinus, then took up the struggle, but by the end of the century, of all the states of the Balkans, Greece included, only Montenegro, safe in her mountain fastnesses, had not yielded to the Turk. Venice made accommodations which allowed her to trade in eastern waters, but the Republic had to give up some ports on the Adriatic. The Turkish sultan, Muhammad II (1451–81), followed his military successes with administrative expansion, evidently determined on a policy of consolidation of his conquests. His last military project was an attempt in 1480 to capture Rhodes, which, in the hands of the Knights of St. John, stood guard over the eastern Mediterranean. The attack was a failure, and Muhammad died the following year. His successor, Bayazid II (1481–1512), was a mild, unenterprising ruler. His younger brother Djem was driven into exile and took refuge with the Grand Master of the Knights of St. John, who treacherously accepted pay from Bayazid to keep him prisoner for eight years. Pope Innocent VIII and after him Pope Alexander VI with equal cynicism took over the arrangement with Bayazid. Djem died of a fever in 1495 in the train of Charles VIII, then occupying Naples. The French at least were not involved in the crass treachery. For a number of years thereafter, except for naval engagements between the Turks and Venice, there was relative peace in the Balkans. On the Danubian front Christian resistance had stiffened, and the Turks' drive was at a standstill. Furthermore, the Turks were occupied with troubles with the Persians on their eastern frontier, and to the south Egypt had taken some Turkish border cities.

Selim I, the son of Bayazid, came to the throne (1512) after defeating in battle and then executing his brothers and cousins. He was anxious for action and glory, saturnine of temper, and properly called Selim the Grim. He took vigorous and successful measures in the east, and by 1517 had brought peace from Egypt to Persia. Rhodes was next on his schedule, but just when he was ready to attack, Selim died of the plague (September 1520). Europe felt great if premature relief. Selim's son and successor, Suleiman the Lawgiver (also known as the Magnificent) was as determined as Selim to expand and secure the frontiers of his empire. He besieged and took Belgrade (1521), thus opening the upper Danube. Then he returned to the problems of still defiant Rhodes, which he took after a siege of over three months, giving generous and honorable terms to the Knights, who had, by their tough defense, won his deep respect. The two bastions of the Christian world, Belgrade and Rhodes, had fallen. The papal *curia* and the courts of Europe were full of plans for a crusade to avenge these humiliations. But little help was forthcoming. King Louis of Bohemia and Hungary, young, inexperienced, and hardly suited by temperament either to rule or to fight, had to bear the brunt of organization and preparation. He was able to collect a motley force of only 30,000 troops, which engaged a Turkish host of over 100,000 seasoned soldiers on the field of Mohács, south of Buda (August 29, 1526). There could have been only one result, annihilation of the Christian forces. King Louis' horse slipped into a stream as the king was leaving the field of battle, and Louis was drowned. The victory of Suleiman meant the consolidation of the rule of the Ottomans in the whole Balkan area. The history of central and western Europe was deeply affected in all its development for hundreds of years thereafter because of this one afternoon's disaster.

It is obvious and proper that we should here make some comparisons between the world of Dante (Chapter 1) and the Europe of Machiavelli, in order to estimate what had taken place in these two and a half centuries. The two Italys—that of 1275 and that of 1525—were vastly different. The French Angevins, who, allied with the Papacy and the Guelphs, were so dominant in the time of Dante, had almost disappeared from the internal affairs of Italy by the later date. The French effort, under Charles VIII, Louis XII, and Francis I, to recover their lost hold in Italy by military conquest, served only to unite Italian sentiment against them. The house of Aragon, on the contrary, was readily accepted by the Italians, wherever they set firm foot, in Sicily, Naples, and Milan. Italy's earlier great diversity in principalities and free communes had settled into a more stable structure of five leading powers, Naples, Florence, Venice, Milan, and the Papacy. Lesser states had survived by attaching themselves to one of their larger neighbors. The Papacy, now in effect a lay state, as warlike and cynical as any Italian despotism, had lost most of its spiritual temper.

Outside Italy, the focus of most political as well as cultural activity in Europe, great changes had taken place. Spain had achieved a high degree of unity, at least in the persons and policies of the Catholic Kings, and had gained a global empire whose fabulous wealth would enable a hitherto poor land to dominate European developments for another century and a half. France, not yet aware of her unity in 1300, after suffering the ravages of over a century of war, had by the time of Francis I become a rich, united, and articulate nation, able to survive even the foolish adventures of a Charles VIII. The Empire, which in the time of Dante was still a European idea and remained for some time thereafter a hope of universal peace, had become a purely German skeleton, disunited even in Germany, and, as long as it remained in the hands of German rulers, thoroughly impotent. Only the wealth of Spain and the Lowlands and the dedication of the Spanish king to the proposition that it was God's will that he should use that wealth to maintain the Empire, had kept it alive as a European concept.

About the middle of the fifteenth century two new and aggressive powers, Russia and Ottoman Turkey, appear in the East. The impact of their pressure upon the Western European states will profoundly affect almost all political and economic development for centuries. No Western court will dare to neglect the effect of any political move upon the policies or actions of the Sultan. With this change in the East, the discoveries across the Atlantic, and commercial imperialism in Africa, India, and the Far East, there begins the Europeanization of the whole world, and although at the same time Europe herself diminishes in relative size, yet her every movement and idea has repercussions around the globe.

SUGGESTIONS FOR FURTHER READING

See bibliography for Chapter 8.

COMMYNES, PHILIP DE, *Memoirs*. 2 vols. London, 1885–86
MACHIAVELLI, *The Art of War* (with other works). New York, 1891
MACHIAVELLI, *The Discourses*. Many editions; in Modern Library
MACHIAVELLI, *History of Florence*. London, 1871. Bohn Library (includes some letters)
MACHIAVELLI, *The Prince*. Many editions; in Everyman's and Modern Library

BATIFFOL, L., *Century of the Renaissance*. London, 1916
BUTTERFIELD, H., *The Statecraft of Machiavelli*. New York, 1956
CHABOD, F., *Machiavelli and the Renaissance*. London, 1958
DAVIES, R. T., *The Golden Century of Spain, 1506–1621*. London, 1954
FISHER, H. A. L., *Political History of England, 1485–1547*. London, 1906
GREGOROVIUS, F., *Lucrezia Borgia*. London, 1901 (Phaidon, 1952)
HYMA, A., *Renaissance to Reformation*. Grand Rapids, 1951
KIRCHNER, W., *Rise of the Baltic Question*. Newark, 1954
KITCHIN, G. W., *History of France*, Vol. II. Oxford, 1877
MACKIE, J. D., *The Earlier Tudors, 1485–1558*. Oxford, 1952
MERRIMAN, R. B., *Rise of the Spanish Empire*, Vol. I. New York, 1918
POLLARD, A. F., *Wolsey*. London, 1929
PRESCOTT, W., *Ferdinand and Isabella*. Philadelphia, 1872
RAGG, L., *Crises in Venetian History*. London, 1926
RANKE, L. VON, *Latin and Teutonic Nations*. London, 1887
ROSCOE, T., *Life of Leo X*. 2 vols. London, 1846. Bohn Library
SCHEVILL, F., *History of Florence*. New York, 1939
SCHEVILL, F., *The Balkan Peninsula and the Near East*. New York, 1922
WALSH, W., *Isabella of Spain*. London, 1932
WILLIAMS, C. H., *England under the Early Tudors*. London, 1925

BAETHGEN, F., *Europa im Spätmittelalter*. 1951
DE BOOM, G., *Marguerite d'Autriche*. 1946
DELABORDE, H. F., *L'Expédition de Charles VIII en Italie*. 1888
GITERMANN, V., *Geschichte Russlands*. 3 vols. 1949
HAUSER, H., and A. RENAUDET, *Les Débuts de l'âge moderne*. 1946
KASER, K., *Deutsche Geschichte im Ausgang des Mittelalters*, Vol. II. 1912
LEMONNIER, J.-H., *Les Guerres d'Italie*. 1903
RENAUDET, A., *Préréforme et humanisme à Paris pendant les premières guerres d'Italie*. 1953
RITTER, G., *Die Neugestaltung Europas im 16. Jahrhundert*. 1950
ULMANN, H., *Kaiser Maximilian I*. 2 vols. 1884–91

CHAPTER SIXTEEN

ON THE EVE OF
THE REFORMATION

GERMANY was the scene of the most dramatic events of the Protestant Reformation. The leading personalities of this cataclysmic movement spent the greater part of their lives within the boundaries of the "Holy Roman Empire of the German Nation": Charles V, the Dutch-born Emperor, steadfast defender of the faith; Martin Luther, Saxon monk and convinced reformer of the Church; Philip Melanchthon, sensitive scholar and reluctant successor to Luther; Frederick the Wise, Elector of Saxony and staunch supporter of his brash Wittenberg professor; Philip of Hesse, courageous if not always stable leader of the Protestant princes—all these and many more played their roles on the soil of Germany in this short half-century that decided the ecclesiastical and religious complexion of the Western world for at least the subsequent four centuries. The German Reformation, led by Luther and Melanchthon, was not the only reformation that took place in Europe in this middle period, nor indeed was it the first. It was not acceptable to several other nations not comprised within the Germanic group of peoples. Yet by its magnitude, by its success, by the clarity of the issues it raised, and by the compelling formulation of its thought, the German Reformation may claim prior importance among all the reform movements. We will, in the course of our story, observe how broadly based the Lutheran revolt was and how deep its roots reached into German life, far beyond the ecclesiastical or purely theological issues Luther and his colleagues raised. While emphasizing the dynamic personality of Luther and his tremendous impact upon his time, we shall also see how, paradoxically, the Lutheran movement was a relatively conservative movement. It is therefore proper that we should first examine the soil out of which this movement grew, in order to understand its involvement in the social, economic, political, and cultural movements of the time.

GERMANY AT THE TURN OF THE CENTURY

VISITORS to Germany in the latter part of the fifteenth century very frequently remarked upon the generally high level of prosperity they found. Aeneas Silvius Piccolomini, a much traveled and acute observer, wrote in 1458 that "Germany has never been richer or more prosperous than today. She surpasses all other nations in wealth and power. On every side we see cultivated farms, fields of grain, vineyards and gardens. Handsome buildings, walled cities are everywhere, and the farmers are well off." Testimonies to the high degree of material comfort in the cities abounded, at least for the next half-century. It was a period of marked economic expansion. Before the explorations of the Portuguese and the Spaniards brought great wealth to Europe, the German merchants had flourishing commercial relations with Venice, where the *Fondaco dei Tedeschi* (Agency of the Germans) was the focus of the trade from the German cities into the Mediterranean area. From Augsburg, the most active center of south German trade, Nürnberg, hardly less active, and Ulm lines of commercial activity reached to all the principal marts of Europe: to the Hanseatic cities, to the Lowlands, down the Danube and into Switzerland, and as far west as Lisbon.

In the late fifteenth century two south German business firms emerged from among many as the most enterprising and successful: the Welsers and the Fuggers. Both houses began as trading companies, but the Fuggers early restricted themselves to banking. Their opportunity was the need of the Habsburg house for ready cash to implement its expansionist policies. In 1487 Archduke Sigismund of the Tyrol gave a mortgage to Jacob Fugger on the Tyrolean silver mines for an advance of 24,000 florins. The next year another advance of 150,000 florins was given against the whole silver output of the Schwatz mines in the Tyrol, the most productive silver mines then known in Europe. The Fuggers soon acquired control of the copper mines in Hungary under similar conditions. Emperor Maximilian I, the worst financier of all the Habsburgs, obtained many advances from the Fuggers and some Nürnberg bankers, being obliged, with each transaction, to give some imperial security—mines, taxes, plate, or anticipated revenue. The Fuggers drove hard bargains and grew fabulously rich and powerful. In one period of seven years they are reported to have increased their capital by 13,000,000 florins. They remained the leading banking house of Germany until the end of the century, when losses in Spain weakened the firm's credit noticeably.

The Welsers, on the other hand, preferred to stick to trade, and were not so exclusively a family enterprise as the Fuggers, allowing other business houses or individuals to participate in some of their larger ventures. They thus spread their risks, and took more modest profits. In addition to the head office at Augsburg, they maintained factories in Nürnberg, Lisbon, Venice, Genoa, Antwerp, Vienna, Danzig, Saragossa, Milan, and Rome. They extended fewer loans than the Fuggers, but, like the latter, owed their ultimate decline to losses from unrecoverable advances made to princes.

These two firms, the Fuggers and the Welsers, were only the most prominent among many venture enterprises in Germany. A spirit of commercial and
financial prosperity was in the air. The expectation of heavy profits stimulated
ventures which would take advantage of increased demands for goods and a
general atmosphere of financial optimism. It was a period when bigness was
an ideal. Many associations of merchants in similar or related businesses were
formed, aimed at controlling the market and raising prices. These monopolies
were hard on the small merchant and on the common consumer. Many complaints against their practices were registered in Diets and in the literature of
the time. The Landtag at Innsbruck in 1518 resolved that "The great companies have monopolized everything and cannot be borne any longer. . . . All
sorts of goods, silver, copper, steel, sugar, spices, corn, cattle, wine, meat,
tallow and leather, are now in their hands. . . . They raise prices arbitrarily
when it suits them. . . . They are a great harm to our country." The steep rise
in prices before and after 1500, due not only to the increase in the amount of
coined specie but also to monopolistic practices and the high profits demanded,
had a twofold significance; it was not only a reflection of the prosperity of the
merchant class who took the profits but also an indication that the peasantry
and the artisan class were worse off than before. Their income tended to remain
static, while the prices of consumer goods might double or treble within a few
years.

The Peasantry

THE peasantry was still tied to an agricultural economy that responded only
slowly to the boom of commerce and finance, which enriched the cities
and particularly the capitalist class. The peasants had sensed for some time that
they were being driven still lower on the economic scale. They saw the luxury
in which the capitalist class was living and noted the growing disparity between that luxury and their own poverty. There were many attempts by peasant
groups in the fourteenth and fifteenth centuries to bring their plight to the
attention of the princes and the Diets. Little if any help came from that source,
and open revolt was inevitable. The first substantial peasant revolt was that of
the three forest cantons of Switzerland and Lucerne in the mid-fourteenth century. This was followed by another Swiss peasant confederacy early in the
fifteenth century, known as the Graubund. These earliest uprisings were directed against the feudal overlords, but in increasing measure the peasantry
included the clergy in the ranks of their oppressors. The news of the successes
of the Swiss peasantry and mountaineers spread rapidly throughout southern
Germany, where, in the fifteenth century, hardly a decade passed without an
uprising of a lower class against oppression. In Gotha in 1391 the resentment
was directed against the Jews of the town who demanded heavy interest for
loans. The Hussite wars (1419–34) occasioned sympathetic unrest among the
unfree classes, as the impression spread that the struggle lay between the Czech
peasants and the German nobility who wished to enslave and oppress them.
By the middle of the century the Church, a wealthy feudal landowner demanding tithes and services from the peasantry, was identified with the nobility and

the capitalistic merchants in the towns as responsible for the woes and failures of the peasantry, who by this time had a long list of grievances which grew heavier with every passing season.

Most of the uprisings were spontaneous, lacking in leadership, and easily put down by force of arms. The position of the peasants was likely to be worse after the revolt than before. In 1476, however, a natural leader, Hans Böheim (Böhm) appeared in southern Germany. Motivated by a deep conviction and gifted with natural eloquence, he is reported to have held crowds of twenty to thirty thousand spellbound. He denounced all priests, attacked the Emperor for supporting the parasitic nobility, and ridiculed the Pope and the whole ecclesiastical establishment. He exhorted his hearers to refuse to pay taxes and demand the rights to hunt and fish and make free use of common pastures and meadow lands. Böhm remained unmolested only a few weeks. The bishop of Würzburg had him apprehended and, after a sort of trial, burned. Böhm had given a religious, almost evangelical, turn to his message. This was a new manifestation in the movement for peasant liberation, and one which the Church could not be expected to endure.

A development which in its origins had nothing specific to do with the rise of the spirit of revolt did, ultimately, contribute to the bitterness with which the nobility and the princes were regarded, both by the depressed classes and by the intelligentsia, who sympathized with their plight. From about the middle of the fifteenth century more and more complaints were heard about the enforced introduction of Roman law to replace traditional Germanic law. German students went to Italian law schools in increasing numbers and, on their return, were given positions at the courts of the princes and as judges in princely and imperial law courts. Resentment at the invasion of non-Germanic legal ideals was general, but there was little that could be done about it. Roman law favored the ruler and put a premium on meticulous legalism. The knights, the artisans, and the peasants were helpless in the face of the new legalistic dictatorship, and throughout the second half of the century and on into the sixteenth voiced their opposition. Sebastian Brant at Basel in 1494 spoke of the lawyer who "finds a well-off peasant, and with legal documents roasts him. . . . They corrupt the law to make a living." The humanist John Cochlaeus wrote about the same time "I only lament over the general evil which has come from that Thracian fellow Justinian whose code has been the cause of all the trouble." Jacob Wimpheling asserted "The Roman lawyers are overwhelming us. . . . They minister to the interests of the princes by curtailing the freedom of the people. . . . The jurists at the sovereign courts suck the blood of the people by the new taxes which they justify with such fine words as 'We must curb the too forward peasantry.'"

In 1491 and 1492 there was open revolt against the exactions of the abbot of Kempten, near Lake Constance. This revolt began as an uprising of the peasantry but it was soon joined by the working classes of the town of Kempten. Religion seems to have played only a minor role in this manifestation. The next year, 1493, saw a more widespread revolt in Alsace. Here again the peasantry and the town workers united—7000 men and 400 women—to demand alleviation of their burdens. Furthermore, they stipulated, the new Roman law must be abolished in favor of ancient Germanic law and custom, the property of the Church must be reduced, and both the priests and the Jews must be kept within bounds. The movement of opposition to Church and feudal nobility and the monopolies adopted a common emblem, the device of a peasant's shoe, tied with a string, commonly called *Bundschuh*. This device, which had first appeared as the insignia of a peasant uprising in 1443 near Basel, was to appear henceforth, beside a white cross and a picture of the crucifixion, on the flags of almost all the lower-class uprisings in Germany.

From 1501 there were almost yearly uprisings within the Empire. The most ambitious was the revolt which broke out in the region around Speier in 1502. Its leaders called for loyalty to the Emperor but rejected all princely and ecclesiastical jurisdictions and appealed to peasants and oppressed townsfolk throughout the Empire to join them. Most of the leaders were caught and summarily dispatched. One of those who escaped to Switzerland, Joss Fritz, laid plans for a revival of the movement. In 1512 the plans were discovered and he had to escape again, with the flag of the *Bundschuh* wrapped around his waist. In 1513 the peasants and townsfolk of Freiburg im Breisgau, organized by Fritz, revolted. The following year a revolt of peasants and townsfolk broke out in Württemberg against the tyranny of Duke Ulrich. It was ruthlessly suppressed. Then in 1517 Fritz led another, better planned and organized uprising in the Upper Rhine area. He operated with a network of "agents" among all the poor and oppressed of southern Germany, and the authorities were able to stifle the outbreak only with the greatest difficulty. By now it was evident that the peasantry and the townsfolk were in dead earnest in their demands: the abolition of serfdom (*Leibeigenschaft*), the relaxation of rents and taxes, rights to fish, common pasture, the reform of the Church, and the limitation or abolition of the exemptions enjoyed by both clergy and nobility. The religious overtones in the demands of the peasantry and the townspeople were as prominent as their conviction that what Germany needed was a strong central government under a single ruler, the Emperor. This peasant insistence on religious reform struck at the roots of the wealth and luxury of the clergy. The political idea, a rejection of the intermediate jurisdiction of the princes, was naturally unwelcome to the landed nobility. Both these factors will appear relevant when we consider the vindictive brutality with which the most dangerous of all peasant revolts, that of 1525, was crushed in blood.

The German Nobility

AS WE look forward toward the German Reformation and strive to understand its success, we find that some factors not basically religious were of peculiar significance in the ultimate acceptance of its aims and principles by a great part of the German people. We have seen above (Chapter 15) that the upper nobility, both secular and ecclesiastical, led by Berthold, Archbishop Elector of Mainz, tried to reform the organization of the Empire and at the same time to strengthen their position as essentially independent princes. The Emperor struggled against this trend with varying success. The end result, however, was that the great princes within their territories were essentially independent of imperial control. Furthermore, the adoption of the Roman law code, which exalted the ruler and repressed the ruled, only tightened the hold of the magnates upon their subjects. Politically, as we shall see when following the course of Luther's thought, this centralization of control within each electorate or principality in the hands of the rulers was of crucial importance. On the one hand, the princes were able to defy the Emperor; on the other, they controlled the Church in their lands and could dictate whether their subjects should remain faithful to the established church or accept the new teachings of the monk of Wittenberg. Thus a constitutional question had a significant bearing upon a religious development.

Just below the greater princes of the Empire was a class difficult to categorize with any accuracy—the imperial knights. The origins of this class go back to the days when the knight in armor was of some real use. The rise of the city, its industry and commerce, and the money economy which brought with it a transfer of power from the law of the fist (*Faustrecht*) to the law of contract and enterprise, made the knight obsolete. In Germany these scions of old and noble houses, failing to adjust to the change in society, frequently became robber knights (*Raubritter*), living off raids on cities and monasteries or outright highway robbery. Nevertheless, some among them showed staunchly patriotic tendencies and, whenever admitted to the Diet of the Empire, knights of this turn of mind supported the imperial cause as against the magnates. They may have been motivated by jealousy of their more successful fellow nobles and the patriciate of the towns, but as a class they opposed fragmentation of the Empire.

A number of these knights made common cause with the peasantry and appeared as their military leaders in several uprisings. The best known of these were Franz von Sickingen (1481–1523) and Götz von Berlichingen (1480–1562). For most of his life von Sickingen held strong imperialist convictions. The rich cities and the great princes were particular objects of his hatred. At various times he warred on Worms, Metz, and Frankfort, the duke of Lorraine, and the landgrave of Hesse, forcing all of them to buy him off with large indemnities. He served the French king against Emperor Maximilian, then reversed his stand and entered the Emperor's service as a field commander, only at the end to be deserted by his allies and laid under the ban of the Empire for taking up arms against the Archbishop Elector of Trier. He decried the introduction of Roman law into Germany and proclaimed himself a defender of the ancient and real Germany and an unrelenting opponent of new ideas and non-German novelties. Apart from his unquestioned German nationalism, he resembled more than anything else an Italian *condottiere*. Götz von Berlichingen, called Götz of the Iron Hand, was very like von Sickingen. He also warred on numerous Rhenish cities, as well as on the bishops of Würzburg and Mainz, and took part in many other feuds. He lost his right hand in a war against Nürnberg in 1504, and replaced it with an iron hook, whence his sobriquet. He was frequently allied with von Sickingen; like the latter, he was at various times on both sides of the issue of prince versus people. He sided with Duke Ulrich of Württemberg against the Swabian League, and after joining the peasants in 1525, deserted them before the decisive battle. Often imprisoned, he was able by promises or purchase to obtain his release. Goethe's romantic drama *Götz von Berlichingen* (1773), based on the misleading autobiography rather than on the historical documents, depicts the knight as the heroic foe of priest and prince, defender of peasant and oppressed. In fact Götz was at times a very ambiguous, not to say slippery character.

Ulrich von Hutten (1488–1523) will cross our path at a number of junctures in the early days of the Reformation. Of an old and honored knightly family in Franconia, he was, probably because of frail health and scholarly proclivities, destined for the Church and sent to school at Fulda. He found theology uncongenial, and, against his father's wishes, left the monastery in 1505 to devote himself to the new humanistic learning. Without family support, undernourished, and ill, he nevertheless won a name as a poet and scholar. In 1511 he spent some time at the imperial court in Vienna, which, under the favor of Maximilian, was a center of art and letters. The next year found him studying law and the classics at Bologna. Unable to make a livelihood by letters, he became for a while a not very successful mercenary soldier. What he saw of the Church on a short trip to northern Italy in 1512 and particularly of the warlike Pope Julius II so shocked him that his pen grew bitter against the Pope, "pest of the world," "scourge of mankind." Hutten remained in Germany for several years thereafter. In 1515 a cousin was murdered by Duke Ulrich of Württemberg. This murder of a noble by a prince aroused all the pride and indignation of the whole knightly class. Hutten burst out in verse and satire, constituting himself the voice of the noble knighthood of Germany. Classical studies had sharpened his naturally invective pen. As a result of the charges against him the duke was laid under the ban of the Empire, but was able to squirm out of it, much to the disappointment of Hutten. While engaged in these polemics Hutten began to collaborate with Crotus Rubeanus in the *Letters of Obscure Men* (see above, p. 335). In disgust at the outcome of his struggle against Duke Ulrich, he left again for a second stay of two years in Italy (1515–17), this time mostly in Rome and Bologna. From what he saw in Rome he conceived an even deeper hatred for the whole papal institution, which he now regarded as the source of the woes of all Christendom and particularly of Germany. The first part of the *Letters of Obscure Men* was published in 1515 while Hutten was in Italy. His share in this part of the satire was not as great as it had been in part II of the *Letters,* which, published in 1517, was predominantly the work of Hutten. Its popularity was immediate, and set all literate Germany laughing at the pompously crude ignorance of the obscurantists who were attacking learning in the person of Reuchlin. On his return from Italy in 1517 Hutten was crowned with the laurel wreath of the poet by Emperor Maximilian. He heartily approved Luther's attack on the indulgences later that year; in the remaining years of his life he continued to awaken Germany to her mission and the dangers threatening German liberty from the Papacy. His literary production, increasingly in German from 1517 to his death in 1523, was prodigious and remarkably effective. In 1520 he wrote to his humanist friend Capito at Mainz: "Wake up. My patience is at an end, for the Roman lions thirst for blood. But unless I am wrong, they will first bleed themselves and will have to wear the shackles with which they threaten me." His belligerence offended some of his friends, and Erasmus refused to see him in 1522. At the end it was only Zwingli who gave him refuge on an island in Lake Zurich.

Hutten, as a forerunner of the German Reformation, as an awakener of

Germany to a national consciousness, occupies a very prominent place. To the extent that the Reformation was a nationalistic and patriotic movement—and, as we shall see, this motive forms a clearly discernible part in the revolt against the Church—Hutten, as well as the other imperial knights who sided with him, exercised a powerful influence on the course of German history. Hutten was in himself an anomaly. Two German patriots warred in one breast: the humanist and the knight. Neither alone could have brought about the much needed reform in religious life, much less German unity. There was, furthermore, no possibility that they would be successfully combined. The humanist was antifeudal; the knight represented the last refuge of an outdated feudal society. It would take a German monk to break the power of the Church in Germany with the weapon of religion and the language of the nation.

The Universities

WE HAVE noticed above (Chapter 12) how, late in the fifteenth century, humanism came to some centers in Germany—the courts of several enlightened

Ulrich von Hutten, an engraving by E. Kieser, frontispiece of *Letters of Obscure Men*, original in the British Museum [PIERPONT MORGAN LIBRARY].

princes and several south German cities. These scattered focal points of the new learning were significant, yet they were too few to have more than a limited impact on the total cultural life of Germany. University education came late to the Empire, but once the way was shown the institution flourished. Before the outbreak of the Reformation the region east of the Rhine was blessed with a respectable number of moderately well-supported universities. The following list reveals the spread:

1348	Prague, founded by Emperor Charles IV
1364	Cracow, by King Casimir III of Poland, papal bull of 1365
1365	Vienna, by ducal charter and papal bull
1379, 1392	Erfurt, by papal bulls
1385	Heidelberg, by electoral grant and papal bull
1388	Cologne, by municipal action and papal bull
1409	Leipzig, by papal bull
1419	Rostock, by ducal charter, city council, and papal bull
1456	Greifswald, by papal bull
1455–56	Freiburg im Breisgau, by papal bull and ducal charter
1459	Basel, by city council and papal bull
1459, 1472	Ingolstadt, by papal bull and ducal charter
1476	Mainz, by archiepiscopal charter and papal bull
1476	Tübingen, by papal bull and imperial charter
1502	Wittenberg, by imperial charter
1506	Frankfort on the Oder, by imperial grant and papal bull.

All these universities were the scenes—in varying degrees of intensity—of conflict between the *via antiqua,* the revived scholasticism of St. Thomas, and the *via moderna,* the more widely accepted nominalism of William of Ockham. This conflict arose out of purely philosophical differences within the scholastic tradition; but in the latter half of the fifteenth century the humanistic tendencies that filtered northward from Italian centers introduced a new conflict, between those who held to the older method and curricula and those who desired to study the more humane subjects (*humaniora*). The two battles were not infrequently being fought at the same time at the same university. The campaign against the old curriculum and methods of teaching and even the degrees given under the old system was waged with increasing success in the last decades of the century. Aeneas Silvius, on one of his many trips to Germany, had remarked caustically on the pointlessness of the university instruction he found there, and his judgment was frequently echoed by Germans of the new school. We have seen (see above, p. 329) that Peter Luder had begun to lecture at Heidelberg in 1444 on the Latin authors, but he created no school and had no significant followers. At the University of Basel Johann Heynlin von Stein, intermittently professor of philosophy and theology, from 1464 until his death in 1496, was sympathetic to the humanistic studies and managed to reconcile the newer disciplines with his defense of Plato and fervent evangelical preaching. One of his students, Johann Amerbach, was a devoted humanist who founded (1478) one of the most successful printing firms of the century. There poured from this press in a steady stream editions of the Bible and the Fathers of the Church, Greek and Latin, as well as carefully prepared works of the Latin and Greek classics. In 1492 he brought Johann Froben into his firm as a partner. The humanist tradition at Basel was continued by Heinrich Loriti of Glarus, known as Glareanus (1488–1563). Of a mettlesome temperament, he was often at odds with the university authorities; as a teacher and as a scholar, both of Greek and Latin, he was effective and respected. He was almost unique among humanists in his Swiss patriotism. Most of the Swiss humanists either prided themselves on their indifference to such petty foibles as local patriotism or tended to identify themselves with their German colleagues. Glareanus by contrast made a respectable specialty of Swiss geography and the history of the arts in his native land.

At the University of Tübingen, a late (1476) foundation, humanism had little determined opposition from scholastic traditionalism. Conrad Summenhart (1450–1501) was the dominant personality on the faculty. He was by nature and training a conservative, both in theology and in philosophy, but was anxious to avoid controversy. He decried the worldliness of the Papacy and the luxury of the clergy, and urged upon his students a careful study of the Bible. A younger colleague of Summenhart was Heinrich Bebel (1472–1518), who was an ardent protagonist of pure classical form. He found the models of Latin that were used in class instruction full of faults, ridiculed all medieval Latin authors, and praised such Italian humanists as Petrarch, Filelfo, Panormita, and Aretino for their obedience to the classic rules. He made himself unpopular among his German colleagues by asserting, quite objectively (as he thought), that no German could write decent Latin.

The University of Cologne, one of the older German universities, was essentially an outgrowth of a vigorous school of Dominican theology dating back to the thirteenth century, and its curriculum showed this scholastic tradition. Humanistic studies, therefore, met heavy resistance. Hermann von Busch (1468–1534), a pupil of Rudolf Agricola, had traveled and studied widely in Italy. He taught the classics at Cologne from 1495 to 1500, then at other universities for seven years, returning to reside at Cologne from 1507 to 1516. He was involved in the Reuchlin-Pfefferkorn controversy and, with Hutten and Crotus Rubeanus, in the composition of the *Letters of Obscure Men*. As early as 1518 he was an adherent of Luther. His most significant work, *Vallum humanitatis (The Rampart of Humane Studies)*, published in 1518 in Cologne, became the standard defense of the new learning. He contended, from history and logic, that the study of the classic authors, particularly the poets, could only be useful and profitable to the young.

Cologne was also the center for the activities of Ortwin Gratius (1491–1545), who, almost alone among humanists, supported Pfefferkorn and attacked Reuchlin. It is not easy to understand Gratius' motivation. A reasonably well-trained humanist, his scholarly production was hardly in the scholastic tradition. His best-known work, the *Fasciculus rerum expetendarum ac fugiendarum (Collection of Things That Should Be Rejected and Avoided)* (1535), is a collection of the texts of violent attacks on the Papacy in recent centuries. The work certainly helped the opponents of the Church more than its defenders. At the end of his life he reversed his position, praising Reuchlin and sponsoring a work of Hutten. There were at Cologne other "poets," as the humanists were called, who were sought out by many students. Most of them had studied in Italy. This ancient center of conservative scholasticism thus showed the confusing influence of the new learning as it acted upon established currents of thought and broadened the horizons of the younger generation who were unconsciously being prepared for the shocks of the Protestant Reformation.

The university at Erfurt had a history very similar to and almost contemporary with that at Cologne, save that the *humaniora* received official recognition earlier than at most other German universities. Peter Luder was on the faculty in 1460, and soon thereafter there arose a split among the "poets" into a moderate and an aggressively active party. The moderates would have been content to accept the older scholastic curriculum, grafting onto it classical studies. The "activists" wanted to abolish the whole medieval program and initiate a radically new curriculum based exclusively on the Latin and Greek classics. The leading representative of the moderate party was Jodocus Trutvetter (1460–1519), who was later one of Luther's teachers. A nominalist, he wrote some quite medieval commentaries on Aristotle. Yet he was favorable to the new studies, and sincerely urged his students to study the classics, while he himself quoted them often with approval. The "activists" were led by Conrad Mutianus Rufus (1470–1526), who had studied at Deventer with Erasmus and earned a law degree at Bologna. From 1503 to the end of his life he had a canonry at Gotha but spent much of his time with the Erfurt circle of humanists, students as well as teachers. He, too, was on Reuchlin's side in the case of the books, and probably took part in the composition of the *Letters of Obscure Men*. Strongly imbued with the ideals of Italian humanism, he was eager, persuasive, and a popular if demanding teacher. He wielded his greatest influence through his voluminous correspondence. Trutvetter came to occupy a position of leadership beside Reuchlin and Erasmus in the whole German humanistic movement. His was a dedicated leadership; he never relaxed his demands for moral as well as stylistic excellence on the part of his colleagues and followers. His religion was perhaps closer to that of the Platonic Academy of Florence than to current Catholicism; yet, while rejecting the rigors of Luther's teaching, he did not lack deep religious feeling. He once wrote to a friend concerning the Eucharist: "He who takes this memorable and healing Eucharist in a devout frame of mind is doing something of a godlike deed. The true body of Christ is peace and concord and there can be nothing more holy than to love one another."

The Renaissance Papacy

SOME of the most violent language Martin Luther used, in the whole course of his battle with the papal system, was directed against the luxury and cynical immorality of the *curia,* the cardinals, and the popes at Rome. He had been in Rome for about a month, December 1510–January 1511, during the pontificate of Julius II, and had seen much with his own eyes. But what he saw was only a confirmation of the evil repute the papal *curia* had won in the last half of the fifteenth century. The evidence of the deep degradation into which the Papacy had fallen was only too graphically clear.

Pope Pius II (Aeneas Silvius Piccolomini) had come to the papal throne after a long career as a humanist. As Pope he repented quite sincerely of a lurid past, and for the six years of his pontificate (1458–64) strove to lead the Church devoutly and, for that time, relatively honestly. His control over the hierarchy and particularly the cardinals was very slight. His project of a crusade against the Turk, to recapture Constantinople, savored of the days of medieval chivalry, but at least he made the effort, and as he lay dying saw his few caravels slowly move out of the lagoons of Venice. They turned back as soon as his death was known, and the idea of the crusade died with him.

The cardinals chose one of their number, Pietro Barbo, a Venetian, to succeed Pius II. As Paul II he reigned from 1464 to 1471, enjoying the wealth and power his high office brought him. Fond of display, he entertained the Roman populace with fêtes and carnivals, horse races and footraces, of which the later Roman emperors could have been proud. No humanist himself, Paul suspected the humanists at Rome of plotting against him and dissolved the Roman Academy, then headed by Pomponio Leto, whom he imprisoned for a time. On the other hand, he collected coins, vases, and jewels, and was not opposed to the spread of printing, which first appeared in Italy (1467) during his pontificate, though not at his order or expense. Paul was well served by most of the cardinals who had elected him and lived a moderate and even simple life. He was guilty of extensive nepotism, but the relatives he elevated to high positions in the Church served well and fairly honestly. On balance, he is generally regarded as a transitional character between the essentially medieval Pius II and the popes of the Renaissance who followed him.

The successor of Paul II was the Franciscan Cardinal Francesco della Rovere, who took the name of Sixtus IV (1471–84). He had had a distinguished career as a professor at several Italian universities and had earned wide recognition as a scholar and orator. Though not, in the true sense of the word, a humanist, he nevertheless had artistic interests, supported painters and sculptors, built gracefully, and restored many bridges and buildings in Rome. The Sistine Chapel in the Vatican is his best-known monument. Yet no sooner was he firmly seated in the chair of St. Peter than he began to surround himself with nephews and grandnephews. He had sixteen of them, and his two brothers and four sisters, with their children, all had to be richly provided for. Eight of his nephews and grandnephews became cardinals. One of them, Peter Riario, was showered with wealthy benefices and lived in such luxury and ostentation as to be the wonder of Rome. He died at twenty-eight, the victim of his excesses. Another nephew, Jerome, was the author of a plot to kill Lorenzo and Giuliano de' Medici in the cathedral in Florence in 1478. The Pope approved of the plot (see above, p. 413) and, when Lorenzo survived, excommunicated him as a "son of iniquity." Most of the thirty-four prelates now raised to the cardinalate were extremely worldly men, and the total impression the college gave was one of cynical venality. It is in retrospect difficult to understand Sixtus' mania for indulgence of his worse than worthless nephews. The outside world, seeing the wanton wasting of the contributions of the faithful, held the Pope personally responsible. In Germany, particularly, resentment at the heavy papal taxation resulting from the extravagance of the *curia* was high and vocal. In 1479 an assembly of the clergy at Coblenz formulated a long list of complaints against papal exactions and sent it to Rome. Yet with all his forced levies from all over Europe Sixtus left a huge debt for his successor to wrestle with.

The degradation of the Papacy grew steadily more notorious. The papal elections of 1484 and 1492 have been called by Pastor, the great Catholic historian, "among the most deplorable in the annals of Church History." The election of Innocent VIII was the result of a vigorous and callous campaigning for the purchase of votes by Cardinal Giuliano della Rovere, to whom the new Pope was deeply indebted. Anarchy ruled in Rome for weeks after the election, and throughout his pontificate Innocent was unable to bring any real order into the city. Churches were plundered, pilgrims and Romans robbed or murdered, and "justice" was bought and sold. Counterfeited papal bulls were peddled openly in the streets; spiritual offices in the *curia* were marketable commodities. The Pope himself set an example—eighteen papal secretaryships brought 62,400 ducats and the price of the office of *plumbator,* an official who affixed the lead seal to a papal bull, was currently 2500 ducats. Innocent was party to the retention of Djem, brother and rival of Bayazid, son of Sultan Muhammad II. Bayazid had won out in the struggle for the sultanate, and when Djem fled to the Christians, was willing to pay generously to have him kept a prisoner in the West. Innocent, glad to accommodate the Sultan, kept Djem in luxury, collecting 45,000 ducats a year for his custodianship (see above, p. 433). The sight of the successor of St. Peter acting as jailer for the Muslim sultan, the despoiler of the tomb of the Savior, aroused no little indignation in the Christian community. On the death of Innocent VIII in 1492 the repute of the Papacy throughout all of Christendom had sunk lower than it had been since the days of the dissolute Benedict IX in the middle of the eleventh century. But worse was yet to come.

As the result of a scandalous campaign of barter and bribery—the king of France deposited 300,000 ducats in Italian banks to ensure the election of his candidate, Giuliano della Rovere, only to be outbid—Cardinal Rodrigo Borgia was chosen Pope under the pontifical name of Alexander VI. Alexander was magnetic and imposing. He was likewise dissolute, venal, cynical, and guilty of the most shameless nepotism and simony. What is perhaps more serious is that he was generally thought at the time and in Rome to be an acceptable, even good, head of the Church. The best-known of his many children by various mistresses were Cesare and Lucrezia Borgia. Cesare, as his father's political and military chief of staff, set out, by war, diplomacy, and deceit, to build a papal empire in central and northern Italy (see above, p. 416). He was able and ruthless, and, until the death of Alexander in 1503, successful. He was commonly charged with the murder, out of jealousy, of his younger brother the duke of Gandia, in 1497. A list of those he dispatched by poison or the dagger would be long. His father, who knew of almost all of these murders, remained unconcerned. His sister Lucrezia has been variously depicted, on the one hand as a fiend and a licentious murderess, on the other as a paragon of filial and wifely virtue. The truth probably lies somewhere between

Pope Alexander VI, detail from *The Resurrection,* fresco by Pinturicchio, in the Borgia apartments, the Vatican, Rome [ALINARI].

the extremes. Her first husband was divorced for impotency; her second was murdered by Cesare; with her third she lived in apparent happiness until her death in 1519. Of the rule of the Borgias in Rome, a cardinal, Egidius of Viterbo, who was a young man during the pontificate of Alexander VI, has left a vivid judgment:

Everything was hidden in darkness and stormy night . . . never were more terrible revolts in the cities of the ecclesiastical state, more sacks and more bloody deaths.

Never were robberies committed with such impunity in the streets; never was Rome so full of criminals; never was the multitude of informers and robbers so audacious. People could neither leave the gates of the city nor dwell within it. To own money or valuable property was equivalent to being guilty of high treason. There was no protection either in house, sleeping-room or tower. Justice was effaced. Money, power, and lust governed everything.*

The facts of the indescribable shame to which the Borgias brought the Papacy were known throughout Christendom. Particularly the pilgrims who came from all of Europe to the City of the Martyrs in the jubilee year of 1500 were, on their return to their homes, eloquent in their condemnation of the rampant vice that disgraced the Church and almost destroyed its usefulness among the people. Of these pilgrims many were Germans, traditionally loyal to the line of Peter, whose revulsion against what they saw and heard in Rome became common knowledge in Germany.

Under his father's successor, Julius II (1503–1513), Cesare Borgia's power quickly evaporated and with it some of the amoral tone of the Papacy. Julius, known best as the "warrior pope," was a rugged character who had a certain concept of integrity. Vice did not flourish under him, though he was guilty of the sale of benefices and indulgences. Nevertheless, he restored to the Papacy some of the dignity it had long since lost. The Fifth Lateran Council which he called in 1512 to undertake reforms dragged on for five years, well into the reign of Julius' successor Leo X (1513–21), but its actual results were negligible, as the Pope gave no thought to spiritual matters, and without his active support the hierarchy was in no mood to assume the trammels of austerity. One bull which Julius issued, the *Liquet omnibus* (January 11, 1510), was further evidence of the crass commercialization to which the *curia* was committed. This bull extended the sale of indulgences to cover almost every conceivable case over which the Church could claim jurisdiction. The bull was so worded as to enable the pardoners (*penitentiarii*) to represent the indulgence as covering both *poena* (punishment) and *culpa* (guilt). Intended to raise money for his wars and diplomacy as well as for the projected rebuilding of St. Peter's, this bull in fact was a further degradation of the spiritual mission of the Church. It was received with indignation in many quarters in Germany. The *Ten Complaints of the German Nation* (*Decem gravamina germanicae nationis*) of 1510 may be attributed directly to the callous cupidity of the *curia,* which, in this bull, showed itself willing to sell any spiritual grace for money. This list of complaints, first clearly formulated in 1456 at the Frankfurt Diet, originally stemmed from the Council of Constance, and had often been appealed to by German princes and prelates in their dealings with the Papacy. Resentment against the exactions of the *curia* among the German princes and higher clergy in the later years of the fifteenth century became at times very bitter; there was much talk of a pragmatic sanction which would have given the German hierarchy and the Emperor control over benefices and the income of the Church. The favorable position of the French clergy under the Pragmatic Sanction of Bourges (1438) was well known

* F. Gregorovius, *History of Rome in the Middle Ages* (London, 1900), VII, 528–29.

and envied in Germany. In its later form (1511), which was the work of the humanist Jacob Wimpheling at the order of Emperor Maximilian, the *Gravamina* was used by the Emperor in his dealings with the Papacy. In 1521 the Diet of Worms employed the *Gravamina,* now expanded to 102 specifications of papal abuses, to document its policy toward the Vatican. The phrases of the *Gravamina* echo and re-echo through German history for the next century. Julius II and his equally mercenary if less warlike successor Leo X must take some blame for giving painful substance to many of the complaints which had hitherto been vague and only partly justified.

Leo X (Giovanni de' Medici) was the second son of Lorenzo de' Medici, the Magnificent. Giovanni, tonsured at seven, nominated Archbishop of Aix at eight, had been made a cardinal-deacon at the age of thirteen and became Pope at thirty-seven. He was a completely Renaissance pope, not specifically un-Christian, yet quite convinced that the head of the Church should not live the simple and austere life of Christ and the apostles. The magnificent ceremonies of his coronation were intended as a foretaste of the display and

Pope Julius II, by Raphael, in the Uffizi Gallery, Florence [ALINARI].

splendor the world should expect from his reign. Leo was indeed a great contrast to Julius II. The latter had been firm, determined, frugal in financial matters, austere in his own life, whereas Leo was a sybarite, pleasure-loving, inconsistent and uncertain in policy, weak in execution, extravagant in his tastes and his largess to his relatives. The *curia* was soon after his election packed with members of the Medici family, either as ecclesiastics or in various lucrative positions in the administration of the States of the Church. Leo is reported to have said: "As God has given us the Papacy, let us enjoy it." And enjoy it he did. Feasts, masques, the company and adulation of humanists and artists—these he relished to the full. His concept of Christianity was rather that of the Platonic Academy, in whose atmosphere he had spent formative years, than that of a monk or a theologian. He was amiable, generous, and tolerant to a fault, probably because he had very vague, if any, beliefs.

Germany and the Papacy

UNDER Leo X the relations of Germany with the Papacy did not improve over what they had been under Julius II. Maximilian was indeed reconciled with Leo in 1513, but this was a purely political and tactical move on the Emperor's part, calculated to take advantage of Leo's well-known desire for peace. The opposition of the German people to Rome and the exactions of the *curia* was, if anything, more bitter and vocal than under Julius. The most obvious as well as burdensome tax in the Empire was the annates, the first year's revenue of a bishopric or headship of a monastery. As this sum was sent to Rome, the bishop would have to collect its equivalent for his own expenses, so that the people of the diocese had eventually to pay a double tax for that year. If the vacancy occurred frequently, as often happened, the burden became unbearably heavy. In addition, a newly appointed archbishop had to pay Rome heavily for the pallium, the symbol of archiepiscopal authority. The cost in Mainz, for example, was 20,000 gulden.* At this high level vacancies might occur frequently, as it was to the *curia*'s profit to collect on each change of incumbency. In Mainz there were vacancies in 1505, 1508, and 1513, and each time the people of the archdiocese had to produce the amount, under pain of ecclesiastical discipline. Beyond these extraordinary and irregular levies, the people had regular fees to pay, not only to their parish clergy but also to separate and irregular or mendicant monks, which, for all of Germany, have been estimated at more than a million gulden annually. Every German parishioner knew of some of the conflicts with Rome. Bishops or abbots who went to Rome to win some lightening of the load on their people were either completely frustrated in their efforts or forced to expend great sums in bribery to get even a consideration of their cases. The stories of these exactions spread among the people by word of mouth and were commonplaces of the popular literature and lore of the day.

By the early years of the sixteenth century the Papacy had long since lost

---

* In buying power this sum would be the equivalent of roughly half a million dollars today.

the confidence of the common people in Germany. The deeply ingrained loyalty of the Germans to Rome, strengthened by the tradition of a Holy Roman Empire of the German Nation and by the fact that the German Emperor was supposed to be crowned by the Pope in Rome, had gradually lost its substance. The Avignonese Papacy, in systematizing and commercializing its control of the means of grace, had begun the process of weaning Germany from the establishment. The Schism carried the process further, and the sad spectacle of the struggle between Pope and Council from 1409 to 1448 was undeniable evidence of the Papacy's inability or unwillingness to reform the evil abuses of its spiritual power "in head and members." Thus from about 1450 to the Lutheran outbreak in 1517, the voices raised in Germany against the Papacy in Rome, its agents and adherents in Germany, on every conceivable aspect of the Church's action, grew continually more critical. The Church was accused of hypocrisy in religion, of violation of solemn engagements, of raw cupidity, of disregard of all Christian principles of justice and mercy, of blatant cynicism in political action, and of callous immorality in every other regard. The evidence supporting this judgment was overwhelming. Every German had seen with his own eyes, heard with his own ears, or had had to pay out of his own pocket, and the Church stood condemned.

Religion and the German People

THE low repute of the Church among all classes of the German people was strangely dissociated from the common interest in religion. It has often been said that the German people have always been deeply religious. Whether this be true as a generalization or not, certainly in the fifteenth and early sixteenth centuries the prevalence of this general interest in the things of the spirit is indisputable. We have the evidence of Italian travelers to Germany in the fifteenth century and particularly of the humanists, who consistently remarked upon the evident piety of the people and their respect for religion. The undoubted fact that a large proportion of this interest fell within the bounds of what later ages would call superstition does not modify the basic conclusion. What is noteworthy is that so much of this religiosity was simple, direct, evangelical, and rooted in family piety. We are sufficiently well informed about the practice and teaching in typical German homes. Luther tells much, in his various references to his early years, of the piety of his parents; and we know that he was taught the Lord's Prayer, the Creed, and the Ten Commandments in the German language. His parents were at that time not able to afford one of the Bibles in German translation which were already in print; he recalls, in his *Table Talk,* first having seen such a Bible when he was almost twenty and hoping he would some day be able to own one himself.

The *Seelenführer,* or *Guide of the Soul,* a popular manual for parents, appeared in printed form in 1498. Its admonitions to parents may be assumed to represent the temper and practice of the time. Though the main emphasis in the *Guide* is upon aims and methods in the schools for the young, it is made quite clear that the home was regarded as the most important factor in the training of children. Parents are told firmly how they should initiate their children in religion:

Children are the hope of the Church. Let parents therefore see to it that their children grow up in Christian fear and piety. Christian mother, when you hold your child, made in the image of God, on your knee, make the sign of the Cross on his forehead, on his lips, and on his heart, and as soon as he can talk, teach him to say his prayers. Take him along occasionally to confession, and teach him what he needs to confess properly. Fathers and mothers should set their children a good example, and should take them to mass, vespers, and to hear the preaching on Sundays and saint's days as often as they can.*

There were other similar manuals, in Germany and in Austria, and collections of sermons, such as those of Johann Nider, in all of which great stress was laid on a simple faith, reaching directly to God for guidance, a belief in the mercy and forgiveness of God toward His children and in the efficacy of the saving work of Christ. There was thus, in the minds of the people of Germany, a large reserve of what is perhaps best called an evangelical Christian faith, realized through early family training and maintained by the earnestness of many sincere parish priests. The wide spread of the printing press —a German invention—was a contributing element of great force since, by furnishing at very moderate cost and in German translation religious tracts, sermons, catechisms, hymn books, and the Bible, in whole or in parts, it made evangelical piety easily communicable.

In this century before the outbreak of the Reformation the German people showed their religious bent in a more concrete form than the mere training of their children. More churches and other religious establishments were built in the century before Luther's entrance into German public life than at any other time in German history. There seemed no limit to the eagerness of the Germans, both in the towns and in the country, to erect cathedrals, chapels, convents, monasteries, and beguine and beghard houses. The records of the building of many of these structures and their endowment illustrate the pious participation of the whole community in the enterprise. At Xanten on the Lower Rhine we find that the master of the works got his pay in kind, from one a bed, from another a measure of grain, from someone else a coat, from another a cow, all to be used or sold for the building. One citizen offered his jewelry, others brought coats of mail, and the masons gave back half their wages. The churches were a common enterprise; the fervor of the common religious aim cannot be missed. This zeal for building to the glory of God may seem to us to have reached extremes. Cologne, an archiepiscopal see of perhaps 30,000 population, about the year 1500 could boast of 11 large churches, 19 parish churches, over 100 chapels, 22 cloisters, 12 hospitals, 76 convents, and 106 Beguine houses. In Brunswick, a much smaller city, there were 15 churches, over 20 chapels, 5 monasteries, 6 hospitals, and more than a dozen beguine houses. Throughout Germany and Austria there was a rapid growth in religious establishments of all sorts. The churches in the larger towns

* Quoted in J. Janssen, *History of the German People* (London, 1896), I, 31.

blazed with rich decoration, pictures, tapestries, stained-glass windows, and treasures of one sort or another from the parishioners. It seemed as if the people sought ever new ways of showing their loyalty and devotion.

One of the more obvious developments in the church life of the later Middle Ages was the increased attention paid to preaching. The two mendicant orders, the Franciscans and the Dominicans, had won their great following among the common people by their mastery of preaching techniques and their responsiveness to the popular demand for a fresh presentation of the Gospel. The rise of printing spread this new art and, at the same time, by making available the Bible and religious books of all sorts to any who could pay the reasonable prices, layman and cleric alike, tended to raise the quality of pulpit performance. By about 1500 at least 10,000 different sermons were available in print—mostly in Latin. The best-known collections were those of John Geiler of Kaisersberg (d. 1510), whose sermons were often reprinted and sold by the thousands; the *Postillae* of the Franciscan Nicholas of Lyra (d. 1340) and Luther's mentor, John Staupitz (d. 1524). The names of John Herolt, Henry of Hesse, and William of Paris as authors of sermon collections are also frequently met with. There were, furthermore, anonymous manuals for the preacher, called *Plenarien,* which brought together relevant texts from Scripture, the Fathers of the Church, and Church liturgy that could be used by the parish priest in preparing his sermon or by the pious layman in his private devotions. The manuals and the sermon collections were in Latin, but the preachers translated them into German as they went along. It is estimated that the usual sermon was about an hour in length, although on some occasions such as special feast days the priest may have preached, with slight interruptions, for five or six hours.

The general tenor of these sermon collections, and therefore of the popular concept of religion, was ethical rather than doctrinal. Everybody's morals—those of the layman as well as of the cleric—were subjected to candor, sarcasm, and even vitriol. The people enjoyed the performance immensely. The net result of this resurgence of interest in the spoken explanation of Scripture and Christian tradition, even on a largely ethical basis, was to be favorable to the later attack of the reformers on the doctrinal foundations of the Church. The documents of the Christian faith, the Scriptures and the great Fathers of the early Church, were better known from having been quoted so often by so many preachers. The reformers could base their work on the preparatory education the later medieval preachers had given their generations.

Religious Movements among the Laity

ONE of the more remarkable religious manifestations of the period before Luther's movement broke out was the various aspects of specifically lay interest in religion. We have seen how the common people participated in the tremendous building activity of the time, and, before that, how the family had come to occupy a substantial position in the creation of an atmosphere of piety. But beyond this, there was a considerable movement among laymen to organize for religious exercises outside the clergy-controlled ecclesiastical institution.

In the course of the latter half of the fifteenth century a number of lay princes made arrangements to control the administration of charitable funds, an area where the monastic orders and the secular clergy had hitherto ruled unquestioned. In some instances town councils made and enforced regulations concerning the handling of funds for the poor and of homes and hospitals previously in the control of the town clergy. But the field of activity of the laity extended even farther into religion than just the control of "good works." The clergy's religious ministrations were evidently not satisfying. Beginning in the fourteenth century associations had been formed in Germany by laymen for the express purpose of praying together and joining in the singing of Gospel hymns. The best-known such association was the "Brotherhood of the Eleven Thousand Virgins," also known as "St. Ursula's Little Ship," established early in the fifteenth century, first at Cracow, then at Cologne. All over Germany these religious lay brotherhoods sprang up. They were usually attached to a church or a chapel, not infrequently led by a priest sympathetic to the devout spirit of the brotherhood; but as frequently they had their own building or chapel named after a patron saint of their choice, where they held prayer meetings or social gatherings in a religious atmosphere with no priest present. Lübeck had almost seventy such associations, Cologne eighty, Hamburg over a hundred. The Lowlands and northern Germany were the centers for what was known as the *Kalendsbruderschaften,* or brotherhoods, that met regularly on the first of the month, originally for prayer and Gospel singing, later for a common meal and a social gathering. The craft guilds, as well as the merchant guilds, were not unaffected by the spreading feeling that the laity had a right to worship in their own way, without benefit of clergy. Their meetings came to be led in prayer by a member of the guild, and a religious atmosphere for lay activities was accepted as normal and proper. Quite naturally the great popularity of the movement led to a deterioration in the spirit; simultaneous membership in a number of such brotherhoods for reasons of social prestige or "contacts" was not uncommon by the early years of the sixteenth century. Nevertheless, this movement indicated the growing interest of the laity in religion, and its capacity to undertake and carry out religious exercises without the help of the priesthood became clear. By the end of the fifteenth century high officials of the Church, among them Cardinal Nicholas Cusa, disturbed by the trend, were making strenuous efforts to combat its progress. The Church could hardly be expected to approve a religious development over which it had no control and to run the risk of being found unnecessary and therefore dispensable.

The rise of the movement known as the Brethren of the Common Life, which began in the Lowlands in the mid-fourteenth century and spread thence all over Germany, has been related (see above, pp. 168–71). The impact of this movement upon German society remained strong well into the sixteenth century. Its attention to sound learning, through the schools in Germany founded or directed by the graduates of the mother colleges at Deventer, Zwolle, and 's Hertogenbosch, commanded great respect among the burgher class. This type of education bridged a gap between that of the humanists, which many Germans regarded as pagan, and the conventional scholastic methods and aims still dominant at most of the universities, which had begun to lose their appeal. The moderate and sincere religiosity of the Brethren, on the other hand, satisfied the needs of the devout laity which the luxury and cynicism of most of the secular and regular clergy had offended.

There was yet another element in the religious life of Germany, particularly in the southern and central parts of the land, which contributed to the anti-clericalism of the pre-Reformation era. The Hussite wars in the early part of the fifteenth century had made a deep impression on all Germans. They knew that the imperial armies sent against the Hussites had been repeatedly humiliated by the hymn-singing "Warriors of God," and the fervor of the Hussite faith had become a legend among Germans of all classes. After the wars were over Hussite ideas had found root in the middle classes. The anti-clerical, nationalistic, and anti-Roman teachings of the Hussites, their emphasis upon Scripture and the free preaching of the Word, pleased the German, who found the demands of Rome exorbitant and resented the power the clergy sought to exercise over his life and thought.

German Reformers before Luther

AMONG the many men who, in the period immediately preceding the Protestant Reformation, showed a clear grasp of the issues at stake and voiced the common rejection of the dominant ecclesiasticism of the hierarchy, two stand out as reformers: John of Wesel (*ca.* 1400–81) and John Wessel of Gansfort (1419–89). Wesel, born near Mainz, took the degrees of master of arts (1445) and doctor of theology (1456) from the University of Erfurt, and stayed on as professor for a few years. In 1461 he was professor at Basel, only to leave in less than three years to accept the post of cathedral preacher at Worms. Wherever he taught or preached his sermons caused offense to the Church authorities. On several occasions he was haled before ecclesiastical courts and was finally condemned to repentance for life and virtual imprisonment in an Augustinian monastery, where he died. The doctrine and practice of penance and indulgences were the particular object of his attacks. He asserted that the absolution given by the priest was only a ministry, the implication being that *per se* it had no real efficacy. He held the indulgence to be valueless and favored marriage of the clergy and communion in both kinds, the latter a Hussite doctrine. He conceived of the Church as the body of the faithful, whose number and persons were known to God alone. This and others of his teachings were dangerously close to the thought of Wyclyf, Hus, and Augustine. Transubstantiation, an accepted doctrine of the Church since the Fourth Council of the Lateran (1215), he regarded as unscriptural. In one of his later works he asserted: "I despise Pope, Church and councils. I love Christ. Let the word of Christ dwell in you abundantly." Luther was, as we shall see, a student at Erfurt, and he related how, when studying for his master's degree, he had read the writings of John of Wesel.

John Wessel of Gansfort was born in the Lowlands, and early became associated with the Brethren of the Common Life. He spent seventeen years with the Brethren at Zwolle, proceeding thence in 1449 to Cologne. Later he spent sixteen years in study and teaching at Paris, attaining a high proficiency in Hebrew and Greek and achieving the status of a respected humanist. About

1470 he was in Rome with Cardinal Bessarion, returning to Zwolle in 1479, where he died. His last words were: "I know none but Jesus Crucified." Gansfort was a gentler soul than Wesel, but not thereby less effective. He was strongly attracted to the thought of St. Augustine, and almost all his teaching was permeated with Augustinian phraseology and thought. To Gansfort salvation was a free gift of God's grace. This doctrine, though strongly emphasized by the later reformers, can of course be found frequently in the Middle Ages. But Gansfort went much further. He held that the Church consisted of the "saints," known to God alone; thus the Pope and the visible Church are not necessary. They are certainly not infallible, since the Scriptures, not the Church, provide the rule of faith. In ecclesiastical matters Gansfort attacked indulgences and the sacrament of penance, and regarded the power of the priest as scarcely more efficacious than that of the pious layman. While this body of doctrine falls short of full Reformation thinking, it is at sharp variance with the teaching of the established ecclesiastical organization in its estimate of the place and power of the Church in the scheme of salvation.

It is a commonplace to assert that the Protestant Reformation did not come unheralded onto the European historical scene. It had a long preparation. Every failure to remove the abuses that had crept into the Church only made it more certain that the effort would have to be repeated in a more forceful manner. If any of the reform endeavors—for example, those of the councils, the mystics, certain progressive popes or cardinals, the reformers within the older orders, the reform-minded laymen, or the humanist reformers—had succeeded, the Protestant Reformation would probably not have occurred, or at least it would have been postponed for a long period of time. But all these and other similar movements did in fact fail, leaving the ills exposed but unhealed. Resentment among the people against ecclesiastical abuses at all levels of the organization deepened and became more explosive. Yet the list of attempts to bring order and propriety into Western Christendom is not exhausted by the many movements and men we have just described. One last effort before the Lutheran explosion must be presented: the combination of learning, education, satire, and mild Christian teaching which was fused in the person and thought of Erasmus of Rotterdam.

ERASMUS OF ROTTERDAM

Few men in the history of Western culture have been more diversely treated by contemporaries or posterity than Erasmus. He was largely responsible for this diversity (or misunderstanding) by his own actions and words. Luther, as have many Protestants after him, accused him of inconsistency, lack of courage, time-serving unwillingness to follow the dictates of his conscience and the logic of his own findings. It is true that after attacking the Church from parish priest to pope, he nevertheless stayed within the fold to the end of his life. Catholics have, on the other hand, held him partially responsible by his writings, for the Protestant conflagration, as he gave much ammunition to the enemies of the Church, and himself, with all the prestige of his position as the leading scholar of all Europe, set the style of the disastrous attack and encouraged those of lesser fame to carry on the campaign. Both sides are to a certain degree right. There is even another position, taken by those who sympathize with his temperament. This group has regarded him as the Great Liberal, fighting to propagate the gospel of culture and moderation in a world gone mad with sectarian extremism. His career and his personality eminently deserve careful study.

Erasmus was born, the younger of two sons of a certain Gerard at Rotterdam, in Holland, sometime between 1466 and 1469; the exact date remains in doubt as at various times he himself gave three dates. His mother was a widow, Margaret, the daughter of a physician of Zevenberghen, a small town not far from Rotterdam. His father took orders, probably in 1467, and the liaison appears to have been broken off. After several years of primary and not very successful schooling at Gouda, he was sent in 1475 to the school of the Brethren of the Common Life at Deventer, where he remained until 1484. The training, largely medieval, was thorough and severely administered. Erasmus was far from a brilliant student. Only at the end of this period was any "breath of some better learning," as Erasmus called it, brought to the school in the person of two humanist teachers, Zinthius and Hegius. The estate left by the father on his death in 1484 was soon dissipated or mismanaged by the executors, and the two sons were pressed into the monastic profession. Erasmus entered the convent of the Augustinian Canons at Steyn, near Gouda, probably in 1487. The monastic life at Steyn seemed very pleasant, largely because he was left free to read the pagan Latin writers, and he found the humanist writers, such as Aeneas Silvius, Agricola, and Valla, satisfying and inspiring. His letters and some poetry written in these impressionable years reveal a sensitive and fastidious young man. While at Steyn he wrote much, usually on the same theme: the barbarousness of monastic learning and, by contrast, the beauty of Latin letters. His repute for facility in writing was in all probability responsible for an offer, in 1492, to become the secretary of the bishop of Cambrai. In order to qualify for a career in the ecclesiastical world, Erasmus was ordained priest at Utrecht on April 25, 1492. He remained with the bishop for three years. Little is known about his life during this period; he may not have been happy immersed in an atmosphere of officialdom. In 1495 he obtained permission from the bishop to matriculate at the University of Paris. The arid Scotist scholasticism which then permeated the curriculum at Paris elicited his sarcastic amusement. In a letter to an English friend, Thomas Gray, Erasmus told of a lecture concerning the Greek philosopher Epimenides who, it was reported, fell asleep in the midst of a logical discussion and slept for forty-seven years, and added:

As far as I am concerned, I think Epimenides extraordinarily fortunate to have awakened even that late, as most theologians never wake up at all. . . . But just consider, what do you think Epimenides dreamed of all those years. . . . I am told here that if you have any Latin style you cannot understand the mysteries of this science. So I write nothing elegant or precise, indeed I write as badly as I can, and I make famous progress.*

* Nichols, *Letters of Erasmus,* I, 143–44.

As a Lowlander Erasmus had joined the Collège de Montaigu, one of the colleges which, originally little more than dormitories, had come to function as teaching units, presided over by an eminent professor. John Standonck, a Fleming of great ability who had been trained by the Brethren of the Common Life at Gouda, had been regent of the College of Montaigu since 1475, and had built it into an influential if small institution within the Paris community. Erasmus was repelled by the extreme austerity of the life and discipline, and even more by the poor food and unsanitary quarters. He fell ill and had to return to the Lowlands for a time to regain his health. Back in Paris, he was unwilling to return to Montaigu; he joined the household of an English student he was tutoring and enjoyed for a while a measure of comfort. His friends were of various temperaments, but almost exclusively from the group of humanists. Robert Gaguin, an older French historian and humanist, was a man of sober and austere mien. Erasmus sought and won his friendship, and one of his first serious writings was a laudatory preface to Gaguin's *History of France*. Faustus Andrelinus, an Italian scholar at Paris, on the other hand, was a complete pagan in manners and morals, yet Erasmus admired him and became his fast friend.

Erasmus' material resources were irregular and uncertain. He tried to make a living by tutoring, and he had hopes of winning a patron who would support him and allow him to continue a life of scholarship. He thought he had

Erasmus of Rotterdam, by Hans Holbein the Younger, in the Louvre, Paris [ARCHIVES PHOTO-GRAPHIQUES].

found such a Maecenas when one of his English pupils, William Blount, Lord Mountjoy, asked him (May 1499) to accompany him to England. During this sojourn of less than eight months Erasmus won the friendship of John Colet, then lecturing on the Epistles of St. Paul, and of Thomas More, at that time a young and brilliant lawyer. He was presented to the young Prince Henry, the future Henry VIII, and to his two sisters. At Oxford Erasmus was welcomed by Colet and encouraged in his studies. Colet's more religious nature had a great influence on Erasmus, who, at this early stage of his development, would have been attracted rather by the purely literary and rhetorical aspects of any text or writing than by its spiritual content.

Early in February 1500, Erasmus was back in Paris, after having his money confiscated by the English customs officials, an indignity which rankled for years. But in order not to wound his English friends, against whom Erasmus' acquaintances expected him to be resentful, he hastily put together a collection of *Adages,* 878 apt sayings culled from the Latin writers, and published it the same year with a dedication to Lord Mountjoy. The work won immediate public acclaim and was often reprinted in successively enlarged editions. The last edition compiled by Erasmus contained 3260 adages. Almost one hundred separate reprints or editions of this guide for pleasant Latin usage have appeared since the first modest version in the summer of 1500.

Although this work brought him fame, he was still struggling with poverty. He wrote epitaphs, orations, and letters for rich clients. The compensation was uncertain, and precious time was lost from his beloved work with the ancients. Convinced that Paris was unprofitable for him, later in 1500 he went to Orléans, only to return to Paris in 1501 and eventually settle down to what he thought would be his great work: to master Greek and to edit St. Jerome. He did, in fact, make remarkable progress and drew numerous friends into serious study of the Greek and Latin fathers. From this period and these associations comes Erasmus' gentle *Enchiridion militis christiani (Handbook of the Christian Soldier).* This warmly written praise of Christian ideals separates the inner from the outer man, contrasts external observances with inner righteousness, and exalts sincerity, simplicity of heart, and love of one's fellow man. First printed in 1503, it did not match the immediate popularity of the *Adages,* but was eventually translated into ten languages, including Czech and Russian, and had a deep influence on both Catholic and Protestant leaders in the sixteenth century.

In the late summer of 1505 Erasmus was again in England, led by the hope of obtaining a prebend from Henry VII which would put an end to his financial concerns. Invited to Cambridge by John Fisher, bishop of Rochester and vice-chancellor of the university, he planned to study for the doctorate in theology. He began preparation of a series of lectures on Paul's Epistle to the Romans. But suddenly, in the summer of 1506, he left Cambridge and accepted a post as tutor on a trip to Italy to the two sons of the Italian physician of Henry VII. On the way the party stopped off in Turin, where Erasmus was granted the degrees of master and doctor in theology by the archbishop of Turin, honors of which Erasmus never boasted. The party passed through the great cities of the Italian Renaissance, yet Erasmus had almost nothing good to say of Italian culture, and he made keenly unfavorable comments on the luxury and worldliness of the Papacy. He spent, on the way back from Rome, almost a year at Bologna, where the scholarly atmosphere was congenial to him, and in November 1507, on invitation of Aldus Manutius, the renowned humanist printer of Venice, spent the next eleven months in the city of the lagoons, eight of them as a guest in the house of Aldus. The latter printed a new and enlarged edition of the *Adages;* on his part, Erasmus worked hard on classical and patristic texts which Aldus wanted to publish. The physical conditions, particularly the meat and drink, all skimpy and stale, displeased Erasmus immensely, and in the late autumn of 1508 he was on the move again. He had been given the post of tutor to the young Alexander Stuart, a natural son of James IV of Scotland, who had already been named archbishop of St. Andrews. This tutorship took him to various Italian cities, and he was again in Rome early in 1509. He found little to admire in the Holy City, save the freedom he enjoyed in the use of the libraries and the friendship of writers and scholars to be found at the papal court.

But once again the hope of a rich preferment drew him to England. The young and brilliant Henry VIII had just (May 22, 1509) ascended the throne, and Erasmus' friend Mountjoy urged him to come and enjoy the golden age of letters then dawning. Erasmus, reaching England late in the autumn of 1509, went straightway to the house of Thomas More to await his books and recover from an attack of lumbago. While waiting he wrote, in a few days, the satire with which his fame has been most closely connected—the *Encomium Moriae,* better known under its English title, the *Praise of Folly.*

Satire was popular in this age, and Erasmus had models such as the *Ship of Fools* of Sebastian Brant, but the *Praise of Folly* is perhaps the most sweeping and devastating attack on human foibles of the whole century. Folly is represented as a loquacious, impulsive lady who delivers the most sublimely naïve judgments in a simple language to which there is no answer. The basic position is that Folly is at the root of every human action.

No society, no intimacy can be pleasant or enduring without folly; so much so that a people could not stand its prince, nor the master his man, nor the maid her mistress, nor the tutor his pupil, nor the friend his friend, nor the wife her husband for a single moment more, if they did not from time to time make the same mistakes, then flatter one another, now connive together, now cover themselves with some honey of folly. . . . Every profession, every calling, every art is tinged or permeated with folly. What more stupid than the scholar who glories in the discovery of a worthless writing, or a new manuscript of something old and useless? What more stupid than the monk who devotes his life to doing nothing with unction and ceremony, and makes ignorance a virtue? The scientists too, who think they have done something wonderful when they see another star or think they have solved the riddle of the ages, are, in the face of the real wonders of Nature, ridiculous. The statesman, the merchant, the theologian, the poet, all chase unattainable goals or take pride in acts and writings that are vain and pointless.*

Although written in the summer of 1509 the work was not printed until 1511, when Erasmus went to Paris to see it through the press. Its reception was generally enthusiastic, and new editions were quickly called for. By 1522 twenty

* *Praise of Folly,* §§ 9–10.

thousand copies had been sold, and translations into other European languages had begun to appear. Churchmen were divided in their opinion, some, perhaps the majority, regarding it as too pointed. Luther had reservations as to how much good it might do, while almost all humanists read it with delight. Pope Leo X laughed and remarked: "I am glad our Erasmus is in the *Moria.*" It has remained for subsequent generations a delightfully sharp mirror of the age; whereas, to the men of Erasmus' time, it had the added piquancy of showing them the foibles and excesses of which they themselves were in some degree guilty.

When, in 1514, Erasmus sailed up the Rhine to Basel, where he was to spend many years of his life, he met a number of the leaders of the German humanistic circles. He was universally greeted as the most eminent scholar of the day. The *Adages,* the *Enchiridion,* and the *Praise of Folly* were only the most popular of his writings. These scholars knew of his editions of the classics and the Church Fathers, and his wide correspondence had spread the awareness of Erasmus' deep and broad learning. At Mainz he met Ulrich von Hutten (see above, p. 443). He was immediately attracted by the younger man's enthusiasm and was informed by Hutten of the course of the Pfefferkorn-Reuchlin controversy. Erasmus, as might have been anticipated, took Reuchlin's side in the dispute, and in the course of the next year wrote against Pfefferkorn, although his own nature was not that of a militant crusader in any cause. Further south, at Strassburg, he probably met Sebastian Brant, who was the head of the humanist circle in that city. At Basel Erasmus made friends with the great printer Johann Froben, who, with his partner Johann Amerbach, was to print many of Erasmus' scholarly works until the death of the printer in 1527.

In 1516 he completed a work for which he had been preparing himself for over ten years: a textual study of the New Testament. In its final form it was an edition of the Greek text of the New Testament. He had found the Vulgate Latin text then current unsatisfactory by reason of the many errors that had crept into the manuscript tradition, and had decided, probably about 1510, that it would be necessary to make an edition of the Greek text direct from the manuscripts. He used ten Greek codices, the oldest of which he judged to have come from the first or second century. Paleographers now assign it to the eleventh century. The first edition of his Greek text of the New Testament was published in February 1516 by Froben in Basel. Erasmus had probably heard of the imminent publication of a Greek New Testament edited by Cardinal Ximénes in Spain, which had in fact been set up in print by January 1514, but had not been published. Erasmus' work, judged by modern standards, suffers from haste and even more from the inadequacies of the manuscripts he used. A second edition, with four hundred corrections, introduced after consultation of additional manuscripts, was issued in 1519. Two further revisions appeared soon thereafter. By the time of Erasmus' death in 1536 sixty-nine printings of the revised Greek text had been issued. The work was warmly received in all humanist and liberal circles in Germany, the Lowlands, and Switzerland. Luther's work of translation of the Bible into German would hardly have been possible without Erasmus' previous textual labors. Pope Leo X wrote a letter of approval; his successor, Adrian VI, asked Erasmus to do a similar text of the Old Testament. Nevertheless, Erasmus was bitterly attacked by conservatives, particularly for his omission of I John 5:8, which in the Vulgate was used as a proof-text for the doctrine of the Trinity. He had left it out simply because he did not find it in his Greek manuscripts. He inserted it in the third edition (1522) on finding it in a single, late manuscript. In his later editions the Greek text was accompanied by a Latin paraphrase. This practice was also sharply criticized, as he was represented as implicitly rejecting the traditional Vulgate. In answer to these charges Erasmus could reply that his paraphrases carefully avoided delicate doctrinal questions. But he did refer often to his "philosophy of Christ" and ridiculed the artificial accretions of usage and ceremony in the Church, which he felt had obscured the original Christian message and spirit. In all his exchanges with his critics Erasmus came off best, but he enjoyed none of the polemic. The letters of Erasmus in these years reveal him as irritable, inclined to regard himself as persecuted, and convinced that he alone was right. Most of the time from 1516 until 1521 Erasmus spent in the Lowlands, living with friends at Brussels, Antwerp, or Louvain. In Louvain he was, though an object of great respect, not infrequently attacked by conservative theologians.

Erasmus and the Beginning of the Lutheran Reforms

IN THE middle of Erasmus' stay in Louvain Luther's ninety-five theses were nailed on the north door of the Castle Church at Wittenberg, marking the outbreak of the Protestant Reformation. It was inevitable that Luther and Erasmus should have something to say to each other. Erasmus had for years stood on the side of the liberals who, aware of the deficiencies of the established Church, were anxious for reform in morals and doctrine. Luther was bent on reforming that same Church. They had a common object for their actions, but they were not at one in spirit.

The matter of Luther's theses against indulgences (October 31, 1517) made little impression on Erasmus, though he did approve their general intent. When, early in 1519, Luther wrote Erasmus, asking him in a delicate way for some indication of sympathy for the new movement, Erasmus delayed answering for almost two months, then politely declared himself to be neutral, "the better to assist the new flowering of good learning, and it seems to me that more can be done by unassuming courtesy than by violence." His attempts to remain neutral, at peace with both sides, were not successful. He was under pressure from both sides of the controversy. The papal party urged him to take a stand against the heretic. Luther and Luther's partisans, gaining hourly in numbers, demanded that he have the courage to acknowledge his own earlier position calling for reform. Louvain soon became a center of anti-Lutheran thought. The pressures upon Erasmus, from his conservative friends in Louvain on the one hand and from his German and Swiss humanist friends on the other, urging him to declare for one or the other side, grew so great that he decided to leave. On October 28, 1521, he set out for Basel, ostensibly to see the third edition of the Greek New Testament through the press, actually to preserve the independence of mind he so deeply treasured.

Basel was Erasmus' home for the next seven and a half years, 1521–29. For the most part he enjoyed freedom from worry and bitter controversy, and he was able to give his whole mind and energy to his varied scholarly projects: new editions of the New Testament and the *Adages,* editions of works of Church Fathers, among them Cyprian, Hilary, Ambrose, Jerome, Augustine, and a Latin translation of John Chrysostom. The sum of this labor was a tremendous corpus of very high quality editing; much of it was done while he was suffering from the pains of gout. He polished off his *Familiar Colloquies,* some of which had been composed as early as 1500. A collection of his *Colloquies,* which he had not intended for publication, had been printed by a friend in Basel in 1518, much to Erasmus' irritation. Rather than disown authorship of the as yet unpolished dialogues, he revised and added to the collection which he had Froben publish in 1519. Its popularity was immediate, and within three years twenty-five editions appeared from many presses. From almost all of these reprintings Erasmus received nothing. Erasmus succeeded in producing in the form of lightly satirical storytelling a distinctly moral treatise, only less obviously so than the *Enchiridion militis christiani.* Since many persons were named in the *Colloquies,* the work became forthwith the center of rabid controversy. Erasmus' frequent disclaimers that he had no desire to engage in polemics did not convince. His naturally sharp pen was always stinging some one, and retaliation in kind was to be expected. For years he had to defend himself against attacks from many quarters where his satire had struck home. In 1523 he engaged in a quarrel with his former friend, the dying von Hutten, and later, under steady pressure from friend and foe in England and the Lowlands, with Luther himself.

The Break with Luther

FROM the beginning of Luther's break with the Church, Erasmus was sympathetic with a large part of the reformer's program. He had avoided taking an open stand in his favor, probably in the honest conviction that he could be of greatest help as an influential neutral who could appeal to both sides of the controversy for calm consideration of the deeper issues of Christian morality, the primacy of the Scriptures, and the advance of Christian tolerance and justice. He had followed the movement with great interest and had intervened with the highest authorities, both in Church and state, in favor of a fair hearing for Luther and his followers. But as, even before the Diet of Worms in April 1521, the tempo of Luther's revolt increased and his attacks on the institutions of the Church became more irrevocably violent, all efforts at arbitration or compromise seemed vain, and Erasmus felt regretfully obliged to withdraw even his measured support. He refused an invitation to attend the Diet, declaring that he preferred "being a spectator rather than an actor in the drama." For a few more months he was on the fence and consequently sharply criticized by both sides. The final and open break with Luther was made in November 1521, when Erasmus published a collection of *Epistolae ad diversos* (*Letters to Various Persons*) which made clear Erasmus' loyalty to Rome and desire to have nothing to do with Luther and his reforming associates at Wittenberg. But although he wished to break with the reformers, he could not yet bring himself to accede to urgent requests from the side of the Church, from Henry VIII of England and Duke George of Saxony, and especially from his friend and fellow countryman Pope Adrian VI, that he write openly against

Luther. It was two full years before he could so far repress his natural disinclination to controversy as to attack a cardinal doctrine of Luther, the doctrine of predestination.

In September 1524, he published with some misgivings the *De libero arbitrio* (*Diatribe on Free Will*). The fact that Erasmus was preparing such an attack was known to the reformers many months in advance of its publication. They were not therefore taken by surprise. Erasmus' tone was moderate, but there was no doubt that Luther, or, indeed, any predestinarian, would be unable to accept the conclusions. Erasmus' argument was principally an appeal to Scripture, the writings of the Fathers, and human experience to the effect that man's will is free. Else how could man be responsible for his actions or how could God's justice be assumed? Luther, though disgusted with the work, felt it necessary to reply, late in 1525, in a long and vehemently written polemic, *De servo arbitrio* (*On the Bondage of the Will*). His approach is diametrically opposed to that of Erasmus. Whereas the latter had begun from human experience, Luther set out from the assumption of God's omnipotence and man's impotence. He therefore accepted the implications of divine determinism, a doctrine which leaves little room for man's freedom. Of the two treatises, Erasmus' was more suave and "reasonable," Luther's more dynamic and convincing. Compromise between the two positions was virtually impossible. The purposes and tempers of the two men were likewise almost beyond reconciliation. In a letter to Luther written soon after receiving a copy of the latter's work Erasmus said: "You treat the evangelic cause so as to confound in one mass all things sacred and profane, as if it were your main purpose to prevent the tempest from ever becoming quiet, while it is my greatest aim that it should die down." Yet in spite of his protestations of a pacific intent Erasmus did not refrain from adding fuel to the flames of controversy. In March 1526, he published *Hyperaspistes,* a stout and voluminous defense of his earlier *Diatribe,* which added little to the substance of the dispute. By this time, furthermore, the Reformation movement had gone far beyond the bounds of reasoned discussion on such fine points of theology as the exact degree to which God's grace cooperated with man's will to effect salvation. The firm and fervent conviction of the reformers, that there was no substitute for an acceptance of the doctrines of grace and God's omnipotence, was by now too widely current to admit of any logical or "reasonable" contradiction. Many of Erasmus' friends had cast in their lot with the reformers' cause, and he felt somewhat isolated and deserted.

Erasmus must go down in history as the great exponent of the middle way, of moderate conservatism in word and action, at a time when a moderate position no longer held any appeal either to the learned or the common people. Not only had most of the liberal scholars of Germany rejected the neutralism of Erasmus toward the reform ideals; he found himself out of sympathy with the humanists who were in the Italian tradition. These latter had nothing in common with Erasmus' sincere Christianity. Their paganism revolted him. Just as he had attacked Luther for neglecting the evidence of human experience as to the freedom of man's will, so he attacked the pagan humanists in the *Ciceronianus,* a colloquy written in 1528, in which he ridiculed their artificiality and perversion of the spirit of "good letters." The barbs in this colloquy must have struck home, for several French humanists, over the next few years, wrote strident replies which Erasmus wisely ignored. The general judgment of the learned world favored Erasmus in this controversy.

In February 1529, the city of Basel suddenly accepted reformed doctrines and formally suppressed Catholic services. The leading spirit in the move was Oecolampadius, earlier a friend and admirer of Erasmus, although since Erasmus' break with Luther their friendship had cooled. With Oecolampadius at the head of the dominant reform party in the city, Erasmus' position became embarrassing. Determined to protect his independence, aging and ill, he left Basel for Freiburg im Breisgau, where he was warmly welcomed as an honored guest and named a professor at the university. In 1531 he bought a house and prepared to enjoy his scholarly pursuits, his wide correspondence, and the pleasant surroundings of the town. He did not soften his views of Luther and his movement. Quite the contrary: he ridiculed the coarseness and antiliteracy of the whole group around Luther, whom he called the "pseudo-evangelicals."

Events in the world of affairs were moving too fast in the early 1530's for Erasmus to keep up. He felt his time too short to waste on attention to circumstances he could no longer influence. There were, however, tasks he wanted to finish before laying down his pen. During his stay at Freiburg he completed—in 1533—his vast study of the art of preaching, *Ecclesiastes,* which the house of Froben printed in 1535. He had intended to dedicate this, his most voluminous work, to his friend John Fisher, bishop of Rochester. On June 22, 1535, Fisher was executed at the command of Henry VIII (see below, p. 586) for remaining faithful to his ideas of the unity of the Christian Church. Two weeks after Fisher, Thomas More, Erasmus' other dearest friend, mounted the scaffold. Erasmus, who had returned to Basel barely in time to learn of the execution of his two friends, was deeply grieved. "In More I seem to have died, so much did we have one soul." With most of his old friends dead, he felt painfully alone. The new Pope, Paul III, answered cordially a letter of congratulation which Erasmus had written him and invited him to help in the unifying work of the forthcoming council. Already bedridden, he worked to the end. His will had long been written, and an accurate inventory of his possessions was drawn up in 1534. He died on July 12, 1536, in great pain. His last words were in his native Dutch, "Lieve God" (Dear God).

Erasmus has been condemned and reviled by both Catholic and Protestant authorities. His works have been put on the Index. Protestants have complained of his unwillingness to come out openly for the Reformation cause, while the reformers of the first and second generations borrowed from him copiously and shamelessly. Between these extremes Erasmus has found many zealous defenders and followers. Perhaps he needs no defense. The grandeur of the monument of Christian learning he left to posterity, the valor of his struggle against bigotry and cant, ignorance and sloth, the courage he displayed throughout his life in refusing to be forced to take a position on one side or the other, neither of which he could honestly accept—these are enough in themselves to warrant history in regarding him as one of the greatest characters of his century.

Whether he was a voice from the past, or the prophet of a new age; whether in retrospect we judge him as an ineffectual advocate of colorless neutralism in a period of crisis when history demanded that her sons stand up to be counted, or as a noble champion of tolerance and reasonableness—these are decisions each viewer of the past must make for himself. Erasmus would have asked no more.

SUGGESTIONS FOR FURTHER READING

See bibliography for Chapter 15.

BRANT, S., *Ship of Fools,* trans. E. H. Zeydel. New York, 1944
ERASMUS, *Complaint of Peace.* Chicago, 1917
ERASMUS, *Familiar Colloquies.* Many editions
ERASMUS, *Manual for a Christian Soldier.* London, 1905
ERASMUS, *Praise of Folly.* Many editions
HUTTEN, U. VON, *et al., Letters of Obscure Men,* trans. F. G. Stokes. London, 1925
HYMA, A., *Erasmus and the Humanists.* New York, 1930
LUTHER, M., *Primary Works, Table Talk, Letters.* See bibliography for Chapter 17
NICHOLS, F. M., *The Epistles of Erasmus.* 3 vols. New York, 1901–08

ALLEN, P. S., *The Age of Erasmus.* Oxford, 1914
ALLEN, P. S., *Erasmus: Lectures and Wayfaring Sketches.* Oxford, 1934
Cambridge Modern History, Vol. I. Cambridge, 1903
FLICK, A. C., *Decline of the Medieval Church,* Vol. II. New York, 1930
FROUDE, J. H., *Life and Letters of Erasmus.* New York, 1896
GILMORE, M. F., *The World of Humanism 1453–1517.* New York, 1952
GREGOROVIUS, F., *History of the City of Rome in the Middle Ages,* Vol. VII. London, 1900
HOLBORN, H., *Ulrich von Hutten and the German Reformation.* New York, 1937
HUIZINGA, J., *Erasmus of Rotterdam.* London, 1952
JANSSEN, J., *History of the German People at the Close of the Middle Ages,* Vols. I–III. London, 1896–1900
MILLER, E. W., and J. W. SCUDDER, *Wessel Gansfort, Life and Writings.* 2 vols. New York, 1917
New Cambridge Modern History, Vol. I. Cambridge, 1957
PASTOR, L. VON, *History of the Popes,* Vols. I–VII. London, 1891–1900
RANKE, L. VON, *History of the Reformation in Germany.* London, 1905
SCHAFF, D. S., *History of the Christian Church,* Vol. V. New York, 1920
SCHAPIRO, J. S., *Social Reform and the Reformation.* New York, 1909
SMITH, P., *Erasmus.* New York, 1923
STRAUSS, D. F., *Ulrich von Hutten.* New York, 1914
ULLMAN, C., *Reformers before the Reformation.* 2 vols. Edinburgh, 1855

ANDREAS, W., *Deutschland vor der Reformation.* 1932
AUBENAS, R., and R. RICARD, *L'Eglise et la renaissance (1449–1517).* 1951
BATAILLON, M., *Erasme et l'Espagne.* 1937
BEZOLD, F. VON, *Geschichte der deutschen Reformation.* 1890
GUIRAUD, J., *L'Eglise romaine et les origines de la renaissance.* 1921
KASER, K., *Deutsche Geschichte im Ausgange des Mittelalters (1438–1519).* 1905, 1912

Renaudet, A., *Erasme et l'Italie.* 1954
Rodocanachi, E. P., *Erasme: sa pensée religieuse.* 1926
Rodocanachi, E. P., *Etudes érasmiennes.* 1939
Sombart, W., *Der Moderne Kapitalismus.* 4 vols. 1926

CHAPTER SEVENTEEN

LUTHER AND LUTHERANISM

T HE truth of the expression that a movement is the shadow of a man has never been better illustrated than in the case of Luther and the German Reformation. We have amply seen in the preceding chapter that the roots of anticlericalism and lay religion, which underlay the great religious and social movements of the sixteenth century, ran deep into the soil of the fifteenth and even the fourteenth century. But, with all due allowance for this substantial base in the life and thought of the German people, the fact remains that, as far as we can judge at this distance in time, no other person could have precipitated the movement as Luther did. No one of his contemporaries compares with him in zeal, in vigor of expression, in understanding of the heart and temper of the German people, in power to convince and inspire a whole generation, in courage to face the consequences of a break with a universally accepted institution. His force and personality have challenged scholars for centuries, and there seems little likelihood that the interest in his thought and development will die down, either in Germany or in the rest of the Western world, where the effects of his movement have had such far-reaching consequences for more than four centuries. It is therefore altogether proper that we should follow closely his life and career. The story of the early days of the Reformation is to a great extent the story of the crisis in Luther's own thought. We shall first trace his personal development to the point where that crisis arose.

The Beginnings

IN 1482, in the western reaches of the Electorate of Saxony,* in and around the Thuringian village of Möhra, a large family, almost a clan, by the name of Luder (or Ludher), had been living for some generations. In that year a member of the leading family of Möhra, Hans Ludher, and his bride Margarete

---

* Saxony, the possession of the house of Wettin, was divided in 1485 between the brothers Ernest, made Elector of Saxony, and Albert, who kept the title of duke. We shall hereafter refer to Electoral and Ducal Saxony as the case may be.

Ziegler, desiring to build their own future in the larger world, moved with their first-born son to Eisleben, forty miles east of Möhra, where the growing copper-mining industry afforded opportunities to a strong and ambitious young man. A second son was born to them on November 10, 1483. The next day, the feast of St. Martin, the boy was baptized in St. Peter's church and given the name of the saint of the feast. The next year Hans Ludher moved to Mansfeld, deep in the Harz mountains, where an intensive mining industry offered greater rewards for initiative and hard work than he could find in Eisleben. The Ludhers experienced poverty in these early years; it was not until the boy Martin was ready for school that Hans had achieved any financial independence at all. Martin tells, in later years, how his mother carried wood on her back. Of itself this would not indicate extreme poverty, as almost all working people did the same, yet the boy's memories are of very difficult times. When Martin was eight, in 1491, we find Hans chosen as one of four citizens of Mansfeld to represent their fellow burghers on the city council. Hans continued to climb, and in a few years could be called a capitalist. By 1502 he was leasing and operating mines and furnaces, and a five-year contract of this sort was renewed in 1507. By this time Hans had become part-owner of six shafts and two furnaces.

The schooling that Martin, with his brothers and sisters, gained in the town school at Mansfeld was elementary. Reading, writing, Latin, and singing were about the size and sum of it. The methods were stilted and mechanical, and pointed solely toward training for the lower clergy. Luther in later life complained of the dull instruction and the absence of history, yet he had in fact gained a mastery of the elements of language, which served him well in his own career. The piety of his home was sincere, but both his father and mother were not much above the general level of belief in witches and evil spirits which prevailed at the end of the fifteenth century all over Europe. They followed scrupulously the priest's directions for using the power of the Church to protect them against the evil spirits: consecrated herbs against witchcraft, sprinkling of holy water over the hearth and the lintel, and other such devout practices. Piety was not far removed from superstition or the witchcraft it was used to exorcise. Hans and Margarete were not indulgent parents; neither were they inordinately severe. It is certain that Hans was master in his own house, and the children were taught to obey. After he became a father himself, Martin's judgment of his parents' discipline was quite mild, even favorable.

When Martin was thirteen and had gone as far as he could in the Mansfeld school, Hans decided to send him to a well-known school at Magdeburg, some forty miles to the north. The cathedral was the center of an active religious life at Magdeburg, and the year Martin spent at the cathedral school, taught by several Brethren of the Common Life, made a deep impression on him. It was while he was there that he saw Prince William of Anhalt walking, emaciated and barefoot, through the streets, begging alms. This picture remained vivid in his memory for his whole life.

Martin stayed only a year at Magdeburg, returning to Mansfeld for Easter 1498, then going on to Eisenach, a small city of about 2100 inhabitants, to attend the St. George's School, then under the direction of John Trebonius, an able and dynamic teacher. Martin was now old enough to profit by association with maturer people. He was welcome in the home of the well-to-do merchant Henry Schalbe, a pious and intelligent host who encouraged him both to study and to meditate on holy things. He was also a frequent guest in the home of Frau Ursula Cotta, a cousin of Schalbe, and may indeed have lived in her home for some months. Martin seems to have been happy in Eisenach and made great progress in his studies. He was soon ready for the next step in his education, the university. Hans had prospered and was able to finance the further training of his talented son. After much thought, father and son decided upon the University of Erfurt, which then enjoyed a high repute as an intellectual center.

At the University of Erfurt

LUTHER matriculated at Erfurt in the spring of 1501, and began study for the bachelor of arts degree under the direction of Dr. Jodocus Trutvetter, widely recognized as an eminent scholar and teacher. The university counted about two thousand students; the city was a busy commercial and ecclesiastical center of about twenty thousand inhabitants. Luther became a member of the *bursa* or college of St. George. Each of the various *bursae* had its regulations, specifying clothes to be worn inside the dormitory and on the streets, hours of study and mealtimes, rules which, in general, were strictly enforced. Luther would appear to have conformed without noticeable misconduct. His roommate, the later humanist Crotus Rubeanus, testified to Luther's reputation among his fellow students for scholarship. He finished his bachelor's course in the minimum time in September 1502, standing about the middle of a class of fifty-seven. From the bachelor's degree he went on immediately to the three-year course leading to the degree of master of arts. This advanced course he finished in February 1505, ranking second in a group of seventeen.

The University of Erfurt was one of the more progressive of the German universities. At various times such well-known humanists as Peter Luder, Conrad Celtis, and Jacob Wimpheling had held posts on the faculty. Trutvetter, Luther's own favorite professor, was familiar with the classics, and urged his students to read the great Latin poets and prose writers. Luther must have complied to a degree, for his own writing shows a sound acquaintance with Cicero, Virgil, Ovid, Livy, Terence, Juvenal, and Horace. But at this stage of his studies, he knew little Greek and no Hebrew. Furthermore the spirit of classical humanism was foreign to him as a student, and would remain so for the rest of his life. On the other hand, the scholasticism which was the substance of the required courses, both for the bachelor's degree and beyond, was hardly more congenial to his temperament. The reigning philosophy at Erfurt was the *via moderna* of Ockham as interpreted by D'Ailly and Gabriel Biel, which, while accepting in principle the findings of science, assumed that for matters of faith, revelation and not science was determinative. The ecclesiastical implication of this position was that the Church, the custodian of revelation, had a perfect knowledge of these matters. This general approach met with Luther's approval, and in later life he called himself an Ockhamist.

With his master's degree, Luther could have embarked on a career as a university professor. On April 23, 1505, he did in fact begin the series of lectures in the faculty of arts which were required of him as a new master of arts.

Further study of some sort was, however, expected. Urged on by friends, and probably also by his father, he decided to go on to a law degree. The profession of the law was the door to many important and lucrative posts. Within six weeks of enrollment in the law faculty he had an experience that shook him. In a sudden shower and electric storm, as he returned, on June 20, to Erfurt from a short visit to his parents at Mansfeld, a bolt of lightning struck near him, knocking him to the ground. Panicked, he made a vow to St. Anna: "Help, dear Anna, I will become a monk." It is obvious that such a radical decision must have had behind it a considerable period of inner tension, doubts, and reflection. The storm was only a precipitant of the decision. He remarked later that he soon repented having made the vow, and that his friends tried to dissuade him from carrying it out. But he stood firm; on July 17, 1505, he asked to be admitted to the order of the Hermits of St. Augustine in Erfurt. This order had earned a high reputation for its devotion to the ascetic ideal, and it is quite probable that this fact influenced Luther's choice. His father was at first enraged, declaring he wanted nothing more to do with such an un-grateful son; but he later relented and approved, "with reluctance and sad-ness." After a period of two months, during which he was allowed to reflect on his decision, and, if need be, recall it, Martin was received into the order in September as a novice. As such, he had to learn monastic attitudes and be-havior, maintaining almost complete silence. To test his character he had to perform menial tasks, scrub his floor, and occasionally beg from door to door. Reading, the regular services of the day, confession, and instruction from the tutor of the young monks occupied the rest of the carefully apportioned time.

His doubts and concerns, he found, had not abated. An older friend even had to tell him once: "God is not angry with you. You are angry with Him." Luther's piety and earnest pursuit of the means of grace impressed his fellows, and when, at the end of his year's novitiate, he took the monastic vows of chastity, obedience, and poverty, the whole convent rejoiced with him. The next step was ordination, as subdeacon, deacon, and finally, on April 4, 1507, as priest. He invited his father to his first Mass, and Hans brought with him a party of twenty friends and relations from Mansfeld. The young priest was so deeply awed by the seriousness of the power he possessed in "making the body of Christ" in the sacrament that he almost failed to get through the ritual. His doubts still unsatisfied, Luther did eagerly everything required of him. The order, ambitious for its members and impressed by Luther's previous academic success, destined him for the professorate in theology. He began his studies in 1507, and in March 1509 became *baccalaureus in bibliam*.

At Wittenberg

THE progress toward the doctoral degree was interrupted by several events. In 1508 he was sent to Wittenberg, where he lectured on moral philosophy. He found the town dirty and unattractive. He wondered why the Elector Frederick had chosen this crude electoral capitol as the site of a new (1502) university intended to rival Leipzig. Frederick, being economy-minded, was glad to accept on the faculty two Augustinian professors, to whom, because of their vow of poverty, he would not have to pay any salaries. The vicar-general of the Saxon province of the Augustinian Order, John von Staupitz, had held one of these professorships, that in theology, since 1502. The other post, in moral philosophy, was held by Brother Martin Luther from 1508 to 1509. The autumn of 1509 saw Luther back in Erfurt, promoted to *sententiarius,* lecturing on the *Sentences* of Peter Lombard. In October 1510, he was commissioned by Staupitz to go to Rome on business of the order. Many stories have grown up about his experiences and reflections while in Rome. The business on which he had been sent was settled in Germany while Luther was in Rome. It is hardly likely that this trip had any crucial influence on his religious development. He admitted that he was anxious to take advantage of all the indulgences offered to pilgrims, and piously wished that his parents were dead so that he could get them out of purgatory. While he suffered any earnest Christian's reaction to the worldliness of the Italian clergy, this did not affect his loyalty to the Papacy. By February he was back in Germany, where new responsibilities awaited him. He was sent back to Wittenberg and given his doctorate by the university on October 19, 1512. The Elector Frederick of Saxony, after defraying the costs of the promotion, asked that he be named professor of theology at the University of Wittenberg.

The dean of the faculty, Andreas Carlstadt, was seldom in residence at the university, and Luther was free to teach as he thought best. He chose to lecture on the text of the Bible. He began with the Psalms, rejecting the customary method of lecturing on commentators on the text of the Bible. At this early stage in his growth the methods of medieval allegory are very evident. But what is more evident is the direct appeal to Scripture, which was a new departure in biblical exposition, destined to affect profoundly the development of the whole Reformation. Furthermore, we find thus early in his career deep concern with the problem of justification. To the biblical scholar the Latin term *justitia* is susceptible to two translations: the justice with which God judges and punishes the sinner, or the righteousness of God which He imputes to the believer through grace. This distinction came to Luther in his study in the tower of the cloister in Wittenberg as he was considering the sentence in Paul's letter to the Romans, I: 7, "For therein is the righteousness (*justitia*) of God revealed from faith to faith." He says of this discovery: "So my soul was lifted up. For the justice of God is that by which we are justified and saved through Christ. Then I felt a greater joy in these words. The Holy Ghost revealed the Scriptures to me in this tower." But study and inspiration were not the only factors in Luther's development. His friend and superior, Staupitz, was also his mentor and guide, a fact which Luther always acknowledged with gratitude. To him Luther took his doubts and questions. The older man urged Luther to look to the mercy and love of God, to center his thought on the person and mission of Christ, apart from scholastic arguments and human "logic."

Luther continued to lecture on the Psalms until the summer of 1515. In that year he was made director of studies for the Wittenberg convent of his order, and also district vicar for a three-year term. In the latter position he had under his supervision eleven Augustinian cloisters in Thuringia and Meissen, including Dresden, Gotha, Erfurt, and Magdeburg. His supervisory responsibilities were accordingly heavy, yet he maintained his lecturing and preaching at the university. In these years he was at work on his next great series of lectures, on Paul's Epistle to the Romans. By this time his acquaintance with George Spalatin, who had been a fellow student at Erfurt and had gone on to be librarian, chaplain, and secretary to the Elector Frederick, had ripened into deep and understanding friendship. There are extant 430 letters in Luther's hand addressed to Spalatin, covering an amazingly broad range of subjects. As Luther had taken the side of Reuchlin in the controversy with Pfefferkorn, there were, for several years—from 1514 to about 1517—cordial relations between the young professor of theology and the German humanists.

In the meantime Luther had increased his own scholarly equipment by acquiring a reasonable mastery of Greek and some Hebrew, so that he was able to approach the exegesis of St. Paul's letter to the Romans with a sound technical background. When Erasmus' edition of the Greek New Testament appeared in 1516, Luther was in an ideal position to compose a commentary which would satisfy him. He drew more on Augustine than on any other source, and as one reads Luther's work, whole sections seem to echo the thought of the eloquent bishop of Hippo. In freshness of expression and originality of thought the work is far superior to the work on the Psalms. His main concern now was with man's ineradicable sinfulness, the inefficacy of works, and the incapacity of the human will to will good. The corollary of this position is the absolute need of man for God's merciful forgiveness and the free, because unearned and unmerited, gift of grace.

In 1516, while engaged in the study of the Epistle to the Romans, Luther came upon the sermons of John Tauler, whose mysticism had a great influence on him. Later that same year he discovered the *German Theology,* which at first he thought also by Tauler (see above, Chapter 7). He liked it so much that he published it with an enthusiastic introduction. In this way Luther appropriated for himself a potent portion of the German spiritual legacy. The fact that it was easy for him to do so only emphasizes Luther's consonance with the German tradition. These lectures show an increasingly critical attitude toward the clergy and the abuses in the Church. This may not have been unusual among the more conscientious circles of the monastic orders and in the universities; it was, in fact, rather expected by the general public. But Luther's language was strong and the examples he cited were matters of common knowledge.

His theological ideas were growing more clear; his confidence in his own position, arrived at partly by emotion and intuition, partly by scholarly study and logic, was becoming a certainty. By the late summer of 1516, he had come to the point of rejecting publicly the primacy of Aristotle and his scholastic followers, particularly as they claimed to present Aristotle as a guide for Christian theology. After finishing the lectures on Romans in September 1516, he chose to begin a new series on a very similar if more uncompromising letter of St. Paul, the Epistle to the Galatians. This commentary, begun on October 27, 1516, was finished in March 1517. It was a more hurried product than the lectures on Romans, but done with great fervor. Sure of his conviction that salvation is not affected by good works, that faith alone brings justification, Luther found the thesis of St. Paul and St. Augustine, that faith frees the sinner from the shackles of his sin and free grace makes him righteous in the sight of God, wholly acceptable. To him it became the essence of the Gospel.

His public preaching, which was well attended by townspeople as well as the university students, followed the same line of thought, a mingling of the mysticism of Tauler and the *German Theology* with his newer thinking on salvation by faith. The whole university community was being profoundly influenced by Luther's presentation, as much by his fervor and conviction as by their own intellectual assent to his doctrine. Furthermore, his name and reputation were beginning to be known in other parts of Germany; the widening circle of his correspondents during 1516 and 1517 reflects his growing repute. He was already easily recognized as the most eminent member of the faculty of the university. When, in March 1517, he had finished the lectures on the Epistle to the Galatians, he chose to lecture on the Epistle to the Hebrews. These lectures lasted until April 1518. But by that time Luther had become involved in the controversy over indulgences to which we must now turn.

Indulgences and the Ninety-Five Theses

THE indulgence, remitting to the penitent some or all of the temporal punishment (*poena temporalis*) incurred on account of sin already forgiven by God, scarcely appears before the time of the Crusades, and was not generally used as a source of income to the Papacy until well into the thirteenth century. There is, however, much evidence that during the thirteenth century it was already common practice to proclaim remission of the punishment (*poena*) and the guilt (*culpa*) to whoever paid for an indulgence.* After Boniface VIII's profitable employment of indulgences for the jubilee of 1300, their use spread widely. The "treasury of merits" of Christ and the saints, in the custody of the Church, was drawn upon to make up the deficiency of the penitent's pious works. The Council of Constance (1415) tried to curb papal use of the system, particularly as there was some lingering theological objection to the general extension of the coverage of the indulgence to remit the *guilt* of the penitent, hitherto considered to be beyond the canonical jurisdiction of the temporal Church, by use of the important phrase *a poena et a culpa* (from punishment and from guilt). Later popes, however, continued to employ the indulgence, and during the fifteenth century the coverage was further extended to the souls of the departed. The indulgence in this form required nothing from the person who acquired it beyond the payment of a certain sum of money. It must be pointed out, however, that there was some difference between the dogmatic explanation of the indulgence by many theologians, as a part of the sacrament of penance, and opinions held by the majority of the common people. These latter believed without question that the indulgence freed them from the punishment and the guilt their sins had incurred, while the "pardoners," or professional hawkers of indulgences, made no effort to disabuse them of the error of their opinions.

Late in 1514 Pope Leo X organized a campaign to raise money for the rebuilding of St. Peter's in Rome, begun by his predecessor, Julius II. The

* N. Paulus, *Geschichte des Ablasses in Mittelalter,* II, 141–42.

sale of indulgences was the surest means of raising the vast sums necessary. Albert of Brandenburg, Archbishop Elector of Mainz, was commissioned to raise the funds allotted to north Germany. Albert had but recently borrowed 30,000 ducats from the banking house of the Fuggers in Augsburg, 20,000 for the pallium of the archbishop, 10,000 for the right to occupy the archbishopric of Magdeburg.* The Fuggers in turn then (1515) arranged with the Pope to handle the collection of the indulgences for that area, agreeing to accept half the proceeds in payment of Albert's debt to them and to send the other half to the Pope. The agreement was not formally concluded until May 1517.

Since the matter of the indulgences was in large degree a religious operation, a priest had at least to direct it. John Tetzel, a Dominican monk, was chosen by the archbishop to organize and lead the campaign. Tetzel, who had been Inquisitor for Saxony from 1504 to 1510, had had extensive experience in raising funds through the sale of indulgences. He had collected generous sums of money for the Teutonic Knights for several years, from 1507 to 1509, and the next year was employed by Elector Frederick the Wise of Saxony to raise money by the sale of indulgences, permitting the holder of the indulgence to eat milk-foods on fast days. No amateur in preaching indulgences, he knew all the tricks of the trade. His instructions to his subordinates, including model sermons for the purpose, were thorough and effective. Tetzel began to preach the indulgences in the spring of 1517. The Elector Frederick had forbidden the sale of indulgences in his territories, not out of any scruples as to the right or wrong of the practice, for he had previously benefited from their sale, but simply because he had no part in the deal between the Fuggers and Albert. News of Tetzel's promises traveled fast. The more Luther heard of what the Dominican was doing and saying, the more convinced he became that the whole system was wrong.† The doggerel verse credited to Tetzel and his preachers,

> Just when the coin in the coffer rings
> The soul from purgatory springs

illustrates the spirit of the campaign. When Tetzel came as close as he could to Saxon territory, at Jüterbog in Thuringia, just twenty miles from Wittenberg, parishioners of Luther crossed the border, bought indulgences, and brought them proudly back to Wittenberg.

Luther refused to accept these indulgences in the confessional in lieu of repentance and penance, but, for a time, made no open attack on Tetzel. For several months he studied the matter of indulgences closely. He made the discovery, or so it seemed to him, that penance in ecclesiastical practice was taken to mean satisfaction for sin committed; whereas repentance, which was the intent of Scripture, was a change of mind and heart. This to Luther was a profound distinction. On a basis of his studies he decided, late in October, to bring the whole matter out into the open by calling for a public academic disputation on indulgences. Carefully preparing his case, he made a list of ninety-five propositions, on the general subject of penance and indulgences,

---

* These figures are approximate. The sources do not agree.
† On at least two occasions—late in 1516 and early in 1517—before he heard of Tetzel's preaching, Luther had attacked indulgences as subversive of morals and Christian faith.

Pope Leo X with Cardinals Giulio de' Medici and Luigi de' Rossi, by Raphael, in the Pitti Gallery, Florence [ALINARI].

which he was willing to debate. About noon of All Saints' Eve (October 31, 1517), he nailed them, in printed form, on the doors of the university church. The theses began as follows:

A disputation of Martin Luther, Theologian, for the clarification of the validity (*virtutis*) of indulgences.

With the aim and desire of bringing out the truth, the following matters will be disputed at Wittenberg, under the presidency of the Reverend Father Martin Luther, Master in Arts and Sacred Theology, and reader in ordinary at the same University. Wherefore he asks those that cannot discuss these matters orally that they do so in writing. In the name of Our Lord Jesus Christ. Amen.

1. Our Lord and Master Jesus Christ, when he said Repent ye, etc., intended that the whole life of the faithful should be repentance.

Luther sent a copy of the theses, with a covering letter, to Archbishop Albert at Mainz, and separate copies to the bishop of Brandenburg and to other high clerics in and around Wittenberg. In their stiff and scholastic Latin form, their explosive nature at first escaped notice. But the cumulative effect of all the questions these raised as to the grounds for the power of the Church was tremendous. Within a matter of weeks all Germany had either seen copies of the theses or heard what the monk of Wittenberg was doing. As reports got back to the university town, many of Luther's friends begged him, in the interests of peace, to drop the dispute.

A few of the Ninety-Five Theses will illustrate the tenor of the whole document.

5. The Pope has neither the will nor the power to remit any penalties except those which he has imposed by his own authority or by that of the canons.

8. The penitential canons are imposed only on the living, and no burden ought to be imposed on the dying, according to them.

20. Therefore the Pope, when he speaks of the plenary remission of all penalties, does not mean simply of all, but only of those imposed by himself.

24. Hence the greater part of the people must needs be deceived by this indiscriminate and high-sounding promise of release from penalties.

27. They preach man who say that the soul flies out of purgatory as soon as the money thrown into the chest rattles.

32. Those who believe that, through letters of pardon, they are made sure of their own salvation, will be eternally damned along with their teachers.

37. Every true Christian, whether living or dead, has a share in all the benefits of the Church, given him by God, even without letters of pardon.

47. Christians should be taught that the Pope's pardons are useful if they do not put their trust in them, but most hurtful if through them they lose the fear of God.

56. The treasures of the Church, whence the Pope grants indulgences, are not sufficiently named nor known among the people of Christ.

86. Why does not the Pope, whose riches are at this day more ample than those of the wealthiest of the wealthy, build the basilica of St. Peter with his own money, rather than with that of the poor believers?

The letter to the archbishop of Mainz and a copy of the theses were forwarded to Rome, and various efforts were made to persuade the German hierarchy to take measures against the "rash monk of Wittenberg." Neither move had any immediate effect. Pope Leo and the *curia* regarded the matter as a "monks' quarrel"; the German clergy, sensing that the Elector of Saxony was supporting Luther, preferred to take no action.

Meantime Luther was carrying on his lectures at the university, conscious that the eyes of Germany were becoming fixed on him. The Elector was probably influenced by his chaplain, Spalatin, in Luther's favor; while it was known that the archbishop of Mainz was planning heresy proceedings against him at Rome. Finally, in March 1518, Pope Leo appointed a committee of inquiry under a learned Dominican, Mazzolini, better known as Prierias. The latter wrote, in the form of a dialogue, a rather superficial reply to Luther's theses which he thought would demolish the ignorant monk. Luther republished the dialogue with his answer to it in August 1518. In his reply Luther declared that popes and councils could err and that only the Scriptures were free of error. When Prierias wrote a second pamphlet Luther published it also, adding advice to Prierias not to make himself ridiculous by writing any more books. Luther was summoned to Rome to answer charges of heresy, and the Elector Frederick was ordered to deliver him to Rome.

Cardinal Cajetan, newly appointed apostolic legate to Germany, was charged with the task of uprooting the Hussite heresy and gaining German support for a crusade against the Turks. He reached Augsburg, where the Diet was already in session, in July 1518. The cardinal found a mixed welcome. The German princes, with much experience of papal demands for money, were cool to the legates, and Cajetan reported to the Pope that the Germans should not be pushed too far. The legate had been ordered by the *curia* to declare Luther a heretic and to summon him to a hearing in Rome on pain of excommunication. The Elector Frederick, however, unwilling to have Luther leave Germany, arranged for an interview between Cajetan and Luther at the Diet, still in session. In the meantime Luther had published his *Explanations of the Ninety-Five Theses,* late in August 1518, and the issues at stake were thus somewhat clarified. In the three meetings between Cajetan and Luther (October 12, 13, and 14), the legate was at first "fatherly"; but, when Luther refused to retract his "errors" and admit the infallibility of the Pope, the legate threatened him with excommunication and the interviews were broken off with both Luther and Cajetan in bad humor. Luther published a report of his side of the controversy and made a public appeal, first, from the Pope "badly informed to the Pope to be better informed," and, a month later, from the Pope to a general council.

The attempt of Cajetan to silence Luther had obviously failed. The *curia* tried another approach. Pope Leo sent his nuncio and chamberlain, Karl von Miltitz, a Saxon nobleman of some diplomatic experience, to placate Elector Frederick and to deal with Luther. He met Luther in Spalatin's house on January 6, 1519. Miltitz, without really understanding the issues upon which Luther stood, was persuasive, and, with tears in his eyes, urged Luther to consider the peace of the Church and refrain from further provocation or attacks upon the spouse of Christ if his opponents would cease to attack him. Luther agreed and wrote a conciliatory letter to the Pope, yet without retracting his convictions, so hard come by. The letter apparently was never delivered to the Pope. Luther was at the time quite sure nothing would come of the engagements entered into.

The Leipzig Debates, Excommunication, and the Diet of Worms

UPON the death of Emperor Maximilian on January 12, 1519, the whole European situation underwent a radical change. The coming imperial election was the focus of attention for the next few months. Luther was left in relative peace, since the Pope, needing the support of the powerful Elector Frederick in the diplomatic maneuvering for the election to the imperial throne, had no wish to antagonize him further. Miltitz was still in Germany, but he had lost most of his earlier prestige; Luther even called him "ludicrous."

The peace agreed upon by Miltitz and Luther was broken by the Church party. Dr. Johann Eck, professor of theology at the University of Ingolstadt and a facile speaker with a distinguished academic record, had challenged Luther's colleague Carlstadt to a public debate in November 1518. While arrangements for the debate dragged on through the spring, Eck published *Twelve Theses,* concerned mostly with penance. The *Twelve Theses* were obviously aimed more at Luther than at Carlstadt. Thesis Twelve, particularly, was an attack on specific statements of Luther concerning papal sovereignty. The debate with Carlstadt was set for Leipzig, beginning June 27, 1519, and was opened with much ceremony in the presence of Duke George of Saxony. For the first week, June 27 to July 1, the disputation was between Eck and Carlstadt alone, with Luther as a mere spectator. Carlstadt, unable to withstand Eck's facility and overbearing manner and deprived of his notes and books of reference at Eck's demand, made a poor impression on the audience. Eck, enjoying his apparent victory, called upon Luther to debate the *Twelve Theses* with him beginning July 4; that debate lasted until July 14. Luther was cool and confident under fire. He knew the Scriptures and the early Fathers, both Greek and Latin, better than Eck, and was his equal in repartee and quickness of perception. The issue at stake between them, essentially chosen by Eck, was the primacy of the pope. Eck found occasion to charge Luther with holding the errors of John Hus on the constitution of the Church. Though Luther protested against being classed with the Hussites, whose heresies he deprecated, he did assert that "among the articles of John Hus or the Bohemians there are many that are plainly quite Christian and evangelical which the universal Church cannot condemn." Eck was convinced, and with him many of the audience, that he had proven Luther to be guilty of a great heresy. Luther was not happy at his own performance, though discerning observers were stirred by his appeals to Scripture and the evangelical tone of the "new theology." A considerable number of Leipzig students, evidently attracted by Luther's sincerity, moved to Wittenberg the next year. The questions involved received a thorough airing. The best and most balanced analysis of the issues was the summary of the debate written by Luther's young colleague, Philip Melanchthon, professor of Greek at Wittenberg, who had attended the disputations from the beginning. For months after the debates the air was thick with charges and countercharges, explanations and refutations, claims and counterclaims of victory from Luther and his friends as well as from Eck and his party. It is easy to see, by comparison of Luther's statements after Leipzig with his pre-Leipzig pronouncements, how his thinking had progressed beyond his position at the time of his *Explanations of the Ninety-Five Theses* or even of the discussions with Cajetan. His theology was being hammered out in the heat of controversy, and with each new challenge to his declarations he discovered, as it were, new reasons in Scripture justifying his instinctive expression. This is typical of the man and his development, and is a measure of the predominance of the religious element in his nature over the purely rational.

In the spring of 1520, urged on by a conviction that there was no hope of any honest reform from Rome and aware, furthermore, of rumors that his enemies in Germany and at the *curia* were preparing a bull of excommunication against him, Luther gave what time he could spare from a heavy teaching and preaching schedule to study of the Bible and the history of the Church. He took aid and comfort from Hutten, Spalatin, and Melanchthon. He was also heartened by the number of students who flocked to Wittenberg to hear the "new theology."

The Three Primary Works: 1520

THE expected bull of excommunication, *Exsurge Domine* (Arise, Lord), was issued in Rome on June 15. It was published in Leipzig on September 29 and in Wittenberg four days later. Long before publication its contents were widely known. In it Luther was ordered to recant in writing or appear personally in Rome within sixty days, on pain of being declared an obstinate heretic. Before the text of the bull was known to him he had written his *Address to the Christian Nobility of the German Nation,* which was in print by August 18. This was an appeal in the full vigor of the vernacular tongue to the princes of Germany to throw off bondage to Rome. Luther denounced the pope's claims to temporal and spiritual sovereignty and declared, on the contrary, that the Christian laity possesses a valid and universal priesthood. He called for a general council to remove the abuses in the Church, listing, in twenty-seven articles, the abuses that a council should consider. It was so savage an attack on the whole ecclesiastical institution that some feared it might set off a civil war.

But Luther had just begun. He ended the *Address* with the words: "I have still another song to sing concerning Rome. If they wish to hear it I will sing it to them and sing with all my might. Do you understand, my friend Rome, what I mean?" This second "song" was the treatise *On the Babylonian Captivity of the Church.* Published by October 6, it was a detailed attack on the sacramental system, which, he contended, was in actuality a captivity for the Church, preventing the believer from receiving God's free sacramental grace. He rejected the withdrawal of the cup from the laity—in this agreeing with Hussite doctrine, opposed the official doctrine of transubstantiation, and the sacrifice of the Mass. In his declaration that the power of the Church rested completely on its control of the sacraments, the means of grace without which the ordinary sinner could not hope for salvation, lay the radical significance of this attack. Luther accepted fully only two sacraments as of divine origin, baptism and the Lord's Supper. A third, penance, was on the borderline. The other four might be useful institutions but they were not really sacraments. As to the Lord's Supper, he insisted that faith was the important thing in this sacrament, not the power or the words of the priest. His thought on the scholastic theory of transubstantiation was not yet clear. He retained throughout his life his belief in the real presence of Christ in the sacrament, but he also insisted on the persistence of the physical elements of bread and wine. This doctrine is popularly known as consubstantiation, although, as we shall see, the term must be used with care.

Later in October Luther wrote a third treatise, *The Liberty of the Christian Man,* which from many points of view is the best and certainly the most attractive of all the reformer's writings. It appeared as an open letter to Leo X, prefaced by a conciliatory dedication to the Pope. The Christian is, Luther writes, by reason of his faith, lord of all, yet, by virtue of love, the servant of all. Faith frees man and then justifies him. Good works are not rejected; they are only put in their proper place as the fruit of justifying faith. This little book was certainly the product of Luther's immersion in Augustine and the medieval mystics. There was no talk of recantation; Luther spoke to the Pope as an equal, even with a touch of condescension. It is not known whether Leo ever received or read the pamphlet and the dedication.

The Burning of the Bull: The Diet of Worms

BY NOW Luther felt the need of a drastic gesture which would signalize his choice to break irrevocably with the Roman cause. The bull of excommunication had become widely known and made Rome's decision quite clear. As the bull had ordered his books to be burned, he chose a similar course. On December 10, 1520, he threw a copy of the bull, along with the papal decretals, a copy of canon law, and some writings of his enemies, into a fire just outside the eastern gate of Wittenberg. A crowd of students joined in the ceremony with enthusiasm. Luther defended his act in several writings, on the grounds that the pope was Antichrist and the canon law a tissue of lies making the pope into God on earth. The answer of the Papacy was the pronouncement of the ban (January 3, 1521) against Luther and his followers and an interdict on whatever place might give him shelter.

Three weeks later the young Emperor Charles V opened the first Diet of his reign at Worms. He was immediately faced with a demand from the Pope that he accept and re-enforce the bull of excommunication of Luther. Charles discovered that the princes were inclined to Luther's cause—for political and patriotic rather than religious reasons—and decided to proceed in a moderate and legal manner. On April 2, in obedience to a summons from Charles to present himself before the Diet, under an imperial safe-conduct, Luther set out for Worms with three companions. He was enthusiastically greeted on the way by students, citizens, and officials of the towns through which he and his party traveled. But some friends feared for him, and, reminding him of the fate of Hus who had also relied upon an emperor's safe-conduct, tried to dissuade him from going to Worms. Luther went on. The Elector Frederick had him met at Worms by an escort of Saxon noblemen and provided for his safe lodging. The populace was obviously disposed in his favor.

Luther was brought before the crowded Diet on April 17, the day after his arrival, and, in the presence of the Emperor and a pile of his writings on a table in front of him, was asked "first, whether you have written these books and others appearing under your name, and secondly, will you recant or will you stand by them?" To the first, he acknowledged his authorship. To the second, he asked for a day's grace to consider his answer. The evening of the next day he addressed the Diet at some length, explaining that some of the books he had written were not even criticized by his adversaries as they were straightforward commentaries on Scripture or the Fathers. These he could hardly recall. In others, he admitted being guilty of acerbity, but their substance he could not in conscience withdraw without being shown wherein they were in error. The Emperor, finding Luther's statement too involved, asked for a plain answer "without horns." Luther replied: "Well, then, since His Imperial Majesty wants a plain answer I shall give him a plain answer, without horns and teeth . . . I cannot and will not recant anything, since it is unsafe and wrong to go against my conscience." In the confusion attending the discussion after this "plain answer," Luther is reported to have said to

Martin Luther, aged forty-six, from the studio of Lucas Cranach the Elder, in the Art Gallery, Dessau [BILDARCHIV FOTO MARBURG].

485

the Emperor, who was on the point of leaving the hall: "I cannot do otherwise. Here I stand. God help me. Amen."

During the following week Luther, with a few of his friends, was called before several commissions, whose aim was to gain from him some concessions which might be acceptable to the Emperor and the papal legate. No compromise was possible; on April 26, under the safe-conduct and with the permission of the Emperor, who honorably resisted urgings by his councilors to disregard the safe-conduct he had given to a heretic, Luther left the city to return to Wittenberg. By popular request he preached several times in towns through which he passed. On May 4, as he was riding through the forest south of Eisenach, a troop of armed horsemen suddenly surrounded him and took him as prisoner to the castle of the Wartburg, belonging to the Elector Frederick, which they reached about midnight. The Elector or his brother John had thought out the whole plan and Luther was let into the secret the night before leaving Worms. The purpose was twofold: to protect Luther's person and to prevent him from further irritating the Emperor and the papal party. News of his disappearance spread like wildfire over all Germany, and it was generally believed that papal agents were responsible for the outrage. Cardinal Aleander at Worms thought his own life was in danger from popular indignation.

The Wartburg: The Reformation Confirmed

ON MAY 8 an edict was issued by Aleander, on the Emperor's order (and signed by the Emperor only on May 26), giving legal force to the papal ban of excommunication of Luther, ordering the burning and forbidding the printing or sale of his works, forbidding anyone to feed or shelter him or his followers, and demanding that he be immediately handed over to the Emperor. On reading the edict, Ulrich von Hutten wrote: "I am beginning to be ashamed of my fatherland."

In the Wartburg Luther discarded his monastic habit, put on a sword, and was known as Sir George, taking part in the usual activities of a medieval castle. He did much writing, especially on his commentary on the Psalms and his sermons on the Gospels and Epistles, and kept in touch with his friends in Wittenberg by frequent letters. In December, having heard that Archbishop Albert, again in financial difficulties, had announced a new sale of indulgences, Luther, without telling him where he was but subscribing the letter "from my desert," wrote the archbishop a letter warning him that he was not dead, and that if he did not call off the announced sale within fourteen days, he would attack him openly. The archbishop wrote an immediate letter of apology and called off the sale. That same month Luther visited Wittenberg secretly.

From discussions with his friends there over the future of the "new theology," it became clear to Luther that, for the movement to have a secure support among the people, they would have to have the Scriptures in their own tongue. After his return to the Wartburg he began the translation of the New Testament, using Erasmus' 1518 revision of the Greek text as a basis. Within three months the translation was essentially completed. Its superiority to all previous German translations lay in its accuracy and in the thoroughness with which Luther had captured the spirit of the New Testament. His own closeness to the German soil and the fervor with which he felt the message of the Gospel combined to make the translation a monument of German literary expression. When the work was done he decided he had been absent from the scene of action long enough, and planned to return to Wittenberg after Easter.

In his absence from the university town the implications of his earlier talk about liberty together with the critical attitude toward the ancient institutions and the liturgy which he had preached had found wide acceptance. He heard as early as October 1521 that priests were marrying, monks were marrying nuns, priests were celebrating the sacrament of the altar in plain clothes without requiring preliminary confession or preparation; images were being smashed, and students were leaving the university because endowments were being withdrawn. Carlstadt, Melanchthon, and the other colleagues whom he had left in charge of the movement were being led by events and were not showing firm leadership.

To add to the confusion, three enthusiastic laymen from Zwickau had come to Wittenberg just after Christmas. They had been associated with Thomas Münzer and claimed to be prophets having special revelations directly from God on a number of matters. Melanchthon, impressed by their zeal, had not withstood them. Luther's presence was necessary; in March he returned to Wittenberg, preached eight sermons which disposed of the special claims of the "prophets," and straightened out the doctrinal points they had raised. A firm hand was again at the helm. The radical changes in practice that Carlstadt had permitted were softened so as to strike a moderate compromise with the ancient liturgy.

King Henry VIII of England, anxious to show his piety and to strengthen England's connection with the papal-Habsburg coalition, had written in May 1521 an attack on Luther's *Babylonian Captivity* under the title *Assertio septem sacramentorum* (*A Defense of the Seven Sacraments*). The reformer, busy with preaching and visitation of churches in Saxony, only reluctantly took the time to answer the royal theologian. Henry had used unregal language against Luther and Luther finally answered in kind. The difference was that the German's vocabulary of invective was richer than Henry's, who now thought it best to let the matter drop. Luther then, with Melanchthon and other helpers, devoted himself almost exclusively for several years to his translation of the Bible, revising the text of the New Testament and continuing the work on the more difficult and voluminous Old Testament. By 1524 the historical works of the Old Testament, in addition to Job, the Psalms, and the writings attributed to Solomon, were completed. Other labors intervening, the rest of the Old Testament was not finished until 1532 nor the Apocrypha until 1534.

The work of reforming and reorganizing the public worship of the Church engaged Luther steadily from early in 1523. This work of organization was usually in answer to a request from a priest or even a bishop who, already in sympathy with what he knew of Luther's theology and ideas on worship, wanted further guidance in putting these reforms into practice in his own chapel or church. Luther's basic approach was one of moderation; he urged that what was not contrary to the Word of God in the old service should be retained. He gave much importance to the sermon, and, in order to make the people more active participants in the worship, introduced hymns in which the whole congregation should join. The first evangelical hymn book appeared in 1524, containing eight hymns, of which Luther had written four. In other songbooks turned out about the same time for choir use and family worship, Luther was the author or composer of almost three-fourths of the hymns. He wrote the classic *"Ein feste Burg ist unser Gott,"* known in English as "A mighty fortress is our God," in 1527.

In the meantime Pope Adrian VI (1522–23), a Fleming and the last non-Italian to be a pope, urged in vain that the Edict of Worms against Luther be enforced. His successor, the Medici Clement VII (1523–34), tried to induce successive Diets, both through the Emperor and directly through letters and legates, to reaffirm and enforce the Edict, but found the German princes, and particularly the Elector Frederick, resolutely inclined to protect German freedom in the person of Luther. The Lutheran cause, however, did not have to be content with victories of passive resistance to the Papacy such as that of the German princes. In 1522 Luther was in correspondence with leaders of the Hussites in Bohemia. As far away as Danzig in Poland, Buda in Hungary, Königsberg in Prussia, Vienna, Uppsala, Riga in Livonia, Louvain, Brussels, and Strassburg, Luther's doctrines were being preached, and there were by 1523 several martyrs to this "new theology." A positive gain for the cause was the requests from numerous German princes and cities, among them Magdeburg, Hamburg, Mecklenburg, Hesse, Brandenburg, Königsberg, and Strassburg, calling for Luther's friends or pupils to occupy pulpits or head schools.

MELANCHTHON

THE educational achievement of the Lutheran Reformation was of only slightly less enduring significance than its religious effects. Luther was deeply convinced that if his movement were to succeed the German people must be reached through the written word, and he realized that the educational system then prevailing was woefully inadequate. He was, therefore, from the very first, glad to offer advice and encouragement to any who sought his counsel on the improvement and broadening of schools or school systems. He was fortunate in having as his colleague and co-worker a younger man whose scholarly capacities were greater than his own, and whose genius for educational organization was such as to give him the honored title of "Praeceptor Germaniae" (Teacher of Germany). Philip Melanchthon was Luther's right-hand man and was to be his successor as recognized leader of the German Reformation.

Philip Schwarzerd was the son of a well-known armor-maker of the Palatinate, his mother being a niece of the humanist Reuchlin. Born in 1497, he matured early, and received his master's degree at Tübingen at the age of seventeen. Thus precociously he enjoyed a wide reputation for brilliance in Greek and Latin. Within four years he had published scholarly editions of Terence and Plutarch, a Latin translation of Aratus, and a Greek grammar.

Erasmus had already publicly acknowledged the extraordinary performance of the youthful scholar who, by the time he was twenty, had been invited to the faculties of three universities. He accepted the offer from Wittenberg to become professor of Greek. His inaugural address (August 29, 1518), "On the Improvement of the Studies of the Young," is generally regarded as marking an epoch in the history of German education. In the happy combination of the humanistic passion for learning with the Christian purposefulness of study lay the secret of the effectiveness which the German Gymnasium curriculum has, since the time of Melanchthon, enjoyed.

In the summer of 1519 Melanchthon attended the Leipzig debates between Carlstadt, Luther, and Eck, and was of great help to the Wittenbergers in refuting and correcting Eck's glib, frequently inaccurate quotations. Melanchthon published a report of the debate which, by careful delineation of the issues and the arguments, did much to reverse the general opinion that Eck had been the winner. In 1521 he published the first edition of his *Loci communes*

Philip Melanchthon, from the studio of Lucas Cranach the Elder, in the Staatliches Museum, Berlin [BILDARCHIV FOTO MARBURG].

theologorum (*Commonplaces of the Theologians*). Although more a statement of his own beliefs than a textbook, it nevertheless served as a semiofficial platform for the whole reform party. While Luther was at the Wartburg Melanchthon was left as his lieutenant in Wittenberg. When the Zwickau "prophets" raised issues he was not able to handle, he had to ask Luther to return. The rough and tumble of a public fracas did not fit his retiring and scholarly nature. He was at his best in the quiet of the study, in gentle discussion, and in apt and tactful formulation of doctrinal beliefs. It was his *Epitome doctrinae christianae* (*Epitome of Christian Doctrine*) that won Philip, Landgrave of Hesse, in 1524, to the Lutheran position. He stood beside Luther loyally in many trying situations from these early times on; in a very real sense the history of the Lutheran movement is, from about 1524 to the end of Luther's life, the story of Luther *and* Melanchthon. One without the other would have been lost, and Luther would have been, and indeed was, the first to recognize the great need he had for Master Philip's rare qualities. In 1529 Luther wrote:

I am rough, boisterous, stormy and completely warlike. I am born to fight against innumerable monsters and devils. I must remove stumps and stones, cut down thistles and thorns, and clear the wild forests. But Master Philip comes along softly and gently, sowing and watering with joy, according to the gifts which God has abundantly bestowed upon him.

Social Disturbances: The Peasants' Revolt

IN 1522 Luther had quickly silenced the Zwickau "prophets" by eight vigorous sermons. Carlstadt, a colleague and friend, had not opposed the "prophets" and had committed himself to the cause of extreme reform. He was soon (1523) allied with Thomas Münzer, an even more enthusiastic mystic and revolutionary. Münzer, after studies at the universities of Leipzig and Frankfurt, had become pastor at Zwickau upon Luther's recommendation. Expelled from that town in 1521 for his counsels of violence, he fled to Prague. Driven from Bohemia, he returned in 1523 to Germany as pastor in Alstedt, near Eisleben. His learning and eloquence gave him a certain prestige. But when he urged the Elector to found a new kingdom of the godly, declaring that he had thirty squads ready to slaughter the ungodly, the Elector expelled him from Saxony. Luther felt impelled to issue warnings against the extremes to which Carlstadt and Münzer had gone; and, sometime in 1524, Carlstadt parted company with Münzer. Münzer, regarding himself as the voice of the oppressed, openly preached rebellion against all authority, religious as well as secular, spreading his ideas of social and religious revolt in middle and southern Germany. In these areas, as we have seen, the early years of the sixteenth century were frequently disturbed by revolts of peasantry and townfolk. There were warnings of a recurrence of peasant rebellion in the very years that Münzer and Carlstadt were attacking the established order on religious grounds. The Peasants' Revolt of 1525, in which Luther was involved, is therefore a movement in which both social and religious issues became for a time fused.

The revolt first appeared in Swabia in the summer of 1524, then, increasing in violence and irresponsibility on into 1525, spread all over southern and middle Germany. Early in 1525 the peasant leadership published their program, the *Twelve Articles,* which might appear to us quite moderate. They demanded:

1. The right to choose their own pastors.
2. Relief from the small tithe of cattle. [They were willing to pay the great tithe of grain.]
3. Abolition of serfdom.
4. The right to hunt and fish, and to the protection of their crops from wild animals [until then, reserved for the nobility's hunting and sport].
5. Use of forests for domestic fuel.
6. Restriction of excessive compulsory services.
7. Payment for extra work beyond the conditions of their feudal contract.
8. Reduction in rents beyond what the holdings would justify.
9. Cessation of unlawful punishments, and return to old written [Germanic] law.
10. Restriction of pasture lands to communes which formerly owned them.
11. Abolition of heriot (*Todfall*), which deprived widows and orphans of their inheritance.
12. Scriptures to be the test of the justice of their demands and any further demands they might be impelled to make.

The repeated appeal to Scripture as a basis for their demands gave a strong color of justice to the whole document and to their cause in the eyes of the people of the rest of Germany. Luther's first reaction (April 1525) to these demands was an admission that they were reasonable, and he criticized the princes and the bishops for their oppression of the peasantry and their disregard of the law of Christ. He also urged the peasants to patience and peace. But as news of the actions of groups of peasantry—burning, murder, destruction of property, and the profaning of churches and convents—came in, Luther changed his opinion. Disorder and violent license he would not endure. As civil war threatened all of Germany early in 1525, Luther hurriedly wrote a pamphlet, *Against the Rapacious and Murdering Peasants,* which was published on May 5. His language was brutal: he urged the nobility to "cut, stab, strangle" the stupid and stubborn peasantry. "If you die in the struggle, you die in obedience to God's word and command." The nobility were only too glad to accept the reformer's cruel suggestion. They collected troops and forced the peasantry and the considerable contingents of the burghers of the smaller cities, who had joined the peasantry under Münzer's orders, to engage in a decisive battle at Frankenhausen (May 15, 1525). The superior equipment and discipline of the nobility easily won the battle. Over five thousand peasants and burghers lay dead on the field; three hundred more were beheaded before the town hall. Münzer was caught and executed on May 27. There were several other pitched battles, always with the same results. In all, it is calculated that well over 100,000 lives were lost during the Peasants' Revolt: mostly peasants, but in tragically large numbers monks and nuns in the convents that were destroyed, and members of the nobility whose castles were sacked and razed.

Luther's severe stand against the peasantry in this struggle for humane conditions of life was widely attacked and has remained a dark blot on his record.* However, he never regretted the position he took; he even consistently defended his conduct as the will of God. He must have weighed the alternatives: if the peasants, led by Münzer, were to win, his moderate reform would be completely lost. Better a few lives lost now than the souls of untold thousands later, for lack of hardihood at one moment. A case for Luther's consistency in the matter, as opposing rebellion in any form against the civil magistrates appointed by God, can be made; but it is not self-evident. Melanchthon stoutly defended Luther's position. It is perhaps less easy to understand how so gentle and pacific a person as Melanchthon could approve the brutality of the suppression of the revolt than it is to excuse Luther, who was a stormier nature and felt a more urgent compulsion to protect his movement from a disaster he saw as threatening it.

Ten days before the battle of Frankenhausen the Elector Frederick died. He had supported Luther, whom he had never met, though he never ceased to be a devout Catholic. Without his protection it is unlikely that the reformers could have laid the foundations of the movement. His brother and successor, John the Constant (1525-32), continued the policy of support of Luther, becoming an open adherent of the reformed faith.

The year 1525 was a memorable date in Luther's life for another event. He married (June 13) Catherine von Bora, an escaped nun, for whom he had first tried to arrange marriage with a friend. It was a happy union; the home life they enjoyed with their six children (two of whom died young) has been told in intimate and amiable detail by many friends and pupils who enjoyed their hospitality, as well as in many letters and in the *Table Talk*.

The Princes, the Emperor, and the Reformation

THE social revolution in Germany, of which the Peasants' Revolt was the most palpable indication, brought about an increasingly sharp division between the leaders of the Roman party and those leaning to the side of the reformers. The peasants' appeal to Scripture gave some plausible excuse for connecting the rebels with the Lutherans, and, despite Luther's condemnation of the violence of the peasantry, the Catholic princes were only too ready to regard rebellion and Lutheranism as identical. On this issue the Catholic princes could and did unite "for mutual defense" in July 1525. The princes who supported the Lutheran movement were somewhat slower to combine, but by the time of the opening of the Diet at Speier in the summer of 1526 even they had an understanding to work together.

Archduke Ferdinand, the younger brother of Emperor Charles, presided over the Diet when it opened, June 25, 1526. The breach between the German princes who had aligned themselves with Luther, the Elector of Saxony, Philip, Landgrave of Hesse, and some imperial cities on the one side, and the Emperor and those remaining loyal to the Catholic cause on the other, had become wide and clear. The Emperor had defeated his bitter enemy Francis I of France in battle at Pavia (February 24, 1525) (see below, Chapter 19) and,

* Luther's conflict with Münzer, Carlstadt, and the peasantry influenced his attitude toward the Anabaptists, a more moderate though still radical group.

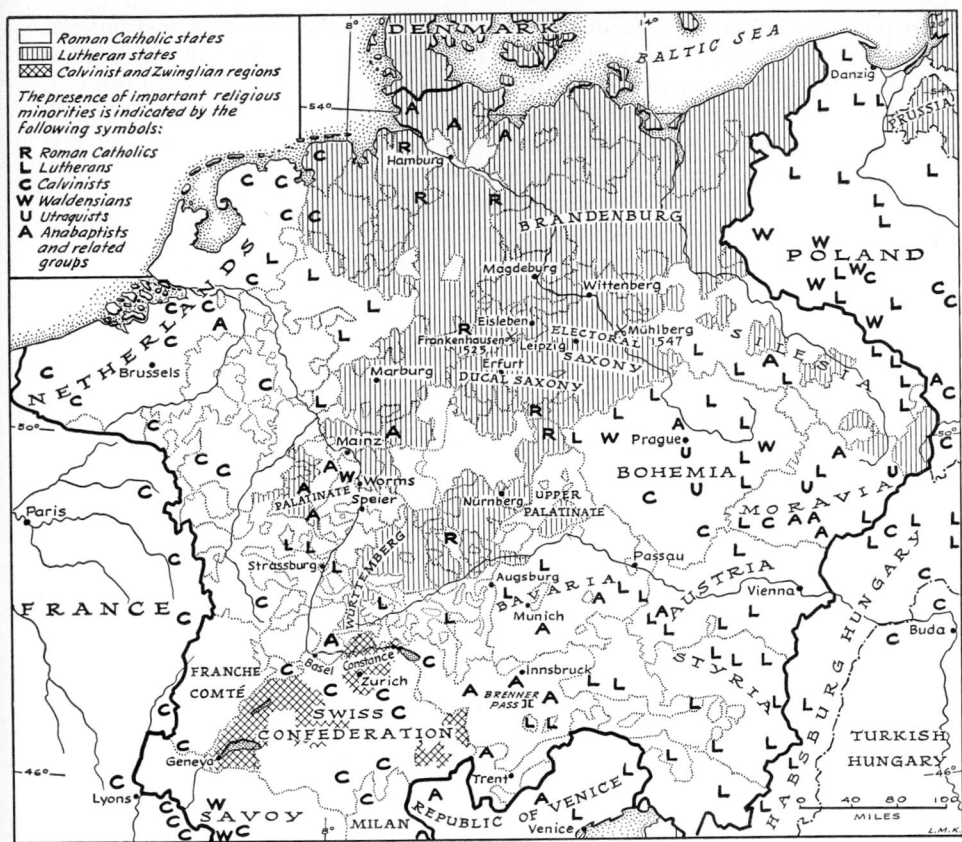

Germany during the Reformation

having extorted from him the humiliating treaty of Madrid (January 14, 1526), found himself the virtual dictator of Italy. Pope Clement VII could ill afford to have any one beside himself dominate the peninsula; he immediately joined Francis in an alliance against the Emperor, known as the Holy League of Cognac. When, to the untoward circumstance of the antagonism between the leading Catholic powers, the Empire and the Papacy, was added the threat to Christendom, and particularly the Empire, from the advance of the Turks up the Danube after their victory over Christian forces at Mohács, Charles, on the defensive, was obliged to accept an armistice in Germany with the pro-Lutheran princes at the Diet of Speier, concluded at the end of the Diet, August 27, 1526. According to the terms of this agreement, a general council was called for and each prince and state was left free to "live, rule, and act as he may hope and trust to answer before God and His Imperial Majesty." This temporary concession was utilized to the full by the reform party. Without doing violence to the facts, we can see in this agreement the first formalization in Germany of the principle of territorial ecclesiastical sovereignty which was to prove so important a factor in the spread of Lutheranism. The Emperor, frustrated in Germany by the failure of the Diet to enforce the Edict of Worms and, in Italy, by the defection of the Pope to the side of his enemy, Francis I, struck back—or at least allowed imperial troops, to the number of twenty thousand, to besiege and sack Rome (May 6-14, 1527) in scenes of bestiality, rapine, and debauchery which the Vandals could not have surpassed.

The second Diet of Speier met in March 1529. The Catholic party was then in the ascendant and revoked the temporary concessions made in 1526. Outnumbered and divided among themselves, the Lutheran princes presented to the Diet a formal *Protest* (April 19, 1529) rejecting the decisions of the Catholic majority. This *Protest,* from which the term "Protestant" stems, was presented to the Emperor, then in Italy; but he refused the courtesy of a hearing to the delegation which brought it to him. Luther and Melanchthon were pleased at the courage of the signers of the *Protest,* though they were opposed to the military resistance which most of the princes were preparing to organize.

In the meantime both Luther and Melanchthon were busily occupied with details of church organization and the preparation of manuals of instruction for the new ecclesiastical order. Pastors in outlying districts of Saxony and neighboring states were in some confusion as to how much of Catholic usage and liturgy they should keep. Melanchthon and Spalatin made several visitation trips in 1526 and 1527 and, aided by the experience thus gained, they prepared "Visitation Articles" which, later revised by Luther and supplemented by two catechisms, formed the basis for the organization and instruction of the Lutheran church.

Since 1519 a reform movement in Zurich, quite independent of Luther and his Wittenberg colleagues, had been active and successful. The leading character in this Swiss reform was Huldreich Zwingli (see below, Chapter 18), whose humanistic training caused him to lean to the positions of Erasmus, but who was also a convinced evangelical. As this movement progressed, gaining the adherence of neighboring Swiss and south German cities, Philip of Hesse, the most astute statesman of the Lutheran princes, fearing that the Protestants would be permanently outnumbered by the Catholics as at the second Diet of Speier, became convinced that he should try to bring the Swiss and Lutheran movements together. Against the reluctance of both Luther and Melanchthon, a meeting was arranged which took place in the Landgrave's palace in Marburg from September 30 to October 5, 1529. Each party to this "Marburg Colloquy" was well represented. Fifteen important articles of Christian faith as seen by the reformed theologians were drawn up. Outside the group of participants, great hopes were entertained that the two parties would come to an agreement which would unite the whole reform movement. All recognized they had to deal with a united Catholic party and that their own divisions might be fatal. On fourteen of these fifteen Luther and Zwingli came to quick agreement, and they signed the articles formally. The fifteenth, on the nature of the sacrament of the Supper, presented apparently insuperable difficulties to complete agreement. On the ministration of the sacrament in both kinds (bread and wine) they agreed, but Luther insisted on the real presence of Christ in the sacrament, while Zwingli was equally firm in his belief that the word *is* in the words of consecration, "This is my body," meant "signifies." The difference in point of view—Luther here a literalist and Zwingli a symbolist—was basic, and despite urgings from Landgrave Philip no agreement was possible. Yet, in sum, the Colloquy achieved a united front on fourteen and a half of fifteen heads of reformed faith, and was of some psychological value for the future. In the various conferences Luther was less courteous than Zwingli and, in the opinion of the audience, lost some face by his overbearing and uncompromising attitude, whereas Zwingli gained greatly. The Landgrave, impressed by the latter's manner and temper, even asked him to come to Hesse to direct the reform in his lands.

The Augsburg Confession and the Schmalkaldic League

THE next German Diet met at Augsburg on June 20, 1530. The Emperor Charles, attending in person, was hopeful that he could bring an end to the religious troubles of the Empire. He found, however, that the Protestant princes had no intention of accepting his direction. Luther, under the ban of the Empire, was not allowed to be present. The Elector John of Saxony had him stay at his palace at Coburg, some thirty miles from Augsburg, where he was in frequent communication with Melanchthon, in Luther's absence the leading Protestant theologian. The Saxon chancellor, speaking for the Protestant princes, read a statement of the faith they were committed to, in the form known as the *Augsburg Confession (Confessio Augustana)*. Melanchthon had had a hand in the preparation and polishing of the *Confession,* but it represented fully the thought of the princes. It was in two parts, the first a statement of the beliefs of the signers of the document, the second listing the errors of the Catholic Church which they deplored and rejected: enforced celibacy, the Mass as a sacrifice, auricular confession, monastic institutions, and the mingling of political and spiritual power in the hands of the bishops. The Swiss and the Strassburgers brought in separate confes-

The Augsburg Confession, 1530, by Herreneisen (1601), in the city hall, Windsheim in Franken [HANS RETZLAFF].

Rejection of the Reformers, detail from Herreneisen's *The Augsburg Confession, 1530* [HANS RETZLAFF].

sions, but they were of less moment than the *Augustana* of the Lutherans.

The document, in Latin and in German, was presented to the Emperor. He turned it over to his theologians, who wrote a *Confutation* to the Emperor, which he immediately pronounced as superior to the *Confession*. Melanchthon then wrote an *Apology,* seven times longer than the *Confession*. This *Apology* the Emperor refused to receive. Charles had made up his mind that, one way or another, the Protestant movement would have to be crushed. But it was not so simple to decide just how such strong and determined princes should be forced into line. After the *Confession* and the *Apology,* the Protestant princes left Augsburg, and soon (December 22, 1530) met at Schmalkald in southern Electoral Saxony to organize their resistance to the Emperor's threats to destroy them by force of arms. The result of their consultations, the Schmalkaldic League, at first counted only seven princes of northern Germany, the Elector of Saxony, the Landgrave of Hesse, two dukes of Brunswick-Lüneburg, the prince of Anhalt, the two counts of Mansfeld, and the cities of Magdeburg and Bremen. Gradually others joined, and by 1532 the League was so strong that Charles did not dare move against it. In thus organizing on politico-confessional lines the princes virtually assumed the dual functions of bishops and princes, confirming the tendency already evident toward the territorial church (*Landeskirche*). The Protestants in turn, more loyal to the Empire than the Catholics, gave Charles substantial support in his campaign against the Turks threatening Vienna. In 1532 the Pope again drew closer to Francis I of France, who was allied with the Sultan Suleiman, and Charles was once more in difficulty. For the next three years the Protestants were able to consolidate their gains without the threat of interference from the Emperor. The Schmalkaldic League took the lead in German politics, and, under the guidance of Philip of Hesse, brought about the reinstatement (1534) of Ulrich as duke of Württemberg,* who promptly declared his large duchy for Protestantism. Protestant prestige was high. When the Swabian League was dissolved in 1534, the Schmalkaldic League remained the strongest group of states and cities in all of Germany. The Protestant pastors of southern Germany, encouraged by the success of the political union of the League, asked to meet with Luther and arrive at a formula which would make it possible to avoid conflicts in the future. The resultant agreement, composed by the subtle Melanchthon after discussions and conferences lasting almost a year and known as the *Wittenberg Concord* (May 29, 1536), brought nearly all the German Protestants together. On the controversial question of the real presence the final wording allowed both sides to believe they had made their points.

The desire on the part of the various Protestant elements, lay as well as clerical, for unity was sharpened by the knowledge that the Emperor's insistence on the calling of a general council was being received with increasing favor by the new Pope, Paul III (1534-49). Such a council was actually called for May 23, 1537, at Mantua, to which the Protestants had been invited to send representatives. But the Protestant churchmen, their church organization and teaching already established, felt that little could be gained by attendance at a pope-dominated council. John Frederick, the Elector of Saxony, however, thought it best to be prepared, and asked the theological faculty of the University of Wittenberg to provide him with a statement which he could present and defend before the council when it should convene. As it turned out it was Luther alone who composed a statement (January 1537), later known, somewhat inaccurately, as the *Schmalkald Articles.* This statement, in twenty-one articles circulated among the theologians and friends of the Elector in February, is more uncompromising in its Protestantism and antipapalism than Melanchthon's *Augsburg Confession,* and posits a separate and independent Saxon territorial church, with its own theology and church organism. The Elector was very happy at the tone and the implications of the document. The *Articles* were not, however, accepted by all the theologians then present in Wittenberg. The princes did not sign the *Articles.* Instead they formally refused to attend the council called by the Pope. The superiority of the *Articles* to the *Augsburg Confession* and the *Apology* was not recognized until later. Coming late in the Reformation movement, they made a clearer distinction between the papal and the reformed position than Melanchthon had made in 1530. In the revised and polished form which Luther gave them in 1538 they came to be accepted as one of the official statements of Lutheran faith, the product of Luther's most mature thought.

The Protestant cause seemed by about 1538 to have won its independence.

* Ulrich was forced to resign his duchy in 1516, after murdering a cousin of Ulrich von Hutten. See above, Chapter 16.

It had achieved a great measure of theological unity; it had competent political leadership, and its enemies were unable to arrest its growth. Luther himself was less in the forefront of the battle than he had been in the first fifteen years after the Ninety-Five Theses. There were younger men whom he had trained well able to carry the burden. From about 1535 his health was worsening and he was content to remain at Wittenberg, lecturing, writing, and building up a body of theology which he could leave as his testament to future generations. He would have preferred to end his days in peace, but this was not to be. He became involved in several unfortunate matters which were to cause much embarrassment to the whole movement.

The best political mind of the whole Lutheran party was Philip, Landgrave of Hesse. He was, furthermore, completely loyal to Luther. He was also a man who found it difficult to control his passions. Married in 1523 at nineteen years of age to the daughter of Duke George of Saxony, he came to dislike her profoundly, and sought satisfaction in occasional liaisons. He met at court, in the entourage of his sister, a seventeen-year-old girl, Margaret von der Saale, whom he chose to be his second wife. The girl's mother insisted that Philip should get approval for the marriage from several scholars and theologians. After obtaining his wife's consent, Philip asked Luther and Melanchthon for their approval, but he did not tell Luther all the details of the arrangements and promises he had made. Luther's concurrence was conditioned on keeping the marriage secret, and he justified it on the ground that bigamy was valid in the Old Testament and not expressly forbidden for the laity in the New Testament. Luther acted rather as if he were a confessor back in the monastery, with power to grant dispensations from canon law. Obviously both Luther and Philip behaved inexcusably. The marriage took place early in 1540, in the presence of Luther and Melanchthon. The latter became ill with shame and indignity, but Luther was not so easily upset. The secret, in any case, was soon out. Luther counseled Philip to deny the fact of the marriage with "a good stiff lie." The whole unsavory incident was a catastrophe for the reformed cause. The Catholics greeted the news with glee, the Protestants with stunned humiliation.

The Emperor now had a powerful weapon with which to weaken the Schmalkaldic League. By imperial law, for the crime of bigamy Charles could have deprived Philip of his lands and title. He chose to force him (1540) to engage to prevent the young duke of Cleves, owner of a territory close to Charles' Lowlands, from joining the Schmalkaldic League. When, in 1543, the Emperor attacked the duke and took part of his lands, the League, weakened by Philip's forced defection, had to stand by idly. Charles could cling to the hope that he could, by dividing the Protestants, win a predominance in Germany by diplomacy instead of war.

Yet the Emperor was not immediately free to use his advantage to the fullest. A fourth war with Francis I of France (1542–44) was not going well for Charles, and, in the east, Charles' brother Ferdinand was calling for help against the Turks, then again threatening Austria. But by patience and diplomacy, in both of which he was well schooled, Charles rode out his ill luck and in September 1544, in the treaty of Crépy, he obliged Francis to give up some territorial claims and join him against the Turks and the German

Protestant princes. By the end of that year Charles was once more in a strong position, while the Protestants were in such difficulties that they thought it wise to offer help against the Turks and Francis I, their former ally. The Pope, however, now complicated matters by opening the long-promised and frequently postponed Council at Trent on March 15, 1545; and Charles' published intention to bring before the Diet, set for May 16 at Worms, a Christian reformation through a German council was partially frustrated. The Pontiff, anxious to prevent further cooperation between Charles and the German Protestants, made the Emperor a large grant of 100,000 ducats to support the war against the Turks, and in June added another 100,000 ducats, 12,500 soldiers, and the right to sell Spanish church lands to the extent of 500,000 ducats. Once the Pope and the Emperor were thus reconciled, the Protestants could no longer delude themselves with the hope that they could keep the two Catholic powers at odds with each other.

The fact that the Council was called for Trent, close to Italy, meant that Italian bishops would outnumber all others and that any Protestant representation would get short shrift. The Protestants therefore rejected the Council from the beginning. The feeling was general in Germany that the only solution of the impasse was war. During the fall and winter of 1545–46 both sides were busy with diplomatic and material preparations for a conflict which they knew would have to be decisive. The Emperor's situation improved during these six months, while that of the Protestants, because of divisions and petty jealousies, worsened. They were to suffer two major blows before war actually broke out. Luther died in Eisleben on February 18, 1546, full of fears and despondent over the turn of events within the Protestant camp, yet without any weakening in his personal faith and conviction that the reformed church would survive. Then Maurice, duke of Saxony, a professing Lutheran, went over to the Emperor's camp in return for a promise that the electoral title would be taken from the Ernestine branch of the house and given to him as head of the Albertine branch (see above, p. 471*n*).

The war that followed was quickly over. The Protestants, divided and stunned by Maurice's defection and attack upon his cousin John Frederick, the Elector of Saxony, were unable to offer adequate resistance to Charles. The Protestant cities of southern Germany would not fight. Philip of Hesse did practically nothing. John Frederick the Elector, however, showed unexpected vigor and not only repelled the forces of Maurice but overran parts of Ducal Saxony. The Emperor marched straight across Germany to meet the Elector's weakened forces at Mühlberg on the Elbe on April 25, 1547, and won a quick and decisive victory. With the Schmalkaldic League dead on the field, Charles was, for the first time, really master of Germany, albeit less by his own merits than by the divisions and shortcomings of the Protestant princes. That Charles was unable to consolidate his victory was due partly to the chronic fluidity of political power in Germany, partly to the fact that even the Catholic princes were somewhat dismayed at the implications of the victory of the Emperor, but probably in larger measure to the depth to which the ideas of princely independence inherent in the Lutheran Reformation had penetrated the German mind.

The Augsburg Interim to the Peace of Augsburg

THE Lutheran princes, their League, and their political morale were crushed, their leader dead. But the Lutheran movement was still very much alive. The Pope, alarmed at Charles' predominance and fearful lest he might attempt to control the Council, transferred that body from Trent to Bologna, while Charles angrily ordered the German and Spanish delegates to remain at Trent (see below, Chapter 21). The Emperor was therefore in a mood of moderation toward the Protestants when he met the Diet at Augsburg, September 1, 1547. A religious and political compromise known as the *Augsburg Interim* was drawn up at Charles' suggestion, passed by the Diet, and proclaimed by the Emperor as a provisional law of the Empire on May 15, 1548. As a compromise, attempting to bring something resembling Protestant doctrine into workable harmony with Catholic practice, it obviously could satisfy neither side. The Protestant leaders, even John Frederick, then Charles' prisoner, refused to accept it, and the cities, despite measures of enforcement at the Emperor's orders —four hundred Lutheran pastors were expelled from their homes for non-acceptance of the *Interim*—offered active resistance. The Elector Maurice had Melanchthon, now recognized as Luther's heir and successor, modify the *Interim* so that it would be more acceptable to the reformed party, then published it as the *Leipzig Interim* (December 21, 1548).

The *Augsburg Interim,* however, soon became a dead letter, for the most part because of Charles' attempts to force compliance with its provisions by the use of Spanish troops. It had served one purpose: it had alienated Germany from Charles. His resources exhausted, his unpaid Spanish soldiers deserting in great numbers, he was really beginning to despair of ever bringing religious unity to Germany. Furthermore, he had angered the princes by trying to force them to accept his son Philip as Emperor. Philip and the electors found each other uncongenial. He increased his unpopularity by expressing distaste for German beer, and the relief with which he left Germany was shared by the princes. To cap the climax of Charles' frustrations, Maurice of Saxony decided at this point (1551) to desert the Emperor and head up the Protestant opposition. He had been well paid for his first treachery of deserting the Schmalkaldic League. His second he did not live long enough to enjoy. He allied with Henry II of France in the treaty of Chambord, January 15, 1552, and attacked the Emperor's troops in March. He almost captured the Emperor in a wild race from Innsbruck over the Brenner Pass, but it may be that he was careful to keep his pursuing horsemen just far enough behind not to reach Charles' company. The Emperor would have been an embarrassing prisoner. On August 2, 1552, by the peace of Passau, Charles practically abandoned his policy of maintaining imperial power in Germany. He released the second of the two Protestant princes he had held captive, Philip of Nassau, and agreed that the religious affairs of the Empire should be decided by the imperial Diet.

The Diet which finally made this settlement met at Augsburg from February to September 1555. The lines of the agreement had in reality been hammered out over the past thirty years of conflict and negotiation. Both parties knew by now what the opposition wanted and would fight for, and what would be acceptable to the mass of the German people. Territorialism had come to stay; any idea of an over-all unitary monarchy had been proven completely vain. On the confessional issues the principle of toleration was recognized, but in a very narrow sense. Just two possibilities were open to a prince: he could choose Roman Catholicism or Lutheranism for his lands. Those of his subjects who found his choice unacceptable could quite freely move elsewhere. Neither Zwinglianism, Calvinism, Anabaptism, nor any other sect was recognized. All Church lands in Lutheran hands before the peace of Passau of 1552 were to remain in Lutheran possession. Whenever, thereafter, a high prelate, archbishop, bishop, or landed abbot became Lutheran the lands formerly in his name should revert to the Catholic Church. This last provision, the Ecclesiastical Reservation, encountered heated opposition from the Lutherans. In the cities, where there had already been much practice in the tolerance of several confessions, Catholics and Lutherans had learned to live together in a measure of peace.

There was much to criticize in the Peace of Augsburg; for example, its refusal to recognize the principle of full confessional tolerance, or specifically the rights of Calvinists, Zwinglians, and other sects to full and unfettered exercise of their faiths. Yet the Peace did bring order to the Empire by ending the religious wars. It was also a clear warning to Ferdinand, Charles' brother and soon to be his successor as Emperor, that he could not control the princes as Charles had tried to. The use of force, either by the Church or by a civil ruler, no matter how powerful, to bring about changes in the religious convictions of their subjects, was soon to be a thing of the past.

Lutheranism Led by Melanchthon

SINCE the death of Luther in 1546, on the eve of the Schmalkaldic War, the leadership of the Lutheran movement had fallen upon the slender shoulders of Philip Melanchthon. The compromises he had agreed to at the time of the *Augsburg Interim* (1548) and the *Leipzig Interim* had brought forth complaints from many Lutheran pastors. His answers urged the brethren not to be unduly concerned over *adiaphora* (things indifferent), but to emphasize the really important doctrines of grace and salvation by faith. One of the most determined and vocal opponents of Melanchthon's tendency toward compromise was Matthias Flacius Illyricus, a native of Illyria, who had studied and traveled widely and was a fervent opponent of anything papal and Roman. With a number of like-minded scholars he carried on a bitter campaign against Melanchthon's leadership. He objected to any subservience of the church to the princes, and to compromise of any sort on doctrine. Flacius' attack on Melanchthon was in fact scurrilous and in some respects dishonest. Melanchthon endured it in silence for a while, but in October 1549 he replied in a general and open letter, taking up each of Flacius' charges and explaining his actions or denying the truth of the allegations. Flacius should have been silenced, as Melanchthon's defense was calm, clear and, to almost everybody, convincing. Melanchthon had to endure yet more calumny and venomous attacks; he found his position of leadership an uncomfortable honor.

The Protestant princes, having been invited, were now toying with the idea of going to the Council of Trent themselves, or of sending representatives. Melanchthon, consulted, advised against attendance, but prepared a new statement of the reformed faith, *The Confession of the Doctrine of the Saxon Churches, (Confessio saxonica)* which reaffirmed the articles of the *Augsburg Confession* and refuted some statements already accepted by the Council at Trent. A number of leading Protestant princes and their theologians signed the *Confessio,* which Melanchthon took, quite properly, as a vindication of his conduct in the face of the calumnies of Matthias Flacius.

Melanchthon was once more, in 1552, on the point of being sent to Trent to present the Lutheran cause, and indeed traveled as far as Nürnberg, but as other Protestants, although invited, had not received a hearing at the Council, Melanchthon returned to Wittenberg. It was at this point that Maurice of Saxony, finally realizing how firmly his subjects were devoted to the Lutheran faith, had reversed himself, deserted the Emperor, and forced from him the treaty of Passau which relieved the pressure on Lutheran pastors, many of whom had had to flee from Saxony. With these pressures abated, for a short time it appeared that Melanchthon would be able to enjoy the peace and quiet of his study. But a fellow Lutheran, Osiander of Nürnberg and Königsberg, was stirring up trouble. He had some irregular ideas on the dual nature of Christ; when Melanchthon declined to endorse these ideas, he attacked him and his books violently, promising to "spill his blood all over Germany." Osiander died late in 1553, but the controversy was carried on, from various quarters, for several years longer.

By the time the Diet of Augsburg opened in February 1555, the Protestants, victorious politically, were engaged in bitter controversies among themselves on almost every cardinal tenet of the reformed faith, although the principal controversies were over the Eucharist and the manner of presence of Christ in the elements of bread and wine. Melanchthon opposed the rabid literalists who contended that Christ's body was consumed "corporeally, dentally, gutturally and stomachically," but he tried to stay out of a controversy which he thought would lead nowhere. Calvin, from Geneva, urged Melanchthon to fight back, and even expressed doubt as to Melanchthon's courage. An attempt in 1556 to reconcile Melanchthon and Flacius failed. Flacius set such terms as would have humiliated Melanchthon irretrievably. Flacius' rigidity and readiness to vilify anyone who did not accept his extreme Lutheranism weakened his position and sent some of his adherents to the side of Melanchthon. The Protestant princes, appreciating the harm the open polemics were doing their cause, sought to bring peace. They issued in March 1558 a statement called the *Frankfurt Recess,* which stated the Lutheran faith in sufficiently general terms to which, they hoped, all Lutherans could subscribe. Flacius and the rigid party rejected the *Recess* immediately, and the split was widened. There was some irony in the situation, as Melanchthon himself had the humor to see. Flacius and his followers continually appealed to the Augsburg *Confession* and the *Apology.* But, as Melanchthon remarked: "I wrote the *Confession* and the *Apology* from which they quote. Now they want to throw out the author of these same formulae." The last years of his life were steadily embittered by the continuation of this controversy. At every turn Flacius and his followers hurled charges and epithets against Melanchthon, who, although he refused to dignify much of it with replies, nevertheless had to correct and answer some of the scurrility. In the last year of his life the Jesuits had appeared in Bavaria and threatened the gains of the Lutheran as well as the Reformed * faith in southern Germany. One of the last things Melanchthon wrote was a marginal note in a book he was reading in which he looked forward to Heaven to free him from the raging of the theologians. He died April 19, 1559, and was buried beside Luther in the churchyard of the chapel at Wittenberg. With his death the German Reformation entered upon its period of compromise and amalgamation, culminating in the *Formula of Concord* (1577) and the *Book of Concord* (1580). From other points of view this third period was a time during which the reformed thought was already becoming scholastic. The original fervor and dynamic conviction which had fired Luther and Melanchthon had cooled to a noticeable degree in their followers; in their stead there was organization and, within the limits of the Augsburg Peace of 1555, security. Security, for any movement which is built on emotion or conviction, is always a dubious good. It proved so in this case.

THE THOUGHT OF LUTHERANISM

Thus far we have given our attention to the rise, establishment, and growth of the movement in Germany that goes by the name of its founder, Martin Luther. The half-century thus traversed was one of the most crowded in all Western history. It was hardly to be expected that in the midst of a virtual social and spiritual tempest anyone, least of all the leader of the revolt, should be able to erect a rationally integrated system of thought. Such a structure must be worked out in quiet and serene surroundings. Luther, furthermore, was not a systematic thinker. He was quite aware of his limitations. Like many a religious genius, he felt religious truths first and put them into words afterward. This is not the way of the philosopher or the systematic theologian.

It might be possible to make a coherent and balanced system of doctrine, in the formal sense, out of Luther's own voluminous writings. But it would require a selective method, which would do some violence to the truth because certain inconsistencies or changes in his thinking brought about by inner spiritual development would have to be overlooked. Luther grasped the full implications of his own construction of the Gospel only gradually and over a period of at least twenty years, from about 1515 to about 1535. In the course of his development he spoke and wrote prodigiously. He wrote as he thought and felt at the moment under the impact of his conviction or in answer to heavy attacks from many quarters. Polemic is never conducive to clarity of thought or consistency in its formulation. The Lutheran movement without any question owed its existence and its force to Luther himself. But it owed most of its intellectual organization to Luther's younger colleague, Philip Melanchthon. In the following attempt to describe what Lutheranism as a totality held and put forth on the important matters in dispute, we shall have to draw in about equal meas-

* The term "Reformed" in its historic sense refers to those churches which trace their origins to Zwingli or to Calvin. With a small "r," its meaning is broader, including the Lutheran and Anglican traditions.

ure from Luther and from Melanchthon. This task is somewhat complicated by the fact that there was not infrequently a difference of opinion between the two friends. These differences were sometimes only matters of phraseology, but at other times the differences ran deeper and may never have been completely reconciled.

Of the four classic "heads" of theology—theology (the nature and attributes of God and His creation), soteriology (the person and work of Christ the Savior), anthropology (the nature of man), and ecclesiology (the Church and the sacraments), Lutheranism was close to Roman Catholicism on most points of the first three. The Fatherhood of God, the Trinity, the full deity and humanity of Christ, the reconciling ministry of the Holy Spirit—these were fundamental to the reformers. It was in the application of the doctrine of salvation that Luther departed from emphases current in the Roman Church of his time.

Luther was convinced from his own experience of the inability of man to effect, in the slightest degree, his own salvation. "Works" were vain. Human merit, he believed, was worthless. Sin was so deeply rooted in man that only the vastness of God's freely given grace could make man righteous in His sight. Man lays hold of this gift of grace by faith. Faith forms the link between man and God, for without that faith in God's mercy and Christ's power to save, man stands outside God's mercy. But how can man gain so necessary a faith? Luther would answer, as he did in the *On the Bondage of the Will* (*De servo arbitrio*), that by himself he cannot possibly obtain saving faith. It must have been determined by God, by a decision in which the sinner has no active part at all. It is all in God's hands. To Luther predestination was a corollary to his principal doctrine of salvation by faith alone (*sola fide*). This latter, so prominent in Luther's thought, has come to be known as the "material" principle of the Reformation, and is contrasted with the teaching of the medieval Roman Church that salvation was conditioned upon faith *and* good works. Beside this "material" principle is conventionally placed the "formal" principle of the Reformation, the primary authority of Scripture over the authority of the Papacy and Church tradition. The medieval Church had not intended to teach anything contrary to Scripture, but had reserved interpretation to specially designated organs within the Church. The reformers regarded Scripture as the living word of God, by which He spoke to believers. Luther's work of translation was based on the conviction that all Christians should be able to hear God speaking directly to them. Luther also felt free to judge the books of the Bible according as they presented doctrine which he held to be true. The Epistle General of James, for example, he regarded as an "epistle of straw, as it has in it nothing whatever of the Gospel."

In his teaching concerning the Church, Luther departed sharply from the Roman tradition. It was at the Leipzig debates with Dr. Eck (1519) that he was first driven to see where his thinking on the sacrament of penance and the control of the Church over the life of the believer had already led him, and he was thus early forced to acknowledge the closeness of his ideas on the nature and membership of the Church to those of the heretic John Hus. The Church became for Luther the community of the predestinate, the Church invisible, a spiritual body united through a common faith and the sacrament of baptism. It is the "communion of saints" in the original sense of the Creed. The claims of Rome to papal absolutism Luther rejected as blasphemous and mad. The visible Church was not, as many Catholics contended, the source of grace or a unique route to salvation. The hierarchy was not divinely instituted, nor even necessary. Luther and his associates held, furthermore, not only that the clergy was not an exclusive priesthood, but that all believers possessed the gift of priestly rights and privileges. The "universal priesthood of believers" was a point of cardinal emphasis to Luther and Melanchthon. Within and through the visible Church, which assumed for Luther the form of a spiritual community (the German word *Gemeinde* was a favorite with him), the revelation of the forgiving love of God in Christ was made known to the believer. The Church was then the indispensable agent and means used by God to effect the salvation of the believer.

Although Luther was clear in his own mind concerning the essentially spiritual nature of the Church and its mission, he was less perceptive in his conception of how such a spiritual community should cooperate with secular authority. He succeeded in freeing the German church from the control of Rome, but, after 1525, he relied upon the power of the German princes for the reconstruction of a visible German church. Whether the substitution of the power of secular princes for that of a nominally spiritual and universal *curia* was a gain or not may be debated. But it is certain that Luther tied the church in Germany to the power of the civil prince. It is also true that the civil princes seldom meddled in doctrinal and purely religious matters; and in this respect the church enjoyed more freedom than it had under Rome. Yet the development within the Lutheran church was to be conservative in doctrine and subservient toward the princes until very recent times.

On no aspect of Catholic faith and practice was Luther so outspoken as on the doctrine of the sacraments. It was Tetzel's blatant and crass preaching on the indulgences in 1516 and 1517 that first brought Luther from his study into the public eye. Since the indulgence was connected with the sacrament of penance, Luther began to give thoughtful attention to the scriptural and historical warrant for the whole sacramental system. The results of his investigations were formulated in his work *On the Babylonian Captivity of the Church* (August 1520). He rejected four of the orthodox seven sacraments, accepted two as of divine institution—baptism and the Eucharist or the Lord's Supper— and regarded a third, penance, as sacramental but in essence only a ceremony indicating a return through repentance to the purity gained at baptism. He never departed from the position thus early proclaimed. The Lord's Supper called for frequent discussion because of the importance attached to the doctrine by the Roman Church and the centricity of the miracle of the Mass in the life of the people.

Consistent with the desire common to all the reformers to re-examine every teaching as well as every practice of the Church which they had set out to reform, Luther gave much thought to the manner in which the body and blood of Christ were present in the Eucharist. The Fourth Council of the Lateran, held by Pope Innocent III in 1215, had decided that at the repetition by the priest administering the sacrament of the words of Christ, *"Hoc est corpus meum,"* in some mysterious way the substance of the bread and the wine changed into the substance of the body and blood of Christ. This has since remained the teaching of the Church. It was accepted, in consequence, that the substance of the bread and wine were no longer there. The accidents—that is, taste, weight, size, color, appearance, and so on—of course remained. Luther accepted the presence of Christ's body and blood, but insisted that the substance of bread and wine also remained. He saw no great logical contradiction in the double presence, using the figure of heat in iron. This position is usually, if somewhat too readily, called consubstantiation. Luther's explanation was simply that the mode of the presence of the risen Christ was different from the mode of presence of a physical substance like bread or wine. Luther, it will be remembered, at the Colloquy of Marburg in 1529 (see above, p. 494) stood adamant against Zwingli in his (Luther's) conviction that Christ was truly (*vere*) present in the bread and wine and actually eaten by the communicants. Ten years later Melanchthon modified the phraseology of the *Augsburg Confession* (in the edition of 1540) to read that "with the bread and the wine the body and blood of Christ are truly *exhibited* to those that eat in the Lord's Supper." Both Zwingli and Calvin, who held to the symbolical presence of Christ in the Eucharist, could almost have accepted this statement. Luther, although he would have preferred to keep the early and stronger statement of the actual presence, did not repudiate Melanchthon's modification. The final official position of Lutheranism, however, as stated in the *Formula of Concord* of 1577, is rather a restatement of Luther's view and a rejection of Melanchthon's compromise. It was the princes and not the theologians who forced the return to Luther's "consubstantiation" against the moderate sacramentarians.

As a reformer Luther was a conservative. His doctrinal divergence from the established Church was relatively modest. The ancient creeds he accepted without hesitation. He continually claimed that he wanted to bring the Church back to its primitive purity of belief and practice. There was little in his theology that was original, and parallels even to his emphases have been found in his predecessors, in St. Paul, St. Augustine, and the scholastics. What was new and original, creative and revolutionary, was the intensity and the energy with which he believed what others had only accepted, and applied what others had only stated. The application was to men of a new age and came at a propitious moment.

Luther's basically conservative temper was nowhere better illustrated than in his treatment of social and economic questions. We have seen how, after counseling both the peasantry and the nobility to moderation and restraint, he finally turned against the peasants and sided with the nobility. Similarly, in his occasional writing on economic questions he took the side of the established order. His thinking was conditioned by his peasant and monastic background rather than by any reasoned appreciation of the economic revolution that was taking place before his eyes. The Fuggers, he thought, should be curbed. Interest should, for the most part, be forbidden. The whole world of individual enterprise, profit, and the accumulation of capital was the invention of the devil, therefore wrong and conducive to sin. He held to the idea of the "just price" as fervently as had St. Thomas Aquinas and canon law. It has not infrequently been said that Protestantism is indissolubly related to the rise of a capitalist society. There may, under some conditions, be some truth in this statement. But it is certainly not true of Luther and the Lutheran movement. Capitalist enterprise in the German cities antedated Luther, and economic imperialism on a national scale first appeared in the strongly Catholic countries of Spain and Portugal. In social ethics it is difficult to accuse Luther of departing far from the best of Catholic and medieval thinking, at the same moment that he rejects the authority by which the Church had established and propagated that system. Canon law and papal authority, Luther asserted, were quite unnecessary. The Scriptures and his own conscience were enough to guide the believer in all temporal matters. But the rules of conduct which Luther discovered in the Scriptures were remarkably close to the ethical demands of the very canon law which he rejected.

SUGGESTIONS FOR FURTHER READING

LUTHER, *Table Talk*. New York, 1893

Luther's Primary Works, ed. J. Wace and C. H. Buchheim, London, 1896

Luther's Works, ed. H. T. Lehmann. 55 vols. Vols. XXXI–XXXIV, *Career of the Reformer*. Concordia, Mo., 1957–60

Three Treatises by Martin Luther. Philadelphia, 1943

CURRIE, M. A., *The Letters of Martin Luther*. London, 1908

HYMA, A., *Luther's Theological Development from Erfurt to Augsburg*. New York, 1928

KERR, H. T., *A Compend of Luther's Theology*. Philadelphia, 1943

FOSDICK, H. E., *Great Voices of the Reformation*. New York: Modern Library, 1952

SCHAFF, P., *Creeds of Christendom*. 3 vols. Vol. III, *Evangelical Creeds*. New York, 1877

SMITH, P., and G. M. JACOBS, *Luther's Correspondence*. 2 vols. Philadelphia, 1913, 1918

WOOLF, B. L., *Reformation Writings of Martin Luther*. 2 vols. New York, 1953, 1956

BAINTON, R. L., *Here I Stand: A Life of Martin Luther*. New York, 1951

BOEHMER, H., *Luther in the Light of Recent Research*. New York, 1915

BOEHMER, H., *Road to Reformation*. Philadelphia, 1946

FIFE, R. H., *The Revolt of Martin Luther*. New York, 1957

GRISAR, H., *Luther*. 6 vols. St. Louis, 1914–17. One vol. ed., St. Louis, 1935

JACOBS, H. E., *Martin Luther, Hero of the Reformation*. New York, 1898

LINDSAY, T., *A History of the Reformation*. Vol. I, *Germany*. 2 vols. New York, 1906

MACKINNON, J., *Luther and the Reformation*. 4 vols. London, 1925–30

McGIFFERT, H. C., *Life and Letters of Martin Luther*. Boston, 1914

RANKE, L. VON, *History of the Reformation in Germany*. London, 1905

RICHARD, J. W., *Philip Melancthon, The Protestant Preceptor of Germany*. New York, 1898

SCHWIEBERT, E. G., *Luther and His Times*. St. Louis, 1950

SMITH, P., *Life and Letters of Martin Luther*. New York, 1911

BORNKAMM, H., *Luthers Geistige Welt*. 1947

DENIFLE, H., *Luther und Luthertum*. 3 vols. 1904–09

HAUSRATH, A., *Luthers Leben*. 2 vols. 1914

JOACHIMSEN, P., *Die Reformation als Epoche der deutschen Geschichte*. 1951

KIDD, B. J., *Documents of the Continental Reformation*. Oxford, 1911

RITTER, G., *Luther, Gestalt und Tat*. 1943

SCHEEL, O., *Martin Luther*. 2 vols. 1921, 1930

SEEBERG, E., *Luthers Theologie*. 2 vols. 1929, 1937

STROHL, H., *L'Evolution religieuse de Luther jusqu'en 1515*. 1922

STROHL, H., *La Pensée de la réforme*. 1951

CHAPTER EIGHTEEN

THE REFORMATION OUTSIDE GERMANY

I N THIS chapter it will become evident that the word "Reformation" must be used with some discrimination. Generally we must distinguish in any given land between the impulses toward reform in the church which were completely native and those coming from abroad. The native movements may have arisen out of local conditions, perhaps precipitated by a single earnest individual or a group or school of those who were aware of the low state to which religious thought and action had fallen. These movements in almost every case antedate the Lutheran outbreak and are essentially quite independent of any foreign movement. Furthermore, they were almost universally orthodox in intention, led by men and women who desired to remain in the church of their birth. The idea of a break with the established institution came only gradually. In other cases we may trace quite clearly the course and route of importation of reform doctrine. The most forceful such reform movement was, of course, that headed by Luther, which brought students and clerics to Witten-berg from all over Europe. The influence of these adventurous souls after their return to their native lands was tremendous.

THE ZWINGLIAN REFORMATION

H ARDLY less vigorous was the Zwinglian reformation, and, because it was somewhat less intolerant than the Lutheran movement, in some cases it had more appeal than the latter. On the other hand, the vitality of native re-form trends must not be underestimated. The imported doctrines were often adopted by the national leadership, then subjected to considerable modification, as demanded by local traditions and needs. In the second generation of the Reformation Calvinism had, as we shall see, a wide influence, perhaps wider than either Lutheranism or Zwinglianism, precisely because of its emphasis on individualism and its freedom from any nationalistic bias.

Zurich

NEXT to Wittenberg Zurich was the most important center of thought and action in the first generation of the Reformation. Much of this importance stemmed from the looseness of the political framework of Switzerland, which permitted each canton to follow its own convictions in religious matters. The other large factor in the German-Swiss contribution to the reform movement was the personality and work of the leader of the movement in Zurich, Huldreich Zwingli (1484–1531).

Switzerland was a federation whose origins went back to the formation of the Perpetual League among three forest cantons, Uri, Schwyz, and Unterwalden, for permanent mutual defense against the Habsburg Emperor, Rudolf I, in 1291. Victorious in its initial defense, this League defeated the imperial forces again at the battle of Morgarten in 1315, and in the course of the next century and a half ten other Swiss cantons joined the League. Soon other leagues were formed among the mountain peasantry on the model of the Perpetual League. Of the various cantons, Zurich, an active commercial and manufacturing center, was democratic in structure, whereas Bern, farther west, was almost aristocratic. In all the cantons, whether forest or town, the bishops claimed more power than the people, through their assemblies or elected magistrates, were willing to grant. This local independence had been exercised so long that it had come to be almost an article of belief. Not included in the territories of the thirteen cantons which constituted Switzerland were lands known as "common territories" or "free bailiwicks," which were made use of or administered either alternately or jointly by adjacent cantons.

The victories of the Swiss leagues over Charles the Bold of Burgundy at Grandson, Morat, and Nancy in 1476 and 1477 (see above, p. 263), against the Habsburgs at Nafels in 1488, and against the Emperor Maximilian in 1499 gave the Swiss soldiery such prestige that they were in great demand as mercenaries by neighboring rulers. France and the Papacy, at the turn of the century, were continually in need of fighting troops, and the Swiss youth found easy and lucrative employ fighting for pay on either or both sides in the intermittent wars then being waged. In this way much needed ready money poured steadily into Switzerland, with regrettable results for the morale of the Swiss youth and hardly less for the whole population. This deleterious effect of foreign-paid military service upon Swiss morals was, as we shall see, partly responsible for the Reformation in German-speaking Switzerland.

Zwingli: Beginnings

HULDRYCH ZWINGLI, the leader of the Swiss reform movement, was born in Toggenburg, a high Alpine village in the canton of St. Gall, on January 1, 1484, seven weeks after the birth of Martin Luther. His father was the chief magistrate of the village. His paternal uncle, dean of the chapter at Wesen, the nearby episcopal seat, took charge of Huldrych's early education, and when the boy was ten sent him to a Latin school in Basel. The lad's capacities for learn-

ing were evident, and after four years of thorough instruction in the rudiments
he was sent (1498) to a college at Bern of which the leading Swiss humanist,
Heinrich Wölflin, was head. After two years at Bern, Huldrych went to the
University of Vienna, then enjoying a period of brilliance under the patronage
of Emperor Maximilian. In 1502 Huldrych returned to Basel to teach Latin in
St. Martin's school. Not satisfied with his education, he enrolled at the university, receiving his bachelor of arts degree in 1504, his master of arts degree in
1506. In that same year he was ordained priest and named pastor at Glarus, a
post which he retained for ten years (1506–16). In 1513 and 1515 he accompanied the Swiss contingent on short campaigns in Lombardy, and in the
latter year was a chaplain of the Swiss troops at the battle of Marignano. At
Glarus he took advantage of what leisure he could command from his pastoral
duties to learn Greek and Hebrew, reading avidly in the Greek and Roman
masters, for whom he conceived a warm admiration. He preached against the
evils of the traffic in mercenary military service to any power but the Papacy
so earnestly as to arouse the animosity of several influential parishioners who
had profited from the business. When his position became untenable in 1516,
he accepted a call to Einsiedeln, a short distance away. His reading and his
wide experience had already begun to unsettle his acceptance of many Church
practices. His reading of Erasmus, particularly, convinced him that the Bible,
and not the Church, was the source of Christian truth. His temperament was
close to that of Erasmus; his natural emphasis was upon Christian teaching as
a high moral philosophy rather than a consuming belief in the saving effects
of God's free grace. After two years at Einsiedeln he was called to be *Leut-
priester* (people's priest, i.e., preacher and pastor) at the Great Cathedral in
Zurich. He was also to teach Greek in the cathedral school. In his preaching
he took a strong line against the service of Swiss young men in foreign armies
and emphasized the Scriptures as the source of Christian faith and practice.

In the summer of 1518 a Franciscan monk of Milan, Bernhardin Samson,
arrived in Switzerland with a papal commission to sell indulgences. Early in
1519 he came to Zurich, where Zwingli immediately organized opposition. The
town fathers supported Zwingli, and even the bishop of Constance, who would
have been willing to sell indulgences himself, opposed Samson. The Roman
curia, still shocked by the furor raised by Tetzel's sale of indulgences in Germany, was unwilling to make an issue of Samson in Switzerland, and he was
recalled. No effort was made to discipline Zwingli, as the bishop was on his
side. Anyway, the sale of indulgences was by now in ill favor. Later in that
year, and on into 1520, Zurich was ravaged by a plague which killed over 2500.
Zwingli attended the sick and dying without concern for his own health, and
was finally taken sick, but recovered. The months of stress and convalescence
turned his thoughts to the deeper implications of his religious life. There was
not, in his case, any such crisis or sudden religious conversion as Luther had
experienced. His development was gradual. It was, however, not the less certain; both in his sermons and in his poetry the gradual deepening of his piety
and consecration was manifest. The years from 1519 to 1522 especially were
marked by this growth in spirituality. His pleas for reform in the Church were
focused on externals—the treatment of the poor, fasting in Lent, the language

of the liturgy, and the marriage of the clergy; and he was careful to win the support of the magistracy of the city before leading a public campaign.

By the end of 1523, Zwingli was ready for a more basic step. On January 29, 1523, he presented, for public debate in the Zurich town hall, sixty-seven theses, covering a much wider range of topics than Luther's ninety-five. At the conclusion of the meeting the magistrates ordered him to continue to preach as he had in the past. A few of Zwingli's theses will illustrate the trend of his thought:

7. Christ is the head of all believers who are his body; but without him the body is dead.

15. Who believes the gospel shall be saved; who believes not shall be damned. For in the gospel the whole truth is clearly contained.

16. From the gospel we learn that the doctrines and traditions of men are of no use to salvation.

19. Christ is the only mediator between God and us.

27. All Christians are brothers.

28. Whatever God permits and has not forbidden is right. Therefore marriage is becoming to all men.

34. The spiritual power, so called, has no foundation in the Holy Scriptures and the teaching of Christ.

50. God alone forgives sins, through Jesus Christ, our Lord alone.

57. The Holy Scripture knows nothing of a purgatory after this life.

At a second public disputation before about 900 persons, including over 300 clergymen, Zwingli defended his reformed position on the Mass and images. As a consequence of this presentation the magistrates ordered that the people of Zurich be instructed in the Gospel truth concerning images and the Mass by a committee which included Zwingli and several of his colleagues. Opposition to these measures came from the bishop of Constance, and the Swiss Diet expressed regret that Zurich had gone so far as apparently to side with the Lutheran religion. But the people of Zurich decided, by popular choice, to follow their own leadership; and in the spring of 1524 by popular consent the old order of worship was rejected. Crucifixes, relics, altars, candles, and pictures were removed from the churches, and precious paintings and sculpture were destroyed. It was orderly, but it was destruction. From Easter of 1525 the Lord's Supper was celebrated in the Great Cathedral according to Zwingli's new liturgy; symbolically, the Reformation was established in Zurich.

The social disturbances in Germany which reached their peak in the Peasants' Revolt of 1525 had their repercussions in Switzerland, but the Swiss peasants were less demanding than their counterparts in Germany, while the authorities, because they were not of the feudal nobility, were more progressive. For Zwingli, however, the years 1523 to 1526 were made additionally difficult by his conflicts with the radicals in the reform camp. The Swiss Anabaptists, a group of earnest souls who founded, in February 1525, an informal association which called itself the Swiss Brethren, caused Zwingli the most trouble. The question of infant baptism had been discussed among the reform-minded leaders in Germany as well as in Switzerland for some years. Gradually opinion divided into two sections: those who accepted traditional infant baptism as adequate, and those who felt that baptism should be performed only after a conviction of its need had been arrived at by a mature person.

The leader of the Anabaptists, Conrad Grebel, originally a follower of Zwingli, had broken with the latter over the Mass as early as the October 1523 disputation, and in the summer of 1524 had opposed Zwingli's acceptance of traditional infant baptism. A public disputation according to Swiss practice, on January 17, 1525, resulted in the town council's decision against Grebel and his colleagues, and made infant baptism obligatory. Nonacceptance of the magistrates' decision was punishable by expulsion from the canton. As the Brethren persisted in their beliefs and practices, sterner measures were taken; between 1527 and 1532, six Anabaptists were executed, all by drowning. Zwingli seems not to have taken a leading part in the persecution, but he did

Zwingli, from an engraving by Tobias Stimmer [STAATLICHE GRAPHISCHE SAMMLUNG].

not openly oppose it. Zwingli had little more directly to do with the Brethren after their expulsion from Zurich.

In the meantime, the Zurich reformation was arousing firm opposition among the other members of the Swiss Confederation. The issue of reform was brought before several meetings of the Diet, in 1524 and 1525, but most of the cantons feared disturbing innovations, until the 1526 meeting in Baden when, in Swiss style, the whole matter was the subject of a long-drawn-out disputation. From May 21 to June 8, Dr. Eck, who had participated in the Leipzig debate with Carlstadt and Luther, upheld the Roman case with confident eloquence. Since Zwingli was not allowed by the Zurich magistracy to go to Baden, John Oecolampadius of Basel and Berthold Haller of Bern presented the reform position. The decision by the audience, swayed rather by the volume of Eck's voice than by the substance of his argument, went to the Roman side. Zwingli was excommunicated and all innovations were forbidden. Like the Leipzig "victory" of Eck in 1519, this was only a temporary conquest for the Roman party. On sober second thought several cantons declared for reform. Bern, until this time consistently conservative and reluctant to accept the leadership of Zurich and Zwingli, was the first canton to come out for the new faith. After an open disputation (January 6 to 26, 1528) the decisions of the Baden Diet were reversed for Bern, and *Ten Theses,* revised by Zwingli, were adopted as the formula of faith for the church in the canton. The jurisdiction of the bishops was rejected; reformed worship and discipline were authorized.

Basel and Oecolampadius

BASEL was doubtless influenced by the Bern decision to accept the reformed principles. But the work of the preacher of the Church of St. Martin and professor of theology at the university, John Oecolampadius (1482–1531), was even more decisive. A brilliant and precocious scholar in Latin, Greek, and Hebrew, he became a close friend of both Erasmus and Melanchthon. He was called to the pulpit of the cathedral in Basel in 1518, and in 1519 moved to Augsburg, where he remained until forced to flee because of his pronounced reform preaching. He urged reform in the Church, and was attracted to Luther by his early works. In 1522 he was back in Basel as professor of theology. His theological position was somewhere between Zwingli and Luther. No firebrand, he won a considerable following among the citizens, and the Council gave him steady support in the modifications he introduced into the service of the Church. On the Eucharist he took Zwingli's position of a figurative interpretation of the words "This is my body," and attended the Marburg Colloquy (1529) at Zwingli's side. In other points of theology he was closer to Calvin than to Zwingli or Luther. Bern's decision (January 1528) to adopt the reform was followed by commotions in Basel directed against the pro-Roman leanings of the city council, but there was no bloodshed. Oecolampadius was named superintendent of the church in the city and head preacher of the cathedral. The transition from Roman to Protestant usage was kept by his influence from going to excesses of iconoclasm and demagoguery. He lived only two years after Bern became Protestant. Next to Zwingli, Oecolampadius was the most important of the Swiss reformers.

The Reformation in Zurich, 1529–66

BY FEBRUARY 1529, Basel had accepted the Reformation; soon thereafter Schaff-hausen, St. Gall, Mühlhausen, and the Free Bailiwicks followed. Several cantons were divided, among them Appenzell and Glarus, where Zwingli had begun his preaching ministry in 1516. The Grisons (Graubünden) in south-eastern Switzerland had had a rule of tolerance of both Roman and reformed preaching since 1526. Now the lines were being drawn between the two sides. The Protestant cantons, led by Zurich, formed, on combined religious and political lines, the Christian Civic League (*Das christliche Bürgerrecht*) to which Strassburg and Constance, both outside the Swiss Confederation, were invited. This League had the effect of splitting the Confederation. When the Catholic cantons, Lucerne, Schwyz, Uri, Unterwalden, and Zug, with Austrian support, formed a defensive league, to which they gave the name of Christian Union as an answer to the Civic League, a war along religious lines seemed inevitable. Bern counseled peace and conciliation, but Zurich would not modify its demands for control of the lands of the rich Abbey of St. Gall. After the city had moved its troops into the field, Zwingli's plans for quick action, which would, if followed energetically, have certainly brought a decisive victory to the Civic League, were sidetracked for mediation. The first peace of Kappel (June 25, 1529) stipulated hardly more than a truce. The Catholics (the Five Cantons) gave up the Austrian alliance and paid a war indemnity. Since the freedom of preaching in the Five Cantons was not clearly defined, the seeds of future trouble were implicit in the treaty.

Two and a half months later Zwingli, with his associates Oecolampadius of Basel and Bucer and Hedio of Strassburg, went to Marburg to confer with Luther and Melanchthon (see above, p. 494) in the hope of joining with the Wittenberg reformers in a doctrinal statement which would be a prelude to a religious-political alliance of all Protestants against the Romanists. Zwingli, primarily a statesman, earnestly desired to unite all Protestant forces everywhere in Europe, in order to match the effective unity which he saw in Catholic action. In such breadth of vision, Luther was not Zwingli's equal. In other respects it is possible he may have been his superior. This attempt to form a united Protestant front was defeated by Luther's refusal to yield the slightest ground in a matter of words at which, even later in his own life, he would not have boggled.

The year 1530 marked the high point of the Zwinglian reformation. Within Zurich Zwingli's position of influence and leadership was predominant. Many cities of southern Germany found the political democracy of the Zwinglian organization more acceptable than Luther's dependence on the princes, the traditional enemies of the cities. Zwingli was active in several synods in Swit-zerland, where he was able to impress upon reform beginnings in other cantons his own clear formulations of faith and practice. But 1531 saw a decline in the aggressive spirit of the Zurich reformation. As the Five Catholic (Forest) Cantons had regained their will to resist reform, and were seeking aid again from Austria and the Emperor, the diet witnessed scenes of bitter recrimina-tion between the two parties. The chief object of contention was the control of the common territories or free bailiwicks of the Confederation. There seemed no solution which would find general acceptance. Zwingli thought that only a war would settle anything. Bern suggested a blockade of the Forest Cantons, which might starve them into submission without the shedding of blood. The Protestants accepted this policy over Zwingli's protests (May 15, 1531).

The resultant starvation of men, woman, and children was indeed more cruel than a war between soldiers would have been. Zwingli had premonitions of disaster, caused by a decision against which he had protested. He resigned his post as head of the church in Zurich (July 26, 1531), but his resignation was refused. The appearance of Halley's comet for three weeks, from mid-August to early September, caused widespread consternation. Many, Zwingli included, regarded it as a sign of God's anger. The Forest Cantons, reduced to desperation, gathered their forces—8000 men—and marched on Zurich (October 9, 1531). The city was split by dissension and indecision, and only 1200 men could be mustered. Zwingli went with the little army to the battlefield, to urge them on. He did not use his weapons. The battle lasted the whole afternoon of October 11, and at the end over 500 of the Zurichers lay dead or dying on the field, Zwingli among them. Several of his relations and many of his best friends died with him. The Catholics had the sheriff of Lucerne quarter his body and burn it for heresy. The war was soon over; the second treaty of Kappel (November 20 and 24, 1531) sealed the division of Switzerland into Protestant and Catholic. With Swiss Protestantism now set on a course quite separate from that of Lutheran Protestantism, the south German cities, seeing that Zurich was weaker than they had thought, turned to the Schmalkaldic League for support. Zurich, held responsible for failure to defend the reformed faith, lost its position of leadership in Swiss Protestantism to Bern, where the solid work of Oecolampadius had, as we have seen, prepared the city for its new task.

Although Zwingli's death and the defeat of the Zurichers by the Forest Cantons was a grievous setback for the Reformation in Switzerland, it was not catastrophic. The rights of the cantons of both parties to keep their respective faiths were recognized, and the Catholic minorities in the bailiwicks were protected from any pressure to force them to accept Protestantism. All foreign alliances, on both sides, were forbidden. The net result was as follows: seven cantons, Lucerne, Uri, Schwyz, Unterwalden, Zug, Freiburg, and Solothurn, remained Catholic; four, the most populous—Zurich, Bern, Basel, and Schaffhausen—confirmed their Protestantism; five cantons, Glarus, Appenzell, Aargau, Thurgau, and St. Gall, were about evenly divided between Catholicism and Protestantism, and the bailiwicks remained, by a small majority, Catholic.

In Zurich the work of Zwingli was carried on by his son-in-law, Henry Bullinger (1504–75). Educated by the Brethren of the Common Life and at the University of Cologne, Bullinger was early attracted by the writings both of Luther and of Melanchthon. He taught school at Kappel from 1523 to 1529, during which time he joined forces with Zwingli and attended several disputations with him. After Zwingli's death at Kappel in October 1531, Bullinger was chosen people's preacher at the cathedral, a post he held until his death forty years later. He felt that Church and state should be mutually independent. His position on the Eucharist was perhaps closer to that of Luther than Zwingli's, as he was anxious to give due consideration to the effect of Christ through the sacrament upon the believer, whereas Zwingli limited himself to the memorial, subjective aspect of the participation. Bullinger was one of the principal authors of the *First Helvetic Confession* (1536), which was an official statement of the beliefs of the Swiss Protestants, intended to be used as the basis of discussions at the general council, then thought to be imminent. Furthermore, it was hoped that Luther would find it acceptable and thus make common cause with the Swiss before the Council. Luther did in fact praise the Christian character of the formula, but he found the statements on the Lord's Supper lacking in precision and evangelical firmness.

From this time on the Reformation in the eastern and German-speaking parts of Switzerland departed more decisively from Lutheranism and drew closer to the Reformation in Geneva under Farel, Calvin, and Beza. In 1549 Bullinger and Calvin worked out together the *Consensus Tigurinus* (*Zurich Accord*) which was soon approved by the other Swiss Reformed churches. It was explicitly anti-Lutheran in expression; and, though it did not contain Calvin's doctrine of predestination in its fuller form, yet it was an acceptable compromise serving to show that doctrinal unity was consonant with political liberty. The *Second Helvetic Confession* (1566) was Bullinger's work alone. It was more complete than any previous reformed creed, clear in its opposition to the Roman positions, recently elaborated by the Council of Trent, and moderate in differing from the Lutheran doctrines.

Strassburg

AFTER Zurich, Bern, and Basel, Strassburg was the most significant city in the reform movement in the south German region. As a free imperial city it adopted the Reformation teachings in 1523 without any outside interference. Among the Protestant leaders who labored there at various times were Martin Bucer, Wolfgang Capito, Caspar Hedio, Matthias Zell, and John Calvin. The spirit of Strassburg Protestantism was conciliatory and, in the best sense, compromising. Luther's extreme positions were listened to but not adopted, and efforts were continually being made by Strassburg leaders to find formulae which might bring the reformers together. The city was well known as a refuge for Protestants driven out of other countries, particularly France, for their beliefs. There were about five hundred such refugees in Strassburg to whom John Calvin, expelled from Geneva, ministered from 1538 to 1541.

THE REFORMATION IN THE LOWLANDS

THE Lowlands had had, in the two centuries before the Reformation, a very irregular history. Sovereignty over much of the territories of the area had been in dispute between France, the Empire, the local nobility, the commercial cities, and the dukes of Burgundy. Under Philip the Good (1419–67) some progress toward consolidation had been made, but it was not until the defeat of Charles the Bold of Burgundy by the Swiss in 1477 that the history of the Lowlands began to take clear shape. Charles' heiress, his daughter Mary, married (1477) Maximilian of Habsburg, later (1493) Emperor of the Holy Roman Empire. Of this marriage a male heir, Philip the Handsome, was born in 1478. This young prince, also known as Philip of Austria, was married in 1496 to the daughter of Ferdinand and Isabella of Spain, called Joanna the Mad. The son of Philip and Joanna, Charles, born in Ghent in 1500, eventually inherited Spain and the Spanish empire beyond the seas from his mother, and the Burgundian inheritance, including the Lowlands, from his father.

From the death of his father in 1506 to 1515, when Charles came of age, the Lowlands were ruled by his aunt Margaret of Austria as sole regent. Thereafter, until her death in 1530, she ruled as regent when Charles was absent. The task of ruling the Burgundian lands was an extremely difficult one. In the south and west the lands were fiefs of the French king; the northern and eastern states were a part of the Empire. The currents of thought that arose in both France and Germany were bound to cross and recross in the Lowlands. There were, furthermore, the local traditions, reaching back for several centuries, of local liberties, a free bourgeoisie, anticlericalism, and active mysticism, which were to complicate any political and religious settlement during the coming century.

Some of the appeals of Luther, such as that to German nationalism in his *Address to the German Nobility,* had no relevance for the Lowlanders. On the other hand, his attacks on the abuses of indulgences, the heavy exactions of the Church, and the abuses of ecclesiastical power found a quick and sympathetic response. The intellectuals of the Lowlands had long read the works of their countryman Erasmus with lively interest. His lofty urgings to reform and freedom only added fuel to the fire of dissatisfaction with the Church as it was. A measure of the emotions aroused by Erasmus' influence would be Aleander's statement to the Pope in 1525 that he was amazed that the Pontiff should allow Erasmus, who was responsible for all the ills of the Empire, to live. The theologians of the University of Louvain had declared open war on Erasmus and all his sect.

Luther's works were widely circulated in the Lowlands, where a number of translations of the Bible or parts of it in Dutch, Flemish, or French were current. Aleander, papal nuncio to the Empire, in October 1520 visited the Lowlands before going to Worms for the meeting of the Diet. He was shocked to find many Lutheran writings in open circulation. At Louvain he had eighty Lutheran and "harmful" books publicly burned; ten days later he repeated the ceremony at Liége. Soon Charles issued for his ancestral lands severe edicts against the new doctrines. In July 1521, Aleander burned four hundred more copies of Luther's writings at Antwerp and found the Augustinian monastery in that city infected with Lutheran ideas. More stringent measures were necessary to halt the spread of this heresy. In 1522 Charles brought the Inquisition to the Lowlands. As might have been expected of a Spanish ruler, he regarded the Inquisition as an arm of the civil government; the man he put in charge of it, Francis van der Hulst, was a crude and tactless court-jurist who quickly antagonized both clergy and laity. Several persons were forced to retract opinions favorable to Lutheranism; Henry of Zutphen, prior of the Augustinians in Antwerp, who had preached Lutheran doctrines publicly, escaped death in 1522 only by being rescued from prison by a sympathetic crowd of several thousand angry citizens. It was not long before the Inquisition exacted the death penalty. Two Antwerp Augustinians, Henry Voes and John Esch, were the first victims. They were burned alive in the public square in Brussels on July 1, 1523, for Lutheran beliefs, while the Augustinian cloister in Antwerp that had nurtured this reforming pestilence was razed to the ground. The preaching of the "new gospel" was strictly forbidden within the city. A certain Nicholas of Antwerp who dared to disobey this order was sewed in a sack and drowned in the moat. Charles' determination to keep his hereditary lands free from the curse of the new heresies was, for a time, effective in the south. Antwerp was cowed by the severity of Charles' measures. In the northern provinces of the Netherlands, however, the flame of the reform movement burned steadily. The first of a long line of martyrs in the northern provinces was a layman, Willem Dirks, who had spread abroad Lutheran teachings on penances, celibacy of the clergy, pilgrimages, and the office of the pope. He was martyred in Utrecht on July 10, 1525. Both in Utrecht and in Groningen Erasmus' "reasonable" Christian spirit and the devout humanism of John Wessel of Gansfort were deeply rooted in the regular and the secular clergy. Charles found it difficult, in spite of his support of a strict and ruthless Inquisition, to alter this basic disposition toward an intelligent evangelicalism.

In another and very important direction Luther's influence coalesced with that of Erasmus. Both earnestly desired to have the Bible in the hands of the common people. By 1522 seven editions of separate gospels, translated into Dutch, were available in the Lowlands. Other books of the New Testament followed in 1523, and late in that year a Dutch rendering of Luther's New Testament was published in Antwerp, where it sold out quickly. A second edition appeared in Antwerp in 1524, a third immediately thereafter in Amsterdam. Other editions followed rapidly (twenty-three in six years), and by 1527 three translations of the whole Bible, based partly on Luther's German translation, partly on Erasmus' *Paraphrases,* and partly on the Vulgate, had appeared. Many of the translators and publishers suffered martyrdom at the hands of the Inquisition. Such repression seemed only to spread the heresy.

The Emperor Charles, beside employing the inquisitional object lessons of executions by fire, burying alive, strangling, drowning, and simple hanging, issued regular "placards" or public warnings against Lutheran teachings and those infected with Lutheran ideas. In 1527 the first Anabaptists appeared in the Lowlands in sufficient strength to deserve punishment. Three Anabaptists were roasted on a slow fire in The Hague in that year, compared with sixty ordinary heretics—that is, Lutherans—who were victims of the Inquisition.

In 1530 Margaret of Austria died and Mary, Charles' half sister and queen-widow of Hungary, succeeded her as regent of the Lowlands. The better to instruct her clearly in her new duties Charles wrote to her (October 17, 1531): "If I had a father, mother, brother, sister, wife or child who were infected with Luther's heresy, I would treat them as my worst enemies." Charles was not the only persistent persecutor of the heretics. Charles Egmont, duke of Guelders, and Philip, duke of Burgundy, each in his lands, strove to root out all taint of Lutheranism. In Friesland the administration of the Inquisition was somewhat more moderate, and many young Frisians who went to Wittenberg to study were allowed to return and remain unmolested. In the rest of the Lowlands, however, not a year passed without numerous executions for disobedience of the "placards." The specifications and the records of the trials often show that in the Lowlands Lutheran and Anabaptist teachings had, by about 1532, become somewhat mingled, so that it was difficult to make clear distinctions between them. The Inquisition was obviously faced with an alarming spread of the two heretical tendencies, and it did not know which to attack the more drastically. There was, furthermore, no single inspiring leader of either evangelical party, such as Luther in Germany or Zwingli in Switzerland, whose removal or death might have caused the movement to wither and die. By this time the martyrs were men and women of all walks of life, especially the common folk, who asked only to witness to their belief in the person and grace of Christ. With each execution the number of adherents of the reformed faith, in one form or another, grew and spread. In this regard the Reformation in the Lowlands presents a somewhat special aspect.

From 1532 to 1540 the Anabaptist faith seemed to predominate among the common people. Melchior Hoffman, a Swabian mystic who had won from Luther a letter of approval and had preached in Latvia and Schleswig, gradually becoming more radical, had already brought enthusiasm and direction to the Anabaptists in Friesland before returning to Strassburg in 1533. A pupil of Hoffman's, Jan Matthiisen, a Haarlem baker, took over the leadership of the movement; he or his associates baptized thousands within a short period in 1534. Since the spirit of Matthiisen was more aggressive than that of Hoffman, the period from 1532 to 1540 was the period of Anabaptist predominance in the Lowlands. In 1540 the Emperor Charles returned to a Ghent that had defied his orders and his officials. The city was deprived of all its earlier liberties, and new and even more drastic "placards" were issued against Lutheran and Anabaptist heresies. Houses were searched for forbidden books; delations were encouraged and well rewarded. Many of all ages and stations were executed in Ghent and in other cities of the Lowlands, and for the next sixteen years—to the end of the rule of Charles—the persecution never lessened. The "placards" were frequently reproclaimed, while publication of any book at all was forbidden without specific permission.

In 1540 John à Lasco (1499–1560), a Polish nobleman, settled in East Friesland with his Dutch wife. He had known Zwingli and Erasmus and the other reformers well. In Poland he had been raised to the Roman Catholic bishopric, but, finding it impossible to do what he desired for the Church, had left for East Friesland, then known for its religious freedom. Catholics, Lutherans, Zwinglians, and Anabaptists lived, as it were miraculously, side by side in peace. The countess of East Friesland asked à Lasco to become superintendent of the Church in her lands. During the six years of his work there he infused a spirit of moderation and cooperation in the clergy of varying shades of opinion that was remarkable for the age and left its stamp on the whole of northwestern Germany. In 1548, after Charles' defeat of the Protestants at Mühlberg, à Lasco was called to England by Edward VI to minister to the German and Dutch émigrés in London.

In 1550 Charles proclaimed, in a new "placard," the institution of the Inquisition. The name only was new. The Office had in actuality functioned in the Burgundian lands for thirty years. The foreign merchants in Antwerp, many of them Lutherans or Zwinglians, quickly left the city. The regent, Mary, Charles' sister, also departed and wrote from Augsburg urging him to withdraw the "placard." He made the concession of substituting the words "spiritual judges" for "inquisitors." As Charles' agents, these "judges" were zealous and efficient, and the executions multiplied. Informers were rewarded with a portion of the goods of the condemned. But still the heresy flourished, whether Lutheran, Anabaptist or, by now, Calvinist. We have seen that the humiliation which Charles had suffered in 1552 when Elector Maurice of Saxony had almost captured him as he fled over the Brenner Pass was confirmed by the Peace of Augsburg in 1555. It was probably at this time that Charles decided to abdicate the imperial crown. There was some poetic justice that the first ceremony of abdication should take place (October 25, 1555) in Brussels, the capital of Charles' hereditary lands. The enfeebled Charles, leaning on the shoulder of the young prince of Orange and followed by his son Philip, entered the great hall of the dukes of Brabant in Brussels and turned over the rule of the Lowlands to Philip. Charles was surrounded in Brussels not only by the pomp and ceremony of the house of Burgundy, but by the ghosts of tens of thousands of his Lowland subjects whom he had had drowned, buried alive, hanged, or broken on the wheel for their religious beliefs. It was one of the accomplishments of his forty years' reign that was not recited on that day.

FRANCE BEFORE CALVIN

IT HAS been seen above (Chapter 17) that a large element in Luther's appeal to the German people was the fact that the Roman *curia* controlled a considerable portion of German church wealth and made exorbitant demands on German clergy which were then passed on to the laity. This is the burden of the message in Luther's *Address to the German Nobility*. This factor was lacking in France. From the Pragmatic Sanction of Bourges of 1438 to 1516, the French church was virtually a national church, controlling most of the important appointments and disposing of most of its own income. In 1516 Francis I, after a military victory at Marignano over allied Italian and Papal forces, by the Concordat of Bologna with Pope Leo X made himself master of the French church, displacing the French clergy who had ruled the church in France since 1438. The nationalistic appeal which Luther could and did make to the German clergy and the princes could not be duplicated in France, where the church was ruled either by the French clergy or by the French king and where the voice of the Pope was barely heard. Thus the French church had had almost a century of functional independence of Rome. We may therefore expect to find the beginnings of the Reformation to be different in France from what they had been in Germany.

The closing decades of the fifteenth century had witnessed a growing demand for reform in the French church. It was not so violent as in Germany, nor, perhaps, so widespread. It found its clearest expression at the royal court, among the highly literate laity and some of the clergy and the humanists. In 1484 the Estates General at Tours had demanded the reform of the Church. At that time neither the crown nor the hierarchy wished to disturb the actual situation, and the problem of clerical discipline and morality was not really attacked. It was commonly recognized that the religion of the people was relatively more pure and active than that of the monastic orders and the parish clergy. The University of Paris, traditionally the leader of French opinion and the training school for the clergy, was in the intellectual doldrums, infected by the indifference and disorder of the whole French church. The curriculum was restricted to a repetitious scholasticism which neither stimulated nor indeed permitted any fresh thinking. Theology was nothing more than an exercise in scholastic method. The nominalism of William of Ockham ruled the university. Original and useful in the fourteenth century, Ockhamism had, in the intervening century and a half, become a treadmill. Several efforts to break out of this dry and fruitless constraint had met with only minor success. It was not until the invasion of a group of Italian humanists that Paris began again to be a center of intellectual activity. First, Gregory Tifernates came to Paris in 1456 to lecture; then a French scholar, Guillaume Fichet, who had gone to Italy in 1469 and 1470, helped to establish a printing press at the Sorbonne. In 1470 the dispute then raging in Italy between the Aristotelians and the Platonists was brought before the University of Paris. For most of the Parisian professors the dispute was beyond understanding, but the exercise was useful and many eyes were opened to the larger world of Greek philosophy and Italian learning. Cardinal Bessarion, invited by Louis XI, visited France. In subsequent years there came to Paris, for shorter or longer stays, such humanist scholars as Filippo Beroaldo of Bologna, George Hermonymus of Sparta, Paolo Emilio of Verona, Pico della Mirandola, Faustus Andrelinus of Forlì, and many others. They found congenial association with a group of native French scholars already active in the pursuit of the "humane letters." Among the leaders of this circle were Robert Gaguin (d. 1502) and Jacques Lefèvre d'Etaples (1450–1536). With Lefèvre we enter the period of the early French reform. The scholarly humanistic preparation from which the movement later drew so much of its strength was more Italian than French, whereas the religious direction which it took under the influence of late fifteenth-century orthodox mysticism was distinctly and solely French in origin.

In the meantime the demands pronounced at the 1484 meeting of the Estates at Tours had not been completely disregarded. A few courageous prelates urged higher morals and a more serious clergy. Among these reforming clergy the most prominent were Olivier Maillard, vicar-general of the strict Observantists of the Franciscan order and a forceful preacher who had great influence at the court of Charles VIII; and John Standonck, head of the Collège de Montaigu, a product of the school of the Brethren of the Common Life at Gouda in the Lowlands. The combined influence of these men and their friends and followers in the last decade of the fifteenth century and the opening decade of the sixteenth was considerable, primarily in Paris but also in the provinces, among both the secular and the regular clergy. A general atmosphere of spiritual awakening was being prepared, to such a point that by the end of the century "reform" had almost become a popular slogan. What resistance there was came from the conservative clergy and those whose interests would be affected by a cleaning of the clerical stables: the clergy-related families of the nobility who held rich prebends or several abbacies or bishoprics in violation of laws against pluralities. It was in these years of intellectual and religious ferment that Erasmus studied at Paris and came to know the leaders of both the older and the younger generations of humanists. His *Enchiridion* (*Handbook of the Christian Soldier*) could be regarded as the manifesto of the French humanistic reform in its appeal to the ancient and simple ideals and illumination of the mind through the Scriptures.

Lefèvre d'Etaples

GAGUIN died in 1502 and Standonck in 1504. The reform movement soon after the death of these leaders of its first generation took on another aspect. The change could be signalized in the religious experience of Lefèvre d'Etaples in 1509, when he suddenly became convinced of the beauty of "divine studies." "They seemed to me," he said, "to give off a perfume whose sweetness was beyond compare . . . beside them all human studies are fog and shadow. . . . Since their study has been neglected, the monasteries have fallen into ruin, piety is dead and true religion has been snuffed out." His reputation as a savant had been built upon his numerous translations, editions of and commentaries on the moral and philosophical works of Aristotle and, more recently, of Nicholas of Cusa and other late mystics. His new dedication to biblical studies resulted in his commentary on the letters of St. Paul (1512), novel in its simple appeal to the sense of Scripture and its avoidance of the artificialities of scholastic exegesis. He did not reject human liberty, although he emphasized the priority of grace, and he attempted to reconcile grace and free will. He did not put forward the predestination of the elect or the damned. He minimized the special merits of works, but did not specifically reject any Roman doctrine. Without rejecting pilgrimages, veneration of relics, and the cults of the Virgin and the saints, he subjected some of the lives of the saints to rigid criticism. While the intention, quite clearly, is that of a Catholic revival and a return to pure Christianity, Lefèvre's insistence on the primacy of Scripture anticipated the teaching of Luther, and his Erasmian approach to tradition soon made him suspect to the conservative theologians of the Sorbonne.

The course of the polemic between Reuchlin and Pfefferkorn in Germany, which grew bitter in 1512 and 1513, was followed with great interest in France. Reuchlin wrote at length to Lefèvre, in August 1513, asking him to pass the letter around among his friends and to explain his side of the quarrel. The French humanists were solidly behind Reuchlin, but when the case was brought by the Dominicans at Cologne before the theological faculty of the University of Paris (1514) the majority of the theologians condemned Reuchlin and demanded that he make a public retraction.

A former pupil of Lefèvre, William Briçonnet, bishop of Meaux, had appointed him librarian of the ancient Benedictine Abbey of St. Germain des Prés. This position made it possible for him to keep abreast of all the latest developments in the world of religion. It also exposed him to suspicion and attack from the scholastics. In 1518 he was accused of heresy before the theological faculty; two pamphlets he had written in 1517 and 1518 on Mary Magdalen were condemned on November 9, 1521. Noël Bédier, syndic of the faculty and arch heretic-hunter, would have proceeded against Lefèvre if Francis I and his sister, Marguerite of Navarre, had not intervened in his behalf.

By this time Luther's works were being widely read in France, and Lefèvre was in communication with the monk of Wittenberg. With Bédier pressing for Lefèvre's condemnation, discretion dictated that he leave Paris. He took refuge with Briçonnet and, in 1523, was made vicar-general of the diocese of Meaux. Two years later, deprived of the king's favor during his imprisonment in Spain, he fled to Strassburg. The careers of Briçonnet and Lefèvre, closely related until this flight, diverge at this point, never to cross again. Briçonnet's role in the early period of the French reform is of sufficient interest to call for some description.

Reform at Meaux

BRIÇONNET was descended from a wealthy and influential noble house of Touraine. First made bishop of Lodève, then abbot of St. Germain des Prés in 1507, he was several times in Italy and, appointed bishop of Meaux in 1516, was sent by Francis I as an envoy to Rome. The immorality he witnessed in Rome led him, on his return, to try to reform his own diocese. He divided the diocese into thirty-two districts, for each of which he named a preacher who should urge reform. He convoked synods which made anti-Lutheran pronouncements. Among the thirty-two evangelical preachers he called in, the most effective were Lefèvre, Gérard Roussel (Marguerite of Navarre's chaplain), Michel d'Arande, and William Farel. Briçonnet's own position was equivocal. He wished to avoid any charge of heresy; yet at the same time he protected these preachers and scholars, the so-called group of Meaux (of whom the four above-named were the best known), who were all at least Erasmians, while many of them were in sympathy with Luther's attacks on indulgences and Roman control of the Church. But as the Sorbonne heretic-hunters pushed their campaign, it became increasingly dangerous for anyone to hold openly any doctrine that might be called Lutheran. In 1523 Briçonnet, realizing that it was dangerous even to be accused of favoring Lutheran ideas, declared his open opposition to anything Lutheran; then, to give effect to this attitude, he withdrew from Farel and his friends the right to preach in his diocese. At a diocesan synod in October 1523, he condemned everything Lutheran and ordered Luther's books burned. The next year a woolcarder of Meaux was burned alive at Metz for destroying several statues of saints. The attack of the Sorbonnists continued, now supported by the Order of the Cordeliers, Briçonnet's ancient enemies. The bishop was summoned before the Paris *parlement* to answer charges of heresy. He defended himself successfully and returned to his diocese to pursue, with great circumspection, the cause of upright clerical morals and more zealous preaching. The last years of his episcopate are obscure. The cause of reform which had thrived in the early years in Meaux was completely estopped, and had to seek outlet elsewhere.

One of the most brilliant and attractive women of the whole sixteenth century played a leading part in this early stage of the French Reformation. Marguerite, duchess of Alençon, younger sister of Francis I, was educated at the court of her guardian, Louis XII. She showed unusual brilliance in theology, philosophy, and languages, ancient and modern. She was married to the duke of Alençon in 1509, and later kept at court by her brother Francis, who valued her judgment and her company. She gathered around her humanists and evangelicals and was in correspondence with most of the reformers from the beginnings of the movement in Switzerland and Germany. Lefèvre, William Briçonnet, William Farel, the poet Clément Marot, were her friends; and on several occasions she was able, either by herself or through her brother the king, to get them freed or offer them the security of her court. Her first husband, the duke of Alençon, died in 1525. Two years later she was married to Henry d'Albret, king of Navarre, some years younger than herself. He shared her interest in religious reform, and their mountain kingdom became an asylum for Protestants expelled from other lands or in danger from the Inquisition. The German Protestants regarded her as the hope of the cause in France.

Marguerite of Navarre, by François Clouet, in the Louvre, Paris [GI- RAUDON].

Francis was, for most of his reign, willing to give her his protection, but from 1533 he turned against the whole reform cause and joined the persecutors. Marguerite, indignant but helpless, left Paris for her capital, Oléron. Her literary activity, aside from a heavy correspondence, was significant. In her *Les Marguerites de la Marguerite, Le miroir de l'âme pécheresse* and in her separate verses she showed a full acceptance of evangelical teaching on salvation by faith and the sacraments, and an equally firm rejection of many Catholic usages: indulgences, confession, and prayer to the saints. All these works were attacked by the Sorbonnists. The *Miroir* was particularly objectionable to them because there was in it no mention of purgatory or the saints.

Francis I, in his relations with the Protestants, had followed a very flexible course, depending somewhat upon his need for the help of the German Protestant princes in his wars with Charles V. He had intermittently favored or burned Lutherans and other Protestants in his lands. The incident of the "placards" (October 18, 1534) led to the most determined persecution of the reformed faith in France. Broadsides spread all over Paris—one was even tacked on the door to the king's bedchamber—coarsely attacking the Catholic Mass. There was general revulsion at the crudity of the act, and a rigorous campaign intended to uproot heresy from the kingdom was undertaken. Hundreds of Protestants or persons suspected of holding Protestant views were imprisoned; at least twenty-three were burned alive within a few months. In the meantime a very important person had made a fleeting appearance on the stage. On November 1, 1533, the new rector of the university, Nicolas Cop, having to make a formal rectoral address in Latin and wishing to produce something different from the usual platitudinous performance on such occasions, asked a young and promising humanist to help him in the composition of his speech. The result created a sensation. The address was an elaborate defense of the doctrine of justification by faith. The king was furious, the Sorbonne in arms. The young humanist was John Calvin, who, with Cop, thought it best to leave Paris immediately. A year and four months later this same Calvin published the first edition of his *Institutes of the Christian Religion,* dedicated to Francis I. The publication of this work may be regarded as the beginning of the second generation of the Reformation.

ITALY AND SPAIN

NEITHER in Italy nor in Spain was the reform movement as we have observed it in Germany generally a popular movement, in spite of the fact that there were many conditions in the Church and in society which resembled conditions north of the Alps, and in spite of early publication or importation of some of Luther's earlier works. When we refer to "Reformation" in Italy as well as in Spain it must be observed that there were many high-ranking churchmen, as well as many scholars and pious men in more modest positions of responsibility and leadership, who, deeply conscious of the need for reform in the Church, were struggling to raise the level of clerical morals and to revive a piety of which the Church all over Europe stood in such great need. Even at the time of the Church's deepest depravity—under Alexander VI and Julius II—

there were those at the *curia* in Rome who went against the current of relaxation and sought means to revive the best Christian spirit they could conceive. We shall deal with some of these "reforming" men and movements when we follow the story of the Catholic Reformation, also known as the Counter-Reformation. But it can be remarked here that the ideals for which these men strove were almost without exception ideals of medieval monastic piety and purity. They had not the slightest desire to re-examine doctrine or the practices of the Church as to indulgences, worship of the saints, clerical celibacy, and the general involvement of the Church in secular affairs. Of these movements, therefore, we can hardly use the formal term "Reformation," though they were sincere attempts toward reform in the Church.

In Italy there were three principal centers where the Lutheran teachings found a welcome: Venice, Naples, and the northwestern principalities. Venice, a great commercial center, was frequently visited by German merchants and was ideally situated to keep abreast of events north of the Alps. As early as 1520 several of Luther's principal works were on sale in Padua and in Venice, where the Patriarch of Venice, on orders from the Pope, endeavored to enforce the papal bull condemning Luther and his works; but the Senate of Venice obstructed the execution of the bull. Many copies of Luther's works were smuggled into Venice, and Melanchthon's *Loci Communes,* printed in an Italian translation as by "Messer Ippofilo da Terra Santa," was widely sold in Venice and as far away as Rome. Other reformers' works were similarly printed under fictitious or misleading names in the following years. The buyers and readers of these heretical books were mostly churchmen. First, in 1530, Caraffa, a member of the Oratory of the Divine Love in Rome, then Jerome Aleander in 1532, were sent to Venice as nuncios with firm instructions to stamp out growing Lutheranism. They both failed to make any headway against the Venetians' tolerance of heresy. Many clerics of high and low degree were suspected of holding heretical doctrines or were found in possession of books by the reformers, and a not inconsiderable number of them were tried and imprisoned. Nevertheless, despite the urgings of the nuncios and the personal appeals of the Pope, the heresy advanced. Melanchthon, perhaps overestimating the reform movement in Venice, wrote to the Senate in 1539, hoping to establish closer relations with a great Italian state; Luther, in 1543, was also in hopeful correspondence with the Venetians. The Inquisition, however, by imprisonment, mutilation, and determined pursuit of those who showed any sympathy with Lutheranism or any deviation whatsoever associated with it, succeeded in driving the movement out of the Republic soon after 1550.

In the Piedmont, where the Waldensians had taken refuge several centuries before the sixteenth, there was a constant and growing coalescence of their spirit with that of the reformed faith. In 1538 Calvin wrote a confession of faith for these Piedmontese Waldensians. In the duchy of Milan (the Milanese), there were many, both clergy and laity, who incurred the wrath of the Inquisition by smuggling in Lutheran or Calvinist writings and spreading the heretical infection.

From the year 1528 the name of Valdés begins to appear in circles interested in the reform movement. The Valdés twins, Alfonso and Juan, born in Spain, were well connected at the court of the young king Charles and held positions of trust there as well as at the papal court at Rome. Alfonso wrote a dialogue on the sack of Rome blaming the Pope for the sad event, which, though attacked as "ultra-Lutheran," surprisingly enough escaped condemnation by the Inquisition. Alfonso's thought focused primarily on political issues as they were affected by the corruption in the Church. He died on a diplomatic mission in Vienna in 1532. Juan, remaining at the Spanish court, had written several dialogues loyal to the Catholic faith but stressing the need for reform in the Church. One of these dialogues, *On Christian Doctrine,* published anonymously in 1529 in Spain, was strongly Erasmian in tone. He traveled to Mantua and to Rome in 1531 and 1532, and in 1534 entered the service of the Gonzaga in Naples. While there he became the friend and spiritual counselor of the brilliant and beautiful Giulia Gonzaga, recently widowed. To console and inspirit her, he wrote in 1536 the *Alfabeto cristiano (The Christian Alphabet),* a series of dialogues on Christian piety in the spirit of Erasmus' *Handbook of the Christian Soldier.* Their main theme was the need of true believers to love God above all things. The implication, that the individual believer could attain Christian perfection through personal piety, was certain to arouse the suspicion of the hierarchy. Equally suspect was the author's view on confession: he held that the sinner is forgiven not because of his confession to the priest but because of his sincere belief in Christ. He died in 1541, at the moment when persecution of the Protestants and those suspected of harboring any evangelical doctrines was at its height.

As Juan de Valdés passed from the scene, another bright light of spiritual revival appeared. The most eloquent and moving preacher in Italy at this time was the Capuchin monk Bernardino of Ochino (1487–1564). Because of his abilities and moral qualities he was, in 1538, elected to the high position of vicar-general of his order. Often in Rome he came into contact with members of the circle around Juan de Valdés, and was attracted by Valdés' spirit and the Erasmian ideas of reform which the whole group so enthusiastically avowed. By 1540 he was counted one of them and was reading widely in the works of Luther and Melanchthon. In his sermons he frequently discussed justification by faith, the futility of indulgences without real contrition and, by clear implication, the fallibility of the pope. Before long, the Inquisition was preparing to discipline him. Summoned to Rome in 1542, he decided to flee Italy. We find him in Geneva, preaching to the Italian exiles there, in Augsburg, in Zurich, in Basel, and then, from 1547 to 1553, in England, as a guest of Cranmer under Edward VI's strongly Protestant rule, preaching, writing and teaching. When the Catholic Mary succeeded to the English throne, Ochino returned to Geneva. Next, we find him in Zurich, then in Poland, then finally, in the year of his death, 1564, in Moravia. The Inquisition had by this time gained control of heresy in Italy and there were Italians of evangelical views in almost every city in Europe who had found it necessary to flee their native land. The Reformation in the Lutheran or Zwinglian sense was never able to gain enough of a foothold to defy the Inquisition. The peninsula had, furthermore, too long accepted the Papacy as both spiritual and secular head. Periodic efforts for reform could count on a measure of popular support for a short while among certain sections of the clergy, the intellectuals, and even some of the bourgeoisie; but it was vain to expect any sustained rejection of the rule of the Church in

Rome or the widespread acceptance of religious deviations which had originated in a non-Latin country.

Spain

IN SPAIN the Inquisition was a well-organized and efficient corrective for heresy many years before the rise of the Protestant Reformation. Its first objective had been the uprooting of the Islamic faith among Spaniards, then the conversion or expulsion of the Jews, and only thereafter the crushing of movements for reform, either of mystical tendency or those which had relations with Erasmus or the Protestant reformers. By about 1500 the first two objectives had been attained. The third was more difficult, as the mystics and the "enlightened" (*alumbrados* they called themselves) were usually good Catholics. A Franciscan, Ximénez de Císneros, confessor to Queen Isabella from 1492, archbishop of Toledo and Primate of the Spains from 1495, Inquisitor-General from 1506, raised to the cardinalate in 1508, twice regent of the kingdom, died eight days after Luther affixed the Ninety-Five Theses on the Wittenberg Chapel door. For the last twenty years of his life, he was the most important person in Spain. He was a zealous reformer, on Franciscan lines, an enthusiastic and imaginative scholar, an exceptional administrator, and a passionately loyal subject of the kings of Spain. In 1492 Queen Isabella had asked him to plan the continuance of the reform of the Spanish church begun earlier in the century. Against much opposition he carried through drastic reforms in the monastic orders and among the secular clergy. As a result of his labors the Church in Spain was, even before the outbreak of the Protestant Reformation, in less need of reform than anywhere else in Europe. Ximénez had, beyond his interests in religious administration, high cultural aims. The first great project to which he gave his energy and interest was the foundation, in 1500, of a new university at Alcalà de Henares, whose doors were opened in 1508. The earliest instruction was a sort of compromise between humanism and Christian *devotio*. Ximénez chose his professors from among the ablest humanist scholars, particularly those competent in Greek and Hebrew as well as several Latin grammarians who had been trained in Italian humanistic centers. The cardinal assigned to this group the next great task that was dear to his heart: an edition of the Bible in the original languages. This Bible, known as the *Complutensian* (from *Complutum,* the Latin name for Alcalà) *Polyglot,* was finished in stages. The first, the New Testament, was printed in 1514, but left stacked in the printshop until its publication was finally approved in 1520. It will be remembered that Erasmus hurried his own edition of the Greek New Testament to forestall the *Complutensian*. Erasmus was already well known in Spain. Some of his works were read and translated into Spanish, and many Spanish scholars were proud to count themselves correspondents of the great master. The first translation of any work of Erasmus (the *Enchiridion*) appeared in 1525 over the Inquisitor's *imprimatur*. Certain friars began to attack Erasmus, and soon a battle was raging between his followers, the *erasmistas,* and his opponents, the *antierasmistas*. For some years the former were victorious; but from 1534 the Inquisition was able to control and finally crush the movement.

The careers of the two Enzinas brothers illustrate the vicissitudes of Protestantism in Spain after the demise of Erasmianism. Francisco de Enzinas (*ca.* 1510–52), of a rich Burgos family, studied at Louvain and Paris, then at Wittenberg under Melanchthon. At the reformer's suggestion, the young Spaniard translated the New Testament into Spanish. He took it to the Lowlands, where in 1543 he had it printed and published, then presented it to the Emperor Charles. The Emperor's confessor thought the translation highly dangerous, and Enzinas was imprisoned. Escaping (February 1, 1545), he took refuge in Wittenberg and other Protestant centers. For two years he was in England. His older brother Jaime, after studying theology and Hebrew at Paris, prepared a Protestant catechism in Spanish and was burned at Rome as a heretic in 1547.

Within Spain the Inquisition had been able to prevent any considerable sale and dissemination of Lutheran books. Yet some Reformation ideas and doctrines found adherents in the peninsula. In Seville a certain nobleman, Rodrigo de Valer, was a profound student of Scripture and influenced many friends, one of whom, a priest, Juan Gil by name, preached justification by faith. He was imprisoned and forbidden to preach or say Mass. According to the records of the Inquisition there were, about 1550, over 130 members of a heretical community in Seville. The treatment was severe. The *auto da fé* of September 24, 1559, at which fourteen persons were burned as heretics, marks the real end of the evangelical movement in Seville.

The corresponding movement in Valladolid did not last so long. It was also ended by an *auto da fé* (May 1559) at which, of the forty-four accused of heretical opinions, fourteen were burned. (Some of these latter were, as a special dispensation, strangled before being burned.) In October of the same year thirteen more went to the stake, this time honored by the presence of King Philip II. A few years later the archbishop of Toledo, Bartolomé de Carranza (1503–76), a confidant of Charles I (V) and highly respected by the Spanish hierarchy, was brought before the Inquisition (1559) and accused of holding heretical doctrines on justification. He spent seventeen years in prison and was condemned, on the basis of a book which the Council of Trent had previously declared orthodox and blessed with its express approval. Such was the zeal of the Inquisition in Spain that it was more orthodox than the Papacy. Of another Spaniard who dared to disagree with the establishment, Michel Servetus, we shall speak when we describe the theocracy at Geneva.

By about 1560 Protestantism, whether native as in the case of the Valdés brothers, or foreign-inspired as in the case of the Enzinas brothers, was in reality uprooted and destroyed in Spain. The effectiveness of the earlier purge of the Church in Spain, the support given reform by the Catholic Kings, and the identification, in the minds of the Spaniards, of the Catholic faith with Spanish patriotism, had prepared the way for a popular rejection of any ideas which could be called heretical. To the Spaniard, heresy was tantamount to an attack on his beloved country. The Spanish Inquisition, thus generally regarded as the custodian of the honor of the Spanish kingdom, was more effective in its protection of the national faith than any branch of the Inquisition in any other country of Europe.

SCANDINAVIA

THE Reformation in the Scandinavian lands was more related to political issues than in any other area. The issues of an aggressive Danish policy, opposed to Swedish nationalistic resistance, complicated by the intense rivalry between leading families in Sweden, loom much larger than any widespread conviction that reforms in the life of the Church were needed. These convictions did exist, and there had been since the time of St. Birgitta (1303–73) frequent appeals for higher ideals and morals among the Scandinavian clergy. There was, furthermore, a growing ground swell of grumbling at the exactions of the Roman *curia*. But to a marked degree the Reformation in these northern lands exhibits a certain character of political accident.

We have described in Chapter 15 the conditions in Scandinavia at the time of Christian II and have seen how the Church in Sweden was involved in the struggle for Swedish independence from Denmark. The Blood Bath of Stockholm (November 1520) not only confirmed the Swedes' determination never to suffer the rule of a Danish monarch, but, from a religious point of view, prepared the Swedes to reject the Roman hierarchy, which had stood throughout on the side of the foreign monarch.

The Protestant Reformation in any precise sense was an importation into Sweden, made possible by the joint labors of four Swedes: Gustavus Vasa (1496–1560), the two brothers Olaus (1493–1552) and Laurentius (1499–1573) Petri (also known by their Swedish names of Olaf and Lars Petersen), and Lars Andersen (1470–1552). Gustavus had escaped from his Danish prison to Lübeck and thence, in May 1520, to a remote corner of Sweden, where he began organizing resistance to the Danes, particularly among the peasantry. His cool resourcefulness and narrow escapes from the police sent to capture him at all costs gave heart to his followers and made him a legend. With untrained peasant forces he almost captured Stockholm in the summer of 1521; a few months later he was accepted as Administrator of the kingdom by a council of nobles in East Gothland. After other successes in the field, a Swedish Diet (the *Riksdag*) elected Gustavus king in Strangnås on June 4, 1523. It was on this occasion that he met the two Petersen brothers and recognized their potential importance for the national movement. Olaf, who had taken his master of arts degree at Wittenberg in 1518, was a warm supporter of Luther and Melanchthon. Since his return to Sweden in 1520 he had declared the primacy of Scripture over the Church and preached against indulgences, celibacy of the priesthood, and the temporal power of the pope. Late in 1521 Gustavus had Olaf called to the headship of the church in Stockholm with the title of Rector, and made his brother Lars a professor of theology at the University of Uppsala. In 1524 Olaf was named secretary of the city of Stockholm. His influence as principal preacher and secular official of the city was understandably great.

In 1523 Gustavus named the most respected prelate in the kingdom, Laurentius Andreae (Lars Andersen), chancellor of the realm. As Andersen had already been won to the new teachings, the firm trend of the king's policy was clear. In public debates in 1524 the Protestant divines, appealing to the Scriptures alone, bested the Catholic defenders, whose appeals lay to canon law and Church tradition. The king asked the archbishop of Uppsala to have the New Testament translated into Swedish so that the people could judge the truth of the Christian religion for themselves. To demands from the Catholic side that he should prohibit the sale of Luther's works, the king replied that he did not see how he could "until we hear them condemned by impartial judges, especially since books against Luther are brought into the country. It seems, therefore, according to our poor understanding, that one side as well as the other should have a chance to be read." Gustavus' policy, moderately favoring the Protestant side, was the object of attacks from the Catholic bishops and clergy, but he sensed that the temper of the people was against the wealth and immorality of the clergy, and stood firm in his course. Petersen's translation of the New Testament in 1526 bore the king's coat of arms on the last page.

From about 1526 the king leaned more and more toward an openly Lutheran position. Gustavus met opposition, particularly in the delicate matter of control of Church property, from several Catholic bishops. To settle the dispute he called a meeting of the *Riksdag* (diet) to meet at Västerås in June 1527. In anger at the indecision of the diet and the opposition of the Catholic bishops, particularly Bishop Brask of Linköping, Gustavus burst out:

For all Our labor for you We have no other reward than that you would gladly see the axe at Our neck, and none of you but would gladly grasp its handle. Who would be your king on such terms? Not the lowest devil in hell, much less a man. Return to me what I have laid out of my own, release me from ruling over you, and I will leave and never set foot again on this ungrateful fatherland.

He then abdicated and retired to his palace. The diet, coming to an awareness of its futility without royal leadership, quickly passed decrees accepting the king's demands, then begged him to withdraw his abdication. The Västerås Recess, as these decrees collectively are known (June 24, 1527), granted the king income and control of the lands and property of the Church (beyond what was absolutely necessary for their maintenance), recognized the "new" preaching as fully Christian, and demanded that "the Word of God be preached in its purity."

Armed with the triumph of his firmness at Västerås, Gustavus brought the church in Sweden under the control of the crown. The new sanction of his authority and of the position of the monarch was so significant that he was now willing to accept formal coronation. At this ceremony, which took place in the Cathedral of Uppsala in January 1528, the crown was conferred by no person, cleric or layman. It rested on the high altar, from which Gustavus took it and placed it on his own head, thus making clear his opinion that the crown of Sweden came from heaven and certainly not from the Church. Immediately after the ceremony he marched to Dalecarlia with fourteen thousand men to crush decisively the resistance of a Sture pretender. In 1530 the king declared himself a Lutheran, and in 1531 he called an assembly of the clergy of the whole kingdom which named Lars Petersen archbishop of Uppsala. Soon all the bishoprics were filled by men acceptable to the king and in favor of the Swedish brand of Lutheran teaching and practice.

The Swedish Reformation had, up to this time, been a slow and moderate movement toward Lutheranism. The Swedish Bible (1541) was almost a literal translation of Luther's version, and the catechisms and manuals were usually based on those of Luther and Melanchthon. The responsibility for the moderation of the Swedish Reformation may be divided between the king and his three principal advisers, the Petersen brothers and Lars Andersen, although the prime reason was certainly the character of the monarch. There was, for example, no martyr of the Swedish Reformation in an age which saw much shedding of blood for religious convictions in Germany, the Lowlands, France, Spain, and England. The king's advisers were men of learning who were more prone to rely on instruction than coercion, and the king shared this temper with them.

Late in the 1530's events beyond the seas began to have their repercussions in Sweden. Henry VIII of England had (1531) taken the title of "singular protector . . . and supreme head of the English Church and clergy," and Gustavus heard from an intriguing German visitor how the German princes ruled their churches without episcopal interference. For long suspicious of the bishops, Gustavus was taken in, and, in his pique at what was left of the power of the Swedish bishops, turned against Olaf and Lars Petersen and had them tried on charges of fomenting rebellion (1540) and deposed on charges that were at best flimsy, at worst shamefully false. Henceforth Gustavus intended to rule the Swedish church through a superintendent responsible only to him. A peasant revolt in Smaland in 1542 received much local support before the king was able to suppress it in the summer of 1543. The last years of Gustavus' reign were mostly years of quiet and peaceful prosperity. He ruled firmly, but he was not capricious and he was in close touch with the spirit of his people. The Reformation was a national political event. On the other hand, Gustavus' interest in reform and morality was, even if compounded with a conviction that the church was the servant of the state, an honest interest.

Denmark and Norway

IN SWEDEN Christian II had been opposed as a foreign oppressor. In Norway and in Denmark he was opposed by the nobility and the clergy for several quite different reasons: he had favored the peasantry and the burghers; in church matters he had criticized the established hierarchy and encouraged and supported Wittenbergers, some of whom had come to Copenhagen at his invitation. Christian, learned and sympathetic to the humanist movement, maintained connections with many Western scholars. He furthered the interests of the humanistically inclined scholars at the University of Copenhagen, which already boasted of a number of eminent foreign scholars on its faculties. In 1517 Christian gave the Carmelite Order in Copenhagen a chapel and a hospital building for its college on condition that the order provide a professor of theology at the university. The order chose Paul Eliaesen (Paulus Helie), a well-known and able theologian and preacher, as the principal of the college. Three years later Paul angered the king by a remark in a court sermon which the monarch took as criticism of his policies and had to flee. But his teaching had already had a great effect upon the young. From 1517 Christian was, in fact, in clear sympathy with the Wittenberg program, and on a trip to the Lowlands in June 1521, he took along a box full of Luther's books. The Emperor Charles may have cooled Christian's enthusiasm for Luther at that time, but there was at least no reversal on the king's part.

In 1521 Christian issued a code of regulations (the *Landretten,* ecclesiastical laws, and *Byretten,* civil laws), which subjected the Danish church to Danish law, forbade appeals to Rome, urged marriage for the clergy, enforced residence upon them, and demanded morality and education from them at all levels. This code, if carried out, would have reformed and nationalized the Danish church without affecting doctrine. Had Christian remained much longer as king in Denmark, this code might indeed have created a national Danish church. It was his severity and impatience, his heavy taxes and raised tolls on the Sound that brought about his downfall.

When Christian fled to the Lowlands in 1523, his uncle Frederick I (1523–33) was elected king by a coalition of magnates and prelates. The choice of Frederick signified a sort of reaction against the humanist and Lutheran tendencies of Christian II. Frederick, by nature and experience conservative and cautious, took at least two years to realize that the Danish people were disposed to reject the leadership of the higher clergy and to accept the freer air of the Lutheran faith. The peasantry, who had supported Christian II because he was an enemy of their oppressors (the nobility, the prelates, and the monastic orders), were willing to give their allegiance to any person or movement which would alleviate the conditions of their life. The Lutheran doctrines of freedom and individualism were therefore congenial to them. In 1526 Frederick arranged the betrothal of his daughter to Albert, duke in Prussia, who had but recently espoused the Lutheran faith. This move was taken as a sign of Frederick's turn to the new order. In December 1527, the Danish diet (the *Rigsraad*) met at Odense. The Catholic bishops demanded that the king protect the Church, forbid marriage of the clergy, and cease to encourage the new (Lutheran) doctrines. The king insisted that men's souls were free, that marriage was "their own business," and that he would continue to allow the Gospel to be preached. The Recess of Odense of 1527, though no formal acceptance of Lutheranism by the Danish diet, was significantly parallel to the Swedish Recess of Vesterås of June 1527, in which, in fact, tolerance for the spread of Lutheran teaching in Sweden was won. For the next six years, in increasing numbers, Danes who had studied at Wittenberg and north German Lutherans found posts as teachers or pastors in Danish cities. The University of Copenhagen gave the appearance of a Lutheran center. Lutheran books were published, manuals of devotion in Danish translated from Luther's or Melanchthon's German appeared, and German hymnbooks were translated.

The king's eldest son and heir, duke Christian, already an open Lutheran, actively furthered the teaching and organization of the Wittenberg reformers in the two duchies of Schleswig and Holstein. Whereas the king would never go so far as to repress the older teachings, Duke Christian was more zealous for the new faith and practice, and occasional outbreaks of violence disturbed the provinces he ruled. Some of the nobility and Catholic clergy opposed his succession to the throne. In the event, it was the common people, not the nobility or the ecclesiastical hierarchy, that determined the victory of Protestantism in

Denmark. The resentment of the workers and the peasants at the wealth of monastic orders was even more vocal than the envy of the nobility. The two motives, resentment and envy, brought about the gradual suppression of most of the monasteries in the kingdom.

In 1530 about twenty of the leading Lutheran pastors of Denmark were invited to a meeting of the diet in Copenhagen. Without premeditated cooperation with the German princes at Augsburg, these Danish pastors composed a confession of faith in forty-three articles which, though not presented to the Estates, was widely published and discussed. In 1532, the last year of Frederick's reign, the Catholic archbishopric of Lund changed hands. The new incumbent, Torben Bilde, promised the king he would permit the preaching of "the true Word of God." Thus, by gradual infiltration, the Lutheran primacy of the Scriptures won free course.

For three years after the death of Frederick (April 10, 1533), the succession was in dispute. There were three parties in the *Rigsraad,* the strict Catholics, a Lutheran group, and, the most numerous, a middle group. Compromises were suggested, but unanimity proved unattainable. One group would have supported the reinstatement of Christian II, then a prisoner in Sonderbog. The view that Duke Christian, the oldest son of the late king, was the most acceptable candidate finally prevailed, though not without a civil war. Christian entered Copenhagen as conqueror on July 29, 1536. The Catholic bishops, who had obstructed Christian's election to the throne, were imprisoned, and the ancient episcopate virtually ceased to exist. The people supported the king and quickly accepted his offer of a new electoral charter or contract between the king and the Diet to regularize the incorporation of Norway under the Danish king, and the primacy of the crown both over the bishops and the church.

Christian III, a sincerely religious ruler, keenly aware of the confusions that had arisen during the past fifteen years to plague the Church and disturb religious thought and practice, asked for help from the Elector of Saxony. The Elector sent a friend and co-worker of Luther, John Bugenhagen (1485–1558), a Pomeranian who had had much experience in church reform and administration under Luther and Melanchthon. Bugenhagen promptly appointed seven provincial superintendents, clergymen already known for their reforming zeal. His second step in giving the Danish reformed church a reserve of learning and literate personnel was the revitalization of the University of Copenhagen, which had sadly declined in recent years. In 1537 new professors were named and installed and adequate income set aside from lands and customs dues. The third, perhaps the most significant, step in the construction of the Danish reformed church, was the composition of the Church Ordinance of 1537. Many sources were drawn upon in the construction of the Ordinance: the Forty-Three Articles of 1530 and several writings of Luther and Melanchthon. The draft was sent to Luther for his approval, signed by the king, and finally adopted at a later meeting of the diet at Odense, June 14, 1539. The Ordinance has, with slight modifications, remained the constitution of the Danish church to this day. Many Church clergy accepted the new order; those who did not were not persecuted. In 1559 there were only ten monasteries still under Catholic ecclesiastical control. Since recruitment to the monastic life was no longer possible, the ultimate disappearance of these monastic founda-

was only a matter of time. Within the space of twenty years, from 1519 the Ordinance of 1537–39, the whole structure of Danish ecclesiastical life was changed from Catholicism to moderate Lutheranism. It was a national, throne-encouraged movement, yet rooted in and supported by the common people, against most of the clergy and the nobility. Herein lies a difference from the process by which Lutheranism spread in Germany, and perhaps a partial explanation of the fact that, whereas the Catholic Counter-Reformation had some success in Germany, it had almost none in Denmark. The gentler process of growth and open discussion which the Danish monarchs favored allowed the public to make up and express its own mind, whereas Luther's reliance on the princes brought an element of coercion into the decisions any German individual might make, thus opening the way for possible reaction.

POLAND

THE Protestant Reformation found a particularly warm welcome in Poland. Largely because of distance from Rome and the fact that the Eastern Orthodox Church on Poland's eastern reaches made the Roman Church unwilling to exert any pressure that might drive the Poles into the arms of the Eastern Church, the Church in Poland had a long tradition of virtual independence from Roman domination. Many Polish rulers had, at various times, blandly and with impunity disregarded Roman directives, and the clergy had stood behind their kings.

The Hussite movement in Bohemia in the early part of the fifteenth century had aroused Polish sympathy; at the Council of Constance the Polish delegation had sided with Hus and the Bohemians. Many Polish soldiers fought on the side of the Hussites against the crusaders of the Emperor Sigismund. A Polish-Lithuanian prince, Korybut, was accepted by the Bohemians as regent of the kingdom for some years. The nationalistic, anti-German, antiecclesiastical ideas of the Hussites were so popular in Poland, in the period from 1415 onwards, that King Jagiełło (Władysław II) issued the severe edict of Wieluń in 1424 against the Hussite heresies. It was apparently not successful, as he issued a second edict in 1433 threatening those who held such ideas with even more dire punishments than before. The Hussite "heresies"—the cup for the laity, liturgy and preaching in the vernacular, marriage of the clergy—spread not only among the common people but perhaps even more noticeably among the nobility and the Polish bourgeoisie, and not only in the south along the Bohemian frontier but in western and northern Poland along the Baltic coast. Furthermore, recent research has revealed that Hussite doctrines found adherents among the German minorities in Polish commercial centers such as Cracow, Warsaw, Poznań, and Danzig.

A second factor favoring the cause of the Reformation was the flowering of the Renaissance in Poland, which took place in the late fifteenth and early sixteenth centuries. Many Polish students traveled to Italy after the Council of Constance, and, on their return, occupied posts of influence in the Church or at court. After the defeat of the Teutonic Order in the wars ended by the two treaties of Toruń (1411 and 1466) had brought peace and prosperity to the

Commonwealth, a cultural flowering was natural. The royal court and the clergy in the latter half of the fifteenth century were all affected by the Italian trends and favored Renaissance ideals. In pursuance of a policy of westward orientation, King Sigismund I (the Old, 1506–48) married a gracious and gifted Italian princess, Bona Sforza of Milan. She brought with her numerous humanistically trained clerks and friends, and during her life maintained intimate contacts with her learned friends in Italy, Switzerland, and France. Partly as a result of these stimuli the first half of the sixteenth century in Poland was a period of intellectual brilliance when, wherever one turned, there was humanist competence, patronage of letters, enthusiasm for learning, and substantial scholarly productivity. Erasmus, who corresponded with a number of Polish scholars, several times expressed his amazement at the high level of Polish culture. So far, then, as the humanistic Renaissance may be regarded as a preparation for the Reformation, Poland was in a position favorable to the reception of reformed ideas.

A third factor favorable to the Reformation in Poland was the presence of a large German population on Polish soil. The lands of the Teutonic Order, Prussia and the southeastern Baltic shore, had, since the second treaty of Toruń in 1466, been a part of the Polish Commonwealth. The Grand Master of the Order gave feudal homage to the king of Poland. The Germans in Prussia as well as those of inland Polish cities were in close touch with friends and events in the Empire. The Hanseatic towns on the Baltic coast, centers of German culture, were among the first to receive the news of Luther's attack on indulgences. The transmittal of the news and ideas to Polish cities was natural and immediate.

A fourth factor favorable to the reform in Poland was the low level of morality and literacy of most of the native clergy, whether German or Polish. Since the higher positions in the Church had gravitated into the hands of the nobility, the impulse to keep the lower clergy in line had almost disappeared, and the common people, as in Germany and elsewhere, had openly expressed their dissatisfaction with their spiritual ministrants.

Lutheranism

THE first open preaching of Lutheran doctrine occured in Danzig. James Knade, a Dominican monk and popular preacher who had accepted Luther's positions soon after hearing of the Ninety-Five Theses, had the city in an uproar by the summer of 1518. Imprisoned by the orders of the bishop, he soon escaped and took refuge with a friend near Toruń. Peace prevailed for a few years, but the writings of Luther were brought into Danzig in considerable quantities. Other commercial cities followed Danzig's lead. The best evidence for the presence of Luther's works in these centers was the king's edict of July 1520 prohibiting their importation. In July 1522, James Hegge, a secular preacher, opened the question of reform along moderate Lutheran lines, only to be faced with an active radical group who wished to carry the reform to the extreme of rejection of all traditional practices. The result was, in 1525, a revolution in the city government and the abolition of all Roman practice and jurisdiction.

.g Sigismund took effective measures to quell the movement, beheading
.n of the leaders of the uprising. Yet the quick restoration of Catholicism
.s essentially superficial. Beneath the surface, the ideas of Luther gained
ground steadily and quietly. Other towns where there were German merchants
heard Lutheran doctrines preached and possessed writings of the reformer. The
Grand Master of the Teutonic Order, Albert of Brandenburg, after visiting
Nürnberg and Wittenberg in 1522, had been won to the cause of reform. He
was advised by Luther to secularize the lands of the Order and to proclaim the
reform in his territory. In 1525 he carried out Luther's suggestion and took
the title of Duke in Prussia. Königsberg, Albert's capital, was henceforth to be
the center of Reformation publishing, both Polish and German; and many
Polish students came to the University of Königsberg to study under Lutheran
professors.

Meanwhile, in spite of their German origin—normally certain to make them
unpopular with the Poles—the new ideas were making headway in central and
southern Poland. At the Jagiellonian University in Cracow, by 1521, Luther's
works were widely known and discussed. Contact with Saxony was close and
frequent; merchants as well as students followed the ancient commercial route
from Leipzig and Dresden by way of Breslau in Silesia to Cracow and the
east. The repressive measures of Sigismund and the hierarchy slowed but did
not stop the growth of interest in the reform program. In the next few years
adherents of Luther's teaching appear among Poles of every class, the clergy,
high and low, the nobility, and the Polish burghers.

Typical of the career and caliber of many of the Poles of reforming tendencies
is the case of John à Lasco, illustrious scion of one of the great families
of Poland. His uncle was archbishop of Gniezno, Primate of Poland, and
John was destined for high office. He was sent to Bologna, Padua, and Rome
to study canon law and humane letters. After five years (1514–19) in Italy he
visited Switzerland, France, and Germany, meeting the leading churchmen
and scholars wherever he went. Returning to Poland, he was given a Church
position and made secretary to King Sigismund. On a trip to France and
Switzerland in 1524 he met Marguerite of Navarre, William Briçonnet, and
Lefèvre d'Etaples, all deeply imbued with ideals of Christian humanism and
hopes of reform through education. Going on to Basel, à Lasco met Erasmus,
to whom he became deeply attached and from whom he learned to appreciate
the high value of critical scholarship for the foundations of the whole Reformation movement. From 1526 to 1539 à Lasco was involved in politics and diplomacy, but he became so unhappy over the course of events in Poland that he
decided to go to Wittenberg to consult Melanchthon. In 1538 he resigned his
episcopal title and declared for the Protestant faith. Impelled to give up his
Erasmian gradualism, he turned to an active evangelical course, accepting a
post in East Friesland, as we have seen (see above, p. 520), as superintendent of
the reformed church. After 1548 until his death in 1560, he was intermittently in
England, Germany, Denmark, and Poland, guiding, advising, organizing,
reconciling—all tasks at which he was adept and convincing. Yet at the end he
felt he had failed, that the cause of the true Gospel was not victorious.

The life-span of à Lasco covered the most important developments in the
history of Polish Protestantism. The best proof of the spread of the Lutheran

heresy was the repeated demands of the higher clergy and various pr.
synods in the late 1520's and early 1530's that the king should support ef
measures against those who taught the new doctrines. In 1534 the nobilit,
Great Poland requested that the Bible be made available for general use .
Polish. In that same year Sigismund prohibited Polish students from attending
foreign universities that were at all suspect of heretical leanings and ordered
the recall of those then studying at such universities. Other repressive measures
were proclaimed at subsequent synods, or by the king in separate edicts; but
enforcement became increasingly difficult. The Polish nobility and the burghers,
both German and Polish, simply refused to be deterred. The diet of Cracow
in 1543 formally reversed Sigismund's edict of 1534 and granted the right to
study at any foreign university to all Polish subjects.

Humanism

THE intellectuals were scarcely less attracted to the evangelical movement than
the nobility and the burghers. At the University of Cracow there grew up, in
the 1530's, a secret society of eminent scholars, led by the Italian Franciscan
Francis Lismanini, chaplain and confessor to Queen Bona, who gathered regularly to discuss the theological and political problems raised by the writings
of Luther, Melanchthon, and the Swiss reformers. The society aroused the
suspicions of the bishop of Cracow, who had Lismanini's library searched; but
the wily Franciscan, warned, had removed all heretical books from his study
in time. The influence of this society spread and grew, and early in the 1540's
many Roman Catholic usages were being openly attacked by professors and
clergy. The positions and prestige of the members of the society were so high
among the people that they could not easily be affected by simple ecclesiastical
discipline; while, as the influence of their known sympathies with the new
teachings spread, an increasing number of the lower clergy publicly accepted
the reformed faith.

Calvinism and the Bohemian Brethren

AT ABOUT this time Calvinistic writings began to spread in Poland. The appeal
of the Genevan teaching lay in the fact that it was French, not German, in
origin and less involved in imperial politics than the Lutheran movement.
Furthermore, it had a greater intellectual appeal than Lutheranism. A number
of leading Polish families and many university men declared their preference
for Calvinistic Protestantism. The three greatest Polish literary characters of
the sixteenth century, Nicholas Rey, poet, Andrew Frycz Modrzewski, political
theorist, and John Kochanowski, poet and essayist, were strongly influenced
by Calvinistic ideas. King Sigismund, toward the end of his life, after years of
futile edicts against the Lutheran heresy, gave up; from 1544 to his death in
1548 he made no further effort in that direction. The Protestants used the respite to consolidate their gains. In 1548, just as the young Sigismund Augustus
ascended the throne amidst rumors that he was secretly a Protestant, a large
group of Bohemian Brethren, expelled from their native land by Ferdinand I,
crossed over to Poland from Bohemia. They were welcomed so heartily by the

...ants of Poznania that the bishop of Poznań persuaded the king to order ...expulsion. They then went on to Prussia, where Duke Albert received ...m gladly. Their devoutness, their firm faith, and their congregational hymns ...uring their short stay in Poland, left a lasting impression upon the Poles.

More and more individuals from the clergy and the nobility identified themselves with reformed doctrines in the early years of the reign of Sigismund Augustus. Yet the Protestants may have overestimated the strength of their position or underestimated the strength of their opposition. When Nicholas Oleśnicki, lord of Pińczów, converted a convent into a Protestant church and held Calvinist services in it, he was summoned before king and senate. He escaped punishment, but the Catholic clergy, aroused, instituted numerous prosecutions of priests and nobility for heresy. In 1551 a priest, Nicholas of Kurow, was martyred. Others suffered imprisonment and torture. Several noblemen were put on trial. Ancient Polish traditions of personal freedom were, however, too strong to permit any general persecution for beliefs that so many shared. Indignation at the determination to persecute was mounting throughout Poland from 1549 to 1552 when, at a meeting of the diet, it was decided that the Church should have no jurisdiction in any civil or political matter. The Church could pronounce a given teaching to be heresy, but such a pronouncement would have no civil or political consequences; and the Church could prescribe no temporal punishment. The king issued this decree over his signature, thus in effect establishing religious liberty in Poland. As the Church sought to evade the provisions of this edict, it was repeated in more precise terms by other diets, in 1562, 1563, and 1565.

In the meantime the Protestant cause had been strengthened by preliminary formulation of a catechism (1543), a Confession of Faith, composed by Seklucyan (1544), and the first translation of parts of the New Testament into Polish, also by Seklucyan, in 1551. Three years later the whole New Testament in Polish was in print. In 1555 the Calvinistic churches united with the groups of Bohemian Brethren which had survived the earlier expulsion or had returned from Prussia. The diet of 1555 demanded from the king virtually the same program of religious liberty which Charles V had been obliged to grant the Lutherans in the Peace of Augsburg, save that a complete and organic separation from Rome was not stipulated. Nevertheless, it was most evident that the desire for a national church was general. The presence of a tactless papal nuncio, Lippomano, in Poland only heightened Polish distrust of Rome.

In 1559 there occurred almost unobserved an incident which was to have great significance for Poland's later history. Two Jesuit priests, Canisius and Mengini, came to Cracow incognito to survey the field of the later activity of their order (see below, Chapter 21). On the Protestant side, efforts to bring the Calvinists and the Bohemian Brethren together were partially successful, and in 1557 these two groups resolved to seek union with the Lutherans. Actual agreement was some years away, but a degree of cooperation and the awareness of a common cause were achieved. By 1565 almost half the members of both houses of the Diet were open Protestants, and in voting they could count on scattered support from some nominally Catholic lords. In 1570 Lutherans, Calvinists, and Bohemian Brethren came to an agreement at Sandomierz, known as the *Consensus sandomirensis,* which, while not a union on ecclesiastical or doctrinal lines, was an expression of their intention to work to₂ politically against Catholic repression and in mutual tolerance and underst. ing with each other. Soon after 1565 the Protestant cause lost momentt. and was overtaken by a revived Catholic Church. How this remarkably suc den reversal took place will be discussed when we describe the whole Catholic Reform.

BOHEMIA

THE Hussite traditions of opposition to Rome and of a democratically organized national church had for over a century set Bohemia apart from all the rest of Christendom when Luther came on the public scene in Wittenberg. His writings were soon being eagerly read among the Utraquists and the less numerous Unity of Czech Brethren. He came into direct contact with the Unity after the Leipzig debates in 1519, and in 1520 he read Hus' great treatise *On the Church* (*De ecclesia*) with amazed approval. In that same year he had the work printed in Germany and said publicly that it was high time the Czechs and Germans forgot their ancient enmity and worked together for the furtherance of the Gospel. In the next few years a large proportion of the Germans in Bohemia became Lutheran; both Utraquists and the Brethren considered on what terms they might cooperate with Luther and his followers. In the long history of Czech-German conflict this common opposition to Romanism constituted a period of peace and amity.

Upon the death of the young King Louis II at the battle of Mohács against the Turks (1526), Ferdinand of Austria, the younger brother of the Emperor Charles V, was elected to the Bohemian throne. He was known to be a loyal son of the Church; but the Bohemian Estates, whether Czech or German, feeling that their ancient rights were adequately protected, had no fear that Ferdinand would interfere with their religious creed and practice. They may have been too confident. Ferdinand was astute. He found, on the one hand, that Catholicism was weak in Bohemia. He found also that the opponents of Catholicism, although constituting a majority of the population, were divided or suffering from uncertain leadership.

Luther's relations with the Unity were free of invidious personalities, and from the beginning the approaches were sincere on both sides. Luther admired the evangelicalism and faith of the Unity: they in turn admired his courage and devotion to the Gospel. Nevertheless, in spite of much correspondence, no agreement was possible on the sacraments or on Luther's doctrine of justification by faith. In 1524 the correspondence broke off. In 1532 John Augusta, the newly installed bishop of the Brethren, had a new confession of faith composed, of which he sent a copy to Luther, with a request for comment. Luther gladly obliged and relations were resumed. Luther, more considerate than he had been in 1524, welcomed the Brethren's steadfast adherence to their concept of the Gospel. The confession was sent to King Ferdinand in 1535, who did not like it but would tolerate the Brethren as long as they remained loyal subjects. Augusta and a companion went to Wittenberg (1536) to discuss union of the Unity with the Lutheran movement, but there were doctrinal points on which side would yield. At the end of several months of friendly discussion ~r said: "So be it. You be the Bohemian reformers; we will be the re- .ners in Germany. You work for Christ where you are; we will do the same ~re."

Luther's relations with the Utraquists, from whom he had expected so much, turned out even less satisfactory than those with the Brethren. A petty and unreliable Prague priest who had acted as intermediary was expelled from Bohemia by the king in 1529. This misfortune prejudiced Luther's hopes of cooperation with the Utraquists. More serious was the fact that the Utraquists were split among themselves, the conservative wing leaning toward Catholicism, whereas the leading personalities in the sect were Erasmian and averse to evangelical zeal by nature. There were, on the other hand, some who would have accepted certain Lutheran teachings. The stricter Utraquists were nationalistically minded and guarded their Hussite tradition jealously. The Germans in Bohemia were, by 1530, predominantly Lutheran, although some powerful German families did remain loyal to the Catholic cause.

In this confusion Ferdinand was obliged to utilize his support among the various strata of Bohemian society with great care. In 1537 he declared that he would uphold the *Compactata* of 1436, which recognized only two faiths: the orthodox Roman faith and the Utraquism of Hussite times. This would of course mean, provided the king were able to carry out his will, the elimination of Lutheranism and the Unity, which, having arisen after the *Compactata*, were not mentioned in the document. This confusion was momentarily increased. Ferdinand had shown his hand. Yet the basic situation was not much changed, simply because the country was, in so preponderant a majority, if not united, at least anti-Catholic.

Attempts by both the Utraquists and the Unity to gain support from Wittenberg for their Protestantism having had no positive results, about 1538 leaders of both groups began to look elsewhere. The reformers in Switzerland and southern Germany had been in correspondence with leading evangelical Utraquists and Brethren, and the fact that their doctrine was not German gave them a certain advantage among the Czechs. From about 1540 the Strassburg reformers and particularly Calvin gained popularity in Bohemia. In addition to the non-German origin of the teaching, Calvin's symbolic doctrine of the Eucharist was more congenial to the Czechs than Luther's insistence on the real presence; and personal relations between Calvin and leaders of the Unity were established.

The victory over the Schmalkaldic League at Mühlberg in 1547 had put Charles V in a strong position; Ferdinand, having recently suppressed an uprising of the Protestant Bohemian nobility who refused to join him in the war against the League, took advantage of the fact to initiate a campaign against the Unity. In 1548 he ordered the preachers of the Unity to cease their preaching and drove the Brethren from four of their leading cities out of Bohemia. The Utraquists he had to treat more carefully because of their greater numbers and their legal position under the *Compactata*. In 1561 Ferdinand was able to re-establish the Catholic archbishopric in Prague, which had been "administered" without an archbishop since 1421. Anton Prus, Grand Master of the Order of the Crusaders and bishop of Vienna, was chosen as archbishop. With

Ferdinand's support Prus gained from Pope Pius IV in 1564 the concession that Catholics in the lands of the Emperor Ferdinand and Albert of Bavaria might partake of the sacrament in two kinds. This concession was intended to weaken the hold of Utraquism upon the people. As a further means of combatting Utraquism and evangelicalism Ferdinand welcomed a small group of Jesuits to Prague in 1555, giving them his personal protection.

The position of the Protestants was only slightly improved under Ferdinand's successor, Maximilian II (1564-76). The new King-Emperor strengthened his hold over the Utraquist ruling body, the Consistory, and refused the request of the Unity for a written statement specifically including them in the terms of the Peace of Augsburg. In self-defense the various Protestant groups arrived at sufficient harmony to agree on a common Bohemian confession of faith (*Confessio bohemica*) in 1575. This confession they presented to the king at the meeting of the diet in May, as evidence of the strength of Protestantism in the kingdom. It was a composite document, including certain statements of clearly Lutheran inspiration, others of apparent Calvinist origins, and some no less unmistakably native Hussite. This confession is perhaps the high point of Bohemian Protestantism; although Maximilian refused the demands of the evangelicals that it be recognized by him, in a formal document, as of equal validity with the Augsburg Confession, he nevertheless promised orally to accept it for Bohemia. The Protestant Estates pinned their hopes for religious toleration perhaps too optimistically on the Emperor's oral promise to honor the Confession.

HUNGARY

CONDITIONS in the Church in Hungary in the fifteenth century were similar to those in Germany. King Mathias had made a number of efforts to improve clerical morals, and some members of the hierarchy had projected reform along humanist lines. Early in the sixteenth century the work and spirit of Erasmus were known and applauded in enlightened quarters. As early as 1520 the name of Luther and his early conflicts with the Roman Church were familiar to a few scholars and princes, but the full impact of the Reformation came later. After the Battle of Mohács, when the allied Bohemian and Hungarian forces were defeated by the Turks, the kingdom was partitioned into three parts: the southern third came under the direct rule of the Sultan, a narrow strip along the north was in the hands of Ferdinand, and Transylvania, under its Prince John Zapolya (d. 1540), gave formal homage to the Sultan. A major portion of the Hungarian diet elected Zapolya king of Hungary, while a smaller group of magnates elected Ferdinand to the same office. The close ties Mathias Corvinus had established with the West prepared the way for the early transmission of Lutheranism to Hungary. The writings of Luther were avidly read among the Saxon Germans of Transylvania and by them further spread among the Hungarian bourgeoisie and nobility. The Turks were quite willing to allow Lutheran writings to circulate, since they regarded the Catholic Church and the Habsburgs as their principal enemies.

The conversion to Lutheranism of Mathias Devay (1500-45), a Catholic priest, educated first at Cracow, then at Wittenberg, provided the energy and impetus the movement needed at its beginning. He was at Buda in 1531 as minister to the reformed congregation, and the next year at Kassa, where his zeal and consequent effectiveness earned him imprisonment and several trials. After two further imprisonments he found a protector in the Palatine, Count Nadasdy, then had several of his works published in Germany. Melanchthon's influence on him was strong, and he became convinced that the reform movement needed schools and a literature. He wrote a treatise on Hungarian orthography and several religious manuals in Hungarian, modeled on Luther's catechisms. About 1541, on a visit to Switzerland, Devay accepted the Calvinist teaching on the Eucharist and on other points of doctrine deserted Luther.

In 1543 the Lutherans were allowed free exercise of their faith in Transylvania. In 1545 five cities in Upper Hungary (Slovakia) at the first Protestant synod in Erdöl published their *Confessio pentapolitana* (*Confession of the Five Cities*), which was modeled on the Augsburg Confession. By about 1550 it was clear that, in general, Germans preferred Lutheranism and the Magyars Calvinism. Debrecen prided itself on the epithet the "Hungarian Geneva." Catholicism was supported mostly by those who favored the Habsburgs; it became almost the patriotic duty of any Hungarian to accept one or other of the Protestant confessions.

An interesting and indeed almost typical case of the confusion inherent in the Reformation in Hungarian lands is the case of Francis David (*ca.* 1515–79). First a Catholic priest, then a Lutheran superintendent, he soon turned to Calvinism; in 1564 he became superintendent of the Calvinist congregations and court preacher to the prince, John Sigismund Zapolya. The current of Unitarian thought from Italy and Switzerland attracted him, and in 1566 he attacked in public debates at the University of Kolozsvar (Klausenburg) the doctrine of the Trinity. He was able to gain the prince's recognition of Unitarianism in 1568, and in 1568 he became its bishop. He contended that the doctrine of the Trinity was an invention of the third and fourth centuries not to be found in the New Testament. The declarations of Zapolya decreeing religious freedom in Hungary, on three separate occasions, in 1557, 1563, and 1568, were attributable to the influence of David. His success, however, was short-lived. On the death of John Sigismund Zapolya (1571), his successor, Stephen Báthory, a staunch Catholic, removed all Unitarians from court and suppressed their writings. David's extreme position, approaching Judaism, was rejected even by other Unitarians, who brought charges of blasphemy and "innovation" against him. Convicted, he was imprisoned for life in the royal castle of Deva, where he died, probably of natural causes. He had professed all four "accepted" or legal faiths and had been a bishop, or the equivalent, of three of them. Such a career could have been possible only in a land where principles of freedom and tolerance prevailed. Subsequent Unitarianism owed much to David, and both Lutheranism and Calvinism were the better for having had to face his attacks on their doctrines.

By the end of the sixteenth century the four faiths, Catholicism, Lutheranism, Calvinism, and Unitarianism, were all active in the several parts of Hungary; the Hungarians were predominantly Calvinist, among the Saxons and the Slovaks Lutheranism was favored, while Catholicism had deep roots among those of whatever race who favored the Habsburg cause. Unitarianism appealed to certain groups of the intellectuals.

SUGGESTIONS FOR FURTHER READING

BROMLEY, G. W., ed., *Zwingli and Bullinger,* Vol. XXV in *Library of Christian Classics.* Philadelphia, 1953
JACKSON, S. M., ed., *Selected Works of Huldreich Zwingli.* Philadelphia, 1910
JACKSON, S. M., *et al.,* eds., *The Latin Works and Correspondence of Huldreich Zwingli.* 3 vols. New York, 1912–26
WIFFEN, B. B., *Life and Writings of Juan de Valdés,* with a translation by J. T. Betts from the Italian of his *Hundred and Ten Considerations.* London, 1865
WIFFEN, B. B., ed., *Alfabeto cristiano* from the Italian. London, 1861
WILLIAMS, G. H., ed., *Spiritual and Anabaptist Writers.* New York, 1957

BERGENDORFF, C., *Olavus Petri and the Ecclesiastical Transformation in Sweden.* New York, 1928
BROWN, G. K., *Italy and the Reformation.* Oxford, 1933
DALTON, H., *John à Lasco.* London, 1886
DUNKLEY, W. H., *The Reformation in Denmark.* London, 1948
FOX, P., *The Reformation in Poland.* Baltimore, 1924
JACKSON, S. M., *Huldreich Zwingli: The Reformer of German Switzerland.* New York, 1900
LEA, A. C., *History of the Inquisition of Spain.* 4 vols. London, 1906–07
LINDSAY, T. M., *History of the Reformation.* Vol. II, *The Reformation in the Lands beyond Germany.* New York, 1907
MERTON, R., *Cardinal Ximenes and the Making of Spain.* London, 1934
MEYRICK, F., *The Church in Spain.* London, 1892
TURBERVILLE, A. S., *The Spanish Inquisition.* New York, 1932

ALTMEYER, J. J., *Les Précurseurs de la réforme aux Pays-Bas.* 2 vols. 1896
BAINTON, R. H., *Bernardino Ochino, esule e riformatore.* 1940
BATAILLON, M., *Erasme en Espagne.* 1937
CIONE, E., *Juan de Valdés, la sua vita et il suo pensiero religioso.* 1938
HOLMQUIST, H., *Die schwedische Reformation.* 1925
IMBART DE LA TOUR, P., *Les Origines de la réforme,* Vol. II. 1946
RENAUDET, A., *Préréforme et humanisme à Paris pendant les premières guerres d'Italie.* 1916. 2nd ed., 1953
RODOCANACHI, E., *La Réforme en Italie.* 2 vols. 1920, 1921
RUFFINI, F., *Studi sui reformatori italiani.* 1955
VIÉNOT, J., *Histoire de la réforme française,* Vol. I. 1926

CHAPTER NINETEEN

HABSBURG AND VALOIS:
FRANCE FIGHTS ENCIRCLEMENT

T HE struggle between the ruling house of France, the Valois, and the rulers of Spain and the Spanish possessions in Europe and beyond the seas was the most bitter, inveterate conflict of the century. Generally regarded as beginning with the election of Charles I of Spain to the imperial throne as Charles V in 1519, and lasting forty long years to the Treaty of Câteau-Cambrésis in 1559, it was in reality a much more drawn-out and irrepressible conflict, of which the forty years of Charles' reign were only the first open and sanguinary phase.

Encirclement Takes Shape

WE HAVE sketched in an earlier chapter (16) the process of the unification of Spain carried out by the Catholic Kings, Ferdinand and Isabella, which, for the first time, placed a major power on France's southern frontier. We have also seen (Chapter 13) how, as it were accidentally, these same monarchs came into possession of a vast empire beyond the seas, with resources which soon began to pour rivers of gold into the Spanish treasury. Equally, perhaps more, important for the peace of Europe and the security of France was the marriage in 1496 of Joanna, the daughter of Ferdinand and Isabella, to Philip the Handsome of Austria, son of the German Emperor Maximilian and Mary of Burgundy. This was one of the most fateful marriages in European history. The alliance sealed thereby could eventually place the northern and eastern borders of France in the same hands that held the southern frontier. A simple glance at the map will make the precarious position of France in the center of these potential pressures quite evident. That it was possible for France to be eventually encircled and strangled was clear as early as 1490, when negotiations for an alliance between France's neighbors were as yet only tentative. Nevertheless, at that time and for some time to come the French were not unduly concerned. Marriage alliances in the past had frequently failed to achieve their aim; the chances of failure in these negotiations were more than even.

546

But when, in 1500, a son and heir was born to Juana and Philip while a further marriage alliance between Spain and England was confirmed, to be followed, in 1501, by the marriage of Catherine of Aragon to Arthur, eldest son of Henry VII, the danger in France's position became obvious to everyone.

The Italian campaigns of Louis XII in the years 1499 to 1504 and 1509 to 1512 should be understood in the light of this encirclement, although it is not certain that Louis was completely aware of what he was doing in these terms. He did certainly know that he had to combat the power of Spain by arms as well as by diplomacy. His claims, by descent from Valentina Visconti, to the duchy of Milan, justified, to him at least, his conquest of the duchy in 1499–1500. His easy conquest of Naples (1501) was quickly lost; his other Italian wars, against Genoa, Venice, the Swiss, Ferdinand of Aragon, Emperor Maximilian, and the Papacy, only resulted (1512) in the loss of everything he had won. He retired to pine and die.

Louis was succeeded by his cousin, Francis I (1515–47), young, chivalrous, ambitious, confident, witty, and unfortunately volatile. The first four years of his reign were remarkably successful. Immediately after the resplendent coronation festivities, Francis set out to regain the duchy of Milan, which Louis had lost and renounced. His preparations were both diplomatic and military. He warmed up the old friendship with Venice, made peace with Henry VIII of England, promised Charles of Austria, soon (1516) to be king of Spain, to aid him in the future, and protested on every side that he was interested only in what had long been French territory. The army he gathered to make good his claims shared his optimism, and, with luck and some clever staff work, was soon on the plains near Milan. The Swiss garrison of Milan attacked the French near Marignano, a village ten miles from the city, late in the afternoon of September 4, 1515. The battle dragged on through the night, with the French nearer defeat than the Swiss realized. But the next morning the French, reassembled and inspirited, drove the Swiss before them. Milan was once again in French hands. Pope Leo X, impressed and a little dismayed, was anxious to make peace on Francis' terms. King and Pope met at Bologna, where, amidst pomp and persiflage, they agreed to revise the Pragmatic Sanction of Bourges of 1438. By the new arrangement, the Pope would receive the annates, the first year's revenue from French bishoprics, while the king would have the right of naming archbishops, bishops, and abbots. In essence the French church was now in the control of the king, and the Papacy had accepted the Gallican claims which Philip IV had enforced two centuries before. On the French side, there was opposition by the university and the *parlement* of Paris, as well as the higher French clergy, who now saw that their convocations were without power to control or even to influence appointments to the highest offices in the Church. The king and his advisers were firm, and the opposition was helpless. The French church, from this point on, tended to become an agent of royal policy.

The Emperor, Maximilian I, was old and feeble, and the succession was a subject of discussion in all the courts of Europe. Francis' military and diplomatic successes encouraged him to be a candidate for the imperial crown. He had the electors sounded, his agents talking in terms of large gratuities and marriage alliances. The electors were graciously interested in the talk of gifts. The candidacy of Henry VIII was never taken seriously by anyone save perhaps Wolsey. The dying Emperor, desirous that his grandson Charles, ruler of the Burgundian lands since 1504, and king of Spain since 1516, should succeed him, persuaded the Augsburg bankers, the Fuggers and the Welsers, to loan Charles over 500,000 gold florins to bribe the open-minded electors. Charles added another 350,000 of his own. Thus bribed by both candidates, the electors were able to make an impartial choice. They chose unanimously the Habsburg heir, who, they thought, living far away in Spain, would be less likely to interfere in their local affairs than a powerful and ambitious monarch like Francis, who was just next door.

The Election of Charles V and Completion of Encirclement

WITH the announcement of the election on June 28, 1519, the first overt phase of the Habsburg-Valois struggle opened. Both Charles and Francis knew that war between them was inevitable, and each began the diplomatic moves preliminary to armed conflict—the securing of allies or the neutralizing of potential enemies. At right angles, as it were, to the axis of tension, reaching from Madrid through France to the Empire, were the two most powerful rulers outside the principal protagonists: Henry VIII of England, to the north, and the Medici Pope, Leo X, to the south. Francis wanted to be sure that if he had to fight in Italy his northern flank would be safe from attack. Henry, obviously realizing the importance of his own position, allowed himself to be wooed by both sides. Early in June 1520, Henry met Francis in the neighborhood of Calais, on what is known as the Field of Cloth of Gold. Before a numerous and splendid concourse of both courts, the two young monarchs vied with each other in lavish entertainments and athletic contests. A good time was had by all, but no alliance resulted. Henry, on his return to Calais, met Charles at Gravelines, where they concluded an agreement binding Henry not to join Charles' enemies, and in the event a war should break out between Charles and Francis, Henry engaged to act against the aggressor. Henry was delighted to be holding the balance between the two powers, but at this stage he leaned to the side of his nephew Charles. Charles was on his way from Spain to Germany to be crowned King of the Romans at Aachen and to preside at the Diet of Worms, where he was to put the ban of the Empire on a Saxon monk by the name of Martin Luther.

Charles' experience at Worms with the complex problems of the Empire led him to realize that he would have to make provisions for its governance in his own absence. He therefore appointed (April 21, 1521) his younger brother Ferdinand as his lieutenant, turning over to him the Habsburg Austrian lands of Austria, Carinthia, Styria, Carniola, and Tyrol. Not the least factor in Charles' decision was the growing menace of Turkish aggression from the south. Ferdinand was thus delegated to be the eastern guardian of the Empire's frontiers, a task which assumed more serious proportions when news of the capitulation of Belgrade (August 28, 1522) to Suleiman the Magnificent reached Vienna.

In the meantime, and in Charles' absence from Spain, the revolt of the townsmen (the *comuneros*), had broken out, and Charles' regent, Adrian of

Francis I, by François Clouet, in the Louvre, Paris [CAISSE NATIONALE DES MONUMENTS HISTORIQUES].

Utrecht, was imploring the king to return to avoid losing his throne. The opposition to Charles on the part of the towns and urban nobility of Castile and Aragon had been open since 1518. Charles' Flemish and French advisers were resented, the king's scanty knowledge of Spanish disappointed his Spanish subjects, and in some cases the towns flatly refused to pay the levies he laid on them. They demanded, furthermore, that the king marry immediately in order to assure the succession to the throne. Hardly had Charles left Spain for the Lowlands and Germany in May 1520 when the storm broke. The rebels took Toledo and set up a separate government. With other towns following suit, among them Salamanca, León, and Valladolid, a sort of league of *comunidades* was formed. The rebels went so far as to take possession of Charles' mother, Joanna, and tried to inveigle her into declaring herself the queen and accepting their junta as the government. Joanna, then in one of her sane periods, refused to cooperate against her son and retired to her castle. For some time Charles, busy with imperial affairs in Germany and the Lowlands, left matters in the hands of Adrian and his military staff. The junta, to whom many of the clergy had rallied, sent Charles in Worms a long list of demands. If he had accepted them, or even a part of them, he would have been a captive, not a king. Instead, he rejected the demands in their entirety and imprisoned the leader of the delegation for treason. From Germany he ordered vigorous measures against the leaders of the revolt, and gradually the force of the uprising began to decline. The royal troops met the rebels at Villalar on April 23, 1521, and crushed them decisively. When several leaders were promptly beheaded the revolt was over. In August Charles granted the rest of the rebels amnesty. The proud spirit of Spanish independence, however, was not so easily extinguished; in the course of his long reign Charles had often to hear from his Spanish subjects words of firm objection to if not defiance of his demands for increased subsidies to maintain his imperial obligations.

Francis saw in Charles' absence from Spain and the internal disturbances in that country an opportunity, and in the spring of 1521 sent across the Pyrenees an army which seized Spanish Navarre. Charles reacted quickly; a Spanish army met and defeated the French and retook the mountain kingdom. The war then broke out on the Flanders front, and in Italy Milan was taken. Francis' army in Italy, composed mostly of Swiss mercenaries under Lautrec, was defeated at Bicocca, north of Milan, on April 27, 1522, and the French were virtually driven out of northern Italy. To add to his humiliation, Francis heard from Henry VIII that the latter was actively allied with Charles by the treaty of Windsor (June 19, 1522) and would soon invade France. The invasion amounted to no more than ravaging of the coast of Normandy, but it was nevertheless discouraging for Francis to see Charles and Henry acting together against him from two directions. Furthermore, the Pope and Venice soon followed Henry's course, so that Francis could say to the *parlement* of Paris: "All Europe has joined together against me. Very well then, I shall have to fight all Europe."

This was the juncture at which the duke of Bourbon, Constable of France, chose to go over to Charles. The treason had been planned for some time. He was the richest peer of France, but was afraid, with some justification, that his vast lands in the south and west of France might be taken by Louise of Savoy, Francis' mother, or by Francis himself. Yet this fear, by itself, would hardly have justified the act of treason. Bourbon felt he had not been treated by Francis as well as his wealth and position called for, and when Charles, knowing of the friction between Bourbon and Francis, offered the duke the hand of his sister Eleanor and his support in holding his French inheritance,

Bourbon decided to join Charles. When the plot and his decision were discovered, he had no choice but flight. Francis, bitter at the desertion, declared all Bourbon's property reverted to the crown. Bourbon escaped to Italy and was given a responsible post in the imperial army. He brought with him no troops; only his sword and his name were added to the Emperor's cause.

The year 1523, although it was one of Charles' most successful years, turned out less badly for Francis than he had anticipated. French opinion, outraged by Bourbon's treason and Henry's raiding, was all on Francis' side. Pope Adrian VI, formerly Charles' tutor, died, and the political inclinations of his successor, Clement VII, though reputedly pro-Charles, were not yet completely known. English aid to Charles in Flanders was turning out to be almost a liability, while the English alliance with Spain was cooling to the extent that Wolsey was even negotiating with French agents for a French alliance. Tudor commercial policy and the aims of Charles, as long as he remained the ruler of the Lowlands, could with difficulty avoid an ultimate clash. Charles was having difficulties in raising the money needed to maintain forces in Lombardy, where the natives found Spanish troops unwelcome guests.

The next year, 1524, was indecisive. Charles had planned to take Provence

Emperor Charles V, by Bermart van Orly, in private collection, Budapest [BILDARCHIV FOTO MARBURG].

and the port of Marseilles, which would have assured control of Genoa, which in turn would have guaranteed Charles ready access to the Lombard plain from the Mediterranean Sea. Charles, however, had troubles with his allies, and the great Genoese sea captain, Andrea Doria, then in French pay, by dominating the Ligurian coast easily kept the Spaniards at bay. Francis, on the other hand, although he suffered some spring reverses in Lombardy, was able in September to drive Bourbon out of Provence. To complicate matters further, Clement VII had left the side of the Emperor and was trying to act as peacemaker between the rivals. In December Francis was able to conclude a "holy" alliance with the Pope and Venice against Charles. At this moment Wolsey, having deserted the Spanish alliance, was seeking tangible encouragement to shift England's weight to the side of France. For a short while it appeared that events were moving in a direction favorable to the French cause. But before anything substantial could come out of Francis' changed fortunes, catastrophe struck.

Pavia and the Treaty of Madrid

FRANCIS had seen the imperial armies retreat from Provence; he followed them out onto the Lombard plain. On October 26, 1524, he recaptured Milan, then moved a part of his army to lay siege to Pavia, at that time held by Charles' general de Leyva. Well defended, the city withstood siege for three months, until, in mid-January 1525, imperial forces, under Bourbon and Lannoy, came to its relief. The two armies faced each other for three weeks; battle was finally engaged on the night of February 24. Maneuvering proved difficult and confused at night in a wooded park. Francis and his nobles fought gallantly and coolly against odds, some of the great names of France falling at their king's side. When at last the French king was wounded and almost alone, his mount fell, pierced by a spear, leaving him helpless. He refused to surrender his sword to Bourbon, but he was a prisoner; the cause of France had been lost in a few hours of fighting. Francis was put under heavy guard in a nearby fortress to await Charles' disposition. He wrote to his mother, Louise of Savoy, "My honor and my life are all that remain to me."

This complete victory was more than Charles had dared hope for. When the news was brought to him, he was at first dazed, then retired to his chambers to think out alone how to make the best use of the great good fortune God had granted him. Henry VIII wanted a part of the victory, and presented his bill: either the crown of France, long claimed by the kings of England, or at least the ancient provinces owned by the Plantagenets. This, with what Charles and Bourbon between them might have taken, would have removed France from the map of Europe. Charles' advisers were opposed to any aggrandizement of the king of England and pointed out that there was still a French people and a French government to take into account, under the leadership of the regent, Francis' mother, Louise of Savoy. Charles decided to consolidate the results of his victory in Italy and to force Francis to accept severe but not impossible terms on matters in dispute between them.

Francis, brought to Spain in June 1525, was in Madrid by August. Charles repeatedly refused to receive him, until, in September, he heard that his captive was dying. Since a dead French king would be of little use to Charles, he rushed to Francis' bedside, with protestations of fraternal encouragement and affection. Francis' beloved sister, Marguerite of Angoulême, came to care for him and to act as an intermediary in negotiations for the settlement which had to be made. The French officials hoped that her feminine charms might soften the heart of Charles. But negotiations dragged on. The English claims were not taken too seriously either by the French or by the Spaniards. Charles said he was willing to continue the war if Henry would pay for it. This was enough to quiet any further talk on this line by the Tudor. Other extreme claims were put forward, only to be smiled out of court. On one important point Charles would not budge: France would have to give up, not only Flanders and Artois, but Burgundy, which Louis XI had taken from Charles' ancestor, Charles the Bold. The French negotiators, faced with Charles' firmness and the imprisonment of their king, were at a bargaining disadvantage.

Francis, restive in confinement, formally abdicated in favor of his son the dauphin; while Charles, by his refusal to accept alternative terms of peace suggested by Louise, prolonged negotiations to such a point that the fruits of victory began to vanish. Louise made a separate settlement with Henry; Venice, the Pope, and Florence, unwilling to see Charles become the dominant power in Italy, were glad to accept French suggestions for the return of the Sforza to Milan. Charles, however, refused to be deflected, and Louise, finally worn out by the tension of governing under such trying conditions, counseled acceptance of the Emperor's terms. The treaty was finally signed by the envoys on December 19, 1525. It called for Francis to marry Charles' sister Eleanor, widowed queen of Portugal; to give up Burgundy, Flanders, and Artois, and all his claims in Italy; to restore to the duke of Bourbon the lands and dignities taken from him; and to join the Emperor on a crusade against the Turks. Francis' two sons were to be left with Charles as hostages of his good faith. On the night of January 13, 1526, before the ceremony of signing the document with Charles, Francis called together the French plenipotentiaries and affirmed to them that the agreement he was going to sign on the following day had been wrung from him by force and was in violation of his honor as king. He regarded himself as not bound by its conditions and wished them to be witnesses to his intentions. On March 17, 1526, Francis was exchanged, in the middle of the Bidassoa River, for his two sons. When the terms of the Peace of Madrid were made public, the general reaction throughout Europe was one of indignation. The Pope voiced the general opinion when he said there was no good reason why an agreement reached under such conditions of constraint should be regarded as valid. Charles had overreached himself. Francis, on French soil, refused to ratify the treaty, and when Charles' envoy, de Praet, demanded that he live up to the terms of his solemn engagement the king's Council informed de Praet that it was impossible even to consider separating Burgundy from the kingdom of France. Charles, defied, with the great victory of Pavia completely nullified, had now to begin all over again. The two sons of Francis were roughly treated, kept in dark prisons, barely

The Empire of Charles V, 1526

clothed, and badly fed. As this cruelty became widely known, the Emperor suffered further loss of esteem throughout Europe.

French diplomacy found the Italians, afraid of imperial hegemony in Italy, ready to align themselves against Charles. The Pope, indeed, took the lead in forming a coalition—the Holy League of Cognac, consisting of France, the Papacy, Venice, Florence, and the duchy of Milan (May 22, 1526). The king of England was invited to be the "protector" of the League. Had Francis acted with decision at this point, the power of Charles might have been broken. Instead, he chose to engage in the pleasures of outdoor sports and the boudoir, to the exclusion of serious business. The League of Cognac was ineffective and soon ceased to figure in international relations.

Ottoman Expansion: Mohács

IN ADDITION to the two rival powers of Habsburg and Valois, a third power, the Ottoman Turks, under aggressive and determined leadership was moving into the Habsburg area of vital interest. After the capture of Belgrade in August 1521 and Rhodes in December 1522, Suleiman had turned his attention southward to bring order and efficient administration to Egypt. Just before Christmas the Knights of St. John on the island of Rhodes capitulated to Suleiman after a five months' siege. This was a defeat for all of Christendom, but, because of his Mediterranean interests, was most acutely felt by Charles. Suleiman spent the year 1525 in extensive preparations for resuming his conquests in the Danubian basin. He properly analyzed the extent of the rivalry between Francis and Charles, and concluded an actual if not explicit understanding with France on the very simple basis that they both had the same enemy, the Habsburgs, wherever they might be found. In April 1526, Suleiman moved against Hungary. By August he had reached the plain of Mohács, where he awaited the Christian host. The young Louis II, Jagiellonian king of Hungary and Bohemia, had been able to muster fewer than 20,000 troops in defense of his kingdom against Suleiman, with 100,000. John Zapolya, prince of Transylvania, with 80,000 troops, did not join the king as agreed on, but rather sent a messenger urging Louis to fall back. The king, however, decided to make a stand (August 29, 1526). He ordered a charge up a slight slope against the Turkish line. The Turks gave way, and the Hungarians found themselves directly facing the Turkish artillery, waiting for them. The massacre was terrible. The king fell, and with him the flower of the Hungarian feudality.

In two and a half hours the fate of the Danube basin for two centuries was decided. The death of Louis without an heir made his brother-in-law Ferdinand the nearest claimant to both crowns. The Hungarian magnates, however, treasured their electoral rights; instead of Ferdinand, a majority of the nobility elected John Zapolya as king in November 1526. A year later Ferdinand's claim to the throne was accepted by a small assembly of nobility at Pozsony (modern Bratislava); Zapolya, in flight, appealed to the Sultan for help. The Sultan, only too glad to oblige, declared his support of Zapolya. The ancient lands of Hungary were, in effect, divided into three parts: a narrow, crescent-shaped strip of land stretching from the Adriatic coast to the tip of the Carpathians; Transylvania, under Zapolya as elected king, technically tributary to the Sultan, but essentially independent; and the southern circle under direct Turkish administration.

The Christian West was humiliated and frightened. The Habsburg cause was discredited. The Emperor was, for the moment, obliged to be lenient with the Lutherans in Germany; in the face of the precarious hold of Ferdinand on Vienna and Upper Hungary, Charles' position toward Venice and the Papacy was weakened. Military victory or defeat had a way, in the sixteenth century, of being as indecisive as diplomatic conclusions, as was true in this case. The treaty of Madrid had become, within a few months, a dead letter. Within a few months after Mohács, in the face of Ferdinand's failure to gain the throne of all of Hungary, and with the coalition of Cognac against him, Charles was once more master of Italy and the Papacy.

The Sack of Rome

IMPERIAL troops, mostly German *landsknechte* under Frundsberg, and elements under Bourbon were gathered near Piacenza in February 1527. Ill paid and ill fed, they demanded pay or booty. A truce concluded by Pope Clement VII on March 15 forecast further inaction, and the clamor for remuneration was overpowering. Frundsberg had an apoplectic stroke as he was urging the *landsknechte* to be patient, and Bourbon had to yield before the demands of the soldiers for action. He decided to lead them south. Florence, willing to fight, was bypassed, and the unruly mob moved on toward Rome. As the Pope had, after the truce, disbanded his troops, there was a mere skeleton of defense when the army reached the city on May 5. When Bourbon was killed scaling a wall, the prince of Orange took command of an imperial army that obeyed no commands. The Pope reached the safety of the Castel Sant'-Angelo only a few minutes ahead of his German pursuers. The sack of the city lasted eight terrible days. *Landsknechte,* mostly Lutheran, enjoyed pillaging the papal citadel; ravage and rapine went unchecked. When the inhabitants, priests and nuns, nobles and church dignitaries, offered no further resistance, the soldiers fought among themselves. It is estimated that four thousand people perished in this sack of Rome. Since there was no one to rescue the Pope, he had to accept whatever terms were offered. He paid 400,000 ducats ransom and gave up a number of cities near Rome, as well as Piacenza and Modena, which had heretofore acknowledged papal suzerainty. Clement's Medici nephews were expelled from Florence and a model republic under Savonarola established. The imperial troops, now somewhat sated with their savage attack on the city, remained in Rome, barely under military discipline for nine months more. The humiliation of the Pope was perhaps more drastic than the Emperor and Clement's other enemies may have desired. A broken pope would be a weak ally. Charles may have been too successful in his anti-papal campaign.

The question was asked then, and still may be, how responsible was Charles for this shameful and basically pointless outrage. Clement, by his duplicity in dealing with Francis and Charles at the same time, and by his callous disregard of his own word, may have helped to bring the disaster on himself; but Charles could have withdrawn his troops from Rome much sooner than he did. On the surface, Charles had added another crushing victory to his long list of defeats of his enemy Francis. Henry VIII and Francis I were again allied (treaty of Westminster, April 30, 1527) and anxious to free the Pope from Charles' control. Francis desired most of all a withdrawal by Charles of his claims to Burgundy and the release of Francis' two sons, hostages in Madrid. The French king applied two kinds of pressure: an army in the Milanese which moved south to Naples in cooperation with Andrea Doria, the powerful Genoese admiral, and an offer of cash. Charles at this point refused the cash offer, and the military expedition had to withdraw from Naples when the plague decimated the army and Doria, deserting the French, offered his services to the Emperor.

The Treaty of Cambrai

NEGOTIATIONS for peace had been going on all this time. The first agreement reached was between Charles and the Pope (treaty of Barcelona, June 25, 1529) by which the Medici were re-established in Florence, and Charles returned the lands Venice had taken from papal control. The more important settlement was that between Charles and Francis, the epochal treaty of Cambrai, August 3, 1529, called "the Ladies' Peace" (*La paix des dames*) because it had been negotiated by Margaret of Austria, Charles' aunt and his regent in the Lowlands, and Louise of Savoy, Francis' mother. By this arrangement, Francis renounced his claims in Italy and his feudal rights of suzerainty in Flanders and Artois. Charles, on his part, agreed to drop his claims to Burgundy; Milan was given to Francesco Sforza; Francis was to marry Eleanor, Charles' sister and widowed queen of Portugal, and pay Charles two million écus for the ransom of his two sons. Across the Channel the English people were only too glad to see the end of a war out of which they got nothing and which had disturbed their profitable trade with the Lowlands.

When, finally, the terms of the treaty of Cambrai were carried out, and Eleanor, the new queen-to-be, accompanied by the two sons of Francis, crossed the Bidassoa River and stepped onto French soil (July 1, 1530), the second phase of the rivalry between the two great ruling houses of Europe had come to an end. Charles had been crowned by Clement on February 24; his brother Ferdinand, having driven the Turks from the gates of Vienna, was soon to be formally elected King of the Romans, thus assuring to the Habsburgs the continuance of the imperial prestige. The Papacy was now surrounded by Spanish territory. Charles had Italy in his hand. Milan, Florence, and Naples were his, and the lands beyond the seas. To all appearances Charles was the undisputed head of Christendom. Martin du Bellay, an adviser of Francis and brother of the cardinal, wrote, in 1532, concerning the results of the peace of Cambrai: "Most people thought that this was peace for our time, but there were those who, reflecting on long experience with matters of this sort, did not agree." There followed almost a decade of hesitation, avoidance of conclusions, contradictory alliances on all sides. There was no doubt in anyone's mind that, for a generation at least, the Italian issue had been decided and Spain had won that conflict. The treaty of Cambrai was followed by six years of "peace" between Charles and Francis. But it was only a truce. Both parties to the conflict were, in 1530, near exhaustion. Continuance of the war would have been impossible.

Peace Interlude, 1530–36

FRANCIS took advantage of the "peace" to prepare for a final decision which he hoped profoundly would be favorable to him. He set about building a diplomatic network which would eventually break Charles' tight hold on Europe. He sent agents to all the courts of Europe where there was any latent or real animosity toward the Emperor, to the various courts of Italy, to the Swiss, to Denmark, to Hungary, to the *curia* at Rome, and to the court of Henry VIII.

At all these courts the overwhelming power of Charles aroused feelings of deep foreboding, and Francis' emissaries were welcomed. At the court of the Turkish Sultan Francis' overtures for an active and aggressive alliance had been anticipated by parallel military action. Francis and Suleiman had a common enemy, the Habsburgs, and their alliance was easy and natural, without equivocation on either side.

Charles, for his part, found that the Lutherans in Germany were so strong that he could not act in imperial matters against their will. Next to the religious question, which he realized had to be held in abeyance, the threat of Turkish aggression demanded more resources than Charles and Ferdinand could, on their own, put in the field. Charles was therefore in the position of having to ask the Protestant princes for help.

The second Diet of Speier, which met in March 1529, was, in a majority, Catholic. In the absence of Charles in Italy, Ferdinand presided. He was less pliant in religious matters than Charles would have been, and his rigorous attitude led to the *Protest* of April 19, signed by the leading Lutheran princes present at the Diet and by fourteen cities. A few months later Vienna was under siege by the troops of Suleiman. In September the Turks withdrew, but they did not go far, and no one in Europe doubted that they would return. Ferdinand's need for substantial help remained acute. In the meantime the Protestant issue pressed for a solution. Charles met the Diet at Augsburg in June of 1530. There lay before him three possible approaches to the Protestant issue: he could attempt to solve it by force, by waging war against the recalcitrant Protestant princes—thus, if he won, forcing their submission; he could negotiate, and thus perhaps win some of the princes by fair words and liberal promises and isolate the more stubborn of them; he could oblige the Pope to call a council at which the issues at stake could be smoothed out and German unity in the face of Turkish attack be achieved. Charles tried both persuasion and the promise of a council. After five months of argument at the Diet neither Charles nor the Protestant leaders were willing to give an inch. Charles had written to Pope Clement VII twice, urging the calling of a council at which the Protestants would be heard and doubtless brought back into the fold of Mother Church. The Pope was unalterably opposed to a council. There the matter rested for some time.

The peace of Europe was, in these years, very precariously balanced. The Protestant princes of Germany, warned by Charles' unbending stand at Augsburg that their faith was in danger, formed, between December 1530 and March 1531, a league at Schmalkald, which brought them together into a political unity supported by military and financial resources so substantial that they were convinced the Emperor would have to reckon with their power. In December 1530, Margaret of Austria died, and in September 1531, Louise of Savoy followed her to the grave. With the two makers of the treaty of Cambrai removed from the scene Francis could more openly let it be known that he did not intend to be bound by its provisions much longer. He could at the same time take advantage of the tension between Charles and the German princes. In May 1532, Francis signed the treaty of Scheyern with some German princes, in which he engaged to fight "for the defense of German liberty." In return he was given the right to recruit soldiers in Germany. Francis favored the Swiss Protestants against the Catholic cantons, and refused to join Charles in suppressing heresy in Switzerland, thus bringing comfort to the Protestants.

Henry VIII had, on balance, from the beginning of his reign, been on the side of Spain in the Habsburg-Valois struggle, partly because of his marriage to a Spanish princess, partly because France and England were traditional enemies. Francis, however, had never given up hope that he might be able either to win Henry to his side, or at least to neutralize him in the struggle against Charles. Queen Catherine's failure to produce a male heir had led Henry to seek a divorce. Francis knew of the project and saw in it possible advantages for himself. If Henry put away his Spanish wife the ancient Anglo-Spanish alliance would be shaken if not broken, and, if Francis could wean England from Spain, France would be proportionately strengthened. From 1529 on, Henry was open to the French friendship. The University of Paris, among other universities, was asked to approve the divorce on the grounds that the papal dispensation to marry his brother's widow violated canon law. The favorable decision of the university was in large part the result of pressure from the French royal court. Francis watched the course of the relations between the English king, the Emperor, and Pope Clement VII with great interest, and on several occasions during these years instructed his agents at Rome to support Henry against Charles. Henry and Francis met at Boulogne in October 1532 on the friendliest of terms, and although nothing formal was concluded beyond a meaningless treaty against the Turks, Henry was from this time effectively neutralized. Francis had won a diplomatic victory and was free for further action in Italy or elsewhere.

Clement VII had, since the sack of Rome, never been happy at being held in Charles' leading strings. He had, furthermore, family interests that were dear to his heart. Not only did he want to keep Florence in Medici control, but he desired a royal marriage for his niece Catherine. There were many suitors for her hand; as early as 1524 Francis had offered his third son as a candidate. In 1529, after the peace of Cambrai, as a part of his diplomatic campaign to strengthen his position against an eventual decisive struggle with Charles, the French king saw the papal-Medici connection as more important than before, and this time offered his second son, Henry, as a bridegroom for Catherine. Charles supported the candidacy of the duke of Milan, Francesco Sforza. After long negotiations Clement met Francis at Marseilles in October 1533, and Catherine and the young Henry were married in the grand style. Apart from the magnificent marriage ceremonies, the Pope and the king found that their common fear of and enmity for Charles had brought them together on many points. Francis could congratulate himself that he now had either won to his side or neutralized two of the great powers of Europe, England and the Papacy, and had established friendly relations with a third powerful group, the Protestant princes of Germany. If all the factors in the combination had persisted, it would have been a considerable achievement. But the Pope died in September of the next year, before Francis could profit from the alliance. The French monarch now had to build his diplomatic fences all over again.

The Franco-Turkish Alliance and Charles

THERE remained the Turks. After almost a decade of friendly if informal relations with Suleiman, Francis decided to formalize the alliance. In November 1534, the lieutenant of Suleiman in the West, Grand Admiral Kheir-ed-Din Barbarossa, after capturing Tunis from the Moorish king, an ally of Spain, sent an embassy to Francis. Francis reciprocated by sending an envoy to Tunis to express the king's thanks for his offer of help, then on to Constantinople (May 1535). On the return of Suleiman from his campaign against the Persians, Francis' envoy concluded (February 1536) in the name of His Most Christian Majesty, Francis I, a commercial treaty very favorable to French merchants in the East. The most important result of the negotiations, a military and political alliance, was not committed to paper. Francis and Suleiman understood each other perfectly. Their common enemy, Charles, assured their cooperation. In some quarters French opinion was scandalized at an alliance with the Infidel, but for the most part the French need for whatever help the king could muster from any source against the "rapacity" of Charles was accepted as ample justification.

As ruler of Sardinia, Sicily, the kingdom of Naples, and the Balearic Islands, in addition to the southern and eastern coasts of Spain, Charles had great responsibilities in the Mediterranean. While the Turks were engaged in the Danube basin and Charles was fighting France in the Lowlands and in northern Italy, there was little activity on the Islamic sea. But, once the peace of Cambrai gave Charles a respite in the north, he turned his attention to the expansion of Suleiman's empire in north Africa, which threatened the Spanish lines of sea communication between Spain and Italy. With the aid of Andrea Doria Charles went on the offensive against Turkish holdings. In 1532 Doria captured Coron in the Peloponnese and drove the Turks out of the Gulf of Corinth. The next year, as we have seen, Barbarossa took Tunis from the Moors. Tunis was too close to Spain for Charles to forego an attempt to wrest it from the Turks. In June 1535, Charles set out from Sardinia with 30,000 men in 400 ships. To get to Tunis it was necessary to capture the fortress of Goletta, which guarded the entrance to the Lake of Tunis. After almost a month of bombardment and assaults Goletta was taken. Then the wells which lay outside the city were seized in fierce hand-to-hand battle. Within the city, almost twenty thousand Christian captives suddenly rose, overpowered their guards, and turned on the Turks. In the turmoil the city was easily taken by the Spanish troops. Barbarossa, who had received help from Francis, escaped with most of his army to Algiers. Charles' capture of Tunis was a signal accomplishment, but Barbarossa's escape and quick retaliatory attack on the island of Minorca essentially nullified the Christian victory.

Charles was well aware of Francis' aims and of most of his diplomatic moves during these years of "peace." During the war that broke out soon after Francesco Sforza of Milan died heirless on November 1, 1535, Charles made several efforts to placate the king. Ancient French claims to Milan inevitably collided with imperial plans in Italy, and war resulted as a matter of course.

The duke of Savoy, allied to Charles, resisted the French march through his territory, but Turin was taken by the French in April 1537. Charles made an offer during the campaign to invest Francis' third son, Charles, duke of Orléans, with the duchy of Milan on condition that he marry Sforza's daughter and that Francis also join the Emperor in a crusade against the Turk. Francis found the offer unacceptable. He wanted the Milanese without any conditions. Charles sent an army of twenty thousand men to Francis' rear, up the Rhône valley. The French general, Anne de Montmorency, avoided contact, but left no grain or forage for the Spanish army, which soon had to retire. Marseilles defended itself successfully and Charles, frustrated, had to withdraw his depleted forces to Italy. Neither side was gaining anything, and a three months' truce was signed at Monçon in November 1537.

At the end of seven months the representatives of the king, the Emperor, and the Pope met at Nice in June 1538, there to agree on a further truce for ten years, each side to retain what it then occupied. Francis kept two-thirds of Piedmont, Charles the rest and the Milanese. It was a slight gain for Francis, but no victory. A month later the two monarchs met at Aigues Mortes, apparently completely reconciled like two loving brothers. They jointly declared their firm intention of furthering the Catholic faith and combatting the Turk. Nothing was said about the Milanese or the Church council which Charles desired so much. France, like Spain, rejoiced at peace; a monarch at war made heavy demands on the pockets of his subjects. Francis' allies, however, felt they had been tricked. Henry VIII considered recalling his ambassador to France, while the German Protestants were deeply concerned, and not entirely without reason, lest Francis should now join with Charles to crush them. The reconciliation with Charles, indeed, coincided with Francis' persecution of the French Protestants. Until about 1535 the king's sister Marguerite had been able to influence him in favor of tolerance. From that time, however, he became increasingly more severe. In 1540 the Edict of Fontainebleau established the principles of an inquisition. In 1545, at Francis' orders, three thousand Albigensians in the mountains of Provence and Savoy were massacred, and twenty-five towns and villages were destroyed.

In 1538 Francis raised Anne de Montmorency, the general who had foiled Charles' attack on Provence, to the position of Constable of France, giving him full power over the finances, and generally over all the king's affairs. This was to put the direction of the affairs of the whole kingdom into the constable's hands. It explains the notably relaxed attitude of France toward Charles for the next few years. Montmorency, antipathetic toward anything resembling aggressiveness, persuaded Francis to follow a line of appeasement toward Charles. The full extent of this change of heart was revealed by the revolt of the city of Ghent. The city had refused to pay a tax levied on it by Charles in 1537, and in 1539 the citizens revolted against imperial rule. They asked Francis' help, appealing to his oft repeated claim to be the suzerain of Flanders. Francis refused to interfere, and when Charles asked permission to cross France in order to visit the Lowlands, primarily to suppress the revolt, Francis not only gave his permission but welcomed him at Paris with open arms and gala festivities (January 1540). This performance was also on Montmorency's initiative. Just what Francis may have hoped to win by falling in with his minister's policy of rapprochement is not completely clear. It is fair to assume that in his own mind he had not given up his desire to win back the Milanese and even the Lowlands. The basic situation between the two houses had not changed; the tension between a France encircled and a Spain that controlled positions surrounding France remained. At all events the honeymoon was over soon after the Paris meeting. The issues, French security on her three eastern fronts —the Lowlands, the Franche Comté, and the Milanese—were still burning bright.

Francis' envoy to Constantinople, Antonio Rincón, had at first great difficulty in persuading the Sultan and his advisers that the French king's recent agreements with the Emperor were not genuine. But the Sultan's understanding of the fundamental opposition between the Habsburgs and France, in which a temporary and superficial reconciliation was only a breathing space before the renewal of the conflict, saved the Turkish alliance, and, in the end, preserved France from disaster.

Despite certain vague suggestions made by Charles to Francis at Paris toward a solution of the dispute over the Milanese, it soon became evident that the Emperor had no idea of letting the duchy out of his control. With the failure of the policy of appeasement for which Montmorency had been responsible, the constable fell from power. The major adversaries were almost back where they had been fifteen years before, after Pavia. England had come to occupy a neutral position. Catherine had died, and Charles was willing to make friends with Henry. Henry, on the other hand, had grown to enjoy his role as the middle power, and for the rest of his life preferred to have a free hand, veering now to one side, now to the other. Charles, having failed to convince Francis to accept a compromise settlement of the thorny question of the Milanese, conferred the duchy on his son Philip (November 1540), thus making French claims thereafter illegal. To Francis this was an unbearable insult. Then, when in July 1541 two of Francis' envoys, Rincón, accredited to Constantinople, and Fregoso, to Venice, were arrested at Milan and murdered, war became certain.

Renewal of the War, 1541–44; the Peace of Crépy

THE opening blows of this, the third war between Charles and Francis, were exchanged at sea. Charles planned to take Algiers, thus weakening Francis' ally, the Sultan. The Emperor set out with his fleet in October 1541, rather later than his advisers thought wise, and storms on the African coast almost annihilated his fleet, forcing him to withdraw to Spain. Francis, meantime, was having some successes in Brabant, Luxemburg, and Hainault; but Charles' forces were able to hold Perpignan and strike back in Cleves and Luxemburg. Henry of England, taking advantage of Francis' troubles, made a secret treaty with Charles in February 1543, and in July landed a small army near Boulogne, threatening Paris. Charles would have liked to see Henry come closer to Paris; Henry, however, had no intention then of playing the Emperor's game for him. The campaigns of 1543 were, taken all together, inconclusive. In the spring of 1544, the young Duke d'Enghien won a victory, more brilliant than significant, over the imperial forces at Ceresole in the Piedmont, but Charles was able to balance this victory by some successes in Champagne. It was known that Charles and Henry had planned to have their armies meet before the walls of Paris, Charles marching westward from Château-Thierry and Henry south from Boulogne. It would have been possible for them to do so, but Henry, distrustful of Charles, laid siege to Boulogne instead of marching on to Paris. Boulogne capitulated with the honors of war on September 14, 1544. Four days later Francis, hard pressed, accepted the terms offered by Charles at Crépy (without consulting his ally Henry).

This peace provided that Charles, duke of Orléans, should marry a niece of the Emperor who would bring the Milanese as her dowry; Charles renounced Burgundy; Francis renounced Flanders, Artois, and Naples. Henry continued his private war for another year, but finally promised to give up Boulogne at the end of eight years for two million crowns (peace of Ardres, January 1546). Francis and Henry each had another year to live, which they spent in peace and misery. Charles, stubborn and imperial, outlived his royal companions by twelve years: they were not to be years of peace.

The series of wars, truces, and peaces we have followed from Francis' victory at Marignano in 1515 is usually called the Italian Wars. It is, however, both more and less than that. It is more because Italy was the setting of only a part of the struggle. The Danube, the Near East, north Africa, the western basin of the Mediterranean, the Pyrenees, the Lowlands, the Rhine valley, the northern coast of France, Savoy, and, indeed, the German *Reichstag,* these were all involved in a Europe-wide conflict which saw France, the richest and most centralized state in Europe, fighting for her life against the stranglehold of the Habsburg house, in the person of Charles V. The term "Italian Wars" is less than accurate by reason of the fact that the beginnings of the struggle between Valois and Habsburg preceded Marignano by another two decades and continued for fifteen years after the treaty of Crépy. One might even connect some features of the Thirty Years' War (1618–48) and the wars of Louis XIV with the marriage of Philip of Austria and Juana of Spain in 1496. Major issues in history have long roots and equally long branches.

Before we follow this struggle through its next significant stage, to the Peace of Câteau-Cambrésis in 1559, it will be helpful to examine the administrative and financial structure of the main protagonists in the conflict. Ferdinand and Isabella had striven toward centralization of power in the several Spanish kingdoms of which they were monarchs. They had had singular success, but there remained many pockets of local and regional liberties which they had been unable to eliminate. They had set up a Royal Council (*Consejo real*) which was to exercise royal power. This was in turn divided into four administrative councils, for the various functions of government. The professional personnel of these councils were chosen by the monarchs, and were therefore dedicated to the strengthening of the powers of the king. Charles on his accession accepted this system, increasing the number of councils slightly to handle the increasingly complicated affairs of a greater state. At the head of his system was the Council of State (*Consejo de estado*). When he became king in 1556, Philip made no change in structure, only raising the number of councils to twelve, as the business of a vast and growing empire called for more bureaucracy. The rulers of Spain were all hard-working administrators, unwilling to delegate authority. There was no such person as a first minister, such as Wolsey or Cromwell in England. Charles had his Flemish tutors, Chièvres and Adrian, who guided his early years of ruling, but there never was any doubt that Spanish policy and action were Charles' own decisions. Philip gave a measure of confidence to Cardinal Granvelle, who acted as chief minister in the Lowlands both for him and for his regent, Margaret of Austria, but he never relaxed his personal and direct control over Spanish policy.

French Governmental Structure

THE steady tendency of French governmental organization before the time of Francis I had been toward centralization to such an extent that Francis must be called an absolute monarch. Louis XI, taking advantage of the disturbed conditions of government which had been the legacy of the Hundred Years' War, had so firmly and effectively consolidated the power of the crown that the feeble rules of Charles VIII and Louis XII had not weakened the position of the king. Absolutism suited Francis' temperament, and he gathered around him ministers and advisers who shared his taste for power. In France, as in Spain, the monarch governed through a council. This body changed somewhat from ruler to ruler. Francis instituted a Council of Affairs (*Conseil des affaires*) consisting of five or six intimates whom he consulted regularly on matters of high policy, war and peace, and finance. Apart from this select and intimate group there was the traditional Great Council (*grand conseil*), formalized by an ordinance of Charles VIII of August 2, 1493. This was a larger group of officials who might be called upon by the monarch as professionals to handle appeals from lower courts or administrative referrals, ecclesiastical matters and concerns arising out of the Concordat, disputes referred by the provincial *parlements*. Francis, finding this body useful and subservient, increased, during his reign, the range of matters handled by the Great Council. This body sometimes functioned through a financial section. We find several references to a Council for Financial Matters (*Conseil pour le fait des finances*) during Francis' reign. The *parlement* is a unique and traditional French institution, whose functions and powers are difficult to define with any precision. The seven provincial *parlements* of the sixteenth century, Toulouse, Grenoble, Bordeaux, Aix, Rouen, Dijon, and Rennes (1553), in theory formed, with the *parlement* of Paris, which was the most powerful of all, one *parlement* of the king. The members of the *parlement* were magistrates, judges, lawyers, lay and cleric in equal numbers, and, since 1467, unremovable. Their independence was thus assured. Their primary function was the registration of royal edicts. But, as officials who realized that edicts had to be workable or should conform to national needs and traditions, they had exercised the right to suggest amendment or correction. The kings had frequently welcomed such practical suggestions, but if a monarch did not approve the suggestions he was not bound to accept them. He then held a public *lit de justice* and declared the royal edict registered. There was no appeal from that decision. As all edicts came before the *parlement* its involvement in all aspects of government—not solely judicial —was recognized.

The costs of war and government were less for Francis than for Charles. The French king could move on internal lines, whereas Charles had to transport his soldiery over greater distances to the far limits of his imperial interests. The Emperor was continually in financial straits, and, at the end, left Spain bankrupt and broken. Francis, wasteful and extravagant as he was, was also usually spending beyond his revenues. Yet he had, from early in his reign, some sense of the need to provide for the expensive campaigns he planned, and, with more authority in his hands than Charles, he ordered (1523) a complete reorganization of the finances of the kingdom. He set up a Treasury of Economy (*Trésor de l'épargne*) and increased its power to centralize various sources of royal income in subsequent ordinances. He placed final responsibility for the administration of the budget and disbursement on the Royal Council. Thus the ancient sources of income, the *taille,* the *aides,* duties on imports, sales of offices, the *gabelle* (on salt), the royal domain, confiscations and fines, the tenth of the clergy, other special ecclesiastical income such as "grants" and "loans," "gifts" from cities, hitherto unsystematic and uncertain, were channeled through one agency; the government could, in theory at least, know where it stood in financial matters. Obviously no such drastic reform could work perfectly on short notice, nor was petty graft obviated. None the less, the reforms of Francis were the basis for the centralized financial structure of the kingdom throughout the seventeenth and eighteenth centuries and explain, in large measure, the important fact that in these centuries the French monarchy had the reputation of being the richest land in Europe.

CHARLES AND SPAIN:
PROSPERITY AND DECLINE

THE situation with which Charles had to deal was quite different. He never had the almost complete control over the national finances which Francis enjoyed, and this lack of control made it impossible for him to use efficiently what resources the *Cortes* of the separate Spanish kingdoms might put at his disposal. We have seen that the imperial crown cost Charles 850,000 florins, all of it borrowed. The economy of Spain, before bullion began to pour into the peninsula from the New World, was largely dependent on the *mesta,* the guild-like organization of the grazing industry, and its wool. Ferdinand's involvement in Italian affairs forced him to borrow money from Spanish tradesmen, so that Charles' additional borrowing to purchase the imperial crown, added to Ferdinand's debt, represented a substantial deficit before he began the wars with Francis. Yet at this time Spanish credit was good. In the course of the decade from 1520 to 1530 bullion imports were low. The mines of the Americas had not yet begun to produce heavily.

From about 1530 the trend of bullion reception in Spain was noticeably upward. Before the abdication of Charles it reached well over $5,000,000 a year. The most direct result of this heavy import of gold and silver bullion was a more drastic rise in prices than in national income. Prices trebled during the reign of Charles. An industrial revolution began to take place as a result of the increased circulation of specie and the growing demand for manufactured goods. At Seville three thousand weavers were employed in the silk mills, while Toledo was reported to have counted twice or three times as many in the textile industry. At Saragossa sixteen thousand looms were in use. There was so much demand for manufactured goods that there was a shortage of Spanish labor, and thousands of skilled artisans from France and Italy came in to ply their trades. Manufacturers of chinaware, worked steel for arms, luxury fabrics, and soap produced in exportable quantities paid heavy taxes into the royal treasury. But the boom period of industrial prosperity was short-lived. The decline began well before the end of the reign of Charles, and by 1565 industrial output had dropped to an average of two-thirds of what it had been in 1550. Thereafter, the output dropped still more rapidly. The explanation lies partly in the import of bullion which raised prices so noticeably, partly in the temper of the Spanish people and their attitude toward manual labor. Everyone wanted to be a *hidalgo,* too proud to indulge in vulgar money-making, whose status would allow him to be a gentleman without engaging in commerce. Foreigners were soon in control of industry, and profits had a way of leaving the country. Then, when the government, in response to the demands of the nobility, forbade not only the export of fine cloth but even its manufacture in order to force the merchants to import cloth from Flanders, the increased flow of money out of Spain was assured. All this of course meant that the normal royal income, which had profited from business even when carried on by foreigners, was less by the amount lost from taxes and the *alcabala* (a 10 per cent sales tax), and because the international bankers and money lenders knew of the declining royal income, the interest rate on moneys borrowed to carry on the wars against France, the Turks, and the German Protestants was raised substantially.

There were several accompanying circumstances related to the great influx of bullion into Spain. As prices rose the exportable products of Spanish industry competed more unevenly with the products of countries receiving no colonial bullion; as export dropped, output also declined, and again the royal revenue suffered. Philip, remaining in Spain as his father's regent, was hard put to it to raise the sums Charles demanded for his wars in Italy and the Lowlands. Philip wrote Charles in 1546 that taxation fell so heavily on the king's humble subjects that they were ceasing to go into trade entirely. The crown, in order to maintain its army and expensive diplomacy, had to raise tax rates already confiscatory and find new sources of revenue. The nobility, the *hidalgos,* were, as commonly in Europe, exempt from most taxes, so that those best able to pay contributed nothing. Apart from the monopolies like salt and mineral products, the *alcabala,* inherited from the Moors, was the most fruitful single source of revenue. But, since it was collected with each transaction, it could easily amount to 30 or 40 per cent and sometimes more of the original value of a commodity before it reached its final destination. The obvious result of such a tax is the virtual elimination of turnover.

As the needs of Charles increased with his involvements all over Europe, his income from Spain, the only source of revenue he could rely upon, decreased. He was therefore obliged to borrow, and by the end of his reign every single source of royal income was overpledged some years in advance. Whereas, at the beginning of his reign he had been able to borrow large sums at 6 to 8 per cent interest, in 1557 Philip was offering to pay up to 40 per cent for loans and had the greatest difficulty in finding takers. It is easy to see why, in that year, Philip had to take the drastic step of issuing the "First Decree," which suspended payments to creditors out of royal revenue, and issuing in their stead *juros,* a sort of life annuity paying 5 per cent interest. The device was an admission that the government was not able to pay its debts, and its effect on government credit was equivalent to a limited bankruptcy. All the gold and silver the mines of the New World could produce—three hundred tons a year —was unable to keep Spain solvent. The ambitions of Charles in the end not only watered the battlefields of Europe with the best blood of Spain, Italy, and the Lowlands, but ruined the economy and drained the spirit of the Spain he loved so much. The Emperor won most of the wars against his bitter rival the king of France; yet, whereas France emerged stronger at the end of almost a half century of war than at the beginning, Spain lay bankrupt and almost crushed.

France and Henry II

THE death of Henry VIII and of Francis I within two months of each other early in 1547 left only Charles of the trio of bright young monarchs who had contested the imperial title almost thirty years before. Henry was succeeded by his frail nine-year-old son, Edward VI, under a Protestant Protector. Francis' heir was his oldest surviving son, the somber and taciturn Henry II. Henry II had not agreed with his father in all matters, and had almost withdrawn from court during the last years of Francis' reign. But once on the throne he followed the same anti-Habsburg policy which had motivated his father for over thirty years, only more systematically and, for a decade, more successfully. He recalled Constable Anne de Montmorency, who had been out of favor with Francis for some years, and filled the *Conseil des affaires* with men whom Francis had not trusted. Henry II was robust and athletic rather than intellectual. His marriage to Catherine de' Medici had been a political match, arranged by Pope Clement VII to counter Charles V's predominance in Italy. He treated her with respect, appreciating her dignity and high political intelligence. Her conduct both before and after the ascension of Henry to the throne was admirable. Childless for the first ten years of the marriage, she thereafter bore the king ten children. The court of Henry, under Catherine's guidance, was brilliant and certainly more decorous than it had been under Francis. The king was deeply attached to Diane de Poitiers, a noblewoman whose husband had died in 1531. She was twenty years his senior, but he remained faithful to this attachment until his death; she, in turn, was considerate of the queen's feelings and prerogatives. It was due largely to her influence that he persecuted the Protestants so cruelly.

Henry may not have been as politically talented as his father, but he more than compensated by organizing French policy, something Francis had never done. Henry set up a department of foreign affairs in four sections under Montmorency, so that policy and diplomacy on France's several frontiers might be coordinated. Henry was guided in his foreign and domestic policies by a deep hatred of Charles V, a carry-over from the years of his brutal imprisonment in Madrid, and only slightly less strongly by a hatred of Protestantism. One of his first acts was to summon Charles V to his coronation as a vassal for

French fiefs. The Emperor answered that he would be glad to come—at the head of fifty thousand armed men. Neither side was ready to attack so soon in the new reign, but it was obvious that the treaty of Crépy had run its course. Henry would need all the ability he could command from any source to follow a policy of enmity against this wily and determined antagonist.

Montmorency brought with him to power a number of his relatives, the family of the Coligny. His sister Louise, by her first marriage, had a grandson, known to history as the prince de Condé, who was destined to be an important figure during the coming Wars of Religion. Her second marriage was to Gaspard de Coligny, marshal of France. Two of the children of this union later led the Huguenot cause: Odet, cardinal of Châtillon, and Gaspard II de Coligny, admiral of France. These men, closely bound by family ties and traditions, gave Montmorency valuable support in the years of transition from the rule of Francis to that of his sons. Montmorency was brusque, not tolerant of disagreement, and considered avaricious. He needed support from those who were more urbane and pliable. At the same time another powerful and ambitious house was making its bid for influence and position at the French court, the Guise family. The head of this house was Claude, duke of Lorraine and peer of France, married to Antoinette of Bourbon. His brother was Cardinal John of Lorraine, member of the Royal Council since 1530. Claude had six sons and four daughters. The oldest son, Francis, married to Anna d'Este, granddaughter of Louis XII and therefore connected with the royal house of France, succeeded Claude as head of the house of Guise in 1550. His brother Charles became cardinal of Lorraine,* and a third brother, also in the Church, became the cardinal of Guise. The oldest sister, Marie, married James V, king of Scotland, whose daughter Mary Stuart was beheaded at Queen Elizabeth I's order in 1588. Thus related to two royal houses, of France and Scotland, the Guises naturally sought high place in France. Among them were men and women of great ability. Duke Francis was a military commander of stature. Charles, cardinal of Lorraine, was an adept politician and ecclesiastical administrator. The history of France for the next forty years is to be in large measure affected by the rivalries between these two powerful families, the one loyally Protestant, the other passionately Catholic. In the ultimate struggle, neither family won out; a third, related by marriage to the Montmorency-Coligny-Châtillon group, ascended the throne in the person of Henry IV.

When Henry II came to the throne in 1547, Boulogne was still in English hands. Mary Stuart, the six-year-old daughter of Marie de Guise (Lorraine), was queen of Scotland under the regency of her mother. At the threat of an English invasion Marie de Guise asked Henry II for help. Fearing the English might carry out their rumored plan to marry Mary Stuart to the young Edward VI, Henry sent a fleet and six thousand troops to Scotland and brought the child safely to France (August 20, 1548). Soon thereafter Henry and Montmorency easily took Boulogne; the government of Edward VI, in trouble at home and on the Scottish border, gave up the port for 400,000 écus (treaty of Boulogne, March 29, 1550). Henry II had peace on the English front until the death of Edward VI in 1553.

* The term, inexact in itself, was in common use.

The imperial front, at the beginning of Henry's rule, was not encouraging. Charles had crushed the Protestant forces of the Schmalkaldic League at the battle of Mühlberg (April 24, 1547) and had taken John Frederick, Elector of Saxony, prisoner. In Italy Charles' position was favorable; Florence and Milan were strongholds of his influence. There were, however, weak spots in the Habsburgs' armor.

A continual source of concern to Charles was the imperial succession. The Emperor had always envisaged the maintenance of Habsburg power in the hands of one ruler as the best guarantee of European peace and the Christian faith. He wanted to have his son Philip named by the electors as Ferdinand's successor. There was nothing unusual in a return to the hereditary principle. Ferdinand, however, objected strenuously to Philip's succession; and he knew what Charles seemed never to realize, that the Germans hated the Spanish and had resented Charles' Spanish advisers and the Emperor's efforts to tie Germany to the kingdom of Spain. The family quarrel was public knowledge and Charles' sister Mary was asked to bring peace between the brothers. Her success was only moderate; in the end the decision of the brothers as to the succession proved pointless. The electors, having no intention of abdicating their powers or responsibilities, in 1562 elected Maximilian to succeed Ferdinand as King of the Romans, to become Emperor two years later.

Charles and the Papacy

THE Emperor's relations with Pope Paul III were bad. On few occasions in his life did Charles lose his equanimity, but when it came to discussions with the papal legate (the Pope's grandson) and the nuncio, his temper grew very short. He accused the Pope of working for the French; he complained that the few Italian troops the Pope had sent to help him in his war with the Protestant League were criminal scum and robbers; he was bitter that the Pope had transferred the Council from Trent to Bologna (see below, Chapter 21) in order to keep it under his control, thus removing any possibility of gaining Protestant attendance or adherence; the Pope had refused permission for Charles to take half of the ecclesiastical plate and of the annual repair fund of churches and monasteries in Spain for his military needs against the Protestants. After one of these conferences the nuncio wrote: "I have never heard the Emperor use such biting language."

The Pontiff, on his side, had some grounds for complaint. He was angry with Charles for having given in to the German princes by the Augsburg Interim of 1548. All the Pope's overtures for peace and all the efforts of his legates to win Charles' support for the Council were spurned by Charles' envoys. The crowning incident was the assassination of the Pope's son, Pier Luigi Farnese, despot of Piacenza, at the orders of the imperial viceroy of Milan, Ferrante Gonzaga (September 1547). Charles may not have ordered or even permitted the murder, but he did not disavow his viceroy, nor did he apologize to the Pope. He certainly shared some responsibility. The Pope immediately assumed that Charles was involved in the crime, and was determined to get a revenge which would have as its justification Charles' opposition to papal policy in Italy, particularly in Piacenza, as well as the murder of his son. Unable of his own power to punish Charles, he sought help from France and Venice as well as from the Swiss, and the Medici in Florence were approached. This all took time, and the Emperor, away at the Diet of Augsburg, seemed not to be disturbed at the thought that his many enemies might band against him. It is more than likely he fully realized that the interests of the various powers were so different and conflicting that they would never be able to form any effective coalition against him. Much time was frittered away by Paul III in negotiations with possible allies; at the time of the Pope's death, November 10, 1549, the predominance of Charles in Italy was still unquestioned.

Charles V and Henry II

ALTHOUGH Charles was at the height of his power in 1548 and 1549, because of his victory over the German Protestants and his strong position in Italy, he was not without depressing experiences. He was so ill with the gout that he found it advisable to write a long testamentary letter to Philip, much in the manner of a father who feels his end near. To add to his woes, he and his brother Ferdinand had several sharp disagreements over the handling of the Turkish threat prompted by Ferdinand's repeated calls for help to conquer Transylvania. The Emperor was also kept informed of the diplomatic and military preparations of the young Henry II for a final decision with Spain. It was clear that Henry was determined to take up the war where his father had left it, and Charles dreaded the continuation of a bitter struggle which he thought he had already won.

There were small irritations on both sides, but the real cause for the renewal of the struggle was Henry's initiative in supporting the German Protestants against the Emperor. Negotiations began in 1550, after England and France had settled the matter of Boulogne. Henry's agents signed with Maurice, Elector of Saxony, known to be ready to leave the imperial camp, a preliminary secret agreement at Lochau in October 1551. Other German Protestant princes were approached later that year, with the result that Henry was asked officially to provide aid against the aggressive actions of the Emperor. Henry agreed to help them "to recover the liberty of their German fatherland." Signed at Chambord, January 15, 1552, this treaty put Henry, a fervent Catholic and a persecutor of Protestants in France, openly on the side of the German Protestant princes and cities. He engaged, furthermore, to provide a substantial subsidy for their use. In return for his help he was to receive the cities of Cambrai, Metz, Toul, and Verdun, as "vicar of the Empire." Both sides, while protesting a fervent desire for peace, were gathering troops and munitions in hurried preparation for war.

The war which everyone knew was inevitable had broken out first in Italy. It was war by indirection. The specific object of the Italian phase of the war was Parma, a papal fief of which Ottavio Farnese, an ally of Henry II, was in possession. On May 22, 1551, Julius declared Farnese to have forfeited the fief. Farnese invaded the Papal States, but was defeated in a battle by papal troops, who then joined the imperial army under Ferrante Gonzaga, whereupon the latter took full command of the combined papal and imperial operations. Both

Henry and Charles piously protested that they had not violated the peace of Crépy and were only acting in support of their respective allies. Julius III was not the man to handle a war as confused as the one upon which he had entered, and his treasury was empty. He was easily persuaded to try to negotiate his way out of his predicament. Henry's envoy, Cardinal Tournon, a shrewd and firm diplomat, obtained favorable terms for a two years' armistice. Parma remained in Farnese's hands (April 29, 1552).

The Italian operations were, from the point of view of Henry's basic plans, camouflage, or at best diversionary. Henry had in his own mind given up the Italian dreams of his ancestors. But it could hardly hurt to make the demands anyway. He planned, very wisely, to concentrate on the northern and eastern frontiers, where chances of ultimate victory or of territorial gains were better. He set out for his eastern lands with an army of forty thousand. He was welcomed at Toul and Nancy, and took Metz by a ruse. Instead of stopping there, according to the terms of the treaty of Chambord, he marched on to the Rhine. Strassburg refused him entry; at Speier he was told he could come in alone to see the city as a tourist. Henry correctly understood the signs of German antagonism to further French progress and discreetly withdrew. In the meantime, at Ferdinand's urging, Charles was reluctantly coming to a temporary agreement with the Lutherans at Passau (August 2, 1552), the better to be able to turn all his forces against France. He ordered troops gathered on the Upper Danube, while he stayed at Augsburg. Henry, divining the plans of Charles to recover the four imperial cities, sent Francis, duke of Guise, to defend Metz, a large city at the confluence of the Moselle and the Seille rivers and well situated for defense. With the aid of engineers and practiced artillerymen he made the city almost impregnable. He had a garrison of ten thousand troops, well provisioned and of high morale. The duke of Alva camped outside the city on October 19, 1552, and was soon reinforced by Albert of Brandenburg, a mercenary brigand with 18,000 soldiers and 40 cannon. The Emperor joined the attack on November 20 with additional troops, bringing the total of besiegers to about 75,000 men. The defense was firm and well handled, and the besiegers could not break it. Charles, in despair, lifted the siege on December 26. His losses, from artillery fire, desertion, disease, and exposure, were exceedingly heavy. In Guise a new and heroic figure came upon the scene. He had conducted the French defense against much larger forces confidently, intelligently, and coolly.

Henry's generals in Italy, operating for the most part in support of his Italian allies, had minor successes and some defeats, but mostly their purpose was to irritate Charles and immobilize parts of his armed forces. The real war was on the northeastern frontier of France. Montmorency had there an army of fifty thousand but, in his usual way, avoided any decisive engagement. A siege of Valenciennes was precipitately raised when the imperial forces made a sortie in strength. The next year, 1554, near Brussels, the Constable retreated before an imperial army led by Emmanuel Philibert of Savoy. In August the Emperor lost heavily at Renty in Artois, which he was trying to relieve. For the French it was an empty victory for which, furthermore, Montmorency was in no wise responsible. It was again a personal victory for the duke of Guise. Popular opinion was indignant at the conduct of Montmorency. The Venetian ambassador spoke of him as "pusillanimous and craven," diplomatic words for "cowardly." Henry's repute was intimately involved because he retained Montmorency in supreme command against everybody's better judgment when he had so often proven himself incapable. The Emperor, tired, sick, and frustrated, was already contemplating abdication. He went from Renty to Brussels, where he arrived on October 18. Henry, on his part, harassed by intrigues at court and loud protests against the heavy taxes which he had to levy on a country whose commerce was depressed, uncertain as to the results of French involvement in imperial affairs, was ready to talk peace. Envoys of the Emperor and Henry met in the late summer of 1555. Both sides were stubborn. Peace was finally arrived at only in February 1556 at Vaucelles. Henry's principal negotiator, tough, bland, and wily, was Montmorency's nephew, Gaspard de Coligny, now admiral of France and governor of Picardy and Artois. The peace was essentially a five-year truce, each side leaving the other in possession of its holdings as of the date of its conclusion.

The Abdication of Charles

THE Charles who had agreed to the peace, at fifty-three years of age, was an infirm and feeble man, painfully crippled by the gout, his hands so afflicted that he was hardly able to open a letter. At court rumors had been for some time rife that he was planning to turn over many of his arduous duties to Philip. In September Philip arrived in Brussels from London, where he had just recently married Queen Mary Tudor. On October 25 Charles turned over the sovereignty of the Low Countries to his son. He waited three months before transferring to Philip the crowns of Spain, Sicily, and the Spanish possessions beyond the seas (January 16, 1556). At the Brussels ceremony, solemn and impressive, Charles leaned on the shoulder of the young William of Nassau, who, as William the Silent, prince of Orange, was to wrest the freedom of the northern Lowlands provinces from Charles' son. Charles retained the title of Emperor while the real governance of the Empire, so far as there was any governance, was in the hands of Ferdinand. Charles sailed for Spain and the monastery of Yuste, where he died two years later (September 21, 1558). He had been, in the estimate of friend and foe, one of the greatest rulers in history, worthy to be classed with Augustus and Charlemagne.

With the abdication of Charles the pressure on France was somewhat relieved. To a large extent the aggressive diplomacy of Henry II, in allying in 1552 with the German Protestant princes and cities, the flexibility of French policy in Italy, and the diminution of the English threat under the strongly Protestant rule of Edward VI, brought France in the mid-1550's to a strong position. In 1552 Pope Julius III began to veer away from his earlier pro-imperial policy; when he died (1555), he was succeeded * by Paul IV (Pietro Caraffa), a Neapolitan and a bitter enemy of Spain. Henry thus had an ally in Italy where before had been an enemy. The new Pope soon called for French help against the Spaniards, "that scum of the earth," as he called them.

* The intervening pontificate of Marcellus II of twenty days, April 11–30, 1555, had no political significance.

His chances of success thus improved on his southern front, Henry had the duke of Guise take an army across the Alps in late December 1556, and a fortnight later Coligny attacked the Spanish around Douai. Action having already been begun at the two extremes of the front, Italy and the Lowlands, war was declared on January 31, 1557. The truce of Vaucelles had lasted barely a year. In Italy Guise rapidly approached Rome, and the Spanish withdrew. The Pope, taking advantage of the presence of French troops which put the Spaniards on the defensive, made a separate peace with the Spanish in September 1557. Guise, baffled and disgusted by Italian intrigue, was recalled to France, where, in the meantime, a decisive military engagement had taken place.

St. Quentin

MILITARY action in the north of France from the rupture of the truce of Vaucelles in the winter of 1556 had been rather tentative on both sides. Philip II's wife, Mary Tudor, declared war on France on June 7, 1557, and put 8000 soldiers at Philip's disposal. In July Emmanuel Philibert of Savoy, one of the ablest of Philip's generals, with an army of 60,000 men, began maneuvering. He first laid siege to the town of Guise in Picardy, then suddenly moved southwest to St. Quentin, on the Somme River. Coligny, with a small force, entered the city to defend it. The constable, Montmorency, came to his aid with a considerable army, but handled the movement and transport of his units so awkwardly as to expose his whole force to the rapid flanking attack of Emmanuel's well-drilled cavalry (August 10, 1557). The result was a massacre: 3000 French dead, 4000 to 5000 wounded and prisoners. Montmorency, who was responsible for the catastrophe, and other high-ranking French officers were captured. It was feared and expected that Philibert would move directly on Paris. There seemed to be nothing in his way. But he did not leave the environs of St. Quentin, probably because of the lack of provisions in enemy territory.

Coligny, meanwhile, was still defending the battered city. The walls had been breached in a dozen places by the big siege guns, and food and supplies soon ran short. The mayor and most of the seven thousand citizens of the city were loyal and tenacious, but bravery was not enough. On August 27, two weeks after the defeat of Montmorency, the weakened and beleaguered city was taken by a sudden assault in force. The usual brutalities of pillage and murder by the attacking Spanish troops followed. The long defense of the city was not, however, completely lost; it had given Henry time to gather around Paris a new army which was to be put under the command of the duke of Guise, recently recalled from Italy. Henry had spent his last sou, but the city of Paris immediately voted the king 300,000 livres and enthusiastically undertook its own defense. Guise arrived in Paris on October 6 and took charge as lieutenant-general of the kingdom with wide powers. At this point the family of Montmorency-Coligny and the Bourbons was painfully in eclipse, while the Guises were riding the crest of royal and public favor.

Guise decided on a counterblow which would soften the sting of the disaster of St. Quentin. Calais was still in English hands. The idea of taking it from the ancient enemy was not new, but the execution of it was the merit of Guise.

He planned every detail of the action himself, over a period of two months—November and December 1557—and on the last day of that year his troops surrounded the city. The English commander had warned Queen Mary that the French preparations were under way, but no attention was paid to his warnings. The first outlying fort was taken on January 1, 1558; three days later the citadel of the city was in French hands, and on the seventh the English commander surrendered. On the twentieth Guines, a smaller town five miles inland, south of Calais, was taken, and the English were finally and completely out of France. There was jubilation throughout the kingdom; both Guise and the king were the heroes of the nation.

The Treaty of Câteau-Cambrésis

IT SEEMED a good time to make peace with Spain. Both the principal adversaries, France and Spain, were tired of war and, furthermore, in great financial straits. The last engagement of the northern phase of the war was the battle of Gravelines (April 22, 1558) between the combined Spanish and Dutch forces under the dashing Flemish general, Count Egmont, and a French force under de Termes. Flemish steadiness won the day. The French army was annihilated and the French general captured. The main French force under Guise was not, however, involved, and the Spanish victory at Gravelines, although humiliating to the French, was only the last of a string of French defeats. Beyond providing a precipitant for a peace, it did not greatly alter the course of negotiation then under way.

The preliminary negotiations, during which everybody jockeyed for position, had been long drawn out. It was not until September 1558 that all the envoys met face to face. The principal envoys for Spain were the duke of Alva, William of Orange-Nassau, and Cardinal Granvelle; for France, the Constable Montmorency, Marshal St. André, and Cardinal Guise of Lorraine, the former two recently released from prison to represent the French king. Mary Tudor sent envoys, but their influence was not noticeable, and after her death (November 28, 1558) her successor, Elizabeth, replaced them with men of her own choosing. The first knotty problem was Calais, just recently captured from the English. France was anxious to have Calais unconditionally. The result of this part of the discussion was a compromise (April 2, 1559), accepted by Elizabeth. France was to hold Calais for eight years, at the end of which time the city was to be returned to England or France would pay a compensation of 100,000 gold crowns. The next day agreement was reached on the larger question at issue. The total settlement is known as the Treaty of Câteau-Cambrésis. A number of dynastic marriages were arranged. Elizabeth, Henry II's young daughter, was to marry Philip II, recently widowed by the death of Mary Tudor. Marguerite, Henry's sister, was to marry Emmanuel Philibert, taking with her as her dowry Piedmont and Savoy, then occupied by French troops. France recovered St. Quentin and other north French cities but gave up a few strongholds on the Flemish frontier. Although they were imperial cities and did not therefore concern Spain, Henry insisted on retaining the three bishoprics, Metz, Toul, and Verdun, and Ferdinand finally yielded. In Italy France gave up Siena to the Medici duke of Tuscany, and withdrew completely from the duchy. France ceded Corsica to Genoa and withdrew from Montferrat, the Milanese, and the Piedmont, but was to keep garrisons in Turin and four other fortresses. The Savoy settlement was accommodated in the marriage between Philibert and Marguerite. In all, France gave up 189 fortified posts in Italy. French opinion, while relieved at the conclusion of a peace, was generally indignant at what seemed so broad a surrender and blamed Montmorency and St. André for making such large concessions to the Spaniards in order to assure their personal freedom from imprisonment. Neither side could, in fact, have pursued the war through another campaign.

This treaty is one of the most significant in French history. By it a momentous decision was made. France had decided to accept the Savoyard Alps as her southeastern boundary and to give up her Italian dreams. Spain, on the other hand, also accepted the limitations of her natural peninsular frontiers while retaining her predominance in Italy. Yet Italy, in a degree, also gained. Her territorial, peninsular, if not her political, unity was recognized. The peninsula was yet to be the scene of much political strife, but two of the foreign contestants for control of part or all of Italy had essentially withdrawn: the Empire and France. Henceforth there was to be only one dominant foreign power, Spain, and several native powers, Milan, Venice, Tuscany, Naples, and the Papacy. The course of this intrapeninsular struggle is, for the moment, less significant for us than the withdrawal of the two great northern powers, France and the Empire, and the consequent realignment of the factors in the struggle for the European balance of power.

Hardly less important than the consolidation and delimitation of the territory of France was the related straightening of the boundaries of the Netherlands. Late in the following century a successor of Henry II, Louis XIV, was to attempt to push French possessions beyond these limits, but until that time the French-Dutch frontier was generally constant. A not unimportant feature of the treaty was the fact that the Empire was not a party to it. The whole period of the struggle between the Habsburgs and the house of Valois had been marked by Charles' use of his imperial power to attempt to crush France. His abdication marked the failure of that policy and plan, and from 1556 France could breathe easier. The peace of 1559 was a further gain in security as it became evident that the Empire and Spain not only no longer obeyed one will, antagonistic to French interests, but frequently had opposing interests, and France could profit by helping to widen the breach.

Apart from the political and military agreements in this momentous treaty there was another area of agreement between Philip and Henry that was closely related to the religious wars which were to plague France and the Lowlands in the second half of the century. The two monarchs prefaced the whole treaty with the declaration that they were mutually determined to devote their energies henceforth to the maintenance of the Holy Catholic faith and the uprooting of the increasingly pestilential heresy of Protestantism. To assure fulfillment of the many conditions of the treaty, Philip gave into Henry's hands four hostages: William, prince of Orange, the duke of Alva, the count of Egmont, and the duke of Aerschot. It would have been difficult to choose individuals whose futures were more dramatically bound together than the first three of these noblemen. Shortly thereafter, during a royal hunt in the Bois de Vincennes near Paris, Henry II was riding beside William. Assuming that William, known to be close to Philip as a royal councilor, was informed of the plans the two monarchs had agreed on to exterminate heresy and the heretics, Henry launched into a detailed description of ways and means of accomplishing the purification of Henry's France and Philip's Lowlands. William, from whom the plans had been kept by Philip, listened attentively, leading Henry on by question and apparent agreement until he had the whole story. The revelation shocked him, but it also determined the course of his life and the ultimate loss to Spain of the Lowlands. By his careful restraint on this occasion William gained the sobriquet of "the Silent." Philip was to have adequate reason to regret the indiscretion of his brother monarch.

It has been remarked above how events in Europe entered a new phase about the year 1547, when, within a short while, a group of important characters were removed from the scene by death: Martin Luther, Henry VIII, Francis I, and Pope Paul III. From some points of view the year 1558–59 was an even more important watershed of history. Charles V died in the monastery of Yuste on September 21, 1558. A month later his sister, Mary of Hungary, died on the way to take up again her duties as regent of the Lowlands. On November 17 Mary Tudor of England and Cardinal Reginald Pole both passed to their reward within a few hours of each other, and with them expired the English Catholic revival. On July 10, 1559, Henry II died of a splinter from a broken lance which had pierced his brain in a joust. The extermination of heresy which Henry and Philip had mutually sworn to bring about was going to have to wait some time in France. In Spain Philip was having notable success. In Valladolid on October 8 he burned fourteen heretics alive. A few days later in Seville, he burned fifty more. It was a beginning. It appeared that the very forces that brought a political peace to western Europe were destined to usher in a period of bitter religious persecution and equally bitter resistance.

SUGGESTIONS FOR FURTHER READING

ADY, C., *Milan under the Sforza*. London, 1907

ARMSTRONG, E., *Emperor Charles V*. 2 vols. London, 1902

BATIFFOL, L., *The Century of the Renaissance*. London, 1916

BRANDI, K., *Charles V* (Vol. I of German original), trans. C. V. Wedgwood. London, 1939

CHUDOBA, B., *Spain and the Empire, 1519–1643*. Chicago, 1952

DAVIES, R. T., *The Golden Age of Spain*. London, 1937

MERRIMAN, R. B., *Rise of the Spanish Empire*. Vol. II, *The Catholic Kings;* Vol. III, *The Emperor*. New York, 1925

MORETON-MACDONALD, J. R. M., *A History of France*. New York, 1915

MOWAT, R. B., *A History of European Diplomacy, 1451–1789*. London, 1928

RANKE, L. VON, *The History of the Popes*. 3 vols. London, 1913

RANKE, L. VON, *The Latin and Teutonic Nations*. London, 1887

ROBERTSON, W., *A History of the Reign of the Emperor Charles the Fifth*. Philadelphia, 1902

Habsburg and Valois: France Fights Encirclement

SETON-WATSON, R. W., *Maximilian I*. London, 1902
TYLER, R., *The Emperor Charles V*. London, 1956

BABELON, J., *Charles-Quint*. 1947
BRANDI, K., *Kaiser Karl V: Werden und Schicksal einer Persönlichkeit*. 2 vols. 1941
BRAUDEL, F., *La Méditerranée à l'époque de Philippe II*. 1949
CARDAUNS, L., *Paul III, Karl V und Franz I, 1535–1536*. 1908
COSCI, A., *L'Italia durante le preponderanze straniere (1530–1789)*. 1875–78
FUETER, E., *Geschichte des europäischen Staatensystems von 1492–1559*. 1915
HAUSER, H., *La Prépondérance espagnole 1559–1660*. 1933
HAUSER, H., and A. RENAUDET, *Les Débuts de l'âge moderne*. 1929
KALKOFF, P., *Die Kaiserwahl Friedrichs IV und Karls V*. 1925
MIGNET, F. M. W., *Rivalité de François Ier et Charles V*. 2 vols. 1875
QUAZZA, R., *Preponderanza spagnuola*. 1950
RASSOW, P., *Die Kaiser-Idee Karls V*. 1932
ZELLER, G., *Henri II et Charles-Quint, 1552–1555*. 1940

CHAPTER TWENTY

ENGLAND AND THE REFORMATION: CALVIN AND FRENCH PROTESTANTISM

Thε revolt against the Catholic Church took varying forms in the several countries of Europe, depending largely upon the background of opposition or loyalty to the established ecclesiastical organization. This, in turn, depended upon many factors: proximity to Rome, as in Italy; the personal convictions or loyalties of the ruling house, as in Spain; traditions of independence from external control, as in Bohemia; a single dynamic personality who might by himself precipitate or quell a religious revolt, as, in part at least, in Germany. We shall, in this chapter, see how the spiritual and intellectual crisis that we call the European Reformation developed in two of the strongest countries of Europe, England and France. In both countries, political and social forces had significant influence within and upon a movement that was ostensibly religious and theological.

ENGLAND AND THE REFORMATION

In 1453 England was driven from the continent of Europe, save for the port of Calais, by a resurgent and reinvigorated France. For thirty years thereafter, England was prevented by civil strife from participating in Continental affairs. But the ascension of the Tudor dynasty to the throne in the person of Henry VII ushered in a new era in European political history. From 1485 to the death of Elizabeth I in 1603, almost without interruption, England, safe in her island fortress, wielded even more power than she had when an English monarch had ruled half of France. Henry VII, faced with the strong and ambitious France created by Louis XI, chose to ally with Spain. After his death, his son, Henry VIII, maintained the alliance against France until the growing strength of Charles V made such an alignment dangerous. Henry then cooled toward Spain and drew closer to France.

The flexibility which allowed England to maintain the balance of power in Europe has been the guiding thread of English policy from Henry's time to the present. It was more than a policy; it became a national temperament. It was manifested in English commerce, in the adaptation of changes in Continental institutions to England's needs, in her own constitutional development, in her literature and art, and, far from least, in her religious and ecclesiastical life. It is this last, so prominent in the days of the Tudors, with which we are here concerned. However, it should be pointed out in passing that all phases of English life and institutions—art, letters, constitutional structure, commerce and industry, society, and even philosophical thought—were closely inter-involved in the English Reformation during the Tudor age, as, in fact, they have been throughout English history.

The Church in England

THE English church on the eve of the Reformation was not greatly different in structure from the Church in other countries, under the Pope at Rome. After the decisive suppression of the Wyclyfite and Lollard movement early in the fifteenth century, the supremacy of the Roman see in matters of dogma was unchallenged. On the other hand, since William the Conqueror, the crown had gradually built up a tradition of firm if unprovocative control of the English church through its virtually unquestioned right to nominate bishops. The Papacy, disturbed and weakened by the Conciliar Movement and rising nationalism on the Continent, was in no position to press for a stronger foot-hold in England. Any papal claim to temporal sovereignty in an England which had successfully repudiated the Peter's Pence and was proud of its statutes of *Provisors* and *Praemunire* would have been treated with contempt. It is necessary to appreciate this situation in order to understand how Henry VIII was able to bring about a revolution in the relations between state and Church with such relative ease.

The interference of the Papacy in the internal affairs of the Church was markedly less in England than in Germany. Nevertheless, reformers found much to attack within the English church. The laity was generally at the mercy of the clergy, which, judging from the complaints frequently voiced on the floor of Parliament, often used their canonical powers arbitrarily. Objections to the luxury and immorality of the clergy were too insistent to be disregarded. The clergy were numerous and the Church wielded great economic influence, owning at least one-third of the land of England and perhaps one-fifth of the nation's total wealth. The clergy were not subject to the ordinary civil courts; if apprehended in a crime, they were handed over to a bishop, whose sentence would certainly be lighter than that of a royal court. This exemption from civil jurisdiction—"benefit of clergy"—naturally bred resentment among the people, resentment which grew as the burghers gained in position and substance. Men who had won financial independence by their own aggressive efforts now wanted commensurate legal and social recognition. If the Church and its canon law stood in the way, so much the worse for the Church.

But their relative independence from and, in certain quarters, resentment toward the Church did not mean that the English were opposed to religion. Foreign visitors to England in the early sixteenth century remarked upon the piety of the common people. The parish churches were well attended; the interiors of the chapels and churches were amply supplied with crucifixes, silver and gold vessels, censers, and other evidences of the devotion of the parishioners to the local center of their religious life. This devotion was probably not on a high intellectual level; the religious literacy of the laity in England at this time was fairly low, judging from the fact that there was no translation of the Bible printed in England before 1535, whereas in Germany there were at least seventeen printings of the Bible in German before Luther's New Testament in 1522. There were, of course, religious books published in England before the outbreak of the Reformation, but these were pietistic in nature—e.g., legendary lives of saints and collections of homilies for the use of priests who were unable or unwilling to write their own sermons. Yet, all in all, the religious disposition in England was sufficiently widespread and deep-rooted to respond enthusiastically, when the time came, to the appeal of a popular ruler such as Henry VIII. From the numerous instances of trials for heresy recorded before the outbreak of the Reformation, some of which are clearly vestigial Lollardy, we may reasonably deduce that the evangelicalism of Wyclyf had left some traces among the common folk.

The hierarchy of the English church was in large measure political in nature. Many of the bishops and abbots were university graduates and men of great learning, but their advancement tended to depend on their potential usefulness to the crown rather than on their learning or piety. A few, under Henry VII, were chosen from noble families or relatives of the monarch, but most of the prelates were members of the yeomanry or the gentry class who, by diplomatic and administrative ability, had risen to positions of responsibility and trust. The lucrative positions in the Church were given them as compensation for their services; the crown thus paid its highest civil servants with Church appointments. Since these dignitaries were quite likely to continue to serve the interests of the prince who had appointed them, the monarch had the potential support of a great majority of the dominant personalities of the English church. There were exceptions in the course of the Reformation, but in general the relation between the higher clergy and the crown was one of *quid pro quo,* payment for services rendered.

Echoes of Lutheranism in England

THE Lutheran outbreak in Germany in 1517 did not go unnoticed in England. Some of Luther's works soon spread widely, and in some quarters aroused great enthusiasm. From Germany, whose trade with England was heavy, and also from the Lowlands, a traditional home of religious radicalism, news of the German struggle against the Church filtered into England. The king himself, paradoxically, helped to disseminate Luther's ideas and to emphasize the importance of his break with Rome by writing and publishing (1521) an extensive reply to Luther's *On the Babylonian Captivity of the Church,* which was widely circulated both in Latin and in English. As a reward for Henry's learned orthodoxy, Pope Leo X conferred on him the title "Defender of the Faith." Luther's answer was phrased in such vigorous terms that Henry felt it beneath his royal dignity to reply; however, he asked Sir Thomas More to do so. More, under a pseudonym, wrote (1523) in terms fully as scurrilous as those Luther had used. John Fisher, bishop of Rochester, entered the fray on the side of orthodoxy in treatises published in Paris and Cologne. The exchange focused the attention of all England upon the importance of doctrine in the dispute, and for several years thereafter all the points of Lutheran teaching in conflict with orthodox Catholicism were heatedly discussed.

It was at this time that William Tyndale suddenly became a prominent factor in English religious evolution. Tyndale was an Oxford don who moved to Cambridge, where he came into contact with a group of scholars who had begun to discuss the new ideas from across the sea. They met informally and irregularly at the White Horse Inn; the nature of their discussion was such that the Inn was soon called "Little Germany." Tyndale, rebuffed in England, left in 1524 for Germany. In Wittenberg he translated the New Testament into English, basing his work on Erasmus' text. Some six thousand copies were printed, with interruptions, at Cologne and Worms in 1526. The prologues to each of the books of the New Testament are essentially translations from those of Luther, so that English readers were presented with the Gospel in a Lutheran framework. The translation was an immediate best seller. Tunstall, the humanist bishop of London and keeper of the Privy Seal, condemned the author and the work from the pulpit. As a group, the bishops condemned, bought up, and burned the book. Like most such campaigns, this one made the book even more sought after; pirated editions, printed in the Lowlands, sold faster than the bishops could buy them up. Booksellers and colporteurs were willing to take great risks to realize the profits from so popular a piece of merchandise. The appeal to the Scriptures, similar to that of Luther in Germany, may not have been highly theological, but it was effective. There was a certain anomaly in the position of a Christian bishop presiding over the burning of the Christian Scriptures that could hardly have escaped the simplest peasant. Other works of Tyndale were pursued with equal rigor, and Cardinal Thomas Wolsey thought him important enough to request the government of the Lowlands to extradite him to England. Nothing that he wrote or said, however, was so effective as his translation of the New Testament in preparing the way for the English Reformation.

The peculiar conditions of conglomerate Germany which influenced Luther's thought were absent in insular and essentially united England. Yet there were circles in England in which Lutheran teachings were congenial. In the 1520's criticism of the Church increased and there was growing popular support for a movement of reform. On the other hand, the ancient autonomy of the English church, English isolation from the Continent and its disturbances, plus a traditional disposition on the part of the English to settle their own affairs combined to offset the impact of Lutheran and Continental reform ideas. It is possible that England would have remained, like France, within the fold of the Roman Catholic Church had it not been for the attempts of Henry VIII, beginning in about 1527, to dissolve his marriage to his brother's widow, Catherine of Aragon.

Henry VIII's Divorce

IN THAT year, Henry first brought up the subject in a message to Pope Clement VII asking that the marriage be dissolved on the ground that it had been contrary to the Scriptures and canon law, since Catherine had been his brother's wife and was therefore his own "sister." Of the several children Catherine had borne him, only a girl, Mary, had survived. Henry came to look upon his lack of a male heir as Heaven's judgment against his marriage to his "sister." It is quite probable that Henry's conscience did in fact trouble him, but there were other and no less compelling factors in his decision to dissolve his marriage to Catherine. The Tudor line had only a short history, preceded by a century of dynastic troubles culminating in the bitter Wars of the Roses. Any doubt as to the succession in a line which owed its position to the fortunes of the battlefield might bring a recurrence of civil war. Henry therefore felt that he had to have a male heir—and soon, so that he could be properly trained for his task as his father's successor and accepted by the English people. Since Catherine was apparently unable to give him a son, Henry was determined to become free to marry someone who could.

Henry's minister, Cardinal Wolsey, conceived the strategy by which Henry hoped to achieve his ends with papal approval, but his plans became involved in a maze of European diplomacy and power politics. After the sack of Rome by imperial forces in May 1527, Pope Clement VII was not a free agent and could not grant so drastic a request even if he had wished to do so. Charles V, who, as Catherine's nephew, naturally opposed Henry's plan, was the master of Italy and Clement's virtual jailer. The Pope was thus caught between Henry's demands and Charles' power. Cardinal Wolsey then effected a realignment of England and France, and in April 1528, when French arms were for a time successful in Italy, the Pope appointed Wolsey and Cardinal Campeggio as legates to hear Henry's suit in London. Campeggio was under secret orders from the Pope to delay matters as long as possible.

The favorable political atmosphere on the Continent lasted only a short time. The French armies in Italy were soon retreating, and with them vanished the value to England of the French alliance. The Pope was again in Charles' camp, with Henry's opponents, and the likelihood that the king's suit would have a favorable outcome before the legatine court in London diminished. The suit dragged on through the spring and summer of 1529. Catherine, fighting for her rights as queen, defended herself nobly and forthrightly, then withdrew from court. Henry's legal case depended on the validity of the dispensation by Julius II which had permitted the marriage in the first place, and this point could not be agreed upon. Before the course of the suit could force him to make a decision, Campeggio suddenly (July 23, 1529) suspended the court and adjourned it until October, when it was to meet in Rome, far from English influence. Henry thus lost his last chance to obtain the annulment within the framework of the Roman Church. He had already, through his envoy at Rome, hinted that England might withdraw her support from the Papacy. The events of the preceding twelve years in Germany, when much of the Empire had broken from Rome, made such a threat, however veiled, a serious one.

Campeggio's reports from London to the *curia* reveal his astonishment at the overt currency of Lutheran literature and views at the royal court and the familiarity of the English public with events in Germany. He reported conversations in which it was suggested that the crown might take over the Church's property. The king had even quoted to him—with obvious approval—Lutheran doctrines on the primacy of the prince over the Church. His point was not lost on the cardinal, who relayed it immediately to Rome.

Until the removal of the legatine court from London, Henry had proceeded as a good and obedient Catholic prince. He now became an open and determined enemy of the Church. The peace of Cambrai (August 3, 1529) among Francis I of France, Charles V of Spain and the Empire, and the Pope was an alliance of Henry's enemies and meant that Wolsey's strategy, aimed at preserving the balance between France and Spain, had failed. Consequently, Henry's divorce from Catherine would have to be obtained—if, indeed, it could be obtained at all—on English soil and with English means. Since Wolsey's policy had failed, it was clear that its author would have to be removed. On October 9, 1529, Wolsey was indicted in the King's Bench under the act of *Praemunire,* which forbade any English subject to accept an appointment from the Papacy in derogation of the king's authority. The cardinal was summarily dismissed from the office of chancellor. Ironically, it was Henry who had obtained the position of legate for him. Wolsey asked the king to take all his land and wealth to compensate for his failures. A move to punish him further by an act of attainder was unsuccessful; Henry did not want or need to go so far. Wolsey retired to the Archbishopric of York, whence he was summoned, in October 1530, to answer charges of high treason. He died on the trip to London, at Leicester Abbey. His famous words on learning of the fate in store for him—"If I had served God as diligently as I have served the King, He would not have deserted me in my grey hairs"—as a commentary on his career, do not do him complete justice. Although he was a high-placed churchman, he was so occupied with secular affairs that he had no time for his ecclesiastical duties. He labored brilliantly and loyally for the aggrandizement of his master, who turned upon him when plans and plots which Henry had himself approved and participated in went awry. His undoubtedly great qualities, which might have been directed toward higher aims for England's welfare, were largely wasted in pursuit of Henry's goal of divorcing Catherine and siring a male heir. Yet in spite of obvious shortcomings, Wolsey's work was in large measure responsible for the concentration of powers in the hands of the crown. This concentration, in turn, was the real contribution of the Tudor monarchy to England's greatest period. England rose from a second-rate to a first-rate power in this century, and much of the credit for this surge must be given to Wolsey.

The next step in Henry's attempt to ensure the continuance of the Tudor line was to seek extraclerical confirmation of the illegality of the dispensation under which he had married Catherine. Following the suggestion of Thomas Cranmer, then only a Cambridge don, the king proceeded to solicit opinions from the leading universities of Europe. Oxford and Cambridge were obliged to support the king's position. The University of Paris, over some opposition, was forced by Francis I, once again at outs with Charles, to give an opinion favorable to Henry. Some Italian academies, no friends of the

Papacy, were cajoled or bribed to follow suit. Henry, thus fortified in his quest, had the collection of documents sent to the Pope (July 1530), who promptly (September 1530) rejected the appended demands and the king's open threat to "seek our remedy elsewhere" in case of refusal.

When it became clear that the Pope would not, under any circumstances, be of any help, Henry turned to an agency that stood ready to hand. Within two weeks of Wolsey's fall, in October 1529, writs had been issued for the body known in English history as the Reformation Parliament. It was to be in session for six years and to complete, under Henry's guidance and pressure, the severance of England from Rome, the establishment of the Church of England, and the formalization of Tudor absolutism. Henry, now assisted by Thomas Cromwell, had much to say in the selection of members of the Commons; to a great extent it was a "packed" Parliament. With Parliament now behind him, Henry was ready to bring the clergy into line. In 1531 he forced the Convocation of the clergy to pay a heavy fine (£100,000) for having accepted Wolsey as legate and thus having violated *Praemunire*. He gained from them recognition of his title as "Supreme Head" of the Church of England.

The Reformation Parliament was anticlerical in temperament, as Henry had intended it should be, and Cromwell had little difficulty in getting the Commons to issue complaints against the prelacy and to ask the king to limit the powers of the bishops, particularly in the extent of their jurisdiction and rights to issue decrees under canon law. It was somewhat more difficult to persuade the Commons to attack the prerogatives of the Papacy. It had long been customary all over Europe for new appointees to any bishopric or higher preferment in the Church to pay the total first year's income to the *curia*. This payment, known as the annates, was an important part of the papal exchequer. In 1532 Parliament passed an act for the Conditional Restraint of Annates, suggesting that only 5 per cent of the first year's income be sent to the Pope. The king was asked to take the matter up with the papal authorities, which indicates that, at least at this point, the suggestion was regarded as a bargaining measure. Convocation, when presented with this and other acts of Parliament intended to curb ecclesiastical prerogatives, replied: "We, your most humble subjects, may not submit the execution of our charge and duty, certainly prescribed by God, to your highness' assent." Henry, not satisfied with Convocation's submission of the previous year, presented to Parliament a simple issue: Was the clergy, by obeying the Pope, guilty of treason to the English crown? To the question so stated there was of course only one answer for clergymen who wished to remain English subjects. The medieval concept of the separability of spiritual and temporal powers had allowed the two to coexist with only occasional friction. Henry was demanding that they be united in one *imperium,* the civil, with himself as unquestioned head. There was in his demand much that was distinctly English in character. One could almost surmise that Henry had been reading Wyclyf's work *On the Office of the King (De officio regis),* in which suggestions not greatly dissimilar were made. It is doubtful that the issues could or would have been similarly stated anywhere on the Continent.

In the fall of 1532 events occurred which were to hasten the development of the English Reformation. Anne Boleyn, whom Henry had already selected as Catherine's successor, was created Marquess of Pembroke. She had withstood Henry's advances until he promised her marriage and the title of Queen, but in December 1532 she became pregnant. The necessity of ensuring the legitimacy of Anne's child—who might be Henry's fervently desired male heir—meant that the marriage with Catherine would have to be dissolved, and that with Anne solemnized, within seven or eight months. The sequence of events is therefore of some importance. First, Thomas Cranmer was nominated Archbishop of Canterbury in September 1532, and the Pope was persuaded to issue (February 1533) the necessary bulls to make him a fully ordained and properly consecrated Roman prelate. On January 25, 1533, Henry and Anne were secretly married. On May 23, after a hearing, Archbishop Cranmer declared Catherine's marriage null and void from the beginning, and on June 1 Anne Boleyn was crowned queen of England in Westminster Abbey. The future Queen Elizabeth I was born on September 7.

In the meantime, Parliament and Convocation had moved quickly and decisively to make the break clean and the supremacy of the king unquestioned. In February 1533, Parliament passed the Act in Restraint of Appeals, which declared the king to have "preëminence, authority, prerogative, and jurisdiction to render and yield justice and final determination to all manner of folk . . . without restraint or provocation to any foreign princes or potentates." The Act specified that no cases in spirituality might go beyond the archbishop's court except cases involving the king, for which the Upper House of Convocation was to be the court of last jurisdiction. In short, it completely and finally denied the jurisdiction of Rome. We do not know whether Henry had in mind an irrevocable split with Rome at this point, but it is certain that the legal basis for a step was now at his disposal.

The annulment of Catherine's marriage and the coronation of Anne Boleyn were outright violations of canon law. Clement VII promptly declared the marriage of Anne and Henry void and excommunicated the king, allowing a suspension of the sentence until September. This action initiated a new stage in the English Reformation, which was to last until 1540. In the earlier stage, from 1529 to 1533, the issues of religious reform and theological revolt were hardly involved; the "movement," if such it can be called, revolved around a political and dynastic matter; the Papacy entered in only as a legal obstacle to the attainment of the king's desire for a male heir to assure the continuity of the Tudor dynasty. Ecclesiastical administration and, to a lesser degree, theological formulation did appear in the second phase of the English Reformation, but, as will be seen, they still did not provoke the interest or attention evinced in Germany, Switzerland, or France.

Parliament Legislates the Reformation

IN THE early months of 1534, Parliament took a number of significant actions: (1) it passed a new Act on Annates forbidding payment to Rome of any first fruits at all; (2) in the Act against Papal Dispensations, it transferred the pope's power to dispense to the Archbishop of Canterbury and abolished the

Peter's Pence; * (3) it made it no longer heresy to criticize the Bishop of Rome; (4) in the Act for the Submission of the Clergy, it formalized the king's control of Convocation and canon law, which he had in fact exercised since 1532; (5) in the Act of Succession, it gave final legal sanction to the dissolution of Henry's first marriage and the validity of his second. Refusal to accept these decisions was made treasonable. In November Parliament passed the Act of Supremacy, which declared Henry to be "taken, accepted, and reputed the only supreme head on earth of the Church of England." Another act declared it treason to deny the royal supremacy of Henry or his heirs.

Cromwell was a master at guiding Parliament to leave no loopholes which might allow power to escape the monarch. In the six years of this Parliament, thirty-two acts having directly or indirectly to do with the king's control of the Church were passed, and Cromwell was behind them all. His policy in these years faithfully reflected the desires of his master. The Tudors had an uncanny gift for sensing what the people wanted and for finding and emphasizing the parallel between the will of the royal house and that of the realm.

Henry's firm determination to carry out the Acts of the Reform in Parliament is illustrated by the classic case of Sir Thomas More. More (1478-1535), the leading mind of Tudor England, a close friend of Erasmus, Holbein, and most of the Christian humanists, and the author of *Utopia* (1516),† became Speaker of the House of Commons in 1523 and Lord Chancellor of the Exchequer in 1529, succeeding Wolsey at Henry's request. He remained in the office of chancellor for three years and then handed the insignia of office over to Cromwell (May 1532), not without a certain sense of relief. Despite his previously cordial relations with the king, More found himself unable to accept in conscience the Act of Supremacy, as well as that part of the Act of Succession that declared the marriage of Henry and Catherine to be illegal. He was therefore charged with high treason in 1534 and sentenced to death. Despite some opposition in Parliament to the wide construction of the royal power in the Treasons Act, acts of attainder were passed against More and also against John Fisher, bishop of Rochester, a man almost equally eminent and respected for his learning and probity. The property of both men was confiscated. Fisher was beheaded on Tower Green on June 22, 1535; More followed him to the scaffold a fortnight later, July 6, 1535.

The grandeur of More's character may have obscured the simplicity of the issue. He was fighting for the conviction that the kingdom of God on earth was inviolate and supranational and that the Christian could not, therefore, bow his head to the secular ruler in matters of faith or accept him as supreme head of the Church. Henry and Cromwell, on the other hand, were convinced that the secular ruler in general and Henry VIII in particular was appointed by God to rule the people of England in spiritual as well as in temporal matters, without exception. In medieval terminology Henry was claiming control of the two keys. Archbishop Cranmer shared this view. Thus the medieval conception of the Church collided with the new secularism. Henry's revolution was carried through with such speed and adroitness that there was no time for

---

* The Peter's Pence had been a dead letter for over a century, but it was still in the statute books.

† Henry had profited from More's support against Luther in 1523. See above, p. 581.

Sir Thomas More, by Hans Holbein, in the Frick Collection, New York [FRICK
COLLECTION].

doubt or caution to crystallize into organized resistance. Certainly no single
man, such as More or Fisher, could stand against the combination of royal will
and the acquiescence of Parliament and the people.

With these victories safely won and incorporated into the law of the land,
the king went on to extend his control of the church. Henry's Continental
wars and involvements had been costly and his treasury was continually de-

pleted. Money was his first need. Since Wolsey had suppressed a few monasteries and turned their revenues to other than religious purposes, there was precedent for such action on a greater scale. To give it a show of justification, Cromwell appointed a commission early in 1535 to investigate the abuses in the monastic establishments throughout the kingdom. That there were abuses, scandals, and widespread laxity in the monastic orders is supported by much evidence ante-dating the time of the commission. It is equally certain that there were monas-teries with fewer inmates than they should have had and at the same time larger incomes than comported with the ideals of the religious life as the monastic constitutions described it. On the other hand, the commissioners knew what they were supposed to find and found it, sometimes even when it was not there. Their reports were in Cromwell's hands by January 1536; in February Parliament passed an act suppressing the monastic houses having an annual in-come of less than £200. Their property was given to a new royal court to be administered for the king. The monks and nuns thus displaced were per-mitted to go to the larger houses, still functioning, or to become seculars. Many chose the latter course. In the next year some of the larger houses were dis-solved, and by early 1540 the last considerable abbey, Waltham, was in royal hands. The wealth of the almost six hundred establishments that were dis-solved went to enrich some of the king's supporters. The royal treasury bene-fited substantially, for much of the confiscated property was sold to the highest bidder. The dissolution was not accomplished without opposition. In 1536 there was a series of demonstrations among the country folk in the north of England which was known as the "Pilgrimage of Grace." Parish priests, some of the gentry, and plain yeomen from the land participated, all protesting loyalty to the king, but demanding that dissolutions cease and that no new taxes be imposed. The leaders were not rebels; they wanted merely to present their views to the king. But Henry would brook no opposition. The leaders, more than forty of them, were hanged and almost two hundred others were executed, while the dissolution of the monasteries proceeded more rapidly.

When Anne Boleyn also failed to produce a male heir, Henry decided on a third queen. Anne was tried, condemned, and executed on flimsy and unsupported charges (May 19, 1536), and Jane Seymour, lady in waiting to Catherine of Aragon, immediately became the next queen. She succeeded in bearing Henry a son, Edward, on October 12, 1537, and died immediately thereafter. Since he now had a male heir, Henry's later marriages—to Anne of Cleves (annulled six months later), Catherine Howard (1540), and Katherine Parr (1543)—lacked the urgency that accompanied the earlier pursuit. The largely political and dynastic factors in the first stage of the Tudor Reforma-tion gradually gave way to the legal consolidation of the second stage. And, as the legal framework of the new church-state was perfected, a new atmosphere developed in which the theoretical implications of the many constitutional changes were freely examined.

During the years in which Henry had been struggling with the Papacy, there had been some communication between English humanists and theo-logians and their counterparts in Germany, Switzerland, and France. By 1536, when England's separation from the Papacy was finally consummated, there were six English bishops who could be called "reformers" in that they were sympathetic to Continental Protestantism. In October 1535, Miles Coverdale's translation of the Bible appeared, with the approval of Cromwell. It gave rise to much discussion of the concept of the Scriptures as the basis for faith and practice. Convocation in 1536, under the leadership of the reforming bishops, drew up the Ten Articles of Faith. The Articles, which showed strong Lutheran influence, were an obvious attempt to put the English church in a position to collaborate with the Lutherans. Only three of the seven Catholic sacraments were mentioned (baptism, the Eucharist, penance); the statement on the Real Presence was equivocal, adaptable to an interpretation of either transubstantiation or the Lutheran consubstantiation; justification by faith was asserted, but in a manner that Catholics could not find offensive. It was a document of compromise and some ambiguity.

In 1538 a committee of Lutheran leaders visited England, and a sort of concord was reached. Henry, however, was never enthusiastic about any political or confessional alliance with the Germans, and his short-lived marriage to Anne of Cleves (to whom, he later said, he had taken a dislike as soon as he saw her) hardly helped the situation. In 1539 Henry asked Parliament to attempt to bring unity to English religion, and the Six Articles of 1540, whose final form the king considerably influenced, were conservative, even traditional, that is, closer to Catholic doctrine than to Protestantism. Some mild declarations of the Ten Articles of 1536 were expressly repudiated. It is difficult indeed to analyze Henry's theological position for the last seven years of his reign. He had several Lutherans burned and allowed some of the reforming bishops to resign; yet he kept Cranmer, as reforming as any, in his post as Archbishop of Canterbury and in the royal confidence.

In 1540 Cromwell fell from power and was beheaded. In 1543 the *King's Book* was issued as a doctrinal guide for the English clergy. It was conservative and even Catholic, yet it contained certain Lutheran phrases and ideas which Henry had found acceptable. In 1544 Cranmer was allowed to bring before Convocation certain reforms in the service, and Henry discussed with him further reforms both in liturgy and in matters of doctrine as late as 1546. Equally significant was the fact that Henry gave the education of Edward, Prince of Wales, to tutors who were openly Protestant. Apparently, in the years since 1535, the king had gradually come to the conclusion that Protestantism was not a real threat to the throne and that the Lutheran approach, which he disliked, was not the only species of Protestantism available to England. His primary goal was a religious formulation that could bring national unity and thereby assure the stability of the crown. For that purpose he was avowedly an opportunist; had he lived longer, he would almost certainly have been open to suggestions for further changes in the direction of Protestantism. Much of England's strength in the following centuries may be credited largely to Henry's careful opportunism.

Edward VI and Extreme Protestantism

LATE in December, a month before his death on January 28, 1547, Henry appointed a Council of Regency for his son and heir, then nine years old.

The Council consisted of sixteen nobles and high officials, predominantly Protestant. Edward Seymour, an uncle of the Prince of Wales, was chosen by the Council soon after Henry's death as Protector of the Realm and Governor of the King's Person. Seymour took the title of Duke of Somerset and ruled England as Protector for two and a half years. He was moderate where Henry had been firm and preferred to rule by persuasion where Henry would have forced compliance. Somerset repealed the treason and heresy laws which had legalized Henry's absolutism and was surprised at the discussion and resistance which broke out in Parliament. Henry's ruthless conservatism had only postponed discussion of doctrinal issues. Somerset's parliaments became scenes of tempestuous debates and bitter discord on questions of liturgy, orders, the right to preach, the Mass and the Eucharist, and confession. Parliament approved a *First Prayer Book*, largely the work of Cranmer, which was an abridgement and simplification of the old Latin service books. Introduced in the spring of 1549, it soon encountered opposition and provoked a rebellion in Devon and Cornwall by country folk who demanded their accustomed Latin services. They did not profess to understand the Latin services, but they were at least used to them. Somerset would have dealt with the rebellion in sweet reasonableness, but other members of the Council, without his knowledge, had it put down with arms. Somerset's very moderation was the cause of his fall. He was ahead of his time. The radicals were against him because he would not go so far as they demanded in the direction of Protestantism. The Catholics and conservatives attacked him because, they said, he had gone too far. The incidence of a state of war with France was an additional source of disaffection and an opportunity for his enemies.

In October 1549, the earl of Warwick took advantage of Somerset's troubles to engineer a plot to remove him from power. The coup was successful; Somerset was arrested and sent to the Tower, and Warwick ruled England thereafter (as duke of Northumberland) until the death of Edward in 1553. He loudly proclaimed Protestant views, although privately he leaned to Roman Catholicism, and took a more aggressively reform line than Somerset. In 1550 Warwick felt strong enough to make the gesture of releasing Somerset from the Tower and allowing him to resume his position on the Council for a while, but Somerset's popularity was so great as to become a threat to Warwick. In January 1552, the former regent was executed on trumped-up charges of treason.

Both Somerset and Northumberland, though personal enemies, were strongly Protestant in their policies, and the Reformation during their rule was in full swing. Several conservative bishops were obliged to vacate their sees, and the new appointments were openly reformist. In 1548 *The Order of the Communion*, with prayers in English, was issued for general use by parish priests. In January 1549, Parliament passed the first Act of Uniformity, which made the *First Prayer Book* of Edward VI, essentially Cranmer's work, the official form of worship. These early formulations and measures were still characterized by compromise and conservatism. The heritage of Henry VIII's successful *via media* was not lost on the English people. But after Northumberland's ascent to power the swing to Protestantism was accelerated. A number of Continental reformers, among them John à Lasco, Pietro Vermigli, Bernardino Ochino, and Martin Bucer, came to England and aided in the campaign to bring

English Protestantism into line with the movement on the Continent. The *First Prayer Book* was revised along more Protestant lines (1552), and the Second Act of Uniformity presented this revision for universal use in the English church. Cranmer was responsible not only for the form of the revision but also for the content of the *Forty-Two Articles of Religion,* which were uncompromisingly Protestant in the acceptance of justification by faith alone and in the denial of the Real Presence of Christ in the Eucharist. These Articles never went into effect, for they were not published until the spring of 1553, when Edward's health was failing and a crisis over the succession was impending.

Mary Tudor, 1553–58

BY THE will of Henry VIII, Mary was to succeed her half brother Edward. Since Mary was staunchly Catholic, Northumberland wished to prevent her accession. He found a counterclaimant in Lady Jane Grey, granddaughter of Henry VIII's younger sister, Mary, and prevailed upon the dying Edward VI to sign a decree naming her as his successor. Northumberland's enemies rallied around Mary, and the English sense of legitimacy defeated the usurpation. Northumberland's support melted away, and he himself changed sides at the last minute. It was too late; the Tower and the execution of Northumberland were the end of the Edwardian Reformation.

Queen Mary, a strong-minded, energetic ruler, was fervently attached to the Catholic faith. Almost all the strongly Protestant legislation of the preceding six years was quickly repealed and the leaders of the reform wing of the English church, as well as many whole groups, were encouraged to leave England. Thousands left to form congregations in Frankfurt, Basel, Strassburg, and Geneva. Under Mary's rule, Parliament went a long way toward a Roman Catholic restoration; yet by occasionally refusing to do as she asked, it made clear that the Parliament of England was not a mere creature of the monarch. When Mary's marriage to Philip of Spain was being negotiated, Parliament advised the queen against the union. The independence of action which Henry VIII had won for England was precious to every Englishman, and the possibility of having a Spanish king met with a very cool response.

Mary's first moves were moderate and tolerant. She was at first content with Parliament's decree restoring religious services as they had been in the last years of the reign of her father. When Mary wished to restore papal supremacy in place of Henry's doctrine of royal supremacy in the church, Parliament balked. With patience and time, she might have succeeded in restoring such Catholic institutions as clerical celibacy, Latin services, and the seven sacraments. But her insistence on the unpopular Spanish marriage, which took place on July 25, 1554, was more than Parliament could accept; even Mary's Catholic advisers were opposed to it. Philip from the beginning of his stay in England was aware of the feeling against him and showed great tact in his dealings with English officials.

Parliament was then persuaded to revoke almost all of Henry's legislation after 1529, on the Pope's promise, given through Cardinal Reginald Pole, the papal legate, not to interfere with the transfers of church property and offices that had taken place in the meantime. This was the high point of Mary's popularity. The settlement under Henry had found a wide acceptance among the English people; it was a sensible compromise between the old and the new and discouraged fanaticism and extremes on either wing. Mary seems not to have understood the basic views of the people. When, with the victory of the restoration of pre–1529 religion in hand, she demanded more, her popularity began immediately to wane.

It is an interesting sidelight on this conservative counterrevolution that what Parliament had put down, only Parliament could restore. It was Parliament that had expelled the pope from England, Parliament that brought him back into the English church, and Parliament that set the theological as well as the fiscal conditions on which he was again a part of the ecclesiastical structure of the land. Fundamentally, the English people, speaking through Parliament, were their own church and continued to be even when they once more accepted Roman Catholicism.

Mary Tudor is widely known for her persecution of Protestant dissenters. The fires did not start until February 1555, and the change which then took place, from tolerance to persecution, was Mary's own idea. The victims were from all classes; the grounds for "relaxation to the secular arm" were heresy, essentially as defined in the Middle Ages. The popular reaction to the campaign of persecution of humble Englishmen for Christian views honestly held was one of angry resentment. From 1555 Mary sank greatly in the esteem of the people. The leading Protestant bishops, Latimer, Ridley, and Hooper, and the Archbishop of Canterbury, Thomas Cranmer, had gone to the fires by the fall of 1555, adding to Mary's unpopularity. Other unfortunate actions worked against her. She declared war on France in 1558 to help her husband Philip in his war against Henry II and in consequence lost Calais in January 1559. English pride was deeply wounded by this loss. Mary was unable to work out satisfactory relations with Pope Paul IV, whose sudden refusal to accept Cardinal Pole, papal legate under the preceding pontiff, as his legate to England left England isolated from the papal *curia*. The English people as a whole would without much doubt have accepted the reversal of the extreme Reformation under Edward, but when Mary attempted to undo the work of her father and to restore the pre–1529 situation, she was going too far. At the end Mary knew her reign was a failure and died in frustration and despair in November 1559.

CALVIN AND FRENCH PROTESTANTISM

THE net result of the labors of the first generation of reformers in France had been, on the surface, discouragingly little (see above Chapter 18). By 1535 the few pioneers of the Reformation were in flight, in prison, or in hiding. The king, Francis I, had rejected his sister Marguerite's policy of benevolence toward reforming preachers and humanists and in 1534 declared open war on the whole movement. At the moment that the reformers' hopes were at their lowest ebb, the escape of John Calvin to Geneva, beyond Francis' power to interfere, meant the rebirth of the French reform movement on more congenial soil.

Calvin is regarded as the central figure of the second generation of Continental reformers, and particularly as the leader of the French Reformation. He is of the second generation not only chronologically (he was born in 1509, twenty-five years after Luther), but in the more significant sense that he brought to the Reformation movement what Luther, Melanchthon, and Zwingli had been unable to bring and what the movement deeply needed: a systematic theology. The importance of this function will become increasingly clear as we see in the next chapter how the Catholic Church used its traditional theology as a weapon in the campaign to regain ground lost to the Protestants. The success of the Council of Trent and the whole Catholic Revival (more familiarly known as the Counter-Reformation) was in great measure dependent upon the restatement of patristic and medieval theological formulations. Revitalized Catholicism found its most formidable obstacle in Calvin's imposing theological system. If ever a system or a movement was the reflection of a man, Calvinism was the image of John Calvin. It is of importance, therefore, to trace the career and development of the man and his thought in some detail.

John Calvin: To 1536

JOHN CALVIN was the fourth son of Gérard Cauvin, notary apostolic and procurator fiscal and solicitor-secretary to the bishop of Noyon, in Picardy, and of Jeanne Lefranc, daughter of a well-to-do innkeeper of nearby Cambrai. Through his own ability, Cauvin had risen to a position of some importance in Noyon. In 1497 he acquired the rights of a bourgeois of the city. A year later he was elected to the city council. He was on good terms with the leading family of the region, the de Hangests, from whom the bishops of Noyon had for generations been chosen. John's early years were uneventful. There is evidence that he was a good student and of a religious bent. In 1521, when the boy was twelve years old, he received, through his father's offices, a benefice from the chapter of the cathedral, which was equivalent to a scholarship to encourage further study for the priesthood. This and two other small benefices that were given him later he was expected to relinquish at the age of twenty-five if he did not enter the priesthood. His teachers soon recognized his great gifts, and it was taken for granted that he would study at Paris. When, in 1523, the young son of the de Hangest family was sent to Paris to study, John Calvin went along.

In Paris, John, now fourteen, was enrolled in the Collège de la Marche, part of the University of Paris. The Collège de la Marche enjoyed only a mediocre repute among the colleges in Paris, but John was fortunate in his teacher of Latin grammar, Mathurin Cordier, one of the better scholars of France. Soon Calvin moved to the Collège de Montaigu, which Erasmus and Rabelais had attended before him. The head of the college was Noël Bédier, an enthusiastic enemy of the new learning, Luther, and all reform ideas. The curriculum was rigorous and the demands on the students were incredibly severe. From four in the morning to six in the evening, with hardly a minute free, the pupils worked under a rigorous regime of study.

Calvin found Paris in religious turmoil. The group of Christian humanist reformers, led by William Briçonnet, bishop of Meaux, had for some years been under attack from the conservatives at the Sorbonne, led by Bédier. Since the Sorbonne's condemnation of Luther's Latin works (April 15, 1521), Briçonnet had had gradually to withdraw his support of men whom he had invited into his diocese for the purpose of reforming it. Although we know little about Calvin's years at Montaigu, Luther's name and the ideas of the Reformation beyond the borders of France must have been familiar to him and must have been presented to him by his own professors in a very dark light. In these years, he may even have had access to some of Luther's works, for a few editions were published in Paris under pseudonyms, against the prohibitions of the Sorbonne, and were available in the bookstores.

Early in 1528 Calvin took the degree of master of arts, a natural step toward the pursuit of theology and an ecclesiastical career. But it appears that his father had in the meantime changed his mind about the ultimate value of an ecclesiastical career for his son and persuaded John to turn his course of study in the direction of the law. In 1528, therefore, he transferred from Paris to the University of Orléans, which at that time had the most respected school of law in France. It was, as well, a center of humanistic studies, a feature which was already attractive to the young scholar. He remained at Orléans for eighteen months, then, in 1529, left for Bourges, capital of the duchy of Berry. Here Calvin began the study of Greek under Melchior Wolmar, a German humanist and follower of Luther.

In 1531 Calvin's father had gotten into difficulties with the chapter of Noyon and, excommunicated, died soon after. Calvin, freed from his father's pressures, was now able to make his own choice of a career. He returned from Bourges to Paris to continue his study of Greek and begin that of Hebrew. He believed he had found the interest to which he wished to devote his life—humane letters in the spirit of the new learning. His first scholarly production was a commentary on the *De clementia* of Seneca, which he published at his own expense in Paris in 1532. It shows his interest in political ethics in the light of Christian faith. For example, he disagreed with Seneca on "mercy"; Seneca repudiated it as a vicious weakness, while Calvin regarded it as necessary for a good ruler. The tenor of the commentary, however, is classical rather than Christian; it was not intended to be an original contribution. The Latin is smooth, and the work reveals a marked power of organization and vigor of presentation. It was the last product of this period of his life, for sometime between the publication of the *De clementia* and 1534 Calvin experienced what he later called a "sudden conversion," the details of which remain unknown. He dated his later religious activity from this crisis.

During or shortly after the period of his conversion, a friend, Nicolas Cop, was rector of the University of Paris. His formal rectorial address delivered on November 1, 1533, was interpreted as a defense of Marguerite of Navarre * and the reform group around her. At the same time it attacked the obscurantists and detractors of the new spiritual trend in the Church. Calvin, who was known to be in complete accord with the intent of the address, may have been consulted in its composition; he may even have helped to write it. Because of the speech, *parlement* indicted Cop for heresy, at the insistance of the Sorbonne,

---

* Marguerite d'Angoulême, sister of Francis I of France, widowed duchess of Alençon, married Henry II (d'Albret), king of Navarre, in 1527.

and Calvin was included in the indictment. Cop fled to Basel and Calvin escaped to Noyon, disguised as a vine dresser. His books and papers, left behind in his haste, were seized by the officers who came to arrest him. The furor soon died down, and Calvin returned to Paris for a short stay. He next went for a period of rest and study to Saintonge, where he stayed with a school friend who had inherited a rich library. It is generally thought that the reading and some of the writing for the *Institutes* were done at Saintonge.

In April 1534, Calvin met Lefèvre d'Etaples for the first time at Nérac, Marguerite's capital, and had a long talk with the aged dean of the French reform humanists. Lefèvre's cautious methods of reform from within the Church had obviously failed. Should not a direct and bolder approach be attempted? In Calvin's own life he had experienced the inefficacy of medieval religious resources. The evidence that multitudes of others also had grave doubts of the capacity of the established religion to satisfy man's heart and mind was all around him in the earnest discussions and troubled consciences of his friends. Calvin felt called to find a solution.

Returning to Noyon in May 1534, he gave up his benefices and thereby severed any formal connection with the Roman Church. The following year he spent in flight and hiding, at Angoulême under Marguerite's protection, at Poitiers, at Orléans, and, for a short but eventful stay, back in Paris. In each place, frequently under the assumed name of Charles d'Espéville, he was the guide and inspiration of small groups of earnest people, from various walks of life, who were finding their way into Protestantism. The movement was not Lutheran; its impulse came from purely native sources. The relations Calvin established at this period of his life with these widely dispersed groups and individuals go far to explain the later expansion of the French Reformation. They were the first French Calvinists.

On October 18, 1534, the incident of the "placards" occurred. Some extremists among the reform party in France imported placards coarsely attacking Catholic doctrine and practice and posted them in prominent places throughout the city. One was affixed to the door of the king's bedchamber at Amboise. Francis was furious and ordered immediate reprisals, declaring, falsely, that he was proceeding against Anabaptists and seditious persons. Those Protestants who could do so left Paris and France. Many others were imprisoned, tortured, or burned at the stake. Calvin was among those who escaped in time, again using his assumed name of d'Espéville. Traveling by way of Strasburg, he arrived in Basel in February 1535.

Francis' misrepresentation of the facts precipitated Calvin's decision to publish a treatise which he had been working on for some time and which had been intended as an outline of the new and reformed doctrine. It would serve, he felt, as a defense and justification of the whole movement. This modest Protestant *apologia et instructio* appeared in Basel in March 1536 under the title *Institutes of the Christian Religion (Christianae religionis institutio)*. In subsequent editions it was expanded to almost five times its original size, but the organization and basic positions remained the same. The first edition contained a dedicatory letter to Francis I in which Calvin tried to convince the king that the Protestants he had been persecuting were not subverters of Christian doctrine or of the king's authority but, rather, sincere Christian men and women endeavoring to live according to the Scriptures as loyal, law-abiding subjects of a just monarch.

When the *Institutio* appeared, Calvin was in Italy, at the court of Renée, duchess of Ferrara. Renée, a daughter of Louis XII and a cousin of Francis I, was known to be friendly to Frenchmen and Italians of evangelical views. Her court had become a center and a refuge for such men. Calvin was welcomed by this vital group and found Renée receptive to his ideas. Renée's husband, Ercole d'Este, however, became uneasy at the presence of so many French and Italian refugees, suspect in their own lands, and the period of tolerance for reformation ideas soon came to an end. Calvin left in June 1536, and during a short period of Francis' tolerance, returned to Noyon to settle the family estate. His destination then was Strassburg, which on a former visit he had found congenial to his scholarly tastes and receptive to his ideas of reform. Since war between Charles V and Francis I had just broken out again, the direct road to Strassburg was closed by the rival armies; Calvin was therefore forced to detour by way of Geneva. During his stopover there he was approached by William Farel with an urgent appeal to join him in organizing the reform in Geneva. Farel's strong appeal, coupled with a fiery threat that God would punish Calvin if he refused His call, so "terrified and shook" Calvin, as he himself said later, that he gave up the journey he had undertaken and accepted the post of professor of the Holy Scriptures in the Genevan church. Thus began an epoch in the history of the Reformation.

Calvin and Farel at Geneva, 1536–38

WILLIAM FAREL (1489–1565) led a most active life. As an enthusiastic and evangelistic pupil of Lefèvre, he had had to leave France in 1523. He was at first welcomed at Basel, then expelled at Erasmus' request. He wrote a number of books on the forms of reformed worship and held successful ministries at Neuchâtel and several lesser towns in western Switzerland. He came to Geneva in 1532 and entered with fervor and some success into the heated political and religious discussions then going on in the city. The opposition was strong and in October 1532 he was expelled from Geneva for fourteen months but was back in the city, preaching and disputing, in December 1533.

Despite some victories in public debates, Farel found it difficult to bring Geneva completely into the Protestant camp. It was this difficulty and feeling of inadequacy that prompted him to demand that Calvin stay and help him. He sensed that Calvin's abilities might be especially useful in Geneva's peculiar situation.

Geneva had recently (January 1536) emerged victorious from a struggle to achieve self-rule, a three-cornered conflict involving the bishop of Geneva, the duke of Savoy, and the burghers of the city. The victory belonged to the burghers, supported by the free cities of Bern and Fribourg, over the bishop and the duke in alliance.

The city was ruled by a mixed hierarchy of councils. The broad basis of authority was the General Council of the whole citizenry, in existence since 1409. The administrative functions of this General Council or Commune were exercised by a Little Council of twenty-five. In 1457 the conduct of foreign relations, which, for so commercial a city, were important and complex, was entrusted to a Council of Fifty (after 1502 the Council of Sixty). After protracted struggles with the bishop and the duke of Savoy had assured the city virtual independence from any outside sovereignty, a Council of Two Hundred was established. The powers of this group were at first vague, but during this period they steadily increased. It was the Council of the Two Hundred that made almost all the important municipal decisions in our story.

Calvin's first position in Geneva was simply that of a public teacher and lecturer on the Bible. He was, however, soon preaching regularly, along with other leaders of the reform group, and was paid a regular but inadequate salary as "Professor of Sacred Letters." The question of the organization of the reformed group and its services was a leading problem which Farel had been unable to solve. In January 1537, the company of pastors presented a plan for the church's organization, which emphasized the regular and orderly administration of the Lord's Supper and specifically provided for the right of exclusion (excommunication) by the proper authorities. Men of upright life were to be chosen in each ward of the city to oversee the morals of the citizens. This plan was probably Calvin's work. His primary aim, and that of Farel, was to protect the sacrament from profanation by the participation of evil persons, but the reintroduction of authorized "snoopers" was an unfortunate return to inquisitional methods. Several official visitors from other Protestant centers came to Geneva and spoke publicly against the innovations. Calvin and Farel were accused by preachers at Lausanne and Bern of having denied the doctrine of the Trinity. After public and acrimonious hearings, they were finally exonerated, but the attacks left their mark and encouraged their opponents in Geneva. To add to the concerns of Calvin and Farel, Anabaptist missionaries from the Lowlands to Switzerland were spreading doctrines that had to be refuted.

These irritations slowed the work of reform, but in the summer of 1537 Calvin and Farel were again concentrating on their program of instruction and organization. A Confession of Faith and a Catechism were prepared, and the Council decreed (September 19) that failure to accept these two basic documents on oath could incur banishment. This extreme measure brought a storm of protest and many absolute refusals. At the annual elections in February 1538, the party of opposition to Calvin and Farel had gained much strength. When the matter of the Confession and the Catechism came before the General Council, the preachers were instructed to preach the Gospel and to avoid political matters. It was further decreed that services should be conducted according to the Bernese rite. The preachers rejected the competency of the Council to decide matters of theology and refused, on Easter Sunday 1538, to administer the communion according to the forms of Bern. The Council would not suffer such defiance and on April 23 ordered Calvin and Farel to leave the city within three days. The reformers promptly departed and presented their case to a synod of Protestant cantons at Zurich, then to the Council of Bern, whose intervention in Genevan politics had been partly responsible for the expulsion. They won some support, but the Council at Geneva would not change its decision and Calvin and Farel were again reformers without a field of action. They had been much too precipitate. The discipline they wished to impose was too strict for any free-minded people to accept after so short a period of education and preparation. They had, furthermore, on many occasions disobeyed the dictates of common courtesy, to say nothing of tact. Calvin, recalling this experience in later years, admitted that he had expected too much and had acted rashly and at times rudely.

Calvin and Farel went on to Basel, where they were welcomed. Farel soon accepted a call to Neuchâtel, where he had been a pastor before going to Geneva. Calvin hoped to return to his studies, but his friend Bucer, who had been the spiritual guide of Strassburg since 1523, prevailed over Calvin's reluctance and persuaded him to come to that city. In September 1538, he became the minister to a congregation of about four hundred French Protestants who had been banished from France by Francis I and had settled in Strassburg, which had a tradition of moderation and tolerance.

The next three years, during which he remained in Strassburg, were, in spite of straitened circumstances, the happiest of his life. In addition to his pastoral duties, Calvin taught at the Gymnasium and found time to write and publish his *Commentary on Romans,* manuals for church worship, collections

John Calvin, artist unknown, in the Bibliothèque de Genève [BIBLIOTHÈQUE DE GENÈVE].

of Psalms put to music, and, most significant of all, a thorough revision and expansion of the *Institutes,* which appeared in 1539. After frequent urging by Bucer, who pointed out Calvin's need for a helpmate in his pastoral work, Calvin finally decided to marry Idelette de Bure, a widow with two young children. It was a happy marriage, but her health was not robust; she died some years after Calvin's return to Geneva, in 1549, and he did not marry again.

Calvin was too well known to remain hidden for long as a simple preacher and teacher in Strassburg. He was invited to represent the city at several conferences of Lutheran Protestants and Catholic divines—at Frankfurt in 1539, at Hagenau and Worms in 1540, and at Regensburg in 1541. He begrudged the time spent away from his work in long-drawn-out discussions, yet through these conferences he came to know the German reformers. He was particularly drawn to Melanchthon, although he felt that the German was too ready to give in on important points to the Catholic emissaries.

In the meantime things were not going well in Geneva. The preachers chosen to replace Farel and Calvin were not their equals and were unable to impose any unity on their congregations. The factions in the city were once again at each other's throats, and bloodshed not infrequently ensued. Relations with the city of Bern had deteriorated almost to the point of war. Some of Calvin's bitterest opponents on the Council were thrown out for being troublemakers, and former adherents of the reformers pressed for the recall of Calvin and Farel. The first overtures Calvin quickly rejected; he had suffered more than enough from Geneva and wanted no part of it again. Farel and other friends, however, managed, over the course of a year, to persuade him that Geneva needed him and that Geneva's need was the voice of God. When he finally returned to Geneva on September 13, 1541, he was greeted warmly by the Council and the people.

Return to Geneva, 1541–64

CALVIN undertook his second ministry in Geneva with no little apprehension. He knew quite well that, despite his warm reception, opposition and unpleasantness would follow. His project for the organization of the church in Geneva, worked out in collaboration with a committee of the Council, was passed by the General Council in a slightly amended form on November 30, 1541, and issued as the Ecclesiastical Ordinances. It has been the basic document for the organization of all Calvinistic bodies since that time, and many of its features have been taken over by other, political organizations. It is in substance a system of parallel and interlocking jurisdictions, which is purported to be based completely on Christ's prescriptions for His Church. Four classes of officers were recognized, pastors, teachers, elders, and deacons, each with appropriate functions: the pastors to teach, preach, and administer the sacraments; the teachers to serve as repositories of pure doctrine as transmitted through the ages from the fountainhead, Christ Himself; the elders to be the link between the pastor and the laity, with coordinate and equal power to decide on heresy and discipline; the deacons to administer the charitable funds of the church to the sick and needy. The pastors and the elders made up the Consistory, which was the final court of appeal in the church.

The Council's acceptance of the Ordinances did not signify an end to Calvin's troubles. For the next eight years he was in constant difficulty of one kind or another. His former opponents were no less determined than before to break his power and were able to gain in strength as one or another of the issues at stake divided public and official opinion. The basic issue, of course, was the strictness with which the Consistory tried to govern the lives of the Genevese. Time and again the recorded proceedings of the Council report violent attacks on Calvin's rigor. Men high in the city's life, members of the Council, at one point the Captain-General, objected defiantly to the austere restrictions on their public and private behavior. The opposition, who came to be called Libertines, comprised both highly placed men acting on principle and riffraff whose lives would not bear close scrutiny. Calvin was able to gain a favorable decision in most of these cases and get the Council to discipline or restrain the malcontents. The Council was generally, but not unanimously, on Calvin's side, but in 1548 it was clearly against him. Yet even when he could not command a majority in the Council the suggestion that he be driven from the city again would not have found wide support. He had become too important a person on the European stage for Geneva to risk affronting the good opinion of her neighbors. On other occasions his enemies played into his hands by indiscreet declarations or overt violation of laws of the city. Calvin's colleagues among the pastors and in the Consistory were often lukewarm in his support. The campaign to make Geneva a pure and thoroughly reformed city in the end devolved mostly on Calvin himself. He wrote to Farel in 1548 that not a week passed without conflict of some sort.

Castellio and Servetus vs. Calvin

BEFORE his ultimate triumph over his enemies he had to undergo many crucial tests of his strength and his policies. The best known were the cases of Jerome Bolsec, Sebastian Castellio, and Michel Servetus. Bolsec, a charlatan doctor, had come to Geneva in the fall of 1551 and challenged Calvin's doctrine of predestination. To Calvin this was tantamount to challenging the majesty and omniscience of God, who, in his view, decreed salvation for whom He chose, from all eternity. Other Protestant cities, asked to comment on the issue, supported Calvin rather halfheartedly. Bolsec was banished from Geneva by the Council, returned to France, and died a good Catholic in 1584.

Calvin's conflict with Castellio was more serious and lasted many years. Castellio, a trained humanist, had embraced the reform movement and at one time had been a member of Calvin's household, training for the ministry. Given the headship of an academy at Geneva, he had proven himself a successful teacher. He began a translation of the New Testament which Calvin found to contain errors. Calvin objected to Castellio's admission to the ministry on the basis of the latter's rejection of the canonicity of the Song of Solomon and that article of the Creed which reads "He descended into Hell." The issue of the complete authority and inspiration of the Bible was to Calvin the cornerstone of the whole Reformation movement, and he could not allow it to be questioned. Castellio left Geneva in 1544 with letters of recommendation from Calvin for his excellent teaching of academic subjects and settled in Basel as a printer's proofreader, but continued his scholarly activity. His most important work was the *Treatise on Heretics* (1554), a defense of the right of Christians to disagree.

Servetus was a Spaniard, trained in law and medicine, who came to have quite original ideas about the Bible. In 1531 he published an attack on the orthodox doctrine of the Trinity which caused a sensation among theologians, Catholic as well as Protestant. Having come into conflict with authorities in various Protestant centers, he changed his name to Villeneuve and for a time devoted himself to the practice of medicine. He appears in histories of medicine as having approached the discovery of the circulation of the blood. In 1538 he left Paris after an altercation with the medical faculty, and in 1544 we find him as physician to the archbishop of Vienne, just south of Lyons on the Rhône River. From 1545 Servetus, using his pseudonym of Villeneuve, was writing to Calvin, trying to instruct the reformer in Christian doctrine and offering to come to Geneva to help in the good work. He sent Calvin a copy of the *Institutes* with copious marginal notes that corrected Calvin's "errors," and in 1553 he published a large volume setting forth his reconstruction of Christianity and of Calvinism (*Restitutio christianismi*). Again the doctrine of the Trinity was violently attacked, and in addition he denied original sin and the practice of infant baptism. When a friend of Calvin informed a relative at Lyons of the nature of the book and the identity of the author became known, Servetus was arrested, tried, and found guilty of heresy. He managed to escape from jail, whereupon the authorities at Vienne sentenced him to be roasted alive over a slow fire if he ever came within their jurisdiction again. For some strange reason Servetus came to Geneva and attended the church where Calvin was preaching. He was recognized, imprisoned, and charged with heresy on forty counts. Throughout a long trial, highly technically theological at times, Servetus defended himself stoutly. At the end of the trial the churches of Basel, Bern, Schaffhausen, and Zurich, asked for their opinion, quickly pronounced Servetus' views heretical. On October 26, 1553, with the replies of the four cities before them, the Council condemned Servetus to death by burning. Calvin tried in vain to have the sentence commuted to the more merciful death by the sword. Faithful to his convictions, Servetus refused to recant despite the last-minute urgings of Farel.

Most of Christendom approved the execution. The denial of the ancient doctrine of the Trinity was an attack upon one of the most sacrosanct points of Christian belief. Nevertheless, there were voices raised against Calvin for his part in the trial and condemnation. Calvin thought it necessary to offer a defense of the trial in January 1554, but it was not very convincing. The most telling attack on Calvin was Castellio's *Treatise on Heretics,* published under a pseudonym, which received wide attention. The *Treatise* was a plea for tolerance of sincere differences of opinion on doctrine. Since Calvin had not prevented the execution of Servetus, Castellio claimed, to that extent he was responsible for it. Calvin's warmest admirers admit that the Servetus affair is a blot on his record. Locally, however, the Servetus affair aided Calvin's cause. His opponents had sided with Servetus, and because, by the standards of the time, there was no doubt that Servetus was a heretic, they were discredited along with him.

The next year, 1555, was decisive. The old and established families had resented the great ingress of French refugees into Geneva. Once admitted, they were almost uniformly sympathetic to Calvin's leadership. A somewhat crude attempt was made to organize this resentment into a revolution that would unseat Calvin. The older families and the Libertines * found common cause in opposition to Calvin and his French supporters. A riot broke out in May 1555, which was easily put down. The leaders fled to Bern, thus giving an appearance of guilt. They were tried *in absentia* and sentenced to death as traitors. Some of their underlings who had not fled were tried, and a few were executed. The identification of the Libertines and the other opponents of Calvin with lawlessness and disorder was the final sanction for Calvin's leadership of the city. In a very real sense Calvin was fortunate in his opponents. They almost always backed the losing cause.

From 1555 to Calvin's death in 1564, Geneva was regarded by sympathetic observers as a holy city, governed by Protestant saints under the inspiration of the Holy Spirit. The Ordinances of 1541 were revised in 1560 so as to give the Consistory virtual independence of the Council and to oblige the civil authorities to support the ecclesiastical organization. It was in effect a theocracy, or rather an autocracy of the clergy. John Knox, who came to Geneva in 1557, called the city "the most perfect school of Christ that ever was on earth since the days of the apostles." Some of the Swiss Protestant cities, however, had less favorable opinions. Bern, a traditional ally of Geneva, found many points of friction, and relations between the two cities were frequently strained. There was an Italian colony, made up of those who, compelled to flee the Inquisition in their homeland, had taken refuge in Geneva. At first received with open arms, they soon found the regimen stricter than they had anticipated. Some were put on trial for heresy and a number of their eminent members moved on to more congenial climes.

The Thought and Writing of Calvin

CALVIN, no less than Melanchthon and Luther, attached great importance to education as a means of undergirding and directing the reform movement. His whole life was indeed spent in instructing his parishioners and the world that could read his commentaries in the basic tenets of the Protestant faith. The Lutheran movement had started in a university and had grown and spread in large measure because of its academic leadership. Geneva, the leading Protestant city of the second generation, had schools but no university; Calvin decided that that lack should be remedied. At his suggestion and according to his plan, a college was inaugurated in 1559 which soon became the University of Geneva. The college was fortunate in having Theodore Beza come from Bern to be its first rector and other eminent scholars from Bern and Lausanne to grace its faculty. By the time of Calvin's death there were fifteen hundred students at the university, many of them from Italy, France, the Lowlands, Germany, England, and Scotland.

Calvin published his final edition of the *Institutes* in 1559. His doctrines had

* The Libertines were a group of religious fanatics originating in northern France. They appeared in Geneva soon after Calvin's return. He first attacked them in 1545.

Reformation monument, in Geneva, showing, left to right, Farel, Calvin, Beza, and Knox [P. BOISSONNAS, GENEVA].

changed only slightly since the twice-revised edition of 1543. There is no question that Calvin owed much to Luther and a great deal to Melanchthon, whose *Loci communes* he had read most carefully. His contribution was his systematization of the thoughts of his mentors, his persistent emphasis on the terrible demands of the sovereign majesty of God, and his insistence on the utter inability of man to affect God's decrees or bring about his own salvation. Man has a sense of God, but his will is enslaved, because of his inheritance from Adam and the taint of his fall. Mankind, therefore, is under a general sentence of death which God alone can, as He chooses, remit. He has chosen certain ones, the elect, by an immutable decree from all eternity, and they alone will be saved. The individual cannot have the gift of faith unless God gives it to him, nor can faith originate in the heart of man. Election is thus the cause of faith. It seemed logical to Calvin that God's omnipotence and omniscience were inseparable in His unified person. This is, in essence, Calvin's doctrine of predestination. It is a doctrine for the strong, not for the gentle or the weak. The other reformers accepted predestination in principle but were more prone to emphasize other attributes of God—His mercy, love, justice, and truth—and de-emphasize His sovereignty and majesty. There was criticism of Calvin's reasoning from the Protestants even during his lifetime, and some gaps in his logic were never successfully bridged. How, for example, if God made Adam perfect, in His own image, could Adam have committed the catastrophic sin that involved all mankind in its effects? Or again, if we take Calvin at his word and ascribe to God omniscience and omnipotence, should we not blame God for being the cause of sin? Despite these and other objections, the system that Calvin presented had a tremendous impact upon the Europe of his day and still gives rise to provocative thinking and austere and elevated religious sentiment.

Of the seven sacraments of the Catholic Church, Calvin accepted only two as scripturally warranted, baptism and the Eucharist. In his teaching on the sacraments, he stood somewhere between Zwingli and Melanchthon. He emphasized the spiritual content of the sacrament of the Lord's Supper. For him it was not a mere commemoration, as Zwingli had described it, nor was there any special sacredness attached to the bread and the wine in themselves, as in the Roman doctrine of transubstantiation and in Luther's doctrine of impanation. Rather, it was a spiritual experience in which the participant accepted the elements as if they were in fact the body and blood of Christ and united his heart in mystic communion with the risen Christ. The union was not less real because it was spiritual. Calvin stood in awe of the mystery of this sacramental union of the believer with Christ and never arrived at an exposition which could be called explicit.

Hardly less significant than his theology for the world in which he lived and for posterity was Calvin's ethical thought, which clearly stemmed from his theology. It has often been claimed that the doctrine of predestination justifies libertinism. If we are saved or damned already, the argument goes, it makes no difference what we do, so let us enjoy ourselves now. This "reasoning" would have amazed Calvin. The job of the professing Christian was to act as if he were saved. The Kingdom of God must be served. Each man is to serve God in and through his calling in life; in the world, not by withdrawal from it. The honor of God is the greatest good of all society. Calvin's thoughts as to the nature and aim of the social organism fitted admirably into the growing industrialism of the sixteenth and seventeenth centuries. The pursuit of worldly success, if undertaken in the proper spirit, could honestly hope for the blessing of God. Money, as such, was neither good nor evil, and its accumulation depended on the spirit of the person who amassed it. Calvin's years in Geneva and Strassburg, communities which lived by trade, certainly had an effect upon his thinking, though at no point in his formulations does he subordinate the theological and religious to the social or the economic.

Protestantism, as we have seen, had roots in France that were independent of Luther and his movement. In the uncertain years of the rule of Francis I, the success of Lutheranism in Germany was a source of encouragement to its French sympathizers, but the king's repressive measures kept French Protestantism in close check. Under him no Protestant congregation was able to exist. Nevertheless, French Protestantism survived beyond Francis' reach. The community at Strassburg to which Calvin ministered from 1538 to 1541, and the increasing number of French immigrants into Geneva after his return, were more significant than their feeble numerical strength would have indicated. They all maintained contact with friends and relatives who remained in France, almost a catacomb and martyr church. Henry II's open persecution seemed to have an effect opposite to what he intended. The Edict of Châteaubriand (1551) was as severe as the king could make it and the Burning Chamber (*Chambre ardente*) which he set up expelled the ashes of hundreds of victims. Despite all this, Protestantism in France grew and reached into the royal family. Reaction against Henry's severity was inevitable. Even the *parlement* of Paris objected to the Inquisition which Henry brought in in 1555, and royal judges, growing lenient, had to be forbidden to exercise mercy toward Protestants brought before them. Calvin was in constant touch with these developments, Frenchmen trained in Geneva were returning to France to minister to newly established congregations. The name Huguenots, probably from *Eidgenossen* (bound by an oath), was applied to the French Protestants from about 1556. In 1559 the first synod of Protestant churches of France met in Paris. Almost fifty churches were represented by laymen or pastors or both. There were probably as many more which were not able to send delegates. The Geneva Ordinances and Catechism were accepted as a matter of course by this group as a basis for their organization and worship. The Protestants, now bearing the mark and name of Calvin, had suddenly become a powerful force in France.

The transfer of Calvin's thinking and the ideal of his theocratic city to other areas in Europe and America have been of great moment in the history of liberty. Even Calvin's bitterest enemies, pointing to the rigidity and intolerance of the regime he established in Geneva, have not been able to deny that his followers in other lands have been leaders in the struggle for political and religious freedom. He set up certain instruments which were intended to provide for the expression of the people's will. The fact that he hoped to form that will into something appropriate to a "City of God" did not alter the fact that the organisms for the attainment of freedom were there. The contribution of Calvinism to the growth of democracy in the Western world has probably been out of proportion to the number of its adherents, and all thinking on representative government today owes much to the formulations of John Calvin (see below, Chapter 22).

SUGGESTIONS FOR FURTHER READING

ALLEN, J. W., *A History of Political Thought in the Sixteenth Century*. London, 1928

BASKERVILLE, G., *English Monks and the Suppression of the Monasteries*. London, 1937

BURNET, G., *A History of the Reformation*. 7 vols. London, 1865

CONSTANT, G., *The Reformation in England*. 2 vols. London, 1934, 1941

GAIRDNER, J., *The English Church in the Sixteenth Century*. London, 1912

HACKETT, F., *Henry VIII*. New York, 1929

HUGHES, P., *Rome and the Counter-Reformation in England*. London, 1942

MACKIE, J. D., *The Earlier Tudors, 1485–1558*. London, 1950

MOZLEY, J. F., *William Tyndale*. London, 1937

PARKER, T. M., *The English Reformation to 1558*. London, 1950

POLLARD, A. F., *Henry VIII*. New York, 1902

POLLARD, A. F., *Wolsey*. London, 1929

POWICKE, F. M., *The Reformation in England*. London, 1942

READ, C., *The Tudors*. New York, 1936

ZEVBELD, W. G., *Foundations of Tudor Policy*. London, 1948

BAIRD, H. M., *History of the Rise of the Huguenots of France*. 2 vols. New York, 1879

CALVIN, J., *Institutes of the Christian Religion*. 2 vols. New York, 1928. Other editions

CALVIN, J., Vols. XX–XXIII of the *Library of Christian Classics* contain various principal works of Calvin, newly translated into English. Philadelphia, 1953–58

DAKIN, A., *Calvinism*. London, 1941

D'AUBIGNÉ, M., *History of the Reformation in Europe in the Time of Calvin*. 8 vols. New York, 1863–79

HUNT, R. N. C., *Calvin*. London, 1938

MACKINNON, J., *Calvin and the Reformation*. London, 1936

McNEILL, J. T., *The History and Character of Calvinism*. New York, 1954

TAWNEY, R. H., *Religion and the Rise of Capitalism*. New York, 1926

TROELTSCH, E., *Social Teachings of the Christian Churches*. 2 vols. New York, 1931

WALKER, W., *John Calvin*. New York, 1906

WARFIELD, B. B., *Calvin and Calvinism*. New York, 1931

BOHATEC, J., *Calvins Lehre von Staat und Kirche*. 1937

BUISSON, F., *Sébastien Castellion (1515–1563)*. 1891

DOUMERGUE, E., *Jean Calvin: Les Hommes et les choses de son temps*. 7 vols. 1899–1927

IMBART DE LA TOUR, P., *Les Origines de la réforme*. 4 vols. 1905–35

LOBSTEIN, P., *Etudes sur la pensée et l'oeuvre de Calvin*. 1927

VIÉNOT, J., *Histoire de la réforme française*. Vol. I, 1926

WENDEL, F., *Calvin: Sources et évolution de sa pensée religieuse*. 1950

CHAPTER TWENTY-ONE

CATHOLIC REFORM AND COUNTER-REFORM

HE rise and spread of the Protestant Reformation was so dramatic and eventful and, in its effects, so catastrophic for the Roman communion that the efforts of the Church toward reform tend to be forgotten. Indeed, one might easily gain the impression that the Protestants were the only group interested in structural reform of the Church and in purification of the morals of the clergy or of the laity. That impression, however, would be false to the facts. It will be remembered that the express purpose of the whole Conciliar Movement of the fifteenth century was to reform the Church "in head and members," from the pope and the *curia* to the humblest parish priest. The purposes of the Conciliar Movement were at first almost unanimously supported by European opinion. There was no doubt in anyone's mind that the Church needed reforming. As the popes of Avignon and the Schism had failed to do anything effective about it, the whole European community, it was widely felt, should assume the task and set up norms and procedures by which reform could be carried out and its benefits assured. The important decree *Frequens* (1417) of the Council of Constance, calling for the convocation of a general council of the Church every ten years, whose task it would be to examine the activity of the *curia* and the course of the implementation of the reform measures previously decreed, became the document to which, in subsequent decades, protagonists of reform, as well as opponents of the Papacy, appealed. The Papacy was, on the other hand, determined to annul this decree and thereby restore to itself a complete initiative in matters of doctrine and morals. The bull *Execrabilis* (1462) of Pius II did in fact condemn the doctrine of conciliar supremacy and attempted to prevent the further use of *Frequens* by opponents of papal supremacy. His successors, particularly Paul II, Sixtus IV, Innocent VIII, and Julius II, followed the same policy of opposition to a council, in spite of frequent fair words concerning reform.

Not a small factor in papal opposition to a general council which might have inherited its motif from *Frequens* was the fact that the whole issue of a reforming council became a tool of political blackmail. Louis XI of France used the threat of a council most frequently in his many disputes with successive popes, and even the Emperors Frederick III and Maximilian I, who had nothing to gain from a council, supported Louis' threats on several occasions. The king of Bohemia, George of Poděbrady, a Hussite and therefore anathema to the *curia,* on two occasions, before as well as after he was formally excommunicated by Pius II in 1462, called for a general council and entered into negotiations with other princes of the Empire for its convocation. Charles VIII and Louis XII of France both found the threat of a council useful in their Italian ventures. They could wring from the pope approval of a conquest or his participation in an alliance by the pressure of a threat they seldom had any intention of carrying out. In Italy the many princes and despots realized they had little to gain from a general council which might raise embarrassing questions of legitimacy and justice. Their dungeons and gallows would ill bear the light of day. Nevertheless, we find both Florence (1478) and Venice (1483, 1509) appealing to a future council for reform of the Papacy. Both were quite sure their appeals would not have any concrete result and therefore felt quite safe in making them. The Catholic Kings of Spain, secure in their power over the Church in their realms, did not in general indulge in this game of ecclesiastical threat for political concessions. Furthermore, at about the time that the Papacy reached its lowest ebb and needed reform the most, the Church in Spain, quite independently of Rome, was undergoing a thorough and vigorous reform in spirit and substance under the leadership of Cardinal Ximénez.

The reason why the princes called for a council along lines of Constance or Basel, in spite of the fact that they were not really interested in reform, was simple. The Church did in fact need reform, the Papacy and the *curia* most, but the lower clergy scarcely less. Everybody knew that there was "something rotten" about the institution to which they all belonged, and everybody agreed that it was getting worse. The humanists, the monastic reformers, the mystics, and the many loyal and orthodox preachers all told their respective audiences that the situation was intolerable and must be corrected. The common people hoped that a council of all Christendom, powerful, honest, and devout, with a mandate from king, peasant, and pious priest, could and would bring a return to apostolic purity. The princes were aware of this popular feeling and were relying upon it to support their formal, if usually cynical, appeals to a council against the pope.

The demand for a reforming council, however, was wider than the intrigues of princes. We have seen (see above, pp. 274–75) that the University of Paris in the late fourteenth century was the home of the theory of conciliar supremacy over the pope. Paris continued to advocate the conciliar solution of the woes of the Church throughout the fifteenth century, and, with its prestige, carried with it some of the leading universities of Europe. At various times, the universities of Vienna, Cracow, Cologne, Leipzig, and Erfurt supported the demands for a council during the fifteenth century. The Italian universities, however, were in a difficult situation. Their generally legalistic approach to the Church and its discipline would have led them to favor the representative authority of a council expressed in ecumenical decrees, arrived at by canon lawyers; whereas proximity to the Papacy and dependence upon papal favor tended to keep them silent. Officially they remained discreetly neutral, while individual professors did in some cases openly advocate the calling of a council to bring health to the body ecclesiastic.

Pre-Reformation Councils and Efforts at Reform

THERE were in fact three councils called in the period between the inglorious end of the Council of Basel in 1449 and the outbreak of the Lutheran revolt. Two of these were called in direct opposition to the Pope, the third was called by Pope Julius II. Cardinal Zamometic, an eminent scholar and diplomat, had in 1481 voiced open criticism of Pope Sixtus IV and his nephew. He was promptly imprisoned for his pains. Released, and burning with resentful hatred, he fled to Basel and in April 1482 issued a call for a council to prevent the Pope from ruining the Church. He summoned the Pope to appear before this council to answer specific charges. He counted on the support of the northern princes, who had themselves so glibly threatened to call a council. The response to his call was negligible, and in the face of Sixtus' quick and energetic actions, the city of Basel, although traditionally pro-conciliar, finally put Zamometic in prison. The whole project evaporated. It was evident the time was not yet ripe for so drastic a solution to the Church's problems.

The second pre-Reformation attempt to convoke a reform council had a slightly greater success. Julius II, primarily political and military in his thinking, had won for himself many enemies, among whom France and Louis XII were most prominent. As Julius had invaded the field of international relations Louis felt justified, on his side, in invading the field of ecclesiastical polity. Julius had sworn to drive the "barbarian" French out of Italy. Louis' answer was to summon a meeting of French prelates (July 1510) which would formalize the royal attack on the Pope. Within a few months five cardinals, three of whom were not French, joined Louis, and in February 1511 decided to call a council. The call, proclaiming a state of emergency in the Church, was issued in May over the signature of the five cardinals and with the tacit approval of four more. The council was to meet at Pisa on September 1, 1511. The Emperor, Maximilian I, joined Louis in supporting the call. Julius circumvented the Pisan Council by calling, in July 1511, a council to meet at the Lateran in Rome on April 19, 1512. As the Pope was completely within his canonical rights in calling a council, and as the minority group who had called the Pisan Council had, in the process, made several legal mistakes, it soon became evident that the Pisan meeting would not command broad support. It nevertheless began its sessions on November 1, 1511, with attendance almost exclusively French. Pope Julius degraded (October 24, 1511) the five cardinals who had initiated the Pisan Council, which he was canonically justified in doing, and the prestige of the *conciliabulum* of Pisa (as it came to be called with contempt), now moved to Milan under Louis' direct protection, collapsed. It had been conclusively shown that an ecclesiastical instrument could not command any wide support in European opinion when used for political purposes by a lay prince. By the countermeasure of calling a council himself, Julius had given some satisfaction to the insistent cry for reform by way of a general council, and the lingering hope that the council thus called would do something about the abuses in the Church was just enough to postpone the crisis for a few years. Julius died soon after the first session of the Council, and it dragged on for five more years, finally disbanding without accomplishing anything of any lasting importance, significantly in the year of Luther's entrance upon the European scene.

Appeals for reform from laymen and clerics and attempts by pious individuals and groups to remove abuses and recover the purity and zeal of primitive Christianity had been frequent all through the fifteenth century. Of the mystics and of Cardinal Nicholas of Cusa we have spoken before. Their efforts to inspire their age with religious fervor by calling upon each Christian to dedicate himself anew to the fear and worship of God were not without result. The response among the common people was substantial. The Catholic Church found room for these manifestations of religious zeal and allowed and indeed often furthered the foundation of sodalities and orders, clerical and lay, within the framework of the Church's far-flung and manifold organization. Furthermore, as corruption seemed to increase, abuses to multiply, and evidences of a general moral deterioration to emerge on every hand, men and women of good will and determination began to go about reform systematically, not depending on guidance or help—of which there was little—from the *curia* but operating on the level of local or diocesan synods, individual orders, or, indeed, individual convents. The total energy put into this kind of independent and orthodox reform effort before the time of Luther, and often in spite of the *curia* at Rome, was most impressive.

In France the Estates General of 1484 formally protested against the corrupt practices in the administration of the French church which were responsible for the degradation of the clergy and superstition among the people. The next year a provincial synod at Sens, perhaps shamed by the pronouncement of the Estates General, promulgated a program of correction of abuses in monastic and clerical life. John Standonck, the energetic and influential head of the Collège de Montaigu at Paris, became the center of a group of clerics and scholars demanding reform in the French church. Not a few higher churchmen, men of lofty ideals, saw hope in this initiative and gave it their active endorsement. At the general assembly of the French clergy at Tours in 1493 the condition of religion in France was brought out openly and in detail, together with measures for improvement. The king, Charles VIII, supported the efforts at reform and persuaded Pope Alexander VI (1492–1503) to help. The Pope, limiting himself to one religious order, appointed three abbots to visit the French houses. The tide seemed to have turned; various bishops and even whole orders, particularly that of Cluny, made serious and to a degree successful efforts toward reform on a local scale. Cardinal d'Amboise, as papal legate and supported by Louis XII, began a strict reform of the mendicant orders in 1501. His methods were drastic, involving at times the employment of armed soldiery. The cardinal favored the more austere Observant branch of the Franciscans, whose reputation for purity of life and religion among the people was high. This correspondence between the temper of official action and public opinion was of itself fortunate, as it assured the popular approval of the cardinal's reforms and thus the permanence of the results. D'Amboise was for nine years, until his death in 1510, virtual dictator of the Church in France. His vigorous action must be remembered when we consider that many of the abuses which Luther found and attacked in the Church as he knew it in Germany were already on the way to abolition or correction in contemporary France. We know, for example, that at the same time that requirements for ordination to the clergy were being stiffened and a higher level of education was being demanded, the number of ordinations was steadily increasing in the years before 1520. Reform was in the air. On the other hand, not all the clergy shared the impulse toward pure religion. There had been much opposition to Cardinal d'Amboise on the part of the regular clergy whom he was determined to reform. Vested interests in property, lands, privileges, exemptions, and status remained even after d'Amboise's death. It was these interests in France and elsewhere as much as the reluctance of Pope Leo X (1513–21) to act decisively in favor of reform that caused the Lateran Council to give up its feeble ghost in 1517 without any significant accomplishment.

A further aspect of the general attitude toward religion is related to what has been said in a number of connections concerning the appetite of the common people for religious literature (see above, pp. 454–59). The printing press, a recent innovation, made it possible for a widening public to choose and own books. The fifteenth century was *par excellence* the period of the dissemination of the Greek and Roman classics, but it is probably true that as many copies of sermons, the *biblia pauperum,* the Vulgate Bible, and works of devotion were printed and bought. The flood of religious literature increased in volume in every country of Europe after the turn of the century, and by the early years of the Lutheran revolt had already established channels of exchange of ideas between like-minded "progressives" from the Baltic to Sicily. It was an international society of men and women who found a common interest and firm purpose in deepening their own religious knowledge and experience and thereby furthering their common faith.

One of the latest fruits of the movement for reform was the foundation of a number of religious orders or groups dedicated to specific tasks within the general program. In 1497 an "Oratory of Divine Love" was founded at Genoa by a cultured layman, Hector Vernazza, who rejected monastic retirement in favor of the practice of private devotions and charitable work among the poor, the orphans and the sick. Soon thereafter Vernazza founded a similar group at Rome, and in both places he was able to attract into the small group men of eminence, mostly laymen. Among the group at Rome were several future cardinals and one future pope. No effort was made to increase the membership, but almost spontaneously, as if in response to a hitherto unnoticed need, affiliated groups sprang up in Florence, Brescia, Milan, and then Venice. At this last center a young nobleman from Vicenza, Gaetano da Thiene, joined the group. He conceived the idea of an organization of clerics living, under a rule, a life of complete poverty, deep devoutness, dedicated to works of mercy, preaching, and teaching. These were, in distinction from the mendicants, not allowed to beg. This body, an outgrowth of the Oratory, under the guidance of da Thiene and Gian Pietro Caraffa of Naples, the later Pope Paul IV, became the Order of the Theatines, and received papal sanction in 1524. Other orders, less numerous or well known, founded in this and the next decade, were further evidences of the pressing demand for a religion that had meaning and intensity. They were spontaneous foundations, not yet intended as counters to Protestant heresy. That purpose was hardly to appear, as we shall see, until the time of Ignatius Loyola and the Society of Jesus.

PRELIMINARIES OF THE COUNCIL OF TRENT

IT IS at about this point, the early 1520's, that the two currents of Catholic thought which we have been describing, the politico-ecclesiastical reform in the control of princes and the *curia* on the one hand, and the personal reform, rising out of the thought of the mystics, the devout laity, and the moral humanists, on the other, begin to flow in parallel lines or to coalesce.

Luther had appealed to a council as early as November 1518. The Emperor Charles V, a fervent Catholic, made the calling of a council a primary condition of support of the Papacy. The Estates of the Empire in 1523 demanded a "free Christian" council which should meet in Germany. The papal legate to Germany, Aleander, exclaimed in 1520: "The whole world shouts 'Council, Council!'" Churchmen from every country in Europe, some anticurial, others strongly procurial, proclaimed the necessity of a council. The net result of a few years of such agitation from all sides was, first, papal embarrassment, then, a reluctant decision to comply with a universal demand. The sack of Rome in 1527 by imperial troops and the consequent predominance of Charles V in Italy precipitated the admission by the vacillating Pope Clement VII that a council should be called as soon as possible. But again the affair dragged on in the face of political maneuvering by both sides, until, in June 1532 at Ratisbon in Germany, the Catholic Estates demanded that a general council should be called; if it were not called within a year either by the Pope or by the Emperor, there should be a German national council to reform the Church and settle points in dispute between the Catholics and the Protestants. The Pope, however, was now in alliance with Francis I of France, who was consistently sabotaging the council because the Emperor was promoting it, and negotiations with the Germans and the Emperor were fruitless. The final judgment on Clement VII must be severe; it was well expressed by Peter Bloomeven, prior of the Charterhouse of Cologne in 1532: "Many Catholics are of the opinion that the Pope shrinks from a council in order to save himself from reform." Clement VII died in July 1534, and Alessandro Farnese was chosen Pope in October, taking the pontifical name of Paul III. Hopes arose that now at last something would be done. In January 1535, the convocation of a council was decided upon and legates were sent to the principal courts of Europe to gain the assent of the secular rulers to the holding of such a council and, hardly less important, agreement as to the place of meeting. Francis was evasive and reluctant; the Protestant princes refused to meet on the Pope's terms; and not a few of the Catholic princes and prelates offered objections to place or agenda. Only Ferdinand I, king-elect of the Romans, was favorable. Henry VIII of England, having already broken with Rome, was not even asked. Finally, after heroic negotiations on the part of the Pope's legates, a number of favorable replies were obtained and Paul issued, on June 2, 1536, a call for a general council to meet at Mantua on May 23, 1537, with the express purpose of reforming morals, extirpating heresy, preparing a crusade against the infidel, and bringing peace to Europe. By the date set for the council to meet, Charles V and Francis I were already locked in their third war.

In the meantime, in order to inform himself of the needs and progress of reform, the Pope had appointed in 1536 a commission of prelates to study the whole matter and report to him. This commission was made up of men known to be firm advocates of reform, among them Cardinal Contarini, and three reformers, soon to be raised to the cardinalate, Gian Pietro Caraffa, the Englishman Reginald Pole, and Jacopo Sadoleto. The result of their deliberations was the devastatingly candid *Consilium de emendanda ecclesia* (*Plan for Reforming the Church*), presented to the Pope in March 1537. It laid the blame for the sad predicament of the Church squarely on the popes, who had by laxness or greed furthered the vices of simony and nepotism, had shown flagrant disregard for the spiritual welfare of the faithful, had appointed to spiritual office men unsuitable for such charges, and, in general, had seemed to hold the theory that the property of the Church was their personal possession. They had "imagined that their will is law; that they are the owners of all benefices, so that they are free to dispose of them as they please without taint of simony." The recommendations were equally drastic. Appointments to bishoprics must be for merit and suitability, not to provide some favorite or relative with an income; expectatives and reservations, by which the best candidate may be eliminated from consideration by the whim of the *curia,* must be given up; distant bishoprics or benefices must no longer be bestowed on cardinals who could not possibly serve their dioceses; priests inadequately prepared should not be ordained. These and similar abuses rooted in greed and vanity—of which there was a long and detailed list—would have to be removed, or the Church would not be able to fulfill its function of the cure of souls. The document was widely circulated. Within the Catholic obedience it was both approved and criticized, the latter on the ground that it was unrealistic and, if followed, would wreck the whole administrative system of the Papacy. The Pope had the document read and discussed in his presence but left action to the coming Council. Luther published a German translation of the *Consilium* with sarcastic comments. In 1538 the *curia* forbade its publication, but in spite of the prohibition, thirteen editions appeared within the next twenty years.

The invitations to the forthcoming Council were sent out in proper form to those entitled to attend. Getting them to attend was another matter. French prelates followed Francis' lead and made excuses. Many German Catholic princes or prelates found themselves unable to leave their lands. The duke of Mantua, on whose territory the Council was to meet, made such difficulties that the Pope had to postpone the Council until November 1, 1537, and to try in the meantime to arrange for a more suitable place of meeting. Vicenza, on Venetian territory, was decided on and a further postponement of the opening of the Council to May 1, 1538, was decreed. The only prelate to be in Vicenza on May 1 was Archbishop John Magnus of Uppsala, who had been expelled from his see by the Reformation and was living in Italy. The council was thereupon postponed for a third time, without a date being set for its meeting. There followed other frustrations and two further prorogations, increasing the general distrust of the Pope's real intentions.

The Pope, however, was not completely discouraged. Urged on by his advisers, Cardinals Morone and Sadoleto, and by the Emperor, he convoked, on May 22, 1542, the Council to meet at Trent * on November 1, 1542. The choice of Trent was as fortunate as any could have been. It was barely within the borders of the Empire and yet largely Italian in population and tradition. Objections to Mantua or Vicenza as under papal influence, or against Nürnberg or any other German city, under imperial influence, could not hold against Trent. By the time set for the Council to open, the negotiations at Worms in 1540 and Ratisbon in 1541 between papal envoys and Protestant leaders on the subject of reunion, undertaken under pressure from the Emperor, had ended in complete deadlock and failure. The ultimate irreconcilability of German Protestant convictions with Catholic doctrine was made painfully clear. Thenceforth it was accepted on all sides that any future council called by the Pope would not be attended by the Protestants.

War between Francis and Charles having broken out—for the fourth time—in July 1542, it became obvious that the work of the Council would suffer under conditions of war between the two leading princes of Christendom. Nevertheless, the Pope sent to Trent his three legates, who, arriving on November 22, 1542, found a bare handful of delegates, uncertain whether to remain or return home. For months nothing was accomplished, while Francis and Charles were at war, and in July 1543 the Council was suspended. When war was concluded by the peace of Crépy (September 18, 1544), the subject of the Council again came up, and, with the consent of both Charles and Francis, the Pope reconvoked the Council for March 25, 1545. The Pope appointed three cardinals, del Monte, Cervini, and Pole, as his legates, empowering them to open the Council and preside in his place. Delegates began, slowly, to arrive in Trent, so slowly in fact that the opening of the Council had to be put off again. The formal opening took place only on December 13, 1545.

The Council of Trent: First Assembly, 1545-49

THE Council of Trent (*Concilium Tridentinum*), one of the most important synods in the history of the Church, was technically in session over a period of eighteen years, 1545 to 1563. It met in three Assemblies: the first, of eight sessions under Pope Paul III, from December 1545 to March 1549; the second under Pope Julius III, sessions X † to XVI, from January 1551 to April 1552; the third Assembly under Pope Pius IV, sessions XVII to XXV, from January 1562 to December 1563. In the course of these eighteen years the Church formulated its doctrine in the light of the attacks made upon it by Protestant and Catholic alike, and along lines of conservative scholasticism. The break between Protestant and Catholic was recognized as completely and finally irrevocable. The change from Catholic Reform to the Counter-Reformation took place, and the Church went from the defensive onto the attack, with new weapons, new leadership, and a new spirit.

This new and aggressive posture, however, was not achieved without an

---

* In Latin *Tridentum,* hence the adjective Tridentine, referring to the city and the Council.

† Session IX was simply a motion to reconvene the Council.

inner struggle, much bitter squabbling, and some loss of dignity. From the very first it was evident that powerfully entrenched interests and policies would contend for dominance in the decisions of the Council, largely carried over, of course, from the pre-Council period. The Emperor, always in need of the support of the German Estates, either for help in his Turkish wars or for financial reasons, often seemed to be acting as a protagonist of Protestant interests. On another side, the Spanish church was under his jurisdiction, although its undisputed orthodoxy and generally high moral level gave the Spanish delegates to the Council a weight their numbers alone could not have won for them. The fact that they were frequently in opposition to the Papacy laid upon Charles the obligation to protect them from papal reprisals. Then, as the master of much of Italy, Charles had interests which often conflicted sharply with those of the Papacy. With these various interests to reconcile, it is only natural that Charles' policy must, at times, have concealed inner conflicts. The more glaring antagonisms, however, were between the avowed advocates of reform and the defenders of the *curia*. The strength of the latter group lay in numbers. Italy had more and smaller bishoprics than any other part of Europe, and their bishops were usually dependent on the pope's favor. It was easier for them to attend the Council than it was for a French or a German bishop whose pastoral cares were more onerous. Throughout the Council the Italian prelates were in a majority. Their majority was never, however, unanimous, as some of them were subjects of the Emperor, while some of the reform party were also Italian and frequently voted against the *curia*. Yet a large block of the Italians voted consistently as the *curia* wanted them to.

It was understood that the legates of the Pope should preside over the deliberations of the Council. Voting privileges were restricted to those of episcopal rank or above and to generals of orders. The Emperor earnestly wanted the Council to take up first the question of reform. He felt it would show the world, and particularly the Germans, that the Papacy was serious in its announcement of plans of reform. The curial party, on the other hand, wanted to formulate doctrine, which would put the Church in the strong position of being able to accept or reject Protestant "innovations" by simple reference to an established theology. Between Charles' wish and that of the curialists a compromise was effected. The Council voted to divide its membership into three classes or special congregations, which should discuss a question assigned to it by a preliminary committee of theologians. The formulations of these congregations would then be presented to a "General Congregation," whose reformulation would be voted on at a subsequent plenary session. At the same time it was decided to take up doctrine and reform concurrently. But the result of the division of labor and subject matter was that doctrine actually received more attention than reform.

The rule of faith was first defined so as to put Scripture and Tradition on an equal basis, to be received by the Church *pari pietatis affectu et reverentia* (with an equal pious devotion and reverence). This definition was completely contrary to the basic Protestant doctrine that the Christian faith rests exclusively upon Holy Scripture and that Tradition is valid only when it conforms to Scripture. The Council then further rejected Protestant doctrines on original sin and justification by faith. There were members of the Council whose view on justification by faith was so Augustinian as to sound very much like Luther's, and the debates in the long sessions on this subject were frequently lively. The condemnation of the Lutheran doctrine of justification by faith alone was perhaps the most significant as well as most carefully elaborated doctrinal pronouncement of the whole Council. It exalted the need of grace in the work of salvation, but also affirmed the cooperation of man's free will in its achievement and expressly condemned Luther's doctrine of salvation by faith alone. Late in the session the doctrine of the seven sacraments, essentially in its medieval form, was stated, and the objective nature of the sacraments was plainly asserted: they are effective, not by reason of the person of the ministrant, but because, in themselves and by virtue of Christ's intention and institution, they work in the believer what Christ and the Church have promised.

In matters of administration and reform the Council urged the bishops to institute reform in their dioceses and establish schools for training the clergy. It accepted the Vulgate as the official text of the Scriptures, ordered bishops and other prelates to preach in their dioceses or provide for substitutes to preach, and prescribed that the regular clergy obtain permission from the bishop before preaching in his diocese. In reform this was not a bad beginning, but it was also not more than a beginning. In doctrinal matters the Council took a strongly anti-Protestant position; in reform very tentative and mild recommendations were put forward, whose primary purpose seemed to be to strengthen the power of the bishops and the *curia*.

Early in 1547 the tension between the Emperor and Pope Paul III had risen to the point where there was some fear in the Council that the Emperor might allow his troops to move into Trent. The excuse of an epidemic was used to justify leaving the city, and on March 11 the Council voted to move its seat to Bologna. Charles, at war with the Schmalkaldic League, was angry at having the Council removed from imperial territory, and ordered the fourteen prelates loyal to him to remain in Trent. But the first Assembly of the Council was over. The Emperor's victory at Mühlberg (April 24, 1547) left him master of Germany. Without the Emperor's support or at least compliance, the Council would have no real significance. Since he firmly refused to allow these fourteen prelates to go to Bologna, no compromise was possible.

The Council of Trent: Second Assembly, 1551–52

ON SEPTEMBER 10, 1547, the Pope's son, Pier Luigi Farnese, upon whom the Pontiff planned to confer the duchies of Parma and Piacenza, was assassinated at the orders of Ferrante Gonzaga, governor of the Milanese and a dependent of the Emperor. The Pope did not directly accuse Charles of complicity in the crime, but he initiated immediately the formation of a short-lived Holy League against the Emperor. Charles' favorable terms to the Protestants in the *Interim* of Augsburg (May 15, 1548, see above, p. 500) gave the Pope further justification for his plans to diminish imperial power in Italy. All this time the Council was necessarily in abeyance and the work of reform at a standstill. The prelates assembled at Bologna were released on September 17, 1549. The Pope died of old age two months later.

After a long and tightly locked conclave of seventy-one ballotings, Cardinal

The Council of Trent, by Titian, in the Louvre, Paris [ALINARI].

del Monte was elected Pope (February 7, 1550) and chose to be called Julius III (1550–55). He urged the Emperor Charles and Henry II of France to live in peace and reconvoked the Council, to meet at Trent on April 29, 1551. This second Assembly of the Council of Trent, which lasted until April 1552, was poorly attended. There were fewer than twenty voting prelates present at the opening session and no French bishop among them. Henry II had taken an antagonistic attitude toward the Council. The Council's accomplishments were limited to decrees on the Eucharist, reaffirming the doctrine of transubstantiation and the sacrifice of the Mass, and on penance. In these discussions and formulations two clerics took part who were to represent a new force in the Church and to influence its future policies: Diego Laynez and Alfonso Salmerón of the Society of Jesus. In these decrees and others less controversial the views of the Protestants were specifically and carefully anathematized. The suspension of the Council in April 1552 was explicitly for a period of two years, but the affairs of the Church were so deeply involved in international politics that the two years stretched out to ten. These were the years of the gradual slackening of the Emperor's efforts to win the Protestants back to the Catholic fold. Henry II of France had decided on suppression of the heretics by force and saw no need for the endless discussions in a *conventus* controlled by the *curia.* Within the *curia,* by this time, all hope of conciliation had vanished, and to a degree that argument for conciliar action had lost its force. The increasing effectiveness and impressive record of the new order of the Jesuits led many curialists to the conviction that, accepting the existence of the Protestants, the best thing to do would be to fight them with their own weapons: preaching, teaching, missionary evangelism, reform in administration and morals. It is to the origins and growth of that order that we must now turn.

IGNATIUS LOYOLA AND THE SOCIETY OF JESUS

IN ORDER to place the Society of Jesus in its proper perspective it will be necessary to retrace our steps some years to the early decades of the sixteenth century. We have noted at least two illustrations of the commonplace that great movements are the shadows of great men: Luther and Lutheranism, Calvin and Calvinism. It is fully as true of Ignatius Loyola and the Society of Jesus, of which he was the founder and first General, and has remained the inspiration and model. His person and peculiar genius are so significant as to call for detailed attention.

Don Iñigo Lopez de Recalde * was born in 1491, the thirteenth child of a Basque nobleman, Beltrán de Loyola, at the family castle of Loyola in the northern province of Guipúzcoa. He passed his boyhood as a page at the court of Ferdinand the Catholic, in an atmosphere redolent of the centuries-long Christian crusade against the infidel, with all its accompaniments of devout knighthood and gallant adventures in honor of the saints. He later served with two brothers in the army of his family's overlord, the duke of Najera, for a number of years; in the defense of the citadel of the city of Pampeluña against the French in 1521, his right leg was shattered by a cannon ball. The primitive surgery to which he was subjected by the French doctor and a later attempt to repair the damage lamed him for life. During convalescence he asked for his beloved romance of chivalry, *Amadís de Gaula,* but at the family castle the only books available were lives of the saints and the *Life of Christ* by Ludolph of Saxony. Loyola became, in spite of himself, interested in the characters of St. Francis and St. Dominic and readily transferred his military experience and imagery to the new subject matter. He visualized the Virgin Mary as the Lady of his heart and regarded the Christian quest as a military campaign: on the one side the hosts of the Lord, on the other the minions of the Devil, flying the flags of Lucifer. Thus spiritualizing knighthood and chivalry, he found a new outlet for his devotion and energy.

When, early in 1522, he was well enough to travel, he went to the Dominican monastery of Montserrat, where he made his declaration and his vows as a pilgrim, exchanging his knightly apparel and weapons for the rags of a beggar. Shortly thereafter (March 24, 1522) he went into the nearby monastery at Manresa. Here he made a detailed confession of his sins which took three days to write, performing the severe acts of a penitent, long fasts, and rigorous self-examination. It was some time before he found peace. According to his followers it was after a vision lasting eight days, in which the whole organization and program of his Society and the plan of the *Spiritual Exercises* were revealed to him. It is certain that it was at Manresa that, in his reading, he came upon a work of García de Císneros, former abbot of Manresa, the *Exercitatorio de la vida espiritual (Book of Exercises of the Spiritual Life)*, published in

* The name appears variously. The most likely form is Iñigo de Oñaz y Loyola.

1500, and similar works of the Lowland mystics, which served to induce him to commit to paper the broad lines of his own *Exercises*.

After ten months of prayerful and humble vagrancy Loyola left Manresa for Barcelona, on the way to fight the infidel in his own camp, Jerusalem, with the spiritual arms of the Christian knight. He landed first in Italy, went to Rome, obtained the papal blessing for his pilgrimage to Jerusalem, then walked on to Venice, begging his bread. He begged passage to the Holy Land on a ship of the Republic to Cyprus, thence on a specially built pilgrim ship to the shores of Palestine. In September, six months after he had left Barcelona, he stood in the footsteps of Christ. The Franciscans, guardians of the Holy Places, found Ignatius' enthusiasm unwelcome. His eagerness to convert the native Moslems might disturb the uneasy truce under which Christians lived in Palestine. He was asked to leave. Begging his passage back to Venice, by foot or by boat, he returned to Barcelona in March 1524.

On the way he had decided he would have to acquire a formal education if he were to carry out his mission. At thirty-three he went to grammar school with boys of eight and ten and struggled with Latin paradigms. After two years of schooling by day and begging by night he went to Alcalá and attended all the free lectures at the university that he could, particularly on Aristotle and Peter Lombard. He would pass on to any who would listen the *Spiritual Exercises,* which by now he had greatly revised. Three disciples joined him, living at the same hospital (or almshouse) where he now made his home. The four of them aroused suspicion, and inquisitors from Toledo subjected them to a long investigation. It was feared they were of the *alumbrados* or *illuminati,** of whom the Inquisition was especially distrustful. They were cleared of any heresy, but ordered to change the color of their garments from brown to black to conform to the usual religious habit. In 1527 Ignatius was imprisoned for a while, then released but forbidden to teach for three years. To avoid so hard a restriction the four left Alcalá and moved to Salamanca, where their talk again brought them to prison and long questioning. Reluctantly, Ignatius had to decide that he and his friends could no longer study in Spain. It would be better to go to Paris, where they could study theology without such unreasonable restrictions. Driving ahead of him a donkey loaded with his few books, he limped to Barcelona, then on to Paris, where he arrived on February 2, 1528.

Ignatius entered the Collège de Montaigu, famous for its dour scholarship and discipline, as an external student. He was not sufficiently advanced in elementary grammar to be admitted as a regular "internal" student. John Calvin had left but a few months before. It is interesting to speculate that the two may have met in the course of the next five years, as Calvin visited the city frequently until 1533, but neither mentions any such meeting. Ignatius studied at Paris, first at Montaigu, later at the Collège de Sainte Barbe, for seven years. He gained the master of arts degree in 1534, then began study toward the bachelor of divinity degree. By the time he left Paris in 1535 he had around him nine disciples, four Frenchmen and five Spaniards, all of whom took the master's

---

* The *alumbrados* were a group of highly spiritual persons in Spain whose emphasis on private prayer and contemplation had led the Inquisition to doubt their conformity to Church doctrine. See also above, Chapter 18.

degree and went on to study theology. The best known of his early disciples were Francis Xavier, Diego Laynez, and Alfonso Salmerón. In 1535, on a physician's advice, Ignatius left for Spain, in hopes of recovering in his native air the health that his self-imposed privations had so seriously impaired. It was planned that he should go from Spain to Venice, where his nine companions, coming directly from Paris, would meet him. From there they would set out for the Holy Land. They met in Venice early in January 1537. While awaiting appropriate passage to the Holy Land they worked in hospitals and preached in the streets. Five of their number received ordination as priests.

By this time Ignatius had perfected, to his satisfaction, the program of spiritual discipline, the *Spiritual Exercises* which form the backbone and strength of the order he was to found. This manual prescribes instruction for four weeks of self-examination and control. The first week, the *via purgativa,* was intended to lead the believer to a recognition of his deep sinfulness and the cleansing of his conscience through contemplation of the sinful nature of man; the second week, the first part of the *via illuminativa,* is devoted to an understanding of the mission of the Redeemer and the battle against Satan, described as facing one another in feudal battle array; the third week continues the "illuminative way" to a consideration of the suffering of Christ on the Cross and His death; the fourth week, the *via unitiva,* completes the meditation, leading the believer to a conviction of oneness with God, a complete surrender of his will and mind to God in Christ. This exercise, repeated after the completion of the education of a member of the Society, was recommended, in an abbreviated form, by several popes to clergy and laity alike. Its inspiring discipline has played a large part in maintaining piety in the Church.

War made passage to Palestine impossible and the group decided to go to Rome to get the Pope's blessing and instruction for further activity. They encountered difficulties and suspicion in Rome, but Pope Paul III extended them his favor. Their consciousness of their need for organization grew with action and thought, and Ignatius drew up a brief preliminary constitution which he submitted to the Pope in September 1539. They added to the usual monastic vows a special vow of paramount obedience to the pope, to undertake any mission, anywhere, which he might assign to them, asking no compensation of any kind. The Pope gave this vow his canonical approval in the bull *Regimini militantis ecclesiae* of September 27, 1540. He stipulated the quasi-military organization of the order, approved the *Spiritual Exercises* and the general plan of organization, and limited the membership to sixty, a limit which he later withdrew.

From Papal Approval to Death of Loyola: 1540–56

THE first successes of the Society were in Italy. The membership scattered to various parts of the peninsula to preach and teach, combatting heresy, whether native Italian or imported Lutheran, laboring among the poor and the sick, establishing schools and, within a few years, colleges. In 1550 Ignatius established at Rome the most important of the early colleges, the *Collegium Romanum,* which within a very short time had graduated and sent out over a hundred priests trained in the rigorous discipline of the order. In 1552 the

Collegium Germanicum was also established at Rome, especially planned to train members of the Society for the recovery of Germany from Lutheranism. The order was strong in Spain, divided into three provinces with eight colleges, though it also met opposition from the Dominicans and the Inquisition, and even from the crown. We have seen before how the Spanish crown was traditionally opposed to papal interference (see above, Chapter 6) in the affairs of the Spanish church, and the Jesuits bore direct allegiance to the pope. In spite of the opposition, the order won popular approval and made a notable impression at the universities. Portugal was more congenial, and the work of Xavier, who went as a missionary to the Portuguese possessions in India, was deeply appreciated at the Portuguese court.

The early emissaries to Germany had a most difficult path ahead of them. The years of freedom from the *curia,* added to a basic distrust of the Papacy, had made even loyal Catholics reluctant to believe that any good thing could come out of Rome. By 1542, however, three of Ignatius' companions were active and established in northern and southern Germany. Bavaria offered an especially fertile soil for their labors. Peter Canisius was the member of the Society who was primarily responsible for the final victory of Catholicism in

Ignatius Loyola, in the University Church, Seville [BILDARCHIV FOTO MARBURG].

southern Germany. His particular merit was the preparation of catechisms which were adapted to combat effectively the catechism of Luther, and it was he who later guided Ferdinand in his policy of catholicizing his court at Vienna and the Austrian nobility. In return Ferdinand supported Canisius to the extent of endowing several colleges and a seminary, not only in Vienna but also in Bohemia.

Four of Ignatius' ablest companions, Laynez, Salmerón, Lejay, and Canisius, were present at the second Assembly of the Council of Trent (1551–52) as consultants and theologians for the papal legates. Laynez was entrusted by Cardinal legate Cervini with the task of making a list of all the dogmatic errors which would have to be condemned by the Council. The order was young, and the work of these Jesuits, aside from a memorable three-hour speech by Laynez against Lutheran tendencies in a proposed decree on justification, was not spectacular. It was, however, invaluable experience for them to see the Church functioning at such an important juncture in its history.

By about 1550 Ignatius had elaborated the rules and organization of the order in the form of the definitive *Constitution,* by which it is still governed. The structure is strictly military. A General, elected for life, has almost absolute power. The membership is made up of three ranks of members, first of novices who, after a short period of testing, remain in that probationary status for two years. They may then be released or be allowed to advance to the second rank, the status of scholastic, lasting at least seven years, covering a thorough study of philosophy and theology—the most numerous class of the Society. The next advance, which only a few achieve, is to the status of spiritual coadjutors or professed who, alone, in addition to the usual vows of chastity, poverty, and obedience, take a special vow of obedience to the pope. The result was a highly disciplined, flexible, and loyal élite group whose effectiveness was the envy of other and older orders and often the despair of the Protestants.

By the death of Ignatius in 1556 the Society counted 1500 members, with active provinces in every country of Europe and in Asia, many colleges, and an impressive record of achievement, doctrinal, diplomatic, and missionary. Pope Paul IV, that same Caraffa who had been one of the members of the Oratory of Divine Love in the early 1520's, was ill disposed to all things Spanish, remarking that Charles V was "the worst man born into the world for a thousand years," and calling the Spaniards "the dregs of the earth." The Society, therefore, Spanish in origin, had some difficulties with the Pope, most particularly in electing a successor to the founder. Finally, in July 1558, Laynez was chosen General of the order in time to participate, as a voting head of a monastic organization, in the third and last Assembly of the Council of Trent.

In these intervening years great changes had taken place in the world as well as in the personnel of the Council. The Emperor Charles V had abdicated his crown, retired to the monastery of Yuste, and died in 1558. The unity of the Habsburg domains was broken, never to be recovered. Ferdinand, king of Bohemia and Hungary, inherited the imperial title, and his nephew Philip II ruled Spain, the Low Countries, and the Spanish possessions beyond the sea. Nephew and uncle frequently differed in their relations to the Council as well as to the Protestants. The king of France, Henry II, had died (1559) of a tragic accident after a reign of twelve years, and was succeeded by his son, Francis II, who ruled under the influence of the queen mother, Catherine de' Medici, and of the Guises. England, which in 1553 had been started on the way back to the fold when the Catholic Mary Tudor came to the throne, was now ruled by Elizabeth, whom the papal *curia* deeply distrusted. She had surrounded herself with advisers openly Protestant in sympathy. France and Spain, after decades of war, signed the peace of the Pyrenees in 1559. Issues which had led to war were either buried or settled; the Papacy no longer found it easy to play the two kingdoms against each other and thus disturb the balance of power.

THE ROMAN INQUISITION

WITH the name of one of the most forceful popes of the century, Paul IV (1555–59), is inevitably connected the growth of the power and range of interest of the Roman Inquisition. The Inquisition as an institution had been in existence for many centuries. Since 1216 it had been the particular charge of the Dominican Order, and had been favored by kings and emperors. The Catholic Kings found it useful in their task of unifying Spain, against Moslem and Jew, and it became in Spain a peculiarly effective national disciplinary organ. Thousands were burned at the stake. Caraffa, as papal nuncio to Spain, observed the effectiveness of the Inquisition and, returning to Italy, set it up there on the Spanish model. At his urging, supported by Ignatius Loyola, Pope Paul III instituted the Roman Inquisition by the bull *Licet ab initio* (July 21, 1542). Six cardinals, Caraffa being mentioned first, were to constitute a Commission of Inquisitors-General, with wide discretion and authority. Men in high place were its first victims. The Vicar-General of the Capuchins, Bernardino Ochino, was charged with heresy, and fled to Geneva in 1542. Anyone who had ever been on friendly terms with Juan Valdés in Naples was suspect and ultimately imprisoned. Fear gripped whole sections of the Italian people, paralyzing intellectual life. The University of Modena dissolved in 1546. When, in 1555, Caraffa became Pope Paul IV, the Inquisition had freer rein than before. Cardinal Pole came under suspicion and was removed from his post as legate to England. He was realistic enough not to return to Rome. In Italy no opposition to the tyranny of the Inquisition was able to stand. Renée, duchess of Ferrara, who had leanings toward reformed doctrines, had to leave the country. Cardinal Morone was imprisoned and other bishops and prelates were arrested, still others charged with heresy were burned.

The Papacy and Spain split on many issues, but on the need for an austere and powerful Inquisition with authority to investigate and discipline anyone of any station in civil life or in the Church, they were in complete accord. Philip II was a firm and aggressive supporter of the Inquisition, regarding it as an agency calculated to bring uniformity in society. The severity of the administration of the Inquisition varied from pope to pope, temperate under Pius IV (1559–65), harsh under Pius V (1566–72), himself formerly Inquisitor-General, who made executions, by strangling, beheading, or burning, the common thing in Rome, with the clergy required to attend. As the great Catholic historian Ludwig Pastor wrote, "The Inquisition sealed the fate of Protestants in Italy." Had the Inquisition not been so effective and convincing in eliminating heresy and the heretics from Italian society, it is doubtful if the Counter-Reformation would have been successful, even granted the substantial work of the Council of Trent and the brilliant labors of the Society of Jesus.

Last Sessions of the Council, 1559–63

IT WAS indeed a new world in which Pius IV (1559–65) convened the Council of Trent for April 8, 1561. This reconvened Council was immediately concerned with the question as to whether it was a new council or a continuation of the previous two Assemblies. The latter construction was favored and all previous decrees and canons simply accepted as part of the whole conciliar program. The question of whether the papal legates merely presided over the Council or had the power to propose action, thus depriving the Council of the power of initiation, was hotly contested. It was the old struggle between pope and council in a new guise. The Papacy won out and the legates gained the right to "propose" measures for conciliar approval. The *Index* of prohibited books, founded by Paul IV in 1559, was revised. Significantly, the delegates were now discussing whether the commands to bishops to reside in their dioceses were of divine origin or of ecclesiastical obligation only. If the residence commands were of divine origin, the Pope could not exempt any bishops from the obligation. After bitter debate, and in spite of the fact that a majority was really in favor of divine obligation, the decision was made, in order to avoid an open rupture in the Council, to refer the matter to the Pope. Once again the cause of curial centralization had won.

Another issue which caused sharp divisions among the delegates was whether the cup, at Mass, should be given the laity. The imperial delegates, bearing in mind the popular demand for the cup in Germany, Bohemia and Hungary,* urged the concession; the papal and Spanish parties, with the temporary support of the French king, successfully evaded the issue. The Mass was decreed to be a sacrifice, Christ's offer of Himself as a living oblation at the Last Supper and upon the Cross.

The last sessions of the Council were stormy. The clash between the curialists and the Ultramontanes—that is, those representing the Emperor, the French and others outside Italy—was keen and persistent. For the curialists, the Jesuits Salmerón and Laynez were among the abler speakers, although at times they overstated the case for papal supremacy. Papal victory was ultimately achieved by singleness of command and purpose, division and manipulation of the opposition, aided by the general fatigue of the delegates. Agreement had been reached in a few matters of importance to the welfare of the Church, particularly in the decrees on the sacrament of ordination. Clear statements were made as to the qualifications for the bishopric, which were set high enough to prevent some of the worst abuses of papal power in the pre-Reformation period. Episcopal supervision of the lower clergy was stipulated. Most important for the real revival of Catholic vigor, seminaries were decreed for every diocese to provide adequate preparation for the clergy. An educated clergy, it was reasoned, would be the best answer to Protestantism. By July 1563, the leader of the French legation, Cardinal Guise of Lorraine, had been

* Ferdinand I had been titular king of Bohemia and Hungary from 1526.

won over to the papal side by the offer to make him Legate Apostolic in France. The Spanish stood almost alone for substantial reform, resisting to the end the curialist policy of minimizing the need for active attention to the ills in the Church. Whatever was accomplished in this direction in this third Assembly of the Council was their doing. Some decrees on doctrine were rushed through in the last months of 1563 and were generally moderate in tone. On December 4, 1563, the Council held its last session. The official acts of the Council were signed by 255 prelates, of whom 189 were Italian.

The function of the Council, as Charles V, who had been most active in bringing it about, had intended, was to have been to offer a basis for the reunion of the Protestants with the Church. The result was in fact the opposite. The position of the Catholic Church was now so defined as to make it impossible for the Protestants to rejoin it without giving up virtually everything they had fought for. On the other hand, by formulating Catholic doctrine, revising their own organization, and confirming the central authority of the pope in matters of doctrine and practice, the fathers at Trent clarified the issues between Protestant and Catholic upon which the religious wars of the next century and beyond—on the field and in the study—should be fought. The Council of Trent was a landmark, not only in the history of the Catholic Church, but in the whole history of the European idea.

THE POST-TRIDENTINE COUNTER-REFORMATION

ARMED with a crisp, aggressively formulated statement of its traditional doctrine, confident of success and proud of having rediscovered its soul, the Catholic Church now went on the offensive against Protestantism and heresy in every form in all the lands where it had lost its predominance. At its command were two powerful agencies of conquest: the Society of Jesus and the Roman Inquisition. It was, furthermore, to profit in some areas from a new Catholic spirit of mystic devotion and a new urge in literature and art. Seen in retrospect, in view of this impressive display of vigor and discipline, there is reason to wonder how Protestantism, divided into many sects and dedicated to principles of individualism, eschewing any degree of central controls, managed to maintain itself as well as it did.

The popes of the Tridentine and post-Tridentine period were, for the most part, men of exceptional merit and ability. Paul IV had energetically undertaken and carried through reform within the *curia* and the States of the Church. He sent back to their dioceses over a hundred bishops who were at Rome without good reason. He disciplined severely his own nephews who were living in Rome in scandalous luxury, and he stopped the traffic in benefices at heavy cost to papal income. His high morality was a tonic for Rome and an inspiring preparation for the final Assembly of the Council. He increased the power of the Roman Inquisition and established the *Index* of prohibited books. Paul's successor, Pius IV, was less rigorous and firm, and in other times might have allowed the *curia* to return to its Renaissance laxness. But the spirit of reform had gained strength, so that under the guidance of his nephew Charles

Borromeo, one of the great ecclesiastical statesmen of the century, he maintained the Inquisition and supported the activity of the Council. There was a reaction from his relative moderation in the direction of the austerity of Paul IV in the election of Ghislieri, former Inquisitor-General, as Pius V (1566–72). This Pope planned a league of Christian princes against Islam and supported energetically and with papal naval components the expedition of Don Juan, Philip II's half brother, which resulted in the defeat of the Turks at Lepanto (October 7, 1571). In Rome he was responsible for many executions in public *autos da fé* of those guilty of deviation in theology. His personal life was spotless, his efforts toward reform were sincere and well conceived, and his services to the Church in rooting out Protestantism in Italy were noteworthy. He was later canonized by the Church.

The work of maintaining the program of reform was carried on by Pius V's successor, Gregory XIII (1572–85), who had had wide experience in papal administration and diplomacy under the three previous popes. Influenced by Borromeo, he demanded of the *curia* and the episcopate a sincere adherence to the decrees of Trent and furthered the foundation of seminaries to provide a learned priesthood. He initiated the system of residential colleges at Rome for priests from various countries, and the great Gregorian University at Rome was also his foundation.

Gregory's successor, the Franciscan Sixtus V (1585–90), continued the tradition of vigorous and able administrators endued with great personal piety. In his five years it is possible he introduced too many innovations. His pontificate gave an impression of feverish activity, some of it ill considered. To repair the loss of income which the austerity of his predecessors had incurred, Sixtus established prices for the purchase of papal offices and honorific titles. But the city of Rome was beautified by him, the administration of the business of the *curia* completely reorganized, and the number of cardinals fixed at seventy, where it was to remain for almost four centuries. His appointees to the College of Cardinals were men of high ability and character. In foreign relations he was fairly adroit and successful in strengthening the diplomatic position of the Papacy. A major undertaking of his was the publication of an edition of the Latin Vulgate. Done too hurriedly, it was sharply criticized even during his lifetime.*

Clement VIII (1592–1605) accepted and continued the foreign policies of Sixtus V, but did not distinguish himself in efficient administration or in the maintenance of the tradition of reform in the Church. An important event during his pontificate was the conversion of Henry IV of France to the Catholic faith. Although he proceeded cautiously in accepting Henry's conversion, the Pope realized that he needed French support if the Papacy were to win independence from Spain, which was his fixed policy. The loss of France to Catholicism would have been an almost fatal blow to the Church's prestige. Clement issued a revised edition of the Vulgate Bible published by Sixtus V which was to be the Church's official text of the Scriptures until the present time.

The jubilee year of 1600 brought many thousands of pilgrims to Rome. In

* The next three popes, Urban VII, Gregory XIV, and Innocent IX, together reigned hardly more than a year.

retrospect, Catholics could in general take satisfaction in the successes the Church had won in all areas of its interest during the preceding half-century. The pontificate of Paul V (1605–21) covers the period of the gathering storm of the Thirty Years' War. The activities of this Pope in the political maneuvering that led up to that sad conflict will be touched upon later. We are here concerned with his place in the development of reform and the Counter-Reformation. He enforced episcopal residence, chose able and conscientious cardinals, obliging them to perform the functions of their local sees, gave impetus to the reform of liturgical music, and formed or approved several orders intended to convert Protestants to the Catholic faith.

The Counter-Reformation North of the Alps: The Empire

UNDER the leadership of an exceptionally able and determined group of popes, the Church made great strides in the half-century after Trent in its campaign to recover lost ground. Within the Empire where, from about 1560, Lutheranism had lost much of its earlier enthusiasm, the missionaries of the revised and reformed Church made their most spectacular gains in Bavaria. Taking a leaf from Luther's appeal to the princes, the Church adroitly used individual princes who might be susceptible to the call of tradition to bring their subjects and lands back into the fold. The Peace of Augsburg, by formalizing the principle of *cuius regio, eius religio,* had secured this right to all princes. The Protestants had frequently used the right, but as often as not it worked to the advantage of a Catholic. This was particularly the case in Bavaria, under Duke Albert V (1550–79). Albert consistently resisted the spread of Protestantism in his lands and firmly supported Catholic reform. A Jesuit college was founded at Ingolstadt in 1556 and affiliated with the local university. The ever effective Canisius was a frequent adviser of the duke; the high-minded efficiency of the Jesuits and indeed of the whole reform effort made a great impression upon the people. As early as 1554 Albert asserted that over ten thousand of his subjects had voluntarily returned to the Church. In 1563 the Jesuits, under the protection of the bishop of Augsburg, Cardinal Otto Trucksess, took over the University of Dillingen.

Canisius, traveling prodigiously, seemed to be everywhere at once. He founded colleges on the Jesuit model at Cologne, Würzburg, Nijmegen, Vienna, and Innsbruck. Perhaps the most effective weapon in the Catholic armory was the catechism of Canisius, which, in clear language and succinct form, presented the Catholic faith. First published in 1555 in Vienna, it was often republished in Germany and adopted in other lands. It is estimated that there have been over four hundred editions of the original Latin edition and its many translations. In 1556 Canisius was appointed provincial of the Society of Jesus for Upper Germany, including Austria, Tirol, Bohemia, and Bavaria. In 1559 Cardinal Trucksess attached Canisius to his cathedral at Augsburg as a regular preacher, a connection which he retained until 1566, in addition to his duties as provincial of the order and frequent special missions to other parts of the Empire or Rome. His preaching, firm and moderate, was largely responsible for reviving Catholicism in Augsburg. Empty churches became full, and hundreds were baptized.

The Protestant princes were unable or unwilling to present a united front to this determined and concerted Catholic attack. Not only were there doctrinal differences among the Protestants, Lutheran, Zwinglian, and Calvinist, but dynastic and territorial ambitions and squabbles further divided them. The Jesuit advisers of the Catholic princes were extremely adept at exploiting these gaps in Protestant defenses. In Saxony, Swabia, the Palatinate, Württemberg, Brandenburg, and most of northern Germany, the Catholic offensive made few or no gains. But in Austria, Bavaria, along the lower Rhine, and in the three ecclesiastical electorates of Trier, Mainz, and Cologne, Catholic success was significant. Emperor Ferdinand I, personally a good Catholic, was interested in reforming the Church more to attract the Protestants than to comply with demands of the Pope, with whom he had frequent sharp disputes. His successor, Maximilian II (1564–76), was friendly to the Protestants but stayed within the Church. His son, Rudolf II (1576–1612), was raised by Jesuits and remained under their tutelage all his life. We shall discuss his reign in some detail in connection with the background of the Thirty Years' War.

Bohemia

BOHEMIA, technically a part of the Empire but occupying a unique and almost autonomous position under the Emperor, was the scene of interesting developments. Ferdinand had been sovereign, since 1526, of a kingdom which had been Hussite, that is, anti-Roman, for over a century. The Estates, made up of nobles of German blood as well as of the Czech nobility and towns, were sympathetic to the Lutheran revolt and, later, to the Calvinistic teachings. From about 1560 to early in the seventeenth century the Protestant or pro-Protestant element could count on a majority of 90 per cent in the Diet. Ferdinand, as king, had had to walk very carefully in religious matters. His court was Catholic and he made no secret of his own preferences, but there was no possibility that he could force any change in the religion of his subjects. He had, in fact, to allow the cup to the laity and marriage of the priesthood. In his dealings with the Papacy he insisted on these concessions to his Bohemian subjects. On the other hand, he did what he could to strengthen Catholicism in the land. When, in 1555, Canisius came to Prague with several companions, none of them Czech, Ferdinand extended him every possible assistance, assigning him the church of St. Clement near the Charles Bridge. The results of the work of the Jesuits among an antagonistic population were, for long, meager. It was years before they could count a single convert, and by the end of the century a bare dozen native members of the order was their reward. Their teaching, however, was their best recommendation, and Hussite and Lutheran families sent their sons to the Jesuit college in considerable numbers. Favorable results in the form of conversions had to await the second generation.

Poland

THE recovery of Poland for the Catholic faith was, at first sight, one of the most remarkable reversals of a basic trend in the history of the Counter-Reformation. Protestantism in its various forms had swept the Catholic

Church before it. The *szlachta* (nobility) welcomed the independence it gave them; the towns, where Germans were numerous, had accepted Lutheranism or Calvinism with astonishing rapidity. King Sigismund I (1506–48) remained a Catholic, but was unable or unwilling to go against the current. The membership of the Polish diet by about 1555 was more than half Protestant. The trend began to change soon after that, and by the end of the century Protestantism had been reduced to a remnant. The credit for the change must be given almost solely to Stanislaus Hosius (1504–79), cardinal and bishop of Ermeland. After studying canon law in Italy, he became in 1538 secretary to the king, took orders in 1543, and was given the bishopric of Chełmno (Kulm) in 1549. The new king, Sigismund Stanislaus Augustus (1548–72), had at first leaned to Protestantism but was won over to the Catholic cause by a papal nuncio, Martinengo, and chose Hosius as his adviser, sending him on crucial diplomatic missions to the Emperor Charles V and later to Ferdinand I. Hosius was transferred to the important bishopric of Ermeland in 1551 and took the lead in the campaign against Protestantism. In that same year he led the decisive Catholic synod of Piotrków, which adopted his Confession of Faith as its guide and platform of reform and reconquest.

The ubiquitous Canisius came to Poland in 1558, accompanying a papal nuncio. At a colloquy with the Protestants, Canisius had an opportunity to assess the situation in Poland and to plan the Jesuit strategy, which was to recover Poland from the Protestants. Cardinal Hosius had gained great prestige

Peter Canisius, artist unknown, Vienna National Library, Vienna [DEUTSCHE FOTOTHEK DRESDEN].

in Poland by his activities at the last Assembly of the Council of Trent, and, on returning to Poland, increased the tempo of his anti-Protestant campaign. At his urging, the king in 1564 ordered the acceptance of the decrees of Trent. Canisius sent Sigismund in 1565 at his request ten Jesuits, who founded colleges at Płock, Vilna, Braunsberg (in Prussia), and Poznań. The efforts of the Protestants to combat the Catholic progress by composing the *Consensus* of Sandomierz in 1570 were vitiated by two things: their dissensions and the fact that many of them had been attracted by the antitrinitarian doctrines then being spread in Poland by the followers of Lelio Sozzini. A confused creed does not lead to aggressive propagation or determined defense. One result of the divisions was an atmosphere of toleration. The Polish Diet of 1573 proclaimed toleration for "dissidents," but the organized and ably led Catholics were those best able to take advantage of the toleration. The Protestants, divided into three main groups, could offer no organized resistance. The result was certain Catholic predominance.

In 1573, some time after the death without heirs of Sigismund II, the last of the Jagiellonian line, Henry, duke of Anjou, son of Catherine de' Medici, was elected king. A Catholic alliance seemed desirable in view of the fact that Poland's immediate neighbors to the west, Silesia and Brandenburg, were Protestant. He arrived in Cracow only in February 1574. Six months later, on hearing of the death of his brother Charles IX, the new king suddenly left Cracow by night for Paris and the French throne. The Poles were indignant, and the papal nuncio and leaders of the Catholic party were reviled and openly charged with responsibility for a national humiliation. Out of the confusion there came a new election which was a mixture of comedy and chaos. Stephen Bátory, prince of Transylvania, won out over the Habsburg candidate. The papal nuncio left Warsaw before Stephen entered in triumph. Bátory was a perfectly good Catholic, but the Catholic cause, by its commitment to the Habsburg candidate, had lost some prestige with the people. The Jesuits, however, had avoided involvement in the nuncio's schemes, and Stephen came to rely upon them in matters of education and the execution of his foreign policy. Stephen had a master plan: to bring Hungary, western Muscovy, and Poland together in order to drive the Turks from Europe. Only the Jesuits had the vision to see the soundness of his plan. In return for their support he extended to them great privileges and allowed them to establish colleges in Cracow, Riga, Dorpat, and Lublin, in addition to the four at Poznań, Vilna, Braunsberg, and Płock. The king remained personally tolerant, and Protestants as well as Catholics lived in the enjoyment of their faiths.

It was under his successor, Sigismund III (1587–1632), that the Catholic cause won complete dominance. The Jesuits had control of education, and occupied key positions of influence at court. The years of patient conduct of well-managed schools paid large dividends. The judges, the administrators, and the leaders in every section of Polish life had gone through Jesuit schools. By the beginning of the seventeenth century there were flourishing in Poland seventeen Jesuit colleges; there were over 450 members of the Society in the Polish province, and an especially selected group of Jesuits was on fixed duty at the royal court for whatever task the king might entrust to them. The Counter-Reformation had won a decision that has never been reversed.

Scandinavia

THE course of the Counter-Reformation in Scandinavia is soon told. The Lutheran faith was firmly implanted in all three countries in the 1520's and was almost universally accepted by both crown and people from that time on. The first Vasa kings of Sweden were loyal Lutherans. Eric XIV (1560–68) was deposed by his brother John III, who ruled from 1568 to 1592. John's wife, the daughter of Sigismund II of Poland, was a Catholic and influenced the king toward sympathy with the Roman faith. Cardinal Hosius sent several very competent Jesuits, the first in 1574, two more in 1576, to guide the king in his efforts to bring the Protestant and Catholic faiths closer together. They traveled and gave lectures pretending to be Lutheran theologians, urging the substitution of Canisius' catechism for that of Luther. The king put forward, at their suggestion, a *Red Book,* a Catholic liturgy, to replace the Lutheran liturgy then in use. The Swedish clergy, under some pressure, agreed in 1577 to accept the *Red Book,* but Pope Gregory XIII then demanded a more open procedure, and John, uncomfortable under the pressure, broke off negotiations. The Jesuits had to leave the country in 1583.

Sigismund III of Poland, son of John III, became king of Sweden (1592–99) on the death of his father. As an earnest Catholic he desired to bring his northern kingdom back into the fold. This purpose was known to the Swedes who, in solemn assembly at Uppsala in 1593, under the influence of Duke Charles Vasa, Sigismund's uncle, swore to remain true to the Augsburg Confession. The *Red Book* was forbidden. The clergy chose as archbishop of Uppsala an outspoken opponent of the policy of concession to Catholicism. Sigismund III was forced to swear approval of these anti-Catholic measures, although the Swedes doubted his word, with good reason. The tension between a Lutheran people and a Catholic king became a matter of Europe-wide interest. Spain, England, France, and the Empire were all watching the outcome of the Swedish struggle closely. Duke Charles, who represented the national opinion, finally won out. It came to a trial by arms and Sigismund was defeated (1598), and formally deposed from the Swedish throne in 1599. Charles then became regent and, in 1604, king. Sweden remained enthusiastically Lutheran. The Counter-Reformation thus met defeat in the North.

The Spanish Netherlands

IN THE Spanish Netherlands the early history of the Counter-Reformation is the record of the efforts of the Society of Jesus to gain freedom of action from imperial authority. Charles V quite correctly regarded the Society as an arm of the Papacy; since he and the Papacy were seldom on terms of mutual trust, the Society was never, so long as Charles ruled the Netherlands, formally allowed. Nevertheless, Peter Lefèvre and Canisius (a Lowlander) were active at Louvain and elsewhere in the Burgundian domains. A number of young students at the University of Louvain were won for the order. The secular clergy in the Netherlands were strongly opposed to the Society, and the bishop of Cambrai, Robert de Croy, forbade them to perform any ecclesiastical functions in his diocese. Their progress was, however, substantial. The abdication of Charles V in 1555 seemed a fortunate development to Loyola, who sent Ribadeneira to Brussels to consult with Philip II and urge him to allow the Jesuits a freer hand in the Netherlands. Philip, aware of the general opposition to the order on the part of the clergy, both secular and regular, as well as the citizenry, was reluctant to grant the request. A year later (1556), urged by his aunt Mary, who had resigned as regent in 1555, he gave a conditional permission to the Jesuits to work in Flanders. Margaret of Parma, Philip's half sister, whom he left as regent of the Netherlands in 1559, was an admirer of the Society and had chosen her confessor from their ranks. In 1560, against the protests of the Estates of both Flanders and Brabant, she permitted the Society to establish colleges in Louvain and Antwerp. In both centers young students of theology were attracted into the Society, and the aristocracy seemed anxious to have Jesuits for confessors. The common people noticed these trends with ill-concealed anger; as late as 1578 the Jesuits were being driven out of their houses in Antwerp, Douai, Maastricht, Bruges, and other cities by popular demonstrations. These were years of high emotions in the Low Countries, and the expulsions were not unconnected with political and military events, but the general animosity against the Jesuits needed hardly any external irritant to bring it to the surface. From about 1565 the religious aspect of the Counter-Reformation in the Spanish Netherlands was submerged in the struggle for independence from Spain, led by William the Silent. The work of the Jesuits in Flanders and Brabant was largely responsible for the fact that the southern provinces chose, in 1579, to remain Catholic.

France

THE movement for reform of abuses in the French church in the early decades of the sixteenth century had its own tradition, quite independent of the Protestant Reformation. Lutheranism, partly because it was of German origin, had met with only moderate sympathy. Calvinism, coming later as a purely French movement, received a warmer welcome and spread widely among the upper classes as well as among the bourgeoisie and the peasantry. In the latter years of the reign of Francis I the leadership of the Church in France became aware of the dangerous inroads Calvinism was making among the French laity. With the support of the king severe measures were taken against all "heretics." In September 1546, a Calvinist group at Meaux were surprised by soldiers in the midst of celebrating the Lord's Supper and carted off to Paris, where fourteen were burned alive. Elsewhere in the kingdom similar arrests and punishments took place. Henry II and his advisers were firmly convinced of the necessity to repress all such heresies. The *Chambre ardente* (Burning Chamber), established by the king in 1547, lived up to its name, in two short years condemning five hundred "heretics" to death at the stake. This rigorous policy, however, did not stop the spread of Protestantism. In June 1551, Henry issued the Edict of Châteaubriand, which provided that there should be no appeal from the judgments of the ordinary courts in matters of heresy. But the Calvinist heresy continued to spread and flourish.

The year 1555 saw an especially active diffusion of Calvinism in France, mostly by young Frenchmen returning to their homes after spending a year or more at Geneva under Calvin's direct guidance. While some were caught by the king's agents, many succeeded in their mission and there grew up a network of affiliation among groups, now formed into churches and synods according to Calvin's organization, stretching from Lorraine to Brittany and from Marseilles to the borders of the Netherlands, all in close contact with Calvin. The Catholic hierarchy were deeply worried about the continued growth of Protestantism and certainly exaggerated the number of its adherents. The Cardinal Guise of Lorraine asserted in 1559 that the heretics had won over two-thirds of the king-dom. The situation was never so serious as that. Nevertheless, the number of Protestants, mostly Calvinists, was considerable, probably a determined and convinced minority of 10 per cent by the year 1560.

By 1556 Henry II had begun to share the concern of the Church at the growth of Protestant heresy. Cardinal Caraffa, on a diplomatic mission to France, told the king that the Pope wished to help in the extermination of heresy by estab-lishing the Inquisition in France, and gave a glowing account of its success in Spain and Italy. At that time the king was unwilling to go so far, but in the course of the next year he was won over to a policy of rigorous repression. In May 1557, he named three French cardinals as Grand Inquisitors. Three months later the king issued the Edict of Compiègne, whereby all cases of heresy were to be handled by the bishops, without the intervention of civil judges, and a single penalty, death, was prescribed for the crime of holding Protestant views. After accepting the Peace of Câteau-Cambrésis with Philip II of Spain, April 2 and 3, 1559, the king issued letters (Edict of Ecouen) to the provincial judges, ordering that all "Lutherans" be destroyed. A few days later, he asked the advice of the *parlement* as to how heresy could be crushed. Several speakers suggested that stringent measures be postponed until the General Council (Trent) could treat the question. These speakers were sent forthwith to the Bastille on the king's order. A bare month after this incident Henry II died (July 10, 1559) of a tourney accident. In May of 1559, the first national synod of the reformed churches had met in Paris, and by the end of that year there were seventy-two organized Calvinist congregations in France. The Catholics, at home and abroad, were stunned by the untimely death of the king just at the point when the extermination of heresy and heretics seemed to be going so well.

It might appear that the Counter-Reformation in France consisted of royal edicts and stern repressive measures by the government. Politics and religion were indeed closely related in France, but there were other agencies also at work in defense of the Catholic faith and in answer to complaints against the abuses that still persisted in the establishment.

The group of early reformers at Meaux (see above, pp. 523–24) had had to flee the country under the persecution of Francis I. From Geneva and Strassburg, many years later, their ideas returned to France to disturb Francis' successor, Henry II. But that was not the only current of religious revival. Ignatius Loyola had won his first disciples in Paris in 1530, and that city was always close to his heart. As soon as possible after organization of the order was fixed, he sent a small group of his disciples, mostly Spaniards, to Paris to carry on their work. At first poor and unrecognized, they later were able to move to comfortable quarters at the College of the Lombards. When, at the beginning of Francis' fourth war with Charles in 1542, all Spaniards were ordered to leave France, the Jesuits departed hurriedly for the Spanish Netherlands and, arriving at Louvain, formed the nucleus of the later Belgian province of the Society.

Back in Paris the few French and Italian Jesuits left continued their work. Shortly afterward at the Council of Trent, Guillaume du Prat, bishop of Clermont, an active advocate of reform, both in his own diocese and at the Council, met the Jesuit Lejay and was impressed by him and the activities of the Society. He offered the Paris Jesuits the use of his house for a residence. The house gradually evolved into a college for the secular youth. The college led a precarious existence, beset by poverty and annoyance from the university and the bishop of Paris. The sin of the order, of course, was twofold: it was international in membership and its members were devoted to the Papacy. In the strongly nationalistic France of the mid-sixteenth century, these were unpardonable sins.

Forbidden by the bishop to preach or hear confession, the Jesuits moved in 1556 to Auvergne under the protection of Bishop du Prat, and established the Collège de Billom, with a teaching staff of seven Jesuits and five hundred pupils. Within a few years the student body grew to 1600. The repute of the Jesuits for success in missionary work and in teaching brought appeals from other parts of France for help in counteracting ignorance and heresy. In the county of Foix the queen of Navarre's sympathies for Calvinism were alienating some of the population from the Catholic Church. The bishop of Pamier called in the Jesuits to counteract this pernicious tendency. The Huguenots later drove out the Jesuits, but the effort had been made and the Jesuits were not easily discouraged. Meantime in Paris the order had found favor with the Cardinal Guise of Lorraine, who influenced Henry II in the Society's favor. However, opposition from the conservative and nationalistic party, i.e., the Sorbonne and *parlement,* to this group reached such a point that in December 1554 the Faculty formally condemned the Society as "disturbers of the peace of the church," causing "contentions, hatreds, rebellions, and schisms among the people," and therefore "dangerous to the faith." On the other hand, the powerful prior of the Benedictine Abbey of St. Germain des Prés stood firmly behind the Jesuits, allowing them to preach and teach in the monastery, and thus the Society contrived a limited existence. For years, in spite of orders from the king and letters from the French cardinals and the queen mother, Catherine de' Medici, and the *parlement,* the bishop of Paris refused the Society any legal status. Finally, however, yielding to the persistence of the Jesuits and the obvious need of the Church for whatever aid it could command, the bishop allowed the Society to function, provided that it change its name to something less pretentious and accept the complete supervision of the bishop of Paris. *Parlement* was less accommodating, stipulating that the Society get the approval of the General Council which was soon to reassemble at Trent. Much of the history of the Catholic reform in the period from 1559 to 1565 is directly related to the beginning of the French Wars of Religion, and will be recounted in that connection. The strivings of the Society of Jesus for legal existence and freedom of action in France until that date have been recorded here as a continuation of the earlier struggles of the order.

In the midst of the battle for power at court between the strongly Catholic Guise family and the Bourbon-Châtillon connection (see above, p. 568) the Jesuits played only a minor role. After the Tumult or Conspiracy of Amboise in March 1560, the queen mother leaned for a while to the Bourbons as a counterpoise to the temporary predominance of the Guises, and called for a conference in which both sides, Protestant and Catholic, would be heard and, she hoped, some reasonable and acceptable arrangement be reached. The result was the Colloquy of Poissy, September 9–October 14, 1561. The Protestant case was eloquently and impressively presented by Theodore Beza, Calvin's second in command, who had been specially brought from Geneva for this conference. The Cardinal Guise answered him. As might have been expected, neither side changed its views in the slightest degree. Laynez, now General of the Society of Jesus and theological adviser to the Pope's legate to the Council of Trent, came from Rome. His participation was limited to advising Catherine de' Medici to leave all such efforts at compromise to the Council of Trent, soon to be again in session. At this point it became clear that the conflict was three-sided, involving: (1) traditional Gallicanism, which was deeply imbedded in French thought and ecclesiastical practice; (2) French Protestantism, which represented the demand of the bourgeoisie, large segments of the peasantry, and some of the clergy for a complete renovation of religious organization; and (3) the Ultramontanes or the party that clung to the central authority of Rome as the best guarantee of an effective religious life. The Jesuits were the foremost protagonists of the ultramontane, papal cause. As the Ultramontanes were only a small minority among French Catholics, no pro-papal decision could be reached to which a majority could subscribe. Laynez was listened to with no little impatience by most of the delegates to Poissy. When we perceive, furthermore, that the principal participants in this three-cornered struggle were motivated by personal and family ambitions, we can better understand how the next thirty years were a period of confusion, of battles that brought no victory, and of peaces that brought no peace.

The great and obvious need of the Catholic party for any help it could get in its fight against the spread of Protestantism, together with the failure of the Colloquy of Poissy and the urging of the queen mother and the chancellor of the realm, Michel de l'Hôpital, won for the Jesuits in Paris the permission so long refused them. On February 15, 1562, the Society was grudgingly given legal existence at Paris under the title of the Society of the Collège de Clermont. Classes began in February 1564. The shining light of the college was Juan Maldonado, a brilliant scholastic recently at Salamanca. Students flocked to his lectures, until other jealous rival lecturers caused the college, at one point, to lose its academic privileges. The Jesuits in France, as papalists and foreigners, were always confronted by the Gallican antipathy to anything non-French. Antagonism resulted in a lawsuit (March 1565) brought by the university against the Jesuits. A decision adverse to the Society precipitated street fights and protests, and was finally revoked, leaving the college in comparative peace. From this date the Jesuits were accepted as on the side of the Catholic Church. Catherine de' Medici, the University of Paris, and the Guises employed them in diplomacy, in controversy, and in education, tasks for which their training and discipline eminently fitted them.

Catholic Reformation in Spain

IT HAS been briefly mentioned above that by 1560 Protestantism had been virtually uprooted in Spain through the determined and decisive work of the Spanish Inquisition. The Inquisition had, in Spain as everywhere, a negative effect; it could not be called a constructive organization. But Spain was also possessed of positive factors which, after the work of the Inquisition is fully allowed for, gave free play to deep native religiosity. The reforms of Cardinal Ximénez and Adrian of Utrecht prepared the organized church for the great display of religious sentiment which characterized Spain's *siglo de oro* or Golden Age.

The Christian humanism of Erasmus was very popular in Spain. His devotees at the many Spanish universities through the early decades of the sixteenth century spread his ideas and his works with enthusiasm. He was, on the other hand, sharply criticized in some quarters for the liberal trend of his theology. The Inquisition, after a period of indecision, began, about 1535, to take an antagonistic position, and soon thereafter his works were forbidden.

Mysticism ran deep in the Spanish soul. The fifteenth century in Spain had been rich in the mystics. There was much of the mystic in Ignatius Loyola; the *Spiritual Exercises* encourage the contemplative way and end in the inculcation of the way of union with God (*via unitiva*). The *alumbrados,* the "enlightened ones," were a peculiarly Spanish manifestation which the Inquisition regarded as dangerous precisely because it appealed to the mystic motif in the Spanish nature, so prone to get out of institutional control.

Two of these many sensitive souls may properly represent to us the essence of Spanish religiosity in this century: St. Teresa de Jesus (1515–82) and St. John of the Cross (1542–91). St. Teresa was born in Ávila in Old Castile of a family with a noble military history. As a child she was imbued with the knightly ideals of the crusades against the Moors. From 1531 to 1534 she was in residence at an Augustinian monastery at Ávila and in the latter year she left to become a nun in the Carmelite monastery of the Incarnation in the same city. Her life for the next seventeen years was one long experience of prayer and contemplation. Her reading was in the *Confessions* of St. Augustine, the letters of St. Jerome, the lives of the saints, and the *Spiritual Exercises* of Loyola, all of which confirmed her in her pursuit of an immediate knowledge of God through prayer and meditation. She had visions, vivid details of which she has left in her *Life*. Her ecstasies and visions she discussed with her confessors, at first Jesuits, later an eminent Franciscan mystic, St. Peter of Alcántara. In obedience to a vision she founded a monastery to St. Joseph at Ávila in 1562, and followed this with other similar foundations in Castile. In her travels she met a young Carmelite monk, St. John of the Cross, and with his help founded a monastery for discalced (unshod) Carmelites from which other monastic foundations were to follow. St. Teresa did not achieve all this work of initiation without opposition. At one point (1577) a papal nuncio, influenced by the calced (unreformed) Carmelites, made such difficulties for her that for four years her work was greatly impeded. Philip II took her part, and during the last year of her life, 1581–82, she was able to establish four more monasteries. Her life combined in a remarkable way the contemplative and the active, illustrating the truth of the oft-repeated remark that the mystics are usually the most active and creative of persons. Her autobiography is a detailed record of her ecstasies, true in their depiction of struggles and pain, as well as of her raptures and thoughts. The journeys of her soul are told in her other books as well—the *Foundations,* the *Interior Castle,* and the *Way of Perfection.* She owed nothing to the Renaissance or to the Reformation. Intellectualism or the aggressive spirit of the Protestant reformers was completely alien to her. She was purely medieval. In her were fused devotion, joy, and good sense, without pretense or loss of dignity.

Her younger friend, Juan de Yepes, better known as St. John of the Cross (1542–91), was much like her. He too came from Ávila and was educated at the Jesuit college at Medina del Campo. At twenty-one he joined the Carmelite Order in the same city, then went to Salamanca to the university. He first met St. Teresa in 1568, and, inspired by her, undertook to reform his order. He founded a college at Alcalá de Henares in 1571 and preached and taught reform of the order from that pulpit. The order was not anxious to be reformed; for most of a year (1577–78) he was in prison, where he began to write poetry. In the next few years, in the midst of heavy duties as prior of a number of monasteries, he continued to write pages that are among the most beautiful in all the rich literature of Spain; *The Spiritual Canticle, The Ascent of Mt. Carmel, The Lively Flame of Love, The Dark Night of the Soul.* His poetry, regarded as the loftiest among all Spanish mystic verse, is natural, rhythmical, and rich in imagery. The great Spanish scholar Menéndez y Pelayo called it "angelic, celestial and divine." The poet and the man seem almost to disappear and the intense reality of the spiritual world comes clear. His prose, commentaries on his verse, is less notable, but eloquent enough, direct and forceful.

Intellectual Leaders of the Counter-Reformation

ALTHOUGH St. Ignatius Loyola was without doubt the most important and effective individual of the Catholic Counter-Reformation, at least three other dignitaries of the Church deserve to be mentioned almost in the same breath: Cardinals St. Charles Borromeo (1538–84), Caesar Baronius (1538–1609), and St. Robert Bellarmine (1542–1621). Eminent and effective in different ways, each contributed markedly to the success of the Church's efforts to regain lost territory or defend its doctrine and traditions.

St. Charles Borromeo

BORROMEO was born of a noble family in the Milanese and educated at Milan and the University of Padua, where he took the doctorate in civil and canon law in 1559. When his uncle, Giovanni de' Medici, became Pope Pius IV (December 1559), young Charles was immediately summoned to Rome to assume responsible duties. The Pope raised him to the cardinalate in 1560 and shortly thereafter named him archbishop of Milan. Kept at Rome, he was made

Apostolic Protonotary and put in charge of papal legations to lands of the Patrimony in Italy, then Protector of the crowns of Portugal, the Low Countries, the Catholic cantons of Switzerland, and of several monastic orders, and finally chairman of the commission that handled all the civil administration of the Papal States. This rapid advancement of a nephew of the Pope caused much adverse comment at a time when the Papacy was talking reform of abuses and the abolition of nepotism. But it soon became evident that the young man was the right person in the right position. His austere life and refusal to accept the income of more than one of the offices he held changed criticism into praise.

He was in Rome for five years, from 1560 to 1565, guiding or helping to guide papal policy in times of extremely delicate and uncertain strain. Poland had almost slipped from Rome's grasp. France was recalcitrant and her Gallicanism rampant. England, where the return to Catholicism under Mary had been repudiated under Elizabeth, gave the *curia* deep concern. At least half of Germany was lost, and what was still Catholic was very unsure. The Emperor Ferdinand I was, or so Rome thought, so liberal toward his Protestant and Hussite subjects as to be unreliable. Spain, though passionately Catholic, was perpetually antipapal. Borromeo was involved in all these areas, negotiating, suggesting, planning, encouraging; resourceful, patient, sure, consistent, and incorruptible. He was largely responsible for convening the third Assembly of the Council of Trent (1562–63), at which he led the papal delegation, and brought the Council of Trent to what the *curia* at least thought was a successful conclusion. Afterward he was influential in following up its decisions, and the Tridentine catechism is largely his work. By this time, 1564, he seems to have begun to feel that he had had enough curial administration. In that year he sent a trusted friend, Nicola Ormaneto, to his titular archdiocese of Milan to ascertain its condition, which he had found from reports to be bad, and to institute a program of reform and revival. He entered the city for the first time as archbishop on September 23, 1565. Pope Pius IV, his uncle, died several months later, and Borromeo, unwilling to be a candidate for the papal tiara, threw all his influence to the candidacy of Ghislieri, who was elected as Pius V. Returning to Milan, he began a long career to his death in 1584, as a reforming archbishop. This was probably the happiest period of his life. He was able to put into practice among the clergy and among the people of his archdiocese the decrees and principles of the Council of Trent. He made full use of the zeal of the new orders, the Theatines, the Capuchins, and particularly the Jesuits. He rebuilt churches that had fallen into decay and built new ones, and established many seminaries for the training of the clergy and a college for Swiss youth. He visited throughout his diocese, encouraging or correcting as was necessary. He held eleven diocesan and six provincial synods, the most effective means to apprise the clergy of new developments and to raise the level of pastoral care. His concern for the welfare of his people was not limited to their souls. During the plague and drouth of 1576–77 he was everywhere, exposing himself to all the perils of disease without stint. Borromeo had opponents, as any reformer would have. He had critics, as any man of decision and action must have. Yet no one can contest that he was a leading champion and executor of the Counter-Reformation.

Caesar Baronius

BARONIUS, frequently called by Protestants as well as by Catholics the "father of ecclesiastical history," was of a noble family of Tuscany. He took the doctor's degree in jurisprudence at Rome in 1561 and took orders three years later. He joined the Oratorian order and divided his time between active, humble pastoral work and the study of church history. In 1583 he was sent to Naples to take charge of a campaign against an influential heretical group. The next year he was named deputy of the Congregation of the Oratory and prefect of the Great Oratory. In 1589 he was offered the bishopric of Teano by Pope Sixtus V, but declined. In 1593 St. Philip Neri, superior of the Oratorians, designated Baronius as his successor. The next year Pope Clement VIII chose him as his confessor and gave him increasing confidence and responsibilities. Baronius was consulted by Clement in the important matter of papal acceptance of the conversion of Henry IV of France. In 1595 he was named Apostolic Protonotary, and the next year he was raised to the cardinalate. His honors and responsibilities had not, even by that recognition, reached their limit. In 1597 he was made librarian of the Vatican and charged with the Congregation of Rites and the conduct of the papal publishing house. He served on diplomatic missions under Clement VIII, and on the Pope's death in 1605 he missed election as his successor by a narrow margin. If it had not been for the flat veto of Spain he would undoubtedly have been elected.

This was a distinguished career of work and recognition, yet it does not reveal Baronius' most significant place in the Counter-Reformation. All during his ecclesiastical career he had been amassing historical material with which he planned to confute the *Magdeburg Centuries,** a work of tremendous if biased learning edited by Matthias Flacius Illyricus in 1559. The *Centuries,* a Lutheran version of the history of the Church to 1400, were bitterly anti-Catholic in their selectivity, yet there had been no attempt thus far to present the Catholic answer. Baronius set out, from early in his career, to fill that gap. The result was the vast work *Annales ecclesiastici,* the first volume of which appeared at Rome in 1588. As left by Baronius it covered the story of the Church, year by year, up to the pontificate of Innocent III (1198). There have been twenty-one editions and many abridgements and translations of all or parts of the *Annales.* It was attacked by Catholics as well as by Protestants, one Catholic historian claiming he had discovered eight thousand errors in the work. Baronius asserted that he had found in the Church of the thirteenth century the identical institutions of the Church of the Apostles. He frequently used sources in such a way as to obscure their meaning and not infrequently simply neglected to mention sources that did not fit his central theme. Any idea of development of thought was quite foreign to him. The annalistic method does not lend itself to the development or analysis of trends and movements. On the other hand, in view of the mass of material with which he worked alone, without collaborators, it is amazing that there were not more errors. As to his central theme,

* The first edition of this work, which appeared at Basel from 1559 to 1574, bore the title *Ecclesiastica historia. . . .* The third edition (Nürnberg, 1757) appeared under the title *Centuriae Magdeburgenses,* by which it has since been generally known.

the correspondence of the Roman Papacy to the ideals of Christ, he might reasonably claim that it was as valid as the opposite theme of the *Centuries,* which condemned almost everything the Papacy had ever done as inspired by the Devil in person. The *Annales* should be used with caution, but the work still has to be used by scholars working in the history of the Papacy. It was a memorable achievement and heralded another phase in the Counter-Reformation: the appeal to documented tradition.

St. Robert Bellarmine

THE Jesuit Cardinal Bellarmine is known as the leading theological defender of Catholicism in the period of the Counter-Reformation. His family was of the Tuscan nobility, his mother a sister of Pope Marcellus II. Robert entered the Jesuit order in 1560, at the age of eighteen, and studied philosophy at the Roman college of that order, going thence to teach at its colleges in Florence and Mondovi. His promise as a scholar-theologian caused him to be sent to the University of Padua and then, in 1569, to the University of Louvain, where he was assigned the post of Latin preacher to the students. His eloquence attracted large audiences and students came from far away to hear him. In 1570, ordained as a priest, he began to teach scholastic theology at Louvain. Six years later he was chosen "director of controverted questions" at the Roman college. He remained at this post for twelve years, and out of his study and lectures there came the works on which his fame and significance justly rest: *The Controversies*. The first volume appeared in 1586. Some of the positions Bellarmine took touching on the theory of the power of the pope were not in accord with the ideas of Pope Sixtus V, who placed the book on the *Index* until it should be corrected. When Sixtus died in 1590 that tentative condemnation was lifted. In 1589 Bellarmine was sent to France as the theologian of a mission to combat the Huguenots. In 1590 Gregory XIV (1590–91) appointed him to the commission for revision of the Vulgate that Sixtus V had published in 1590. It was a delicate matter to revise, so soon after publication, a text which had been issued by a previous pope as the official text of the Bible yet was obviously in need of serious correction. Bellarmine, in his introduction to the revision, asserted that Sixtus V had noticed the errors and wished to eliminate them. This effort to absolve Sixtus of a responsibility which all informed persons around the *curia* knew was the Pope's subjected Bellarmine to severe charges of fabrication. He certainly must have known what everyone else knew, that Sixtus V had been extremely careless. The revision, published in 1592 by order of Clement VIII (1592–1605), was called the Sixtine-Clementine text of the Vulgate.

In 1592 Bellarmine became rector of the Roman college of the Jesuits, and headed the commission to revise the *Ratio studiorum,* the educational program of the order. Charged with other tasks and responsibilities by Clement VIII, he was made a cardinal in 1599 and his influence grew. Named archbishop of Capua in 1602, Bellarmine labored for three years in his archdiocese with exemplary devotion. Pope Paul V (1605–21) called him back to Rome, where his knowledge and talents were needed in controversies with Protestant powers and within the Church. Again, as in the case of Baronius, Bellarmine's distinguished career as an active churchman had less significance for the cause of the Counter-Reformation than the spirit and text of his writings. In all subsequent disputes between Catholic and Protestant, his opinions and arguments were certain to be cited. His disciplined logic, his broad learning, his fervent loyalty to Rome always offered support and comfort to the Church and difficulties to the Protestants.

By the end of the sixteenth century, the positions of the contesting parties, Protestant and Catholic, were consolidated. The Protestants had almost run away with Europe in the first half of the century. The reaction of the Catholic Church in the second half was almost as rapid. The agencies by which it achieved this speedy recovery—the Council of Trent, the Society of Jesus, the Inquisition and the mystic-moral revival—have been sketched in this chapter. In the end, certain areas in northern Europe were irretrievably lost to Rome, while southern Europe had rejected Protestantism fully as decidedly. With minor modifications this was to be the situation of the Continent in the following centuries.

SUGGESTIONS FOR FURTHER READING

See the bibliographies to Chapters 17 and 18.

IGNATIUS LOYOLA, *Spiritual Exercises.* Many editions
The Life of Saint Teresa of Ávila by Herself. Penguin, 1957

BOEHMER, H., *The Jesuits.* Philadelphia, 1928
BREMOND, H., *Literary History of Religious Thought in France,* Vol. I. London, 1928
BRODRICK, J., *The Origin of the Jesuits.* London, 1940
BRODRICK, J., *Progress of the Jesuits (1556–79).* London, 1946
BRODRICK, J., *Robert Bellarmine: Saint and Scholar.* London, 1961
DANIEL-ROPS, H., *The Catholic Reformation.* New York, 1962
FROUDE, J. A., *Lectures on the Council of Trent.* New York, 1896
HARNEY, M. P., *The Jesuits in History.* New York, 1941
HUGHES, P., *Rome and the Counter-Reformation.* London, 1944
JANELLE, P., *The Catholic Reformation.* Milwaukee, 1949
JEDIN, H., *Girolamo Seripando.* 2 vols. St. Louis, 1947
JEDIN, H., *A History of the Council of Trent.* 2 vols. London, 1957, 1961
KIDD, B. J., *The Counter-Reformation.* London, 1937
LEA, H. C., *History of the Inquisition of Spain.* 4 vols. London, 1906–07
PASTOR, L. VON, *History of the Popes,* Vols. VIII–XV. London, St. Louis, 1923–28
POLLARD, A. F., *The Jesuits in Poland.* London, 1902
SEDGWICK, H. D., *Ignatius Loyola.* New York, 1923
SYMONDS, J. A., *The Catholic Reaction.* New York, 1887
VAN DYKE, P., *Ignatius Loyola.* New York, 1926
WARD, A. W., *The Counter-Reformation.* London, 1889

CAPASSO, C., *Paolo III.* 2 vols. 1924
CRISTIANI, L., *L'Eglise à l'époque du concile de Trente.* 1948
FOUQUERAY, H., *Histoire de la Compagnie de Jésus en France.* 25 vols. 1910
FRIEDENSBURG, W., *Kaiser Karl und Papst Paul IV.* 1932

HEFELE, C. J., and H. LECLERCQ, *Histoire des conciles,* Vols. VIII–X. 1917–38
PIAGET, E., *Histoire de l'établissement des Jésuites en France.* 1893
RIESS, L., *Die Politik Pauls IV und seiner Nepoten.* 1909
TACCHI-VENTURI, P., *Storia della Compagnia di Gesù in Italia.* 1931
WILLAERT, L., *La Restauration Catholique, 1563–1648.* 1960

CHAPTER TWENTY-TWO

THE ECONOMIC REVOLUTIONS:
THEORIES OF THE STATE

T HE period from about 1400 to the early years of the eighteenth century is frequently described as the age of economic revolution, a period during which Europe developed from a predominantly agrarian and feudal economy to a capitalistic system. There is good reason for accepting this periodization. Yet, on closer examination of the changes that took place in the methods of production and distribution in the various parts of Europe, one finds that these changes were so differently involved in local conditions or in movements and events in other parts of Europe that a clear picture of precisely what was cause and what was effect in economic development is not obtainable. Economic realities were then, as now, deeply involved in all other activities of mankind. Politics and international relations, population growth, discoveries, fashions and morals, the church and society, education and art, all had their effects upon and were in turn influenced by the production and distribution of goods, the expansion of credit, and the amassing of capital.

Capitalism was not unknown in the Middle Ages. The rising cities of Italy, especially Florence, Genoa, Venice, and Milan, began as early as the twelfth century, and increasingly in the thirteenth and fourteenth centuries, to exhibit the marks of commercial capitalism: individual accumulations of money used to control markets and increase capital loans and profitable venture investments. The cities of the Lowlands, well situated to take advantage of growing trade in northern Europe and along the northern coasts, were not far behind the Italian cities in organizing trade and industry so as to derive profit from the production of saleable goods—mostly textiles—and the trading of other goods for which the Lowlands were a useful marketplace. The people of the Lowlands were, in a sense, driven to become traders, precisely because their land, small and lacking in many products necessary for an adequate livelihood, could not support them. Forced to add to their local income, they found trade the simplest and at the same time most profitable recourse. Aside from the enterprise of the German cities bound together in the Hanseatic League, there was little commercial capitalism in the rest of Europe at the beginning of the fifteenth century. Europe was still predominantly agrarian. The system of fairs, both local and international, while it was responsible for a considerable distribution of merchandise, and some traders became wealthy, was not a permanent, year-around, urban-connected institution. The unmistakable tendency in Europe was toward urbanism. The city as a unit of competitive production and distribution was already on its inexorable way, just as the agrarian economy was inevitably on the decline.

We could, however, go too fast and too far in proclaiming the demise of the agrarian economy of the Middle Ages. Those who wielded political and social power in Europe around 1500 rested their power in control of the land. Their income came almost exclusively from the peasantry who worked for them on various bases of tenurial contract, and the satisfaction of both sides to the contract was general if not universal. The needs of the seigneur, the lord of the manor, were met by the labor of the peasants, who received in return security, the administration of justice, and, in time of need, exceptional paternalistic assistance. The fourteenth and fifteenth centuries witnessed a further development favorable to the peasant. Whereas, in the Middle Ages, the peasant was typically bound to the soil, that is to the estate of a given seigneur, by the end of the fifteenth century, in many parts of Europe—in France, in England, in Italy, and in parts of Germany—the ties between lord and serf had been or were being relaxed, and the free peasant was increasingly able to move from place to place, and to contract freely to rent land of his own choosing. The disaster of the Black Death in the middle of the fourteenth century, by creating a scarcity of labor, naturally increased the tempo of peasant liberation.

The Cities

THE remarkable growth of the cities in the fifteenth century looms large in the rise of modern capitalism, but the fact remains that the economic basis of society was still the land and was to remain so for several centuries. Figures for urban population are notoriously only approximate. In spite of the fact that scientific censuses did not yet exist, it is still possible to use the approximations for comparison between cities and as indications of growth or decline. By 1500 only a few cities counted 100,000 souls: Venice, Paris, London, Palermo, and Florence. Bruges, Ghent, and Milan had populations between 40,000 and 60,000. Louvain, Brussels, and Liége in the Lowlands had populations between 20,000 and 30,000. In Germany Cologne had around 30,000 and Lübeck, Strassburg, Danzig, Nürnberg, and Ulm around 20,000, while Augsburg and Erfurt had no more than 18,000. A century later the figures for most of these cities were much higher. In 1600 Paris reached 180,000 and London 250,000. At the beginning of the seventeenth century the population of Madrid was almost 200,000. Venice, on the other hand, had dropped to hardly more than 50,000, because of the loss of some of her Eastern trade. The number of towns which had been mere villages in 1500 and had reached substantial size a century later was considerable. This general increase in urban population has to be seen from two points of view: (1) the over-all increase of the population in any given country, which, during the sixteenth century, in spite of wars and other disasters, was probably in the neighborhood of 30 to 40 per cent; (2) the increase specifically for the urban centers, which was, on the average, probably more than 100 per cent. Thus the percentage of population living in the towns may be assumed at least to have doubled and perhaps trebled in this century. Certain cities, however, lost in population from the effects of famine or diversion of trade. Ragusa, for example, lost 20,000 in one year.

Capitalism

THE general increase in population was certain to strengthen the demand for all kinds of goods. An expanding market offered numerous opportunities for profit, and in the latter half of the fifteenth century many merchants of northern Europe with initiative and a little luck were able to become moderately wealthy. A few, indeed, amassed great fortunes. In southern Germany the Fugger family, the Welsers, the Ruckers, and the Imhofs accumulated whole industries and spread their branches throughout the Empire and neighboring states. In France there was the legend of Jacques Coeur, who, in the fifteenth century, by speculation and initiative had become the wealthiest man in the kingdom, owning fleets and mines in France and abroad, before he was banished by the king. The establishments of these "new men" surpassed the courts of kings in luxury and elegance, and fashions in bourgeois mansions and dress were taken from this new banking-commercial class. With the increase in opportunities for making money and the gradual expansion of a money economy, the way for the price revolution of the early and mid-sixteenth century was being prepared.

France: The Transition from Feudal to Bourgeois Economy

POLITICAL events of the fifteenth century were also creating conditions favorable to capitalism. In France the Hundred Years' War, which called upon the French people to repel the foreign invader, had at the same time weakened the power of the nobility. The war had been fought mostly by the feudal nobles, who had lost much of their best blood, while the expense of maintaining themselves and their detachments had been so heavy that land and feudal privileges had had to be sold or commuted for money payments. Ready money was to be found almost exclusively among townsmen. The bourgeoisie grew in freedom and wealth, and the nobility were on the way to impoverishment. Louis XI, whose great achievement was the consolidation of French royal power, favored the bourgeoisie, encouraged industrial and commercial enterprise, and, when in need of ready cash, as he often was, depended on the bankers and merchants to provide, with or without interest, the substantial sums required for his growing bureaucracy, his imaginative diplomacy, and his wars. Sometimes he raised "loans" from a city such as Lyons, the banking center of France, more often from one or more of the Florentine banking firms which did business in France. In the last years of the fifteenth century the volume of business, both banking and commercial, between Italy (mostly Florence) and France increased substantially. Business brought specie, and an increase of money in circulation led to both a further growth of venture enterprise and a rise in prices. Commercial capitalism was already a reality, functioning on an international basis.

Fundamentally agricultural, France, after the end of the Hundred Years' War, encountered difficulties similar to those in England, where enclosures disturbed the relations between large landowners and the peasantry. In France, under the system of triage (the division of communal lands into three parts), the seigneurs demanded and took, sometimes by force, land which the peasantry needed for pasture. Despite a royal decree of 1576 which forbade the system of triage or even the sale of such communal lands to the seigneurs, the practice continued well into the seventeenth century. The result was obviously an impoverishment of the peasantry, later to become so serious that the government decreed in 1659 the return of all such properties to their communal ownership.

Although France's economy was predominantly agricultural, based on a rich soil and adequate water, the country was deeply engaged in developing commerce and industry. Some of the leading cities were international markets. Paris, Lyons, Dijon, and Orléans were busy centers of exchange where branches of Italian banking houses handled large sums of money. Through numerous ports—Bordeaux, Boulogne, Dieppe, Nantes, and others—many kinds of commodities moved in and out of France. France sold grain to Spain as well as to England and Portugal, wine and fruits in season to England, Flanders, and Switzerland. French linen cloth was in demand in England, Spain, northern Italy, and north Africa. The excess of salt could be sold in England. Yet France had to import many articles: metals, leather goods, furs, ham, cheese, spices, horses, and fish came from Germany. From Italy France imported linens, silk, crystal, jewels, and arms, some of which had come to Italian merchants from farther east. France got much gold, silver, lead, tin, and also leather, wool, and fish from England. From Spain, even in times when the two kingdoms were at war, came money coined from bullion which had in turn been brought to Spain from the New World. From Portugal came spices, precious stones, perfumes, and drugs. This list indicates that France was not yet as industrialized as her neighbors from whom she had to obtain much of the manufactured goods to satisfy the demands of her markets.

What industry there was in France was in the hands of the traditional medieval guilds, known as corporations, consisting of masters, companions (or journeymen), and apprentices. These corporations remained much as they had been in the Middle Ages: strictly graduated and exclusive societies. Francis I made some efforts to curb the power of the masters of these guilds, but with only indifferent success. The king had no special leaning toward the laboring man. In 1539 a royal edict suppressed the "confraternities" of artisans which had grown up as a counterbalance to the power of the masters. When, in that same year, the journeymen in the numerous printing establishments in Lyons struck for over a year for higher wages and better living conditions, the king took the side of the masters and made no concessions whatever to the demands of the workers.

The protectionism which was traditional in France was continued throughout the sixteenth century. Italian merchants in particular and their goods were subjected to rigorous restrictions; these, however, were frequently evaded by the

French merchants anxious to have merchandise to sell, of whatever origin, with little concern for edicts from Paris. The expansion to the Far East and the New World which was in full swing in Spain and Portugal, and to a lesser degree in England, during the time of Francis I also caught popular fancy in France. By 1530 French expeditions, usually financed by individual merchants or adventurous noblemen with commercial connections, had set out from Atlantic or Mediterranean ports for the Indian sea and the Spice Islands. Two large ships reached Sumatra in 1529. In 1530 a merchant of Dieppe organized a company to trade in spices "for the good and profit of the common weal." Other similar companies and enterprises followed in steadily increasing number. But it was not until the voyages of Jacques Cartier that French exploration became significant. Francis I financed Cartier's first expedition to the New World in 1534. He reached Newfoundland, Labrador, and the Gulf of St. Lawrence. On a second expedition in 1535 he went up the St. Lawrence River to the Lachine rapids. Taking possession of the land in the name of the king of France, he remained until the following spring. A subsequent (1541) attempt at colonization failed dismally. France was not to make another such venture until Champlain settled Quebec in 1608. Obviously French commerce was not destined to gain from westward expansion or colonization in comparison with Spain or England.

At home the French government and publicists had long boasted of their self-sufficiency. The chancellor of the realm opened the Estates General of 1484 with a speech in which he said: "Can we find a land better provided with all the riches necessary for man's wants?" In 1557 a royal edict echoed the same conviction: "The inhabitants of the Kingdom of France have no need to seek the aid and assistance of neighbors or of foreigners for the necessities nor for other things made necessary by common usage." If it is barely possible that France may have been sufficient unto herself in 1484, it was certainly not true by 1557. The royal treasury was emptied, and, along with Spain, France was bankrupt. Without gold or silver mines Francis I and his successors had had to borrow heavily from Florentine or Antwerp bankers in order to defray the expenses of war against the Habsburgs, an extravagant diplomacy, and a luxurious court. The French defeat at St. Quentin in 1559 was only the last straw for the French treasury. The Estates General of 1560 were told that the debt of the crown was in the neighborhood of forty million livres. For the next thirty years France was torn by civil and religious strife. The peasantry suffered terribly from the ravages of the war. Lyons ceased to be a financial center; there were years of famine and unemployment in cities where industry had begun, before the war, to flourish. The nobility, when the peasantry did not produce, were forced into deeper debt to maintain any kind of respectable standard of living. Furthermore, for much of these thirty years large stretches of the kingdom were not under the control of the king of France, and law and order were not honored. The Huguenots maintained the pattern of fiscal administration for their own profit alone. France was painfully divided, not only politically and religiously, but economically and administratively.

The final victory of Henry IV was greeted with a deep sigh of relief by the vast majority of Frenchmen. At last they could get back to work and repair the damages of three decades of chaos. Henry's most urgent task was the restoration of fiscal and financial order. It was the good fortune of Henry IV and of France that he had a minister, Sully, whose primary motivation was financial morality and governmental economy. He faced a permanent annual deficit of 36,000,000 livres. France was pulled out of the morass of mismanagement and bankruptcy only by stringent economy, self-denying austerity, and vast resourcefulness. Henry must be given credit for an appreciation of the need for a superhuman effort and for directing and supporting the extreme measures of Sully. He turned over to his successor a solvent kingdom, with the public debt reduced from 350,000,000 to 224,000,000 livres. The annual income of the kingdom was almost doubled and in 1609 there was in the treasury a cash reserve of 41,000,000 livres. Henry was not content with merely being economical at home. In 1604 commercial treaties with the Hanseatic League, with Sweden and Denmark were concluded. French salt, wines, cloth, and paper were in steady demand on the foreign market. The traditional political alliance with Turkey aided French trade with the Levant, and French merchants were able to meet the competition of Dutch and English traders in the eastern Mediterranean on a favorable basis. By the end of the reign of Henry IV, France had regained most of the economic ground lost during the Wars of Religion and was taking her place as a leading world commercial power.

The rapid economic recovery which took place in France under Henry IV could hardly have been accomplished if it had not been for the economic teaching and practice of Calvinism. The theoretical opposition of the Catholic Church to usury had in actuality been largely outdated by the middle of the century. But Calvinism went much farther than practice; it proclaimed the moral rightness of individual effort and justified putting money to work. Whereas the older assumption of canon law had been that money was a dead thing, the reformed teaching held that it was potentially alive, and could morally be used to increase its substance. Profit, in the capitalistic sense, if honestly achieved, was an indication that a man had used his talents wisely and well. The spread throughout France of this attitude toward money in the latter half of the century laid a solid basis for an economic revival. The merchant class had now a philosophy of individualism and the added sanction of a highly respectable religious motivation, something which Catholic canon law had withheld from them. The prosperity which made the "Great Century" of Richelieu and Louis XIV possible was rooted in this redirection of economic theory which was taking effect even during the devastation of the Wars of Religion, and was consolidated during the too short reign of Henry IV.

Italy: Economic Separatism and Decline

THE Italy of the sixteenth century never approached unification, being divided along economic as well as political lines. Yet, in comparison with other parts of Europe which were showing remarkable signs of economic expansion, all Italy shared a common experience of decline. The Republic of Venice, with a population of almost 200,000 around 1500 spread between the city of the lagoons and its mainland dependencies, was not apparently aware of her imminent decline. Her stations in the Levant suffered from the rerouting of trade around Africa and to the New World as well as from the growth of Ottoman power which drove her from some points in the eastern Mediterranean. When the competition of Western powers—France, the Lowlands, and England—broke in on Venetian monopolies, the proud city did not adjust to the new situation. Nevertheless, Venice remained an important financial center, and, before the end of the century, had found another outlet for Venetian talent: the application of art to industry. Woodcarving, artistic ironwork, bronze and stone statuary, cabinet work, gold- and silversmithing, inlay, fine leatherwork and other luxury trades, and of course fine printing, became Venetian specialties, sustaining the city's reputation through the sixteenth and into the seventeenth century.

Genoa, having lost her earlier maritime supremacy to Venice in a centuries-long struggle, yet had, in spite of short periods of French conquests by Louis XI and Louis XII, clung to her traditions of independence. The government was in the hands of the rich bourgeoisie and the nobility. The *popolo minuto,* the laboring and craft classes, never attained a position of political power. Genoa lost her trading outposts in the Levant, while her ocean trade suffered in competition with French and Portuguese merchants. On the other hand, her bankers were notably successful; Charles of Spain asked the Bank of St. George of Genoa to manage the repayment of his loans from the Low Countries. Aside from these operations, Genoa's best source of income in the sixteeenth century was the mercenary service of her fleet under the naval genius Andrea Doria, who served with equal effectiveness, at different times, both Francis I and Charles V.

Florence under the benevolent despotism of the Medici had been the most prosperous land power in Italy at the end of the fifteenth century. After Savonarola's theocracy failed in 1498 the Medici returned to power and in 1532 a Medici became hereditary duke of Florence. The days of brilliant initiative seemed to be over, as a period of comfort and peace set in. Nevertheless, the basic industries of Tuscany—wool, silk, pottery, and ironwork—continued to prosper. Toward the end of the century, guild restrictiveness began to have its inevitable effect and industry was on a sure decline. The Papal States led a quite irregular economic existence in the sixteenth century. In some of the cities, such as Bologna or Faenza, which lay within the territory ruled by the Papacy, there was a viable economy of mixed domestic and capitalistic enterprise. But Rome itself, as the center of papal administration and the recipient of pilgrims' gifts and the vast sums that came to the papal treasury from the sales of indulgences, dispensations, and offices, was economically unproductive and, strictly speaking, a parasite on the industry and commerce of the rest of the Christian world.

The kingdom of Naples, under Spanish rule since early in the fourteenth century, was an agricultural region. In some parts agriculture gave way to sheep-raising, which greatly increased during the sixteenth century. The nobility entered this industry more actively and gained more profit from the tolls levied when sheep changed pastures than they would have made from farming. The number of sheep in the kingdom increased during the century from 600,000 to 5,000,000. Productive farming dropped proportionately. The movement of herds of sheep was catastrophic for field crops and great numbers of the farmers left the land to join the city proletariat. In a few towns there was some trade with foreign merchants, and an incipient silk industry, sporadically encouraged by Spanish kings, kept some workers busy, but the steady trend of this sector of the economy was downward.

Milan, a beehive of industry and trade since Roman times, had suffered a variety of Italian despotism and foreign rule. But in spite of an extravagant court and political turbulence, industry and banking prospered. The country around Milan, well watered and fertile, supplied the basic needs of the population. Milanese craftsmen in many highly competitive skilled trades ranked among the best in the known world. Gold- and silverwork, glass, silks, and fine brocades produced in Milan were in demand at all European trading centers. Branches of Lombard banks were active from Lisbon to the Hanseatic cities on the Baltic. Although the rise of manufacturing centers and banking houses in France and Germany did cut into Milan's business, during this century at least the city was energetic and prosperous.

On balance and in spite of several spots that looked bright, such as Florence (that is, Tuscany) and the Milanese, Italy presents by the end of the sixteenth century a picture of decadence. Her divisions and internal rivalries, the policies of the popes which brought wars onto Italian soil, the prevalence of foreign and especially Spanish rule, as in Naples and Milan, and, perhaps most significant of all, the transfer of Europe's commercial center of gravity from the Mediterranean to the Atlantic, relegated Italy to a secondary place in the total European economy.

Spain: From Prosperity to Poverty

SPAIN was an economic anomaly. The Iberian peninsula until 1492, the date of the reconquest of Granada, was generally prosperous and operating on a relatively balanced economy. There were industries based on highly skilled craftsmanship. Cordova produced leather highly prized all over Europe; Toledo, metalwork and weapons of a steel famed for quality. From the middle of the sixteenth century on, silk was shipped from Jaen to France to compete successfully with French and Italian products. Craftsmen even came from France and Italy to work and at times settle in Spanish towns where the crafts were advanced and work plentiful. Saragossa, Barcelona, Granada, Valencia, and Cádiz were busy industrial and commercial centers. In agriculture, Spain benefited by the native aptitude of the Spanish Moors for working the soil. These, before their expulsion in 1492, were responsible for the bulk of exports of olive oil, wine, fruit, and grain. About 1530 the receipt of gold and silver bullion from the Spanish possessions in the New World began to be very substantial. In the course of the century the average annual production of silver bullion was about three hundred tons. The immediate effect of the reception of this bullion in Spain was to raise prices within the kingdom; then, more often than not, the gold and silver took flight and ended up in France, in the coffers of the bankers of Antwerp or London, or in the hands of the populations in the regions where the Spanish armies were encamped or on the march. Within Spain, at any event, from the beginning of the sixteenth century to the early years of the next century, the general level of prices more than trebled. From an economic point of view, from the beginning of the century, coincident with the arrival of the precious metals, Spain was on the decline: the richer the kingdom became in specie the more rapid was her economic deterioration. The reasons for the decline, manifold and at the same time quite obvious, are of several orders: political, social, fiscal, demographic, and certainly moral.

Two factors in Spanish economic history must be understood before the decline can be grasped. The first is of a purely economic order; the second is partly social and partly moral. The organization of the sheep raisers, the *mesta,* had, in the course of the fifteenth century and well into the seventeenth, become so strong as to be able to dictate to the government in matters of economic policy. They obtained exemptions from taxation and concessions to use waste tracts of land exclusively for mobile grazing. The *cañada,* a strip of land running from north to south, was taken completely out of cultivation and reserved for the movement of sheep from summer grazing in the north to winter grazing in the south. Farmers on the edge of this strip were unable to protect themselves from the wandering of herds over their ploughed or seeded fields. Many royal measures during the sixteenth century extended further concessions to the sheep farmers. Then, when agricultural produce began to be heavily taxed later in the century, farmers were further discouraged and an exodus from the land set in. The loss to Spanish agriculture was almost irreparable and imports of food became necessary. The population decreased as many farmers, in desperation, left for France or Italy. By early in the seventeenth century many formerly productive areas looked like deserts.

The influx of gold and silver bullion into Spain did not reach the root of the matter. In addition to the great loss to the state through graft at ports of entry, the cost of maintaining a lavish court, an expensive foreign policy, and armies in Italy, the Lowlands, and the Empire was more than mere occasional shipments of bullion could sustain.

The second social and moral factor which figured so largely in Spain's decline was partly the result of the success of the *reconquista.* The Spanish nobility, the *hidalgos,* were proud of having driven the infidel Moor from the sacred soil of Spain. They felt they had earned repose and the rewards of a noble achievement. Work and commerce were for menials. This depreciation of labor went deep into Spanish character and was not easily eradicable. The Moors had done this sort of despised work and Spain had prospered. When the Moors were driven out the work was no longer done. The laziness reached down into the craftsman class, to such an extent that by the reign of Philip II Spaniards had lost much of the desire to work. The craftsmen in the land were in large measure Frenchmen and Italians who came to Spain to work as carpenters, iron mongers, brick makers, or knife grinders, stayed a few years, accumulated a small treasure, and returned home, leaving Spain poorer than before.

These two diverse circumstances drove the rulers of Spain to extreme measures to raise revenue to defray their political and military outlay. Charles I, for example, absent for most of his reign in the Empire, at war with Francis I, the German Protestants, or the Turks, demanded from Philip, his son and regent in Spain, large sums of ready cash. Philip had to levy taxes on such things as wagon wheels and windows, and a 10 per cent sales tax, the *alcabala,* on all transactions. So high a sales tax had the inevitable effect of punishing trade and drying up sources of government income. Even the *mesta,* during the reign of Philip II, suffered a diminution in the number of sheep it grazed from seven million to two million.

Spanish colonization in the New World, instead of providing a growing market for Spanish merchandise, drained Spain of much of her best blood. Into the armies that fought in Flanders, along the Rhine, or in Italy went much of the rest of Spain's best youth. The Spanish birth rate was certain to suffer from the absence of tens of thousands of the most vigorous of her men. A further sad fact in this "Golden Age" (*siglo de oro*) in Spanish history was the power of the Spanish Inquisition. It stifled freedom of thought, it severed any connection of the Spanish cultured classes with the rest of Europe, and it burned or drove out some of the finest minds of the country. The stranglehold the Inquisition had on the Spanish mind reduced Spain to intellectual impotence for centuries.

The Empire

IN THE Empire economic life developed along several lines. The course of the Lutheran reformation emphasized the position of the princes, and the gradual weakening of imperial power obliged them to strengthen their hold on the cities which had, in previous centuries, gained a great measure of liberty. The Hanseatic League cities, hard pressed by competition from English and Scandinavian merchants who had behind them the vigorous support of their governments, were frequently further weakened by tension or friction between member cities. In addition, the herring shoals moved from the closed Baltic to the open North Sea in the fifteenth century, depriving the League of one of its largest sources of revenue. The cities of southern Germany had, all during the later Middle Ages, served as distribution centers for merchandise from Venice and ports in the Adriatic. The *fondaco dei tedeschi,* the German depot at Venice, through which German merchants doing business in Venice conducted their affairs, preserved a substantial trade for the German market well into the sixteenth century. As Venetian trade shrunk, however, German cities such as Ulm, Nürnberg, Regensburg, and Vienna saw their income diminish. The big banking houses, notably the Fugger, the Welser, and the Imhof, continued to prosper, but they owed their prosperity to international financial manipulation quite independent of local industry or the usual commercial dealings. The city of Augsburg, with a population estimated at hardly more than twenty thousand soon after 1500, favorably situated both for trade originating in the south and for commercial and banking relations with the north, was the richest city in the Empire. Its luxury and ostentation were famous throughout Europe. Not only was it a trade and banking center, but it had a large textile industry, importing cotton from Italy and flax from Swabia, combining linen and cotton into a cloth called fustian. The peasant in sixteenth-century Germany suffered most from the general European rise in prices and the increased power in the hands of the princes. The influence of Roman law, which favored the landlords, laid heavier burdens on the peasant and reduced him to virtual serfdom.

The Peasants' Revolt of 1525 was only the most violent of the outbreaks of the oppressed peasantry against the nobility. The peasant movement was sup-

Christoph Fugger, by Christoph Amberger, in the Pinakothek, Munich [BAYERI-SCHE STAATSGEMÄLDESAMMLUNGEN].

pressed in blood, and afterward their condition was worse than before. In south-west Germany a real serfdom (*Leibeigenschaft*) was reimposed upon the peasant class. The towns and their industries involved in the resultant depression of a large class were soon impoverished and thus unable to buy, and economic deterioration became general.

England: Prosperity through Peace and Royal Initiative

IN ENGLAND the situation was to a degree similar to that in France. The disaster of the Black Death had reduced the number of agricultural laborers, and grain-raising gave way to sheep-herding. The latter industry demanded fewer hands, a situation which in turn gave rise as early as the first quarter of the fifteenth century to the enclosing of adjacent lands where herds could graze, the nobility being in general the enclosers. Enclosures meant that some peasants had to be evicted. The towns were their only refuge. There they swelled the labor market, and were eventually fed into the factory system. Henry VII tried in vain to stop the flight from the land, but the trend toward enclosures and pasturing continued. Sir Thomas More shared the prevalent regret at the spread of enclosures when he wrote, in the *Utopia,* that "Sheep have become so great devourers and so wild that they eat up and swallow down the very men themselves."

After the English were driven out of France in 1453 a civil war between the rival royal houses of Lancaster and York almost wiped out the old feudal lines. The townsfolk had remained mostly unaffected by the war, but were prepared and willing to profit by the elimination of a class that had blocked their growth. The first Tudor monarch, Henry VII (1485–1509), was a royal economist. His reign opened a new epoch in English economic policy. He favored the expansion of industry and commerce, and made it a cardinal point of his policy to join politics and economics. This was particularly evident in the favor he showed the woolen industry and in his political support of the Merchant Adventurers. England's wealth, from the fourteenth century on, had come in great measure from the woolen industry, which, from the early years of Edward III (1327–77), had been under the special protection of the crown. Flemish weavers and dyers were enticed to England by promises of franchises and safe-conducts. The policy of protection was followed by successive English monarchs until Henry VII. The English woolen industry prospered, satisfying all home demands, but customs duties were laid on exports of cloth as well as on raw wool exported from England. In 1437, 56,000 broadcloths were shipped abroad, and just before Henry's rise to the throne the figure reached 62,000. The prosperity in the woolen industry generally gave rise to a form of industrial capitalism. Many traders or growers contracted with weavers and fullers to produce cloth, frequently on looms belonging to the clothier, which was then marketed either at home or abroad. Henry VII, and after him all the Tudors, realizing the value to England of the woolen industry, favored and defended the weavers and the clothiers, sometimes against one another, sometimes against capitalist manipulators seeking to take over control of a lucrative industry.

Since the middle of the fifteenth century the system of craft guilds had been on the wane, largely because of the rise of the domestic system by which the merchant capitalist turned raw materials over to families or individual masters to finish, paying them by the piece for their labor. He then marketed the finished product through his own connections. Henry VII disliked the restrictive features of the craft guild and favored the domestic system, finally bringing the craft guilds under royal control. The Act of 1504 decreed that the guilds should submit their ordinances to certain high royal officials. Other restrictive ordinances followed, making governmental control almost complete. This was not the end of the craft guilds, but it allowed the more capitalistic domestic system to gain acceptance.

From the middle of the fifteenth century competition between English and

Flemish finished woolen cloth was sharp, each side restricting or prohibiting the import of cloth from the other. England, during the sixteenth century, attracted many skilled craftsmen from the Continent. The Massacre of St. Bartholomew in 1572 brought to England many French Protestant craftsmen who devoted themselves mostly to the manufacture of silk. The weaving industry became so prosperous as to call for governmental regulation. In 1555 the Weavers' Act restricted the exercise of the trade to those who had been practicing it theretofore and in towns where cloth had been made for the preceding ten years.

Henry VII took personal charge of England's foreign trade, concluding commercial treaties with France, the Lowlands, and the Empire. With the Lowlands he negotiated the *Intercursus magnus* in 1496, according to which English cloth could be freely sold in the Netherlands. Further conventions abolished all duties on English cloth in Burgundy (except Flanders) and for a while permitted English cloth to be sold wholesale in Flanders. The Hanseatic merchants were obliged to give up some of their exclusive rights in English ports, while the English traders gained access to Scandinavian, Baltic, and north German markets, with resulting increase in English commercial confidence and prestige. Henry supported the expeditions of the Cabots to the New World, hoping to add to England's trade; in 1506 an organization of Bristol merchants under the name of the Company Adventurers into the New Found Lands received his blessing as well as his financial interest. Henry set the style of economic management of the royal treasury and, while taking advantage of every royal prerogative to collect fines, levy taxes, or redeem royal demesne, he scrutinized most carefully every expenditure from the exchequer. At the end of his rule, he left a full treasury to his successor. What had been good for Henry had, indeed, been good for England.

The economy of a country is frequently measured by the soundness of its coinage. By such a measurement Henry VII's rule was successful. He coined, for the first time in 1489, the gold sovereign (twenty shillings). He also minted a number of silver and copper coins. The coinage was scrupulously pure as to weight and fineness of metal, and, after the first few mintings, the design showed a certain artistic stateliness hardly matched elsewhere in Europe. The debasement of the coinage began only under Henry VIII, when the purity of both gold and silver coins was reduced on an average about 15 per cent, a factor contributing to the rise of prices as the later debased money drove the older and sounder money out of circulation. In the last three years of his reign Henry VIII profited from the debasement of the coinage in the amount of £363,000. He still had to borrow money to carry on his diplomacy and threats of war, and the Antwerp bankers, knowing that the king was in difficulties, demanded interest as high as 14 per cent, even then insisting on guarantees from Italian banking houses doing business in London. Edward VI, Mary, and Elizabeth I strove, firmly and courageously, to restore the coinage to the standard of Henry VII.

Another index of English economic growth in this century would be the customs receipts of the port of London, the leading port of the realm. In 1506 the port of London brought in £12,000. By 1581, late in the reign of Elizabeth, the corresponding figure was £35,000. The other English ports had in the meantime declined slightly. The figures for the export of woolen cloth were perhaps even more accurately indicative of the growth of capitalistic enterprise. Under Henry VIII the export rose from 85,000 cloths per annum to over 120,000 near the end of his reign. On the other hand, the export of wool showed a decline of 45 per cent from 1509 to 1547, and as the customs on cloth was light and that on wool was high, a drop in total income for the treasury was the result. Henry VIII, although not unaware of the need for diplomacy to support commerce, was yet less systematic and more casual in execution than Henry VII.

The solid basis laid by Henry VII, both for the wool industry at home and for commercial expansion abroad, was the necessary foundation for Britain's greatness in subsequent centuries. At times in the sixteenth century much of English commerce on the high seas was barely disguised piracy. Seamen like Sir John Hawkins and Sir Francis Drake engaged profitably in the slave trade and blithely captured ships belonging to nations with whom England was at peace. The booty was sent on to England, the royal treasury, more likely than not, receiving its slice of the treasure. From the slave trade through piracy to a knighthood and an admiral's hat was a natural progress. Such men and exploits, as well as honest and sagacious trade, built English commercial supremacy.

Henry VIII continued his father's general policies of protection for English commerce and industry and the combination of diplomacy and economic interests, but an expansionist diplomacy forced Henry VIII to desert the conservatism of his father's monetary policy. In a time of economic change the government naturally sought to preserve stability, both in agriculture and in the towns. Much of the legislation of Henry VIII was restrictive toward capitalistic expansion; at the same time it brought the ancient craft guilds under government control. The expenses to which Henry VIII was put in preparation for the defense of England against threats of war at the time of his break with the Church forced him and his ministers to find new sources of income. The suppression of the monasteries (1535–38) and the confiscation of their lands and properties was the answer. This measure added about £30,000 to the royal revenue, a sum which was soon found to be inadequate to bridge the gap between income and outgo.

The reigns of Edward VI and Mary were hardly long enough to alter in any fundamental way the economy of England. Both rulers strove to restore the fiscal and commercial soundness of the reign of Henry VII and, especially in the matter of currency, made progress toward a sound basis. Some of Henry VIII's coins were demonetized and better coinage issued in their place.* Nevertheless, the years of Edward's reign were years of economic disturbance. Prices were high, the inheritance of Henry VIII's extravagance, while the land did not produce enough food to feed a growing population. The effect of the enclosures was beginning to make itself felt. In 1549 there were uprisings in Somerset and Norfolk, spreading to many other counties in the midlands and southern England, demanding that the enclosures be laid open. The Protector, Somerset, issued a proclamation condemning enclosures, which had no effect.

* Elizabeth demonetized all the base currency in circulation in 1561 and thereafter English currency—gold, silver, and copper—was completely sound, all issued from the royal mint in London.

There was, however, the bright spot of trade and industry. London was prospering and the merchants were accumulating substantial fluid capital which tended to free the government from having to borrow money abroad. In 1553 London merchants financed an expedition of three ships for "the discovery of the Northern part of the world." One of the ships reached Archangel, and in 1555 a Muscovy Company was chartered with a monopoly of Russian trade. Under Elizabeth this connection was maintained and even expanded, overland to Persia. Imports from Russia—oil, tallow, hides, tar, hemp, and wax—were valuable for England's maritime growth. The commercial aggressiveness of the Merchant Adventurers brought about, in 1564, a break with the merchants of Antwerp, and the English company moved the center of its activities to Germany, where the Hansards offered severe competition. The break with Antwerp, which lasted until 1585, was one of the factors in the commercial decline of that city. In addition to the Merchant Adventurers, who were consistently favored by royal diplomacy, an Eastland Company was chartered in 1579 to compete with the Hansa in Scandinavia and the Baltic. English cloth was the commodity for which northern raw materials were exchanged.

The English were determined to break into the Far Eastern market. The Muscovy Company tried at least twice (1556, 1580) to reach the Pacific through the northeast passage, north of Russia, while other expeditions attempted the northwest passage. Frobisher made three expeditions in three years, 1576–78, but got only as far as the modern Frobisher Strait. Another captain, John Davis, in 1579 reached latitude 73 north, beyond Greenland, the farthest north in the sixteenth century. Both Frobisher and Davis missed Hudson Strait; this had to wait another thirty years to be discovered by Henry Hudson. Other English merchants opened the markets of Turkey and the Levant. Portugal had been England's source for spices, an indispensable commodity for seasoning and preserving food. When, in 1580, Portugal was taken over by England's enemy, Philip II of Spain, England had to obtain her spices directly from the East. In 1581 a joint-stock company of London merchants obtained a charter from Queen Elizabeth to trade with Turkey, the queen investing £40,000 of her own in the venture. In 1583 an expedition of merchants reached Goa and there divided forces. One member of the party went on to Burma and the Malay Peninsula.

Magnificent as these exploits were they did not provide an adequate outlet for English industry. England needed more markets. The Continental market was hedged about with restrictions and heavy competition for English products. Colonization in America offered an unexplored opportunity. In 1578 Sir Humphrey Gilbert obtained a patent from Queen Elizabeth to "plant" America. He chose to try to colonize Newfoundland, the venture ending in tragedy and failure in 1583. Two attempts by Sir Walter Raleigh, with patents from the queen, in 1585 and 1587, to settle on the coast of Virginia were also disastrous. It is possible that colonization was the aim of Sir Francis Drake's voyage around the world (1577–80). He may have been instructed to establish a base for colonization on the California coast. Thus far the ventures of English merchants, colonizers, and captains had not brought any commercial success. But in 1591 a trading expedition to India foretold an altered policy, that of trading without attempting to colonize. Late in 1599 the East India Company was chartered by the queen; the next year five ships loaded with English cloth set sail for Sumatra and Java. England's empire in the East had begun.

Tudor economic nationalism fostered many new industries, frequently brought to England by craftsmen and entrepreneurs who had fled France or the Lowlands for one reason or another, political, economic, or religious. But, as it was an age of transition in economic and industrial integration, there were bound to be periods of maladjustment, unemployment, and distress for the laborer. The Statute of Apprentices of 1563 attempted to protect the poor, the trades, and the general public by controlling conditions of entrance into productive industry and by setting wages. For the support of those who could not work, the Poor Laws, from 1563 to 1601, made provision by organizing contributions from the church and from those able to pay.

Although the prosperity of Tudor England was unevenly distributed, its impact on society was tremendous. New styles, new standards of dress and living, new ideals of success, a new literature, new butts of humor and ridicule, new fashions in shoes, hats, and haircuts, occupied the attention of all classes— the newly rich, the aristocracy, the new bureaucracy, and the hangers-on. It was a lusty age, clearly portrayed on its own stage and in its literature. Shakespeare is only the best and the most finished representative of the end of that age.

The Lowlands: Free Enterprise

THE most genuinely prosperous and, from the viewpoint of economics, the most effectively organized land in Europe has been left to the last. The Low Countries looked four ways: to France, with whom economic ties only confirmed ancient feudal relationships; to Germany, where both commerce and, for much of the Lowlands, a legal and constitutional position within the Holy Roman Empire created a framework favorable to commerce; to England, whose wool and carrying trade were indispensable to the economic health of the Lowlands; to a lesser degree, to the Hanseatic League which, in spite of a certain decline in prestige and economic power, still carried on a valuable sea trade with Scandinavia, the Baltic, and northeast German cities. Before our period Bruges had been the leading city of the Lowlands. But in the latter half of the fifteenth century ports along the nearby coast began to silt up and the larger ships, necessary to carry the increasing sea trade of the age of discovery, sought wharves easier of access. Antwerp, on the Scheldt, was ready to take over the burden of being the leading Dutch center. In 1505 the Fuggers moved their branch offices from Bruges to Antwerp, and in 1545 the Hanseatic cities followed their lead, Antwerp becoming the money and trade center of northern Europe. Henry VIII had a permanent agent, Sir Thomas Gresham, in residence at Antwerp to handle his financial arrangements with Continental bankers. All the leading German and Italian bankers had headquarters in the booming city. It reached a population of 200,000 by 1560, acting as host to two large world trade fairs each year, where merchants and commission agents from all parts of the known world—from Muscovy to Angola and the Spice Islands—came and traded. A hundred or more ships docked or left the wharves daily. Guicciardini, the Florentine historian, reported that spices and sugar imported from Portugal amounted to 1,500,000 ducats a year, gold and silk embroideries from Italy to 3,000,000 ducats, grain from the Baltic to 1,500,000, wines from France and Germany to 2,500,000, and all imports from England to 12,000,000.

Antwerp was not only a money and commercial center; it had also become the leading center for the industries of the Lowlands. The manufacture of all kinds of cloth, wool, cotton, velvet, and satin, carpets, glass and ceramics, mining and metallurgy brought great prosperity to the capitalist entrepreneurs. Ghent, Liége, and Brussels shared in this prosperity. The working classes, however, did not fare so well. The old guilds were unable to adapt themselves to the boom conditions and rapid expansion of industry and, in spite of frequent uprisings, could not present a united front against the exploitation of those dependent on their wages for their daily bread. The city reached the height of its prosperity in 1566. After that time the oppressive rule of Philip II and the repressions of the duke of Alva hampered free commerce and drove many craftsmen and merchants out of the land, some to England, some to the northern provinces of the Lowlands, which were then winning their independence from Spain. The "Spanish Fury" of 1576 was disastrous for the spirit of the people. Seven thousand inhabitants were put to the sword; pillage and fire made a shambles of the busiest part of the city. After another access of Spanish temper in 1586 the population dropped to 85,000; four years later it was only 55,000. In 1598 Philip II decreed that no trade from America or the Indies should enter Antwerp. For decades this was a "ghost city," and the southern provinces under Spanish rule ceased to be a factor of any significance in European commerce.

The northern provinces, free from the Spanish yoke in 1581, took over much of the commercial importance of Antwerp and Ghent. The north had never been predominantly industrial; its prosperity was based on agriculture, shipping, sea trade, and fishing. The Dutch sailors were reputed to be the best in the world, and their enterprise and reliability brought the carrying trade of all Europe to their ports. It was said of the Dutch that "Norway is their forest, Prussia and Poland their granaries, the Rhine, the Garonne, and the Dordogne their vineyards, Germany, Spain, and Ireland their sheep fold." From 1585 to 1595 the population of Amsterdam, the leading Dutch port, nearly doubled from the emigration of merchants, craftsmen, and Protestant citizenry from Antwerp. In 1620 the population was reckoned at 105,000. The enterprise of the Dutch stretched to the southeastern seas. In 1602 the Dutch East India Company was founded, financed on a sharing basis by subscription from the Estates General, towns, and private business concerns. It carved out an empire in the East Indies which was to last for over three centuries.

Maintaining their agricultural tradition the Dutch improved their methods of production, recovered thousands of acres from the sea, improved and increased their dairy stock, and continued to produce cheese for domestic use and for export. Advances in social welfare, the foundation and maintenance of hospitals, almshouses, and schools marked the adventurous and progressive thinking of the whole people. When, in 1609, peace was finally concluded with Spain, the northern provinces were on the eve of a golden age of expansion and prosperity. The southern provinces, still under Spanish domination, went into a steady economic decline which was to last for many generations.

To add to their glory, the United Provinces became the refuge of the persecuted in other lands. Jews, Huguenots, Protestants fleeing the Inquisition in Italy, Spain, Austria, or France found safety and sympathy under the flag of the house of Orange. The list of the names of those who came to Holland for asylum would include many of the greatest minds of the late sixteenth and seventeenth centuries. From this policy of liberality and tolerance the Dutch profited both economically and spiritually. The loss of the persecutors was Holland's gain.

POLITICAL THOUGHT

PERIODS of political disturbance and crisis have always called forth suggestions for change and improvement or the justification and re-establishment of the old order. The sixteenth century was an era of constant political turmoil, in almost every land of the Continent; and it was consequently a time when men everywhere were seeking answers to the questions of the relation of the individual to the state, the ordering of the organs of government, the relation of the state to the church, political justice and its implementation, monarchy, autocracy and democracy, tyrannicide and rebellion. There is hardly a basic political problem in our modern world which was not discussed by some thinker somewhere during this crucial century.

Italy

ITALY was the most fragmented of all the European lands. It was cursed by the greatest variety of government of any part of the Continent. Despotism, royalty, democracy, aristocracy, theocracy, anarchy—all could be found in Italy of this century and several of them in one city or duchy within a short period of time. It was a political kaleidoscope that defied precise description or reliable analysis. Yet out of this welter of experiment, oppression, rejection, and acceptance by the populations there arose one observer whose realistic thought has given his name to a whole segment of political philosophy in our Western tradition, Niccolò Machiavelli (1469–1527).

In two quite different works, *The Prince* and the *Discourses on Livy,* Machiavelli presented the results of his experience and analysis of Italian and European statecraft. It was as if he were saying: "This is what I saw, and these were the results." He was not interested in abstract concepts of truth and right, but rather in the portrayal of what measures, political or military, brought a stable victory. He delineated sharply the permanent separation of ethics from politics. This had not been done before in the Latin-Christian tradition. In the *Discourses,* obviously, he was writing not from experience but from historical sources. Machiavelli attempted, not always successfully, to draw historical parallels and to formulate some rules of political behavior. He had preferences in political organization, favoring a republican form of government over personal rule, whether by legitimate dynasties or by princes who rose by their own *virtù.* Yet he never went so far as to project a system or a theory of government, for he was not nor did he intend to be a political philosopher. Intensely patriotic, he must have harbored a hope that Italy would one day be united, probably under the leader-

ship of Florence or of some powerful personality who would be as realistic as
the Prince he so vividly portrayed, from the model he knew, Cesare Borgia.
He implied, in the *Discourses,* that the chaos from which Italy chronically suffered was due, as much as anything else, to the fact that the rulers and powers
of the peninsula acted on preconceived ideas, generally theological, as to the
functions of the state, or on unrelated concepts of good and evil. He intended to
brush away these vagaries and to present political motives and actions as they
really were. This was a revolution in political thought and, although he offered
no finished system, he did present a fresh attitude to the consideration of political action. His work had no immediate effect. It did not win for him the favor
of the Medici; *The Prince* and the *Discourses* were not even printed until 1531,
four years after his death. His work had no discernible influence in political
literature until about 1560. In spite of this slighting by his contemporaries
Machiavelli has to be treated as of his own time, for he truly mirrors the changes
that were taking place in Italy in the early years of the century. After mid-
century, however, his popularity grew, and the thinking of the *Politiques* in
the French wars of religion found suggestive support in Machiavelli's realism.
The Prince had many powerful readers. Charles V and his son Philip II
studied it. Catherine de' Medici brought it with her to France, and her son
Henry III had it read to him. A copy was on Henry IV's person when he was
murdered.

After the peace of Câteau-Cambrésis in 1559 the Spanish Habsburgs dominated the Italian peninsula. There was then an end to the squabbles of the petty
despots and minor states. Theorizing on politics during the latter half of the
century aroused little interest. Two scholars, however, who lived in territories
not under Spanish rule, deserve to be mentioned. Paolo Paruta of Venice, a
studious dilettante, published in 1579 a collection of conversations between himself and his cultured Venetian friends entitled *On the Perfection of Political
Life.* The principal point of the work is to show that the high-minded citizen
should participate in the political life of his city or state. Paruta prefers an aristocratic constitution: democracy leads to anarchy, monarchy to tyranny. The
Church hardly enters into his consideration at all. The assumptions on which he
proceeds are completely secular.

Giovanni Botero, a Piedmontese priest and secretary to Cardinal Borromeo,
published in 1589 a book *On the Reason of State,* and in 1596 a study *Of the
Causes for the Greatness of States.* In his detachment from any moral or moralizing approach to political questions he was close to Machiavelli. He intended
merely to describe the functioning of politics as he had observed it in action,
paying close attention to economic and climatic factors in government, probably as a result of reading Bodin's *Republic.* Hereditary monarchy appeared to
him as the best form of government, and he emphasized the utility of religion
in preserving the loyalty and obedience of the subjects to their king. Deprecat-
ing war in general, he blamed its frequency on the petty ambitions of too many
monarchs, each anxious to expand his territory. This observation led Botero to
advocate a universal monarchy with, hopefully, a universal language and a universal currency. Paruta and Botero, both distinctly of the second rank, were the
best that Italy, a seedbed of political action, could produce in the latter half of
the century.

Northern Europe

LONG before Machiavelli became a by-word for the ideas of deceit, chicanery, and calculated disregard of natural law and justice, new ideas of the state and the individual had begun to circulate in Europe. True, none of these was as revolutionary as Machiavelli's elevation of cynical realism to a principle of state-craft; but none the less the medieval idea of a universal society under the cover of a universal church was as surely yielding, north of the Alps, to the modern concept of separation of church and state as it was in Italy.

Luther

MARTIN Luther was no more of a systematic theologian than Machiavelli was a political scientist. The revolution he led was mostly religious and only in-cidentally political. But that minor degree of political involvement yet had seri-ous repercussions. Luther's early appeal to the German nobility (1520) was a sort of political manifesto. It was antipapal, nationalistic, and aristocratic, but in no way systematic. He rejected the control which the Roman *curia* exercised over Germany and sought to substitute for that centralizing role the disparate rule of the German princes, under the overlordship of the Emperor. When Luther realized, from about 1521, that Charles V was determined to hold Ger-many fast to the Papacy, he had to recast his earlier hopes and countenance resistance to a monarch. In 1523 he wrote *On Secular Dominion (Von welt-licher Obrigkeit)*, in which he declared the independence of the church from secular princes, for whom he had contempt. Yet he demanded that the secular princes secure the reform of the church and thereafter protect the church's freedom of action. The state, to Luther, was primarily an agency established by God to assure the safety and work of the church, yet without the right to the slightest interference in matters of doctrine or the sacraments. In 1526 he wrote: "The hand that wields the secular sword is not a human hand, but the hand of God . . . it is God who wages war." The secular magistrate must be obeyed. Rebellion against the magistrate is forbidden by Scripture. The situation in which the magistrate attempted to coerce the church created a dilemma for Luther which he never clearly resolved. He made, at various times, clearly contradictory statements on the subject. In fact, Luther never entirely faced up to the question of the boundaries between secular and ecclesiastical power, choosing rather to leave the decision to the Scriptures. Early in his career he spoke vehemently for toleration in religious concerns, even declaring at one point that the Anabaptists should be allowed to preach. After 1531 he came to believe that the reformed faith should be maintained by force. It is not possible to make Luther into a consistent political thinker from whose writings we can construct a coherent or reasoned concept of the state, the church, the duties of the prince, or the rights of the subject. While Luther and his movement certainly had an effect on the German state, it was not in the direction of cohesion or the formulation of a clear political doctrine. The connection between Luther's elevation of the secular ruler over the church to more recent German political developments, from Frederich II to Hitler, has frequently been pointed out.

Melanchthon

MELANCHTHON, who was so useful to Luther in bringing a degree of order into the theology of the German Reformation, was scarcely less vague than Luther in the field of political thought. He emphasized the necessity of obedience to the magistrate, discountenanced rebellion against the established prince, favored, perhaps more consistently than Luther, the duty of the prince to protect and maintain religion, but at the instigation and according to the direction of the church. Instead of allowing the magistrate to decide matters of discipline and doctrine, he proposed that they be under the jurisdiction of a council composed of qualified lay and clerical persons. In theory, Melanchthon accepted the principle of the divine right of princes, at the same time recognizing the right of tyrannicide against a notoriously unjust ruler. This conflict in logic only illustrates the difficulties inherent in the effort to work out a new concept of the state, after rejecting the combined and cooperative universalism of both Papacy and Empire.

The radicals of this century tended to minimize the importance of the state. While some preferred to ignore it, others regarded it as evil and the magistrate as an offender against the law of God. Coercion of any sort was to them absolutely wrong. There was some communism among scattered groups of Anabaptists, but its extent has been exaggerated. At Münster in 1534-35, under militant leadership and wartime conditions, communism of a sort was enforced, but it was not a matter of doctrine. As the Anabaptists envisaged a theocracy on earth, the concept of equal participation in God's gifts to His children overrode the urgency of private ownership.

Calvin

COMPARED with the inconsistencies and confusion which plagued the political thinking of the early reformers, John Calvin's thought was orderly and clear. One whole chapter (22) of Book IV of the *Institutes* is devoted to civil government. Calvin accepts the separation between church and state as normal and even necessary and condemns those (the Genevan Libertines are obviously intended) who imagine that Christian liberty allows them to live without legal restraints: "They think that nothing will be safe until the whole world is changed into a new form, when there will be neither courts, nor laws, nor magistrates, nor anything of the kind to interfere, as they suppose, with their liberty." Calvin holds that, given the present condition of "the community of men," law, courts, and magistrates are necessary, and "it is perfect barbarism to think of exterminating civil government." Calvin assigns to civil government not only the task of providing order and honesty among the citizenry but also that of protecting "true religion, contained in the law of God." Civil government consists of three parts: "the magistrate who is president and guardian of the laws, the laws according to which he governs, and the people, who are governed by the laws and obey the magistrate." The magistrates' duties extend to both civil and religious concerns, since their office is ordained by God. The people owe them not only obedience but honor, as "ministers and ambassadors of God." The advocates of the theory of the divine right of kings could claim support from this position. Calvin earnestly urges obedience to properly constituted magistrates, even to the point of suffering harshness, though there are exceptions: "We are subject to the men who rule over us, but subject only in the Lord." Orders contrary to the law of God may be disregarded, but active resistance Calvin consistently rules out. The magistrate is responsible to God, and Calvin adduces many instances in the history of the Children of Israel where God, in His own way, removed a ruler who was evil or disobedient to His law.

Almost alone among the reformers Calvin was able to put his political theories into practice. The organization of the Genevan state after 1555 was essentially a theocracy along Calvin's lines. The citizenry of Geneva was under a double regime, of both church and state. The ecclesiastical framework was headed by the Venerable Company, made up of the ministers and theologians, and the Consistory, consisting of the ministers and twelve lay elders. The ministers dominated both groups. As a civil regime, the state was theoretically ruled by a series of coordinating councils; in practice the whole system was highly aristocratic. The discipline for the citizens was severely puritanical. As long as Calvin lived the system worked, if not without opposition. The inherited separation of church and state was gradually abandoned, and the Genevan state came to be dominated by the clergy. A direct consequence of this theocratic solution of the church-state dilemma was intolerance of heresy and its qualification as a crime against the state. Indirectly, however, through the discussions that followed upon the trial and death of Servetus, the rigidity of the Genevan discipline led to its own modification. Within the next generation, when the Huguenots themselves suffered persecution under Catherine de' Medici, their devotion to the principle of toleration became even more marked.

Huguenots and Politiques

THE Massacre of St. Bartholomew in August 1572 precipitated an avalanche of Huguenot pamphleteering against the royal party. Among the publicists who were disciples of Calvin, the most significant were Theodore Beza (1519–1605), Francis Hotman (1524–90), and the author of the *Vindiciae contra tyrannos*, probably Philip Duplessis-Mornay (1548–1623). The three differ among themselves, but all shared Calvin's legalism, respect for authority, and dislike of violence. Beza, in his *On the Rights of Magistrates over Their Subjects*, written in 1573, vaguely voices the concept of contract between ruler and people. While he relies on God to punish the tyrannical ruler, as Calvin had argued, he appeals to the law of nature and the rights of Christians against usurpers and tyrants. He demands that resistance be not an individual matter, but be led by the appropriate representatives of the people. If this restraint on tyranny fails, Beza, alone among the Huguenots, allows recourse to tyrannicide.

In 1573 there appeared Francis Hotman's *Franco-Gallia*. Hotman, a patriotic French jurist, was anxious to prove that France had never, in all her history, been an absolute monarchy, but that sovereignty had always rested in a general assembly of the nation. The king was thus responsible to the people and could be removed for violating the contractual conditions of his election. This appeal to constitutional history, buttressed by a show of great learning, remained an important document to republicans and Huguenots.

The *Vindiciae contra tyrannos,* published in 1579, is an eloquent and closely argued attack on the absolute monarch. The argument is focused around four questions, to which unequivocal answers are given: (1) Subjects are not bound to obey a ruler whose commands are contrary to God's law. (2) Subjects have the right to resist a ruler who goes contrary to the law of God or persecutes His church. This conclusion is based on the concept of a covenant between God, ruler and people. Capricious rebellion is ruled out; only the appropriate leading classes or representative organizations, the Estates, the nobility, an elective assembly, have the right to resist a tyrannical ruler. (3) Since the people were prior to the king and gave assent to his rule, only on carefully stipulated conditions, whereas he must promise absolutely and unconditionally to rule justly and according to the contract, the people are immediately released from their obedience by the ruler's violation of his promises. It is then their duty through their representatives to depose him. (4) It is the duty of rulers to interest themselves in the affairs of their neighbors, and, in case of tyranny or persecution of God's people or His church, to interfere. The relation of this line of argument to the political situation of the Huguenots under Charles IX and Catherine de' Medici is obvious. Beyond that, the fourth point was clearly intended to justify the aid and comfort extended the Huguenots by Elizabeth of England and some German Protestant princes. The effect of the whole treatise was to justify resistance to a tyrant or a ruler persecuting or perverting the faith of his subjects. Rebellion must be led by the representatives of the people. Individual rebellion is not excusable. This was a common Huguenot position.

George Buchanan (1506–82) was a friend and collaborator of John Knox, but spent most of his mature years in France. He may thus be treated along with the French Huguenot thinkers. In 1568 he composed a work, *On the Law of Kingship among the Scots (De iure regni apud Scotos)*, which was intended to show that the deposition of Mary Queen of Scots in the previous year was right and proper. The book was not published until 1579. Mary, the author argued, had been deposed because she was a tyrant, not a proper ruler. The task of the princes is to administer the law, which is made by the people acting through their representatives. When a ruler perverts the law to his own will he becomes a tyrant. Buchanan here advances beyond the theories of passive obedience of Luther and Calvin. He concludes that a tyrant must not only be resisted; he may, in the last resort, be justly killed.

The idea that the relationship between a ruler and his people was a contract was generally accepted in the latter half of the sixteenth century. It was not restricted to the Protestant publicists. The Catholics were also ready to employ the idea in their polemics with rulers who did not support the Church. The Sorbonne declared in 1587 that the people of France were freed from their obedience to Henry III because he had violated his pact with them by siding with the Huguenots; and Jean Bouchier, Prior of the Sorbonne and a prominent member of the Catholic League, published in 1589 a book *On the Just Abdication of Henry III,* in which he argued that as kings were chosen by the people they could also be deposed by the same body. Hereditary rights to a throne, he argued, are baseless; and other Catholic publicists expressly sanctioned, like Knox from the Protestant side, the killing of a heretic ruler.

These legalists, intent on proving that monarchs received their powers from the consent of the governed, were not alone in formulating answers to political problems that would suit their needs. There was, however, a current of opinion in an opposite direction. The catastrophic civil wars in France from 1560 to Henry IV (1590) led some to think that the only way to bring and maintain order in the kingdom was for the ruler to be recognized as absolute, consecrated and fortified by God as His special agent. For these advocates of absolute rule and the divine right of kings, resistance to the will of God's anointed was rebellion against the Deity. The number of those who sought the nation's security in absolutism was as yet not great, but the current was already discernible in the days of Henry III (1574–89). Those who advanced this idea were for the most part members of the Catholic League.

A far more numerous and indeed representative group was that of the *politiques*. Their number grew after 1572, when the Massacre of St. Bartholomew convinced many loyal Frenchmen that the suicidal internecine strife was only ruining France and the Christian religion. La Noue, the Protestant general who at the last served Charles IX, remarked: "Our wars of religion are making us forget our religion." The quick consolidation of Huguenot strength after the failure of the royal army to take La Rochelle in 1573 made it clear that a decisive victory over the Protestants was impossible. The alternative of mutual tolerance began to appear as the only solution to the woes of a divided France.

In Michel de l'Hôpital (1507–73), chancellor of the kingdom of France from 1560 until a few weeks before his death, the cause of tolerance found a great and noble advocate. Trained as a lawyer, and by inclination a humanist, de l'Hôpital accepted the divine origin of kingship and the obligation of the subjects to obey a king who is a supreme lawgiver and is himself above the law. Rebellion was wrong and tyrannicide detestable. Only under such presuppositions could there be peace and order in the kingdom. So far, de l'Hôpital agreed with many advocates of absolutism. But his temperament rebelled at the extreme application of his theory, and, in a France split on religious issues, he faced the practical problems involved and declared that only by toleration on the part of the government could civil war be avoided. Not alone in this view, he was, by reason of his position and prestige, its most effective protagonist. In 1561 he published his *Exhortation to the Princes and Lords of the King's Privy Council,* in which he proposed the recognition of two churches in France, declaring simply that the Huguenots were too strong to be crushed without destroying the integrity of the kingdom and urging the elimination of names of sects and factions. Instead, he urged, "Let us use again the name of Christians." A government which would effect uniformity of belief by overpowering force would suppress all liberty and weaken the realm beyond recovery.

The *politiques* were not an organization; they were a focus of tolerant opinion. The most significant of their political ideas was that France could exist and even prosper with two religions. The long dominant opinion that there had to be unity of belief in a state in order for that state to function and progress was seen to be false. The next step was a certain scepticism about religious professions and a growing doubt as to the sincerity of the leaders of both sides of the Wars of Religion. Henry of Navarre, in 1585, voicing the conviction of a great part of the French people, declared: "Provided that the basis of good conscience is present, diversity in religion does not prevent a good ruler from being able to command the service and loyalty of his subjects." Any *politique* could have subscribed to this sentiment; indeed, almost all of them soon did.

Bodin

THE most original political thinker of France in the latter part of the century was Jean Bodin (1530–96). He studied law and was a professor of jurisprudence at the University of Toulouse, then moved to Paris in 1561 and began to write. In 1566 he wrote *A Method for the Easy Understanding of History,* which rejected the medieval Christian divisions of history and projected a universal and even comparative history covering all peoples and all ages. Two years later, in *The Response to the Paradoxes of M. de Malestroit,* he explained the great rise in prices by the depreciation of currency and the influx of specie from abroad. The facts were of course known but no one before him had presented them so effectively. In 1571 he was taken into the service of the duke of Anjou, the future Henry III. At the time of the St. Bartholomew massacre he was sought as a Huguenot, probably because he was known to have advocated toleration. He escaped from Paris, to reappear early in 1573. Intermittently he enjoyed royal favor until 1584, when he retired to Laon as procurator general until his death of the plague in 1596. His most significant work was the *Six Books of the Republic,* published in French in 1576. The events of St. Bartholomew had doubtless induced him to order his thoughts on the nature of the state, sovereignty, and the sovereign.

Bodin argues that the family is the germ of society and thence of the state. He begins his treatise with the definition: "A state is an association of families and their common possessions, governed by a sovereign power and by reason." Since liberty is restricted within the family, there is no absolute liberty in society or the state. All voluntary associations involve the exercise of authority and the infringement of individual liberty. Authority must be concentrated in one person, the sovereign, in order for the state to be "well ordered," since, obviously, good government (*droit gouvernement*) demands sovereign power (*puissance souveraine*). Nevertheless, he contends, "sovereignty does not reside in the someone or few [to whom supreme power has been granted] but in the people at whose pleasure they hold their power." The people do not surrender their power, they only entrust it to an individual or individuals for a limited time or at their pleasure. The woes of a harassed and divided France would have led him to this conclusion, and his legal training gave him the logic by which he reached his formulations. It never seems quite clear how far the sovereignty he discusses extends, but it is certain that it was limited by the law of nature, the disposition of the subjects, and the ancient laws attached to the crown of that particular land. The idea of a constitution to limit the power of the sovereign, however, is foreign to Bodin. As a loyal Frenchman, he found monarchy in general the best state, and French monarchy in particular the ideal type of government. The sovereign is such by virtue of divine grace, and therefore inviolable. On many points Bodin's thought was vague, even self-contradictory. It is certain, for example, that some confusion must have arisen between his two statements: that the sovereign is released from obedience to laws (*legibus solutus*) and that "nothing should be sanctioned which is contrary to God's laws or the laws of nature," since, as Althusius (see text below) pointed out, nearly all positive law is merely a declaration of natural law. On other points Bodin's thought was quite unoriginal. Nevertheless, he must be given credit for being the first to bring the concept of sovereignty into clear focus. Montesquieu's *Spirit of the Laws* was deeply indebted to Bodin's treatment of sovereignty and the state in the *Republic*.

Political developments precipitated political discussion or polemic in almost every part of Europe in the sixteenth century. It has been noticed above that neither Luther nor Melanchthon was a systematic political thinker, being too close to the revolution they had precipitated to be able to analyze the changes that had taken place. Indeed, no Lutheran Protestant was to make any positive contributions to political theory.

Germany

THE MOST significant German political thinker of this period was John Althusius (1557–1638). Raised in Calvinist circles in Westphalia and Nassau, he was educated in Geneva and, from 1586 to 1604, was professor of jurisprudence at the University of Herborn. In 1604 he was called as syndic to Emden, where he remained until his death in 1638. In 1603 he published his *Politica methodice digesta (Politics Systematically Treated)*, of which he issued two revisions (1610, 1614).

In Althusius' view all rights of sovereignty reside in the people. They are needful for social existence. These rights may properly be administered by a magistrate, yet remain the property of the whole people who unite in the state. Althusius manufactured a Latin term *consociatio* (hardly translatable as consociation) to describe the association of people into a body, a community, or a corporation which has the right and the will to work together, to assign its rights to a magistrate for specific, limited exercise. Influenced by Calvin's thought, Althusius accepted ecclesiastical organization by presbyteries and synods, parallel to the civil structure of the peasantry, the bourgeoisie, and the gentry. The state consists of cities and provinces, which, assembled, constitute the state endowed with supreme power on earth to do what it must to preserve order. Bodin had given this state absolute supreme power. Althusius kept the state subject to God's will. Tyranny has no right to exist. A people can resist, depose, and, if necessary, kill a tyrant. Whereas Bodin had advanced the idea of a contract between people and ruler by which the people subject themselves to the prince's rule, Althusius does not even place the magistrate in a position of contractual equality with the people. Rather, the magistrate is a servant of the people and administers or rules only at their order.

Poland

IN POLAND, the trend of constitutional development in the fifteenth century was toward greater liberties for the nobility (*szlachta*) and less power in the hands of the monarch. The Polish gentry were proud of their rights and of the fact that their kings were elected only after confirming these privileges and perhaps adding to them. It was a feast of freedom, and chaos in government. Into this anomalous situation there came an acute and high-minded observer, Andrew Frycz Modrzewski, known by his latinized name of Modrevius (1503-90). He studied at the University of Cracow, then at Wittenberg, where he became a close friend of Melanchthon. Later he was in the employ of the Laski family, and in 1546 he became a secretary to Sigismund Augustus, the heir to the throne, remaining in the prince's employ after he ascended the throne in 1548. In 1551 his great work *De republica emendanda* (*On the Reform of the Republic*) began to appear in Cracow. It was planned in four books. The fourth book, "On the Church," was so critical of the established institution that it was not allowed to be published in Poland. The whole work appeared in Basel in 1554, first in Latin, later in a German translation—interestingly enough the first treatise on political theory to be published in German.

The work of a Christian humanist, largely influenced by Melanchthon and Erasmus, the *De republica* based political structure on issues of moral rectitude. Modrzewski approved the Polish elective monarchy, and accepted the differentiation between the classes, but he also insisted that all men, from peasant to magnate, should be equal before the law. Punishments for the peasant should be identical with those for the nobleman, and justice should be available to the humblest laborer on an equal basis with the aristocrat. In other connections he rejected the hereditary serfdom that subjected the peasants to the perpetuation of their hopeless condition. To enforce justice for the serfs, he proposed royal censors or inspectors of morals, whose function it would be to assure the peasantry justice under the law. Obviously the whole of the Polish nobility would regard such suggestions as a direct and dangerous attack on their class and privileges, and Modrzewski was bitterly hated. Like all humanists he was a pacifist, allowing war only as a defense of the homeland. Taxes intended to support campaigns for conquest he would have abolished, thus striking at the source of much of the income of the nobility. In the fourth book he called for a broader doctrinal approach than the orthodox could accept. Modrzewski's doctrine was in fact moderate Lutheranism, with a few traces of Hussitism and Calvinism. He wanted marriage of the clergy, abolition of pluralities, the liturgy in the vernacular, and the opening of high offices in the Church to men of capacity and learning regardless of their birth. The king, Sigismund Augustus, had explicitly commissioned him to write this book on the Church. In spite of this royal patronage he was persecuted by the Catholic hierarchy and, for several periods of time, imprisoned as a heretic. Modrzewski, throughout his projected reforms, placed great reliance on the man of letters, the humanist, and the professor, elevating the teaching function almost above the priesthood. At the end of a sustained attack on the two strongest elements in Polish life, the Church and the nobility, he would fain have created a republic of letters, equality, and reason. Poland, on her way to dissolution, was hardly prepared for any such miracle of benign charity.

Spain

THE Jesuit Juan de Mariana (1536–1624), after humanistic studies in Spain, Sicily, and France and profound research into the history of his own country, wrote a treatise *On Kingship and the Education of a King,* dedicated to Philip III of Spain in 1599. For him, society arose out of man's weakness and need for security. Monarchy was to him the best system of governance and hereditary monarchy the optimum, but society must be protected from tyranny. The people, in granting power to a ruler, reserve the right to control legislation, taxation, and succession to royal authority, that is, to election and removal. Mariana denies to the ruler any control over religion. The higher clergy must be allowed complete autonomy in their sphere. The ruler, ultimately, is subject to three constraints: the authority of God, the honor and honesty to which all human beings are bound, and the opinion of the citizenry, formulated in positive laws and traditions. Mariana was almost alone among the Jesuits in his opposition to absolute monarchy, and in 1606 the French Jesuits even expressly repudiated his work.

A younger contemporary of Mariana, likewise a Spanish Jesuit, Francisco Suarez (1548–1617), was, for most of his active life, a professor of philosophy and theology at the universities of Rome, Alcalá, and Coimbra. He is usually regarded as the greatest theologian of the Jesuit order. Among his voluminous writings, one treatise, *On the Laws and on God the Lawgiver* (1612) was a commentary on nineteen relevant questions arising out of Thomas Aquinas' pronouncements on the origin of law, both natural and divine. Suarez broadens the treatment to cover natural and international law. While Suarez favors monarchy as the best kind of government, he would have the monarch rule in fulfilment of a contract with his subjects, who form a moral unity whose power rests in the whole society. The people are the source of the law by which the monarch rules them. But, "once the king is legitimately constituted, he holds supreme power on all the points for which he has received it." To the question then deeply disturbing Spain, already on the decline and in chronic financial difficulties, as to the right of the monarch to impose taxes without the consent of the taxed, Suarez holds that the monarch has this right. The power to rule implies the power to tax. Obviously Suarez' acceptance of an almost absolute monarchy would meet with a more open approval in Spain than Mariana's emphasis on the right of the subjects to revolt. The Jesuit Society everywhere accepted and spread Suarez' teachings with alacrity.

The dynamic course of the history of the sixteenth century was almost matched by the variety and freshness of the theorizing about the state which responded to events. By the end of the century three significant political conceptions emerged: (1) sovereignty, (2) the state, and (3) the international community. Sovereignty, rooted in the institution of the head of the family, then extended to the larger social group, had eventually to be prescribed and focused either in a single person or in a supposititious entity, the state. The state, or the republic, as a result of a long evolution was a nexus of obligations and privileges, framed by location, language, and race. The synthesis of capacities and functions, carefully nurtured by the "legislator," was harmonious and satisfying. The international community was not yet, in the sixteenth century, a firm concept. European rule over the natives of the East and the New World had not been a reality long enough for an idea of the interworking of several peoples at different levels of social and political development to take clear shape. The Church's idea of universality, dominant for so many centuries, died slowly, and the concept of empire, which places one nation above other nations, failed to inspire a ruling people to regard other peoples as equals. Internationalism dawned in this century in the writings of Suarez and a few others of like mind, but it was not to become dominant for some centuries after the time of these pioneers.

SUGGESTIONS FOR FURTHER READING

CHEYNEY, E. P., *An Introduction to the Industrial and Social History of England.* New York, 1923

CLOUGH, S. B., and C. W. COLE, *Economic History of Europe.* New York, 1948

DAY, C., *A History of Commerce.* New York, 1938

EHRENBERG, R., *Capital and Finance in the Age of the Renaissance.* New York, 1937

FAYLE, C. E., *A Short History of the World's Shipping Industry.* New York, 1933

HÄBLER, K., *Das wirtschaftliche Blüte Spaniens im 16ten Jahrhundert.* 1888

HAMILTON, E. J., *America's Treasure and the Price Revolution in Spain, 1501–1650.* Cambridge, Mass., 1934

HANNAY, D., *The Great Chartered Companies.* New York, 1926

HANNAY, D., *The Sea Trader.* London, 1912

HARING, D. H., *Trade and Navigation between Spain and the Indies.* Cambridge, Mass., 1918

HAUSER, H., *Travailleurs et marchands dans l'ancienne France.* 1920

HEATON, H., *Economic History of Europe.* New York, 1948

HECKSCHER, E., *Mercantilism.* 2 vols. London, 1935

HYMA, A., *Christianity, Capitalism, and Communism.* Ann Arbor, 1937

JEANNIN, P., *Les marchands au XVIᵉ siècle.* 1957

KLEIN, J., *The Mesta.* Cambridge, Mass., 1920

KULISCHER, J., *Allgemeine Wirtschaftsgeschichte des Mittelalters und der Neuzeit.* 2 vols. 1928

LIPSON, E., *The Economic History of England.* 2 vols. London, 1937

MONROE, C. A., *Readings in Early Economic Thought.* Cambridge, Mass., 1924

NEF, J. U., *Industry and Government in France and England, 1540–1640.* Compass Paperback

NELSON, B. N., *The Idea of Usury.* Princeton, 1949

News and Rumor in Renaissance Europe. The Fugger Newsletters. New York: Capricorn, 1959

NUSSBAUM, F. L., *A History of the Economic Institutions of Modern Europe.* New York, 1933

RENARD, G., and G. WEULERSSE, *Life and Work in Modern Europe: Fifteenth to Eighteenth Centuries.* New York, 1926

SÉE, H., *Histoire économique de la France,* Vol. I. 1939

SÉE, H., *Modern Capitalism: Its Origin and Evolution.* London, 1937

Strieder, J., *Studien zur Geschichte kapitalistischer Organisationsformen.* 1925
Tawney, R. H., *The Agrarian Problem in the Sixteenth Century.* London, 1912
Tawney, R. H., *Religion and the Rise of Capitalism.* New York, 1928
Troeltsch, E., *Social Teachings of the Christian Churches.* 2 vols. London, 1931
Usher, A. P., *An Industrial History of England.* Boston, 1920
Weber, M., *Protestant Ethic and the Spirit of Capitalism.* London, 1930

Allen, J., *A History of Political Thought in the Sixteenth Century.* New York, 1928
Braudel, F., *La Méditerranée et le monde méditerranéen à l'époque de Philippe II.* 1949
Carlyle, A. J., *A History of Medieval Political Theory in the West,* Vol. VI. London, 1936
Coker, F. W., *Readings in Political Philosophy.* New York, 1914
Dunning, W. A., *A History of Political Theories from Luther to Montesquieu.* New York, 1918
Hauser, H., *Ouvriers du temps passé: XVe et XVIe siècles.* 1927
Hearnshaw, F. J. C., *Social and Political Ideas of Some Great Thinkers of the Renaissance and Reformation.* 1925
Hearnshaw, F. J. C., *Social and Political Ideas of Some Great Thinkers of the Sixteenth and Seventeenth Centuries.* London, 1926
Mesnard, P., *L'Essor de la philosophie politique au XVIe siècle.* 1936
Murray, R. H., *The Political Consequences of the Reformation.* London, 1926
Parry, J. H., *The Spanish Theory of Empire in the Sixteenth Century.* Cambridge, 1940
Sabine, G., *A History of Political Theory.* New York, 1950

CHAPTER TWENTY-THREE

LATE HUMANISM:
THE NATIONAL LITERATURES

The intellectual movement we call the humanistic Renaissance was, at its beginning, largely of Italian origin. We have followed the course of its growth and spread until the early years of the sixteenth century in Chapter 12, and have seen how it reached its highest expression in Erasmus of Rotterdam, a Dutchman who was equally at home in England, France, the Lowlands, Switzerland, Italy, and Germany. He had congenial correspondents in all the other countries of Europe. Humanism had by the first quarter of the sixteenth century become a Europe-wide movement, its ideals widely accepted, its standard-bearers generally respected. In some universities, it is true, the conservatives, loyal to medieval scholasticism, still raised obstacles to the pursuit of the "new learning," but this resistance was clearly on the wane. Humanism, as an appeal to the standards of classical literature in form and content, and as an expression of confidence in the high potentialities of man in all aspects of his life and thought, was from this time on an integral part of our Western cultural tradition.

The earlier humanists had written Latin; not the Latin of the Church and the schools, but an idiom modeled on the great writers of Roman antiquity. Several generations of practice produced a respectable imitation of classical rhetoric, and the next goal was a mastery of Greek. By the middle of the fifteenth century most of the Italian humanists were competent in both Latin and Greek, and some were beginning to learn Hebrew. A few of these multiple-trained scholars deigned to write some prose or poetry in the vernacular, but for the most part the humanists regarded the vernacular as lacking the traditional dignity and beauty possessed by Latin and Greek.

Italy, the birthplace of the whole movement, had offered hospitality to visiting scholars from north of the Alps. When, their days of study and travel over, they returned home, they took with them the ideals and the disciplines they had learned in Italy. Thus we find native Germans, Frenchmen, and Englishmen, after years of study and wandering in Italy, returning to their countries imbued with humanist learning and eager to spread the good word. Furthermore, we soon find many Italian scholars invited as teachers, tutors, or professors by monarch, noble, or city north of the Alps. Frequently the chair of Greek in a northern university was occupied even by a native Greek. On the other hand, in Italy, by the end of the fifteenth century, the enthusiasm for classical learning was beginning noticeably to wane; the scholarly output was losing in quality at the very time that, across the Alps, France's age of glory in humanist learning was dawning. In Italy, Latin and Greek were giving way to Italian; while literary subjects were, in increasing measure, being drawn from medieval legends. In France tough problems of classical scholarship were being tackled and mastered. Unlike the earlier Italian humanists, who, for the most part, preferred to write in Latin and tended to scorn the vernacular, the leading French humanists wrote both in Latin and in French. As a partial result, the French language gained from its use by trained classicists and the total literary product of French writers was the richer, both in expression and in content. This conscious utilization of both languages may explain why the leadership in the traditional humanistic learning passed from Italy to France in the sixteenth century. In vernacular literature, as we shall see, primacy of quality and depth is not so easy to decide.

THE FRENCH LITERARY RENAISSANCE

THE art of printing, so important for the rapid and cheap dissemination of books and ideas, came rather late (1471) and slowly to France. The first few books printed in that country were texts of the classics or of Italian humanists. The Italian campaigns of Charles VIII and Louis XII brought certain Italian influences to France, but before 1500 Greek had been taught in Paris by only three scholars, all native-born Greeks, none of whom gained much of a following. In 1507 the first Greek text printed in France appeared in Paris. The next year Jerome Aleander, an Italian, began to teach Greek and perhaps Hebrew at the University of Paris, where he remained until 1517. The popularity of Greek and Latin classics grew steadily from about 1520, and a number of French printers turned out Greek texts notable for their beauty and accuracy. One of the glories of France in the first half of the century was Guillaume Budé (1467–1540), a wealthy bourgeois and a royal secretary and diplomat who gave himself to the study of Greek and Latin with such success that his reputation for learning came to rival that of Erasmus. In 1515 there appeared his study of Roman coinage, *De asse* (*On Money*), of which ten editions were exhausted during his lifetime. His greatest work was his *Commentarii linguae graecae* (*Commentaries on the Greek Language*), which appeared in 1529. This voluminous work was intended to clarify the complicated legal terminology found in both Greek and Latin writings. In 1530 he founded, at the order of Francis I, the Corporation of Royal Readers, at which Latin, Greek, and Hebrew language and literature were to be taught. This academy was to become in time the Collège de France. Budé illustrates well our observation that the French humanists wrote both in Latin and in the vernacular. In 1516 he wrote *De l'Institution du Prince* (*On the Education of the Prince*), which was not published until

1547. In this work he urged that every ruler should be thoroughly versed in Greek and Latin if he is to deal satisfactorily with men.

A younger colleague, the scholar-printer Robert Estienne (1503–59), known by the latinized form of the name as Stephanus, published his *Thesaurus linguae latinae* in 1532, and again in an expanded form in 1543, and the following year began the issuance of a number of Greek texts. These editions were justly famous for the beauty of their typography as well as for the precision of the text. Estienne's son Henry (1528–98) maintained the family tradition and turned out, among his many separate editions of the Latin and Greek classics, a massive *Thesaurus graecae linguae* in 1572 to accompany his father's Latin lexicon. These two works are of great scholarly value to this day. France was the scene of the activity of other scholars known for their contributions to classical learning: Julius Caesar Scaliger (1484–1558), a naturalized Italian, attacked Erasmus scurrilously, but was himself an industrious and capable classical philologist. Etienne Dolet (1509–46), after some years of study in Italy, returned to France to compose commentaries on Cicero which were highly regarded by his contemporaries. He also attacked Erasmus, but the latter refused to honor the attack with a reply. Dolet composed and published, besides much else, French translations of several works of Cicero, of the New Testament, and of some works of Plato. He was burned for heresy in 1546. With Budé and Dolet we enter the period when French humanism speaks in French as well as in Latin and Greek. The influence of the classics both upon the French language and upon the

Guillaume Budé, French school of the sixteenth century, in the Museum of Versailles [ALINARI].

content of the literature was pervasive. The high and formal classicism of the seventeenth century may be traced to these beginnings. After their use of the vernacular had proven acceptable, other humanists, sometimes encouraged by Francis I, dared to translate from Greek or Latin into French, and the vernacular was used for original composition, both prose and poetry.

The French literary revival of the sixteenth century was a broader and deeper movement than "humanism," significant as that was. Many of the writers who wrote exclusively or almost exclusively in French knew and used Latin models and motifs. Jean Lemaire de Belges (1473-1525) was born in the Low Countries, but spent most of his life in or near Paris, in royal or princely employ. He was one, and perhaps the best, of the "Great Rhetoricians" (*Grands Rhétoriqueurs*), a school of poets whose distinctive mark was an elaborate formalism with excessive affectation of classical imagery, alliteration, and onomatopoeia. Some of his poetic compositions are strongly medieval and imitative of such works as the *Roman de la Rose*. His most significant work was his *Illustrations de la Gaule et Singularitez de Troie* (1512-13), which forms a link between the twelfth-century *Roman de Troie* and the *Franciade* of Ronsard (see below, p. 678). Lemaire traces in long historical narratives, with much show of learning, the origins of France back to ancient Troy. The historians as well as the mythologists of antiquity, Greek and Latin, were heavily drawn upon. The taste for antiquity, in almost any dress, had become popular.

A younger contemporary of Lemaire, Clément Marot (1497-1544), spent most of his mature life in trouble or, freed from prison, in writing remorseful or bitter verse about his woes. He became *valet de chambre* to Marguerite of Navarre, then to her brother Francis I, was suspected of heresy, took refuge at the court of Renée of Ferrara, and died in exile at Turin. He wrote much for pure entertainment—witty rondeaux, many epigrams, epitaphs, and occasional poems. He translated into French fifty psalms, which were later incorporated into the Huguenot hymnbook. This Protestant association was a count against him in the eyes of Francis and the rigid Sorbonne. Marot was facile rather than serious, pleasant and tuneful rather than profound. He created a style, later to be imitated by a few lighter poets, but it fell short of greatness.

The native vigor of the French language and the French spirit could not long be confined to formal scholarship along classical lines. Contemporary with the scholars Budé, the Estiennes, Scaliger, and Dolet, two writers represented, as it were, the two poles of the French literary Renaissance, Rabelais and Calvin—the learned, naturalistic humanist, and the systematic theologian, the master of precise formulation.

François Rabelais (*ca.* 1490-1553) was trained, at his father's orders, to be a monk. He left the strict order of the Cordeliers and became a Benedictine monk in 1523 at Ligugé. The Benedictine Order was more tolerant of his devotion to classical learning than the Cordeliers had been. Yet, two years later he renounced his monastic vows to become a secular priest and move from place to place in search of knowledge. At Montpellier in 1530 he was studying medicine; the next year saw him at Lyons as a practicing medical doctor. His reputation as a physician was great, and he edited or translated several Italian, Latin, and Greek medical treatises. The urge to write and entertain was as strong as his medical curiosity, and in 1532 he published at Lyons *The Great and Estimable*

Chronicles of the Great and Enormous Giant Gargantua. In 1533 he brought out the *Pantagruel,* a complement. The success of this work moved him to revise and expand the theme of the *Chronicles,* these two forming the first and second books. The third book appeared in 1547 and the fourth in 1548, but the work remained incomplete. He traveled to Rome as personal physician to Cardinal du Bellay, returning to Lyons in 1534; thereafter his restlessness and curiosity led him into a great variety of activities. He had returned to the Benedictines in 1536, and the next year took a doctorate in medicine at Montpellier. He never lost his restlessness, never remaining in one city longer than a year. The fourth book of *Gargantua et Pantagruel,* after revision and recasting, appeared in 1552, the year before his death. The fifth book (if, indeed, it is his work) appeared only in 1562. The whole work is a monument of prodigious buffoonery. Every action is exaggerated, every motive ridiculous. The author defies, with delirious laughter, all conventions of precise and realistic organization and narrative. Rogues are lovable, monks coarse; the braggart is amusing, the illogical welcome. The theme of the book, besides the general satire of the society of Rabelais' day, was the motto of the Abbey of Thélème, where much of the action and dialogue of the first book takes place: *fay ce que voudras* (do as you please). This reaction to medieval order and restraint is, of course, not new. There was much of it in vernacular literature from the *Roman de la Rose* to Villon, but Rabelais' freshness and robust vulgarity brought a new element into the temper of the age.

François Rabelais (?), artist unknown, in the Museum of Versailles [GIRAUDON].

In 1549, only five years after the death of Marot, there appeared a revolutionary prose treatise, the *Défense et illustration de la langue française* of Joachim du Bellay. It was the manifesto of a party, a group of young poets that came to be called the Pléiade. They set out to reform French poetry on Greek and Roman models. Aware of what Italian poets and scholars had done with poetry since Petrarch, they were determined to do as much for France. Du Bellay argued enthusiastically, in defense of the French language, that it was as capable as Latin and Greek of expressing lofty ideals; he was indignant that so many French writers were content to use their noble tongue only in frivolous ballads and light entertainment. The language, he urged, should be enriched by imagination and imitation, both in its stock of words and genres of expression, from the classics and from Italian.

The Pléiade consisted of seven principal members, of whom du Bellay and Pierre Ronsard (1524–85) were the most significant. By the age of eighteen Ronsard had had much experience at the royal court and in diplomacy, and was an intimate of the future Henry II. With his early penchant for languages and literature, he had become a member of a group of young nobles enthusiastic over the new learning. His first works were translations from Latin, but in 1550 he published four books of *Odes,* adding a fifth in 1553. Some of his first work appeared in this collection. There followed love poems (*Les Amours*), epigrams imitated from classic authors, eclogues, and, in 1560–64, the *Discourses,* largely political pieces, some satirical, others passionately patriotic. In 1572 he published four cantos of what he obviously intended to be his master work—the *Franciade,* an epic tracing the history of France to Francus, son of Hector of Troy, and advancing as far as Charles Martel. This epic was never completed. From 1574 to his death in 1585, Ronsard returned to writing elegies and retouching some of his earlier poems, sometimes to their detriment.

Ronsard frequently followed Petrarch or some Latin model too closely. His style often obscured instead of clarifying his thought. On the other hand, he was largely responsible for the vogue of the ancients, from whom any literary age could learn much. By his life and his writings he propagated the idea that the poet is important to a culture. His reputation, high during his lifetime, began to decline soon after his death, to revive early in the nineteenth century with the rebirth of Romanticism. The influence of the Pléiade diminished after the turn of the century, though it was manifest in Agrippa d'Aubigné (1572–1630), a Huguenot nobleman and author of the *Tragiques,* eloquently depicting episodes in French history, of some love poems and satirical works. Exceptionally for a poet of this age, d'Aubigné composed a prose *Universal History,* essentially a heavily documented history of France from 1550 to 1601 which, despite the author's Huguenot convictions, was notably impartial.

Calvin's *Institutes* in the French version of 1541 has been spoken of as "the first book that was really *composed* in the French language." Calvin certainly created a new vocabulary for ideas and concepts previously conveyable only in Latin. His subject called not for colorful phrasing but for precision, logic, structure, and great erudition, qualities Calvin had in full measure.

His colleagues and disciples also wrote effectively in the vernacular. Theodore Beza, Calvin's successor at Geneva, wrote vigorously both in Latin and in French. His French *History of the Reformed Churches of France* was widely read and for long exercised a profound influence on Protestant historiography. He was also the author of many hymns. During the Wars of Religion there was much polemic, in French, from both sides. Among the political thinkers, Duplessis-Mornay wrote, in addition to the *Vindiciae contra tyrannos* (1581), a treatise, *De la vérité de la religion chrétienne,* which is a masterly defense of Christianity against the *libertins.*

On the Catholic side, M. François de Sales (1567–1622), a nobleman of Savoy educated by the Jesuits, began his ministry by attempting to reclaim his district (the Chablais) from the Protestants. He became Bishop-Coadjutor of Geneva and spread his benign influence through his books and a wide correspondence. His *Introduction to the Life of Devotion* (1608) and *Treatise on the Love of God* (1616) stressed his conviction that the root of Christian life is love, which, suffused through all man's actions and thoughts, leads naturally to the Christianization of society. His French was clear and flexible.

French humanism, in the broadest sense of the term, culminated in Michel de Montaigne (1533–92), son of a wealthy merchant of Bordeaux who had risen to the *noblesse de robe.* Well founded in Latin, he studied at the University of Toulouse, served several years as a magistrate at Périgueux and in the *parlement* of Bordeaux, then resigned from public service to study and write. In 1581, while absent on a trip to Italy, he was elected mayor of Bordeaux, and reelected two years later. In the Wars of Religion he refused to join either party, suffering abuse from both sides as a consequence. He left public life in 1585 to labor in his beloved library and revise his life work, the *Essays.* The *Essays,* though they discuss many and varied subjects—education, religion, the law, study and letters, the art of learning, friendship, conscience, experience—were in essence a self-portrait. Montaigne wanders far afield in his discussions, using examples and descriptions from history, from his travels, meditations, conversations with friends to serve as a loose framework for his moralizing philosophy. Order and organization were not his forte. His style, spontaneous and full of imagery, was personal and intimate. In the introduction, he said "I wish to be seen in my simple and natural way, just as I am, without study or artifice; for it is I that I depict. I am myself the subject of my book." Though he died as a good Christian, his thought was closer to that of the Stoics than to Christian doctrine; and his all-pervasive scepticism lies in the tradition of Voltaire and Renan rather than in that of Calvin and Pascal. The succeeding age of classicism could regard him as its initiator.

The age of Henry IV brought forth a new crop of writers, differently motivated and conditioned by the release from the long-drawn-out tension of the Wars of Religion. We no longer speak of men of the Renaissance. Yet it was the latter who had prepared the way and hammered out the language for the coming revival of classical antiquity.

ITALY: THE SILVER AGE

T HE sixteenth century was a period of less vigor and originality in literary production throughout the Italian peninsula than the two preceding centuries. Nevertheless, it was a time of serious activity, justly called the "silver age," following upon the "golden age" of the great Florentine trio and the glorious *quattrocento*. Machiavelli, whose literary activity falls within the early decades of this century, we have discussed above (Chapter 15). He need only be mentioned here to point out that the date of his death roughly corresponds to that of the dire Italian catastrophe: the sack of Rome in 1527 by imperial troops and the virtual subjugation of the whole peninsula to Spanish power. Principalities and republics survived, but, in the face of Spanish dominion, these curbed all thought of independence, their energies going into other channels. To this diversion of energy and interest we owe most of the literature, art and music which add luster to the century. Where, previously, a relative peace through balance of power had been achieved by Italian powers among themselves, now the same quality of peace was imposed by the presence of Spanish troops. The cities were no longer allowed to war on one another. Left without this outlet, the soldier class, the nobles and the courtiers intensified their life at court; and this way of life became more complicated, more hedged about with rules and protocol, increasingly involved with manners and modes and susceptible to description and formalization.

The numerous Italian courts became centers of intellectual and social intercourse; court life, in the course of the century, grew more stylized and further removed from actuality. Deprived of the distractions of war, the Italians compensated themselves by talking and writing about wars that had become legendary. Tales of King Arthur and his knights, medieval legends of Charlemagne, of Alexander the Great, of the Crusades, these became the common fund out of which scholars and poets spun their stories to amuse, inspire, and edify.

Poetry

AT THE court of Ferrara, Matteo Maria Boiardo (1441–94), a well-trained humanist, left behind him on his death the unfinished *Orlando Innamorato (Roland in Love)*. This was a Carolingian epic, romantic, courtly, embellished with a mixture of heavy classical learning and the excessive chivalric trappings of medieval legend. Though not free from stylistic defects, it showed the direction Italian literary taste was taking. Its successor, the *Orlando Furioso (Roland Insane)* of Ludovico Ariosto (1474–1533), was also its supplanter. Son of the commander of the Este citadel at Ferrara, Ariosto was employed on diplomatic missions by several of the lords of Ferrara. Like Boiardo, he began to write as a humanist, but in 1506 he decided to complete Boiardo's unfinished *Orlando Innamorato*. The result, the *Orlando Furioso,* was superior to the work of Boiardo: it drew on a wider treasury of classical poetry, on humanistic polish and native Italian versions of the Arthurian romances. The opening lines of the epic recall Virgil's "Arms and the man I sing":

> I sing of ladies, knights, arms and loves,
> Of courtesies and daring deeds.

The principal scene of the epic is laid in and around the Paris of Charlemagne, under siege by the Saracens. Roland hears that his Angelica has fallen in love with a Saracen soldier, has married him and set out with him for Cathay. This situation gives rise to pursuits, shipwrecks, sieges, and duels between Saracen and Christian heroes until the pagans (paynims) are defeated and Christendom is again at peace. Ariosto arranges to have the Este family count its descent from one of the champions of his story. Ariosto's poem quickly won wide favor throughout Italy. Its beauty and its ironic humor, perhaps more than its appeal to the nostalgia of ancient chivalry, found an eager response among the courtly class in an Italy now anxious to avoid the rigors of war.

The best illustration of this new taste for the polite and the courtly is the work of Baldassare Castiglione (1478–1529), *The Courtier* (*Il Cortegiano*). It is also a work of pronounced literary merit. As a young gentleman, Castiglione was trained at the courts of the Sforza at Milan and of the Gonzaga at Mantua. In 1508 he joined the court of the Montefeltro family at Urbino, moving, after five years, to Mantua, and then to Rome. At all these courts he was employed by the princes on diplomatic missions; at Rome he was entrusted by the Medici Pope, Clement VII, with an important mission to Charles V in Madrid. The Emperor admired him greatly and treated him as an honored guest, but coolly deceived him as to his own purposes. Castiglione, deeply hurt by this deceit, died, probably of a broken heart, only two years later (1529). *The Courtier,* the most important of his works, was written between 1508 and 1516 as an attempt to describe the ideal court life he found at Urbino. In the form of a dialogue between nobles and ladies at the court, it treats the qualities of the ideal courtier, who should be of noble blood, physically versatile, fluent in several languages, well read, and able and willing to discuss literature and the arts. He should avoid being a specialist in anything; a gentleman first and last, he should be loyal to his prince, modest and moderate in all things, and careful of his reputation. As for the court lady, she should be a good manager, well educated and gracious. The ideal court and courtier presented by Castiglione could hardly have been found in all Italy outside his imagination, though the court at Urbino was a close approximation. Nevertheless, the work had much effect, both in Italy and, by translation into many languages, outside the peninsula. It influenced manners and morals throughout Europe well into the eighteenth century.

Echoes of the Petrarchian spirit and style were to be heard all during the century. Bernardo Tasso (1493–1569) of Bergamo spent most of his life at the court of Salerno. In 1531 he composed a whole book of *Amori,* sonnets in the Petrarchian style. He then tried his hand, with considerable success, at odes in the style of Horace. Many lines could have come directly from classical models. His most ambitious work was the *Amadigi,* begun in 1542, finished only in 1560. It was modeled after the Spanish prose romance of chivalry *Amadis of Wales* (*Amadís de Gaula*). Involved, repetitive, and verbose, it cannot be compared with the *Orlando Furioso* of Ariosto, yet it is significant as an indication of the popular demand in Italy for a recovery of the glamor of medieval chivalric society.

Bernardo's son Torquato (1544–95) was superior to his father. At the age of eighteen, while still a student of the classics at the University of Padua, he published the *Rinaldo,* a romantic epic in twelve cantos. It was promising, but not yet great poetry. Cardinal d'Este took him into his personal service at Ferrara in 1565. While at that court he wrote, among other serious works, the *Aminta,* a pastoral intended to amuse or to hold the reader in suspense. His greatest work was the *Gerusalemme liberata* (*Jerusalem Freed*), completed, after long years of labor, in 1575. It was the story of the Christian capture of the Holy City in the First Crusade in 1099. The ostensible hero of the story is Godfrey of Bouillon. The poetic hero is Rinaldo d'Este. The poet pays his debt to his noble patron by making his hero an ancestor of the dukes of Este. The imaginary hero is, as might be expected, enamored of a Saracen princess, who, in turn, spirits him away to the Fortunate Isles, whence Godfrey has to recall him to his Christian duty. History and imagination, medieval chivalry and classic nobility, mingle to create a tremendous and heroic whole. In addition to these major works, Torquato wrote over two thousand lyrics. The last years of his life were shadowed by periods of insanity and deep depression. At the end he was held in high honor and justly, but when Clement VIII was arranging to give him the laurel crown of the poet Tasso fell ill and died. The *Gerusalemme* was popular immediately on publication, not only in Italy but also in England (where Milton used it copiously) as well as in France and Spain.

Tasso's uncontrollable temper caused him to be thrown into prison at Ferrara in 1579. His successor as court poet was a former professor of philosophy at Ferrara who had come into the service of Duke Alfonso. This scholar-diplomat-poet, Giovanni Battista Guarini (1538–1612), nine years later also broke with the duke, and passed the rest of his life at various courts, highly appreciated but troubled by bitter squabbles with his sons. His most important work was a pastoral tragi-comedy, *Il Pastor fido* (*The Faithful Shepherd*). The plot is complicated; essentially it is the story of frustrated love, prophecy, fate, near tragedy, and the final victory of true love. The work was hardly more than an imitation of Torquato Tasso's *Aminta,* somewhat more artificial in style and plot.

In the second half of the sixteenth century tastes in courtly entertainment began to develop away from the stereotypes of epic romances, set in scenes of medieval chivalry or pseudo-classical mythology. Two new genres appeared, the *opera in musica* and the *commedia dell'arte*. There arose in Florence, late in the sixteenth century, a group of musicians known as the *camerata,* who experimented in putting drama to music. The first successful sustained effort of this sort was the *Dafne* of Ottavio Rinuccini (1562–1621), a moderately well-known poet, first produced in 1594. The music was composed by Peri, who said he was trying "to imitate a speaking person in song." The authors and players mistakenly thought they were reproducing the Greek drama. In these early operas, at first called melodramas, the principal characters, mythological or pastoral, sang their parts; choruses of shepherds and nymphs were inserted in order to clarify the plot and explain the action. Other performances of the *Dafne* and new operas took place in the next few years. With Claudio di Monteverdi (1567–1643), whose first *opera in musica,* the *Orfeo,* was performed in 1607 in Mantua, the opera as we know it broadened the range of its subject matter and gained vastly in popularity. It reached both the eye and the ear of the spectator.

An equally popular if less aristocratic sort of entertainment was the *commedia dell'arte,* which might best be translated "professional comedy." This type of drama became popular in the second half of the sixteenth century, retaining its appeal well into the eighteenth. It was imitated and translated far beyond the limits of Italy. The play was essentially quite simple. Actors portraying certain stereotyped personages—the lady, the lover, the servant, the doctor, the loud-mouthed captain—each dressed or masked appropriately so as to be easily recognizable, agreed upon a certain plot, and thereafter improvised as instructed by a director. No two performances were ever the same. The success of the *commedia* depended upon the quick wit of the actors, the humor, usually rough, of the players, and the "gags" or *lazzi* which the servants provided. It was, more often than not, unadulterated slapstick.

Prose

THE courtly literature of sixteenth-century Italy, whether prose or poetry, had, in the course of that century, gradually lost its classical humanistic flavor and framework, and had come to represent the taste of everyday people. Thus the humanistic Renaissance steadily and surely lost its hold on the Italian mind. Imitation of Petrarch and Boccaccio and of their classical models gave way to the art of the street and the marketplace. Aside from this courtly poetry, there was much vigorous prose written during this period. Machiavelli's limpid prose represented the best Florence could produce at the beginning of the century, and better or more vital and eloquent Tuscan has hardly ever been written. Besides the well-known *Prince, Discourses,* and *History of Florence,* he employed his talent on some poetry, a dialogue concerning the Italian language, and several comedies in prose. One of these latter, the *Mandragola (The Mandrake),* is a political satire in which bourgeois ethics and priestly cynicism are tellingly pilloried. Perhaps the most successful feature of the piece is the deftness of personal characterizations. The *personae dramatis* come alive for the reader. Machiavelli's younger Florentine contemporary, Francesco Guicciardini (1483–1540), was primarily a political analyst, commentator, and historian. His *Memoirs* are a collection of political aphorisms, astute and clear, prompted by the experiences of his life. His most important work, the *History of Florence* from 1378 to 1509, is without doubt the best portrayal of the glorious age of the Medici. His *History of Italy,* however, was more than good. It was revolutionary, being the first serious and consistent effort to recount the story of the whole of the Italian peninsula as a unit. Italians were used to thinking only in very local terms: Florence, Venice, Milan, Mantua, Naples, and so on. The concept of one Italy was new. Others soon took it up, but Guicciardini set forth a pattern of Italian unity which was not to be actualized for over three centuries.

One of the most informative writers of the century was Giorgio Vasari (1511–74). He was a successful and competent architect and painter, who, at the suggestion of a friend and prominent historian, Paolo Giovio, wrote a compendious *Lives of the Most Excellent Painters, Sculptors, and Architects.* First published in 1550, it is our most valuable single source of information about the works and techniques of the two hundred artists he treats. His own high competence as an artist and his familiarity with the problems the artist faced make his *Lives* of priceless importance for the historian of art.

The *Autobiography* of Benvenuto Cellini (1500–71), goldsmith, soldier, libertine, storyteller, is the frank and refreshingly boastful story of a great artist who had at the same time a genius for narrative equal to that of Boccaccio. His *virtù,* his quarrelsomeness, his painstaking care for detail in his art, his valor with the sword, and his prowess with the ladies of high and low estate, his candid admission of his own superiority over all other artists, his bitter vindictiveness toward his enemies, all these qualities are portrayed in living lines and in the strong speech of sixteenth-century Italy. Here indeed was another "universal man"—half the universality was genius, the other half human nature.

There remain four Italian writers of prose whose importance reached far beyond the peninsula: Giordano Bruno (1548–1600), Paolo Sarpi (1552–1623), Giovanni Domenico Campanella (1568–1639), and Galileo Galilei (1564–1642). Bruno joined the Dominican Order at the age of fifteen, but soon found himself at odds with the discipline, and, in 1592, under suspicion by the Inquisition, he fled the monastery. For twenty years he had no fixed abode, becoming steadily more heterodox in his views. For a few years he was a professor at the University of Toulouse, then, 1579 to 1583, at Paris and thereafter in England for a while. Various of his pantheistic treatises had meanwhile been published and his views were well known. After more wandering, in 1591 he accepted an invitation to Venice. His host soon denounced him to the Inquisition. He was taken to Rome, kept in prison for seven years, and in 1600 burned at the stake for heresy. He wrote much, his more important productions being *Gli eroici furori* (*Heroic Inspirations*) and *On the Infinite Universe and Its Worlds.* He was excited by the new astronomy of Copernicus and Kepler, and, while they were still on the *Index,* defended them vigorously. He went farther, contending that there were other worlds beyond the solar system. Since the Church could not endure this overt challenge to her authority, his punishment was certain. Bruno wrote both in Latin and in Italian, and to the same intent. His own theology was more vivid and true than the, to him, very limited doctrine of the Church. He felt that a deity who lived and moved in many solar systems was greater than one limited to mankind's single, puny system. But the Church held otherwise. Bruno's Italian was intense, tempestuous, and imaginative, as if his ideas were so exciting and came to him so fast that he could not keep them clear and ordered.

Paolo Sarpi of Venice was a member of the Servite Order. Studious, he devoted himself to theology, law, history, and the sciences. He early had difficulties with the Inquisition; he was tried three times and each time acquitted. In 1606 he became special counselor to the city of Venice; when, in that year, Venice and the Pope had a sharp disagreement, Sarpi conducted the Venetian defense. A gang of cutthroats, in papal hire, set upon him in October 1607 and left him for dead, bleeding from fifteen knife wounds. They escaped to Rome and Sarpi recovered. He wrote an account of the dispute and, led by his study to examine papal claims, came to the subject of the Council of Trent, of which he proceeded to write a full history. His *History of the Council of Trent,* which took him eight years to write, from 1610 to 1618, was his greatest work and a remarkable achievement. He did not pretend to be unbiased, but he recounted the story with heavy documentation, with such clarity and perception both of issues and of personalities that it remains to this day a monument of informative historical writing.

Giovanni Campanella entered the Dominican Order as a boy, but much reading led him to formulate a philosophical system quite at variance with that of the Church. The Inquisition imprisoned him several times, subjecting him to torture. For twenty-seven years, from 1599 to 1629, he was in prison, often in danger of death. He later fled to France, dying there in 1639. Much of his literary work has been lost, but enough of his Italian lyrics remains to show him to be a highly sensitive metaphysical poet, perhaps too analytical, yet certainly honest and noble. His best-known work, the *Città del sole* (*The City of the Sun*), written in 1602 in prison, is the description of an imaginary utopia. His ideal city is situated on a large island at the center of seven concentric rings. Society is organized on a basis of common ownership of all property, and the vices of pride, intrigue and jealousy have no reason for existence. The city is ruled by Sun, who is both philosopher and priest, aided by three high officials, with jurisdiction over the chief activities of the citizenry. Elaborate provision is made for education in letters and the sciences, theoretical and applied, at all levels. Of the wide range of Campanella's thought, in broad sweep and in detail, there is no doubt. Of his hopefulness that great numbers of men and women could or would long follow the austere and demanding monastic principles he prescribes we speak with charity.

Galileo Galilei, whose name marks an epoch in the history of science, was also a writer of masterly Italian prose. He began his university education in 1581 at Pisa as a student of medicine, but soon shifted to mathematics and physics, yet without neglecting current literature. One of his earliest writings was a critical essay on Tasso's *Gerusalemme liberata*. At the age of twenty-eight he became a professor of mathematics at the University of Padua, and while there invented a telescope with a magnification of thirty. His researches in physics and astronomy both affirmed and corrected the ideas of Copernicus, while profiting from the patient calculations of the Danish astronomer Tycho Brahe and the German John Kepler. In 1632 Galileo, aware of his obligation to present his findings to a broader public than his professional colleagues, after long preparation and with a remarkable combination of practical experiment and *a priori* deduction, published *Dialogues Concerning the Two Principal Systems of the Universe*. The dialogue was a common literary device which Galileo used most effectively. Over a period of four days one person, Simplicio, presents and defends the traditional Ptolemaic view of the universe with scholastic arguments drawn from Aristotle. A second interlocutor, Salviati, presents Galileo's own views. The third person, Sagredo, holds the balance between the two antagonists, representing the layman's common sense. At the end, naturally, the new ideas of Salviati-Galileo triumph. Soon after publication he was called before the Inquisition, forced to retract his errors and retire from active life. He became blind in 1638, but the next year he published, in Italian in Holland, his *Dialogues of the New Science,* a popular presentation of Galileo's revolutionary theories of mechanics, motion, inertia, and gravity. He was an effective popularizer and a fearless polemicist, his expository prose being among the clearest and most direct of the whole period in Italy. At some distance from the height of classical humanism, he yet, in the conveyance of revolutionary ideas and discoveries to the broad masses of the people, stands among the first-rank writers in the Italian language.

SPAIN: THE GOLDEN AGE

IN 1283, after the bloody Sicilian Vespers, the island became a part of the possessions of the house of Aragon, maintaining regular commercial and military relations with mainland Spain. The rest of the ancient Kingdom of the Two Sicilies, Naples, remained in the hands of the Angevins. In 1443, however, Alfonso V, the Magnanimous, of Aragon entered Naples as conqueror, and from that time until the nineteenth century Spain and southern Italy were to be closely related. The movement of men and ideas, in both directions, was free and mutually acceptable. It is thus possible to speak of the Spanish influence over Italy as well as of Italian influence over Spain. As, at the time of Alfonso V, Italy was experiencing the height of the humanistic *quattrocento,* it was natural that the enthusiasm for the new learning should be transmitted to a Spain still deep in the Middle Ages. Although Spanish intellectual life in the mid-fifteenth century was somnolent, the infiltration of Italian influences, books, and scholars was warmly welcomed, so that soon the Spanish universities were live centers of humanism, while at the courts of the nobles Italian models in poetry and drama were eagerly followed, translated into Spanish or imitated. In this way men of letters had before them both kinds of models: the purely classical, and the native Italian. Without doubt this twofold inspiration goes far to explain why the Spanish forms of poetic expression, particularly the lyric, were so nearly perfect. There was, however, some determined resistance to the invasion of the Italian style and themes in poetry. It was feared that the native Spanish poetic art might be smothered. The resistance was of itself good, since it tended to force a fusion of the best elements of each. Among others, Jorge de Montemayor (1520–61) wrote excellent lyrics in both styles. In his *Diana,* a pastoral novel, mingled prose and verse, shepherds and shepherdesses, court society, spirits, magic mountains, and some classical mythology all appeared in some sort of a composite. It was extremely popular in the sixteenth and seventeenth centuries, and parts of it were borrowed by Shakespeare for his *Two Gentlemen of Verona.* In our terms, it was a kind of escapist literature, giving some relief from the rigors of war and the uncertain crudities of colonial existence. The ballad (*romance*) was a form of poem native to Spain. It was popular, short, usually anonymous, varied in form and content, transmitted almost exclusively by oral tradition, only later—in the early sixteenth century—to be collected into a group called a *romancero.*

The "golden century" of Spain was rich in monuments in prose. The novel appeared in several forms: the pastoral novel, such as the *Diana* of Montemayor, romances of chivalry, modeled after the *Amadís de Gaula* and frequently purporting to be its continuation, and the picaresque novel. This latter, focused around the life and adventures of the *pícaro* (the rogue), his master, and his confederates, was a distinctly Spanish genre. The first appearance of this type of writing was the anonymous work purporting to be an autobiography, the *Life of Lazarillo de Tormes, and of His Fortunes and Adversities. (Vida de Lazarillo de Tormes y de sus fortunas y adversidades*), first published about 1550. More than an individual rogue or adventurer, the *pícaro* was a type who symbolized the decadence of Spanish court and town life at the middle of the century. There were thousands like him, living by trickery, deceit, theft, by taking advantage of the pride or misfortunes of courtiers or townsmen. The very popularity of the novel indicated how low the general ethical standards had fallen by mid-century.

The second half of the century saw growth in several directions. Epic poetry experienced a remarkable flowering. Pride in their incredible empire, a conviction that Spain had been chosen by God to bring the Faith to the whole world, the ambition to equal or surpass the poetic achievement of Italy, by now known and absorbed in Spain, all combined to assure the popularity of the epics. There were many authors and many epics, some religious, some of pure adventure; the most famous being the *Araucana* of Alonso de Ercilla y Zuñiga (1533–94). It is the story of the revolt of the natives of southern Chile against their Spanish conquerors. Other events are recounted, and some romantic touches intrude, but for the most part it remains historical narrative, highly vivacious and imaginative. In the area of religious inspirational writing, this period is perhaps the richest in all Spanish history. Mysticism had long been native in Spain, and the connections with southern Italy and Sicily from the thirteenth century only accentuated this native mysticism, giving it a larger field of influence. Ignatius Loyola had been deeply influenced by the *Spiritual Alphabet* (*Abecedario espiritual*) of Francisco de Osuña; many other clerics wrote as effectively of prayer, meditation, and union with God. St. Teresa de Jesus (1515–82; see above, p. 636) in her *Autobiography* (*Libro de su vida*), written between 1562 and 1566, recounted her inmost spiritual experiences, and, in her other mystical writings, described the mystic ecstasy of the soul striving for annihilation in God. Her Castilian style, flowing, ardent, and individual, has been admired for its purity and strength.

A great Spanish author, Lope de Vega (1562–1635), almost defies classification. Everything he wrote—poetry, pastoral, religious, or historical epic, romance, the drama, particularly his finest creation, the *comedia española*—was memorable. His life was as varied as his talents. A prodigy in his adolescence, a soldier of the Great Armada, a secretary, a member of several monastic orders and ordained a priest; twice a husband, often a lover, involved in lawsuits, in prison seven years for slander, Lope de Vega is one of the wonders of literature. Most of his work has disappeared, but what remains is prodigious in quantity: a total of almost 470 dramas, filling over 30 volumes. He asserted that he had written 1500 dramas. His best prose work was the *Dorotea,* a novel in the form of a drama. His nondramatic work fills twenty-one volumes, and an amazing proportion of it is pure genius. He was the culmination of a century of development in Spanish dramatic art.

Cervantes

A SLIGHTLY older contemporary of Lope de Vega was destined to enjoy a repute farther from his native soil, not for versatility and prodigious production, but for a single book. Miguel de Cervantes Saavedra (1547–1616) was almost self-educated. He early felt the urge to write verse, but it was not distinguished. He then tried the life of a courtier in the suite of an Italian cardinal. The Renaissance spirit he found in Italy impressed him deeply. As a soldier in the fleet of Don Juan at the Battle of Lepanto in 1571, he was so severely wounded as to lose the use of his left hand. He afterwards referred to himself with some pride as *el manco de Lepanto* (the maimed of Lepanto). On the return to Spain his ship was captured, and he was a prisoner of Moslem pirates in Algeria for five years before ransom brought him back to his native land. His life thereafter was uncertain. Often in financial trouble, twice tried on charges of peculation, he was never able to keep any post of responsibility. He was probably a poor businessman. He wrote, and occasionally was able to publish, some indifferent pieces—lyric poetry, pastoral novels, short stories, and a few dramas. He began his great work, *Don Quijote de la Mancha,* in 1604. The first part was published in 1605. Although it was immediately successful, he derived little profit from it. He was never far from abject poverty. In 1613 the *Exemplary Novels,* a collection of twelve short stories, was published, and two years later, shortly before his death, the second part of the *Don Quijote.* If it had not been for the *Don Quijote,* Cervantes would have ranked as hardly more than just another man of letters. The *Exemplary Novels* were good, but not the work of genius. The *Don Quijote* on the other hand is one of the greatest prose novels of the Western world. Critics have found in it many and varied esoteric meanings. It is better to regard it as delightful storytelling, composed by a sincere and loyal Spaniard who believed with all his heart in the purity of the chivalric ideal, yet was close to the common man. To see conscious social satire in the work is probably vain. The two leading characters, Don Quijote and Sancho Panza, consistently complement each other. Together they represent Spain, the romantic and the coarse, the idealist and the common realist, the dreamer and the cynic. Essentially Spanish, romantic, dreamy, even eccentric, the work is at the same time human and universal.

We may not leave the Iberian peninsula without noticing the great Portuguese epic poet, Luis de Camoens (1524–80). Well grounded in Latin literature and familiar with the Italian poets from Petrarch to Ariosto, he spent some years at court in Lisbon, then became a soldier and spent several years of undistinguished service in India. He was in frequent difficulties and several times in prison on various charges. Returning to Lisbon in 1570, he brought with him the manuscript of his epic *The Lusiads,* published two years later. The reception was cool. Camoens died in 1580, several months before Portugal was conquered by Philip II and became a part of the Spanish domains. The theme of the poem is the heroic building by the Portuguese of a magnificent global empire. The first canto opens with the voyage of Vasco da Gama to India; the tenth closes with the return of da Gama to his beloved Lisbon. Camoens, who had seen and lived through this proud achievement, shows his patriotic ardor in every line. He claimed for the story of Portuguese conquest of the East more honor and glory than Virgil claimed for Aeneas.

> Let us hear no more then of Ulysses and Aeneas and their wanderings
> Nor of Alexander and Trajan and their well chronicled victories;
> I sing of the daring and the fame of the Portuguese
> For to them Neptune and Mars render due glory.

The poets and the heroes of yesterday have had their praise,
Another and a more noble valor we must now proclaim.

Proem to CANTO I

In Camoens we find an excellent example of the Renaissance mingling of classical form and framework with the national fire of the age of discovery and imperial vision.

GERMANY: LITERARY STAGNATION

T HE fourteenth and fifteenth centuries, the age of Italy's creative glory, were for Germany relatively dull and empty. The coarse poetry and drama of a retarded feudal age seemed to satisfy German taste. The end of the fifteenth century, however, brought across the Alps the fresh and exciting air of Italian humanism, and many German students and scholars visited Italian centers of learning to see and hear for themselves. When these free souls returned to Germany the old *Minnesong* and the lyrics of chivalry appeared to them outmoded and even ridiculous. The rising bourgeoisie, enriched by growing commerce and enlightened by travel, were both willing to support the new learn-

Cervantes, by Juan de Jauregui (1600) in the Instituto Valencia de Don Juan, Madrid [MAS, BARCELONA].

ing and happy to have their sons become its devotees. Church and court ceased to be the dictators of taste and style. In their place the burgher and the town hall came to dominate. The Easter cycle of plays portraying biblical scenes and acted on the steps of the cathedral or of the parish church was transformed into a secular carnival on the main square and in the town streets, with only the slightest lip service to its religious origins. It was into this secularized and anticlerical atmosphere that there came what has been called Germany's first real contribution to world literature, Sebastian Brant's *Ship of Fools (Das Narrenschiff)*. Brant (1457–1521) was well schooled in the new learning and as a young man composed verses in Latin. The *Ship of Fools* was published in Basel in 1494. It was a collection in crudely rhymed verse of satires on almost every craft, trade, profession, and class. Brant was a moralist and his judgments were sharp, but he had no remedy for the ills of his time. He made some show of learning by quoting from Latin poets, yet his was not the humanist spirit. He had a successor and continuator in Thomas Murner (1475–1536), a Franciscan friar, who spent most of his life in Strassburg, but traveled widely, writing verse satires and sermons in the style of the *Ship of Fools,* only with more finish and venom. He went beyond Brant in demanding reform in the Church and in blaming the clergy for their vice and laziness, yet without any thought of a break with the establishment. In 1522 he attacked Luther with one of his most violent satires, *Of the Great Lutheran Fool (Von dem grossen Lutherischen Narren)*. The *Fool* was the Reformation, which Murner, in the poem, brings to a ridiculous end.

The greatest humanist of them all, Erasmus (see above, Chapter 12), was a Dutchman, but wrote nothing in the vernacular. Nevertheless, his influence on German literature was profound. Lesser men, writing both in Latin and in German, borrowed from him and popularized his ideas on education, religion, and the Reformation.

The pre-eminent figure in German literature of the century was Luther himself. His translation of the Bible, the New Testament in 1522 and the Old Testament in 1534, was probably the most important event in the history of the German language. It gave the German people a language which brought the many dialects into a single speech. His attention was fixed upon the speech of the common people, which he sensed had an inner vitality no scholar's language could match. Luther's hymns, his *Catechism,* and his sermons further helped to impose the speech of the Saxon court and of the common people on German literature for centuries to come.

The devotees of humanism were enthusiastic in their advocacy of Latin as a literary medium, and, supported by the burgher class anxious to assist culture, revived the Latin comedy. This genre was widely used as a teaching tool in schools, where the students were taught to learn by acting. Plays by Terence and Plautus were presented, sometimes abridged, often in their entirety. Later original plays, based on or imitating their classical models, were composed and staged. German humanism had its fruits and its influence, yet it produced no great literature. Since most of the humanists scorned the vernacular, they were partially cut off from the spirit and life of the common people. Somewhat surprisingly, the leading dramatist of the century, Hans Sachs (1494–1576), was an apprentice tailor in Nürnberg who became a shoemaker. Goethe called him

"Our dear Master." Kind, shrewd, honest, whimsical, he brought to his plays the eternal truth of the common things of life. In 1523 he apostrophized Luther in a poem as "the Wittenberg Nightingale," but he never seemed to have realized what a world-shaking event he was witnessing in the Reformation. Whereas he could tell a story or point a moral as artfully as Boccaccio, he did not realize that the world could never be the same again after Luther. His productivity was enormous. In the course of his long life he wrote 4275 Master-songs (*Meistergesänge*) and 1773 poems, over 200 of them intended as dramatic pieces. His art was natural, unaffected by the Renaissance; no new form or concept marked his work. In actuality the greatest Meistersinger of the sixteenth century, he yet remained essentially medieval and national or local in his outlook and spirit.

This century saw the formal rise of the prose novel, though its roots may be traced in the folk literature of the later Middle Ages. The medieval romances of chivalry gradually went out of style, but there remained a strong demand for stories of adventure. In line with the changed social situation, the rise of the bourgeoisie, stories in which the poor peasant or apprentice rises by thrift, cleverness, and honesty to fat fortune, to marry a nobleman's daughter, became popular. Jörg Wickram (*ca.* 1510–60), an Alsatian, wrote a number of such success stories between 1540 and his death. His gift lay in his understanding of the changes taking place in contemporary society and in his ability to mirror the mind and spirit of the rising middle class. In 1555 he published a collection of short stories, most of them humorous, some slightly risqué, in his *Anthology for Stage-Coach Reading* (*Das Rollwagenbüchlein*). Another satirist, perhaps more benevolent than Wickram, certainly more diffuse, was Johann Fischart (*ca.* 1550–90). Born in Strassburg, he had traveled to Italy, France, and England and took a law degree at Basel. An ardent defender of the Reformation, he began to attack the Catholics in 1570. He was a talented writer, smooth and resonant in verse, brilliant in prose. One of his most important works was an adaptation (in 1575) of Rabelais' *Gargantua and Pantagruel.* Only an inveterate satirist could have transmitted into the German idiom the ludicrous enormities of the French original. The adaptation is much longer than Rabelais' text. Fischart also translated the French *Amadis of Gaul,* as well as a work of Jean Bodin on *Demonomania.* In view of his notable gifts, his failure to create is surprising. The decline of the German mind had set in, perhaps due to psychic fatigue after the tension and stress of the religious disputes in the earlier decades of the century.

The last significant literary event of this troubled century was the publication in 1587 of the People's Book (*Volksbuch*) entitled *History of Dr. Johann Faustus, the Famous Magician and Master of the Black Arts.* The tradition of the Wittenberg scholar who sold his soul to the devil in return for twenty-four years of power and sensual pleasure was current at least as early as the first decades of the century. The anonymous author, probably a Lutheran clergyman, depicted Faust as a rebel against God, who made the iniquitous pact with the devil out of an evil desire to know and experience more than God intended him to, and who suffers justly horrible retribution at the end. There is little artistry in the work. Sophistication has not replaced superstition; no ray of contemporary scientific light is at any point visible. The devil, Mephistopheles, is incredibly unseductive. Yet, in spite of these drawbacks, the story exercised a strong hold on the imagination of the German people. The English dramatist Marlowe finished and refined the story within a few years, but it remained for Goethe, in the eighteenth century, to give it drama and the terror inherent in the legend. For a generation after *Dr. Faustus* almost nothing of real worth appeared in German. It was a sterile and unimaginative age. Recovery was to come only after the bloodletting of the Thirty Years' War.

Looking back upon the period of the Reformation and its aftermath, we must conclude that in Germany it was, aside from Luther himself, a period of literary mediocrity and decline. The humanistic Renaissance that meant so much to the leaders of Italian thought and, to a slightly different degree, stimulated in France a spirit of creativeness and initiative, had almost no repercussions in Germany. It is probable that the dynamic of the Lutheran Reformation in the early decades of the century was too absorbing of energy and attention, just at the time when the humanistic movement might, undisturbed, have directed German thought and effort into channels of literary and artistic vigor. When the religious strife was stilled, after the Peace of Augsburg in 1555, humanism was no longer a living movement anywhere in Europe, and other possible stimuli to greatness, such as nationalism, were impossible in a Germany divided on religious issues and fragmented by political separatism.

ENGLAND: THE TUDOR RENAISSANCE

THE attraction of the new learning had been slow to reach England. During the Hundred Years' War communication with Italy was tenuous, and the Wars of the Roses left those Englishman who were interested in scholarship little opportunity for tranquil travel or study. Nevertheless, in 1499 we find Erasmus in England enjoying the companionship of men whose knowledge of Latin and Greek he could admire. The intimate association with Thomas More, John Colet, William Grocyn, William Lyly, Thomas Linacre, John Fisher, and their circle remained with him as a sweet and satisfying memory for the rest of his life. The contacts thus established increased in the subsequent decades; books and scholars from the Continent found enthusiastic welcome in England, while many English scholars visited centers of learning in Italy, Germany, the Lowlands, and France. There grew up a sort of supranational guild of humanistically inclined scholars whose common, enthusiastic aim was the furtherance of the new learning and the dissemination of classical ideals, both in the ancient languages and in translations into the vernacular. As long as he lived Erasmus was the recognized dean of these scholars, though the English leaders stood not far below him in the esteem of their colleagues. The atmosphere of free inquiry inherent in the new learning had a strong influence on the early stages of the English Reformation. There were, in the Parliament that obeyed the requests of Henry VIII for power to take over the Church in England, men who had heard sermons and lectures by Colet, Fisher, Grocyn, Tyndale, or Richard Croke, First Reader of Greek at Cambridge, and had read as much of Erasmus as they could get their hands on. The antiquity of the authority of the medieval Church could carry little weight with men avid for free examination and discussion.

The first stage in the transfer of the humanistic spirit to England is the mastery of Latin and Greek on the high level by this time normal in Italy and France. This step was soon achieved. By about 1530 there were many scholars who used Greek easily, and by about 1560 England could be favorably compared with any Continental center for the excellence and spread of Greek studies. During these same years a large number of Englishmen traveled to the Continent, particularly to Italy, establishing friendships with Italian scholars and imbibing the ideals and tastes of the mature Renaissance. Many of the books which they brought back with them, whether in Italian, Latin, or Greek, were translated into English. The cultured Englishman of the latter half of the sixteenth century was quite familiar with the themes and motifs of Italian Renaissance literature and was likely to have in his private library works of Petrarch, Boccaccio, Castiglione, Ariosto, or Matteo Boiardo, some of whose writings appeared in English translation before the end of the century. Literally scores of translations of Latin and Greek works were in fact printed in England before 1600. All of the great names of the English Renaissance, through the age of Elizabeth, were deeply indebted to classical sources for their ideas. Thomas Wyatt (1503–42), Christopher Marlowe (1564–93), Edmund Spenser (1552–99), and Sir Philip Sidney (1554–86), to list only a few, while remaining essentially English, all drew on the classical tradition for much of the form or content of their writing. The greatest of all, William Shakespeare (1564–1616), while not a formally educated man, was so deeply rooted in the humanist heritage that more than half of his work is either on classical themes or is set in Renaissance Italy or Greece—e.g.: *The Merchant of Venice, Two Gentlemen of Verona, Julius Caesar, Timon of Athens, Romeo and Juliet.* He was perhaps the most successful of all English authors in grafting this classical and humanistic tradition onto a sturdy English trunk, to produce an all-European tree of genius.

However, these two stems, the English and the classical humanist, do not make up the totality of the English sixteenth-century culture. The translation of the Bible into English and the Book of Common Prayer are events whose influence on the English mind and language is incalculable. The Wyclyfite translations (*ca.* 1380–88) were known to only a restricted circle. William Tyndale (1484–1536), educated at Oxford in classical studies and devoted to the ideas of the Reformation, felt obliged to go to Germany to get his translation of the New Testament printed (1525). Copies he sent to England aroused ecclesiastical opposition, and when he openly opposed the divorce of Henry VIII, he was sent to the stake in 1536. His translation had high literary merit, and the version by Miles Coverdale (1488–1568) in 1535 was greatly dependent upon it. Indeed, the Westminster divines who translated the whole Bible from the original Hebrew and Greek at the order of King James I in 1611 reproduced much of Tyndale's text. The rapid spread of the use of the Bible and the frequent printing of various editions during the century had an obvious and pervasive effect upon the language spoken by the common people. The Book of Common Prayer, the work of Thomas Cranmer (1487–1556), heard in all services of the church week in and week out, approached the Bible itself in the influence it exercised upon standards of fine prose style. Cranmer's English prose has seldom been equalled and never excelled. The Book of Common Prayer, which has quite justly endured to this day, was a worthy companion to the elegance of the English Bible.

England is almost unique among the countries of Europe in the evenness of balance between the three roots of literary inspiration: the classical, both Latin and Greek, the Italian humanistic, and the native. The vigor of the Elizabethan age, perhaps the most glorious in all the long history of English culture, is in large measure traceable to the variety of its roots and the enthusiasm with which these three diverse traditions were adapted and appropriated.

POLAND: A GOLDEN AGE

THE loyalty of Poland to Western ideas has never been lessened by the proximity to the East. The Poles have, on the contrary, always regarded themselves as defenders of Western culture against the pressure on their eastern border, from Mongols, Muscovites, Turks, or an expanding Russia. The sixteenth century was no exception to this rule; it witnessed a rich flowering of literary productivity inspired, in great measure, by the Italian Renaissance, and known as the golden age of Polish cultural history. During the preceding century many young Poles had gone to Italy to study and travel, bringing home their classical manuscripts and books and their enthusiasm for the new learning. As many of them gained positions of influence in the Church and at court, the ideas to which they were devoted spread among their friends and colleagues. In at least one notable case the current flowed in the opposite direction. Philip Buonaccorsi of Rome was invited to Poland by the influential Gregory of Sanok, later archbishop of Lwów. In a few years Buonaccorsi became tutor to the sons of King Casimir the Jagiellonian. He made Poland his home from 1470 to 1496, spread humanistic ideals, organized at Cracow a club of like-minded scholars, the *Societas Vistulana,* and by his enthusiasm and geniality won for the new learning a high repute among the elite of the kingdom. This broad background served as a useful preparation for the fruitful activity of the sixteenth century.

The court of Sigismund I (1506–48) offered a favorable setting for Renaissance ideas. The king, educated at the cultured court of Hungary, was a patron of the arts. His second wife, Bona Sforza, sister of the duke of Milan, was a learned person in her own right who brought in her suite a number of polished Italian humanists. The vice-chancellor of the kingdom was Peter Tomicki, bishop of Cracow. Under his protection, the Jagiellonian University in Cracow became a center of the classical languages and literatures, of Roman law, and of the fine arts. In the course of the century Poland produced many eminent men of letters, some preferring Latin to Polish, others equally at home in both languages, still others who wrote by preference in the vernacular—all well trained in Latin literature and some in Greek. Since many of them were familiar with recent Italian and French writing, the literary atmosphere of the country was extremely cosmopolitan, perhaps in a higher degree than in some lands of the West.

Among many eminent men of Renaissance temper, four at least may be noticed. Nicholas Rey (1505–69), Jan Kochanowski (1530–84), Andrew Frycz Modrzewski (Modrevius) (1520–89), and Peter Skarga (1536–1612). Rey supplemented a limited formal education with keen observation, closeness to nature, and a robust nationalism. He wrote both poetry and prose, choosing his subjects from everyday life, with marked preference for the rural scene. Technically his poetry was somewhat heavy, but his prose was strong and, for that age, smooth and flexible.

Jan Kochanowski, unlike Rey, was a thoroughly trained humanist, with, in addition, four years at the University of Padua and extensive travel in France. He began by writing poetry in Latin but became convinced that he would be most effective and useful if he wrote in the vernacular, with due respect for classical models and the great works of the French and Italian schools. For some years Kochanowski was at the royal court as secretary to the king. In this period he wrote *The Trifles,* a collection of stories and incidents, somewhat similar to the *Facetiae* of Poggio Bracciolini. Many of his *Songs,* a collection of poems about life in the country, were modeled on the *Odes* of Horace; some are direct translations, others are love poems or occasional poems of a religious or patriotic nature. The most popular work of Kochanowski was his version of the Psalter (1579). It is rather a paraphrase of the Latin than a translation. He sensed the deeply poetic nature of the Psalms and his transformation of the text of the Vulgate into living Polish was a work of genius. His *Threnodies* (1580), prompted by the death of a dearly loved daughter, plumbed the depths of the afflicted human soul, and brought the genre, the lament for the loss of a loved one, to a high degree of artistic perfection. His religious temper was unquestionably Roman Catholic. The struggles of Protestantism which split Poland until the last years of the century find no echo in Kochanowski's writing. He remained the devout, cultivated, loyal gentleman to the end.

Modrzewski was a humanist whose interest in the law led him to criticize the legal structure of Poland, which favored the gentry (*szlachta*) over the peasantry. He wrote only in Latin, but his greatest work, *On the Reform of the Republic* (*De republica emendanda,* see above, Chapter 22), was translated into Polish in 1577 before his death, and was widely read among the bourgeoisie. Long before Grotius he proposed means of avoiding wars by international arbitration and even suggested a supranational force to hold warlike nations in check. While his social consciousness appealed to liberal elements in the population, the hierarchy opposed bitterly his ideas of a national Polish church.

Peter Skarga is remembered as the eloquent preacher of the Polish Counter-Reformation. He was a university man but had no leanings toward humanism or Protestantism. On the contrary, he went to Rome and joined the Jesuit order in 1568 and, on his return, became a leader in the campaign of reconversion to Catholicism of those who had defected to the Protestant faith. He was extremely effective. He became rector of the Jesuit university at Vilna in 1579, then, for the next twenty years, was court chaplain to King Sigismund III. His preaching was emotional to the point of fanaticism. He would, if it had been possible, have forced Catholicism upon the whole population, though he would not have approved the rigors of the Inquisition upon non-Catholics or the lapsed. He attacked the Edict of Tolerance of 1573, as we might expect of any religious zealot in the sixteenth century. Most of Skarga's significance for the literary history of his country lay in his sermons, both those orally delivered and those printed; but he wrote, in addition, lives of the saints and other popular religious works. His sermons are full of criticism of Polish vanity and lawlessness. Some of his jeremiads must have been embarrassing for the nobility to hear or read.

These are only a few of the great writers of Poland's golden age, who, while loyal and patriotic Poles, were yet highly cultured Europeans, drawing upon the best sources of Western culture to produce a language and a literature notable for flexibility, expressiveness, and cosmopolitan content.

BOHEMIA: HUSSITISM AND HUMANISM

THE sixteenth century saw two principal streams of literary tradition developing in Bohemia: the Hussite-Utraquist religious strain, and the humanist, secular current of thought. About 1460, in reaction against the pale religiosity of the moderate Utraquists, a movement began, inspired by Peter Chelčický and his successor Gregory the Tailor, which took the name of the "Unity of Czech Brethren," frequently spoken of as "The Brotherhood." Ascetic, evangelical, pacifist, the group was soon subjected to suspicion, then persecution, first by the Utraquists and later by the Jagiellonian and Habsburg courts. Gregory has left, in Czech, an account of these years of trial which was preserved by the Brethren almost as the letters of the Apostle Paul were treasured by the primitive Christians. The death of Gregory in 1474 was followed by some years of disunion in the Unity until the personality of a certain Brother Lucas of Prague (1460–1528) came to dominate the scene. Writing almost exclusively in Czech, he covered a broad range of religious and theological questions, attacking, at various times, the teaching of Luther, of Zwingli, the Catholic apologists, and even criticizing Chelčický. To him, the Unity was the modern version of the primitive Church. He was the greatest theologian of the brotherhood, and it is probable that his ordering of its thought, as well as his reorganization of the Unity, was responsible for the strength it later showed in severe adversity. A later bishop of the Unity, Jan Blahoslav (1523–71), was almost as prolific as Lucas, and, for a curious posterity, more informative. A competent humanist, at home both in Latin and in Greek, he traveled in Austria, Germany, and Switzerland and was personally acquainted with many scholars outside Bohemia. His experiences abroad only enforced his nationalism and his devotion to his native tongue. He wrote many hymns for the services of the Unity, a Czech grammar, and, among many other works, some of which are lost, an *Origins of the Unity*. He also translated the New Testament into Czech, basing his text on the Greek original and the most authoritative commentaries.

One of the monuments of the Czech language is the Bible of Kralice. A group of scholars within the Unity began, soon after the death of Blahoslav, to make a translation of the whole Bible into Czech. Blahoslav's translation of the New Testament was accepted almost in its entirety. The Old Testament had yet to be translated on a comparable level. The cooperative task was begun in 1577 and finished in 1593, when the whole Bible was published at Kralice in

Moravia. This Bible has remained the guide and companion of the Czech and Slovak Protestants until the present time. In the words of a leading historian of Czech literature, the Bible of Kralice "crowned the unification of the Czech language."

Another leader of the Brethren, Václav Budovec of Budov (1547–1621), illustrates the change that took place in the leadership of the Unity at the end of the century. A nobleman, Budovec traveled even more widely than Blahoslav, to Germany, the Netherlands, France, Italy, and England, and in 1577, as a member of an imperial diplomatic mission, to Constantinople. It was he, principally, who persuaded Rudolf II to sign the Letter of Majesty of 1609, granting religious liberty to the Brethren. He played a prominent role in the events leading up to the Bohemian Revolt in 1618. Chosen a Defender, he was, after the defeat of the White Mountain in November 1620, executed by Ferdinand II in Prague, June 21, 1621. In Budovec, a man of high culture and impressive dignity, the religious fervor of the Unity and the national spirit of the Hussite tradition were united.

The greatest, if at the same time the most puzzling, figure of the Unity was yet to come. John Amos Komenský, better known as Comenius (1592–1670), was the last bishop of the Brotherhood. He looms large on the whole European scene, as educator, philosopher, humanist, and religious spirit. He studied and traveled in Germany and the Lowlands, returned to Moravia in 1616, married, and soon lost his wife and children from the plague. His early work, the *Labyrinth of the World,* is very similar to the *Pilgrim's Progress,* and came to be regarded as almost a sacred book by members of the Unity, who, in 1627, had to flee Bohemia. Comenius joined a group at Leszno in western Poland, and from then until his death was almost always a wanderer: to the Lowlands, to England, where he was offered the presidency of Harvard College, to Prussia, to Hungary. He became widely known for his "pansophy," an attempt to bring together all science and all learning under the aegis of an academy of the most learned men of all lands, conversing in a universal language. The impracticability of these plans was soon evident to all but Comenius. His real and lasting contribution lay in his humane spirit and in techniques of graded education. He remains a noble figure in the Hussite tradition of brotherly love and Christian hope.

The secular, humanistic current of thought in Bohemia had also its distinguished figures. In its earlier stages, when humanism was new, the vernacular speech was held in contempt. Bohuslav Hasištein of Lobkovice (1460–1512) studied at Bologna and Ferrara, imbibing the spirit, together with the limitations, of his Italian colleagues. Disappointed in his hopes for the bishopric of Olomouc, he retired to his hereditary castle, his correspondence, and his books. He identified himself with the staunch Catholic party and was, toward the end of his life, isolated from many of his humanist friends who were, in a great majority, opposed to the Roman Church. He wrote copiously and exclusively in Latin, thus his influence on Czech cultural development was not remarkable. Among his friends was another humanistically trained scholar, Viktorin Kornel of Všehrd (1460–1520), Bohuslav's equal in his Latinity and superior in character and influence. The two friends quarreled, probably on religious grounds, as Všehrd was a member of the Czech Brethren. Thereafter Všehrd wrote in the vernacular, translating works from Greek and Latin, both classical and patristic. He justified his changed course in these words:

Let others, writing in Latin, write new books, and, bringing water to the sea, bring honor to the Roman tongue, but I, translating the writings and works of the best ancient authors, prefer to enrich the poor rather than risk being scorned and held in contempt by a rich man to whom I bring gifts of no value of which he has no need. . . . I could, just as well as any of my colleagues, write in Latin; nevertheless, realizing that I am a Czech, while I master Latin, I want to write and speak Czech.

His most important work was the result of the five years he spent as director of records in the law courts in Prague. His *Nine Books on the Laws, the Courts and the Registers of Land* is a mine of information concerning the laws and customs of Bohemia at a critical stage in the constitutional development of the kingdom. During the Habsburg rule from 1526 on, the work was frequently appealed to by the Czech Estates in their struggle to protect their rights against the dynasty.

The new learning gained in popularity throughout the first half of the century. Not only were works of many ancient authors translated into Czech, but some works of Renaissance humanists appeared in the vernacular. Erasmus was especially popular. His *Praise of Folly* was translated into Czech in 1513, the *Handbook of the Christian Soldier* in 1519. A number of Czech humanists were in frequent correspondence with the author. The work of translation had the specific advantage of markedly improving the native tongue by forcing it to express concepts and distinctions that arose out of the more sophisticated Latin world of ideas.

In the second half of the century we meet several competent men of letters, whose capacities were on a European level and whose performance was, by any standard, substantial. Adam Daniel Veleslavín (1545–99) and his son Adam Samuel Veleslavín (1592–1628?) were, almost like the Aldus family in Venice, printers and lexicographers. The father published the *Silva quadrilinguis* and *Nomenclator quadrilinguis,* dictionaries in four languages, Czech, Latin, Greek, and German. The importance of lexicons for the growth of any language in precision and standardization is of course paramount. The son, until he went into exile in 1621, continued the editorial work of the father and in 1613 published an edition of the Czech Bible.

This period was not notable either for poetry or for the drama. What there was of both genres was borrowed or derivative from the Latin or the Italian. On the other hand, the writing of history and the compilation of chronicles was popular throughout the whole century. Great events occurred in or near Bohemia and the national historical sense was sharply perceptive of their significance. The teaching of Hus was itself an appeal to history, and his followers, both Utraquists and the Brethren of the Unity, carried on the tradition. Bartoš Pisář (Bartholomew the Scribe) (1470–1535) wrote a *Chronicle of Prague* which covered the years 1524 to 1534. He was a small businessman, without a university degree, who wrote from a strongly bourgeois and moralistic point of view. He was scrupulously honest, so that his facts are in general reliable.

A most important historical source that contains almost as many errors as truths was the *Czech Chronicles* of Hajek of Libočan (*ca.* 1500–53). Hajek was a Catholic priest whose *Chronicles,* dedicated to Ferdinand I, were about the only history of Bohemia allowed under the Habsburgs until the end of the eighteenth century. He was long known as the "Czech Livy," but historical research over the past century has shown him to be quite unreliable, and frequently a deliberate falsifier. One of the leaders of the Unity, Charles the Elder of Žerotín (1564–1636), the leading noble of Moravia, was a scholar of considerable eminence. He had traveled and studied abroad and served for a while in 1591 as a soldier under Henry IV of France. He maintained a copious correspondence, at home and abroad, but is best known for his *Apologia* or *Defense,* in which he eloquently defended himself from attacks made by his friends because he had withdrawn from active political life. Ciceronian in its smooth and urbane persuasiveness, it remains a model of classic Czech prose.

By the end of the century the Czech language had absorbed what humanistic learning and the Latin language could offer. Both streams of thought, the Hussite religiosity of the Unity of Czech Brethren and the more secular humanistic tradition, had found their own level; the techniques of the latter and the patriotic spirit of the former had joined to form a literary and cultural medium impressive in its completeness and expressive of the troubled and divided spirit of the people. The black night of Habsburg conquest—the aftermath of the Battle of the White Mountain—was to obscure and stifle whatever life might have come from the union of these two currents. The darkness was to last a full three centuries.

HUNGARY: HUMANISM AND PROTESTANTISM

In no country of Europe was the mingling of the two strains of religion and secular learning better illustrated than in Hungary of the sixteenth century. The humanistic tradition had been brought in directly from Italy early in the fourteenth century and propagated by King Mathias Corvinus late in the fifteenth. Soon after the Lutheran movement became established in the Empire it was widely known in Hungary, both among the German and the Magyar population. At this point, however, there enters a catastrophic third factor, destined to darken all Hungarian thought and its literary expression. The tragedy of the Hungarian defeat by the Turks at the Battle of Mohács in 1526, the death of the king on the field, the subsequent capture by the Moslems of the capital city of Buda, and the partition of the kingdom into three parts all combined to wound deeply the Hungarian spirit, which thereafter betrays a pervading melancholy in all its expression.

Hungarian prose profited in a measure from the Reformation. Transylvania, though nominally a vassal of the Sultan, enjoyed a large degree of independence, and polemics between Protestants, whether Lutheran or Calvinist, and Roman Catholics brought forth some vigorous writing. The constant Protestant appeal to the Scriptures inevitably led to a demand for the Bible in the vernacular. A translation of the New Testament had been made late in the fifteenth century but had not been widely copied or used. In the sixteenth century, when printing simplified dissemination, several scholars translated parts of the Scriptures, until finally the whole Bible was translated and published in 1590 by a Protestant pastor, Gaspar Karolyi. It became as normative for Hungarian prose as Luther's translation was for the German, and has since reappeared in hundreds of editions. The Catholics, unwilling to accept Karolyi's text, soon produced one of their own. As in all lands where the Reformation took root, church music in the vernacular assumed new life, and with it religious poetry appeared. While much of this poetry remains anonymous, several lyric poets gained national repute. Sebastian Tinodi (d. 1559) was hardly more than a wandering minstrel, but he preserved in an age of war, defeat, and depression reliable accounts of many of the tragic events of his time and depicted the spirit of heroic devotion to the land. The literate background of Hungarian culture is reflected in some of his other work, where themes from the Bible are employed. Elsewhere he draws on classical mythology for his subjects and motifs.

A later poet, Valentine Balassa (1551–94), superior to Tinodi in talent, was the greatest Hungarian lyric poet until modern times. His was a restless, violent, and romantic nature, undisciplined, adventurous, and unaccountable. His verse is full of religious feeling, but he adds to that an element new to Hungarian poetry, a marked sensitivity to the beauties of nature, and frames it all in graceful rhyme. The continual struggle of the Hungarians against their Turkish oppressor gave rise to a multitude of heroic stories in verse. Others, inspired by foreign themes, such as the *Decameron* of Boccaccio or other Renaissance-classical models, were also current. An educated foreigner visiting northern Hungary or Transylvania at the end of the sixteenth century would have found literary themes and the general intellectual climate very similar to that in most of Germany or Bohemia. The ancient and traditional connection with the Adriatic and Italy lingered on in the Hungarian memory.

The tremendous movements of the sixteenth century in the arenas of politics, religion, and economics, were quickly reflected in the literature of the time. We find some men writing out of devotion to new ideals, out of hatred of their enemies, or out of hope for the future victory of their faith. There were others whose motives were more prosaic: to amuse, to educate, to curry the favor of a patron, or, as we must believe of Montaigne, to understand themselves and, through themselves, their fellow men. In the final result, as we survey the total picture, we see that, apart from the motives behind the writing, there came together and coalesced the two main streams of native tradition and of the humanistic Renaissance. The Renaissance brought to the man of the sixteenth century two things he found he needed: the form, tried and perfected, of classical antiquity; and a rich mine of material themes and subjects which, to the northern European, were new and usable. Native motifs and traditions had only to be clothed in this dress or adapted to the classic themes in order to take on a new life. The transfer of classical form to native material called only for competence in Latin or Greek, a competence relatively easily attained. The educated man of the sixteenth century, whether Spaniard, Pole, or German, continued to read the classics in their original languages, but, in increasing measure, wrote in his mother tongue. What he wrote was partly native and his own creation, partly classical, Renaissance, and borrowed. The degree of perfection of the result depended on the writer's absorptive powers, and upon how true he remained to the ideas and ideals of his own people. This fusion, difficult to achieve and maintain, occurred frequently in the century. Torquato Tasso, Calvin, Rabelais, Montaigne, Modrzewski, Thomas More, and the giants Cervantes and Shakespeare, achieved it most effectively. The sixteenth century is unique in our Western history in this creative experience.

SUGGESTIONS FOR FURTHER READING

BLANCHARD, H. H., *Prose and Poetry of the Continental Renaissance*. New York, 1949

BRANT, S., *Ship of Fools,* trans. E. H. Zeydel. New York, 1944

CAMOENS, L., *The Lusiads*, trans. W. C. Atkinson. Penguin, 1960

CASTIGLIONE, B., *The Courtier*. Everyman's Library

CELLINI, B., *Autobiography,* trans. J. A. Symonds. Many editions

CERVANTES, *Don Quixote*. Everyman's and Modern Library. Many other editions

COMENIUS, *Labyrinth of the World and Paradise of the Heart*. Temple Classics, London, 1924

ERASMUS, *Institution of a Christian Prince,* trans. L. K. Born. New York, 1936

GALILEO, *Dialogues Concerning Two New Sciences*. New York, Dover, 1949

MONTAIGNE, *Essays*. Many translations

RABELAIS, *Gargantua and Pantagruel*. Many translations

VASARI, G., *Lives of the Most Excellent Painters, Sculptors and Architects*. 8 vols. Temple Classics, London, 1900

FRANCE

LANSON, G., *Histoire de la littérature française*. 1918

MORÇAY, R., *La Renaissance*. 1933

NITZE, W. A., and E. P. DARGAN, *History of French Literature*. New York, 1938

TILLEY, A., *Dawn of the French Renaissance*. Cambridge, 1918

TILLEY, A., *Studies in the French Renaissance*. Cambridge, 1922

ITALY

BELLONI, A., *Il Seicento*. 1929

HALL, R. A., *A Short History of Italian Literature*. Ithaca, N.Y., 1951

SYMONDS, J. A., *Italian Literature*. 2 vols. London, 1910

TOFFANIN, G., *Il Cinquecento*. 1935

WILKINS, E. H., *A History of Italian Literature*. Cambridge, Mass., 1954

SPAIN AND PORTUGAL

BELL, A. F. G., *Portuguese Literature*. New York, 1922

BURTON, R. F., *Camoens*. London, 1881

FITZMAURICE KELLY, J., *Historia de la literatura española,* 7th ed. 1950

FORD, J. D. M., *Main Currents of Spanish Literature*. New York, 1919

HURTADO Y PALENCIA, A. G., *Historia de la literatura española*. 1921

NORTHUP, G. T., *Introduction to Spanish Literature*. Chicago, 1925

GERMANY

FRANCKE, K., *A History of German Literature as Determined by Social Forces*. New York, 1913

HERFORD, C. H., *Studies in the Literary Relations of England and Germany in the Sixteenth Century.* Cambridge, Mass., 1886
ROBERTSON, J. G., *History of German Literature.* London, 1902
THOMAS, C., *History of German Literature.* New York, 1909

ENGLAND

BAUGH, A. C., *A Literary History of England.* New York, 1948
Cambridge History of English Literature. 15 vols. Cambridge, 1907–17

POLAND

BRÜCKNER, A., *Dzieje literatury polskiej.* 2 vols. 1907
BRÜCKNER, A., *Geschichte der polnischen Literatur.* 1901
KRIDL, M., *Survey of Polish Literature and Culture.* New York, 1950

BOHEMIA

JAKUBEC, J., *Dějiny české literatury.* 2 vols. 1929, 1933
JELINEK, H., *Histoire de la littérature tchèque.* 1930
LÜTZOW, F., *History of Bohemian Literature.* London, 1907
PRAŽÁK, A., ed., *Pisemnictví* (Vol. VII in *Československá Vlastivěda*). 1933

HUNGARY

KONT, I., *Histoire de la littérature hongroise.* 1900
RIEDL, F., *A History of Hungarian Literature.* London, 1906
TOTH, V., *A magyar iradalom története.* 1960

CHAPTER TWENTY-FOUR

NATIONAL SOLUTIONS:
ENGLAND, SCOTLAND,
AND THE LOWLANDS

THE religious and political tensions which developed in the countries of Europe as a result of the Reformation movements on the one hand, and the evolution of political concepts and structures on the other, were resolved in diverse fashions. Germany maintained its political separatism and yet reached an agreement to be half Protestant and half Catholic. This was an uneasy balance, as we shall see when we follow the course of the Thirty Years' War. Spain, under a fervently Catholic dynasty, with the help of the Inquisition, chose political absolutism and unified Catholic orthodoxy. Italy, the arena for much of the diplomatic and military action of foreign powers, remained politically chaotic, religiously Catholic. Poland, by the end of the century, had confirmed her loose political structure, but had preferred the uniformity of Catholicism to a Protestantism that meant further sectarian fragmentation. Switzerland found that her federal form of government allowed an acceptable freedom of religious choice: Zwinglianism in the north and east, Catholicism in the south, Calvinism in the west. France's decision to remain a Catholic land did not come until the end of the century, and we shall follow that development in subsequent chapters, as well as that of Bohemia, which changed, against its will, from a Protestant to a Catholic country as a result of the Thirty Years' War. In the present chapter we shall briefly trace the decisions reached in England, Scotland, and the Low Countries in the latter part of the century, a decision in each case partly political and partly religious and, in growing measure, partly economic, thus indicating, once again, the close interlacing of the factors of politics, religion, and economics in sixteenth-century Europe.

ENGLAND AND SCOTLAND

Elizabeth I: 1558–1603

THE attempt to return England to the Catholic faith ended in failure with the death of Queen Mary Tudor, November 17, 1558. She was succeeded by her half sister Elizabeth, daughter of Henry VIII and Anne Boleyn. Elizabeth, labeled a bastard by the Roman *curia,* was hardly likely to follow the faith of her sister. An impressive young woman of twenty-five, she had already had much experience of survival, and her native shrewdness had translated experience into wisdom. She could be calculating, dissembling, patient, or decisive as the situation demanded. These qualities, so necessary to a ruler, were all put to the service of her primary passion: the welfare of the realm of England. To that welfare every other consideration had to yield. When to this fortunate combination of qualities was added a long rule of forty-five years, from 1558 to 1603, it is no wonder that the age of Elizabeth is perhaps the greatest period in the long annals of England.

Elizabeth did not ascend the throne of a happy kingdom. Calais had recently been lost. The treasury was empty, and there was a heavy debt of a quarter of a million pounds, payment of which was being demanded. The land was suffering from years of capricious misgovernment at the top, and the bureaucracy in direct contact with the mass of the people was uncertain and inefficient. The king of France had not only taken England's last possession on the Continent, he was virtual ruler of Scotland through the regent, Mary of Guise, and England thus lay within the jaws of the French vise. After losing Calais, England was a less valuable ally to Spain, and if that counter to French power were lost, England would be left to her own weakened resources. Most pressing of all for the new queen was the religious problem. What would happen to the church in England? Was England to remain Catholic as Mary had made it, Protestant as under Edward VI, or Anglican as under Henry VIII?

Elizabeth moved firmly yet without undue haste. She chose as her secretary Sir William Cecil, a moderate Protestant with experience under Somerset and Northumberland, and discreet enough to have been employed for a time by Mary Tudor. All new appointments to the Council were Protestants. Other changes were clearly Anglican in intent, but not drastic. When Parliament met on January 25, 1559, the trend of Elizabeth's policy emerged: firm moderation and the tranquillity of the realm were her obvious aims. Catholic opposition in both houses was heard and had some influence on the wording of bills brought forward by the queen's ministers. The Convocation of the clergy declared for the Catholic doctrines of transubstantiation and the sacrifice of the Mass. The majority of the bishops were Mary's appointments, and there was no doubt the higher clergy would not suddenly become Protestant of their own volition. Elizabeth saw that reformation of the clergy would have to be effected through Parliament. By the Act of Supremacy which came out of the animated debate in both houses, late in April 1559, the statutes of Henry VIII were substantially restored, and the Second Prayer Book of Edward VI, slightly revised, was prescribed. The clergy and all judges and royal officials were required to take the oath accepting the supremacy of the crown over the church, on pain of loss of office. Advocacy of the authority of any foreign prince or prelate was high treason, punishable by death. Along with the Act of Supremacy went the Act of Uniformity, which applied to the whole of the nation, laity as well as clergy. A fine of twelve pence penalized every absence from religious service. Elizabeth had already taken the title of "Only Supreme Governor of this realm, as well as in all spiritual and ecclesiastical things or causes as temporal," thus avoiding the touchy term "Supreme Head of the Church," which Henry and Edward had used, yet sacrificing none of the substance of power. The deprivation of bishops appointed by Mary came only during the summer when they refused to take the oath of supremacy. The lower clergy was much more compliant, and only a very small minority, in the north and northeast of England, refused the oath and were deprived of their livings. This compliance notwithstanding, a substantial remnant of the population remained Catholic at heart while conforming outwardly to the new regime. Elizabeth and her ministers were well aware of this fact and chose not to aggravate opposition by demanding complete obedience.

When the second Parliament met in 1563, complaints arose that many justices and sheriffs were not being sufficiently vigorous in enforcing the terms of the Act of Supremacy. Parliament, therefore, had to pass laws re-enforcing the Act, broadening its coverage and tightening its administration. While this Parliament was sitting, Convocation gave the Protestant restoration its doctrinal form. The Forty-Two Articles of Edward VI were revised by Archbishop Parker and received Elizabeth's approval. In 1570 they were further slightly revised and became the Thirty-Nine Articles which have remained the middle-of-the-road Anglican formula of belief to the present time. Their most prominent characteristic is their avoidance of fine creedal definitions. Transubstantiation is expressly denied, as is the symbolistic theory of Zwingli. The resultant definition leaves much room for private interpretation. Scripture is declared to contain "all things necessary to salvation." The creeds are valid because founded in Scripture. Predestination is mentioned with approval, but it seems far from the Calvinist understanding. The sovereignty of the monarch is clearly declared. Protestantism in a most moderate form was thus adopted for a land and a people who had suffered from violent changes from Catholicism to Protestantism and back to Catholicism within the memory of many.

The Papacy was undecided as to how to proceed against Elizabeth. England had been torn from Rome's grasp by a queen regarded by the *curia* as of illegitimate birth. Many around Pope Paul IV urged the severest measures: excommunication and the interdict. But this procedure had had no effect on Henry VIII, and it might quite well fail again; a second failure would weaken the instrument for any other use. Furthermore, Philip II counseled patience. He reasoned simply that he could not afford to lose the possible alliance with England against France, a common enemy; furthermore, English trade was essential to the prosperity of the Lowlands. While there was, if not peace, at least no open war from the side of Rome, troublous clouds were gathering in the north. James V of Scotland died in 1542, leaving an infant daughter, known as Mary Stuart, as titular queen. Turmoil and civil strife for the regency followed for twelve years, when, with help from her brothers the Guises, the widow of

James, Mary of Guise, became regent. The "auld French alliance" was revived in full force, yet it was not so popular with the nobility and the people as it had been in the past. The presence of French troops and a growing feeling among the people that their land was being ruled for the benefit of the king of France brought a reversal of opinion that came to a head in 1558, when the young queen came of age.

This radical change of political atmosphere coincided with the work of a certain John Knox. This fiery Scot had been sent to the galleys for his Protestant beliefs in 1547, had been released, had returned to England, then, in 1553, had fled to Geneva, where he became an ardent and effective disciple of John Calvin. He appeared in Scotland in 1555, but returned to Geneva again the next year, leaving behind him in Scotland a large number of hopeful converts among the clergy and the nobility as well as the common folk. His preaching had a distinct national cast. The fact that the French king was persecuting the Calvinists put Calvinism, in the minds of many, on the side of Scottish patriots. Late in 1557 a group of nobles and influential burghers signed a "Covenant" which demanded the rejection of the Catholic Church, that "congregation of Satan." Mary Stuart was married to the French dauphin, who, on the death by accident of his father Henry II in July 1559, became king of France as Francis II. Mary was thus queen of France as well as of Scotland, and her uncles, the Guises, were the actual rulers of France.

Happy in the sparkling life at the French court, Mary was content to encourage her uncles to rule France through her weak husband. The Scottish movement of resistance to a French ruler whose primary interests were in Catholic France grew, and, now that its tenor was predominantly Protestant, sought the aid of Elizabeth. Knox was again in Scotland, rousing the people to action against a "Jezebel" living in luxury at a distant and enemy court. Elizabeth, glad of an opportunity to strike a blow at her declared enemies, the Guises, engaged to help the Protestant nobility in Scotland to drive out French troops and the French influence. She sent troops by land and a fleet to the Firth of Forth. The result was a complete victory for the English-Scottish forces. By the terms of the treaty of Edinburgh (July 6, 1560) the French withdrew from Scotland. Then Elizabeth exhibited her wisdom. She withdrew her English troops immediately, asking no booty, no payment for her help. She had, by one act of restraint, healed the wounds to Scottish pride and the resentment at repeated claims of English sovereigns to suzerainty over the kingdom of Scotland. In August of that year, the Scottish Parliament rejected papal authority and abolished the Mass. The rapid progress of the Reformation in Scotland astonished even its advocates. It may have been the absence of the queen that allowed so sudden a switch in church form and organization.

On December 5, 1560, Francis II of France died; Mary was a childless queen-widow at eighteen. The Guises were, for the moment at least, out of power. There was no reason for Mary to remain in France to face another queen-widow, Catherine de' Medici, now ruling for her second son, Charles IX. In August 1561, Mary returned, a Catholic, to her Protestant kingdom of Scotland. Her first steps were careful and moderate. No religious fanatic, she showed no inclination to force Catholicism on her subjects. What she did most ardently covet, however, was recognition as Elizabeth's successor in England, since she too was a granddaughter of Henry VII. This desire of Mary was to cloud her relations with Elizabeth for many years. The succession to the English throne was of interest to Parliament, and there were almost yearly petitions by Parliament to Elizabeth to marry and assure a normal succession. Mary, on the other hand, was a marriageable widow and much sought after. Mary chose to marry her cousin, Lord Darnley, in 1565. Faced with open rebellion by the Protestant nobility, Mary sought Spanish and papal aid to restore Catholicism in the country. Help was promised but none came. The jealous Darnley had Mary's Italian secretary, Rizzio, killed before the queen's eyes (March 9, 1566). Three months later a son James was born to Mary. Her husband was slain on February 10, 1567, probably with her connivance. Soon thereafter she married the earl of Bothwell, who was generally believed to have murdered Darnley. The Scottish lords determined to arrest Bothwell for regicide, but he escaped; Mary then surrendered and was imprisoned. Elizabeth's efforts to get Mary freed were vain, and the rebellious Scottish lords forced her to abdicate (July 24, 1567) and had the five-year-old prince James crowned king. Mary escaped from her prison (May 2, 1568) and fled to England, throwing herself on Elizabeth's mercy, hoping indeed that her cousin would help her to recover her throne. Restoration was impossible, but the presence on English soil of a possible rival for the crown of England was almost a continual threat to Elizabeth's peace of mind for the next nineteen years.

Foreign Relations under Elizabeth

WE MUST return to the story of Elizabeth's handling of domestic and foreign affairs. Serious civil war had broken out in France in 1562 and Huguenot leaders had appealed to Elizabeth for help. Hoping to recover certain ancient English strongholds on the French coast, she dispatched some troops to Normandy. When the Huguenots and the court signed the peace of Amboise in March 1563, Elizabeth was left engaged with the royal French forces around Le Havre. It was not until April 1564 that she made peace with France, on condition that she renounce all claims to Calais. Her participation in the French war was on the side of the Protestants, yet not wholeheartedly so. Rather she saw some possible advantage to England in case the Protestants were able to make an effective show of strength. In the end the Protestants were defeated; Elizabeth's part in the war was made to appear to the French as the selfish aggression of a grasping foreigner against the kingdom of France.

The relations of Elizabeth with Philip II of Spain went through several stages. Upon her accession he made a polite offer of marriage, which she as politely declined. Undaunted, he made it clear he would like to be friendly, particularly in view of his need for an ally in his tug of war with France. English interest in trade with the Lowlands involved Elizabeth, as a Protestant, in the struggle of the Lowlanders against Philip and Spanish rule of the seventeen provinces. For years Elizabeth was careful not to give open aid to the Dutch Protestants, but she nevertheless had agents in the Lowlands, agitating against Spanish rule, and welcomed thousands of Dutch and Flemish fugitives to

England, allowing them to practice their trades. Elizabeth's later open intervention on the side of William of Orange in the Dutch struggle for independence will be sketched below.

England met Spain on the wider field of economic expansion. Spanish colonies in the New World were producing gold and silver and precious goods that were a substantial support for Philip's international position. Elizabeth's England was vigorous and inevitably expansionist. Captain John Hawkins, in 1562, first brought English attention to the possibilities of the situation by venturing to trade in Spanish colonial ports, with great profit to himself and the English economy. He was soon joined by Sir Francis Drake and other captains, and the combination of barely veiled piracy and commercial enterprise paid high dividends in which the queen had a share. About 1570 the tension between Spain and England brought about, in large measure, by English "enterprise" on the high seas and Elizabeth's support of the rebellious and heretical Lowlanders reached the dimensions of a crisis. Philip's envoy to England thought his function to be the overthrow of Elizabeth and the establishment of Mary Stuart on the throne, and with this purpose in mind he fomented a plot of malcontent English nobles against Elizabeth's life. The plot reached its height in 1569 at the same time as a rebellion in the north of England broke out. Both plot and rebellion, based on an overoptimistic analysis of the opposition to Elizabeth, failed dismally. Thereafter Elizabeth's position at home was stronger than ever.

Pope Pius V, influenced by reports that the 1569 rebellion in the north of England was the beginning of the end for Elizabeth, concluded that, with only slight encouragement, the whole of England, essentially loyal to the ancient Catholic faith, would rise up and drive her and her government into the sea. He could hardly have been more wrong. On February 25, 1570, he issued a bull of excommunication and deposition, urged rebellion against her authority and, by clear implication, invited other powers to put the bull into effect. The last charge failed completely. Philip of Spain and the Emperor were angry at the Pope for his stupidity in issuing a bull based on wrong information; the French were too busy with civil strife to be interested in anything across the Channel. In England, beyond normal precautions against papal emissaries, the bull was regarded as vacuous. The English Catholics in general may have been somewhat confirmed in their faith, and instances of Catholic recusancy (the refusal to attend Anglican services) increased slightly. Yet the bull had only to be issued to fail, revealing how strong Elizabeth's position actually was.

A more significant factor in the life and behavior of English Catholics was the missionary work of the graduates of the Catholic College of Douai, who began to return to England about 1571 to revive loyalty to the faith and the Church among known Catholics. The college had been founded in 1568 by William Allen on the Jesuit model. The young students were taught that martyrdom was the highest aim of the dedicated Christian. The Pope and Philip of Spain gave the college their support, quite unaware of the fact that the reports given them of the number of the faithful that would rise against Elizabeth in favor of a Catholic insurrection were grotesquely exaggerated.

Gregory XIII (1572–85), who succeeded Pius V, set the recovery of England for the Catholic faith as the primary aim of his pontificate. To accomplish this he supported both religious and military measures. A harebrained plan by an English soldier of fortune, Sir Thomas Stukeley, to strike at Elizabeth by way of Spain, Portugal, and Ireland was taken up by the Pope, who financed it, only to see it dissolve as soon as the group of adventurers reached Lisbon. It had been ridiculous from the beginning, but so much noise had been made about the plans all over Europe that the failure was bound to affect the position of all Catholics in England. These were soon regarded by the rest of the population as parties to the plan. Then two Jesuits, Edmund Campion and Robert Persons, who came to England in 1579 on a purely religious mission, were, in common opinion, linked with the Irish expedition. Campion, a noble and winsome figure, was executed (1581). Persons fled the country and was engaged in plots against Elizabeth for the rest of his days.

Catholics and Puritans

A CATHOLIC life within the Anglican Church continued to grow and prosper. Many of the richer families kept Catholic chaplains and held secret Catholic services in their homes after attending Anglican services. Elizabeth and her ministers were not unaware of this underground activity and made sporadic efforts to keep it under control. Recusancy, originally punishable by a fine of one shilling per Sunday, later brought down upon the guilty a fine of £20, a very large sum. The government came to regard recusancy not only as a religious offense, but also as a political crime and thus treasonous. On the scaffold Campion had said: "If you esteem my religion treasonous then am I guilty." To be a Catholic meant acceptance of the papal bull of 1570 which asked for the deposition of Elizabeth. The Pope's responsibility for the identification of political action and religious faith was as great as that of Elizabeth. Church and state were then explicitly identified, which is a mark of the Tudor monarchy. This was the Elizabethan "persecution" of Catholicism. In the last twenty years of Elizabeth's reign it is estimated that 250 Catholics were executed for treason. In five years of Mary Tudor's reign something over three hundred Protestants were burned or hanged on a similar charge.

While Elizabeth was struggling with the recusants as well as the revival of Catholicism after the papal bull of 1570 her establishment was being attacked by those who thought she had not departed far enough from the Roman system. The Presbyterians, or Puritans, disagreed with the Anglican positions on several vital points: whereas Elizabeth insisted on the union of church and state, the Puritans regarded the church as a free and voluntary assembly of those who shared the faith. Elizabeth had taken over much of the Roman ceremonial and vestments. The Puritans demanded severe simplicity, and exalted the sermon as the center of religious worship. The Anglican system retained a hierarchy of the clergy, apart from the laity, from deacon to archbishop. The Puritans proclaimed "parity" among the clergy, and accepted the system of presbyters, selected laymen who would share in the governance and discipline of the church.

From some points of view the differences between Puritanism and Anglicanism were greater and more radical than those between Anglicanism and Catholicism. The Puritans, furthermore, were loud in their complaints against the corruption, simony, and worldliness which were allowed to persist even after the parliamentary action of 1559. Archbishop Parker had to face a wide diversity of opinion among the clergy, and much confusion arose. In 1566 he published a *Book of Advertisements,* intended to bring some degree of uniformity into the services of the church, but he found it impossible to enforce the uniformity he desired. Hardly more than a third of the clergy accepted his instructions. The opposition to Elizabeth's conservative Anglicanism was strengthened by the return of the five hundred and more "Marian exiles" who had spent the five years of the rule of Mary Tudor on the Continent. Having worshiped in various congregations, they had returned convinced of the rightness of Calvin's ideas on predestination, church organization, and austere ethics, and eager to put these ideas into effect in England. A few of them, risen to positions of eminence in church and university, had had to be removed and disciplined. Others, more moderate in their expression, went on to exercise influence and spread Calvinistic views.

The early leader of the Puritan movement was Thomas Cartwright, a fellow of Trinity College, Cambridge, and professor of divinity in the university. He appealed to Scripture for his Calvinistic views of church government. The vigor of his statements led Elizabeth to order his removal from his post as professor in 1570, and in 1574 he was deprived of his fellowship at Trinity College. He fled to the Continent, there to continue his battle for the purification and reorientation of the church in England by an active campaign of propaganda on a highly intellectual level. This campaign found a sympathetic response among many members of Parliament; several petitions were introduced in the House of Commons, as in 1566 and in 1571, asking the queen to inquire into abuses in the church and the general inadequacy of the clergy. Elizabeth promptly told the Commons that the church was not within their competence, but was her especial concern. The Puritan sentiment in Parliament was not thereby lessened. A pamphlet debate between Cartwright, safely writing on the Continent, and Whitgift, dean of Lincoln and soon to be elevated to the Archbishopric of Canterbury, brought out two *Admonitions to the Parliament* (1572). Whitgift urged Parliament to take in hand a reform of the clergy and changes in the prayer book. The Puritan criticisms had enough factual basis to command broad approval, and Elizabeth and her minister Cecil were deeply concerned. In Parliament two Wentworth brothers, Peter and Paul, bore the brunt of the attack on the establishment. Peter as early as 1572 had objected to the queen's refusal to allow Parliament any discussion of religious questions. He was later sent to the Tower and the Commons apologized to the queen for impinging on her prerogatives. The issue of free speech in Parliament, however, was not so easily quieted. In 1587 Peter again demanded that Parliament be allowed to discuss the matter of religion; he was hustled to the Tower, where he eventually died. The Puritans were men of their time. They demanded freedom of speech and worship, but for themselves alone. Catholicism was to them the work of the devil; the Pope in their eyes was Antichrist.

The twenty years of his archbishopric (1583–1604) were used by Whitgift to enforce uniformity and episcopal authority in the church. His rigor was so extreme as to elicit the comment from Lord Burghley that it "savored of the Spanish Inquisition." In 1586 he set up a censorship of books by which he could control criticism. The spirit of Puritanism was, however, too strong and deeply rooted to be erased from English life by such means. In 1588 the Martin Marprelate tracts began to appear, attacking in scurrilous language individual bishops and practices in the church. There was enough truth in these broadsides to make it almost impossible to answer them on the same level. Recourse was had to legislation, and in 1593 Parliament passed an Act against Seditious Sectaries that formally forbade nonconformity or Puritanism under pain of exile. Many did in fact leave and take refuge in Holland, where they were welcomed with open arms. The Act was passed by a Parliament that did not dare go counter to the queen's will, but public opinion in the land was very lenient toward evasion of the letter of the law. There were many who conformed outwardly while inwardly remaining Calvinist. By the end of Elizabeth's reign there was a great measure of external obedience, both in practice and in doctrine, to the Act of 1593, which had been formulated loosely enough to allow general adherence. This uniformity was more apparent than real, as the history of the next century was to show. All three confessional tempers, Catholic, Anglican, and Puritan, were still alive and active and were to remain so for decades.

In the meantime the drama of Mary Stuart, queen of Scots, was being played to its tragic end. From the time she took refuge in England both Parliament and Convocation, realizing the threat she bore to the stability of the kingdom by virtue of being a claimant to the throne, urged Elizabeth to allow Parliament to attaint Mary of treason. But Elizabeth shrank from so treating a fellow monarch, a cousin and a woman. At times the pressure on Elizabeth to have done with the thorny problem was almost irresistible. Mary's defiance and arrogance, as well as her involvement in plots against Elizabeth and her treasonous correspondence with Spanish, French, and papal agents, gave Elizabeth more than sufficient cause for action.

One of the first fruits of the papal bull of 1570 calling for the deposition of Elizabeth was the Ridolfi plot. Roberto Ridolfi, an Italian merchant resident in England with wide Continental connections, conceived the idea that, with a little help from Spain, the Empire, and the Papacy, Elizabeth could be driven from the throne and Mary put in her place. Philip of Spain was willing to cooperate, although the duke of Alva, Philip's governor-general in the Lowlands, branded the plot as nonsense. Pope Pius V was enthusiastic. The duke of Norfolk was the leading English personage in the plot. By the summer of 1571, the government was aware of what was afoot and, in a few months, had the leaders in custody. Norfolk was tried and executed for treason; Mary, whose guilt was glaringly manifest, lost much prestige and sympathy. For the next twelve years she was kept in secure confinement in Sheffield, continually plotting and continually protesting her innocence. Enough of her correspondence was intercepted to establish her persistent guilt. Her agents were active in France, in the Lowlands, at Rome, and at Madrid, but the end result of their plotting was only to confirm Mary's guilt and the need for her elimination. The Babington Conspiracy, so called from the principal agent, was hatched in 1586, calling for the murder of Elizabeth and the enthronement of Mary. Elizabeth's minister, Sir Francis Walsingham, broke the conspirator's cipher and in a few months had all details necessary to quash the plot, along with the names of the principal conspirators in Mary's own hand. Elizabeth, when the unanswerable proof was presented to her, was still reluctant to allow the law to take its course. Mary was a queen widow of France, and her son James VI, king of Scotland, was the heir apparent to the English throne. Elizabeth finally appointed a mixed commission to try and judge Mary. Mary conducted her own defense, with spirit and a consistent denial of obvious facts that elicited the admiration if not the credence of her judges, who passed on their findings to Parliament. The conclusion was foregone. Elizabeth postponed making a decision, but finally signed the warrant for the execution. Mary died February 8, 1587, more nobly than she had lived. There was almost universal relief and rejoicing in England at the removal of a threat to the stability of the government. There was indignation in France, in Rome, and in Spain, but no foreign government could do much about a legal execution for treason on English soil.

Philip II and the Armada

BY NOW Philip II had many scores to settle with Elizabeth. She had aided the rebels in the Netherlands in their fight against Spanish rule. Her sea captains, Hawkins and Drake, had brazenly attacked Spanish shipping on the high seas and in the Americas; cargoes of treasure ships destined for the king's coffers had a strange way of being docked and unloaded in London. Now Elizabeth had murdered a Catholic queen. Preparations for the Great Armada which was to punish Elizabeth were speeded up. Philip had entertained the idea of the Armada since 1585, and in anticipation England took defensive measures, guarded ports, or organized a home guard. By 1587 Philip's preparations were well advanced and even in detail were public knowledge. Drake set course for Cádiz in April of that year, coolly sailed into the port, burned many ships, sank the Spanish admiral's galleon, and sailed out again unscathed. He reported to Elizabeth that he had "singed the king of Spain's beard." Philip levied more taxes on a bankrupt country and continued with his plans. The new fleet was ready in the spring of 1588, and under the duke of Medina Sidonia, who had had no naval experience whatever, 130 ships sailed forth the last day of May. The Spanish plan was to use the fleet as a cover and transportation for a land army from the Lowlands to England under the duke of Parma. A naval engagement was not sought. It was hoped that the fleet, sticking together, might skirt the French coast through the Channel and reach a suitable port in the Low Countries.

The English had prepared an appropriate welcome. Admiral Howard and Drake planned to meet the Spanish fleet as far to the west in the Channel as possible. On July 21 contact was established. There ensued a running engagement that lasted ten days. The English did not fight as the Spanish thought they should. With superior guns, both in range and weight, they put Spanish ships out of commission without themselves being touched. Sidonia, pressed to the southern coast of the Channel, lost some ships which were driven by the winds onto the shoals near Nieuport, and five other of his principal units were

The Trial of Mary Queen of Scots, artist unknown, Additional MS. 48027 in the British Museum, London [BRITISH MUSEUM].

put out of action from English gunfire. The English superiority was painfully evident, and Sidonia fled northward with what ships were still manageable. He sailed around Scotland, thence southward along the rocky Irish coast, losing more ships on the way. He put into Santander late in September, having lost more than half the original complement of the Great Armada. The victory had not cost the English a ship or a man in combat. Danger from Spain was not completely eliminated, but Spanish prestige had suffered a serious blow, while English confidence and pride of performance were heightened.

The defeat of the Armada was not, however, the end of a war: Philip did not give up that easily. He redoubled his efforts and improved the defenses of the sensitive spots in the Spanish Empire. English expeditions against Spain, Portugal, and the Americas were only occasionally successful, while several of them were very costly failures. The outfitting was, on the average, certain to cost more than the royal portion of the booty turned out to be. Spain was still England's principal rival. In 1589 when, by the death of Henry III of France, the Protestant Henry of Navarre became Henry IV of France, Philip assumed the task of "protecting" the crown of France from falling into the hands of a heretic. Elizabeth, who had helped Henry against the Guises and the Catholic League with troops and money, was sure to continue her aid against her old enemy Philip. Spanish troops in Normandy and Brittany quite justifiedly frightened the English. There was no break in Elizabeth's alliance with Henry after he accepted Catholicism in order to rule over a unified France. Elizabeth, of all people, understood what a political decision involved for a ruler.

The Last Years of Elizabeth

THE last decade of Elizabeth's long reign was clouded when droughts brought on five near famine years. Prices of corn trebled, quadrupled, and in 1592, 1602, and 1603 epidemics made grievous inroads on the population. A dramatic attempt at a *coup d'état* by the earl of Essex, upon whom Elizabeth had showered honors and her favor, led to his condemnation and execution in 1601. His vanity and insatiable ambition brought him to his doom, while his treason saddened the queen.

Her reign ended on a more modern and constructive note than she may have realized. Parliament had begun to attack the system of monopolies, privileges granted to certain persons, nobles or burghers, to control a product or a process, resulting, normally, in raising the cost of the commodity. The monopolies were given by the crown, and were profitable to the royal treasury. Elizabeth listened to the complaints, then, to the surprise of the petitioners, promised to reform the system and conduct it according to law. The novelty lay in the acceptance of a rule of social responsibility by a monarch who was in fact almost absolute. The problem of the people, driven by enclosure from the land to the towns, there to become almost permanently unemployable, had plagued all the rulers of the earlier part of the sixteenth century. Successive efforts to handle the problem by various poor laws had fallen short of a satisfactory solution. By a broad statute of 1598 the problem of beggars, vagabonds, the indigent, and unemployable was at last, for this age at least, systematically attacked. Almshouses, hospitals, the financing and administration of controlled aid to the poor were provided for by a stipulated levy "on every inhabitant." The responsibility of the whole society for its unprofitable or maladjusted members was acknowledged and implemented.

On December 31, 1599, after a series of not very successful experiments in the organization of overseas trade in the Americas, the East India Company was chartered. Granted a monopoly of all trade with the region we now call the southeast Pacific and the Indies, it was destined to bring fabulous wealth to Britain and have a determinative impact upon her philosophy of empire.

James VI of Scotland and I of England

FROM the time of the execution of Mary Stuart it was universally accepted that her son, James VI of Scotland, should succeed Elizabeth on the throne of England. James' career of forty years as king of Scotland had given him an opportunity to grow up to kingship. He had come to the throne as a child of five years of age, and the government had been carried on by regents. The nobility was not used to being ruled, and three of the four regents had either been murdered or executed. In 1582 James was taken prisoner by the Protestant party, only to become, the following year, a virtual prisoner of the Stuarts, the party of Queen Mary. The situation was reversed again the following year. By this time James was beginning to take hold, and for the ensuing nineteen years, until he left for London and the throne of England, he was king of Scotland in fact as well as in name. While he did not share his mother's Catholic leanings, he found the Calvinistic Kirk of Scotland scarcely more to his liking. The Kirk as Knox had organized and left it on his death in 1572 was constitutionally quite independent of the state, and strong by reason of the representation of the laity in its councils. The Kirk did not hesitate to criticize the anarchy and immorality of the nobility as well as the laxness of the king in putting up with it. James, never friendly to the Kirk, nevertheless found it the stronger element in Scottish life, and allied himself with it. In 1592 he signed the act establishing the Presbyterian church as the Kirk of Scotland. For the next ten years he was often in conflict with the Presbyterian clergy, and frequently irritated by their meddling in political affairs. He perforce learned much Calvinist theology, of which he admitted being an accurate exponent. Finding the clergy determined to be politically active, he endeavored to attach enough responsibility to their rights of criticism to make them conscious of political realities. Had he stayed in Scotland instead of leaving for England in 1603, his plans might have had more success. He was, however, glad to leave behind him in Scotland the Calvinist theologians turned politicians.

The reign of Elizabeth began with a platform of religious settlement, the Acts of Supremacy and Uniformity. The queen was convinced that her realm could not survive half Catholic and half Protestant: it would have to be united and English. In these two acts she delineated what was meant by the broad English way, then insisted that her subjects stay within the bounds of this program. For the forty-five years of her reign, in spite of many trials and difficulties, she adhered to this policy. Its rightness was shown by the fact that England has ever since found Elizabeth's broad religious settlement satisfying and healthy. England's notable progress in other areas of national life during the queen's lifetime and in the subsequent century was largely due to the fact that her subjects were able to accept that settlement and go on to other tasks. Adaptation joined to firmness spelled national success.

715

THE LOW COUNTRIES

THE Burgundian Netherlands, which Charles V left to his son Philip in the solemn ceremonies of abdication at Brussels in 1555, were then enjoying relative quiet and prosperity. Bourgeoisie and nobility, both vigorous, were in political and economic balance. The government at Brussels, firm in the interest and support of the Emperor, a native of Ghent, was well equipped to maintain that balance. Nevertheless, the equipoise was delicate; it could be easily disturbed by the injection of new governmental politics, disregard of the temper of the people, or the neglect of trends and forces that might introduce new tensions. Philip II managed, within a very few years, to commit all these faults. The result was the revolt of the Netherlands, the defeat of the military and political might of Spain, and the formation of a new Protestant state.

King Philip, speaking only Spanish, and with no native sympathy with the Netherlanders, chose his advisers and high officials from those with whom he could communicate—mostly Spaniards—and seemed to regard the land as an adjunct to his Spanish dominions or as a support for his French policy. In March 1556, he demanded from the Estates General of the seventeen provinces a grant of 1,300,000 florins to meet obligations, largely inherited from his father. He suggested two kinds of levy, one of 1 per cent on immovables (real estate) and a second of 2 per cent on movables. The Estates, offended by the manner of the demand, refused point-blank to make any such grant. Philip, temperamentally incapable of negotiating or winning a point by discussion and persuasion, had to accept a flat grant of a fraction of what he had asked for. His father had received frequent grants as large as Philip asked for and was refused, but Philip managed to antagonize the Estates from the first days of his rule.

Charles had been adamant in his resistance to the growing tide of Protestant "heresy" sifting into his lands from Germany and even from France. He had introduced the Inquisition and had burned hundreds of heretics. The Inquisition was so unpopular with his own officials that he resorted to the issuance of "placards" decreeing death for anyone who should read, copy, sell, or spread heretical books, or in any way disseminate heretical doctrines. Thousands had perished under these decrees without thereby stopping the spread of Lutheran and, after about 1545, Calvinist teaching and worship. Charles laid upon his son, as a special task, the extirpation of the plague of heresy. Philip gladly accepted the charge, reissued Charles' last and most severe placard, that of 1550, and gave new and sweeping powers to the Inquisition. The people chose to regard the whole plan of the repression of heresy as a foreign imposition, and hated it the more for that reason.

The Church in the Lowlands was administered by three bishoprics, completely inadequate from the viewpoint of administrative efficiency. Charles had planned to increase the number of bishoprics to six and straighten the boundary lines to correspond to a few of the political boundaries. Philip decided there should be fourteen bishoprics—on its merits, a sound decision. Yet, because the people distrusted the king and saw in the increase a sinister plan to tighten the Spanish control of the Church and fasten the Inquisition on their necks, they protested bitterly, while hatred of the ruler grew immeasurably.

William of Orange

AS SOON as the campaign against France was victoriously completed and the Treaty of Câteau-Cambrésis signed (February 1559), Philip prepared to return to Spain. He appointed his half sister Margaret, duchess of Parma, as regent, to rule with the advice of three councils, of which the Council of State was by far the most significant. The members of this Council were Granvelle, bishop of Arras, later archbishop of Malines and cardinal, Viglius, president of the Privy Council, Barlaymont, president of the Council of Finance, the count of Egmont, soldier, diplomat, and stadtholder of Brabant and Artois, and finally William of Nassau, prince of Orange. Having appointed these Councilors, Philip left the Netherlands in August 1559 for Spain, never to see the Lowlands again.

Of the five members of the Council, Granvelle was from the first the most influential. Since he had had the confidence of Charles V and Philip trusted him to carry out his wishes, Margaret was instructed to put her faith in him. Viglius and Barlaymont consistently followed Granvelle's lead. Egmont and William of Nassau found themselves excluded from the inner circle, and soon perceived that they were on the Council solely to allay the suspicion of the native population. From the moment of Philip's departure from the Lowlands an ultimate clash between Spanish rule and the free spirit of the Lowlanders was certain. The person around whom this spirit crystallized and who directed the struggle was William of Orange (1533–84), known to history as William the Silent.

The house of Nassau had a long history of eminence in the region of the lower Rhine. Joined with the Dillenburg family in the fourteenth century, in the course of the next two centuries it acquired substantial holdings in the Lowlands, especially in Brabant, as well as lands in northwestern Germany. Charles V, who had regarded the father of William, though a Lutheran, with especial affection, took the oldest son into his court at an early age, often having the boy by his side at meetings of the Council of State. The title of prince of Orange came to William in 1544, on the death of an uncle. Orange, a small principality on the Rhône River, gave William the title of prince, but its most famous ruler never set foot on its soil. William early showed talent as an administrator and a diplomat. At the age of twenty-one he was in command of an army. The next year, at the abdication ceremonies, Charles walked down the aisle of the cathedral leaning on William's shoulder. Philip kept him on at court as a counselor, conferred upon him the Order of the Golden Fleece, the highest honor in the Burgundian realm, and named him the principal envoy of the Spanish monarch for the Treaty of Câteau-Cambrésis. He was one of four hostages for the fulfillment of Spain's obligations under that treaty, and as such went on to Paris, where he was treated with great respect by Henry II. The story of his gaining the sobriquet "the Silent" has been told above (p. 575).

The Beginning of William's Resistance to Spain

RETURNING to the Lowlands, William set out upon a policy of defending the autonomy of the country, which, beginning as simple constitutional opposition to Spanish encroachments upon ancient local rights, ended in open and complete rejection of Spanish rule, a war which lasted eighty years and resulted in Dutch independence. William headed the opposition in the Estates General, but acted and spoke within the bounds of tradition on behalf of the rights which Charles V had approved. The withdrawal of Spanish troops from the territory of the provinces was the initial request, to which Philip answered with an indignant refusal.

The regent Margaret was so obviously bound by the aggressive policy of Granvelle that her own judgment was not allowed to soften the harshness of Philip's orders. Sullen resentment met her and her government on all sides. In 1561 William and Egmont wrote to Philip, telling him that things were being done of which they could not approve and asking permission to resign from the Council of State. What William did not know at that time was that it was not Granvelle who was dictating the policy of rigorous repression of Lowlands liberties and religious freedom, but Philip himself. William realized, however, that the policy must be resisted.

At about this time he was arranging his second marriage. His first wife had died, and he decided on a connection with a Protestant state. His marriage to Anne of Saxony, a Lutheran princess, took place at Dresden in August 1561. It was destined to cause him much grief and humiliation, though its political gain was not completely lost. William was active in the efforts to convince Philip that the opposition to Granvelle by the noblemen and burghers of the provinces was justified, but Philip made it quite clear that Granvelle had his complete confidence. In July 1563, William, Egmont, and Hoorn, the last a recent addition to the Council of State, asked Philip to dismiss Granvelle from his post. Margaret, for reasons explicitly rooted in Granvelle's overbearing personality, also asked Philip for his removal. The king was finally persuaded to relieve Granvelle, now a cardinal, from his offices in the Lowlands (February 1564), but in such a way as to save face for Granvelle and give no great satisfaction to his enemies. There was peace in the Lowlands for a while, as William, Egmont, and Hoorn again appeared in the Council of State and Margaret seemed glad to have their counsel.

In the late summer of 1564, Philip ordered that the decrees of the Council of Trent be published and accepted in the provinces. The opposition to the decrees was universal among the people. The Council of State, backed by the Privy Council, decided to suspend the decrees, hoping meantime to persuade Philip to relax his pressure for compliance. Philip's refusal was categorical. On these scores, the enforcement of the placards, the reactivation of the Inquisition, and the decrees of the Council of Trent, the free-spirited Lowlanders felt their ancient liberties were being violated; popular resentment threatened to flare up in violent demonstrations against Spanish rule. In the Council William of Orange insisted that candid representations be made to Philip about the temper of the people and that the king be urged to provide for a radical reform of his administration in the country. This last suggestion obviously meant that Spaniards in important offices in the provinces should be sent home and the government left in the hands of native-born officials. These recommendations were brought together in a memorandum which Egmont personally took to Madrid. Philip promised him blandly to make reforms along the lines sug-

William the Silent, by Anthony Moro, in Het Prinsenhof, Delft [PRINSENHOF].

gested, at the same time secretly ordering his officials in the Netherlands to execute his decrees to the letter. This decision became public and declared policy in November 1565. Many magistrates refused to obey the orders; many others resigned their posts in protest. Confusion was general, boding no good for law and order.

About this time a group of younger nobles, one of whose leaders was Louis of Nassau, William's younger and more militant brother, banded together to resist the royal repression. They all signed a document called the *Compromise of the Nobles* early in April 1566, setting forth their objections to the royal government by foreigners, to the Inquisition, the placards, and the decrees of Trent, and indicating their determination to oppose this oppression by every means. There were more than two thousand signers of the *Compromise,* Catholics as well as Protestants, burghers and noblemen. William was not ready at this time to take so open a stand against Philip, preferring to hope that something might yet be done through legal and constitutional means to regain the ancient liberties upon which Philip had encroached. Many of the older heads among the nobles were afraid that the *Compromise* and subsequent proclamations of the "Young Bloods" went too far on the dangerous path toward treason. Yet the fact remained that the *Compromise* accurately reflected general opinion among the population. The young nobles, now known as the Young Bloods, asked the regent to receive a *Request* from them to pass on to King Philip their strong recommendation that, in order to preserve peace in the land, the Inquisition and the placards be withdrawn. On the occasion of the presentation of the *Request,* one of the Catholic members of the Council of State referred contemptuously to the Young Bloods as "these beggars" (*ces gueux*). The epithet stuck and was adopted with pride by the party of opposition. While another embassy sent to Philip in the summer of 1566, with the same requests to mitigate the severity of the placards and the Inquisition, seemed only to harden Philip's determination to crush heresy, Protestantism increased by the arrival of thousands of Lutherans and Calvinists, whose preachers held services in public places, in defiance of the placards and the Inquisition. Antwerp particularly was the scene of serious disorders.

At Margaret's request William used his influence to restore a measure of order. But when, on April 19, William left Antwerp to attend, at the regent's command, a meeting of the Order of the Golden Fleece, the storm broke; for five days, Catholic churches and chapels, convents, every place that reminded the people of the Inquisition, the placards, or the Council of Trent, were sacked and sacred relics burned. William had once more to bring order. The excesses of the rioters, composed partly of Protestant fanatics, partly of irresponsible or criminal elements, brought a reaction in favor of the regent and legality. A great loss to the national cause was the defection of Egmont and Hoorn in October. Never realistic in their judgment of the plans of Philip, even in 1566 they were still persuaded that the king would eventually treat the Netherlands with loyal and understanding fairness. William was unable to make them appreciate Philip's real intention. They and the prince of Orange parted political company in October 1566.

William now renewed his efforts to gain outside support. He suggested a German league against Catholic oppression in the Lowlands. The responses were evasive, and while no help resulted from William's *démarches,* the more headstrong element among the young nobles broke out in open rebellion (March 1567). Margaret with veteran troops put down the rebellion quickly, and most of the confederates perished. William bent every effort to prevent a sympathetic uprising in Antwerp which he was certain would result in the death of thousands and further damage to the cause. He had decided, however,

The Duke of Alva, by Anthony Moro, in the Royal Museum, Brussels [A.C.L., BRUSSELS].

to withdraw from a position where he was using his prestige to defend the legal theory of royal authority, and in April left Antwerp and the Lowlands for his ancestral home, Dillenburg, on German soil. He did not leave too soon. Philip had chosen the duke of Alva, a trusted disciplinarian, to quell the rebellious spirit of the native Lowlanders. He entered Brussels with over ten thousand veteran troops on August 22. Margaret, now deprived of any real power, soon asked to be relieved of a task she had never really relished.

The next six years, from 1567 to 1573, are among the most tragic and the most heroic in the annals of modern nations. Alva's record of unalloyed cruelty has no match among civilized peoples from the sixteenth century until the barbarism of Hitler. Egmont and Hoorn, expecting recognition for their continued loyalty to Philip, were surprised, two weeks after Alva's arrival, to find themselves arrested and imprisoned. The country was stupefied at this action. Alva next set up a Council of Troubles, soon to be known as the Council of Blood, with authority superior to that of the Council of State, controlled by two Spanish blackguards, who answered only to Alva. There were mass arrests and executions, capriciously reaching into all classes of society. There were judicial murders intended to "teach" the inhabitants the laws under which they now lived. There were mass confiscations of land and property, by which Alva raised money for his troops. William of Orange was summoned to answer charges of treason. When he answered from Dillenburg that Alva had no jurisdiction over him, his properties in the Lowlands were confiscated and his son, a student at the University of Louvain, was arrested and sent to Spain, never to see his father again.

Egmont and Hoorn, long kept in solitary confinement, were finally subjected to a hearing, charged with treason and rebellion. Pleas for clemency from many quarters, the Emperor, some German princes, and even Granvelle, were disregarded and the two were executed, both serene and noble in the face of death, in the public square of Brussels on June 5, 1568. Alva apparently thought that the execution would be an object lesson to the "men of butter" he had so contemptuously promised to master. The results were just the opposite of what he hoped. He had failed to understand the temper of the people he had been sent to rule. The hatred of the Lowlanders for the Spanish oppressor was sealed with the blood of those Alva murdered, among whom Egmont and Hoorn occupied a place of honor.

As Alva continued on his blood-spattered way William was active in his efforts to clarify for his people the issues for which they should strive, and at the same time to awaken world opinion to the need for support of their cause. In 1568 there appeared his *Justification,* in which he defended his past conduct and blamed Spanish officials, particularly Granvelle, for the troubles of the land. A three-pronged military expedition planned by William against Spanish strongholds ended in ignominious failure, in spite of a bold action of his brother Louis at Heiligerlee which redeemed in part the darkness of the defeat. William, undaunted, sought help from French Huguenots, to whose interest it was to discomfit Philip and the Catholics at any price, and his two brothers Louis and Adolphe fought with distinction on the side of the Huguenots in several battles against the League in this year. Help was not yet forthcoming from the French Protestants. Although William's military efforts were failures, they were not completely in vain. Alva had been obliged to keep troops in the field, and that was expensive. He was running short of funds. Two ships carrying 450,000 ducats intended for Alva's army were seized by Queen Elizabeth and retained in the port of Plymouth. Alva, desperate for funds, demanded of the Estates General in March 1569 three levies totaling 16 per cent of assessed valuation, including a 10 per cent sales tax on all immovables, corresponding to the *alcabala,* a Spanish tax which had helped to ruin Spanish commerce. The Estates opposed the levies stubbornly. In reprisal Alva took to quartering Spanish soldiery on the citizenry, assuring himself of further unpopularity.

William's agents made much of Alva's brutality and, circulating quietly among the people, particularly in the northern provinces, kept alive the spirit of resistance. More effectively, William began to issue letters of marque to Dutch sea captains which gave a show of legality to what might otherwise look like free-booting or simple piracy. Alva could get supplies and money only by sea, and the slow Spanish galleons were no match for the Dutch "Sea-Beggars." By February 1570, about three hundred Spanish ships had fallen into the hands of these gay ruffians. At first William derived no direct profit from their action, but by 1571 he had imposed on them both organization and a measure of discipline and laid down the rule that one third of the booty should go into his war coffers. The first land conquest for which they were responsible was the capture of the port of Brill (April 1, 1572). The action had begun as a simple quick raid; almost prankishly the leader decided to hold the city as a port and evidence of political connection with William, whose flag was raised over the city hall. Then Louis of Nassau took the port of Flushing; suddenly the trend of defeat which had long been the lot of William and the national cause was reversed. The cities of the five northern provinces, Holland, Zeeland, Guelders, Utrecht, and Friesland, asked William to be their leader. The German princes changed their tune, allowing William to recruit troops in their lands. Elizabeth of England permitted him to raise money in London. The immense popularity which Louis had won by his charm and valor among the French Huguenots seemed about to bear the fruit of French support of the Nassau cause.

William, with money, troops, allies, and popular favor, entered Dutch territory on July 9, 1572, hopefully determined to drive out the hated Spanish oppressor. His plan of campaign called for him to march from the north toward Brussels, and for his Huguenot allies to move northward toward the same point, thus catching Alva between the two jaws of the vise. The plan was excellent. The reality was a tragic blow to William. On the night of August 24, the eve of St. Bartholomew, as William was directing the march of his troops across Guelders, the massacre of the Huguenots broke on Paris, and William's hope of Huguenot help against Alva vanished. On the other hand, Alva's situation was not much improved. The sullen hatred of the natives of the provinces for the Spanish remained. A bold attempt to capture William in his own camp was only foiled by the warning bark of his pet dog. Louis was compelled to surrender at Mons (September 19), and Alva's troops took some northern cities which they brutally sacked. Nevertheless, William now safely held important territory in the north and was accepted as stadtholder by the Estates of Holland and Zeeland, with broad backing elsewhere in the land. Alva, a resolute and crafty soldier, struck several telling blows at William's growing strength. Spanish troops took and sacked, amid scenes of incredible butchery, the cities of Zutphen and Noorden, and laid siege to Haarlem, surrounded by water. This city resisted all attacks for over seven months, surrendering only when the inhabitants were reduced to eating shoe-leather, roots, and rats. The 1600 men of the garrison, all that remained of the 4000 who had begun the defense, were slaughtered in cold blood by the Spaniards. Four hundred citizens were executed. William had tried desperately to rescue the city, but successive expeditions had been cut to pieces by the Spanish professional soldiers.

The Tide Turns: Alva Retires

THE fall of Haarlem had cost Alva much in men—twelve thousand of his troops were lost in the effort—in time and in treasure. The Sea-Beggars had defeated a Spanish fleet and captured Alva's admiral. His soldiers, unpaid, were ready to mutiny, if they were not already out of control. Alva's mission had not succeeded; in November 1573, he was replaced by Don Luis Requesens, who brought talk of a compromise with William. But William had gone too far toward his ultimate aim of independence for the Lowlands to risk all for fair words, and the war was on again. Louis was killed in an engagement near Maestricht, to the deep grief of William, who was passionately fond of his gay, reckless, and loyal brother.

By this time William had made his religious position quite clear. In October 1573, he had openly declared his acceptance of the Calvinist faith, although much of this creed and many of its adherents were not to his taste. No religious fanatic, he would have been content to stay a Catholic or a Lutheran and let others have their faith in peace. But as the struggle for the freedom of his people unfolded, he found that the Calvinists were the only ones who represented the forces of freedom and the only group upon whom he could rely. The firmness of their faith and the fervor of their patriotism had a great effect upon William, and from 1573 he may be counted a Calvinist. He would, however, never depart from his principle of religious toleration.

In May 1574, Leyden was under siege by Requesens' troops, who sat down before the walls to starve it into surrender. William decided that the only way to relieve the city was to cut the dikes twenty miles away and drive the Spaniards out. This meant a great sacrifice to owners of land that would be flooded by salt water. William won their consent, and the dikes were cut. The water moved over the land, but slowly, and the city was on its last very tight rations, with disease raging, before the Spaniards withdrew (October 3, 1574), bedraggled and mud-soaked, and the Dutch barges floated into the city with food and supplies. William established the University of Leyden to commemorate the heroic defense of the city.

Until the following summer there was a sort of armistice between Requesens and the Lowlanders. William's second wife, Anne of Saxony, had caused him such embarrassment by her excesses and adulteries that she had had to be divorced. In need of both a consort and a helpmate, he married (June 1574) Charlotte of Bourbon, a former nun. It was, unlike the previous match, a happy marriage of affection.

Requesens broke the uneasy peace in September 1575 with a bold attack on two key islands of Zeeland. One was quickly taken, and by the following summer the second was in Spanish hands. The Spaniards had thus gained an outlet on the sea of which the Sea-Beggars had deprived them since 1572. This was a setback for William. Had it not been for the sudden death of Requesens in March 1576, the total advantage might have been on the side of the Spanish. William's diplomatic activity, however, was persistent. In April the two states of Holland and Zeeland signed an act of federation, and broad authority was conferred on William as "Sovereign and Overlord." The Protestant Reformed faith was declared to be the state faith, but William had no intention of persecuting Catholics. To succeed Requesens Philip sent his half brother Don Juan of Austria, who, reluctant to assume a post which had brought only frustration to previous commanders, delayed his coming. His delay worked to William's advantage.

Spanish troops, as usual unpaid, mutinied in a number of posts, and popular resentment at their excesses ran high. This was William's opportunity. He arranged for a meeting between representatives from united Holland and Zeeland and from the southern fifteen provinces at Ghent in October. While the congress was discussing the terms of federation, the news of the sack of Antwerp by the Spanish garrison reached them (November 4, 1576). This brutal sack, known as the "Spanish Fury," was more ferocious and devastating than anything in the history of the Lowlands. Seven thousand inhabitants were murdered and uncounted treasures destroyed, burned, or stolen. Indignation against the Spanish brought an immediate signature of the treaty provisionally agreed on at Ghent by the Estates General of the provinces meeting at Brussels and by William. It is known as the Pacification of Ghent. William was recognized as Governor, but he realized that the Pacification was not a union of the north and the south. Don Juan, about to cross Luxemburg, was refused admittance by the Estates, save on condition of accepting the Pacification and the removal of all Spaniards from the land. By his commission from Philip Don Juan was unable to grant any such conditions.

The southern provinces, where there was a strong Catholic tradition, formed a separate Union of Brussels in January 1577, which, while recognizing Philip's royal authority, yet approved the Pacification and insisted on the expulsion of all Spaniards from the provinces. Don Juan finally accepted these conditions and signed an agreement known as the Perpetual Edict (February 12, 1577). William's position was thus, ironically, confirmed by royal authority, although it was an approval that William knew to be of very dubious value. From this point Don Juan's position was in fact merely nominal, and he soon found it humiliating. When, in pique, he brashly captured Namur with Spanish troops (June 24), thus showing that he had no intention of being bound by his promises in the Edict, he lost all credit with the populace. William's doubts as to Don Juan's sincerity were now completely justified. In January 1568, the young Archduke Matthias, a Habsburg, came peaceably yet noisily to assume the authority Don Juan had failed to maintain. William welcomed and used him under the terms of the Perpetual Edict, retaining for himself the practical exercise of power.

The Spanish cause seemed fatally weakened; but Philip was not yet willing to give up. He had never wanted to remove troops from the Lowlands; under urging from Don Juan, he sent one of the ablest of his generals, Alexander Farnese, duke of Parma, with twenty thousand seasoned troops to bring the

Lowlands back to their senses and their Spanish obedience. The first engagement went in Parma's favor, and the country was in a panic lest all their struggle for autonomy be in vain. William sought outside help. In answer to his appeal, French troops under the duke of Anjou crossed the frontier from the south, and John Casimir, heir to the Palatinate, crossed from the north. The pro-Catholic south and the Calvinist north were inevitably separable on the religious issue, and when, on the death of Don Juan in October 1578, Farnese replaced him, the north-south differences were brought out into the open. Farnese used these differences with supreme tact, the fanatic behavior of certain Calvinists in Ghent strengthening his hand. The religious differences between north and south soon came to outweigh whatever antipathy to Spanish rule the two sections may have had in common. The upshot was the formation of a league of three southern and Catholic provinces: Hainault, Artois, and Douai, by the treaty of Arras (January 1579), looking to a return to Philip's sovereignty provided only he accept the Pacification of Ghent and the Union of Brussels.

The Union of Utrecht

THE Protestant northern provinces of Holland, Zeeland, Friesland, Guelders, Groningen, Overyssel, and Utrecht some two weeks later joined in a Protestant Union of Utrecht. The division of the land into two separate unions was a heavy blow to William, who had long striven for a more inclusive unification free of Catholic or Protestant labels, and allowing religious toleration in all provinces. But the centrifugal forces of religious differences aided by Spanish intrigue and bribes were stronger than William's diplomacy. When William rejected Spanish offers of payment of his very large debts and the return of his lands and honors, he was placed under the ban by Philip and a reward of 25,000 crowns of gold and a title of nobility for his capture or assassination was proclaimed. This decree William answered with the *Apology,* a long and detailed story of his dealings with Philip published in four languages and sent to all the courts of Europe.

The seven northern provinces, in the Manifesto of The Hague (July 1580), proclaimed Philip a tyrant and repudiated their obedience to him as justified "according to the laws of nature." Meantime, Farnese was capitalizing on the divisions between the Catholic south and the Protestant north, and, in another effort to counteract these successes, William called in the duke of Anjou who, at the moment, was courting Queen Elizabeth of England. The help of France, re-enforced by Elizabeth's benign interest, would be a formidable counter to Spanish arms. In February 1582, at William's instance, Anjou was accepted as duke of Brabant in elaborate ceremonies at Antwerp. A month later William was seriously wounded in the first attempt at assassination since Philip's open sanction of political murder. In July William had Anjou accepted as duke of Guelders, count of Flanders, and lord of Friesland. This did not satisfy the stupidly ambitious duke, to whom the perfidy of attacking a trusting population seemed quite in order. Suddenly, on January 17, 1583, his soldiers ran berserk in the streets of Antwerp, crying: "Long live the Mass! Long live the duke of Anjou!" The population resisted stoutly. The "French Fury" was quelled; 2000 French were killed and 1500 taken prisoners. William was widely blamed for having supported the French duke, but he was convinced the Lowlands could not win and maintain their independence without outside help, and that the French alliance was the only alternative to submission to Philip. William retired to the northern provinces in order to strengthen their union against ever pressing Spanish action in the south. He had not resigned himself to the idea of a final split between the north and the south. In the midst of his labors as head of the government he was fatally shot at his home in Delft (July 10, 1584) by an assassin who gained access to his house on the plea that he needed a pass to the French lines.

With the assassination of William of Orange there died also the last chance for a united Lowlands. No other person could possibly succeed where he had failed, in guiding the two parts of the Burgundian heritage, Catholic south and Calvinist north, into an organic union. Farnese had been able to win the south back to Spanish allegiance; the northern seven provinces, fervently Calvinist, were determined to go their own way, to win complete independence from Spanish rule. To that extent the work of William of Orange had been completed. This did not mean, however, that their independence was won or recognized by Philip. The Dutch did not feel strong enough to stand alone against Farnese's sixty thousand veteran troops. The French alliance had been a bitter disappointment. A return to hopes of help from Elizabeth of England, whose relations with Philip were known to be rapidly deteriorating, followed as a matter of course. Her previous answers to the Dutch appeals had been evasive or noncommittal. She might now, they hoped, be in a more propitious mood. But she drove a hard bargain for her help, demanding custody of three Dutch cities to guarantee the refunding of her expenses before sending her favorite, the earl of Leicester, with six thousand troops. The Dutch welcomed him wildly, and he accepted, against Elizabeth's explicit instruction, the title of Governor General. It was an inauspicious beginning to a sad chapter of ineptitude and misjudgment. Gradually, in the face of Leicester's inadequacy, John Oldenbarneveldt, advocate of the province of Holland, assumed a position of predominant influence. Representing the party favoring the constitutional superiority of the burgher Estates, he could point to the fact that the traditions of burgher patriotism and initiative had been responsible for the successful resistance to Spanish tyranny. After William the Silent, Oldenbarneveldt may be regarded as the founder of the Dutch Republic. Upon the departure of the baffled Leicester in 1587, Oldenbarneveldt became the acknowledged leader of the state.

Maurice of Nassau; the Death of Philip

BY HIS side stood a remarkable son of a remarkable father. Maurice of Nassau, son of William, was seventeen at the time of his father's murder, but was quickly named Stadtholder of Holland and Zeeland, Utrecht, Guelders, and Overyssel, Captain-General and Admiral of the Union. He was a military genius, deeply grounded in the science of warfare, calculating and at the same time daring. For many years the cooperation between Maurice and Oldenbarneveldt was close and confident. The military successes of the Spaniards, which Leicester's incompetence had permitted, were brought to an end, and in 1590 the tide turned. Maurice began capturing border towns from the Spaniards, taking the key city of Nymegen in October 1591, other cities in 1592 and 1593, and, in 1594, Groningen. Farnese had died in disgrace in 1592. Spanish resources were exhausted, and for a while in 1595 Philip was anxious to talk peace. Now, however, the northern provinces were thinking of formal independence of Philip's sovereignty, and no peace was possible. With France again at war with Spain, the Dutch states assumed new political significance and value. France and England made an alliance in 1596 with the states, recognizing them as the United Provinces, an independent state. The next year Maurice won many brilliant victories, adding much territory to the states, whose foreign repute now stood high. France signed a separate treaty with Spain at Vervins, but Elizabeth continued the war with Philip. Until his death in September 1598, Philip was planning the reunion of all seventeen provinces under a member of the Habsburg house. The thought that any province should want to withdraw from under the beneficent rule of so glorious a dynasty was beyond his powers of comprehension.

The death of Philip brought about a new situation. His sovereignty, reaching back to his father's personal rule, had some sentimental substance. His successor, Philip III, had no such connection. This break in continuity, coming at a time when the northern provinces were at the height of their prosperity from foreign trade and war booty and had tasted a few years of military success, gave them a formidable international position. They had become desirable partners. In 1600 war broke out again between the Habsburg rulers of the southern provinces and the Dutch Estates General. Maurice won several spectacular battles, but Ostend, the most southerly seaport in the hands of the Estates, gallantly defended by Dutch and English troops, after a siege lasting three years was captured at great cost by the Spanish under Spinola (September 20, 1604). Meanwhile, the Dutch had held and fortified a better port, Sluys, and maintained their strong position on the sea.

In foreign relations the good luck of the Dutch took a turn for the worse. Whereas Elizabeth had been favorable to the Dutch cause, her successor, James I, leaning toward a Spanish alliance, withdrew that support. Henry IV of France, at peace with Spain abroad and with the Catholics at home, had no longer any need for a Dutch alliance. The Dutch had then to rely upon themselves alone. Their commercial successes in the Indies, on the African coast, and in the North Sea demanded a continuation of peace and brought about negotiations with the Habsburgs. Oldenbarneveldt was more anxious for the conclusion of a treaty than Maurice, who, although suspicious of Spanish intentions and the value of any agreement they might sign, was finally won over to acquiescence by Jeannin, Henry's envoy, and by the desire of the Dutch delegates for peace. In the negotiations the northern provinces were accepted as "free provinces and states" for the purposes of concluding a peace, and an agreement was reached (April 4, 1609). Known as the Twelve Years' Truce, the treaty made no mention of tolerance of Catholics in the northern provinces, providing simply for a cessation of hostilities for twelve years and for freedom of trade "wherever it might be carried on," without specific mention of the East Indies, where the Dutch had begun to break into the Spanish monopoly. For the Dutch it was a diplomatic victory with very practical results, allowing them to consolidate their strong position on the sea and rationalize their government at home.

After a half-century of conflict, certain manifest results had changed the lines of the ancient Burgundian heritage. A religious and a political struggle had split the Lowlands irrevocably. The southern eleven provinces (approximately modern Belgium) had remained loyal to their Spanish Habsburg rulers and to their Catholic faith. The northern six provinces, mostly Dutch-speaking, had thrown off the Spanish yoke and rejected Catholicism. The southern provinces were perhaps more industrial, the northern provinces more marine and commercial. Protestants found themselves in difficulties in the south; most of them migrated to the north or to England. The northern republic proclaimed religious toleration and maintained the principle throughout the next century, to become a haven for free spirits and a center for intellectual venture in modern times. The northern republic accepted as a tradition the leadership of the house of Nassau; it was fortunate in the heritage of a family which produced men and women of remarkable wisdom and devotion to duty. The family, at first merely stadtholders in an oligarchical republic, were later given the royal title. In the seventeenth century the Dutch, by reason of their energy, drive, and sagacity, were the nearest rivals to the English as a great naval power. Their alliance was sought and their enmity feared. Their liberties were envied, their learning imitated, and their Calvinism exported.

SUGGESTIONS FOR FURTHER READING

GEE, H., and W. H. HARDY, *Documents Illustrative of English Church History*. London and New York, 1896

HAKLUYT, R., *Principal Navigations*. Everyman's Library

HOOKER, R., *Ecclesiastical Polity*. Everyman's Library

KNOX, JOHN, *The History of the Reformation in Scotland*. London, 1899

TANNER, J. R., *Tudor Constitutional Documents, 1485–1603*. London, 1922

BLACK, J. B., *The Reign of Elizabeth*. Oxford, 1936

CREIGHTON, M., *Queen Elizabeth*. London, 1899

FRERE, W. H., *The English Church in the Reigns of Elizabeth and James*. London, 1904

FROUDE, J. A., *The Reign of Mary Tudor*. Everyman's Library

LINKLATER, E., *Mary Queen of Scots*. London, 1952

NEALE, J. E., *Elizabeth I and Her Parliaments, 1559–1581*. London, 1953

NEALE, J. E., *Queen Elizabeth I*. London, 1958

PERCY, E., *John Knox*. London, 1937

POLLEN, J. H., *The English Catholics in the Reign of Queen Elizabeth*. London, 1920

READ, C., *Mr. Secretary Walsingham and the Policy of Queen Elizabeth*. 3 vols. Oxford, 1925

WAUGH, E., *Edmund Campion*. London, 1935

WILLIAMSON, J. A., *The Age of Drake*. London, 1938

BLOK, P. J., *The History of the Netherlands*. New York, 1912

GEYL, P., *The Netherlands Divided*. London, 1936

GEYL, P., *Revolt of the Netherlands.* London, 1932
LANG, A., *John Knox and the Reformation.* London, 1905
MOTLEY, J. L., *History of the United Netherlands.* 4 vols. New York, 1867
MOTLEY, J. L., *The Rise of the Dutch Republic.* 3 vols. New York, 1880
PIRENNE, H., *Histoire de Belgique,* Vol. IV. 1911
VAN DER ESSEN, L., *A Short History of Belgium.* Chicago, 1920
WEDGWOOD, C. V., *William the Silent.* New Haven, 1944. London: Penguin

CHAPTER TWENTY-FIVE

THE CATHOLIC POWERS:
FRANCE AND SPAIN

THE characteristic movement of the sixteenth century—at least from the point of view of the political evolution of the state systems under which the peoples of Europe lived—is the break of many states from the universalist conception of a supranational church comprehending all men everywhere. We have seen how large parts of Germany, most of Switzerland, all of England, Scotland, and the northern provinces of the Netherlands joined Bohemia in separation from the Papacy. The stimulus to these movements for independent political existence came in large measure, though not wholly nor solely, from Protestant ideology. Nevertheless, Protestantism did not triumph in the Latin countries. Italy remained Catholic in form and substance; Spain, which produced the Dominican Order, the Spanish Inquisition, Ignatius Loyola and the Jesuit order, and such mystics as Saint Teresa of Ávila and Saint John of the Cross, gave Protestantism a very poor welcome. There was no Protestant political party to cause the monarch any trouble.

FRANCE:
WARS OF RELIGION AND HENRY IV

IN CHAPTER 20 we followed the course of the Protestant movement in France to the tragic death of Henry II in July 1559. By that time, in spite of Henry's determined repression of Protestantism in all its forms, the Calvinists had grown in strength and boldness. The first "reformed" church in Paris was organized in September 1555; others elsewhere followed quickly. By 1559 the number of their French adherents was estimated at almost half a million, and the first national synod took place in Paris in that year. By 1561 the growth of the movement had been so rapid, in the face of a policy of royal repression, that there were almost 2500 churches throughout the kingdom. Henry II and his advisers had good reason to be dismayed at the vigor of the heresy.

Henry's successor was his fifteen-year-old son, Francis II, frail, adenoidal, experiencing puppy love for his seventeen-year-old wife, Mary Stuart. Mary's uncles, the Guises, efficient, ambitious, confident, were only too glad to take charge of the routine drudgery of government and allow the young royal couple to frolic. The queen mother, the widow Catherine de' Medici, who had never been politically active during the lifetime of her husband, and, because of her Italian origin, never popular at court, was in no position to offer any resistance to the masterful Guises. These latter divided up the work of governing among themselves. The duke of Guise, Francis, justly enjoyed high repute as a military leader and took charge of the armed forces and military policy. His brother, the cardinal of Lorraine, was a capable bureaucrat who applied his energy to the finances and internal affairs. The Constable, Montmorency, had been in the full confidence of Henry II. The new regime had no place for him, and he retired discreetly from court, leaving a void which the Guises hastened to fill. The Guises' great rivals, the Bourbon-Châtillon group, whose relations and sympathy with the reformers were well known, were relegated to the background. It was not to be expected that so impressive a group, princes of the blood, would accept such demotion passively. Antoine de Bourbon, king of Navarre, was delegated by his relatives to approach the queen mother and protest against the Guises' assumption of power. The timid Bourbon was received coolly by the young king, who had been coached by his uncles, and warily by Catherine de' Medici, still feeling her way in the midst of court intrigues. One effect of this formal rejection of the Bourbon claims was to push the whole group farther toward the Calvinist camp, and finally to give to the "reformed" party its royal and noble leadership.

The severe anti-Calvinist edicts issued by the Guises, calling for the imprisonment of every Calvinist, had the same effect as the measures taken by Henry II against the "heretics": to increase the numbers and power of the Protestants. A highly respected member of the *parlement* of Paris, Anne du Bourg, nephew of a former chancellor of France, dared to defend the Protestants on the floor of *parlement*. He was arrested on the king's order, tried, and condemned to death (December 1559). His dignified conduct on the scaffold was reported by an eye-witness chronicler to have "done more harm to the Roman Church than a hundred ministers could have done." Protestant opinion was consolidated and confirmed in its opposition to the royal policy. The Bourbon-Châtillon group, disappointed and embittered at the treatment meted out to the king of Navarre by the Guises, met again at La Ferté, the home of the king's brother, Louis de Bourbon. It was there decided to join their cause with that of the Protestants, who were suffering specific persecution from the Guise-controlled court. Late in December Coligny made open profession of his Calvinist faith. Thus the issue was joined: the strongly Catholic Guises in control of the royal cause were faced by a powerful coalition of princes of the blood, allied with and soon to be the political and military leaders of the Calvinist cause in France. Both sides were aware that severe tensions might lead to armed conflict, yet for a few months neither wished to precipitate a civil war.

On the Protestant side an adventurer, Jean de Barry, known as La Renaudie, began to organize a conspiracy to gain possession by a sudden coup of the person of the young king Francis. Condé, the leading Huguenot with political and military prestige, was doubtless the real moving force behind the project.

Calvin, consulted in distant Geneva, had counseled against violence of any sort. Inevitably news of the conspiracy reached the Guises; when the plot was about to be put into action at Amboise, where the court was temporarily (March 1560) in residence, the conspirators were arrested. Punishment was quick and sanguinary. Two hundred conspirators were hanged. The Protestants called for vengeance: the Civil Wars, or the Wars of Religion, were the direct result. If not this so-called Tumult of Amboise, something else would have precipitated the struggle. Both sides prepared for conflict on a military and on a propaganda basis, each publishing defenses of their position and appealing to public opinion for understanding and support.

The Civil Wars were to last, with interruptions, truces, and so-called peaces, for over thirty years. We shall see that there were what may be called eight separate "wars," each ended by a kind of peace, either of fatigue or of stalemate. Victories on the field of battle seemed to mean very little; an army defeated "decisively" in the field often melted away, only to reappear later, almost intact. Foreign powers, Spain, England, the German princes, frequently sent forces to aid one side or the other, without thereby breaking off diplomatic relations with each other. Issues were confused. Many Catholics resented the

Catherine de' Medici, from the French school of the late sixteenth century, in the Walters Art Gallery, Baltimore [WAL-TERS ART GALLERY].

fact that their cause seemed to depend upon the support of foreigners, the Spanish king or the Pope at Rome, while the strength of the Guises of Lorraine in the making of royal policy was regarded as foreign intervention by many Frenchmen. On the other hand, many loyal subjects of the king of France, who would have been glad to accept principles of toleration of Protestantism, were affronted by the presence of foreign troops, English or German, on the Protestant side. Out of the confusion there early arose a large group, representing probably the most numerous segment of French opinion, who shared the views neither of the extreme Calvinists nor of the extreme Catholic party headed by the Guises. This group came to be called the *politiques*. As the wars dragged painfully on, this moderate group became the deciding factor; but for a time the wars were being fought on French soil, between three parties: the Catholic party, led by the Guises, the Protestants, called Huguenots from the mid-1560's, led by Henry de Bourbon, king of Navarre, and the *politiques,* led at various times by Catherine de' Medici or her son Henry III. At no time, however, were the lines of allegiance or division clearly discernible, and there was much shifting of opinion and loyalty before a solution to the French civil conflict was achieved in the victory of Henry of Navarre—a victory which was itself the result of a compromise between the position of the Huguenots and the ideas of the *politiques.*

On December 5, 1560, after seventeen months as king, Francis II died without issue, and was succeeded by his younger brother, Charles IX. Since Mary Stuart was no longer a reigning queen, her uncles the Guises lost their predominance at court. The queen mother, Catherine de' Medici, as guardian of her minor son, had increased influence and became regent. She had not been in agreement with the policies of stern repression of the Protestants which the Guises had followed, and, as soon as her position at court was clear, the chancellor, Michel de l'Hôpital, with her approval issued the Edict of January, which gave the Protestants certain rights of assembly, stipulating that they should hold their meetings outside the cities, that royal officials be allowed to attend, that synods be held only with royal permission, and that the Huguenots obey royal edicts on holidays and enroll no troops.

The earlier policies of repression had, however, been supported by a substantial proportion of the population, and adherents of the Guises were ready to speak and write provocatively against the "heretics." The Huguenots were eager to respond with equal asperity. Under such circumstances there arose disorders, some serious, some of only local import. On Sunday, March 1, 1562, a Huguenot service was being held in the town of Vassy, in accordance with the provisions of the Edict of January, when the duke of Guise with a considerable retinue entered the town. His followers broke into the service; the Huguenots objected, shots were fired, and soon over sixty Huguenot worshipers lay dead. Guise rode on to Paris and began to gather troops. The prince de Condé went first to Meaux, thence (April 2, 1562) to Orléans, where Huguenot soldiers flocked around him. Thus began the first civil war.

There was much action on a small scale throughout France, but the battle of Dreux (December 19, 1562), which followed the siege of Rouen by the Catholics, was the only large-scale engagement of this war. The battle was bitterly fought; Condé was taken prisoner, and the Catholic Marshal St.

André was killed by a Huguenot. The Calvinists, losing about six thousand of their troops, were forced to retire. Guise, given credit (probably rightly) for the victory, offered amnesty to all Protestants who would surrender; when there was no response to his offer, he laid siege to Orléans, then the Huguenot capital. In the absence of Condé, Admiral Coligny took command of the Protestant forces. On February 24, as the siege of Orléans was being pressed, a young and ardent Calvinist fanatic assassinated Guise. The loss of their ablest and most aggressive general was a serious blow to the Catholic party, and for a while it appeared that the Protestant cause might prevail. Catherine, however, freed from the constant pressure of the Guises, was anxious to adopt a moderate line, which she was convinced would serve the good of the whole kingdom better than alignment with either party. She was able to persuade both sides to agree to the peace of Amboise on March 19, 1563.

The terms of the peace were very similar to those of the Edict of January: a general amnesty for the Huguenots, who were to have a city in each county except Paris, where their faith could be openly practiced, the Calvinist nobles could freely exercise their faith in their own castles, and priests of each confession were to desist from provocative attacks on the other faith. The conditions had, as we shall see, a certain resemblance to the terms of the Edict of

Michel de l'Hôpital, from the French school of the late sixteenth century, in the Musée Condé, Chantilly [GI-RAUDON].

Nantes of 1598, which was to come after more than thirty years of bitter struggle. In 1563 they were idealistic and, in the heated atmosphere of confessional struggle, unenforceable, but they corresponded to the aims both of Catherine and of her chancellor, de l'Hôpital. Protests from the Pope, from Philip of Spain, and, more significantly, from French cities, the *parlement* of Dijon and the Estates of Burgundy, over the toleration of heresy in which Catherine had become involved, warned the queen mother that the way of the mediator was hard.

In an effort to win popular opinion to her side Catherine made a prolonged state tour of France, taking with her the young king. The trip lasted from March 1564 to the end of 1565. She gained the registration of the peace of Amboise by the Paris *parlement,* hoping thus to further the cause of peace and toleration. At Bayonne, near the Spanish border, in June 1565, her daughter Elizabeth, third wife of Philip II of Spain, met her, accompanied by the duke of Alva. We are not informed about everything that took place at this conference, but we do know that Alva, speaking for his master, rebuked Catherine for her tolerant attitude toward the Huguenots and urged her to join Philip in his effort to crush heresy, and particularly to support him in his war against the rebels in the Low Countries. Catherine's answers to these urgings were evasive or ambiguous. In later years the Protestants were sure that the massacre on St. Bartholomew's day was arranged and agreed upon at this meeting. There is no evidence that this was true.

The Second War of Religion, 1567

HOSTILITIES on a limited scale broke out again in September of 1567, but there were no decisive engagements in this second phase of the wars. German troops, loaned to the Huguenots by John Casimir, Elector of the Palatinate, saw no effective combat, though they increased the Protestant potential striking power. The Huguenots gained the city and port of La Rochelle, henceforth to be a Protestant citadel. On balance, the Protestants had gained slightly in the year's campaigns; the peace of Longjumeaux, which ended hostilities in March 1568, repeated the essential provisions of the edict of Amboise of 1563. Neither side was satisfied with the peace. To the Huguenots, it did not allow a broad enough toleration; to the extreme Catholics and Philip of Spain, it went too far in its acceptance of the right of heresy to exist. The court was turning against toleration. De l'Hôpital, who had consistently advocated a policy of moderation, persuaded that he could no longer count upon the support of the court and of Catherine, gave up his position and left the court. The impression was universal that the peace was only a truce, and indeed the truce was to last only a few months.

The Third War of Religion, 1567-70

THE Guises, again dominating the court, began the third war in the autumn of the same year. The first engagements between small detachments were indecisive. In the spring of 1569, when military operations were again possible, the main armies met at Jarnac (March 14, 1569), the Huguenots under Admiral

Coligny and Condé, the Catholics under the duke of Biron, Marshal Tavannes, and the duke of Anjou. The Huguenots, defeated, had to withdraw; Condé was captured, then shot dead by the captain of Anjou's guard. Like many other such military victories, this one brought no decision, and soon a Huguenot army, made up of the same soldiers and leaders which had just dissolved as an army, was assembling at Cognac. The young son of the queen of Navarre, Henry, duke of Vendôme, was declared titular head of the Huguenot party. Son of the late king of Navarre, Antoine de Bourbon, he was a direct descendant of the French king St. Louis IX, and thus a potential claimant to the throne of France.

Both sides to the conflict recognized that they were too evenly matched for any military decision to be reached; and both parties sought outside assistance, the Catholics from Alva, the Huguenots from German and Dutch Protestants. At this point, the summer of 1569, we find William of Orange and his brother Louis in the Huguenot army under Admiral Coligny in central France. In July the Protestants laid siege to Poitiers, only to raise the siege early in September when the Catholic army came to its relief. In a subsequent pitched battle at Montcontour (October 3, 1569), the issue was decided against the Huguenots by a charge of Swiss mercenaries, and the Protestants lost their supply train and artillery. The Huguenots, though badly defeated in this battle, still controlled most of the south of France. The war went on into the spring and summer of 1570. The Huguenots had by then recovered some territory, and among the Catholics, particularly the nobility, the dissatisfaction with the Guise dominance was growing. The queen mother, irritated by the arrogant dictation of the Catholic leadership, began to lean toward compromise. The later course of this war, for the moment at least, marked a change in governmental policy. Catherine was cooling toward Philip of Spain and his demands for an unrelenting prosecution of the war against heresy, as well as toward the Guises.

On the Huguenot side Admiral Coligny had, by superb handling of both the military and diplomatic phases of the Protestant cause, gained prestige for himself and the Huguenots. The Protestants were therefore able to negotiate from strength, and the terms they finally won at the peace of St. Germain-en-Laye (August 8, 1570) came nearer meeting their demands for freedom of organization and worship than at any time since the death of Henry II. In addition to liberty of conscience throughout the kingdom, they were assigned for two years four "cities of security": La Rochelle, Cognac, Montauban, and La Charité, where they could have Huguenot garrisons and magistrates.

This changed situation, a virtual recognition of the legal parity of the two sides, Catholic and Protestant, led to the revival of an earlier plan, which, it was thought, by uniting the two leading houses, Bourbon and Valois, might lead to peace. It was suggested that the young Bourbon prince Henry of Navarre, who was in the line of succession to the French throne, marry Marguerite of Valois, the youngest daughter of Catherine de' Medici. At the same time negotiations were under way for the possible marriage, first, of the duke of Anjou, then for his younger brother, the duke of Alençon, to Queen Elizabeth of England. Catherine's principal object seemed to be to demonstrate her independence of Spanish dictation or even influence. These marriage projects for two of Catherine's children with Protestants, Navarre and Elizabeth, both of whom were helping Philip's Lowlands subjects in their war against him, were certainly an affront to the Spanish king. It was by now impossible to separate the wars in the Lowlands from the struggle for power in France.

The king, Charles IX, within the past two years had become devoted to Admiral Coligny, and was inclined to follow his advice even against that of his mother. Coligny favored a war against Spain, an active alliance with England, and a partition of the Lowlands. This policy would have constituted a sharp deviation from Catherine's careful maintenance of the balance of power, and Catherine, reacting against Coligny's line, was impelled to swing to the Guise party in an effort to return France to its earlier middle position. For the moment, however, Coligny appeared to have gained the upper hand. In May 1572, Charles IX and Elizabeth of England made a defensive alliance, and Charles allowed Louis of Nassau to lead an army on French soil to the capture of Mons.

It appeared that the Protestants had won royal approval, or at least benevolent acceptance of their basic aims. Coligny obviously would have wished for France to go still farther along the Protestant line and even join in a partition of the Low Countries. Coligny's great influence with the king made it quite possible that France might be committed to an active anti-Catholic policy. This would have meant war with Philip, and to Catherine an open war with Spain was a catastrophic prospect. Facing this dread alternative, she determined that Coligny and his influence with Charles must be eliminated. In the summer of 1572, she was again working with the Guises, who had never given up their ideas of revenge for the assassination of Duke Francis nor of the extermination of the Protestant heresy. Catherine and the Guises, for the moment united, began the task of convincing Charles IX that he should agree to the death of his admired friend and minister. The king resisted the pressure of his mother and the Guises as long as he could, but finally gave in. The Guises took over the job of the actual assassination with relish.

St. Bartholomew's Eve Massacre and the Fourth War, 1572–73

THE festivities attendant upon the marriage of Henry of Navarre with Marguerite of Valois continued for four days after August 18, 1572, the day of the ceremony. On the twenty-second Coligny was returning to his house from the palace of the Louvre. Just as he reached his entrance a shot from a nearby house, known to belong to a partisan of the Guises, hit him, carrying away a finger of one hand and breaking the other arm. The news excited the whole city. The festivities had attracted great numbers of Huguenots, noblemen and men at arms, and for a moment it looked as if civil war would break out in the streets of Paris. Catherine called a meeting of her advisers. It was decided that the best way to avoid such a catastrophe would be to kill all the leaders of the Huguenots, then conveniently in Paris.

Early in the morning of the twenty-fourth, St. Bartholomew's day, the church bells suddenly began to toll and henchmen of the Guises began murdering all the Huguenots they could find. The duke of Guise personally led a band of armed men to the house of Coligny, where the wounded man was run through with a pike; the body was then thrown out of the window at the feet of Guise. The Paris mob did its part. About 3000 Huguenots were massacred in the city, and as the fever spread to the provinces another 10,000 were killed. Henry of Navarre and the young prince de Condé, then in the royal palace, were spared on condition of abjuring their Protestant faith. A few leaders of the Huguenots, learning of the massacre in time, managed to escape from the city on horseback. Most of Europe was horrified at the brutality of the slaughter. Pope Gregory XIII had a *Te Deum* sung and a medal struck to commemorate the great Catholic victory. Philip II was deeply gratified. He is reported to have laughed for the first time in many years. Charles was stricken with remorse from which he did not recover. Elizabeth of England expressed shock, but did not break off negotiations for her projected marriage to the duke of Alençon.

Whether the decision to make the elimination of Huguenots so wholesale was a sudden one, taken under conditions of panic after the failure of the attempted assassination of Coligny, or whether it was an act long planned as a part of a considered policy may never be known. A lapse of over thirty-six hours between the attack on Coligny and the beginning of the general massacre could account for the fact that in cities many miles from Paris the murder of Huguenots began at almost the same time as in the capital itself. There are however certain facts which can hardly be explained on any other basis than that the massacre had been planned for at least several weeks before St. Bartholomew's day. Catherine's responsibility for the massacre is indisputable, but she had fervent support from the Guises for the pressure she put upon her weak son Charles to agree to the act.

The Huguenots throughout France, deprived of most of their leadership, showed a remarkable steadiness and resourcefulness. The leadership devolved in large degree upon the individual pastors, who displayed an understanding of the needs of the situation which surprised the Catholics. The government was determined to take the cities then in Huguenot hands. Thus began the so-called fourth war. La Rochelle resisted royal siege for eight months, and by its stubbornness gained a peace (June 1573) only slightly less favorable than that of St. Germain.

In the meantime the natural revulsion of moderate men to unreasoned violence was having its effect. After St. Bartholomew many Frenchmen began to find their sympathies lying with the *politiques;* these, in turn and increasingly, were rallying to the defense of the Huguenots—not on confessional grounds, but in the interests of tolerance and peace. Tolerance of itself was as yet a quite novel concept. To the first generation of reformers, not less than to their opponents, the idea of toleration scarcely occurred. The middle of the century witnessed several cases of Protestant intolerance—Luther and the Anabaptists, Calvin and Servetus—which set honest men to thinking, while the Council of Blood in the Lowlands, the Inquisition in Spain, and finally the Massacre of St. Bartholomew contributed to raise the basic question of tolerance in an acute fashion. By about 1570 Western Europe was ready for the principle of religious toleration, and the *politiques* began to see the Huguenot struggle for freedom to exercise their faith as an instance of the larger concept. From this point on, the Guises and the extreme Catholic partisans were fighting a losing battle against a combination of parties and ideas: (1) the Huguenots and (2) the average Frenchman's sense of justice. These were formidable adversaries.

In May 1573, after long negotiations, the younger brother of Charles IX, Henry, duke of Anjou, was elected king of Poland and set out for Cracow (see above, p. 630).

The Fifth War, 1574–76

MEANWHILE, as the French Protestants recovered strength, aided by some *politiques,* the fifth civil war was being prepared. It broke out in the early spring of 1574 and seems to have been more confused as to the aims and intrigues of all parties than any of the other wars. The king, long failing in health, died on May 30, and Henry, in distant Cracow, succeeded to the French throne as Henry III.

On his return to France, Henry began to negotiate with the Huguenot leaders, La Noue, du Plessis-Mornay and with the leading *politique,* Marshal Damville, who now controlled a large part of southern France. Then, in quick succession, he allied himself with the Guises by a marriage and surrendered actual control of affairs to Catherine. As the culmination of a long story of intrigue with the Huguenots, the ambitious duke of Alençon, Catherine's youngest and favorite son, now, by the death of Charles, dauphin of France and bearer of the title "Monsieur," escaped from court and joined La Noue in Huguenot territory. Catherine, already embarrassed by the king's inattention to affairs of state and the parlous condition of royal finances, feared that Alençon might become leader of the Huguenots and was persuaded that every effort should be made to avoid a decisive war. She was therefore willing to make concessions to the Protestants. The "war" was ended by the edict of Beaulieu (May 6, 1576), which became known as the "Peace of Monsieur." The Protestants gained a diplomatic victory by the confirmation of the liberties they had previously won. The Catholics, on the other hand, remained obstinately determined to crush the heretical movement. The Guises were as active as ever, and the early renewal of the conflict was certain.

One of the consequences of the fifth war of religion and the Peace of Monsieur was the sudden rise to prominence of the Holy League, a grouping of conservatively minded personages and associations devoted to the royal cause and the Catholic faith. Their propaganda was directed by the Jesuits and their natural leader in the early stages of the movement was the duke of Guise. Henry III, sensing that the movement, under Guise's aggressive leadership, might get out of hand and dictate royal policy, proclaimed himself the head of the League (December 6, 1576).

The Sixth and Seventh Wars, 1577–80

AT THE next meeting of the Estates on January 1, 1577, the king repudiated the edict of Beaulieu, and Alençon, now become the duke of Anjou, soon declared his support of the king. As the sixth war began, Damville had swung from neutrality to the royal cause and the Huguenots were again on the defensive. Nevertheless, with some help from Elizabeth of England, the Protestants were able to negotiate for a peace (of Bergerac, September 17, 1577), which left them a measure of religious tolerance and civil status for a few years.

Hostilities began again in 1580, virtually at the insistence of the Catholic clergy. It was more a show of individual valor and horsemanship than a war and brought no change in the positions of the combatants. The laity, who had to fight and pay for the war, would have preferred an uneasy peace to yet another costly and indecisive conflict. Both Henry III (of Valois), the king of France, and Henry III, king of Navarre, were glad to bring hostilities to an end by the peace of Fleix (November, 1580), which restored the conditions of the peace of Bergerac. The Protestants had about held their own. On the other hand, the League and the party of the Guises suffered something of a rebuff when the king rejected their demands for a war of extermination against the Huguenots. Anjou, meanwhile, in addition to paying court to Queen Elizabeth of England, had since 1576 been scheming for the crown of the Netherlands and had been closely cooperating with William of Orange in his struggle against Spain. Consequently, relations between France and Spain were strained. Both Henry III and Catherine realized that the interests of Spain in the Low Countries and the security of France in the north must inevitably clash. Anjou's participation in the wars in Flanders at the head of Huguenot troops and his acceptance, in 1578, of the title "Defender of the liberty of the Low Countries" and, in 1582, of that of duke of Brabant and count of Flanders, did not run counter to the interests of France. Any weakening of Spain's position in the Lowlands would be a gain for France. Anjou's failure to avail himself successfully of the opportunity thus presented to him was attributable, as we have seen, to his faults of character (see above, p. 000). He returned from Flanders and died of consumption in June 1584. Henry III had no children, so that by the death of Anjou, Henry of Navarre became the heir apparent to the French throne. Three weeks after the death of Anjou, William of Orange was assassinated. The Lowlands and France were henceforth to follow divergent paths.

The Catholic League took advantage of the death of Anjou to assume the leadership of the anti-Protestant forces. In January 1585, Philip II of Spain joined with the League in a commitment (made concrete by a large contribution in cash) to accept the cardinal de Bourbon as successor to Henry III, instead of Henry of Navarre. Henry III had no desire to be the tool of the Guises, whom he hated, or of Philip, whom he distrusted, yet was unable, by his own strength, to recapture from the League the effective leadership of the Catholic cause. The duke of Guise's aggressive leadership of the League foretold the complete overshadowing of the king and the reversal of his policy of toleration in the interests of national unity. In July 1585, the king was compelled, much against his will, to sign a treaty at Nemours making Guise and the League the real masters of France. The Protestants became a proscribed sect. The Pope, working in concert with the League, soon declared Henry of Navarre ineligible for the crown of France and formally excommunicated him. Neither the Protestants, for obvious reasons, nor the *politiques* could accept such a solution to the nation's problem, which violated all principles of legitimacy.

The Eighth War: The War of the Three Henries

UNDER these conditions of confusion and conflicting claims and interests, a renewed resort to arms was inevitable. The eighth civil war was on its way, to be known as the War of the Three Henries. Of the leaders, Navarre was a brilliant field general, and had on his side not only the Protestants but most of the moderates of France. The king's forces, on the other hand, offered only halfhearted support to the actions of the League, of which the king was still the nominal head. Paris was ruled by a revolutionary Committee of Sixteen, acting under orders from the duke of Guise. In May 1588, Guise entered Paris in arrogant disregard of the king's express command that he not set foot in the city. The king left Paris a few days later, almost a fugitive from his own capital.

The military successes of the Huguenots and the defeat of the Spanish Armada by England (early August 1588) gave Henry III a respite from the pressure of the League. The Estates met in October, and while it continued in session the cause of the king seemed to be gaining some support. The king had long been determined to eliminate the Guises from the scene. On December 23 the duke was assassinated in the royal castle, and his brother the cardinal was killed the next day. Henry told his mother: "I have killed the king of Paris. I am now king of France." Her reply was to ask if he had made sure of the other French towns. The League, even without the Guises, remained strong, and Henry was still far from secure. He opened negotiations with Henry of Navarre, and a truce was arranged early in April 1589; by the end of the month the forces of the two kings, of France and Navarre, were acting together against the forces of the League. The royal cause was strengthened still further when Pope Sixtus V summoned Henry III to appear in Rome. This summons was, to most Frenchmen, an intolerable interference in French affairs. Out of resentment some of the moderate Leaguers came over to the side of the king. When the royal military campaign seemed on the point of success Henry III was fatally stabbed by Jacques Clément, a Jacobin monk under orders from the League.

Before he died (August 2, 1589), the king designated Henry of Navarre as his successor. The latter was immediately acknowledged as king of France, not only by his own Huguenot followers but by some of the late king's adherents. Navarre was urged, from many sides, in the interests of French unity, to return to the Church of Rome. Unwilling to make so drastic a move at that time, Henry saw himself obliged to continue with depleted forces the war against the League. Most of the soldiers of the late king chose to regard their contract with Henry III as dissolved by his death. In September Navarre met the superior forces of the League at Arques in an engagement which was at least a moral victory. After this showing Henry, reinforced by four thousand English troops from Elizabeth and by other troops attracted to his colors by the promise of success, marched toward Paris. In a pitched battle at Ivry in March 1590, Henry, again with fewer men than his opponents, roundly defeated the army of the League under the duke of Mayenne. Navarre now dominated the field. Paris, however, defied capture, and without the capital a king of France was not fully a sovereign. His siege of Paris was at the point of success as famine within the city weakened resistance, but in September the duke of Parma, Philip II's great general, came to the rescue and Henry had to raise the siege. Henry, realizing that he could not defeat the League upheld by the resources of Spain, called upon England and the German Protestants for substantial help. On the other hand, the Leaguers and, in Paris, the Sixteen were appealing to Philip for more assistance, going so far as to ask him to appoint a ruler for France.

In the meantime, in 1591 and 1592 Henry had a number of successes in the provinces with corresponding increase in his support among the people of France. The League's main ally, the duke of Parma, died in December 1592, and without his aid the League was soon compelled to demand an armistice. Simultaneously Henry declared his readiness to be "instructed" in the Catholic faith. In July the archbishop of Bourges received him into the Church. Henry made no secret of his reasons for leaving the faith in which he had been reared. "Paris is worth a mass" is the expression credited to him. There is little doubt he could have taken Paris by force of arms and crushed the League; but it is not so clear that he would then have ruled over a united France. The spirit of the League and the problem of the Guises would have lingered on to trouble his reign. For years he had witnessed the devastating effect of civil religious war that left France exhausted. He wanted to give her a chance to recover from protracted fratricidal strife. The great majority of the French people were Catholic. He was convinced he could best rule them by being of their confession. He could protect his former co-religionists, the Huguenots, by specific provisions guaranteeing them freedom of worship. Toleration had finally become a respectable principle on which a state could take its stand. Henry next set his hand to the task of reuniting France. By persuasion, bribery, the restrained show of superior force (which he now easily commanded), or by promises of offices in his government, he gradually won over to his side the governors or generals who had, in the chaos of the wars, come to rule over the separate parts of France like petty monarchs. Those who had been *politiques* were naturally the first to join Henry and accept his assurances of nonretaliation. But soon even the young duke of Guise made peace with the king, in return for a bribe of almost four million livres. Paris cost the king 1,700,000 livres. Rouen and its surrounding territory cost even more. Other towns which had resisted Henry were granted remission of taxes in various amounts. In the king's view these sums were well justified, measured by the peace and unity they brought as aids to the security of his throne. Events proved his judgment to be correct. In March 1594, Henry entered Paris in triumph, and by the end of the year most of France acknowledged him as king.

Henry IV in Paris: The Treaty of Vervins and the Edict of Nantes

HENRY did not forget that Philip of Spain had done everything possible to prevent his accession to the throne of France. There were, furthermore, Spanish troops still in France. Henry would not be king of all of France until the Spanish were driven from French soil. Early in 1595 he began the campaign to expel the Spanish. The first fruits of the war were the reconquest of Burgundy. In 1596 the duke of Mayenne, the titular head of the League, came to terms, and Philip, having lost his strongest ally within France, found that all loyal Frenchmen, now behind Henry, regarded the king of Spain as a foreigner and an enemy of the people of France. But though Philip was rejected by Frenchmen as a foreigner, there were many of Henry's former Huguenot co-religionists who resented his conversion to Catholicism and refused to help him in the war with Spain. He was, during this war, often in severe difficulties. The help from Elizabeth and the German Protestants was meager and uncertain. The victory he finally achieved was almost completely his own.

Philip, sensing the futility of further conflict, began to negotiate for peace in October 1597. The Treaty of Vervins between France and Spain was finally signed in May 1598. France recovered everything she had possessed at the Treaty of Câteau-Cambrésis in 1559 and a foothold in Brittany. At about the same time Henry fulfilled his earlier promise to the Huguenot leaders of protection of their faith by issuing the Edict of Nantes (April 13, 1598) confirming previous concessions, guaranteeing liberty of worship in those places where it had actually been exercised by 1597, complete equality of Huguenots and Catholics before the law, and access for Protestants to all public offices. Furthermore, as a guarantee of the execution of these terms, for a period of eight years the Huguenots received one hundred "places of security," which were to be ruled by Huguenot magistrates and garrisons. Only in Paris and for five leagues outside the city were the Huguenots forbidden to assemble or hold religious meetings. The Edict of Nantes was opposed by the assembly of the clergy and the *parlements*. The *parlement* of Paris registered the edict in April 1599, but it was not until 1600 that Henry was able to secure its registration by the *parlements* of Aix and Rennes. The principle of freedom of the individual conscience was not completely new. The edict of 1577 (peace of Bergerac) had proclaimed it in a less precise form. Nevertheless, its formal implementation and guarantees marked a notable advance in the struggle for human freedom. France was alone among the great powers of Europe in accepting the principle. Elsewhere, in Spain, the Empire, and England, it was taken as a matter of course that the ruler had the right to determine the faith of his subjects. The Peace of Augsburg of 1555 remained the classic statement of this assumption: *cuius regio eius religio* was its theme, generally accepted by the governed and the rulers. France must be given credit for an innovation that was ultimately to release the dynamic of religious liberty in the Western world. The fact that the decree had in it dangerous seeds, that it created a kingdom within a kingdom and, by combining qualified religious liberty with excessive local autonomy, crystallized a schism within the French nation was not, at the time, clearly realized. This fault was to cause the successors of Henry, his son Louis XIII and the latter's great minister, Richelieu, serious difficulty.

Peace and Recovery

THE year 1598 marks the end of the first period of Henry's reign. The two important documents signed in that year, the Edict of Nantes and the Treaty of Vervins, ended the internal religious struggles of France and signified the renunciation by Philip II of his hopes to rule, directly or indirectly, the French kingdom. Once these two objectives were attained, Henry was free for the task which, for all of his brilliant military and diplomatic successes, was dearest to his heart, the healing of France's wounds and the restoration of her economic health. Henry's own assessment of what France needed was sound. He was, furthermore, exceptionally fortunate in his choice of an agent to carry out his plans. He found in the Huguenot baron de Rosny, after 1606 the duke de Sully, a servant who was intelligent, resourceful, energetic and incorruptible. Henry made him Superintendent of Finances, then Grand Master of Artillery and Administrator of Roads and Communications. In each post he cut down waste, increased revenue, carried out reforms and made the will of the king effective over a larger sector of French life than had been done since Louis XI. He raised the royal revenue from 23,000,000 livres in 1597 to 39,000,000 in 1609; he recovered much royal domain that had been pledged for loans or allowed to get out of royal control. Petty graft, the traditional vice of bureaucracy, was repressed; industry and trade were encouraged. Roads, canals, and bridges were built, cleared or repaired, ports activated, colonization projected and attempted. Military affairs received careful attention. The peacetime army was reduced in size, arms and personnel were carefully reviewed, and, at a time when most European armies consisted largely of foreign mercenaries, the soldiers in Henry's army were almost all native Frenchmen.

Henry, in the effort to establish his rule and the unity of France, had adopted a policy of leniency toward former enemies, members of the League, even those who had been in the pay of the king of Spain. He had forgiven his enemies much, in the calculated hope that once the cause of France was proven safe in his hands, patriotism would win out over factionalism and fanaticism. His own generosity and honesty were large factors in bringing conviction and confidence to those he was trying to win. In almost every case his judgment of men and his consistent fairness dressed in humor and charm—were proven correct. The exception was the treason of a former companion in arms on whom he had conferred the highest honors in his gift. The duke de Biron, son of a marshal of France, had fought beside Henry, who had twice saved his life. Biron had been made admiral, marshal, governor of Burgundy, and a peer of France by Henry. It was not enough. Biron contracted great gambling debts and, approached by agents of Philip II and later by the duke of Savoy, entered into a conspiracy to take parts of the kingdom of France to form an independent territory. Henry intercepted some of the correspondence and, confronting Biron with his suspicions, sought to get a confession from his friend. He would willingly have forgiven him, in the name of their long comradeship. Biron, arrogant and defiant, refused to confess his guilt. If Henry wished to show he could be firm as well as forgiving, there was nothing for him to do but turn Biron over to the courts and let justice take its course. Biron was executed in July 1602.

The second period of Henry's reign was from 1598 to his untimely death in 1610. During these twelve years Henry was engaged in only one substantial military operation, a short war with the duke of Savoy over a frontier territory between Savoy and France. Henry had some difficulties with his former co-religionists, who wanted more privileges and exemptions than he had given them in the Edict of Nantes. In 1603, in the face of opposition from many Huguenots and some of his advisers, Henry allowed the Jesuits to return to centers from which they had been expelled by *parlements* in 1594. He answered the objections to their return with the remark that he would feel better if he had them in France where he could watch them; in any event he would rather have them as friends than as enemies. He felt that their excellent educational capacities should not be wasted. In his foreign relations Henry maintained the English alliance, though he found both Elizabeth and James I difficult and unpredictable allies. He consistently supported the United Provinces in their struggle against Spain, and on his other frontiers in Italy, Savoy, and around the Mediterranean, he maintained his diplomatic pressure against Philip II and Philip III. Venice was encouraged in her traditionally anti-Spanish attitude; Pope Clement VIII, fretting under Spanish predominance in the peninsula, was given to understand he could rely on French support.

By the last years of his reign Henry had in his control a powerful and enthusiastic nation. Precisely what he planned to do with the efficient machinery of a revived, united and prosperous France is not, to this day, clear. His correspondence indicates his determination that the Protestant powers, England, the Lowlands, and the German Protestant princes, should work together to prevent the Habsburg monarchies in Spain and in the Empire from retaining any vestige of their previous European hegemony. The diplomatic foundation for such a strong Protestant coalition was, in large measure, laid some years before his death. But just how Henry would have proceeded from that point will never be certain. Sully, in his *Memoirs,* written some years after the death of the king, ascribed to Henry a vast plan, the "Grand Design," for a sort of league of European states, of which France, naturally, should be the leader. It is generally agreed that Sully's imagination was more responsible for this "plan" than was Henry, but that Henry was capable of conceiving such a scheme is certain. He was also clear-sighted enough to realize that Europe was not ready for such a submersion of individual aims and interests in a federation for the good of France.

In 1609 Henry became involved in a dispute over the succession of the duchies of Cleves-Jülich, a small group of territories straddling the lower Rhine and therefore of great strategic importance both to the Lowlands and to France. There were several claimants, among them the Habsburg Emperor. Henry succeeded only partially in uniting the Protestant powers against imperial pretensions. The conflict, diplomatic and military, dragged on for many years after the king's death. He was in the midst of preparations for active military action against the Habsburgs when, returning from a conference in the Louvre on March 14, 1610, he was stabbed to death by François Ravaillac, an ardent Catholic who declared he was acting in the interests of the Faith and for the good of France.

Henry's death, in the prime of life, was a staggering blow to France. He had already accomplished almost a miracle, bringing peace with hope for the future to a sadly troubled people. He was without doubt one of the sanest and wisest of the rulers of France. He made some mistakes—the institution of the *paulette,* the system by which government offices could be purchased and handed over to an heir like private property, was a serious error—but there is every likelihood that had he lived much longer he would have corrected some of these mistakes or provided safeguards against abuses arising from them. He had enemies during his lifetime, and at times the bitterness of their attacks on him caused him deep pain and despair. But in the memory of the French people he became, very soon after his death, a symbol of the best that France could produce. His charm, his candor, his humor, his tolerance, even his love affairs, endeared him to the common people of the kingdom. His military valor and his successes, often dramatically won by coolness or craft, accompanied by a dry quip, against odds and superior forces, became legends to the Frenchmen who took pride in a ruler who was such a symbol of victory and glory. On all these grounds Henry was great and fortunate, and was understood by his people. Yet he was even greater as a statesman. His diplomacy, clever, resourceful, patient, imaginative, was dedicated to the task of giving France peace and stability with honor. He knew when to concede, when to demand. He understood the relation of economics to diplomacy, of religion to public morale. A victorious general, he yet dedicated his policies to the avoidance of pointless war and to the attainment of security for his subjects. He remarked once to Sully, "France owes me much. I work hard for her." In Henry the genius of France was personified. It is no wonder the French people mourned his passing. He had restored to them their most precious possession, pride in their country.

Regency and Civil Faction under Louis XIII

THE next fourteen years, until the emergence of Richelieu as principal minister of Louis XIII, constitute one of the sad periods of French history. The assassination of the king was a grievous blow to France's hope for consolidation and political health. Henry's son and heir, Louis XIII, was only nine years of age at the death of his father, and the regency was entrusted to Henry's widow Queen Marie de' Medici. She had none of the qualities necessary for a ruler. She was lazy, avaricious, unintelligent, and completely in the hands of her intimate friend Leonora Galigaï, who, in turn, was subservient to her scheming husband Concini. The ministers of Henry IV were retained in office for a while, but without the king's energy and vision to guide them their administration lacked direction. Neither the queen nor the young king could provide any valid leadership. France was suddenly a country without a head.

The greater nobles saw their opportunity and began to recover from the crown prerogatives and positions which they had lost under Henry's vigorous rule. The first notable break in the anti-Habsburg tradition, now well over a century old, was the arrangement in 1612 by which the young Louis was betrothed to Anne of Austria, daughter of Philip III, and Louis' sister Elizabeth to the Spanish *infante*. Spain thus gained a place in French politics which Henry and his predecessors had carefully prevented since the beginning of the previous century.

The nobles, now well agreed among themselves and against the regent and her court, made strong demands of Marie and obtained concessions from her which made serious inroads on the power of the crown. The queen attempted to buy them off with large bribes out of the treasure Henry had so carefully amassed, but at the Estates General, called in October 1614, the demands by the nobles that the *paulette,* which allowed members of the Third Estate to rise to the nobility by buying high offices, be abolished led to a sharp conflict between the nobility and the Third Estate. Out of this struggle there arose a new alignment of forces in French politics. The Third Estate proclaimed the theory of the supremacy of the king: "holding his crown from God alone, there is no power on earth, spiritual or temporal, which has any right over his kingdom." Since the clergy and the nobility generally voted together, an alignment of court and Third Estate against nobility and clergy was in the making. The nobles were led by the prince de Condé, young and showy, the bearer of a great name but brutal and unprincipled. The royal cause, unfortunately, was led by the queen's hated minister Concini, now governor of Normandy and marshal of France.

The young king, deeply resentful of the scorn with which Concini treated him, decided to rid himself of the minister. On April 24, 1617, a captain of the royal guards, obedient to Louis' suggestion, arranged the assassination of Concini at the entrance to the Louvre. The populace rejoiced. The queen mother was sent out of Paris; the nobles, who had hated Concini, declared for the king; Louis' friend and confidant, the duke de Luynes, appeared to have taken over the governance of the state. In reality it was the Council of State, older ministers, who determined policy. The great nobles, unstable save in their own interests, soon broke out in rebellion against the court. A rebellion in which the Protestants and the queen mother were implicated was foredoomed to failure. The king showed firmness and wisdom in meeting and dispersing the rebels at Pont de Cé (August 1620). The treaty which resulted from this encounter was negotiated, for the queen, by the bishop of Luçon, better known as Richelieu. The preponderance of France in modern Europe owes much to this frail cleric.

Richelieu

SINCE his first appearance in public life at the meeting of the Estates General in 1614, and a short period as a secretary of state for war and foreign affairs in the Royal Council from November 1616 to April 1617, Richelieu had played a very careful role, usually on the side of the queen mother. At the same time he was careful not to close all means of access to de Luynes and the circle around the king. The king had no personal regard for the bishop but recognized his great abilities. Richelieu's dominant idea, early as well as late in his career, was the unity of France. He was persuaded that the queen mother, for all her faults of selfish pettiness in the period after the death of Concini, best represented that ideal. He knew that the circle of fawning courtiers around the king were bitterly and uncompromisingly opposed to a strong central authority. Realizing that the nobility were the enemies of the crown, he strove to bring the queen mother and Louis together to make common cause for a strong France. The reconciliation that took place in 1619 between them was his work, for which he was made a cardinal and principal minister of the king. His career from this point to his death in 1642 belongs to modern history and we shall not follow it further here. Richelieu was the continuer of the work and principles of Henry IV; he was in essence a modern statesman, cool, realistic, foresighted, dedicated to his state, ruthless in pursuit of his goal, the glory of France.

SPAIN: PHILIP II AND PHILIP III—
GRANDEUR AND DECAY

IN THE eyes of the man of the sixteenth century Spain had all the aura of glory, power, and success that a European state could boast. Her hand was in every political action in the known world; her interests were in every land and on every sea; her triumphs were accepted as inevitable; her displeasure was universally feared; her wealth was legendary. Yet we now know that long before the sixteenth century had run its course Spain was a hollow shell, her economy in ruins, her land desolate, her population reduced to penury and decrepitude, her political system a travesty, her religion a show, her morale a pompous sham. Such a tragic descent, continued on into the seventeenth century, cannot have come by natural causes. Great peoples do not wish themselves into sudden and drastic decline. They have to be helped into obscurity by rulers who labor at the job of ruining a nation. The judgment of history has been that Philip II of Spain, called by his contemporaries Philip the Prudent, was in great measure responsible for the decline of Spain in the latter half of the sixteenth century. Had he not been so "prudent," so hard-working and conscientious, so persistent and, by his lights, so nobly motivated, Spain might have recovered from the exhaustion brought on by the decades during which the land had to support the imperial ideas and responsibilities of Charles V.

Philip, the only legitimate son of Charles V, had been carefully trained for his life work by his father. His mother, Isabella of Portugal, had died in 1539 when Philip was only twelve years old. His boyhood had already been grim. He had not been allowed the normal give and take of youthful play. His companions knew that punishment for laying a hand on the prince would be severe. He was put in the hands of several private tutors, no one of whom was either particularly firm or successful. Spanish remained the only language he really knew. His political education came from his father; but in retrospect, adroit as Charles was in practice, his son learned from him only to command, and not to persuade or to lead.

In 1543, when Charles had to leave Spain for Germany, he appointed the sixteen-year-old Philip as regent of the kingdom, and from that moment until ascending the throne in 1556, whether as titular regent or merely as the *infante,* Philip had as his daily concern the affairs of the kingdom and its vast possessions around the world. He became duke of Milan in 1546. In 1548 Charles took him to Germany and the Netherlands, in the hope that the electors might be favorably impressed and disposed to elect him to the imperial throne. Philip, unable to speak German, made a poor impression. He made no secret of his abhorrence of German conviviality and, after two years, he was as glad to leave Germany as the princes were to see him go. In 1554 Charles conferred on him the throne of Naples, so that when, that same year, Philip married Mary Tudor and became by parliamentary grant titular king of England, he was already a king in his own right. By Charles' decree he became vicar of the republic of Siena in 1554, thus manifesting increased Spanish interest in the

Italian peninsula. In October of the next year Charles, with great ceremony, transferred to Philip the suzerainty of the Netherlands, the seventeen provinces of the Burgundian inheritance which lay between France, the Empire, and England. The crowns of Castile and Aragon came to him shortly thereafter (January 1556). By the time he returned to Spain in 1559, never again to leave that sacred soil, he ruled an empire on which the sun never set, whose untapped wealth was his to order and to use for whatever ends he might choose.

The ends he chose are easily discernible. His father's intense devotion to the preservation of the Catholic faith had been transmitted to the son undiminished. Of his sincerity in this matter there has never been any doubt. He was always an obedient son, who admired his father above all other men. But along with Philip's high religious devoutness there ran an absorbing conviction that the cause of God and the Catholic Church was best identified with the cause of Spain. Thus equating Spain and the Christian faith he not infrequently disregarded or indeed opposed the Papacy. He was convinced that his own commission from God had priority over any other. He was persuaded that there was adequate support for this stand in his father's career. Seldom in history have father and son, ruling over a great people, been so similarly motivated or so disastrously certain that the voice of the king was the voice of the Almighty.

Philip's first task was the liquidation of the war with France. France was tired of a profitless conflict, her king anxious to be free to crush the pestilence of Protestantism. England, party to an alliance with Spain carried over from Mary's marriage to Philip, was now ruled by a calculating and realistic Protestant, Elizabeth, and aside from claims to Calais, had nothing to gain from a war on the Continent. The Peace of Câteau-Cambrésis (April 1559) was a welcome conclusion to a war which none of the combatants wished to prolong. It formalized what had been fact for some time: France's withdrawal from Italy and Spanish hegemony in the peninsula. This peace concluded, Philip was at liberty to give his attention to his kingdom and the problems of his global empire.

Philip II Rules the Spanish Empire, 1559–98

PHILIP, no innovator by temperament, on assuming power in 1559 began to rule with the administrative organs left by his father. It was a government of councils, at the top of which stood the Council of State (*Consejo de estado*), consisting simply of officials chosen by the king. They were not hereditary grandees, of whom Charles was always very suspicious, but rather bureaucrats or soldiers, chosen for their personal loyalty and dependence upon the king. The Council was purely consultative; it had no executive responsibility whatever. That power Philip never let out of his hands. It suited Philip's purposes to allow the membership of this Council to be split into two factions. If one faction favored a course of action, the other would certainly oppose it. Out of the discussion Philip felt confident he would have both sides fully explained, and would then make his own decision. Below (in rank though not related in structure or organization) the Council of State were the other Councils: of Castile, Aragon, Italy, Portugal, the Indies, Justice, the Inquisition, the Military

Orders, the Crusade, the Treasury—all of them purely consultative and without more discretionary power than that of recommending action to the king.

Administration in all its branches was Philip's care. It seems incredible that one man could have read reports and recommendations from all over the world, let alone from one kingdom like Castile, and not been crushed under the load. But Philip's marginal annotations are in the documents; his labors were herculean and often futile. Many decisions were handed down months and years after the crisis at the source had been reached and passed. The suppliants or the disputants not infrequently died before Philip got around to their cases, thus making the royal decision an academic matter. Philip was quite aware of these possibilities, yet he consistently refused to delegate authority. Events

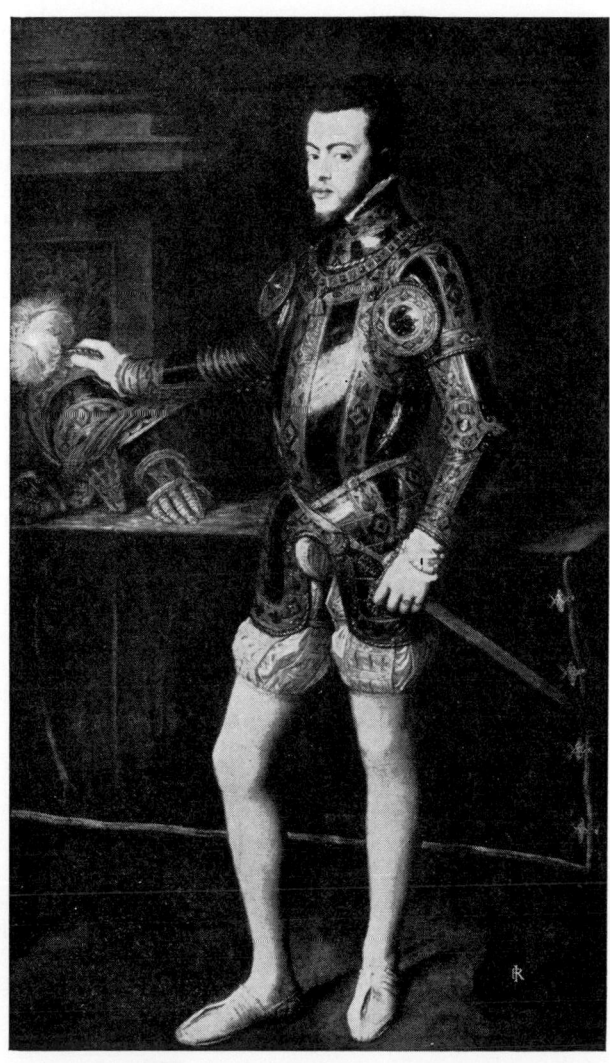

Philip II of Spain, by Titian, in the Prado, Madrid [ANDERSON, ART REFERENCE BUREAU].

could wait until he had read the documents himself and made a royal and therefore correct decision. His secretaries were nothing more than copyists who transcribed his instructions or messengers who brought to him reports of council meetings. The king was above being influenced by a powerful minister; he was also above getting things done. He was far from unintelligent. He simply tried to do what no human being could do under the circumstances. His failure was tragic for Spain.

The Spanish empire—Italy, the Mediterranean, the Netherlands, the lands in the Americas and in the Far East—with its manifold points of friction, posed a whole complex of problems for its ruler. The Spain to which Philip returned in 1559 was seriously in need of quiet, recuperation and guidance toward recovery. Spanish interests touched upon and brought into focus the whole Mediterranean area, the Turks, England, France, the Papacy, the as yet free states of Italy, the Balkan principalities, the Empire, and Protestantism all over the world.

From Charles V Philip inherited a debt that was staggering. Charles' imperial wars and diplomacy were perforce paid for, in great measure, by Castile and Aragon. In 1557 Philip, as regent, had had to fund the debt of approximately seventy million ducats by issuing new interest-bearing *juros* or certificates to creditors. This was the "first decree," which virtually admitted that the government could not meet its obligations from regular revenue. Thereafter lenders demanded higher interest rates and the spiral of decline of government credit thus induced led, in 1575, to the "second decree," suspending all grants of royal revenue. This arbitrary if necessary measure ruined many foreign bankers who had accepted the royal grants as security for their loans, while at the same time making it almost impossible for Philip to borrow money for his wars and diplomacy.

Why did vast amounts of gold and silver bullion brought regularly to Spain from the New World fail to keep Philip's government solvent? Graft and theft eroded this wealth before delivery to the royal treasury. Furthermore, Philip was spending money on military campaigns far from Spain and was obliged to supply his commanders in distant lands with cash to pay their soldiery. Finally, the *alcabala*, a 10 per cent turnover tax, throttled commerce; as the nobility and the Church were exempt from taxation, the weight of taxes fell on a middle class that had no protection and a peasantry already reduced to abject poverty.

The second bankruptcy, that of 1575, precipitated the turn in events we have witnessed in the Lowlands, which enabled William the Silent to unite the provinces in the Pacification of Ghent; it also aroused Philip to an unaccustomed policy of adventure. He added Granvelle, whom he trusted, to the Council of State; he took possession of Portugal (1580) with its rich colonies and assumed a more active attitude toward the internal affairs of France. Philip established Madrid, a city without a distinguished history, as his capital, and in 1563 began to build his own headquarters, the monastic castle El Escorial, a scant thirty miles northwest of Madrid, from which he governed his empire until his death. The liberties of the kingdom of Castile had been radically clipped by the Catholic Kings and by Charles V. Philip had therefore little trouble with the Castilian *Cortes*. Aragon, however, was more obdurate. The

Palace of the Escorial, built by Philip II of Spain [ANDERSON].

Aragonese had had a long history of independent glory, and stubbornly defended their traditions. These rights and liberties were tested in the affair of Antonio Pérez. Pérez, until 1577 a trusted secretary of Philip, was involved in the assassination of a rival, Escobedo. Under trial for irregularities in his handling of royal favors, Pérez was first found guilty and then tried for murder. In 1590 he escaped to Aragon. Unable to extradite him from Aragon to Castile, Philip had to bring charges against him all over again in the Aragonese court. When this procedure failed, Philip called upon the Inquisition. The Aragonese resented this move more than the long legal pursuit, and a revolt against the royal agents, the *Justicia* (Supreme Court of Aragon) and the Inquisition allowed Pérez to escape and take refuge in France (September 1591). The incident shows clearly that up to this time in Aragon the king had none of the absolute power he enjoyed in Castile. Philip took quick action against the insurrection and put it down, forcing the *Cortes* to revise the constitution so as to give the king more, though not yet absolute, authority in governing the land, replacing in essence the power of the higher nobility, who had hitherto ruled the land at their own pleasure. But the spirit of noncompliance remained strong in Aragon.

A young and headstrong king of Portugal, Sebastian, died in an ill-planned and badly led crusade against the Moors in 1578. The next of kin, his aged grand-uncle Cardinal Henry, succeeded to the throne. The next in line was Philip of Spain, through his descent from his mother, Isabella of Portugal. There were, however, other native-born Portuguese claimants, and the natural antipathy of the Portuguese, noble and commoner alike, to being ruled by a Spanish monarch made it necessary for Philip to proceed cautiously if he wished to avoid bitter resistance. The cardinal favored Philip, but died (1580) before any decision could be reached. Philip prepared a military expedition by sea and by land under Alva's command, which, he was sure, would convince the Portuguese, and quickly disposed (July 1580) of the mob assembled to defend Portuguese liberty. The country submitted almost immediately. The Spanish troops were held in tight restraint by Alva, and Philip was in Lisbon in August. Portugal was to be under a Spanish king for the next sixty years. Scrupulously respecting Portuguese sentiment, Philip governed the land through Portuguese officials. Thus, between his conquest of Portugal and the suppression of Aragonese "liberties," Philip brought a high degree of unification to the Iberian peninsula. The commercial aspects of the union of Spain and Portugal in the person of the monarch were not lost on Philip or on his enemies. The Portuguese colonial empire was almost as rich as the Spanish, and to have the ports and produce of both empires available to one European ruler was a fact which England, France, and the Dutch contemplated without pleasure.

It was Philip's most sincere hope that all of his subjects should share the boon of his religious faith. He supported the Inquisition with enthusiasm, rejoicing in its successes and in the *autos da fé* at which the bodies of Protestants or other heretics were burned to save their souls. He had another problem regarding the purity of the faith: the Christianized Moors living in the region of the ancient kingdom of Granada. When they had submitted to conquest in 1492 they had been promised toleration for their faith. Soon toleration had given way to proselytism and enforced baptism. Their Christianity was without much doubt barely skin deep. The Inquisition knew this, and because the Moors worked hard at their agriculture and were rich, their Spanish neighbors, less energetic and therefore less successful, discovered the fact. Repression and annoyance followed, to such a point that in 1568, the Moriscos broke out in rebellion against Spanish persecution. Philip took quick and ruthless vengeance. Thousands of Moriscos were murdered, other thousands reduced to slavery and dispersion (1570). The Morisco "problem" in Granada was temporarily solved and Spain was immeasurably poorer for the loss of the prosperous segment of her population.

Probably no event in Philip's long life has aroused more interest than the story of his first son and heir, Don Carlos, born to Philip's first wife, his cousin Maria of Portugal, in 1545. Carlos was malformed, excitable, and unsteady from his early years, and as he grew older caused Philip many embarrassments. He was abnormally and sadistically cruel to animals and to his servants. A trepanning operation at one point is reported to have saved his life. In the hope that he might recover, Philip had the *Cortes* of Castile accept him as heir to the throne and even began negotiations for his marriage. In 1565, convinced he was being persecuted, Carlos planned to escape from Spain. Obviously Philip could not allow such an unstable hostage to fall into the hands of any of his enemies, and in January 1568, the king personally arrested the boy and had him imprisoned in the royal castle. Six months later Don Carlos was dead, probably from his own excesses or abnormalities. All manner of elaborations upon the known facts have arisen, such as that Philip gave his son a slow poison or had him strangled or beheaded. What is certain is that the Spanish empire could not be allowed to come under the control of an insane monstrosity. Philip had no need to do more than imprison such an offspring. The succession could thereafter be easily arranged. Philip's four marriages were all directly related to Spanish foreign policy. The first, to Maria of Portugal, was later used to justify the conquest of Portugal. The second (1554–58), to Mary Tudor, was an outcome of Charles' anti-French policy. The third (1559–68), to Elizabeth of Valois, was intended by Philip as a check on French ambitions. The fourth (1570–80), to Anne of Austria, was an attempt to bind the Habsburg family and interests together.

Philip's Foreign Relations

PHILIP quickly found that Spain's success and prowess, earned by Charles V, brought her enemies. He was surrounded by them. His foreign policy was, in the main, a constant effort either to keep one enemy at war with another, or to ally with one or the other in order to maintain Spanish hegemony. A third and more expensive recourse was war. Philip, who had made peace with France in 1559, followed the course of the French wars of religion with deep interest. Regarding the Huguenots as his enemies, he sided with the Guises and the League from the beginning. In 1565 Granvelle, acting for Philip, met Catherine de' Medici at Bayonne and tried to revive the plan of having the two great Catholic powers, France and Spain, follow a single policy of extermination of Protestant heresy. Catherine was sagacious enough to see that under such conditions France would be playing Philip's game. She remarked drily: "I see that the duke of Alva wants the whole world to dance to his master's tune" and refused Philip's demand for a war of extermination of the Huguenots. Philip was encouraged by the Massacre of St. Bartholomew's day (1572) to think that at last France would be safely in the Catholic fold. His agents in France even frequently advanced his claims to the French throne in the name of his Valois wife. Henry III, angered by Guise dominance and swagger, had the duke of Guise murdered (December 1588). The next year Henry himself was assassinated and the Catholic party seriously thought of Philip as Henry III's successor; Philip himself played with the idea, but the firm and adroit diplomacy as well as success in the field of Henry of Navarre forced Philip to drop any thought of obtaining the crown for himself. Instead, he considered marrying his daughter Isabella, a granddaughter of Henry II and therefore niece of the last three kings of France, to a French prince and even having her declared queen. The Estates General of France of January 1593 heard Philip's envoy clumsily present the case for Isabella and rejected it quickly. Thereafter the possibility of a Spanish monarch on the French throne steadily diminished. Yet, by his interference Philip had cast a definite weight in the balance of the French religious settlement. His support of the League had made it certain that France would not turn Protestant. Had not Henry of Navarre become a Catholic it is quite probable that the Spanish line, in one form or another, would have been on the French throne. Philip's failure in France was, in that case, only half a failure. By the Treaty of Vervins (March 1598) Henry gave

Philip a certain consolation for his setbacks, in that the latter's daughter, the *infanta* Isabella, was recognized, jointly with the Austrian Archduke Albert, cardinal archbishop of Toledo, as heiress of Flanders. The *infanta* and the archduke were to marry, and in the event they had no issue, the title should revert to the crown of Spain.

The position of Spain as a Mediterranean power was critically exposed. Charles V had had only a qualified success in defending the Spanish interests in Italy, the isles of the western Mediterranean and the seaboard of Spain, and his defense had cost him dearly. In 1556 Tripoli had been captured by the Turks from the Knights of St. John. Philip planned to recapture Tripoli for Christianity and thus, between Sicily, Malta, and Tripoli, control the passage from the eastern to the western Mediterranean. A naval expedition sent against the Turks in March 1560 was humiliated and five thousand men taken prisoner. The Turks then attacked Malta (summer of 1565) but were beaten back by the gallant defense of the Knights of St. John. In 1570 the Turks attacked Cyprus and took two key cities. Pope Pius V, regarding the struggle as a common Christian defense against the infidel, induced Philip to join with the Venetians and the Papacy in an anti-Turkish Holy League (1571). Don Juan, Philip's half brother, was named to command the combined fleet, which, when assembled, counted 208 galleys, 6 galleases, 24 other ships, and almost 30,000 troops. On October 7, 1571, the fleets, about equally matched, met in the Bay of Lepanto in the Gulf of Corinth. Don Juan immediately attacked, and, after three hours of fierce hand-to-hand combat on the decks of ships grappled together, every Turkish ship but one was taken, burned or sunk. Over 10,000 Christians, held as galley slaves on the Turkish ships, were freed. Eight thousand Turkish sailors were killed, another 8,000 were taken captive. It was a proud victory. Cervantes, who lost the use of his left hand from an arquebus shot, spoke of it as "the noblest occasion that past or present eras have seen or the future may hope to see." The Christian allies lost 7500 men and over a dozen ships. Some, perhaps most, of the possible benefits from the victory were canceled by Philip's withdrawal from the alliance, but not less by the willingness of Venice to come to an accommodation with the Turks. A clear gain was the knowledge that the Turks could be soundly beaten. The myth of their invincibility was exploded. Philip took Tunis in 1573 and the western Mediterranean was thereafter safe from Turkish control.

Philip's relations with the Papacy were conditioned on the two foci of their contact: Italy, where Philip was the most powerful secular sovereign, and Spain, where Philip, not less than Henry VIII in England, regarded himself as head of the Church. During the last days of the Council of Trent the Spanish delegates on Philip's instructions had stood firm against papal control of the Council, and the king incurred thereby the strong dislike of both Paul IV and Pius IV. On many issues throughout the long reign of Philip II the Papacy and the king differed sharply. The Papacy frequently accused the Spanish Inquisition of violating proper canons of procedure, yet was unable to enforce its censure. Philip always supported the Inquisition. In spite of the tension resulting from the presence of the Spaniards both north and south of the Papal States and Spanish independence of papal guidance in religious and ecclesiastical policy, the Papacy had to accept the fact that Spain was the great bulwark of the Catholic faith and the only power upon whose permanent fidelity the Church could count.

Philip's relations with England passed through several stages. The Anglo-Spanish alliance, favored and arranged by Charles V and realized in the bizarre marriage of Philip and Mary Tudor in 1554, was obviously aimed at Charles' Continental rival, France. After Mary's death in 1558 and Philip's return to Spain, he was realistic enough to wish to maintain as long as possible the essence of the alliance in spite of the fact that Mary's successor, Elizabeth, was a Protestant. So long as France remained a threat to Spanish hegemony in Europe, the English alliance was wise. After the Treaty of Câteau-Cambrésis (1559) brought the two Catholic powers together in a crusade against Protestantism, England became less necessary to Spain's fortune. Yet Philip continued to maintain friendly relations with Elizabeth. The gradual estrangement followed upon Philip's marriage to Elizabeth of Valois (the daughter of Catherine de' Medici), and his increasing interest in the cause of Mary Stuart, whom he came to support as Elizabeth's successor and even supplanter on the throne of England. This development coincides with the growth of the conviction in England and in the mind of Elizabeth that England would eventually have to support the cause of William of Orange against Philip and Spanish rule in the Low Countries.

Relations between Spain and England became gradually more strained, until in 1568 Elizabeth's ambassador to Madrid was expelled from the country. War was barely avoided, while on the high seas and in the Spanish Americas Elizabeth's sea captains, mainly Drake and Hawkins, raided ports and captured Spanish vessels bearing treasure which soon turned up in England, some of it in Elizabeth's coffers. For years there were mutual recriminations and harassments, more or less serious; yet neither side wanted or could afford open war. Nevertheless, as Elizabeth increased her aid to the rebellious Dutch and the French Huguenots, Philip's advisers pressed him to conquer England for the Church and to release Mary Stuart from her imprisonment and put her on the throne. In June 1586, Mary formally accepted Philip as her heir to the English throne, and Philip decided upon an expedition to crush the heretic Elizabeth. The Grand Armada was the result. Its story and its sequel have been told (see above, p. 712). After this humiliation Philip subsided for a while, but in 1595 he returned to the attack, this time hoping to damage England through support of the Irish rebels. But before an expedition could be organized, an English fleet attacked Cádiz (June 1596), destroyed all shipping in the port, and sacked the city. In spite of the third bankruptcy of Spain, which struck the country in this year, Philip continued his war against France until, by the Treaty of Vervins, a peace of exhaustion was welcomed by all participants. As peace was being made Philip lay dying in agony in the gloomy palace of the Escorial. He had, laboring incessantly and with unexampled courage and devotion, devastated Spain, isolated the peninsula from the intellectual currents of Europe, broken whatever spirit of freedom may have been left alive by his father, fastened the Inquisition upon his people, driven out of the land many of its best elements, by his long wars deprived the home population of its best blood, and helped to fix the political framework of Europe for the next three centuries.

Philip III, 1598–1621

PHILIP II was succeeded by his son Philip III, then twenty years of age, who turned the ruling of Spain and his empire over to his favorite, the duke of Lerma. The new actual ruler adopted a more active and spectacular policy than Philip had followed, and met with some singular humiliations. The war in the Netherlands, in spite of the brilliance of Spain's great general, the Genoese Spinola, was carried on with little gain and at great expense. The war with England on the sea resulted in the loss of several large Spanish fleets, and the expeditions to aid the Irish rebellion, begun with some hope of success, ended in defeat and costly withdrawal. Henry IV of France regarded the Treaty of Vervins as a mere truce, and, still encircled by Spanish lands (the Spanish Lowlands, Milan, and Spain), was waging a diplomatic war in preparation for a military effort which he hoped would break Spain's power. Only his death in 1610 saved Spain from this attack. In Henry Spain had to deal with a formidable soldier as well as an astute diplomat. It may be idle to speculate on the outcome of such a conflict between Henry IV and a decaying Spain, but it is difficult to imagine Henry in the role of a defeated general.

The accession of James I to Elizabeth's throne in 1603 brought a change in England's attitude toward Spain. James had no personal reasons to hate Spain, as had Elizabeth, the frequent object of plots against her life financed by Spanish gold. James was interested in peace and in marriage alliances that would strengthen the position of England in Continental politics. He bestowed a daughter on the Elector of the Palatinate and hoped to marry his son Charles to a Spanish princess. From 1604, when a treaty ended the long war with Spain, England and Spain were at peace. This was perhaps more to the profit of Spain than of England, but it was in any event a gain for both. The Dutch, still at war with the Habsburg rulers in the Lowlands, were soured by England's defection from the Protestant cause.

A Spanish war against the duke of Savoy, Charles Emmanuel, who had seized the marquisate of Montferrat, situated at an important crossroads in the Savoy Alps, had an indifferent success. Montferrat was of strategic interest to neighboring Milan, and Spanish troops, according to their custom, defeated the duke of Savoy (1616). The peace of Pavia (1617), under French pressure, returned Savoy's lands to the duke, but Montferrat was given to the duke of Mantua. Venice, which had been gradually expanding westward in the Po valley, was an inevitable enemy of Milan. Venice had a long tradition of alliance with France, and Henry IV had been glad to support Venetian claims as the Republic of Venice moved westward toward the Spanish-held Milanese. The Spanish lifeline for the transit of troops and supplies from the Mediterranean bases to Habsburg Tyrol and imperial seats of war, ran through the Val Telline, northeast of Milan. Spanish interests demanded that this lifeline not be cut or placed at the mercy of the enemies of Spain. The threat of friction at this point was chronic; on several occasions there was actual if undeclared war between Venice and the Spanish governors of Milan. The question of the control of the Val Telline was not to be finally settled until 1631, by the diplomacy of Richelieu, and then in France's favor.

In 1601, in a specious effort to bring prosperity to a desolated part of Spain, the duke of Lerma had the capital moved from Madrid to Valladolid in Old Castile. The benefits of the move went mostly into Lerma's pocket. He had vast properties in and around Valladolid which he sold to courtiers after selling them empty offices and titles which permitted them to remain at court and continue as useless appendages to an already overloaded bureaucracy. Apart from the display and extravagance of Lerma and his family and friends, which further burdened Spain with debt beyond her power to redeem, the expulsion of the Moriscos was the most significant event in Spanish internal affairs during the rule of Philip III. Lepanto had put an end to Turkish claims to rule the Mediterranean, but it had not arrested piracy nor stopped Moorish and Berber corsairs from making raids upon the Spanish coast. Several more expeditions, between 1601 and 1604, outfitted at great expense, against Algiers, the center of Moorish piracy, failed, owing to incompetent leadership or cowardice, so that Spanish arms were for a time regarded with contempt. Another expedition, in 1608, was more successful, defeating a pirate fleet in the Gulf of Tunis. But this victory won only a temporary respite. The coasts of Spain were not yet safe from corsairs, and the daring of the Moors kept the southeastern ports of Spain in a state of continual terror. The population of Spain's southern and eastern coasts was in large part of Moorish extraction, and the raiders could count on sympathy, information and even active assistance. Measures of persecution taken under Charles V and Philip II in Granada had indeed moved many thousand Moriscos inland, but in the neighboring kingdom of Valencia and Andalusia there remained, nominally Christian, over half a million subjects of Moorish blood, enough to form an unassimilable alien and anti-Spanish core, dangerous in time of war, in time of peace so prosperous as to excite the envy and hatred of their pure Spanish neighbors. As a part of his perpetual warfare with the Habsburgs, Henry IV of France had given some aid to the Morisco plans for revolt. They had thus become an international liability to Spain. On September 22, 1609, a royal edict decreed expulsion to north Africa of the whole Moorish population of Valencia. Their properties were confiscated and they were allowed to take with them only what they could carry. Estimates vary as to how many Moriscos actually were deported, but a conservative judgment would put the number at 200,000 from Valencia alone. Lerma and his family and hangers-on profited handsomely from the sale of Morisco property he confiscated, but Spain lost, once again,* an energetic and productive segment of her population. Lerma extended the expulsion to the other provinces of Spain, thus increasing his share of Spanish booty and impoverishing the land. The total expulsions must have reached between 200,000 and 500,000 "new" Christians. The economic loss, in addition to the social and moral damage such an act of fanatic violence did to the Spanish state, is beyond calculation. It was a factor in the increasingly rapid decline of Spain as a world power that followed the expulsion.

One thing may be said in favor of Lerma's regime: he was fond of show and spectacle, but not of war. He concluded peace for Philip III where Philip II would have hung grimly on, win or lose. The sense of religious obligation which characterized Philip II was completely lacking in Philip III and Lerma.

* For the expulsion of the Jews in 1492, see above, p. 420.

Spain, therefore, enjoyed more peace under them than under Philip II, and the vast burden of war expenses was, for the time being, lessened. In 1618, after twenty years of virtual control of Spain, Lerma fell from royal favor and was allowed by Philip to retire with a cardinal's hat. His son, the duke of Uceda, who had conspired to remove his father from power, took his place and, in turn, enriched himself and his friends at the expense of the commons and the nobles of Spain.

The social, political, moral and economic picture of Spain in the last years of the sixteenth and the first decades of the seventeenth century is somber and depressing. Yet in literature and the arts the period is still a part of the Golden Century (*siglo de oro*) of Spanish civilization. This remarkable manifestation of vitality and genius is discussed in another connection (see below, Chapter 26). Any concurrence of genius and decay has always attracted the attention of analysts of cultural vigor and decline. Here we must simply point out that by the death of Philip III in 1621 Spain, though still regarded as the first power of Europe, the arbiter of causes, the protagonist of internal Catholicism and the great defender of the faith once delivered to the saints, was in reality a crumbling façade. Twelve years of relative peace under Philip III were not enough to repair the ravages of a century and a half of drain and strain.

SUGGESTIONS FOR FURTHER READING

ARMSTRONG, E., *French Wars of Religion*. Oxford, 1904

BAIRD, H. M., *History of the Rise of the Huguenots*. 2 vols. New York, 1909

BATIFFOL, L., *The Century of the Renaissance*. New York, 1920

GRANT, A. F., *The French Monarchy, 1483–1789*. Cambridge, 1905

MARIÉJOL, J. H., *La Vie de Marguerite de Valois, reine de Navarre et de France*. 1928

McKINNON, J., *Rise and Decline of the French Monarchy*. New York, 1902

PALM, F. C., *Religion and Politics in Sixteenth-Century France*. Boston, 1927

SEDGWICK, H. D., *Henry of Navarre*. London, 1930

SEDGWICK, H. D., *The House of Guise*. New York, 1938

THOMPSON, J. W., *The Wars of Religion in France*. Chicago, 1909

VAN DYKE, P., *Catherine de Medicis*. 2 vols. New York, 1923

WHITEHEAD, A. M., *Gaspard de Coligny: Admiral of France*. London, 1904

ALTAMIRA Y CREVEN, R., *A History of Spanish Civilization*. London, 1930

BALLESTEROS Y BERETTA, A., *Historia de España y su influencia en la historia universal*, Vol. IV. 1927

CASTRO, A., *The Structure of Spanish History*. Princeton, 1954

DAVIES, R. T., *The Golden Century of Spain, 1501–1621*. London, 1954

HAUSER, H., *La Prépondérance espagnole (1559–1660)*. 1940

HUME, M. A. S., *Spain: Its Greatness and Decay (1479–1788)*. Cambridge, 1898

LOTH, D. G., *Philip II of Spain*. New York, 1932

MARAÑON, G., *El Conde-duque de Olivares*. 1952

MARIÉJOL, J. H., *Philip II, the First Modern King*. New York, 1933

MERRIMAN, R. B., *The Spanish Empire*, Vol. IV. New York, 1934

PEERS, E. A., *Spain: A Companion to Spanish Studies*. London, 1929

SLOCOMBE, G., *Don John of Austria, the Victor of Lepanto (1547–1578)*. London, 1935

TURBERVILLE, A. S., *The Spanish Inquisition*. London, 1932

YEO, M., *Don John of Austria*. London, 1934

CHAPTER TWENTY-SIX

SCIENCE, EDUCATION, AND ART

HE scholars of the fifteenth century were primarily interested in the recovery of the thought and atmosphere of classical antiquity. The discovery and copying of manuscripts of the works of Latin and Greek
authors challenged their attention to the exclusion of almost any other subject.
With the invention of printing by movable type soon after 1450 the concentration on the mere manual labor of copying began to taper off. The interest in
things classical, however, remained, and the printing press provided easily accessible texts of ancient writings. With the reproduction of the great works of
Greek science, the curiosity of the Renaissance scholar as to the universe about
him and what the giants of the past had thought about it was assuaged. Pliny's
Natural History was printed in Venice in 1469, the *Botany* of Theophrastus in
1469, the *Writers on Life on the Land* (*De re rustica*) in 1472, also in Venice,
Frontinus' *On Aqueducts* at Rome in 1486, Dioscorides, in Latin translation at
Venice in 1499. Euclid appeared in a Latin translation in Venice in 1482 and
frequently thereafter. A Latin abridgement of Ptolemy's *Almagest* was published in Venice in 1496. A complete text of Aristotle and Theophrastus' *On
Plants* appeared in 1495 and 1496, a collection of *Ancient Astronomers* in 1499,
all in Venice. A Latin translation of Galen's medical works came out in
Venice in 1490 and again in 1541, and frequently elsewhere during the sixteenth
century. It appeared in the original Greek in Venice in 1525. Strabo's *Geography*
appeared in Latin translation at Venice in 1516; Hippocrates in Latin translation in Rome in 1525 and in the Greek original at Venice the following year.
The *Physics* of Archimedes was published in Basel in 1544. These and many
other editions of scientific works of antiquity were at the disposal of scholars
during the last years of the fifteenth and the early years of the sixteenth centuries. A knowledge of what the ancients had said about natural phenomena
was, of course, interesting and at times suggestive, but by itself did not answer
many scientific questions. Experimentation, facilitated by advanced techniques,
was necessary to further development of all the sciences. In increasing
measure this was to be the contribution of the sixteenth and following
centuries.

SCIENCE

THE turbulent events of the early Reformation and the wars of the Habsburg-Valois conflict may help to explain the fact that little progress in original scientific research and discovery was made from about 1450 to about 1540. Men's minds were occupied with the events and concerns of a world in tense confusion.* Yet we must allow also for the fact that the powerful tradition of authority which the ancient writers enjoyed over the thought of Renaissance man had not yet been broken. Their teachings were revered, and it was simply assumed that they were right. Their works were therefore read and studied avidly, uncritically. In this acceptance of authority the Renaissance man resembled his medieval predecessor. The authority of the Church and of Aristotle had merely given place to that of classical authors. Doubt as to the validity of the conclusions of the Greek and Latin writers was impermissible. It would take more than this century to convince Western thinkers that the whole of the physical universe had to be looked at afresh, with new instruments and on new assumptions.

The period that followed this Renaissance area from 1450 to the middle of the sixteenth century was to be infinitely more productive in the areas of physical science than its predecessor. It would produce many men of unmistakable genius. True, most of the progress ran against the current of established thought, entrenched in the Church and hardly less in the educational institutions. But progress was made; the Church and the vested interests had to yield. We shall concern ourselves here only with those fields in science which produced great changes and advances in theory and techniques: notably astronomy, physics, mathematics, biology, and medicine.

In any history of Western culture and thought the year 1543 looms large. Two revolutionary books were published: Copernicus' *On the Revolutions of the Celestial Bodies* (*De revolutionibus orbium celestium*) and Vesalius' *On the Structure of the Human Body* (*De fabrica humani corporis*). Copernicus made comprehensible to the mind of man the vast panoply of heavens. Vesalius led man to look within himself at the wonders of his own body.

Astronomy: The Copernican Revolution

NICHOLAS COPERNICUS (1473–1543) was born in Toruń (Thorn) in Poland, the son of a Polish father and a Polish-speaking German mother. His uncle, before becoming bishop of Ermeland (Warmia) in Prussia, had studied at Bologna. Realizing the capacities of the boy, the bishop sent him to the University of Cracow, where he was attracted to the study of astronomy, which was, at this point, a mixture of Aristotelian authority and astrological mumbo jumbo. In

---

* It is not here intended to minimize the work of Leonardo da Vinci (1460–1529). He anticipated much of the work of Galileo. But he appeared to his time as a clever mechanic and artist rather than as a theoretician dealing with basic scientific concepts. See above, pp. 396–98.

1496 Copernicus returned to Toruń; then, at his uncle's behest, he set out for Bologna to prepare for an ecclesiastical career. Although ostensibly studying canon law, he became a friend of the professor of astronomy and probably lived in his house. While at Bologna he was made a canon of his uncle's cathedral, so that he had a sufficient income to continue his studies in Italy. He spent the year 1500 in Rome, from whence he went to Padua to study medicine. He returned to Ermeland in 1506 and for the next six years the tower of Heilsberg Castle, his uncle's episcopal residence, was his observatory and his home. Upon the death of his uncle in 1512 he moved to Frauenberg, the seat of the bishopric, and lived near the cathedral. He was a busy and responsible member of the chapter, which had frequent occasion to make use of his fine legal training.

Copernicus spent most of his time in one of the turrets of the castle, since known as Copernicus' Tower. It was there he made his observations and developed his ideas. His instruments were essentially similar to those used by Ptolemy sixteen hundred years before, and any real accuracy was out of the question. He could measure the meridian altitude of the sun and the altitude of bodies in the sky, but hardly more. Competent in a number of fields, as physician, as acting administrator of the diocese, in currency reform, and in the reform of the calendar, his greatest work was in rethinking on a basis of his observations the question of the centricity of our planetary system. Since the time of Ptolemy of Alexandria in the second century A.D., it had been accepted that the sun and the planets revolved about the earth. Copernicus became convinced

Copernicus, copy of self-portrait, by Tobias Stimmer (1571) on the astronomical clock tower, cathedral of Strassburg [PHOTO OEUVRE NOTRE-DAME, STRASBOURG].

that such a theory was untenable. He saw too many objections to a geocentric system. The irregularities in the orbits of the five planets, besides the sun and the moon, had necessitated the addition of scores of separate transparent spheres within which the planets were supposed to move. To Copernicus this recourse to additional spheres seemed unreasonable. He came to believe that the sun, not the earth, was the center of our planetary system. On this assumption the eccentric orbits of the planets, including the earth, could be understood and accurately calculated. He spent thirty years on a book describing this discovery. A brief and preliminary discussion appeared in 1530, but the major treatment was barely finished before his death thirteen years later. A copy of the final work (printed in Nürnberg) was put in his hands on his deathbed. Great and revolutionary as the work was, it contained much that was medieval. Copernicus accepted much from Aristotle and his Arabic commentators: no little part of the data he used was old and inaccurate. His theory was his contribution; its simplicity, as opposed to the intricate multitude of spheres of the Ptolemaic system, was its charm. A whole century would pass before his theories were completely documented and even longer before they were universally accepted. The first edition included a preface written by a Lutheran pastor into whose hands the manuscript had fallen, which represented the new theory as only a suggested alternative to the accepted Ptolemaic construction. Thus at first opposition was less determined than might have been expected.

Inevitable inaccuracies and inadequacies in Copernicus' data impeded ready acceptance by men of science. A Danish astronomer, Tycho Brahe (1546–1601), after years of observation and study at an observatory he had built on an island between Denmark and Sweden, published a description of his ingenious astronomical instruments in 1598; another work, listing the position of 777 (later raised to 1000) fixed stars, was published by John Kepler after Tycho's death. Whereas Tycho had the sun and moon revolving around the earth, Kepler had the five planets revolving around the sun, a strange compromise between Ptolemy and Copernicus. The data Tycho so carefully assembled were to be used by Kepler and Galileo to corroborate Copernicus' heliocentric theory and to correct it in detail. The carefulness of his observation and calculation may be judged from the fact that he estimated the length of the solar year within one second. Without electronic devices such accuracy is amazing.

When Tycho left Denmark to settle in Germany and, for a while, in Prague, he had as assistant a young Württemberger, John Kepler (1571–1630), who had hoped to become a Protestant pastor. Trained to close and patient observation by Tycho Brahe, Kepler was later appointed Tycho's successor as imperial mathematician and excelled his master in his imaginative search for mathematical formulae. He defended Copernicus and gave the theories of the Pole a substantial observational basis. His imagination, however, sometimes went wild, giving rise, along with intuitions that were brilliantly correct, to much scientific nonsense. He wrote to Galileo, for example, that there could be only six planets because there were only five regular polyhedrons which could describe their orbits and the distance between them. His great work may be summed up in his famous three laws of which two were given to the world in 1609 in his *New Astronomy:* First, the planet's orbit is an ellipse, of which the sun is one focus. Second, planets do not move at uniform speeds, but a straight line between the planet and the sun sweeps out equal areas in equal periods of time. Third, the squares of the periods of revolution of any two planets around the sun are proportional to the cubes of their distance from the sun. The third law was published ten years later (1619) in his *Epitome of Copernican Astronomy*. These laws were not based on flights of the imagination, but were deduced from the patient observations of Brahe, which Kepler inherited from his master, supplemented by his own. The laws of mechanics which would explain why a planet moved in an ellipse and not in a circle were still hidden from Kepler. Science moves forward by measured steps, one gain at a time.

Kepler was also interested in the phenomena of optics, and wrote a book on *Dioptrics* discussing refraction and propounding the first correct theory of vision. His greatest contribution lay in the application of hypothesis to observation and the persistent investigation into mathematical relations between theory and "actual" and observed phenomena.

His contemporary, the Florentine Galileo Galilei (1564–1642), was a combination of ingenious mechanic and mathematical philosopher. He studied at the University of Pisa, where he was more interested in the things around him than in the authorities who resided in books. He became a professor of mathematics at the university in 1589, but in 1592 he moved to Padua, where he was a professor at the university for eighteen years. Well before 1596 he had become an adherent of the Copernican heliocentric theory and was in frequent correspondence with Kepler at Prague. His first scientific interests had been in mechanics and dynamics. Early in his academic life he found some of Aristotle's physical theories untenable, particularly those concerning falling bodies. In 1591 he is reported to have shown his students at Pisa, by dropping two objects, one of one pound the other of 100 pounds, which reached the ground simultaneously, that Aristotle's statement that rate of fall was related to the weight of the falling object was false.* Pursuing this line of critical investigation, Galileo laid the foundation of modern dynamics, dealing with acceleration and deceleration, projectiles and their trajectories, the composite of forces. The final statement of these discoveries was to be the work of Isaac Newton (1642–1727), but Galileo provided the data and in many cases almost the precise formulation of the relations between force, motion, and inertia.

In 1609 he constructed a telescope which magnified thirty times, enabling him to discover many stars hitherto invisible to the naked eye. When, in 1610, he announced that he had discovered four of the satellites of Jupiter, the professors in Florence refused to look through his telescope. He also constructed a crude microscope with which he observed the anatomy of insects.

In 1616 Galileo was ordered by the Inquisition to forsake his opinion that the earth revolved around the sun, the immovable center of the planetary system. At the same time Copernicus' *On the Revolutions* was condemned "until corrected." Galileo refrained from any open violation of the order; he had much in other fields to occupy his time and mind. Yet he was not completely silenced. He published in 1623 *Il Saggiatore* (*The Balancer* or *The Assayer*), in which

---

* This incident is reported by his earliest biographer. It is now generally accepted that it never took place, at least in these circumstances. The facts may have seemed to him too commonplace to need such a dramatization. He does, however, describe in the *Discourses* the experiment of rolling a brass ball down an inclined plane to measure acceleration.

he expounded his belief that the secret of understanding nature in any of her manifestations was measurement. "But I hold," he said, "that there exists nothing in external bodies for exciting tastes, smells and sounds, but size, shape, quantity and motion." In 1630, after years of painstaking labor, he finished his great *Dialogue Concerning the Two Systems of the Universe, the Ptolemaic and the Copernican.* His principal point was an insistence that nature, that is, the physical universe, must be understood as functioning on a basis of uniformity. Similar causes will have similar effects. Published two years later, it was regarded as a massive and aggressive defense of the Copernican theory. Its sale was almost immediately prohibited and the author was again summoned before the Inquisition in Rome. He recanted; but as the whole world knew that the recantation was forced, no one paid much attention to it. He was sentenced to silence and perpetual imprisonment. He retired to Florence to study; in 1638 his last and definitive work, the *Discourses on the Two New Sciences,* appeared in Amsterdam. In this work Galileo summed up his best thought on dynamics and included everything that he had discovered of use to the engineer or the physical scientist. Soon thereafter he went blind, and his research was greatly restricted, but in the last years of his life he enjoyed the recognition that came to him from scholars in Italy and abroad. The Inquisition was able to obstruct the spread of Galileo's views in Italy; elsewhere his findings found general acceptance and his prodigious scholarship was generously praised. In the final analysis, his concept of the universe as a machine, obeying fixed laws of force which had only to be understood by observation and mathematical rationalization, was to influence not only astronomy and physics but all other sciences as well.

Biology: Vesalius and Harvey

IN BIOLOGY and medicine this tremendous influence coalesced with a previous tendency toward more careful observation and description. The herbals of the later Middle Ages already showed a high accuracy of observation, and the early printed herbals continued the trend. In Conrad of Megenberg's *Book of Nature* (first printed in 1475), woodcuts gave the reader a visual guide to the written description of plants and animals. Another German, Otto Brunfels (d. 1534), published in 1530 an herbal with illustrations made by a pupil of Albrecht Dürer. Jerome Bock of Strassburg (d. 1554) produced in 1539 an improved illustrated book of plants in the region, which showed a more mature scientific approach. No effort was made to compare German flora to the ancient Greek, a comparison that could lead only to confusion. Three years later a Tübingen professor and practicing physician, Leonard Fuchs (d. 1566), published in Basel a catalogue of plants arranged alphabetically, illustrated by 515 woodcuts. He contributed nothing to scientific classification, but his illustrations were more accurate as well as more realistic than those of his predecessors. These pioneers in descriptive botany had numerous followers, and the latter part of the century was rich in treatments of all phases of biological science. This was a period when observation had taken the place of authority, and in this respect parallels the development we have noticed in astronomy, physics, and mechanics from Copernicus to Galileo.

The most brilliant of the biological observers was the Fleming Andreas Vesalius (1514–64), the accurate detail of whose anatomical illustration marked an epoch in the history not only of human anatomy but of all descriptive biological study. Dissection of the human body had been legalized at the University of Salerno in the thirteenth century, to take place as a public exercise once in five years. In 1308 the medical faculty at Padua was allowed to dissect one body a year. At this rate progress in the study of human anatomy was certain to be fairly moderate. By the time of Leonardo da Vinci control was further relaxed, and Leonardo alone dissected over thirty bodies. His purpose was partially artistic, partially scientific. His notebooks, containing his drawings and descriptions, were not published until 1898, and consequently had no influence upon the science of the sixteenth century. There were, however, several competent and careful anatomists between Leonardo and Vesalius; but the work of the latter was so far ahead of theirs that they may be passed over without affecting the continuity of our account.

Vesalius was early interested in anatomy, and when at eighteen years of age he left his native Belgium to study at Paris, he was already expert in what was then known on the subject. He had hardly matriculated at the medical faculty of the University of Paris when, impatient with the awkward dissecting of the barber illustrating a professor's lecture, he brushed him aside and proceeded to perform the dissection as he thought it should be done. Returning to Belgium after three years, he was an army surgeon for a while, then went on to Padua, the most famous school of medicine in Europe. His ability was quickly recognized and he was appointed to teach anatomy. His methods were new. Where, previously, professors had taught by reproducing the text of Galen, Vesalius taught anatomy from the body on the table which he personally, and not some clumsy barber, would deftly dissect before the students' eyes.

He began to write his great work at the age of twenty-three; by his twenty-eighth year it was completed. *The Structure of the Human Body (De fabrica humani corporis)*, published in 1543, correcting some two hundred errors of Galen, fixed for all time the study of the structure of human anatomy, which is at least half of the study of the human organism. It met a mixed reception. He was accused of plagiarism, and, because he found the same number of ribs on both sides of the male body, he was charged with denying the dogma that Eve had been created out of one of Adam's ribs. Even a former teacher, Sylvius, defending Galen, attacked Vesalius bitterly. Vesalius, deeply hurt by the attacks, resolved to give up his researches. He became court physician to Charles V, then to Philip II. He left that service in 1563 to make a pilgrimage to Jerusalem —probably to escape boredom at court—and died on the return trip. Vesalius' greatness lies in the photographic accuracy of his representations and in the sincerity of his method of presenting what he saw and not what Galen had seen centuries before. This freedom from an original bias is in the noblest tradition of science.

Vesalius had successors, if not equals. His pupil, Gabrielle Fallopio (1523–62), succeeded him at Padua and improved on some details of Vesalius' teaching in tracing connections in the nervous system and in the genito-urinary system. Jerome Fabrizzi, known by the Latin form of his name as Fabricius (1539–

1619), made important observations of the functioning of the veins in his work *On the Valves of the Veins* (1603), but, fully as important, he is reckoned the founder of the science of embryology.

The next eminent name in the history of medicine and biology is that of an Englishman, William Harvey (1578–1657). A Cambridge graduate in the classics, Harvey went on to Padua in 1597 to study under Fabricius for five years, then returned to England to lecture and to be physician to James I (1618). In 1628 there appeared in Frankfurt his great work *On the Motion of the Heart and Blood*. He had labored on this treatise for at least sixteen years, checking and rechecking his conclusions many times. The work complements Vesalius' *Fabrica*. The latter was structural and descriptive, whereas Harvey's was concerned with the functioning of the body. Vesalius was an anatomist, Harvey a physiologist. Harvey thought through the relation of the heart to the circulation of the blood; he traced the movement of the blood in the veins and away from the heart in the arteries. He found that the quantity of blood pumped out of the left cavity of the heart in a half hour is more than the total amount of blood in the whole body: it must therefore come back into the heart. Harvey's explanation that the total circulation of the blood through the whole arterial and venal system is caused by muscular contraction of the heart is quite different from the circulation suggested by Michel Servetus, whom we have met as an antitrinitarian caught in Geneva and executed with Calvin's permission (see above, p. 600). Servetus had described the circulation of the blood through the lungs from the right to the left side of the heart, known as the "lesser circulation." Further research and the advance of technology were to refine some points in the explanation, but the basic problem of the functioning of the heart and the movement of the blood was now clarified. Modern medicine and surgery were made possible by the fundamental labors of Vesalius and Harvey.

Chemistry: Paracelsus and Helmont

CHEMISTRY lagged far behind its sister sciences of physics, astronomy, and physiology. The reason was partially that techniques of measurements of gases and liquids had not yet been perfected to a point at which profitable experimentation could be undertaken. A Swiss who boasted the impressive name of Aureolus Philippus Theophrastus Bombastus von Hohenheim (*ca.* 1493–1541), better known by the Latin name Paracelsus, mercilessly attacked current chemical dogmas of Galen and Avicenna, yet his own pronouncements were frequently as unsubstantiated. He was, in much of his thinking, as bound to medieval alchemy and astrology as those he criticized. But he did believe in and call for close observation of the action of nature, and probably discovered ether, yet without realizing its later beneficent use. A pupil of Paracelsus, van Helmont (1577–1644), who gave the name "gas" to various substances hitherto uncategorized, reduced all the four conventional elements—earth, air, fire, and water—to water, but was uncertain as to how the reduction actually took place. There were others in the field, largely concerned with chemistry as a branch of medicine, hence called iatro-chemists or medicinal chemists, yet it was not until the following century that real advances in techniques and experimentation with the gases and the liquids began to be made.

Mathematics: To Descartes

THE field of mathematics did not see the revolutionary and sensational developments that made astronomy and physics so dramatic in the period of the Renaissance and the Reformation. Nevertheless, from the invention of printing (about 1450) to the publication of Descartes' work on geometry in 1637, significant progress was made. In arithmetic the system of decimal fractions was introduced. In algebra, which had labored under the handicap of an inadequate system of symbols, new symbols for known and unknown quantities and for processes came to be accepted. The simple signs $\times, \div, +, =, (\ ), \sqrt{\quad}$, made speed in calculation possible, and negative and imaginary roots could now be handled. The various branches of mathematics had been used for practical purposes, business accounts, construction of many sorts, the calendar, and of course astronomy.

With the increase in flexibility through improved signs and symbols, mathematics began to have an interest for the thinker. This heightened abstract interest inevitably produced results in the substance of the discipline. Trigonometry, used by the engineer, the astronomer, and the mapmaker, began to cover a larger area and develop its own appeal. In 1614 a Scotsman, John Napier, published a careful treatise on logarithms which substituted addition and subtraction for multiplication and division. Elaborate tables by other scientists were soon on the market. Eminence in mathematical research and adventure was shared by men of all nations. Michael Stifel, a German, improved the algebraic notation, while Niccolò Tartaglia, an Italian, solved equations involving the cube of the unknown quantity and other arithmetical puzzles. Lodovico Ferrari, another Italian, solved equations of the fourth degree. François Viète, a French court lawyer, produced the first work on symbolic algebra and made significant contributions to the solution of cubic equations. Lastly, René Descartes, an eminent French philosopher and educator, produced, at the age of sixteen, an epochal treatment of conic sections. The cumulative result of the work of these scholars and their many colleagues and pupils was to provide for all other sciences the tools with which they solved their technical and theoretical problems during the next great century of science.

Although the sixteenth century cannot be said to have made specific advances or discoveries of revolutionary significance in every science, it did make a frontal attack on the spirit of obedience to authority which was its legacy from both the medieval era and the men of the humanist Renaissance. The former bowed before the authority of the Church; the latter revered and accepted the ancients as their final authorities. The sixteenth century declared its independence from these restrictions and, in so doing, prepared the way for the discoveries and inventions of the next centuries which, free to observe, experiment and reason, changed the aspect of the universe and of the atom.

EDUCATION

THE educational system throughout Europe at the beginning of the sixteenth century was basically unchanged from what it had been a century earlier. The medieval university, concerned with Aristotle, the trivium, and the quadrivium, had, in the course of the three centuries or more since Paris, Oxford, and Bologna, become the model and had undergone virtually no modification. It will be remembered that the leading humanists, from Petrarch to Erasmus, had usually refused to accept posts at universities which would have obliged them to fit themselves into a system of which they disapproved (see above, chapters 4 and 12). Those humanists who did join university faculties usually met antagonism from their conservative colleagues, and on occasion were in difficulty with the Inquisition. Yet the humanists were, as a rule, deeply interested in the problems of education—so interested that they wanted to reform the whole system. Moved by a missionary zeal on behalf of the new learning, these scholars produced many books on the education of boys and girls.

More enlightened rulers frequently asked well-known humanist scholars to compose guide books for the education of their heirs or children, or even employed such a scholar to be the tutor of their offspring. Peter Paul Vergerio composed in 1404 for Ubertino, son of Carrara, lord of Padua, a treatise *On the Liberal Arts* (*De ingenuis moribus*), which pioneered the humanist curriculum and enjoyed great popularity for many years. A few years later Guarino da Verona was employed by Marquis Niccolò d'Este of Ferrara as tutor to his son Leonello. Aeneas Silvius Piccolomini, later Pope Pius II, wrote a treatise *On the Education of Children* which was widely read and justifiably influential. The eminent humanist educator Vittorino da Feltre was employed to tutor the three sons of Gianfrancesco Gonzaga, lord of Mantua. A generation later Erasmus was tutoring the natural son of James V of Scotland and was writing voluminously on the theory of education. His treatise *On the Education of a Christian Prince,* written in 1516, was intended for the young Charles I of Spain. It was a thoughtful survey of the methods of inculcating a desirable spirit in a ruler while he was still educable. In the same year Guillaume Budé, the leading French humanist, composed a work on the education of a prince for the young Francis I of France. Four years later Erasmus was asked to be tutor to Charles' younger brother Ferdinand. The humanists may have been cold-shouldered in most of the universities of the time, but their capacities were certainly not disregarded by the rulers.

To all of these humanist scholars the standard pattern for the cultured man was the ideal of Cicero and Quintilian. A mastery of both Latin and Greek, urbanely absorbed and decorously exhibited, was the goal so patiently sought. Christian ethics were desirable and in most cases sincerely urged. The classical disciplines, including appropriate and seemly physical exercise, were certain to make a man appreciative of the finer things in life and letters. This was not democratic education in any sense. It was for those who could afford good private tutors, which were rare and expensive. The bourgeoisie in general could not yet pay for such a luxury. However, the demand for an education suited to the age was on the increase. The universities, mostly adhering to a scholastic curriculum that was out of date, were in no real position to satisfy that demand. It is in large measure this lack in the educational structure that gave rise to much independent thought and experimentation in the late fifteenth and sixteenth centuries.

The Lowlands

ONE of the notable and very successful efforts toward a better and more relevant education than that offered and controlled by the Church and the tradition-bound universities was the schools set up by the Brethren of the Common Life (see above, Chapter 7). At first emphasizing simple lay piety, the group, open-minded and unburdened by traditions, began to organize their schools into eight annual classes carefully graded between the student's sixth and sixteenth years. Their success in the Netherlands brought invitations to set up schools elsewhere in the area of the lower Rhine, and individual teachers were called to head city grammar schools far from Deventer. Alexander Hegius, who headed the school of the Brethren at Deventer from 1465 to 1498, was responsible for broadening their curriculum to include Greek and a humanistic approach to Latin. Erasmus, who studied under Hegius, owed much to the training he received from the Brethren. The school at Deventer counted among its alumni virtually all the important educators of northern Germany well into the sixteenth century. The educational work of the Brethren was a large factor in the preparation of the soil for the Lutheran Reformation.

Germany

THE Lutheran Reformation itself was a further stimulus to thought and innovation in schools and universities. Early in his public career, in the face of opposition from university circles, Luther saw the clear necessity to take his message to the people; at the same time he realized that the Reformation could get nowhere if the public were illiterate. His message was essentially an appeal to the written word, and his campaigns and polemics depended for their success on the ability of the masses to read and understand what he and his friends said in answer to their enemies, who were also using the printing press to spread their message. In 1524 Luther published an open letter to burgomasters and councilmen of all the cities of Germany on the subject of public schools, and throughout his life he remained a fervent advocate of public education. He wanted the new church to perform the same task the old one had done, only to do it better and for more students, for girls as well as for boys. Maintained at public expense, these schools would teach languages, history, music, and other arts. The aristocratic selective approach of the humanists he rejected, differing sharply on this point from Erasmus. Luther had no faith in the motives of an artificially created élite.

His friend and lieutenant, Philip Melanchthon, was more academic-minded than Luther. Where Luther proclaimed broad principles and general aims, Melanchthon was able to elaborate a detailed educational system to fit a special situation, then write appropriate textbooks to achieve the optimum results. He reorganized many municipal school systems, initiated others, and gained, for his forty years of active educational work, the title "Preceptor of Germany." As might have been expected from a trained humanist, Latin grammar was the basic discipline. To a degree, his insistence on Latin as a base, to the exclusion of German, countered Luther's primary concern that the broad masses of the population be trained to read and use the vernacular tongue. In fact it was Melanchthon's Latin curriculum that became stodgy and scholastic soon after his death; whereas Luther's appeal to the national language and national spirit brought into existence a course of study which continued to be resilient and responsive to the changes effected by time and social development up to the present day.

Within the German-language area, the person who, after Melanchthon, exercised the most influence on schools and education in general was a younger friend of the reformer, John Sturm (1507–89). He reorganized and headed for forty-five years the Gymnasium at Strassburg. He had studied under the Brethren of the Common Life at Liége, and later at Paris and Louvain. Leaning toward Christian humanism, he held up as the three-fold object of teaching "piety, knowledge, and the art of expression." A distinctive feature of his school was the grading of his students into ten annual classes within the eleven years from the student's sixth to his seventeenth year. Later he imposed a further five years of advanced studies upon the secondary school, which eventually became the University of Strassburg. Sturm's system was copied by nearby cities and was for long extremely influential in ordering the educational framework in southern and western Germany.

Geneva

NOT far from Strassburg lay a still more active center of educational thought and practice. John Calvin, scholar before he was a reformer, knew perfectly well that the teaching function lay at the root of any success his reform might achieve. He was didactic and systematic by nature, and his theological masterpiece, the *Institutes of the Christian Religion,* can be called a highly effective textbook in Christian thought. In 1559, after a visit to Sturm's school in Strassburg and with the support of the city fathers of Geneva, he formally founded the College of Geneva, later the University of Geneva. The followers of Calvin from the first were enthusiastic about education and were committed to the support of a complete school system, democratic, liberal, bilingual (Latin and French), and comprehensive. Wherever Calvinism spread, it set up schools and maintained a high level of literacy among its adherents. In the Lowlands, in England, among the Huguenots in France, and particularly in Scotland, the ideals of Genevan education were adopted. John Knox, who had spent ten years in Geneva, within a year of Scotland's rejection of Rome published in *The First Book of Discipline* what was essentially an outline for a national system of church-state education: "Of necessity we judge it that every several church shall have a schoolmaster appointed, such a one as is able, at least, to teach grammar and the Latin tongue, if the town be of any reputation." Colleges to teach the arts, and universities whose task was to be more specialized, were planned for. "All must be compelled," said Knox, "to bring up their children in learning and virtue."

England

QUITE apart from the two great English universities of Oxford and Cambridge, England was relatively adequately provided with schools on a primary and secondary level before the Tudors came to the throne. There was a respectable number of endowed grammar schools in existence even before the outbreak of the Wars of the Roses. The Tudors had a special interest in education, and from the time of Henry VII through the reign of Elizabeth we hear of the establishment of new schools and of careful and at times generous provision for the support of teachers and scholars throughout the whole kingdom. The fashion of support for education was not limited to the royal house but spread widely among the prelates and the nobility. The curriculum in most of these schools tended to be humanistic. The scholars were taught from Livy, Terence, Ovid, Cato, Cicero, Sallust, and Horace, as well as from some of the standard medieval authors and the works of selected Italian humanists.

Henry VIII, one of the best educated of all English monarchs, took particular interest in the schools of his kingdom. Cardinal Wolsey's efforts to further education met with Henry's full approval. At the dissolution of the monasteries in 1536 and 1539 a few of the schools which had been connected with them may have ceased to function. It is certain, on the other hand, that many new grammar schools were founded and school endowments increased with funds taken over by the crown from the dissolution. The statutes which Henry issued for the cathedral school at Canterbury are typical of many others which he decreed.

That piety and good letters may in our church aforesaid for ever blossom, grow and flower, and in their time bear fruit for the glory of God and the advantage and advancement of the commonwealth, we decree and ordain that there shall always be in our church of Canterbury elected and nominated by the Dean or in his absence the Sub-dean and Chapter, fifty boys, poor and destitute of the help of their friends, to be maintained out of the possessions of the church, of native genius as far as may be and apt to learn; whom however we will shall not be admitted as poor boys of our church before they have learnt to read and write and are moderately learned in the rudiments of grammar in the judgement of the Dean or in his absence the Sub-dean and Head Master.

The headmaster, who had to be competent in Greek as well as in Latin, and his assistants, normally trained only in Latin, were frequently laymen. The earlier schools were typically connected with the church or the cathedral; the headmaster, whether a canon or a priest, being under the jurisdiction of the vicar of the dean of the cathedral chapter. The foundations of Henry VIII and of Wolsey changed the style, and in the 1520's many "free" schools with no specific ecclesiastical connection began to be established. Some were founded by private individuals, some by guilds, others by town corporations. As a result it is estimated that there was one grammar school for every 5500 of the population, a higher proportion than would be reached until the end of the nineteenth century.

The two universities, Oxford and Cambridge, had shared in the disturbances of the Wars of the Roses, but at the end of the century both were again flourishing, and the intellectual atmosphere, according to Erasmus, who visited England in 1499, was exciting and erudite. Greek had been taught for some years at Oxford; at Cambridge the new learning was sponsored by John Fisher, bishop of Rochester and chancellor of the university; it made somewhat more substantial progress than at Oxford, which was still suffering under the cloud of its earlier adherence to Lollard heresy. Henry VIII and his grandmother, the Lady Margaret, extended their favor to both Oxford and Cambridge, and Cardinal Wolsey, always anxious to further the cause of learning, was a generous patron of both universities. At Oxford three new colleges were founded under the Tudors in the course of the sixteenth century: Brasenose College in 1515, Corpus Christi College in 1517, Cardinal College, later Christ Church College, by Wolsey in 1525. At Cambridge five colleges were founded or refounded in the same period: Jesus College (1496), Christ's College (1505), St. John's College (1511), Magdalene College in 1542, and Trinity College, refounded by Henry VIII in 1546. The Chantries Act of 1548, intended to transfer funds from the suppressed chantries to the king for the use of schools, had not in fact worked well. The funds were used for other purposes and consequently many elementary schools had to close. Queen Elizabeth later made a conscious effort to reestablish these schools, but she had to call upon wealthy laymen to help in founding and maintaining schools in towns near their family seats.

Political pressures, mostly connected with the Reformation, and the need felt by the Tudors for academic approval of their policy toward the Roman Church, tended to make the universities subservient to the crown. This tendency had some advantages for the universities, such as royal support and gifts. On the other hand, there was the distinct disadvantage that the universities lost much of their independence. Under Edward VI the universities marked time; but under Mary the loss in independence and the visitations, intended to assure a full return to Catholic doctrine and practice, brought humiliation to the universities and forced many scholars into exile. The three martyrs burned at Oxford in 1555, Latimer, Cranmer, and Ridley, were all Cambridge men, whence the expression "Cambridge educated the martyrs and Oxford burnt them." Queen Elizabeth demanded conformity and acceptance of the Act of Supremacy from fellows, many of whom were expelled for refusal to conform. The general intellectual level of the universities in the first decade of Elizabeth's reign was low. Nevertheless, it was inevitable that the stability and good sense of Elizabethan England should be reflected in the life of the intellectual centers of the country. The number of students steadily increased, able scholars were appointed to endowed chairs, new statutes governing the administration of the universities were enacted, though not without opposition from within the teaching bodies, and accepted by the queen. Libraries were enriched and the new colleges worked themselves into the corporate life of the institutions. On the debit side there were bitter encounters between the Puritans and those who leaned to the romanism of Mary Tudor. The strict enforcement of the Act of Conformity of 1580 forced many excellent scholars and schoolmasters out of their positions, to the detriment of the cause of education.

A bright and shining light of learning during the early years of the reign of Elizabeth was the gentle and amiable Roger Ascham (1515–68). A Cambridge graduate and fellow of St. John's College, he was chosen public orator of the university because of his superb command of both Latin and Greek. He was for two years (1548–50) tutor to the Princess Elizabeth, then secretary to the English ambassador to the court of Emperor Charles V, in which post he came to know scholars and rulers on the Continent. Returning to England, he became Latin Secretary to Queen Mary, who allowed him to remain Protestant without any restrictions. When Elizabeth came to the throne she called to her service her former tutor, and showed him her favor and gratitude the remaining ten years of his life. He was held in high regard by nobles and prelates, and his advice and assistance in cultural matters was sought by the great. The earl of Leicester, favorite of Elizabeth and patron of letters, leaned upon Ascham for counsel and help, as did Elizabeth's minister, Lord Burghley.

While Ascham contributed to the advance of the cause of humane learning, by his correspondence and personal advocacy, his treatise, *The Scholemaster,* published in 1570, two years after his death, was the manifesto of English humanistic education. In this work, written in flowing and vivid English, Ascham advanced, along with suggestions for the discussion of broad principles of a disciplined upbringing of the young, the "double translation" method of learning Latin and Greek. The teacher, after clearing the ground and explaining unfamiliar terms and concepts, has the student translate the Latin passage into equally stately, finished English. Once this is satisfactorily accomplished, the English then is to be translated back into Latin. This exercise will form in the student an improved control of his native tongue and increase his facility in Latin. Ascham never ceased to be proud of Queen Elizabeth's excellent Latin and Greek and of the fact that she had learned these languages under his tutelage. Dr. Samuel Johnson two centuries later said of *The Scholemaster* that it contained "the best advice that was ever given for the study of languages."

Among the earnest and resourceful schoolmasters of the reign of Elizabeth, Richard Mulcaster (1530–1611) is eminent. He was headmaster of Merchant Taylors' School in London for twenty-five years, and thereafter, for twelve years, of St. Paul's School, once headed by John Colet. In 1581 he published his thoughts on elementary education in the *Positions,* and the next year, in the *First Part of the Elementarie.* Essentially, he was calling for thorough discipline in reading, writing, music, and drawing, up to the age of twelve, and in English for all, rich and poor. He would begin Latin in the grammar school only at twelve years of age, and then only for those, whether rich or poor, who had shown themselves capable of further study. Mulcaster further called for special training for teachers, having found that not a few of these were unable to convey their knowledge to younger minds. English interest in the educational process and the gradual creation of an English school tradition continued through the Elizabethan era well into the next century. Francis Bacon (1561–1626) had a good deal to say about education in his *Advancement of Learning* and in his correspondence; he felt that English education could profit from a study of Jesuit and French educational methods.

France

THE University of Paris dominated French education at the beginning of the sixteenth century, as it had for the three preceding centuries. When Erasmus came to Paris as a student medievalism still dominated the curriculum, but with the difference that the voices of humanism and the French Reformation were already audible. Humanistic studies had been pursued at Paris since the middle of the fifteenth century, yet without fanfare or substantial following. The native reform movement, led by the group at Meaux and Marguerite of Navarre, indicated an increase in the tempo of revolt against the scholasticism still ruling in the Sorbonne. These currents of revolt combined in the foundation by Francis I in 1530 of the Collège de France as an academy independent of the University of Paris. The Sorbonne opposed the foundation on the grounds that the six professors in the Collège, three for Hebrew, two for Greek, and one for mathematics, would not be competent to engage in theological disputations. Four years later a chair of Latin was added. The Collège was dedicated to the proposition that a thorough knowledge of the ancient languages and literatures was the best guarantee of a high national culture. Classical humanism had thus an institution and royal favor to counterbalance the stubborn medievalism of the university. This opposition was to persist for over a century, until the foundation of the French Academy by Richelieu in 1634 sealed the commitment of the government to the cause of secular and vernacular letters.

During this century, among many educators and scholars concerned with the problems of educating the young, three names stand out: François Rabelais (1490–1553), Peter Ramus (Pierre de la Ramée) (1515–72), and Michel de Montaigne (1533–92). We have met Rabelais as a wandering scholar and scientist, a man of letters and satirist of his times (see above, p. 697). Several chapters in his *Gargantua and Pantagruel* are devoted to the education of the young. In describing the upbringing of Gargantua, Rabelais apparently advocates an ambitious schedule of universal learning which would barely have left time for sleep. All meals were accompanied by didactic reading, and no activity was allowed to go without its educational by-product. Even games and sport were to be educational. This was humanism with a vengeance. One suspects that Rabelais was mixing some irony with his serious instructions. Because the work was widely read, its pedagogic aspect must have had a great influence on the curriculum in French schools.

Ramus was a serious educational revolutionary. He went through the University of Paris, finding both its spirit and its letter thoroughly distasteful. Criticism was a commodity the professors found unwelcome, and his master's thesis, built on the assertion that "everything that Aristotle has said is false," was a shock to his examiners. Ramus opposed the servile acceptance of authority and the obstacles placed in the way of free inquiry. His first two books, both published in 1543, *The Institutes of Dialectic* and *Animadversions on Aristotle,* were condemned by royal decree. Under Francis' successor, Henry II, however, Ramus was restored to favor, and in 1551 was appointed to a professorate of eloquence and philosophy in the Collège de France. From his rostrum he proclaimed his reforms of the basic trivium and quadrivium. He wrote Latin and Greek grammars which, he contended, made the mastery of these languages simpler and more effective. He broadened his interests to include mathematics and physics, translated works of Archimedes and Proclus from the Greek, wrote textbooks on mathematics in Latin and in French. By 1561, the year of the outbreak of the Wars of Religion, he had gained a great reputation for tact and persuasiveness and was used by the university to present its complaints to the king. Shortly after this he became a Protestant, and in 1562 he presented to the king and queen an *Advice on the Reformation of the University of Paris.* The core of the *Advice* was the suggestion that the university should have only a limited number of professors, named by the king, instead of the hundreds of masters of arts who had the right, if not the competence, to teach. Throughout the *Advice* Ramus' devotion to the principle of simple and direct logic applied to natural and obvious physical data brought him to conclusions shocking to the professorate. His enemies multiplied in proportion as his suggested reforms pointed to their superfluity, and the Jesuits were now added to their number.

Seeking above all peace in which to work, in 1568 Ramus asked the king for a leave of absence. He went to Switzerland and Germany, refusing many offers of teaching posts from German and even Hungarian universities. His ideas of educational reform were everywhere listened to with deep attention, though at times he was strenuously opposed and student-faculty demonstrations against him were staged. After returning to Paris in 1570 he was removed from his posts, then reinstated by the influence of the cardinal de Bourbon so that he could continue his study and writing quietly. The third day of the Massacre of St. Bartholomew (August 1572) Ramus was killed in his study by assassins hired by his bitterest enemy, his body hacked to pieces and thrown into the Seine. His great contribution was not exactly an innovation, though his emphasis on mathematics was both new and prophetic, but lay rather in his appeal to simplicity, nature, and a rational system. The encrustations of scholastic complexity he strove to cut away in order to make learning both useful and interesting.

Michel de Montaigne we have also met before (see above, p. 679), as an observer of man and his thought, largely seen through himself by patient and objective analysis. Montaigne occupies a respectable niche in the development of educational theory. As a man of affairs and experience in the world he was interested in the preparation of the young of his class, the bourgeoisie, for the tasks that awaited them. For this purpose the purely classical education advocated by the conservative humanists seemed to him as useless as the scholastic curriculum still followed in the clerical schools. In his essay "On the Education of Children" he urged that children be taught by action from the "book of the world."

They keep us four or five years understanding words and stringing them together in clauses, as many more putting them together in a long diatribe, precisely divided into four or five parts, then another five or more learning how to mix them briefly and interlace them into some subtle fashion. Let us leave this to those who make a special profession out of it.

Montaigne was a powerful advocate of the practical, the sensible, and the judicious. In the education of the young to be good citizens in a reasonable society, he urged training in judgment, independence, individualism, and justice.

Spain

SPAIN produced Juan Luis Vivés (1492–1540), but he left for Paris when only seventeen years of age and the rest of his life was spent abroad, partly in England, as a protégé of Queen Catherine of Aragon, but mostly in the Netherlands, at Bruges, and at Louvain. A friend of Erasmus, he was in many ways a follower and continuer of his humanistic ideals. His influence, like that of Erasmus, was of international scope. He subjected the current educational practices and theories to severe criticism, finding them corrupt. As he saw the situation, Latin and Greek were badly taught, logic was misused, the natural sciences were ignored, the law was taught by outworn methods and for false and degenerate purposes. The psychology of learning interested him deeply and he applied his findings, new for his time, to the problems of education. The term "associational" might properly be used of his theorizing. He favored education for girls as well as for boys and provided a similar if not identical curriculum for them. His requirements for the teaching profession were so high that it would have been difficult to find many, then or now, who could meet them. He would indeed have produced an educational élite. There was as yet no serious thought of a democratic or universal educational system.

In addition to Vivés, strictly a humanist educator, Spain produced Ignatius Loyola, the founder of the Jesuit order (see above, p. 618), which established more schools and colleges and had more influence on the young than any other group in this period. Pope Paul III spoke, in the bull recognizing the order in 1540, of their teaching "boys and uncultivated people (*personas rudes*) those truths which are necessary to the formation of the Christian." Spurred on by the success of the Protestant appeal to learning, Ignatius and his colleagues were convinced that higher, as opposed to primary, education needed emphasis; the Jesuit program of education henceforth followed that conviction. Before Loyola's death in 1556 over 100 colleges * and higher institutions had been established, and by 1600 their number had grown to almost 200. Forty years later there were 372 Jesuit colleges and universities in operation. The Jesuit system became almost the official educational program of the Catholic Church. The Council of Trent, in prescribing diocesan seminaries, was greatly influenced by Diego de Laynez (see above, p. 622) and, by so remarkably improving the quality of the clergy, made its greatest single contribution to the revival of the Church.

Jesuit educational policy and method took shape only gradually. In the Constitution of 1540 much detailed attention was given to education. Principles were outlined upon which Jesuit schools functioned for many years. Laynez, who followed Loyola as General of the order, was an extremely able educational statesman who maintained the tradition of progress and experiment with great profit to the Jesuit college system. The ultimate result of this experiment and experience was the document known as the *Ratio studiorum*. The fifth General of the order, Aquaviva, named an international committee of six Jesuit fathers in 1584 which issued, two years later, a tentative list of suggestions in-

---

* The term "college" includes Latin secondary schools, preparatory to advanced professional training on the university level. Normally a student could finish college at sixteen or seventeen.

tended as a basis for discussion by teaching members of the order. Five years later a second, revised, edition appeared which was subjected to further use and emendation. In 1599 a final version appeared, the result of the discussion and experience of the whole Society. In this form the *Ratio* was the official educational guide of the Society until its suppression in 1773.

The *Ratio* presented essentially a conservative program of higher education. Emphasis lay upon mastery rather than breadth. A few well related subjects were to be taught; thoroughness, exemplified and instilled by a dedicated teacher, was demanded. The primary aim was the training of the mind, not merely the acquisition of disparate facts. Depth of understanding and flexibility of interest and perception were more important than practical skills. The Latin language in its Ciceronian form was the medium of instruction; even Greek was to be taught through Latin. The *praelectio,* an adaptation of the medieval professor's lecture, was the Jesuit contribution to classroom techniques. By this method, the basic Latin text of the work under consideration was carefully read to the class, difficult or obscure passages were briefly explained, then the passage was subjected to interpretation—this all in Latin—whereupon the whole was translated into the vernacular. Finally there came the *eruditio,* a sort of historical, geopolitical or ethical commentary upon relevant parts of the text.

It was characteristic of the whole Jesuit system that there was no provision for the teacher or the students to venture upon new subjects or new methods of instruction. Herein lay much of its strength. The uniform discipline was effective in creating a body of men similarly trained and responsive to direction along lines already well inculcated. On the other hand, this very uniformity had its drawbacks. There was no flexibility and little room for individual initiative. The rise of the scientific temper in the seventeenth century fostered demands upon the educational systems of Europe which Jesuit rigidity could not or would not satisfy. This failure to keep in touch with the spirit of the age, in spite of the inherent excellence of the instruction they gave, contributed to the repudiation and suppression of the order in 1773. In all fairness, it should at the same time be pointed out that the Lutheran educational system, both at the lower and at the higher levels, suffered from a similar sterile attitude toward the dynamic development of European culture in these decades.

ART

ART, in any of its many forms, never stands still. We have seen how the revival of learning in the fifteenth century was reflected in the sculpture, the architecture, and the painting of the fifteenth century, culminating in creativity of special power and brilliance in the work of versatile men of genius, of whom Leonardo da Vinci and Michelangelo are perhaps the best known. It is a commonplace of art history that Florence, in spite of the achievements of the painters of Venice, Siena, and Milan, was the seedbed of more artistic creation than any other Italian center. This judgment holds true until well toward the end of the fifteenth century, but this artistic hegemony began to give way in favor of Rome about the turn of the century. The popes of the later Renaissance, almost without exception enthusiastic and discerning patrons of the arts, called many eminent artists to the Holy City. Under Sixtus IV (1471–84), so many of the best masters were in the employ of the Pope that Rome was for a short while the undisputed center of artistic production in the peninsula. This early leadership was only temporary. However, a few years later, in 1505, under Julius II (1503–13), Michelangelo and Bramante settled in Rome and in 1508 Raphael brought his atelier to the city, and in the same year the Pope called the painters Signorelli, Pintoricchio, and Sodoma to Rome. All these artists were soon planning and creating for the Papacy. Other masters of lesser note followed.

For a period of roughly two decades, the period commonly called the High Renaissance, under the inspiration and at the urging of the papal *curia* the city of Rome took on a new and monumental appearance. Cardinals built palaces, had them richly decorated; popes ordered monuments of Rome's past cleaned up and rebuilt; bankers and rich merchants vied with the high clergy for splendor in their dwellings and patronage of the arts, commissioning murals, portraits, statuary, public fountains, and sarcophagi. The majesty of ancient Rome re-emerged in the city of the popes. Splendor, beauty, naturalism—these were the motifs of the time. They grew out of the *quattrocento;* but they went a step beyond the precision, the Christian austerity, the memory of a severe ethic, which had still restrained the artists of the mid-fifteenth century. This change, from a vestigial concept of art as a manifestation of a Christian ethic to a more relaxed naturalism inspired by classical models and ideals, should be kept in mind when we approach the next noticeable change, to what has come in recent years to be called Mannerism. We shall find that even when the subject was religious, as was often the case, the treatment followed freer and more emotional, at times capricious, lines.

The High Renaissance

THE artists of the High Renaissance were attracted by the appeal of physical beauty. Leaving behind them the medieval antipathy to the sensual and, as a second rejection, the coldness of classicism, they embraced the thought that physical beauty and spiritual elevation could be joined in one person. On this basis, suddenly, the prophets, the evangelists, the apostles, and the saints appeared in stone and on canvas as handsome, majestic, fulsome types. Their beauty was worthy of the rich garments they wore. The similarity of this concept in the plastic arts to the ideal courtier of Castiglione, urbane, confident, serene, suitably turned out, is only too obvious. It will be remembered that Castiglione's *Courtier* was written between 1508 and 1516, precisely at the zenith of the period we call the High Renaissance.

This spirit found expression in architecture as well as in sculpture and painting. Donato Bramante (1444–1514), after a long and successful career as a painter and architect in Florence and Milan, moved to Rome in 1499 and soon had more commissions than he could handle. The Tempietto (Little Temple), which he designed and began to build in 1502, illustrates the new artistic motif. It is a small circular temple with Doric columns topped by an entablature, a drum, and a dome. Erected on the spot where St. Peter was supposed to have been crucified, it is perfectly, severely classical, simple, and without decoration, thus symbolizing anew the complete secularization of the Papacy. In 1506 Pope Julius II engaged Bramante to design and rebuild St. Peter's basilica. Julius was responsible for accepting the general plan, a floor design of a Greek cross, with four apses, in itself a revolutionary departure from the traditional Latin longitudinal cruciform design. But the details and the implementation of the grandiose conceptions of space, proportion, majesty, and power—these were Bramante's. The changes that later architects, including Michelangelo, made in the plans and construction did not substantially alter Bramante's original conception.

Mannerism

THE High Renaissance, a period when classical models and motifs were accepted and absorbed, came to an end with the third decade of the century. In all probability the sack of Rome in 1527 was responsible for its demise. If the city of the Caesars and the "capital of the world" was not safe from the frenzy and the barbarism of imperial soldiery there was no such thing as security. This shock to the Church, added to the disaster of the Reformation and the defec-

The Little Temple (*Tempietto*), by Bramante, in Rome [ANDERSON].

tion of Germany from obedience to the *curia,* was more than a mere trend in the fine arts could bear. The harmony, security, and balance of classicism were gone beyond recall and any appeal to that spirit was bound to find a very uncertain response. The artists, congenitally sensitive to shades of security and turbulence in the world about them, looked around and within themselves for new sources of guidance. There was experimentation, a wider range of imitation and adaptation, greater individualism and personalism. Some of this took the form of richer embellishment, more curvilinear designs, more freedom in mingling or varying the classical orders, freer play with tradition, a more feverish search for satisfaction in originality, to learn if by any means the specters of chaos and moribund art might be exorcised. This was Mannerism. Basically it was healthy; it is not enough to say simply that it was a transition between classicism and the Baroque of the seventeenth century, for it was much more. It was a courageous outreaching for artistic salvation, a noble effort to bridge the gap that had opened up between form and content, between truth and its conveyance, between religion and life.

It is most appropriate that this move covered the period of the convalescence of the Catholic Church, when it was literally picking up the pieces after catastrophe. When the Church again felt sure of itself, after the Counter-Reformation had restored unity and pride, by the end of the century, a new, vigorous, even enthusiastic current governed building and decoration. The Baroque style, ebullient and outgoing in all areas of life, letters, politics, dress, and the plastic arts, befitted a society sure of itself and its future. It had, again, a harmony, this time not borrowed from the past as that of the Renaissance had been, but growing out of trial and tribulation, disaster, courage, and recovery, its own creation and its proper pride.

The courts of Europe in general welcomed Mannerism. Court painters imitated the latest work of Michelangelo, whose *Last Judgment* (1534-41) and much of the ceiling in the Sistine Chapel present perfectly the disharmony which so eloquently mirrors the bewilderment and insecurity of that generation. Mannerism flourished not only in Rome but elsewhere in Italy and even as far away as the French court. Michelangelo had many imitators, but Tintoretto (1512-94) was more—he was his artistic heir. This Venetian became the most typical painter of the Catholic Counter-Reformation. His subjects were chosen from the tragic and dramatic scenes of biblical and sacred history, from the *Temptation of Adam in the Garden of Eden* to the *Massacre of the Innocents.* His treatment was free and ebullient. He was the first to employ the *chiaroscuro* in order to portray by varying half-shadows, sudden light, or a peculiarly suggestive darkness, moods of emotion, hope, despair, or inspiration. All the Venetian painters, particularly his contemporaries Titian and Veronese, were colorists, but Tintoretto added to color poetry and the control of intensity which lifted his work from the merely decorative to the passionate and the sublime.

As Bramante, Michelangelo, Raphael, and their pupils dominated the architecture of central Italy well into the second half of the century, Andrea Palladio (1518-80) of Vicenza represents and typifies the modification of Renaissance classicism which from about 1550 captured the fancy of north Italy. He was a careful student of Roman architecture and his book, *Architettura,* first

Church of the Gesù, by Giacomo Barozzi (da Vignola), in Rome [GABINETTO FOTO-GRAFICO NAZIONALE].

published in 1575, showed on every page his indebtedness to Vitruvius' *De architectura*. Palladio favored broad, balanced façades, wide curved colonnades and porticoes, and monumental stairways. Public buildings and, as a new subject of the architect's art, the spacious country villa of the gentleman were his primary interest. His influence, widely propagated through his book, reached to seventeenth-century England and from there even to America. Both the Mount Vernon home of George Washington and Thomas Jefferson's Monticello show the clear influence of Palladio's architectural ideas.

Spain

THE Spain of the Golden Age witnessed notable artistic creativity. The plateresque (*platero* in Spanish means silversmith) style in architectural decoration, ornate, imaginative, almost grotesque, was pleasing for a time, but endured little more than half a century. The reaction to this exaggeration was in the direction of a cold and severe classicism, which in turn lasted as a dominant style hardly more than fifty years. The native Spanish desire for color and ornament, by the early decades of the next century, was demanding more decoration and graceful lines. Thus the Baroque of the seventeenth century found a warm welcome in Spain and her lands beyond the seas.

It was in painting that Spain produced her most original art, in the work of a Cretan, Domenico Theotocopuli (1545–1614), better known as El Greco. First at Rome, then in Venice as a pupil of Titian, he absorbed the passion for color and tension that marked Michelangelo and the Mannerists. Soon after moving to Spain he was employed (1580) by Philip II to paint in the Escorial, and thereafter settled in Toledo. His high emotionalism dominated all his work —rich color, elongated proportions, giving an impression of great tension, sharp transitions from light to dark, nervous movement—these all united to portray extreme Catholic ecstasy.

France

NORTH of the Alps, in France, the Netherlands, and Germany, there were native motifs, but the influence of Italy was clearly discernible. France produced no great school of art, in any of its branches, in this century. In architecture Italian masters and models were followed. The artists imported from Italy by Louis XII and Francis I enjoyed high favor, and building and decoration were largely turned over to them. The châteaux and the public buildings constructed under the Valois kings were essentially French Gothic modernized and decorated in Italian Renaissance style. The other arts advanced very little in the sixteenth century. Only in portraiture could the French be called creative. Jean Clouet (d. 1539) and his son François (d. 1572), of Flemish origin, were court painters successively to Francis I and Henry II. The portraits they executed are noted for their detail and finesse and a precision of line almost photographic in its accuracy. Ronsard called François Clouet "the honor of our France," and he was undoubtedly the best painter France could boast. Yet he lacked the fire and the passion, the grand conception and the conviction which greatness demands and which many Italians had in abundant measure.

The Lowlands

ART in the Low Countries passed through several confusing stages. The earlier fifteenth century had witnessed a vogue of French and Italian influence. Many Flemish artists had traveled to Italy, then returned to imitate and perpetuate Italian artistic ideals. But by the end of the century, foreign inspiration having about run its course, we may observe a national school arising. Engelbrechtsen (d. 1533) and Lucas of Leyden (1493–1533), although obviously under Italian influence, produced paintings and engravings that show originality in the attention paid to native scenes of common life. In the northern provinces the influence of German art began to predominate; the south tended to draw closer to France and share in French dependence on Italian models, both in painting and in sculpture.

Hieronymus (Jerome) Bosch (1450–1510) and Quentin Metsys (1460–1540) were both psychological realists of great technical virtuosity. Bosch painted scenes of diabolical horror, intended to show the ghastly depravity of which the human spirit is capable. He invented loathesome, creeping creatures to represent the suffering or the cruelty of his human subjects. Metsys' work shows Italian influence; while psychological analysis is intended, the result is less violent and dramatic than the work of Bosch.

The strong individualism and psychological naturalism of these men led to the work of Peter Brueghel the Elder (1525–69). Brueghel took the landscape as his background, filling it with people at work, at play, or at rest. His powers of observation caught the most minute detail, yet the total picture makes a nat-

St. Martin and the Beggar, by El Greco, in the Art Institute of Chicago, gift of Mr. and Mrs. Chauncy McCormick [ART INSTITUTE OF CHICAGO].

ural whole. He was not malicious, as Bosch often was; he was close to the soil and the common things of life: he saw in the seasons, the sowing and the harvest, marriage feasts, the domestic chores, life's meaning as essentially the acceptance of the order of a benevolent God. He lived through the early period of the wars against the Spaniards, and in his *Massacre of the Innocents,* which shows Spanish soldiers killing inhabitants of a small snow-decked Flemish village, women and children, in cold blood, he reveals his Flemish national resentment at the rule of the hated foreigner. Nature in her bare truth and man in his struggle for life are Brueghel's constant inspiration and theme.

Germany

ALL during the fifteenth century the influence of the mature and vigorous art of the Low Countries had been spreading up the Rhine. Traffic of ideas and of men went both ways, up as well as down the river. Thus we find many recorded cases of artists from Swabia, Württemberg, Westphalia, or the Palatinate, who at some time or other in their lives spent a period of months or years in the Low Countries. In the reverse direction, many Flemish and Dutch artists or artisans were employed in cities of northwestern, central, and southern Germany. This exchange was to be expected in the Burgundian lands of which Brussels was the natural capital, but it will be remembered that after the defeat and death of Charles the Bold in 1477 the possessions of his family were broken up, with a consequent increase of French influence in the southern and western parts of the ancient lands of the Burgundian house. At the same time the free flow of artists between the Low Countries and southern and central Germany continued unabated. The influence of Flemish and Dutch artistic expression upon the German schools may be traced all through the sixteenth century and well into the seventeenth. The decoration of the castle of Heidelberg, the leading example of German monumental architecture of the sixteenth century, was the work of a Flemish artist. In painting, portraiture, church and domestic decoration, copper engraving, statuary in stone or in wood, book illustrations, the art of the gold- and silversmith, tapestry, and the minor arts and crafts German art owed much to its northern neighbor. Cologne, an active center of Gothic art in the later Middle Ages, yielded its leadership to the Swabian school in the late fifteenth century. Ulm and Augsburg become thereafter the focal points of south German art. Martin Schongauer (d. 1488), a competent painter showing Flemish influence, was also a bold innovator in the art of copper engraving. Ulm continued to lead Swabian art for a generation after his death, until the rise to prominence of Hans Holbein the Elder (1460–1524) in Augsburg. The subjects of his paintings were still mainly religious. Beset by misfortune, he traveled all over southern Germany, leaving his works of art in many monasteries and churches. His painting was marked by appreciation of beauty, mastery of detail, a striking delineation of character, a warm use of color, and very acceptable *chiaroscuro.*

While the Flemish and Dutch influence was remarkably strong in all forms of German art, it was only one of the sources of artistic inspiration in sixteenth-century Germany. The native Gothic school retained much of its vigor, and in many parts of Germany it was the strongest single tradition. In the south, however, especially along the routes of trade and travel, the Italian "manner" was warmly welcomed. The most notable piece of sculpture in Germany of this century is the tomb of the Emperor Maximilian at Innsbruck. The sarcophagus of the Emperor is surrounded by twenty-eight bronze statues, several of the best of which are the work of Peter Vischer (d. 1529), a productive sculptor and metal worker whose style was profoundly influenced by Italian realism.

Albrecht Dürer with Hans Holbein the Younger, the son of Hans Holbein the Elder, stand as the two glories of the German artistic Renaissance. Dürer (1471–1528) was trained by his father, a respectable if not superlative goldsmith of Hungarian origin, in the finesse of the gold- and silversmith's art. At fifteen he was apprenticed to a well-known Nürnberg painter with whom he remained over three years. Thereafter he traveled widely in Germany, to Holland, to Basel, and to Italy. The stay in Italy made a deep impression on him; it has been said with only slight exaggeration that the Northern Renaissance should properly be dated from his return from Italy in 1495. Nürnberg was his home until his death. He was patronized by emperors, nobles, clerics, and rich bourgeois. In two branches of his craft he excelled: engraving and portraiture. In each he passed through several distinct periods, alternating between imagination and realism. He was of a devoutly religious nature and the events

Self-portrait, by Albrecht Dürer, in the Pinakothek, Munich [BAYERISCHE STAATSGEMÄLDESAMMLUNGEN].

of the Lutheran Reformation affected him deeply. Many of his subjects were from the Bible and the lives of the saints, such as his *Passion of Christ,* the cycle of the *Apocalypse,* a series of fifteen woodcuts, and the *Life of the Virgin,* also a series of engravings. His most mature work was, significantly enough, done after his second trip to Antwerp in 1520, where he was strongly attracted by the French and Italian artists then resident in Flanders. His *St. Jerome* and *Melancholy,* done in 1524, are in his imaginative style. He was equally at home in oil, engraving on copper or in wood, but from 1520 until his death in 1528 he specialized in portraits in copper plate and achieved a mastery of the medium unequaled by any artist of his time or since. Unlike many artists, Dürer was interested in formulating his views on the theory of art; over some years and with many revisions, he wrote a number of specialized treatises on human proportion and on geometry as well as on the fortification of cities and castles.

Hans Holbein the Younger (1497–1543) was born in Augsburg. Most of his life was spent abroad, in Switzerland, France, and England, and he can be called German only in a limited sense. His earliest creations were produced in Basel. His portraits exhibit qualities of composition, realism, warmth and control of line and detail. His favorite subjects were religious and historical portraits, but he branched out later into monumental wall-painting and, under the influence of the Italian colorists, added to grand conceptions a mastery of *chiaroscuro* and delicate shading. In 1523 he painted three portraits of Erasmus. His most powerful work in this period was the *Dance of Death* which depicted Death as the great interrupter of human life and hopes. In 1526 Holbein came to England for the first time and was welcomed by Sir Thomas More, whose portrait he painted. After four years back in Basel (1528–32), he returned to England, where he was kept occupied with commissions for portraits of the great and the near great, notably Henry VIII and lords and ladies of the court. In addition to large portraits he worked in miniatures. From the work of Leonardo da Vinci and the French portraitist Jean Clouet he learned much, though he was perhaps their superior in analysis and portrayal of character. He began several large wall-paintings in London in 1542, but died of the plague (1543) before he was able to complete them.

After Dürer and Hans Holbein the Younger there were many competent artists in Germany, yet the following generation produced none who could match them for intensity of genius, force of portrayal and ability to convey the highest emotions with conviction and clarity. Toward the end of the century all the arts, architecture, painting, sculpture, and the minor arts, underwent the trend toward the Baroque, whose heaviness replaced finesse and simplicity, while affectation took the place of directness.

Poland

POLAND was subjected to influences from all sides. Late in the fifteenth century Italian Renaissance ideals were already being realized in the construction of the inner arcaded courts and in façades of castles and public buildings. French and Flemish influences were, around the turn of the century, rivaling the German in painting and church monastic decoration. Cracow, a commercial and cultural crossroads, developed its own school of painting and architecture. The subjects were for the most part events and persons from the Bible. It was in architecture that the Renaissance ideas were most freely used. The beautiful royal castle of the Wawel in Cracow, as well as the Cloth Hall on the large market square in the same city, or the town hall in Poznań, could have been built in northern Italy in the sixteenth century. The ruling monarchs, Sigismund the Old (1506–48), whose second wife was Bona Sforza of Milan, and his son Sigismund Augustus (1548–72), both patronized Italian artists, and much of the credit for the acceptance of foreign inspiration must be given to them.

Bohemia

THE sixteenth century was for Bohemia the age of the Renaissance, in the sense that Italian influences were extremely strong. Architects and sculptors in considerable numbers came to Prague and other leading cities of the kingdom, there to design and execute churches and chapels, town houses of the aristocracy and public buildings for the crown or the state. Ferdinand I, a Habsburg who became king in 1526, was particularly anxious to get away from the dominant Czech Gothic, and built on a grand scale, employing, along with some German and Czech architects, many Italian builders and artists to design and decorate in the new style. The Belvedere in the royal garden on the Hradčany and arcaded castles at Litomyšl and Opočin are perhaps the best examples of this new trend.

In the various branches of art the sixteenth century saw Italy still the leading center of inspiration, experimentation, and technique. Italy had never really had a Gothic age; but in the countries of northern Europe, where the Gothic spirit had ruled for from two to four centuries, Italian Renaissance ideals, the humanist faith, the pleasures of line and curve, of color and shade, profoundly influenced all artistic expression. The artist became, in reality, the voice of his time and of the people of his generation. The overlap of religious austerity imposed by a universal church was weakened; the delights of sense and the potentialities of the individual broke through. The modern world was being born.

SUGGESTIONS FOR FURTHER READING

See also bibliographies to Chapters 13 and 14.

BUTTERFIELD, H., *The Origins of Modern Science*. London, 1949
CROMBIE, A. C., *Augustine to Galileo*. London, 1952
DAMPIER, W. C., *A History of Science*. Cambridge, 1952
HALL, A. R., *The Scientific Revolution, 1500–1800*. Boston, 1952
PLEDGE, H. T., *Science since 1500*. New York, 1959
SARTON, G., *History of Science and the New Humanism*. New York, 1937
SEDGWICK, W. T., and H. W. TYLER, *A Short History of Science*. New York, 1917
SINGER, C. J., *A Short History of Science*. Oxford, 1941
TATON, RENÉ, ed., *La Science moderne*, Vol. II, *De 1450 à 1800*. 1958
THORNDIKE, L., *A History of Magic and Experimental Science,* Vols. V–VII. New York, 1923

Wolf, A., *A History of Science and Technology in the 16th and 17th Centuries.* New York, 1950

Brodrick, G. C., *History of the University of Oxford.* London, 1894
Cubberley, E. P., *History of Education.* New York, 1920
Cubberley, E. P., *Readings in the History of Education.* New York, 1920
d'Irsay, S., *Histoire des universités françaises et étrangères.* 2 vols. 1933, 1935
Kaufmann, G., *Geschichte der deutschen Universitäten.* 2 vols. 1888
Mallett, C. E., *History of the University of Oxford.* 3 vols. London, 1924, 1928
Mullinger, J. B., *History of the University of Cambridge.* London, 1888
Quick, R. H., *Essays on Educational Reformers.* New York, 1912
Smith, P., *History of Modern Culture,* Vol. I. New York, 1930

Anderson, W. J., and A. Stratton, *The Architecture of the Renaissance in Italy.* London, 1921
Beccherucci, L., *L'Architettura italiana del cinquecento.* 1936
Benesch, O., *The Art of the Renaissance in Northern Europe.* New York, 1945
Faure, F., *History of Art.* Vol. III, *Renaissance Art.* New York, 1921–30
Fletcher, B., *History of Architecture on the Comparative Method.* 14th ed. London, 1948
Gardner, H., *Art through the Ages.* 4th ed. New York, 1959
Hauser, A., *The Social History of Art.* New York, 1957
Hoffmann, H., *Hochrenaissance, Manierismus, Frühbarock.* 1938
Pevsner, N., *An Outline of European Architecture.* London, 1951. Pelican
Pijoan, José, *A History of Art.* 3 vols. New York and London, 1927 and 1933

CHAPTER TWENTY-SEVEN

THE EMPIRE AND THE
THIRTY YEARS' WAR

THE religious Peace of Augsburg of 1555, which ended temporarily more than thirty years of tension and war between the Emperor Charles V and the German Protestants, was a result of fatigue on both sides perhaps more than a sincere composition of the issues. Charles had come to see that he could neither force his Lutheran subjects to return to the Church nor decisively defeat them in the field. It was no settlement, only a truce. Both sides realized the nature of the truce and were firmly determined to advance their cause by any possible means and on every possible issue. The very terms of the peace provided occasions for renewal of tension. The Calvinists were excluded from the tolerance provided for Catholic and Lutheran rulers in the Empire; the Ecclesiastical Reservation stipulated that if an ecclesiastical prince, archbishop, bishop, or abbot changed his confession from Catholic to Lutheran, he must give up his office with all its lands and properties. The strenuous objections of the Protestants to the Reservation forecast trouble in the future, since, in the fluid conditions of the times, changes of confession were certain to occur. The arrangement that in free and imperial cities ecclesiastical property should be divided between Catholic and Lutheran communities was to give rise to local friction, especially since populations not infrequently changed through immigration or emigration, and property once possessed under an earlier proportional adjustment would not willingly be given up when the population changed.

There was, however, in the midst of the uncertainties for which the Peace was largely responsible, one certain result: the princes, Catholic or Lutheran, had gained in power in their own lands. The principle *cuius regio eius religio* confirmed the independence of the princes from the Emperor. This independence from imperial control had, as its reverse side, heightened dominance of the princes over the estates of their lands, over their subjects, and over those cities which had imperial status, thus continuing a trend already a century old, which, fortified by the importation of Roman law, had made the princes of Germany virtual kings in their little realms. When Charles V retired from the affairs of the Empire just prior to the Peace of Augsburg and formally abdicated as Emperor in 1558, he increased the tempo of decentralization.

Habsburg Emperors: Ferdinand I and Maximilian II

CHARLES' successor, his younger brother Ferdinand I, was rooted in his Austrian lands and, since 1526, elected king of Bohemia and of a rump of Hungary. He had to defend Europe against the apparently invincible Turks. Obliged to ask the Diet for large grants for this purpose almost every year, he found himself a suppliant, dependent on the good will of the German princes, Protestant as well as Catholic. He had perforce to balance a double policy, Austrian and imperial. When the princes of Germany now came to doubt the Emperor's interest in the Empire as a whole, there began that prolonged cleavage in sentiment and loyalty between the Habsburg emperors and the princes and Diet of Germany which marks the succeeding century.

Ferdinand, anxious to gain and retain the acquiescence of the Protestants, granted, in 1556, the use of the cup to the laity, and marriage of the clergy was a permitted practice. In a secret "declaration" Ferdinand promised the Protestants that they would not be disturbed in the possession of ecclesiastical properties of which they had already established ownership. So far had Ferdinand gone in concessions to the Protestants that the decade from Augsburg to about 1565 would have seemed to a casual traveler in Germany a period of Protestant predominance. Of the four secular electors only the Emperor himself, as king of Bohemia, was a Catholic. The electors of Saxony and Brandenburg and the Count Palatine were professing Lutherans. Of the cities only a few were Catholic.

These were apparent and visible signs of Protestant strength. In the scales against Protestantism there were weighty factors, some within the reformed faith itself, some external to it. The Peace of Augsburg made provision for only one kind of reformed faith—Lutheranism. But from the middle of the century Calvinism made great gains in western and northern Germany. Determined opposition to its spread came from Lutherans perhaps more openly than from Catholics. Protestantism was thus bitterly divided within itself. Furthermore, divergent political aims made broad cooperation among Lutheran princes almost impossible. An equally significant factor in the ultimate arrest of Protestant growth was the vigorous campaign waged by the Jesuits for the recovery of Germany for the Church, from their introduction into Germany in 1544. Armed with the decrees and spirit of the Council of Trent and their own effective organization and discipline, the order won city after city which had Protestant majorities, came to occupy posts as chaplains and tutors at princely courts, and gave new tone and direction to higher education in all of Germany. The Jesuits were strongest in Bavaria, where Duke Albert V, son-in-law of Emperor Ferdinand I and educated by the Jesuit order, gave them every facility and encouragement. In 1569 he introduced a strict Catholic censorship. In 1570–71 he ordered all Protestant preachers out of his domains, setting a precedent of direct action soon followed in the ecclesiastical electorates of Trier (1572) and Mainz (1574).

Maximilian II (1564–76), the son of Ferdinand I, was an amiable, cultivated, and capable person. His long-standing sympathies with the reform movement were public knowledge, so much so that many Protestants hoped and many Catholics feared that he would accept the Protestant faith openly. Early in his reign he was antipapal and anti-Spanish, but after the death of Philip's son Don Carlos in 1568, when there was a possibility that Maximilian, as the eldest nephew of Charles V, might inherit the Spanish throne, he changed his tune and spoke with respect of Philip and Spain. Maximilian's many good qualities did not include that of field generalship. In 1566 he had at his command a well-equipped army of seventy thousand troops to meet the advance of the Turks into Hungary. In October of that year Suleiman died, and Maximilian, who should have attacked, failed to take advantage of the situation. Instead he ended an inglorious campaign by signing a treaty leaving the Turks in possession of what they already had, and he promised to continue the tribute of thirty thousand ducats. In 1575, already decrepit at forty-five years of age, he was a candidate for the throne of Poland. The Polish Senate accepted him; but the whole Diet, led by the great chancellor, Jan Zamojski, would have no German ruler over them and elected Stephen Báthory, prince of Transylvania, instead. Báthory's great advantage in the eyes of the Poles was that he had just waged a successful war against the Turks. In the last *Reichstag* of his reign, at Regensburg in 1576, Maximilian was faced with the demand of the Protestants that he publicly approve and accept the "declaration of Ferdinand," guaranteeing Protestants freedom from molestation in the exercise of their religion. With Catholic princes outnumbering the Protestants in the *Reichstag,* Maximilian was able to avoid complying with the embarrassing demand. A few months later he was dead and his son Rudolf II succeeded to the throne.

Calvinism in the Empire

THE twenty years from the Peace of Augsburg to the death of Maximilian II witnessed the establishment and growth of Calvinism on imperial soil. Otto Henry became Elector of the Palatinate in 1555 and almost immediately declared for Lutheranism under the terms of the Peace of Augsburg. The University of Heidelberg thereupon took a leading position in the Protestant movement, enlivened by debates between visiting Calvinists and resident Lutheran students and professors. Otto Henry was succeeded by Frederick III (1559–76). In 1561 a conference of Protestant princes met at Naumburg. The immediate purposes of the meeting were to formulate a united policy toward the Catholic Church and, specifically, toward the Council of Trent, and to choose between the strict Lutheranism of Flacius Illyricus, as demanded by John Frederick, Elector of Saxony, and a position more nearly in accord with Melanchthon's moderate program. Frederick III supported the moderate side. One of the theologians speaking for the Melanchthonian party was Zacharias Ursinus (Bär). Frederick, greatly impressed by the personality and talent of Ursinus, took him back to Heidelberg as his adviser. In 1563 Ursinus and another professor at Heidelberg, Olivian, a pupil of Calvin, at the Elector's request composed the Heidelberg Catechism, which was soon in use in Nassau, Hesse-Cassel, Anhalt, and Bremen. In 1564 Frederick reorganized the church of the Palatinate according to the Calvinist model. From this time the Palatinate, surrounded by Catholic states, was, with short interruptions, the determined center of German Calvinism.

Frederick's open espousal of Calvinism obliged Maximilian to raise the question whether under the terms of the Peace of Augsburg, which recognized only Lutheranism as Protestant, Frederick was legally a Protestant. The question was brought up at the *Reichstag* at Augsburg in 1568. Frederick defended himself eloquently and successfully, and Maximilian's decree, ordering Frederick to cancel his Calvinistic measures, had to be withdrawn. Frederick supported William the Silent in Holland with a loan and troops, sent substantial contingents of troops to Condé and Coligny in France, and participated in the peaces of Longjumeau (1568) and St. Germain (1570) on the side of the Huguenots. The principality of Nassau became Calvinist in 1574. Others were to follow under the rule of Maximilian's son and successor Rudolf II (1576–1612).

While Calvinism was making some modest gains in western Germany, Lutheranism was suffering from division and dissension. The two wings of the movement, the stricter party, followers of Flacius Illyricus, and the Philipists, or followers of Melanchthon, were brought together by the Elector Augustus of Saxony as early as 1576. The document which resulted from this effort at conciliation, the *Formula of Concord,* was issued in 1580. Augustus was particularly anxious to exclude Calvinism from the benefits of the Peace of Augsburg, and the *Formula* accurately reflected this purpose. In the final analysis the actual result of the *Formula* was only to make more evident the split between the strict party and the moderates. The latter would have been inclined to accept the Calvinists as fellow Protestants and to forget their minor differences.

The influence of the Calvinist minority was, at about the same time, strengthened by the arrival in Nassau, the Palatinate, Jülich, Cleves, and other Rhenish areas of Protestants recently forced to leave the Spanish Netherlands. These refugees were almost without exception Calvinists. The very fact of their growing strength alarmed their Lutheran opponents. One of the leading Lutheran theologians, Polycarp Leyser, wrote a pamphlet under the title *Whether, How, and Why We Should Prefer to Consort with and Trust Papists Rather Than Calvinists.* German Protestantism was thus in effect split three ways: at one extreme the strict Lutherans, headed by the Elector of Saxony, at the other extreme, the Calvinists, led by the Elector Palatine. In between were the moderate Lutherans, influenced by Melanchthon's conciliatory temper and variously called Philipists or Crypto-Calvinists. The middle group could obviously not be counted on by either side in any political or military struggle.

The Counter-Reformation in the Empire

WHILE Protestantism was thus wasting its energy in internal strife, Catholicism was showing new vitality. The Counter-Reformation, led by the Jesuits and favored by the Habsburgs and the duke of Bavaria, was recovering for the Church great areas of the Empire. Protestant holdings were being attacked on every front. In 1582, at the *Reichstag* at Augsburg, the Protestant Joachim

Frederick of Hohenzollern, who had been since 1566 administrator of the arch-bishopric of Magdeburg, was prevented from taking his seat because he had not been confirmed in his office by the Pope. Gebhart Trucksess, who had been elected archbishop of Cologne in 1577 and confirmed by Pope Gregory XIII, declared himself a Lutheran in 1582. Under the terms of the Ecclesiastical Reservation he would of course have to give up his lands and privileges. If, however, the Protestant electors had supported him he would in all probability have been safe in his post. Instead they sided with the Emperor against their fellow Protestant. On the Catholic side, following an aggressive and well-conceived policy of attacking on all fronts, Ernest of Bavaria, a Jesuit-trained member of the Wittelsbach family, collected bishoprics: Freising (1566), Hildesheim (1578), Lüttich (1581), and Münster (1585). After the deposition of Trucksess Ernest was raised to the electoral archbishopric of Cologne (1583).

Aachen Rewon to Catholicism

THE imperial city of Aachen (Aix-la-Chapelle), close to the Dutch frontier, had been gradually losing its Catholic character. In addition to a growth in the Lutheran population, Calvinist émigrés from Holland came into the city in such numbers that finally, about 1580, Protestants were in a majority. They took over the city government in spite of the Emperor's intervention and later ban (1582). The Catholic majority in the *Reichstag* of 1582 forbade the exercise of Calvinism in the city, the officials were punished and deposed and the city heavily fined. Ultimately, in 1605, all non-Catholics were expelled. These few instances may be taken to illustrate the reason why the Protestants lost ground in Germany in the second half of the sixteenth century: the terms of the Peace of Augsburg which made no provision for Calvinism; the narrow antipathy of Lutheran rulers toward any version of Protestantism but their own; the consistent firmness and legalism of the Habsburg rulers; the brilliant leadership and effective labors of the Jesuits and, what has not hitherto been specifically mentioned, the failure of non-German Protestant powers, principally England and the Huguenots in France, to come to the aid of their co-religionists in Germany. It was indeed, from the Protestant standpoint, a tragedy of errors.

The Protestants were divided and unlucky. But the Habsburgs, the leaders of the Catholic party, were not by any means free from troubles. The Turkish wars demanded their constant attention and great sums of money. Ferdinand and Maximilian had been almost continually and unsuccessfully at war with the Turks. Rudolf, too, had had to fight on the Transylvanian front, and Matthias, as Rudolf's lieutenant, fought the Turks for thirteen years (1593–1606) before concluding an acceptable peace. During all this half-century, from 1556 to 1606, the emperors, in need of grants of money from the *Reichstag,* could ill afford to take an aggressive line against princes of the Empire, whether Lutheran or Calvinist. Although the Lutheran and the Calvinist princes were at odds among themselves, yet they would usually unite to protect the independence of their order from imperial aggression or interference. Not until the Turkish wars were over did the imperial party feel itself strong enough to devote its full energy to the task of suppressing Protestantism, that "dog's creed," as Matthias called it.

Donauwörth

THERE were many minor incidents between Catholics and Protestants in the last years of the century leading up to the withdrawal of the Protestant princes from the *Reichstag* of 1598. Spanish troops had on several occasions been used to settle disputes in favor of the Catholic party, and popular resentment against the foreign soldiery ran high. A single incident broke the uneasy peace. The little town of Donauwörth on the Danube was a free imperial city whose population was, in a great majority, Protestant. The few Catholics remaining in the town were restricted in the public exercise of their religion. The Jesuits decided to win the city back to Catholicism, and, from 1602, revived old ceremonies, processions, and public burials. When the Protestant magistrates (in 1605) took action to "abate the nuisance," the case was brought before the imperial court which forthwith, without examining the facts, ordered the magistrates to desist from interfering with Catholic exercises. In the city itself there was violence, and the Emperor commissioned the duke of Bavaria to bring order. The duke was only too glad to oblige. After being occupied by Catholic troops (1607) Donauwörth lost its freedom and was forcibly catholicized.

Throughout the Empire the Protestants took alarm at this violent action; in fear lest the new policy of Habsburg force be applied more widely, a number of them banded together in a "Union" (May 14, 1608) of which the leading spirit was Christian of Anhalt, acting as minister of Frederick V, Elector of the Palatinate. There were Lutheran as well as Calvinist members of the Union. The almost immediate answer to this defensive gesture was the formation (July 10, 1609) of a Catholic League under the leadership of Maximilian of Bavaria. Neither the Emperor nor any Habsburg prince joined the League. Both groups sought outside alliances: the Union with France, the Netherlands, and England; the League with Spain.

Germany had, throughout the preceding centuries, witnessed the formation of many leagues and their early disappearance. Although there was exceptional bitterness behind these latest alignments, the situation did not yet threaten war. Many of the participants still hoped for peace and conciliation.

The Cleves-Jülich Crisis

HOPES for peace were, however, shaken by the outbreak of the Cleves-Jülich crisis. The ruler of this important complex of strategically situated territories on both sides of the lower Rhine—Cleves, Jülich, Berg, Mark, and Neuburg—died in March 1609 without a direct heir. Claimants sprang up on all sides, among whom the most impressive were the Elector of Brandenburg and the Count Palatine of Neuburg. These two reached an agreement to divide the lands about evenly between them. Because of the strategic importance of these territories all Europe was interested. The Emperor wanted a Catholic prince to possess the lands. Henry IV of France was determined that no Habsburg prince should control the Rhine, while the Spanish, in view of the proximity of these lands to Holland and their own Netherlands, wanted no Protestant to border Spanish territory. The Union sent troops to support Brandenburg and the count of Neu-

Germany and the Thirty Years' War

burg and made a treaty with Henry of France for French troops to enter the conflict on the Protestant side. Spanish troops under the Archduke Leopold were driven out, and Protestant success seemed to call for more energetic League action. The Catholic League armed, and, on the Protestant side, Dutch troops under Maurice of Nassau entered Jülich. War was very near, but at this critical juncture the League decided not to precipitate it, and by the autumn of 1610 the danger passed.

It was unfortunate for the cause of peace that the settlement of a German question had been enforced by foreign military intervention. It was, further-more, an uneasy peace, since the two "possessor princes" quarreled and split, one, the Brandenburger, becoming a Calvinist, and the other, the count of Neuburg, a Catholic. In 1614, by the treaty of Xanten, the territories were formally di-vided between the two princes—the only solution short of open hostilities that met any acceptance whatever. First it had been Cologne, then Aachen, then Donauwörth, and now the Cleves-Jülich crisis. In every case the issue resolved itself into a matching of forces between Protestant and Catholic. The question whether Europe could avoid a total armed conflict much longer was in every-body's mind, when lightning struck from an unexpected quarter.

Bohemia and the Habsburgs

BOHEMIA had a long history of religious and political independence. It was predominantly Hussite, that is, anti-Roman Catholic, when the Habsburg Ferdi-nand I was elected to the throne in 1526. For the most part the Habsburgs treated Bohemian (both Czech and German) anti-Catholicism with great deli-cacy. Maximilian, originally sympathetic to Bohemian religious independence, in 1575 agreed orally to allow the Bohemian Confession to be practiced in the kingdom. Maximilian's son and successor, Rudolf II, a more fervent Catholic, gave eager support to the Jesuits, who made noticeable gains at court and among the nobility. By the year 1600 there were two hundred Jesuits in the kingdom, yet, despite their activity and court favor, the country remained steadfastly Prot-estant. The Estates were probably nine-tenths Protestant. It was, however, a strange Protestantism: partly Lutheran, partly Utraquist, partly Calvinist, and the whole influenced by the austere Hussite tradition of the Bohemian Brethren. Whatever it was, it was national, combining both Bohemian Germans and native Czechs, one of the few instances in the history of the country when German and Czech thought worked together. A royal order of 1602, directed against all Protestant clergy, was almost completely disregarded throughout the country.

From about 1595 Rudolf had been suffering from melancholia, and the Habs-burg family wished him to name a successor who would rule when the Emperor was indisposed. Rudolf refused and was at virtual war with his brother Mat-thias, who was the choice of the family, for the next nine years. In 1609, when Matthias brought his army close to Prague, Rudolf, pressed for recognition of their faith by the Protestant Estates (without whose support he could not stand against Matthias), granted the Letter of Majesty (*Majestätsbrief*). In this docu-ment the Bohemian Confession of 1575 was recognized as the law of the land, and tolerance was guaranteed by the constitution. Protestant and Catholic lords, knights and royal cities were allowed freedom of worship and the right to build churches and schools on royal lands. Thirty "Defenders" could be named by the Estates to watch over the execution of the decree. The Consistory of the church in Prague, as well as the university, the ancient and traditional center of Bo-hemian cultural and national life, were to be in the hands of the Protestants.

The Protestant majority had gained what they thought was their *magna charta* and rejoiced. The Catholics were in consternation. The Jesuits ordered all the faithful to pray steadily for forty hours that God might protect the faith and exterminate the heretics. The determined Catholics at court, led by the Spanish ambassador Zuñiga, bent every effort toward getting the king to with-draw his approval of the Letter, or, failing that, to force the Protestants to com-pliance. War loomed close in the summer and early autumn of 1609. However, cooler councils prevailed and both parties settled down to prepare for the struggle which all were convinced was now inevitable.

Relations between Rudolf and Matthias, whom Rudolf knew the Habsburg family favored to succeed him, were uneven but mostly bad. In 1611, after Mat-thias forced Rudolf to turn over to him the crown of Bohemia, Rudolf retired, bitter, ill and broken in spirit, to the Hradčany, retaining for himself the title of Emperor, by now an empty honor. Matthias, soon after Rudolf's death in 1612, was elected Emperor without opposition. When he quickly confirmed the Letter of Majesty, the Protestants felt prematurely confident that the battle of religion was won. The most important person in the Emperor's entourage, in the formulation of policy and in its execution, was thenceforth to be Melchior Khlesl, who became chancellor in 1612 and was given a cardinal's hat in 1615. Matthias was not robust, but in his determination to win back what prestige the crown had lost in Bohemia through Rudolf's weakness and vacillation he was firmness itself. On Khlesl's advice he removed known Protestant officials from posts in the royal gift and appointed vigorous Catholic prelates and officials in their place. So brisk and efficient were Matthias' moves that the Protestant Estates, caught unprepared, were unable to make effective protests or plan counteraction. To add to the concern of the Protestants the question of the ailing Matthias' successor was being discussed. His marriage had remained childless and his cousin Ferdinand of Styria was regarded as the most likely candidate. Ferdinand was known as a pupil of the Jesuits and a fanatical exponent of the Counter-Reform. The Bohemian nobility and townsmen regarded his candidacy with perturbation. The Estates clung to the tradition that the crown of Bohemia was elective, not hereditary, and other possible candidates were discussed in Protestant circles quite openly. In the event, however, not only was no other candidate put up, but by their indecision the Estates were forced into the position of "recognizing" or "accepting," instead of "electing," Ferdinand as heir to the throne (June 1617). This action had the effect of approving the Habsburg contention that the dynasty had a hereditary right to the crown of Bohemia. Ferdinand accepted the Letter of Majesty and was crowned with great pomp on July 1, 1617. From this time it was Ferdinand who ruled. Matthias' death in March 1619 was scarcely noticed.

At the very time of Ferdinand's "acceptance" by the Bohemian Estates two disputes involving the principles of the Letter of Majesty were coming to a head. Since 1611 the Lutheran inhabitants of the little Czech town of Broumov (Braunau) had been building a chapel in accord, as they thought, with the terms of the Letter of Majesty, on land belonging to the local monastery but commonly regarded as crown land. The abbot (later elected archbishop of Prague) ordered the church closed and locked. At Hrob (Klostergrab) the local Calvinists were building a small church on land belonging to the archdiocese of Prague. Again the parishioners assumed that ecclesiastical land was a part of the royal domain. The archbishop ordered the church demolished, stone by stone (December 1617). Popular indignation at the violation of the Letter of Majesty ran high. The Defenders called a meeting of the Estates, as they were allowed to do under the terms of the Letter. The Estates met in Prague on May 5, formulated their complaints against the royal lieutenants, and set the next meeting for May 21, allowing time for a royal answer to their gravamina. The streets were full of knights and burghers from outside Prague, the air was full of rumors and threats. The Bohemian leadership talked of the rights of the crown and the treason of the king's counselors. The royal answer, composed on Khlesl's advice, forbade the meeting of the Estates and threatened all participants with the royal displeasure. On the twenty-second the Bohemian leaders had already decided on the punishment the royal lieutenants were going to suffer. On the twenty-third, early in the morning, the Estates met in the Old Town, armed and confident, then marched in a body across the Charles bridge and up to the castle on the hill (the Hradčany). There they met the king's officials, listened to the letter they had just received from the king in Vienna, replied by charging them with high treason, and threw the two they regarded as most guilty, Martinic and Slavata, out of the window into a moat seventy feet below. An inconspicuous imperial secretary who ventured to object to this harsh treatment of His Majesty's trusted counselors was thrown after them. Miraculously, or so it seemed, only one of the three was seriously injured. The sloping stone wall, their armor, and a pile of brush and manure at the bottom broke their fall. They got up, found horses, and fled to Vienna. War had been declared.

The Bohemian Revolt

THE war, of which the Bohemian revolt was the precipitant, was to last for thirty years and involve almost all the states and princes of Europe. It is notorious for the havoc and devastation it wrought and for the shock it caused to the social and moral structure of the Western world. It is also known as the final phase of the religious wars between Charles V and the German princes and cities that followed Luther. There is no question that the Bohemian Estates broke with the Habsburgs largely on grounds of religious differences—the Bohemians demanding religious freedom, some for their Lutheranism, some for Calvinism, and some for Hussitism in one form or another. The Habsburgs, on the other hand, guided and supported by Jesuit advisers and the voice of Spain, were determined to root out heresy and force their Bohemian subjects, German or Czech, to accept the Catholic faith. These differences were basic, and it is difficult to see how war in Bohemia could have been avoided. Nevertheless, once war was joined, the religious aspect tended to become mixed with purely political and dynastic issues so that, at any given moment after the defeat of the Bohemians at the Battle of the White Mountain (Bilá Hora) outside Prague on November 8, 1620, the student can easily trace political aims and issues, in varying degrees, in the negotiations and shifts of the several powers. By the end of the war, as we shall see, political and dynastic issues dominated the scene; religion was never again to hold the dominant place in European diplomacy, as it had at the outbreak of hostilities. To this extent the Thirty Years' War marks a watershed in European history. It is the end of the religious age and the beginning of the age of secularism.

The course of the war may best be treated in three periods. The first, from 1618 to 1629, from the Bohemian revolt to the peace of Lübeck, marks the collapse of native German Protestantism and the victory of the imperial cause. The second period, from 1630 to the peace of Prague, 1635, covers three significant changes in the balance of power in Germany: the revival of Protestant prestige by Swedish military intervention, Maximilian of Bavaria's capture from the Emperor of the leadership of the Catholic cause, and the entrance of France into German affairs through a Swedish alliance. The third period, from 1635 to 1648, covers the implementation of the strange alliance of France and Sweden, whose purpose was to block Habsburg hegemony within the Empire, strengthen forces of separatism in Germany, and permit both allies to expand their borders at German expense.

The Winter King: Protestant Failure

IMMEDIATELY after the defenestration the Bohemian Diet set up a Directory of Thirty Defenders to defend and administer the country. The chosen Defenders and military leaders began a diplomatic campaign to gain allies and outside support. The Emperor at the same time sent his envoys to the courts of Europe to hold or win allies. The Bohemians had counted, optimistically as it turned out, on the support of Protestants everywhere and on that of enemies of the Habsburgs, of which there were many. The Emperor's cause was represented as that of legitimacy and the repression of rebellion. The Bohemians presented the cause of an injured and suppressed people, deprived of their ancient liberties, subjected by force and deceit to a faith they did not accept and a government against their constitution. The Hungarian Diet, in a majority Protestant, expressed sympathy with the Bohemians and urged them to make peace with the Emperor. The Moravian Estates, led by Charles of Žerotín, a highly respected Hussite, answered the Bohemian appeal by urging peace upon the Emperor. John George, Elector of Saxony, although a Protestant, rejected all overtures from the Bohemians, even when the crown was dangled before his eyes. In his view too many of the Bohemians were Calvinists, and to him Calvinism was worse than Catholicism. He could not countenance rebellion, and let it be known that his sympathies lay with the Emperor and the cause of legitimacy. The Elector of Brandenburg, also Protestant, remained neutral. Silesia, out of enmity for the Habsburgs, sided with the Bohemians and the Estates voted to send six thousand soldiers to their aid. The most enthusiastic response to Bohemian calls for help came from the Palatinate, whose ruler, Frederick, guided by Christian of Anhalt, aspired to be the effectual leader of Protestantism in Germany. From Charles Emmanuel, duke of Savoy and a bitter enemy of the Habsburgs, came substantial help. Ernest of Mansfeld, a professional soldier in the duke's employ, was sent with four thousand men into Bohemia in September and laid siege to Pilsen, a city with a Catholic tradition, loyal to the Emperor. Its capture in November 1618 was the first military success of the Bohemian side, won by a German soldier in the pay of a French prince.

In the meantime the imperial court had secured promises of support or of neutrality from Spain, Poland, Bavaria, Saxony, and Brandenburg, while the Protestant Union, of which Frederick of the Palatinate was the president, rejected his pleas to join him in his support of the Bohemian Estates (September 1618). After the death of Matthias in March 1619, the Bohemian Estates claimed that Ferdinand had not been legally invested with the crown and formally deposed him (August 17, 1619), leaving the throne vacant. A few days later (August 26) Frederick of the Palatinate was elected king of Bohemia in Prague. On the twenty-eighth Ferdinand was elected Emperor in Frankfurt.

In 1619 there was military action on many fronts. The Bohemian army under Count Thurn struck south toward Vienna in the spring but withdrew for lack of siege equipment. Mansfeld was attacked and defeated by the imperial general Bucquoi; Bethlen Gábor, the Protestant prince of Transylvania and traditional enemy of the Habsburgs, approached Vienna from the east but was unable to remain because of severe winter conditions. The year's campaigning ended indecisively, with both sides planning for the spring. Denmark, Sweden, the United Provinces, and the Venetian Republic recognized Frederick as king, and hope sprang up that help would be forthcoming from these countries. Frederick's father-in-law, James I of England, opposed to rebellion of any sort, gave no help save long letters of pointless advice. On the other hand, the Catholic cause gained adherents and position with the spring. Maximilian of Bavaria, having led the League to diplomatic advantages over the Union, was at the gates of Pilsen. New generals and armies began to press against the Bohemians: Spinola, a Genoese commander of Spanish troops from the Netherlands, Tilly, an able general in the pay of the League, Bucquoi from Austria, and a Saxon army under John George against Lusatia. Spinola took the Palatinate; Frederick, daily losing popularity in Prague and incapable of military or diplomatic command, was unable to counter at any point along the line.

The Bohemian revolt had become a war involving the Empire and Spain. The Catholic forces, from three directions, bore in upon Prague. Near the city, at a prominence known as the White Mountain, the three imperial armies joined on November 8, 1620, facing the Bohemian troops. The Protestant armies were badly led and the victory of the Catholic forces was clear and decisive. Frederick fled the land with his wife and a few followers, earning the epithet of the Winter King. He took refuge at The Hague while most of his Palatinate was occupied by imperial troops. On January 22, 1621, Ferdinand put him under the ban of the Empire and deprived him (with more than doubtful legality) of his lands and titles. Frederick was personally almost helpless, but still he represented to a certain degree the cause of the princes of the Empire, and there was some sentiment among the German nobility in his favor. Mansfeld, with sixteen thousand troops, kept up resistance to imperial occupation for a time in the Upper Palatinate while an English regiment defended Frederick's cause in the Lower Palatinate. In 1621 two Protestant leaders, the margrave of Baden and the warlike administrator of the bishopric of Halberstadt, Christian of Brunswick, took the field against Tilly and the Spanish troops. A war of siege and movement dragged on through the winter. Divided command could lead only to defeat, and by the summer of 1622 the Palatinate was safely in the hands of the imperialists. The capital Heidelberg surrendered to Tilly on September 19.

In 1621 Spain and Holland had renewed their war. The Twelve Years' Truce of 1609 expired in that year and a new conflict, Catholic against Protestant, had come to imperial soil and was to complicate the issues within the Empire. Hereafter one may expect the Dutch to be interested in supporting the Protestant cause in Germany and the Spanish to be committed to support of the Catholic side. There were times when it was not certain whether this support was given to the Habsburgs or to the Catholic League, but for the most part Spain and the Emperor worked closely together. It was easier to cooperate with one person, such as the Emperor, than with a group of uncertain and divided counsels, such as the League.

Meanwhile in Bohemia Ferdinand was reaping the fruits of victory. The Bohemian leaders were captured and tried, and twenty-seven of them, nobles and burghers, were beheaded on the Old Town Square in Prague on June 21, 1621; their heads were stuck on pikes at prominent places throughout the city as a warning to the population that resistance to the Habsburgs was dangerous. Ferdinand slashed the original of the Letter of Majesty across its face to show it was no longer valid, and the systematic confiscation and expulsion of the Protestants began. The Bohemian phase of the war was over. For the Protestant cause it had been disastrous, and for the Winter King it was worse. In February 1623, Ferdinand paid his debt to Maximilian of Bavaria by transferring to him, quite unconstitutionally and against the protestations of the other electors and even the Spanish ambassador, Frederick's electoral dignity. Maximilian would live to regret an action which went contrary to the interests of the princes and at the same time strengthened the power of the Emperor. If the Emperor could depose one elector he could depose any other who might oppose him. The constitution of the Empire was being gravely weakened. The Protestant electors of Saxony and Brandenburg, hitherto conciliatory toward the Emperor, were now convinced that the imperial side meant to crush Protestantism by any possible means and that resistance to the death was their only choice. Hereafter they might be neutral at any given moment, but their general leaning was to the Protestant cause.

The War in Northern Germany: Denmark

THE fever of war had affected northern Germany, and as the Protestants north of the Main realized the extent and implication of the Catholic victories in Bohemia, Bavaria, and Austria, sentiment in the Palatinate grew for an appeal to arms. James I of England, influenced by his rash son Charles and the latter's even more reckless favorite Buckingham to reverse his stand of five years earlier, decided to support a move to retake the Palatinate, restore Frederick, and strike a blow for the Protestant faith. France had already seen the necessity of opposing the Spanish-Habsburg coalition—Spain in Italy and the Low Countries and a victorious imperial army sweeping into northern Germany. In 1623 Louis XIII was negotiating with Mansfeld to campaign in northern Italy. In 1624 Richelieu came to power in France and the anti-Habsburg trend in French policy became a fixture, well articulated and brilliantly executed. At this point in French history Richelieu was neither obliged nor inclined to have France enter the fray with troops in Germany. France was divided religiously and the Huguenots were strongly entrenched in their cities. In view of this limitation, at least of the moment, Richelieu substituted for troops a diplomacy which took advantage of common interests, and in the course of 1624 aided in bringing together France, the Dutch, the Elector of Brandenburg, Denmark, Sweden, England, Savoy, and Venice into a linkage of alliances designed to arrest Habsburg expansion in northern Germany. In the north it was obvious that Richelieu preferred to have his allies do the fighting. To the south, however, Richelieu could actively participate in the obstruction of Spanish re-enforcements to the Emperor at the point of passage over the Alps—the Val Telline on the southern slope of the mountains. In 1625 this route was blocked by French and Savoyard troops and France was in effect fighting on the side of the German Protestants, though her heavy military involvement had to wait for some years upon the settlement of the Huguenot question at home.

Christian IV of Denmark, a lusty, energetic, and withal able ruler, took the lead in 1625 in the Protestant cause. As duke of Holstein he was a prince of the Empire and thus legitimately interested in the course of the struggle for power within its bounds. The allies, who had been brought together in the previous year, found for various reasons that their several contributions to the cause would have to be small. The winter was severe, disease was rampant, and unpaid soldiers ravaged the countryside. Gustavus Adolphus of Sweden, then at war with Poland, was invited to lead the Protestant military effort, but, not provided the troops or the money that he thought he would need to achieve victory, refused the invitation and returned to his Polish war. The English Parliament, cool to James I's plans and his successor Charles I's ambitions, refused to make any further grants to the Protestants of northern Germany. John George, Elector of Saxony, hoping to stay on good terms with the Emperor, refused to help his fellow Lutheran, the king of Denmark. Richelieu in 1626 had to face a Huguenot revolt at home and found himself so heavily engaged that he was unable to offer any assistance to Christian. The king of Denmark was thus left to face on his own the imperial armies under Tilly. His only aid was to come from Mansfeld, a very uncertain and even unlucky general. The Emperor, on his side, had enemies: Bethlen Gábor threatened from the east and France was a menace in the west.

At this crucial point Albrecht Waldstein,* duke of Friedland, a rich Bohemian nobleman with a genius for organization, offered his services to Ferdinand as a recruiter and general. He asked no mercenary pay, only the right to administer the lands he conquered for the Emperor. The Emperor accepted the conditions and soon Waldstein was in undisputed possession of broad areas in northern Germany. A conflict between Christian and the two imperial generals was only a matter of time. The first battle was at the bridge of Dessau over the Elbe (April 25, 1626), where Mansfeld was badly defeated by Waldstein. Mansfeld was fortunate to escape. He went to join Bethlen in Silesia to annoy Ferdinand from the east. In August Tilly met the army of King Christian at Lutter in Thuringia. The Danish army fought bravely and well but lacked the staying power of Tilly's veterans reinforced by 1900 cavalry and 2400 infantry sent by Waldstein. Christian withdrew to the north. The Protestant side had thus twice been decisively defeated in six months. The Catholic side, however, was having its own difficulties. The League and the Emperor were sharply divided on aims and means. Waldstein's very virtues made him an object of envy and suspicion to the Catholic League. The population of the lands he had squeezed for tribute distrusted and feared him. Yet the Emperor needed a successful general, and Waldstein was showered with rewards. In 1627 he took Silesia, then, with Tilly, drove Christian out of Holstein. He pursued him northward through Schleswig into Jutland, and Danish resistance was at an end.

* Incorrectly known as Wallenstein.

Protestant Defeat: The Treaty of Lübeck

WALDSTEIN had by now certainly formed a plan for the subjection, in the name of the Emperor, of all of northern Germany, including the southern coast of the Baltic. His enemies at the court in Vienna cast doubt on the honesty of his motives, but the Emperor was not yet ready to accept their suspicions as justified. Waldstein was granted by the Emperor the two duchies of Mecklenburg and appointed Admiral of the Baltic, while the Hanseatic towns were urged to accept his leadership. They refused, but Waldstein soon had almost all the coastal cities in his hands. Stralsund, however, refused to admit him and his troops. Waldstein, unable to endure defiance, laid siege to the city. For four months in the summer of 1629, the city withstood attack. At the end of that time, unable to break the spirit of the defenders, Waldstein, realizing that the inhabitants, encouraged by Swedish and Danish help filtering into the city from the sea,

Count Wallenstein, by Van Dyck, in the Pinakothek, Munich [BAYERISCHE STAATSGEMÄLDESAMMLUNGEN].

were growing more hopeful the longer the siege lasted, withdrew in disgust. This, his first failure, showed at least that he was not invincible. Protestants throughout Germany, Austria, and the north breathed easier. The Protestant cause in the rest of Europe, however, suffered from two related setbacks. La Rochelle, the principal Huguenot stronghold in France, at odds with the king, had sought and received the support of Charles I of England. France, at war with England, could hardly permit such an alliance to exist. Richelieu besieged the port, and after a bitter and exhausting investment by land and by sea lasting almost twelve months, the city surrendered. This Protestant humiliation, in addition to the failure of the English to bring any effective help to the beleaguered city, tended to counterbalance the moral victory of Stralsund. As the year ended almost everyone realized that no clear-cut victory for either side was in sight.

The Emperor, pressed by Maximilian and the Jesuits at court, determined to make the most of some recent minor victories of Waldstein and decreed, in the Edict of Restitution (March 6, 1629), that all ecclesiastical and conventual properties in the Empire which had, since the treaty of Passau of 1552, been taken over by Protestants should be restored to the Catholic clergy. By this device two rich archbishoprics, Magdeburg and Bremen, twelve bishoprics, and over 120 other ecclesiastical foundations were lost to the Protestants in northern Germany. The terms of the Edict were so drastic that full enforcement was out of the question. Two and a half months later (May 22, 1629), Waldstein made peace with Christian of Denmark at Lübeck. By the terms of the peace the Danish king gave up his claims to territories in the Empire and, in return, was restored to his hereditary Danish lands and titles. This treaty may be taken as marking the end of the predominantly German and religious phase of the war. France, England, Spain, and Sweden had been skirting the edge of the conflict, but not actually or seriously participating. The issues were still essentially related to questions of religious loyalty, and foreign influences, though at times strong, were not determinative. After the Edict of Restitution and the treaty of Lübeck the position of the Emperor was, on paper, exceedingly strong. It was in fact too strong, and there was much dissatisfaction among the princes, both Catholic and Protestant, at Ferdinand's grab for power. There was little the German princes feared more than imperial centralization.

Protestant Revival: The Peace of Prague

DEMANDS for the removal of Waldstein, the main instrument of Ferdinand's power, became more insistent than ever before, and early in September 1630, the Emperor announced his dismissal. The internal peace the Emperor thought he had won by giving in to the princes was almost immediately banished by war from the north and the south, from Sweden and from France. These were opponents who would not be susceptible to arguments of imperial unity or loyalty, nor could the Emperor reach the roots of their strength in their homelands.

Only a month before the dismissal of Waldstein, Gustavus Adolphus, having composed a peace with Sigismund of Poland and thinking the hour ripe for entering the struggle for power in Germany, landed near Stettin, then proceeded to clear the coast of Pomerania and Mecklenburg of all imperial garrisons. In the meantime Richelieu was winning a diplomatic and military victory over the Emperor in the dispute over the Mantuan succession. It was natural that Richelieu and Gustavus, fighting a common enemy, even if for quite different reasons, should find common ground for action. On January 23, 1631, the treaty of Bärwalde was concluded between France and Sweden. France subsidized Sweden to restore Germany to the situation of 1618. The alliance was to be for five years. The German princes, with a record of distrust of the Emperor and his gains, were invited to join, but, fully as suspicious of France and Sweden as of Ferdinand, they remained cool to Richelieu's proposals. It is probable that Richelieu underestimated Gustavus both as to his ability and as to the honesty of his Protestant principles. He certainly never quite comprehended the mixed motives of the German princes; and least of all could he grasp the thought that princely independence was a constant and perhaps benign factor of German history. Gustavus was motivated by two principal aims. In the first place he was a convinced if tolerant Lutheran and, realizing that no German then on the scene could unify the Protestant cause, saw himself as the only one able and willing to create a united Protestant Germany powerful enough to withstand Spain, Austria, and the Papacy. In the second place he sought a firm territorial hold on the southern shore of the Baltic which would protect Sweden's predominance on that sea. These aims could be pursued at the same time, by the

Gustavus Adolphus of Sweden, by J. Hoefnagel, in the National Museum, Stockholm [SWEDISH INFORMATION BUREAU].

same methods: military power, diplomatic dexterity, and administrative efficiency. In all those areas he had no superior in Europe of the seventeenth century. Short though his life was—he died in his thirty-eighth year—he is recognized as the greatest military strategist of the century; he was more than Richelieu's match as a statesman and Waldstein's superior in benevolent administration. Added to all this he was a man of unquestioned uprightness and moral courage, certainly one of the greatest kings of modern times. The five-year period from Gustavus' landing on German soil in 1630 to the treaty of Prague in 1635 was dominated by the personality and policies of Gustavus, even after his death on the battlefield of Lützen in November 1632.

This middle period of the Thirty Years' War was marked by much military action. At first the two Protestant electors, John George of Saxony and George William of Brandenburg, refused Gustavus their support. They were finally convinced that they should change their position. Brandenburg was persuaded by the Swedish troops, Saxony by the horrors of the sack and burning of Magdeburg at the hands of the drunken troops of Tilly in May 1631. Gustavus could have saved the city if he had not been held up by his negotiations with the two electors. There were only 5000 survivors out of a population of 30,000. In cold rage at the useless slaughter Gustavus made it clear to the reluctant electors that he would argue no more with them at the cost of Protestant blood. The troops he received from the electors were of little use, but at least they were not fighting on the imperial side. Gustavus was able to bring the imperial forces, led by Tilly and Pappenheim, into an engagement in September of 1631 at Breitenfeld near Leipzig in Saxony. The Saxon allies of Gustavus broke and ran under attack and Gustavus won the seven-hour battle with his own steady Swedish infantry and artillery. The imperialists lost eighteen thousand in dead, wounded, and prisoners. Gustavus then marched toward the Rhine, occupying in quick succession Erfurt, Würzburg, Hanau, Aschaffenburg, Frankfurt-on-the-Main, and, a few days before Christmas, Mainz. His ally, Bernhard of Saxe-Weimar, took Mannheim. All Protestant Germany hailed Gustavus as the conquering Lion of the North, while the Emperor and the court at Vienna quivered in dire fear lest he march on the defenseless city of the Habsburgs. Richelieu, Gustavus' ally and paymaster, was perplexed: the Swedish king was not supposed to be so successful. He was now, in any case, too close to French territory for the cardinal's comfort. For the Emperor, it was not a matter of comfort, but rather of desperation. Something had to be done and quickly. Waldstein was the only hope for the Catholic side. It took three begging letters from the Emperor to bring Waldstein back into his service, and then, even after having made terms which gave him almost royal power in northern Germany, the general was deliberate about putting troops in the field.

In the spring of 1632 Gustavus marched south and east, crossing the Danube at Donauwörth. When Tilly died in April from wounds received in a minor engagement, Waldstein was about the only general of major stature left on the Catholic side. He was soon on the move; there followed several months of marching and countermarching by armies of both Waldstein and Gustavus, each hoping to exhaust or out-maneuver the other, all played out on a background of diplomatic negotiations which got nowhere. Finally, in September the two armies faced each other in battle array near Nürnberg. Neither was quite ready for a decision, and Waldstein withdrew to Saxony, closely followed by Gustavus. On November 16 Gustavus attacked near Lützen. The king died in the battle, but Waldstein withdrew from the field. The Lion of the North was victorious only in death, and it was an empty victory. His plans for a confederation of Protestant princes, the *Corpus Evangelicorum* as he called it, could not be brought into being by any lesser man. Royal Swedish authority was exercised by Gustavus' faithful friend and chancellor, Axel Oxenstierna, but, able as he was, he was not Gustavus. Waldstein, his armies still intact and powerful, weaned the Elector of Saxony from the Protestant alliance and was in a fair way to dictate peace. The duke held to the position that the imperial cause still had in its favor the principles of legality, and, now alone as military commander, in his own person he gave this policy the strength of unity. Once again, however, Waldstein's success—in surviving and in negotiating with the Protestants—brought his enemies, particularly the Spanish ambassador Oñate, out into the open and complaints at his great power and greater plans poured in upon the Emperor. His correspondence with the Emperor's enemies, Sweden, France, and Saxony, was partly known, partly suspected. Now that Gustavus was dead, Waldstein had ceased to be so necessary, and in January 1634, for the second time, Ferdinand dismissed the man who had saved his Empire. But this was not enough. Charges of high treason were brought against the general. Waldstein withdrew to Pilsen, thence to Eger at the western frontier of Bohemia, and, depending on the loyalty of some of his higher officers, hoped to be met by Bernhard of Saxe-Weimar, Oxenstierna's second in command. But, before Bernhard reached Eger, hired assassins murdered Waldstein's generals at a banquet, then proceeded to his quarters. An Irish adventurer, Captain Devereux, stabbed him where he stood (February 15, 1634). His career and death illustrate perhaps better than any single event or series of events the incredible maze of intrigue and deceit, of frustrated ideals and ambitions, of meanness and greatness through which all men in high places during this century had to tread.

Later this year Bernhard, with seriously diminished forces, was forced to fight the imperial army at Nördlingen and was badly defeated. The gains of Gustavus were thus at one stroke hopelessly lost and the Protestant cause was again in distress. The Elector of Saxony, like a weathercock, made his peace with the Emperor. At the subsequent peace of Prague (May 1635), territories were restored to their owners, Protestant or Catholic, as of 1627, a settlement which favored the Catholics. The Elector of Saxony was rewarded with Lusatia for his desertion of the Protestant cause, and his son was made administrator of the archdiocese of Magdeburg. Lutheranism, but not Calvinism, was recognized and tolerated. There was thus no real gain on this front. There was little any Protestant prince could do but accept the conditions for the time being.

France Dominates the War: The Peace of Westphalia

THE signing of the treaty did not bring the expected peace, although both sides were exhausted. The cities and countrysides through which the armies had passed were barren and deserted. Disease, famine, despair, and death were everywhere, and hope was nowhere. The cruelties of war left their mark on all men. Outrage, murder, robbery, brutalization of all humane instincts—these were the legacy of a war that had begun as a struggle for religious principles. Peasant and townsman alike had given up counting on a better day to come. The longer the war lasted the worse it got. The lot of the poor was to reach a new low in the years after the peace of Prague.

The years from 1635 to the conclusion of the Peace of Westphalia in 1648 are a more dismal period of German history—if that be possible—than the sad years before the treaty of Prague. In part, the deterioration of the struggle was attributable to a lowering of the plane on which the issues lay. After fifteen years of bitter and devastating war, motives had become so blurred, so many compromises had been made and unmade, personal convictions had so often wavered and failed, that it was no longer possible for any party to the strife to maintain the fiction of consistency or of adherence to principles. The Empire had become the loot over which two gangs of thieves fought: Austria and Spain against France and Sweden. Other powers were involved at various times, but these played only minor roles in the drama.

Richelieu had long been planning for the moment when Germany would lie exhausted. He knew what he wanted. He saw on the map of Europe the need for France to break the line of communication between Spanish possessions in Italy and the Spanish Lowlands. This encirclement was similar to that faced by previous French rulers. For Richelieu the primary enemy was Spain, and if Spain was allied with Austria, then Austria too was the enemy.

The Swedish defeat at Nördlingen convinced Richelieu that France should pass from indirect war to open hostilities, and that the previous arrangements in support of Sweden would have to be reinforced. First taking over from Oxenstierna the Swedish positions in Alsace, Richelieu then declared war (May 19, 1635) on Spain. His first military measures were failures, and Spanish troops were on French soil at Corbie within the next year. French spirit rallied, the king, Louis XIII, took the field in person, and the Spanish were driven out by November. Swedish successes in Brandenburg encouraged the Protestants further, but 1637 saw a resurgence of Habsburg fortunes. Ferdinand II died in February 1637 and was succeeded by his son Ferdinand III, distinguished by his piety as well as his parsimony. It was not until 1638 that Alsace, the objective so important to Richelieu, was won. Bernhard of Saxe-Weimar, with a small but well-disciplined army, captured Breisach, on the right bank of the Rhine. The victory, although it broke the Spanish line of communication between Italy and the Spanish Netherlands, was not entirely welcome to France. Bernhard wanted to create a German principality out of Alsace and leave it in the Empire, whereas Richelieu had plans to make Alsace French. The sudden death of Bernhard in July 1639 allowed the French to take control of Alsace without further military action and without embarrassing tension with their German allies.

Spain's other connection with her Lowlands was by sea. Until Richelieu Spain had been France's superior on the sea; but the cardinal had built a navy and in 1638 went on the offensive. In 1639 Richelieu's allies, the Dutch, destroyed a large Spanish fleet off the coast of England and Spain's days as a naval factor in the war were ended. Richelieu's careful and patient preparation for a final reckoning with Spain in military as well as diplomatic affairs paid off in the wars in Germany. France won a military victory in 1641 against an imperial army at Wolfenbüttel and again in 1642 at Kempten near Augsburg. By this time it was well known that Spain's part in the war was less, her subsidies to the Emperor diminished and irregularly paid. In July 1641, Sweden and Brandenburg had signed a truce. It was evident that the imperial cause was losing important support and that the will to peace throughout the Empire was becoming more insistent. The Emperor put the best possible face on his situation and at the Diet of Regensburg in October agreed to the calling of a general conference to discuss terms of peace. The negotiations moved very slowly, while French and Swedish commanders scored minor military successes along the Rhine, in Thuringia, in Silesia, and in Moravia. War broke out again in 1643 between Sweden and Denmark, two Protestant states, which weakened for a while the anti-Catholic alignment. The death of Richelieu in December 1642 and of his master, Louis XIII, six months later brought no change in French policy. His successor as minister, Cardinal Mazarin, maintained the Swedish alliance and pressure on the imperialists.

From 1643 military action was, if frequently spectacular and on a grand scale, not the most important factor in the final settlement. France had her Turenne and Enghien, two of the great captains of French history; Sweden produced both Banér and Torstensson, able heirs of the tradition of Gustavus. Imperial armies suffered several defeats. The Spanish infantry, the famous *tercios,* regarded as invincible through the sixteenth and early seventeenth centuries, were fairly defeated at the battle of Rocroi (1643) by Condé. Maximilian, hitherto secure in his precious Bavaria, was humbled by Turenne and forced to sign a separate truce at Ulm (March 1647). But none of these battles between soldiers was of itself decisive. While the common folk were being ravaged and starved, the diplomats were tortuously preparing the peace. The important thing for Europe was the complex of negotiations which were to result in the Peace of Westphalia.

Several fundamental facts conditioned the course of these negotiations. The first was the exhaustion of Germany under the heels of conquering foreign armies—Spanish, Swedish, Dutch, and French. The second was France's emergence around 1638 as the most powerful single factor in German politics. The third was the virtual disappearance, partly through emotional fatigue and partly because of the exigencies of power politics and survival, of religion as a primary issue. From 1635 a Catholic power, headed by a cardinal of the Church, was leading Protestant forces, and Protestant princes were occasionally fighting on the side of the Catholic Habsburgs. While confusion reigned within confessional lines, political alliances were not more firm, each prince keeping his eyes and ears open for a more advantageous connection than the one to which he was bound at the moment. It is ironic that almost the last military actions of the whole war took place in Prague, where, thirty years before, the war had broken out on a purely religious issue. In July 1648, a Swedish force occupied the left bank (Malá Strana) of the Moldau at Prague, and the right side of the river (the Old Town) was under siege for three months, to be relieved only at news of the conclusion of the peace at Osnabrück. But everything had changed in the intervening thirty years: issues, resources, personalities, and loyalties. The most pressing fact was that finally Europe realized it must have peace.

The Treaty of Westphalia, in reality two treaties, of Osnabrück and of Münster, was a landmark in European history. It was the first peace in which all the important Continental powers participated. It set boundaries and political alignments which were accepted as basic for the next century and a half. During that period the treaties of the Pyrenees, of Utrecht, of Paris in 1763, were regarded as modifications of the broad lines drawn at the Peace of Westphalia. The religious issues at the root of the war in 1618, carried over from the mistakes of the Peace of Augsburg, itself an attempt to bring some political order out of the cataclysm of the Reformation, were, as we shall see, only partially settled. But they were not disregarded, and a *modus vivendi* was worked out, acceptable to the vast majority of the population in an age which had become more secular than a century before. Men were beginning to learn to live with differences in religious expression, of itself a great step toward a free and vital society.

Peace Negotiations

THE peace conference was long in coming. As early as 1635 Pope Urban VIII, known to be pro-French, was urging negotiations that would lead to a permanent peace. The Emperor was willing to discuss the project, but Richelieu was not ready for peace. His aims had not been attained. Several years later the proposals were renewed; this time Sweden was unwilling to treat. Various suggestions were made. Christian of Denmark offered his services as mediator. But the Swedes distrusted him. Other lesser princes offered their mediation, but all, for one reason or another, were rejected. For several years envoys of all participants in the war, France, Sweden, Brandenburg, Saxony, Spain, the Emperor, the Dutch, and the Papacy, were busy talking and intriguing, jockeying for position and striving to undermine one another. The very futility of their "diplomacy" brought about a conviction that only a general Europe-wide peace conference could end the strife. As a start in the right direction a preliminary treaty was signed on December 25, 1641, between envoys of the Emperor and of France, which provided for parallel meetings of representatives of the Emperor and his allies on the one hand, and France and Sweden and their allies on the other, to take place concurrently at two neighboring Westphalian towns, Osnabrück and Münster. As a matter of diplomatic reality, four wars had been going on at the same time: (1) between the Emperor and his allies on one side and France (France avoided war with Bavaria, the leading ally of the Emperor); (2) between the Emperor and Sweden; (3) between Spain and Holland; and (4) between France and Spain. As alliances weakened or strengthened, the parties to one or more of these wars changed. Diplomacy and international usage were hard pressed to keep abreast of developments. It was not always clear just who was fighting whom.

Representatives of the Protestant princes and cities met in Osnabrück, those of the Catholics in Münster. The first meeting was called for July 11, 1643, but the envoys were late in showing up and no real work was accomplished until a year later. The leading personality of the whole conference was Count von Trautmansdorff, the Emperor's chief envoy. Hard-working, respected by all, flexible, well versed in law and diplomacy, he was able to present the Emperor's case so cogently that he obtained for his master better conditions than the imperial military failures of the years between 1643 and 1648 would appear to have justified. The Dutch war for independence from Spain was concluded by a separate peace treaty, the treaty of Münster, on January 30, 1648. Spain, in order to have freedom of action, both military and diplomatic, against France, acceded to almost every demand of the Dutch. This terminated the third of the four wars. The fourth war, between France and Spain, did not end until 1659, and need not, therefore, concern us here.

In the meantime the terms of settlement of the various knotty problems were being painfully worked out. France, as the dominant party in the last period of the war, had definite demands to make of the Emperor. Alsace had been occupied for some years by French troops, and it was assumed that France would demand the left bank of the Rhine. After much debate all the rights of the Emperor in Alsace and the ten imperial cities of the province were given to France in full sovereignty, and not as an imperial fief. The latter title would have brought France into imperial politics as a member of the Diet. The king of France would have been an uncomfortable vassal of a Habsburg emperor. The transfer had the support of Maximilian of Bavaria. As so often happened in a century not yet free of feudal complexities, it was not made clear just what "rights" the Emperor had before he transferred them to the king of France. The wording of that article in the treaty was ambiguous and destined to cause dispute in the future, particularly under Louis XIV of France. The bishoprics of Metz, Toul, and Verdun, with their lands long in French possession, were ceded outright, as was the city of Breisach on the right bank of the Rhine. This agreement, known as the Münster treaty, ended the war between France and the Empire.

Sweden demanded satisfaction on two levels, in territory and in cash as indemnity for the expenses of her armies on imperial soil. In the final settlement, known as the Osnabrück treaty, Sweden was given Western Pomerania as a fief of the Empire, the territories of the archbishopric of Bremen and the bishopric of Verden, the islands of Rügen and Poel, and the ports of Stettin and Wismar. For her soldiery Queen Christina demanded six million dollars and settled for five. To compensate for territories yielded to Sweden, Brandenburg was given the reversion of the rich archbishopric of Magdeburg and two bishoprics near Brandenburg holdings. Other lesser German houses received bishoprics or the right to election as administrators. In the case of Brunswick-Lüneburg it was stipulated that the bishopric of Osnabrück should be occupied alternately by a Catholic and a Protestant. Some other territorial disputes of long standing were left unsettled. In 1623 the duke of Bavaria, who had twice threatened to desert the Emperor and side with France, had been awarded the electoral title which Ferdinand II had taken from Frederick of the Palatinate. At the peace table there were insistent demands, from many quarters, that Frederick's heir, Charles Louis, should be restored to his father's electoral dignity. Since Maximilian was too powerful to be deprived of the electorate a compromise had to be reached: Maximilian was to keep the title and the Upper Palatinate to accompany the dignity, while Charles Louis was given a new (the eighth) electorate and restored to his ancestral land of the Lower Palatinate. Maximilian was never fully forgiven by the princes of Germany for taking the land and title of a fellow prince. Possession of secular lands reverted to the individual or family in possession in 1618. In deciding whether a church or church lands should be restored to Protestant or Catholic authority the year 1624 was accepted as the test of possession. The Confederation of Switzerland, which had avoided participation in the war, was declared free from Habsburg suzerainty.

Religious Questions

THE achievements of the peace congress in the controversial area of religious liberty, while not revolutionary, were not insignificant. Religious questions were handled in the Osnabrück treaty, which settled the war between Sweden and the Empire. Complete toleration was not to be expected. The old principle of *cuius regio eius religio* was deeply ingrained in the princely class. Now, however, Calvinists were tolerated and the princes were expressly enjoined not to interfere in the religion of their subjects. In the Diet, it was stipulated, on matters of religion a mere majority was of no effect. Protestant or Catholic representatives could simply get up in a body and walk out—the so-called *ius eundi in partes,* or right of going out. The matter in dispute would then be referred to a committee consisting of Protestants and Catholics in equal representation. Under certain conditions private worship at home was protected, along with the right of an individual to send his children outside the country for education in another faith. In his personal domain of Austria, Ferdinand III would not even discuss toleration for Protestants of any stripe. Many of the religious stipulations seem vague, but the negotiators were well aware of the seriousness of the questions of religion. So far as they were able they were making some effort to avoid rigidity and constriction in political arrangements having to do with religion.

The treaty in its entirety was proclaimed by the Emperor and thus took its place as a constitutional document alongside the Golden Bull of Charles IV. As such it has several curious aspects. It provided that any Estate, acting independently of the Emperor, might contract alliances with nonimperial powers as well as with other German states. There were over three hundred such political entities in the Empire. It is hard to imagine the possible complexities to which such freedom of action might expose the Empire, but it is not difficult to see that the Emperor had lost control of all of the Empire save his family lands. Another fact which almost escapes notice in any running account of the issues and the conflict is the inconspicuousness of the Papacy, not only in the wars being waged, but in the peace negotiations. The popes of the time, from Paul V (1605–21) to Innocent X (1644–55), were deeply concerned over the war. Urban VIII, who was Pope for twenty-one of the thirty years of war (1623–44), was anti-Habsburg and supported Richelieu's policy of alliance with Sweden. He is even reported to have said a private mass for the repose of the soul of Gustavus Adolphus. His influence was not great. His successor, Innocent X, took the opposite position, supporting the Habsburg cause. The Peace of Westphalia was negotiated without the Papacy, and Innocent, unhappy at concessions to the Protestants, issued a bull condemning those articles in the treaty that were harmful to the Catholic faith. No attention was paid by either side to this protest. The days of ecclesiastical influence in international relations were well-nigh over.

Results of the War and the Peace

IT WOULD not be possible to assess the results, either of the Thirty Years' War or of the making of the peace, in a short space. These results lay not only in the field of political life, frontiers, sovereignties, and dynastic ambitions; they touched every class and stratum of society: the peasant, the beggar, the soldier, the townsman, the parish priest, the prelate, the prince, and the banker. Social order was disrupted; the loss and dislocation of population put a premium on the labor of the peasant, but it did not lead to his emancipation. The ruling classes passed laws keeping the peasant where he was in 1618. The bourgeoisie, ruined by taxes, the disruption of trade by ravaging armies, and the migration of the population, could gain no ground. German culture in the broader sense suffered tragically. The universities were greatly depopulated; some closed altogether. Music and art survived only in isolated courts. Hardly a significant monument of German literature can be found issuing from this period. Along with some changes in the attitudes of Germans toward themselves and their neighbors, we can trace a heightened German nationalism. For years the German natives had heard and seen Danes, Swedes, Frenchmen, Dutchmen, and Spaniards, soldiers and generals, marching noisily and haughtily over their precious German soil, and their reaction was a perfectly natural one: hatred of the foreigner and a sharpening of their German national consciousness. Coupled with this development came a growing distrust of the Habsburgs, whom the common man in Germany held responsible for bringing in Spanish troops and using German resources to fatten the lands and possessions of the dynasty. Much of the historic German-Austrian tension may be traced from this time.

The destruction wrought by the Thirty Years' War has been generally termed as catastrophic, the population described as decimated. Modern historical opinion has modified this extreme judgment. Some towns suffered more than others. There was shocking famine and disease in many places. Crops were damaged, and in some areas the farmers refused to plant, knowing that their crops would either be destroyed or stolen. Many handsome cities were piles of rubble. Yet large parts of the Empire escaped such depredations altogether, and some cities continued to prosper. One might hazard the guess that Germany lost a quarter to a third of her population. The work of reconstruction was quickly and energetically undertaken by the princes, and within a remarkably short time, from two to six years after the peace, Germany was again functioning almost normally.

Whatever the results of the war for Germany and the Germans, and whatever may have been its significance for the future of Europe, the fact remains and must be clearly stated that the war arose out of the tensions and animosities engendered by the Protestant Reformation, coupled indissolubly with the Catholic Counter-Reformation. Both movements cast their shadow upon all secular thought and political life; and, once this influence was realized, the whole Pandora's box of ambition, greed, deceit, and cynical opportunism was open.

Religious at the beginning, the conflict became cruelly dynastic and expansionist toward the end. The Thirty Years' War was the prolongation and realization of issues but dimly seen in the preceding century. It was the tragic fulfillment of an era as well as the opening act of an age of imperialism and secularism.

SUGGESTIONS FOR FURTHER READING

AHNLUND, N., *Gustav Adolf the Great*. New York, 1940
BOULENGER, J., *The Seventeenth Century*. New York, 1920
Cambridge Modern History. Vol. IV, *The Thirty Years' War*. Cambridge, 1906
CLARK, G. N., *The Seventeenth Century*. Oxford, 1929
DAVIES, R. T., *Spain in Decline*. London, 1957
GARDINER, S. R., *The Thirty Years' War*. London, 1912
GEYL, P., *The Netherlands Divided, 1609–1648*. London, 1936
GEYL, P., *The Netherlands in the 17th Century*. London, 1961
GINDELY, A., *The Thirty Years War*. 2 vols. New York, 1884
GREEN, M. A. E., *Elizabeth Electress Palatine and Queen of Bohemia*. London, 1909
MacMUNN, G. F., *Gustavus Adolphus*. New York, 1930
MOTLEY, J. L., *The United Netherlands*. 4 vols. New York, 1895
READE, H. G. R., *Sidelights on the Thirty Years' War*. 3 vols. London, 1924
ROBECK, M., *Gustavus Adolphus: A History of Sweden, 1611–1632*. 1913
WATSON, F., *Wallenstein, Soldier under Saturn*. New York, 1940
WEDGWOOD, C. V., *The Thirty Years War*. New Haven, 1939. Also Penguin

DENIS, E., *Fin de l'indépendance bohême*. 2 vols. 1890
DENIS, E., *La Bohême depuis la Montagne Blanche*. 2 vols. 1903
GINDELY, A., *Geschichte der Gegenreformation in Böhmen*. 1894
PAGÈS, G., *La Guerre de Trente Ans, 1618–1648*. 1949
PEKAŘ, J., *Bilá Hora*. 1922
PEKAŘ, J., *Wallenstein, 1630–1634*. 2 vols. 1937
RITTER, M., *Deutsche Geschichte im Zeitalter der Gegenreformation und des Dreissig-
    jährigen Krieges*. 3 vols. 1889–1905
TAPIÉ, V.-L., *La politique étrangère de la France et le début de la Guerre de Trente
    Ans*. 1934
WERTHEIM, A., *Der tolle Halberstadter Herzog, Christian von Braunschweig*. 1929
WINTER, G., *Geschichte des Dreissigjährigen Krieges*. 1893
WITTROCK, G., *Gustav Adolf*. 1930

APPENDIXES

CHRONOLOGY OF IMPORTANT EVENTS

1250 Death of Frederick II of Holy Roman Empire.
1260 Niccolò Pisano finishes Baptistry at Pisa.
1265 Birth of Dante. First English Parliament.
1266 Battle of Benevento. Charles of Anjou becomes king of the Two Sicilies.
1273 Election of Rudolf of Habsburg to imperial throne.
1282 Sicilian Vespers.
1285 Philip the Fair becomes king of France.
1300 Jubilee at Rome.
1302 Bull of Boniface VIII, *Unam sanctam*. First meeting of French Estates General.
1303 Assault on Boniface at Anagni.
1306 Extinction of line of Přemyslids.
1308 Henry of Luxemburg becomes Holy Roman Emperor. Papacy settles in Avignon.
1312 Suppression of the Knights Templar.
1321 Death of Dante.
1323 Outbreak of struggle between Louis of Bavaria and John XXII.
1324 Marsilio of Padua's *Defender of the Peace*.
1337 Opening of Hundred Years' War.
1338 Edicts of Rense and *Licet iuris*.
1341 Petrarch receives laurel crown of the poet in Rome.
1346 Election of Charles of Luxemburg as emperor.
1347 Outbreak of Black Death. Ascent of Cola di Rienzo to power in Rome.
1348 Spread of Black Death. Death of Petrarch's Laura.
1353 Boccaccio finishes the *Decameron*.
1356 Golden Bull of Charles IV. Battle of Poitiers.
1357 Etienne Marcel in power in France.
1358 The Jacquerie.
1360 Peace of Brétigny.
1367 Urban V moves to Rome.
1370 Urban V returns to Avignon. Death of Casimir the Great of Poland.
1374 Death of Petrarch. Beginning of Wyclyf's opposition to Papacy.
1377 Gregory XI returns Papacy to Rome.
1378 Elections of Urban VI and Clement VII and beginning of Schism. Ciompi revolt in Florence.
1381 Peasant revolt in England.
1386 Marriage of Jadwiga of Poland and Jagiello of Lithuania.
1397 Union of Kalmar.
1399 Deposition of Richard II.
1409 Council of Pisa and election of a third pope, Alexander V.
1410 Poles defeat Teutonic Knights at Tannenberg (Grunwald).
1414 Opening of Council of Constance.
1415 Hus burned at the stake. Deposition of John XXIII. Battle of Agincourt.
1420 Treaty of Troyes. Thomas à Kempis writes the *Imitation of Christ*.
1431–49 Council of Basel.

1434 Advent of Cosimo de' Medici to power in Florence.
1438 Pragmatic Sanction of Bourges. Union of Eastern and Western Churches at Council of Ferrara-Florence.
1447 Election of Nicholas V: a humanist papacy.
1450 Vatican Library established.
1455 42-Line Bible probably completed; first major book to be printed from movable metal type invented by Gutenberg.
1458 Aeneas Silvius elected pope as Pius II. Mathias Corvinus becomes king of Hungary. George of Poděbrady elected king of Bohemia.
1461 Louis XI becomes king of France.
1464 Establishment of Platonic Academy at Florence.
1466 Birth of Erasmus.
1467 Charles the Bold becomes duke of Burgundy.
1469 Lorenzo de' Medici assumes rule of Florence. Marriage of Isabella of Castile and Ferdinand of Aragon.
1477 Death of Charles the Bold at Nancy.
1478 Inquisition established in Castile.
1482 Torquemada becomes Grand Inquisitor of Spanish Inquisition.
1483 Birth of Martin Luther. Death of Louis XI and accession of Charles VIII.
1485 Henry VII becomes Tudor king of England.
1485–89 Grocyn, Linacre, and Latimer go to Italy.
1486 Cape of Good Hope passed by Bartholomew Dias.
1491 Savonarola Prior of San Marco, Florence.
1492 Death of Lorenzo de' Medici. Election of Alexander VI (Borgia). Fall of Granada to the Catholic Kings.
1493 Papal bull of demarcation between Spanish and Portuguese claims. Maximilian elected Emperor.
1494 Charles VIII invades Italy. Medici expelled from Florence.
1495 Formation of Holy League against Charles VIII.
1496 French expelled from Naples. John Cabot reaches Labrador and Newfoundland.
1497 Vasco da Gama reaches Calicut around Africa. Leonardo da Vinci finishes *The Last Supper*.
1498 Louis XII becomes king of France. Savonarola executed. Erasmus in England.
1500 Louis XII takes Milan.
1502 Cesare Borgia at height of his power in northern Italy. Erasmus publishes his *Handbook of the Christian Soldier*.
1503 Fall of Cesare Borgia.
1505 Luther enters Augustinian Convent.
1507 Ximénez becomes Grand Inquisitor.
1508 League of Cambrai against Venice.
1509 Death of Henry VII and accession of Henry VIII. Birth of John Calvin. Michelangelo at work on Sistine Chapel.
1511 Holy League against France.
1512 Restoration of Medici in Florence.
1513 Machiavelli writes *The Prince*.
1514 Greek New Testament printed (but not published) at Alcalá at orders of Ximénez. First volume of *Letters of Obscure Men*.
1515 Death of Louis XII and accession of Francis I. French recapture Milan. Battle of Marignano.
1516 Death of Ferdinand and accession of his grandson Charles. Erasmus' Greek New Testament published. Sir Thomas Moore's *Utopia* published. Concordat of Bologna.

1517 Publication of Luther's Ninety-Five Theses at Wittenberg.
1519 Death of Maximilian and election of Charles V as Emperor.
1519–21 Magellan's ship circumnavigates the world.
1521 Diet of Worms. Excommunication of Luther. Belgrade taken by Turks.
1522 Rhodes falls to the Turks.
1523 Gustavus Vasa, king of Sweden.
1524 Outbreak of Peasants' Revolt in southern Germany.
1525 Battle of Pavia. Francis I taken prisoner to Madrid.
1526 Treaty of Madrid. Battle of Mohács. *Spiritual Exercises* of Ignatius Loyola. Ferdinand succeeds to thrones of Bohemia and Hungary.
1528 The *Courtier* of Baldassare Castiglione published.
1529 Diet of Speier. Turkish attack on Vienna repulsed.
1530 German Protestant princes declare faith in *Augsburg Confession*.
1531 Henry VIII assumes title of Supreme Head of Church in England. Battle of Kappel; death of Zwingli.
1534 Society of Jesus founded by Loyola.
1536 Publication of first edition of Calvin's *Institutes of the Christian Religion*. Lesser monasteries in England suppressed.
1538 Calvin expelled from Geneva.
1540 Society of Jesus approved by papal bull.
1543 Copernicus' *On the Revolution of the Celestial Bodies*. Vesalius' *On the Structure of the Human Body*.
1545 Opening of Council of Trent. Spread of Calvinism in Poland.
1546 Death of Luther. Schmalkaldic War.
1547 Battle of Mühlberg, Protestants defeated by Charles V. Death of Henry VIII and of Francis I. Accession of Edward VI and Henry II.
1548 *Augsburg Interim* proclaimed by Charles V.
1549 First English *Prayer Book*. Act of Uniformity.
1552 Treaty of Chambord. *Second Book of Common Prayer*. Treaty of Passau.
1553 Execution of Michel Servetus in Geneva. Mary Tudor becomes queen of England.
1554 Marriage of Mary Tudor and Philip II.
1555 Diet of Augsburg. Abdication of Charles V.
1556 Death of Ignatius Loyola. Ferdinand becomes Emperor. Jesuits in Prague.
1558 Fall of Calais to French. Death of Mary Tudor and accession of Elizabeth I.
1559 Death of Henry II. Treaty of Câteau-Cambrésis. Knox returns to Scotland. Protestant Synod at Paris.
1560 Tumult of Amboise. Regency of Catherine de' Medici.
1561 Colloquy of Passy.
1562 Beginning of French Wars of Religion.
1563 Thirty-Nine Articles. End of Council of Trent.
1564 Death of Calvin. Death of Michelangelo.
1565 Inquisition introduced in Netherlands.
1567 Revolt in Netherlands. Alva assumes rule. Council of Blood.
1568 Execution of Egmont and Hoorn. Jesuit seminary founded at Douai.
1569 Union of Poland and Lithuania effected at Lublin.
1571 Battle of Lepanto. Báthory becomes prince of Transylvania.
1572 Massacre of St. Bartholomew. Capture of Brill by "Sea Beggars."
1573 Duke of Anjou elected king of Poland. Alva recalled from Netherlands.
1574 Anjou flees Poland to accept French crown.
1575 Báthory elected king of Poland. Accession of Rudolf to imperial throne. *Confessio Bohemica*.
1576 Sack of Antwerp. Pacification of Ghent. Jean Bodin's *Six Books of the Republic*.

1579 Treaty of Arras. Union of Utrecht.
1580 Jesuits Campion and Parsons arrive in England.
1583 French fury in Antwerp. William of Orange made hereditary count of Holland and Zeeland.
1584 Assassination of William of Orange.
1585 War of the Three Henries in France.
1586 Death of Báthory.
1587 Execution of Mary Queen of Scots. Drake raids port of Cádiz.
1588 Defeat of Spanish Armada.
1589 Henry IV victorious at Arques. Death of Catherine de' Medici.
1590 Battle of Ivry.
1592 Clement VIII issues revision of Vulgate of Sixtus V. Military successes of Maurice of Nassau.
1593 Henry IV accepts Catholic faith.
1598 Peace of Vervins. Death of Philip II. Edict of Nantes.
1600 East India Company receives charter from Elizabeth.
1601 Dutch East India Company chartered.
1602 Rudolf decrees banishment of Protestants from Bohemia.
1603 Death of Elizabeth I. Accession of James I.
1604 Galileo discovers laws of gravitation and the pendulum.
1605 Calvinism established in Hesse-Cassel.
1606 Death of Bocskai, king of Hungary. Cervantes publishes *Don Quijote*.
1607 Violence at Donauwörth.
1608 Union of Evangelical Estates founded.
1609 Death of duke of Cleves-Jülich opens question of succession. Catholic League formed. Twelve Years' Truce between Spain and United Provinces. Rudolf II grants Letter of Majesty.
1610 Murder of Henry IV. Archduke Matthias ruler of Habsburg lands. Galileo constructs the telescope.
1612 Death of Rudolf II.
1618 Defenestration at Prague. Outbreak of Thirty Years' War.
1619 Frederick V of Palatinate elected king of Bohemia.
1620 Defeat of Bohemian forces at White Mountain.
1624 Richelieu becomes Chief Minister under Louis XIII.
1625 Christian IV of Denmark enters war in north. Sweden and Poland at war. Waldstein in command of imperial forces.
1628 Siege of Stralsund. Richelieu takes La Rochelle.
1629 Edict of Restitution. Peace of Lübeck.
1630 Gustavus Adolphus lands in Pomerania. Emperor dismisses Waldstein.
1631 Gustavus defeats Tilly at Breitenfeld.
1632 Waldstein recalled to lead imperial forces. Battle of Lützen and death of Gustavus.
1633 Condemnation of Galileo.
1634 Assassination of Waldstein at Eger. Battle of Nördlingen. Treaty of alliance renewed between France and Sweden.
1635 Peace of Prague. Foundation of French Academy.
1639 Death of Bernhard of Weimar.
1640 Portugal revolts against Spanish rule. Frederick William, elector of Brandenburg.
1642 Swedish victory at Breitenfeld. Death of Richelieu.
1643 Victory of French over Spanish troops at Rocroi. Death of Louis XIII.
1643–48 Negotiations leading to Treaties of Münster-Osnabrück (Westphalia).

POPES OF THE PERIOD OF THE
RENAISSANCE AND THE REFORMATIONS

For Italian popes the family name and place of origin are given, for non-Italian popes the family name or the place of origin. Antipopes of the Schism or the Conciliar line are indented. (* restored; † deposed.)

1243–1254	Innocent IV (Fieschi, GENOA)
1254–1261	Alexander IV (Segni, ANAGNI)
1261–1264	Urban IV (TROYES)
1265–1268	Clement IV (ST. GILLES)
1271–1276	Gregory X (Visconti, PIACENZA)
1276	Innocent V (TARANTAISE)
1276	Adrian V (Fieschi, GENOA)
1276–1277	John XXI (LISBON)
1277–1280	Nicholas III (Orsini, ROME)
1281–1285	Martin IV (de Brie)
1285–1287	Honorius IV (Savelli, ROME)
1288–1292	Nicholas IV (Masci, ASCOLI)
1294	St. Celestine V (Angeleri, ISERNIA)
1294–1303	Boniface VIII (Gaetani, ANAGNI)
1303–1304	Benedict XI (Boccasini, TREVISO)
1305–1314	Clement V (de Got)
1316–1334	John XXII (d'Euse)
1328–1330	*Nicholas V (Rainalucci)
1334–1342	Benedict XII (Fournier)
1342–1352	Clement VI (Roger)
1352–1362	Innocent VI (Aubert)
1362–1370	Urban V (Grimoard)
1370–1378	Gregory XI (de Beaufort)
1378–1389	Urban VI (Prignano, NAPLES)
1378–1394	Clement VII (GENEVA)
1389–1404	Boniface IX (Tomacelli, NAPLES)
1394–1424	Benedict XIII (de Luna)
1404–1406	Innocent VII (Migliorati, SALMONA)
1406–1409	†Gregory XII (Corraro, VENICE)
1409–1410	Alexander V (Filargi, CANDIA)
1410–1415	†John XXIII (Cossa, NAPLES)
1417–1431	Martin V (Colonna, ROME)
1424–1429	Clement VIII (Muñoz)
1431–1447	Eugenius IV (Condulmeri, VENICE)
1439–1449	Felix V (SAVOY)
1447–1455	Nicholas V (Parentucelli, SARZANA)
1455–1458	Calixtus III (Borgia, SPAIN)
1458–1464	Pius II (Piccolomini, SIENA)
1464–1471	Paul II (Barbo, VENICE)
1471–1484	Sixtus IV (Della Rovere, SAVONA)
1484–1492	Innocent VIII (Cibo, VENICE)
1492–1503	Alexander VI (Borgia, SPAIN)
1503	Pius III (Piccolomini, SIENA)
1503–1513	Julius II (Della Rovere, SAVONA)
1513–1521	Leo X (Medici, FLORENCE)
1522–1523	Adrian VI (UTRECHT)
1523–1534	Clement VII (Medici, FLORENCE)
1534–1549	Paul III (Farnese, ROME)
1550–1555	Julius III (dal Monte, ROME)
1555	Marcellus II (Cervini, MONTEPULCIANO)
1555–1559	Paul IV (Caraffa, NAPLES)
1559–1565	Pius IV (Medici, MILAN)
1566–1572	St. Pius V (Ghislieri, BOSCO)
1572–1585	Gregory XIII (Boncampagni, BOLOGNA)
1585–1590	Sixtus V (Peretti, GROTTAMARE)
1590	Urban VII (Castagna, ROME)
1590–1591	Gregory XIV (Sfrondati, CREMONA)
1591	Innocent IX (Fachinetti, BOLOGNA)
1592–1605	Clement VIII (Aldobrandini, FLORENCE)
1605	Leo XI (Medici, FLORENCE)
1605–1621	Paul V (Borghese, ROME)
1621–1623	Gregory XV (Ludovisi, ROME)
1623–1644	Urban VIII (Barberini, FLORENCE)
1644–1655	Innocent X (Pamphili, ROME)

EMPERORS OF THE HOLY ROMAN EMPIRE

KINGS OF BOHEMIA

The titular numbers refer to the imperial title only. Many emperors bore separate royal titles.

1250–1254	Conrad IV (Hohenstaufen)
1247–1256	William of Holland
1257–1271	Richard of Cornwall
1257–1273	Alfonso of Castile
1273–1291	Rudolf I, of Habsburg
1292–1298	Adolf of Nassau
1298–1308	Albert I, of Habsburg
1308–1313	Henry VII, of Luxemburg
1314–1347	Louis IV, of Bavaria
1314–1325	Frederick of Austria (Habsburg)
1346–1378	Charles IV, of Bohemia (Luxemburg)
1378–1400	Wenzel of Bohemia (Luxemburg)
1400–1410	Rupert of the Palatinate (Wittelsbach)
1411–1437	Sigismund of Hungary (Luxemburg)
1438–1439	Albert II, of Habsburg
1440–1493	Frederick III, of Styria (Habsburg)
1493–1519	Maximilian I, of Burgundy (Habsburg)
1519–1556	Charles V, of Spain (Habsburg)
1556–1564	Ferdinand I, of Austria (Habsburg)
1564–1576	Maximilian II, of Austria (Habsburg)
1576–1612	Rudolf II, of Austria (Habsburg)
1612–1619	Matthias of Austria (Habsburg)
1619–1637	Ferdinand II, of Inner Austria (Habsburg)
1637–1657	Ferdinand II, of Austria (Habsburg)

1230–1253	Václav (Wenzel) I (Přemyslid)
1253–1278	Přemysl Ottokar II (Přemyslid)
1283–1304	Wenzel (Václav) II (Přemyslid)
1305–1306	Václav (Wenzel) III (last Přemyslid)
1306–1307	Rudolf of Habsburg
1307–1310	Henry of Carinthia
1310–1346	John of Luxemburg
1346–1378	Charles I (IV of the Empire; Luxemburg)
1378–1419	Václav IV (Wenzel of the Empire; Luxemburg)
1419–1437	Sigismund (of the Empire and Hungary; Luxemburg)
1438–1439	Albert of Habsburg
1440–1457	Vladislav Posthumous (Habsburg)
1458–1471	George of Poděbrady
1471–1516	Vladislav II (Wladislas II of Hungary)
1516–1526	Louis II (Jagiellonian)
1526–1564	Ferdinand I (Habsburg)
1564–1576	Maximilian I (II of Empire; Habsburg)
1576–1612	Rudolf II (Habsburg)
1612–1619	Mathias (Habsburg)
1619–1620	Frederick of the Palatinate
1619–1637	Ferdinand II (Habsburg)
1637–1657	Ferdinand III (Habsburg)

RULERS OF ENGLAND

KINGS OF FRANCE

PLANTAGENET LINE

1216–1272	Henry III
1272–1307	Edward I
1307–1327	Edward II *
1327–1377	Edward III
1377–1399	Richard II *

HOUSE OF LANCASTER

1399–1413	Henry IV, of Bolingbroke
1413–1422	Henry V
1422–1461	Henry VI

HOUSE OF YORK

1461–1483	Edward IV
1483	Edward V
1483–1485	Richard III

HOUSE OF TUDOR

1485–1509	Henry VII
1509–1547	Henry VIII
1547–1553	Edward VI
1553–1558	Mary
1558–1603	Elizabeth I

HOUSE OF STUART

1603–1625	James I (VI of Scotland)
1625–1649	Charles I †

CAPETIAN HOUSE

1226–1270	Louis IX (St. Louis)
1270–1285	Philip III, the Bold
1285–1314	Philip IV, the Fair
1314–1316	Louis X, the Quarrelsome
1316	John I, the Posthumous
1316–1322	Philip V, the Tall
1322–1328	Charles IV, the Fair

HOUSE OF VALOIS

1328–1350	Philip VI
1350–1364	John II, the Good
1364–1380	Charles V, the Wise
1380–1422	Charles VI, the Well Loved
1422–1461	Charles VII, the Victorious
1461–1483	Louis XI, King Spider
1483–1498	Charles VIII

Orléans-Valois

1498–1515	Louis XII, Father of His People

Valois-Angoulême

1515–1547	Francis I
1547–1559	Henry II
1559–1560	Francis II
1560–1574	Charles IX
1574–1589	Henry III

HOUSE OF BOURBON

1589–1610	Henry IV
1610–1643	Louis XIII
1643–1715	Louis XIV

* deposed.   † executed.

RULERS OF HUNGARY

1235–1270	Béla IV (Árpád)
1270–1272	Stephen V (Árpád)
1272–1290	Wladislas IV (Árpád)
1290–1301	Andrew III (last Árpád)
1301–1304	Wenzel (Václav III of Bohemia)
1305–1308	Otto (of Bavaria)
1308–1342	Charles I (Charles Robert of Anjou)
1342–1382	Louis I, the Great (Angevin)
1382–1395	Maria (Angevin)
1385–1386	Charles II (Durazzo)
1387–1437	Sigismund (Luxemburg)
1437–1439	Albert (Habsburg)
1440–1444	Wladislas I (Jagiellonian; Władysław III of Poland)
1444–1457	Wladislas Posthumous (Habsburg)
1458–1490	Mathias I (Corvinus)
1490–1516	Wladislas II (Jagiellonian; Vladislav II of Bohemia)
1516–1526	Louis II (Jágiellonian)
1526–1540	John Zapolya
1526–1564	Ferdinand I (Habsburg)
1564–1576	Maximilian (Habsburg)
1576–1608	Rudolf (Habsburg)
1608–1619	Mathias II (Habsburg)
1619–1637	Ferdinand II (Habsburg)
1637–1657	Ferdinand III (Habsburg)

RULERS OF POLAND

PIASTS

1227–1279	Bolesław V, the Modest
1279–1289	Leszek VI, the Black
1289–1291	Bolesław, prince of Masuria, Henry IV, prince of Breslau
1291–1292	Władysław IV, prince of Sieradz, Henry IV, prince of Breslau
1295–1296	Przemysław I, prince of Posen and Pomerania
1297–1299	Władysław IV, the Short (second time)
1299–1305	Václav I (II of Bohemia)
1306–1333	Władysław IV, the Short (third time)
1333–1370	Casimir III, the Great (the last Piast)
1370–1382	Louis (I of Hungary; the Great)
1384–1399	Jadwiga

JAGIELLONIANS

1386–1434	Władysław II (Jagiełło of Lithuania)
1434–1444	Władysław III, surnamed Warneńczyk (Wladislas I of Hungary)
1447–1492	Casimir IV
1492–1501	John Albert
1501–1506	Alexander
1506–1548	Sigismund I
1548–1572	Sigismund II, Augustus (the last Jagiellonian)
1574–1575	Henry of Valois
1576–1586	Stephen Báthory (of Transylvania)
1587–1632	Sigismund III, Vasa
1632–1648	Władysław IV
1648–1668	John Casimir

RULERS OF SPAIN

The kingdoms of Navarre and Granada are not represented in this list. From 1580 to 1640 the Spanish kings also ruled in Portugal.

CASTILE AND LEÓN

1217–1252	Ferdinand III, the Saint *
1252–1284	Alfonso X, the Scholar
1284–1295	Sancho IV, the Brave
1295–1312	Ferdinand IV, the Summoned
1312–1350	Alfonso XI, the Judge
1350–1369	Peter I, the Cruel
1369–1379	Henry II of Trastamara, the Bastard
1379–1390	John I
1390–1406	Henry III, the Suffering
1406–1454	John II
1454–1474	Henry IV, the Impotent
1474–1504	Isabella the Catholic

ARAGON

1213–1276	James I, the Conqueror
1276–1285	Peter III, the Great
1285–1291	Alfonso III, the Liberal
1291–1327	James II, the Just
1327–1336	Alfonso IV, the Benign
1336–1387	Peter IV, the Ceremonious
1387–1395	John I, the Hunter
1395–1410	Martin I, the Humane
1410–1416	Ferdinand I, of Antequera
1416–1458	Alfonso V, the Magnanimous
1458–1479	John II
1479–1516	Ferdinand II (V of Castile), the Catholic

1504–1516   Joanna the Mad †

HABSBURG LINE

1516–1556	Charles I (V of the Empire)
1556–1598	Philip II, the Prudent
1598–1621	Philip III
1621–1665	Philip IV

* Ferdinand III inherited Castile through his mother, Berengaria, in 1217. In 1230 Ferdinand succeeded his father, Alfonso VIII, as king of León, thus reuniting Castile and León.

† Joanna the Mad inherited Castile and León from her mother, Isabella, in 1504. She ruled until the onset of her madness, brought about by the death of her husband, Philip the Handsome of Austria, in 1506. From that date to his death in 1516, her father, Ferdinand, ruled for her as regent.

A BIBLIOGRAPHICAL NOTE

THE selective reading lists appended to most of the separate chapters of this book have been designed to serve several purposes. The first of the groups into which these lists are divided records English translations of works referred to in the text, usually available in college and university libraries. The second group lists standard modern monographic works in English for collateral reading. The third group offers authoritative studies in foreign languages which advanced students or the instructor may wish to consult. A few chapters have not adapted themselves to this three-fold organization, and the lists for those chapters may seem somewhat mixed. An effort has been made to restrict the bibliography to titles which are generally available. The user of this book is urged to consult current lists of paperback editions of works treating these centuries of Western history as well as of hitherto out-of-print writings from Dante to the Thirty Years' War. The paperback republication of classics of this period has made the task of the teacher who attempts to cover these centuries infinitely easier.

Certain standard works which must be kept in mind for reference throughout the whole book may not appear on any of the lists. The *Cambridge Medieval History,* particularly volumes VI–VIII, the *Cambridge Modern History* (old edition), volumes I–III, the *New Cambridge Modern History,* volumes I and II, the *Histoire de France,* edited by Ernest Lavisse, volumes IV–VI, Louis Halphen and Philippe Sagnac's *Peuples et Civilisations,* volumes VII–IX, and the *Propyläen-Weltgeschichte* make distinguished contributions to an understanding of the period covered by this book. Of the American series, "The Rise of the Modern World," E. P. Cheyney's *The Dawn of a New Era* and Myron P. Gilmore's *The World of Humanism* are useful; the volume on the Reformation has not yet appeared. All these works, excepting, regrettably, the *New Cambridge Modern History,* contain helpful bibliographies. For more complete bibliographical detail for Germany one may always consult F. C. Dahlmann and Georg Waitz's *Quellenkunde der deutschen Geschichte* or Karl Schottenloher's monumental *Bibliographie zur deutschen Geschichte im Zeitalter der Glaubensspaltung* (6 vols.) and, for France, H. Hauser's *Les sources de l'histoire de France: Le XVIe siècle,* 4 vols., Paris, 1906–15. The Clio publications, *L'Élaboration du monde moderne* (Paris, 1949), by J. Calmette, *Le XVIe siècle,* by Henri Sée and Armand Rébillon (1934), and *Le XVIIe siècle,* by Edmond Préclin and V.-L. Tapié (1934), carry rich bibliographies. For ecclesiastical history the volumes thus far published of the *Histoire de l'Église,* edited by Augustin Fliche and Victor Martin, relevant to this period, i.e., volumes XIII, XV, XVI, XVII, XVIII, and XIX, are not only full as to detail but provided with excellent, critical bibliographies of the latest scholarship.

Of the encyclopedias the best for the Latin world is the *Enciclopedia italiana,* though the Spanish *Enciclopedia universal ilustrada* should not be underestimated. The *Schaff-Herzog Encyclopedia of Religious Knowledge,* with two supplementary volumes recently published (1955), and the *Catholic Encyclopedia* are especially valuable for our study. For ready reference two recent one-volume encyclopedias are most satisfactory: H. Rössler and G. Franz, *Sachwörterbuch zur deutschen Geschichte* (1958) and the same editors' *Biographisches Wörterbuch zur deutschen Geschichte* (1953).

This period has not, in recent years, so far as I am aware, been the object of many attempts to treat it as a whole. There was the pioneering work of George Lincoln Burr, which was retouched and published as *Renaissance and Reformation* by E. M. Hulme in 1915 (revised in 1920). Some years later (1934) Henry S. Lucas published *The Renaissance and the Reformation,* a text which has held the field for almost thirty years. This text, somewhat revised, appeared in a second edition in 1960. For political history the Methuen series has several excellent volumes: C. W. Previté-Orton's *A History of Europe: 1198–1378* (3rd ed., 1951); W. T. Waugh's *Europe: 1378–1494* (3rd ed., 1949); A. J. Grant's *A History of Europe: 1494–1610* (5th ed., 1951). The *Renaissance and Reformation* of V. H. H. Green (1952) limits itself to the period between 1450 and 1660, and would appear to disregard the significance of the principal personalities of the Renaissance movement. More recently H. J. Grimm has published a full length text, *The Reformation Era*, covering the period from 1500 to 1650. This work has a helpful selective bibliography. R. H. Bainton published in 1935 a valuable *Bibliography of the Continental Reformation* which restricts itself to materials available in English. This bibliography lists works out of print and hard to obtain and is a most valuable guide to what has been written in England and America on the sixteenth-century religious movements. The revised (1961) edition of the *Guide to Historical Literature*, published by the American Historical Association, will be found helpful. The material is arranged by countries, not by periods.

At the risk of some duplication, we add a brief selective list of works which may be regarded as national histories. Reference is made to the lists at the end of chapters 5, 6, 8, 9, 10, 15, and 25, in which national history was the substance of the story.

ITALY

RANKE, L., *History of the Popes*. 3 vols. London, 1908
SEDGWICK, H. D., *Short History of Italy*. Boston, 1905
VERNON, MRS. H. M., *Italy, 1494–1790*. London, 1909

FRANCE

BATIFFOL, L., *Century of the Renaissance*. New York, 1925
BOULENGER, J., *The Seventeenth Century*. New York, 1920
GRANT, A. J., *The French Monarchy 1483–1789*. London, 1914
KITCHIN, G. W., *History of France*. 2 vols. Oxford, 1877–81
MORETON-MACDONALD, J. R., *History of France*, Vols. I–II. Oxford, 1915
See also the bibliography to Chapter 25.

GERMANY

HOLBORN, H., *History of Modern Germany*, Vol. I. New York, 1957
TUTTLE, H., *History of Prussia*, Vol. I. Boston, 1883
See also the bibliography to Chapter 6.

ENGLAND

GREEN, V. H. H., *The Later Plantagenets*. London, 1955
LUNT, W. E., *History of England*. New York, 1938

SCANDINAVIA

BIRCH, J. S. H., *Denmark in History*. London, 1938
HALLENDORFF, C., and A. SCHÜCK, *History of Sweden*. 1929
LARSEN, K., *A History of Norway*. Princeton, 1948
STROMBERG, A. A., *History of Sweden*. New York, 1931

POLAND

BAIN, R. N., *Slavonic Europe*. Cambridge, 1908
Cambridge History of Poland. 2 vols. Cambridge, 1941, 1950
HALECKI, O., *A History of Poland*. New York, 1941

BOHEMIA

Lützow, F., *Bohemia: A Sketch.* Everyman's Library
Seton-Watson, R. W., *History of the Czechs and Slovaks.* London, 1943
Thomson, S. H., *Czechoslovakia in European History.* Princeton, 1953

HUNGARY

Kosary, D., *History of Hungary.* Cleveland, 1940
Sinor, D., *History of Hungary.* New York, 1958
Zarek, O., *History of Hungary.* London, 1939

SWITZERLAND

Bonjour, E., W. S. Offler, and G. R. Potter, *A Short History of Switzerland.* Oxford, 1952
Oechsli, N., *History of Switzerland.* Cambridge, 1922

LOW COUNTRIES

Blok, P. G., *History of the Dutch People.* New York, 1898 1912
Edmundson, G., *History of Holland.* Cambridge, 1922
Motley, J. L., *Rise of the Dutch Republic.* 3 vols. New York, 1883
Motley, J. L., *The United Netherlands.* 4 vols. New York, 1895
Boulger, D. C., *History of Belgium.* 2 vols. New York, 1900, 1911
Van der Essen, L., *Short History of Belgium.* Chicago, 1920

INDEX

A

Aachen, 795
Abélard, Peter, 76–77
absolute monarchy: in France, 564, 665–66; in Spain, 670
absolution, 31–32
Achaia, 10
Acts of Supremacy and Uniformity, 590–91, 704–05, 715, 774
Adolf of Nassau (Holy Rom. Emp.), 105, 139
Adrian VI (Pope), 464, 466, 488, 551, 564
Adrian of Utrecht, 548–50, 636
Aeneas Silvius, see Pius II (Pope)
Africa, 82, 87, 88
Africa, 560, 562; explorations in, 356–58
Agincourt, battle of, 251, 253; map, 251
Agricola, Rudolf, 330, 446
agriculture, 664; technical advances and, 350–51
Ailly, Peter d', 161–62, 178, 275, 284, 288, 289, 292, 473
Albania, 10, 212
Albergati, Cardinal, 305–06, 317
Albert (archduke) of Austria, 756
Albert of Bavaria, 543
Albert V (duke) of Bavaria, 627, 792
Albert of Brandenburg (Archbishop Elector of Mainz), 478, 480–81, 486
Albert of Brandenburg (duke of Prussia), 538, 540
Albert the Great, 154, 156, 165, 345
Albert I of Habsburg (Holy Rom. Emp.), 38, 57, 139
Albert II of Habsburg (Holy Rom. Emp.), 152, 194–95, 206, 210, 308, 487
Albert of Mecklenburg, 183, 185, 187
Albert II (prince-archbishop) of Riga, 189
Albert of Saxony, 354
Albert (duke) of Saxony, 471*n*.
Albert Achilles of Brandenburg, 428
Alberti, Antonio degli, 95, 310
Alberti, Leone Battista, 326, 392, 393, 407–08
Albertus Magnus, see Albert the Great
Albigensian heresy, 171
Albigensians, 162–63, 561
Albizzi family, 315–16, 413

Albornoz, Gil, 63, 72, 73
Albret, Charles d', 251
Albret, Henry d' (king of Navarre), 525
Albret, Jean d' (king of Navarre), 421
Albuquerque, Alfonso de, 363–64
Alcalá, University of, 619
alcabala, 566, 651–52, 752
Alcántara, Order of, 134–35
alchemy, 346
Alcuin of York, 343
Aleander, Jerome, 486, 518, 527, 612, 676
Alençon, duke of, see Anjou, Francis, duke of
Alessandria, 14, 15
Alexander III (Scotland), 113
Alexander IV (Pope), 182
Alexander V (Pope), 287
Alexander VI (Pope), 360, 416, 418, 429, 434, 449, 610; illus., 450
Alexander (Grand Prince) of Lithuania, 196, 433
Alfonso V (Aragon; I of Naples and Sicily; the Magnanimous), 132, 299, 314, 324–25, 418–19, 686
Alfonso VIII (Castile), 127
Alfonso X (Castile; the Scholar), 103, 128–29, 132, 137; illus., 129
Alfonso XI (Castile), 130, 131
Algiers, 562, 759
Allen, William, 708
Almeida, Francisco de, 363
Almohades, 127
Alsace, 440, 810, 813
Althusius, John, 668
alumbrados, 529, 619, 636
Alva, duke of, 574, 575, 659, 711, 721–24, 736, 737, 754; illus., 721
Amboise, George d', 423, 610–11
Amboise, peace of, 707, 735–36
Amboise, Tumult of, 635, 733
Amedeus IV (count) of Savoy, 14
Amedeus VI (count) of Savoy, 14
Amerbach, Johann, 445, 464
America, exploration of, 358–62, 365–66, 647, 657
Amiens cathedral, 399; illus., 399
Amsterdam, 519, 659
Anabaptists, 512–13, 519–20, 597, 663

E

F

H

I

K

L

EUROPE in 1648

0   100   200   300   400   500 MILES